Lecture Notes in Artificial Intelligence   11671

Subseries of Lecture Notes in Computer Science

More information about this series at http://www.springer.com/series/1244

Abhaya C. Nayak · Alok Sharma (Eds.)

PRICAI 2019: Trends in Artificial Intelligence

16th Pacific Rim
International Conference on Artificial Intelligence
Cuvu, Yanuca Island, Fiji, August 26–30, 2019
Proceedings, Part II

 Springer

Editors
Abhaya C. Nayak ⓘⅅ
Department of Computing
Macquarie University
Sydney, NSW, Australia

Alok Sharma ⓘⅅ
RIKEN Center for Integrative
Medical Sciences
Yokohama, Japan

ISSN 0302-9743   ISSN 1611-3349   (electronic)
Lecture Notes in Artificial Intelligence
ISBN 978-3-030-29910-1   ISBN 978-3-030-29911-8   (eBook)
https://doi.org/10.1007/978-3-030-29911-8

LNCS Sublibrary: SL7 – Artificial Intelligence

This Springer imprint is published by the registered company Springer Nature Switzerland AG
The registered company address is: Gewerbestrasse 11, 6330 Cham, Switzerland

Preface

These proceedings in three volumes contain the papers presented at the 16th Pacific Rim International Conference on Artificial Intelligence (PRICAI 2019) held during August 26–30, 2019, in Yanuca Island, Fiji. PRICAI started as a biennial conference inaugurated in Tokyo in 1990. It provides a common forum for researchers and practitioners in various branches of artificial intelligence (AI) to exchange new ideas and share experience and expertise. Over the past years the conference has grown, both in participation and scope, to be a premier international AI event for all major Pacific Rim nations as well as countries from further afield. Indeed, the growth has merited holding PRICAI on an annual basis starting this year.

Submissions to PRICAI 2019 were received through two different routes: (1) some papers were directly submitted to PRICAI as in earlier years, and (2) in a special arrangement with IJCAI 2019, authors of submissions that narrowly missed out being accepted were encouraged to resubmit to PRICAI, along with the reviews and meta-reviews they received. The submissions of the first category underwent a double-blind review process, and were reviewed by the PRICAI Program Committee (PC) members and external reviewers against criteria such as significance, technical soundness, and clarity of presentation. Every paper received at least two, and in most cases three, reviews. Submissions of the second category were not subjected to further review, keeping in mind the workload of the reviewers in the community.

Altogether we received 311 high-quality submissions (with 265 submissions being of the first category) from 34 countries, which was impressive considering that for the first time PRICAI was being held in consecutive years. The program co-chairs read the reviews, the original papers, and called for additional reviews if necessary to make final decisions. The entire review team (PC members, external reviewers, and co-chairs) expended tremendous effort to ensure fairness and consistency in the paper selection process. Of the 265 submissions under the first category, 105 (39.6%) were accepted as full papers for the main-track, and 6 as full papers for the industry-track. A small number of papers were also accepted as short papers for the main-track (6), short papers for the industry-track (7), and as posters (6) – with the understanding that papers in the last category will not be included in these proceedings. The papers are organized in three volumes, under three broad (and naturally overlapping) themes, "Cognition", "Investigation", and "Application."

The technical program consisted of two workshops, five tutorials, and the main conference program. The workshops and tutorials covered important and thriving topics in AI. The workshops included the Pacific Rim Knowledge Acquisition Workshop (PKAW 2019) and the Knowledge Representation Conventicle (2019). The former was co-chaired by Prof. Kouzou Ohara and Dr. Quan Bai, while the latter was organized by Dr. Jake Chandler. The tutorials focused on hot topics including Big Data in bioinformatics, Data Science, Cognitive Logics, and Identity Management. All papers at the main conference were orally presented over the three days in parallel, and in thematically organized sessions. The authors of the posters were also offered the opportunity to give short talks to introduce their work.

It was our great honor to have four outstanding keynote/invited speakers, whose contributions have pushed boundaries of AI across various aspects: Prof. Hiroaki Kitano (Sony Computer Science Laboratories Inc. and The System Biology Institute, Japan), Prof. Grigoris Antoniou (University of Huddersfield, UK), Prof. Mary-Anne Williams (University of Technology Sydney, Australia), and Prof. Byoung-Tak Zhang (Seoul National University, South Korea). We are grateful to them for sharing their insights on their latest research with us.

The success of PRICAI 2019 would not have been possible without the effort and support of numerous people from all over the world. First of all, we would like to thank the PC members and external reviewers for their engagements in providing rigorous and timely reviews. It was because of them that the quality of the papers in this volume is maintained at a high level. We wish to thank the general co-chairs, Professors Abdul Sattar and MGM Khan for their continued support and guidance, and Dr. Sankalp Khanna for his tireless effort toward the overall coordination of PRICAI 2019. We are also thankful to various chairs and co-chairs, namely the industry co-chairs, workshop co-chairs, the tutorial co-chairs, the web and publicity co-chairs, the sponsorship chair, and the local organization chair, without whose support and hard work PRICAI 2019 could not have been successful. We also acknowledge the willing help of Kinzang Chhogyal, Jandson S. Ribeiro, and Hijab Alavi toward the preparation of these proceedings.

We gratefully acknowledge the financial and/or organizational support of a number of institutions including the University of the South Pacific (Fiji), Griffith University (Australia), Macquarie University (Australia), Fiji National University (Fiji), RIKEN Center for Integrative Medical Sciences (Japan), University of Western Australia (Australia), Australian Computer Society (ACS), and Springer Nature. Special thanks to EasyChair, whose paper submission platform we used to organize reviews and collate the files for these proceedings. We are also grateful to Alfred Hofmann and Anna Kramer from Springer for their assistance in publishing the PRICAI 2019 proceedings in the *Lecture Notes in Artificial Intelligence* series, as well as sponsoring the best paper awards.

We thank the Program Chair and the Conference Chair of IJCAI 2019, Professors Sarit Kraus and Thomas Eiter, for encouraging the resubmission of many IJCAI submissions to PRICAI 2019. Last but not least, we thank all authors and all conference participants for their contribution and support. We hope all the participants took this valuable opportunity to share and exchange their ideas and thoughts with one another and enjoyed their time at PRICAI 2019.

August 2019   Abhaya C. Nayak
                                                                     Alok Sharma

Organization

Steering Committee

Tru Hoang Cao	Ho Chi Minh City University of Technology, Vietnam
Xin Geng	Southeast University, China
Guido Governatori	Data61, Australia
Takayuki Ito	Nagoya Institute of Technology, Japan
Byeong-Ho Kang	University of Tasmania, Australia
Sankalp Khanna	CSIRO, Australia
Dickson Lukose	GCS Agile Pty Ltd., Australia
Hideyuki Nakashima	Sapporo City University, Japan
Seong-Bae Park	Kyung Hee University, South Korea
Abdul Sattar	Griffith University, Australia
Zhi-Hua Zhou	Nanjing University, China

Honorary Members

Randy Goebel	University of Alberta, Canada
Tu-Bao Ho	JAIST, Japan
Mitsuru Ishizuka	University of Tokyo, Japan
Hiroshi Motoda	Osaka University, Japan
Geoff Webb	Monash University, Australia
Wai K. Yeap	Auckland University of Technology, New Zealand
Byoung-Tak Zhang	Seoul National University, South Korea
Chengqi Zhang	University of Technology Sydney, Australia

Organizing Committee

General Co-chairs

Abdul Sattar	Griffith University, Australia
M. G. M. Khan	University of the South Pacific, Fiji

Program Co-chairs

Abhaya C. Nayak	Macquarie University, Australia
Alok Sharma	RIKEN Center for Integrative Medical Sciences, Japan

Local Co-chairs

Salsabil Nusair	University of the South Pacific, Fiji
A. B. M. Shawkat Ali	Fiji National University, Fiji

Workshop Co-chairs

Nasser Sabar   La Trobe University, Australia
Anurag Sharma   University of the South Pacific, Fiji

Tutorial Co-chairs

Min-Ling Zhang   Southeast University, China
Yi Mei   Victoria University of Wellington, New Zealand

Industry Co-chairs

Duc Nghia Pham   MIMOS Berhad, Malaysia
Sankalp Khanna   CSIRO, Australia

Sponsorship Co-chairs

Andy Song   Royal Melbourne Institute of Technology, Australia
Sabiha Khan   Fiji National University, Fiji

Web and Publicity Co-chairs

Mahmood Rashid   Victoria University, Australia
Benjamin Cowley   Griffith University, Australia

Local Arrangements

Priynka Sharma   University of the South Pacific, Fiji
Gavin Khan   University of the South Pacific, Fiji
Wafaa Wardha   University of the South Pacific, Fiji
Goel Aman Lal   University of the South Pacific, Fiji

Program Committee

Eriko Aiba   University of Electro-Communications, Japan
Patricia Anthony   Lincoln University, New Zealand
Quan Bai   Auckland University of Technology, New Zealand
Yun Bai   University of Western Sydney, Australia
Blai Bonet   Universidad Simón Bolívar, Venezuela
Richard Booth   Cardiff University, UK
Zied Bouraoui   CRIL – CNRS, Université d'Artois, France
Arina Britz   CAIR, Stellenbosch University, South Africa
Rafael Cabredo   De La Salle University, Philippines
Longbing Cao   University of Technology Sydney, Australia
Lawrence Cavedon   RMIT University, Australia
Siqi Chen   Tianjin University, China
Songcan Chen   Nanjing University of Aeronautics
                                  and Astronautics, China
Wu Chen   Southwest University, China
Yingke Chen   Sichuan University, China
Wai Khuen Cheng   Universiti Tunku Abdul Rahman, Malaysia

Krisana Chinnasarn	Burapha University, Thailand
Phatthanaphong Chomphuwiset	Mahasarakham University, Thailand
Dan Corbett	Optimodal Technologies, USA
Célia da Costa Pereira	Université Côte d'Azur, France
Jirapun Daengdej	Assumption University, Thailand
Xuan-Hong Dang	IBM T.J. Watson, USA
Abdollah Dehzangi	Morgan State University, USA
Clare Dixon	University of Liverpool, UK
Shyamala Doraisamy	Universiti Putra Malaysia, Malaysia
Atilla Elci	Aksaray University, Turkey
Vlad Estivill-Castro	Griffith University, Australia
Eduardo Fermé	Universidade da Madeira, Portugal
Christian Freksa	University of Bremen, Germany
Katsuhide Fujita	Tokyo University of Agriculture and Technology, Japan
Naoki Fukuta	Shizuoka University, Japan
Marcus Gallagher	University of Queensland, Australia
Dragan Gamberger	Ruđer Bošković Institute, Croatia
Wei Gao	Nanjing University, China
Xiaoying Gao	Victoria University of Wellington, New Zealand
Yang Gao	Nanjing University, China
Xin Geng	Southeast University, China
Manolis Gergatsoulis	Ionian University, Greece
Guido Governatori	CSIRO, Australia
Alban Grastien	Data61, Australia
Fikret Gürgen	Boğaziçi University, Turkey
Peter Haddawy	Mahidol University, Thailand
Bing Han	Xidian University, China
Choochart Haruechaiyasak	NECTEC, Thailand
Kiyota Hashimoto	Prince of Songkla University, Thailand
Tessai Hayama	Nagaoka University of Technology, Japan
Jose Hernandez-Orallo	Universitat Politècnica de València, Spain
Juhua Hu	University of Washington, USA
Sheng-Jun Huang	Nanjing University of Aeronautics and Astronautics, China
Xiaodi Huang	Charles Sturt University, Australia
Van Nam Huynh	JAIST, Japan
Masashi Inoue	Tohoku Institute of Technology, Japan
Sanjay Jain	National University of Singapore, Singapore
Jianmin Ji	University of Science and Technology of China, China
Liangxiao Jiang	China University of Geosciences, China
Yichuan Jiang	Southeast University, China
Hideaki Kanai	JAIST, Japan
Ryo Kanamori	Nagoya University, Japan
Byeong-Ho Kang	University of Tasmania, Australia

C. Maria Keet	University of Cape Town, South Africa
Gabriele Kern-Isberner	Technische Universität Dortmund, Germany
Sankalp Khanna	CSIRO, Australia
Frank Klawonn	Ostfalia University of Applied Sciences, Germany
Sébastien Konieczny	CRIL - CNRS, France
Alfred Krzywicki	University of New South Wales, Australia
Young-Bin Kwon	Chung-Ang University, South Korea
Ho-Pun Lam	CSIRO, Australia
Jérôme Lang	CNRS, LAMSADE, University Paris-Dauphine, France
Roberto Legaspi	RIKEN Center for Brain Science, Japan
Gang Li	Deakin University, Australia
Guangliang Li	University of Amsterdam, The Netherlands
Li Li	Southwest University, China
Ming Li	Nanjing University, China
Tianrui Li	Southwest Jiaotong University, China
Yu-Feng Li	Nanjing University, China
Beishui Liao	Zhejiang University, China
Jiamou Liu	University of Auckland, New Zealand
Qing Liu	CSIRO, Australia
Michael Maher	Reasoning Research Institute, Australia
Xinjun Mao	National University of Defense Technology, China
Eric Martin	University of New South Wales, Australia
Maria Vanina Martinez	Universidad de Buenos Aires, Argentina
Sanparith Marukatat	NECTEC, Thailand
Michael Mayo	University of Waikato, New Zealand
Brendan Mccane	University of Otago, New Zealand
Thomas Meyer	University of Cape Town and CAIR, South Africa
James Montgomery	University of Tasmania, Australia
Abhaya Nayak	Macquarie University, Australia
Richi Nayak	QUT, Australia
Kourosh Neshatian	University of Canterbury, New Zealand
M. A. Hakim Newton	Griffith University, Australia
Shahrul Azman Noah	Universiti Kebangsaan Malaysia, Malaysia
Masayuki Numao	Osaka University, Japan
Kouzou Ohara	Aoyama Gakuin University, Japan
Hayato Ohwada	Tokyo University of Science, Japan
Mehmet Orgun	Macquarie University, Australia
Noriko Otani	Tokyo City University, Japan
Lionel Ott	University of Sydney, Australia
Maurice Pagnucco	University of New South Wales, Australia
Hye-Young Paik	University of New South Wales, Australia
Laurent Perrussel	IRIT, Université de Toulouse, France
Bernhard Pfahringer	University of Waikato, New Zealand
Duc Nghia Pham	MIMOS Berhad, Malaysia
Jantima Polpinij	Mahasarakham University, Thailand

Mikhail Prokopenko	University of Sydney, Australia
Chao Qian	University of Science and Technology of China, China
Yuhua Qian	Shanxi University, China
Joël Quinqueton	LIRMM, France
Fenghui Ren	University of Wollongong, Australia
Mark Reynolds	University of Western Australia, Australia
Ji Ruan	Auckland University of Technology, New Zealand
Kazumi Saito	University of Shizuoka, Japan
Chiaki Sakama	Wakayama University, Japan
Ken Satoh	National Institute of Informatics and Sokendai, Japan
Abdul Sattar	Griffith University, Australia
Torsten Schaub	University of Potsdam, Germany
Nicolas Schwind	National Institute of Advanced Industrial Science and Technology, Japan
Nazha Selmaoui-Folcher	University of New Caledonia, New Caledonia
Lin Shang	Nanjing University, China
Alok Sharma	RIKEN Center for Integrative Medical Sciences, Japan
Chuan Shi	Beijing University of Posts and Telecommunications, China
Zhenwei Shi	Beihang University, China
Daichi Shigemizu	NCGG, Japan
Yanfeng Shu	CSIRO, Australia
Guillermo R. Simari	Universidad del Sur in Bahia Blanca, Argentina
Tony Smith	University of Waikato, New Zealand
Chattrakul Sombattheera	Mahasarakham University, Thailand
Andy Song	RMIT University, Australia
Markus Stumptner	University of South Australia, Australia
Xing Su	Beijing University of Technology, China
Merlin Teodosia Suarez	De La Salle University, Philippines
Thepchai Supnithi	NECTEC, Thailand
Michael Thielscher	University of New South Wales, Australia
Shikui Tu	Shanghai Jiao Tong University, China
Miroslav Velev	Aries Design Automation, USA
Serena Villata	CNRS, France
Toby Walsh	University of New South Wales, Australia
Kewen Wang	Griffith University, Australia
Qi Wang	Northwestern Polytechnical University, China
Wei Wang	NJU, China
Paul Weng	UM-SJTU Joint Institute, China
Peter Whigham	University of Otago, New Zealand
Wayne Wobcke	University of New South Wales, Australia
Brendon J. Woodford	University of Otago, New Zealand
Chang Xu	University of Sydney, Australia
Guandong Xu	University of Technology Sydney, Australia
Ming Xu	Xi'an Jiaotong-Liverpool University, China
Shuxiang Xu	University of Tasmania, Australia

Xin-Shun Xu	Shandong University, China
Bing Xue	Victoria University of Wellington, New Zealand
Hui Xue	Southeast University, China
Bo Yang	Jilin University, China
Ming Yang	Nanjing Normal University, China
Roland Yap	National University of Singapore, Singapore
Kenichi Yoshida	University of Tsukuba, Japan
Chao Yu	University of Wollongong, Australia
Yang Yu	Nanjing University, China
Takaya Yuizono	JAIST, Japan
Yifeng Zeng	Teesside University, UK
Chengqi Zhang	University of Technology Sydney, Australia
Dongmo Zhang	Western Sydney University, Australia
Du Zhang	Macau University of Science and Technology, China
Min-Ling Zhang	Southeast University, China
Minjie Zhang	University of Wollongong, Australia
Qieshi Zhang	Chinese Academy of Sciences, Australia
Rui Zhang	University of Melbourne, Australia
Shichao Zhang	Guangxi Normal University, China
Wen Zhang	Beijing University of Technology, China
Yu Zhang	Hong Kong University of Science and Technology, SAR China
Zhao Zhang	Hefei University of Technology, China
Zili Zhang	Deakin University, Australia
Zongzhang Zhang	Soochow University, China
Li Zhao	MSRA, China
Yanchang Zhao	CSIRO, Australia
Shuigeng Zhou	Fudan University, China
Zhi-Hua Zhou	Nanjing University, China
Xiaofeng Zhu	Guangxi Normal University, China
Xingquan Zhu	Florida Atlantic University, USA
Fuzhen Zhuang	Chinese Academy of Sciences, China

Additional Reviewers

Shintaro Akiyama
Yuya Asanomi
Mansour Assaf
Weiling Cai
Rohitash Chandra
Jairui Chen
Armin Chitizadeh
Laurenz A. Cornelissen
Emon Dey
Duy Tai Dinh

Bayu Distiawan
Shaokang Dong
Steve Edwards
Suhendry Effendy
Jorge Fandinno
Zaiwen Feng
Chuanxin Geng
Sayuri Higaki
Jin B. Hong
Yuxuan Hu

Paul Salvador Inventado
Abdul Karim
Karamjit Kaur
Sunil Lal
Ang Li
Haopeng Li
Weikai Li
Yun Li
Yuyu Li
Shenglan Liao
Shaowu Liu
Yuxin Liu
Wolfgang Mayer
Kingshuk Mazumdar
Nguyen Le Minh
Risa Mitsumori
Taiki Mori
Majid Namaazi
Courtney Ngo
Aaron Nicolson
Lifan Pan
Asanga Ranasinghe
Vahid Riahi
Maria AF Rodriguez
Manou Rosenberg
Matt Selway
Cong Shang

Swakkhar Shatabda
Manisha Sirsat
Fengyi Song
Yixin Su
Adam Svahn
Trung Huynh Thanh
Yanlling Tian
Qing Tian
Jannai Tokotoko
Nhi N. Y. Vo
Guodong Wang
Jing Wang
Xiaojie Wang
Yi Wang
Yuchen Wang
Yunyun Wang
Shiqing Wu
Peng Xiao
Yi Xu
Wanqi Yang
Heng Yao
Dayong Ye
Jun Yin
Zhao Zhang
Zhu Zhirui
Zili Zhou
Yunkai Zhuang

Contents – Part II

Social and Information Networks

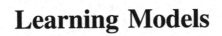

Learning Models

Local Uncorrelated Subspace Learning

Bo Li[1,2(✉)], Xin-Hao Wang[1,2], Yong-Kang Peng[1,2], Li Chen[1,2],
and Sheng Ding[1,3]

[1] School of Computer Science and Technology,
Wuhan University of Science and Technology, Wuhan 430081, China
liberol@126.com
[2] Hubei Province Key Laboratory of Intelligent Information Processing
and Real-Time Industrial System, Wuhan, China
[3] Fujian Provincial Key Laboratory of Data Intensive Computing,
Quanzhou, China

Abstract. In this paper, we present a supervised manifold learning based dimensionality reduction method, which is titled local uncorrelated subspace learning (LUSL). In the proposed LUSL, a local margin based on point to feature space (P2S) distance metric is recommended for discriminant feature extraction. What's more, it has been validated that the locally statistical uncorrelation is an important property to reduce the feature redundancy. Hence, a novel locally uncorrelated criterion using P2S distance metric is also put forward, which is taken to constrain the local margin. Finally, by solving both the orthogonality and the local uncorrelation constrained objective function using an iterative way, a low dimensional subspace will be explored for pattern recognition. Compared to some related subspace learning methods, the effectiveness of the proposed LUSL have been shown from experimental results on some benchmark face data sets as AR and FERET.

Keywords: Dimensionality reduction · Local uncorrelation ·
Point to feature space distance metric

1 Introduction

So far, dimensionality reduction is still a hot issue either in the field of machine learning or in the fields of data mining because so many data in these fields always display property of high dimensions, thus dimensionality reduction has to be adopted to avoid the curse of dimensionality problem.

As a widely used linear dimensionality reduction method, principal component analysis (PCA) explores a low dimensional subspace through unsupervised learning, which can be approached by modeling an objective function to maximize the covariance of all the original data [1]. Unlike PCA, linear discriminant analysis (LDA) exploits data label information to construct a between-class scatter and a within-class scatter, which are taken to characterize the between-class data apartness and the within-class data compactness [2]. Both PCA and LDA focus on digging linear information in the original data and nonlinear features are neglected, which are also very helpful to

© Springer Nature Switzerland AG 2019
A. C. Nayak and A. Sharma (Eds.): PRICAI 2019, LNAI 11671, pp. 3–11, 2019.
https://doi.org/10.1007/978-3-030-29911-8_1

final data classification. Under such circumstance, some kinds of nonlinear learning models have also been brought forward.

During last decade, manifold learning methods have been focused on including isometric mapping (ISOMAP) [3], locally linear embedding (LLE) [4], and Laplacian eigenmaps (LE) [5], etc. It must be noted that manifold learning desires to find low dimensional embeddings of the original data via locality preserving, which can always be approached using k nearest neighbors criterion. However, in these traditional manifold learning methods, point to point (P2P) distance metric is employed for neighborhood selection. It has been validated that other distance metric such as point to feature space (P2S) will benefit to explore more discriminant features and to improve the final classification performance. Uncorrelated discriminant nearest feature line analysis (UDNFLA) uses point to feature line distance metric to seek a feature subspace with a uncorrelated constraint [6]. Nearest feature space embedding (NFSE) define a local between-class scatter and a local within-class scatter with P2S distance metric to find a subspace [7].

The methods mentioned above are looking forward to finding a low dimensional subspace which is spanned by those vectors under orthogonal constraint. Recently, the statistical uncorrelated characteristic between vectors is also favored by researchers to reduce redundancy compared to those just under orthogonal constraint [8]. A vector uncorrelation criterion about the covariance of all the original data was presented by Yu [9]. Later, the criterion was extended using feature line distance metric by Lu [6]. Moreover, we can find that these statistical uncorrelated constraints only pay attention to the global uncorrelation of the original data. However, since data geometry information can be locally explored especially in manifold learning methods, it will be vital to select that locally statistical uncorrelated discriminant information for classification. Thus locally statistical uncorrelated criterions are worth studying. Chen proposed a locally uncorrelated dimensionality reduction approach for face recognition, which is titled local uncorrelated discriminant Projection (LUDP) [10]. Later, Li presented a new locally statistical uncorrelated constraint, which is related to the intra-class scatter using the locally linear reconstruction technique [11].

In this paper, we also propose a local uncorrelated subspace learning (LUSL) method for local uncorrelated discriminant feature extraction, where P2S distance metric is also contained. Firstly, class information is taken into account, by which an intra-class nearest feature space and an inter-class nearest feature space for any point will be determined, respectively. Then, the projections of any point in its intra-class nearest feature space and its inter-class nearest feature space will be obtained, which will result in the corresponding P2S distances. Then a local intra-class scatter and a local inter-class scatter can be constructed with P2S distance metric. Similar to classical maximum margin criterion (MMC) [12], a local margin based on P2S distance metric is also reasoned. Moreover, we also model a new local uncorrelated constraint that shows close relation to the local intra-class scatter with P2S distance metric. Thus the local uncorrelated discriminant subspace will be explored by maximizing sum of all the local margins under both the orthogonality and the local uncorrelation constraints.

2 Local Uncorrelated Subspace Learning with P2S Distance Metric

In NFSE, an objective function with Fisher form is constructed to explore a subspace, where P2S distance metric is introduced. However, out-of sample problem still appears to NFSE when the scale of the original data is smaller than their dimensions. In addition, NFSE formulates a local learning model to search subspace with orthogonal constraint. If a local correlation is also appended, it will benefit to mine more discriminant features. Thus in the following, a local margin and a novel local uncorrelated criterion based on P2S distance metric will be proposed, based on which a constrained objective function can be constructed for subspace location.

2.1 Local Margin Based on P2S Distance Metric

MMC was presented to avoid out-of-sample problem by Li [12], which is deduced from traditional LDA by deriving its objective function from ratio to difference between the between-class scatter to the within-class scatter. Thus in this paper, just like the transformation from LDA to MMC, we also define a P2S distance metric based local margin from NFSE, which is stated below:

$$
\begin{aligned}
S_M &= S_B^{(p)} - S_W^{(p)} \\
&= \sum_i (X_i - f_B^{(p)}(X_i))(X_i - f_B^{(p)}(X_i))^T - \sum_j (X_i - f_W^{(p)}(X_i))(X_i - f_W^{(p)}(X_i))^T
\end{aligned}
\tag{1}
$$

where S_M denotes the defined local margin, $S_B^{(p)}$ and $S_W^{(p)}$ are P2S based between-class scatter and P2S based within-class scatter, respectively. Moreover, $f_B^{(p)}(X_i)$ and $f_B^{(p)}(X_i)$ are the projections of point to its nearest between-class feature space and point to its nearest within-class feature space. For any point, the projection to its nearest feature space can be expressed to:

$$
f^{(p)}(X_i) = \sum_{j=1}^k l_j X_j
\tag{2}
$$

$$
\sum_{j=1}^k l_j = 1
\tag{3}
$$

where $X_j(j = 1, 2, \ldots, k)$ denote points composed the nearest feature space and $l_j(j = 1, 2, \ldots, k)$ are the linear representation coefficients.

2.2 Local Uncorrelated Constraint Based on P2S Distance Metric

In order to reduce the redundancy and improve the discrimination of the extracted features, a local uncorrelated criterion will be learned from P2S distance metric based local within-class scatter. The original local uncorrelation can be stated to:

$$\int A_i^T(X_i - L(\bar{X_i}))(X_i - L(\bar{X_i}))^T A_j dX_i = 0 (i \neq j) \tag{4}$$

where $L(\bar{X_i})$ represents the local neighborhood mean of point X_i, A_i and A_j are two different uncorrelated vectors.

From Eqs. (2) and (3), we can find that the projection of any point X_i in its within-class nearest feature space is obtained by the linear combination of k within-class nearest neighbors of point X_i, moreover, the sum of these linear combination weights are one. Hence, we can take the projection of any point X_i in its within-class nearest feature space as the desired local mean. Then the local uncorrelation will change into:

$$\int A_i^T(X_i - \sum_{j=1}^{k} l_j X_j)(X_i - \sum_{j=1}^{k} l_j X_j)^T A_j dX_i = A_i^T \int (X_i - \sum_{j=1}^{k} l_j X_j)(X_i - \sum_{j=1}^{k} l_j X_j)^T dX_i A_j$$

$$= A_i^T \{ \sum_i (X_i - \sum_{j=1}^{k} l_j X_j)(X_i - \sum_{j=1}^{k} l_j X_j)^T \} A_j = A_i^T \{ \sum_i (X_i - f_W^{(p)}(X_i))(X_i - f_W^{(p)}(X_i))^T \} A_j$$

$$= A_i^T S_W^{(p)} A_j = 0$$

$$\tag{5}$$

2.3   Local Uncorrelated Subspace Learning

Based on above defined the local margin and the local uncorrelation using P2S distance metric as well as the orthogonal constraint, we can construct an objective function of the proposed LUSL, which is stated as follows:

$$\max(A^T S_B^{(p)} A - A^T S_W^{(p)} A)$$
$$s.t. \begin{cases} A^T A = I \\ A_i^T S_W^{(p)} A_j = 0, i \neq j \end{cases} \tag{6}$$

Thus LUSL wants to find a low dimensional discriminant subspace which is composed of some orthogonal vectors. Meanwhile, they should also be locally uncorrelated about the local within-class scatter each other. Above all, it is in the subspace that the P2S distance metric based local margin can be maximized, which is defined to be difference between the local between-class scatter to the local within-class scatter.

The solutions of the above objective function cannot be easily obtained. It should be solved with an iterative way. In order to obtain its solutions, we firstly get the first discriminant vector A_1, which is the eigenvector regarded to the top eigenvalue of the following objective function just with the orthogonal constraint.

$$\arg\max_{A^TA=I}(A^TS_B^{(p)}A - A^TS_W^{(p)}A) \tag{7}$$

However, for other vectors $A_i(i = 2, 3, \ldots, d)$, which are composed of other bases of the expected subspace, the property of local uncorrelation about the local with-class scatter will be seriously considered. Namely, these vectors should maximize the P2S distance metric based local margin not only under orthogonal constraint but also under local uncorrelated constraint. On the basis of the first vector A_1, we can obtain other discriminant vector A_i using Lagrange multiplier. Then we have:

$$L(A) = A^TS_B^{(p)}A - A^TS_W^{(p)}A - \lambda(A^TA - I) - \sum_{i=1}^{d}\mu_iA^TS_W^{(p)}A_i \tag{8}$$

where $A = [A_1 A_2 \ldots A_{i-1}]$.

Let $\partial L(A)/\partial A = 0$, we get

$$2S_B^{(p)}A - 2S_W^{(p)}A - 2\lambda A - \sum_{i=1}^{d}\mu_iS_W^{(p)}A_i = 0 \tag{9}$$

Multiply A_i^T to Eq. (9), due to $A_i^TS_W^{(p)}A = 0$, it is

$$2A_i^TS_B^{(p)}A - 2\lambda A_i^TA - \sum_{i=1}^{d}\mu_iA_i^TS_W^{(p)}A_i = 0 \tag{10}$$

So we obtain

$$\mu_i = 2(A_i^TS_W^{(p)}A_i)^{-1}(A_i^TS_B^{(p)}A - \lambda A_i^TA) \tag{11}$$

Then, substitute Eq. (11) into Eq. (9), we have

$$2S_B^{(p)}A - 2S_W^{(p)}A - 2\lambda A - 2S_W^{(p)}\sum_{i=1}^{d}A_i(A_i^TS_W^{(p)}A_i)^{-1}A_i^T(S_B^{(p)}A - \lambda A) = 0 \tag{12}$$

Denote $H = [A_1 A_2 \ldots A_d]$, $D = diag(A_1^TS_W^{(p)}A_1, A_2^TS_W^{(p)}A_2, \ldots, A_d^TS_W^{(p)}A_d)$, it will be

$$A_i(A_i^TS_W^{(p)}A_i)^{-1}A_i^T = HD^{-1}H^T \tag{13}$$

Continue to mark $B = I - S_W^{(p)}HD^{-1}H^T$, it is

$$\begin{aligned}
S_B^{(p)}A - S_W^{(p)}A - \lambda A - S_W^{(p)}HD^{-1}H(S_B^{(p)}A - \lambda A) \\
= (I - S_W^{(p)}HD^{-1}H)S_B^{(p)}A - S_W^{(p)}A - \lambda(I - S_W^{(p)}HD^{-1}H)A = 0
\end{aligned} \tag{14}$$

Finally, it can be deduced to the following generalized eigenvector decomposition.

$$(BS_B^{(p)} - S_W^{(p)})A = \lambda BA \tag{15}$$

Therefore, for those local uncorrelated discriminant vectors, which consist of the linear projection matrix $A = [A_1 A_2 \ldots A_i](i = 1, 2, \ldots, d - 1)$, their next vector A_{i+1} is the eigenvector related to the maximum eigenvalue of above mentioned generalized eigen-decomposition.

3 Experiments

In order to validate the performance of the proposed LUSL, some related dimensionality reduction methods such as uncorrelated discriminant locality preserving projection (UDLPP), nearest feature space embedding (NFSE), locally uncorrelated discriminant projection (LUDP) and constrained discriminant neighborhood embedding (CDNE) are introduced for comparisons. All these algorithms and the proposed LUSL have some points in common. Among these algorithms, NFSE is a local version of traditional LDA, where P2S distance metric based local between-class scatter and local within-class scatter have been used to form the local margin in LUSL. Both UDLPP and LUSL aim to find a uncorrelated discriminant subspace. However, the vectors spanned the subspace explored by UDLPP is global uncorrelated. LUDT, CDNE and LUSL contribute to extract local uncorrelated discriminant features. But either in LUDT or in CDNE, P2P distance metric is applied as measurement. In addition, the proposed LUSL can also be viewed as a new extension to NFSE with a local uncorrelated constraint. It is believed that local correlation contributes to extracting features with the minimum redundancy and P2S distance metric benefits to learn more discriminant information from the original data. Thus compared to UDLPP, LUDT, NFSE and CDNE, LUSL shows its superiority either from using P2S distance metric or from the locally uncorrelated constraint.

Moreover, Experiments are carried out on AR and FERET face data to evaluate the performance of LUSL. In the experiments, the number k of nearest neighbor points, which consist of nearest feature space, will be set individually. Let l denote training samples per class, we set $k = l - 1$ for AR and FERET. Then we perform UDLPP, LDUP, NFSE, CDNE and the proposed LUSL on these data to extract features, whose class labels will be predicted by using the nearest neighbor classifier.

3.1 Experiment on AR Face Data

Among AR face data, 120 persons' face images including 65 men and 55 women are selected, which can be divided into two sessions by taking photos on separated two weeks. Each session has 13 color images, which can also be transformed to gray images. In this experiment, AR14 (without glasses and scarf) is chosen, respectively. The example images of one person in AR face data subset are shown in Fig. 1.

In the experiment, 6, 7 and 8 images per individual are randomly selected for training subsets and the rest 8, 7 and 6 images as test, respectively. Thus k will be set to

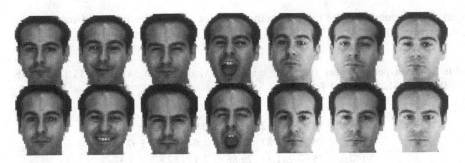

Fig. 1. Some samples from one person in AR face dataset.

5, 6 and 7, respectively. In addition, all the experiments have been repeatedly carried out 10 times, where the training samples per person are randomly selected. The statistical experimental results are shown in Table 1, from which we can find that LUSL superiors to UDLPP, LUDT, NFSE and CDNE no matter how many training samples per person are selected.

Table 1. Mean performances (%) with standard deviations using UDLPP, LUDT, NFSE, CDNE and LUSL on AR face data

Methods	6Trains	7Trains	8Trains
UDLPP	92.70 ± 1.23	94.38 ± 1.58	96.78 ± 1.54
LDUP	93.45 ± 1.92	95.75 ± 1.27	97.15 ± 0.96
NFSE	93.91 ± 4.94	97.49 ± 0.80	98.06 ± 0.52
CDNE	95.19 ± 1.82	97.12 ± 1.89	97.98 ± 1.56
LUSL	97.13 ± 2.21	98.52 ± 0.94	98.97 ± 1.21

3.2 Experiment on FERET Face Data

In this experiment, a subset is selected from the original FERET data. It contains 200 individuals, each of which has seven images. All the images in the subset are cropped to 64 × 64. Figure 2 displays one person's example images in the FERET face data set.

Fig. 2. Sample images of one person in the FERET database

In the experiment, 3, 4 and 5 individual images are chosen as trainings. Moreover, we also test the performance statistically, i.e. each experiment is repeated ten times by randomly selecting 3, 4 and 5 samples as trainings, respectively. Table 2 shows the mean performance and the corresponding variance, where the proposed method outperforms the others.

Table 2. Mean performances (%) with standard deviations using UDLPP, LUDT, NFSE, CDNE and LUSL on FERET face data

Methods	3Trains	4Trains	5Trains
UDLPP	78.64 ± 1.52	80.76 ± 0.95	82.37 ± 1.21
LDUP	79.21 ± 1.83	81.37 ± 1.94	83.28 ± 0.96
NFSE	75.67 ± 1.83	79.88 ± 2.12	82.87 ± 1.32
CDNE	80.43 ± 1.25	82.78 ± 1.56	84.54 ± 0.87
LUSL	81.56 ± 1.13	83.75 ± 0.78	86.12 ± 0.56

4 Conclusion

This paper presents a supervised manifold learning method named local uncorrelated subspace learning (LUSL) for discriminant feature extraction from the following two aspects. Firstly, compared to P2P distance metric used in most of dimensionality reduction methods, P2S distance metric shows more contribution to mine discriminant features. Thus in the proposed LUSL, P2S distance metric is introduced to learn a local margin which is defined to be difference between the local between-class scatter to the local within-class scatter. Moreover the P2S distance metric based local margin can be used to characterize the separability of between-class data. Secondly, local uncorrelation benefits to reduce the redundancy in the features. Hence combining to the property of locality learning in manifold, a local uncorrelation criterion is also reasoned, which can be deduced to locally uncorrelated about the local within-class scatter based on P2S distance metric. Then we can formulate an objective function with orthogonal and local uncorrelated constraints, by which a local uncorrelated subspace will be explored with the maximum margin. By making comparison to some related methods as UDLPP, LUDT, NFSE and CDNE, experimental results on CMU PIE, AR and FERET display the performance of the proposed LUSL.

Acknowledgments. This work was partly supported by the grants of National Natural Science Foundation of China (61572381, 61273303 & 61375017) and Fujian Provincial Key Laboratory of Data Intensive Computing (BD201805).

References

1. Jolliffe, I.T.: Principal component analysis. Springer Series in Statistics, 2nd edn, p. 488. Springer, New York (2002). https://doi.org/10.1007/b98835
2. Kim, T.K., Stenger, B., Kittler, J., Cipolla, R.: Incremental linear discriminant analysis using sufficient spanning sets and its applications. Int. J. Comput. Vision **91**(2), 216–232 (2011)
3. Tenenbaum, J.B., de Silva, V., Langford, J.C.: A global geometric framework for nonlinear dimensionality reduction. Science **290**, 2319–2323 (2000)

4. Roweis, S.T., Saul, L.K.: Nonlinear dimensionality reduction by locally linear embedding. Science **290**, 2323–2326 (2000)
5. Belkin, M., Niyogi, P.: Laplacian eigenmaps for dimensionality reduction and data representation. Neural Comput. **15**(6), 1373–1396 (2003)
6. Lu, J., Tan, Y.P.: Uncorrelated discriminant nearest feature line analysis for face recognition. IEEE Signal Process. Lett. **17**(2), 185–188 (2010)
7. Chen, Y.N., Han, C.C., Wang, C.T., Fan, K.C.: Face recognition using nearest feature space embedding. IEEE Trans. Pattern Anal. Mach. Intell. **33**(6), 1073–1086 (2011)
8. Jin, Z., Yang, J.Y., Tang, Z.M., Hu, Z.S.: A theorem on the uncorrelated optimal discriminant vectors. Pattern Recogn. **34**(10), 2041–2047 (2001)
9. Yu, X., Wang, X.: Uncorrelated discriminant locality preserving projections. IEEE Signal Process. Lett. **15**, 361–364 (2008)
10. Chen, Y., Zheng, W.S., Xu, X.H., Lai, J.H.: Discriminant subspace learning constrained by locally statistical uncorrelation for face recognition. Neural Netw. **42**(1), 28–43 (2013)
11. Li, B., Lei, L., Zhang, X.P.: Constrained discriminant neighborhood embedding for high dimensional data feature extraction. Neurocomputing **173**(1), 137–144 (2016)
12. Li, H., Jiang, T., Zhang, K.: Efficient and robust feature extraction by maximum margin criterion. IEEE Trans. Neural Networks **17**(1), 157–165 (2006)

DLENSO: A Deep Learning ENSO Forecasting Model

Dandan He[1,2], Pengfei Lin[3(✉)], Hailong Liu[3], Lei Ding[1,2],
and Jinrong Jiang[1(✉)]

[1] Computer Network Information Center,
Chinese Academy of Sciences, Beijing, China
hedandan_ucas@163.com, dinglei2017@cnic.cn,
jjr@sccas.cn
[2] University of Chinese Academy of Sciences, Beijing, China
[3] State Key Laboratory of Numerical Modeling for Atmospheric Sciences
and Geophysical Fluid Dynamics, Institute of Atmospheric Physics,
Chinese Academy of Sciences, Beijing, China
{linpf,lhl}@mail.iap.ac.cn

Abstract. El Niño-Southern Oscillation (ENSO) phenomenon is the strongest
signal in the interannual time scale of global climate, and has a significant
impact on the global short-term climate (temperature, precipitation, etc.). Every
year, researchers around the world would predict ENSO for the coming year,
and have been studied new forecasting methods all the time, including
numerical methods, statistical methods and deep learning methods. The existing
deep learning methods are only for the ENSO index or single-point meteorological elements forecasting and rarely involve forecasting of specific regions. In
this paper, we formulate a deep learning ENSO forecasting model (DLENSO) to
predict ENSO through predicting Sea Surface Temperature (SST) in the tropical
Pacific region directly. DLENSO is a sequence to sequence model whose
encoder and decoder are both multilayered Convolutional Long Short-Term
Memory (ConvLSTM), the input and prediction target of DLENSO are both
spatiotemporal sequences. We explore the optimal setting of this model by
experiments and report the accuracy on Niño3.4 region to confirm the effectiveness of the proposed method. Moreover, it can be concluded that DLENSO
is superior to the LSTM model and deterministic forecast model, and almost
equivalent to the ensemble-mean forecast model in the medium and long-term
(4–12 months ahead) forecast. This model will pave a new way of predicting
ENSO using deep learning technology.

Keywords: ENSO · Sea surface temperature · Deep learning ·
Sequence to sequence

1 Introduction

Short-term climate changes include the monthly scale, seasonal scale and interannual
scale, which all have been spotlighted for their significant impacts on people's production and life. Among them, ENSO is particularly concerned as an interannual

© Springer Nature Switzerland AG 2019
A. C. Nayak and A. Sharma (Eds.): PRICAI 2019, LNAI 11671, pp. 12–23, 2019.
https://doi.org/10.1007/978-3-030-29911-8_2

climate change. El Niño is a phenomenon of periodic increase of SST, and the Southern oscillation describes a bimodal variation in sea level barometric pressure between the western and eastern Pacific. In 1969, Bjerknes [1] claimed that El Niño and Southern Oscillation were two different manifestations of the same physical phenomena in nature, which were embodied in the ocean as an El Niño phenomenon and reflected in the atmosphere as a Southern Oscillation phenomenon.

Since ENSO was a global ocean-atmosphere interaction, it had a huge impact on crop yields, temperature and rainfall [2] on the earth. The surface air temperature over the Chinese mainland reached record highs and the precipitation was significantly reduced in the summer of 2015 owing to the strong impact of ENSO [3]. Moreover, corn and wheat yields were obviously affected by ENSO-induced changes in maximum temperature, solar radiation, and rainfall in the southeastern United States of America, East and West Africa, Mexico and Indonesia [4].

Since ENSO has a tremendous impact on the global climate, scientists in various countries have been committed to the prediction research of ENSO since the 1980s. Since the decorrelation time scale of SST variability is about one year over much of the tropical Pacific Ocean, where ENSO events dominate the variability [5], and occurrence of the ENSO phenomenon is reflected by the anomaly of SST, predicting the ENSO phenomenon is equivalent to predict the sea surface temperature anomaly (SSTA). At present, ENSO forecast models mainly include statistical forecast models and numerical forecast models such as Intermediate Coupled Model (ICM), Hybrid Coupled Model (HCM) and Coupled General Circulation Model (CGCM) [6], and the predictions have reached a reliable forecast of 6–12 months. In addition, Niño3.4 is the most common index used to measure ENSO phenomenon in all indexes, and Niño3.4 index is the average SSTA in the region bounded by 5°N to 5°S, from 170°W to 120°W.

Because of the uncertainty of the initial conditions, in reality, most numerical forecast models are having difficulty with simulating the average annual variation of SST, so they cannot reach the perfect level [7]. In addition, due to the great variability and diversity of the temporal and spatial evolution of ENSO, there are still great uncertainties in predicting ENSO with traditional methods [8]. In recent years, with the rise of artificial intelligence (AI), machine learning, and deep learning have once again come into people's sight. Some scholars began to use machine learning or deep learning techniques to predict meteorological elements (wind speed, temperature, etc.) or ENSO phenomenal, and obtained ideal results [9].

Silvestre and William [9] proposed two kinds of nonlinear regression models, Bayesian neural network (BNN) and support vector regression (SVR), to predict the tropical Pacific SST anomalies. More recently, Zhang and Wang [10] formulated the SST prediction problem as a time series regression problem, and adopted Long Short-Term Memory (LSTM), the special kind of recurrent neural network (RNN), as the main layers of network architecture. As for ENSO forecasting, Feng [11] proposed a toolbox called "ClimateLearn", which was used to predict the appearance of El Niño and Niño3.4 index by combining some machine learning methods. Peter [12] combined a classical Autoregressive Integrated Moving Average technique with Artificial Neural Network to predict ENSO index.

However, existing machine learning models for SST prediction rarely can predict a regional SST directly. To our knowledge, these models are based on time series of a certain latitude and longitude point to perform prediction. They make the same prediction on all points on a certain grid area, thereby obtain the SST of the specific region. Considering that temperature is an element with both temporal and spatial information, this single-point prediction method obviously ignores the spatial information of temperature, which may destroy the continuity of the temperature distribution.

In 2016, ensemble-mean forecast model is developed for modeling the model errors of an ICM for ENSO prediction [13]. Ensemble model showed better performance than deterministic ICM in ENSO forecasting. To demonstrate the effectiveness and efficiency of our work, our model will be compared with LSTM neural networks, ensemble-mean forecast model and deterministic forecast model in predicting accuracy. Finally, we will use our trained model to make an actual ENSO forecast and compare the forecast results with the existing statistical forecast models and numerical forecast models in the word.

In this paper, two contributions are made: (1) Sequence to Sequence model with ConvLSTM layers are properly designed to predict ENSO through regional SST. The regional SST will preserve the continuity of temperature distribution and the ConvLSTMs can handle the spatiotemporal data. (2) We focus on the Niño3.4 regional SSTA, and a get more accurate prediction than deterministic forecast model and ensemble-mean forecast model.

2 Methodology

2.1 Problem Formulation

The Pacific region where the ENSO phenomenon occurs is generally divided into grid regions by latitude and longitude. Every grid has values of meteorological elements (such as SST, surface wind speed, flow velocity, etc.) at every time step, and the horizontal distribution of these elements is two-dimensional (2D). Hence, the SST for a period is three-dimensional (3D) with the time dimension.

We build a neural network model named DLENSO to solve the regression problem of predicting the 3D SST according to the historic meteorological elements. Simultaneously, given SST values and other closely related meteorological elements of h months, the prediction problem can be abstracted to get the SST values for $h + 1$ to $h + t$ months, here, the t represents the lead months.

2.2 Convolutional Long Short-Term Memory (ConvLSTM)

ConvLSTM is the LSTM that combined with convolution operation. In 2015, ConvLSTM was put forward by Shi and Chen et al. [14] to predict precipitation in a local region over a period, and input and output were both 3D tensors.

LSTM is a special form of RNN, which was proposed by Hochreiter [15]. Then, after improved and promoted by Alex Graves [16], they performed remarkably in language translation, robot control, document summarization, speech recognition, etc. The LSTM cell was designed specially with three gates to solve the long-term dependence problems.

The ConvLSTM was designed for solving the 3D prediction problem, and the cell could receive matrix, or even higher dimension input at each time step. The crucial improvement was the Hadamard product between the weight and input was replaced by convolution operation as Eq. (1), the ○ denoted the Hadamard product and the * denoted convolution operator.

$$f_t = \sigma\left(W_{xf} * X_t + W_{hf} * H_{t-1} + b_f\right)$$
$$i_t = \sigma(W_{xi} * X_t + W_{hi} * H_{t-1} + b_i)$$
$$\tilde{C}_t = tanh(W_{xc} * X_t + W_{hc} * H_{t-1} + b_c) \tag{1}$$
$$C_t = i_t \circ \tilde{C}_t + f_t \circ C_{t-1}$$
$$O_t = \sigma(W_{xO} * X_t + W_{hO} * H_{t-1} + b_O)$$
$$h_t = o_t \circ tanh(C_t)$$

3 The Model

Since the performance of sequence to sequence model is effective and impressive in sequence prediction problem, and the ConvLSTM layers are designed to handle 3D data, we combined these two to predict regional SST, that is: replace the RNN-related units in the traditional sequence to sequence model with ConvLSTM, Fig. 1 shows our model architecture I. Where blue rectangle is the input data, and parameter before @ is the kernel number, ? represents the kernel number will change with number of input variables, parameter behind @ is the kernel size, the purpose of using CNN layer is to make the output variable only SSTA. Furthermore, total input length is 12, t_1–t_{11} are for Encoder input, and t_{12} is for the initial input of the Decoder. The Decoder output length is 12.

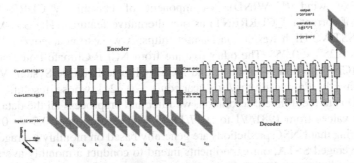

Fig. 1. Architecture I: chronological input order at the encoder side, the encoder and decoder are both two layers of ConvLSTM.

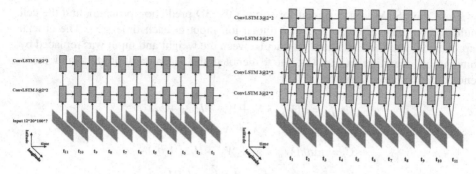

Fig. 2. Architecture II: reverse input order at the encoder side.

Fig. 3. Architecture III: bidirectional ConvLSTM at the encoder side.

In addition, Sutskever et al. [17, 18] found that putting the input sequence into the encoder in reverse order could achieve better results than putting in chronological order in the task of machine translation. And bidirectional LSTM was also well represented in Natural Language Processing (NLP) tasks because it considered context information at the same time. Therefore, this paper also considered the use of reverse input order and bidirectional ConvLSTM at the encoder side of the sequence to sequence model whose architecture are shown in Figs. 2 and 3.

4 Experiments

We run our experiments with single NVIDIA Tesla P100 GPU, and our model is implemented using Python 3.5 with TensorFlow.

4.1 Dataset

We use SSTA, sea surface pressure (P_SURF), v-component of wind (V_WIND), u-component of wind (U_WIND), v-component of current (V_CURRENT), u-component of current (U_CURRENT) as our alternative features. The SSTA is from NOAA OI SST V2 High Resolution Dataset (https://www.esrl.noaa.gov/) [19] whose resolution is $0.25° \times 0.25°$. The other five are from NCEP Climate Forecast System Reanalysis (CFSR) 6-hourly Products and NCEP Climate Forecast System Version 2 (CFSv2) 6-hourly Products(https://rda.ucar.edu/) [20, 21] whose resolution are $0.5° \times 0.5°$. Due to the different resolution, we filter and preprocess all the data, and get 13235 daily values from 1981/9/1 to 2017/11/25 with resolution of $0.5° \times 0.5°$.

Considering that ENSO predictions are generally based on monthly averaged SSTA or weekly averaged SSTA, our experiments intend to conduct a monthly average SST forecast for predicting the ENSO events. We use the 30-day sliding window method to amplify the dataset mentioned above and get 13207 monthly datasets from 1981 to 2017 over the Niño3.4 region (20×100). Then the dataset is divided into training set and test set in a ratio of 8:2.

4.2 Evaluating Metrics

Root Mean Square Error (RMSE) and Correlation (Corr) coefficient were used to test the prediction performance of our experiments.

RMSE and Corr respectively measures the difference and correlation between the predicted value (the output of the model) and the observed value. The formula for calculating the RMSE and Corr are shown in Eqs. (2) and (3), where y_{obs} is the observed value and y_{pred} is the predicted value.

$$RMSE = \sqrt{\frac{\sum_{i=1}^{n}(y_{obs,i} - y_{pred,i})^2}{n}} \tag{2}$$

$$Corr = \frac{\frac{1}{n}\sum_{i=1}^{n}(y_{obs,i} - \overline{y_{obs,i}})(y_{pred,i} - \overline{y_{pred,i}})}{\sqrt{\frac{1}{n}\sum_{i=1}^{n}(y_{obs,i} - \overline{y_{obs,i}})^2}\sqrt{\frac{1}{n}\sum_{i=1}^{n}(y_{pred,i} - \overline{y_{pred,i}})^2}} \tag{3}$$

4.3 Determination of Architecture

Contrast experiments are adopted to select the best architecture from architecture {I, II, III} for our prediction task. The comparison results of the three kinds of models on the training set and the test set are shown in Table 1.

It can be seen that the performances of these three models on the training set are all much better than test set. This phenomenon should be caused by the difference between the training phase and the testing phase at the decoder side.

From the perspective of model comparison, the performance of these three models on the training set are basically indistinguishable. While on the test set, in the mid-term and long-term predictions the input with the chronological order obviously generates better result than the other two, and its advantage is more obvious with the increase of the lead months. From a meteorological point of view, ENSO is an annual cycle of event, which will be affected by the chronological meteorological elements, so more effective information will be obtained. Hence, the model with encoder chronological sequence input is the most suitable, so DLENSO model is designed as architecture I.

To train the neural network, some critical parameters of a neural network model need to be set to initial values in advance, such as optimizer, learning rate and batch size. The batch optimization method can make the gradient descend faster to accelerate the convergence of the network. We set Adadelta as the initial optimizer, and batch size as 16. The size of convolution kernels of ConvLSTM layers are set as 2×2.

Table 1. Comparison of metrics of different architectures in different lead months

Architecture	Metrics	Lead months				
		1	3	6	9	12
I_train	RMSE	**0.234**	**0.239**	**0.241**	**0.244**	**0.310**
	Corr	**0.963**	0.937	**0.958**	**0.945**	**0.903**
II_train	RMSE	0.234	0.251	0.247	0.253	0.315
	Corr	0.962	**0.940**	0.925	0.914	0.900
III_train	RMSE	0.235	0.256	0.302	0.311	0.314
	Corr	0.963	0.942	0.944	0.904	0.897
I_test	RMSE	0.307	**0.484**	**0.621**	**0.607**	**0.711**
	Corr	**0.955**	**0.874**	**0.730**	**0.726**	**0.608**
II_test	RMSE	**0.305**	0.484	0.692	0.709	0.791
	Corr	0.953	0.781	0.726	0.615	0.481
III_test	RMSE	0.309	0.485	0.687	0.710	0.763
	Corr	0.902	0.796	0.727	0.611	0.509

4.4 Parameters Contrast

Input Variables. The variability of SST in the tropical Pacific Ocean is mainly caused by ENSO events [7], that is to say, SST is the best variable to judge the occurrence of ENSO. We calculate the correlation coefficient between the other five variables and SSTA to determine the inputs of the model, shown in Table 2. And it can be seen that the P_SURF and U_WIND are more related to SSTA. Thus, contrast experiments with three different inputs are conducted, the first one has only one input variable (SSTA), the second one has three input variables (SSTA, P_SURF, U_WIND), the last one has all six variables. The result is shown in Table 3.

From Tables 2 and 3, we can get the following information: the performances of the model with different inputs are similar in the short-term prediction (lead month is less than 3). With the increase of lead month, the model with all input variables occupies some advantages in the medium-term prediction (lead months is from 3 to 6). However, when lead month continues to increase, the advantages of the model using three variables are becoming more and more obvious and gradually achieve the best performance. In conclusion, the input of three variables generates the most remarkable performance.

Table 2. Correlation coefficient between variables and SSTA

Variables	Correlation coefficient
P_SURF	−0.457
U_WIND	0.577
U_CURRENT	−0.027
V_WIND	−0.055
V_CURRENT	−0.101

Table 3. Comparison of metrics of different variables in different lead months

Variables	Metrics	Lead months				
		1	3	6	9	12
one-var	RMSE	0.354	0.505	0.613	0.595	0.672
	Corr	0.923	0.832	0.741	0.701	0.624
three-vars	RMSE	**0.312**	0.501	0.544	**0.550**	**0.652**
	Corr	**0.923**	0.852	**0.813**	**0.785**	**0.671**
six-vars	RMSE	0.346	**0.452**	**0.461**	0.566	0.714
	Corr	0.921	**0.856**	0.774	0.703	0.618

Decay Function. During training, the decoder of the sequence to sequence model has current state and previous token, while at inference, the unknown previous token is replaced by a token generated by the model itself. To solve this problem, we use scheduled sampling approach [22] to gradually reduce the previous token of the decoder in the training phase, so as to smooth the transition to the inference phase. Three kinds decay functions (linear, exponential and inverse sigmoid decay functions) and no decay function are examined here by comparing the RMSE and Corr, which is shown in Table 4. Obviously, the exponential decay function is the best choice for our model, the reason may be the exponential decay function can reduce the probability of choosing the previous token rapidly, making the letter part of the training phase very similar to the inference phase.

Table 4. Comparison of metrics of different decay functions in different lead months

Decay function	Metrics	Lead months				
		1	3	6	9	12
no_sampling	RMSE	0.814	0.820	0.841	0.924	1.163
	Corr	0.763	0.586	0.427	0.209	0.188
exp_sampling	RMSE	**0.342**	**0.533**	**0.617**	**0.605**	**0.771**
	Corr	**0.975**	**0.902**	**0.809**	**0.811**	**0.625**
linear_sampling	RMSE	0.348	0.534	0.622	0.724	0.719
	Corr	0.975	0.806	0.798	0.621	0.581
inverse_sigmoid_ sampling	RMSE	0.349	0.542	0.620	0.715	0.782
	Corr	0.974	0.881	0.795	0.606	0.567

Optimizer and Learning Rate. Considering that different optimizers and learning rates interact with each other, we conduct comparison experiments in two steps. First, the corresponding optimal learning rate of different optimizers are found. Then, the RMSE and correlation coefficients of the different optimizers at optimal learning rates are compared.

Figure 4 shows the RMSE and correlation coefficients of different optimizers at their optimal learning rates. Four optimizers are experimented here: Adam, Stochastic Gradient Descent (SGD), Adadelta, and Adagrad, while different optimizers perform slightly differently with different learning rates. On the whole, it is better to learn with a learning rate of 0.05. The reason that the model performs poorly when the learning rate is large, is that the excessive learning rate causes the gradient to fall, always near the minimum value of the function, and thus cannot convergence to a smaller value. As for the Adadelta and Adagrad optimizers, it is obvious that the optimal learning rates are 1 and 0.1 respectively.

Table 5 shows experimental results of the RMSE and correlation coefficients of the four optimizers at their respective optimal learning rates. What we can get that the Adam optimizer is the best, and its optimal learning rate is 0.02.

Table 5. Comparison of metrics of different optimizers at respective optimal learning rate in different lead months

Optimizer	Metrics	Lead months				
		1	3	6	9	12
Adam-0.02	RMSE	0.356	0.470	**0.521**	**0.591**	**0.603**
	Corr	**0.985**	**0.872**	**0.765**	**0.680**	**0.625**
SGD-0.05	RMSE	0.396	0.491	0.627	0.601	0.611
	Corr	0.971	0.844	0.698	0.649	0.624
Adadelta-1	RMSE	0.318	**0.463**	0.624	0.622	0.720
	Corr	0.909	0.842	0.743	0.576	0.553
Adagrad-0.1	RMSE	**0.312**	0.474	0.612	0.594	0.726
	Corr	0.913	0.840	0.752	0.643	0.517

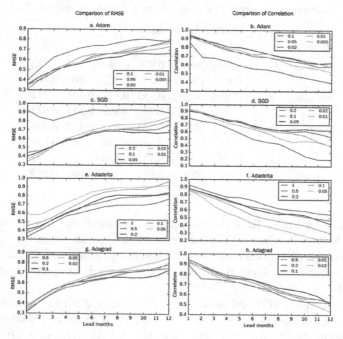

Fig. 4. The RMSEs and Corrs of different optimizers and different learning rates.

5 Result and Conclusion

5.1 Result

We use 3D dataset of Niño3.4 region to do these experiments and get the region SSTA prediction. Then we compare DLENSO model to the traditional numerical models, such as ensemble forecast models and deterministic forecast models. Our model parameters are as following, Optimizer and learning rate are set to Adam optimizer and 0.02, no L2 loss and use exponential decay function.

Figure 5 displays the horizontal distributions of the anomaly RMSE between the observed and predicted SST anomalies at 1 to 12 months of lead time. The RMSE in the central equatorial Pacific is below 0.6 when the lead time is less than 6-month, and in the eastern equatorial Pacific, the RMSE is stable at 1.1 for all the lead times. According to the whole figure, the predicting skill does not drop much in the eastern equatorial Pacific and has only a slight decrease in the central equatorial Pacific with the increasing of lead time. As a whole, the RMSE of eastern region is higher than other regions. Since our DLENSO model is an end-to-end learning approach, it is much more accurate to capture the information that comes out of the data.

The Niño3.4 index of comparison as shown in Fig. 6. The ensemble-mean model and deterministic model are initialized from the same initial conditions, and the LSTM model has the same hyper-parameters as DLENSO. The RMSE of LSTM model is higher than other three models at all lead months, and when the lead months is equal to 7, the result of DLENSO model is more accurate than that of deterministic forecast model and when the lead months is larger than 8, the result of our model is better than that of ensemble-mean forecast model. What's more, the trend of correlation curve

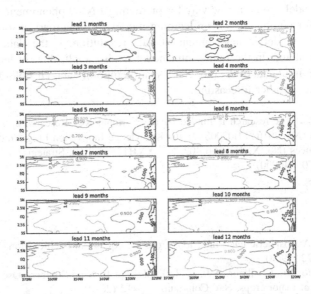

Fig. 5. Horizontal distributions of the anomaly RMSE between the observed and predicted SST anomalies at 1, 2, 3 to 12 months of lead time. The result was obtained by the prediction of the training set which during 1981–2017.

between LSTM model and DLENSO is the same, and the correlation coefficient of DLENSO is higher than deterministic forecast model when the lead months is larger than 4. By analysis, the poor boundary (upper boundary in the RMSE and lower boundary of the correlation coefficient) should be related to the "Spring Predictability Barrier (SPB)" phenomenon [22].

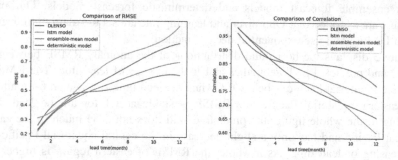

Fig. 6. The comparison of RMSEs and Corrs of different models.

5.2 Conclusion

In this paper, a ConvLSTM based sequence to sequence model name DLENSO is formulated to predict ENSO event through predicting regional SST of Niño3.4. We conduct experiments to set the suitable parameters and the input variables. This is the first time to predict regional SST using deep learning methods as we know, and the prediction accuracy is higher than the deterministic forecast model in the medium and long-term forecasts and almost equivalent to the ensemble-mean forecast model.

DLENSO model can be a new way for predicting ENSO phenomenon, and builds the foundation for combining a deep learning model and a numerical forecast model. Furthermore, the model is independent of data resolution, if the data with higher resolution are available in the future, our model is also applicable. In terms of scalability, due to the input data of the model are spatiotemporal data, DLENSO can be used in intelligent grid weather forecasting.

Acknowledgments. The research is funded by the National Key Research and Development Program of China (No. 2016YFB0200800), the Knowledge Innovation Program of the Chinese Academy of Sciences (No. XXH13506-402, No. XXH13506-302), Strategic Priority Research Programme (XDC01040000).

References

1. Bjerknes, J.: Atmospheric teleconnections from the equatorial Pacific. Mon. Weather Rev. **97**(3), 163–172 (1968)
2. Iizumi, T., Luo, J.J., Challinor, A.J., et al.: Impacts of El Niño Southern Oscillation on the global yields of major crops. Nat. Commun. **5**, 3712 (2014)
3. Shuai, J., Zhao, Z., Sun, D.Z., et al.: ENSO, climate variability and crop yields in China. Clim. Res. **58**(2), 133–148 (2013)

4. Zhai, P., Yu, R., Guo, Y., et al.: The strong El Niño of 2015/16 and its dominant impacts on global and China's climate. Meteorol. Res. **30**, 283 (2016)
5. Goddard, L., Mason, S.J., Zebiak, S.E., Ropelewski, C.F., Basher, R., Cane, M.A.: Current approaches to seasonal to interannual climate predictions. Int. J. Climatol. **12**(9), 1111–1152 (2001)
6. Yuzhu, W., Jinrong, J., et al.: A scalable parallel algorithm for atmospheric general circulation models on a multi-core cluster. Future Gener. Comput. Syst. **72**, 1–10 (2017)
7. Jin, E.K., Kinter, J.L., Wang, B., et al.: Current status of ENSO prediction skill in coupled ocean-atmosphere models. Clim. Dyn. **31**(6), 647–664 (2008)
8. Jiang, J., Wang, T., Chi, X., et al.: SC-ESAP: a parallel application platform for earth system model. Procedia Comput. Sci. **80**, 1612–1623 (2016)
9. Aguilarmartinez, S., Hsieh, W.W.: Forecasts of tropical Pacific sea surface temperatures by neural networks and support vector regression. Int. J. Oceanogr. **2009**, 1687–9406 (2009)
10. Zhang, Q., Wang, H., Dong, J., et al.: Prediction of sea surface temperature using long short-term memory. IEEE Geosci. Remote Sens. Lett. **14**, 1745–1749 (2017)
11. Feng, Q.Y., Vasile, R., Segond, M., et al.: ClimateLearn: a machine-learning approach for climate prediction using network measures. Geosci. Model Dev. Discuss. 1–18 (2016)
12. Nooteboom, P.D.: Using network theory and machine learning to predict El Niño. Earth Syst. Dyn. **9**, 969–983 (2017)
13. Zheng, F., Zhu, J., et al.: Improved ensemble-mean forecasting of ENSO events by a zero-mean stochastic error model of an intermediate coupled model. Clim. Dyn. **47**(12), 3901–3915 (2016)
14. Shi, X., Chen, Z., Wang, H., et al.: Convolutional LSTM network: a machine learning approach for precipitation nowcasting, vol. 9199, pp. 802–810 (2015)
15. Hochreiter, S., Schmidhuber, J.: Long Short-term memory. Neural Comput. **9**(8), 1735–1780 (1997)
16. Graves, A.: Supervised sequence labelling. In: Kawakami, K. (ed.) Supervised Sequence Labelling with Recurrent Neural Networks. Studies in Computational Intelligence, vol. 385, pp. 1735–1780. Springer, Heidelberg (2012). https://doi.org/10.1007/978-3-642-24797-2_2
17. Sutskever, I., Vinyals, O., Le, Q.V.: Sequence to sequence learning with neural networks (2014)
18. Plank, B., Søgaard, A., Goldberg, Y.: Multilingual part-of-speech tagging with bidirectional long short-term memory models and auxiliary loss (2014)
19. NOAA ESRL: NOAA OI SST V2 high resolution dataset. https://www.esrl.noaa.gov/psd/data/gridded/data.noaa.oisst.v2.highres.html
20. Saha, S., et al.: NCEP climate forecast system reanalysis (CFSR) 6-hourly products, January 1979 to December 2010. Research Data Archive at the National Center for Atmospheric Research, Computational and Information Systems Laboratory, Boulder, CO (2010)
21. Bengio, S., Vinyals, O., Jaitly, N., et al.: Scheduled sampling for sequence prediction with recurrent neural networks. In: Proceedings of the International Conference on Neural Information Processing Systems (2015)
22. Luo, J.J., Masson, S., Behera, S.K., et al.: Extended ENSO predictions using a fully coupled ocean-atmosphere model. J. Clim. **21**(1), 84–93 (2008)

Transfer Learning for Financial Time Series Forecasting

Qi-Qiao He[1], Patrick Cheong-Iao Pang[2], and Yain-Whar Si[1(✉)]

[1] Department of Computer and Information Science,
University of Macau, Taipa, Macau
`fstasp@umac.mo`
[2] School of Computing and Information Systems,
The University of Melbourne, Parkville, Australia

Abstract. Time-series are widely used for representing non-stationary data such as weather information, health related data, economic and stock market indexes. Many statistical methods and traditional machine learning techniques are commonly used for forecasting time series. With the development of deep learning in artificial intelligence, many researchers have adopted new models from artificial neural networks for forecasting time series. However, poor performance of applying deep learning models in short time series hinders the accuracy in time series forecasting. In this paper, we propose a novel approach to alleviate this problem based on transfer learning. Existing work on transfer learning uses extracted features from a source dataset for prediction task in a target dataset. In this paper, we propose a new training strategy for time-series transfer learning with two source datasets that outperform existing approaches. The effectiveness of our approach is evaluated on financial time series extracted from stock markets. Experiment results show that transfer learning based on 2 data sets is superior than other base-line methods.

Keywords: Transfer learning · Financial time series · Forecasting · Artificial neural networks

1 Introduction

Time-series forecasting is one of the challenging tasks in data analytics and artificial intelligence area. Time-series prediction plays a crucial role in plethora of applications such as forecasting sales, marketing, finance, and production planning etc. Traditional statistical methods in time-series forecasting include autoregressive integrated moving average (ARIMA) [16] for non-stationary data, simple exponential smoothing (SES) [9] for predicting time-series, and Holt and Damped exponential smoothing [10]. Besides, Conventional machine learning techniques have been used in time series forecasting, such as support vector regression (SVR) [19] and various hybrid methods [12]. However, time-series

© Springer Nature Switzerland AG 2019
A. C. Nayak and A. Sharma (Eds.): PRICAI 2019, LNAI 11671, pp. 24–36, 2019.
https://doi.org/10.1007/978-3-030-29911-8_3

forecasting is a challenging task when limited data is available for training the machine learning models.

Recently, the success of deep learning models in image and Natural Language Processing (NLP) applications becomes a driving force behind the adoption of deep learning model for time-series forecasting. The information obtained during the learning processes is used for interpretation of data such as text, images and sound. The learning process also allows the computer to automatically extract the pattern features. It also integrates the feature learning into the process of modeling and therefore reduces the incompleteness caused by artificial design features. Three techniques, namely, a large number of hidden units, better learning algorithms, and parameter initialization techniques, have contributed to the success of deep learning approach [6]. However, when the dataset does not have sufficient data, deep learning approach could result poor forecasting performance [26].

In order to alleviate insufficient data problem, transfer learning is commonly used in majority of deep learning model [29]. Transfer learning is shown to be effective in computer vision [3] and NLP [23]. Despite its promising results in computer vision and related applications, transfer learning has been rarely used in deep learning models for time series data. Recently, Fawaz et al. [8] investigate how to transfer deep convolutional neural networks (CNNs) for Time Series Classification (TSC) tasks. Ye et al. [27] propose a novel transfer learning framework for time series forecasting. Most of these studies were designed to transfer features from a source dataset to a target dataset. However, in certain cases it may be necessary for the model to learn features or patterns from different source datasets when the target dataset is insufficient. This research problem has been widely considered in developing multilingual speech technologies. Most of these works focus on transferring features between languages because of the limited resources available for the target language [15]. In the time series forecasting, Hu et al. [14] combine wind speed information from multi-sources to build a deep neural network (DNN). In their model, the hidden layers are shared across many farms while the output layers are designed to be farm dependent. In their approach, the shared hidden layers can be considered as a universal feature transformation.

Motivated by these recent findings, in this paper, we investigate whether or not transfer learning can be effectively used for financial time series forecasting. Specifically, we evaluate the effectiveness of transfer learning with more than one source dataset for stock price prediction. In a more detailed case study, we also evaluate the effect of choosing different source datasets based on a similarity measure. Besides, a new training strategy for transfer learning with two source datasets is also proposed in this paper. To the best of authors' knowledge, our work makes the first attempt to investigate transfer learning for financial time series forecasting problem. Our contributions are two-fold:

- We propose a new training strategy for transfer learning with two source datasets.

– We propose a similarity based approach for selecting source datasets for training the deep learning models with transfer learning for financial time series forecasting.

The rest of the paper is structured as follows. In Sect. 2, we describe some background knowledge and review existing work on transfer learning for time series forecasting. In Sect. 3, we describe our proposed training strategy used in this paper. In Sect. 4, we present our experiment setups and discuses the result. Finally, in Sect. 5, we conclude the paper with future work.

2   Background and Related Work

2.1   Financial Time Series Forecasting

Financial time series forecasting is a challenging task due to the noise and volatile features of the underlying market situations [24]. Several technical indicators used for time-series prediction include auto-regression (AR), moving-average(MA), ARIMA, Holt-Winters Exponential Smoothing (HWES) and so on. However, with the development of deep learning models, DNN, recurrent neural network (RNN) and CNN have been extensively researched in time series forecasting area. Deep learning can successfully learn complex real-world data by extracting robust features that capture most useful information [13]. Ding et al. [7] combine the neural tensor network and deep CNN to predict the short–term and long–term influences of events on stock price movements. Yoshihara et al. [28] also adopted deep belief networks in financial market forcasting. However, Makridakis et al. [18] conclude that when the available data is insufficient for training, the performance of deep learning can be poorer than simple statistical methods.

2.2   Transfer Learning in Time Series Forecasting

Transfer learning aims to extract knowledge from one or more source tasks and applies the knowledge to a target task [20]. The study of Transfer learning is motivated by the fact that people can intelligently apply knowledge learned previously to solve new problems faster or with better solutions. Karl et al. [25] have defined the transfer learning as follows: *"Transfer learning for deep neural networks, is the process of first training a base network on a source dataset and task, and then transfer the learned features (the network's weights) to a second network to be trained on a target dataset and task"*. Transfer learning has been used in computer version and nature language processing. These cases include application of transfer learning in visual application by Amaral et al. [3] and initialization of the language model's weights with pre-trained weights by Ramachandran et al. [21]. Recently, transfer learning was also adopted for time series analysis. For example, Ye et al. [27] propose a novel transfer learning framework for time series forecasting. To calculate the similarity as the guideline of selecting source datasets, Fawaz et al. proposed a dynamic time warping (DTW) based algorithm in [8].

In [14], Hu et al. proposed an approach for the prediction of the wind speed for the new farm by transferring information from several old farms. In [14], the authors use the time series data of several old farms to pre-train a two-layers DNN model. The parameters of the model are then shared with all wind farms. The model can be considered as a universal feature transformation. In contrast to the approach proposed by Hu et al. [14], in our training strategy, a source dataset is used for training the first layer of the DNN only and the second layer is trained by using both source datasets. In addition, the parameters of these layers are not shared among the layers. Therefore, the model from our strategy not only have the universal features but also the specific features. In addition, Hu et al. [14] did not compare the performance of the model based on one source dataset with model which is built from multi-source datasets.

3   Method

In this paper, we aim to answer several questions related to transfer learning in time series prediction:

- Is transferring features from two source datasets better than transferring from one source dataset?
- What is the effect of transfer learning when the ratio for training is increased while the size for the testing is fixed in the target dataset?
- Whether or not the similarity measure of two data sets can be used as an indicator for selecting source datasets?

3.1   Training Strategy

In the context of multi-domain transfer learning, Hu et al. [14] proposed a strategy in which a learned shared model from a set of domains is adapted for each individual target domain. The shared hidden layers can be considered as a universal feature transformation that works well for many domains. However, all source domains may not have the same influence on the performance of target domain. In this paper, we extend shared-parameters strategy proposed in [14]. In our approach, the parameters of the hidden layers not only contain the universal features, but also maintain specific features of the source domains.

The architectures of the proposed strategy is shown in Fig. 1. Assume that D_s^1 and D_s^2 are two different source datasets and D_s^1 is more similar to the target dataset D_t than D_s^2. In our approach, the first layer of the proposed architecture will learn the features of D_s^1 and the second layer will learn the features of both D_s^1 and D_s^2. The proposed strategy has three steps:

1. First, we use the first source dataset to pre-train the deep learning model.
2. Next, we freeze the first layer of the model. Then we use the second source dataset to train the model.
3. Finally, we use the target dataset to fine-tune the whole deep learning model. The process of training model is similar to stack auto-encoder [4].

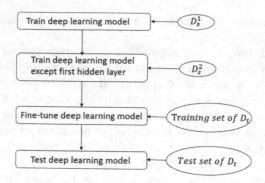

Fig. 1. Our proposed training strategy.

3.2   Network Architecture

The deep learning model used in our approach comprises of an input layer, two hidden layers, and an output layer. The model is designed to be a generic model meaning that it can be replaced with a DNN or a Long Short-Term Memory (LSTM) model. Note that our training strategy proposed in the previous section is independent of the chosen network architecture.

Hu et al. [14] used two hidden layers and each number of each hidden layer contains 100 nodes. In [14], Sigmoid function is used as the activation function. Similar to their approach, in DNN model, we also used two hidden layers and increased the number of nodes in each layer to 256. Besides, we choose Tanh as activation function because it gives better training performance for multi-layer neural networks [17]. The output layer contains one unit with Linear activation function. The network is shown in Fig. 2. The LSTM model used in our approach consists of two LSTM cells with Tanh as activation function and one output layer of a neuron with Linear activation function. Each LSTM layer has a 256-dimensional state vector. LSTM solves the gradient explosion and vanishing problem of RNN. The LSTM network used in this paper is shown in Fig. 3.

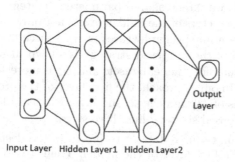

Fig. 2. Two-layers DNN network.

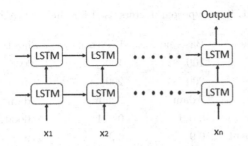

Fig. 3. Two-layers LSTM network.

4 Experiments

4.1 Experiment Setup

During the experiment, we used DNN and LSTM models for forecasting. We implemented our network using open source deep learning library Keras [1] with the Tensorflow [2] back-end. We run our experiments on Octal Core Intel(R) Core(TM) i7-6700 CPU @ 3.40 GHz. In this paper, we have compared five strategies for testing the effectiveness of different transfer learnings in financial time series forecasting. These strategies are numbered from M1 to M5.

- M1: Training the neural network model without transfer learning.
- M2: Transfer learning from source dataset D_s^1 to target dataset D_t.
- M3: Transfer learning from source dataset D_s^2 to target dataset D_t.
- M4: Transferring learning from source datasets D_s^1 and D_s^2 to target dataset D_t with shared parameter strategy.
- M5: Transferring features from source datasets D_s^1 and D_s^2 to target dataset D_t with our proposed strategy.

The first strategy is to train the model with the target dataset without transfer learning. We denote this strategy as the baseline approach. In the second and third strategies, the model is pre-trained by only using one of the source datasets and subsequently fine-tuned by using the target dataset. In the fourth strategy, the model is pre-trained by using two source datasets with shared parameters [14] and subsequently fine-tuned by using target dataset. In the last strategy, the model is pre-trained by using two source datasets with our proposed training strategy from Sect. 3.1. In the experiments, we adopt similar Hyper-parameters from [8] except that the epochs and batch size are set to 100 and 200 respectively. Besides, the learning rate of fine-tune step is also set to 0.00001. The Hyper-parameters used for the models are listed in Table 1.

4.2 Evaluation

After the learning process, the output of the model are inverse-normalized before computing the indicators. In this paper, we choose three classical indicators

Table 1. The hyperparameters used for the experiments.

Hyperparameter	Baseline	Pre-train	Fine-tune
Epochs	100	100	100
Batch size	200	200	200
Optimizer	Adam	Adam	Adam
Learning rate	0.001	0.001	0.00001
First moment	0.9	0.9	0.9
Second moment	0.999	0.999	0.999
Loss function	Cross-entropy	Cross-entropy	Cross-entropy

($MAPE$, $RMSE$ and R^2) to measure the predictive accuracy of each model. The definitions of these indicators are as follows:

$$MAPE = \frac{100\%}{n} \sum_{i=1}^{n} \left| \frac{y_i - \hat{y}_i}{y_i} \right| \tag{1}$$

$$RMSE = \sqrt{\frac{\sum (y_i - \hat{y}_i)^2}{n}} \tag{2}$$

$$R^2 = 1 - \frac{\sum (y_i - \hat{y}_i)^2}{\sum (y_i - \overline{y}_i)^2} \tag{3}$$

In these equations, y_i is the actual value and $\hat{y}_i$ is the predicted value. n represents the prediction period. $MAPE$ measures the size of the error. $RMSE$ is the mean of the square root of the error between the predicted value and the true value. R^2 is used for evaluating the fitting situation of the prediction model. The lower the $MAPE$ and $RMSE$, the better the model in forecasting. In contrast, higher the R^2, better the trained model.

4.3 Datasets

In the experiments, we use the stock market data from Yahoo Finance (https://finance.yahoo.com/). We choose three different groups of source and target datasets. The first group of datasets include Hang Seng Commerce & Industry (HSNC, 1000 time points) and Hang Seng Properties Index (HSNP, 1000 time points) as source datasets and Hang Seng Finance Index (HSNF, 1000 time points) as target dataset. The second datasets contain Dax Performance-Index (DAX, 5000 time points) and CAC 40 (CAC, 5000 time points) as source datasets and FTSE 100 (FTSE, 4000 time points) as the target dataset. Third datasets include S&P 500 (GSPC, 10000 time points) and Nasdaq (IXIC, 10000 time points) as source datasets, and Dow 30 (DJI, 8000 time points) as target dataset. These groups are different in size and we label them as small, mid-size, and large datasets.

Time series data are preprocessed before they are used for deep learning model. First, we drop missing and abnormal values. We also transform the time series into acceptable data format by the DNN and LSTM. For a given timestamp t (day), the input vector x consists of 90-day historical stock price: $\mathbf{x} = [p_{(t)}, \ldots, p_{(t-89)}]$ and the output vector y consists of 1-day stock price from time t: $\mathbf{y} = p_{t+1}$. We trained the model using 90 days for the lookback and 1 day for the forecast horizon. The value of time series are min-max scaled to [-1, 1] interval. During the experiments, we used the 70% and 30% of the target dataset for training and testing. The test size of target dataset of HSNF, FTSE, DJI are 273, 1173, and 2373 respectively.

4.4   Results and Discussion

In the experiments, we compare the performance of our strategy with the shared parameter strategy for multi-source datasets. We also examine the effect of transfer learning when the ratio for training is increased while the size for the testing is fixed in the target dataset. The experiment results are listed in Table 2. From these results, we can observe that the model with transfer learning have significant impact on time series forecasting. Besides, transfer learning with two source datasets (M4 and M5) is better than transfer learning with one source dataset (M2 and M3). Our proposed strategy (M5) achieve good results in majority of the cases.

Table 2. Experiment results for different transfer learning strategies.

D_s^1	D_s^2	D_t	Strategy	DNN			LSTM		
				MAPE	RMSE	R^2	MAPE	RMSE	R^2
HSNC	HSNP	HSNF	M1	1.2445	622.0425	0.9569	1.5868	801.2603	0.9291
			M2	1.0356	522.7943	0.9698	1.0088	511.6846	0.9711
			M3	1.0297	518.9767	0.9702	0.9899	507.3583	0.9716
			M4	0.9944	505.0655	0.9718	**0.9618**	494.5743	0.9730
			M5	**0.9851**	**499.9882**	**0.9724**	0.97348	**492.6246**	**0.9732**
DAX	CAC	FTSE	M1	0.9380	79.9719	0.9718	0.7254	63.7207	0.9835
			M2	0.7020	62.6288	0.9841	**0.6533**	**58.6790**	**0.9861**
			M3	0.6832	61.3956	0.9847	0.6817	60.3091	0.9853
			M4	**0.6708**	**60.4791**	0.9852	0.6750	59.8770	0.9855
			M5	0.6752	60.5211	**0.9852**	0.6675	59.4312	0.9857
GSPC	IXIC	DJI	M1	0.9287	212.3614	0.9978	1.2121	289.9345	0.9959
			M2	0.7428	172.5451	0.9985	0.7162	166.7077	0.9986
			M3	0.7023	168.2734	0.9986	0.7469	174.1719	0.9985
			M4	0.9489	210.1081	0.9979	0.6807	159.6134	0.9987
			M5	**0.6858**	**158.5243**	**0.9988**	**0.6787**	158.7363	**0.9988**

The experiment results for the effect of transfer learning when the ratio for training is increased while the size for the testing is fixed in the target dataset are shown in Figs. 4, 5, and 6. The experiment settings for testing with different ratio of target training dataset for fine-tuning is similar to previous experiments except that we use 20%, 40%, 60%, 80%, 100% of target training dataset for fine-tuning. In these experiments, the size of test datasets for target dataset of HSNF, FTSE, DJI are kept constant at 273, 1173, and 2373 respectively. From 4, 5, and 6, we can observe that DNN model with transfer learning is better than the model without transfer learning regardless of the size of training dataset. We also found that M5 (LSTM) gained good result in majority of the cases.

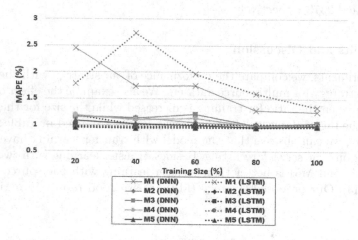

Fig. 4. The MAPE of HSNF dataset.

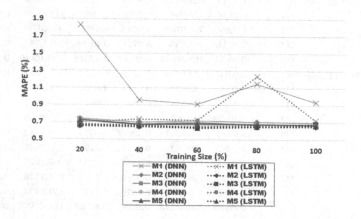

Fig. 5. The MAPE of FTSE dataset.

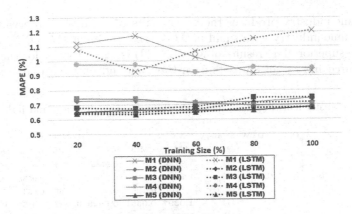

Fig. 6. The MAPE of DJI dataset.

4.5   Additional Experiment with Similarity Measure for Source Datasets

Rosenstein et al. [22] empirically showed that if two datasets are dissimilar, then brute-force transfer may negatively effect the performance of the target dataset. Such effect is also labeled as negative transfer by [22]. In this section, we further examine the effect of similarity between the source and target datasets on the overall results of transfer learning strategies. In this paper, we adopt Dynamic Time Warping (DTW) [5] algorithm to calculate the similarity of two time series (two datasets). DTW does not require that the two time series to be in the same length. DTW also permits time shifting between the two time series. Therefore, in the following four experiments, we use the mean value of two DTW distances as the main criteria to find potential source datasets for a given target dataset. The equation of $mDTW$ (mean DTW distance) is defined as follow:

$$mDTW = \frac{DTW(D_s^1, D_t) + DTW(D_s^2, D_t)}{2} \tag{4}$$

The smaller the mDTW, the more similar between the source and target dataset. In the four experiments, time series of Bank of China (BOC) is used as the target datasets for all transfer learning strategies. Source datasets for the experiments include China Construction Bank Corporation (CCB) and Industrial and Commercial Bank of China Limited (ICBC), Alibaba (BABA) and Lenovo Group (Leveno), Hang Seng Bank Limited (HSB) and Bank of America (BOA), Tencent and CLP Group (CLP). In experiment 1 and 3, the source datasets are selected from the same industry (i.e. Finance). In experiment 2 and 4, the source datasets are selected from the different industries. In Experiment 1 and 2, we evaluate the effect of small distance ($mDTW = 0.6$) between source and target datasets and Experiment 3 and 4 are designed to evaluate the effect of larger distance ($mDTW > 0.15$). The results of the experiments are listed in Table 3. From these results, we can observe that selecting the source and target datasets from the same industry produces the best results. We can also observe that for the case of same industry with small $mDTW$, the results of M4 (DNN) and M5 (LSTM) are superior. The results of M5 (LSTM) is also superior for the case of selecting source and target datasets from the same industry with large $mDTW$ value.

Table 3. Transfer learning strategies for different DTW distance and industry.

Exp	D_s^1	D_s^2	D_t	mDTW	Strategy	DNN			LSTM		
						MAPE	RMSE	R^2	MAPE	RMSE	R^2
Exp1	CCB	ICBC	BOC	0.06	M1	1.3095	0.0672	0.9735	1.3271	0.07107	0.9705
					M2	1.1568	0.0609	0.9783	1.0011	0.0558	0.9819
					M3	1.1419	0.0592	0.9795	0.9765	0.0543	0.9828
					M4	**1.0397**	**0.0551**	**0.9823**	0.9817	0.0551	0.9823
					M5	1.0631	0.0560	0.9817	**0.9780**	0.0547	0.9825
Exp2	BABA	Lenovo	BOC	0.06	M2	1.1499	0.0601	0.9789	1.0264	0.0567	0.9812
					M3	1.2798	0.0656	0.9749	1.4130	0.0768	0.9656
					M4	1.0769	0.0585	0.9800	1.0060	0.0561	0.9816
					M5	1.0927	0.0586	0.9800	1.0070	0.0552	0.9822
Exp3	HSB	BOA	BOC	0.15	M2	1.1989	0.0634	0.9766	1.1064	0.0601	0.9790
					M3	1.2582	0.0648	0.9755	1.0459	0.0563	0.9815
					M4	1.1565	0.0613	0.9781	0.9861	0.0548	0.9825
					M5	1.1287	0.0597	0.9792	0.9828	**0.0542**	**0.9829**
Exp4	Tencent	CLP	BOC	0.17	M2	1.2217	0.06404	0.9761	1.4027	0.0734	0.9685
					M3	1.1988	0.0613	0.9781	1.0334	0.0560	0.9817
					M4	1.1434	0.0599	0.9790	0.9899	0.0556	0.9819
					M5	1.1119	0.0585	0.9800	1.0019	0.0563	0.9815

5   Conclusion

In this paper, we propose a new training strategy for transfer learning with two source datasets. The experiment results reveal that the model with transfer learning has positive impact on financial time series forecasting. The experiment results also reveal that transfer learning with more source datasets is superior than using a single source dataset. In addition, the proposed training strategy (M5) achieve good results in majority of the cases. Although the proposed strategy is tested with only 2 source datasets, it can be extended for training more datasets after additional hidden layers are added to the network architecture. A similarity based approach based on DTW for selecting source and target datasets for training the deep learning models with transfer learning for financial time series forecasting is also proposed in this paper. Experiment results show that the transfer learning with similar (i.e. smaller $mDTW$) source datasets from the same industry is superior than selecting source datasets from different industries. In the paper, we use the DTW distance to calculate the similarity of two time series. As for the future work, we are planning to investigate the effect of other distance functions on the transfer learning strategies. In addition, we are also planning to test the effect of more than two source datasets on the training outcome. We are also conducting experiments for the deep learning neural networks with varying number of hidden layers.

Acknowledgement. The research was funded by the Research Committee of University of Macau, Grant MYRG2018-00246-FST.

References

1. Keras (2015). https://keras.io/
2. Abadi, M., et al.: TensorFlow: a system for large-scale machine learning. In: 12th USENIX Symposium on Operating Systems Design and Implementation (OSDI 2016), pp. 265–283 (2016)
3. Amaral, T., Silva, L.M., Alexandre, L.A., Kandaswamy, C., de Sá, J.M., Santos, J.M.: Transfer learning using rotated image data to improve deep neural network performance. In: Campilho, A., Kamel, M. (eds.) ICIAR 2014. LNCS, vol. 8814, pp. 290–300. Springer, Cham (2014). https://doi.org/10.1007/978-3-319-11758-4_32
4. Bengio, Y., Lamblin, P., Popovici, D., Larochelle, H.: Greedy layer-wise training of deep networks. In: Advances in Neural Information Processing Systems, pp. 153–160 (2007)
5. Berndt, D., Clifford, J.: Using dynamic time warping to find patterns in time series. In: KDD Workshop, vol. 10, no. 16, pp. 359–370 (1994)
6. Deng, L., Yu, D.: Deep learning for signal and information processing. Found. Trends Signal Process. **2–3**, 197–387 (2013)
7. Ding, X., Zhang, Y., Liu, T., Duan, J.: Deep learning for event-driven stock prediction. In: Proceedings of the 24th International Conference on Artificial Intelligence, pp. 2327–2333. AAAI Press (2015)
8. Fawaz, H.I., Forestier, G., Weber, J., Idoumghar, L., Muller, P.A.: Transfer learning for time series classification. In: 2018 IEEE International Conference on Big Data (Big Data). pp. 1367–1376. IEEE (2018)
9. Gardner Jr., E.S.: Exponential smoothing: the state of the art. Int. J. Forecast. **4**(1), 1–28 (1985)
10. Gardner Jr., E.S.: Exponential smoothing: the state of the art–part ii. Int. J. Forecast. **22**(4), 637–666 (2006)
11. Glorot, X., Bordes, A., Bengio, Y.: Domain adaptation for large-scale sentiment classification: a deep learning approach. In: Proceedings of the 28th International Conference on Machine Learning (ICML-11), pp. 513–520 (2011)
12. Haque, A.U., Nehrir, M.H., Mandal, P.: A hybrid intelligent model for deterministic and quantile regression approach for probabilistic wind power forecasting. IEEE Trans. Power Syst. **29**(4), 1663–1672 (2014)
13. Hinton, G.E., Salakhutdinov, R.R.: Reducing the dimensionality of data with neural networks. Science **313**(5786), 504–507 (2006)
14. Hu, Q., Zhang, R., Zhou, Y.: Transfer learning for short-term wind speed prediction with deep neural networks. Renew. Energy **85**, 83–95 (2016)
15. Huang, J.T., Li, J., Yu, D., Deng, L., Gong, Y.: Cross-language knowledge transfer using multilingual deep neural network with shared hidden layers. In: 2013 IEEE International Conference on Acoustics, Speech and Signal Processing, pp. 7304–7308. IEEE (2013)
16. Hyndman, R., Khandakar, Y.: Automatic time series forecasting: the forecast package for R. J. Stat. Softw. **27**(3), 1–22 (2008)
17. Karlik, B., Olgac, A.V.: Performance analysis of various activation functions in generalized mlp architectures of neural networks. Int. J. Artif. Intell. Expert Syst. **1**(4), 111–122 (2011)

18. Makridakis, S., Spiliotis, E., Assimakopoulos, V.: Statistical and machine learning forecasting methods: Concerns and ways forward. PLOS One **13**(3), 1–26 (2018)
19. Ortiz-García, E.G., Salcedo-Sanz, S., Pérez-Bellido, Á.M., Gascón-Moreno, J., Portilla-Figueras, J.A., Prieto, L.: Short-term wind speed prediction in wind farms based on banks of support vector machines. Wind Energy **14**(2), 193–207 (2011)
20. Pan, S.J., Yang, Q.: A survey on transfer learning. IEEE Trans. Knowl. Data Eng. **22**(10), 1345–1359 (2009)
21. Ramachandran, P., Liu, P., Le, Q.: Unsupervised pretraining for sequence to sequence learning. In: Proceedings of the 2017 Conference on Empirical Methods in Natural Language Processing, pp. 383–391. Association for Computational Linguistics (2017)
22. Rosenstein, M.T., Marx, Z., Kaelbling, L.P., Dietterich, T.G.: To transfer or not to transfer. In: NIPS 2005 Workshop on Transfer Learning, vol. 898, pp. 1–4 (2005)
23. Vu, N.T., Imseng, D., Povey, D., Motlicek, P., Schultz, T., Bourlard, H.: Multilingual deep neural network based acoustic modeling for rapid language adaptation. In: 2014 IEEE International Conference on Acoustics, Speech and Signal Processing (ICASSP), pp. 7639–7643. IEEE (2014)
24. Wang, B., Huang, H., Wang, X.: A novel text mining approach to financial time series forecasting. Neurocomputing **83**, 136–145 (2012)
25. Weiss, K., Khoshgoftaar, T.M., Wang, D.: A survey of transfer learning. J. Big Data **3**(1), 9 (2016). https://doi.org/10.1186/s40537-016-0043-6
26. Wu, D.D., Olson, D.L.: Financial risk forecast using machine learning and sentiment analysis. In: Wu, D.D., Olson, D.L. (eds.) Enterprise Risk Management in Finance, pp. 32–48. Springer, London (2015). https://doi.org/10.1057/9781137466297_5
27. Ye, R., Dai, Q.: A novel transfer learning framework for time series forecasting. Knowl. Based Syst. **156**, 74–99 (2018)
28. Yoshihara, A., Fujikawa, K., Seki, K., Uehara, K.: Predicting stock market trends by recurrent deep neural networks. In: Pham, D.-N., Park, S.-B. (eds.) PRICAI 2014. LNCS (LNAI), vol. 8862, pp. 759–769. Springer, Cham (2014). https://doi.org/10.1007/978-3-319-13560-1_60
29. Yosinski, J., Clune, J., Bengio, Y., Lipson, H.: How transferable are features in deep neural networks? In: Advances in Neural Information Processing Systems, pp. 3320–3328 (2014)

3DTI-Net: Learn 3D Transform-Invariant Feature Using Hierarchical Graph CNN

Guanghua Pan, Peilin Liu, Jun Wang, Rendong Ying[✉], and Fei Wen

Shanghai Jiao Tong University, Shanghai, China
rdying@sjtu.edu.cn

Abstract. Recently, emerging point cloud dedicated deep learning frameworks, such as PointNet and PointNet++, have achieved remarkable advantage in both accuracy and speed over traditional handcrafted ones. However, since the point coordinates of point clouds are represented in various local coordinate systems, most existing methods require additional preprocessing on raw point clouds. In this work, we design an efficient transform-invariant framework (named 3DTI-Net) for point cloud processing without the need of such preprocessing. 3DTI-Net consists of a transform invariant feature encoder as the front-end and a hierarchical graph convolutional neural network as the back-end. It achieves transform invariant feature extraction by learning inner 3D geometry information based on local graph representation. Experiments results on various classification and retrieval tasks show that, 3DTI-Net is able to learn 3D feature efficiently and can achieve state-of-the-art performance in rotated 3D object classification and retrieval.

Keywords: Point cloud · Rotation invariance · 3D deep learning · Hierarchical graph CNN

1 Introduction

Recently, 3D deep learning has achieved much progress in many computer vision analysis tasks [29]. Due to its importance for many computer vision applications, a number of methods have been proposed for 3D deep learning. For example, the works [16,30] propose to convert 3D shapes to voxel and perform convolution on 3D grids with 3D weight kernels, whilst [14,24] propose to project 3D objects into different image planes and learn features with 2D convolutions. While the former represents 3D data in a sparse way which is memory consuming and inefficient, the latter relies on heavy computation and needs additional view rendering.

Point clouds provide a flexible and scalable geometric representation of 3D objects, which can be easily acquired from range sensors such as LiDAR and depth camera.

The first deep network consumes point cloud directly is PointNet [6], which uses a transform net to align 3D shapes and utilizes a max-pooling as a global symmetric function to handle unordered point clouds. Though efficient, PointNet

© Springer Nature Switzerland AG 2019
A. C. Nayak and A. Sharma (Eds.): PRICAI 2019, LNAI 11671, pp. 37–51, 2019.
https://doi.org/10.1007/978-3-030-29911-8_4

cannot make full use of local structure information since it treats each point individually. To address this limitation, PointNet++ [19] and DGCNN [28] achieve local structure information exploitation via taking neighbor points into account. However, since the coordinates of the points are represented in various coordinate system, these methods require the orientation of the training and test sets to be similar to achieve stable accuracy in recognition tasks.

While translation invariance can be simply achieved by re-centering a point cloud to its centroid, rotation invariance remains a challenge in 3D deep learning.

Most existing point cloud processing methods can only tackle it by data augmentation. Very recently, the methods [7,31] propose to solve this problem by projecting 3D points onto a unit sphere and perform spherical CNN to learn SO(3) equivalence 3D features. Though effective, these methods require preprocessing and are time-consuming.

To efficiently address the transform-invariant problem in 3D point cloud processing, we propose a transform-invariant 3D deep net, called 3DTI-Net, which directly take point clouds as input. It is mainly composed of two parts, a transform-invariant feature encoder as the front-end and a hierarchical deep net based on Edge-Conv [28] as the back-end. Through experiments on classification and 3D retrieval tasks, 3DTI-Net is shown to be able to tackle rotation invariant problem without data augmentation and is computationally efficient. Our model does not require pre-training and can directly consume point clouds without any preprocessing like sphere rendering or voxelization.

The key contributions of our work are as follows:

(1) We propose a transform invariant feature encoder and a DGCNN based hierarchical deep network to effectively learn transform-invariant 3D geometry features from graph signals.
(2) We design a fast and effective pooling method and a dynamic graph update strategy to achieve multi-resolution learning on graphs.
(3) We establish theoretical guarantee on the transform-invariant property of our method, and explain the meaning of it in Euclidean domain.
(4) We present various test results to show that, compared with existing representative methods, 3DTI-Net can achieve state-of-the-art performance in rotated 3D shape classification when using fewer parameters, smaller input size, and no pre-training.

To the best of our knowledge, our work is the first to propose a graph-based transform-invariant 3D feature extraction network for 3D point cloud learning, along with established theoretical guarantee on the transform-invariant property.

2   Related Work

3D Geometry Feature

Generally, 3D feature descriptors can be classified into two classes, handcrafted features and learned features. Traditionally, handcrafted 3D features descriptors have been widely used in various tasks, such as segmentation, matching and classification [1]. Such descriptors include spin images [13], shape context [3] and histogram based approaches [20,21,27]. Handcrafted features based methods have reached a bottleneck in challenging tasks, especially in handling noisy and low-resolution data. Moreover, such methods were designed for specific applications and, hence, are hard to adapt to different applications and situations.

Very recently, benefited from the powerful deep CNN, data-driven methods using learned 3D features have achieved overwhelming advantage over traditional handcrafted features based ones. Learned 3D features have made much progress since the introduction of 3D deep learning. It has been shown in [32] that, by leveraging the vast amounts of correspondences obtained from RGB-D reconstructions, learned 3D descriptors outperforms traditional handcrafted features by a significant margin. Furthermore, to achieve rotation invariance, an auto-encoder is employed in [9] with a collection of point-pair-features combined with the points and normals within a local vicinity.

Deep Learning on Point Clouds: Qi *et al.* [6] firstly designed a novel deep network, named PointNet, to process point clouds. PointNet provides a unified architecture for various 3D based applications, such as object classification, part segmentation, and scene semantic parsing. In order to better exploit local structure information, the authors further proposed an improved PointNet++ architecture [19]. PointNet++ applies PointNet recursively on a nested partitioning of the input point set, by which geometric features in local point sets can be well exploited. As a consequence, PointNet++ has achieved state-of-the-art performance on various benchmark tasks. Inspired by these pioneer works, many deep learning based methods for point clouds analysis have been proposed recently, e.g, [15,28].

Graph Signal Processing: Graph signal processing is an emerging field, which aims to generalize fundamental signal operations defined on regular data to that for irregular data represented by graphs.

A comprehensive overview of graph signal processing is given in [17], which summarizes recent development of basic graph signal processing tools, including methods for sampling, filtering and graph learning.

Graph Convolution Neural Network: Convolution on graphs is originally defined in the spectral domain [4]. Though effective, the computation cost is high due to the eigen-decomposition of the graph Laplacian matrix. An improvement through fast localized convolutions has been proposed in [8], where Chebyshev expansion is employed to approximate graph Fourier transform. Graph convolution networks have achieved remarkable performance on learning irregular data from non-Euclidean domains, e.g., point clouds [26]. However, for methods defined on the spectral domain, since the Laplacian eigenbasis is domain-dependent, spectral filters learned on one shape may not generalize to others. To address this problem, DGCNN [28] proposed an Edge-Conv operation working on spatial domain, which showed superiority over previous methods.

Rotation Invariant 3D Features: Rotation invariance is a fundamentally desired property for 3D feature descriptors. To achieve rotation invariance, [7, 10] proposed to project 3D objects to a unit sphere and use the spherical convolutional network to achieve global 3D rotation equivariance. Some early methods use the spatial transformer [12] to learn a canonical transformation of the original input. Recently some methods try to encode coordinates of point clouds to transform invariant representation, Deng *et al.* [9] proposed point pair feature and a deep net based on PointNet to achieve rotation invariance. Similar to [9], our 3DTI-Net proposes a feature encoder to transform the coordinates of point clouds to rotation invariant feature representation. However, 3DTI-Net can better aggregate local features of different scale, and, as a consequence, outperforms previous arts with a significant margin.

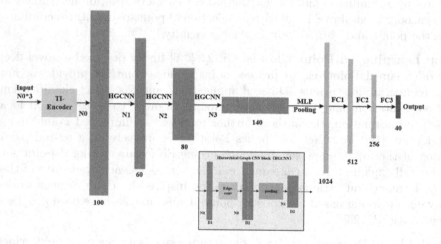

Fig. 1. 3DTI-Net model architecture, the left part is the front-end, the input of which is a point cloud with coordinates, a graph is then constructed with these points, The point cloud coordinates X can be encoded as high dimensional transform-invariant feature $X' \in \mathbb{R}^{N \times F_0}$ by rotation invariant feature encoder. The right part is the back-end, which is composed of dynamic edge-convolution layers and graph pooling layers to aggregate local features on different scales, a global max pooling is then applied to extract global rotation invariant 3D geometry feature descriptor.

3   Problem Statement

Given a 3D object O represented by point cloud $X \in \mathbb{R}^{N \times C}$, where N is the number of points and C is the number of feature channels (e.g., 3D coordinate, color, normal vector and texture), our first goal is to design a transform-invariant feature encoder (abbreviated as TI-encoder) as the front-end to represent the shape of the 3D object. The encoded features are expected to be able to capture the inner geometric features. Let $H : \mathbb{R}^{N \times C} \rightarrow \mathbb{R}^{N \times F_0}$ denote the TI-encoder, where F_0 is the dimension of the feature space after encoding. The encoded feature can be written as $X' = H(X)$. To achieve transform-invariance, $X' = H(RX) = H(X)$ should be satisfied for arbitrary rotation matrix R.

Based on the output of the transform-invariant encoder, the feature extractor (as the back-end), denoted by $F: \mathbb{R}^{N \times F_0} \to \mathbb{R}^K$ with K be the length of the output feature descriptor, is expected to extract a feature descriptor. The feature extractor F is desired to be computationally efficient, with the output feature be highly discriminative and also be robust to noise and the intensity diversity of point clouds.

4   Method

4.1   Proposed Architecture

Our proposed model is shown in Fig. 1.

The point cloud coordinates are firstly encoded as high dimensional transform-invariant feature $X' \in \mathbb{R}^{N \times F_0}$ by the TI-encoder. Then, Edge-Conv layers are used to extract more abstract features. In order to reduce the number of parameters and to better integrate local features, we perform pooling after each Edge-Conv layer to achieve multi-resolution graph learning. In this manner, the number of nodes is reduced and the information carried by each node becomes more abundant. Subsequently, global max pooling is applied to extract global feature descriptors, followed by three fully connected layers, which outputs the final predicted labels.

4.2   3D Geometry Representation

The absolute coordinates of a point cloud depend on the choice of the 3D coordinate system. Therefore, to achieve rotation invariant geometry feature learning, we need to convert the point cloud coordinates X to another transform invariant representation X'. This transformation should be able to capture informative 3D geometry characteristic in the original 3D shape represented by the point cloud.

The geometric features can be implicitly expressed by the relationship between different points. With a fixed coordinate system, a simple relationship between points can be represented as the difference in coordinate values $(\Delta x, \Delta y, \Delta z) = (x_i - x_j, y_i - y_j, z_i - z_j)$, $i, j \in N$, where x_i, x_j are two points in the point cloud X. This metric represents the relative position in the coordinate system, from which we can get the distance $l = \|\Delta x, \Delta y, \Delta z\|_2$ and the relative direction $\mathbf{n} = (\Delta x, \Delta y, \Delta z)/l$ of two points.

However, if the coordinate system is not fixed, the relative direction will change with the coordinate system, while the distance between points remains unchanged.

At the same time, if the point-pair distance is known, the relationship between two points can be reconstructed in a fixed coordinate system, and the geometric information carried by the two points can also be completely reconstructed except for an additional mirror symmetry uncertainty.

Therefore, the geometric features can be implicitly represented by the connection relationship between points. The graph structure is widely used in describing the relationship between points, where the points serve as nodes and the weighted point-pair connections serve as the edges. There are many ways to represent a graph, such as adjacency matrix A, Laplacian matrix L etc. In this work, we design a transform-invariant feature encoder based on graph.

Graph Signals: We use the coordinates of the point as the original signal, i.e. the signal of node X_i is $x_i = [x_i^x, x_i^y, x_i^z]$, and $X \in \mathbb{R}^{N \times 3}$ denotes the graph signal consisting of all the nodes on the graph.

Graph Construction: We use the Euclidean distance in the 3D space to construct a graph. An undirected k-nearest neighbor graph can be defined as $\mathcal{G} = (\nu, \epsilon, W)$, where ν is a finite set of $|\nu| = N$ verticles, ϵ is a set of edges and $W \in \mathbb{R}^{n \times n}$ is a weighted adjacency matrix encoding the connection weight between verticles.

First, we calculate pairwise distances of the point cloud, then search k nearest neighbors for each point. The knn adjacency distance matrix $W \in \mathbb{R}^{N \times N}$ can then be defined, where $W_{i,j} = \|x_i - x_j\|_2^2$ denotes the Euclidean distance between the i-th and j-th point in the point set and N_i is the neighboring points of the i-th point, the weight between the central point and the neighboring points can then be computed based on the distance matrix:

$$A_{i,j} = \begin{cases} e^{-\frac{W_{i,j}}{\sigma^2}}, j \in Ni; \\ 0, otherwise. \end{cases}$$

$$\sigma = \frac{1}{N} \times \sum_i^N \max\{W_{i,j}, j \in N_i\}, \tag{1}$$

where σ is the self-adaptive normalization parameter, and A is the weighted adjacency matrix, the weight $A_{i,j}$ indicates the connection strength of two nodes. The random-walk normalized Laplacian matrix $L^{rw} = I - D^{-1}A$ can then be calculated, where D is the degree matrix of A.

4.3   Rotation Invariant Geometry Feature on Graphs

Graph filtering is a method that takes a graph signal as raw input and outputs a processed graph signal. Let $S \in \mathbb{R}^{N \times N}$ be a graph shift operator, there are various choices for S in graph signal processing theory (e.g. adjacency matrix A and Laplacian matrix L), when the graph shift operator operates on a graph, the graph signal value of each node is replaced by the weighted average of its neighbors. Each linear translation-invariant graph filter kernel can be written as a polynomial of the graph shift operation [22]:

$$h(S) = \sum_{\ell=0}^{K-1} h_\ell S^\ell = h_0 I + h_1 S + \ldots + h_{K-1} S^{K-1}, \tag{2}$$

where h_ℓ ($\ell = 0, 1, \ldots, K - 1$) represents the filter coefficient, K is the length of the filter. The output of the filtered signal X is $y = h(S)X \in R^N$. Let $S = L = I - D^{-1}A$ and apply the filter kernel L on the graph signal X, the filtered output graph signal can be written as: $X' = h(L)X = h_0 I X + h_1 L X + \ldots + h_{K-1} L^{K-1} X$.

Property 1. Let X be the coordinates of a point cloud recentered to its centroid, define K features on graph as follows: $f_i(X) = \| (h(L)X)_i \|_2^2, i \in 0, \ldots, K - 1$, where $(h(L)X)_i$ represents the i th row of the matrix $h(L)X$, then the $f_i(X)$ is rotation and translation invariant, the proof is provided in Appendix A.1.

TI-Encoder Layer: Given a graph represented by Random Walk Laplacian matrix $L^{rw} = I - D^{-1}A$ together with graph signal $X \in \mathbb{R}^{N \times 3}$, the filtered graph signal is $X' \in \mathbb{R}^{N \times F_0}$, where F_0 is the number of feature map i.e. the dimention of the encoded TI-feature, the polynomial order is K, then the j th output channel of TI layer can be writen as:

$$X_j' = \sum_{i=0}^{K-1} \theta_{ij} \left\| (L^{rw})^i X \right\|_2^2 + b_j, \; for \; j = 0, 1, ..., F_0 - 1, \tag{3}$$

where b_j are the bias of j th channel of the feature map, $\theta_{0j}, ..., \theta_{(K-1)j}$ are K trainable filter coefficients which can be regarded as the convolution kernel.

The encoded features are spatially localized since the graph filter with length K combine information strictly form K-hop neighbors [8], together with hierarchical back-end, 3DTI-Net could learn more flexible local feature on different scales.

Transform Invariant Feature Visualization: Typical visualization result of point cloud features after transform invariant encoding is shown in Fig. 2. The results imply that contours of a 3D object are more informative than the other parts.

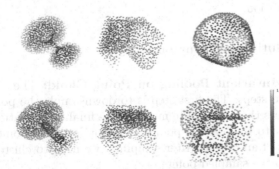

Fig. 2. Visulization of the encoded transform invariant features, each column in the image corresponds to a category, and each row of a column corresponds to two samples in the same class, we reduce the dimentions to 1 with PCA, the value is normalized to [0, 1] for better visulization.

4.4   The Meaning of Rotation Invariant Features in Spatial Domain

As mentioned in Sect. 4.2, when applying the graph shift operator on a point cloud, the weighted average of the neighbor points around the central point are calculated. For Random Walk Laplacian matrix L^{rw}, the sum of each row equals to zero, and for that $L^{rw}X = X - D^{-1}AX$ can be decomposed into two parts: $D^{-1}AX$ calculates the weighted average of the neighbor points around the central point, the weight is calculated by the distance between neighboring points and the central point; $X - D^{-1}AX$ calculate the relative coordinates of the central point to the weighted average point.

Therefore $\|L^{rw}X\|$ denotes the Euclidean distance between the central point and the weighted average point. It provides a more comprehensive understanding of the rotation invariance since the Euclidean distance is invariant in $SO(3)$. We call this distance contour variance.

4.5   Rotation Invariant Convolution on Graphs

In Sect. 4.2, the point coordinates $X \in \mathbb{R}^{N \times 3}$, which is not deterministic on rotation, are converted into a high-dimensional rotation-invariant feature $X' \in \mathbb{R}^{N \times F_0}$ by the front-end. Then, the absolute 3D coordinate value can be transformed into relative rotation invariant feature through the relationship between points. DGCNN uses an Edge-Conv operation working on spatial domain and showed superiority to previous methods. The EdgeConv block takes X' as input, computes edge features for each point by applying a multi-layer perceptron and generates a tensor of shape $N \times F_1$ after pooling among neighboring edge features. Since X' is transform invariant, the output tensor shares the same property, hence the entire feature propagation process is transform invariant.

One weakness of DGCNN is that all the convolution and graph reconstruction operations are performed on full-resolution points, which leads to high computation complexity. Our method follows the Edge-Conv operation but adopts graph pooling in each layer to achieve hierarchical learning, which is much more efficient in computation.

4.6   Multi-resolution Learning on Graphs

Fast Transform-Invariant Pooling on Point Cloud: The pooling operation consists of two steps. The first step is to downsample the point cloud and pick out those points that contribute more on the final classification result after coarsening. Similar to the 'critical points' in PointNet, such points are usually the contour points of an object. After sampling, we need to cluster points that are most similar to the sampled points.

Coarsening on point cloud has been a challenging task, some methods simply treat each point equally and use random downsampling to handle this problem. Such random sampling suffers uncertainty and the sampled points may not be the most informative ones on recognition tasks. Others [9, 19] use furthest points

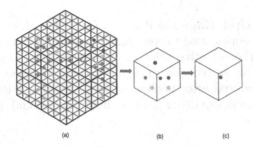

Fig. 3. Coarsening on graphs, column (a) divide 3D spaces to voxel grids and assign each point into associate mini-cell, (b) corsening points in each mini-cell, (c) the point that have the largest local contour variance are picked out in each mini-cell.

sampling but still have the same problem and is far more time-consuming. Pooling is frequently used in deep net, so pooling on point cloud needs to be computationally efficient. Another problem is that after downsampling, the distribution of the point density will be non-uniform, which may lead to the loss of local structure information.

The encoded TI feature is related to the contour variance of a point, i.e. the difference between the central point and its neighbor points, as mentioned in Sect. 4.4. Generally, similar to the edges in 2D images, the contours of a point cloud are composed by the points that are different from their neighboring points.

To solve the non-uniform diversity problem, as shown in Fig. 3, we first divide the spatial domain into uniform grids, then, each point is assigned to a mini-cell, and the point that has the largest local contour variance in each grid cell is picked out. The comparison of our pooling method with others is shown in Fig. 4. it can be seen that, our method can better select the informative points. After coarsening, we search m nearest neighbors of each sampled point in feature space, followed by a local max-pooling to integrate local information.

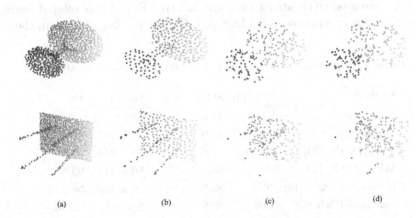

Fig. 4. Coarsening on graphs, column (a) is the raw input point cloud, (b) is the proposed down sampling method, (c) is random sampling while (d) is furthest point sampling

Dynamic Graph Updating: The dynamic graph has three meanings. First, the number of neighbors k used to construct the graph is dynamic in each layer in order to adjust the receptive fields of different layers. Second, the number of nodes of the graph is dynamic since the amount of points used for graph re-construction is reduced after pooling. Third, the connection relationship is determined by the Euclidean distance in the high dimensional feature space [28].

5   Experiment

5.1   Transform Invariance Test

The transform invariance property of our network is tested through 3D shape classification task and 3D retrieval task.

3D Classification. In classification task, given a set of 3D objects with labels, we need to train a function $l = f(X)$ to predict the label of a new object. We choose the ModelNet40 dataset, which is widely used in 3D object classification tasks. ModelNet40 contains 12311 CAD models from 40 categories, for each model, 1024 points are uniformly sampled from the mesh faces and normalized to a unit sphere. Only coordinates of the sampled points are used in classification experiment. We train the model with the origin orientation and test the data with random rotation to show that our model could achieve translation invariance in the classification task.

Implementation Details. (1) Preprocessing: we rescale each training sample with a random scale factor between 0.8 to 1.2 and jitter the points with gaussian noise. (2) Network configuration: the network architecture for classification is shown in Fig. 1. The k nearest neighbor used to construct the graph in front-end is set to 150, for Edge-Conv in the first HGCNN layer, the raw point coordinates are used to construct local graph, other Edge-Conv related configurations are the same as proposed in DGCNN. For the pooling operation, the grid

Table 1. Test result on ModelNet40 (overall classification accuracy).

Method	z/SO(3)	SO(3)/SO(3)	Inp. size	Para
PointNet++ [19]	28.6	85.0	**1024 × 3**	1.7 M
SubVolSup MO [18]	45.5	85.0	20×30^3	17 M
MVCNN 12x [24]	70.1	77.6	12×224^2	99 M
MVCNN 80x [24]	-	86.0	80×224^2	99 M
RotationNet 20x [14]	20.2	80.0	20×224^2	58.9 M
Spherical-CNN [10]	78.6	86.9	2×64^2	0.5 M
Ours	**87.1**	**87.7**	**1024 × 3**	1.2 M[a]

[a]The model size of mode SO(3)/SO(3) is 2.8M

length of each layer is set to [0.06, 0.1, 0.14]. We adopt dropout after fully connected layers and add a regularization term to the total loss to avoid over-fitting. The models are trained using an NVIDIA TITAN GPU, with a batch size of 16 and epoch number of 400.

The result is shown in Table 1, we follow [10] and two settings are considered, z/SO(3) mode means only samples in test set are rotated while SO(3)/SO(3) mode means both training set and test set are randomly rotated. We compare overall classification accuracy, input size and parameter number with state-of-the-arts.

Our proposed method outperforms previous state-of-the-art Spherical-CNN [10] by a significant margin of 8.5%. Previous coordinates based methods could achieve good performance when the orientation of the training data and the test data are aligned, but there is a sharp drop in accuracy when the test data are randomly rotated. This implies that the transform net can only handle minor transform between training set and test set. Multi-View based methods could be regarded as a brute force approach of SO(3) equivariance, they could generalize to unseen orientations [10], still, our method outperforms them with fewer parameters and no pre-training.

Previous point cloud based methods have tried to handle rotation invariance by data argumentation, which requires higher model capacity. As shown in Sect. 5.2, the back-end of 3DTI-Net is also capable of learning the coordinates directly to achieve higher performance in recognition tasks. We trained an additional model with data argumentation using the rotated training set. Then, we concatenate the descriptors learned by the two models and trained a voting network to output the final result. We achieve state-of-the-art prediction accuracy when the training set and test set are all randomly rotated (SO(3)/SO(3) mode).

3D Retrieval. We perform the retrieval experiment on ShapeNet Core55 [5], which is composed of more than 50 thousand models over 55 common categories in total for training and evaluating. We follow the SHREC'17 3D shape retrieval rules [23], which includes random SO(3) perturbations. In our experiment, each query and retrieval results are treated equally across categories, and therefore the results are averaged without re-weighting based on category size.

We use the same model architecture as shown in Fig. 1, and follow the setting of [10], The network is trained for classification on 55 core classes, with an additional loss to minimize the distance between matching categories and meanwhile to pull apart non-matching categories. We use the distance between descriptors for retrieval. The elements whose distance are below a threshold are returned.

As shown in Table 2, our method achieves the best trade-off between the model complexity, input size, and retrieval performance. The result also demonstrates that 3DTI-Net is effective in learning the inner features of 3D objects, and the learned transform invariant features can be widely used in matching and recognition tasks.

Table 2. 3D retrieval result in SHREC'17, including precision, recall and mean average precision.

Mothod	P@N	R@N	mAP	Input size	Params
Furuya [11]	**0.814**	0.683	0.656	126×10^3	8.4M
Tatsuma [25]	0.705	0.769	0.696	38×224^2	3M
Zhou [2]	0.660	0.650	0.567	50×224^2	36M
Spherical-CNN [10]	0.717	0.737	0.685	2×64^2	0.5M
Ours	0.789	**0.771**	**0.702**	1024×3	1.2M

5.2 More Experiments on Modelnet40

Back-End Capability Test. The capability of our model is not limited to effective 3D transform invariant feature extraction. In this subsection, we will show that our back-end is a general network in learning 3D geometry feature represented by graph signal. We train and test the model without rotation, just like most previous point cloud processing models did.

Different form Fig. 1, the TI-encoder are repalced with a transform net [6]. we follow previous point cloud based methods [6,19,28] to train and test without random rotation on ModelNet40, the result is shown in Table 3.

Though there is still a small gap between our method and multi-view based methods, we achieve competitive performance with state-of-the-arts which consume point cloud directly, while our back-end outperforms them by fewer parameters and more effective in computation.

Table 3. Result in coordinates based classification, including overall classification accuracy, forward time, model size and input type.

Method	Overall acc	Fwd time (ms)	Model size	Inp type
MVCNN [24]	90.1	-	99M	Multi-view
RotationNet 20x [14]	**92.4**	-	58.9M	Multi-view
PointNet [6]	89.2	**25.3**	3.5M	Point cloud
PointNet++ [19]	90.7	163	1.7M	Point cloud
DGCNN [28]	92.2	94.6	1.8M	Point cloud
Ours	91.9	52	**1.3M**	Point cloud

Ablation Study. We further investigate the contribution of each component in our model on the overall performance. First, we are interested in whether our graph based TI-encoder is more effective compared with existing transform invariant feature extraction methods. We replace our TI-encoder by the point-pair feature proposed in PPFNet [9] for comparison. Second, we compare our back-end with existing point cloud based Deepnets, including PointNet and DGCNN. Third, we compare our pooling method with existing representative ones, e.g., random sampling (RS) and furthest point sampling (FPS). The result is shown in Table 4. We can conclude that our TI-encoder contributes most to the overall accuracy, while our hierarchical graph CNN makes our method more efficient.

Table 4. Ablation study result, overall accuracy on ModelNet 40 (z/SO(3)).

Front-end	Back-end	Pooling	Overall acc
TI-encoder	HGCNN	RS	86.1
TI-encoder	HGCNN	FPS	86.5
PPF	HGCNN	-	72.1
TI-encoder	PointNet	-	83.2
TI-encoder	DGCNN	-	86.8

6   Conclusion

This work proposed a novel general deep neural network, 3DTI-Net, for point cloud processing. It consists of a transform invariant feature encoder as the front-end, and a hierarchical deep network as the back-end. 3DTI-Net is able to effectively and efficiently exploit both the global shape information and local geometry information of a point cloud. Moreover, 3DTI-Net consumes point cloud directly without any preprocessing and pre-training, and hence has a good generalization ability for various application scenarios. Various test results demonstrated that, 3DTI-Net can achieve state-of-the-art performance in rotated 3D shape classification. Furthermore, compared with state-of-the-art methods, 3DTI-Net uses fewer parameters, smaller input size, and does not need pre-training. The high efficiency of 3DTI-Net makes it suitable for real-time applications, such as semantic SLAM.

A   Appendix

A.1   Proof of Property 1

Proof. Translation invariance can be easily achieved by the re-centering operation, To prove rotation invariance, let $R \in \mathbb{R}^{3 \times 3}$ be an arbitrary rotation matrix, and the rotated point cloud coordinates is XR. Then, the i-th feature satisfies:

$$
\begin{aligned}
f_i(XR) &= \|(h(L)XR)_i\|_2^2 \\
&= \|(h(L))_i XR\|_2^2 \\
&= (h(L))_i XRR^T X^T (h(L))_i^T \\
&= (h(L))_i XX^T (h(L))_i^T \\
&= \|(h(L)X)_i\|_2^2 = f_i(X).
\end{aligned}
\tag{4}
$$

$\square$

References

1. Aldoma, A., et al.: Tutorial: point cloud library: three-dimensional object recognition and 6 dof pose estimation. IEEE Robot. Autom. Mag. **19**(3), 80–91 (2012)
2. Bai, S., Bai, X., Zhou, Z., Zhang, Z., Latecki, L.J.: Gift: a real-time and scalable 3D shape search engine. In: Computer Vision and Pattern Recognition, pp. 5023–5032 (2016)
3. Belongie, S.J., Malik, J., Puzicha, J.: Shape context: a new descriptor for shape matching and object recognition, pp. 831–837 (2000)
4. Bruna, J., Zaremba, W., Szlam, A., Lecun, Y.: Spectral networks and locally connected networks on graphs. In: International Conference on Learning Representations (2014)
5. Chang, A.X., et al.: ShapeNet: an information-rich 3D model repository. arXiv Graphics (2015)
6. Qi, C.R., Su, H., Mo, K., Guibas, L.J.: PointNet: deep learning on point sets for 3D classification and segmentation. In: Computer Vision and Pattern Recognition, pp. 77–85 (2017)
7. Cohen, T.S., Geiger, M., Kohler, J., Welling, M.: Spherical CNNS. In: International Conference on Learning Representations (2018)
8. Defferrard, M., Bresson, X., Vandergheynst, P.: Convolutional neural networks on graphs with fast localized spectral filtering. In: Neural Information Processing Systems, pp. 3844–3852 (2016)
9. Deng, H., Birdal, T., Ilic, S.: PPFNet: global context aware local features for robust 3D point matching (2018)
10. Esteves, C., Allenblanchette, C., Makadia, A., Daniilidis, K.: Learning SO(3) equivariant representations with spherical CNNs. arXiv Computer Vision and Pattern Recognition (2017)
11. Furuya, T., Ohbuchi, R.: Deep aggregation of local 3D geometric features for 3D model retrieval. In: British Machine Vision Conference, pp. 121.1–121.12 (2016)
12. Jaderberg, M., Simonyan, K., Zisserman, A., et al.: Spatial transformer networks. In: Advances in Neural Information Processing Systems, pp. 2017–2025 (2015)
13. Johnson, A.E., Hebert, M.: Using spin images for efficient object recognition in cluttered 3d scenes. IEEE Trans. Pattern Anal. Mach. Intell. **21**(5), 433–449 (1999)
14. Kanezaki, A., Matsushita, Y., Nishida, Y.: RotationNet: joint object categorization and pose estimation using multiviews from unsupervised viewpoints. In: Computer Vision and Pattern Recognition (2018)
15. Li, Y., Bu, R., Sun, M., Wu, W., Di, X., Chen, B.: PointCNN: convolution on x-transformed points. In: NeurIPS (2018)
16. Maturana, D., Scherer, S.: VoxNet: a 3D convolutional neural network for real-time object recognition, pp. 922–928 (2015)
17. Ortega, A., Frossard, P., Kovacevic, J., Moura, J.M.F., Vandergheynst, P.: Graph signal processing: overview, challenges, and applications. Proc. IEEE **106**(5), 808–828 (2017)
18. Qi, C.R., Su, H., Niebner, M., Dai, A., Yan, M., Guibas, L.J.: Volumetric and multi-view CNNs for object classification on 3D data. In: Computer Vision and Pattern Recognition, pp. 5648–5656 (2016)
19. Qi, C.R., Yi, L., Su, H., Guibas, L.J.: PointNet++: deep hierarchical feature learning on point sets in a metric space. In: Neural Information Processing Systems, pp. 5099–5108 (2017)

20. Rusu, R.B., Blodow, N., Beetz, M.: Fast point feature histograms (FPFH) for 3D registration, pp. 1848–1853 (2009)
21. Rusu, R.B., Blodow, N., Marton, Z., Beetz, M.: Aligning point cloud views using persistent feature histograms, pp. 3384–3391 (2008)
22. Sandryhaila, A., Moura, J.M.F.: Discrete signal processing on graphs. IEEE Trans. Signal Process. **61**(7), 1644–1656 (2013)
23. Savva, M., et al.: Large-scale 3D shape retrieval from ShapeNet Core55. In: 3DOR (2017)
24. Su, H., Maji, S., Kalogerakis, E., Learnedmiller, E.G.: Multi-view convolutional neural networks for 3D shape recognition. In: International Conference on Computer Vision, pp. 945–953 (2015)
25. Tatsuma, A., Aono, M.: Multi-fourier spectra descriptor and augmentation with spectral clustering for 3D shape retrieval. Vis. Comput. **25**(8), 785–804 (2009)
26. Te, G., Hu, W., Zheng, A., Guo, Z.: RGCNN: regularized graph CNN for point cloud segmentation. In: ACM multimedia (2018)
27. Tombari, F., Salti, S., Di Stefano, L.: Unique signatures of histograms for local surface description. In: Daniilidis, K., Maragos, P., Paragios, N. (eds.) ECCV 2010. LNCS, vol. 6313, pp. 356–369. Springer, Heidelberg (2010). https://doi.org/10.1007/978-3-642-15558-1_26
28. Wang, Y., Sun, Y., Liu, Z., Sarma, S.E., Bronstein, M.M., Solomon, J.: Dynamic graph CNN for learning on point clouds. arXiv Computer Vision and Pattern Recognition (2018)
29. Wen, F., Chu, L., Liu, P., Qiu, R.: A survey on nonconvex regularization based sparse and low-rank recovery in signal processing, statistics, and machine learning. IEEE Access 1 (2018). https://doi.org/10.1109/ACCESS.2018.2880454
30. Wu, Z., et al.: 3D ShapeNets: a deep representation for volumetric shapes. In: Computer Vision and Pattern Recognition, pp. 1912–1920 (2015)
31. Yi, L., Su, H., Guo, X., Guibas, L.J.: SyncSpecCNN: synchronized spectral CNN for 3D shape segmentation. In: Computer Vision and Pattern Recognition, pp. 6584–6592 (2017)
32. Zeng, A., Song, S., Nießner, M., Fisher, M., Xiao, J., Funkhouser, T.: 3DMatch: learning local geometric descriptors from RGB-D reconstructions. In: CVPR (2017)

Transfer Learning for Driving Pattern Recognition

Maoying Li[1], Liu Yang[1(✉)], Qinghua Hu[1], Chenyang Shen[2], and Zhibin Du[3]

[1] College of Intelligence and Computing, Tianjin University, Tianjin, China
{limaoying,yangliuyl,huqinghua}@tju.edu.cn
[2] UT Southwestern Medical Center, Dallas, USA
chenyang.shen@utsouthwestern.edu
[3] China Automotive Technology and Research Center Co. Ltd., Tianjin, China
duzhibin@catarc.ac.cn

Abstract. Driving pattern recognition based on driving status features (GPS, gear, and speed etc.) is of central importance in the development of intelligent transportation. While it is expensive and labor intensive to obtain a large amount of labeled driving data in real applications. It makes the driving pattern recognition particularly difficult for those domains without labeled data. In this paper, to tackle this challenging recognition task, we propose a novel and robust Transfer Learning method for Driving Pattern Recognition (TLDPR) that can transfer knowledge from other related source domains with labeled data to the target domain. Compared to the traditional supervised learning, one of the major difficulties of transfer learning is that the data from different domains may have distinct distributions. The proposed TLDPR is able to reduce the distribution difference in RKHS between the samples in target and source domain with the same driving pattern, and it can preserve the local manifold structure simultaneously. In addition, an iterative ensemble strategy is implemented to make the model more robust using the pseudo-labels. To evaluate the performance of TLDPR, comprehensive experiments have been conducted on parking lots datasets. The results show TLDPR can substantially outperform the state-of-the-art methods.

Keywords: Transfer learning · Driving pattern ·
Maximum mean discrepancy

1 Introduction

Recently, driving pattern recognition based on driving status features such as GPS, gear, and speed as shown in Fig. 1a has been studied extensively since it is critical to self-driving vehicle and intelligent transportation. However, it is expensive and labor intensive to obtain a large amount of labeled data. Driving pattern recognition without labeled data is very challenging. In general, we assume that the same driving pattern, such as driving in the lane, turning left, turning right as shown in Fig. 1b, should be consistent even for very different scenes, then the

© Springer Nature Switzerland AG 2019
A. C. Nayak and A. Sharma (Eds.): PRICAI 2019, LNAI 11671, pp. 52–65, 2019.
https://doi.org/10.1007/978-3-030-29911-8_5

labeled data in one scene can be very useful for the driving pattern recognition of another. Motivated by [1] that leverages labels of target domain with limited information based on knowledge learned from other auxiliary domains, we focus on incorporating the knowledge learned from other labeled driving scenes to enhance the driving pattern recognition for scenes without label data.

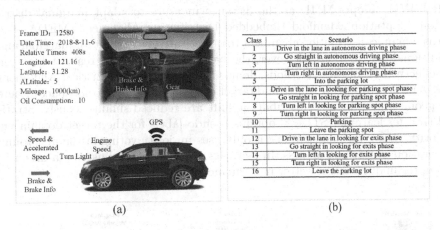

Class	Scenario
1	Drive in the lane in autonomous driving phase
2	Go straight in autonomous driving phase
3	Turn left in autonomous driving phase
4	Turn right in autonomous driving phase
5	Into the parking lot
6	Drive in the lane in looking for parking spot phase
7	Go straight in looking for parking spot phase
8	Turn left in looking for parking spot phase
9	Turn right in looking for parking spot phase
10	Parking
11	Leave the parking spot
12	Drive in the lane in looking for exits phase
13	Go straight in looking for exits phase
14	Turn left in looking for exits phase
15	Turn right in looking for exits phase
16	Leave the parking lot

(a)   (b)

Fig. 1. (a) Driving status features and (b) driving patterns.

Compared to traditional supervised learning, one of the major difficulties of transfer learning is data from different domains may have distinct distributions. In driving pattern recognition, driving status data are recorded for different drivers in various scenes with distinct lane structures which may lead distinct data distributions. Thus, one essential task of transfer learning is to shrink the difference of data among different domains.

To date, remarkable research efforts have been devoted to discover common feature representations to reduce the distribution difference among different domains while preserving important properties in original data. Transfer Component Analysis (TCA) [2] tries to learn some transfer components across domains in a Reproducing Kernel Hilbert Space (RKHS) using Maximum Mean Discrepancy (MMD). Transfer Joint Matching (TJM) [3] reduces the domain difference by not only jointly matching the features but also reweighting the samples across domains. Geodesic Flow Kernel (GFK) [4] exploits the low-dimensional structure to integrate the domains according to geodesic flow kernel. CORrelation ALignment (CORAL) [5] minimizes domain shift by aligning the second-order statistics of source and target distributions. In Landmarks-based Subspace Alignment (LSA) [6], landmarks are selected to reduce the discrepancy between the domains and an efficient subspace alignment is performed. In conclusion, all of these transfer learning methods aim to reduce the global distribution difference between source and target domain.

Elhamifar et al. [7] propose the data from the same class should lay on the same subspace, even if they belong to different domains. Hence, it is necessary to exploit the intra-affinity for each class to overcome the limitation of global domain shift [8]. Existing methods often calculate the intra-class distribution distance with the help of pseudo-labels obtained by standard classifiers. Joint Distribution Adaptation (JDA) [9] and Balanced Distribution Adaptation (BDA) [10] methods jointly adapt both the marginal distribution and conditional distribution simultaneously. Adaptation Regularization based Transfer Learning (ARTL) [11] adopts MMD as the distance measure to adapt marginal distribution adaptation. Manifold Embedded Distribution Alignment (MEDA) [12] learns dynamic distribution alignment to quantitatively account for marginal and conditional distributions. However, the basic classifier has a greater impact on the effectiveness of these methods. Joint Geometrical and Statistical Alignment (JGSA) [13] projects the source and target domain data into two subspaces where the geometrical shift and distribution shift are reduced simultaneously. Stratified transfer learning (STL) [8] obtains pseudo-labels for the target domain via majority voting technique. While it only uses majority voting in the first round of iteration in learning process. In fact, the pseudo-labels adjusted via majority voting technique can get better performance.

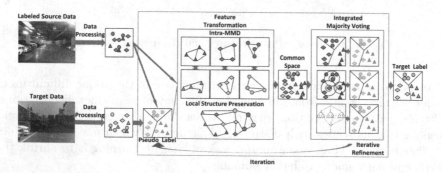

Fig. 2. The framework of the transfer learning for driving pattern recognition. The source data and target data can be transformed to a common space by reducing the intra-MMD distance and preserving the local manifold structure, then the majority voting classifier based on the source data can be used to predict the labels of target data.

To address the issues mentioned above and improve the transfer learning performance for driving pattern recognition, in this paper, we propose a novel and robust Transfer Learning for Driving Pattern Recognition (TLDPR). The complete framework is summarized in Fig. 2. Our contributions are mainly three-fold:

(1) TLDPR is proposed specifically for driving pattern recognition based on the features extracted from driving status. As far as we know, this is the first time to identify the driving pattern using the transfer learning method.

(2) TLDPR can reduce the distribution difference between samples from same class in target and source domain while preserving the local manifold structure. An iterative ensemble strategy is conducted to make model more robust by using pseudo-labels.
(3) Comprehensive experiments for driving pattern recognition on parking lots datasets are conducted to evaluate the performance of TLDPR. Experiments demonstrate the superiority of TLDPR over other state-of-the-art methods w.r.t. classification accuracy.

2   Driving Pattern Recognition

In this section, we will introduce the proposed TLDPR framework. We first present definition of driving pattern recognition, then 3 steps of TLDPR are presented in detail.

2.1   Problem Definition

TLDPR transfers knowledge from labeled samples in source domain to identify the patterns of samples in target domain without label. A domain $\mathcal{D}$ is composed of an m-dimensional feature space $\mathcal{X}$ and a marginal probability distribution $P(\mathbf{x})$, where $\mathbf{x} \in \mathcal{X}$. Given domain $\mathcal{D}$, a task $\mathcal{T}$ is composed of a C-cardinality label set $\mathcal{Y}$ and a classifier $f(\mathbf{x})$, i.e., $\mathcal{T} = \{\mathcal{Y}, f(\mathbf{x})\}$, where $y \in \mathcal{Y}$, and $f(\mathbf{x}) = Q(y|\mathbf{x})$ can be interpreted as the conditional probability distribution. Given labeled source domain $\mathcal{D}_s = \{(\mathbf{x}_1, y_1), \ldots, (\mathbf{x}_{n_s}, y_{n_s})\}$ and unlabeled target domain $\mathcal{D}_t = \{\mathbf{x}_{n_s+1}, \ldots, \mathbf{x}_{n_s+n_t}\}$, we have the source and target data matrices $X_s \in \mathbb{R}^{m \times n_s}$ and $X_t \in \mathbb{R}^{m \times n_t}$ respectively, and the source label vector $\mathbf{y} \in \mathbb{R}^{n_s \times 1}$. Let $X = [X_s \ X_t] \in \mathbb{R}^{m \times n}$ be all $n = n_s + n_t$ samples in the source and target domains. $\mathcal{D}_s$ and $\mathcal{D}_t$ have the same dimensionality and label spaces, that is $\{\mathbf{x}_i\}_{i=1}^{n_s+n_t} \in \mathbb{R}^{m \times 1}$, $\mathcal{X}_s = \mathcal{X}_t, \mathcal{Y}_s = \mathcal{Y}_t$, while the marginal and conditional probability distributions are different, i.e. $P_s(\mathbf{x}_s) \neq P_t(\mathbf{x}_t), Q_s(y_s|\mathbf{x}_s) \neq Q_t(y_t|\mathbf{x}_t)$. The goal is to learn a classifier to classify the unlabeled data in target domain based on information in source domain by explicitly reducing the distribution differences between $P_s(\mathbf{x}_s)$ and $P_t(\mathbf{x}_t)$, $Q_s(y_s|\mathbf{x}_s)$ and $Q_t(y_t|\mathbf{x}_t)$.

2.2   Feature Transformation

In this paper, we propose to reduce the distribution difference by a feature transformation A so that the joint expectations of $\mathcal{D}_s$ and $\mathcal{D}_t$ are matched between domains after transformation. The proposed TLDPR model can be presented under the following framework of unconstrained optimization problem:

$$\min_A \ell(\mathcal{D}_s, \mathcal{D}_t) + \Psi(A), \tag{1}$$

where A indicates the feature transformation function for transfer learning that we need to solve. The data fidelity term $\ell(\cdot)$ can be any loss function which measures the distance between the source data and the target data. The minimization of $\ell(\mathcal{D}_s, \mathcal{D}_t)$ expects to fit the two different domains with the feature transformation. $\Psi(A)$ is the regularization term based on some prior assumptions desired for A. Furthermore, we try to choose proper $\ell(\cdot)$ and $\Psi(\cdot)$ which guarantee the convexity of the model (1), such that the stabilization of the model can be expected. In the following of the paper, the more detailed information of loss term as well as the regularization terms will be given.

Intra-class MMD. It is usually difficult to estimate the probability density of a distribution by parameters, but it is feasible to use statistical information. To reduce the difference between marginal distributions $P_s(\mathbf{x}_s)$ and $P_t(\mathbf{x}_t)$, we follow [8,9] and adopt the empirical MMD as the distance measure to compare different distributions, which computes the distance between the sample means of the source and target data in the k-dimensional embeddings. However, reducing the difference in the marginal distributions does not guarantee the similarity of conditional distributions between domains, while it is known that minimizing conditional distribution difference between $Q_s(y_s|\mathbf{x}_s)$ and $Q_t(y_t|\mathbf{x}_t)$ is critically important for a robust distribution adaptation. Unfortunately, it is not trivial to match the conditional distributions, even by exploring sufficient statistics of the distributions. There are no labeled data in the target domain, so $Q_t(y_t|\mathbf{x}_t)$ cannot be modeled directly. The best approximation is to assume that $Q_t(y_t|\mathbf{x}_t) \approx Q_s(y_t|\mathbf{x}_t)$. This can be executed by applying a classifier f trained on the labeled source data to the unlabeled target data. In order to achieve a more accurate approximation for $Q_t(y_t|\mathbf{x}_t)$, an iterative pseudo-label refinement strategy is developed. Note that the pseudo-label can be predicted by applying some ensemble classifiers trained on the labeled source data to the unlabeled target data. Since the posterior probabilities $Q_s(y_s|\mathbf{x}_s)$ and $Q_t(y_t|\mathbf{x}_t)$ are quite involved, we resort to explore the sufficient statistics of class-conditional distributions $Q_s(\mathbf{x}_s|y_s)$ and $Q_t(\mathbf{x}_t|y_t)$ instead. Now with the true source labels and pseudo target labels, we can match the class conditional distributions $Q_s(\mathbf{x}_s|y_s = c)$ and $Q_t(\mathbf{x}_t|y_t = c)$ w.r.t. each class $c \in \{1, \ldots, C\}$ in the label set $\mathcal{Y}$. Here we modify MMD to measure the distance between the class conditional distributions $Q_s(\mathbf{x}_s|y_s = c)$ and $Q_t(\mathbf{x}_t|y_t = c)$. Let the desired nonlinear transformation denoted as $\phi : \mathcal{X} \rightarrow \mathcal{H}$, where $\mathcal{H}$ is a universal RKHS. The intra-MMD is defined as

$$\left\| \frac{1}{n_s^{(c)}} \sum_{\mathbf{x}_i \in \mathcal{D}_s^{(c)}} A^T \phi(\mathbf{x}_i) - \frac{1}{n_t^{(c)}} \sum_{\mathbf{x}_j \in \mathcal{D}_t^{(c)}} A^T \phi(\mathbf{x}_j) \right\|^2 \tag{2}$$

where $\mathcal{D}_s^{(c)} = \{\mathbf{x}_i : \mathbf{x}_i \in \mathcal{D}_s \wedge y(\mathbf{x}_i) = c\}$ is the set of examples belonging to class c in the source data, $y(\mathbf{x}_i)$ is the true label of $\mathbf{x}_i$, and $n_s^{(c)} = |\mathcal{D}_s^{(c)}|$. Correspondingly, $\mathcal{D}_t^{(c)} = \{\mathbf{x}_j : \mathbf{x}_j \in \mathcal{D}_t \wedge \hat{y}(\mathbf{x}_j) = c\}$ is the set of examples belonging to class c in the target data, $\hat{y}(\mathbf{x}_j)$ is the pseudo(predicted) label of $\mathbf{x}_j$, and $n_t^{(c)} = |\mathcal{D}_t^{(c)}|$. Instead of finding the nonlinear transformation ϕ explicitly, we can transform it as a kernel learning problem [2]. By virtue of the kernel trick, (i.e., $K(\mathbf{x}_i, \mathbf{x}_j) = \phi(\mathbf{x}_i)^T \phi(\mathbf{x}_j)$), the distance between the empirical means of the two domains in Eq. (2) can be written as:

$$\left\| \frac{1}{n_s^{(c)}} \sum_{\mathbf{x}_i \in \mathcal{D}_s^{(c)}} A^T \phi(\mathbf{x}_i) - \frac{1}{n_t^{(c)}} \sum_{\mathbf{x}_j \in \mathcal{D}_t^{(c)}} A^T \phi(\mathbf{x}_j) \right\|^2 = \mathrm{tr}(A^T K M^{(c)} K^T A) \quad (3)$$

$$\text{where } (M^{(c)})_{ij} = \begin{cases} \dfrac{1}{n_s^{(c)} n_s^{(c)}}, \mathbf{x}_i, \mathbf{x}_j \in \mathcal{D}_s^{(c)} \\[2mm] \dfrac{1}{n_t^{(c)} n_t^{(c)}}, \mathbf{x}_i, \mathbf{x}_j \in \mathcal{D}_t^{(c)} \\[2mm] \dfrac{-1}{n_s^{(c)} n_t^{(c)}}, \begin{cases} \mathbf{x}_i \in \mathcal{D}_s^{(c)}, \mathbf{x}_j \in \mathcal{D}_t^{(c)} \\ \mathbf{x}_j \in \mathcal{D}_s^{(c)}, \mathbf{x}_i \in \mathcal{D}_t^{(c)} \end{cases} \\[2mm] 0, \text{ otherwise} \end{cases} \quad (4)$$

and the kernel matrix $K = \phi(X)^T \phi(X) \in \mathbb{R}^{n \times n}$. $A \in \mathbb{R}^{n \times k}$ is the transformation matrix, and the MMD matrix $M^{(c)} \in \mathbb{R}^{n \times n}$ involves the class information. Similar to Pan et al. [2], the orthogonal constraint $A^T K H K^T A = I$ is introduced to avoid the trivial solution ($A = 0$), where $H = I - \frac{1}{n}\mathbf{1}$ is the centering matrix, where $n = n_s + n_t$ and $\mathbf{1}$ the $n \times n$ matrix of ones.

By minimizing Eq. (3), the conditional distributions between domains are drawn close under the new representation $Z = A^T K$. It is important to note that, although many of the pseudo target labels are incorrect due to the differences in both the marginal and conditional distributions, we can still leverage them to match the conditional distributions with the revised MMD measure defined in Eq. (3). The justification is that we match the distributions by exploring the sufficient statistics instead of the density estimates. In this way, we can leverage the source classifier to improve the target classifier.

Regularization Terms. Besides the distance term, we will further force the optimal transformation matrix A to be smooth which can preserve the intrinsic manifold structure. For two samples $\mathbf{x}_i$ and $\mathbf{x}_j$ that are close to each other in the original feature space, we expect that $A^T \phi(\mathbf{x}_i)$ and $A^T \phi(\mathbf{x}_j)$ should be also close to each other after transformation. This fact is referred to local invariance assumption [14] and has been studied intensively in manifold learning and successfully applied in many fields [15, 16].

A ε-nearest neighbor graph is constructed to express the intrinsic geometrical structure, where all n samples are employed as vertices and the edge weight is computed by the heat kernel weight with self-tuning technique [17]: for each sample $\mathbf{x}_i$, $w_{i,j} = w_{j,i} = \exp\left(\frac{-\|\mathbf{x}_i - \mathbf{x}_j\|^2}{\sigma}\right)$ only if an edge is assigned between the sample $\mathbf{x}_j$ and $\mathbf{x}_i$. Otherwise, set $w_{i,j} = 0$ as $\mathbf{x}_i$ and $\mathbf{x}_j$ are not connected. Then $W = [w_{i,j}]$ gives the matrix representation of the ε-nearest neighbor graph, we are able to model the local invariance assumption by utilizing the manifold regularization technique

$$\frac{1}{2} \sum_{i,j=1}^{n} w_{i,j} \|A^T \phi(\mathbf{x}_i) - A^T \phi(\mathbf{x}_j)\|_2^2 = \mathrm{tr}(A^T K L K^T A) \quad (5)$$

where $L = D - W$ is the graph Laplacian of W and $D = [d_{i,i}]$ is a diagonal matrix with each diagonal element is computed by the corresponding column sum of W. To formulate both W and L, it is not necessary to know the label information of samples and therefore, all the samples $X = [X_s, X_t]$ in the feature space can be included. Minimizing Eq. (5) can preserve the local geometrical structure, i.e. mapping $A^T \phi(\mathbf{x}_i)$ and $A^T \phi(\mathbf{x}_j)$ should be close to each other if $\mathbf{x}_i$ and $\mathbf{x}_j$ are similar. Furthermore, Eq. (5) becomes a convex optimization problem if L is a positive semi-definite matrix. Recover that during the construction of W, we set $w_{i,j} = w_{j,i}$ for symmetry of W which guarantees the graph Laplacian matrix L to be positive semi-definite matrix.

Meanwhile, in order to narrow the scope of solution space, Frobenius-norm is introduced to the objective function. Now we are able to incorporate the data fidelity term and smoothness regularization terms to formulate the proposed transfer learning model.

$$\min_A \sum_{c=1}^{C} \operatorname{tr}(A^T K M^{(c)} K^T A) + \beta \operatorname{tr}(A^T K L K^T A) + \lambda \|A\|_F^2$$
$$\text{s.t. } A^T K H(K)^T A = I \tag{6}$$

It is able to learn an optimal mapping function A that can identify and utilize the correlations among labels while preserving the local geometrical structure among the samples in the feature space. Therefore, we can expect that the proposed algorithm can be useful for label prediction in transfer learning.

2.3 Integrated Majority Voting

The integrated classification voting step generates pseudo-labels for the target domain based on several classifiers trained on source domain, which is developed to exploit the knowledge from the crowd. TLDPR makes use of some individual classifiers learned on $\mathcal{D}_s$ to learn the labels for $\mathcal{D}_t$. Let $\hat{y}_j (j = n_s + 1, \ldots, n_s + n_t)$ denote the final result of integrated classification voting on $\mathbf{x}_j$, and $f_r(j)$ denotes the pseudo prediction of the j-th sample by the r-th classifier $f_r(\cdot)$, we have

$$\hat{y}_j = \begin{cases} \operatorname{majority}(f_r(j), r), & \text{if majority holds} \\ -1, & \text{otherwise} \end{cases} \tag{7}$$

where $r \in \{1, 2, \ldots R\}$ denotes the index of classifier. Specifically, $\hat{y}_j$ could be defined as if most classifiers have majority consensus on a sample, we take its label, else we label it '−1'. In theory, the classifiers can be of any type in our framework. Using integrated classification voting, TLDPR can generate pseudo-labels for the target domain.

2.4 Iterative Refinement

After getting pseudo-labels, TLDPR can run feature transformation to reduce intra-MMD distance, and it alternatingly improve the labeling quality until convergence. The framework is shown in Fig. 2, we can obtain better results for target data with TLDPR.

3   Learning Algorithm

3.1   Proposed Algorithm

We aim to minimize the differences of distributions in the class across domains. It leads to the TLDPR optimization problem (6).

According to the constrained optimization theory, we denote $\Phi = \text{diag}(\phi_1, \ldots, \phi_k) \in \mathbb{R}^{k \times k}$ as the Lagrange multiplier, and derive the Lagrange function for problem (6) as

$$O = \text{tr}(A^T(\sum_{c=1}^{C} KM^{(c)}K^T + \beta KLK^T + \lambda I)A) + \text{tr}((I - A^T KHK^T A)\Phi)$$

(8)

Setting $\frac{\partial O}{\partial A} = 0$, we obtain generalized eigendecomposition

$$(\sum_{c=1}^{C} KM^{(c)}K^T + \beta KLK^T + \lambda I)A = KHK^T A\Phi$$

(9)

Finding the optimal adaptation matrix A is reduced to solving Eq. (9) for the k smallest eigenvectors. The overall process of TLDPR is described in Algorithm 1.

Algorithm 1: TLDPR: Transfer Learning for Driving Pattern Recognition

---

Input : Source domain $\mathcal{D}_s = \{X_s, \mathbf{y}\}$, target domain $\mathcal{D}_t = \{X_t\}$, regularization parameter λ and Laplacian regularization parameter β.

Output : The predicted labels of target data.

begin

1: Train several classifiers on $\{(\mathbf{x}_i, y_i)\}_{i=1}^{n_s}$, and get the voting result to initialize pseudo target labels $\{\hat{y}_j\}_{j=n_s+1}^{n_s+n_t}$ of the target data $\{\mathbf{x}_j\}_{j=n_s+1}^{n_s+n_t}$ by Eq. (7).

repeat

 2: Construct MMD matrices $\left\{M^{(c)}\right\}_{c=1}^{C}$ by Eq. (4).

 3: Solve the generalized eigen-decomposition problem in Eq. (9) and select the k smallest eigenvectors to construct the adaptation matrix A.

 4: Train several classifiers on $\left\{(A^T K, y_i)\right\}_{i=1}^{n_s}$, and get the voting result to update pseudo target labels $\{\hat{y}_j\}_{j=n_s+1}^{n_s+n_t}$ of the target data $\left\{A^T K\right\}_{j=n_s+1}^{n_s+n_t}$ by Eq. (7).

until convergence

5: Return the target labels.

3.2   Complexity Analysis

In this section, we will consider the computational cost of TLDPR. The cost mainly contains two parts: eigen-decomposition and the ensemble classifier. The complexity of eigen-decomposition in each iteration is $\mathcal{O}(n^3)$. In our experiments, 1-Nearest Neighbour (NN), Support Vector Machine (SVM) and Random Forest

(RF) are used to be the individual classifiers. Their complexities are $\mathcal{O}(mn)$, $\mathcal{O}(n^3)$, and $\mathcal{O}(mnd)$ respectively, where d is the depth of the tree. In summary, the overall computational complexity of Algorithm 1 is $\mathcal{O}(\tau(n^3 + mnd))$, where τ is the number of iterations.

4   Experiments and Evaluation

In this section, we conduct extensive experiments for driving pattern recognition problems to demonstrate the effectiveness of the TLDPR approach.

4.1   Data Preparation

The proposed approach is tested on five real-world parking lots datasets. The vehicle for data acquisition has many sensors demonstrated in Fig. 1a, we use 13 attributes such as gear, and speed etc. The datasets are collected from five parking lots marked as $A - E$, the numbers of samples in these five datasets are 10047, 9157, 8924, 9765, and 8436 respectively. The datasets from different parking lots have very different distributions, each dataset from one parking lot is used for one domain. After data preprocessing, the source and target domains share the same 13-D feature space and the same label space consists of 16 categories shown in Fig. 1b.

In order to investigate more detailed information during knowledge transfer for driving scene, we perform TLDPR in two scenarios transferring knowledge from one source domain and multiple source domains. In the sequel, we use the notation $A \rightarrow B$ to denote labeling the driving scene of domain B by using the labeled domain A. We conducted 19 tasks, where 16 with one source domain and 3 with four source domains.

4.2   Baseline Methods

We compare our TLDPR approach with 14 baseline methods for classification problem.

- 1-Nearest Neighbor Classifier (NN)
- Support Vector Machine (SVM)
- Random Forest (RF)
- Transfer Component Analysis (TCA) [2]
- Geodesic Flow Kernel (GFK) [4]
- Joint Distribution Adaptation (JDA) [9]
- Transfer Joint Matching (TJM) [3]
- Adaptation Regularization based Transfer Learning (ARTL) [11]
- CORrelation ALignment (CORAL) [5]
- Landmarks-based kernelized Subspace Alignment (LSA) [6]
- Joint Geometrical and Statistical Alignment (JGSA) [13]
- Balanced Distribution Adaptation (BDA) [10]

– Stratified Transfer Learning (STL) [8]
– Manifold Embedded Distribution Alignment (MEDA) [12]

NN, SVM and RF are three classic classification methods. The others are transfer learning approaches, aim to reduce the difference of source and target domains. The codes of all compared methods can be obtained online.

4.3 Evaluation

We use classification accuracy on test data as the evaluation metric, which is widely used in literature [2,4]

$$\text{Accuracy} = \frac{|\mathbf{x} : \mathbf{x} \in \mathcal{D}_t \wedge \hat{y}(\mathbf{x}) = y(\mathbf{x})|}{|\mathbf{x} : \mathbf{x} \in \mathcal{D}_t|} \tag{10}$$

where $\mathcal{D}_t$ is the set of test data, $y(\mathbf{x})$ is the truth label of x, $\hat{y}(\mathbf{x})$ is the label predicted. We run the algorithm 10 times with random initializations and record the average result.

4.4 Experimental Results and Analysis

Effect of Intra-class Transfer. To verify the effectiveness of TLDPR by inspecting the distribution distance, we compared 8 baseline methods which can reduce the MMD distance of source and target domains. Take $ACDE \rightarrow B$ dataset as an example, the MMD distance of each method is shown in Fig. 3a. Compared with other methods, TLDPR can significantly reduce the difference between distributions, that is because it can reduce the difference within each category, and it can iteratively refine the pseudo-labels with the ensemble strategy. To illustrate the performance of reducing the distance within each category of TLDPR, we list the intra-class MMD distance in Table 1. We can see that most of the intra-class MMD distances are reduced, and the classification performances are improved. Moreover, the t-SNE visualizations of all data points before and after transformation are shown in Fig. 3b and c respectively. The red and blue points represent the data from $ACDE$ and B respectively, we can see that the points in the same class from different domains become closer after the transformation. By iteratively updating the pseudo-labels by the ensemble method, TLDPR can reduce the difference in each iteration to improve performance.

Table 1. Intra-MMD/accuracy (%) in original and TLDPR on dataset $ACDE \rightarrow B$.

Class	Original	TLDPR	Class	Original	TLDPR	Class	Original	TLDPR	Class	Original	TLDPR
1	1.66/100	0.03/94	2	9.66/55	2.17/99	3	1.52/17	2.33/15	4	0.04/86	0.03/71
5	4.46/65	3.30/69	6	0.57/30	0.22/78	7	4.33/97	0.38/97	8	0.13/67	0.04/89
9	0.18/55	0.01/95	10	0.06/68	0.04/92	11	3.52/93	2.21/95	12	1.98/66	0.41/77
13	8.93/44	0.04/80	14	0.07/19	0.01/44	15	1.02/55	0.05/65	16	0.04/16	0.03/20

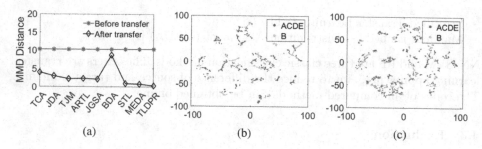

Fig. 3. (a) MMD on dataset $ACDE \rightarrow B$. (b) Data visualization before transformation (MMD = 10.3). (c) Data visualization after transformation (MMD = 0.3).

To verify the effectiveness by inspecting the similarity of embeddings, we compute the 10-nearest neighbor similarity matrix on the embedding $Z = A^T K$ obtained by TLDPR. In order to better demonstrate the results, we only select 4 classes and 25 examples in each class from each domain. The first 100 examples and the last 100 examples are from source and target domain. We also construct the similarity matrices of TCA, JDA and STL using optimal parameter settings. The similarity matrices are shown in Fig. 4, the diagonal blocks of the similarity matrix indicate intra-class similarity in the same domain, the diagonal blocks of the top-right and bottom-left submatrices indicate intra-class similarity across domains, while all other blocks of the similarity matrix indicate inter-class similarity. In this sense, we see that TLDPR can extract higher intra-class similarity and lower inter-class similarity both in the same and across domains.

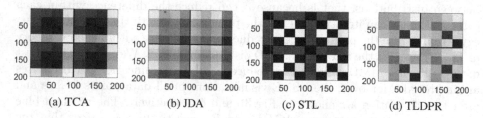

Fig. 4. Illustration of the similarity matrices obtained by (a) TCA, (b) JDA, (c) STL and (d) TLDPR embeddings.

Parameter Sensitivity. The TLDPR approach involves three model parameters: number of subspace bases k, adaptation regularization parameter λ and Laplacian regularization parameter β. We conduct sensitivity analysis to validate that TLDPR can achieve optimal performance under a wide range of parameter values. We randomly select $A \rightarrow D$ and $D \rightarrow B$ as examples to illustrate, while similar trends on all others are not shown due to space limitation. We run TLDPR with varying values of k, λ and β, and plot classification accuracy in Fig. 5. The best results of other baseline methods are marked with dashed lines in this figure. From Fig. 5a, we choose $k \in [10, 20]$ in our experiments. We set the

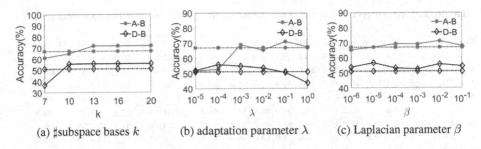

(a) ♯subspace bases k (b) adaptation parameter λ (c) Laplacian parameter β

Fig. 5. Parameter sensitivity for TLDPR on $A \rightarrow B$ and $D \rightarrow B$ datasets (dashed lines show the best baseline results).

adaptation regularization parameter λ by searching $\lambda \in [0.00001, 1]$. Figure 5b shows that we can get optimal parameter values in the range $[0.001, 0.1]$, which indicates that the regularization term is necessary. Figure 5c illustrates the classification accuracy with varying values of Laplacian parameter β, it indicates that Laplacian constraint is useful to retain the local manifold structure, and our model generally does much better than the baselines with a wide range $\beta \in [0.00001, 0.1]$.

Results of All Tasks. The classification results of TLDPR and 14 baseline methods on the 19 tasks are listed in Table 2. We observe that TLDPR achieves much better performance than the baseline methods with statistical significance. The average classification accuracy of TLDPR is 64.7% and the performance improvement is 8.6% compared to the best baseline method. The performances of the standard NN, SVM and RF classifiers are not satisfied, that is because we cannot directly use the classifiers in the source domain to the target domain. TCA, GFK, TJM, CORAL and LSA ignore the intra-affinity between classes which will hinder the performance. Although JDA, ARTL, BDA and MEDA use the pseudo-labels of target data, the initialization of pseudo-label has a great influence to the result. JGSA doesn't perform very well due to the two subspaces. Since the pseudo-label is not iteratively updated via majority voting after the first round of iterations, STL cannot achieve the desired performance. TLDPR avoids these limitations and achieves perform better. This verifies that TLDPR can construct more effective and robust representation for cross-domain driving pattern recognition tasks.

Table 2. Pattern recognition classification accuracy(%) on parking lots datasets.

Task	NN	SVM	RF	TCA	GFK	JDA	TJM	ARTL	CORAL	LSA	JGSA	BDA	STL	MEDA	TLDPR
$A \rightarrow B(1)$	54.4	58.8	41.5	41.5	50.4	66.9	50.0	50.3	43.9	45.5	60.5	59.4	66.0	47.8	**71.1**
$A \rightarrow C(2)$	29.4	39.4	44.9	43.3	28.5	54.7	52.9	53.5	34.3	44.3	56.2	60.5	40.4	41.2	**63.3**
$A \rightarrow D(3)$	19.1	27.9	30.0	45.3	17.7	49.3	44.9	58.0	28.4	39.9	55.9	61.8	30.5	43.3	**64.2**
$A \rightarrow E(4)$	52.8	59.6	57.3	45.1	45.6	74.5	70.4	53.3	48.7	52.6	73.2	70.4	63.2	57.9	**79.6**
$B \rightarrow A(5)$	51.3	54.8	45.5	45.6	39.9	53.0	49.2	54.5	48.3	47.2	43.3	57.3	56.4	45.2	**60.8**
$B \rightarrow C(6)$	56.4	63.9	57.6	47.9	49.4	62.7	59.7	50.3	48.6	52.4	60.3	61.8	65.7	59.3	**68.0**
$B \rightarrow D(7)$	36.6	39.0	43.6	39.1	31.4	54.9	49.0	46.0	24.5	31.0	55.3	56.4	43.3	39.9	**58.2**
$B \rightarrow E(8)$	30.5	30.2	18.0	34.9	24.1	46.1	33.7	47.6	23.6	20.0	52.6	50.5	37.9	35.4	**54.0**
$C \rightarrow A(9)$	25.5	33.1	31.4	38.8	19.7	54.1	58.1	54.0	38.9	44.5	60.7	59.6	36.8	37.7	**64.5**
$C \rightarrow B(10)$	50.6	62.9	44.1	41.2	49.3	61.8	56.6	50.0	49.3	59.8	60.6	60.2	59.1	55.0	**63.9**
$C \rightarrow D(11)$	42.4	45.0	42.9	41.6	38.6	49.4	50.0	50.1	54.0	44.2	58.2	55.8	46.9	50.4	**64.8**
$C \rightarrow E(12)$	18.0	25.2	31.3	43.7	18.1	50.6	37.5	48.9	33.8	34.3	47.3	53.8	22.9	39.6	**57.3**
$D \rightarrow A(13)$	21.3	40.6	53.0	46.2	19.3	48.9	50.1	40.4	42.7	51.3	53.5	46.1	43.7	51.0	**57.3**
$D \rightarrow B(14)$	37.9	43.4	55.1	41.3	35.5	47.7	47.3	42.8	37.2	41.0	51.1	42.8	46.8	43.9	**55.7**
$D \rightarrow C(15)$	41.9	45.0	47.5	48.9	40.9	53.6	57.3	49.3	41.8	54.6	50.1	59.7	44.5	56.4	**60.0**
$D \rightarrow E(16)$	34.9	44.2	45.1	50.4	32.5	60.8	62.4	**65.3**	40.5	53.3	56.0	62.8	44.0	43.0	61.4
$ACDE \rightarrow B(17)$	68.5	75.2	80.3	74.9	57.0	81.9	81.8	66.8	68.6	66.7	79.3	76.3	78.5	67.8	**82.9**
$ABDE \rightarrow C(18)$	35.0	41.1	39.9	60.4	25.4	69.4	68.3	60.5	56.4	58.0	62.8	69.8	40.2	44.0	**70.8**
$ABCE \rightarrow D(19)$	26.0	33.3	29.6	47.6	17.2	58.6	54.8	35.4	58.9	54.2	51.0	67.4	33.9	37.4	**70.6**
Average	38.6	45.4	44.1	46.2	33.7	57.8	54.4	54.4	43.3	47.1	57.3	59.6	47.4	47.2	**64.7**

5 Conclusion

In this paper, we propose a driving pattern recognition method based on transfer learning. TLDPR aims to adapt intra-class distributions in an iterative ensemble procedure. Experiments show TLDPR is effective and robust for driving pattern recognition task, and can significantly outperform several state-of-the-art adaptation methods on the parking lots datasets. In future, we will consider inter-class differences of distribution.

Acknowledgments. This work is supported by the NSFC under Grant No. 61732011, 61702358, the Beijing Natural Science Foundation under Grant No. Z180006, and Key Scientific and Technological Support Projects of Tianjin Key R&D Program under Grant No. 18YFZCGX00390.

References

1. Pan, S.J., Yang, Q.: A survey on transfer learning. IEEE Trans. Knowl. Data Eng. **22**(10), 1345–1359 (2010)
2. Pan, S.J., Tsang, I.W., Kwok, J.T., Yang, Q.: Domain adaptation via transfer component analysis. IEEE Trans. Neural Netw. **22**(2), 199–210 (2011)
3. Long, M., Wang, J., Ding, G., Sun, J., Yu, P.S.: Transfer joint matching for unsupervised domain adaptation. In: Proceedings of the IEEE Conference on Computer Vision and Pattern Recognition, pp. 1410–1417 (2014)
4. Gong, B., Shi, Y., Sha, F., Grauman K.: Geodesic flow kernel for unsupervised domain adaptation. In: 2012 IEEE Conference on Computer Vision and Pattern Recognition, pp. 2066–2073. IEEE (2012)

5. Sun, B., Feng, J., Saenko, K.: Return of frustratingly easy domain adaptation. In: Thirtieth AAAI Conference on Artificial Intelligence (2016)
6. Aljundi, R., Emonet, R., Muselet, D., Sebban, M.: Landmarks-based kernelized subspace alignment for unsupervised domain adaptation. In: Proceedings of the IEEE Conference on Computer Vision and Pattern Recognition, pp. 56–63 (2015)
7. Elhamifar, E., Vidal, R.: Sparse subspace clustering: algorithm, theory, and applications. IEEE Trans. Pattern Anal. Mach. Intell. 35(11), 2765–2781 (2013)
8. Wang, J., Chen, Y., Hu, L., Peng, X., Yu, P.S.: Stratified transfer learning for cross-domain activity recognition. In: 2018 IEEE International Conference on Pervasive Computing and Communications, pp. 1–10. IEEE (2018)
9. Long, M., Wang, J., Ding, G., Sun, J., Yu, P.S.: Transfer feature learning with joint distribution adaptation. In: Proceedings of the IEEE International Conference on Computer Vision, pp. 2200–2207 (2013)
10. Wang, J., Chen, Y., Hao, S., Feng, W., Shen, Z.: Balanced distribution adaptation for transfer learning. In: 2017 IEEE International Conference on Data Mining, pp. 1129–1134. IEEE (2017)
11. Long, M., Wang, J., Ding, G., Pan, S.J., Yu, P.S.: Adaptation regularization: a general framework for transfer learning. IEEE Trans. Knowl. Data Eng. 26(5), 1076–1089 (2014)
12. Wang, J., Feng, W., Chen, Y., Yu, H., Huang, M., Yu, P.S.: Visual domain adaptation with manifold embedded distribution alignment. In: 2018 ACM Multimedia Conference on Multimedia Conference, pp. 402–410. ACM (2018)
13. Zhang, J., Li, W., Ogunbona, P.: Joint geometrical and statistical alignment for visual domain adaptation. In: Proceedings of the IEEE Conference on Computer Vision and Pattern Recognition, pp. 1859–1867 (2017)
14. Belkin, M., Niyogi, P., Sindhwani, V.: Manifold regularization: a geometric framework for learning from labeled and unlabeled examples. J. Mach. Learn. Res. 7(Nov), 2399–2434 (2006)
15. Zhou, D., Bousquet, O., Lal, T.N., Weston, J., Scholkopf, B.: Learning with local and global consistency. In: Advances in Neural Information Processing Systems, pp. 321–328 (2004)
16. Cai, D., He, X., Han, J., Huang, T.S.: Graph regularized nonnegative matrix factorization for data representation. IEEE Trans. Pattern Anal. Mach. Intell. 33(8), 1548–1560 (2011)
17. Zelnik-Manor, L., Perona, P.: Self-tuning spectral clustering. In: Advances in Neural Information Processing Systems, pp. 1601–1608 (2005)

Towards Meta-learning of Deep Architectures for Efficient Domain Adaptation

Abbas Raza Ali[1]([✉]) [iD], Marcin Budka[1] [iD], and Bogdan Gabrys[2] [iD]

[1] Bournemouth University, Poole BH12 5BB, UK
{aali,mbudka}@bournemouth.ac.uk
[2] University Technology Sydney, Ultimo, NSW 2007, Australia
bogdan.gabrys@uts.edu.au

Abstract. This paper proposes an efficient domain adaption approach using deep learning along with transfer and meta-level learning. The objective is to identify how many blocks (i.e. groups of consecutive layers) of a pre-trained image classification network need to be fine-tuned based on the characteristics of the new task. In order to investigate it, a number of experiments have been conducted using different pre-trained networks and image datasets. The networks were fine-tuned, starting from the blocks containing the output layers and progressively moving towards the input layer, on various tasks with characteristics different from the original task. The amount of fine-tuning of a pre-trained network (i.e. the number of top layers requiring adaptation) is usually dependent on the complexity, size, and domain similarity of the original and new tasks. Considering these characteristics, a question arises of how many blocks of the network need to be fine-tuned to get maximum possible accuracy? Which of a number of available pre-trained networks require fine-tuning of the minimum number of blocks to achieve this accuracy? The experiments, that involve three network architectures each divided into 10 blocks on average and five datasets, empirically confirm the intuition that there exists a relationship between the similarity of the original and new tasks and the depth of network needed to fine-tune in order to achieve accuracy comparable with that of a model trained from scratch. Further analysis shows that the fine-tuning of the final top blocks of the network, which represent the high-level features, is sufficient in most of the cases. Moreover, we have empirically verified that less similar tasks require fine-tuning of deeper portions of the network, which however is still better than training a network from scratch.

Keywords: Computer Vision · Convolutional Neural Networks · Deep learning · Domain adaption · Meta-learning · Transfer learning

1 Introduction

Deep learning has demonstrated tremendous success in various domains, particularly Computer Vision, and Speech and Language Processing (SLP) [26,29],

© Springer Nature Switzerland AG 2019
A. C. Nayak and A. Sharma (Eds.): PRICAI 2019, LNAI 11671, pp. 66–79, 2019.
https://doi.org/10.1007/978-3-030-29911-8_6

where it is consistently outperforming traditional machine learning approaches [2]. Among the key developments in the field of deep learning, Convolutional Neural Networks (CNNs) stand out as the workhorse of Computer Vision. Training a large CNN with millions of parameters is a computationally intensive task which also requires a significant amount of training data. However, several state-of-the-art image classification architectures trained on large image datasets are publicly available, including Visual Geometry Group Network (VGGNet) [21], Inception [23], Residual Networks (ResNet) [9] and Inception-ResNet [22]. These networks are trained on the ImageNet [19] dataset which consists of 1.2 million images and 1000 classes.

Training of these types of deep networks from scratch on a huge dataset is a computationally demanding task, e.g. training of models on each dataset used in this work usually takes a few days of processing time using an Nvidia GTX 1080 GPU. As a result, transfer learning, i.e. reusing parts of the pre-trained models either as-is or as a starting point within the training process, quickly became a de-facto standard in Computer Vision tasks. The general consensus seems to be that the more data one has, the more 'aggressive' the re-training process can be (e.g. re-training more final layers). Conversely, the more similar the new dataset is to the one used to train the original model, the fewer layers need to be fine-tuned. Despite the wide adoption of transfer learning in the context of CNNs, to the best of our knowledge, there is still no principled way of approaching this process. The number of layers to re-train or even the network architectures themselves are chosen in an ad-hoc manner and tested one after the other, which is a computationally inefficient procedure.

This paper proposes and investigates a new approach to adapt pre-trained CNNs to new domains using the Meta-level Learning paradigm. Meta-learning, also known as 'learning to learn', was introduced around three decades ago [25], and was initially limited to classification and clustering tasks [1,12]. Recently, it has also been used in deep learning for the selection of hyper-parameters of a specific architecture. [16] proposed a comprehensive set of global and node level hyper-parameters which are critical to optimizing deep learning architectures through evolution. The use of Reinforcement learning to generate CNN and Recurrent Neural Network (RNN) architectures have been proposed by [3] and [30]. They have used Q-learning to produce new CNN architectures. [7] introduced a simple but powerful approach, model-agnostic meta-learning, which provides an optimal initialization of model parameters that lead to fast learning on new tasks.

Transfer learning has been positioned to effectively adapt pre-trained networks to a new domain by fine-tuning their final layers. Some studies, such as [27] and [20], propose re-training of only final fully-connected (FC) layers of the network which does not guarantee state-of-the-art accuracy, particularly on relatively dissimilar tasks. On the contrary, domain adaptation becomes beneficial by fine-tuning an increasing number of layers based on the complexity and relevance of the new task [28]. Therefore, a question arises as to how many blocks need fine-tuning to adapt to a new domain based on the complexity, size and domain relevance.

The rest of the paper is organized as follows. Section 2 is devoted to elaborating the overall approach of this work. Section 3 outlines the methodology of this study. Section 4 reports the experimental results followed by their analysis. Finally, the paper is concluded in Sect. 5.

2   Methodology

In order to carry out the investigations, a platform has been implemented to conduct experiments with different combinations of pre-trained networks, their hyper-parameters, and image datasets. The experiments have been designed to investigate the relationships among these three key components while fine-tuning the pre-trained networks on new tasks. There are several characteristics which can be considered but the two most important features selected for this study are size and similarity of the new task. The four transfer learning scenarios are based on these two features. A schematic view of transfer learning based is shown in Fig. 1 where Task-A is representing the original problem and Task-B the new problem datasets.

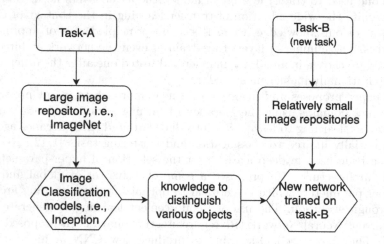

Fig. 1. Schematic diagram of transfer learning

Despite the popularity of transfer learning in computer vision, there is no principled way of finding the relation between characteristics of a dataset and depth of the network that needs to be re-trained. In this work, an effort has been made to find this relationship by identifying a pre-trained network where the minimum number of blocks need to be re-trained to achieve state-of-the-art accuracy. Moreover, instead of learning the general characteristics of the dataset which is usually practiced in shallow learning, e.g. feature statistics [1], a higher level characteristics have been pursued, such as layer activations. The focus of the experiments was to investigate the following key scenarios:

1. If Task-B is small in size and similar to Task-A (e.g. both tasks are concerned with natural images), re-training of the entire network might lead to over-fitting. The higher-level features of the pre-trained network, Task-A, are usually relevant for Task-B. Hence, the re-training of a single or a few final layer(s) becomes very effective.
2. If Task-B is large and similar to Task-A, there is less possibility of over-fitting while fine-tuning more layers of the network.
3. If Task-B is small but less similar to Task-A, there is a possibility that Task-A does not contain relevant features for Task-B. In this case transfer learning might not be very useful, however, re-training of final layers might give reasonable results.
4. If Task-B is large and very different from Task-A, both the training of the network from scratch and initialization of the network with the weights of the pre-trained model would be beneficial.

Figure 2 is summarising the above four scenarios.

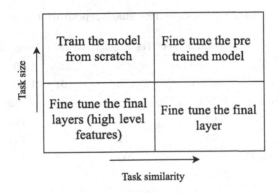

Fig. 2. Transfer learning scenarios

Datasets with appropriate characteristics have been gathered for the experiments to cover the above four scenarios. The network architectures used in this study vary greatly, hence we fine-tune groups of layers rather than individual layers. The rationale for this is that we wanted to avoid e.g. fine-tuning only part of an inception module, which is atomic from the point of view the whole Inception architecture [15]. Please refer to Fig. 3 for the details of how the layers of each architecture have been grouped into what we refer to as 'blocks'.

The pre-trained networks have been fine-tuned on each of the new tasks. The experimental approach was to fine-tune an iteratively increasing number of blocks of each network, starting from the final block, while the lower blocks of the network act as a fixed feature extractor for Task-B. The train and test accuracies have been recorded on every iteration. In some cases, where Task-B is similar, the re-training of only the final layer produces close to the state-of-the-art accuracy. On the contrary, it is hardly applicable when both tasks are very different. In that case, more final layers need to be re-trained. In general, a network learns the hierarchy of features starting from generic ones, e.g., colors, edges, curves, etc., which can be reused for most of the tasks. Conversely, the later layers respond to more specific features of the original task which can only be reusable in case the new task is similar.

3 Experimentation Environment

To further investigate the questions raised in the previous section, a comprehensive experimentation environment has been setup. It comprises of five datasets of different characteristics and three state-of-the-art pre-trained image classification networks. The complexity of the experiments has been calculated as the number of datasets times the number of trainable blocks of all the networks. Therefore, computational power becomes a critical factor to perform these experiments in a reasonable time. There were five GPUs used to train around 200 models.

Table 1. Open-source image repositories

Dataset	Training-set	Testing-set	Classes	Avg. class size
ImageNet [19]	1.2 million	50,000	1,000	1,200
Food [4]	75,750	25,250	101	1,000
Caltech-101 [6]	6,144	2,096	101	82
Chest-Xray [5]	5,943	1,487	2	3,715
Flowers [17]	2,753	917	5	734
Coco-Animals [14]	800	200	8	125

3.1 Datasets

In this work, five publicly available datasets have been used with different domain and characteristics. They can be divided into two categories based on their size and number of classes; large and small as shown in Table 1. The pre-trained networks which are selected for this work are trained on ImageNet. The Food dataset, introduced by [4], is a challenging collection of 101 food categories and 101,000 instances. Likewise, Caltech dataset also has 101 categories with 82 images per category on average [6]. The images are not specific to any particular

Table 2. Benchmarking of various pre-trained image classification models

Network	Layers	Top-1 accuracy	Top-5 accuracy
Inception-v3 [24]	22	78.0%	93.9%
Inception-ResNet-v2	152	80.4%	95.3%
VGG-19 [21]	19	71.1%	89.8%

domain. Chest-Xray [5] is a relatively smaller dataset, originally published with 14 classes. The images were mostly tagged with multiple labels which are converted to two-class problem where every image can be classified as either normal or nodule. This dataset is composed of frontal-view X-ray images of the screening and diagnosis of many lung-related diseases. Similarly, Flowers is another small dataset consisting of five different categories of flower species [17]. Microsoft has gathered a large dataset consisting of 91 categories, known as Common Objects in Context (Coco) [14]. Coco-Animals (Animals) is a subset of the original Coco dataset which is composed of 8 animal categories.

3.2   Pre-trained Image Classification Networks

Three pre-trained image classification and detection CNNs have been used in this work. These networks are trained on ImageNet dataset which consists of 1000 classes [19], however, their internal architecture, depth, and other aspects differ

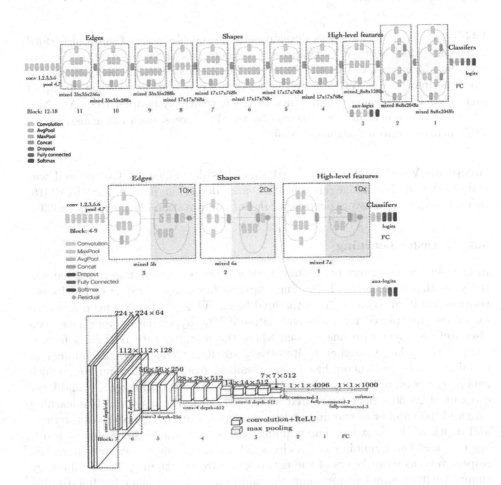

Fig. 3. Schematic view of Inception-v3, Inception-ResNet-v2 and VGG-19 networks where the blue colour is representing a re-trainable layer/block

considerably. The first few layers of the networks capture low-level features of the image like edges, curves, etc. The subsequent layers learned shapes and more abstract features related to the problem domain. The final layers have learned more specific features corresponding to a particular category which is eventually used to classify the images. The pre-trained networks are listed in Table 2 along with number of layers and accuracy in the ImageNet dataset.

Inception-ResNet-v2. Google released Inception-ResNet in 2016 and it became a state-of-the-art image classification network of ILSVRC-2016. Inception-ResNet-v2 is a deeper but simplified version of Inception-v3. The residual connections allow the model to be even deeper, leading to better performance. ResNet relies on micro-architecture modules which consist of building blocks.

A schematic view of different pre-trained architectures can be seen in Fig. 3. The architectures are also labelled with the block numbers, in blue, that can be subject to fine-tuning.

VGG-19. VGG network was developed by Visual Geometry Group of Oxford University which secured first place in the ImageNet ILSVRC-2014. It has two versions which consist of 16 and 19 layers. The 19 layer version has been used in our experiments. The VGG network uses 3×3 convolutions stacked on top of each other in increasing depth which makes it relatively simpler than AlexNet. The convolutional layers are followed by two FC layers, each one consisting of 4,096 neurons, and a Softmax classifier.

Inception-V3. Inception, or GoogLeNet, was developed by Google and was state-of-the-art for image classification and detection in the ILSVRC-2015. Inception-v3 is a 22 layers deep network but computationally inexpensive [23].

3.3 Transfer Learning

In transfer learning three pre-trained networks are re-trained/fine-tuned sequentially on the same task. The training process fine-tunes a range of blocks per training iteration, starting from the final block. This process has been repeated for all the pre-trained networks and datasets. The hyper-parameters have been also updated layer-wise one by one where the learning rate initializes from a comparatively large number to iteratively smaller. Conversely, the number of training epochs parameter has been initialized from a smaller number which gets bigger as more layers need to re-train. The *rmsprop* optimizer [11] and layer dropout of 20–30% have been used while re-training the network. The learning rate and the number of training epochs are dependent on the nature of the tasks and depth of the network. The training begins with the higher value of learning rate and lower number of epochs which gradually decreases and increases, respectively, as more layers of the network require fine-tuning. Their values are changed with a small factor upon the addition of a new layer for fine-tuning.

The idea is to use the lower value of learning rate and higher number of epochs for larger datasets. Table 3 is showing hyper-parameters that are used in our experiments.

Table 3. Hyper-parameters that are used for transfer learning

Datasets	Learning rate	Epochs	Dropout
Food	10^{-3}–10^{-7}	180–1000	20%
Caltech	10^{-4}–10^{-7}	180–1000	20%
Chest-Xray	10^{-3}–10^{-6}	120–800	20–30%
Flowers	10^{-3}–10^{-6}	120–800	20%
Animals	10^{-3}–10^{-6}	120–800	20%

4   Results and Analysis

An extensive set of experiments has been performed to analyze the relationship of size and similarity of a task with the depth of pre-trained network that needs to be fine-tuned. The depth of the pre-trained networks, which is fine-tuned, is varied from 7 to 18 blocks. The layer-wise training and validation accuracies have been reported in Table 4. The table shows accuracies of five datasets against three different architectures and the number of fine-tuned blocks. The top-performing numbers of blocks are in bold. The relationship between the validation accuracy and the number of blocks has been depicted in Fig. 4.

The accuracy of a pre-trained network after fine-tuning every block, also know as block-wise result, is validated with dataset similarity analysis. The networks that are used in this work were originally trained on the ImageNet dataset. Therefore, the validation set of all the datasets have been inferred by the pre-trained networks to compute their similarity with ImageNet. As a result, the maximum of the probability mass function of an image over the 1000 classes, which is referred to as image similarity to ImageNet, and entropy have been calculated and averaged over the number of images N in the dataset. The similarity and entropy are calculated using Eqs. 1 and 2, respectively.

$$\text{similarity} = \frac{1}{N} \sum_{i=1}^{N} \max(\mathbf{f}(x_i)) \tag{1}$$

where $\mathbf{f}(x_i)$ is the probability mass function over classes conditioned on the input image x_i, typically the output of the Softmax layer.

$$\text{average entropy} = \frac{1}{N} \sum_{i=1}^{N} \left(- \sum_{j=1}^{1000} (\mathbf{f}_j(x_i) * \log_2(\mathbf{f}_j(x_i)))\right) \tag{2}$$

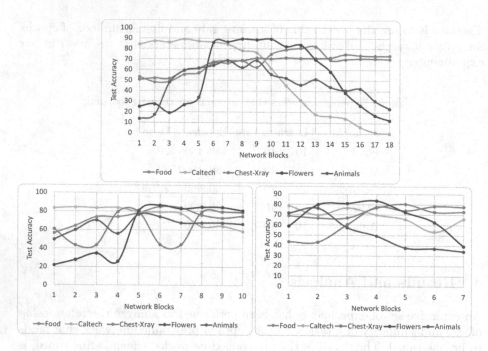

Fig. 4. Transfer learning accuracies of pre-trained networks; (a) Inception, (b) Inception-ResNet and (c) VGG-19 on ImageNet

Table 4. Transfer learning accuracies of the various datasets, classification architectures, and their layers

Dataset	FC	1	2	3	4	5	6	7	8	9	10	11	12	13	14
Inception-v3 network															
Food	85–53	84–48	84–49	72–55	70–57	73–66	73–66	76–68	79–62	84–75	82–79	85–80	**86–82**	79–69	80–70
Caltech	95–84	95–87	96–86	**96–89**	96–87	95–86	93–84	88–78	82–76	69–61	48–45	37–31	24–18	15–16	12–14
Chest-Xray	96–50	96–52	96–52	96–59	96–61	96–67	96–68	96–69	96–71	96–70	96–71	95–71	92–71	78–72	**87–75**
Flowers	84–25	84–27	87–19	88–27	91–34	95–86	96–86	**96–89**	96–88	95–89	92–82	86–83	78–70	56–58	41–38
Animals	54–14	47–17	58–48	81–59	88–61	90–64	**92–69**	91–62	90–69	88–56	81–52	69–46	58–51	47–44	38–41
Inception-ResNet-v2 network															
Food	86–56	86–64	86–74	86–74	87–78	**89–85**	86–84	80–76	71–73	78–75	–	–	–	–	–
Caltech	96–83	**96–84**	95–83	94–84	94–79	93–79	91–78	88–64	79–64	67–59	–	–	–	–	–
Chest-Xray	91–61	89–43	88–44	91–79	91–79	91–44	91–44	91–79	**91–80**	91–79	–	–	–	–	–
Flowers	89–22	89–28	91–35	92–26	93–81	**94–87**	95–83	96–85	96–84	94–81	–	–	–	–	–
Animals	65–49	71–60	77–70	77–56	**82–77**	85–74	86–68	88–68	88–68	85–66	–	–	–	–	–
VGG-19 network															
Food	85–69	85–67	85–67	90–77	**81–80**	77–73	77–73	–	–	–	–	–	–	–	–
Caltech	**79–78**	72–70	80–77	74–70	68–66	66–53	71–66	–	–	–	–	–	–	–	–
Chest-Xray	89–43	87–43	89–61	88–78	89–74	**89–78**	89–78	–	–	–	–	–	–	–	–
Flowers	83–59	81–80	83–81	**86–84**	79–72	79–63	90–39	–	–	–	–	–	–	–	–
Animals	78–71	**79–76**	70–57	74–49	72–38	73–37	79–34	–	–	–	–	–	–	–	–

The header group: Network re-training accuracy (train %–test %) upon fine-tuning a range of blocks, one block per iteration

The similarity of an image from the new domain with the original domain is computed by feeding the image to the original pre-trained network and examining the output probability distribution over the classes. The dataset similarity scores have been recorded in Table 5. The similarity results are correlated with the number of blocks that are needed to fine-tune networks on new tasks. Figure 5(a–c) shows that for tasks where similarity is higher (and the entropy is lower), fewer blocks need to be fine-tuned. On the contrary, more blocks need to be fine-tuned where the datasets are less similar (having low similarity and higher entropy values). This supports our claim that transfer learning is effective for related tasks regardless of their size. However, transfer learning is also useful for dissimilar tasks, i.e., Chest-Xray and Food, but more blocks need to be retrained to get good results. Moreover, similar tasks require fine-tuning of either only fully-connected layer(s) or high-level features block in some cases. Accordingly, less similar tasks require fine-tuning of more deeper layers, i.e., shapes and edges blocks as well based on the similarity of tasks.

Table 5. The similarity and average entropy of different datasets

Dataset	Inception-v3	Inception-ResNet-v2	VGG-19
ImageNet	76.61% – 2.11	78.77% – 1.84	72.7% – 2.23
Food	53.40% – 3.52	59.23% – 3.47	51.24% – 3.83
Caltech	60.41% – 3.27	64.30% – 2.62	57.58% – 2.40
Chest-Xray	40.88% – 4.88	43.25% – 4.40	34.72% – 4.74
Flowers	52.25% – 4.01	60.19% – 3.15	49.72% – 3.12
Animals	54.88% – 3.68	64.87% – 2.68	53.08% – 2.79

Figure 5(d) shows that the size meta-feature has a good correlation with the depth of the network that is fine-tuned. The contribution of the similarity of a dataset dominates over its size when both datasets are similar. However, size becomes critical when both datasets have less similarity between them. It only supports the network to generalize while fine-tuning more deeper blocks of the network, e.g., Food and Chest-Xray dataset. The Food datasets consist of over 100,000 examples with over 100 classes whereas Chest-Xray has around 8,000 instances with only 2 classes. Based on the number of classes both datasets have a reasonable size to class ratio which allow them to fine-tune more deeper networks.

The Food and Chest-Xray datasets' domains are different from ImageNet. Consequently more deeper blocks have been fine-tuned. Transfer learning is more effective than training the model from scratch for these tasks. The maximum validation accuracy of fine-tuned Food and Chest-Xray is closer to the model which is trained from scratch. These accuracies as compared to the training of the network from scratch, reported by various studies, are presented in Table 6. However, transfer learning requires much less effort and resources, in terms of parameter tuning and computation.

Table 6. The state-of-the-art accuracy (training of the network from scratch) versus maximum accuracy from this work

Dataset	Accuracy of the network from scratch	Architecture	Reference	Accuracy from this work
Food	88.28%	InceptionV3	[8]	84.93%
Caltech	91.44%	SPP-Net	[10]	89.00%
Chest-Xray	84.11%	CheXNet	[18]	79.52%
Flowers	91.52%	CNN-SVM	[13]	89.06%
Animals	-	-	-	76.70%

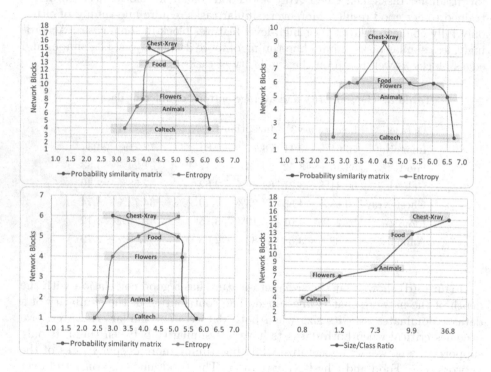

Fig. 5. Datasets similarity with ImageNet for: (a) Inception-v3, (b) Inception-ResNet-v2, (c) VGG-19. (d) Inception-v3 blocks vs dataset size/class ratio. The similarity is normalized to 1–10.

5   Conclusion

This paper presents an empirical study of the relationship between various characteristics describing the similarity of two datasets, and based on that, the amount of fine-tuning required to achieve accuracy close to state-of-the-art. Even though the experiments were limited to only two characteristics, size and similarity with the original task, still as per some studies these are most important in this context. The datasets with both similar and different domains as well as different sizes have been used. Also, three state-of-the-art image classification networks trained on ImageNet were used in the experiments. Extensive experiments have been conducted on different combinations of pre-trained networks (and their blocks), datasets and hyper-parameters. The block-wise results are validated with dataset similarity analysis where the probability of match and entropy of the datasets are correlated with the fine-tuning of the number of blocks. The proposed approach first computes the similarity of the new task with the original one and combines it with the size of the new task to identify which section of the architecture needs fine-tuning.

The experiments were designed around two meta-features where only the datasets having different characteristics were considered. In general, transfer learning is found to be effective for tasks similar to the original one, regardless of the size, where mostly fine-tuning of the final blocks produces close to state-of-the-art accuracy. On the other hand, this work is handy for the tasks having less or no similarity with the original task with very few training examples, i.e., problems related to Medical Imaging [18]. It allows to find the minimum number of blocks a pre-trained network require fine-tuning to achieve the best possible accuracy based on the characteristics of two tasks. It also identifies the portion of the pre-trained network which can be reusable based on the similarity and size among two tasks. The key characteristic of transfer learning is that it saves significant computation and training time while achieving similar accuracy to the networks trained from scratch. This study preserves the key characteristics of transfer learning atleast for less similar tasks which verifies the intuition that one can more effectively reuse pre-trained network.

References

1. Ali, A., Gabrys, B., Budka, M.: Cross-domain meta-learning for time-series forecasting. Proc. Comput. Sci. **126**, 9–18 (2018)
2. Alom, Z., Taha, T.M., Yakopcic, C., Westberg, S., et al.: The history began from AlexNet: a comprehensive survey on deep learning approaches. Computing Research Repository (CoRR) arxiv:abs/1803.01164 (2018)
3. Baker, B., Gupta, O., Naik, N., Raskar, R.: Designing neural network architectures using reinforcement learning. Computing Research Repository (CoRR) arxiv:abs/1611.02167 (2016)
4. Bossard, L., Guillaumin, M., Van Gool, L.: Food-101 – mining discriminative components with random forests. In: Fleet, D., Pajdla, T., Schiele, B., Tuytelaars, T. (eds.) ECCV 2014. LNCS, vol. 8694, pp. 446–461. Springer, Cham (2014). https://doi.org/10.1007/978-3-319-10599-4_29
5. Demner-Fushman, D., Kohli, M.D., Rosenman, M.B., Shooshan, S.E., et al.: Preparing a collection of radiology examinations for distribution and retrieval. J. Am. Med. Inform. Assoc. **23**(2), 304–310 (2016)
6. Fei-Fei, L., Fergus, R., Perona, P.: Learning generative visual models from few training examples: an incremental bayesian approach tested on 101 object categories. Comput. Vis. Image Underst. **106**(1), 59–70 (2007)

7. Finn, C., Abbeel, P., Levine, S.: Model-agnostic meta-learning for fast adaptation of deep networks. In: Proceedings of the 34th International Conference on Machine Learning, vol. 70, pp. 1126–1135. PMLR, International Convention Centre, Sydney, August 2017

8. Hassannejad, H., Matrella, G., Ciampolini, P., De Munari, I., Mordonini, M., Cagnoni, S.: Food image recognition using very deep convolutional networks. In: Proceedings of the 2nd International Workshop on Multimedia Assisted Dietary Management, MADiMa 2016, pp. 41–49. ACM, New York (2016)

9. He, K., Zhang, X., Ren, S., Sun, J.: Deep residual learning for image recognition. In: 2016 IEEE Conference on Computer Vision and Pattern Recognition (CVPR), pp. 770–778 (2016)

10. Hem, K., Zhang, X., Ren, S., Sun, J.: Spatial pyramid pooling in deep convolutional networks for visual recognition. Computing Research Repository (CoRR) arxiv:abs/1406.4729 (2014)

11. Hinton, G., Srivastava, N., Swersky, K.: Overview of mini-batch gradient descent lecture of neural networks for machine learning course (2014). http://www.cs.toronto.edu/~tijmen/csc321/slides/lecture_slides_lec6.pdf

12. Lemke, C., Budka, M., Gabrys, B.: Metalearning: a survey of trends and technologies. Artif. Intell. Rev. **44**, 117–130 (2015)

13. Lin, K., Yang, H.F., Chen, C.S.: Flower classification with few training examples via recalling visual patterns from deep CNN, pp. 41–49. CVGIP (2015)

14. Lin, T., Maire, M., Belongie, S.J., Bourdev, L.D., et al.: Microsoft COCO: common objects in context. Computing Research Repository (CoRR) arxiv:abs/1405.0312 (2014)

15. Mallya, A., Lazebnik, S.: Piggyback: adding multiple tasks to a single, fixed network by learning to mask. Computing Research Repository (CoRR) arxiv:abs/1801.06519 (2018)

16. Miikkulainen, R., Liang, J.Z., Meyerson, E., Rawal, A., et al.: Evolving deep neural networks. Computing Research Repository (CoRR) arxiv:abs/1703.00548 (2017)

17. Nilsback, M.E., Zisserman, A.: Automated flower classification over a large number of classes. In: 2008 Sixth Indian Conference on Computer Vision, Graphics Image Processing, pp. 722–729 (2008)

18. Rajpurkar, P., Irvin, J., Zhu, K., Yang, B., et al.: ChexNet: radiologist-level pneumonia detection on chest x-rays with deep learning. Computing Research Repository (CoRR) arxiv:abs/1711.05225 (2017)

19. Russakovsky, O., Deng, J., Su, H., Krause, J., et al.: Imagenet large scale visual recognition challenge. Int. J. Comput. Vis. **115**(3), 211–252 (2015)

20. Shin, H., Roberts, K., Lu, L., Demner-Fushman, D., Yao, J., Summers, R.M.: Learning to read chest x-rays: recurrent neural cascade model for automated image annotation. Computing Research Repository (CoRR) arxiv:abs/1603.08486 (2016)

21. Simonyan, K., Zisserman, A.: Very deep convolutional networks for large-scale image recognition. Computing Research Repository (CoRR) arxiv:abs/1409.1556 (2014)

22. Szegedy, C., Ioffe, S., Vanhoucke, V., Alemi, A.: Inception-v4, inception-ResNet and the impact of residual connections on learning. In: Proceedings of the Thirty-First AAAI Conference on Artificial Intelligence, 4–9 February 2017, San Francisco, California, USA, pp. 4278–4284 (2017)

23. Szegedy, C., Liu, W., Jia, Y., Sermanet, P., et al.: Going deeper with convolutions. In: Computer Vision and Pattern Recognition (CVPR) (2015). http://arxiv.org/abs/1409.4842

24. Szegedy, C., Vanhoucke, V., Ioffe, S., et al.: Rethinking the inception architecture for computer vision. In: 2016 IEEE Conference on Computer Vision and Pattern Recognition, CVPR 2016, Las Vegas, NV, USA, 27–30 June 2016, pp. 2818–2826 (2016)
25. Vilalta, R., Drissi, Y.: A perspective view and survey of meta-learning. Artif. Intell. Rev. **18**(2), 77–95 (2002)
26. Wang, D., Zheng, T.F.: Transfer learning for speech and language processing. In: 2015 Asia-Pacific Signal and Information Processing Association Annual Summit and Conference (APSIPA), pp. 1225–1237 (2015)
27. Wang, X., Peng, Y., Lu, L., Lu, Z., et al.: ChestX-ray8: hospital-scale chest X-ray database and benchmarks on weakly-supervised classification and localization of common thorax diseases. Computing Research Repository (CoRR) arxiv:abs/1705.02315 (2017)
28. Yosinski, J., Clune, J., Bengio, Y., Lipson, H.: How transferable are features in deep neural networks? In: Proceedings of the 27th International Conference on Neural Information Processing Systems, NIPS 2014, vol. 2, pp. 3320–3328. MIT Press, Cambridge (2014)
29. Zhang, Z., Sun, Z., Liu, J., Chen, J., et al.: An experimental comparison of deep neural networks for end-to-end speech recognition. Computing Research Repository (CoRR) arxiv:abs/1611.07174 (2016)
30. Zoph, B., Le, Q.V.: Neural architecture search with reinforcement learning. Computing Research Repository (CoRR) arxiv:abs/1611.01578 (2016)

Multi-agent Hierarchical Reinforcement Learning with Dynamic Termination

Dongge Han$^{(\boxtimes)}$, Wendelin Böhmer, Michael Wooldridge, and Alex Rogers

Department Computer Science, University of Oxford, Oxford, UK
{dongge.han,wendelin.boehmer,michael.wooldridge,alex.rogers}@cs.ox.ac.uk

Abstract. In a multi-agent system, an agent's optimal policy will typically depend on the policies chosen by others. Therefore, a key issue in multi-agent systems research is that of predicting the behaviours of others, and responding promptly to changes in such behaviours. One obvious possibility is for each agent to broadcast their current intention, for example, the currently executed option in a hierarchical reinforcement learning framework. However, this approach results in inflexibility of agents if options have an extended duration and are dynamic. While adjusting the executed option at each step improves flexibility from a single-agent perspective, frequent changes in options can induce inconsistency between an agent's actual behaviour and its broadcast intention. In order to balance flexibility and predictability, we propose a dynamic termination Bellman equation that allows the agents to flexibly terminate their options. We evaluate our models empirically on a set of multi-agent pursuit and taxi tasks, and show that our agents learn to adapt flexibly across scenarios that require different termination behaviours.

Keywords: Multi-agent Learning · Hierarchcial reinforcement learning

1 Introduction

Many important real-world tasks are multi-agent by nature, such as taxi coordination [10], supply chain management [6], and distributed sensing [9]. Despite the success of single-agent reinforcement learning (RL) [13,17], multi-agent RL has remained as an open problem. A challenge unique to multi-agent RL is that an agent's optimal policy typically depends on the policies chosen by others [16]. Therefore, it is essential that an agent takes into account the behaviours of others when choosing its own actions. One possible solution is to let each agent model and broadcast its intention, in order to indicate the agent's subsequent behaviours [3]. As an example, Fig. 1(a) shows a taxi pickup scenario where taxi A is choosing its next direction. Given the information that taxi B is currently heading towards Q, taxi A can determine passenger P as its preferred option over Q.

Fortunately, hierarchical RL provides a simple solution for modeling agents' intentions by allowing them to use *options*, which are subgoals that an agent aims

A. C. Nayak and A. Sharma (Eds.): PRICAI 2019, LNAI 11671, pp. 80–92, 2019.
https://doi.org/10.1007/978-3-030-29911-8_7

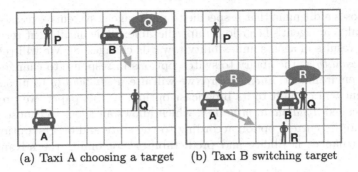

(a) Taxi A choosing a target   (b) Taxi B switching target

Fig. 1. Taxi scenario examples

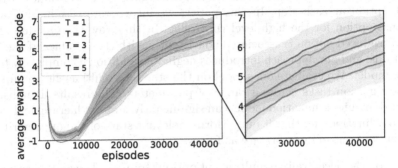

Fig. 2. The effect of terminating options early, i.e., after T steps

to achieve in a finite horizon. Makar et al. [11] proposed *multi-agent hierarchical RL*, where hierarchical agents broadcast their current options to the others. However, despite the advantage brought by using options, there can be a delay in an agent's responses towards changes in the environment or others' behaviours, due to the temporally-extended nature of options, which forbids the agents from switching to another option before the current one is terminated. In the scenario depicted in Fig. 1(b), while taxi A is going for passenger R, taxi B finished picking up passenger Q and also switched towards R. In this case, taxi A will miss the target R, but it cannot immediately switch its target.

A potential solution to the delayed response challenge is to terminate options prematurely. Figure 2 shows the performance of a multi-agent taxi experiment where the agents' current options are interrupted after T timesteps. By reducing T, the agents gain higher flexibility for option switching, which also leads to increasing rewards. This has been studied previously to address the problem of *imperfect options* in single-agent settings, where an agent can improve its performance by terminating and switching to an optimal option at each step [18]. However, this approach may no longer prove advantageous in a multi-agent scenario. When an agent frequently switches options, the broadcast option will be inconsistent with its subsequent behaviour. Consequently, the agent's behaviour becomes less predictable and the advantage of broadcasting options is diminished.

This poses a dilemma that is specific to multi-agent systems: excessive terminations makes an agent's behaviour unpredictable, while insufficient termination of options results in agents' inflexibility towards changes [8]. We will refer to an agent's *flexibility* as the ability to switch options in response to changes in others or the environment. Furthermore, we will use *predictability* to measure how far an agent will commit to its broadcast option. In this paper, we propose an approach called *dynamic termination*, which allows an agent to choose whether to terminate its current option according to the state and others' options. This approach balances flexibility and predictability, combining the advantages of both.

An obvious approach to modelling dynamic termination is to use an additional controller, which decides whether to terminate or to continue with the current option at each step. In this paper, we incorporate termination as an additional option for the high-level controller. In this way, the Q-value of the newly introduced option is associated consistently with the Q-values of the original options, and our approach introduces negligible additional complexity to the original model. We evaluate our model on the standard multi-agent pursuit and taxi coordination tasks across a range of parameters. The results demonstrate that our dynamic termination model can significantly improve hierarchical multi-agent coordination and that it outperforms relevant state-of-the-art algorithms. The contributions of our work are as follows:

1. Based on the decentralized multi-agent options framework, we propose a novel dynamic termination scheme which allows an agent to flexibly terminate its current option. We show empirically that our model can greatly improve multi-agent coordination
2. We propose a delayed communication method for an agent to approximate the joint Q-value. This method allows us to use intra-option learning, and reduces potentially costly communication
3. We incorporate dynamic termination as an option to the high level controller network. This design introduces little additional model complexity, and allows us to represent the termination of all options in a consistent manner

In addition, we adopted several methods that benefits the model architecture and training: deep Q networks and parameter sharing reduce state space and model complexity; adapting intra-option learning [18] to multiple agents yields better sample efficiency; and an off-policy training scheme [7] for exploration.

2   Related Work

Makar et al. [11] appear to have been the first to combine multi-agent and hierarchical RL, through the MaxQ framework [2]. We build on their work, with the following changes: First, the use of tabular Q-learning is insufficient for large state spaces. Therefore, we adopt deep Q networks for parameterizing state and action spaces. Second, we adapt intra-option learning to multi-agent systems [18], which greatly improves the sample efficiency. Third, we adopt a delayed communication channel to prevent costly communication, and joint optimization. And finally, as options cannot be terminated before their predefined termination condition, tasks are limited to the use of perfect options and agents experience the delayed response problem.

Our solution to the delayed response problem is related to works on interrupting imperfect options, i.e., when the set of available options are not perfectly suited to the task, an agent can choose to terminate its options dynamically in order to improve its performance. Sutton et al. [18] introduced a mechanism for interrupting options whenever a better option appears, and Harutyunyan et al. [7] proposed a termination framework which improves upon this idea with better exploration. This is achieved by off-policy learning, which uses an additional behaviour policy for longer options.

Bacon et al. [1] proposed a dynamically terminating model for their Option-critic framework. In comparison, we use the Q-learning framework instead of policy gradient; and we focus on addressing the coordination problems in a multi-agent system. Moreover, our Q-value for dynamic termination does not depend on the currently executing option, which significantly reduces the model complexity and also improve sample efficiency due to off-policy training, i.e., the value of terminating can be learned with any executed option.

In the multi-agent learning literature, Riedmiller et al. [15] proposed the multi-option framework. This is a centralized model in which multiple agents are considered as a single meta-agent that chooses a joint option $\mathbf{o} = (o_1, \ldots, o_n)$. In contrast, our model uses a decentralized scheme where each agent i chooses and executes its own option o_i. This reduces the action space of the high level controller from $|O|^n$ to $|O|$, where O is the set of all options, and n is the number of agents.

Our model also draws upon the independent Q-learning framework proposed by Tan [20], where each agent independently learns its own policy on primitive actions, while treating other agents as part of the environment. Additionally in our model, each agent conditions on the others' broadcast options as part of its observation when choosing the next option. We will discuss the detailed formulation in Sect. 4.

3   Basic Definitions

We first introduce the essential concepts in reinforcement learning (RL), followed by multi-agent RL, hierarchical RL, intra-option learning and off-policy termination.

A *Markov Decision Process* [17] is given by a tuple $\langle \mathcal{S}, \mathcal{A}, R, P, \gamma \rangle$, where $\mathcal{S}$ denotes a set of states, $\mathcal{A}$ a set of actions, P the stationary transition probability $P(s_{t+1}|s_t, a_t)$ from state s_t to state s_{t+1} after executing action a_t, R is the average reward function $r_t := R(s_t, a_t)$, and $\gamma \in [0, 1)$ is the discount factor. A policy $\pi(a_t|s_t)$ is a distribution over actions a_t given the state s_t. The objective of a RL agent is to learn an optimal policy π^*, which maximizes the expected cumulative discounted future rewards. The *Q-value* of the optimal policy conditions this return on an action a_t that has been selected in a state s_t:

$$Q^*(s_t, a_t) = \mathbb{E}\left[\sum_{\tau=0}^{\infty} \gamma^\tau r_{t+\tau}\right] = r_t + \gamma \max_{a'} \mathbb{E}\left[Q^*(s_{t+1}, a')\right]. \tag{1}$$

Q-learning learns the Q-value of the optimal policy by interacting with a discrete environment [22]. Continuous and high-dimensional states require function approximation [17], for example deep convolutional neural networks (DQN) [12,13]. To improve the stability of gradient decent, DQN introduces an *experience replay buffer* to store transitions that have already been seen. Each update step samples a batch of past transitions and minimizes the mean-squared error between the left and right side of Eq. 1.

In multi-agent reinforcement learning, n agents interact with the same environment. The major difference to the single agent case is that the joint action space $\mathcal{A} = \mathcal{A}^1 \times \cdots \times \mathcal{A}^n$ of all agents grows exponential in n. Independent Q-learning addresses this by *decentralizing* decisions [20]: each agent learns a Q-value function that is independent of the actions of all other agents. This treats others as part of the environment and can lead to unstable DQN learning [5]. Other approaches combine decentralized functions with a learned centralized network [14] or train decentralized Actor-Critic architectures with centralized baselines [4].

We now describe some important concepts related to hierarchical reinforcement learning (HRL). The Options Framework [18] is one of the most common HRL frameworks, which defines a two-level hierarchy, and introduces options as temporally extended actions. Options o are defined as triples $\langle \mathcal{I}^o, \beta^o, \pi^o \rangle$, where $\mathcal{I}^o \subseteq \mathcal{S}$ is the initiation set and $\beta^o : \mathcal{S} \to [0,1]$ is the option termination condition. $\pi^o \colon \mathcal{S} \to \mathcal{A}$ is a deterministic option policy that selects primitive actions to achieve the target of the option. On reaching the termination condition in state s', an agent can select a new option from the set $\mathcal{O}(s') := \{o \,|\, s' \in \mathcal{I}^o\}$. A Semi-Markov Decision Process (SMDP) [18] defines the optimal Q-value:

$$Q(s_t, o_t) = \mathbb{E}\left[\sum_{\tau=0}^{k-1} \gamma^\tau r_{t+\tau} + \gamma^k \max_{o' \in \mathcal{O}(s_{t+k})} Q(s_{t+k}, o')\right], \tag{2}$$

where k refers to the number of steps until the termination condition $\beta^{o_t}(s_{t+k}) = 1$ is fulfilled.

To improve sample efficiency, Intra-option Learning [18,19] was proposed as an off-policy learning method which at each time step t updates all options that are in agreement with the executed action, i.e. $\forall o \in \{o \,|\, \pi^o(s_t) = a_t\}$ holds:

$$Q(s_t, o) = r_t + \gamma \mathbb{E}\left[U(s_{t+1}, o)\right]$$
$$U(s, o) = \left(1 - \beta^o(s)\right) Q(s, o) + \beta^o(s) \max_{o' \in \mathcal{O}(s)} Q(s, o'). \tag{3}$$

Here $U(s_{t+1}, o)$ is the TD-target [21]: if o is terminating in the next state, the TD-target will be the value of choosing the next optimal option. If not, the target will be the value of continuing with option o. Updating multiple options vastly improves the efficiency of training. Consider a grid-world navigation case where an agent is going for some goal location, and each coordinate corresponds

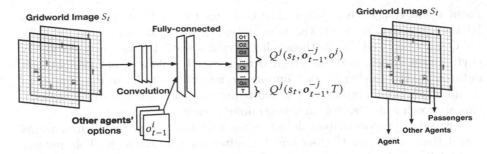

Fig. 3. Dynamic termination Q-value network architecture.

to the sub-goal of an option. When the agent takes a primitive action a_t^j and reaches the next position, all options o^j that would have chosen that action will be updated. Each transition updates therefore a significant fraction of the options, which massively improves sample efficiency.

As introduced by Sutton et al. [18], when the set of available options are not suited to the task, an agent can improve its performance by terminating at each step and switching to an optimal option. Harutyunyan et al. [7] have shown that this approach improves the agent's performance significantly, but has an adverse effect on exploration: temporally extended options can explore the state space more consistently, which is lost by early termination. The authors therefore advocate the use of intra-option learning to update the Q-value off-policy, while executing a different exploration policy that follows a selected option for multiple steps before terminating.

4   Method

In this section we will present our framework for deep decentralized hierarchical multi-agent Q-learning. Our model uses delayed communication to approximate the decisions of a centralized *joint policy*, which avoids many problems usually associated with joint optimization. This induces new challenges such as a *delayed response* of agents, and requires us to define a novel *dynamic termination update equation*.

Delayed Communication: A straightforward application of decentralized multi-agent approaches like *independent Q-learning* (IQL) [20] to the Options framework [18] would yield agents that make decisions independent of each other. Agent j would estimate the Q-value (see Eq. 2)

$$Q_{\mathrm{iql}}^j(s_t, o_t^j) := \mathbb{E}\left[\sum_{\tau=0}^{k-1}\gamma^\tau r_{t+\tau} + \gamma^k \max_{o'^j \in \mathcal{O}^j} Q_{\mathrm{iql}}^j(s_{t+k}, o'^j)\right], \tag{4}$$

and select the option o_t^j that maximizes it. Here other agents are treated as stationary parts of the environment, which can lead to unstable training when those agents change their policy. The best way to avoid this instability would be learn the Q-value w.r.t. the joint option of all agents $\mathbf{o}_t := (o_t^1, \ldots, o_t^n)$, i.e. $Q_{\text{joint}}(s_t, \mathbf{o}_t)$ [15]. While these joint Q-values allow training in a stationary environment, decisions require to maximize over Q-values of all possible joint options. As the number of joint options grows exponentially in the number of agents n, and joint optimization would require a vast communication overhead, this approach is not feasible in decentralized scenarios.

Instead we propose to use a *delayed communication channel* over which agents signal the new option they switched to after each termination. This reduces potentially costly communication and allows each agent j access to all other agents' options of the previous time step $\mathbf{o}_{t-1}^{-j} := (o_{t-1}^1, \ldots, o_{t-1}^{j-1}, o_{t-1}^{j+1}, \ldots, o_{t-1}^n)$. Agents can approximate the joint Q-value by conditioning on this information, that is, by choosing options o_t^j that maximize the *delayed Q-value* $Q^j(s_t, \mathbf{o}_{t-1}^{-j}, o_t^j)$. Note that the approximation is exact if *no other agent terminates at time t*. The optimality of the agents' decisions depends therefore on the frequency with which agents terminate their options.

Multi-agent Intra-option Learning: As introduced in the previous section, the intra-option learning method (Eq. 3) efficiently associates options with primitive actions. In our decentralized multi-agent options model, agent j selects an option according to $Q^j(s_t, \mathbf{o}_{t-1}^{-j}, o^j)$, which is defined as

$$Q^j(s_t, \mathbf{o}_{t-1}^{-j}, o^j) := \mathbb{E}\left[r_t + \gamma U^j(s_{t+1}, \mathbf{o}_t^{-j}, o^j)\right]$$
$$U^j(s_{t+1}, \mathbf{o}_t^{-j}, o^j) := \left(1 - \beta^{o^j}(s_{t+1})\right) Q^j(s_{t+1}, \mathbf{o}_t^{-j}, o^j)$$
$$+ \beta^{o^j}(s_{t+1}) \max_{o'^j \in \mathcal{O}^j} Q^j(s_{t+1}, \mathbf{o}_t^{-j}, o'^j). \qquad (5)$$

We can learn Q^j by, for example, minimizing the mean-squared TD error [17] between the left and right side of Eq. 5. In line with intra-option learning, we update the Q-values of all options o^j that would have executed the same action a_t^j as the actually executed option o_t^j. Note that due to our delayed communication channel, the executed options of all other agents are known after the transition to s_{t+1} and can thus be used to compute the target $U^j(s_{t+1}, \mathbf{o}_t^{-j}, o^j)$, that is, the Q-value of either following the option o^j if $\beta^{o^j}(s_{t+1}) = 0$, or terminating and choosing another option greedily if $\beta^{o^j}(s_{t+1}) = 1$.

Dynamic Option Termination: As mentioned above, the delayed Q-value defined in Eq. 5 only approximates the joint Q-value function. This approximation will deteriorate when other agents terminate, but sometimes agents can also benefit from early termination, as shown in Fig. 1(b). Additionally, options are usually pre-trained and have to cover a large range of tasks, without being able to solve any one task perfectly. Being able to prematurely terminate options can increase the expressiveness of the learned policy dramatically.

The easiest way to use partial options is to modify the termination conditions $\beta^{o^j}(s)$. In particular, we denote choosing the option with the largest Q-value (Eq. 5) at each time step as *greedy termination*. Following [7] we combined this approach with an exploration policy that terminates executed options with a fixed probability $\rho = 0.5$ to allow for temporally extended exploration. During testing the agent is nonetheless allowed to terminate greedily at every step if the Q-value of another option is larger.

Although greedy termination has been shown to improve the performance of individual agents with imperfect options [7], the agent's behaviour will become less predictable for others. In particular, agents that utilize the delayed Q-value of Eq. 5 will make sub-optimal decisions whenever another agent terminates. To increase the predictability of agents, while allowing them to terminate flexibly when the task demands it, we propose to put a price δ on the decision to terminate the current option. Option termination is therefore no longer hard-coded, but becomes part of the agent's policy, which we call *dynamic termination*. This can be represented by an additional option $o^j = T$ for agent j to terminate. Note that, unlike in the Options framework, we no longer need a termination function $\beta^{o^j}(s_t)$ for each option o^j. It is sufficient to compare the value of the previous option $Q^j(s_t, \mathbf{o}_{t-1}^{-j}, o_{t-1}^j)$ with the value of termination $Q^j(s_t, \mathbf{o}_{t-1}^{-j}, T)$. Evaluating $o^j = T$ is computationally similar to evaluating the termination condition β^o. Dynamic termination therefore has a similar cost to traditional termination.

The optimal behaviour for a given punishment δ is the fix-point of the novel *dynamic termination Bellman equation*:

$$Q^j(s_t, \mathbf{o}_{t-1}^{-j}, o^j \neq T) := \mathbb{E}\left[r_t + \gamma \max_{o'^j \in \{o^j, T\}} Q^j(s_{t+1}, \mathbf{o}_t^{-j}, o'^j)\right],$$

$$Q^j(s_t, \mathbf{o}_{t-1}^{-j}, o^j = T) := \max_{o'^j \in \mathcal{O}^j} Q^j(s_t, \mathbf{o}_{t-1}^{-j}, o'^j) - \delta. \tag{6}$$

Similarly to Eqs. 5 and 6 allows intra-option learning and can be applied to all options o^j that would have selected the same action as the executed option o_t^j. Note that the termination option T can always be updated, as it does not depend on the transition.

Deep Q-Learning: A group of n agents can be trained using a deep Q-network Q_θ [12], parameterized by θ. The architecture is shown in Fig. 3: each agent j selects and executes the next option based on the current state (i.e. grid-word image) s_t and the last known options $\mathbf{o}_{t-1}^{-j}$ of all the other agents. A centralized manager is not needed, and the options must only be broadcast after an agent chose to select a new option. The Q-value of choosing an option is updated by *temporal difference learning* with *experience replay*, which is the established standard procedure in deep Q-learning [12]. To reduce the number of parameters, we let all the agents share θ, and the model is thus updated using the experiences collected by all the agents. To differentiate the behaviour of different agents, the presented grid-world image contains a dedicated channel that encodes the current agent's state. These design decisions follow previous work in deep multi-agent learning [4,14] and drastically reduce training time with very little impact on the performance in large domains.

At each transition t, the Q-values of all options o^j, that would execute the same action as the executed option o_t^j, and the termination option T are updated by gradient descent on the sum of their respective losses

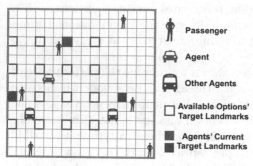

Fig. 4. Example 16×16 grid-world

Table 1. Flexibility and Predictability Results. Near/far refers to whether an agent is within distance $= 4$ to a passenger. Steps to change denotes the number of steps from the new passenger is placed to the agent's option change.

| | Predictability | | | Flexibility | |
| | Option changes | | | Option changes | Steps to change |
	All	Near	Far	All	All
Dynamic	24.1%	28.1%	16.8%	63%	1.61
Greedy	**59.9%**	**57.9%**	**52.8%**	**77%**	**1.15**
Option	10.9%	10.9%	9.5%	3%	6.86

$$\mathcal{L}^o_{j,t}[\theta] := \left(r_t + \gamma \max_{o' \in \{o, T\}} Q_\theta(s_{t+1}, \mathbf{o}^{-j}_t, o') - Q_\theta(s_t, \mathbf{o}^{-j}_{t-1}, o) \right)^2,$$

$$\mathcal{L}^T_{j,t}[\theta] := \left(\max_{o' \in \mathcal{O}^j} Q_\theta(s_t, \mathbf{o}^{-j}_{t-1}, o') - \delta - Q_\theta(s_t, \mathbf{o}^{-j}_{t-1}, T) \right)^2.$$

The total loss for a batch of m transitions with n agents is

$$\mathcal{L}[\theta] := \frac{1}{mn} \sum_{t=0}^{m-1} \sum_{j=1}^{n} \left(\mathcal{L}^T_{j,t}[\theta] + \sum_{\pi^o(s_t) = a^j_t} \mathcal{L}^o_{j,t}[\theta] \right). \tag{7}$$

5 Experiments

We will first evaluate the flexibility and predictability of our dynamically terminating agent, followed by the impact of dynamic termination on the agents' performance.

Experimental Setup: Fig. 4 shows a 16×16 grid-world of the taxi pickup as observed by the green agent, which includes the passengers, the other agents and their broadcast options. The landmarks of distance $L = 3$ show the destinations of options that are currently visible to the agent. This raises our *first challenge*: in order to reach a passenger that stands outside the landmarks, an agent needs to correctly switch between options.

In the *Taxi Pickup Task* m passengers are randomly distributed in each episode. An agent is rewarded $r = 1$ when occupying the same grid as a passenger, and each step incurs a cost of -0.01. Apart from landmark switching, the agents need to interpret others' behaviours to avoid choosing the same passenger, as well as responding quickly to changes such as when a passenger is picked up by another agent.

In the *Pursuit Task* agents try to catch randomly distributed prey by cooperating with others. We refer to the task as k-agent pursuit, where a successful capture requires at least k agents occupying k positions adjacent to the prey, which rewards each participating agent $r = 1$. This task relies heavily on agents coordination. In particular, when close to a specific prey, agents need to observe others and switch between options to surround the prey; whereas when faraway, agents need to agree on and commit to go for the same prey.

Algorithms and Training: Having described the settings, we now introduce the detailed training procedures of the SMDP and option policies, before comparing the four types of agents.

The Policy of Options adopts a local perspective, and navigates the agent to the option's destination. Specifically, we use a DQN of 2 convolutional layers (kernel size 2) with max-pooling, followed by 4 fully-connected layers (size 300). The input is the destination coordinate with the grid-world image, and the output is a primitive action in {N, S, E, W, Stay}.

The SMDP Policies are trained through intra-option learning for all agent types. The inputs are 4-channel grid-world images as in Fig. 3, which represents the agent, the preys (or passengers), the other agents, and lastly, the options broadcast by other agents (except for IQL). The DQN contains 2 convolutional layers (kernel size 3), max pooling, and 4 fully-connected layers (size 512). We use experience replay with a replay buffer of size 100,000.

Self-Play is used in the experiments, and our decentralized agents share the same DQN parameters (not states) [14]. This allows us to scale up the number of agents without additional parameters; and the trained model can directly transfer to more agents during testing. Moreover, self-play creates an important link between the predictability of an individual agent and of the society.

The four types of agents are as follows:

1. *Option Termination Agent* executes its option until the natural termination condition is met.
2. *Greedy Termination Agent* terminates every step and switches to the optimal option. For better exploration during training, an additional behaviour policy is used for experience collection. For fairness of comparison, this exploration policy which terminates with probability $\rho = 0.5$ (tuned for the greedy agent) is applied across all agent types.
3. *Dynamic Termination Agent* is our proposed algorithm that chooses whether to terminate the current option at each step.δ is the termination penalty.
4. *IQL* is independent Q-learning, where agents option broadcasts are disabled. IQL (greedy) and IQL (δ) refers to IQL agents using greedy or dynamic termination.

Results: The delayed response problem reveals that agents need to be flexible enough to change their options when the situation changes, but also predictable enough not to interfere in other agents' plans too frequently. Table 1 shows experimental measurements to showcase these conflicting goals for the investigated termination methods. We measure the agents' *flexibility* in the single-agent taxi domain. 100 episodes are initialized with 5 random passengers. During each episode, one additional passenger is placed near the agent at step T and we observe how quickly the agent adjusts to the new situation. We report the percentage of option changes at step $T + 1$ and the average number of steps till the

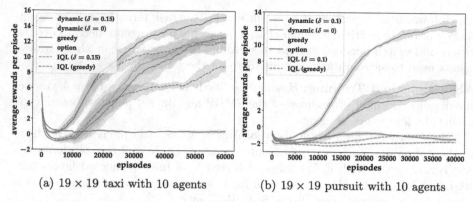

(a) 19 × 19 taxi with 10 agents   (b) 19 × 19 pursuit with 10 agents

Fig. 5. Results from Taxi Pickup and Pursuit Tasks
Note: every point per 500 episode is the testing result averaged over 100 random episodes and 5 seeds. The shaded area shows standard deviation across seeds.

Table 2. Average reward after training for Taxi and Pursuit tasks. n is the number of agents and m is the number of passengers (preys). N × N denotes grid-world size, k agent pursuit denotes the required number of agents for capture, and r is the capture range.

Agents		Taxi			2 agent pursuit			3 agent pursuit	
		n = 5, m = 10	n = 10, m = 20	n = 3, m = 5	n = 10, m = 10	n = 3, m = 5			
		19 × 19	25 × 25	19 × 19	16 × 16 (r = 1)	19 × 19 (r = 1)	19 × 19 (r = 1)	10 × 10 (r = 1)	16 × 16 (r = 2)
Dynamic	$\delta = 0.1$	**7.89**	**5.75**	**15.29**	**10.24**	**9.30**	**12.50**	**6.71**	**10.38**
	$\delta = 0$	6.58	3.28	11.81	6.73	4.07	5.38	5.53	6.54
Greedy		6.62	3.23	12.39	7.36	3.74	4.65	5.89	6.40
Option		−0.32	−0.94	0.52	5.47	−1.82	−1.42	−3.77	5.20
IQL	$\delta = 0.1$	7.11	5.09	12.02	−1.57	−2.29	−0.84	−1.62	−0.59
	Greedy	6.08	2.79	9.06	−2.12	−2.49	−1.64	−2.13	−0.42

agent changes options. Note that dynamic termination allows to react almost as flexible to the changed situation as the greedy termination.

For *predictability*, we measure the average probability to change the option in the multi-agent taxi task for two cases: when the agent is near (within distance 4) or far from its closest passenger. This is an imperfect measurement, as we cannot distinguish the effect of termination on other agents. While options need to change close to a passenger due to imperfect options, the behavior of dynamic termination is much closer to standard option termination when far away. Note that this effect is marginal for the other techniques, which indicates that our method may purposefully refrain from changing to better options to avoid interrupting other agent's plans.

Performance: Fig. 5(a) shows the results from the taxi pickup task. The option termination agent fails due to its inflexibility to switch options. In contrast, our dynamic ($\delta = 0.15$) agent is highly flexible. Moreover compared with greedy and IQL, its high predictability indeed helps the agents to interpret others' intentions and better distribute their target passengers. Figure 5(b) shows the results on the pursuit task, where at least two agents need to surround a prey within capture range = 1. Seen from the IQL agents' low performance, option broadcasting and interpreting others' behaviours are crucial to this task. Our dynamic termination agent ($\delta = 0.1$) significantly outperforms all other agents. Compared with the greedy agents, we can conclude that predictability significantly helps our dynamic agents to stay committed and succeed in cooperation.

Finally, we present the performance of all agents across different tasks and varying parameters in Table 2. Firstly, the option termination agent has difficulty with tasks which require higher level of accuracy and quick responses, such as the taxi tasks and pursuit with capture range = 1. However, it works well with tasks which require coordination but less flexibility, such as the 16×16 3 agent pursuit with capture range 2, which shows the advantage of predictability on cooperation. The performance of greedy termination agents decreases significantly in larger grid-world sizes, and when commitment is essential, such as the 16×16 3 agent pursuit with capture range 2. Our dynamically terminating agent performs well across all tasks, as it balances well between flexibility and predictability. The IQL agents performs well in the taxi task. However, they fail to learn the pursuit tasks where foreseeing others' behaviours is essential to coordination.

6   Conclusions and Future Work

In this paper, we identified the delayed response problem, that occurs when hierarchical RL is combined with multi-agent learning. To address this challenge, we investigated existing approaches of greedy option termination in single agent learning. However, this method introduces a new dilemma specific to multi-agent systems: as an agent broadcasts its current options to indicate its subsequent behaviours, frequent changes in options will result in its behaviour being less predictable by others. Therefore, to balance flexibility with predictability, we introduced dynamic termination, which enables agents to terminate their options flexibly according to the current state. We compared our model with current state of the art algorithms on multi-agent pursuit and taxi tasks with varying task parameters, and demonstrated that our approach outperformed the baselines through flexibly adapting to the task requirements. For future work, we are interested in applying the dynamic termination framework to traffic simulations, such as junction and highway management.

References

1. Bacon, P.L., Harb, J., Precup, D.: The option-critic architecture. In: AAAI, pp. 1726–1734 (2017)
2. Dietterich, T.G.: Hierarchical reinforcement learning with the maxq value function decomposition. J. Artif. Intell. Res. **13**, 227–303 (2000)

3. Foerster, J., Assael, I.A., de Freitas, N., Whiteson, S.: Learning to communicate with deep multi-agent reinforcement learning. In: Advances in Neural Information Processing Systems, pp. 2137–2145 (2016)
4. Foerster, J., Farquhar, G., Afouras, T., Nardelli, N., Whiteson, S.: Counterfactual multi-agent policy gradients. arXiv preprint arXiv:1705.08926 (2017)
5. Foerster, J., et al.: Stabilising experience replay for deep multi-agent reinforcement learning. In: Proceedings of the 34th International Conference on Machine Learning. Proceedings of Machine Learning Research, vol. 70, pp. 1146–1155 (2017). http://proceedings.mlr.press/v70/foerster17b.html
6. Giannakis, M., Louis, M.: A multi-agent based system with big data processing for enhanced supply chain agility. J. Enterp. Inform. Management **29**(5), 706–727 (2016)
7. Harutyunyan, A., Vrancx, P., Bacon, P.L., Precup, D., Nowe, A.: Learning with options that terminate off-policy. arXiv preprint arXiv:1711.03817 (2017)
8. Jennings, N.R.: Commitments and conventions: the foundation of coordination in multi-agent systems. Knowl. Eng. Rev. **8**(3), 223–250 (1993)
9. Lesser, V., Ortiz Jr., C.L., Tambe, M.: Distributed Sensor Networks: A Multiagent Perspective, vol. 9. Springer, Heidelberg (2012)
10. Lin, K., Zhao, R., Xu, Z., Zhou, J.: Efficient large-scale fleet management via multi-agent deep reinforcement learning. arXiv preprint arXiv:1802.06444 (2018)
11. Makar, R., Mahadevan, S., Ghavamzadeh, M.: Hierarchical multi-agent reinforcement learning. In: Proceedings of the Fifth International Conference on Autonomous Agents, pp. 246–253. ACM (2001)
12. Mnih, V., et al.: Playing Atari with deep reinforcement learning. In: NIPS Deep Learning Workshop (2013)
13. Mnih, V., et al.: Human-level control through deep reinforcement learning. Nature **518**(7540), 529 (2015)
14. Rashid, T., Samvelyan, M., de Witt, C.S., Farquhar, G., Foerster, J., Whiteson, S.: QMIX: monotonic value function factorisation for deep multi-agent reinforcement learning. arXiv preprint arXiv:1803.11485 (2018)
15. Riedmiller, M., Withopf, D.: Effective methods for reinforcement learning in large multi-agent domains (leistungsfähige verfahren für das reinforcement lernen in komplexen multi-agenten-umgebungen). IT-Inform. Technol. **47**(5), 241–249 (2005)
16. Stone, P., Veloso, M.: Multiagent systems: a survey from a machine learning perspective. Auton. Robot. **8**(3), 345–383 (2000)
17. Sutton, R.S., Barto, A.G.: Reinforcement Learning: An Introduction. MIT Press, Cambridge (1998)
18. Sutton, R.S., Precup, D., Singh, S.: Between MDPs and semi-MDPs: a framework for temporal abstraction in reinforcement learning. Artif. intell. **112**(1–2), 181–211 (1999)
19. Sutton, R.S., Precup, D., Singh, S.P.: Intra-option learning about temporally abstract actions. In: ICML., vol. 98, pp. 556–564 (1998)
20. Tan, M.: Multi-agent reinforcement learning: independent vs. cooperative agents. In: Readings in Agents, pp. 487–494 (1998)
21. Tesauro, G.: Temporal difference learning and TD-Gammon. Commun. ACM **38**(3), 58–68 (1995)
22. Watkins, C., Dayan, P.: Q-learning. Mach. Learn. **8**, 279–292 (1992)

A Meta-Reinforcement Learning Approach to Optimize Parameters and Hyper-parameters Simultaneously

Abbas Raza Ali[1]([✉])[iD], Marcin Budka[1][iD], and Bogdan Gabrys[2][iD]

[1] Bournemouth University, Poole BH12 5BB, UK
{aali,mbudka}@bournemouth.ac.uk
[2] University Technology Sydney, Ultimo, NSW 2007, Australia
bogdan.gabrys@uts.edu.au

Abstract. In the last few years, we have witnessed a resurgence of interest in neural networks. The state-of-the-art deep neural network architectures are however challenging to design from scratch and requiring computationally costly empirical evaluations. Hence, there has been a lot of research effort dedicated to effective utilisation and adaptation of previously proposed architectures either by using transfer learning or by modifying the original architecture. The ultimate goal of designing a network architecture is to achieve the best possible accuracy for a given task or group of related tasks. Although there have been some efforts to automate network architecture design process, most of the existing solutions are still very computationally intensive. This work presents a framework to automatically find a good set of hyper-parameters resulting in reasonably good accuracy, which at the same time is less computationally expensive than the existing approaches. The idea presented here is to frame the hyper-parameter selection and tuning within the reinforcement learning regime. Thus, the parameters of a meta-learner, RNN, and hyper-parameters of the target network are tuned simultaneously. Our meta-learner is being updated using policy network and simultaneously generates a tuple of hyper-parameters which are utilized by another network. The network is trained on a given task for a number of steps and produces validation accuracy whose delta is used as reward. The reward along with the state of the network, comprising statistics of network's final layer outcome and training loss, are fed back to the meta-learner which in turn generates a tuned tuple of hyper-parameters for the next time-step. Therefore, the effectiveness of a recommended tuple can be tested very quickly rather than waiting for the network to converge. This approach produces accuracy close to the state-of-the-art approach and is found to be comparatively less computationally intensive.

Keywords: Convolutional Neural Networks · Meta-learning · Reinforcement learning · Policy gradients · Hyper-parameter optimization

© Springer Nature Switzerland AG 2019
A. C. Nayak and A. Sharma (Eds.): PRICAI 2019, LNAI 11671, pp. 93–106, 2019.
https://doi.org/10.1007/978-3-030-29911-8_8

1 Introduction

Deep neural networks (DNN) have attained tremendous success by consistently outperforming the shallow learning techniques. However, solving complex tasks need deeper and wider networks which are considered hard to design. Transfer learning, often, works well on simple and more general tasks whereas complex tasks require effort to design a customized network. The network designing process requires specialized skills and numerous trials which is a time consuming and computationally expensive task. The state-of-the-art networks require well-tuned hyper-parameters which often demand numerous computationally intensive trials.

In recent years, Meta-Reinforcement Learning (Meta-RL) has become a de-facto standard to automatically search for optimal hyper-parameters. Therefore, the proposed framework uses Meta-RL to efficiently explore the optimal hyper-parameters of a deep network from the given search space. The exploration happens simultaneously for both the policy network and the DNN. Given a tuple of hyper-parameters that is generated by a policy network, a network is built and trained for a number of steps. The network computes accuracy on hold-out validation-set whose delta is used as a reward. Furthermore, this reward along with the state of the network comprising statistics of probability distribution over number of classes and training loss, are back-propagated to the policy network which generates a tuned tuple for the next time-step. The network is initialized once where different tuples of hyper-parameters are tested on the go without resetting the network. Therefore, a tuple of hyper-parameters is not required to train till convergence of the network which saves a significant amount of computation.

There are a number of recent studies around hyper-parameter optimization using Reinforcement learning. The earliest effort of Meta-RL was made by [3] where a recurrent neural network (RNN) based agent is used to learn the behavior of the environment. The goal of the agent is to learn a policy for learning new policies. The Meta-RL is defined in this work in a way that the agent gets trained once on a problem and transfer learned on similar kind of tasks. Moreover, the idea is a learning policy to learn another policy in a family of similar Markov Decision Processes (MDPs). A Meta-agent adjusts its policy after training for a few episodes and validates on an unseen environment. This approach worked well on both small- and large-scale problems. Another simple, yet powerful Meta-RL approach is Model-Agnostic Meta-learning (MAML) [4]. MAML does not initialize model parameters randomly but rather it provides a good initialization to achieve optimal and efficient learning on a new task. The fine-tuning requires a small number of gradient steps. The key aspect of the MAML is that the model can be trained using a gradient descent including convolutional neural networks (CNNs) with a variety of potential loss functions. Additionally, it is equally effective for regression, classification, and reinforcement learning, where it outperformed a number of previous approaches.

[18] proposed a long short-term memory (LSTM) [8] based approach to train a meta-classifier. The few-shot learning method finds the optimal set of

parameters. However, [5] claims that the MAML initialization of the model parameters is more resilient to over-fitting, particularly, for smaller datasets. Also, it is more effective when the model is dealing with new unseen tasks. Similarly, [1] proposed an effective and efficient domain adaption approach by fine-tuning the final layers of a CNN for both small- and large-scale problems.

Neural Architectural Search (NAS) is another effort towards Meta-RL based network search [24]. NAS uses an RNN based controller that samples a candidate architecture known as child network. The child network is trained till convergence to obtain accuracy on a hold-out validation-set. The accuracy is used as an immediate reward which further updates the controller. The controller generates better architectures over time where the weights are updated by policy gradient. The approach seems quite simple and powerful but it is tested on very small size tasks. Another observation is that the search space of the child network was limited. The reason behind limiting the experiment to small tasks is the inefficiency of the approach. Progressive Neural Architecture Search (PNAS) proposes a different approach to architecture search known as sequential model-based optimization (SMBO) strategy [15]. In SMBO, instead of randomly recommending and testing out the blocks, they are tested and structures searched in order of increasing complexity. Instead of traversing the entire search space, this approach starts off simple and only gets complex when required. PNAS claims to be significantly less computationally expensive than NAS. Another effort to make architecture search more efficient is known as, Efficient Neural Architecture Search (ENAS), proposed by [17]. ENAS allows sharing of weights across all the models instead of training every model from scratch. The idea is to reuse the weights of a block which are already trained. Thus, the system uses transfer learning to train a new model which makes convergence very fast. It is a very effective method and comparatively less computationally expensive than PNAS. The only observation about this approach is that it keeps a large number of architectures in the memory.

[23] proposed a different approach of learning to do exploration in off-policy RL which is Deep Deterministic Policy Gradients (DDPG). The authors compared two different policy gradient RL approaches: (a) On-policy Gradient Algorithms (OPGA) which includes algorithms like Proximal Policy Optimization (PPO), and (b) Trust Region Policy Optimization (TRPO) where a stochastic policy is used for exploration of RL environment. A separate policy has been used instead of a simple heuristic for the exploration. This policy is trained using OPGA methods where the reward for training is a relative improvement in the performance of the exploitation policy network. Experimental results show faster convergence of DDPG with higher rewards. [25] further extended NAS where they also replaced REINFORCE with PPO.

The proposed approach is an efficient form of NAS and ENAS to find optimal neural architecture. The shortcomings of NAS is its limitation to small tasks because it is computationally very expensive. On the other hand, ENAS keeps numerous architectures in the memory so that the new architectures can share the weights of the pre-trained blocks. This work further simplifies architecture search problem which is equally effective for large datasets. The approach tunes the hyper-parameters of the network during training rather than waiting until convergence which saves significant computation time. The effectiveness of a tuple of hyper-parameters is tested by training for a few steps. Further, the feedback of the tuple is used to tune the policy gradient at the same time-step.

This method significantly reduces the computational complexity of the optimal hyper-parameter search problem. Along with minimal computation, the approach requires substantially smaller amount of memory by optimizing a single instance of the network rather than creating and keeping numerous architectures in the memory. The simplicity of the approach does not affect the accuracy of the network and makes it equally effective for more complex and bigger tasks. This is the key contribution of this study.

The rest of the paper is organized as follows. Section 2 is devoted to discussing the methodology of this study. The formulation of REINFORCE, base-learner and stochastic depth algorithms are outlined in Sect. 3. Section 4 outlines the data-sources and different configurations that have been used to conduct various experiments. Section 5 reports the experimental results and their analysis. Finally, the paper is concluded in Sect. 6.

2   Methodology

The primary goal of this study is to efficiently explore the optimal set of hyper-parameters for a given task. This is achieved by optimizing the meta-learner parameters and network hyper-parameters at the same time. Typically, the policy network needs to train for several episodes so that it can start producing effective outcome. In case of hyper-parameter tuning using Meta-RL, the child network needs to be sequentially trained on a task at hand using all the tuples, recommended by the meta-learner, until convergence to conclude their effectiveness. It becomes time and computationally intensive task. Hence, this challenge has been tackled and addressed in this study.

In order to evaluate the proposed approach, a framework is designed using a typical RL setting which consists of two key components: an agent and an environment [20]. The environment can be in different states (S) which are observed by the agent at different time-steps (t). Given its knowledge of the state and a set of available actions the agent chooses an action (A). These actions affect the state of the environment and in return, generate a reward (R). To find the optimal set of hyper-parameters the agent needs to find the actions that lead to maximizing expected reward, see Eq. 1. The γ is a discount factor, which allows the agent to maximize its expected reward on either short- or long-term transitions based on its value. However, the reward is non-differentiable and hence needs a policy gradient method to iteratively update θ as formulated in Eq. 2. The stochastic policy $\pi(a|s)$ describes a probability distribution over the set of actions.

$$R_t \leftarrow \sum_{i=0}^{\infty} \gamma^i R_{t+i}, \quad \gamma \in [0,1] \tag{1}$$

$$\theta \leftarrow \theta + \alpha \nabla_\theta log \pi_\theta(s_t, a_t) r_t \tag{2}$$

The agent generates a tuple of hyper-parameters using an RNN which is known as meta-learner. This tuple specifies a neural network architecture known as base-learner in the framework. The base-learner is trained on a task and evaluated on the hold-out validation-set. The base-learner provides feedback to the meta-learner to get a well-tuned tuple in the next time-step. Figure 1 shows the setting of the proposed Meta-RL framework.

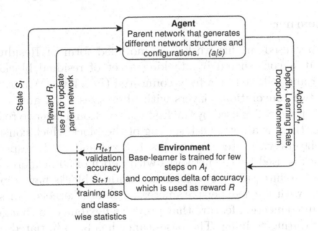

Fig. 1. A typical setting of Meta-RL framework where agent contains a policy gradient and network sits in the environment

2.1 Meta-learner

The Meta-learner consists of a stochastic policy gradient which makes weight adjustments in a direction that lies along the gradient of expected reinforcement. It is a statistical gradient-based approach known as REINFORCE as described by [21]. It makes weights adjustment without explicitly computing gradient estimates with back-propagation. The Meta-learner initializes a base-learner once with the initial values of hyper-parameters from search space except depth. However, the depth is initialized with the maximum value. For instance, if the maximum depth is 34 in the search space, the network is initialized once with the maximum depth. The meta-learner is a two-layer RNN LSTM with 35 neurons per layer. The network is trained with Adam optimizer [11]. An initial learning rate of 0.0006 has been used. The weights are initialized with Xavier-initialization [6]. A discount factor of 0.97 is used to prevent the total reward from reaching infinity. The meta-learner is updated via a policy gradient method which is computed using an immediate reward.

Algorithm 1. Computing immediate reward of an episode

1: $beta = 0.8$
2: Time-step $= t$
3: $episode = e$
4:
5: $reward_t = (accuracy - moving\_accuracy_{t-1})$
6: $reward_t = clip(reward, -0.1, 0.1)$
7:
8: $moving\_accuracy_t = (1 - beta) * accuracy_e$
9: $moving\_accuracy_t += beta * moving\_accuracy_{t-1}$

2.2 Base-Learner

The base-learner used in this work is a modified form of Residual Network
(ResNet) [7]. It is constructed by stacking a set of residual blocks on top of
the input layer and followed by a fully-connected (FC) layer. A block consists of
a sequence of two convolutional layers with filter sizes 1×1 and 3×3, respectively, where a stride of 2 is used by the first convolutional layer to reduce feature
map size. Also, there is a bottleneck setting of the block which consists of three
convolutional layers with filter sizes of 1×1, 3×3 and 1×1, respectively. The
bottleneck block is used for the networks with depth of 50 or more. The benefit
of using ResNet architecture is two-fold: (a) residual blocks have repeated units
of convolutions with fixed hyper-parameters, namely, kernels and strides, and
(b) it has a skip-connection feature that provides flexibility to change the depth
of the network during training. The base-leaner has been initiated once and its
hyper-parameters are modified during the training cycles.

Table 1. Hyper-parameter search space and parameters covering behaviour of the
network that is used as states $t + 1$

Parameters	Values (range)
A. Hyper-parameter search space	
Number of layers (D)	2–50
Dropout Rate (DR)	0.5–1.0
Learning Rate (LR)	0.0001–0.9
Momentum (M)	0.6–0.99
B. Representation of the environment (states)	
Network training loss	0–1.0
Mean entropy of class probabilities	0–1.0
Standard deviation entropy of class probabilities	0–1.0

The meta-learner (RNN) suggests a tuple of hyper-parameters from the
search space which are listed in Table 1(A). The table shows the search space

range of all the hyper-parameters. Based on the suggested hyper-parameters, the existing CNN architecture is trained for 50 steps with a batch size of 32. Furthermore, delta of validation accuracy has been computed which becomes the immediate reward. The reward that is used to update the meta-learner is the delta of validation accuracy of the recent two episodes. The procedure to compute the immediate reward is formulated in Algorithm 1. Apart from the reward few other parameters of the environment are computed at time-step t comprising of network training loss and entropy of probability distribution over number of classes. The entropy is averaged over an episode, see Eq. 3, where x is the output of the softmax layer and N is the size of the episode. Further, the mean and standard deviation of the entropy has been computed over the number of images, N, processed in an episode, see Table 1(B). These parameters are utilized by meta-learner as the state information to generate a tuned tuple for time-step $t+1$. The network is trained with Momentum optimizer with Nesterov momentum [19].

$$\text{entropy} = -\sum_{j=1}^{N}(\mathbf{f}_j(x_i) * \log_2(\mathbf{f}_j(x_i))) \tag{3}$$

$$x_{l+1} = ReLU(x_l + \mathbf{f}(x_l, W_l)) \tag{4}$$

Residual Block with Stochastic Depth. A residual block is composed of convolution layers, batch normalization (BatchNorm) [10] and rectified linear units (ReLU) [16] which is represented as function f in Eq. 4. x_l represents skip-connection path and $f(x_l, W_l)$ is a residual block. A configuration of the base-learner with maximum depth 4 is shown in Fig. 2(a). The meta-learner has recommended a depth size 3 so the last residual block has been disabled for the current episode. Hence, the gradient update of the last block is stopped for the current episode.

The depth of the network is controlled by stochastic depth approach presented by [9]. It leverages the skip-connection path of the residual block x_l to control network depth even during training of the network. The idea of original stochastic depth work, [9], is to randomly skip the residual blocks by letting through only the identity of the raw feature in order to skip a path. In this work rather than randomly skipping the blocks, meta-learner suggests which blocks to skip. Therefore, when a block is skipped, the identity path has been chosen which stops updating the block's gradients.

3   Formulation

The approach to optimize parameters and hyper-parameters simultaneously is outlined in Algorithm 2. It has two components: (a) meta-learner and (b) base-learner. A meta-learner is an RNN which suggests a tuple of hyper-parameters in the form of actions. These actions are applied to the environment which is a base-learner. The base-learner is a CNN which trains the task at hand on the actions of current time-step for a few steps. Furthermore, the network computes accuracy on a hold-out validation-set which is used as an immediate reward at the time-step t. This reward and the state of the network is observed and used to update the weights of the meta-learner that generates new actions for time-step $t + 1$ which are dependent on how well the base-learner performs.

Algorithm 3 shows how stochastic depth approach is modified for this work. The base-learner only updates the gradients of the residual blocks which are less than the suggested depth (D). For the rest of the layers, a skip-connection path has opted. The base-learner is initialized with a maximum value of the depth once and modifies, often, on every episode.

Algorithm 2. Meta-Reinforcement learning algorithm to optimize parameters and hyper-parameters simultaneously

---

1: ▷ META-LEARNER
2: Network depth = D
3: Dropout rate = DR
4: Base-learner's Learning rate = α_b
5: Momentum = p
6: Actions $(a) = < D, DR, \alpha_b, p >$
7: Time-step = t
8: Meta-learner's Learning rate = α_m
9: Reward at time $t = r_t$
10: Differential policy at time t which maps actions to probabilities = $\pi_\theta(s_t, a_t)$
11: Initialize the policy parameter: θ = Xavier-initialization
12: Initialize base-learner CNN: $model \leftarrow ResNet(a)$
13:
14: **for** $episode \leftarrow 1$ to $\pi_\theta : s_1, a_1, r_2, ..., s_{T-1}, a_{T-1}, r_T$ **do**
15:     ▷ policy network
16:     **for** $t \leftarrow 1$ to $T - 1$ **do**
17:         $\theta \leftarrow \theta + \alpha_m \nabla_\theta log\pi_\theta(s_t, a_t)r_t$ ▷ gradient update
18:
19:         ▷ BASE-LEARNER
20:         ▷ Tune the hyper-parameters of network with θ
21:         **for** $s \leftarrow 1$ to $Steps \leftarrow 50$ **do**
22:             $features \leftarrow next\_batch(train, labels)$
23:             **if** $training = True$ **then**
24:                 $fit\_model \leftarrow model.fit(a, features)$
25:             **end if**
26:         **end for**
27:         **if** $testing = True$ **then**
28:             $test\_accuracy \leftarrow fitted\_model(testset)$
29:         **end if**
30:
31:         $r_t = test\_accuracy_t - moving\_accuracy_{t-1}$
32:         $s_t^1 = train\_loss$ ▷ states of t
33:         $s_t^2 = final\_layer\_statistics$
34:     **end for**
35: **end for**

Algorithm 3. Stochastic Depth routine

1: Depth suggested by meta-learner $= D$
2: Maximum depth of a network $= maxD$
3:
4: **for** $block\_no \leftarrow 1$ to $maxD$ **do**
5:     **if** $block\_no >= D$ **then** $x \leftarrow ReLU(x + \mathbf{f}(x, W))$ ▷ residual block
6:     **end if**
7:     **if** $block\_no < D$ **then** $x \leftarrow Identity(x)$ ▷ shortcut
8:     **end if**
9: **end for**

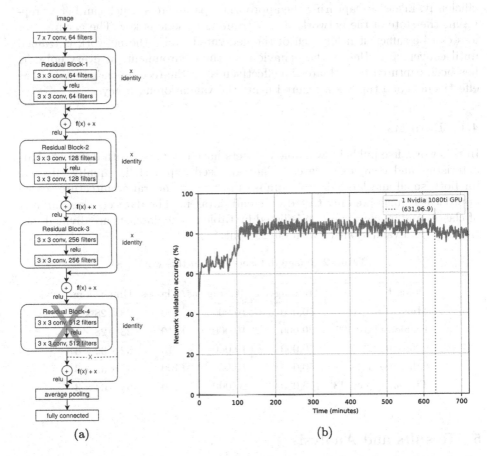

Fig. 2. (a) A schematic view of base-learner with maximum depth 4 and current depth 3. (b) Cifar-10 time taken versus network validation accuracy plot

4   Experimentation Environment

In order to evaluate the proposed approach, a number of experiments have been performed. These experiments use different image classification tasks listed in Table 2. A tuple of hyper-parameters is tested for only a few steps rather than till convergence. Hence, the number of steps the base-learner trains on a tuple of hyper-parameters is a critical parameter. Thus, different values of step-size and batch size have been tested to obtain the optimal values which can evaluate a recommended tuple in the shortest time. The experiments suggest a step-size 50 with a batch size 32 which is sufficient to test a tuple of hyper-parameters efficiently. Likewise, capturing the appropriate parameters which can better represent the state of the network after a training episode is key. The accuracy or loss can be sufficient if for each of the generated tuples the network is trained until convergence. Hence, the behaviour of the environment, at every episode, has been captured to evaluate the effectiveness of the recommended tuple. The effectiveness of a tuple is measured using the validation accuracy.

4.1   Datasets

In this work, five publicly available datasets have been used with different characteristics and complexity levels. The proposed approach is equally effective for both small and large datasets unlike most of the neural architecture search approaches which are only tested on small datasets. The datasets size, number of classes and image resolution is listed in Table 2. The datasets are divided into training- and validation-set with 80–20 split.

Table 2. Image datasets used in this work

Dataset	Training-set	Testing-set	Classes	Dimensions
Mnist [14]	50,000	10,000	10	$28 \times 28 \times 1$
Fashion-mnist [22]	60,000	10,000	10	$28 \times 28 \times 1$
Cifar-10 [12]	50,000	10,000	10	$32 \times 32 \times 3$
Cifar-100 [12]	50,00	10,000	100	$32 \times 32 \times 3$
Tiny-imagenet [13]	100,000	20,000	200	$64 \times 64 \times 3$

5   Results and Analysis

A comprehensive set of experiments is conducted to evaluate the effectiveness of the proposed approach. The experiments were performed on 5 Nvidia 1080Ti GPUs, one dataset per GPU. A comparison of the proposed approach with other architecture search approaches is shown in Table 3. This comparison is only available for Cifar-10 dataset as most of the previous studies used it in their experiments. A plot of validation accuracy against time taken can be seen in Fig. 2(b). The vertical red dotted line is pointing to the top accuracy whose hyper-parameters settings are mentioned in Table 4.

Table 3. Comparison with different architecture search approaches on Cifar-10 dataset

Method	GPUs	Exploration time (days)	Parameters (millions)	Error rate (%)
DenseNet [2]	-	-	26.20	3.46
NASNet-A [25]	450	3–4	3.30	3.41
PNAS [15]	100	1.5	3.20	3.63
ENAS [17]	1	0.60	4.60	2.89
This work (Cifar-10)	1	0.40	4.58	3.11

There are 5 datasets used for experiments with different complexity-levels. The exploration of hyper-parameters for the datasets posses different behaviors in terms of the number of episodes and time. The Mnist, Fashion-mnist and Cifar-10 datasets were comparatively easier to learn. On the other hand, the exploration of Cifar-100 and tiny-imagenet was hard. The complex datasets took many more episodes to explore the optimal parameters from the search space. Moreover, the maximum depth of the architectures was bigger for complex datasets. So a large increase of depth size from one episode to other, particularly in the initial phase, makes the training quite unstable. Figure 2(b) shows a consistent accuracy after 100 min of the training till 630 followed by a spike on a tuple. This tuple produced the maximum accuracy which is reported in Table 4. At the beginning of the training, a much bigger improvement in accuracy has been observed with a tuple which is different than the highest performing hyper-parameter tuple. A network is trained separately from scratch using the highest performing tuple until convergence which produces an error rate of 3.19 which is close to the one mentioned in Table 3. This approach is repeated for the rest of the datasets which produces the accuracy close to the one reported in Table 4 with a marginal difference range of ±0.15. It depicts the effectiveness of the reported highest performing hyper-parameters tuple in the shortest time.

Figure 3 shows the policy loss, reward and network validation accuracy of the 5 datasets. The plots show a vertical line along y-axis representing maximum accuracy. The best hyper-parameters found against each dataset are reported in Table 4 along with the exploration and network accuracy information. The mnist and fashion-mnist tasks took very few episodes to find the top performing hyper-parameters. On the contrary, the complex tasks, cifar-100 and tiny-imagenet, took many more episodes to try different permutations of the hyper-parameters.

The network hyper-parameters are initialized once and tuned after every 50 steps. The policy gradient took more episodes to learn the hyper-parameters for more complex tasks. To evaluate a recommended tuple, 50 steps are very limited, hence the behavior of the network was captured and provided to the meta-learner to more fully observe the impact of the tuple.

Table 4. Accuracy of various datasets including optimal parameters and episodes required to achieve the optimal value

Dataset	Network hyper-parameters $[D, DR, \alpha, p]$	Episodes	Duration (hours)	Network accuracy (%)
Mnist	[4, 0.06, 0.02, 0.95]	720	0.72	98.29
Fashion-mnist	[4, 0.06, 0.02, 0.95]	466	0.36	95.37
Cifar-10	[4, 0.3, 0.006, 0.95]	7,203	10.53	96.89
Cifar-100	[11, 0.2, 0.0007, 0.93]	9,810	19.39	76.94
Tiny-imagenet	[16, 0.25, 0.0004, 0.89]	13,770	36.83	64.39

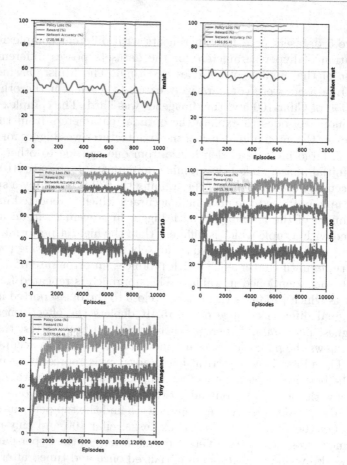

Fig. 3. Statistics of different datasets including policy loss, reward and network accuracy

6   Conclusions

This study has presented an efficient approach to hyper-parameters search of deep models. A Policy-based Reinforcement Learning method is used to generate a tuple of hyper-parameters. The tuple is used by the target network, base-learner, which is initialized once with random hyper-parameters and, often, tunes on every episode. In each episode, a validation accuracy has been computed after training for 50 steps with a batch size of 32. The delta of the accuracy, which is referred to as reward, is fed back to the policy network along with the behavior of the environment. The attributes that represent behavior are training loss and statistics of the target network's final layer outcome. A more refined tuple of hyper-parameters, in return, is generated for the next episode. This cycle tunes the parameters of the policy network and hyper-parameters of the network at the same time which makes the overall process more computationally efficient than the existing approaches.

In conclusion, the proposed approach demonstrates a quick and effective hyper-parameter search approach. Unlike previous studies, it is equally effective for both small and large datasets. Despite, the exploration taking more time if the range of the network depth parameter gets bigger, still using one GPU the exploration takes less than a day for a complex task. This approach is 20% less computation expensive than ENAS with marginally higher error-rate. The depth hyper-parameter is found to be the most effective one where the change of the depth causes a significant jump in the accuracy. There are many possible directions for future work. Currently, only four hyper-parameters are part of the search space which can be enhanced. Accordingly, to evaluate the effectiveness of a tuple of hyper-parameters, state of the intermediary layers of the network can be observed rather than only the statistics of final layer outputs.

References

1. Ali, A., Budka, M., Gabrys, B.: Towards meta-level learning of deep neural networks for fast adaptation. In: Proceedings of the 16th Pacific RIM International Conference on Artificial Intelligence (PRICAI) (2019)
2. DeVries, T., Taylor, G.W.: Improved regularization of convolutional neural networks with cutout. Computing Research Repository (CoRR) arXiv:1708.04552 (2017)
3. Duan, Y., Schulman, J., Chen, X., Bartlett, P.L., Sutskever, I., Abbeel, P.: RL2: fast reinforcement learning via slow reinforcement learning. Computing Research Repository (CoRR) arXiv:1611.02779 (2016)
4. Finn, C., Abbeel, P., Levine, S.: Model-agnostic meta-learning for fast adaptation of deep networks. In: Proceedings of the 34th International Conference on Machine Learning, vol. 70, pp. 1126–1135. PMLR, International Convention Centre, Sydney, August 2017
5. Finn, C., Levine, S.: Meta-learning and universality: deep representations and gradient descent can approximate any learning algorithm. Computing Research Repository (CoRR) arXiv:1710.11622 (2018)

6. Glorot, X., Bengio, Y.: Understanding the difficulty of training deep feed-forward neural networks. In: Proceedings of the Thirteenth International Conference on Artificial Intelligence and Statistics. PMLR (2010)
7. He, K., Zhang, X., Ren, S., Sun, J.: Deep residual learning for image recognition. In: 2016 IEEE Conference on Computer Vision and Pattern Recognition (CVPR), pp. 770–778 (2016)
8. Hochreiter, S., Schmidhuber, J.: Long short-term memory. Neural Comput. **9**, 1735–1780 (1997)
9. Huang, G., Sun, Y., Liu, Z., Sedra, D., Weinberger, K.: Deep networks with stochastic depth. Computing Research Repository (CoRR arXiv:1603.09382 (2016)
10. Ioffe, S., Szegedy, C.: Batch normalization: accelerating deep network training by reducing internal covariate shift. In: International Conference of Machine Learning (ICML) (2015)
11. Kingma, D.P., Ba, J.: Adam: a method for stochastic optimization. In: International Conference on Learning Representations (ICLR) (2015)
12. Krizhevsky, A., Nair, V., Hinton, G.: CIFAR-10 and CIFAR-100. Canadian Institute for Advanced Research
13. Le, Y., Yang, X.: Tiny ImageNet visual recognition challenge. Stanford CS 231N (2015)
14. LeCun, Y., Cortes, C., Burges, C.J.C.: The MNIST dataset of handwritten digits (1999)
15. Liu, C., Zoph, B., Neumann, M., et al.: Progressive neural architecture search. Computing Research Repository (CoRR) arXiv:1712.00559 (2018)
16. Nair, V., Hinton, G.E.: Rectified linear units improve restricted Boltzmann machines. In: International Conference of Machine Learning (ICML) (2010)
17. Pham, H., Guan, M.Y., Zoph, B., Le, Q.V., Dean, J.: Efficient neural architecture search via parameter sharing. Computing Research Repository (CoRR) arXiv:1802.03268 (2018)
18. Ravi, S., Larochelle, H.: Optimization as a model for few-shot learning. In: International Conference on Learning Representations (ICLR) (2017)
19. Sutskever, I., Martens, J., Dahl, G., Hinton, G.E.: Practical network blocks design with Q-learning. In: International Conference of Machine Learning (ICML) (2013)
20. Sutton, R.S., McAllester, D., Singh, S., Mansour, Y.: Policy gradient methods for reinforcement learning with function approximation. In: NIPS (1999)
21. Williams, R.J.: Simple statistical gradient-following algorithms for connectionist reinforcement learning. Mach. Learn., 41–49 (2019)
22. Xiao, H., Rasul, K., Vollgraf, R.: Fashion-MNIST: a novel image dataset for benchmarking machine learning algorithms. Computing Research Repository (CoRR) arXiv:1708.07747 (2017)
23. Xu, T., Liu, Q., Zhao, L., Peng, J.: Learning to explore with meta-policy gradient. Computing Research Repository (CoRR) arXiv:1803.05044 (2018)
24. Zoph, B., Le, Q.V.: Neural architecture search with reinforcement learning. In: International Conference on Learning Representations (ICLR) (2017)
25. Zoph, B., Vasudevan, V., Shlens, J., Le, Q.V.: Learning transferable architectures for salable image recognition. In: Computer Vision and Pattern Recognition (CVPR) (2018)

Learning a Gaussian Process Model on the Riemannian Manifold of Non-decreasing Distribution Functions

Chafik Samir[1,2], Jean-Michel Loubes[2], Anne-Françoise Yao[1], and François Bachoc[2(✉)]

[1] University of Clermont Auvergne, Clermont-Ferrand, France
[2] Institut de Mathématiques de Toulouse, Toulouse, France
francois.bachoc@math.univ-toulouse.fr

Abstract. In this work, we consider the problem of learning regression models from a finite set of functional objects. In particular, we introduce a novel framework to learn a Gaussian process model on the space of Strictly Non-decreasing Distribution Functions (SNDF). Gaussian processes (GPs) are commonly known to provide powerful tools for non-parametric regression and uncertainty estimation on vector spaces. On top of that, we define a Riemannian structure of the SNDF space and we learn a GP model indexed by SNDF. Such formulation enables to define an appropriate covariance function, extending the Matérn family of covariance functions. We also show how the full Gaussian process methodology, namely covariance parameter estimation and prediction, can be put into action on the SNDF space. The proposed method is tested using multiple simulations and validated on real-world data.

Keywords: Gaussian process · Riemannian manifold · Functional data

1 Introduction

In this paper, we consider the problem of learning regression models from a finite set of functional objects. This problem has become very common in several contexts of applications, including science and technology. For example in functional data analysis and medical data it is very common to compare two objects (functions, curves, surfaces, volumes, etc.) in order to find optimal correspondences between their representations. This methodology, is usually refereed to as statistical shape analysis in [13,18,24]. The mathematical formulation leads to a wide range of applications when studying temporal or spatial changes to characterize a population or to build predictive models [11,26]. In particular, we

The authors thank the ANITI program (Artificial Natural Intelligence Toulouse Institute) and the ANR Project RISCOPE (Risk-based system for coastal flooding early warning). JM Loubes acknowledges the funding by DEEL-IRT and C. Samir acknowledges the funding by CNRS Prime.

A. C. Nayak and A. Sharma (Eds.): PRICAI 2019, LNAI 11671, pp. 107–120, 2019.
https://doi.org/10.1007/978-3-030-29911-8_9

are interested in studying variations corresponding to domain deformations in observed objects. For instance, the human heart beating of the same person during a cycle can be different under different circumstances. Hence any regression model should take into account the domain (timing) difference (deformation) in observations when studying them. Consequently, such models will become more realistic, efficient, and parsimonious. Many authors have studied registration methods using dynamic time warping models or semi-parametric deformation models, see for instance [9,10,19].

Gaussian process regression has been successfully applied in many fields. It has been introduced in [15] by Kolmogrov in the 1940s and applied for multivariate regression starting from 1960s. As a supervised learning process, we will refer to a Kriging approach without restriction to any area of research such as geostatistics, time series, etc. The usual Kriging procedure consists in assuming that we observe a random process $Z = (Z_I)$ indexed by an object I living on a compact space $\mathcal{E}$, also called the index space. Hence predicting unobserved values of the process leads to estimating conditional expectation which can be done as soon as a covariance, between the process observed at different locations, can be defined. Actually for I_i and I_j in $\mathcal{E}$, the main issue is to build a proper covariance between Z_{I_i} and Z_{I_j}. In particular, this covariance can define a notion of stationarity for the process. In this work, we consider the case where for any $i = 1, \ldots, N$ I_i is a nonlinear deformation of a common pattern I^*. In this framework, we assume that I_i can be written as $I_i = I^* \circ F_i$ with F_i being a strictly non-increasing distribution, and I being a one-dimensional real-valued function.

In order to capture deformations between observed functions I's and perform optimal predictions for unobserved data, we thus consider a Gaussian Process on the space of distributions functions $\mathcal{F}$ where $Z \sim GP(m, C)$ is defined by a mean function $m : \mathcal{F} \to \mathbb{R}$ and a covariance function $C : \mathcal{F} \times \mathcal{F} \to \mathbb{R}$. To reach such goal we will present properties for the Gaussian process on $\mathcal{F}$ using isometric mappings defined in Sect. 2.2. Indeed, the regression problem on the space of strictly non-decreasing distribution functions will be re-defined as follows. Given a finite set of observations $\{(F_i, y_i) \in \mathcal{F} \times \mathbb{R}, \quad 1 \leq i, \leq n\}$, define a regression model and an estimate of the conditional expectation $\mathbb{E}[y|y_1, \ldots, y_n]$, for a new pair (F, y).

Applications. In this section, we describe some typical applications and explain why they require regression on distribution functions. We consider some applications which belong to the case when the observed curves are real-valued functions (functional data) defined on an interval of the real line. We point out that the choice of application is independent of the proposed method. In particular, we are interested in studying variability in different groups and utilizing full function patterns from such analysis for subsequent classification. An added difficulty in the problem at hand is the fact that the observed objects do not have the same parametrization of the domain. Without loss of generality, we consider that their respective parametrization are deformations (as a convolution with a distribution function) of the unit interval $[0, 1]$. In other words, different individuals will present different amounts of time, and thus, it becomes important to focus on deformations rather than the common pattern. Thus, we require a comprehensive statistical framework for analysis of functional data that allows for statistically analyzing variabilities. There exists a large body of literature on statistical analysis of functions; see for example [14,20,23,26]. When restricting to the analysis of functions that require temporal alignment, the literature is somehow limited [10,12,16,17,24]. Another class of methods are variations of the Dynamic Time Warping (DTW) algorithm that was first applied for speech recognition [22] and has been extended to other engineering and computer science areas [8]. The main differences between our suggested method and those in the literature are: (i) deformations are continuous in our formulations instead of discrete vectors, (ii) we present the asymptotic properties of the regression model, and (iii) our formulation can be extended for other domains' deformations.

1.1 Contribution

The goal of this study is to develop a new set of measures that can enhance classification of functional observations based on distribution functions as element of a Riemannian manifold. To that end, we show how Gaussian process regression works in this setting. Beyond the previous methods, the main contribution of this paper can be summarized in:

- We consider the problem of prediction from a finite set of an observed pattern I^* where the randomness is caused by deformations of its domain. When the deformations are strictly nondecreasing distributions in a space $\mathcal{F}$, we propose to consider a Gaussian process regression on $\mathcal{F}$ with a covariance defined on a Riemannian manifold.
- Since a Gaussian process is determined by its mean function m and covariance function C, we focus on C and we extend the Matérn covariance functions on the SNDF space.
- We study the asymptotic properties of the Gaussian process model, by showing a general microergodicity result.

The rest of this paper is organized as follows. Section 2 describes our framework for Gaussian process models indexed by distributions as well as a reminder for tools needed for our formulation. Section 3 extends the Matérn covariance function to this context, and provides the microergodicity result. Section 4 presents experimental results. In particular, we compare the classification accuracy using different simulations and real medical data. Conclusions are proposed in Sect. 5 while all proofs are postponed to the Appendix.

2 Proposed Method

In this section, we first formulate the problem and then introduce the tools for the manifold Gaussian process regression model.

2.1   Problem Formulation

Let $I_1, \ldots, I_n$ denote a finite set of n observed objects that are non-linear deformations of a specific pattern $I^\star$. By deformation, we mean that for all $i = 1, \ldots, N$ there is a unique distribution $F_i \in \mathcal{F}$ such that

$$I_i = I^\star \circ F_i : \Omega = [0,1] \to \mathbb{R}^d.$$

In this study, we will focus on strictly nondecreasing distribution functions belonging to the space $\mathcal{F} = \{F : \Omega = [0,1] \mapsto [0,1], F(0) = 0, F(1) = 1, \ f > 0\}$, letting $f = \dot{F}$, has been studied to solve statistical shape analysis problem with various applications in medical imaging, computer vision, and mechanics. The space $\mathcal{F}$ can be viewed as a Lie group without topological structures which acts onto the space of objects Is on the right as follows:

$$(I, F) = I \circ F$$

Thus, the notion of dissimilarity between any two objects $I_i = (I^\star \circ F_i)$ and $I_j = (I^\star \circ F_j)$ must be measured with respect to the deformation between these two objects, namely using a proper distance between the two distribution functions F_i and F_j. To reach such goal one needs to consider $\mathcal{F}$ as a Riemannian manifold by putting a Riemannian structure on it in order to define a geodesic distance for our study.

2.2   Background and Space of Representations

We endow $\mathcal{F}$ with the Fisher-Rao metric so that, for any $F \in \mathcal{F}$ and $T_F(\mathcal{F})$ being the tangent space to $\mathcal{F}$ at F we have:

$$< g_1, g_2 >_F = \int_0^1 \dot{g}_1(t) \dot{g}_2(t) \frac{1}{f(t)} dt.$$

for any $g_1, g_2 \in T_F(\mathcal{F})$. Note that $\mathcal{F}$ is now a nonlinear manifold due to boundary conditions and that this metric defines a Riemannian structure on it. As mentioned above, performing Kriging on $\mathcal{F}$ directly is not straightforward. In this work we will use a mapping from $\mathcal{F}$ to another Riemannian manifold and will exploit the isometry to extend the notion of Gaussian process to the space of strictly increasing functions. Indeed, we map each distribution F to the square root of its derivative, the corresponding density function as follows:

$$\Psi : \mathcal{F} \to \mathcal{H}$$
$$F \mapsto \phi = \Psi(F) = \sqrt{f}.$$

Here $\mathcal{H} = \{\phi : \Omega = [0,1] \to \mathbb{R}, \int_0^1 \phi(t)^2 dt = 1, \phi > 0\}$. Note that $\phi = \sqrt{f}$ is well defined since $f > 0$ by definition and that $\Psi(id_{\mathcal{F}}) = 1$ is a constant function.

Following the definition of the metric given above, we assume that the new space of ϕ, denoted by $\mathcal{H}$, is a subset of $\mathbb{L}^2[0,1]$. Then, since

$$\|\phi\|_2^2 = \int_0^1 \phi(t)\phi(t)dt = 1,$$

$\mathcal{H}$ is a subset of the unit Hilbert sphere with a Riemannian structure that will be useful later to ease the analysis of SNDFs. We remind that the geodesic distance on the sphere is given by the length of the connecting arc and that the parallel transport is a rotation. The reader can refer to [6,7] for more details. Furthermore, Ψ is an isometry with the following inverse:

$$\Psi^{-1} : \mathcal{H} \to \mathcal{F}$$

$$\phi \mapsto \left(t \to \int_0^t \phi^2(s)ds = \int_0^t f(s)ds \right).$$

One of the main advantages of this formulation is to exploit the nice properties of the sphere:

-   **Geodesic distance.** Let F_1, F_2 be any two elements $\in \mathcal{F}$ and let $\xi \in [0,1]$, then the geodesic between F_1 and F_2 at time instant ξ is given by the Ψ inverse of the geodesic arc between ϕ_1 and ϕ_2:

$$\eta(\xi) = \frac{1}{\sin(\beta)} \left[\sin(\beta - \beta\xi)\phi_1 + \sin(\beta\xi)\phi_2 \right]$$

    where $\beta = \arccos(< \sqrt{f_1}, \sqrt{f_2} >_2)$.
-   **The exponential map.** Let ϕ be any element in $\mathcal{H}$ and w its tangent vector $w \in T_\phi(\mathcal{H})$, then the exponential map exp is defined as an isometry from $\mathcal{H}$ to its tangent space $T_\phi(\mathcal{H})$ by:

$$w \mapsto \exp_\phi(w) = \cos(\|w\|)\phi + \frac{\sin(\|w\|)}{\|w\|}w.$$

-   **Log map.** As the inverse of the exponential map from $\phi_j \in \mathcal{H}$ to $T_\phi(\mathcal{H})$ is given by $\log_\phi$:

$$\phi_j \mapsto w_j = \log_\phi(\phi_j) = \frac{\beta}{\sin(\beta)}(\phi_j - \cos(\beta)\phi).$$

Therefore and as a special case, we note $\mathcal{E} = T_1(\mathcal{H})$ the tangent space of $\mathcal{H}$ at the constant function one and $\mathcal{V}$ the space of functions v such that $v - 1$ belongs to $\mathcal{E}$:

$$\mathcal{V} = \{ v \in \mathbb{L}(\Omega, \mathbb{R}) : \int_0^1 v(t) = 1, \quad \|v\| \leq \frac{\pi}{2} \}.$$

3   Gaussian Processes on $\mathcal{F}$

Gaussian Processes (GP) are used to provide a probabilistic framework for a large variety of machine learning methods. We refer for instance to [21] and references therein. In this paper, they enable to optimally predict an unobserved value y associated to a deformed curve $I^\star \circ F$, from observed values $y_1, \ldots, y_n$ corresponding to deformed curves $I^\star \circ F_1, \ldots, I^\star \circ F_n$. Here, $F, F_1, \ldots, F_n$ belong to $\mathcal{F}$, so that we focus on constructing Gaussian processes on $\mathcal{F}$.

A Gaussian process Z on $\mathcal{F}$ is a random field indexed by $\mathcal{F}$ so that $(Z(F_1), \ldots, Z(F_n))$ is a Gaussian vector for any $n \in \mathbb{N}$, $F_1, \ldots, F_n \in \mathcal{F}$. We point out that a Gaussian process Z is characterized by its mean function $m : \mathcal{F} \to \mathbb{R}$ and by its covariance function $C : \mathcal{F}^2 \to \mathbb{R}$. The fact that these two functions characterize the Gaussian process is a simplicity benefit, and is one of the reasons for the popularity of Gaussian processes.

In this paper, we consider Gaussian processes with zero mean function and focus on the issue of constructing a proper covariance function for distribution functions in $\mathcal{F}$.

3.1   Constructing Covariance Functions on $\mathcal{F}$

A covariance function C on $\mathcal{F}$ must satisfy the following conditions. For any $n \in \mathbb{N}$, $F_1, \ldots, F_n \in \mathcal{F}$, the matrix $[C(F_i, F_j)]_{1 \leq i,j, \leq n}$ is symmetric non-negative definite. Furthermore, C is called non-degenerate when the above matrix is invertible whenever $F_1, \ldots, F_n$ are two-by-two distincts [4].

The strategy we adopt to construct covariance functions is to exploit the isometric map $\log_1$, based on the tangent space of $\mathcal{H}$ at 1. That is, we construct covariance functions of the form

$$C(F_1, F_2) = K(\|\log_1(\phi_1) - \log_1(\phi_2)\|), \tag{1}$$

where $\|.\|$ is the Euclidean norm in the Hilbert space $\mathcal{E}$ and with $K : \mathbb{R}^+ \to \mathbb{R}$.

We remark that it is common to define covariance functions C_d on $\mathbb{R}^d$ of the form $C_d(v_1, v_2) = K(\|v_1 - v_2\|)$ [21]. These covariance functions are called isotropic. In the next proposition, we show that, for any K so that C_d is a (non-degenerate) covariance function for any $d \in \mathbb{N}$, then C is also a (non-degenerate) covariance function. The next proposition has been partially addressed in [5]. For the sake of completeness, we give a complete statement and proof here.

Proposition 1. *Let $K : \mathbb{R}^+ \to \mathbb{R}$ be such that, for any $d \in \mathbb{N}$, the function $K : \mathbb{R}^d \times \mathbb{R}^d \to \mathbb{R}$ defined by $K(u, v) = K(\|u - v\|)$ is a covariance function. Let C be defined as in (1). Then C is a covariance function.*

Furthermore, assume that for any $d \in \mathbb{N}$ and for any pairwise different $u_1, \ldots, u_n \in \mathbb{R}^d$, the matrix $(K(\|u_i - u_j\|))_{\{i,j\}}$ is invertible. Then C is non-degenerate.

In practice, we can select the function K from the Matérn family [25], letting for $t \geq 0$

$$K_\theta(t) = \frac{\sigma^2(\alpha t)^\nu}{\mathcal{F}(\nu)2^{\nu-1}} K_\nu(\alpha t)$$

for $\theta = (\sigma^2, \alpha, \nu) \in (0, \infty)^3$. We obtain the Matérn covariance functions C_θ on $\mathcal{F}$ defined by $C_\theta(F_1, F_2) = K_\theta(\|\log_1(\phi_1) - \log_1(\phi_2)\|)$ for $F_1, F_2 \in \mathcal{F}$. These functions C_θ are indeed covariance functions and are non-degenerate from Proposition 1, and from the fact that the Matérn covariance function is non-degenerate on $\mathbb{R}^d$ for any $d \in \mathbb{N}$.

3.2 Asymptotic Properties

Consider a parametric set of covariance functions $\{C_\theta; \theta \in \Theta\}$, with $\Theta \subset \mathbb{R}^p$ and where, for $\theta \in \Theta$ and $F_1, F_2 \in \mathcal{F}$, $C_\theta(F_1, F_2) = K_\theta(\|\log_1(\phi_1) - \log_1(\phi_2)\|)$ with $K_\theta : \mathbb{R}^+ \to \mathbb{R}$.

We can see a Gaussian process Z as an application from $(\Omega, \mathcal{M}) \times \mathcal{F}$ to $\mathbb{R}$, with $(\Omega, \mathcal{M})$ a measurable space. For any $\theta \in \Theta$, we can consider a probability measure $\mathbb{P}_\theta$ on Ω so that $Z : (\Omega, \mathcal{M}, \mathbb{P}_\theta) \times \mathcal{F} \to \mathbb{R}$ is a Gaussian process with mean function zero and covariance function C_θ.

Following [25], we say that the covariance parameter θ is microergodic if, for any $\theta_1 \neq \theta_2$ so that $\theta_1, \theta_2 \in \Theta$, the measures $\mathbb{P}_{\theta_1}$ and $\mathbb{P}_{\theta_2}$ are orthogonal.

For Gaussian processes indexed by a fixed bounded subset of $\mathbb{R}^d$, for $d \in \mathbb{N}$, microergodicity is an important concept. Indeed, it is a necessary condition for consistent estimators of θ to exist under fixed-domain asymptotics [25], and a fair amount of work has been devoted to showing microergodicity or non-microergodicity of parameters, for various models of covariance functions [1, 25, 27]. In this section, we extend these types of results to Gaussian processes indexed on $\mathcal{F}$. In the next theorem, we show that the covariance parameter θ is microergodic under very mild conditions.

Theorem 1. *Assume that there does not exist $\theta_1, \theta_2 \in \Theta$, with $\theta_1 \neq \theta_2$, so that $t \to K_{\theta_1}(t) - K_{\theta_2}(t)$ is constant on $[0, \pi/2]$. Then the covariance parameter θ is microergodic.*

In particular, Theorem 1 applies to the Matérn family of covariance functions described above.

3.3 Covariance Parameter Estimation and Prediction

Consider a data set of labeled objects of the form $(I^* \circ F_1, y_1), \ldots, (I^* \circ F_n, y_n)$, with $F_1, \ldots, F_n \in \mathcal{F}$ and $y_1, \ldots, y_n \in \mathbb{R}$. We adopt the point of view of Gaussian processes and assume that, for $i = 1, \ldots, n$, $y_i = Z(F_i) + \epsilon_i$, where Z is a Gaussian process on $\mathcal{F}$ and with $(\epsilon_1, \ldots, \epsilon_n)^t \sim \mathcal{N}(0, \rho I_n)$, independently of ϵ. Here ρ is the observation noise variance, that we assume to be known for simplicity.

Assume that Z has mean function zero and covariance function in the set $\{C_\theta; \theta \in \Theta\}$, for $\Theta \subset \mathbb{R}^p$. Then, θ can be selected by the maximum likelihood, with

$$\hat{\theta} \in \operatorname*{argmin}_{\theta \in \Theta} \log \det(R_\theta + \rho I_n) + y^t (R_\theta + \rho I_n)^{-1} y \qquad (2)$$

where $R_\theta = [C_\theta(F_i, F_j)]_{1 \le i,j \le n}$ and with $y = (y_1, \ldots, y_n)^t$. We remark that alternative estimation techniques exist, for instance cross validation [2,3,28]. Then, for any new object of the form $I^* \circ F$ with $F \in \mathcal{F}$, the corresponding label can be predicted by $\hat{y}_{\hat{\theta}}(F)$, with

$$\hat{y}_\theta(F) = r_\theta(F)^t (R_\theta + \rho I_n)^{-1} y,$$

where $r_\theta(F) = (C_\theta(F, F_1), \ldots, C_\theta(F, F_n))^t$. The prediction $\hat{y}_\theta(F)$ is the conditional expectation of $Z(\mathcal{F})$ given $y_1, \ldots, y_n$, when Z has covariance function C_θ.

The above formulas for maximum likelihood and prediction can be found in [21] for instance. The simplicity of the prediction formula explains the popularity of Gaussian process models. Overall steps of the proposed method are summarized in Algorithm 1.

Algorithm 1. Learning RGP

Input: (I_i, y_i) for $i = 1 \ldots n$
Output: $\hat{\theta}$, $C_{\hat{\theta}}$, $y_{\hat{\theta}}(F)$

1: Compute F_i for every $I_i = I^* \circ F_i$ with $i = 1 \ldots n$
2: Compute $\phi_i = \Psi(F_i)$ with $i = 1 \ldots n$
3: Define the tangent space $T_1(\mathcal{H})$
4: Compute the exponential map $\log_1$ and its inverse
5: Compute the covariance function K_θ in eq 1
6: Find $\hat{\theta}$ that maximizes the likelihood in eq 2
7: Compute $C_{\hat{\theta}}$ and $y_{\hat{\theta}}(F)$

---

4   Numerical Results

We demonstrate the proposed framework for learning a Gaussian process from a finite set of domain deformations. We first represent these deformations by strictly non-decreasing distributions and then consider them as element of a Riemannian manifold using properties detailed in Sect. 2.1. Next, we illustrate the performance of the learned model in terms of classification accuracy using synthetic data and two different real datasets: Berkeley growth study and a medical dataset from a population with arthritis.

Synthetic Datasets. As a sanity test, we simulate two datasets. Some samples are displayed in Fig. 2: class 1 (a) and class 2 (b) from example I and (c & d) these two classes from example II. Each class contains 300 samples for both examples and have been randomly generated from a finite basis of $\mathcal{F}$, see Fig. 1 for few examples of simulated F_i. As a common pattern I^* defined for $t \in [0, 1]$, we used:

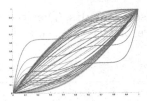

Fig. 1. Examples of F_i from $[0,1]$ to $[0,1]$. The identity is given by the diagonal, an increase appears above the diagonal whereas a decrease appears below the diagonal.

$$\begin{cases} I_1^*(t) = \frac{1}{2} + \sin(4\pi t)\cos(7t) \\ I_2^*(t) = 2(1 + \cos(8t))\exp(-2t^2) \end{cases}$$

to provide flexible enough deformations.

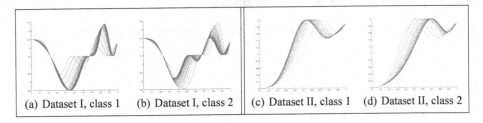

| (a) Dataset I, class 1 | (b) Dataset I, class 2 | (c) Dataset II, class 1 | (d) Dataset II, class 2 |

Fig. 2. Synthetic data: two different synthetic datasets (a &b and c &d), each with two classes.

Real Datasets. We use two different datasets. First, we use Berkeley growth study that records the heights of children at 31 stages from 1 to 18 years (see [20]). It is a typical example of biological dynamics observed over a period of time. The dataset has been widely used as a motivating example to analyze functional data. In our context, all growth curves were represented by their first derivative functions. The common pattern I^* was given as the Fréchet mean of all derivatives. See Fig. 3 top row for examples. The second dataset consists of hand force signals from a population of 80 healthy and 100 patients subject with arthritis. The medical protocol saved the hand force during a continuous period of time where the goal is to study the endurance during test. Thus, members of the healthy group are expected to hold more (less variability in F_i) than patients with pain. See Fig. 4 bottom row for examples of F_i.

- **Hyper-parameter Tuning.** The parameters that require tuning are $\theta = (\alpha, \nu, \sigma)$. We used the gradient descent and a Newton-based optimization to search for optimal values of (α, σ) and a cross-validation on ν to find the maximum likelihood as defined in Eq. (2).
- **Evaluation Method.** The classification accuracy is evaluated using the mean squared prediction error (MSE).

– **Performance Comparison Results.** The accuracy rate is given for Gaussian Process on the space of (I_i) and using the proposed method on the corresponding (F_i).

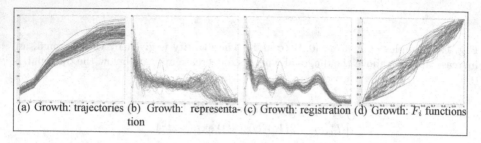

(a) Growth: trajectories (b) Growth: representa- (c) Growth: registration (d) Growth: F_i functions
tion

Fig. 3. Real data: analyzing trajectories from Berkeley growth study. The goal is to characterize the growth rate for boys and girls.

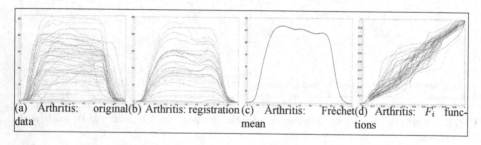

(a) Arthritis: original (b) Arthritis: registration (c) Arthritis: Fréchet (d) Arthritis: F_i func-
data   mean   tions

Fig. 4. Real data: functional signals from adults with and without arthritis. The goal is to learn a regression model for aided diagnostics.

First, we test the efficiency of the proposed method: We learn the model parameters from 75% of the dataset as training and use the rest for test. To compute the classification error, we first compute the estimator and its parameters from the training set. Then, given a new observation F^* for test, we apply the regression model to determine its class logit (y^*), where y^* is the Gaussian process prediction. The subdivision has been performed randomly 20 times and the classification rates are given as a mean. As mentioned above, we evaluate the classification quality using MSE. All scores are summarized in Table 1 for simulated data and Tables 2 and 3 for real data. We note that the regression using a Gaussian process on distribution functions outperforms the Gaussian process on original functions. For a fair comparison, we used the same properties of the Gaussian process such as the Matérn covariance and both gradient and Newton for parameters tuning.

Table 1. Mean squared error with two different hyper-parameters tuning methods on simulated data

Method	Gradient	Newton
Simulation I (F_i)	$3.47e - 9$	$3.47e - 9$
Simulation II (F_i)	$3.23e - 2$	$2.01e - 2$

Table 2. Mean squared error with two different hyper-parameters tuning methods on Berkley growth data

Method	Gradient	Newton
Growth (I_i)	$2.23e - 1$	$1.31e - 1$
Growth (F_i)	$1.10e - 1$	$7.15e - 2$

Table 3. Mean squared error with two different hyper-parameters tuning methods on arthritis data

Method	Gradient	Newton
Arthritis (I_i)	$1.14e - 1$	$1.01e - 1$
Arthritis (F_i)	$7.97e - 2$	$5.29e - 2$

5   Conclusion

This paper presents a novel framework for learning Gaussian process model on strictly nondecreasing distributions. With a Matérn kernel specified as the covariance function in the Gaussian process prior, we have provided the microergodicity of the covariance parameters. The proposed method was successfully tested on both synthetic and read medical data. We showed that the regression model is capable of producing highly meaningful differences on different classes of objects when using their domains' deformations only. A future direction of interest is to build theoretical extension for more complex domains where the distributions could be bivariate or even multivariate for new aspects of manifold learning.

A   Proofs

Proof (Proof of Proposition 1). Let $F_1, \ldots, F_n$ in $\mathcal{F}$. For $i = 1, \ldots, n$, let $g_i = \log_1(\phi_i)$. Consider the matrix $\tilde{C} = (< g_i, g_j >)_{\{i,j\}}$. This matrix is a Grammian matrix in $\mathbb{R}^{n \times n}$ hence there exists a non negative diagonal matrix D and an orthogonal matrix P such that

$$\tilde{C} = PDP' = PD^{1/2}D^{1/2}P'.$$

Let $e_1, \ldots, e_n$ be the canonical basis of $\mathbb{R}^n$. Then $e_i^t \tilde{C} e_j = u_i^t u_j$ where $u_i^t = e_i^t PD^{1/2}$. Note that the u_i's are vectors in $\mathbb{R}^n$ that depend on the $f_1, \ldots, f_n$. We get that

$$< g_i, g_j > = u_i^t u_j,$$

and for any $F_1, \ldots, F_n$ in $\mathcal{F}$ there are $u_1, \ldots, u_n$ in $\mathbb{R}^n$ such that

$$\| \log_1(\phi_i) - \log_1(\phi_j) \| = \| u_i - u_j \|.$$

So any covariance matrix that can be written as $[K(\| \log_1(\phi_i) - \log_1(\phi_j) \|)]_{i,j}$ can be seen as a covariance matrix $[K(\| u_i - u_j \|)]_{i,j}$ on $\mathbb{R}^n$ and inherits its properties. The invertibility and non-negativity of this covariance matrix entail the invertibility and non-negativity of the first one, which proves the result.

Proof (Proof of Theorem 1). Let $\theta_1, \theta_2 \in \Theta$, with $\theta_1 \neq \theta_2$. Then, there exists $t^* \in [0, \pi/4]$ so that $K_{\theta_1}(0) - K_{\theta_1}(2t^*) \neq K_{\theta_2}(0) - K_{\theta_2}(2t^*)$.

For $i \in \mathbb{N}$, let $c_i : [0,1] \to \mathbb{R}$ be defined by $c_i(t) = t^* \cos(2\pi i t)$. Then, $c_i \in T_1(\mathcal{H})$. Let $\tilde{e}_i = \exp_1(c_i)$. Then, for $t \in [0,1]$

$$\tilde{e}_i(t) = \cos(t^*) + \frac{\sin(t^*)}{t^*} t^* \cos(2\pi i t) \geq \cos(t^*) - \sin(t^*) \geq 0.$$

It follows that $\tilde{e}_i \in \mathcal{H}$ and we can let $\tilde{F}_i(t) = \int_0^t \tilde{e}_i(s)^2 ds$. Letting $\bar{e}_i = \exp_1(-c_i)$, we obtain similarly that $\bar{e}_i \in \mathcal{H}$ and we let $\bar{F}_i(t) = \int_0^t \bar{e}_i(s)^2 ds$.

Consider the $2n$ elements $(F_1, ..., F_{2n})$ composed by the pairs $(\tilde{F}_i, \bar{F}_i)$ for $i = 1, \ldots, n$. Consider a Gaussian process Z on $\mathcal{F}$ with mean function zero and covariance function K_{θ_1}. Then, the Gaussian vector $W = (Z(F_i))_{i=1,\ldots,2n}$ has covariance matrix C given by

$$C_{i,j} = \begin{cases} K_{\theta_1}(0) & \text{if } i = j \\ K_{\theta_1}(2t^*) & \text{if } i \text{ odd and } j = i+1 \\ K_{\theta_1}(2t^*) & \text{if } i \text{ even and } j = i-1 \\ K_{\theta_1}(\sqrt{2}t^*) & \text{else.} \end{cases}$$

Hence, we have $C = D + M$ where M is the matrix with all components equal to $K_{\theta_1}(\sqrt{2}t^*)$ and where D is block diagonal, composed of n blocks of size 2×2, with each block $B_{2,2}$ equal to

$$\begin{pmatrix} K_{\theta_1}(0) - K_{\theta_1}(\sqrt{2}t^*) & K_{\theta_1}(2t^*) - K_{\theta_1}(\sqrt{2}t^*) \\ K_{\theta_1}(2t^*) - K_{\theta_1}(\sqrt{2}t^*) & K_{\theta_1}(0) - K_{\theta_1}(\sqrt{2}t^*) \end{pmatrix}.$$

Hence, in distribution, $W = M + E$, with M and E independent, $M = (z, ..., z)$ where $z \sim \mathcal{N}(0, K_{\theta_1}(\sqrt{2}t^*))$ and where the n pairs (E_{2k+1}, E_{2k+2}), $k = 0, ..., n-1$ are independent, with distribution $\mathcal{N}(0, B_{2,2})$. Hence, with $\bar{W}_1 = (1/n) \sum_{k=0}^{n-1} W_{2k+1}$, $\bar{W}_2 = (1/n) \sum_{k=0}^{n-1} W_{2k+2}$ and $\bar{E} = (1/n) \sum_{k=0}^{n-1} (E_{2k+1}, E_{2k+2})^t$, we have

$$\hat{B} := \frac{1}{n} \sum_{i=0}^{n-1} \begin{pmatrix} W_{2i+1} - \bar{W}_1 \\ W_{2i+2} - \bar{W}_2 \end{pmatrix} \begin{pmatrix} W_{2i+1} - \bar{W}_1 \\ W_{2i+2} - \bar{W}_2 \end{pmatrix}^t$$

$$= \frac{1}{n} \sum_{i=0}^{n-1} \begin{pmatrix} E_{2i+1} \\ E_{2i+2} \end{pmatrix} \begin{pmatrix} E_{2i+1} \\ E_{2i+2} \end{pmatrix}^t - \bar{E}\bar{E}^t$$

$$\xrightarrow[n\to\infty]{p} B_{2,2}.$$

Hence, there exists a subsequence $n' \to \infty$ so that, almost surely $\hat{B} \to B_{2,2}$ as $n' \to \infty$. Hence, almost surely $\hat{B}_{1,1} - \hat{B}_{1,2} \to K_{\theta_1}(0) - K_{\theta_1}(2t^*)$ as $n' \to \infty$. Hence, the event $\{\hat{B}_{2,2} \to_{n' \to \infty} K_{\theta_1}(0) - K_{\theta_1}(2t^*)\}$ has probability one under $\mathbb{P}_{\theta_1}$. With the same arguments, we can show that the event $\{\hat{B}_{2,2} \to_{n'' \to \infty} K_{\theta_2}(0) - K_{\theta_2}(2t^*)\}$ has probability one under $\mathbb{P}_{\theta_2}$, where n'' is a subsequence extracted from n'. Since these two events have zero intersection, it follows that $\mathbb{P}_{\theta_1}$ and $\mathbb{P}_{\theta_2}$ are orthogonal. Hence, θ is microergodic.

References

1. Anderes, E.: On the consistent separation of scale and variance for Gaussian random fields. Ann. Stat. **38**, 870–893 (2010)
2. Bachoc, F.: Cross validation and maximum likelihood estimations of hyperparameters of gaussian processes with model misspecification. Comput. Stat. Data Anal. **66**, 55–69 (2013)
3. Bachoc, F.: Asymptotic analysis of covariance parameter estimation for Gaussian processes in the misspecified case. Bernoulli **24**, 1531–1575 (2018)
4. Bachoc, F., Gamboa, F., Loubes, J.M., Venet, N.: A Gaussian process regression model for distribution inputs. IEEE Trans. Inf. Theor. (2017)
5. Bachoc, F., Suvorikova, A., Loubes, J.M., Spokoiny, V.: Gaussian process forecast with multidimensional distributional entries. arXiv preprint arXiv:1805.00753 (2018)
6. Boothby, W.M.: An Introduction to Differential Manifolds and Riemannian Geometry. Academic Press, New york (1975)
7. Dryden, L., Mardia, K.V.: Statistical Shape Analysis. Wiley, Hoboken (1998)
8. Efrat, A., Fan, Q., Venkatasubramanian, S.: Curve matching, time warping, and light fields: new algorithms for computing similarity between curves. J. Math. Imaging Vis. **27**(3), 203–216 (2007)
9. Gamboa, F., Loubes, J.M., Maza, E.: Semi-parametric estimation of shifts. Electron. J. Stat. **1**, 616–640 (2007)
10. Gervini, D., Gasser, T.: Self-modeling warping functions. J. Roy. Stat. Soc. B **66**, 959–971 (2004)
11. Grenander, U., Miller, M., Klassen, E., Le, H., Srivastava, A.: Computational anatomy: an emerging discipline. Q. Appl. Math. **4**, 617–694 (1998)
12. James, G.: Curve alignment by moments. Ann. Appl. Stat., 480–501 (2007)
13. Kendall, D.G.: Shape manifolds, procrustean metrics and complex projective spaces. Bull. London Math. Soc. **16**, 81–121 (1984)
14. Kneip, A., Gasser, T.: Statistical tools to analyze data representing a sample of curves. Ann. Stat. **20**, 1266–1305 (1992)
15. Kolmogorov, A.N.: Wiensche spiralen und einige andere interessante kurven im hilbertschen raum. Doklady Akad. Nauk SSSR **26**, 115–118 (1940)
16. Kurtek, S., Srivastava, A., Wu, W.: Signal estimation under random time-warpings and nonlinear signal alignment. In: Neural Information Processing Systems (NIPS) (2011)
17. Liu, X., Müller, H.G.: Functional convex averaging and synchronization for time-warped random curves. J. Am. Stat. Assoc. **99**, 687–699 (2004)
18. Michor, P.W., Mumford, D.: Riemannian geometries on spaces of plane curves. J. Eur. Math. Soc. **8**, 1–48 (2006)

19. Ramsay, J.O., Li, X.: Curve registration. J. Roy. Stat. Soc. B **60**, 351–363 (1998)
20. Ramsay, J.O., Silverman, B.W.: Functional Data Analysis. Springer Series in Statistics, 2nd edn. Springer, New York (2005). https://doi.org/10.1007/b98888
21. Rasmussen, C., Williams, C.: Gaussian Processes for Machine Learning. The MIT Press, Cambridge (2006)
22. Sakoe, H.: Dynamic programming algorithm optimization for spoken word recognition. IEEE Trans. Acoust. Speech Signal Process. **26**, 43–49 (1978)
23. Srivastava, A., Wu, W., Kurtek, S., Klassen, E., Marron, J.S.: Registration of functional data using fisher-rao metric. arXiv:1103.3817v2 (2011)
24. Srivastava, A., Klassen, E.: Functional and Shape Data Analysis. Springer, New York (2016). https://doi.org/10.1007/978-1-4939-4020-2
25. Stein, M.L.: Interpolation of Spatial Data. Springer Series in Statistics. Springer, New York (1999). https://doi.org/10.1007/978-1-4612-1494-6
26. Tang, R., Müller, H.G.: Pairwise curve synchronization for functional data. Biometrika **95**(4), 875–889 (2008)
27. Zhang, H.: Inconsistent estimation and asymptotically equivalent interpolations in model-based geostatistics. J. Am. Stat. Assoc. **99**, 250–261 (2004)
28. Zhang, H., Wang, Y.: Kriging and cross-validation for massive spatial data. Environmetrics Official J. Int. Environ. Soc. **21**(3–4), 290–304 (2010)

Toward Reciprocity-Aware Distributed Learning in Referral Networks

Ashiqur R. KhudaBukhsh$^{(\boxtimes)}$ and Jaime G. Carbonell

Carnegie Mellon University, Pittsburgh, PA 15213, USA
{akhudabu,jgc}@cs.cmu.edu

Abstract. Distributed learning in expert referral networks is an emerging challenge in the intersection of Active Learning and Multi-Agent Reinforcement Learning, where experts—humans or automated agents—have varying skills across different topics and can redirect difficult problem instances to connected colleagues with more appropriate expertise. The *learning-to-refer* challenge involves estimating colleagues' topic-conditioned skills for appropriate referrals. Prior research has investigated different reinforcement learning algorithms both with uninformative priors and partially available (potentially noisy) priors. However, most human experts expect mutually-rewarding referrals, with return referrals on their expertise areas so that both (or all) parties benefit from networking, rather than one-sided referral flow. This paper analyzes the extent of referral reciprocity imbalance present in high-performance referral-learning algorithms, specifically multi-armed bandit (MAB) methods belonging to two broad categories – frequentist and Bayesian – and demonstrate that both algorithms suffer considerably from reciprocity imbalance. The paper proposes modifications to enable distributed learning methods to better balance referral reciprocity and thus make referral networks win-win for all parties. Extensive empirical evaluations demonstrate substantial improvement in mitigating reciprocity imbalance, while maintaining reasonably high overall solution performance.

Keywords: Referral networks · Reciprocity awareness · Active Learning

1 Introduction

A referral network consists of multiple agents, human or autonomous, who learn to estimate the expertise of other known agents in order to optimize referral decisions when they are unable to solve a problem instance. *Learning-to-refer* in multi-agent referral networks has witnessed recent progress on several fronts, including distributed reinforcement learning algorithms [16], coping with some experts quitting the network and others joining [15], addressing expertise drift [12], e.g., as some experts hone their primary skills over time or others atrophy when disused. Other practical issues addressed include capacity constraints

© Springer Nature Switzerland AG 2019
A. C. Nayak and A. Sharma (Eds.): PRICAI 2019, LNAI 11671, pp. 121–135, 2019.
https://doi.org/10.1007/978-3-030-29911-8_10

on how many problems an agent can address per unit of time [15]. These lines of work, however, implicitly assume altruistic agents, intent on solving problems collectively, rather than maximizing individual gain, where gain is proportional to business volume, i.e., incoming clients and referrals.

An extension beyond implicit altruism is the advent of resource-bounded proactive skill advertisement [11,13,14] among agents, where each agent attempts to maximize gain by attracting the largest number of referrals, assuming incoming referrals for problems an agent can solve result in economic gain. This extension required creating incentive-compatible mechanisms to induce agents to accurately report their skill levels (vs strategic lying), so that local economic gain would align with overall network problem-solving accuracy.

Another extension beyond implicit altruism requires addressing referral reciprocity among agents. Consider a network of physicians who know each other where A and B are dermatologists with different skill levels and C and D are neurologists, also with different skill levels. C might refer all patients with dermatological conditions to A if she believes A is the more skilled dermatologist. If B refers patients with neurological issues to C and D, and after a while notices that C never returns any referrals, a natural reaction would be "Why should I refer anyone to C if she never returns the business?" and henceforth B sends her neurological referrals only to D, even if she may believe D is not the best or most appropriate neurologist. If the reader would prefer to think that physicians act only in the patients' best interests, substitute dermatologists and neurologists with liability and tort lawyers, or with used car salesmen specializing in different auto brands, or with automated agents programmed to optimize their economic benefit. The key issue is reciprocity of referrals, or rather reciprocity imbalance, where an agent, repeatedly slighted by a peer via highly imbalanced referrals, changes her behavior in a manner that may not lead to optimal network referral behavior.

Reciprocity as a means to improve overall multi-agent cooperation has been studied in biological settings [26], economic settings [6], and AI-based multi-agent settings [9,18], but not in the context of referral networks. This paper focuses on reciprocity imbalance (RI) which we define as the divergence from absolute reciprocity in the [0,1] interval. Absolute reciprocity means the referral flow between two agents is identical in both directions, in which case $RI \to 0$. Total lack of reciprocity means that either the first agent receives many referrals from the second agent but never reciprocates or vice versa ($RI \to 1$). The reasons for the arrows is that we measure empirical reciprocity imbalance, and with few data points we regularize it to be close to 0, and adjust upwards if warranted by new observations. Hence, the actual challenge we address in this paper is *learning-to-refer* in a multi-expert distributed setting taking reciprocity of referrals into account. In a broader context, our work is an example of a distributed AI application where a global goal (in our case, network-level task accuracy) is met via self-interested agents locally maximizing their self-interest.

Our work is different from extensive literature on *trust* and *reputation* [22, 23,25] on the following key aspects. First, reputation is trust in aggregate, in contrast for reported work all rewards and referrals are fine-grained, how one agent models another agent's behavior; there is no explicit communication among agents on reciprocity, nor any other requirements for global visibility. Second, unlike trust, reciprocity depends on mutual interaction (concerning referrals, estimated expertise levels and skill complementarities in each agent's subnetwork etc.); an expert can be highly reciprocating to some while being completely non-reciprocating to others.

Key Contributions: First, our extensive analysis on two high-performance referral learning algorithms that include the current state-of-the-art (a frequentist MAB algorithm DIEL [15]), and Thompson Sampling [20] (a well-known Bayesian MAB algorithm) reveals that both algorithms suffer from serious reciprocity imbalance and hence may not be well-suited for practical settings. Second, we propose a simple technique melding dual objectives that allows continual estimation of expertise of the colleagues taking both historical performance and reciprocity into account achieving considerable reduction in reciprocity imbalance at a small cost of overall performance. As baseline, we compared against an algorithmic setting where after observing a certain number of mutual referrals, an expert severs a connection with a colleague if the expert is unhappy with the reciprocal behavior of the colleague and forges a new link with another expert in the network. Our results indicate that such abrupt change in behavior is sub-optimal and achieves less reciprocity and a worse referral-learning performance as compared to our proposed solution. Third, we show that when all experts are reciprocity-aware, strategic deviation to altruism or greed fetches lesser referrals in expectation. Finally, we show that even when we start with the constrained referral-learning algorithm but at a later stage, if we switch to the unconstrained version, the algorithms are able to recover its performance and match the corresponding unconstrained version.

2   Background

2.1   Motivation

We illustrate the effectiveness of appropriate referrals with a small simplified example of a referral network with five experts shown in Fig. 1 (this example is taken from [16]). The nodes of the graph represent the experts, and the edges indicate a potential referral link, i.e., 5 the experts 'know' each other and can send or receive referrals and communicate results. Consider three different topics – call them t_1, t_2, and t_3 – and the figures in brackets indicate an expert's topical expertise (probability of solving a given task) in each of these.

In the example, with a query belonging to t_2, without any referral, the client may consult first v_2 and then possibly e_5, leading to a solution probability of $0.2 + (1 - 0.2) \times 0.2 = 0.36$. With referrals, an expert handles a problem she knows how to answer, and otherwise if she had knowledge of all the other connected colleagues' expertise, v_2 could refer to e_3 for the best skill in t_2, leading to a solution probability of $0.2 + (1 - 0.2) \times 0.8 = 0.84$. The true

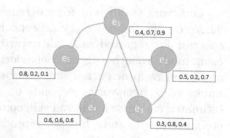

Fig. 1. A referral network with five experts.

topic-conditioned skills of the experts in the network are initially unknown and the *learning-to-refer* challenge is to estimate topical skills of the colleagues in a distributed setting with each expert independently estimating colleagues' topical expertise.

2.2 Preliminaries and Notation

Referral Network: Represented by a graph (V, E) of size k in which each vertex v_i $(1 \leq i \leq k)$ corresponds to an expert and each bidirectional edge $\langle v_i, v_j \rangle$ indicates a *referral link* which implies v_i and v_j can co-refer problem instances.

Subnetwork: of an expert v_i: The set of experts linked to an expert v_i by a referral link.

Referral Scenario: Set of m instances $(q_1, \ldots, q_m)$ belonging to n topics $(t_1, \ldots, t_n)$ addressed by the k experts $(v_1, \ldots, v_k)$ connected through a referral network (V, E).

Expertise: Expertise of an expert/instance pair $\langle v_i, q_l \rangle$ is the probability with which v_i can solve q_l.

Referral Mechanism: For a query budget $Q = 2$, and a given instance, q_l, this consists of the following steps.

1. A user issues an *initial query* to a randomly chosen *initial expert* v_i.
2. The initial expert v_i examines q_l and solves it if possible. This depends on the *expertise* of v_i wrt. q_l.
3. If not, a *referral query* is issued by v_i to a *referred expert* v_j within her subnetwork, with a remaining query budget of $Q - 2$. *Learning-to-refer* involves improving the estimate of who is most likely to solve the problem.
4. If the referred expert succeeds, she sends the solution to the initial expert, who sends it to the user.

The first two steps are identical to Active Learning [19]; step 3 and 4 are the extension to the Active Learning setting. Understandably, with a higher per-instance query budget, the referred expert can re-refer instances to other experts as long as the budget permits. Following [15], in addition to single-hop referral ($Q = 2$), we also considered bounded multi-hop referrals with $Q = 3$ (two-hop) and $Q = 4$ (three-hop). Further details regarding expertise, network parameters, and simulation details can be found in [13,15,16].

2.3   Assumptions

We follow the same set of *assumptions* made in [15,16]. Some of the important assumptions are: the network connectivity depends on (cosine) similarity between the topical expertise, and the distribution of topical-expertise across experts can be characterized by a mixture of Gaussian distributions; for any given instance, we assume that any of the k experts is equally likely to be the initial expert receiving the problem (query) externally. The network connectivity assumption is guided by the observation that experts with similar expertise are more likely to know each other. For topical-expertise distribution, a mixture of two Gaussians is considered. Gaussian distributions are widely used to model real-valued random variables (e.g., height, weight, expertise) in natural and social sciences. A mixture of two Gaussians was used to represent the expertise of experts with specific training for the given topic (higher mean, lower variance), contrasted with the lower-level expertise (lower mean, higher variance) of the layman population.

From the point of view of a single expert, for a given topic, learning referral policy maps to the classic MAB setting where each arm corresponds to a referral choice, and similar to the unknown reward distributions of the arms, the expertise of the colleagues is not initially known. In order to learn an effective referral strategy, depending on the outcome of a referred task, the initial expert assigns a reward to the referred colleague. All our rewards are

- **bounded:** In all our experiments, we considered binary rewards, with a failed and successful tasks receiving a reward of 0 and 1, respectively.
- **i.i.d:** The reward for a given expert on a specific instance belonging to a topic is independent of any reward observed from any other experts and any reward or sequence of rewards belonging to that topic or any other topic by the same expert.
- **locally assigned and locally visible:** $reward(v_i, t, v_j)$, a function of initial expert v_i, referred expert v_j and topic t, is assigned by v_i and visible to v_i only.

2.4   Distributed Referral Learning

In a distributed setting, each expert maintains an action selection thread for each topic in parallel. In order to describe an action selection thread, we first name the topic T and expert v. Let $q_1, \ldots, q_N$ be the first N referred queries belonging to topic T issued by expert v to any of her K colleagues denoted by $v_1, \ldots, v_K$. For each colleague v_i, v maintains a reward vector $\mathbf{r}_{i,n_i}$ where $\mathbf{r}_{i,n_i} = (r_{i,1}, \ldots, r_{i,n_i})$, i.e., the sequence of rewards observed from expert v_i

on issued n_i referred queries. Understandably, $N = \sum_{i=1}^{K} n_i$. Let $m(v_i)$ and $s(v_i)$ denote the sample mean and sample standard deviation of these reward vectors. Additional to the reward vectors, for each expert v_i, v maintains S_{v_i} and F_{v_i} where S_{v_i} denotes the number of observed successes (reward = 1) and F_{v_i} denotes the number of observed failures (reward = 0).

Algorithm 1. DIEL(v, T)

Initialization: $\forall i, n_i \leftarrow 2, \mathbf{r}_{i,n_i} \leftarrow (0,1)$
Loop: Select expert v_i who maximizes
$$score(v_i) = m(v_i) + \frac{s(v_i)}{\sqrt{n_i}}$$
Observe reward *reward*
Update $\mathbf{r}_{i,n_i}$ with *reward*, $n_i \leftarrow n_i + 1$

We next focus on two well-established referral-learning algorithms that have extensive use in other reinforcement learning and MAB contexts. These algorithms are *reciprocity-agnostic*, i.e., they do not consider reciprocity while making any referral decision.

DIEL: Distributed Interval Estimation Learning (DIEL) is the known state-of-the-art referral learning algorithm [15]. First proposed in [10], Interval Estimation Learning (IEL) has been extensively used in stochastic optimization [7] and action selection problems [4,24]. As described in Algorithm 1, at each step, DIEL selects the expert v_i with highest $m(v_i) + \frac{s(v_i)}{\sqrt{n_i}}$ (recall that, $m(v_i)$ and $s(v_i)$ denote the sample mean and sample standard deviation of the reward vector of expert v_i, respectively). Every expert is initialized with two rewards of 0 and 1, allowing us to initialize the mean and variance.

DIEL addresses the classic *exploration-exploitation* trade-off [3] present in MAB algorithm design in the following way. A large variance implies greater uncertainty, indicating that the expert has not been sampled with sufficient frequency to obtain reliable skill estimates. Selecting such an expert is an *exploration step* which will increase the confidence of v in her estimate. Also, such steps have the potential of identifying a highly skilled expert, whose earlier skill estimate may have been too low. Selecting an expert with a high $m(v_i)$ amounts to *exploitation*. Initially, choices made by v tend to be explorative since the intervals are large due to the uncertainty of the reward estimates. With an increased number of samples, the intervals shrink and the referrals become more exploitative.

Algorithm 2. TS(v, T)

Initialization: $\forall i, S_{v_i} \leftarrow 0, F_{v_i} \leftarrow 0$
Loop: Select expert v_i who maximizes
$$score(v_i) = \theta_i$$
Observe reward *reward*
$S_{v_i} \leftarrow S_{v_i} + reward$
$F_{v_i} \leftarrow F_{v_i} + 1 - reward$

Thompson Sampling (TS): First proposed in the 1930's [20], finite-time regret bound of Thompson Sampling (TS) remained unsolved for decades [1] until recent results on its competitiveness with algorithms that exhibit provable regret bounds renewed interest [5,8]. As described in Algorithm 2, at each step, for each expert v_i, TS first samples θ_i from $Beta(S_{v_i}+1, F_{v_i}+1)$ (recall that, S_{v_i} denotes the number of observed successes and F_{v_i} denotes the number of observed failures of expert v_i, respectively). Next, TS selects the action with highest θ_i. When the number of observations is 0, θ_i is sampled from $Beta(1,1)$, which is $U(0,1)$ which makes all colleagues equally likely to receive referral. As the number of observations increases, the distribution for a given expert becomes more and more centered around the empirical mean favoring experts with better historical performance.

3   Incorporating Reciprocity-Awareness

We first introduce a quantitative measure of reciprocity imbalance in referrals starting with the definitions required to formalize the measure.

Interaction: At any given point, *interaction* of a *referral link* $\langle v_i, v_j \rangle$, denoted as $interaction(\langle v_i, v_j \rangle)$, is measured as $interaction(\langle v_i, v_j \rangle) = R(v_j \rightarrow v_i) + R(v_i \rightarrow v_j)$, where $R(v_i \rightarrow v_j)$ denotes the total number of referrals (across all topics) v_j has so far received from v_i. Since $interaction(\langle v_i, v_j \rangle)$ is used as a denominator in *referral share* (defined next), in order to avoid any divide-by-zero boundary condition, $\forall i, j$, $R(v_i \rightarrow v_j)$ is initialized to 1, effectively initializing $interaction(\langle v_i, v_j \rangle)$ $\forall i, j$ to 2.

Referral Share: At any given point, the *referral share* of an expert v_i in a *referral link*, $\langle v_i, v_j \rangle$, denoted as $refShare(v_i, \langle v_i, v_j \rangle)$, is measured as $refShare(v_i, \langle v_i, v_j \rangle) = \frac{R(v_j \rightarrow v_i)}{interaction(\langle v_i, v_j \rangle)}$. In a reciprocal setting, for every expert in a *referral link*, we would like the *referral share* to be close to $\frac{1}{2}$.

Reciprocity Imbalance of a Referral Link: For a given *referral link*, $\langle v_i, v_j \rangle$, the reciprocity imbalance, denoted as $RI(\langle v_i, v_j \rangle)$, is measured as $RI(\langle v_i, v_j \rangle) = |\frac{1}{2} - refShare(v_i, \langle v_i, v_j \rangle)| + |\frac{1}{2} - refShare(v_j, \langle v_i, v_j \rangle)|$.

For every *referral link*, $RI(\langle v_i, v_j \rangle)$ is initialized to zero. For any *referral link*, reciprocity imbalance is bounded within the range [0, 1] with 0 being a case of perfect reciprocity and 1 being the extreme case where one expert in a *referral link* does not receive any referrals from her colleague. Say, v_1 and v_2 have referred 100 instances between each other of which v_2 received 80 instances, the reciprocity of the link will be $|\frac{1}{2} - \frac{80}{100}| + |\frac{1}{2} - \frac{20}{100}| = |0.5 - 0.8| + |0.5 - 0.2| = 0.6$.

Reciprocity Imbalance of a Referral Scenario: The reciprocity imbalance of a *referral scenario* is the average reciprocity imbalance present in its *referral links*.

Reciprocity-Aware Algorithm: We are now ready to define our reciprocity-aware algorithms. For any action selection algorithm $\mathcal{A}$, the corresponding reciprocity-aware (denoted as $\mathcal{A}_{RA}$) variant will only differ in the following way: The reciprocity-aware score of an expert colleague v_i of v for a given topic T, denoted as $RAscore_{\mathcal{A}}^{v,T}(v_i)$, is a function of its actual algorithmic score and referral share.

$$RAscore_{\mathcal{A}}^{v,T}(v_i) = score_{\mathcal{A}}^{v,T}(v_i) + refScore_{\mathcal{A}}^{v}(v_i),$$

where $refScore_{\mathcal{A}}^{v}(v_i) = refShare(v_i, \langle v, v_i \rangle)\ \zeta(interaction(\langle v, v_i \rangle))$, $\zeta(n) = \frac{n}{n+C}$, a factor ramping up to 1 in the steady state and C is a configurable parameter. In all our experiments, we set the value of C to 10^1. Our proposed technique to incorporate reciprocity into existing algorithms melding dual objectives is fairly general; the overall expression of $RAscore_{\mathcal{A}}^{v,T}(v_i)$ depends on the algorithmic score, $score_{\mathcal{A}}^{v,T}(v_i)$. For DIEL, $RAscore_{\text{DIEL}}^{v,T}(v_i) = m(v_i) + \frac{s(v_i)}{\sqrt{n_i}} + refScore_{\text{DIEL}}^{v}(v_i)$, while for TS, $RAscore_{\text{TS}}^{v,T}(v_i) = \theta_i + refScore_{\text{TS}}^{v}(v_i)$, where $m(v_i)$, $\frac{s(v_i)}{\sqrt{n_i}}$ and θ_i all are computed with respect to topic T. Since both the algorithmic score for DIEL and TS and $refScore$ have identical range $[0, 1]$, $RAscore_{\mathcal{A}}^{v,T}(v_i)$ has range $[0, 2]$.

For any algorithm $\mathcal{A}$, if two colleagues v_i and v_j have identical scores $score_{\mathcal{A}}^{v,T}(v_i)$ and $score_{\mathcal{A}}^{v,T}(v_j)$ and *interactions*, the reciprocity-aware variant will select the colleague with greater *referral share* thus favoring colleagues who return the favor more often. As the value of $interaction(v, v_i)$ increases, v becomes more sure of its estimate of the referral share thus putting more weight to referral share in its combined reciprocity-aware score computation. Note that, for a given expert, both $RAscore_{\mathcal{A}}^{v,T}(v_i)$ and $score_{\mathcal{A}}^{v,T}(v_i)$ are computed for a specific topic, however, *refShare* and *interaction* are computed across all topics. While the underlying approach to combine reciprocity with performance is simple, in a distributed multi-agent setting, several such threads of continual estimation and updates of referral shares and expertise of their colleagues are happening in parallel, thus creating a complicated mesh of interaction guided by self-interest, i.e., maximizing incoming referrals.

4   Experimental Setup

Performance Measure: We considered two different performance measures. Following previous literature [12,15], our first performance measure is the overall task accuracy of our multi-expert system. If a network receives n tasks of which m tasks are solved (either by the *initial expert* or a *referred expert*), the overall task accuracy is $\frac{m}{n}$. Q, the per-instance query budget, is set to 2, 3 and 4. Each algorithm is run on a data set of 200 *referral scenarios* and the average over such 200 scenarios is reported in our results section. Similarly, we report the average reciprocity imbalance over 200 *referral scenarios*. We summarize each algorithm's performance with a pair $\langle a, b \rangle$ where 'a' denotes the overall task accuracy at the horizon (5000 samples per *subnetwork*) and 'b' denotes the reciprocity imbalance.

---

[1] Additionally, we present experimental results in Table 3 indicating that the performance is not sensitive to the choice of C over a reasonable set of values.

Algorithm Class, Upper Bound and Baseline: We define an algorithm class, $\mathcal{A} \in \{\text{DIEL}^Q, \text{TS}^Q\}$, with per-instance query budget $Q \in \{2, 3, 4\}$. For a proposed reciprocity-aware algorithm, the upper bound is its underlying reciprocity-agnostic action selection algorithm class, $\mathcal{A}$. We chose this upper bound to answer the following research questions: (a) how much reciprocity imbalance is present in existing algorithms? (b) and to what extent of improvement our modification brings in (in terms of reciprocity imbalance) at what cost of performance (in terms of overall task accuracy)?

For an algorithm class $\mathcal{A}$, we propose the following switching variant, $\mathcal{A}_{switching}$, as baseline. Similar to $\mathcal{A}$, $\mathcal{A}_{switching}$ uses $score_{\mathcal{A}}^{v,T}(v_i)$ (as opposed to $RAscore_{\mathcal{A}}^{v,T}(v_i)$ used by $\mathcal{A}_{RA}$). However, for any referral link, after the *interaction* crosses a certain threshold (expressed through a parameter *interaction*$_{thresh}$), if the *referral share* of any of the participating two experts in the link falls below a threshold (expressed through a parameter *refShare*$_{thresh}$), the expert with smaller *referral share* disconnects and forms a new connection with another expert in the network. Essentially, this means after certain number of interactions between an expert pair, if an expert is unhappy with the reciprocity imbalance, she decides to form a new connection with another expert. Since every time a referral link is deleted a new referral link is formed, at any given point, the total number of referral links in network remains unchanged. For our experiments, *refShare*$_{thresh}$ is set to 0.3 and *interaction*$_{thresh}$ is set to 50.

For any algorithm class $\mathcal{A}$, we compare the performance of three algorithms: our proposed reciprocity-aware variant $\mathcal{A}_{RA}$, a baseline $\mathcal{A}_{switching}$, and an unconstrained upper bound. For instance, for DIEL^2 class, we compare DIEL^2 (the upper bound), DIEL^2_{RA} (proposed reciprocity-aware algorithm) and the switching variant $\text{DIEL}^2_{switching}$.

Data Set: We used the same data set used in [12]. The data set comprises of 200 *referral scenarios*. Each *referral scenario* consists of 100 experts connected through a referral network with a connection density of 16 ± 4.96 and 10 topics (for further details, see, e.g., [13, 15]).

5 Results

Substantial Improvement in Reciprocity Imbalance at Small Performance Cost: As the first step to establish the significance of this work, we need to analyze to what extent reciprocity is lacking in existing algorithms. For each algorithm class, Table 1 summarizes the reciprocity imbalance present in the upper bound, proposed corresponding reciprocity-aware versions and baseline switching variants. We first note that DIEL, the state-of-the-art referral learning algorithm and the upper bound for DIEL algorithm class, exhibits a substantially high reciprocity imbalance. In fact, both algorithms without a mechanism to account for reciprocity suffer from high reciprocity imbalance and this phenomenon is independent of the per-instance query budget Q.

For both DIEL and TS, the improvement in reciprocity imbalance is highly noticeable in its corresponding reciprocity-aware version; each reciprocity-aware

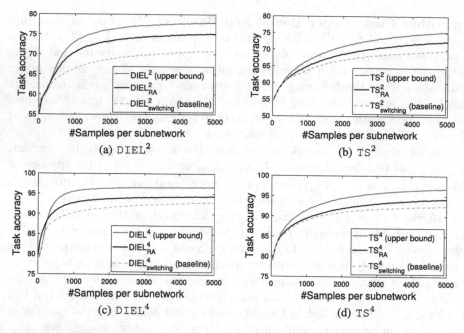

Fig. 2. Performance comparison between reciprocity-aware referral-learning algorithms, corresponding unconstrained counterpart (upper bound) and switching variant (baseline). Qualitatively similar results for per-instance query budget $Q = 3$ are omitted due to space constraint.

version brought about a 2-fold or better improvement in reducing the reciprocity imbalance (a 5x improvement in $DIEL^4$). While the switching variants are in general useful in reducing the reciprocity imbalance, our results indicate that our proposed reciprocity-aware solutions substantially outperform the switching variants. With an increase in query-budget, the imbalance in $\mathcal{A}$ or $\mathcal{A}_{switching}$ show no visible improvement, while $\mathcal{A}_{RA}$'s performance slightly improves. Since referrals are indivisible, with more budget, allocation gets smoother, and this accounts for $\mathcal{A}_{RA}$'s slight performance boost. For $\mathcal{A}_{switching}$, each switch requires estimating the new connection's (and implicitly its subnetwork's) expertise from scratch, which affects the reciprocity.

Understandably, the unconstrained upper bound achieved better task accuracy than our proposed solution as indicated in Fig. 2 and Table 1. However, the performance gap is small and as we have already seen in Table 1, the resulting reduction in reciprocity imbalance is substantial. When compared with the switching baseline, mimicking a realistic algorithmic setting in which slighted peers disconnect from non-reciprocating colleagues and forge new links in the network, we found that our reciprocity-aware versions always performed better than the switching baseline on both performance measures. In terms of task accuracy, a paired t-test reveals that for all $\mathcal{A}$, beyond 1000 samples or more per subnetwork, $\mathcal{A}_{RA}$ outperforms its switching counterpart, $\mathcal{A}_{switching}$, with

Table 1. Performance comparison of referral-learning algorithms. For any given algorithm class, the best task accuracy and reciprocity imbalance are highlighted in bold.

Algorithm class	$\mathcal{A}$	$\mathcal{A}_{RA}$	$\mathcal{A}_{switching}$
DIEL^2	$\langle\mathbf{77.92}, 0.51\rangle$	$\langle 75.13, \mathbf{0.19}\rangle$	$\langle 70.84, 0.33\rangle$
DIEL^3	$\langle\mathbf{92.45}, 0.55\rangle$	$\langle 89.71, \mathbf{0.15}\rangle$	$\langle 86.21, 0.34\rangle$
DIEL^4	$\langle\mathbf{96.67}, 0.55\rangle$	$\langle 94.44, \mathbf{0.11}\rangle$	$\langle 92.95, 0.33\rangle$
TS^2	$\langle\mathbf{75.24}, 0.36\rangle$	$\langle 72.44, \mathbf{0.16}\rangle$	$\langle 69.58, 0.28\rangle$
TS^3	$\langle\mathbf{92.00}, 0.36\rangle$	$\langle 88.30, \mathbf{0.13}\rangle$	$\langle 85.39, 0.29\rangle$
TS^4	$\langle\mathbf{96.64}, 0.36\rangle$	$\langle 94.17, \mathbf{0.09}\rangle$	$\langle 92.47, 0.29\rangle$

Table 2. Performance analysis of different parameter configurations of DIEL$^2_{switching}$. Each row represents a parameter configuration with the left-most two columns indicating the parameter values. P_1 denotes $refShare_{thresh}$ and P_2 denotes $interaction_{thresh}$. The performance of DIEL$^2_{RA}$ and DIEL^2 is presented for reference. The best task accuracy and reciprocity imbalance are highlighted in bold.

P_1	P_2	DIEL$^2_{switching}$	DIEL$^2_{RA}$	DIEL^2
0.35	20	$\langle 68.31, 0.33\rangle$	$\langle 75.13, \mathbf{0.19}\rangle$	$\langle\mathbf{77.92}, 0.51\rangle$
0.35	50	$\langle 68.89, 0.28\rangle$		
0.35	100	$\langle 69.53, 0.33\rangle$		
0.30	20	$\langle 70.83, 0.37\rangle$		
0.30	50	$\langle 70.84, 0.33\rangle$		
0.30	100	$\langle 71.10, 0.36\rangle$		
0.25	20	$\langle 72.15, 0.42\rangle$		
0.25	50	$\langle 72.23, 0.38\rangle$		
0.25	100	$\langle 72.13, 0.39\rangle$		

p-value less than 0.0001. For every referral-learning algorithm class, our proposed solution achieved both better task accuracy and improved reciprocity than the corresponding switching baseline.

Robustness to Parameter Configurations: $\mathcal{A}_{switching}$ has two parameters: $refShare_{thresh}$ (set to 0.3), a threshold for the referral share, and $interaction_{thresh}$ (set to 50), a threshold on the *interaction* of a given *referral link* before the disgruntled expert decides to sever connection. $\mathcal{A}_{RA}$ has only one parameter, C set to 10. Table 2 demonstrates that for DIEL^2, when evaluated across a wide range of configurations, the reciprocity-aware DIEL$^2_{RA}$ consistently outperforms the corresponding switching variant; Table 3 demonstrates that the performance of DIEL$^2_{RA}$ and TS$^2_{RA}$ is not sensitive to choice of C over a reasonable set of values.

Table 3. Robustness to parameter C

C	DIEL_{RA}^2	TS_{RA}^2
5	$\langle 75.15, 0.1893 \rangle$	$\langle 72.25, 0.1604 \rangle$
10	$\langle 75.13, 0.1891 \rangle$	$\langle 72.44, 0.1616 \rangle$
15	$\langle 74.92, 0.1875 \rangle$	$\langle 72.32, 0.1625 \rangle$
20	$\langle 74.98, 0.1879 \rangle$	$\langle 72.45, 0.1633 \rangle$

Table 4. Strategic referral behavior

Algorithm class	F_{greed}	$F_{altruism}$
DIEL^2	1.10	1.16
DIEL^3	1.60	1.12
DIEL^4	1.85	1.08
TS^2	1.08	1.07
TS^3	1.50	1.05
TS^4	1.64	1.04

Reciprocity-Awareness Fetches More Referrals in Expectation: At network level, substantial improvement in reciprocity imbalance can be obtained at a small cost of task accuracy. However, the more important questions are

- What is the individual incentive to meld dual objectives while making referral decisions?
- Can an expert benefit from not following the protocol either by showing extreme altruism or unfettered greed?

Recall that, the reciprocity-aware score melds dual objective by combining algorithmic score and reciprocity:
$RAscore_\mathcal{A}^{v,T}(v_i) = score_\mathcal{A}^{v,T}(v_i) + refScore_\mathcal{A}^v(v_i)$. We now consider two extreme conditions: an expert showing absolute altruism and only using $score_\mathcal{A}^{v,T}(v_i)$; an expert showing unfettered greed and only using $refScore_\mathcal{A}^v(v_i)$. Accordingly, we define the following strategy set of an expert $S = \{altruism, greed, reciprocity\text{-}awareness\}$. For a given scenario $scenario_i$, we first fix one expert, say v_l^i. Apart from v_l^i, all other experts always adopt the same $reciprocity\text{-}awareness$ strategy. Let $R^s(v_l^i)$ denote the number of referrals received by v_l^i in $scenario_i$ when she adopts strategy $s \in S$. We now calculate the following two factors:

$$F_{greed} = \frac{\sum_{i=1}^{200} R^{s=reciprocity\text{-}awareness}(v_l^i)}{\sum_{i=1}^{200} R^{s=greed}(v_l^i)}, \text{ and } F_{altruism} = \frac{\sum_{i=1}^{200} R^{s=reciprocity\text{-}awareness}(v_l^i)}{\sum_{i=1}^{200} R^{s=altruism}(v_l^i)}.$$

Table 4 shows that $\forall \mathcal{A}, F_{greed} > 1$ and $F_{altruism} > 1$. This implies that when all other experts follow the $reciprocity\text{-}awareness$ strategy, deviating to $altruism$

or *greed* fetches lesser number of referrals in expectation. It is straight-forward why *greed* would fetch less referrals as Q increases. Intuitively, if v_l^i adopts *altruism*, and the rest of the field requires reciprocity, connected colleagues will balance reciprocity with those colleagues at v_l^i's expense.

Teasing Apart Different Factors in Learning: In order to separate the effects of learning behavior from reciprocity considerations, we first consider a hypothetical situation where perfect knowledge about expertise is available. Acknowledging both that this situation is unlikely in a real setting and in our work we focus on a much harder problem of joint learning of reciprocity imbalance and expertise, this particular experiment allows us to take a cleaner look at the effect of reciprocity considerations. Specifically, we consider an algorithm, ORACLE^2, where each expert has an access to an oracle that accurately estimates the topical expertise of all expert/topic pairs. The ⟨Accuracy, Reciprocity Imbalance⟩ of ORACLE^2 and corresponding reciprocity aware version ORACLE$_{RA}^2$ are respectively: ⟨79.43, 0.54⟩ and ⟨76.27, 0.24⟩, i.e., we obtained greater than 200% improvement in reciprocity imbalance at 3.98% loss of task accuracy.

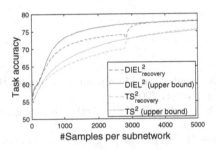

Fig. 3. Recovery performance

Recovery Performance: In terms of task accuracy, the performance gap between $\mathcal{A}$ and $\mathcal{A}_{RA}$ indicates reciprocity comes at a modest performance cost. However, it is important to analyze how much does *learning-to-refer* get affected because of this additional reciprocity constraint. In particular, we were interested in observing the performance of a learning algorithm that starts as constrained $\mathcal{A}_{RA}$, and somewhere in the process abruptly shifts to the unconstrained version $\mathcal{A}$, for instance in a crisis where task performance trumps all other considerations. We evaluate the following research question: can such learning algorithm identify the 'true' expert colleagues as well as a learning algorithm unconstrained from the start? The practical significance of this research question is there could be certain mission critical instances for which the network must find the best expert possible, regardless of reciprocity. If so, how fast can the algorithm match its performance with the unconstrained version? In Fig. 3, after a randomly chosen point in the operation of the algorithm, $\mathcal{A}_{RA}$ switches to $\mathcal{A}$ (we denote this algorithm as $\mathcal{A}_{recovery}$). Our results indicate that neither DIEL$_{recovery}^2$ nor

$TS^2_{recovery}$ had any difficulty in quickly re-establishing the performance of unconstrained $DIEL^2$ or TS^2 from the beginning. Note that, we opted for the same fixed point in time for all experts for clearer visualization; we obtained qualitatively similar performance even when the shifts are distributed across time-steps.

6   Conclusions and Future Work

In this paper, we argue that in the real-world, reciprocity in referral is a crucial practical factor. First we performed an extensive empirical evaluation focusing on two high-performance referral-learning algorithms and found that both of them suffer from substantial reciprocity imbalance. Second, we proposed algorithmic modifications to address reciprocity imbalance and we determined its efficacy empirically. Finally, we have shown our technique is extensible, and without any modification can be effectively applied to other algorithms or settings. Future lines of work include (1) expanding our investigation into other referral settings (e.g., [13]) and other active learning settings involving multiple teachers (e.g., [2,17,21,27]), (2) addressing malicious agents and (3) considering fine-grained referrals.

References

1. Agrawal, S., Goyal, N.: Analysis of Thompson sampling for the multi-armed bandit problem. In: COLT, pp. 39–41 (2012)
2. Ambati, V., Vogel, S., Carbonell, J.G.: Active learning and crowd-sourcing for machine translation (2010)
3. Audibert, J.Y., Munos, R., Szepesvári, C.: Exploration-exploitation tradeoff using variance estimates in multi-armed bandits. Theor. Comput. Sci. 410(19), 1876–1902 (2009)
4. Berry, D.A., Fristedt, B.: Bandit Problems: Sequential Allocation of Experiments. Monographs on Statistics and Applied Probability, vol. 12. Springer, Dordrecht (1985). https://doi.org/10.1007/978-94-015-3711-7
5. Chapelle, O., Li, L.: An empirical evaluation of Thompson sampling. In: Advances in Neural Information Processing Systems (NIPS), pp. 2249–2257 (2011)
6. De Marco, G., Immordino, G.: Reciprocity in the principal-multiple agent model. BE J. Theor. Econ. 14(1), 445–482 (2014)
7. Donmez, P., Carbonell, J.G., Schneider, J.: Efficiently learning the accuracy of labeling sources for selective sampling. Proc. KDD 2009, 259 (2009)
8. Graepel, T., Candela, J.Q., Borchert, T., Herbrich, R.: Web-scale Bayesian click-through rate prediction for sponsored search advertising in Microsoft's Bing search engine. In: Proceedings of the 27th International Conference on Machine Learning (ICML-10), pp. 13–20 (2010)
9. Hütter, C., Böhm, K.: Cooperation through reciprocity in multiagent systems: an evolutionary analysis. In: The 10th International Conference on Autonomous Agents and Multiagent Systems-Volume 1 (AAMAS), pp. 241–248. International Foundation for Autonomous Agents and Multiagent Systems (2011)
10. Kaelbling, L.P.: Learning in Embedded Systems. MIT Press, Cambridge (1993)

11. KhudaBukhsh, A.R., Carbonell, J.G.: Endorsement in referral networks. In: Slavkovik, M. (ed.) EUMAS 2018. LNCS (LNAI), vol. 11450, pp. 172–187. Springer, Cham (2019). https://doi.org/10.1007/978-3-030-14174-5_12

12. KhudaBukhsh, A.R., Carbonell, J.G.: Expertise drift in referral networks. In: Proceedings of the 17th International Conference on Autonomous Agents and Multi-Agent Systems (AAMAS), pp. 425–433. International Foundation for Autonomous Agents and Multiagent Systems (2018)

13. KhudaBukhsh, A.R., Carbonell, J.G., Jansen, P.J.: Proactive skill posting in referral networks. In: Kang, B.H., Bai, Q. (eds.) AI 2016. LNCS (LNAI), vol. 9992, pp. 585–596. Springer, Cham (2016). https://doi.org/10.1007/978-3-319-50127-7_52

14. KhudaBukhsh, A.R., Carbonell, J.G., Jansen, P.J.: Incentive compatible proactive skill posting in referral networks. In: Belardinelli, F., Argente, E. (eds.) EUMAS/AT -2017. LNCS (LNAI), vol. 10767, pp. 29–43. Springer, Cham (2018). https://doi.org/10.1007/978-3-030-01713-2_3

15. KhudaBukhsh, A.R., Carbonell, J.G., Jansen, P.J.: Robust learning in expert networks: a comparative analysis. J. Intell. Inf. Syst. 51(2), 207–234 (2018)

16. KhudaBukhsh, A.R., Jansen, P.J., Carbonell, J.G.: Distributed learning in expert referral networks. In: European Conference on Artificial Intelligence (ECAI) 2016, pp. 1620–1621 (2016)

17. Murugesan, K., Carbonell, J.: Active learning from peers. In: Advances in Neural Information Processing Systems (NIPS), pp. 7011–7020 (2017)

18. Sen, S., Sekaran, M.: Using reciprocity to adapt to others. In: Weiß, G., Sen, S. (eds.) IJCAI 1995. LNCS, vol. 1042, pp. 206–217. Springer, Heidelberg (1996). https://doi.org/10.1007/3-540-60923-7_29

19. Settles, B.: Active learning. Synth. Lect. Artif. Intell. Mach. Learn. 6(1), 1–114 (2012)

20. Thompson, W.R.: On the likelihood that one unknown probability exceeds another in view of the evidence of two samples. Biometrika 25(3/4), 285–294 (1933)

21. Urner, R., David, S.B., Shamir, O.: Learning from weak teachers. In: Artificial Intelligence and Statistics (AISTATS), pp. 1252–1260 (2012)

22. Vogiatzis, G., MacGillivray, I., Chli, M.: A probabilistic model for trust and reputation. In: Proceedings of the 9th International Conference on Autonomous Agents and Multiagent Systems: vol. 1, pp. 225–232. International Foundation for Autonomous Agents and Multiagent Systems (2010)

23. Wang, Y., Singh, M.P.: Formal trust model for multiagent systems. In: IJCAI, vol. 7, pp. 1551–1556 (2007)

24. Wiering, M., Schmidhuber, J.: Efficient model-based exploration. In: Proceedings of the Fifth International Conference on Simulation of Adaptive Behavior (SAB 1998), pp. 223–228 (1998)

25. Yu, H., Shen, Z., Leung, C., Miao, C., Lesser, V.R.: A survey of multi-agent trust management systems. IEEE Access 1, 35–50 (2013)

26. Zamora, J., Millán, J.R., Murciano, A.: Learning and stabilization of altruistic behaviors in multi-agent systems by reciprocity. Biol. Cybern. 78(3), 197–205 (1998)

27. Zhang, C., Chaudhuri, K.: Active learning from weak and strong labelers. In: Advances in Neural Information Processing Systems (NIPS), pp. 703–711 (2015)

A Novel Thought of Pruning Algorithms: Pruning Based on Less Training

Yue Li, Weibin Zhao, and Lin Shang$^{(\boxtimes)}$

Department of Computer Science and Technology,
Nanjing University, Nanjing 210023, China
mf1633021@smail.nju.edu.cn, njzhaowb@gmail.com, shanglin@nju.edu.cn

Abstract. Pre-training of models in pruning algorithms plays an important role in pruning decision-making. We find that excessive pre-training is not necessary for pruning algorithms. According to this idea, we propose a pruning thought—**Incremental pruning based on less training (IPLT)**. We can combine **IPLT** with almost all existing pruning algorithms. Compared with the original pruning algorithms based on a large number of pre-training, the modified algorithms (by **IPLT**) has competitive compression effect. On the premise of ensuring accuracy, the pruning algorithms modified by **IPLT** can achieve 8x-9x compression for VGG-16 on CIFAR-10 and only needs to pre-train few epochs. For VGG-16 on CIFAR-10, we can not only achieve 10x test acceleration, but also about 10x training acceleration. At present, the research mainly focuses on the compression and acceleration in the application stage of the models, while the compression and acceleration in the training stage are few. We newly proposed the thought of **IPLT** that can compress and accelerate in the training stage. It is novel to consider the amount of pre-training required by pruning algorithm. Our results have implications: Too much pre-training may be not necessary for pruning algorithms.

Keywords: Pruning algorithms · Amount of pre-training · Too many

1 Introduction

Deep neural networks have achieved excellent results in many competitions. The outstanding performance of the deep learning model has attracted the attention of academic and industrial circles. From AlexNet [1] to VGG-16 [2], ResNet [3] and InceptionNet [4], it's not hard to see that the superior performance of deep learning models often depends on deeper, wider structures. A deeper deep learning model leads to better recognition accuracy, but it will consume more storage and computation resource. To solve these problems, the researchers proposed a series of model compression and acceleration algorithms.

Most previous works on accelerating CNNs can be roughly divided into three categories, namely, matrix decomposition [5,6], quantization [7,8] and pruning [9,11,27,28,30].

Supported by organization x.

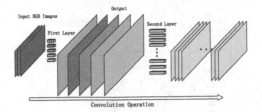

Fig. 1. This picture shows the convolution process of two convolution layers. The convolution network's input is an RGB image. In this picture, each cube in the graph corresponds to a filter. There are five filters in the first layer, so there are five output feature maps in the first layer. We use the same color to show the corresponding relationship between filters and output feature graphs. Notice the first filter in the first layer, which consists of three blocks. In convolution operation, each block corresponds to one input feature map.

As early as 1990, [23] began to pruning the neural network. Before 2016, the pruning algorithm mainly focused on pruning the parameters of the models. In [9], the author determines the importance of the parameter according to the absolute values of the parameters. The author assume the smaller parameters are less important and will be cut off first. The algorithm mentioned in [9] is also used by [10], which greatly compresses the deep learning model.

Then in 2016 and 2017 years, a large number of papers began to focus on the pruning of the deep learning models' filters. Such as [19–22], these papers began to try to slim down the structure of the model. By pruning the filters of the model, the model can be accelerated without relying on specific libraries. We can see the details of the convolution operation and the role of filters in the convolution operation through Fig. 1.

As shown in the left of the Fig. 2, almost all pruning algorithms have a general flow of pre-training models, pruning and retraining. In order to prune better and search for the effective inner structure of the model, the existing pruning algorithms need a long pre-training process for pre-training models, which usually requires hundreds of training epochs. As far as we known, almost all pruning algorithms pruning the models after hundreds of pre-training epochs. In response to this situation, we raised a question: the longer the training, the more effective the pruning decision will be made?

Our Point of View:
The Origin of IPLT: We think that the traditional pruning algorithm pays too much attention to the pre-training process. Previous researchers often believed that the longer the pre-training process was, the more effective the pruning strategy was. Of course, if we were allowed to prune the model only once, it would be wise to do more pre-training. But in the actual pruning process, we focus on the model obtained by pruning, and do not limit the number of pruning. And in many papers, researchers have found that the general iteratively pruning strategy is more effective, that is, the small-step pruning strategy can effectively

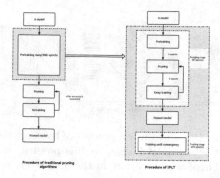

Fig. 2. In this picture, the general flow of the traditional pruning algorithm is on the left, and the general flow of **IPLT** is on the right. It is not difficult to find that the biggest feature of **IPLT** is: first pruning, then training. **IPLT** only trains few epochs to prune the model, and in the training phase of the model, a lot of computing resources will be reduced.

avoid pruning excessive damage to the effective structure of the model.
paginationbreak Therefore, there is a question worth thinking about: if we only prune a small part of the parameters or filters at a time, do we need a lot of pre-training or even training the model to convergence before the first pruning operation? We believe that a small amount of pre-training is enough to complete a small-step pruning on deep learning model. Based on this idea, we propose the thought of **Incremental Pruning Based on Less Training (IPLT)**. In contrast, we can call the thought behind all existing pruning algorithms **Pruning Based on Much Training (PMT)**.

Rough Flow of IPLT. We can use the thought of **IPLT** to improve almost all existing pruning algorithms. The comparison between **IPLT** and traditional pruning thought (**PMT**) is placed on Fig. 2. The biggest difference between **IPLT** and **PMT** is that the model is pruned first and then trained to convergence. As shown in the figure, on the right, **IPLT** is roughly divided into pruning and training stages.

Pruning Stage. We need to set the hyperparameter k. Every time we train k epoches continuously, we prune the network once. When we do the pruning operation, we can utilize any criterion in existing pruning algorithms. Assuming $k = 5$, our ultimate goal is to prune 90% of a layer of network. The pruning ratio list is $[10\%, 20\%, 30\%, \ldots, 90\%]$. We can prune 10% of all filters in network's convolution layer for the first time. At the second pruning, another 10% filters are pruned, the percentage of pruning reaches 20%. Every pruning operation, 10% extra filters are pruned until 90% of filters are pruned.

Training Stage. When pruning reaches the target pruning ratio, we stop pruning, but keep training the pruned network until convergence. By pruning the model step by step, our method achieves the ideal pruning ratio, and avoids the excessive pruning of the model at one time, which affects the performance.

To verify the feasibility of the thought **IPLT**, We utilize our **IPLT** idea to implement two existing pruning algorithms [27,35]. By the contrast experiments, we find the pruning performance of the two modified pruning algorithms is not weaker than original algorithms (**PMT**). For simplicity of expression, we will sometimes use **IPLT** to represent the pruning algorithms modified by the thought of **IPLT**. **PMT** will sometimes be used to represent original pruning algorithms.

The Uniqueness and Contribution of Our Work:

1. Proposing a novel thought **IPLT**. As far as we known, **IPLT** is the first to consider number of pre-training epochs before pruning decision. This thought is different from the thought behind any existing pruning algorithms (**PMT**) and has been proved effective;
2. As far as we know, the two pruning algorithms modified by **IPLT** in this paper are the first two pruning algorithms to optimize the computational complexity during model's pre-training stage. As shown in right of Fig. 2, assuming that we train 300 epochs for the model, the pruning algorithm based on IPLT will finish pruning the model in the first 20 to 40 epochs, and then train the smaller model. Obviously, in 41th to 300th epoch, we train the pruned, small models (the traditional algorithm trains the original model, big). In forward propagation and back propagation, smaller models consume less computing resources naturally. Therefore, **IPLT** make the training of models consuming much less computation resources as original.

2 Related Works

Our algorithm is about pruning. At present, pruning algorithms can be divided into two categories: weight pruning and filters pruning. We classify pruning related content as follows:

2.1 Weights Pruning

Many researchers try to construct sparse convolution kernels by pruning the weight of the network, so as to optimize the storage space occupied by the model. As early as around 1990, both [15] and [23] pruned the network parameters based on the second-order derivative, but this method has a high computational complexity. In [12,16], the author regularize neural network parameters by group Lasso penalty leading to sparsity on a group level. In [9], the author judges the importance of parameters according to their value, and then prune the unimportant parameters. The [10] combine the methods in [9] with quantization, Huffman encoding, and achieve maximum compression of CNNs. [14] regularize neural network parameters by group Lasso penalty leading to sparsity on a group level. In order to prevent overpruning, [11] proposed a parameter recovery mechanism. By pruning the parameters, a sparse model can be constructed. This kind of method can compress the model storage. Because the application of these pruned models always depend on specific libraries, computational optimization is not sufficient. So in the past two years, many researchers have turned their attention to pruning filters.

2.2 Filters Pruning

In the past two years, there has been a lot of work about filters pruning algorithms. Most papers use certain criteria to evaluate filters, and ultimately prune unimportant filters. In 2017, [17] try to use $l1 - norm$ to select unimportant filters. [18] uses the scaling factor γ in batch normalization as an important factor, that is, the smaller the γ is, the less important the corresponding channel is, so that filters can be pruned. [21] proposes a Taylor expansion based pruning criterion to approximate the change in the cost function induced by pruning. In addition to pruning filters through specific criteria, some researchers also proposed new ideas. [28] proposed utilizing a long short-term memory (LSTM) to learn the hierarchical characteristics of a network and generate a pruning decision for each layer. [29] proposed a model pruning technique that focuses on simplifying the computation graph of a deep CNN. In [27], the author proposed a Soft Filter Pruning (SFP) method to accelerate the inference procedure of deep CNNs.

In addition to the above papers, some researchers [12,13] have proposed algorithms that can be used to prune both parameters and filters.

3   Methodology

3.1   Preliminaries

In this section, we will formally introduce the symbol and annotations. We use $\left\{ \mathcal{W}_i \in \mathbb{R}^{O_i \times I_i \times K \times K}, 1 \leq i \leq L \right\}$ and $\left\{ b_i \in \mathbb{R}^{O_i}, 1 \leq i \leq L \right\}$ to denote ith convolutional layer's weights and bias, L is the number of layers. $\mathbf{I}_i$ and $\mathbf{O}_i$ denote the number of input and output feature maps in ith layer, so the input tensor of $i - th$ layer can be represented by $\mathbf{FI}_i$ and its size is $I_i \times H_i \times \mathcal{W}_i$, output tensor of $i - th$ layer can be represented by $\mathbf{FO}_i$ and its size is $O_i \times H_{i+1} \times \mathcal{W}_{i+1}$. Obviously, $\mathbf{FI}_{(i+1)} = \mathbf{FO}_i$, and in CNNs with RGB images $\mathbf{I}_1 = 3$. $\mathcal{F}_{i,j}$ represent $j - th$ filter in CNNs' $i - th$ layer, $\mathcal{F}_{i,j} \in \mathbb{R}^{I_i \times K \times K}$. The convolutional operation of $i - th$ layer can be written as:

$$FO_i = \mathcal{W}_i * FI_i + b_i, 1 \leq i \leq L \tag{1}$$

Equation 2 can be seen as a composite of O_i filters' convolutional operation:

$$FO_{i,j} = \mathcal{F}_{i,j} * FI_i, 1 \leq j \leq O_i \tag{2}$$

where $FO_{i,j}$ is the jth output feature map of $i - th$ layer. Obviously, $FO_i = \{FO_{i,j}, 1 \leq j \leq O_i\}$.

We use R_i to indicate the percentage of filters pruned from $i - th$ Layer to all filters in the same layer. In this case, the number of filters and output feature maps in $i - th$ layer will be reduced to $(1 - R_i)O_i$, so the parameters of $i - th$ layer will be reduced from $O_i \times I_i \times K \times K$ to $(1 - R_i)O_i \times I_i \times K \times K$. Not only the $i - th$ layer's filters pruned but also the $(i+1) - th$ layer will be affected. As shown in Fig. 3, the filters in the $i - th$ layer are pruned, so in the next layer, each filter should be slimmed down. $\mathcal{F}_{i+1,j} \in \mathbb{R}^{O_i \times K \times K}$ should be transformed into $\mathcal{F}'_{i+1,j} \in \mathbb{R}^{(1-R_i)O_i \times K \times K}$.

3.2 How to Select Filters

In the two papers which we choose to make comparison tests, both the authors choose l_p−norm of filters to measure the importance of each filter as Eq. 3. So we choose the same criterion.

$$\|\mathcal{F}_{i,j}\|_p = \sqrt[p]{\sum_{n=1}^{I_i} \sum_{k_1=1}^{K} \sum_{k_2=1}^{K} |\mathcal{F}_{i,j}(n, k_1, k_2)|^p} \tag{3}$$

In their papers, filters with smaller l_2−norm result in relatively small activation values, so they think these filters are even less important to the model. The filters with smaller l_p−norm will be pruned firstly. When we compare the l_p−norm of filters, we can choose either intra-layer comparison (intra-layer mode) or full-network comparison (global mode). The only difference between intra-layer comparison and full-network comparison is whether all filters in the whole network are sorted together (full-network comparison) or within each layer (intra-layer comparison) when filters are sorted in norm value. We show the general procedure of **IPLT** in Algorithm 1.

Algorithm 1. Pruning algorithms modified by **IPLT**

Require: training data:X, training epoches: $epoch_{max}$, incremental pruning sequence:
$\quad L = \{R_1, R_2, ..., R_n\}$, model parametes: $\mathcal{W} = \{\mathcal{W}_i, 1 \leq i \leq L\}$, A CNN model,
$\quad W_l, 1 \leq l \leq L$;
1:
Ensure: Parameters in L layers of the model:$\hat{W}_l, 1 \leq l \leq L$;
2:　Initial: $W_l, 1 \leq l \leq L$; hyper-paramter: k;ind=0;
3:　for $epoch = 1, 2, \ldots, epoch_{max}$, do;
4:　　if epoch%k==0:
5:　　　for $i = 0, 1 \leq i \leq L$, do:
6:　　　　Calculate the importance for each filter $\mathcal{F}_{i,j}, 1 \leq j \leq I_i$ according to certain criterion;
7:
8:　　　　Prune $R_{ind} * \sum_{i=1}^{L} O_i$ filters with minmum importance value in all layers(global) or per layer(intra-layer);
9:　　　　ind = ind+1
10:　　Update model parameters W based on X;
11: Return a pruned and trained model which can be applied directly;

Experiments show that globally sorting filter norms and pruning filters can better guarantee network performance.

3.3   The Thought of Incremental Pruning

Even based on much pre-training, pruning models to targeted ratio within one pruning operation will also have impacts on the accuracy of the model. So we introduce the thought of incremental. For example, according to the sequence $[10\%, 20\%, 30\%, 40\%, 50\%, 60\%, 70\%]$, we will first cut 10% of the filters, then cut off the extra 10% (achieve 20% pruning rate). By gradually pruning, we keep pruning a small number of filters which are not important, and finally achieve the desired pruning ratio.

3.4   Details of Pruning Filters

In Fig. 3, we show the operations performed when pruning a layer.

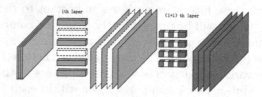

Fig. 3. This picture shows that when we prune filters of one convolution layer, the next layer needs to make some adjustments at the same time. In this picture, each colourful cuboid represent one filter. We pruned the second and third filters in the $i - th$ layer (white), so the second and third output feature maps of $i - th$ layer are also pruned. Obviously, the number of input feature maps of $(i + 1) - th$ layer is reduced. The four filters in $(i + 1) - th$ Layer needn't to consider the second and fourth pruned feature maps. The number of filters in $(i + 1) - th$ layer is still four, but the size of each filter should be modified to $\frac{2}{3}$ of the original (the white part in four blue filters should be pruned also).

In order to facilitate readers to better understand our network compression, we will propose two concepts of pruning rate: 1. Filters Pruning Ratio (FPR); 2. Parameters Pruning Ratio (PPR). FPR represents the percentage of filters that have been pruned to total filters. PPR is the proportion of the number of parameters that are pruned to the total number of parameters in the model. Obviously we can calculate FPR_i, PPR_i for each layer, or the FPR_{all}, $PPRall$ for the whole network. Obviously, whether FPR_{all} or PPR_{all}, the higher the numerical value, the more we prune the network, the more we compress and accelerate the model.

4 Experiments

4.1 Benchmark Datasets and Experimental Setting

Datasets Selection: We empirically apply our methods on two benchmark datasets:MNIST [24], CIFAR-10 [25]. The MNIST dataset consists of 60,000 28×28 black-and-white images. The CIFAR-10 dataset consists of 60,000 32×32 color images. There are 50,000 training images and 10,000 test images. The images in MNIST and CIFAR-10 datasets are both divided into 10 classes, with 6,000 images in each class.

Three Networks: We choose a normal CNN, VGGNet [2] and ResNet to verify the effectiveness of **IPLT**. All the experiments are implemented with PyTorch on one NVIDIA GPU. For the reason of convenience of implementation, we choose to realize the pruning stage in a soft mode—during both pruning stages of **IPLT** and traditional pruning algorithms, we add a mask which consists of 0 and 1 to realize the equivalent effect of pruning. But in **IPLT**, we prune the model after pruning stage in reality. After the pruning stage of **IPLT**, we create a new model with fewer filters is created. We copy the remaining parameters of the modified layers into the new model. Then in training stage of **IPLT**, we will train the actually pruned model.

Selection of Parameters: The hyper-parameters are chosen by several test. We find that the incremental pruning sequence with interval 10% can satisfy the simplicity of pruning without affecting the precision of pruning. In **IPLT**, the number of epochs per pruning operation should be determined according to the complexity of the data set. For example, in the MNIST dataset, k is set to 2, while in the cifar10 dataset, k is set to 5. We find that in **IPLT**, larger k may not necessarily have better pruning operation.

4.2 Contrast Experiments About [35]

In [35], the author choose l_2-norm of filters to measure the importance of each filter. When comparing the importance of filters, the author choose the global mode. The pruning algorithm in this paper choose the filters with smaller l_2-norm values in all layers and pruning them.

We use the thought of **IPLT** to modify the original pruning algorithm. We first set hyper-parameter k (On MNIST is 2 and on CIFAR10 is 5) and pruning ratio list is $[10\%, 20\%, 30\%, \dots]$. Therefore, in modified pruning algorithms (with **IPLT**), we pruning 10% more of filters after every 5(or 2) epochs' training. When we want to prune filters in modified pruning algorithm, we also choose filters by l_2-norm of filters with global mode. We can find the modified pruning algorithm is almost the same as original algorithm in [35] except for the timing to prune. After combined with **IPLT**, the modified pruning algorithm no longer prunes based on too much pre-training.

We make two groups of comparison experiments between original and modified algorithms. One is pruning a normal CNN network on MNIST datasets, as shown in Table 1. The other is pruning VGGNet on CIFAR10 datasets, as shown in Table 2.

The CNN model in Table 1 is a model which we construct randomly. During our experiments, we find that pruning different structures of model on the MNIST datasets always show similar results. We think this is because of the MNIST's complexity. The VGGNet in Table 2 own the same architecture as [35]. Based on Pytorch library, we use 'torch.save(model.state_dict())' to save the VGGNet model before and after pruning.

By comparing the experimental results in the two tables, we can clearly find that combining the pruning algorithm in [35] with **IPLT** will not affect the effect of pruning algorithms. This means that too much pre-training is not necessary for the algorithm in [35]. At least, the thought of **IPLT** is meaningful for the algorithm.

Table 1. Pruning a CNN on MNIST. "baseline" means the model with no pruning. "original_pruning" is the original pruning algorithm in [35]. "modified_pruning" is the original pruning algorithm modified by **IPLT**. "FPR_{all}" represent the percentage of all filters in the model that have been pruned. "PPR_{all}" represent the percentage of all parameters that have been pruned.

Mode	FPR_{all}	PPR_{all}	$Accuracy\,(\%)$
Baseline	0.00	0.00	99.35
original_pruning	60.00	83.05	99.32
original_pruning	65.00	83.05	99.36
original_pruning	70.00	90.65	99.17
modified_pruning	60.00	84.72	99.35
modified_pruning	65.00	87.89	99.31
modified_pruning	70.00	95.47	99.28

4.3   Contrast Experiments About [27]

To further prove the effectiveness of the thought **IPLT**. We did contrast experiments about [27]. In [27], the author set the target pruning ratio first. Then they choose filters with smaller l_2−norm to prune according to the ratio and in intra-layer mode. The "Soft Filters Pruning" in [27] means that the pruning algorithm will choose some filters to be set to 0 after each training epoch but these filters will be updated during the following training stage. The "soft pruning" will continue until the model's convergence.

We modified the "soft filters pruning algorithm" [27] with the thought of **IPLT**. The modified algorithm own two difference from original. First, original algorithm will keep pruning until the end of training. But in modified algorithm, we only prune in the first dozens of training epochs. Second, if the target pruning ratio is 30%, original algorithm will "softly" prune 30% of filters each time. In modified algorithm, we choose filters according to a ratio list like $[10\%, 20\%, 30\%, \dots]$.

Table 2. Pruning VGG-16 on CIFAR-10. "original baseline" is the complete model trained by [35]. "our_baseline" is the complete model trained by ourselves. "original_pruning" is the pruning result of original pruning algorithm in [35]. "modified_pruning" is the original pruning algorithm modified by **IPLT**. "FPR_{all}" represent the percentage of all filters in the model that have been pruned. "FLOPs" refers to the total number of floating-point calculations that the model needs to do when processing a picture. "Pruned FLOPs" refers to how much computation can be saved by the pruned model compared with the original model.

Model	FPR	Model size (MB)	FLOPs	Pruned FLOPs (%)	Accuracy (%)
original baseline	-	-	3.13×10^8	0.00	93.25
original_pruning	-	-	2.06×10^8	34.20	93.40
our_baseline	0.00	58.9	3.13×10^8	0.00	94.33
modified_pruning	60	9.7	1.52×10^8	51.36	94.35
modified_pruning	70	6.0	1.27×10^8	59.54	94.05

In this comparison experiments, we not only adopt the data in [27], but also program the codes to implement original and modified pruning algorithms and show the results in Table 3. From the results, we can easily find that **IPLT** also works for the "soft filters pruning algorithm" [27].

Let's explain column 4 and 5 of the Table 3: because the model's structure is the same, pruning ratio is the same, pruning patterns are all intra-layer mode, the data in the table is repeated.

4.4   Uniqueness of IPLT

As shown in Table 2, the speed of VGG-16 pruned by **IPLT** is about 2.5x faster than original model in theory. In thought of **IPLT**, we finish pruning in first dozens of training epochs. Then in remaining training epochs, the model we train is the pruned model. Training the pruned (smaller) models will consume less computation resource. Therefore, **IPLT** can also achieve about 2.5x acceleration in the training stage.

During the experiments of Table 2, we record the programs' running times. When we want to train the original VGG-16 with 300 epochs on CIFAR10, this procedure will consume 7254 s. But when we use modified pruning algorithm in Table 2, we can get a trained and pruned model within only 5319 s. The difference between two running times may not accurately reflect the acceleration effect of **IPLT** in the training stage. But this difference undoubtedly proves that **IPLT** can optimize the computational cost of training phase.

As far as we known, the pruning algorithms combined with the thought of **IPLT** are the first pruning algorithms which can accelerate the models' training stage.

Table 3. Pruning ResNet-110 on CIFAR-10. "paper's baseline" is the complete model trained by [27]. "our_baseline" is the complete model trained by ourselves. "original in paper" is the pruning result of original pruning algorithm in [27]. "our original" is the pruning result of our codes which implement the original pruning algorithm in [27]. "our modified" is the original pruning algorithm modified by **IPLT**. Other words have the same meanings as shown in Table 2

Model	FPR	Model size (MB)	FLOPs	Pruned FLOPs (%)	Accuracy (%)
Paper's baseline	0.00	-	-	-	94.00
Original in paper	10	-	2.16×10^8	14.60	94.02
Original in paper	20	-	1.82×10^8	28.20	94.34
Original in paper	30	-	1.50×10^8	40.80	93.68
our_baseline	0.00	-	3.9×10^8	0.00	95.17
Our original	10	-	2.16×10^8	14.60	95.07
Our original	20	-	1.82×10^8	28.20	94.89
Our original	30	-	1.50×10^8	40.80	94.93
Our modified	10	-	2.16×10^8	14.60	95.18
Our modified	20	-	1.82×10^8	28.20	95.09
Our modified	30	-	1.50×10^8	40.80	94.96

5   Conclusion

We first focused on the amount of pre-training required for pruning algorithms to make pruning decisions. We made a conjecture: in order make pruning decisions, too much pre-training is unnecessary. Based on this conjecture, we propose the thought of pruning based on less training **IPLT**.

Then we have verified this conjecture by experiments. We modify two existing pruning algorithms [27,35] by **IPLT**. From the experiments' results, we can prove that **IPLT** is at least meaningful to some pruning algorithms. Almost all pruning algorithms need a certain amount of pre-training, so thinking about the pre-training amount of pruning algorithm is meaningful to almost all pruning algorithms. We believe that the amount of pre-training required for pruning deserves further study—based on this kind of research, we can use less computational resources to obtain pruned, trained models.

As far as we know, the two pruning algorithms improved by **IPLT** are the first algorithms that can accelerate the training stage of the deep learning model.

Acknowledgments. This work is supported by the Natural Science Foundation of China (No. 61672276) and the Natural Science Foundation of Jiangsu Province of China (No. BK20161406).

References

1. Krizhevsky, A., Sutskever, I., Hinton, G.E.: ImageNet classification with deep convolutional neural networks. In: Advances in Neural Information Processing Systems, pp. 1097–1105 (2012)
2. Simonyan, K., Zisserman, A.: Very deep convolutional networks for large-scale image recognition. arXiv preprint arXiv:1409.1556 (2014)
3. He, K., Zhang, X., Ren, S., Sun, J.: Deep residual learning for image recognition. In: Proceedings of the IEEE Conference on Computer Vision and Pattern Recognition, pp. 770–778 (2016)
4. Szegedy, C., et al.: Going deeper with convolutions. In: Proceedings of the IEEE Conference on Computer Vision and Pattern Recognition, pp. 1–9 (2015)
5. Jaderberg, M., Vedaldi, A., Zisserman, A.: Speeding up convolutional neural networks with low rank expansions, arXiv preprint arXiv:1405.3866 (2014)
6. Zhang, X., Zou, J., He, K., Sun, J.: Accelerating very deep convolutional networks for classification and detection. IEEE Tran. Pattern Anal. Mach. Intell. **38**(10), 1943–1955 (2016)
7. Zhu, C., Han, S., Mao, H., Dally, W.J.: Trained ternary quantization, arXiv preprint arXiv:1612.01064 (2016)
8. Zhou, A., Yao, A., Guo, Y., Xu, L., Chen, Y.: Incremental network quantization: towards lossless CNNs with low-precision weights, arXiv preprint arXiv:1702.03044 (2017)
9. Han, S., Pool, J., Tran, J., Dally, W.: Learning both weights and connections for efficient neural network. In: Advances in Neural Information Processing Systems, pp. 1135–1143 (2015)
10. Han, S., Mao, H., Dally, W.J.: Deep compression: compressing deep neural networks with pruning, trained quantization and huffman coding, arXiv preprint arXiv:1510.00149 (2015)
11. Guo, Y., Yao, A., Chen, Y.: Dynamic network surgery for efficient DNNs. In: Advances In Neural Information Processing Systems, pp. 1379–1387 (2016)
12. Wen, W., Wu, C., Wang, Y., Chen, Y., Li, H.: Learning structured sparsity in deep neural networks. In: Advances in Neural Information Processing Systems, pp. 2074–2082 (2016)
13. Lebedev, V., Lempitsky, V.: Fast convnets using group-wise brain damage. In: Proceedings of the IEEE Conference on Computer Vision and Pattern Recognition, pp. 2554–2564 (2016)
14. Hu, H., Peng, R., Tai, Y.-W., Tang, C.-K.: Network trimming: a data-driven neuron pruning approach towards efficient deep architectures, arXiv preprint arXiv:1607.03250 (2016)
15. Hassibi, B., Stork, D.G.: Second order derivatives for network pruning: optimal brain surgeon. In: Advances in Neural Information Processing Systems, pp. 164–171 (1993)
16. Scardapane, S., Comminiello, D., Hussain, A., Uncini, A.: Group sparse regularization for deep neural networks. Neurocomputing **241**, 81–89 (2017)
17. Li, H., Kadav, A., Durdanovic, I., Samet, H., Graf, H.P.: Pruning filters for efficient convnets, arXiv preprint arXiv:1608.08710 (2016)
18. Liu, Z., Li, J., Shen, Z., Huang, G., Yan, S., Zhang, C.: Learning efficient convolutional networks through network slimming. In: 2017 IEEE International Conference on Computer Vision (ICCV), pp. 2755–2763. IEEE (2017)

19. He, Y., Zhang, X., Sun, J.: Channel pruning for accelerating very deep neural networks. In: International Conference on Computer Vision (ICCV), vol. 2 (2017)
20. Luo, J.-H., Wu, J., Lin, W.: ThiNet: a filter level pruning method for deep neural network compression, arXiv preprint arXiv:1707.06342 (2017)
21. Molchanov, P., Tyree, S., Karras, T., Aila, T., Kautz, J.: Pruning convolutional neural networks for resource efficient transfer learning, CoRR, arxiv:abs/1611.06440 (2016)
22. Anwar, S., Hwang, K., Sung, W.: Structured pruning of deep convolutional neural networks. ACM J. Emerg. Technol. Comput. Syst. (JETC) **13**(3), 32 (2017)
23. LeCun, Y., Denker, J.S., Solla, S.A.: Optimal brain damage. In: Advances in Neural Information Processing Systems, pp. 598–605 (1990)
24. LeCun, Y.: The mnist database of handwritten digits (1998). http://yann.lecun.com/exdb/mnist/
25. Krizhevsky, A., Hinton, G.: Learning multiple layers of features from tiny images, Technical report. Citeseer (2009)
26. Dong, X., Huang, J., Yang, Y., Yan, S.: More is less: a more complicated network with less inference complexity. In: The IEEE International Conference on Computer Vision (ICCV) (2017)
27. He, Y., Kang, G., Dong, X., Fu, Y., Yang, Y.: Soft filter pruning for accelerating deep convolutional neural networks. In: Proceedings of the Twenty-Seventh International Joint Conference on Artificial Intelligence, IJCAI 2018, 13–19 July 2018, Stockholm, Sweden, pp. 2234–2240 (2018)
28. Zhong, J., Ding, G., Guo, Y., Han, J., Wang, B.: Where to prune: using LSTM to guide end-to-end pruning. In: Proceedings of the Twenty-Seventh International Joint Conference on Artificial Intelligence, IJCAI 2018, 13–19 July 2018, Stockholm, Sweden, pp. 3205–3211 (2018)
29. Ye, J., Lu, X., Lin, Z., Wang, J.Z.: Rethinking the smaller-norm-less-informative assumption in channel pruning of convolution layers, arXiv preprint arXiv:1802.00124 (2018)
30. Zhu, M., Gupta, S.: To prune, or not to prune: exploring the efficacy of pruning for model compression, arXiv preprint arXiv:1710.01878 (2017)
31. Liu, Z., Sun, M., Zhou, T., Huang, G., Darrell, T.: Rethinking the value of network pruning, arXiv preprint arXiv:1810.05270 (2018)
32. Ioffe, S., Szegedy, C.: Batch normalization: accelerating deep network training by reducing internal covariate shift, arXiv preprint arXiv:1502.03167 (2015)
33. Bello, I., Zoph, B., Vasudevan, V., Le, Q.V.: Neural optimizer search with reinforcement learning (2016)
34. Baker, B., Gupta, O., Naik, N., Raskar, R.: Designing neural network architectures using reinforcement learning (2016)
35. Hao, L., Kadav, A., Durdanovic, I., Samet, H., Graf, H.P.: Pruning filters for efficient convnets. In: ICLR 2017

Comparison of Embedded and Wrapper Approaches for Feature Selection in Support Vector Machines

Shinichi Yamada$^{(\boxtimes)}$ and Kourosh Neshatian

Department of Computer Science and Software Engineering,
University of Canterbury, Christchurch, New Zealand
shinichi.yamada@pg.canterbury.ac.nz

Abstract. Feature selection methods are generally divided into three categories: filter, wrapper and embedded approaches. In terms of learning performance, the filter approach is typically inferior compared to the other two because it does not use the target learning algorithm. The embedded and wrapper approaches are both considered high-performing. In this paper we compare the embedded and the wrapper approaches in the context of Support Vector Machines (SVMs). In the wrapper category, we compare well-known algorithms such as Genetic Algorithm (GA), Forward and Backward selection, and a new binary Particle Swarm Optimization (PSO) algorithm. For an embedded approach we devise a new heuristic algorithm based on Multiple Kernel Learning.

Keywords: Binary Particle Swarm Optimization ·
Genetic Algorithm · Multiple Kernel Learning ·
Support Vector Machine

1 Introduction

Feature selection methods are commonly organized into three categories: *filter* methods, *wrapper* methods and *embedded* methods. Filter methods evaluate the relevance among input variables and output labels independent of the classification algorithms. In wrapper methods, a classification learning algorithm is "wrapped" in the search process. During the search, a candidate subset of features is evaluated by projecting the input data onto the selected features, training a classifier using these features, and then measuring the performance of the trained classifier on the validation set. In embedded methods, the search for an optimal subset of features is embedded in the classification learning algorithm. Embedded methods have the advantage that they interact with the classification algorithms, but they are less computationally intensive than wrapper methods (Saeys et al. [1]).

In this article we compare the accuracy of the wrapper approach and the embedded approach. In the embedded approach the relevance (importance) of

© Springer Nature Switzerland AG 2019
A. C. Nayak and A. Sharma (Eds.): PRICAI 2019, LNAI 11671, pp. 149–161, 2019.
https://doi.org/10.1007/978-3-030-29911-8_12

each feature is measured using some indirect quantities such as the size of coefficients of variables. Our question is how accurately these quantities represent the true importance of variables. We answer this question by comparing the embedded approach with the wrapper approach in which the importance of features are measured more directly.

2   Background and Review

In this section, we review common wrapper and embedded feature selection methods. We also review the versatile Particle Swarm Optimization (PSO) algorithm which is commonly used in the wrapper feature selection methods.

In order to avoid confusion, we use the following terminology. A feature subset is a subset of features out of the set of all features. For instance, $\{x_2, x_4\}$ is a feature subset of $\{x_1, \ldots, x_5\}$. In the experiments, we also examine a set of feature subsets and denote it as k subsets of feature. For instance, $\{\{x_2, x_4\}, \{x_1, x_3, x_5\}\}$ is 2 subsets of feature in $\{x_1, \ldots, x_5\}$.

2.1   Wrapper Approach

Feature Selection by Traditional Methods. Sequential forward selection (SFS) methods and sequential backward selection (SBS) methods are two commonly-used wrapper algorithms. SFS starts with an empty subset of features denoted by $\mathcal{F}$. After testing the addition of each feature, SFS adds the feature whose inclusion gives the largest improvement to $\mathcal{F}$. This process is repeated until the addition of a feature does not improve the fitness of $\mathcal{F}$. On the other hand, SBS starts with a set $\mathcal{F}$ of all features. After testing the elimination of each feature, SBS removes the feature whose elimination gives the largest improvement to $\mathcal{F}$. This process is repeated until the elimination of a feature does not improve the fitness of $\mathcal{F}$. Both methods suffer from the problem that once a feature is added (removed), it can not be removed (added), which is called a "nesting effect" (Pudil et al. [2]).

To overcome this problem, Pudil et al. proposed Sequential Forward Floating Selection (SFFS) and Sequential Backward Floating Selection (SBFS) which applies the SFS l times and then the SBS r times and determine the values of l and r automatically. In the case of SFFS, after the inclusion process of SFS, we select the least significant feature among the current set of features except for the last added feature. If the elimination of the (least significant) feature leads to the improvement over the fitness of the subset of features excluding the last feature, we eliminate the feature from the subset and continue the elimination process.

Feature Selection by Particle Swarm Optimization. Both binary PSO and continuous PSO are used for filter and wrapper feature selection methods (Xue et al. [3]). The filter methods evaluate the relevance among input variables and output labels using some correlation measures such as rough sets theory, mutual information, and entropy (Tran et al. [4]).

When continuous PSO is used for feature selection, a threshold ν is usually used to map the real values to $\{0, 1\}$ so that if the real values are larger than ν they are mapped to 1. Tran et al. [5] propose a entropy-based discretization scheme. The threshold ν for each feature is determined so that the divided sub-intervals return the highest information gain. In their model, the threshold ν is chosen from the set of "potential' thresholds which are determined by eliminating the lower values of information gain. Xue et al. [6] firstly introduced the multi-objective scheme (prediction accuracy + number of features) to feature selection in PSO, in which the gbest of each particle is set as one of the highest ranked non-dominated solutions.

2.2 Embedded Approach

Feature Selection by Support Vector Machines (SVMs). Feature (sub-set) selections by SVMs are embedded methods in which features are ranked according to their weights $\mathbf{w}$ in (1).

$$\min \left(\Omega(\mathbf{w}) + C \sum_{i=1}^{n} \ell\left(\mathbf{w}, \varPhi(\mathbf{x}_i), y_i\right) \right) , \tag{1}$$

In the case of linear models $(\varPhi(\mathbf{x}_i) = \mathbf{x}_i)$, $\mathbf{x}_i$ with small $\mathbf{w}_i$ does not have much influence for the determination of the optimal hyperplane. Hence the norm of weight can be used as the criteria for feature ranking (Guyon et al. [7]). If we use an ℓ_1-norm for the regularization function $(\Omega(\mathbf{w}) = \frac{1}{2}\|\mathbf{w}\|)$, the optimization problems (1) return the sparse solutions (Tibshirani [8]). It is known that the ℓ_2-norm shrinks the coefficients of correlated variables evenly. In the extreme case of d identical variables, we get identical coefficients of $\frac{1}{d}$. On the other hand the ℓ_1-norm "picks one and ignores the rest" (Friedman et al. [9]).

In the case of nonlinear models, the coefficients of the linear combination of kernels are used as the criteria for the feature ranking. A set of kernels is pre-pared so that each kernel corresponds to a single feature. Then the information about the relative importance of features is obtained by solving the MKL. As in the linear case, ℓ_1-norm MKL also returns sparse solutions with respect to the coefficients of the kernel (Kloft [10]).

2.3 PSO

PSO is a population-based algorithm where the individuals in the population (or swarm) are called "particles". For each particle i, at time t and along dimension j, $x_{i,j}^t$ represents the current *position*, $v_{i,j}^t$ represents the current velocity, and $p_{i,j}^t$ represents the best position seen so far (**pbest**). The algorithm also keeps track of the best position seen by the swarm thus far (**gbest**), which is, at time t and along dimension j, denoted by g_j^t.

Standard PSO. The original form of the PSO algorithm was first introduced by Kennedy and Eberhart [11], with the following update equations for the elements of the velocity and position vectors, respectively:

$$v_{i,j}^{t+1} = v_{i,j}^t + c_1\, r_{1,i,j}^t \left(p_{i,j}^t - x_{i,j}^t\right) + c_2\, r_{2,i,j}^t \left(g_j^t - x_{i,j}^t\right) \;;\qquad (2)$$

$$x_{i,j}^{t+1} = x_{i,j}^t + v_{i,j}^{t+1}\,,\qquad (3)$$

for $i \in \{1,\dots,n\}$ and $j \in \{1,\dots,d\}$, where $r_{1,i,j}^t$ and $r_{2,i,j}^t$ are random numbers distributed uniformly in $[0,1]$ for each i, j and t; and c_1 and c_2 are constant values.

Shi and Eberhart [12] introduced the inertia weight ω in the velocity update formula, which controls the effect of the velocity in the previous iteration, such that:

$$v_{i,j}^{t+1} = \omega\, v_{i,j}^t + c_1\, r_{1,i,j}^t \left(p_{i,j}^t - x_{i,j}^t\right) + c_2\, r_{2,i,j}^t \left(g_j^t - x_{i,j}^t\right)\,.\qquad (4)$$

This is the most popular form of PSO, which is often referred to as standard PSO.

2.4   Probability-Based Binary PSO

The search space in binary PSO is $\{0,1\}^d$. The goal is to find a bit string of length d that minimizes a given objective function. In this section, we review the probability-based binary PSO proposed by Zhen et al. [13]. In this model, the position vector (a particle) is a point in $[0,1]^d$ which represents the probabilities of corresponding bits being one. The position vector is initialized as follows:

$$\dot{\mathbf{x}}_i^0 = \left(\dot{x}_{i,1}^0,\dots,\dot{x}_{i,d}^0\right) = \left(\frac{1}{2},\dots,\frac{1}{2}\right).$$

All the update equations are identical to those in the original continuous PSO. The elements of the velocity and position vectors are updated according to (2) and (3) respectively, in which x is replaced with $\dot{x}$. The actual outcome of a particle is obtained stochastically as follows:

$$x_{i,j}^t = \begin{cases} 1, & \text{if } r < \dot{x}_{i,j}^t \\ 0, & \text{otherwise}, \end{cases}$$

where r is a uniformly generated random number in the interval $[0,1]$.

In order to avoid premature convergence, the authors also propose a mutation operator that with a probability P_m flips the bits in the outcome:

$$x_{i,j}^{t+1} = \begin{cases} \bar{x}_{i,j}^t, & \text{if } r < P_m \\ x_{i,j}^t, & \text{otherwise}. \end{cases}\qquad (5)$$

We denote this Binary PSO model as PBPSO in the experiments.

3   Proposed Methods

In this section we introduce a new binary PSO method as a wrapper method and introduce a heuristic method based on Multiple Kernel Learning (MKL) which will be used as an embedded method.

3.1   A New Variant of Binary PSO (B-SPSO)

We introduce B-SPSO, a new variant of the probability-based binary PSO which is based on the standard PSO. Probability-based Binary PSO (PBPSO) model in Sect. 2.4 shows that the binary PSO methods can be looked upon as the variants of the continuous PSO and theorems developed for the continuous PSO can be also applied to the binary counter parts. Based on this observation we add two modification to PBPSO:

1. We adopt the standard form of PSO model and use the velocity update formula (4) instead of (2). The inertia weight ω is important to derive the stability condition of PSO (Bonyadi and Zbigniew [14]).
2. In the probability-based Binary PSO (PBPSO) model the particles move in the probability space $[0, 1]^d$. The value of each bit represents the corresponding probability of being 1. If the value of a bit is close to 0 (1), the outcome is likely to take 0 (1). If the value is exactly 0 (1), the outcome is also exactly 0 (1), which leads to a deterministic behavior. Our experiments have shown that we need some additional perturbation factors to let the particles to explore the neighborhood of gbest. While PBPSO used the perturbation formula (5), we introduce a threshold constant ξ ($\xi > 0$) which prevents the value of bit from taking the exact 0 (1):

$$x_j = \begin{cases} \xi & \text{if } x_j < \xi \\ 1 - \xi & \text{if } x_j > 1 - \xi \end{cases} \tag{6}$$

3.2   Heuristic Method Based on MKL (H-MKL)

We introduce a new heuristic method called H-MKL which is based on Multiple Kernel Learning (MKL) method [15]. In MKL, we can use the kernel coefficients to evaluate the relative importance of features. For this purpose, we prepare a set of kernels each of which is constructed using a single feature. After running MKL, the coefficients of kernels tell the relative importance of features.

The heuristic method consists of two parts. In the first part, we choose top k important features out of all d features. We examine all possible $2^k - 1$ subsets (power sets) of k features. We select top l sets of feature subsets out of $2^k - 1$ subsets. In the second part, we select one feature f from the rest of $d - k$ features. We construct $2l$ sets of feature subsets, one is a copy of top l sets of feature subsets and one is a copy of top l sets of feature subsets with the feature f added to each subset. The procedure is described in Algorithm 1.

Algorithm 1. Heuristic method based on MKL

Require: l the number of best features returned; k the number of best features whose power set is examined
1. determine the optimal specification of hyper-parameters in MKL;
2. prepare a set of kernels each of which corresponds to a single feature;
3. run MKL to determine the relative importance of features;
4. select top k features and construct $2^k - 1$ kernels corresponding to the power set of k features;
5. run MKL and select top l subsets of feature;
for each feature f in the rest of $d - k$ features **do**
   1. construct $2l$ kernels which consists of a copy of l sets of feature subsets and a copy of l sets of feature subsets with the feature f added to each subset
   2. run MKL and select top l subsets of feature.
end for

---

4 Experiments

In this section, we conduct experiments for feature selection in a wider scope. Firstly we conduct experiments to compare the binary PSO with GA, which is also a suitable method for the task of feature selection. We use SVM as the classifier algorithm. Then we conduct experiments to compare a traditional feature selection method (SFS and SBS) in Sect. 2. Lastly we conduct experiments to compare a heuristic method based on MKL with the best feature selection method. The former method represents the embedded approach in which we use the coefficients of kernels to evaluate the relative importance of features. The latter method represents the wrapper approach in which we directly evaluate each subset using SVM as the classifier algorithm.

Table 1 lists the 10 benchmark datasets for binary classification from the UCI Machine Learning Repository [16]. In the experiments, a dataset is divided into three parts: training, validation, and test datasets. The validation datasets are used to compute the prediction accuracy during the training phase and for determining the hyper-parameters, while the test datasets are used for the final evaluation. Our strategy is to use larger sizes of validation datasets and test datasets in order to obtain reliable results for the comparison. Experiments are repeated 50 times for each dataset.

4.1 Experiments of Feature Selection (GA vs. Binary PSO)

In the experiment, we use Gaussian kernel:

$$K(\mathbf{x}_i, \mathbf{x}_j) = \exp\left(-\frac{\|\mathbf{x}_i - \mathbf{x}_j\|^2}{\sigma^2}\right) \tag{7}$$

We set the range and the step size of hyper-parameter σ^2 in (7) and C in (1) as follows:

$$\log \sigma^2 = \{-8, -6, \ldots, 10\}$$
$$\log C = \{-8, -6, \ldots, 10\}$$

Table 1. Datasets

Dataset	Instances	Features	(Training/validation/test)	Classes
Default of credit card clients	30000	24	(100/1000/3000)	
Crowd-sourced Mapping Data Set	10845	28	(100/1000/3000)	$= 2$ vs. $\neq 2$
Sensorless Drive Diagnosis	58509	49	(100/1000/3000)	$<= 5$ vs > 5
German	1000	24	(100/400/500)	
Letter	15000	16	(100/1000/3000)	$<= 13$ vs > 13
Optical Handwritten Digits	5620	62	(100/1000/3000)	Odd vs even
Pen-Based Handwritten Digits	10992	16	(100/1000/3000)	Odd vs even
Landsat Satellite	6435	36	(100/1000/3000)	$<= 3$ vs > 3
Segment	2310	19	(100/1000/1210)	$<= 3$ vs > 3
Splice	3175	60	(100/1000/2075)	

At first we run SVM with all features and determine the optimal specifications of σ^2 and C. We then compare the prediction accuracy of GA, PBPSO and B-SPSO.

GA. We use SpeedyGA which is a vectorized implementation of a genetic algorithm in the Matlab programming language with the following settings:

- Crossover is always performed.
- The mutation probability (per bit) is 0.003.
- Sigma Scaling: the fitness value $f(i,t)$ for an individual i is transformed to:

$$f_{new}(i,t) = \begin{cases} \frac{f(i,t) - \mu_t}{\sigma_t} & \text{if } \sigma_t \neq 0 \\ 1 & \text{if } \sigma_t = 0 \end{cases}$$

  where μ_t is a mean of $f(\cdot, t)$ and σ_t is a standard deviation of $f(\cdot, t)$. The purpose of sigma scaling is to prevent a premature convergence (Mitchell [17]).
- Stochastic Universal Sampling (SUS): The roulette wheel sampling often results in a large deviation between the actual allocation and the expected allocation. SUS is proposed to minimize the deviation. Suppose that the population size $= n$. In order to select N parents, SUS divides the $(0,1)$ interval into n parts in proportion to the fitness value of each individual, put N equally spaced pointers in $(0,1)$ and select an individual k times where k is the number of the pointers fall in the portion of the individual (Mitchell [17]).

PBPSO. We use the model described in Sect. 2.4 with the parameter specifications in Zhen et al. [13]. We set $(c_1, c_2) = (2, 2)$ in (2), the maximum of the velocity to 4 and P_m to 0.08.

B-SPSO. We use the model described in Sect. 3.1. We set $(\omega, c_1, c_2) = (0.729, 1.49, 1.49)$. We also set the parameter ξ so that ξ is 0.08 at the first iteration and lineally decreases to 0.01 at the last iteration.

Results. Using the optimal hyper-parameters, we examine three patterns of population size and the number of generations for each method as follows.

- population size = 6 and number of generations = 5
  (Since the GA program (SpeedyGA) assumes that the population size is even, we set it to 6.)
- population size = 10 and number of generations = 10
- population size = 20 and number of generations = 20

Then we record top 100 subsets of feature and report the following results using test data:

- Best: estimated mean for test accuracy of the best feature subset
- Mean$X$: estimated mean for test accuracy of the top X subsets of feature

Table 2 shows the results of the experiments. In each column we emphasize the best result in boldface.

In Table 2, PBPSO and B-SPSO work better than GA in most cases. B-SPSO shows the best results in 69 cells and PBPSO shows the best results in 21 cells among the 90 cells in Table 2.

4.2 Experiments of Feature Selection (SFS, SBS vs. Binary PSO)

We compare the performance of sequential selection methods (sequential forward selection, sequential backward selection) and B-SPSO.

SFS. We use the SFS model described in Sect. 2.1. This method start with a set F_1 which consists of single feature subsets.

$$F_1 = \{\{f_1\}, \ldots, \{f_d\}\}$$

We evaluate each $\{f_i\}$ by running SVM. Let $B_1 = \{f_{i^*}\}$ be the best subset. In the next round, we construct a set F_2 which consists of feature subsets $\{f_{i^*}, f_j\}$ for $j \neq i^*$.

$$F_2 = \{\{f_{i^*}, f_j\} | j \neq i^*\}$$

We evaluate each subset in F_2 by running SVM. Let $B_2 = \{f_{i^*}, f_{j^*}\}$ be the best subset. If the fitness value of B_2 is better than or equal to that of B_1, we continue the process until the fitness value of B_{k+1} is worse than that of B_k or $k \geq d$.

Table 2. Experiments of feature selection (GA vs. Binary PSO)

Dataset	Feature		6×5		10×10			20×20			
			Best	Mean25	Best	Mean50	Mean100	Best	Mean50	Mean100	Mean200
Credit	24	GA	81.56 ± 1.29	79.74 ± 1.02	81.68 ± 1.41	80.90 ± 1.42	80.20 ± 1.33	81.73 ± 1.32	81.44 ± 1.31	81.25 ± 1.36	80.83 ± 1.41
		PBPSO	81.23 ± 1.36	80.24 ± 1.16	81.31 ± 1.34	81.11 ± 1.32	80.49 ± 1.19	81.35 ± 1.31	81.33 ± 1.30	81.32 ± 1.30	81.22 ± 1.30
		B-SPSO	81.59 ± 1.25	80.65 ± 1.14	81.77 ± 1.23	81.53 ± 1.34	80.95 ± 1.26	81.81 ± 1.22	81.79 ± 1.22	81.75 ± 1.23	81.59 ± 1.27
Crowd	28	GA	90.22 ± 1.07	87.55 ± 1.22	90.73 ± 1.10	89.16 ± 1.13	88.26 ± 1.20	90.95 ± 1.12	89.95 ± 0.96	89.60 ± 0.98	89.09 ± 1.01
		PBPSO	90.49 ± 1.02	88.87 ± 1.08	91.17 ± 1.01	90.51 ± 0.79	89.57 ± 0.86	91.54 ± 0.97	91.32 ± 0.88	91.18 ± 0.88	90.93 ± 0.87
		B-SPSO	90.82 ± 1.08	89.17 ± 1.13	91.27 ± 1.09	90.51 ± 1.07	89.69 ± 1.07	91.74 ± 0.87	91.55 ± 0.85	91.40 ± 0.87	91.08 ± 0.89
Drive	49	GA	76.94 ± 2.56	71.72 ± 2.76	78.69 ± 3.29	75.16 ± 2.28	73.27 ± 2.35	79.59 ± 2.97	76.60 ± 2.47	75.87 ± 2.45	74.87 ± 2.48
		PBPSO	77.53 ± 3.35	73.89 ± 2.81	79.44 ± 3.32	77.43 ± 2.73	75.53 ± 2.54	81.37 ± 3.54	80.64 ± 3.19	80.16 ± 2.97	79.15 ± 2.53
		B-SPSO	78.36 ± 3.09	74.96 ± 2.65	80.38 ± 3.68	78.44 ± 2.95	76.39 ± 2.61	82.18 ± 4.22	81.98 ± 4.07	81.68 ± 4.00	80.76 ± 3.74
German	24	GA	72.18 ± 2.37	70.18 ± 1.77	72.58 ± 1.87	71.30 ± 1.68	70.62 ± 1.56	72.54 ± 1.86	71.95 ± 1.74	71.59 ± 1.75	71.11 ± 1.67
		PBPSO	71.69 ± 1.91	70.87 ± 1.63	72.13 ± 1.97	71.75 ± 1.80	71.17 ± 1.65	72.56 ± 1.94	72.27 ± 1.83	72.19 ± 1.80	72.05 ± 1.75
		B-SPSO	72.04 ± 2.44	70.93 ± 1.94	72.75 ± 2.06	72.21 ± 2.16	71.56 ± 2.03	73.16 ± 1.96	72.95 ± 1.71	72.82 ± 1.66	72.49 ± 1.61
Letter	16	GA	71.46 ± 2.19	66.37 ± 2.00	72.29 ± 2.13	69.14 ± 2.04	67.28 ± 2.13	73.50 ± 2.33	71.30 ± 1.75	70.49 ± 1.73	69.39 ± 1.61
		PBPSO	72.54 ± 2.45	68.78 ± 2.11	73.35 ± 2.24	71.22 ± 1.96	69.51 ± 1.82	74.05 ± 2.45	73.05 ± 2.28	72.52 ± 2.26	71.46 ± 2.23
		B-SPSO	72.80 ± 2.42	69.24 ± 1.98	74.26 ± 2.34	71.74 ± 2.01	70.35 ± 1.88	74.64 ± 2.18	73.41 ± 2.04	72.65 ± 2.06	70.93 ± 2.05
Opt Digit	62	GA	93.97 ± 1.37	89.50 ± 5.38	94.36 ± 1.26	92.10 ± 4.36	90.71 ± 5.12	94.56 ± 1.32	93.65 ± 1.32	93.03 ± 1.96	91.98 ± 3.92
		PBPSO	94.34 ± 1.51	91.89 ± 2.95	95.04 ± 1.22	93.96 ± 3.75	92.53 ± 4.83	95.58 ± 1.20	95.37 ± 1.17	95.25 ± 1.17	95.02 ± 1.19
		B-SPSO	94.68 ± 1.35	92.40 ± 2.44	95.16 ± 1.24	94.63 ± 1.28	93.29 ± 1.68	95.52 ± 0.95	95.46 ± 0.98	95.40 ± 1.00	95.23 ± 1.02
Pen Digit	16	GA	94.42 ± 1.24	89.96 ± 2.42	94.74 ± 1.10	92.82 ± 1.38	90.96 ± 1.67	95.20 ± 0.98	94.09 ± 1.08	93.57 ± 1.18	92.68 ± 1.32
		PBPSO	95.01 ± 1.04	92.11 ± 1.65	95.48 ± 0.96	94.56 ± 0.99	93.15 ± 1.25	95.49 ± 1.01	95.22 ± 0.96	95.01 ± 0.95	94.44 ± 1.00
		B-SPSO	94.87 ± 1.17	92.19 ± 1.63	95.36 ± 1.00	94.18 ± 1.03	93.11 ± 1.13	95.49 ± 0.98	95.15 ± 0.94	94.80 ± 0.99	93.48 ± 1.16
Satellite	36	GA	93.13 ± 0.64	92.36 ± 0.77	93.23 ± 0.61	92.84 ± 0.65	92.59 ± 0.72	93.27 ± 0.69	93.08 ± 0.60	92.98 ± 0.60	92.85 ± 0.62
		PBPSO	93.24 ± 0.60	92.85 ± 0.63	93.42 ± 0.64	93.23 ± 0.60	92.98 ± 0.62	93.48 ± 0.61	93.41 ± 0.60	93.38 ± 0.60	93.32 ± 0.59
		B-SPSO	93.27 ± 0.63	92.87 ± 0.63	93.38 ± 0.60	93.25 ± 0.58	93.03 ± 0.60	93.49 ± 0.61	93.45 ± 0.57	93.43 ± 0.57	93.36 ± 0.57
Segment	19	GA	92.56 ± 1.79	87.99 ± 1.99	92.72 ± 1.77	90.58 ± 1.89	88.91 ± 1.93	93.12 ± 1.76	92.11 ± 1.75	91.57 ± 1.83	90.64 ± 1.94
		PBPSO	92.75 ± 1.73	90.20 ± 1.80	93.39 ± 1.80	92.53 ± 1.71	90.86 ± 1.75	93.38 ± 1.65	93.27 ± 1.72	93.08 ± 1.72	92.59 ± 1.75
		B-SPSO	92.45 ± 2.06	90.05 ± 2.33	93.12 ± 1.81	92.14 ± 1.63	90.80 ± 1.65	93.45 ± 1.69	93.23 ± 1.71	92.94 ± 1.72	91.66 ± 1.92
Splice	60	GA	78.56 ± 2.10	70.62 ± 2.30	79.05 ± 1.95	75.31 ± 1.85	72.43 ± 1.94	80.27 ± 1.60	78.09 ± 1.19	77.00 ± 1.24	75.24 ± 1.29
		PBPSO	79.83 ± 2.01	75.29 ± 1.77	81.30 ± 1.54	79.53 ± 1.28	76.76 ± 1.23	82.12 ± 1.26	81.51 ± 1.20	81.21 ± 1.19	80.69 ± 1.19
		B-SPSO	79.66 ± 2.03	75.76 ± 1.81	81.01 ± 1.36	79.96 ± 1.30	77.40 ± 1.18	82.42 ± 1.52	82.14 ± 1.56	81.96 ± 1.53	81.52 ± 1.45

SBS. We use the SBS method in Sect. 2.1. This method start with a set B_0 which consists of all features and proceed as SFS by removing one feature at each round.

B-SPSO. The parameter settings are the same as in the first experiment.

- B-SPSO-5: population size = 5 and number of generations = 5
- B-SPSO-10: population size = 10 and number of generations = 10
- B-SPSO-20: population size = 20 and number of generations = 20
- B-SPSO-30: population size = 30 and number of generations = 30

Results. We report the following results using test data.

- Best: evaluation for the best feature subset estimation
- Mean50(25): mean of the test evaluations for the top 25 subsets of feature for B-SPSO-5 and the mean of the test evaluations for the top 50 subsets of feature for B-SPSO-10, B-SPSO-20 and B-SPSO-30
- Mean100: mean of the test evaluations for the top 100 subsets of feature

Table 3 shows the results of the experiments. The main comparison is Backward versus B-SPSO-20. The best result in each row is emphasized in boldface. If the results between Backward and B-SPSO-20 are significantly different (p-values < 0.05 for the two-tailed paired t-test), (*) is shown beside the number in the column with the better results.

In Table 3, the results of SBS are better than those of SFS in most cases. For the main comparison, the results of B-SPSO-20 are significantly better than SBS for 12 rows and significantly worse than SBS for 4 rows out of 30 rows.

Table 3. Experiments of feature selection (forward selection, backward elimination vs. B-SPSO)

Dataset	Feature		SFS	SBS	B-SPSO-5	B-SPSO-10	B-SPSO-20	B-SPSO-30
Credit	24	Max	**82.00** ± 1.52	81.33 ± 1.27	81.64 ± 1.39	81.71 ± 1.47	81.71* ± 1.32	81.84 ± 1.31
		Mean50(25)	**81.88** ± 1.46	81.32 ± 1.27	80.76 ± 1.30	81.47 ± 1.42	81.72* ± 1.36	81.82 ± 1.30
		Mean100	81.70 ± 1.47	81.29 ± 1.27		80.85 ± 1.21	81.70* ± 1.38	**81.81** ± 1.29
			(206.1)	(168.6)	(25)	(100)	(400)	(900)
Crowd	28	Max	90.07 ± 1.44	**91.56** ± 0.98	90.36 ± 1.32	90.97 ± 1.19	91.46 ± 1.07	91.33 ± 1.05
		Mean50(25)	89.73 ± 1.35	**91.49*** ± 1.02	88.69 ± 1.32	90.25 ± 1.23	91.23 ± 1.07	91.30 ± 0.99
		Mean100	89.18 ± 1.44	**91.42*** ± 1.04		89.37 ± 1.29	91.11 ± 1.09	91.23 ± 1.00
			(305.5)	(134.7)	(25)	(100)	(400)	(900)
Drive	49	Max	80.67 ± 8.89	77.83 ± 2.61	77.15 ± 3.03	78.61 ± 2.45	**81.20*** ± 3.44	80.74 ± 3.27
		Mean50(25)	80.65 ± 8.89	77.81 ± 2.62	74.29 ± 2.67	77.41 ± 2.36	**80.99*** ± 3.16	80.72 ± 3.26
		Mean100	80.62 ± 8.90	77.77 ± 2.63		75.48 ± 2.45	**80.77*** ± 2.98	80.70 ± 3.21
			(673.2)	(733.5)	(25)	(100)	(400)	(900)
German	24	Max	**72.79** ± 2.13	72.55 ± 1.98	72.22 ± 2.52	72.52 ± 2.25	72.47 ± 2.53	72.64 ± 2.09
		Mean50(25)	72.47 ± 1.97	72.39 ± 1.94	71.03 ± 1.86	72.14 ± 2.06	72.50 ± 2.20	**72.68** ± 1.94
		Mean100	72.09 ± 1.91	72.21 ± 1.88		71.52 ± 1.88	72.38 ± 2.09	**72.66** ± 1.95
			(213.8)	(134.8)	(25)	(100)	(400)	(900)
Letter	16	Max	71.41 ± 3.18	74.26 ± 2.45	72.65 ± 2.51	73.81 ± 2.60	74.33 ± 2.43	**74.54** ± 2.51
		Mean50(25)	67.77 ± 4.11	72.96 ± 2.19	68.74 ± 2.08	71.41 ± 2.04	73.31* ± 2.25	**73.70** ± 2.27
		Mean100	65.09 ± 3.06	72.57 ± 2.09		70.11 ± 1.91	72.60 ± 2.17	**73.24** ± 2.20
			(87.3)	(60.7)	(25)	(100)	(400)	(900)
Opt Digit	62	Max	93.89 ± 1.83	**95.62** ± 1.02	94.76 ± 1.13	94.94 ± 1.29	95.57 ± 1.12	95.45 ± 1.15
		Mean50(25)	93.89 ± 1.82	**95.62** ± 1.03	92.72 ± 1.36	94.55 ± 1.32	95.51 ± 1.09	95.45 ± 1.14
		Mean100	93.87 ± 1.84	**95.62*** ± 1.03		93.35 ± 1.39	95.45 ± 1.09	95.43 ± 1.14
			(1109.4)	(863.9)	(25)	(100)	(400)	(900)
Pen Digit	16	Max	94.92 ± 0.97	95.51 ± 0.93	94.79 ± 1.00	95.25 ± 0.96	95.50 ± 0.85	**95.52** ± 0.90
		Mean50(25)	93.46 ± 1.32	95.09 ± 0.91	91.97 ± 1.57	94.05 ± 1.08	95.12 ± 0.80	**95.23** ± 0.82
		Mean100	88.72 ± 2.92	94.98* ± 0.93		92.95 ± 1.22	94.77 ± 0.84	**95.04** ± 0.83
			(120.0)	(55.1)	(25)	(100)	(400)	(900)
Satellite	36	Max	92.55 ± 1.35	93.54 ± 0.61	93.27 ± 0.64	93.45 ± 0.63	93.53 ± 0.67	**93.62** ± 0.58
		Mean50(25)	92.37 ± 1.44	93.52 ± 0.61	92.93 ± 0.71	93.31 ± 0.64	93.46 ± 0.63	**93.57** ± 0.55
		Mean100	92.06 ± 1.86	93.51 ± 0.61		93.09 ± 0.67	93.44 ± 0.63	**93.55** ± 0.54
			(311.5)	(257.5)	(25)	(100)	(400)	(900)
Segment	19	Max	92.65 ± 2.46	93.04 ± 1.50	92.39 ± 1.69	93.02 ± 1.49	93.07 ± 1.54	**93.28** ± 1.52
		Mean50(25)	91.89 ± 2.44	92.69 ± 1.45	89.97 ± 1.70	91.87 ± 1.33	92.91* ± 1.49	**93.10** ± 1.50
		Mean100	88.98 ± 3.42	92.24 ± 1.35		90.55 ± 1.37	92.61* ± 1.45	**92.94** ± 1.44
			(132.1)	(95.3)	(25)	(100)	(400)	(900)
Splice	60	Max	79.84 ± 2.70	80.84 ± 1.41	80.00 ± 1.92	81.56 ± 1.41	82.57* ± 1.39	**83.20** ± 1.46
		Mean50(25)	79.17 ± 3.21	80.77 ± 1.38	75.54 ± 1.87	80.33 ± 1.39	82.36* ± 1.40	**83.08** ± 1.40
		Mean100	78.68 ± 3.94	80.72 ± 1.39		77.62 ± 1.43	82.17* ± 1.35	**82.98** ± 1.38
			(550.1)	(538.9)	(25)	(100)	(400)	(900)

4.3   Experiments of Embedded Method vs. Wrapper Method

We compare the performance of H-MKL which represents an embedded method and B-SPSO as a wrapper method. We use Gaussian kernel and the same specification for the hyper-parameters in the first experiment.

H-MKL. The heuristic method based on MKL:
We set $k = 8$ and $l = 200$ in Algorithm 1.

B-SPSO. The parameter specification is same as the first experiment.

- B-SPSO-5: population size = 5 and number of generations = 5
- B-SPSO-10: population size = 10 and number of generations = 10

- B-SPSO-20: population size = 20 and number of generations = 20
- B-SPSO-30: population size = 30 and number of generations = 30

Results. We report the following results using test data.

- Best: evaluation for the best feature subset estimation
- Mean50(25): mean of the test evaluations for the top 25 subsets of feature for B-SPSO-5 and the mean of the test evaluations for the top 50 subsets of feature for B-SPSO-10, B-SPSO-20 and B-SPSO-30
- Mean100: mean of the test evaluations for the top 100 subsets of feature
- Mean200: mean of the test evaluations for the top 200 subsets of feature

Table 4. Experiments of feature selection (H-MKL vs. B-SPSO)

Dataset	Feature		H-MKL	B-SPSO-5	B-SPSO-10	B-SPSO-20	B-SPSO-30
Credit	24	Best	79.30 ± 1.47	79.68$^{(*)}$ ± 1.68	79.83 ± 1.43	**79.93*** ± 1.55	80.04 ± 1.54
		Mean50(25)	79.06 ± 1.41	79.06 ± 1.44	79.63 ± 1.46	**79.91*** ± 1.55	80.02 ± 1.54
		Mean100	79.05 ± 1.41		79.24 ± 1.35	**79.88*** ± 1.55	80.01 ± 1.53
		Mean200	79.06 ± 1.44			**79.71*** ± 1.55	79.97 ± 1.53
Crowd	28	Best	91.13 ± 2.26	90.83 ± 1.33	91.33 ± 1.01	**91.76*** ± 0.80	91.72 ± 0.97
		Mean50(25)	89.57 ± 1.79	89.42 ± 1.31	90.78 ± 1.08	**91.65*** ± 0.85	91.70 ± 0.94
		Mean100	89.47 ± 1.75		89.98 ± 1.08	**91.53*** ± 0.86	91.64 ± 0.93
		Mean200	89.45 ± 1.66			**91.24*** ± 0.88	91.53 ± 0.94
Drive	49	Best	75.78 ± 2.31	78.33$^{(*)}$ ± 3.02	79.88 ± 2.39	**81.70*** ± 4.18	82.33 ± 3.87
		Mean50(25)	72.96 ± 4.74	75.13$^{(*)}$ ± 2.05	78.34 ± 2.29	**81.46*** ± 3.95	82.32 ± 3.85
		Mean100	73.18 ± 4.39		76.49 ± 1.98	**81.09*** ± 3.75	82.25 ± 3.83
		Mean200	73.24 ± 4.24			**80.19*** ± 3.27	82.03 ± 3.74
German	24	Best	71.58 ± 2.28	71.83 ± 2.25	72.60 ± 2.21	**72.52*** ± 2.13	72.60 ± 2.10
		Mean50(25)	71.31$^{(*)}$ ± 1.74	70.84 ± 1.67	72.01 ± 1.85	**72.36*** ± 1.99	72.53 ± 2.01
		Mean100	71.26 ± 1.71		71.41 ± 1.63	**72.24*** ± 1.93	72.48 ± 2.01
		Mean200	71.23 ± 1.69			**71.94*** ± 1.83	72.39 ± 1.95
Letter	16	Best	71.02 ± 4.21	72.15$^{(*)}$ ± 2.49	73.58 ± 2.50	**73.95*** ± 2.49	74.17 ± 2.51
		Mean50(25)	67.96 ± 2.52	68.58 ± 2.00	70.97 ± 2.31	**72.91*** ± 2.20	73.31 ± 2.21
		Mean100	67.85 ± 2.44		69.61 ± 2.04	**72.14*** ± 2.07	72.84 ± 2.14
		Mean200	67.79 ± 2.43			**70.44*** ± 1.84	71.93 ± 2.03
Opt Digit	62	Best	92.83 ± 3.99	94.58$^{(*)}$ ± 1.09	95.31 ± 0.96	**95.74*** ± 0.90	95.93 ± 0.87
		Mean50(25)	91.39 ± 3.53	92.81$^{(*)}$ ± 1.24	94.76 ± 1.04	**95.68*** ± 0.91	95.87 ± 0.87
		Mean100	91.51 ± 3.33		93.64 ± 1.09	**95.59*** ± 0.92	95.85 ± 0.87
		Mean200	91.58 ± 3.27			**95.35*** ± 0.95	95.79 ± 0.87
Pen Digit	16	Best	94.91 ± 2.03	95.18 ± 0.96	95.50 ± 0.99	**95.69*** ± 1.00	95.73 ± 0.96
		Mean50(25)	92.01 ± 2.15	92.26 ± 1.41	94.23 ± 1.05	**95.34*** ± 0.95	95.44 ± 0.90
		Mean100	91.93 ± 1.94		93.07 ± 1.24	**95.01*** ± 0.94	95.23 ± 0.92
		Mean200	91.89 ± 1.78			**93.63*** ± 1.07	94.75 ± 0.99
Satellite	36	Best	92.26 ± 2.35	93.36$^{(*)}$ ± 0.60	93.52 ± 0.63	**93.51*** ± 0.59	93.53 ± 0.68
		Mean50(25)	91.86 ± 1.95	92.96$^{(*)}$ ± 0.74	93.35 ± 0.62	**93.51*** ± 0.57	93.50 ± 0.62
		Mean100	91.97 ± 1.77		93.10 ± 0.67	**93.49*** ± 0.57	93.49 ± 0.61
		Mean200	92.04 ± 1.70			**93.43*** ± 0.57	93.47 ± 0.60
Segment	19	Best	91.21 ± 2.60	92.34$^{(*)}$ ± 1.56	92.79 ± 1.51	**92.80*** ± 1.58	92.80 ± 1.55
		Mean50(25)	90.12 ± 2.70	90.01 ± 1.90	91.92 ± 1.61	**92.69*** ± 1.59	92.70 ± 1.57
		Mean100	90.16 ± 2.70		90.61 ± 1.65	**92.45*** ± 1.57	92.58 ± 1.56
		Mean200	90.09 ± 2.73			**91.30*** ± 1.67	92.25 ± 1.57
Splice	60	Best	76.01 ± 3.88	79.51$^{(*)}$ ± 2.27	81.25 ± 1.42	**82.30*** ± 1.57	82.84 ± 1.22
		Mean50(25)	75.15 ± 2.55	75.45 ± 2.15	80.14 ± 1.45	**82.12*** ± 1.40	82.77 ± 1.16
		Mean100	75.06 ± 2.43		77.62 ± 1.44	**81.89*** ± 1.38	82.68 ± 1.18
		Mean200	75.08 ± 2.44			**81.38*** ± 1.37	82.52 ± 1.18

Table 4 shows the results of the experiments. The main comparison is H-MKL versus B-SPSO-20. The best result between the two is emphasized in boldface. If the results between H-MKL and B-SPSO-20 are significantly different (p-values < 0.05 for the two-tailed paired t-test), (*) is shown beside the number in the column with the better results. We also compare the performance of H-MKL with B-SPSO-5. If the results between H-MKL and B-SPSO-5 are significantly different (p-values < 0.05 for the two-tailed paired t-test), ((*)) is shown beside the number in the column with the better results.

In Table 4, the results of B-SPSO-20 are significantly better than H-MKL for all datasets. In each run, the total numbers of MKL optimizations (fitness evaluations) in H-MKL is $d - k + 2 = d - 6$. (We set $k = 8$ in this experiment.) The average number of MKL optimizations for the H-MKL method is 25.4 (the average is over various datasets). The total number of SVM optimisations (fitness evaluations) for each run of B-SPSO-20 is $20 \times 20 = 400$. This comparison may not seem fair because for the better performance of B-SPSO-20, a significantly larger number of fitness evaluations are performed. However, even if we compare the result of H-MKL to B-SPSO-5 (where the number of fitness evaluations per run is $5 \times 5 = 25$, the binary PSO method outperforms the heuristic MKL algorithm.

5   Conclusions

In this article, we examined the performance of two categories of feature selection methods in SVMs: the embedded approach and the wrapper approach using a new model of binary PSO. Among the wrapper methods, we compared the performance of binary PSO with GA, SFS, and SBS. The experimental results indicated that the binary PSO is generally more accurate and efficient for feature selection in SVMs.

We then conducted an experiment to compare the embedded approach (a heuristic method based on MKL) with the wrapper approach based on the proposed binary PSO method. The result shows that the wrapper approach outperforms the embedded approach in terms of both, accuracy and efficiency. The wrapper approach is also more flexible so that we can change the size of particles and the number of iterations for each problem. These experiments indicated that the direct measurements by wrapper methods are more accurate than indirect measurements by embedded methods.

References

1. Saeys, Y., Inza, I., Larrañaga, P.: A review of feature selection techniques in bioinformatics. Bioinformatics **23**(19), 2507–2517 (2007)
2. Pudil, P., Novovičová, J., Kittler, J.: Floating search methods in feature selection. Pattern Recogn. Lett. **15**(11), 1119–1125 (1994)
3. Xue, B., Zhang, M., Browne, W.N., Yao, X.: A survey on evolutionary computation approaches to feature selection. IEEE Trans. Evol. Comput. **20**(4), 606–626 (2016)

4. Tran, B., Xue, B., Zhang, M.: Overview of particle swarm optimisation for feature selection in classification. In: Dick, G., et al. (eds.) SEAL 2014. LNCS, vol. 8886, pp. 605–617. Springer, Cham (2014). https://doi.org/10.1007/978-3-319-13563-2_51
5. Tran, B., Xue, B., Zhang, M.: A new representation in PSO for discretization-based feature selection. IEEE Trans. Cybern. **48**(6), 1733–1746 (2018)
6. Xue, B., Zhang, M., Browne, W.N.: Particle swarm optimization for feature selection in classification: a multi-objective approach. IEEE Trans. Cybern. **43**(6), 1656–1671 (2013)
7. Guyon, I., Weston, J., Barnhill, S., Vapnik, V.: Gene selection for cancer classification using support vector machines. Mach. Learn. **46**(1), 389–422 (2002)
8. Tibshirani, R.: Regression shrinkage and selection via the lasso. J. R. Stat. Soc. (Series B) **58**, 267–288 (1996)
9. Friedman, J., Hastie, T., Tibshirani, R.: Regularization paths for generalized linear models via coordinate descent. J. Stat. Softw. **33**(1), 1–22 (2010)
10. Kloft, M.: lp-Norm Multiple Kernel Learning. Ph.D. thesis, Berlin Institute of Technology (2011)
11. Kennedy, J., Eberhart, R.C.: Particle swarm optimization. In: Proceedings of the 1995 IEEE International Conference on Neural Networks, Perth, Australia, vol. 4, pp. 1942–1948. IEEE Service Center, Piscataway (1995)
12. Shi, Y., Eberhart, R.C.: A modified particle swarm optimizer. In: Proceedings of IEEE International Conference on Evolutionary Computation, pp. 69–73. IEEE Computer Society, Washington, DC, May 1998
13. Zhen, L., Wang, L., Wang, X., Huang, Z.: A novel PSO-inspired probability-based binary optimization algorithm. In: 2008 International Symposium on Information Science and Engineering, vol. 2, pp. 248–251, December 2008
14. Bonyadi, M.R., Michalewicz, Z.: Stability analysis of the particle swarm optimization without stagnation assumption. IEEE Trans. Evol. Comput. **20**(5), 814–819 (2016)
15. Yamada, S., Neshatian, K.: Multiple kernel learning with one-level optimization of radius and margin. In: Advances in Artificial Intelligence - 30th Australasian Joint Conference, AI 2017, Melbourne, VIC, Australia, 19–20 August 2017, Proceedings, pp. 52–63 (2017)
16. Dua, D., Graff, C.: UCI machine learning repository (2017)
17. Mitchell, M.: An Introduction to Genetic Algorithms. MIT Press, Cambridge (1998)

Sparse Ordinal Regression
via Factorization Machines

Weijian Ni, Tong Liu[✉], and Qingtian Zeng

College of Computer Science and Engineering,
Shandong University of Science and Technology, Qingdao, China
niweijian@gmail.com, liu_tongtong@foxmail.com, qtzeng@163.com

Abstract. Most existing ordinal regression methods are adapted from traditional supervised learning algorithms (e.g., support vector machines and neural networks) which have shown to work well mostly on dense data. However, the use of existing ordinal regression methods on sparse data has received less scrutiny. This paper proposes to address the sparsity issue arose in many real-world ordinal regression applications by leveraging the feature interaction modeling techniques. Following the popular threshold methodology in ordinal regression studies, we extend Factorization Machines, an effective solution to modeling pairwise feature interactions in sparse feature space, to ordinal regression. The proposed model, namely Factorization Machines for Ordinal Regression (FMOR), combines the ability of threshold methodology in predicting targets of ordinal scale with the advantages of factorization models in handling high-dimensional sparse data. Through extensive experimental studies, we show that the proposed FMOR is both effective and efficient against state-of-the-art baselines.

Keywords: Ordinal regression · Factorization machines · Sparse data

1 Introduction

Ordinal regression is an important type of supervised learning paradigm, which aims to learn predictive models for ordinal targets. Ordinal regression problems are very common in massive domains from social sciences [9] to financial technology [1] and clinical research [23]. In recent years, ordinal regression has experienced significant developments, with many prevalent methods adapted from traditional machine learning algorithms such as support vector machines [3,24], neural networks [2,4,6,13], boosting [11] and discriminant learning [21,22]. These methods have shown to be effective in many scenarios, but unavoidably, retain substantial weaknesses of the original methods. One significant challenge comes from the fact that the feature space can be of very high dimension but sparse in many real-world ordinal regression applications, e.g., collaborative filtering, click-through rate prediction, and computer-aided pathology diagnosis. It is known that the sparse representation problem greatly hinders the performance of traditional machine learning methods, as well as their extensions for ordinal regression [7].

© Springer Nature Switzerland AG 2019
A. C. Nayak and A. Sharma (Eds.): PRICAI 2019, LNAI 11671, pp. 162–174, 2019.
https://doi.org/10.1007/978-3-030-29911-8_13

One successful solution to the sparse representation problem is to model the inherent interactions among features because co-occurrence of features often helps reveal high-level domain knowledge about the task under consideration. One effective approach to model feature interaction is Factorization Machines (FM) [19], which embeds high-dimensional sparse features into a rank-low latent space and learns pairwise feature interactions via the inner product of features' embedding vectors. Although originally proposed in the context of recommender systems, FM has yielded great promise in a wide range of prediction tasks, especially those with very high and sparse feature space [16–18,25]. However, the target variables of traditional FM models can only be either discrete or continuous. Thus, the tradition FM does not yet cater for the ordinal relationship among learning targets. To our best knowledge, there is little work adapting FM for ordinal regression.

In this paper, we propose a novel **F**actorization **M**achines for **O**rdinal **R**egression (FMOR), in which the sparsity issue in ordinal regression is tackled through factorized feature interactions. Motivated by the popular threshold methodology of ordinal regression studies, the proposed FMOR extends the traditional FM by introducing a set of threshold parameters that map real-valued outputs of FM to ordinal labels. We implement the learning algorithm of FMOR based on stochastic gradient descent, and further claim that the ordinal threshold constraint required by threshold-based ordinal regression methods can be automatically satisfied by the derived model. Finally, we perform comprehensive experiments on several benchmark datasets and compare FMOR with state-of-the-art approaches. The results show that FMOR noticeably outperforms all counterparts, especially in case of sparse feature space.

The rest of this paper is organized as follows. Section 2 briefly discusses the literature of ordinal regression. Section 3 gives the details of the proposed factorization machines for ordinal regression. Section 4 reports the experimental results. Section 5 gives some conclusive remarks.

2   Related Work

Generally, ordinal regression methods can be classified into three categories: (i) naive methods, (ii) ordinal binary decomposition methods, and (iii) threshold-based methods.

Naive Methods. Ordinal regression, akin to nominal classification and metric regression, can be simplified into these conventional supervised learning paradigms by either ignoring the ordinal relationship among classes or casting ordinal labels into real values. A more advanced method of this type is to transform ordinal regression as cost-sensitive classification, in which the ordinal information is encoded as misclassification costs [10].

Ordinal Binary Decomposition Methods. The main idea of ordinal binary decomposition methods is to decompose the ordinal classes into several binary pairs, each modeled by single or multiple traditional classifiers. Lin et al. [12] proposed a reduction framework from ordinal regression to binary classification: each sample is extended with a series of ordinal patterns, then a binary classifier is learned for each ordinal class that answers the question: "Is the rank of $\mathbf{x}$ greater than r or not?". Liu et al. [14] made use of triplets with each element from a different rank as samples and a binary classifier is learned for each ordinal class that answers the question: "Is the rank of $\mathbf{x}$ greater than $r-1$ and smaller than $r+1$?".

Threshold-Based Methods. Threshold-based methods have been one popular technique for handling ordinal samples. Threshold-based methods aim to estimate: (i) a latent regression function $f(\mathbf{x})$ that maps the input feature space to a one-dimensional real space; and (ii) a set of thresholds $b_1 \leq \cdots \leq b_R$ that cast the real-valued $f(\mathbf{x})$ into an interval corresponding to an ordinal class. The proportional odds model (POM) [15] is one of the first threshold-based methods and inspires many subsequent studies. Another well-known threshold-based ordinal regression method is Support Vector Ordinal Regression (SVOR) [3,20] that generalize the "large margin" principle adopted by support vector machines to ordinal regression. Two solutions to SVOR have been developed: one maximizes the margin of the closest neighboring classes (called fixed-margin strategy) and one maximizes the sum of margins of all classes (called sum-of-margin strategy). In a recent survey on ordinal regression [5], SVOR is proved to be the best threshold-based methods for its competitive performance on both prediction accuracy and training time.

3   The Proposed Method

In this section, we first give a preliminary introduction to the traditional FM, and then elaborate our proposed FMOR method.

3.1   Preliminary

Factorization Machines (FM) [19] are a generic model class that capable of dealing with high-dimensional and sparse features. Formally, FM takes as input a real valued vector $\mathbf{x} \in \mathbb{R}^d$, and estimates the target by modelling pairwise interactions of sparse features using low-rank latent factors. The model equation of FM is formulated as:

$$\hat{y}_{\mathrm{FM}}(\mathbf{x}; \Theta) = w_0 + \sum_{j=1}^{d} w_j x_j + \sum_{j=1}^{d} \sum_{j'=j+1}^{d} \langle \mathbf{v}_j, \mathbf{v}_{j'} \rangle x_j x_{j'} \qquad (1)$$

where the parameters Θ have to be estimated are:

$$w_0 \in \mathbb{R}; \quad \mathbf{w} \in \mathbb{R}^d; \quad \mathbf{V} = (\mathbf{v}_1, \cdots, \mathbf{v}_d) \in \mathbb{R}^{p \cdot d}$$

In Eq. 1, the first two items are linear combinations of every features with weights w_j $(1 \leq j \leq d)$ and a global bias w_0, and the last item is pairwise feature interactions using a factorized weighting schema $\hat{w}_{jj'} = \langle \mathbf{v}_j, \mathbf{v}_{j'} \rangle = \sum_{k=1}^{p} v_{jk} \cdot v_{j'k}$, where $\mathbf{v}_j$ is factor vector of the j-th feature, and $p \in \mathbb{N}^+$ is the hyper-parameter that defines the dimensionality of factor vectors. Feature factors in FM are commonly said to be low-rank, due to $p \ll d$. Compared with traditional ways (e.g., polynomial SVM) to model feature interactions using separated interaction weights, the factorization schema of FM can reduce the model complexity from $O(d^2)$ to $O(p \cdot d)$, which is a favored property for high-dimensional feature space.

Furthermore, FM is practically efficient for its linear computation time complexity. The model equation of FM in Eq. 1 can be reformulated as:

$$\hat{y}_{\text{FM}}(\mathbf{x}; \Theta) = w_0 + \sum_{j=1}^{d} w_j x_j + \frac{1}{2} \sum_{k=1}^{p} \left(\left(\sum_{j=1}^{d} v_{jk} x_j \right)^2 - \sum_{j=1}^{d} v_{jk}^2 x_j^2 \right) \qquad (2)$$

Equation 2 indicates that the model equation of FM has only linear time complexity in both d and p. In fact, the pairwise feature interaction can be only computed over the non-zero elements of $\mathbf{x}$, i.e., the computation complexity is $O(p \cdot N_z)$. Under sparsity settings, N_z can be much smaller than d, thus the computation of decision function of FM can be very efficient. In brief, FM provides a promising framework for handling high dimensional and sparse data.

3.2 Factorization Machines for Ordinal Regression

We realize Factorization Machines for Ordinal Regression (FMOR) by leveraging the threshold methodology. The basic idea is to introduce a set of consecutive thresholds to partition real line into several intervals which define the boundaries of ordinal classes.

Given an ordinal regression problem with R ordinal classes, OrdinalFM estimates the target of an input vector $\mathbf{x} \in \mathbb{R}^d$ as:

$$\hat{y}(\mathbf{x}) = \underset{r \in \{1, \cdots, R\}}{\arg\min} \{ f(\mathbf{x}) - b_r \leq 0 \} \qquad (3)$$

where $b_1, \cdots, b_R \in \mathbb{R}$ are the R thresholds partitioning real line into intervals, each corresponding to an ordinal class. Besides, the thresholds are required to satisfy the constraint $b_1 \leq \cdots \leq b_R$. For mathematical convenience, b_R is simply set as $+\infty$. $f(x)$ is the latent factor regression function that captures all possible interactions between features (up to second-order, practically):

$$f(\mathbf{x}) = \sum_{j=1}^{d} w_j x_j + \sum_{j=1}^{d} \sum_{j'=j+1}^{d} \langle \mathbf{v}_j, \mathbf{v}_{j'} \rangle x_j x_{j'} \qquad (4)$$

Note that $f(\mathbf{x})$ is the same as the traditional FM model in Eq. 1 except the global bias item. In essence, FMOR extend the traditional FM by introducing a set of thresholds instead of the single global bias. The thresholds are used to map the regression function value $f(\mathbf{x})$ into ordinal targets. Particularly, an input is predicted as r if and only if $b_{r-1} < f(\mathbf{x}) \leq b_r$.

The model parameters of FMOR that have to be estimated are:

$$b_1, \cdots, b_{R-1} \in \mathbb{R}; \quad \mathbf{w} \in \mathbb{R}^d; \quad \mathbf{v}_1, \cdots, \mathbf{v}_d \in \mathbb{R}^p$$

Next, we discuss the learning procedure of FMOR, including the learning objective and the optimization algorithm.

The Learning Objective. Following the traditional supervised learning framework, the parameters Θ are learned from a given training set $\mathcal{D}$ that minimizes the following regularized empirical risk:

$$\mathcal{O}(\Theta, \mathcal{D}) = R_{\text{emp}}(\Theta, \mathcal{D}) + \lambda \Omega(\Theta) \tag{5}$$

where R_{emp} is the empirical risk of an ordinal regression model on the training data, and $\Omega(\cdot)$ is the regularization item. λ is the trade-off between the empirical risk and regularizer of model parameters.

In order to account for the ordinal relationship among targets when calculating the empirical risk, we consider measuring the predicting errors w.r.t. each ordinal class. Formally, give a training set $\mathcal{D} = \mathcal{D}^{(1)} \cup \cdots \cup \mathcal{D}^{(R)}$, where $\mathcal{D}^{(r)} = \{(\mathbf{x}_i, r), \cdots, (\mathbf{x}_{N_k}, r)\}$ $(1 \leq r \leq R)$ is the set of training samples with the class r, the empirical risk of a FMOR model is defined as:

$$R_{\text{emp}}(\Theta, \mathcal{D}) = \sum_{r=1}^{R} \sum_{i=1}^{N_r} \left(\sum_{k=1}^{r-1} \ell(f(\mathbf{x}) - b_k) + \sum_{k=r}^{R-1} \ell(b_k - f(\mathbf{x})) \right) \tag{6}$$

where $\ell(\cdot)$ is the surrogate loss function that penalizes an erroneous prediction. In fact, the empirical risk is contributed over all thresholds, including the lower-grading ones $(k = 1, \cdots, r - 1)$ and the upper-grading ones $(k = r, \cdots, R)$, involved when a predicting error occurs.

Generally, a surrogate loss function is required to be monotonically decreasing in true positives. Moreover, smoothness is a derivable property such that efficient optimization techniques can be applied to estimate model parameters. Here, we adopt the smoothed hinge loss:

$$\ell(z) = \begin{cases} 0 & \text{if } z \geq 1 \\ \dfrac{(1-z)^2}{2} & \text{if } 0 < z < 1 \\ 0.5 - z & \text{if } z \leq 0 \end{cases} \tag{7}$$

As mentioned above, the threshold parameters need to satisfy the ordinal inequality constraint $b_1 \leq \cdots \leq b_R$. Interestingly, the constraint, although not being imposed on the learning procedure explicitly, can be automatically satisfied at the optimal solution of OrdinalFM, as will be shown in the following theorem.

Theorem 1. *Let $\Theta^* = (b_1^*, \cdots, b_{R-1}^*, \mathbf{w}^*, \mathbf{v}_1^*, \cdots, \mathbf{v}_d^*)$ be the optimal solution of the regularized empirical risk minimization problem in Eq. 5, i.e.,*

$$\Theta^* = \arg\min_{\Theta}\{R_{\text{emp}}(\Theta, \mathcal{D}) + \lambda\Omega(\Theta)\},$$

Then we have $b_1^* \leq \cdots \leq b_{R-1}^*$.

Theorem 1 not only establishes a nice property of FMOR but also induces a heuristic that is helpful for finding a better FMOR model. Theorem 1 leads to the following corollary.

Corollary 1. *Given two solution $\dot{\Theta} = (\dot{b}_1, \cdots, \dot{b}_{R-1}, \dot{\mathbf{w}}, \dot{\mathbf{v}}_1, \cdots, \dot{\mathbf{v}}_d)$ and $\ddot{\Theta} = (\ddot{b}_1, \cdots, \ddot{b}_{R-1}, \dot{\mathbf{w}}, \dot{\mathbf{v}}_1, \cdots, \dot{\mathbf{v}}_d)$, where $(\ddot{b}_1, \cdots, \ddot{b}_{R-1})$ is sorted in an ascending order of $(\dot{b}_1, \cdots, \dot{b}_{R-1})$, we have $R_{\text{emp}}(\ddot{\Theta}, \mathcal{D}) \leq R_{\text{emp}}(\dot{\Theta}, \mathcal{D})$.*

Due to space limitation, the proofs will be provided in the full version of the paper.

The Learning Algorithm. We employ the Adaptive Moment Estimation (Adam) [8] algorithm, a popular variant of stochastic gradient descent algorithm that uses adaptive per-parameter learning rates, to solve the regularized empirical risk minimization problem in Eq. 5. The main idea is to iterate over each sample $(\mathbf{x}, r)$ in the training set, and update model parameters towards the direction of negative gradient of the objective:

$$\theta^{(t)} = \theta^{(t-1)} - \eta^{(\theta,t)} \cdot \left(\frac{\partial R_{\text{emp}}(\Theta, \{(\mathbf{x}, r)\})}{\partial\theta} + \lambda\frac{\partial\Omega(\Theta)}{\partial\theta} \right) \tag{8}$$

where $\eta^{(\theta,t)}$ is the individual adaptive learning rate for θ at the t-th iteration.

For the empirical risk in Eq. 6, the gradient is given by

$$\frac{\partial R_{\text{emp}}(\Theta, \{(\mathbf{x}, r)\})}{\partial\theta} = \sum_{k=1}^{r-1} \frac{\partial\ell(f(\mathbf{x}) - b_k)}{\partial\theta} + \sum_{k=r}^{R-1} \frac{\partial\ell(b_k - f(\mathbf{x}))}{\partial\theta} \tag{9}$$

From Eq. 7, the gradient of the smoothed hinge loss is:

$$\frac{\partial\ell(z)}{\partial z} = \begin{cases} 0 & \text{if } z \geq 1 \\ z - 1 & \text{if } 0 < z < 1 \\ -1 & \text{if } z \leq 0 \end{cases} \tag{10}$$

From Eq. 4, the gradient of the factorized-based regression function is:

$$\frac{\partial f(\mathbf{x})}{\partial w_j} = x_j \quad (j = 1, \cdots, d)$$

$$\frac{\partial f(\mathbf{x})}{\partial v_{j,l}} = x_j \cdot \sum_{j' \neq j} v_{j',l} x_{j'} \quad (j = 1, \cdots, d; l = 1, \cdots, p) \tag{11}$$

Through embedding Eqs. 10 and 11 into Eq. 9, we can obtain the gradient used in the optimization algorithm.

One thing to be noted here is gradient-based algorithms, though simple and efficient, are not guaranteed to find the global optimum solution, since the regularized empirical risk minimization problem is usually highly non-convex empirically. Thus the ordinal inequality constraint might be violated in the estimated parameters. Fortunately, according to Corollary 1, we can find better parameters, which not only satisfies the ordinal inequality constraint but also achieve lower regularized empirical risk, by sorting the learned threshold parameters in ascending order.

4   Empirical Study

In this section, we report the results of the empirical studies on the proposed FMOR using several benchmark datasets.

4.1   Experimental Settings

As the proposed FMOR is essentially a threshold-based method, we select several state-of-the-art threshold-based ordinal regression methods as baselines. We also compare FMOR against the traditional FM.

- ORBoost: The thresholded ensemble model for ordinal regression proposed by Lin and Li [11]. The two implementations, namely ORBoost-LR (Ordinal Regression Boosting with Left-Right margins) and ORBoost-All (Ordinal Regression Boosting with All margins), are used as the baselines.
- SVOR: The support vector formulation for ordinal regression proposed by Chu and Keerthi [3]. The two implementations, namely SVOREX (Support Vector Ordinal Regression with EXplicit constraints) and SVORIM (Support Vector Ordinal Regression with IMplicit constraints), are used as the baselines. Both methods are implemented with Gaussian kernel (with kernel width as 1) and linear kernel, respectively.
- POMNN: The ordinal neural network based on the proportional odds model proposed by Gutiérrez [6].
- FM: The original factorization machines proposed by Rendle [19]. The FM model is learned with the regression least-squares loss and the predictions are rounded to the nearest ordinal class.

The ORBoost methods, the SVOR methods and the traditional FM are run using the publicly available implementations provided by the authors[1]. We implemented the POMNN method using TensorFlow. As for the proposed FMOR, we implemented it on basis of LibFM. The hyper-parameters of each method are chosen from a certain range (shown in Table 1) using 5-fold cross-validation within the training set. For other parameters of each method, we use default settings provided by the implementations.

---

[1] http://www.work.caltech.edu/~htlin/program/orensemble/.
http://www.gatsby.ucl.ac.uk/~chuwei/svor.htm.
http://www.libfm.org/.

Table 1. The ranges for hyper-parameter selection

Method	Hyper-parameter	Range
SVOR	Trade-off parameter	{0,0.001,0.01,0.1,1,10}
POMNN	Neurons in the hidden layer	{10,25,50,75,100}
	Learning rate	{0.001,0.005,0.01,0.05,0.1}
FM/FMOR	Dimensionality of factor vector p	{5,10,15}
	Trade-off parameter λ	{0,0.001,0.01,0.1,1,10}
	The general learning rate η	{0.001,0.005,0.01,0.05,0.1}

All the methods are evaluated using the following measures:

1. *MZE*: The Mean Zero–one Error (MZE) is the fraction of incorrect predictions:

$$MZE = \frac{1}{N} \sum_{i=1}^{N} [\![\hat{y}(\mathbf{x}_i) \neq y_i]\!]$$

2. *MAE*: The Mean Absolute Error (MAE) is the average absolute deviation of the predictions from the ground-truth:

$$MAE = \frac{1}{N} \sum_{i=1}^{N} |\hat{y}(\mathbf{x}_i) - y_i|$$

4.2 Prediction Accuracy

In this experiment, we compared the proposed FMOR against the baselines on 9 benchmark datasets which are taken from public machine learning data repositories[2]. All these datasets are real ordinal datasets with a varying number of samples, features and classes. We preprocess each dataset by normalizing every numeric attributes into $[0, 1]$ and transforming every categorical attributes to binary forms with one-hot encoding (one feature per value). As for the *winequality* dataset, we generate one more preprocessed dataset by transforming all attributes, including both numeric ones and categorical ones, to binary forms. To be specific, each numeric attribute in the original dataset is discretized into pre-defined bins and then converted into one-hot vectors. This dataset, denoted as $winequality_{0/1}$ in Table 2, is of high sparsity as each sample is described by a 180-dimension binary feature vector. The characteristics of benchmark datasets are described in Table 2.

---

[2] https://archive.ics.uci.edu/ml/.
  https://www.openml.org.

Table 2. Characteristics of the benchmark datasets

Datasets	#sample	#feature	#class	Class distribution
Balance-scale	625	20	3	288, 49, 288
Car-evaluation	1728	21	4	1210, 384, 69, 65
User-knowledge	258	5	4	24, 83, 88, 63
Eucalyptus	736	89	5	130, 105, 214, 107, 180
School-grades	648	124	14	16, 14, 35, 35, 97, 104, 72, 81, 63, 49, 36, 29, 15, 2
Lecturer-eval	1000	20	5	93, 280, 403, 197, 27
Social-worker	1000	31	4	32, 352, 399, 217
Turkiye-eval	5820	32	5	1902, 1028, 792, 1252, 846
Winequality	4898	11	7	20, 163, 1457, 2198, 880, 175, 5
Winequality$_{0/1}$	4898	180	7	20, 163, 1457, 2198, 880, 175, 5

Each dataset is randomly split 5 times into training and testing sets with ratio 2:1. The averaged MZE and MAE over 5 runs along with the standard deviations are reported in Tables 3 and 4 (best in bold), respectively. From the results, we can see the proposed FMOR beats all baselines 6 of 10 times in terms of both MZE and MAE. Among the datasets that the proposed FMOR performs best, the most significant improvement is obtained on the *winequality$_{0/1}$* dataset of which the feature space is sparser than others. This indicates that the advantage of the proposed FMOR can be more significant as the level of sparsity gets higher. Actually, in these datasets (i.e., *user-knowledge*, *eucalyptus* and *turkiye-eval*) that FMOR or traditional FM fails to outperform traditional ordinal regression methods, the sparsity issue rarely occurs. Taking the *user-knowledge* dataset[3] as an example, the attributes are all numerical ones such as the exam performance or the study time of a student. However, this result does not necessarily mean that the proposed FMOR cannot be applied to the ordinal regression problems with dense feature space. In fact, there is only a small gap between FMOR and the best-performed baselines on these datasets. Also note that the proposed FMOR still achieves the best performance on the dense dataset *winequality*. Among all the baselines, SVOR methods perform best in most cases. We also notice that POMNN does not perform as well as expected. We argue that more advanced techniques for training deep neural networks need to be employed to learn a better neural networks model for ordinal regression.

---

[3] https://archive.ics.uci.edu/ml/datasets/User+Knowledge+Modeling.

Table 3. The MZE results (means and standard deviations over 5 runs) on benchmark datasets

	Balance-scale	Car-evaluation	User-knowledge	Eucalyptus
ORBoost-LR	$0.0208_{\pm 0.012}$	$0.0230_{\pm 0.005}$	$0.1500_{\pm 0.031}$	$0.3696_{\pm 0.028}$
ORBoost-All	$0.0211_{\pm 0.013}$	$0.0249_{\pm 0.004}$	$0.1538_{\pm 0.009}$	$0.3634_{\pm 0.034}$
SVOREX-Gau	$0.0221_{\pm 0.013}$	$0.0191_{\pm 0.003}$	$0.1537_{\pm 0.019}$	$\mathbf{0.3452}_{\pm 0.041}$
SVOREX-Lin	$0.0187_{\pm 0.016}$	$0.0262_{\pm 0.006}$	$0.1431_{\pm 0.024}$	$0.3724_{\pm 0.016}$
SVORIM-Gau	$0.0225_{\pm 0.017}$	$0.0196_{\pm 0.003}$	$\mathbf{0.1362}_{\pm 0.014}$	$0.3655_{\pm 0.029}$
SVORIM-Lin	$\mathbf{0.0185}_{\pm 0.016}$	$0.0242_{\pm 0.004}$	$0.1430_{\pm 0.032}$	$0.3920_{\pm 0.044}$
POMNN	$0.0227_{\pm 0.014}$	$0.0258_{\pm 0.037}$	$0.1501_{\pm 0.018}$	$0.3493_{\pm 0.024}$
FM	$0.0193_{\pm 0.014}$	$0.0243_{\pm 0.019}$	$0.2418_{\pm 0.019}$	$0.4029_{\pm 0.016}$
FMOR	$0.0189_{\pm 0.012}$	$\mathbf{0.0174}_{\pm 0.002}$	$0.1436_{\pm 0.005}$	$0.3643_{\pm 0.026}$
	School-grades	Lecturer-eval	Social-work-decs	Turkiye-eval
ORBoost-LR	$0.8742_{\pm 0.024}$	$0.4030_{\pm 0.004}$	$0.4250_{\pm 0.016}$	$0.8210_{\pm 0.014}$
ORBoost-All	$0.8395_{\pm 0.030}$	$0.4023_{\pm 0.003}$	$0.4261_{\pm 0.014}$	$0.6187_{\pm 0.016}$
SVOREX-Gau	$0.8395_{\pm 0.030}$	$0.3780_{\pm 0.020}$	$0.4260_{\pm 0.013}$	$\mathbf{0.5878}_{\pm 0.012}$
SVOREX-Lin	$0.8332_{\pm 0.030}$	$0.3960_{\pm 0.015}$	$0.4250_{\pm 0.015}$	$0.5885_{\pm 0.013}$
SVORIM-Gau	$0.8240_{\pm 0.027}$	$0.3781_{\pm 0.002}$	$0.4160_{\pm 0.011}$	$0.7833_{\pm 0.012}$
SVORIM-Lin	$0.8257_{\pm 0.041}$	$0.4050_{\pm 0.005}$	$0.4200_{\pm 0.105}$	$0.6361_{\pm 0.035}$
POMNN	$0.8370_{\pm 0.020}$	$0.3671_{\pm 0.003}$	$0.4181_{\pm 0.013}$	$0.6319_{\pm 0.020}$
FM	$0.8381_{\pm 0.085}$	$0.3660_{\pm 0.017}$	$0.4191_{\pm 0.021}$	$0.6732_{\pm 0.028}$
FMOR	$\mathbf{0.7735}_{\pm 0.043}$	$\mathbf{0.3583}_{\pm 0.017}$	$\mathbf{0.3950}_{\pm 0.013}$	
	Winequality	Winequality$_{0/1}$		
ORBoost-LR	$0.5188_{\pm 0.012}$	$0.5194_{\pm 0.018}$		
ORBoost-All	$0.5360_{\pm 0.005}$	$0.5319_{\pm 0.018}$		
SVOREX-Gau	$0.4941_{\pm 0.005}$	$0.5153_{\pm 0.015}$		
SVOREX-Lin	$0.5329_{\pm 0.003}$	$0.5186_{\pm 0.011}$		
SVORIM-Gau	$0.5184_{\pm 0.009}$	$0.5273_{\pm 0.014}$		
SVORIM-Lin	$0.4984_{\pm 0.007}$	$0.5153_{\pm 0.018}$		
POMNN	$0.4816_{\pm 0.012}$	$0.5122_{\pm 0.011}$		
FM	$0.8989_{\pm 0.011}$	$0.5148_{\pm 0.021}$		
FMOR	$\mathbf{0.4839}_{\pm 0.018}$	$\mathbf{0.4767}_{\pm 0.011}$		

4.3 Training Efficiency

In this experiment, we evaluate the training efficiency of the proposed FMOR by comparing training time with other methods. In this experiment, we only consider SVOR methods for comparison for the consistent outperformance over other baselines. All comparison methods were run on a single core of an Intel(R) Xeon(R) CPU E7-4830 processor clocked at 2.13 GHz with access to 24 GB RAM.

Due to space limitation, only the results on the *turkiye-eval* dataset are reported. Figure 1 plots the training time of every comparison methods with varying sizes of the training dataset. It can be clearly seen that the proposed FMOR scales much better than SVOR methods. On large training sets with thousands of samples, training a FMOR model takes only seconds while training SVOR models can take several hours.

Table 4. The MAE results (means and standard deviations over 5-fold cross validation runs) on benchmark datasets

	Balance-scale	Car-evaluation	User-knowledge	Eucalyptus
ORBoost-LR	$0.0307_{\pm 0.019}$	$0.0271_{\pm 0.013}$	$0.1660_{\pm 0.038}$	$0.3966_{\pm 0.050}$
ORBoost-All	$0.0310_{\pm 0.021}$	$0.0258_{\pm 0.013}$	$0.1702_{\pm 0.011}$	$0.3823_{\pm 0.058}$
SVOREX-Gau	$0.0309_{\pm 0.019}$	$0.0206_{\pm 0.013}$	$0.1701_{\pm 0.023}$	$\mathbf{0.3768}_{\pm 0.035}$
SVOREX-Lin	$0.0275_{\pm 0.022}$	$0.0265_{\pm 0.016}$	$0.1583_{\pm 0.029}$	$0.4185_{\pm 0.058}$
SVORIM-Gau	$0.0317_{\pm 0.024}$	$0.0204_{\pm 0.014}$	$\mathbf{0.1507}_{\pm 0.017}$	$0.3816_{\pm 0.046}$
SVORIM-Lin	$0.0283_{\pm 0.024}$	$0.0246_{\pm 0.014}$	$0.1583_{\pm 0.039}$	$0.4197_{\pm 0.037}$
POMNN	$0.0321_{\pm 0.021}$	$0.0272_{\pm 0.020}$	$0.1662_{\pm 0.022}$	$0.3776_{\pm 0.051}$
FM	$\mathbf{0.0248}_{\pm 0.024}$	$0.0248_{\pm 0.020}$	$0.2676_{\pm 0.024}$	$0.4414_{\pm 0.027}$
FMOR	$0.0281_{\pm 0.019}$	$\mathbf{0.0188}_{\pm 0.010}$	$0.1589_{\pm 0.006}$	$0.3784_{\pm 0.037}$
	School-grades	Lecturer-eval	Social-work-decs	Turkiye-eval
ORBoost-LR	$2.7298_{\pm 0.031}$	$0.4369_{\pm 0.016}$	$0.4470_{\pm 0.020}$	$1.3115_{\pm 0.025}$
ORBoost-All	$2.3175_{\pm 0.058}$	$0.4349_{\pm 0.014}$	$0.4511_{\pm 0.018}$	$1.2529_{\pm 0.032}$
SVOREX-Gau	$2.3175_{\pm 0.058}$	$0.4140_{\pm 0.011}$	$0.4360_{\pm 0.017}$	$1.1560_{\pm 0.042}$
SVOREX-Lin	$2.2938_{\pm 0.033}$	$0.4299_{\pm 0.020}$	$0.4380_{\pm 0.060}$	$1.1663_{\pm 0.035}$
SVORIM-Gau	$2.1029_{\pm 0.100}$	$0.4130_{\pm 0.009}$	$0.4290_{\pm 0.012}$	$1.0979_{\pm 0.016}$
SVORIM-Lin	$1.9158_{\pm 0.056}$	$0.4380_{\pm 0.012}$	$0.4330_{\pm 0.052}$	$1.0450_{\pm 0.039}$
POMNN	$2.0764_{\pm 0.091}$	$0.4020_{\pm 0.013}$	$0.4290_{\pm 0.050}$	$\mathbf{1.0297}_{\pm 0.035}$
FM	$2.1595_{\pm 0.035}$	$0.4010_{\pm 0.021}$	$0.4431_{\pm 0.020}$	$1.3324_{\pm 0.042}$
FMOR	$\mathbf{1.8970}_{\pm 0.027}$	$\mathbf{0.3910}_{\pm 0.019}$	$\mathbf{0.4100}_{\pm 0.021}$	$1.1998_{\pm 0.057}$
	Winequality	Winequality$_{0/1}$		
ORBoost-LR	$0.5847_{\pm 0.024}$	$0.5892_{\pm 0.030}$		
ORBoost-All	$0.6107_{\pm 0.015}$	$0.6058_{\pm 0.015}$		
SVOREX-Gau	$0.5545_{\pm 0.015}$	$0.5835_{\pm 0.024}$		
SVOREX-Lin	$0.6074_{\pm 0.013}$	$0.5863_{\pm 0.016}$		
SVORIM-Gau	$0.5870_{\pm 0.016}$	$0.5998_{\pm 0.019}$		
SVORIM-Lin	$0.5574_{\pm 0.017}$	$0.5820_{\pm 0.015}$		
POMNN	$0.5492_{\pm 0.017}$	$0.5820_{\pm 0.016}$		
FM	$2.0390_{\pm 0.055}$	$0.5940_{\pm 0.406}$		
FMOR	$\mathbf{0.5384}_{\pm 0.025}$	$\mathbf{0.5306}_{\pm 0.015}$		

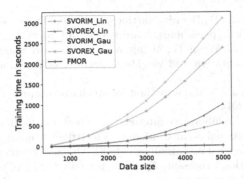

Fig. 1. Training time with varying dataset size

5   Conclusion

In this paper, we put forward Factorization Machines for Ordinal Regression (FMOR), a latent factor model addressing the sparsity issue in ordinal regression problems. Using the factorization machines as the base generic framework for modeling sparse feature space, we incorporate the threshold methodology to handle the ordinal targets in a proper way. We experimentally show that FMOR has the dual advantages of effectiveness and efficiency, and can be applied not only to sparse ordinal data, but competitive results can even be obtained for dense data. Future work includes applying FMOR to model ordinal user preference scores in recommender systems.

Acknowledgement. This work is partially supported by Natural Science Foundation of China (61602278, 71704096 and 31671588), Sci. & Tech. Development Fund of Shandong Province of China (ZR2017MF027), the Humanities and Social Science Research Project of the Ministry of Education (18YJAZH017), the Taishan Scholar Climbing Program of Shandong Province, and SDUST Research Fund (2015TDJH102).

References

1. Alp, A.: Structural shifts in credit rating standards. J. Financ. **68**(6), 2435–2470 (2013)
2. Beckham, C., Pal, C.: Unimodal probability distributions for deep ordinal classification, pp. 411–419 (2017)
3. Chu, W., Keerthi, S.S.: New approaches to support vector ordinal regression. In: Proceedings of the 22nd International Conference on Machine Learning, pp. 145–152 (2005)
4. Goh, C.K., Liu, Y., Kong, A.W.: A constrained deep neural network for ordinal regression. In: Proceedings of the IEEE Conference on Computer Vision and Pattern Recognition, pp. 831–839 (2018)
5. Gutierrez, P.A., Perez-Ortiz, M., Sanchez-Monedero, J., Fernandez-Navarro, F., Hervas-Martinez, C.: Ordinal regression methods: survey and experimental study. IEEE Trans. Knowl. Data Eng. **28**(1), 127–146 (2016)

6. Gutiérrez, P.A., Tiňo, P., Hervás-Martínez, C.: Ordinal regression neural networks based on concentric hyperspheres. Neural Netw. **59**, 51–60 (2014)
7. Huang, X., Zhang, L., Wang, B., Zhang, Z., Li, F.: Feature weight estimation based on dynamic representation and neighbor sparse reconstruction. Pattern Recogn. **81**, 388–403 (2018)
8. Kingma, D.P., Ba, J.: Adam: a method for stochastic optimization. arXiv preprint arXiv:1412.6980 (2014)
9. Koren, Y., Sill, J.: Collaborative filtering on ordinal user feedback. In: Proceedings of the 23th International Joint Conference on Artificial Intelligence (2013)
10. Li, L., Lin, H.T.: Ordinal regression by extended binary classification. In: Advances in Neural Information Processing Systems, pp. 865–872 (2007)
11. Lin, H.T., Li, L.: Large-margin thresholded ensembles for ordinal regression: theory and practice. In: Proceedings of the International Conference on Algorithmic Learning Theory, pp. 319–333 (2006)
12. Lin, H.T., Li, L.: Reduction from cost-sensitive ordinal ranking to weighted binary classification. Neural Comput. **24**(5), 1329–1367 (2012)
13. Liu, X., Zou, Y., Song, Y., Yang, C., You, J., Kumar, B.V.K.V.: Ordinal regression with neuron stick-breaking for medical diagnosis. In: Leal-Taixé, L., Roth, S. (eds.) ECCV 2018. LNCS, vol. 11134, pp. 335–344. Springer, Cham (2019). https://doi.org/10.1007/978-3-030-11024-6_23
14. Liu, Y., Kong, A.W.K., Goh, C.K.: Deep ordinal regression based on data relationship for small datasets. In: Proceedings of the 26th International Joint Conferences on Artificial Intelligence, pp. 2372–2378 (2017)
15. McCullagh, P.: Regression models for ordinal data. J. Roy. Stat. Soc.: Ser. B (Methodol.) **42**(2), 109–127 (1980)
16. Ni, W., Liu, T., Zeng, Q., Zhang, X., Duan, H., Xie, N.: Robust factorization machines for credit default prediction. In: Geng, X., Kang, B.-H. (eds.) PRICAI 2018. LNCS (LNAI), vol. 11012, pp. 941–953. Springer, Cham (2018). https://doi.org/10.1007/978-3-319-97304-3_72
17. Pan, Z., Chen, E., Liu, Q., Xu, T., Ma, H., Lin, H.: Sparse factorization machines for click-through rate prediction. In: Proceedings of the IEEE 16th International Conference on Data Mining, pp. 400–409 (2016)
18. Qiang, R., Liang, F., Yang, J.: Exploiting ranking factorization machines for microblog retrieval. In: Proceedings of the 22nd ACM International Conference on Conference on Information & Knowledge Management, pp. 1783–1788 (2013)
19. Rendle, S.: Factorization machines with libFM. ACM Trans. Intell. Syst. Technol. **3**(3), 57 (2012)
20. Shashua, A., Levin, A.: Ranking with large margin principle: two approaches. In: Advances in Neural Information Processing Systems, pp. 961–968 (2003)
21. Sun, B.Y., Li, J., Wu, D.D., Zhang, X.M., Li, W.B.: Kernel discriminant learning for ordinal regression. IEEE Trans. Knowl. Data Eng. **22**(6), 906–910 (2010)
22. Tian, Q., Zhang, W., Wang, L., Chen, S., Yin, H.: Robust ordinal regression induced by lp-centroid. Neurocomputing **313**, 184–195 (2018)
23. Tran, T., Phung, D., Luo, W., Venkatesh, S.: Stabilized sparse ordinal regression for medical risk stratification. Knowl. Inf. Syst. **43**(3), 555–582 (2015)
24. Wang, H., Shi, Y., Niu, L., Tian, Y.: Nonparallel support vector ordinal regression. IEEE Trans. Cybern. **47**(10), 3306–3317 (2017)
25. Zhu, M., Aggarwal, C.C., Ma, S., Zhang, H., Huai, J.: Outlier detection in sparse data with factorization machines. In: Proceedings of the 2017 ACM Conference on Information and Knowledge Management, pp. 817–826 (2017)

An Approach with Low Redundancy to Network Feature Selection Based on Multiple Order Proximity

Hengliang Wang[✉], Yuan Li, Chenfei Zhao, and Kedian Mu

Peking University, Beijing, China
wanghl@pku.edu.cn

Abstract. Most models for unsupervised network feature selection use first-order proximity and reconstruction loss together as a guiding principle in the selection process. However, the first-order proximity is very sparse and insufficient in most cases. Moreover, redundant features, which can significantly hamper the performance of many machine learning algorithms, have seldom been taken into account. To address these issues, we propose an unsupervised network feature selection model called Multiple order proximity and feature Diversity guiding network Feature Selection model (MDFS), which uses multiple order proximity and feature diversity to guide the selection process. We use multi-order proximities based on the random walk model to capture linkage information between nodes. Moreover, we use an auto-encoder to capture the content information of nodes. As a last step, we design a redundancy loss to alleviate selecting highly-overlapping features. Experiment results on two real-world network datasets show the competitive ability of our model to select high-quality features among state-of-the-art models.

Keywords: Network data · Feature selection · Multiple order proximity · Feature diversity

1 Introduction

With the pervasive use of social media and information networks, network data has become increasingly important in the past decades. The nodes in the network are often accompanied with content information except for link structure. For example, it is possible to extract thousands of profiling features for users in social network. However, these data often have the characteristic of high dimension, which includes many irrelevant and redundant features as well as much noise. This makes it hard for many machine learning algorithms, such as classification and clustering, to achieve better performance. Besides, the capability of many algorithms is limited due to the curse of dimensionality. Feature selection can provide an effective way to address this problem.

Feature selection is the process of selecting high-quality features of the dataset from the original feature set according to some determinate selection

© Springer Nature Switzerland AG 2019
A. C. Nayak and A. Sharma (Eds.): PRICAI 2019, LNAI 11671, pp. 175–187, 2019.
https://doi.org/10.1007/978-3-030-29911-8_14

176   H. Wang et al.

criterion, during which most noise and redundant features are removed. Therefore, feature selection plays a vital role in speeding up the training process and leading to better performance of many machine learning algorithms. Traditional feature selection assumes that data instances are independent and identical distributed (i.i.d), while the data instances on network data cannot satisfy i.i.d. any more. The data instances, which have a connection in the network, tend to be interdependent. As a result, traditional feature selection methods cannot be directly applied to network data. The dependency among data instances is strongly related to the linkage information in the network. For example, friends in Facebook[1] tend to have more common interests. Besides, as in the traditional feature selection, content information is taken into consideration during the selection process. It is challenging to capture linkage information and content information simultaneously.

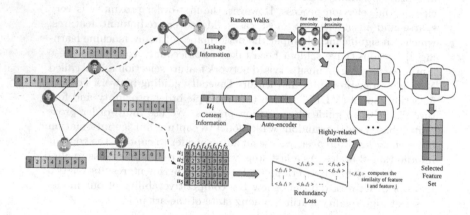

Fig. 1. Illustration of our model. We use random walk-based model and auto-encoder to capture linkage and content information respectively (color indicates feature; size in the cloud block represents importance). Besides, redundancy loss is used to avoid selecting highly-related features (pink). Finally, we get top K features w.r.t the importance. (Color figure online)

Network feature selection algorithms can be categorized into two classes: supervised methods and unsupervised methods, which depend on whether the algorithms utilize the node labels as a guide to select features. Since it is expensive to obtain the node labels, we focus on unsupervised methods in this paper. Some pioneering work has been proposed in unsupervised methods, including POPFS [20], USFS [6], NetFS [7], GFS [19], and LUFS [19].

However, there are two limitations in existing models. Firstly, existing models only take the first-order proximity into consideration. Since the first-order proximity only considers the similarity between neighbors, it is sparse and insufficient in most cases. On the contrary, high-order proximity captures the similarity

---

[1] https://www.facebook.com/.

between a pair of indirectly connected nodes with similar structural contexts [3]. It is well recognized that high-order proximity plays an important role in characterizing network structure [3]. Secondly, since existing models evaluate features individually, the correlation between features is neglected. It is shown empirically that removing redundant features can significantly improve the performance [2].

We propose a network feature selection algorithm, called Multiple order proximity and feature Diversity guiding network Feature Selection model (MDFS) to address the above limitations from three aspects: linkage information, content information and feature redundancy. For linkage information, since high-quality features have a strong connection with multi-order proximities, we apply a random walk-based model in the selection process, which enables our model to capture both first-order proximity and high-order proximity. For content information, it is intuitive that high-quality features are able to preserve the node attributes. We leverage an auto-encoder to guide the selection process. For feature redundancy, redundant features lead to dimensionality unnecessarily and restrict the performance of many machine learning algorithms when facing shortage of data. To alleviate this problem, we design a redundancy loss to penalize overlapping features. We evaluate our model on two real-world network datasets. Experiment results show that our model consistently outperforms the state-of-the-art methods. And the redundancy loss has also been verified to be effective. An illustration of our model is shown in Fig. 1.

Our contributions are listed as follows:

- A network feature selection model, which takes both first-order and high-order proximity into consideration, are proposed.
- We propose a redundancy loss to control the diversity of selected feature set, which contributes to avoid redundant features.
- We conduct experiments on two network datasets, and the experiment results show that our model outperforms the state-of-the-art models.

2   Related Work

2.1   Unsupervised Traditional Feature Selection

Traditional unsupervised feature selection has shown its effectiveness in compressing high-dimension data for many machine learning algorithms. Without label information, there are many alternative criteria to guide the selection process. The criteria can fall into two categories: local discriminative information and data reconstruction error. In LapScore [4], MRSF [24] and SPEC [23], local discriminative information and similarity are directly used as a guiding principle, which indicates the selection process that is supposed to preserve discriminative information and similarity between data instances. The pseudo label is a popular way to access the local discriminative information in unsupervised setting by assigning each node a pseudo label. After that, feature selection algorithms can be learned in a supervised setting. For instance, UDFS [21] applies pseudo label to exploit discriminative information and feature correlations. Li et al.

[11] propose NDFS model, which applies the pseudo label to perform spectral clustering and feature selection simultaneously. UPFS [9] makes use of pseudo label to select personalized features. Moreover, data reconstruction error also plays an important role in guiding the feature selection procedure, which aims at minimizing the error between original feature set and selected feature subset as much as possible. For example, in REFS [8], reconstruction function learning and feature selection are integrated into a coherent model.

2.2   Unsupervised Network Feature Selection

Unsupervised network feature selection gains increasing attention, as it is expensive to obtain node labels. Lots of efforts have been devoted to improving the quality of feature selection on network data in the unsupervised setting. Tang and Liu apply the pesudo label to guide the selection process in LUFS [18]. However, pseudo label based models are indirect and inaccurate [19]. Because pseudo labels are usually generated from attribute of nodes. Wei et al. propose POPFS [20], which utilizes partial order between nodes to extract linkage information from network data. But content information has not been taken into consideration in POPFS. Noticing the relation between latent representations and feature selection on network data, Li et al. introduce USFS [6], an unsupervised streaming feature selection model, by using external latent representations to guide the selection process. Li et al. [7] extend the idea of USFS and propose NetFS. NetFS learns the latent representations and the selected feature set in a joint learning framework instead of using external latent representations. GFS [19] is proposed by Wei et al. GFS uses oracle affinity to take both linkage information and content information into account. However, these works neglect the second and higher order proximity and the overlap between features in the selection process.

2.3   Random Walk-Based Models

Random walk is an efficient way to capture multi-order proximities between nodes for scalable networks [22]. Different sampling strategies are used to generate node sequences. By regrading node sequences as word sentences, Deepwalk [14] learns the latent representations of network through Skip-Gram Negative Sampling model [13]. Node2vec [3], as a variant model of Deepwalk, applies a biased sampling strategy to strike a balance between Breadth-first Sampling (BFS) and Depth-first Sampling (DFS). In order to take structural similarity into account, Struct2vec [15] leverages sampling strategy on a context graph which enables the node sequence to consider both proximity and structural similarity of nodes. DDRW [10], GENE [1] are variant models of Deepwalk for vertex-labeled network presentation learning.

3   MDFS Model

3.1   Problem Statement

Assuming there are N data instances in the network $G = (V, E, X)$ and d features, we use $V = \{v_1, v_2, ..., v_N\}$ to denote the set of linked data instances and $F = \{f_1, f_2, ..., f_d\}$ to denote the set of features. Let $X = (x_1, x_2, ..., x_N) \in \mathbb{R}^{d \times N}$ be attribute matrix of V, the entry $x_{ij} \in X, \forall i \in \{1, 2, ..., d\}, j \in \{1, 2, ..., N\}$ represents the frequency of f_i appeared in v_j. Since there also exists connections among these data instances in the network, the connection relation can be organized by a matrix $E \in \mathbb{R}^{N \times N}$, where $e_{ij} = 1$ if there is a connection between v_i and v_j, otherwise $e_{ij} = 0$.

With the above notation, the problem of unsupervised feature selection for linked data can be formulated as follows:

Given N linked data instances, feature set F, attribute matrix X and connection matrix E, the aim of unsupervised feature selection is to select a feature subset S from F by exploiting attribute matrix X and connection matrix E.

3.2   Transformation Matrix

As the features of nodes are very sparse, it is hard to measure the similarity and correlation between nodes and features. We introduce a transformation parameter matrix $W \in \mathbb{R}^{d \times c}$ to alleviate this issue. W transforms the features of each node into a hidden attribute space, where c is the dimension of hidden space. The norm of $W(i, :)$ means the weight of i-th feature contributing to the latent factors. Thus, the norm of $W(i, :)$ measures the importance of i-th feature. In the first step, we use the matrix to capture both the linkage information and content information in the selection process. Then, redundancy loss is used to avoid redundant features.

3.3   Linkage Information

In network feature selection, linkage information indicates the correlations between nodes. However, the second and higher order proximity, which have seldom been taken into consideration before, play an important role in modeling the linkage information. For example, two papers, which refer to a same paper, are more likely to have similar topics than two random papers. Inspired by this, we introduce random walk-based model to the selection process.

We assume that, a feature is more likely to be informative if the feature can preserve the correlations between nodes. We use a biased sampling strategy S [3], which is utilized to capture the multi-order proximities of nodes, to generate random walks. For a node v_i in a random walk $r = (v_1, v_2, v_3, \cdots, v_n)$ in the random walk set RW, we denote the context nodes of v_i as $C_S(v_i) = \{v_{i-w}, v_{i-w+1}, \cdots, v_{i+w}\} - v_i$, where n is the length of random walk and w denotes the window size. Conditioned on the latent factors of v_i and its context nodes, we try to maximize the log-probability of observing context nodes for node v_i:

$$\max \sum_{r \in RW} \sum_{v_i \in r} \log P(C_{\mathcal{S}}(v_i)|v_i).$$

Following the idea of [3,14], we make two standard assumptions: conditional independence and symmetry in the hidden space, with the help of them, we can factorize the above objective function and model the likelihood of v_i and each context node of v_i as a softmax function parameterized by a dot product of their hidden factors:

$$P(C_{\mathcal{S}}(v_i)|v_i) = \prod_{u \in C_{\mathcal{S}}(v_i)} P(u|v_i) = \prod_{u \in C_{\mathcal{S}}(v_i)} \frac{e^{(Wx_u)^T (Wx_{v_i})}}{\sum_{u \in V} e^{(Wx_u)^T (Wx_{v_i})}}.$$

In the experiment, we use the sampling strategy introduced in [3]. The strategy uses two parameters, returns parameter p, which controls the likelihood of revisiting a node in the walk, and in-out parameter q, which controls the difference between "inward" and "outward" nodes, to smoothly combine the advantage of BFS and DFS. Through this sampling strategy, we generate a random walk set denoted as $RW = \{r_1, r_2, \cdots, r_M\}$. Then, the loss of linkage information is as follows, which is optimized with the help of negative sampling [12].

$$L_{\text{Linkage}} = - \prod_{r \in RW} \prod_{v \in r} P(C_{\mathcal{S}}(v)|v)$$

3.4 Content Information

Besides the linkage information, content information also plays an important role in the selection process. We assume that features are more likely to be informative if they can preserve the information of node attributes in the network data. Thus, we use an auto-encoder [5] to measure the importance of each feature for content information. X denotes the attribute matrix of all nodes. W acts as an encoder, which encodes X into the hidden attribute space. Then, we use a decoder matrix $W_d \in \mathbb{R}^{c \times d}$ to decode the hidden attribute to origin feature space. The reconstruction loss is defined as follows:

$$||X - W_d W X||_F^2,$$

where $|| \cdot ||_F$ denotes the Frobenius norm of a matrix. To avoid overfitting, we add the Frobenius norm of W_d to the content loss. Therefore, the content loss is as follows:

$$L_{\text{Content}} = ||X - W_d W X||_F^2 + \lambda_d ||W_d||_F^2.$$

3.5 Redundancy Loss

In network data, many features of nodes usually are highly-related. However, in many tasks like recommender systems, the diversity between features is encouraged. Inspired by this, we propose a redundancy loss to avoid selecting highly-related features. In our model, we use $\mathbf{S} = X^T X \in \mathbb{R}^{d \times d}$ to represent the similarity matrix of node features. $\mathbf{s}_{i,j}$ denotes the similarity between i-th feature and j-th feature. If the similarity $\mathbf{s}_{i,j}$ between i-th feature and j-th feature is greater than γ, we propose a penalty term to the product of $||W(i,:)||$ and $||W(j,:)||$, which measure the importance of the two features. The redundancy loss is defined as follows:

$$L_{\text{redundancy}} = \sum_{i \neq j} ||W(i,:)||^2 \cdot ||W(j,:)||^2 \cdot \Phi(s_{ij}; \gamma),$$

where $\Phi(s; \gamma) = \begin{cases} s, \text{if } s > \gamma \\ 0, \text{otherwise}. \end{cases}$

3.6 Loss Function

By combining linkage information, content information and redundancy loss in a weighted manner, we can get the objective function as following:

$$
\begin{aligned}
L &= \lambda_l L_{linkage} + \lambda_c L_{content} + \lambda_r L_{redundancy} + \lambda_w ||W||_F^2 \\
&= \lambda_l(- \prod_{r \in RW} \prod_{v \in r} \prod_{u \in C_S(v)} \frac{e^{(Wx_u)^T (Wx_{v_i})}}{\sum_{u \in V} e^{(Wx_u)^T (Wx_{v_i})}}) \\
&\quad + \lambda_c(||X - W_d W X||_F^2 + \lambda_d ||W_d||_F^2) \\
&\quad + \lambda_r(\sum_{i \neq j} ||W(i,:)||^2 \cdot ||W(j,:)||^2 \cdot \Phi(s_{ij})) + \lambda_w ||W||_F^2,
\end{aligned}
$$

where λ_l, λ_c and λ_r are weight parameters to strike a balance among three loss functions. $||W||_F^2$ is the regularization term to control complexity of model and avoid overfitting, and λ_w is weight parameter of $||W||_F^2$.

As a last step, we sort features w.r.t the norm of the row vector of W and output the top K features.

4 Experiment

In this section, we evaluate the feature quality by performing clustering (community detection) on the selected features. First, we introduce two public network datasets with node attributes used in our experiments and summarize the statistics of the datasets in Table 1. Second, we present five important baselines and two evaluation metrics. Finally, we evaluate the selected feature on a clustering task and explain the experiment results.

4.1 Dataset Description

We conduct our experiments on two real-world network datasets: Citeseer dataset and Cora dataset [16]. The statistics of the datasets are summarized in Table 1.

Table 1. Statistics of two datasets

Dataset name	#of instances	#of links	#of features	#of classes
Cora	2708	5429	1433	7
Citeseer	3321	4598	3703	6

4.2 Evaluation Metrics

We evaluate the quality of selected features by their clustering performance. Following the typical setting of evaluation for unsupervised feature selection, we use Accuracy (ACC) and Normalized Mutual Information (NMI) to evaluate the performance of clustering. Accuracy is formulated as following:

$$Accuracy = \frac{1}{n} \sum_{i=1}^{n} I(c_i = map(p_i)),$$

where c_i denotes the real class label of node i, p_i denotes result of node i after clustering, $map(\cdot)$ is a permutation mapping function, which can map p_i to a class label by Kuhn-Munkres Algorithm. Normalized Mutual Information (NMI) is a good measure for determining the quality of clustering. It can be calculated as following:

$$NMI(C, C') = \frac{MI(C, C')}{max(H(C), H(C'))},$$

where C denotes the set of ground truth class label, C' denotes the set of class label after clustering algorithm, $MI(C, C')$ measures the mutual information between C and C', $H(C)$ and $H(C')$ are the entropy of C and C'. The higher the ACC and NMI scores are, the better the feature selection performance is.

4.3 Baseline Methods

We compare our model with following state-of-the-art methods and all features (**ALL**):

POPFS POPFS [20] uses the partial order between nodes to extract linkage information from network data to guide the selection process.

PPOP PPOP [20] is a variant of POPFS, which takes into consideration the correlation between features.

MMPOP MMPOP [20] is another variant of POPFS, which fits POPFS into structural learning framework.

NetFS NetFS [7] learns the latent representations and the selected feature set in a joint learning framework.

GFS GFS [19] uses oracle affinity to take both linkage information and content information into account.

4.4   Results

The parameters in random walk is p, q and sequence length, which are defined as the same as [14], are set to 1, 1, and 100, respectively. And then, in MDFS, the dimension of latent feature is tuned among {50, 100, 150} and selectively set to 100. For content information, λ_d and λ_c are set to 0.1 and 1, respectively. For linkage information, λ_l is set to 1. For redundancy loss, λ_r is set to 0.2. λ_w, which controls the regularization term, is set to 0.1.

Table 2. Results with different feature selection algorithms on Cora dataset

		200	400	600	800	1000
ALL	ACC	0.3650	0.3650	0.3650	0.3650	0.3650
	NMI	0.1549	0.1549	0.1549	0.1549	0.1549
POPFS	ACC	0.3538	0.3809	0.3914	0.4030	0.4335
	NMI	0.1509	0.1911	0.1928	0.2039	**0.2776**
PPOP	ACC	0.3604	0.3954	0.3902	0.4027	0.4023
	NMI	0.1850	0.2266	0.1930	0.2155	0.1376
MMPOP	ACC	0.3639	0.3923	0.3950	0.4068	0.4036
	NMI	0.1644	0.2038	0.1968	0.1462	0.2450
NetFS	ACC	0.3726	0.3904	0.4075	0.4101	0.4085
	NMI	0.1732	0.2185	0.2081	0.2324	0.2085
GFS	ACC	0.3623	0.3997	0.4069	0.4120	0.4122
	NMI	0.1446	0.2025	0.2295	0.2059	0.2113
MDFS	ACC	**0.4025**	**0.4165**	**0.4152**	**0.4159**	**0.4373**
	NMI	**0.2522**	**0.2553**	**0.2319**	**0.2357**	0.2219

In this subsection, we compare the results of our model and other state-of-the-art feature selection algorithms on the two above mentioned datasets. The results are shown in Tables 2 and 3. We vary the number of selected features in the range {200, 400, 600, 800, 1000}. From the results we can observe:

– Feature selection can provide an effective way to improve clustering performance for attributed network data. Compared with using all features, our model improves the accuracy of clustering performance with 10.21%, 9.35% on Cora and Citeseer dataset with 200 features. With the help of linkage information and content information, high-quality features are selected and we avoid selecting highly-overlapping features by using redundancy loss.
– Compared with other unsupervised network feature selection methods, our model has a very competitive performance. Especially, our model gains more improvement when selecting less features. The reason is that through multi-order proximities and content information, our model is more likely to find high-quality features. Besides, taking into consideration redundancy loss makes our model select more discriminative features.

Table 3. Results with different feature selection algorithms on Citeseer dataset

ALL	ACC	0.3880	0.3880	0.3880	0.3880	0.3880
	NMI	0.1582	0.1582	0.1582	0.1582	0.1582
POPFS	ACC	0.3812	0.4082	0.3947	0.4011	0.4188
	NMI	0.1670	0.1827	0.1773	0.1859	0.1897
PPOP	ACC	0.3884	0.4115	0.3923	0.3975	0.4281
	NMI	0.1665	0.1858	0.1858	0.1740	0.2052
MMPOP	ACC	0.3844	0.4076	0.3890	0.3976	0.4399
	NMI	0.1628	0.1836	0.1748	0.1842	0.2076
NetFS	ACC	0.4043	0.4103	0.4139	0.3949	0.4293
	NMI	0.1773	0.1850	0.1882	0.1830	0.2013
GFS	ACC	0.3910	0.4043	0.4052	0.4060	0.4228
	NMI	0.1840	0.1784	0.1824	0.1974	0.2105
MDFS	ACC	**0.4242**	**0.4143**	**0.4197**	**0.4402**	**0.4526**
	NMI	**0.1863**	**0.1896**	**0.1906**	**0.2025**	**0.2150**

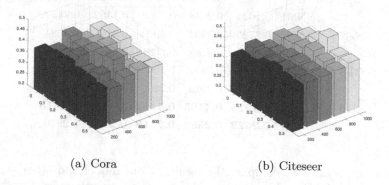

(a) Cora   (b) Citeseer

Fig. 2. The effects of redundancy loss.

4.5   Study on Redundancy Loss

In this subsection, we study the effects of redundancy loss. We fix other parameters and vary the weight of redundancy loss to see how redundancy loss affects the feature selection performance. Figure 2(a) shows the feature selection performance of our model on Cora dataset in terms of ACC when λ_r vary as $\{0, 0.1, 0.2, ..., 0.5\}$. Figure 2(b) reports the results on Citeseer dataset. From the results we can observe that our model achieves its best performance with $\lambda_r = 0.2$ and 0.3 on Cora and Citeseer dataset respectively. For Cora dataset, performance is strengthened by the redundancy loss as λ_r goes from 0 to 0.2. However, when λ_r varies from 0.2 to 0.5, the accuracy goes down. The reason is that our model focus on the correlation between features too much to take into account linkage information and content information.

5   Conclusions and Future Work

In this paper, we propose an unsupervised network feature selection model, called MDFS. Our model takes both linkage information and content information into account to guide the selection process. For linkage information, we leverage the random walk based model to capture multi-order proximities between nodes. An auto-encoder is used to capture the content information of nodes. At last, we design a redundancy loss to avoid selecting highly-overlapping features. From experiments, we can see that our model outperforms other state-of-the-art unsupervised network feature selection models on two real-world network datasets.

However, there are many future work directions for us to investigate. First of all, nodes and edges in our model are homogeneous. That is to say, nodes and edges only have one type. Heterogeneous information networks (HINs) [17] are a powerful tool to represent multi-typed relational data. We would like to extend our work to HINs. Secondly, our model is static. Sometimes, the real-world network may change with time. We also would like to extend our work to dynamic networks in the future.

Acknowledgements. This work was partly supported by the National Natural Science Foundation of China under Grant No.61572002, No.61170300, No. 61690201, and No.61732001.

References

1. Chen, J., Zhang, Q., Huang, X.: Incorporate group information to enhance network embedding. In: Mukhopadhyay, S., et al. (eds.) Proceedings of the 25th ACM International Conference on Information and Knowledge Management, CIKM 2016, Indianapolis, IN, USA, 24–28 October 2016, pp. 1901–1904. ACM (2016)
2. Ding, C.H.Q., Peng, H.: Minimum redundancy feature selection from microarray gene expression data. In: 2nd IEEE Computer Society Bioinformatics Conference, CSB 2003, Stanford, CA, USA, 11–14 August 2003, pp. 523–529. IEEE Computer Society (2003)
3. Grover, A., Leskovec, J.: node2vec: scalable feature learning for networks. In: Krishnapuram, B., Shah, M., Smola, A.J., Aggarwal, C.C., Shen, D., Rastogi, R. (eds.) Proceedings of the 22nd ACM SIGKDD International Conference on Knowledge Discovery and Data Mining, San Francisco, CA, USA, 13–17 August 2016, pp. 855–864. ACM (2016)
4. He, X., Cai, D., Niyogi, P.: Laplacian score for feature selection. In: Advances in Neural Information Processing Systems 18, Neural Information Processing Systems, NIPS 2005, Vancouver, British Columbia, Canada, 5–8 December 2005, pp. 507–514 (2005)
5. Hinton, G.E., Zemel, R.S.: Autoencoders, minimum description length and helmholtz free energy. In: Cowan, J.D., Tesauro, G., Alspector, J. (eds.) Advances in Neural Information Processing Systems 6, 7th NIPS Conference, Denver, Colorado, USA, pp. 3–10. Morgan Kaufmann (1993)
6. Li, J., Hu, X., Tang, J., Liu, H.: Unsupervised streaming feature selection in social media. In: Bailey, J., et al. (eds.) Proceedings of the 24th ACM International Conference on Information and Knowledge Management, CIKM 2015, Melbourne, VIC, Australia, 19–23 October 2015, pp. 1041–1050. ACM (2015)

7. Li, J., Hu, X., Wu, L., Liu, H.: Robust unsupervised feature selection on networked data. In: Venkatasubramanian Jr, S.C., Meira, W. (eds.) Proceedings of the 2016 SIAM International Conference on Data Mining, Miami, Florida, USA, 5–7 May 2016, pp. 387–395. SIAM (2016)
8. Li, J., Tang, J., Liu, H.: Reconstruction-based unsupervised feature selection: an embedded approach. In: Sierra, C. (ed.) Proceedings of the Twenty-Sixth International Joint Conference on Artificial Intelligence, IJCAI 2017, Melbourne, Australia, 19–25 August 2017, pp. 2159–2165. ijcai.org (2017)
9. Li, J., Wu, L., Dani, H., Liu, H.: Unsupervised personalized feature selection. In: McIlraith, S.A., Weinberger, K.Q. (eds.) Proceedings of the Thirty-Second AAAI Conference on Artificial Intelligence, (AAAI 2018), the 30th Innovative Applications of Artificial Intelligence (IAAI 2018), and the 8th AAAI Symposium on Educational Advances in Artificial Intelligence (EAAI 2018), New Orleans, Louisiana, USA, 2–7 February 2018, pp. 3514–3521. AAAI Press (2018)
10. Li, J., Zhu, J., Zhang, B.: Discriminative deep random walk for network classification. In: Proceedings of the 54th Annual Meeting of the Association for Computational Linguistics Volume 1: Long Papers, ACL 2016, Berlin, Germany, 7–12 August 2016. The Association for Computer Linguistics (2016)
11. Li, Z., Yang, Y., Liu, J., Zhou, X., Lu, H.: Unsupervised feature selection using nonnegative spectral analysis. In: Hoffmann, J., Selman, B. (eds.) Proceedings of the Twenty-Sixth AAAI Conference on Artificial Intelligence, Toronto, Ontario, Canada, 22–26 July 2012. AAAI Press (2012)
12. Mikolov, T., Sutskever, I., Chen, K., Corrado, G.S., Dean, J.: Distributed representations of words and phrases and their compositionality. In: Burges, C.J.C., Bottou, L., Ghahramani, Z., Weinberger, K.Q. (eds.) Advances in Neural Information Processing Systems 26: 27th Annual Conference on Neural Information Processing Systems 2013, Lake Tahoe, Nevada, United States, 5–8 December 2013, pp. 3111–3119 (2013)
13. Mu, C., Yang, G., Yan, Z.: Revisiting skip-gram negative sampling model with regularization. CoRR abs/1804.00306 (2018)
14. Perozzi, B., Al-Rfou, R., Skiena, S.: Deepwalk: online learning of social representations. In: Macskassy, S.A., Perlich, C., Leskovec, J., Wang, W., Ghani, R. (eds.) The 20th ACM SIGKDD International Conference on Knowledge Discovery and Data Mining, KDD 2014, New York, NY, USA, 24–27 August 2014, pp. 701–710. ACM (2014)
15. Ribeiro, L.F.R., Saverese, P.H.P., Figueiredo, D.R.: struc2vec: learning node representations from structural identity. In: Proceedings of the 23rd ACM SIGKDD International Conference on Knowledge Discovery and Data Mining, Halifax, NS, Canada, 13–17 August 2017, pp. 385–394. ACM (2017)
16. Sen, P., Namata, G., Bilgic, M., Getoor, L., Galligher, B., Eliassi-Rad, T.: Collective classification in network data. AI Mag. 29(3), 93 (2008)
17. Shi, C., Li, Y., Zhang, J., Sun, Y., Yu, P.S.: A survey of heterogeneous information network analysis. IEEE Trans. Knowl. Data Eng. 29(1), 17–37 (2017)
18. Tang, J., Liu, H.: Unsupervised feature selection for linked social media data. In: Yang, Q., Agarwal, D., Pei, J. (eds.) The 18th ACM SIGKDD International Conference on Knowledge Discovery and Data Mining, KDD 2012, Beijing, China, 12–16 August 2012, pp. 904–912. ACM (2012)
19. Wei, X., Cao, B., Yu, P.S.: Unsupervised feature selection on networks: a generative view. In: Schuurmans, D., Wellman, M.P. (eds.) Proceedings of the Thirtieth AAAI Conference on Artificial Intelligence, Phoenix, Arizona, USA, 12–17 February 2016, pp. 2215–2221. AAAI Press (2016)

20. Wei, X., Xie, S., Yu, P.S.: Efficient partial order preserving unsupervised feature selection on networks. In: Venkatasubramanian, S., Ye, J. (eds.) Proceedings of the 2015 SIAM International Conference on Data Mining, Vancouver, BC, Canada, April 30–May 2 2015, pp. 82–90. SIAM (2015)

21. Yang, Y., Shen, H.T., Ma, Z., Huang, Z., Zhou, X.: $l_{2,1}$-norm regularized discriminative feature selection for unsupervised learning. In: Walsh, T. (ed.) IJCAI 2011, Proceedings of the 22nd International Joint Conference on Artificial Intelligence, Barcelona, Catalonia, Spain, 16–22 July 2011, pp. 1589–1594. IJCAI/AAAI (2011)

22. Zhang, D., Yin, J., Zhu, X., Zhang, C.: Network representation learning: a survey. CoRR abs/1801.05852 (2018)

23. Zhao, Z., Liu, H.: Spectral feature selection for supervised and unsupervised learning. In: Ghahramani, Z. (ed.) Machine Learning, Proceedings of the Twenty-Fourth International Conference (ICML 2007), Corvallis, Oregon, USA, 20–24 June 2007. ACM International Conference Proceeding Series, vol. 227, pp. 1151–1157. ACM (2007)

24. Zhao, Z., Wang, L., Liu, H.: Efficient spectral feature selection with minimum redundancy. In: Fox, M., Poole, D. (eds.) Proceedings of the Twenty-Fourth AAAI Conference on Artificial Intelligence, AAAI 2010, Atlanta, Georgia, USA, 11–15 July 2010. AAAI Press (2010)

Distance Dependent Maximum Margin Dirichlet Process Mixture

Quan Nguyen[✉], Mikko Lauri, and Simone Frintrop

Department of Informatics, University of Hamburg, Hamburg, Germany
{nguyen,lauri,frintrop}@informatik.uni-hamburg.de

Abstract. We propose distance dependent maximum margin Dirichlet Process Mixture (STANDPM), a nonparametric Bayesian clustering model that combines distance-based priors with the discriminatively learned likelihood of the Maximum Margin Dirichlet Process Mixture. STANDPM generalizes the distance-based prior introduced in the distance dependent Chinese Restaurant Process for non-sequential distances and allows modeling of complex dependencies between data points and clusters. The generalized distance-based prior is formulated as an abstract similarity measurement between a data point and a cluster. Empirical results show that the STANDPM model with abstract similarity achieves state-of-the-art performances on a number of challenging clustering datasets.

Keywords: Dirichlet Process Mixture models ·
Chinese Restaurant Process · Gibbs sampling ·
Probabilistic clustering · Uncertainty modelling

1 Introduction and Related Work

Cluster analysis is an unsupervised technique that allows organizing a dataset into groups of similar data points. It has been widely applied to application domains such as data mining (King 2014) and image segmentation (Achanta et al. 2012). Due to the absence of prior information, a number of assumptions on the characteristics of the clusters, such as the number of clusters or the data generation process, are often needed to facilitate the clustering process. Reducing the number of such assumptions and explicitly modeling the uncertainty about the clusters have been one of the main research goals of this field. Several nonparametric Bayesian methods have been proposed to model the uncertainty about the number of clusters (Zhu et al. 2011), the generative model (Neal 2000) or the hierarchy of the clusters (Heller and Ghahramani 2005). One particular class of methods that has remained popular in the last two decades is the Dirichlet process mixture (DPM) models. The DPM models can be constructed using the Chinese Restaurant Process (CRP) (Aldous 1985) which specifies a prior distribution on the structure of the clusters. Viewing clusters as tables and data points as customers in a restaurant, CRP can be intuitively described as follows: a number of customers

A. C. Nayak and A. Sharma (Eds.): PRICAI 2019, LNAI 11671, pp. 188–200, 2019.
https://doi.org/10.1007/978-3-030-29911-8_15

sequentially enter a restaurant, and each of them chooses a table to sit at. If a customer sits at a table, he is said to have a *link* from himself to the table. Each customer can choose to link to an existing table with a probability proportional to the number of customers already sitting at that table, or he can start a new table with a probability proportional to a scaling parameter. The CRP prior works well when the dependencies between customers have no impact on the table configurations. A more complex model for dealing with complex temporal and spatial dependence between data points is the distance dependent Chinese Restaurant Process (ddCRP) (Blei and Frazier 2011). In ddCRP, a customer is linked to a customer instead of a table. In other words, a customer decides on another customer to sit with instead of a table to sit at. The prior probability of linking two customers depends on their pairwise distances.

DPM models often rely on Markov Chain Monte Carlo sampling techniques such as Gibbs sampling to approximate the posterior distribution of clusters. To keep the posterior inference tractable, DPM models are often limited by a number of assumptions such as conjugate prior. It is also challenging for these models to estimate the component parameters of the mixtures, especially for mixtures of high dimensional data (Chen et al. 2016). One recent model that attempts to overcome these limitations of CRP-based DPM models is the Maximum Margin Dirichlet Process Mixture (MMDPM) model (Chen et al. 2016). The MMDPM model turns the Gibbs sampling process into an online learning process that efficiently learns the component parameters of the clusters from high dimensional data. The learning process of MMDPM requires each cluster to be represented explicitly by a vector of component parameters. In contrast, ddCRP-based DPM models require an implicit representation of the clusters so that the clusters can be merged together during the Gibbs sampling process (Blei and Frazier 2011). Consequently, it has remained an open question of how to combine a distance-based prior and a discriminatively learned likelihood.

This paper proposes diSTANce dependent maximum margin Dirichlet Process Mixture (STANDPM) model, a nonparametric Bayesian clustering model that combines the usage of pairwise distances in the ddCRP prior and the learning process for the likelihood in the MMDPM. The central idea of STANDPM is to establish the link from a data point to a cluster via the links from that data point to the existing data points of that cluster. This technique allows STANDPM to use the pairwise distances between data points in the prior and avoid merging clusters during Gibbs sampling. The probability of linking a data point to a cluster in STANDPM depends on a similarity measurement between a data point and a cluster, denoted as *abstract similarity*. The term "abstract" refers to the fact that this similarity measurement is generally not a true distance metric. Figure 1 illustrates an example of the establishment of the links from a data point to two clusters during Gibbs sampling. The abstract similarity allows integrating domain knowledge through the prior function rather than direct regularization of the posterior inference process as in (Chen et al. 2014). Our work here also differs from the distance-based priors in (Dahl 2008) because the prior distribution in our model does not require normalization of

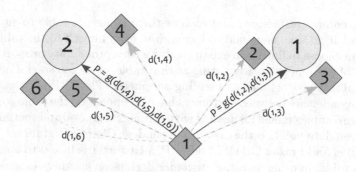

Fig. 1. Visualization of the probabilistic clustering process. The customers (data points) and tables (clusters) are illustrated by squares and circles, respectively. Customer 1 is choosing a table to sit. Customer 2 and 3 are sitting at table 1. Customer 4, 5, 6 are sitting at table 2. The prior probability $p(.)$ (solid arrows) of linking customer 1 to a table is proportional to the abstract similarity $g(.)$ between customer 1 and that table. The abstract similarity is a function of the distances (dashed arrows) from customer 1 to all existing customers of each table.

the customer assignment probabilities. We focus on the integration of pairwise distances into the posterior inference using Gibbs sampling instead of variational Bayesian techniques (Zhu et al. 2011). This paper has two main contributions:

(1) A novel, theoretically justified prior function which allows designing DPM models that have the distance-based clustering effects of ddCRP prior without sacrificing the efficient maximum margin likelihood of MMDPM.
(2) New state-of-the-art clustering performances for Bayesian methods on a number of large, high-dimensional datasets without being given the number of true clusters *a priori*.

2   Unsupervised Clustering with DPM Models

We consider the following problem: Let a set $\mathcal{X} = \{\mathbf{x}_i\}_{i=1}^N$ of N data points in $\mathbb{R}^D$ generated from an unknown number of mixtures in a mixture model and a pairwise distance function $d(i, j)$ measuring the dissimilarity between every pair of two data points be given. Estimate the number of mixtures and generate their corresponding clusters of data points.

The DPM model provides a Bayesian framework for modelling the posterior distribution over all possible clusterings of a dataset. In this framework, the data points can be seen as samples generated from K mixtures in a Dirichlet process mixture model $DP(G_0, \alpha)$ with symmetric DP prior (Chen et al. 2016):

$$
\begin{aligned}
\boldsymbol{\pi}|\alpha &\sim Dir(\alpha/K, \ldots, \alpha/K) \\
z_i|\boldsymbol{\pi} &\sim Discrete(\pi_1, \ldots, \pi_K) \\
\boldsymbol{\theta}_k &\sim G_0 \\
\mathbf{x}_i|z_i, \{\boldsymbol{\theta}_k\}_{k=1}^K &\sim p(\mathbf{x}_i|\boldsymbol{\theta}_{z_i})
\end{aligned}
\tag{1}
$$

where G_0 is the base distribution, α is the concentration parameter, π is the mixture weights, z_i is the cluster indicator and $\boldsymbol{\theta}_k$ is the parameter vector of cluster k.

While the exact computation of the posterior distribution is often intractable, it can be estimated by the samples generated using Gibbs sampling (Neal 2000). Data point $\mathbf{x}_i$ belongs to cluster k if there is a link $z_i = k$ between them. Denote the vector of all such links from all data points by $\mathbf{z}$. Gibbs sampling samples a cluster assignment of each data point from a conditional posterior distribution over z_i, keeping all other variables fixed. The conditional posterior in DPM is

$$
\begin{aligned}
p(z_i &= k|\mathbf{z}_{-i}, \mathbf{x}_i, \{\boldsymbol{\theta}_k\}_{k=1}^{K}, \alpha) \\
&= p(z_i = k|\mathbf{z}_{-i}, \{\boldsymbol{\theta}_k\}_{k=1}^{K}, \alpha) p(\mathbf{x}_i|z_i = k, \{\boldsymbol{\theta}_k\}_{k=1}^{K}) \\
&= p(z_i = k|\mathbf{z}_{-i}, \alpha) p(\mathbf{x}_i|\boldsymbol{\theta}_k)
\end{aligned}
\tag{2}
$$

where $\mathbf{z}_{-i}$ is the link vector $\mathbf{z}$ excluding the ith element. Above, $p(z_i = k|\mathbf{z}_{-i}, \alpha)$ is the prior and $p(\mathbf{x}_i|\boldsymbol{\theta}_k)$ is the likelihood of a data point $\mathbf{x}_i$.

2.1 The Distance-Dependent CRP Prior

Distance-based priors for DPM models have been studied extensively for their advantages in modelling complex relationships between data points. The popular ddCRP (Blei and Frazier 2011) uses the pairwise distances $d(i,j)$ to model the prior probability of linking two data points i and j. Note that ddCRP does not model the links from data points to clusters. Given a DPM model with ddCRP prior, when using Gibbs sampling for posterior inference, the action of merging two clusters is inevitable: any new link between two data points in two clusters will merge two clusters together, resulting in a larger cluster containing all data points from the two original clusters. Merging two clusters is possible in ddCRP because the components of the new cluster can be computed directly from all the data points in the two original clusters without taking into account the components of the two original clusters.

We denote a link from data point i to data point j by $c_i = j$. Let $\mathbf{c}$ be the vector of size N of all such links. The ddCRP prior probability of establishing a link $c_i = j$ is

$$
p(c_i = j|\mathbf{c}_{-i}, \alpha) \propto f(d(i,j))
\tag{3}
$$

where f is a decay function for controlling how distances affect the distribution over clusterings (Blei and Frazier 2011) and $\mathbf{c}_{-i}$ is the vector $\mathbf{c}$ excluding assignment of data point i.

2.2 The Maximum Margin Likelihood

Computing the likelihood for high dimensional data has been a long standing problem because of the intractability in computing the normalizing constants and updating the parameters of the likelihood distribution (Blei and Jordan 2005). The recent MMDPM model (Chen et al. 2016) solves this problem by replacing the generative model in DPM with a discriminative SVM classifier for learning the cluster components. Whenever a data point is assigned to or removed from a cluster, the cluster components are updated with respect to that data point only instead of re-computing the components from all data points in the cluster. The MMDPM model uses the vector of components $\boldsymbol{\theta}_k$ as an explicit representation for cluster k. The likelihood of linking a data point i to cluster k is

$$p(\mathbf{x}_i|\boldsymbol{\theta}_k) \propto \exp(\mathbf{x}_i^T \boldsymbol{\theta}_k - \lambda \|\boldsymbol{\theta}_k\|^2), \tag{4}$$

where λ is a regularization hyper-parameter to avoid trivial clustering results and control the separation between clusters. The MMDPM uses the standard CRP prior which relies only on the size of the clusters:

$$p(z_i = k|\mathbf{z}_{-i}, \alpha) = \frac{n_{-i,k}}{Z} \tag{5}$$

where $n_{-i,k}$ is the number of data points in cluster k excluding data point i, $Z = N - 1 + \alpha$ is the normalization factor. When $n_{-i,k} = 0$, $p(z_i = k|\mathbf{z}_{-i}, \alpha) = \alpha/Z$. In contrast to ddCRP, the CRP prior links data points directly to clusters.

2.3   Combining the ddCRP Prior and the MMDPM Likelihood

We focus on the question of using the prior in Eq. (3) for the conditional posterior in Eq. (2). During each iteration of the Gibbs sampling, the maximum margin online learning process in MMDPM takes each data point and its sampled cluster as a training example. In this training example, the data point is an input and the sampled cluster is the expected output. The component parameters $\{\boldsymbol{\theta}_k\}_{k=1}^K$ are updated only if the signed margin from the data point to its sampled cluster is not maximal among all clusters.

If the ddCRP prior were to be used directly, whenever two clusters are merged, the margins from the data points in the two clusters to all other clusters would have to be computed to simulate the process of linking all these data points to a new cluster. This would add a significant computational cost of $O(N^2 \times K \times D)$ to each iteration of the Gibbs sampling. Furthermore, this merging operation has a reverse effect to the learning process which tries to separate the clusters as much as possible. Since the clusters in MMDPM are explicitly represented and separately learned, merging them directly would be impractical. In this paper, we tackle this challenge by adapting the prior function to the max-margin likelihood learning process.

3   Distance Dependent MMDPM

We present the STANDPM model as an extension of the MMDPM model by replacing the CRP prior in MMDPM with an abstract similarity function. The STANDPM model resolves the challenge of combining the ddCRP prior and the MMDPM likelihood outlined in Sect. 2.3. We show that the abstract similarity generalizes the clustering effects in CRP and ddCRP priors.

3.1 Abstract Similarity in STANDPM

Let $\{\mathbf{x}\}^k$ denote the subset of data points currently linked to cluster k. In our new STANDPM model, the prior term in Eq. (2) is expressed as a function g of the data point i and $\{\mathbf{x}\}^k$:

$$p(z_i = k | \mathbf{z}_{-i}, \alpha) \propto g(\mathbf{x}_i, \{\mathbf{x}\}^k), \qquad (6)$$

where $g \colon \mathbb{R}^D \times \mathcal{X} \to \mathbb{R}^+$ is a non-negative function, $\mathcal{X}$ is a set of points in $\mathbb{R}^D$. If the cluster is new, this prior is set to $\frac{\alpha}{N}$. When $g(\mathbf{x}_i, \{\mathbf{x}\}^k)$ is a function of the pairwise distances, the link z_i is considered being drawn from a distance dependent prior.

We keep the likelihood in our model the same as in MMDPM. Substituting the prior in Eq. (6) and the likelihood in Eq. (4) into Eq. (2), we obtain the general form of the conditional posterior in STANDPM as

$$p(z_i = k | \mathbf{z}_{-i}, \mathbf{x}_i, \{\boldsymbol{\theta}_k\}_{k=1}^K, \alpha)$$
$$\propto g(\mathbf{x}_i, \{\mathbf{x}\}^k) \exp(\mathbf{x}_i^T \boldsymbol{\theta}_k - \lambda \|\boldsymbol{\theta}_k\|^2). \qquad (7)$$

The normalization factor for the prior distribution is

$$Z_i = \frac{\alpha}{N} + \sum_{k=1}^K g(\mathbf{x}_i, \{\mathbf{x}\}^k). \qquad (8)$$

Note that the normalization changes for different $\mathbf{x}_i$. The hyper-parameter α controls the probability of generating a new cluster. In practice, this normalization factor does not need to be computed since in each iteration of the Gibbs sampling, each data point is only processed once.

The function g can be selected so that if the data point i is similar to the set of data points in cluster k, then $g(\mathbf{x}_i, \{\mathbf{x}\}^k)$ will be large and vice versa. In this setting, g can be can be any non-negative function that expresses a similarity measurement from a data point to a cluster of data points, enabling the model to leverage possible structural information of a collection of data points. The prior function of this STANDPM model is defined entirely by the distances between data points and clusters.

Abstract Similarity Based on the Nearest Data point in a Cluster: One possible choice for the abstract similarity is a function of the minimum distances from a data point to the members of a cluster. This setting brings the neighborhood effect in which only a small and diverse set of the nearest neighbors of a data point influences its decision on which cluster to join, thereby encouraging clusters of different sizes instead of always favoring large clusters as the CRP prior.

This similarity measurement from a data point to a cluster is defined as

$$g_{\max}(\mathbf{x}_i, \{\mathbf{x}\}^k) = f(\min_{\mathbf{x}_j \in \{\mathbf{x}\}^k} d(i, j)) \qquad (9)$$

The subscript max reflects the fact that since f is a decreasing function, $f(\min_{x_j \in \{x\}^k} d(i,j)) = \max_{x_j \in \{x\}^k} f(d(i,j))$. We denote an STANDPM model with this g_{max} function *STANDPM-max.*

Abstract Similarity Based on All Data Points in a Cluster: This setting directly integrates the clustering effect of the ddCRP prior into MMDPM. In this case, the abstract similarity is a summation over all the links from a data point to the members of a cluster:

$$g_{sum}(\mathbf{x}_i, \{\mathbf{x}\}^k) = \sum_{x_j \in \{x\}^k} f(d(i,j)) \qquad (10)$$

An STANDPM model with the abstract similarity represented by g_{sum} function is denoted as *STANDPM-sum.*

3.2   Abstract Similarity Generalizes ddCRP and CRP Priors

The CRP and ddCRP priors can both be constructed from the abstract similarity g_{sum}. Recall that in each iteration of the Gibbs sampling, each data point i is processed once to select a cluster k among K existing clusters for linking.

Proposition 1. *Let a DPM model with the CRP prior, a uniform distance function $d(i,j) = \ln(Z)$ and an exponential decay function $f(d) = \exp(-d)$, where Z is the normalization factor in Eq. (5), be given. Then for the data point i and cluster k being processed in an iteration of the Gibbs sampling, $g_{sum}(\mathbf{x}_i, \{\mathbf{x}\}^k)$ is equal to the CRP prior probability of i linking to k.*

This proposition is a straightforward result of applying the given distance and decay functions to Eq. (10) which yields Eq. (5).

Proposition 2. *Let a DPM model with the ddCRP prior, any distance function $d(i,j)$ and decay function $f(d)$ be given. Then for the data point i and cluster k being processed in an iteration of the Gibbs sampling, $g_{sum}(\mathbf{x}_i, \{\mathbf{x}\}^k)$ is proportional to the ddCRP prior probability of i linking to k.*

Proof. Data point i will be linked to cluster k if it is linked to any data point already in that cluster. The probability of i linking to k is the sum of probabilities of links from i to any j in $\{\mathbf{x}\}^k$:

$$p(z_i = k | \mathbf{z}_{-i}, \alpha) = \sum_{x_j \in \{x\}^k} p(c_i = j | \mathbf{c}_{-i}, \alpha)$$

$$\propto \sum_{x_j \in \{x\}^k} f(d(i,j))$$

$$= g_{sum}(\mathbf{x}_i, \{\mathbf{x}\}^k), \qquad (11)$$

where the proportionality is due to Eq. (3).

Proposition 2 shows that the abstract similarity g_{sum} exhibits the same clustering effect as the ddCRP prior: data points whose distances are small will have high prior probability of being in the same cluster.

3.3 Time Complexity Analysis

The time complexity of each iteration in the Gibbs sampling of the proposed model depends on the specific implementation of the abstract similarity g. For g_{max} and g_{sum}, the time complexity of each iteration is $O(N^2 + N \times D^2 \times K)$, larger than the $O(N \times D^2 \times K)$ complexity of MMDPM. In practice, the speed of convergence depends strongly on the speed of reduction in the number of clusters K, so an MMDPM model converging to a large number of clusters might still be slower than a STANDPM model converging to a small number of clusters. In addition, the additional $O(N^2)$ is still orders of magnitude lower than the additional $O(N^2 \times K \times D)$ that would have been required if merging clusters was used. In general, the significance of the abstract similarity is in its ability to model a larger range of clustering effects and to integrate domain-specific constraints naturally for cluster analysis, rather than to reduce time complexity of the inference of a DPM model.

4 Experiments

We study the effectiveness of the two abstract similarity functions g_{max} and g_{sum} by comparing the two models STANDPM-max and STANDPM-sum with a number of baseline methods on several low and high dimensional datasets.

Baselines: The STANDPM is compared directly to three baseline models: ddCRP, DPM and MMDPM. We also include a number of other state-of-the-art clustering methods: Bayesian Nonparametric Kmeans (BN-Kmeans) (Kulis and Jordan 2012), Gaussian Mixture Model (GMM) (McLachlan et al. 2003), Spectral clustering, DP Variable Clustering (DPVC) Palla et al. (2012). Because BN-Kmeans, Spectral and GMM require a pre-defined number of clusters, they **do not** directly solve the problem of interest which involves estimating the number of clusters. In the experiments, they are given the number of ground truth clusters and their performances serve only as upper bounds for their respective approaches. When possible, some results of the baseline methods are taken from (Chen et al. 2016).

Datasets: The models are evaluated on 10 datasets shown in Table 1, including three synthetic datasets Aggregation, Jain and Flame (available online[1]); four small datasets from the UCI Machine Learning Repository: Wdbc, Glass, Iris, Wine[2]; the MNIST dataset[3]; two large datasets Reuters21578 (Cai et al. 2005) and 20 Newsgroup[4]. All datasets are pre-processed and normalized similar to (Chen et al. 2016) for a fair comparison. The Aggregation dataset is generated from 7 Gaussian mixtures and thus the performance of the DPM model is the upper bound for all other methods (Chen et al. 2016). The ddCRP model is not tested on Reuters21578 and 20 Newsgroup since it does not scale to these large datasets, taking more than 12 hours to complete a Gibbs sampling iteration.

---

[1] http://cs.joensuu.fi/sipu/datasets/.

[2] http://archive.ics.uci.edu/ml.

[3] http://yann.lecun.com/exdb/mnist/.

[4] http://qwone.com/~jason/20Newsgroups/.

Evaluation Measure: The clustering performance is measured in F-score (Rijsbergen 1979), V-score (Rosenberg and Hirschberg 2007) (equivalent to the Normalized Mutual Information metric 2011) and Adjusted Rand Index (ARI). F-score belongs to the class of pair-matching metrics which favors a high number of pairs of data points that are in the same clusters in two clustering results (Amigó et al. 2009). On the other hand, V-score belongs to the class of entropy-based metrics which measure homogeneity and completeness of clusters.

Table 1. Number of data points N, dimensionality D and number of classes of all datasets.

Dataset	N	D	#Classes
Jain	373	2	2
Aggregation	788	2	7
Flame	240	2	2
Wdbc	569	30	2
Glass	214	9	6
Iris	150	4	3
Wine	178	13	3
MNIST	2000	784	10
Reuters21578	8293	18933	65
20 Newsgroup	10000	61188	20

Hyper-Parameters Setting: The Euclidean distance metric is used for the computation of the pairwise distances in the prior function. The decay function has the form $f(d) = \exp(\frac{-d}{\gamma})$ where γ is a decay factor, $\min_{i,j} d(i,j) \leq \gamma \leq \max_{i,j} d(i,j)$. The generative model in ddCRP is specified by the Normal-Inverse-Wishart distribution. Similar to (Chen et al. 2016), we find that the hyper-parameter λ has the highest impact on the number of clusters. A random search on the range from 0.001 to 5 is used to tune λ. The number of burn-in iterations in all experiments is $T = 100$. After the burn-in phase, 5 clusterings are sampled and their average score is reported. All experiments are run on a computer with Intel(R) Core(TM) i7-5930K CPU 3.50GHz and 32 GB of RAM.

Results and Analysis

Small Low and High Dimensional Datasets: The clustering performance on the first 8 small datasets are shown in Tables 2 and 3. The STANDPM models

Table 2. Results by **F-score on the first 8 small datasets** of STANDPM and baseline methods. Bold numbers indicate the best scores for each data set. Underlined numbers indicate that the scores of STANDPM are better than or equal to MMDPM.

	ddCRP	BN-Kmeans	DPM	MMDPM	STANDPM-max(ours)	STANDPM-sum(ours)
Jain	0.37	0.57	0.59	0.73	<u>0.76</u>	**0.87**
Aggregation	0.59	0.77	**0.91**	0.79	<u>0.84</u>	<u>0.83</u>
Flame	0.63	0.627	0.43	0.6	<u>0.73</u>	**0.74**
Wdbc	0.61	0.80	0.43	0.85	<u>0.85</u>	**0.87**
Glass	0.39	0.49	0.49	0.51	**0.54**	<u>0.52</u>
Iris	0.75	0.74	0.71	0.75	<u>0.75</u>	**0.76**
Wine	0.33	0.87	0.36	0.68	<u>0.88</u>	**0.90**
MNIST	0.21	0.239	0.18	**0.368**	0.320	0.275

Table 3. Results by **V-score on the first 8 small datasets** of STANDPM and baseline methods. Bold numbers indicate the best scores for each data set. Underlined numbers indicate that the scores of STANDPM are better than or equal to MMDPM.

	ddCRP	BN-Kmeans	DPM	MMDPM	STANDPM-max(ours)	STANDPM-sum(ours)
Jain	0.43	0.46	0.46	0.41	<u>0.47</u>	**0.56**
Aggregation	0.81	0.76	**0.90**	0.75	<u>0.86</u>	<u>0.85</u>
Flame	0.52	0.53	0.41	0.29	**<u>0.63</u>**	<u>0.61</u>
Wdbc	0.003	0.51	0.26	0.57	<u>0.59</u>	**0.62**
Glass	0.03	0.30	0.43	0.38	**<u>0.46</u>**	<u>0.42</u>
Iris	**0.73**	0.71	0.66	0.68	**<u>0.73</u>**	0.67
Wine	0.03	0.78	0.42	0.48	<u>0.81</u>	**<u>0.85</u>**
MNIST	0.12	0.262	0.06	0.389	**<u>0.505</u>**	<u>0.45</u>

consistently outperform ddCRP and MMDPM in both F-score and V-score on all datasets. The clustering results on the synthetic Aggregation dataset are shown in Fig. 2. It can be observed that the separation between two rightmost clusters are captured almost perfectly by STANDPM, while MMDPM fails to do so, suggesting that the abstract similarity helps improving the max-margin likelihood learning process. In the task of character clustering on MNIST dataset, while slightly staying behind in F-score, STANDPM models outperform MMDPM by large margins in V-score. Without access to the true number of clusters, they also outperforms BN-Kmeans on all datasets.

Document Clustering: The Reuters21578 dataset consists of 8293 documents of 65 categories. This dataset is challenging because the distribution of data points into classes is highly unbalanced, with 44.77% of the data in one single class and nearly 80% of the data in the five largest classes. As a result, methods assuming a CRP prior with "richer get richer" effects such as DPM and MMDPM are advantageous over other methods. This advantage is reflected in Table 4 where DPM and MMDPM outperform other methods in F-score and ARI. However, both STANDPM models have higher V-score than MMDPM, indicating that clusters generated by STANDPM have higher degree of homogeneity and completeness simultaneously. We conjecture that the abstract similarity could not capture the imbalance in this dataset as effectively as the CRP prior because the Euclidean distances become less effective for high-dimensional and sparse features (Aggarwal et al. 2001). The same observation can be seen in (Chen et al. 2016) where the deterministic K-means with the true number of clusters failed to compete with MMDPM in F-score and ARI.

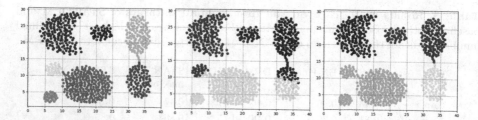

Fig. 2. Visualization of the ground truth (left), clustering output by MMDPM (middle, F-score = 0.79, V-score = 0.75) and clustering output by STANDPM-max (right, F-score = 0.84, V-score = 0.86) for the Aggregation dataset. Notice the data in the two rightmost classes are directly connected and yet the STANDPM is able to find an almost perfect separation between the two classes.

Table 4. Experimental results on **the Reuters dataset** of STANDPM in comparison with baseline methods. GMM and spectral clustering are provided with the ground truth number of clusters.

	GMM	Spectral	DPM	DPVC	MMDPM	STANDPM-max(ours)	STANDPM-sum(ours)
F-score	0.173	0.09	0.484	0.32	**0.507**	0.335	0.379
V-score	0.464	0.432	**0.472**	0.395	0.335	0.372	0.434
ARI	0.123	0.062	0.383	0.211	**0.416**	0.265	0.273

News Article Clustering: To further demonstrate scalability, we perform an additional experiment on the 20 Newsgroup dataset with 18846 documents of 61188 vocabularies. We extract 10000 documents and project them onto 250 most frequent words similar to (Chen et al. 2016). On this large dataset, the STANDPM-max model outperforms MMDPM by a large margin and achieves the best result in V-score; the STANDPM-sum model achieves the best result in F-score, tie with MMDPM. This shows that STANDPM scales up to large datasets. The results are given in Table 5.

Number of Generated Clusters: Figure 3 shows the number of clusters generated by STANDPM and MMDPM in comparison to the ground truth. Since the abstract similarity is less dependent on the size of the clusters, STANDPM tends to generate more clusters than MMDPM. In some cases, this leads to scattered clusters of small sizes. Since the summation in g_{sum} implies that large clusters tend to have higher prior probability, it often generates more clusters g_{max}.

Table 5. Experimental results on **the 20 Newsgroup dataset** of STANDPM in comparison with baseline methods. GMM and spectral clustering are provided with the ground truth number of clusters.

	GMM	Spectral	DPM	DPVC	MMDPM	STANDPM-max(ours)	STANDPM-sum(ours)
F-score	0.088	0.095	0.094	0.09	**0.10**	0.077	**0.10**
V-score	0.104	0.061	0.049	0.02	0.066	**0.18**	0.061

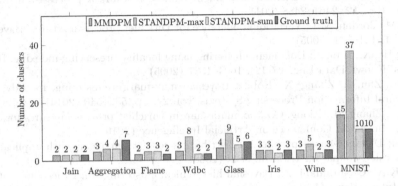

Fig. 3. Number of clusters generated by MMDPM and STANDPM for different datasets.

5 Conclusion

This paper introduces STANDPM model, an efficient and scalable solution to the challenge of integrating of the distance-based ddCRP prior into the max-margin discriminatively learned DPM model. The distances are integrated via the abstract similarity measurement between a data point and a cluster. The abstract similarity can be flexibly chosen so that either only a subset of nearest neighbors of a data point (g_{max}) or the whole set of data points (g_{sum}) contributes to the computation of the prior. We formally show that the abstract similarity can generalize the clustering effects of ddCRP prior and there exists efficient Gibbs sampling inference for its DPM models. Experimental results show that STANDPM models achieve state-of-the-art clustering performance on challenging real datasets without access to the true number of clusters.

References

Achanta, R., Shaji, A., Smith, K., Lucchi, A., Fua, P., Süsstrunk, S.: SLIC superpixels compared to state-of-the-art superpixel methods. IEEE Trans. Pattern Anal. Mach. Intell. **34**(11), 2274–2282 (2012). ISSN 0162–8828

Aggarwal, C.C., Hinneburg, A., Keim, D.A.: On the surprising behavior of distance metrics in high dimensional space. In: Van den Bussche, J., Vianu, V. (eds.) ICDT 2001. LNCS, vol. 1973, pp. 420–434. Springer, Heidelberg (2001). https://doi.org/10.1007/3-540-44503-X_27

Aldous, D.J.: Exchangeability and related topics. In: Hennequin, P.L. (ed.) École d'Été de Probabilités de Saint-Flour XIII — 1983. LNM, vol. 1117, pp. 1–198. Springer, Heidelberg (1985). https://doi.org/10.1007/BFb0099421

Amigó, E., Gonzalo, J., Artiles, J., Verdejo, F.: A comparison of extrinsic clustering evaluation metrics based on formal constraints. Inf. Retrieval **12**(4), 461–486 (2009). ISSN 1573-7659

Becker, H.: Identification and characterization of events in social media. Ph.D. thesis, Columbia University (2011)

Blei, D.M., Frazier, P.I.: Distance dependent chinese restaurant processes. J. Mach. Learn. Res. **12**, 2461–2488 (2011)

Blei, D.M., Jordan, M.I.: Variational inference for Dirichlet process mixtures. Bayesian Anal. **1**, 121–144 (2005)

Cai, D., He, X., Han, J.: Document clustering using locality preserving indexing. IEEE Trans. Knowl. Data Eng. **17**(12), 1624–1637 (2005)

Chen, C., Zhu, J., Zhang, X.: Robust Bayesian max-margin clustering. In: Advances in Neural Information Processing Systems, vol. 27, pp. 532–540 (2014)

Chen, G., Zhang, H., Xiong, C.: Maximum margin Dirichlet process mixtures for clustering. In: AAAI Conference on Artificial Intelligence (2016)

Dahl, D.: Distance-based probability distribution for set partitions with applications to Bayesian nonparametrics. In: JSM (2008)

Heller, K.A., Ghahramani, Z.: Bayesian hierarchical clustering. In: Proceedings of the 22nd International Conference on Machine Learning, ICML 2005, pp. 297–304. ACM, New York, NY, USA (2005)

King, R.S.: Cluster Analysis and Data Mining: An Introduction. Mercury Learning and Information, Herndon (2014)

Kulis, B., Jordan, M.I.: Revisiting k-means: new algorithms via Bayesian nonparametrics. In: Proceedings of the 29th International Conference on Machine Learning, ICML 2012, pp. 1131–1138. Omnipress, USA (2012)

McLachlan, G.J., Ng, S.K., Peel, D.: On clustering by mixture models. In: Schwaiger, M., Opitz, O. (eds.) Exploratory Data Analysis in Empirical Research. Studies in Classification, Data Analysis, and Knowledge Organization, pp. 141–148. Springer, Heidelberg (2003). https://doi.org/10.1007/978-3-642-55721-7_16

Neal, R.M.: Markov chain sampling methods for Dirichlet process mixture models. J. Comput. Graph. Stat. **9**(2), 249–265 (2000)

Palla, K., Knowles, D.A., Ghahramani, Z.: A nonparametric variable clustering model. Adv. Neural Inf. Process. Syst. **25**, 2987–2995 (2012)

Van Rijsbergen, C.J.: Information Retrieval, 2nd edn. Butterworth-Heinemann, Newton (1979). ISBN 0408709294

Rosenberg, A., Hirschberg, J.: V-measure: a conditional entropy-based external cluster evaluation measure. In: Proceedings of the 2007 Joint Conference on Empirical Methods in Natural Language Processing and Computational Natural Language Learning (EMNLP-CoNLL), pp. 410–420 (2007)

Zhu, J., Chen, N., Xing, E.: Infinite SVM: a Dirichlet process mixture of large-margin kernel machines. In: Proceedings of the 28th International Conference on Machine Learning (ICML 2011), ICML 2011, pp. 617–624. ACM, New York, NY, USA, June 2011

Dynamic Re-ranking with Deep Features Fusion for Person Re-identification

Yong Liu[1], Lin Shang[1(✉)], and Andy Song[2]

[1] Nanjing University, Nanjing, China
mg1733041@smail.nju.edu.cn, shanglin@nju.edu.cn
[2] Royal Melbourne Institute of Technology University, Melbourne, Australia
andy.song@rmit.edu.au

Abstract. State-of-the-art (STOA) person re-identification (re-ID) methods measure features extracted by deep CNNs for final evaluation. In this work, we aim to improve re-ID performance by better utilizing these deep features. Firstly, a Dynamic Re-ranking (DRR) method is proposed, which matches features based on neighborhood structure to utilize contextual information. Different from common re-ranking methods, it finds more matches by adding contextual information. Secondly, to exploit the diverse information embedded in the deep features, we introduce Deep Feature Fusion (DFF), which splits and combines deep features through a diffusion and fusion process. Extensive comparative evaluations on three large re-ID benchmarks and six well-known features show that DRR and DFF are effective and insensitive to parameter setting. With a proper integration strategy, DRR and DFF can achieve STOA re-ID performance.

Keywords: Person re-identification · Re-ranking ·
Deeply Learned Features · Features fusion

1 Introduction

Person re-identification (re-ID) [3] is to recognize and associate a person of interest across non-overlapping cameras. It becomes increasingly more important in real world applications but still remains a challenge. Because the same person observed in various cameras may appear different due to the large intra-class variations in illumination, poses, occlusions, and backgrounds. To compensate the appearance variation across cameras, most previous studies focus on two aspects: (1) extracting effective and robust visual features [11,23]; (2) learning an effective metric [5,21]. With the success of deep learning, features learned by this approach, or deep features for short, have demonstrated superior performance against hand-crafted ones and become dominant in the field of re-ID. The typical pipeline of deep feature based re-ID methods consists of two steps: feature extraction and feature matching. It first utilizes a well-trained network as the

© Springer Nature Switzerland AG 2019
A. C. Nayak and A. Sharma (Eds.): PRICAI 2019, LNAI 11671, pp. 201–213, 2019.
https://doi.org/10.1007/978-3-030-29911-8_16

feature extractor and then uses a certain distance metric such as Euclidean distance to identify the same person. Images with score high enough are considered positive.

Re-ranking, especially contextual re-ranking, is an effective step to boost the performance of re-ID [2,16,24]. The rationale behind contextual re-ranking is that images containing the same person should not only be similar in terms of visual content (*content similarity*), but also have similar k-nearest neighbors (*context similarity*) [8], meaning having similar context. Contextual re-ranking takes a distance matrix as input and updates it to be a new metric using the additional contextual information. Once the new metric is obtained, the re-ranking method can be re-applied iteratively. Existing iterative re-ranking methods do not consider the factor that the effectiveness of the new metric changes during the iterations [24]. To tackle this issue, we propose a dynamic re-ranking method named DRR, in which the use of contextual information automatically increases along the iterations so more matches can be considered. Apart from contextual information, diversity of the deep features can also be utilized to improve re-ID performance. Inspired by the idea of "Divide and Fuse" in [24], we introduce Deep Feature Fusion (DFF), which incorporates the diversity information embedded in the deep features by a diffusion process [6,18]. Both DRR and DFF transform the distance metric, they can be integrated. Hence we examine strategy for the integration as well to further improve the effectiveness of re-ID. In summary the three main contributions of this study are:

- Dynamic Re-ranking (DRR), utilizing more contextual information to consider more matches by better exploiting the neighborhood structures.
- Deep Feature Fusion (DFF), integrating diversity information from sub-features to improve re-ID.
- An effective strategy to integrate DRR and DFF to achieve more effective re-ID.

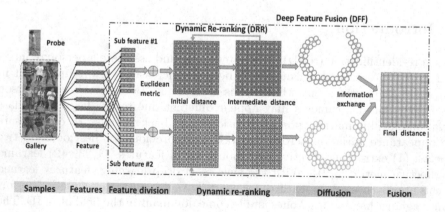

Fig. 1. Overview of the proposed method in the case of S ($S = 2$) sub-features.

2   Related Work

Re-ranking and features fusion are two essential areas of this study, hence the focus of related prior works.

2.1   Re-ranking

Re-ranking contains two main approaches: manifold ranking and contextual re-ranking. In manifold ranking, a similarity or affinity matrix is interpreted as a graph where the weight represents the affinity of two data points. Its key component is the diffusion process which propagates the affinity information on the graph. Compared to the traditional pairwise affinity which measures the similarity between two data points, the diffusion process takes a global view and explores the affinity information among all data points. Manifold ranking can be further divided into two types, diffusion on a single graph [6,22] and on multiple graphs [18,26]. The latter is designed for fusion of features or metrics, named as fusion by diffusion. In particular, each affinity matrix (based on a specific feature or metric) is interpreted as a graph and the affinity information is spread over multiple graphs. Fusion-by-diffusion not only captures the intrinsic manifold structure, but also leverages the complementarity of multiple visual features or multiple metrics. In comparison contextual re-ranking methods achieved excellent performance in recent years [1,24,30]. In contextual re-ranking, the similarity of two data points is re-defined by the similarity of their rank lists for a query. The rank list is usually a short list containing the top k nearest neighbors instead of all data points. The rationale of contextual re-ranking is to utilize contextual information as similar data should have similar neighbors.

2.2   Features Fusion

Features fusion has been proven effective in object retrieval [25,26] and re-ID [12,28]. For example, [28] fuses the hand-crafted features and deep features. But obtaining multiple features can be burdensome. [24] proposed "Divide and Fuse" (DaF) to exploit deep feature information under the framework of features fusion. The basis of [24] is that the characteristics of different parts of a deep feature can be rather diverse [24]. DaF divides a feature into sub-features, then fuses sub-features by a fuzzy aggregation operator. Existing fusion strategies for multiple features [12,28] or multiple sub-features [24] can be classified as weighted linear combination. But they do not utilize the rich diversity information embedded in the data points. The fusion-by-diffusion process mentioned above can address this issue effectively. Therefore we propose a Deep Feature Fusion (DFF) method based on this. It simultaneously leverages "Divide and Fuse" and the fusion-by-diffusion process: fusion of partial deep features.

3   Methodology

The overall architecture of the proposed method is illustrated in Fig. 1. Firstly, each feature obtained through deep learning is split into S sub-features and

S distance metrics are obtained. Secondly, the dynamic re-ranking (DRR) re-defines each metric to a new metric. Thirdly, S re-defined metrics are fused into a single one by the deep feature fusion (DFF) for the final evaluation. The details of DRR and DFF are presented in Sects. 3.1 and 3.2 respectively, while Sect. 3.3 describes the integration strategy.

3.1   Dynamic Re-ranking (DRR)

Consider a probe p from camera a and a gallery set $G = \{g_i | i = 1, 2, \cdots, M\}$ with M images from camera b. The Euclidean distance for an image pair (p, g_i) can be calculated, denoted as $D_E(p, g_i)$. The goal of re-ID is to search in G for images containing the same person with p. Therefore, G is sorted in an ascending order according to their distance to p and the initial rank is obtained:

$$L(p, G) = \{g_{(i)} | i = 1, 2, \cdots, M\} \tag{1}$$

The subscript (i) is enclosed within parenthesis indicating that i is the position in the rank list. Images in top ranks are likely to be the true matches. Most of the false matches can be removed easily with $L(p, G)$. However, some false matches may also be included in the top ranks. Hence, re-ranking is an important step to boost the performance. After re-ranking, the ranks of true matches will rise and the ranks of false alarms will decline. The goal of re-ranking is to learn a function:

$$f : D \to D' \tag{2}$$

It takes a distance metric D (usually Euclidean distance) as input and outputs a more effective one. The core idea is that the distance between two points is replaced by the generalized distance between their k-nearest neighbors. But the k-nearest neighbor relationship is asymmetric since $q_2 \in top_k(q_1) \to q_1 \in top_k(q_2)$, where $top_k(q)$ represents k-nearest neighbors of q. To encode stronger neighborhood information, [13] defines the k-reciprocal neighbor relationship as follows:

$$r_k(q_1, q_2) = q_2 \in top_k(q_1) \ \& \ q_1 \in top_k(q_2) \tag{3}$$

$r_k(q_1, q_2)$ is either 0 or 1, with 1 indicating that q_1 and q_2 are the k-nearest neighbors with each other. The k-reciprocal neighbor relationship is obviously symmetric and encodes stronger neighborhood information than the k-nearest neighbor relationship. Based on the k-reciprocal neighbor relationship, the k-reciprocal feature of the image q_1 can be computed as:

$$R(q_1) = \{q_2 | r_k(q_1, q_2) = 1\} \tag{4}$$

Note that $R(*)$ is a set instead of a vector. Accordingly the distance of a pair (q_1, q_2) is measured by the generalized Jaccard distance. The smaller D_J is, the more co-neighbors between q_1 and q_2 there are.

$$D_J(q_1, q_2) = 1 - \frac{|R(q_1) \cap R(q_2)|}{|R(q_1) \cup R(q_2)|} \tag{5}$$

Most of the re-ranking methods in re-ID use a procedure similar to the above. While in k-reciprocal encoding re-ranking [30], the re-ranking incorporates D_E and D_J to obtain a more robust metric, where D_E represents Euclidean distance. The final distance of an image pair (q_1, q_2) is calculated as below. This is simple yet effective.

$$D_F(q_1, q_2) = D_E(q_1, q_2) + D_J(q_1, q_2) \qquad (6)$$

Because the input and output of re-ranking algorithms are both distance metrics, iterative approach can be adopted naturally. However, the existing iterative re-ranking algorithm [24] in re-ID does not consider the factor that the effectiveness of the distance metric increases along iterations. Figure 2 shows an example of that fact. It gives top-20 ranks for a given query along two iterations. After the first round of re-ranking, there are 10 false matches and most of them receive high ranks. After the second round, only 7 false matches with relatively lower ranks are included in top-20 ranks. Existing iterative re-ranking method, refers to *vanilla version*, sets the number of nearest neighbors to a fixed value, as in Fig. 2, $k = 9$. The parameter k is the amount of contextual information that can be utilized. Excessive contextual information may introduce noises hence harm the performance. Therefore, k is usually set to a small value conservatively as shown in the first round of Fig. 2. However, with careful consideration, the increasing effectiveness of the distance metric along iterations can be utilized to include more contextual information and boost re-ID performance. Therefore, we propose the Dynamic re-ranking method, DRR, in which the k value changes during each round, instead of being a fixed value. As shown in Fig. 2, k is increased to $k + c$ after each iteration:$k_{i+1} = k_i + c$, where c is a constant and set to 1 in this paper. By this approach more matching images can be considered.

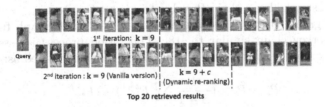

Fig. 2. Example of the Dynamic Re-ranking. Red boxes are false matches. 1st iteration: 10 false matches; 2nd iteration: 7 false matches. (Color figure online)

3.2 Deep Feature Fusion (DFF)

Deep features for re-ID are typically extracted by CNNs. Then the Euclidean distance is used for the final evaluation. In our method, a deep feature vector is split into multiple sub-features and then fuse them similar to [24]. The split generates S sub-features and consequently produces S different distance metrics, denoted as $\tilde{D} = \{D_s | s = 1, 2, \cdots, S\}$. More specifically, there are two stages in the process: graph construction and multi-graph fusion. The rational behind graph construction is to build a special graph to obtain geodesic distances which are better than Euclidean distance in hyper-dimensional space of features.

We first construct a graph for each metric D_s. Each D_s is represented as an affinity matrix. Then a finite weighted graph $G^s = (V_s, W_s)$ can be generated from the matrix, where the vertex set V_s represents all images in the data collection, each vertex corresponding to one image. Edge weight W_s represents the strength of the connection between two given vertices in V_s. A stronger W_s represents higher similarity between a pair of images. The similarity of an image pair can be calculated as:

$$W_s(i,j) = exp(-D_s(i,j)). \tag{7}$$

Based on the graph a Markov chain can be constructed for each graph to obtain the transition probability of the graph as defined below:

$$P_s(i,j) = \frac{W_s(i,j)}{\sum_{n=1}^{N} W_s(i,n)}, \tag{8}$$

where the denominator is the total weight of vertex i over N images. $P_s(i,j)$ represents the transition probability of i to j using the s-th sub-feature. A higher $P_s(i,j)$ value implies a higher probability that images i and j are from the same person. In addition, to reduce the influence of noisy data points, a local transition probability is used:

$$\hat{P}_s(i,j) = \begin{cases} P_s(i,j) & j \in top_n(i) \\ 0 & otherwise, \end{cases} \tag{9}$$

where "local" here refers to the top_n-nearest neighbors. For images outside of the top_n-nearest neighbors, their $\hat{P}_s$ value to i is set to zero.

After the graph construction, the second stage is multi-graph fusion using a mixture Markov chain similar to [18]. The fusion process is essentially an iterative random walk on multiple graphs. The process is defined as:

$$P_s^t = \hat{P}_s \times (\frac{1}{S-1} \sum_{s' \neq s} P_{s'}^{t-1}) \times (\hat{P}_s)^T, \tag{10}$$

where $\hat{P}_s$ is the transition matrix; the component in the first parenthesis is the average status matrix after $t-1$ iterations; and P_s^t is the status matrix under s-th sub-feature after t iterations. The above equation can be viewed as interactions among multiple graphs, hence essentially an information exchange process between sub-features. After t iterations, the overall status matrix is calculated as: $P^* = \frac{1}{S} \sum_{s=1}^{S} P_s^t$. The final distance metric used for re-ID evaluations is computed as $D = \frac{1}{P^*}$.

The effectiveness of DFF is illustrated in Fig. 3 which shows the distance distribution of same person vs. different person, with and without DFF. The baseline is the ID-discriminative Embedding [29] fine tuned on ResNet [4]. DFF significantly improves the distribution compared to the non-DFF counterpart, as the distance between the same person is very small, almost close to zero, while the separation between "same person" and "different person" curves is nice and clear.

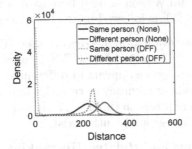

Fig. 3. The distance distributions with and without DFF

3.3 Integrating DRR and DFF

Both DFF and DRR can be integrated together. Figure 4 illustrates two strategies assuming image features are split into 3 sub-features (e.g. $S = 3$):

- DFF-DRR. Three metrics are first fused by the DFF into a single metric. Then the DRR is applied.
- DRR-DFF. Three metrics are re-defined by the DRR separately first. Then three re-defined metrics are fused into the final metric by the DFF.

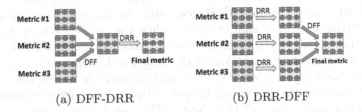

(a) DFF-DRR   (b) DRR-DFF

Fig. 4. Combination strategies of DRR and DFF when $S = 3$. (a) Metrics are first fused and then re-ranked. (b) Metrics are first re-ranked and then fused.

4 Experiments

4.1 Datasets and Settings

Datasets. Three commonly used benchmarks, namely Market-1501 (Market) [27], DukeMTMC-reID (Duke) [14] and CUHK03 [9], are used. Market contains 32,668 images of 1,501 identities taken from six cameras. The training set has 12,936 images of 751 identities and the test set 19,732 images of 750 identities. Duke consists of 1,404 identities captured by eight cameras. The training set contains 16,522 images of 702 identities, the test set 17,661 images of 702 identities. CUHK03 contains 13,164 images of 1,360 identities under two cameras. Two versions are provided, one with manual labels and one with detected bounding boxes. The second version is used here as it is more challenging. The latest evaluation protocol [30] is followed instead of the single-shot protocol [9].

Evaluation Metrics. Two evaluation metrics are used. The first one is the standard Cumulated Matching Characteristics (CMC) curve [19]. The CMC curve shows the probability that a probe appears in different-sized candidate lists. We report the cumulated matching accuracy at rank-1, abbreviated as R-1. The second one is the mean average precision (mAP) [27]. It considers both the precision and the recall when multiple ground truths exist.

Feature Representations and Related Re-ranking Techniques. Six feature extractors are used in the evaluation:(1) the ID-discriminative Embedding [29] trained on CaffeNet (IDE(C) [7]); (2) ResNet-50 (IDE(R)) [4] ; (3) the Pose-Sensitive Embedding (PSE) [15]; (4) the Harmonious Attention CNN (Hacnn) [10]; (5) the Deep Anytime Re-ID (DaRe) [20]; (6) the Part-based Convolutional Baseline (PCB) [17]. In addition, we compare our method with state of the art re-ranking techniques: (i) the sparse contextual activation (SCA) [1], (ii) the k-reciprocal encoding (k-RE) [30] and (iii) the divide and fuse (DaF) [24].

4.2 Evaluation on the Proposed Methods

DRR vs. The Vanilla version: In DRR, we use a dynamic value of reciprocal neighbors, i.e., k, while the vanilla version uses a fixed k. Fig. 5 shows the effectiveness of DRR on Market dataset with different initial k values set as $5, 10, 15, 20$ respectively on IDE(R) features. The R-1 accuracy indicates the ability to retrieve the most similar match, while the mAP indicates the ability to find all true matches [17]. From the four plots we can see that DRR can consistently reach high mAP regardless of the initial k. In comparison, the vanilla version performed poorly when k is as low as 5. When k is 20, the mAP of both methods drops after the 4th iterations due to the negative effect of noisy data. In terms of R-1, DRR also performed better. The best R-1 was achieved by DRR when $k = 5$. This shows DFF allows a re-ranking start from a low k value and reaches optimal performance through the iteration. In addition, DRR is helpful in finding more matches because of its high mAP.

DRR vs. Other methods: Tables 1, 2 and 3, shows the comparisons between DRR, our other methods, Euclidean distance and three SOTA re-ranking methods on three datasets respectively. Both mAP and R-1 are presented on these tables. The best result of each row is highlighted in bold. Note, not all six features are available on these three data sets. We only use existing trained CNNs to extract features to ensure result reproduciblity and fair comparison.

As can be seen, the *DRR Only* column consistently shows better performances than its counterparts on its left, both on mAP and R-1. For example, on the Market dataset, DRR gains a 16% (48.9%–32.9%) increase on IDE(C)

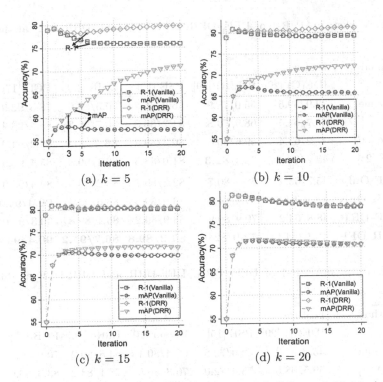

Fig. 5. The R-1 accuracy and mAP along iterations with different initial k: (a) $k = 5$, (b) $k = 10$, (c) $k = 15$, (d) $k = 20$ on Market. The baseline: IDE(R).

features and 17.9% (72.9%–55.0%) increase on IDE(R) features. Such a performance increase can be observed on all six features and all three datasets. In some occasion, DFF achieved the best performance. Such improvement shows DRR is effective in utilizing the contextual information through exploiting the neighborhood structures.

DFF using different splittings: As described early DFF divides features into sub-features. Three splitting modes are evaluated: Even, Hash and Random, denoting an event split, split by a hash table and random split. Table 4 shows the evaluation which is based on the Market dataset with parameter $S = 2$ and $c = 1$. As shown in the table, the three splitting methods are similar on mAP and R-1 except some differences on the PCB feature. In general random split is good hence used in the following evaluation whenever DFF is involved.

DFF vs. Other techniques: DFF as a standalone method is also listed in Tables 1, 2 and 3. DFF yields consistent improvements compared to baseline Euclidean. The improvement here in terms of mAP is in general larger than that in R-1. As mAP characterizes the ability to find all true matches, that means DFF can better utilizes features to identify more matches. More importantly, these results show DFF is effective as it can still achieve competitive performance

Table 1. Market: mAP/R-1 of DFF, DRR, DFF-DRR and DRR-DFF at different features.

Method	Feature				
	IDE(C) [29]	IDE(R) [29]	PSE [15]	DaRe [20]	PCB [17]
Baseline	32.9/59.5	55.0/78.9	65.0/86.3	76.5/89.6	78.5/92.9
SCA [1]	45.7/63.4	68.9/79.8	81.2/88.8	85.7/90.3	89.4/93.4
k-Re [30]	47.2/63.4	69.6/80.6	80.3/89.2	**86.7**/90.9	88.2/94.0
DaF [24]	48.2/**64.3**	72.4/**82.3**	81.0/88.5	86.1/90.8	85.4/91.9
DFF Only	45.2/63.4	68.5/80.7	82.2/89.7	85.2/90.5	89.4/93.9
DRR Only	**48.9**/64.2	71.4/81.3	83.9/89.5	86.6/90.4	**90.4**/94.0
DFF-DRR	48.8/64.2	70.9/80.9	83.9/89.2	86.1/89.8	90.3/94.0
DRR-DFF	**48.9**/64.1	**72.9**/82.0	**84.2/89.8**	**86.7/91.2**	**90.4/94.4**

Table 2. Duke: mAP/R-1 of DFF, DRR, DFF-DRR and DRR-DFF at different features.

Method	Feature				
	IDE(R) [29]	PSE [15]	Hacnn [10]	DaRe [20]	PCB [17]
Baseline	45.0/65.2	62.0/79.8	62.4/80.1	64.5/80.2	70.0/84.5
SCA [1]	59.5/68.5	75.9/82.0	76.3/80.5	78.1/83.2	83.3/86.6
k-Re [30]	56.7/69.8	74.4/82.8	73.3/82.0	**80.0**/84.4	80.9/87.5
DaF [24]	60.2/68.4	76.4/82.2	77.0/81.6	78.7/84.4	79.6/86.5
DFF Only	59.0/69.2	77.0/83.8	76.8/83.2	77.0/84.4	83.9/89.0
DRR Only	61.7/70.6	79.1/83.3	78.5/**83.4**	79.4/84.0	85.2/88.4
DFF-DRR	**61.9**/70.3	79.1/83.0	78.2/82.3	79.2/83.7	85.0/87.9
DRR-DFF	61.8/**71.2**	**79.4/84.3**	**78.7**/83.3	79.9/**84.7**	**85.6/88.5**

Table 3. CUHK03: mAP/R-1 of DFF, DRR, DFF-DRR and DRR-DFF at different features.

Method	Feature			
	IDE(C) [29]	IDE(R) [29]	DaRe [20]	PCB [17]
Baseline	14.2/15.1	19.7/21.3	60.0/64.6	53.9/59.1
SCA [1]	20.5/18.4	26.6/24.7	74.9/72.3	72.2/68.9
k-Re [30]	20.6/19.3	27.3/24.9	71.6/70.6	69.1/67.6
DaF [24]	21.4/19.3	30.3/26.4	74.5/72.0	62.1/60.4
DFF Only	19.8/19.2	26.8/26.7	72.5/71.9	68.2/68.1
DRR Only	21.9/**21.7**	29.6/**26.8**	76.5/75.0	73.6/71.0
DFF-DRR	22.6/19.8	30.4/26.4	76.8/74.9	**74.7**/71.6
DRR-DFF	22.5/21.6	**30.7/26.8**	**76.9/75.3**	74.7/**72.4**

Table 4. mAP/R-1 of DFF at different features and different splitting modes on Market.

Feature	Method		
	Even	Hash	Random
IDE (C)	45.1/63.1	45.2/63.5	45.2/63.4
IDE (R)	68.6/80.1	68.7/81.0	68.5/80.7
PSE	82.1/90.1	82.2/89.8	82.2/89.7
Hacnn	85.0/91.9	85.2/91.8	85.3/92.2
DaRe	85.4/90.9	85.2/90.3	85.2/90.5
PCB	84.0/92.2	89.5/94.1	89.4/93.9

compared with the three SOTA re-ranking methods, SCA, k-Re and DaF, even when re-ranking is not used.

DFF-DRR vs. DRR-DFF: Revisiting Tables 1, 2 and 3, we can see the comparison of two strategies of integrated DFF and DRR on the two right-most columns, DFF-DRR and DRR-DFF respectively. It is clear that DRR-DFF is consistently better than DFF-DRR, meaning sub-feature fusion based on dynamic re-ranking is more effective than re-ranking of fused sub features.

Overall Comparison: In general the methods presented in Tables 1, 2 and 3 are in ascending order from the left to the right in terms of mAP/R-1 performance. DRR appears as competitive method compared to other re-ranking methods. When combined with DFF properly, it can achieve SOTA performance on a given feature.

4.3   Analysis of Parameter S

The number of sub-features S in features splitting is a key parameter. Here we analyze its impact using the baseline feature, IDE(R), and the STOA feature, PCB on CUHK03, the the most challenging dataset among the three. Figure 6 shows the mAP obtained under different S values. The dotted lines are mAPs

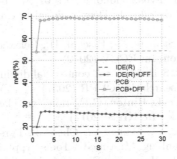

Fig. 6. The impact of the parameters S on CUHK03

using the two features when $S = 1$, effectively no splitting. We can see that splitting does bring significant benefits yet S does not change mAP much when S increases, despite of a minor decline of mAP on IDE(R). That shows DFF is insensitive to S. Such phenomenon can be also observed on other data sets using different features.

5   Conclusion

In this paper we aim to improve re-ID, mainly by better utilizing features generated through deep learning. Firstly we propose a dynamic re-ranking (DRR) to better use of contextual information. Secondly a deep feature fusion (DFF) method is introduced to split and fuse features for better utilization of diverse feature information. The extensive evaluation on six different features and three well known benchmark datasets shows that both DFF and DRR are effective in terms of improving re-ID, especially DRR, which outperformed three STOA re-ranking methods. Moreover when integrating DRR and DFF as a dynamic re-ranking on sub-features, namely DRR-DFF, STOA re-ID performance can be achieved on most cases. In addition, DRR-DFF method is insensitive to parameter setting yet robust in performance. Hence we conclude dynamic re-ranking with deep feature fusion is an effective and highly competitive method to utilize deep learning features for re-ID tasks.

Acknowledgments. This work is supported by the Natural Science Foundation of China (No. 61672276) and the Natural Science Foundation of Jiangsu Province of China (No. BK20161406).

References

1. Bai, S., Bai, X.: Sparse contextual activation for efficient visual re-ranking. IEEE Trans. Image Process. **25**(3), 1056–1069 (2016)
2. Garcia, J., Martinel, N., Micheloni, C., Gardel, A.: Person re-identification ranking optimisation by discriminant context information analysis. In: ICCV (2015)
3. Gong, S., Cristani, M., Yan, S., Loy, C.C.: Person Re-Identification. ACVPR. Springer, London (2014). https://doi.org/10.1007/978-1-4471-6296-4
4. He, K., Zhang, X., Ren, S., Sun, J.: Deep residual learning for image recognition. In: CVPR (2016)
5. Hirzer, M., Roth, P.M., Stinger, M., Bischof, H.: Relaxed pairwise learned metric for person re-identification. In: ECCV (2012)
6. Jegou, H., Harzallah, H., Schmid, C.: A contextual dissimilarity measure for accurate and efficient image search. In: CVPR (2007)
7. Krizhevsky, A., Sutskever, I., Hinton, G.E.: Imagenet classification with deep convolutional neural networks. In: NIPS (2012)
8. Leng, Q., Hu, R., Liang, C., Wang, Y., Chen, J.: Person re-identification with content and context re-ranking. Multimedia Tools. Appl. **74**(17), 6989–7014 (2015)
9. Li, W., Zhao, R., Xiao, T., Wang, X.: Deepreid: deep filter pairing neural network for person re-identification. In: CVPR (2014)

10. Li, W., Zhu, X., Gong, S.: Harmonious attention network for person re-identification. In: CVPR, vol. 1, p. 2 (2018)
11. Liao, S., Hu, Y., Zhu, X., Li, S.Z.: Person re-identification by local maximal occurrence representation and metric learning. In: CVPR (2015)
12. Mirmahboub, B., Mekhalfi, M.L., Murino, V.: Person re-identification by order-induced metric fusion. Neurocomputing **275**, 667–676 (2018)
13. Qin, D., Gammeter, S., Bossard, L., Quack, T., Van Gool, L.: Hello neighbor: accurate object retrieval with k-reciprocal nearest neighbors. In: CVPR (2011)
14. Ristani, E., Solera, F., Zou, R., Cucchiara, R., Tomasi, C.: Performance measures and a data set for multi-target, multi-camera tracking. In: ECCV (2016)
15. Sarfraz, M.S., Schumann, A., Eberle, A., Stiefelhagen, R.: A pose-sensitive embedding for person re-identification with expanded cross neighborhood re-ranking. In: CVPR (2018)
16. Shen, X., Lin, Z., Brandt, J., Avidan, S.: Object retrieval and localization with spatially-constrained similarity measure and k-NN re-ranking. In: CVPR (2012)
17. Sun, Y., Zheng, L., Yang, Y., Tian, Q., Wang, S.: Beyond part models: person retrieval with refined part pooling. In: ECCV (2018)
18. Wang, B., Jiang, J., Wang, W., Zhou, Z.H., Tu, Z.: Unsupervised metric fusion by cross diffusion. In: CVPR (2012)
19. Wang, X., Doretto, G., Sebastian, T., Rittscher, J., Tu, P.: Shape and appearance context modeling. In: ICCV (2007)
20. Wang, Y., et al.: Resource aware person re-identification across multiple resolutions. In: CVPR, pp. 8042–8051 (2018)
21. Xiong, F., Gou, M., Camps, O., Sznaier, M.: Person re-identification using kernel-based metric learning methods. In: ECCV (2014)
22. Yang, X., Koknar-Tezel, S., Latecki, L.J.: Locally constrained diffusion process on locally densified distance spaces with applications to shape retrieval. In: CVPR (2009)
23. Yang, Y., Yang, J., Yan, J., Liao, S., Yi, D., Li, S.Z.: Salient color names for person re-identification. In: ECCV (2014)
24. Yu, R., Zhou, Z., Bai, S., Bai, X.: Divide and fuse: a re-ranking approach for person re-identification. In: BMVC (2017)
25. Zhang, S., Yang, M., Cour, T., Yu, K., Metaxas, D.N.: Query specific fusion for image retrieval. In: ECCV (2012)
26. Zhang, S., Yang, M., Cour, T., Yu, K., Metaxas, D.N.: Query specific rank fusion for image retrieval. IEEE Trans. Pattern Anal. Mach. Intell. **37**(4), 803–815 (2015)
27. Zheng, L., Shen, L., Tian, L., Wang, S., Wang, J., Tian, Q.: Scalable person re-identification: a benchmark. In: ICCV (2015)
28. Zheng, L., Wang, S., Tian, L., He, F., Liu, Z., Tian, Q.: Query-adaptive late fusion for image search and person re-identification. In: CVPR (2015)
29. Zheng, L., Zhang, H., Sun, S., Chandraker, M., Yang, Y., Tian, Q.: Person re-identification in the wild. In: CVPR (2017)
30. Zhong, Z., Zheng, L., Cao, D., Li, S.: Re-ranking person re-identification with k-reciprocal encoding. In: CVPR (2017)

MFAD: A Multi-modality Face Anti-spoofing Dataset

Bingqian Geng[1], Congyan Lang[1(✉)], Junliang Xing[2], Songhe Feng[1], and Wu Jun[1]

[1] Beijing Jiaotong University, Beijing 100190, People's Republic of China
{bqgeng,cylang,shfeng,wuj}@bjtu.edu.cn
[2] Institute of Automation, Chinese Academy of Sciences,
Beijing 100190, People's Republic of China
jlxing@nlpr.ia.ac.cn

Abstract. Face anti-spoofing plays an important role in face recognition system to prevent security vulnerability. It acts as an important step to select the face image to the face recognition system. Previous works have provided many databases for face anti-spoofing, but they either contain too few subjects or contain a single modal. Moreover, due to the limited information of RGB images, the effect of face anti-spoofing is difficult to be further improved, High Dynamic Range (HDR) can be a good choice while many devices now support capturing HDR images. To facilitate further studies on face anti-spoofing, we in this work build a dataset with 50 subjects for face anti-spoofing containing 2100 videos, which containing two different modalities, HDR and Near Infrared Ray (NIR). We further study the influences of different modalities on the performance of face anti-spoofing by extensively experimenting with different combinations of modalities with an end-to-end deep learning model, and find that the HDR information contributes most among different modalities. Finally, we verify these findings on the CASIA-FASD dataset which demonstrates better performance of the proposed model.

Keywords: Face anti-spoofing · High dynamic range · Modalities fusion

1 Introduction

In recent years, biometric systems have been widely applied. Biometric systems recognize a unique person by biometric features such as fingerprint, iris, face, or behavioral characteristics. Face images are very easy to obtain in biometric recognition system. However, with the wide application of face recognition technology using in mobile phones and access control systems, anti-spoofing has become a potential huge security threat. Many people try to pass through face recognition systems by using photos, replay attacks, and 3D masks. Traditional

A. C. Nayak and A. Sharma (Eds.): PRICAI 2019, LNAI 11671, pp. 214–225, 2019.
https://doi.org/10.1007/978-3-030-29911-8_17

face recognition systems are difficult to identify face attacks, so face recognition system is in urgent need of anti-spoofing to ensure its robustness to different kinds of attacks.

In order to build a robust face anti-spoofing system, previous approaches [11, 23] have already explored this issue from multiple perspectives. First, the motion-based method [1,20], which attempts to use motions (such as eye blinking or head motion) to identify live videos. However, this method has two disadvantages. One is that it needs to be judged by special frames of images [5,19], which is sometimes not very fast. The other one is judgment method that can be cheated by video replay attack. Therefore, this kind of judgment method is rarely used in recent years. At present, more researchers try to find the differences between real faces and attacks by analyzing and judging the features of current images using machine learning. This requires a lot of data to train the model. As can be seen from the Table 1, the current datasets exist problems such as insufficient data quantity or large data quantity, less face postures in video and so on.

For the past few years, convolutional neural networks (CNN) have made remarkable achievements in computer vision tasks, especially in image classification and image segmentation. CNN has also been used in face anti-spoofing. CNN has strong ability of feature extraction and information fusion, so it brings new inspiration for face anti-spoofing with multi-modals. Some recent work [18] attempts to train an end-to-end network and uses the multi-modals as auxiliary information for supervised learning. Limited by the dataset, these methods constrain the training of the network by generating different modals from ordinary images or enhancing the data. In [22], they are trying to use near-infrared spectroscopy to do face anti-spoofing. However, all these work is to simulate the effect of multi-mode, and do not fundamentally solve the problem of no corresponding data. So, large multi-modal face anti-spoofing dataset is needed by academics.

To solve this problem, we introduce a new large multi-modal face anti-spoofing database "Multi-modal Face Anti-spoofing (MFA)", which consists of 50 subjects and 2100 video clips with 2 modalities (RGB and IR). It contains 10 real scenes and 11 attack scenes for one subjects. For print attacks, we ensure the scene consistency with the real face recording environments. In order to ensure that recorded videos can be more consistent with the actual situation, we record the real face with large angle changes. When it comes to print attacks, photos are also bent, tilted, rotated, and so on. In [28], HDR is mentioned but not given enough attention. In order to verify the effectiveness of HDR images, we use an HDRCNN [10] network to generate HDR images from ordinary RGB images, classify them and then verify them on the CASIA-FASD dataset [28] to achieve better performance, but the performance is still lower than the native HDR dataset.

We summarize the main contributions of our work in three-fold.

- We release a new database that contains HDR and NIR videos.
- We study the influences of different modalities on the performance of face anti-spoofing.
- We achieve better performance on the CASIA-FASD dataset with HDR images generated.

2   Related Work

We review previous work in the following three relevant groups: datasets,methods and HDR image generation.

2.1   Datasets

Currently, most datasets commonly used in face anti-spoofing only have RGB modality. For example, Replay-attack and CASIA-FASD, the most extensive data used for face anti-spoofing, only have RGB modality. Although many face anti-spoofing algorithms [2] have achieved better results in replay-attack data, the algorithms based on CNN [24] continue to improve performance on the CASIA-FASD dataset.

With the wide application of smart phones, face detection algorithms applied on mobile phones have also attracted attention. Some face anti-spoofing datasets use mobile phones to collect data and simulate the application of mobile phone unlock system, such as Replay-Mobile,MSU-MFSD and Oulu-NPU. But they're also RGB data only.

Table 1. The comparison of the anti-spoofing datasets (* means this dataset only have images)

Dataset	Year	# of subjects	# of videos	Modal types	Pose range	Spoof attacks
Replay-Attack [6]	2012	50	1200	RGB	Frontal	Print 2 Replay
CASIA-FASD [28]	2012	50	600	RGB	Frontal	Print Replay
MSU-MFSD [9]	2015	35	440	RGB	Frontal	Print 2 Replay
Replay-Mobile [8]	2016	40	1030	RGB	Frontal	Print Replay
Msspoof [7]*	2016	21	-	RGB/IR	Frontal	Print 2 Replay
Oulu-NPU [5]	2017	55	5940	RGB	Frontal	2 Print 2 Replay
MFA (Ours)	2018	50	2100	RGB/IR	[−45,45]	2 Print 2 Replay

With the development of attacking methods, the ways of attack become more and more various. A new type of silicone masks [3] easily passes many face anti-spoofing systems. Therefore, we need more effective methods to deal with new types of attacks. Existing methods are difficult to improve due to the limitation of RGB images. Some people have begun to explore the influence of multi-modals on face anti-spoofing systems. Msspoof [7] is a dataset available which includes RGB images and near-infrared images, but only 21 subjects are included. So it is necessary to build a dataset containing both HDR images and NIR images.

We introduce a new large multi-modal face anti- spoofing database "Multi-modal Face Anti-spoofing (MFA)", which consists of 50 subjects and 2100 video clips with 2 modalities (RGB and IR). It has 10 real scenes and 11 attack scenes for one subjects.

2.2 Methods

Most of the previous work uses hand-crafted features, such as LBP [19], DoG [23] and SURF [5] to map face images to low-dimensional feature vectors. Then the extracted feature vectors are fed into the traditional machine learning algorithm to construct face anti-spoofing system. However, hand-crafted features cannot cover all kinds of situations. Therefore, changes in illumination, camera devices and human postures bring great challenges to face detection face anti-spoofing system. Researchers also use color space, Fourier space, optical flow maps and temporal domain to overcome some of these difficulties. But these algorithms are only applicable to small datasets with poor generality.

Another method commonly used in face anti-spoofing is motion detection. Eye-blinking is a useful cue that is mentioned in [20] to detect fake face, but can be poor in a print attack. In [1], Anjos et al. identify fake faces by analyzing the motion relationship between face region and background. However, this algorithm is obviously useless in replay attack. But NIR can identify the different materials of objects. Due to the significant difference between player media surface and skin, NIR can solve this attack well.

In recent years, CNN has demonstrated superior performance in many computer vision tasks. In [12], CNN is trained as a feature extraction network. Through the trained network, the feature vectors of face images are obtained, and the extracted feature vectors are classified by using the traditional classification algorithm. In [22], Sun et al. attempt to use NIR to distinguish face information. In [18], a variety of data such as depth map and rPPG are mixed to train the network as auxiliary information. In [24], Tang et al. further improves his performance on CASIA-FASD. These attempt to extract more modal information from RGB images have inspired us to build a multi-modals dataset.

2.3 HDR Image Generation

High dynamic range images (HDR) can provide more dynamic range and image details than ordinary images. HDR images are obtained through parts of multiple photos with different exposure times. However, our common cameras can only capture ordinary RGB images. In [14], CNN is trained to generate HDR images from a single RGB image. Many face anti-spoofing systems are realized by judging the minutia of face images, while HDR images can provide more detailed parts. Therefore, we believe that the generation of HDR can be effectively used in the face in face anti-spoofing. In the knowledge that we already know, there is few previous work trying to use RGB images to generate HDR images and then determine whether the image is a real person or not. Here, we use the HDRCNN network to produce the corresponding HDR images in CASIA-FASD dataset to verify the effect of HDR image.

3 The Face Anti-spoofing Dataset with HDR and NIR

As can be known from the above, these datasets contain fewer subjects and most datasets only include RGB images. These datasets have promoted the

LED Opened   **LED Closed**

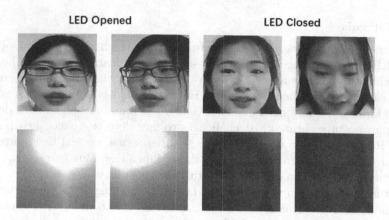

Fig. 1. Examples of images with infrared LED opened or closed in the MFA dataset.

development of face anti-spoofing technology and many researchers have further improved the performance of face anti-spoofing using datasets published at an earlier time. But in the case of high security requirements such as payment and unlock system, the current effect is not very ideal. In order to make better use of multi-modal information, we construct a new dataset of HDR and NIR video for face anti-spoofing. In 2100 videos contains 50 Chinese people. In the dataset we proposed, each subject has 10 live videos and 11 fake videos. In order to make the data more authentic, we select 10 different real locations with different background conditions and lighting conditions. Because the recording is done over a period, the conditions and intensity of sunlight vary. This is more consistent with our real usage environment. In each location we record a live video and a paint attack video. We find that monochrome photos seem to have clearer results in the NIR when the light is dim, so we use half the color photos and half the monochrome ones. For near-infrared images, the acquisition equipment we used has infrared LED lights. When recording the replay attack of video, we partially block the LED light while others turn on the LED light. Comparison results are shown in Figure 1, this makes a big difference in replay attacks. Unlike other datasets, we only have one attack for each location. When different subjects are in the same place, they may attack in different ways. We try to suppress data over-fitting effectively using this method. The attacks we include are given below.

- Color photograph with bending, tilting, and rotating
- Monochrome photograph with bending, tilting, and rotating
- Replay-Attack with infrared LED lights
- Replay-Attack with no infrared LED lights

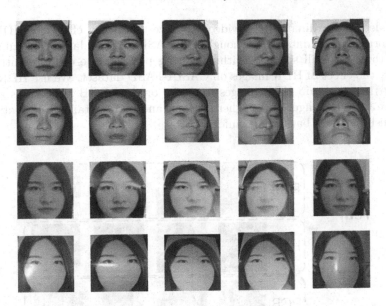

Fig. 2. Examples of different postures in the MFA dataset. The first two lines show different postures in the real image while the other two lines show different postures in the attack image

3.1 Collection Details

We use a special camera to capture HDR images and NIR images at the same time. For the print attack, we print the subjects' color/monochrome photos on A4 paper. During the recording, the human has to do certain actions, such as looking up, looking down, looking left, and looking right to ensure that at least 45 degrees of change have been recorded. The subjects are also asked to open their mouths to talk, blink, smile and so on to ensure that the contents of the dataset are as close to the real world as possible. When recording the print attack, we exhibit a variety of changes to the photos during recording, such as rotation, tilt, bending, etc., to try to simulate the real attack scene. During recording, we use the OpenCV toolbox to record video simultaneously, where both HDR and NIR video have a resolution of 1280 × 720 pixels. There are some examples which are detected by mtcnn [27] (an advanced face detection algorithm) and croped in Figure 2. Unlike the large proportion of men in other datasets, women account for 60% in our dataset. And in order to reflect the real situation, 60% of the subjects in the dataset wear glasses.

4   HDR Versus RGB Images

HDR images contain more detailed information than ordinary RGB images, so HDR images can provide more information for judging whether a face is real or not. But limited by the recording equipment, we cannot simultaneously collect

HDR video and ordinary RGB video. To investigate the effects of HDR, we use a normal RGB dataset. Although the CASIA-FASD dataset is published earlier, there are still some algorithms testing performance on it recently. So, we study the effect of HDR images on CASIA-FASD dataset. We use HDRCNN network [10] to obtain HDR images from the original RGB images. As shown in Figure 3, HDR images have higher contrast and more detailed information to distinguish face and background information.

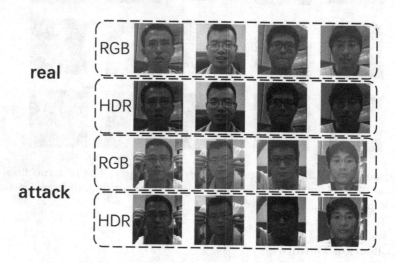

Fig. 3. Examples of RGB images, HDR images generated in CASIA-FASD dataset.

Recently the network ResNet50 [12] proposed by He et al. has a great performance in many areas of computer vision. We believe that this network can perform better. We crop out the face area, then scale the alignment image to 192 × 192 pixels, and then we feed the image into the ResNet50 network, which is pre-trained on the ImageNet [21]. We make the final fc layer output two classes and the kernel for avg-pooling is set as 6 to adapt to the size of the input image. Cross entropy is used to calculate loss. During the training, we set batch size to 80 and initialize the learning rate to 0.001. For HDR images and RGB images, the method we use is only different in the input images.

As shown in Table 2, Resnet50 with HDR images can achieve better performance on CASIA-FASD.

Table 2. Comparison on the CASIA-FASD database

Method	ERR (%)
DOG [28]	17.00
IDA+SVM [9]	12.90
Color texture [4]	6.20
CNN [26]	5.83
DPCNN [17]	4.64
CSURF [16]	4.50
Patch and depth [2]	2.80
MDF [25]	2.22
Resnet50	3.03
HDRCNN+Resnet50	1.68

Fig. 4. The HDR and NIR images in MFA dataset. This is a large multi-modal dataset containing 50 subjects and 2100 videos including HDR and NIR.

5 Benchmark for MFA Dataset

5.1 Data Preprocessing

In order to make the results more robust, we abandon the rich background information and only use face images for the face anti-spoofing. Firstly, we use the most advanced face detection algorithm [27] in HDR image to locate the face. Since the optical axis distance between our HDR and NIR acquisition equipment is 11.2 mm and in the case of a wide angle of view, we ignore the slight difference and argue that the acquired HDR image and NIR image have been aligned. Then we cut out the face image of corresponding frame as the training data and scale them to 224 × 224 pixels as input of our network. The face image and the original image are in Figure 4, where the first and third rows are HDR images while the second and fourth rows are NIR images.

5.2 Experimental Settings

Since face recognition systems are often deployed on terminal devices, we hope to use a relatively simple method to achieve the purpose of face anti-spoofing, so we chose a lightweight network SqueezeNet [13] to build the benchmark. SqueezeNet, with its lightweight, well-structured features, can be deployed in a variety of terminal devices with limited of storage space and computing power. We also try fusion at different levels, including fusion after the original channel fusion and feature extraction. As shown in Table 3, half-way fusion shows better performance. The network structure of halfway fusion is shown in Figure 5. We set the batch size to 64 and initialize the learning rate to 0.001.

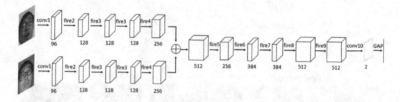

Fig. 5. The halfway fusion net in MFA dataset.

Table 3. Comparison of different Fusion methods on the MFA database

Method	ERR (%)
Channel fusion	0.50
Feature fusion	0.31
Halfway fusion	0.28

Unlike the ResNet50 network we used above, the training of SqueezeNet has become very complicated with the network often failing to converge and the result being volatile. We randomly divide datasets according to the ratio of 1:1:2, and the scale of test sets is the sum of the number of training sets and verification sets. When loss is not changing, we terminate the training. Although in the case of non-convergence, it is possible that the accuracy rate is 0.5, loss still remains unchanged.

5.3 Discussion

It can be seen from Table 4, the EER of HDR is 0.09% which is better than HDR&NIR's score of 0.28% and NIR's score of 0.48%. But there is a significant improvement of TPR at FPR@10^{-3} or FPR@10^{-4}. In [15], TPR has practical application significance only when FPR is at 10^{-3} or 10^{-4}. As shown in Figure 6, NIR can provide higher TPR performance when FPR is small, but with the increase of TPR, NIR performance is exceeded by HDR. Fusion of NIR and HDR results in a stable performance which makes the face anti-spoofing system more robust.

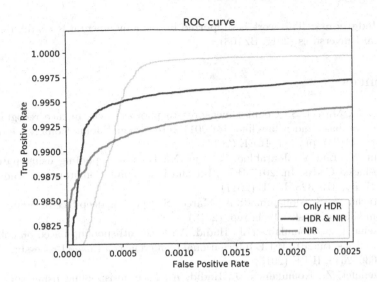

Fig. 6. ROC Curve of HDR and HDR&NIR modals in the MFA dataset.

Table 4. Effect on the number of modalities in MFA dataset.

Method	TPR (%)			EER (%)
	@FPR $= 10^{-2}$	@FPR $= 10^{-3}$	@FPR $= 10^{-4}$	
NIR	0.9927	0.9871	0.9824	0.48
HDR	0.9992	0.9788	0.9646	0.09
HDR&IR	0.9958	0.9870	0.9646	0.28

We also test the model trained on the HDR images of our dataset in CASIA-FASD and get EER = 37.89%. The EER of 41.94% is obtained when training on CASIA-FASD and testing in the HDR image of our dataset.

Although a relatively small neural network SqueezeNet is used in this work, it actually contains 10 layers of convolution, of which 8 layers are fire modules, and fire module contains multiple parallel convolution layers. In order to get more detailed information, the face image is scaled to 224 × 224 pixels, which undoubtedly increases the computational complexity. However, good results have been achieved in our dataset, which makes it possible to apply face anti-spoofing system in unlock, payment and other scenarios.

6   Conclusion

In this paper, we releas a face anti-spoofing dataset of HDR and NIR. This is the largest multi-modalitiy dataset as far as we know. We also verifi the validity of HDR images on the CASIA-FASD dataset. By generating HDR from RGB images, we achiev the better performance on the CASIA-FASD dataset. We also used a lightweight network to train our datasets and get benchmark results.

Acknowledgments. This work is supported by the Fundamental Research Funds for the Central Universities (2017JBZ108).

References

1. Anjos, A., Marcel, S.: Counter-measures to photo attacks in face recognition: a public database and a baseline. In: 2011 International Joint Conference on Biometrics (IJCB), pp. 1–7. IEEE (2011)
2. Atoum, Y., Liu, Y., Jourabloo, A., Liu, X.: Face anti-spoofing using patch and depth-based CNNs. In: 2017 IEEE International Joint Conference on Biometrics (IJCB), pp. 319–328. IEEE (2017)
3. Bhattacharjee, S., Mohammadi, A., Marcel, S.: Spoofing deep face recognition with custom silicone masks. Tech. rep. (2018)
4. Boulkenafet, Z., Komulainen, J., Hadid, A.: Face anti-spoofing based on color texture analysis. In: 2015 IEEE International Conference on Image Processing (ICIP), pp. 2636–2640. IEEE (2015)
5. Boulkenafet, Z., Komulainen, J., Hadid, A.: Face antispoofing using speeded-up robust features and fisher vector encoding. IEEE Signal Process. Lett. **24**(2), 141–145 (2017)
6. Chingovska, I., Anjos, A., Marcel, S.: On the effectiveness of local binary patterns in face anti-spoofing. In: Proceedings of the 11th International Conference of the Biometrics Special Interest Group. No. EPFL-CONF-192369 (2012)
7. Chingovska, I., Erdogmus, N., Anjos, A., Marcel, S.: Face recognition systems under spoofing attacks. In: Bourlai, T. (ed.) Face Recognition Across the Imaging Spectrum, pp. 165–194. Springer, Cham (2016)
8. Costa-Pazo, A., Bhattacharjee, S., Vazquez-Fernandez, E., Marcel, S.: The replay-mobile face presentation-attack database. In: Biometrics Special Interest Group (2016)
9. Di, W., Hu, H., Jain, A.K.: Face spoof detection with image distortion analysis. IEEE Trans. Inf. Forensics Secur. **10**(4), 746–761 (2015)
10. Eilertsen, G., Kronander, J., Denes, G., Mantiuk, R., Unger, J.: HDR image reconstruction from a single exposure using deep CNNs. ACM Trans. Graphics (TOG) **36**(6), 178 (2017)
11. de Freitas Pereira, T., Anjos, A., De Martino, J.M., Marcel, S.: *LBP–TOP* based countermeasure against face spoofing attacks. In: Park, J.-I., Kim, J. (eds.) ACCV 2012. LNCS, vol. 7728, pp. 121–132. Springer, Heidelberg (2013). https://doi.org/10.1007/978-3-642-37410-4_11
12. He, K., Zhang, X., Ren, S., Sun, J.: Deep residual learning for image recognition. In: Proceedings of the IEEE Conference on Computer Vision and Pattern Recognition, pp. 770–778 (2016)
13. Iandola, F.N., Han, S., Moskewicz, M.W., Ashraf, K., Dally, W.J., Keutzer, K.: Squeezenet: alexnet-level accuracy with 50x fewer parameters and <0.5mb model size (2016)
14. Jackson, A.S., Bulat, A., Argyriou, V., Tzimiropoulos, G.: Large pose 3D face reconstruction from a single image via direct volumetric CNN regression. In: International Conference on Computer Vision (2017)
15. Kemelmacher-Shlizerman, I., Seitz, S., Miller, D., Brossard, E.: The megaface benchmark: 1 million faces for recognition at scale. In: Computer Vision & Pattern Recognition (2016)

16. Komulainen, J., Boulkenafet, Z., Hadid, A.: Face anti-spoofing using speeded-up robust features and fisher vector encoding. IEEE Signal Process. Lett. **PP**(99), 1 (2017)
17. Li, L., Feng, X., Boulkenafet, Z., Xia, Z., Li, M., Hadid, A.: An original face anti-spoofing approach using partial convolutional neural network. In: 2016 6th International Conference on Image Processing Theory Tools and Applications (IPTA), pp. 1–6. IEEE (2016)
18. Liu, Y., Jourabloo, A., Liu, X.: Learning deep models for face anti-spoofing: binary or auxiliary supervision. In: Proceedings of the IEEE Conference on Computer Vision and Pattern Recognition, pp. 389–398 (2018)
19. Määttä, J., Hadid, A., Pietikäinen, M.: Face spoofing detection from single images using micro-texture analysis. In: 2011 International Joint Conference on Biometrics (IJCB), pp. 1–7. IEEE (2011)
20. Pan, G., Sun, L., Wu, Z., Lao, S.: Eyeblink-based anti-spoofing in face recognition from a generic webcamera (2007)
21. Russakovsky, O., et al.: Imagenet large scale visual recognition challenge. Int. J. Comput. Vision **115**(3), 211–252 (2015)
22. Sun, X., Huang, L., Liu, C.: Context based face spoofing detection using active near-infrared images. In: International Conference on Pattern Recognition, pp. 4262–4267 (2017)
23. Tan, X., Li, Y., Liu, J., Jiang, L.: Face liveness detection from a single image with sparse low rank bilinear discriminative model. In: Daniilidis, K., Maragos, P., Paragios, N. (eds.) ECCV 2010. LNCS, vol. 6316, pp. 504–517. Springer, Heidelberg (2010). https://doi.org/10.1007/978-3-642-15567-3_37
24. Tang, Y., Wang, X., Jia, X., Shen, L.: Fusing multiple deep features for face anti-spoofing. In: Zhou, J., et al. (eds.) CCBR 2018. LNCS, vol. 10996, pp. 321–330. Springer, Cham (2018). https://doi.org/10.1007/978-3-319-97909-0_35
25. Tang, Y., Wang, X., Jia, X., Shen, L.: Fusing multiple deep features for face anti-spoofing. In: Chinese Conference on Biometric Recognition, pp. 321–330 (2018)
26. Yang, J., Lei, Z., Li, S.Z.: Learn convolutional neural network for face anti-spoofing. arXiv preprint arXiv:1408.5601 (2014)
27. Zhang, K., Zhang, Z., Li, Z., Qiao, Y.: Joint face detection and alignment using multitask cascaded convolutional networks. IEEE Signal Process. Lett. **23**(10), 1499–1503 (2016)
28. Zhang, Z., Yan, J., Liu, S., Lei, Z., Yi, D., Li, S.Z.: A face antispoofing database with diverse attacks, pp. 26–31 (2012)

Deep Learning for Intelligent Train Driving with Augmented BLSTM

Jin Huang[1], Siguang Huang[1(✉)], Yao Liu[1(✉)], Yukun Hu[1], and Yu Jiang[2]

[1] Tsinghua University, Beijing 100084, China
huangjin@tsinghua.edu.cn, 2403107116@qq.com, 892147077@qq.com,
437932979@qq.com
[2] Jilin University, Jilin 130012, China
jiangyu2011@jlu.edu.cn

Abstract. As one of the most important means of transportation, the railway trains in modern society are eagerly approaching automatic driving due to their congenital advantages on operating environments compare to, e.g., road traffics. However, considering the factors of energy-efficiency, punctuality, as well as safety issues, the derivation of railway intelligent train driving process is challenging due to the high dimensionality, nonlinearity, complex constraints, and time-varying characteristics. The time-sequential train control sequences bears similarities to the text streams, which can be studied using Bidirectional LSTM (BLSTM) related methods. In this paper, we propose a dexterously augmented BLSTM model named BLSTM+, which considers both the sequential properties of the time-series and the peculiarities of each control process, for deep learning of control decision making process in such typical industrial control problems. The driving records of experienced human drivers are employed to train the BLSTM+ model. A reinforcement updating mechanism on the BLSTM+ model is also developed to further improve the performance by continuously mining the best-ranked driving records. Experimental results show that an energy saving of over 10% could be achieved under punctuality requirements when compared with the average level of human drivers.

Keywords: BLSTM · Intelligent train driving · Deep learning

1 Introduction

The railway trains are eagerly approaching automatic driving due to their congenital advantages on operating environments compare to, e.g., road traffics. Such technical progress will have advantages on several aspects, e.g., more energy-efficiency and running on time, reducing hard labors, and improving safety. Specifically, the rolling stock is a major source of energy consumption that accounts for 2200 PJ, or 0.6% of global energy consumption and 3.5% of CO_2 emissions in the transport industry [6]. At the present time, except for certain

© Springer Nature Switzerland AG 2019
A. C. Nayak and A. Sharma (Eds.): PRICAI 2019, LNAI 11671, pp. 226–238, 2019.
https://doi.org/10.1007/978-3-030-29911-8_18

short distance light-rail and subway vehicles, rail trains have to be operated by human drivers, whose driving skills have a major impact on the energy efficiency and safety issues. A major feature of train driving is that the route information (e.g. geographic characteristics and speed limit) is known a priori and hence it is possible to derive driving energy-efficient solutions (a set of throttling/braking gear selection) by taking advantage of the undulating terrains along a route. Here the railway intelligent train driving is to reach energy-efficient driving under the time and safety requirements.

Significant research effort has been dedicated to derive the railway intelligent train driving operations. As a unique optimal solution can be derived under certain assumptions on the problem, many analytical solutions were proposed [13,18]. However, the assumptions may not hold under realistic situations. In addition, the operations of trains are under complex constraints in the railway system. To handle the realistic conditions and complex constraints, advanced numerical searching techniques, like the genetic algorithm [7], evolutionary algorithms [17], etc. have been applied to compute the energy optimized driving operation. Such approaches offer high-quality solution but tend to require intensive computation. Online techniques for real-time control were also widely studied [5,16]. However, such techniques suffer from the uncertainty of delivering quality solution. Interested readers should refer to References [3,13,18] for more comprehensive surveys on energy-efficient train driving techniques.

Highly skilled human drivers develop their driving behaviors through years of practice to ensure safety, punctuality and energy efficiency. They intuitively determine the operations based on their knowledge of the terrains and the train parameters. Our statistics proved that highly skilled drivers could save more than 7% energy when compared with the average level of human drivers. Thus, learning the driving behaviors from the highly skilled drivers represents an effective solution to the intelligent train driving problem. The effective extraction of driving experience, however, turns out to be challenging due to the ambiguity and redundancy in the driving records. The driving of train along a given route is realized by a sequence of control operations. Such a sequence bears similarity to the text streams in natural language processing (NLP) problems, which can be addressed by Bidirectional LSTM (BLSTM) related methods [2,9,14]. On the other hand, the train driving problem belongs to the category of the industrial control problem and differs from the NLP problem in the sense that various constraints and domain knowledge have to be considered.

In this paper, we propose an augmented BLSTM model named BLSTM+, which considers both the sequential properties of the time-series and the peculiarities of each control run, to perform deep learning of control decision making process. The driving records of experienced human drivers are employed to train the BLSTM+ model with both forward and backward feature sets designated to represent the context information of running trains. A reinforcement updating mechanism on the BLSTM+ model is also developed to further improve the performance by continuously mining the best-ranked driving records.

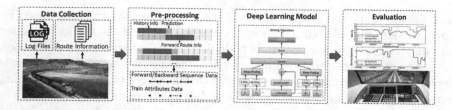

Fig. 1. System design process including data collection, pre-processing, deep learning model design and evaluation parts. First, the train driving log files and route information are collected as raw data. Second, a pre-processing phase using sliding window is carried out to retrieve the sequential data and train attributes for training. Then the deep learning model is implemented with proper evaluations on the performances.

2   Problem Formulation and Background

2.1   Problem Formulation

The motion of a train can be formulated by treating the train position s as an independent variable as follows [13]:

$$
m\rho\frac{\mathrm{d}v(s)}{\mathrm{d}s} = f(s) - R_b(v(s)) - R_l(s),
$$
$$
\frac{\mathrm{d}t}{\mathrm{d}s} = \frac{1}{v(s)}. \tag{1}
$$

where m is the mass of the train, ρ is a factor accounting for the rotating mass, v is the velocity of the train, s is the position (i.e., displacement) of the train, $f(s)$ is the traction or braking force along the position, and is determined by the discrete or continuous level of gear on most modern locomotives, $R_b(v(s))$ is the basic resistance including both roll resistance and air resistance along s, and $R_l(s)$ is the corresponding line resistance caused by track grade, curves and tunnels. These resistance forces are usually formulated as empirical equations with parameters determined experimentally [19].

The objective of the energy-efficient train driving problem is to minimize the energy consumption as well as the time deviation from the time table under various operation constraints, which can be further formulated in the position-dependent form as:

$$
J_E = \int_{s_{start}}^{s_{end}} \phi(f(s))\left(f(s) + \lambda\left|\frac{\mathrm{d}f(s)}{\mathrm{d}s}\right|\right)\mathrm{d}s,
$$
$$
J_T = \left|T - \bar{T}\right|, \tag{2}
$$

subject to the following constraints and boundary conditions

$$
f_{min} \leq f(s) \leq f_{max}, \quad 0 \leq T(s) \leq T_{max}(s),
$$
$$
v(s) \leq v_{limit}(s), \quad s(0) = s_{start}, \quad v(0) = v_{start}, \tag{3}
$$
$$
s(T) = s_{end}, \quad v(T) = v_{end}.
$$

Here, J_E and J_T represent the optimization objective on energy consumption and the time deviation, respectively. $\phi(f)$ stands for a coefficient capturing the gear behavior. $\bar{T}$ is the scheduled time for a train trip and T is the actual time cost for the trip. The maximum allowable velocity $v_{limit}(s)$ is determined by the train model and the route condition. It is usually represented as a piecewise function of the train position s. s_{start} and s_{end} are the train positions at the beginning and ending of a trip, while v_{start} and v_{end} represent the initial and final speeds, respectively. $s(0)$ and $v(0)$ are, respectively, the position and the velocity at the beginning of a trip. The duration of the trip $\bar{T}$ is usually given by the timetable. It must be noted that there is a potential trade-off between the energy consumption and the time deviation during the bi-objective optimization process.

2.2 Patterns in Human Driving

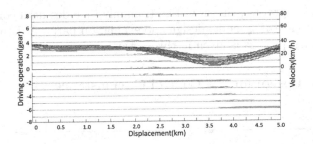

Fig. 2. A snippet of human driving data. Blue and red lines are the velocity and the driving gears, respectively, from a group of drivers. We draw them together to show that distinctive patterns do exist among the driving operations. (Color figure online)

It is extremely hard to derive an optimized solution to the energy-efficient train driving problem due to its high dimensionality, inherent nonlinearity, complex constraints and potential variations of the elements in a sequence of driving operations [18]. On the other hand, human drivers are able to synthesize the multiple factors and anticipate driving solutions in a real-time fashion. As a result, we attack the problem by analyzing the human driving experience.

The intelligent train driving problem can be formulated as a general optimization problem with a discrete driving operations as the output, which can then be exerted to the master controller, by considering factors such as railway properties, train states, train attributes, marshaling information, and various external disturbances. A human driver usually makes decisions of accelerating or decelerating the train according to the lessons learned from their teacher drivers and their experiences accumulated so far. Every operation has an impact on the final energy consumption and punctuality. After reviewing a large number of human driving records, we found identifiable common patterns in the driving behaviors. Figure 2 shows a few representative patterns represented as velocity and driving operations. The driving records contain a wealth of information, for we learn that experienced drivers often have similar locomotive driving patterns. Thus, revealing the hidden patterns of human drivers provides important clues towards an optimized driving solution. This inspired us to apply ourselves to learning potential patterns so as to achieve the same expertise of human drivers or even better driving options.

Driving records are typically sequential data for specific trains. For a given train and timetable information of a specific train route, the train at different timestamps and the railway route at different placements have an obvious timing and location sequential relationship. We shall thus regard the train control problem as processing sequences by taking into account semantic coherence and relevance.

3   Deep Learning with BLSTM+

The whole design process, shown in Fig. 1, mainly includes data collection, preprocessing, deep learning model design and evaluation parts. A detailed description of the design process is given in this section.

3.1   Feature Design for the Control Circumstance

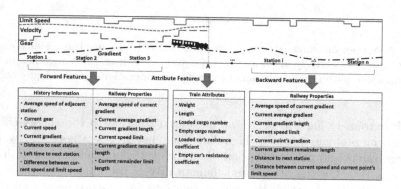

Fig. 3. The designed 27-dimensional feature-set including 13 forward features, 6 train attribute features and 8 backward features.

Considering the context properties discussed above, here we designed a 27-dimensional feature-set, shown in Fig. 3 to capture the sequential properties of the train driving circumstances. In the feature-set, the forward and backward features representing the context of the sequential properties of the running train were designed to incorporate the railway properties in both directions, but include the historical information in the forward direction only. In addition, there are certain train-individual attributes for each run, including the weight and length of the train, the distribution of loaded and empty cargoes, and certain resistance parameters, *etc.* Here we use six such attribute parameters for the control circumstance. This makes the industrial control problem different from the structure of the text streams.

The so-defined forward and backward features, together with the attributes, are used as input data to predict driving operation. The constraints in Eq. (3) are taken as features, *i.e.*, the ones in gray background in Fig. 3. The speed limit is emphasized by features of the 'difference between current speed and limit speed', the 'current remainder limit length' and the 'distance between current speed and current point's limit speed'. The punctuality constraints are represented by the features of the 'left time to next station' and the 'distance to next station'.

3.2 Learning with BLSTM+

The Long Short-Term Memory networks (LSTM) [12] are the variants of Recurrent neural networks (RNN) [?] which address the vanishing gradient problem in RNN and offer great advantages in catching the tendency of sequential data, while the BLSTM [10] is famous for its superiority in scanning text sequences in both directions, forward and backward, and in dealing with natural language processing. Recently, the model has evolved into several variants for different objectives. The multidimensional RNN for handwriting recognition, the subsampling RNN, 2D LSTM and Convolutional LSTM for computer vision research are such typical variants [1, 15].

The above BLSTM models were developed for natural language processing and image processing applications. No variants have been proposed for the problem of control sequence learning. Here we propose the new augmented BLSTM model, called BLSTM+, to accommodate for the requirements commonly found in typical industrial control learning problems, *e.g.*, the train control problem.

We thus propose the BLSTM+ model as an extension of the BLSTM model in order to meet the requirements encountered when dealing with industrial control problems. The BLSTM+ model, as illustrated in Fig. 4, contains the original forward and backward feature-sets, plus a feature set of the attributes of each control run. It can be viewed as a new variant of the standard BLSTM with mainly the following two changes. First, the forward and backward feature-sets are generally asymmetrical. In such case, two independent LSTM are employed to learn the forward and the backward features. A mean pooling layer is added following the LSTM networks to allow for more historical sequential information to be recorded. Second, the proposed BLSTM+ model has 'plus' features of the inherent attributes at each run. Here the 'plus' part of BLSTM+ model mainly refers to those inherent non-sequential attributes in each control process. The autoencoders are added to abstract such attributes. Such attribute features are directly merged with the outputs of the forward and backward mean pooling layers to feed forward to the ReLU and softmax layers for driving operation.

In more details, the BLSTM+ takes a sequence with M tokens $F :< F_1, F_2, ..., F_M >$ as forward-layer inputs and a sequence with N tokens $B :< B_N, B_{N-1}, ..., B_1 >$ as backward-layer inputs. Here, M and N are the unfolded

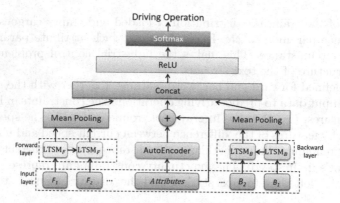

Fig. 4. The two-step unfolded BLSTM+: The input of the BLSTM+ model includes three parts, the forward features, backward features and the inherent attributes features. The inherent attribute features are abstracted by the autoencoder. The output of the forward and backward layers are fed into the mean pooling layer and then concatenated with the output of autoencoder and attributes in concat layer, which then will be used to predict the train driving operation.

steps of the forward and backward layers, respectively. When both directions reach the end of the tokens, the model calculates a fixed dimensional vector that represents the forward and backward information through the mean pooling operations, which will further concatenate the $Attributes :< a_1, a_2, ..., a_K >$ and the autoencoder results to form a new vector $concat$. Then, the resulted $concat$ is used to generate driving operation through ReLU and softmax layers. We train the BLSTM+ in an end-to-end way in a supervised manner. The model is trained by minimizing the cross-entropy error of gear prediction.

For the forward and backward layers the internal hidden states are updated as follows:

$$hf_t, mf_t = LSTM_F(F_t, hf_{t-1}, mf_{t-1})$$
$$hb_t, mb_t = LSTM_B(B_t, hb_{t-1}, mb_{t-1}) \tag{4}$$

where hf_t, mf_t denote the $LSTM_F$'s hidden state and memory state at time step t for the forward layer and F_t denotes the $LSTM_F$'s current input. hb_t, mb_t and B_t are the corresponding parameters for the backward layer. For the $Attributes$ features, the training result is:

$$att_v = [AutoEncoder(Attributes); Attributes] \tag{5}$$

where the att_v denotes the concatenation of $Attributes$ and the abstract result of AutoEncoder. The mean pooling and concat layers processes are as follows:

$$mean_f = Mean(\sum_{i=1}^{M} hf_i), \quad mean_b = Mean(\sum_{i=1}^{N} hb_i)$$
$$concat = [mean_f; att_v; mean_b] \tag{6}$$

where $Mean()$ denotes a mean pooling process of the given features sets hf_i and hb_i. $concat$ is a concatenation of features extracted by $LSTM_F$, $LSTM_B$ and $AutoEncoder$. At last, the $concat$ vector is used to generate driving operation through ReLU and softmax layers:

$$P_g = softmax(ReLU(w * concat + b)) \tag{7}$$

where the w and b are parameters that need to be learned. P_g is a probability distribution over all predicted gears.

3.3 Tuning and Reinforcement Updating

Algorithm 1. BLSTM+ model's Reinforcement updating

1: Initialize BLSTM+ model with random weights;
2: Get the sequential training samples from the top n_{train} trips with the forward, backward and train attribute features be preprocessed and shuffled;
3: **while** $True$ **do**
4:    **if** Not the first loop **then**
5:        Initialize BLSTM's weights with the weights of the last loop;
6:    **end if**
7:    Training BLSTM model with training data;
8:    Get the simulation result with the chosen n_{test} testing trips;
9:    Evaluate the n_{test} trips with $J_i = \alpha \frac{(T_i - \overline{T})}{\overline{T}} + \beta \frac{E_i}{W_i}$; ($T_i, E_i, W_i$ are the corresponding time, energy and train weight for trip i)
10:    Rank the total n_{train} and n_{test} trips with J_i;
11:    Choose the top n_{train} trips to get new shuffled training samples;
12:    **if** Convergence or reach a maximum cycle number **then**
13:        $break$;
14:    **end if**
15: **end while**
16: Save the model.

The above introduced model is essentially for supervised learning, and aims chiefly at the accuracy of the prediction. However, for the intelligent train driving problem, there will always be space for improvement as the process is learning from experienced drivers. In such case, rather than only aiming at the accuracy of the prediction, the evaluation indicators will put more emphasize on the physical aspects such as energy-efficiency and punctuality as well as safety (e.g. under all kinds of running constraints). In order to ensure the universality of the model, the training and simulation data need to tune the weights of some key parameters, e.g., the weight and length of the train. What is more, for the training of BLSTM+ model, the tuning on the size of the network, the parameters setting and the initialization of variables are also necessary. To improve the performance, we perform a reinforcement updating mechanism on the

BLSTM+ model as described in Algorithm 1. In each training cycle, we re-select the top results of the most valid energy-efficient data under punctuality requirements as the next training data for next, and perform iterative training until the BLSTM+ model converges or reaches the maximum number of iterations. The cost function for model updating considers both energy-efficiency and punctuality, and provides a small performance boost on predicting optimal driving operation.

4   Experiments and Analysis

4.1   Experiments Design

The experimental locomotive that we employed has a gear operating with 17 levels in which levels 1 to 8 are for traction, level 0 for neutral, and levels -1 to -8 for braking. Accordingly, the BLSTM+ model is designed to have a 17-class classification labels for the gear. The power characteristics of the locomotive for both traction and braking are shown in Fig. 5, which obviously exhibit different energy consumption per unit time at different power performances [8].

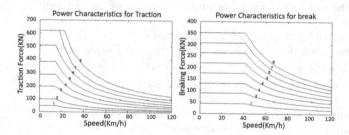

Fig. 5. Power characteristics of the selected locomotives for traction and braking.

Dataset. The datasets that we used for training and testing were originally real datasets that are collected from the Train Control and Management System (TCMS). The collected data mainly contain the driving records of the human drivers and the route information. They were collected from multi-locomotives of the same type on the selected real railway routes of a length of 47.95 Km between 5 stations. We then choose the 400 best valued trips from thousands of records with the weights of the trains be in the range of 3000 to 4000 tons. These selected trips strictly meet the requirements of safety and punctuality. **The data set will go public along with the publication of the paper.** The evaluation of the trips are ranked in an ascending order of the energy amount over weight as E/W. The 400 smallest(E/W) trips were selected as experimental data. We randomly selected 300 trips as training data according to the weight of trains, with the remaining 100 trips for testing and comparison. A total of 1.8 million samplings were collected from the driving records as the base of training data.

Table 1. Performances of different algorithms when compared with the average human drivers.

Algorithm	Predicting accuracy	Energy saving	Average time deviation	Training time (computation)
NSGA-II	NA	6.53%	155.98 s	187.38 h
SVM	57.08%	NA	NA	>48 h
ANN	75.74%	−6.37%	129.62 s	10.40 h
LSTM	90.68%	NA	NA	13.38 h
BLSTM	91.13%	6.73%	47.33 s	37.58 h
BLSTM+	93.26%	8.17%	13.79 s	18.28 h
Re-BLSTM+	**92.28%**	**10.06%**	**11.31 s**	**NA**

Baselines. We compare the proposed BLSTM+ with a batch of popular algorithms, *i.e.,* the numerical optimization algorithm NSGA-II (the computations were implemented in Matlab) [4], as well as the popular machine learning algorithms SVM, ANN, LSTM and BLSTM. For comparison purpose, similar feature sets are employed for the learning algorithms, *e.g.,* the feature sets of SVM and ANN are designed as the sliding-window sequential features of the BLSTM+ model. The LSTM model has the same architecture as the BLSTM+ but without the backward layers and backward features, and the conventional BLSTM model is trained in such a way that the features of inherit attributes are merged into both the forward and backward features. We employ the LSTM model to illustrate the effect of backward features for gear prediction, and the BLSTM model for training time cost comparisons.

Evaluation. We implemented the train driving simulations with the dynamic model in Eq. (1). The simulation environment ensures that the BLSTM+ model predicts constantly the gear until the entire trip is completed. The intelligent train driving problem is a special prediction problem that will accumulate the predicting effects of all steps. The evaluations are designed in four aspects, that is, the predicting accuracy, the energy saving percentage, the average time deviation and the training (computation) time. For energy, the higher the gear, the higher the power, and the higher the energy consumption rate. The relation between them is approximately (but not exactly) in linear, and a certain evaluation model can be fitted through the statistical data. The fitted evaluation model instructs on the amount of consumed diesel in each gear per unit time.

Parameters Setting. For the parameters of the BLSTM+ model, both the forward layer and backward layer have 2 layers with each layer has 100 and 50 cells. The forward LSTM and the backward LSTM unfold 100 and 50 steps, respectively. The ReLU layer has 128 cells. The output layer has 17 cells, corresponding to the 17 gear operations. We use the softmax function as the activation function of the output layer and the cross-entropy as the cost function. The Adam [11]

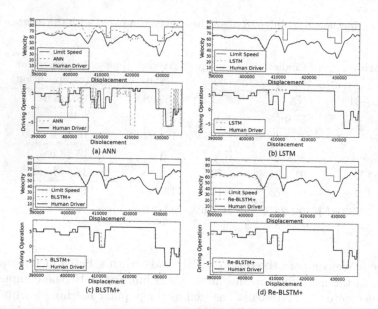

Fig. 6. Illustrative examples of driving trips by ANN, LSTM, BLSTM+ and Re-BLSTM+, respectively, as compared with the reference human driver records. The simulations were performed with a train weighting 3540 tons.

algorithm was selected to perform the gradient descent optimization with mini-batches of size 300. The learning rate was fixed at 0.001. A rate of 0.5 dropout was chosen to avoid over-fitting.

Experiments Results and Analysis. The performance of different algorithms are shown in Table 1. The predicting accuracy indicates the performance of the models in learning human driving behaviors (not applicable to NSGA-II). It can be seen that the BLSTM and its variants with contextual information exhibit more comprehensive information and obtain better results in the predicting accuracy, while the SVM only got a predicting accuracy of 57.08% since it is not good at capturing sequential features. The low predicting accuracy of SVM leads to failures in assessing the simulations due to strong violations of the speed limit. For the energy-saving and punctuality performances, the BLSTM+ works very well and becomes better after 10 round of reinforcement updating (The Re-BLSTM+ in the Table). The numerical searching algorithm NSGA-II got an energy saving of around 6% but with relatively large time deviation and too long computational time. Although the LSTM model is good in its predicting accuracy, which is 90.68%, it fails to finish most of the trips as it can hardly can capture the backward features of the railway. It also can be seen that the BLSTM+ model requires only half of the training time of the BLSTM due to the well refined feature design.

Four instances of the simulation using the trained ANN, LSTM, BLSTM and the BLSTM+ model are shown in Fig. 6(a)–(d), respectively. It can be seen that the ANN model got more gear chattering and occasional speed overstepping, while the proposed BLSTM+ model works very well. The predictions with the LSTM model lead to speed overstepping after missing a key gear change due to its inability to consider future road information (*i.e.*, backward features in BLSTM+).

From Fig. 6(c) and (d) we can conclude that the Re-BLSTM+ model, compare to the BLSTM+ model, predicts slightly lower gears (lower velocity) in some parts of the trip and leads to a slightly better performance in energy consumption.

5 Conclusion

Inspired by the BLSTM in processing the text streams, we proposed the BLSTM+ model that considers both the sequential properties of the time-series and the peculiarities of each control process, for deep learning of control decision making process in the typical industrial control problems. A reinforcement updating mechanism on the BLSTM+ model is also developed to further improve the performance by continuously mining the best-ranked driving records. Experimental results show that an energy saving of over 10% could be achieved compared with the average level of human drivers. The proposed model is applicable to other industrial control problems. Future works can be carried out on exploring more Deep Learning techniques, or even Deep Reinforcement Learning on such industrial control problems.

Acknowledgement. This research is sponsored in part by the NSFC Program (No. 61872217, U1701262, U1801263), the research is also sponsored in part by the Guangdong Provincial Key Laboratory of Cyber-Physical Systems and the National&Local Joint Engineering Research Center of Intelligent Manufacturing Cyber-Physical Systems.

References

1. Byeon, W., Breuel, T.M., Raue, F., Liwicki, M.: Scene labeling with LSTM recurrent neural networks. In: Computer Vision and Pattern Recognition, pp. 3547–3555 (2015)
2. Gehring, J., Auli, M., Grangier, D., Yarats, D., Dauphin, Y.N.: Convolutional sequence to sequence learning. In: Proceedings of the 34th International Conference on Machine Learning, vol. 70, pp. 1243–1252. JMLR.org (2017)
3. Huang, J., Deng, Y., Yang, Q., Sun, J.: An energy-efficient train control framework for smart railway transportation. IEEE Trans. Comput. **65**(5), 1407–1417 (2016)
4. Huang, J., Zhao, X., Chen, X., Sun, J., Yang, Q.: From offline to onboard system solution for a control sequence optimization problem. In: 2014 IEEE Symposium on Computational Intelligence for Engineering Solutions (CIES), pp. 67–73. IEEE (2014)

5. Huang, Y., Li, Y.: Distributed constrained cooperative control of discrete-time high-speed train systems. In: 2018 International Conference on Intelligent Rail Transportation (ICIRT), pp. 1–4. IEEE (2018)
6. IEA, I.E.A., UIC, I.U.o.R.: Railway Handbook 2016 - International Energy Agency. International Energy Agency (2016)
7. Jiang, L., Zhang, J., Hao, X., Xiao, S.y.: Evaluating influence factors of energy consumption for urban rail timetable using an optimized train control method. DEStech Trans. Environ. Energy. Earth Sci. (gmee) (2018)
8. Jin, H., Fan, Y., Deng, Y., Zhao, X., Ming, G.: Human experience knowledge induction based intelligent train driving. In: IEEE/ACIS International Conference on Computer & Information Science (2017)
9. Lipton, Z.C., Berkowitz, J., Elkan, C.: A critical review of recurrent neural networks for sequence learning. arXiv preprint arXiv:1506.00019 (2015)
10. Pratiher, S., Chattoraj, S., Agarwal, S., Bhattacharya, S.: Grading tumor malignancy via deep bidirectional LSTM on graph manifold encoded histopathological image. In: 2018 IEEE International Conference on Data Mining Workshops (ICDMW), pp. 674–681. IEEE (2018)
11. Ruder, S.: An overview of gradient descent optimization algorithms. arXiv preprint arXiv:1609.04747 (2016)
12. Sainath, T.N., Vinyals, O., Senior, A., Sak, H.: Convolutional, long short-term memory, fully connected deep neural networks. In: 2015 IEEE International Conference on Acoustics, Speech and Signal Processing (ICASSP), pp. 4580–4584. IEEE (2015)
13. Scheepmaker, G.M., Goverde, R.M., Kroon, L.G.: Review of energy-efficient train control and timetabling. Eur. J. Oper. Res. **257**(2), 355–376 (2017)
14. Shi, B., Bai, X., Yao, C.: An end-to-end trainable neural network for image-based sequence recognition and its application to scene text recognition. IEEE Trans. Pattern Anal. Mach. Intell. **39**(11), 2298–2304 (2017)
15. Solovyeva, E.: Recurrent neural networks as approximators of non-linear filters operators. J. Phys: Conf. Ser. **1141**, 012115 (2018)
16. Wang, X., Li, S., Su, S., Tang, T.: Robust fuzzy predictive control for automatic train regulation in high-frequency metro lines. IEEE Trans. Fuzzy Syst. **27**(6), 1295–1308 (2018)
17. Xu, X., Li, K., Li, X.: A multi-objective subway timetable optimization approach with minimum passenger time and energy consumption. J. Adv. Transp. **50**(1), 69–95 (2016)
18. Yang, X., Li, X., Ning, B., Tang, T.: A survey on energy-efficient train operation for urban rail transit. IEEE Trans. Intell. Transp. Syst. **17**(1), 2–13 (2016)
19. Zhang, M., Zhang, Q., Lv, Y., Sun, W., Wang, H.: An AI based high-speed railway automatic train operation system analysis and design. In: 2018 International Conference on Intelligent Rail Transportation (ICIRT), pp. 1–5. IEEE (2018)

Neural Networks

Writing to the Hopfield Memory
via Training a Recurrent Network

Han Bao[1,2], Richong Zhang[1,2(✉)], Yongyi Mao[3], and Jinpeng Huai[1,2]

[1] SKLSDE, School of Computer Science and Engineering, Beihang University,
Beijing, China
[2] Beijing Advanced Institution on Big Data and Brain Computing,
Beihang University, Beijing, China
{baohan,zhangrc}@act.buaa.edu.cn, huaijp@buaa.edu.cn
[3] School of Electrical Engineering and Computer Science, University of Ottawa,
Ottawa, Canada
ymao@uottawa.ca

Abstract. We consider the problem of writing on a Hopfield network. We cast the problem as a supervised learning problem by observing a simple link between the update equations of Hopfield network and recurrent neural networks. We compare the new writing protocol to existing ones and experimentally verify its effectiveness. Our method not only has a better ability of noise recovery, but also has a bigger capacity compared to the other existing writing protocols.

Keywords: Hopfield network · Writing protocol · Recurrent network

1 Introduction

Different from conventional memories, associative memories [1] store information in a distributed manner and without an addressing mechanism. With associative memories, message retrieval is content based, which resembles a "recalling" process in response to a query that may represent a partial/noisy version of a stored message. E.g., if the message "The capital of France is Paris" is stored in the memory (superimposed with other messages), then by feeding the memory with "The capital of France is Lyon", the original message may be recovered. Such content-addressable memories are seen as closer to the way human brains store and retrieve information and are arguably an important research subject in artificial intelligence.

Among associative memory models, Hopfield network [9] was conceptualized in 1982. In application, Hopfield neural network was appeared on different fields,

This work is supported partly by China 973 program (No. 2015CB358700), by the National Natural Science Foundation of China (No. 61772059, 61421003), and by the Beijing Advanced Innovation Center for Big Data and Brain Computing (BDBC) and State Key Laboratory of Software Development Environment (No. SKLSDE-2018ZX-17).

A. C. Nayak and A. Sharma (Eds.): PRICAI 2019, LNAI 11671, pp. 241–254, 2019.
https://doi.org/10.1007/978-3-030-29911-8_19

like image processing and optimization [3], economic load dispatch [13], classification task [18], digit recognition [5], social network [4]. Besides, the theoretical studies [7,15,19] and model modification like [11,12,16] have attracted many research interests.

An N-neuron Hopfield network [9] is an undirected weighted graph on N nodes, where each node is referred to as a neuron [14], and the (symmetric) weight matrix W specifies the connectivity strength between neurons. (Negative weights are allowed.) Each neuron i is associated with a state variable x_i taking values in $\{\pm 1\}$. The network has a state-update function $f_W \colon \{\pm 1\}^N \to \{\pm 1\}^N$, defined as

$$f_W(\mathbf{x}) = \mathrm{sign}(W\mathbf{x}), \tag{1}$$

where the sign function is acting element-wise on its input vector, i.e., for all $i \in \{1, \ldots, N\}$, the i-th entry of $\mathrm{sign}(\mathbf{r})$ is equal to 1 if $r_i > 0$ and is equal to -1 otherwise.[1] Using the state-update function, the network updates its state $\mathbf{x} = (x_1, x_2, \ldots, x_N)$ according to

$$\mathbf{x}^{\mathrm{new}} = f_W(\mathbf{x}^{\mathrm{old}}) \tag{2}$$

As an associative memory, a Hopfield network stores a message set $\mathcal{M} = \{\mathbf{x}^1, \ldots, \mathbf{x}^M\} \subseteq \{\pm 1\}^N$ by encoding the message in the weight matrix W. To retrieve a message, when presented with a query/probe $\mathbf{p}$, the network initializes its state vector as $\mathbf{x} = \mathbf{p}$, iterates the update Eq. (2) until convergence or a maximum number of iteration is reached, and declares the state vector as the retrieved message. Usually, the probe $\mathbf{p}$ is a noisy/partial version of one of the message set $\mathcal{M}$ and it is desirable that the retrieved message is equal to the correct message, even when the probe is a severely corrupted version of the message.

The problem of *writing to a Hopfield memory* is then that of designing a weight matrix W for a given message set $\mathcal{M}$. A method of writing is referred to as a *writing protocol*. We note that in the literature, writing protocols are also referred to as "learning rules". In this work, we use the term "writing" instead of "learning" to avoid confusion with another supervised learning problem that will be introduced in a later part of the paper.

Several writing protocols for the Hopfield network are proposed in [10,17] and [8], which are often motivated by practical considerations and the notion of writing capacity. Roughly speaking, the writing capacity is the maximum number of messages that can be written to the memory so that reliable retrieval is possible. Depending on the choice of the message, the amount of noise allowed in the probe, and the precise definition of reliable retrieval, several expressions of writing capacity have been derived, as briefly discussed in the next section. The main drawback of exist writing protocols is either lack of theoretical explanation or

---

[1] More generally, function f_W may take the form $f_W(\mathbf{x}) = \mathrm{sign}(W\mathbf{x} + \mathbf{b})$, where $\mathbf{b}$ is an off-set or threshold vector. In the context of this paper, dropping this offset term $\mathbf{b}$ is without loss of generality.

limitation of capacity. To overcome this drawback, we start with interpretability and propose a new writing protocol which has a bigger capacity. We will describe it in detail on Sect. 3.

2   Existing Writing Protocols

In this section we give a brief review on some existing writing protocols for writing a set of messages $\mathcal{M} = \{\mathbf{x}^1, \ldots, \mathbf{x}^M\}$ into a Hopfield memory of size N. Hopfield's original writing protocol [9], referred to as **HOP** hereafter, accounts for each message by adding its outer-product to the weight matrix, i.e., the weight matrix is defined as

$$W = \sum_{m=1}^{M} \left[\mathbf{x}^m \cdot (\mathbf{x}^m)^T - I_N \right], \tag{3}$$

where I_N is the $N \times N$ identity matrix.

With the energy of a state vector $\mathbf{x} \in \{\pm 1\}^N$ defined as

$$E(\mathbf{x}) = -\frac{1}{2}\mathbf{x}^T W \mathbf{x}, \tag{4}$$

it follows that each message $\mathbf{x}^m \in \mathcal{M}$ is a local minimum of the energy function. (To simplify notation, the dependency of the energy on W is implicit.) Furthermore, the iterative update under Eq. (1) seeks such local minima, i.e.,

$$E(\mathbf{x}) \geq E(f_W(\mathbf{x}))$$

for any $\mathbf{x} \in \mathbb{R}^N$. That is, each message $\mathbf{x^m} \in \mathcal{M}$ is a stable fixed point in the retrieving dynamics.

The **HOP** protocol enjoys two practical properties. Namely, it is local, i.e., W_{ij} depends only on the information available to the i and j-th neurons, and it is incremental, i.e., the writing of a new message depends only on the old W and the new message. The writing capacity of **HOP** protocol for random messages is equal to $\frac{N}{2 \ln N}$ for error free recovery (except for a vanishing fraction of messages) [15] and is approximately $0.14N$ when a vanishing fraction of errors is tolerated [9]. (See [15] for exact definitions and more notions of capacity.)

The pseudo-inverse (**PSE**) protocol is proposed in [10] and is shown to attain a writing capacity of N. In this protocol the (i, j)-th entry of the weight matrix is defined as

$$W_{ij} := \frac{1}{N} \sum_{m=1}^{M} \sum_{m'=1}^{M} x_i^m (Q^{-1})_{mm'} x_j^{m'}, \tag{5}$$

where $Q_{mm'} = \frac{1}{N} \sum_{k=1}^{N} x_k^m x_k^{m'}$ and $(Q^{-1})_{mm'}$ is the (m, m')-th entry of the matrix Q^{-1}.

While the **PSE** achieves a larger writing capacity compared to **HOP**, it loses some of the practically appealing aspects of the **HOP** protocol. A local and incremental protocol with writing capacity $\frac{N}{\sqrt{2 \ln N}}$ is constructed in [17]. We refer to this protocol as **STO**. In this protocol, the (i, j)-th element of matrix W is computed recursively by

$$W_{ij}^m = W_{ij}^{m-1} + \frac{1}{N} x_i^m x_j^m - \frac{1}{N} x_i^m h_{ji}^m - \frac{1}{N} h_{ij}^m x_j^m, \tag{6}$$

where $W_{ij}^0 = 0$, $h_{ij}^m = \sum_{k=1, k \neq i,j}^N W_{ik}^{m-1} x_k^m$, and $m = 1, 2, \ldots, M$. The resulting matrix W^M is then taken as W.

A more recent protocol is the minimum probability flow (**MPF**) protocol [8].

$$K(W) = \sum_{m=1}^M \sum_{\mathbf{x}' \in \mathcal{N}(\mathbf{x}^m)} \exp \left(\frac{E(\mathbf{x}^m) - E(\mathbf{x}')}{2} \right), \tag{7}$$

where $\mathcal{N}(\mathbf{x})$ is the set of state vectors within Hamming distance one from $\mathbf{x}$ and E is the energy of a state as in (4). (Recall that E depends on W.) In effect, the protocol works by designating a W that not only assigns the messages to local minima of the energy function E, but also shapes the region around such local minima so that no state within Hamming distance one from a message attains the same energy level as the message. (Assuming the distance between any two messages in $\mathcal{M}$ is larger than two.)

Our approach to writing on Hopfield networks resembles that of the **MPF**, where in essence we locate the messages as local minima of the energy function and shape the region around such minima. We rely on a simple connection to recurrent neural networks, which casts the writing problem as a supervised learning problem. Contrast to **MPF**, the Hamming radius within which the energy function is shaped is not limited to one, and can be viewed a tunable parameter via the choice of the training set, which will be described in detail in experiments section.

3   TRN Writing Protocol

We regard the writing to a Hopfield network as that of training a recurrent neural network. A *recurrent neural network* (RNN) of length L is a dynamic system that takes a sequence $(\mathbf{u}^1, \mathbf{u}^2, \ldots, \mathbf{u}^L)$ as an input and generates a sequence $(\mathbf{y}^1, \mathbf{y}^2, \ldots, \mathbf{y}^L)$ as an output according to

$$\mathbf{s}^t = f(\mathbf{s}^{t-1}, \mathbf{u}^t) \tag{8}$$

$$\mathbf{y}^t = g(\mathbf{s}^t, \mathbf{u}^t), \tag{9}$$

where $\mathbf{s}^t$ is referred to as the *state* of the network, the first equation as the *state-update equation*, and the second as the *output equation*. Graphically, the structure of a recurrent unit is shown in Fig. 1.

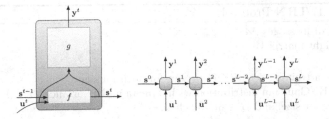

Fig. 1. Generic recurrent neural network of length L. Left: one time step. Right: L time steps.

One of the earliest RNNs [6], often referred to as the Vanilla RNN, specializes the state-update equation to

$$\mathbf{s}^t = \tanh(W\mathbf{s}^{t-1} + U\mathbf{u}^t + \mathbf{b}), \tag{10}$$

where the tanh function is applied element-wise, W and U are matrices of appropriate sizes, and $\mathbf{b}$ is a vector of appropriate size. The output function of Vanilla RNN may vary depending on applications.

Note that in the degenerate case when $\mathbf{u}^t = \mathbf{0}$, for all t, and $\mathbf{b} = \mathbf{0}$, Eq. (10) reduces to (1) with the exception that the sign function in (1) is replaced with the tanh function in (10). As such, a sensible construction of a training set from the set of messages so that, after training, the messages are local minima of a proper choice of a loss function may be viewed as a writing protocol as discussed below.

Given a set of message $\mathcal{M} = \{\mathbf{x}^1, \mathbf{x}^2, \cdots, \mathbf{x}^M\} \subseteq \{\pm 1\}^N$ as in the introduction, a training set can be constructed as $\{(\mathbf{x}^1, \mathbf{p}^{1,k}), \ldots, (\mathbf{x}^M, \mathbf{p}^{M,k}) \mid k = 1, \ldots, K\}$, i.e., for each message we generate K probes, which can be understood as some corrupted versions of the message. (Different noise levels are tried out in the experiments section.) Since the objective is to retrieve a target message $\mathbf{x}^m$ from its probe $\mathbf{p}^{m,k}$, we define the loss function as following,

$$D(W) = \sum_{m=1}^{M}\sum_{k=1}^{K} \|\mathbf{x}^m - f_W^L(W\mathbf{p}^{m,k})\|^2 \tag{11}$$

where f_W^L is the tanh function applied L-times to $W\mathbf{p}^{m,k}$, $\|\cdot\|$ is the euclidean norm. The objective is to minimize the loss function over W, to which end we use the stochastic gradient descent (SGD) [2] to train the RNN. We take the resulting W as the Hopfield weight matrix and refer to the above procedure of obtaining W as the **TRN** writing protocol. The algorithm is summarized in Algorithm 1.

4 Theoretical Results

Two performance metrics, the Message Error Rate (MER) and the Bit Error Rate (BER) are used to evaluate the performance of each protocol. Namely, we define

---

Algorithm 1. TRN Protocol

Input: A set of messages $\mathcal{M} = \{\mathbf{x}^1, \dots, \mathbf{x}^M\}$
Output: Weight matrix W

1: Construct a training set with K probes for each message
2: Initialize W (Gaussian distribution with 0 mean and 1 variance), $r = 1$, $A = M * K$
   is training set size, and B is minibach size
3: **while** $r < 1000$ (maximum number of iterations) **do**
4:   Set $S = 0$, Random sample a minibach $\{(\mathbf{x}^B, \mathbf{p}^B)\}$
5:   **for** $i = 1, \dots, B$ **do**
6:     Computer the gradient of loss on weight W
       $S \leftarrow S + \nabla_W D(W, \{(\mathbf{x}^i, \mathbf{p}^i)\})$
7:   **end for**
8:   $W \leftarrow W - \epsilon \cdot S$ (ϵ is the learning rate)
9:   **for** $i = 1, \dots, A$ **do**
10:    Calculate the loss of every training sample i
       $d_i = ||\mathbf{x}^i - f_W^L(\mathbf{p}^i))||^2$
11: **end for**
12: Calculate the loss and difference: $D(r) = \sum_{i=1}^{A} d_i$, $\Delta D \leftarrow |D(r) - D(r - 100)|$
13: **if** $\Delta D < \delta$ (δ is convergence threshold.) **then**
14:    exit while loop
15: **end if**
16: $r \leftarrow r + 1$
17: **end while**
18: **return** W

$$\text{MER} := \frac{1}{|\widetilde{\mathcal{P}}_{\text{test}}|} \sum_{(\mathbf{x}^m, \mathbf{p}^{m,k}) \in \widetilde{\mathcal{P}}_{\text{test}}} \mathbf{1}(\mathbf{x}^m = f_W^\infty(\mathbf{p}^{m,k})) \tag{12}$$

where $f_W^\infty(\cdot)$ is the retrived message, and $\mathbf{1}(\cdot)$ is the indicator function taking value 1 if its argument is true, and 0 otherwise. Similarly,

$$\text{BER} := \frac{1}{N|\widetilde{\mathcal{P}}_{\text{test}}|} \sum_{(\mathbf{x}^m, \mathbf{p}^{m,k}) \in \widetilde{\mathcal{P}}_{\text{test}}} \mathbf{N}(\mathbf{x}^m, f_W^\infty(\mathbf{p}^{m,k})) \tag{13}$$

where $\mathbf{N}(\cdot, \cdot)$ counts the number of locations at which the correct and the retrived message differ. In this section, we induce that the bound of metrics is related with the memory messages and the noise level of training set in our specific case, which supports our intuition of training the RNN to get the weight of Hopfield network.

Theorem 1. *For a given memory message set $\mathcal{M}$ which is drawn from the Bernoulli (α) sequence of length N, if the weight setting of Hopfield networks is the **TRN** method under training set with noise level β, then the bound of maximum bit error rate (BER) and message error rate (MER) are*

$$BER_i = \phi(\mu_{h_i^1}, \sigma_{h_i}; 0) + [1 - \phi(\mu_{h_i^{-1}}, \sigma_{h_i}; 0)],$$

$$BER_{max} = \max_i BER_i, \tag{14}$$

$$MER = 1 - (1 - BER_{max})^N.$$

$\phi(\mu_{h_i^1}, \sigma_{h_i}; 0)$ *represent the integral larger than 0 with the Gaussian distribution with parameter mean value $\mu_{h_i^1}$ and variance σ_{h_i} larger than 0, where $\mu_{h_i^1}, \mu_{h_i^{-1}}, \sigma_{h_i}$ are:*

$$\mu_{h_i^1} = W_{ii}(1 - 2\beta) + \sum_{k \neq i}^{N} W_{ik}(1 - 2\alpha)(2\beta - 1), \tag{15}$$

$$\mu_{h_i^{-1}} = W_{ii}(2\beta - 1) + \sum_{k \neq i}^{N} W_{ik}(1 - 2\alpha)(2\beta - 1), \tag{16}$$

$$\sigma_{h_i}^2 = \sum_{k \neq i}^{N} W_{ik}^2[\beta^2 + (1 - \beta)^2]4\alpha(1 - \alpha). \tag{17}$$

Proof. Without loss of generality, element i's state for a specific memory message vector X^m is $x_i^m = 1$. Corresponding noise message is Y^m. The i's output can be expressed as $h_i = W_{ii}y_i^m + \sum_{k \neq i}^{N} W_{ik}y_k^m$ approximately, since most noise messages retrieve to the attractor just by one step's evolution, according to the explanation of in Sect. 3.

$$\mathbb{E}(h_i|x_i^m = 1) = W_{ii}(1 - 2\beta) + \sum_{k \neq i} W_{ik}(1 - 2\alpha)(2\beta - 1). \tag{18}$$

Since $R_k = W_{ik}[\beta\bar{X}_k + (1 - \beta)X_k]$, R_k is an independent random variable, each with finite expected value μ_k and variance σ_k^2.

$$\mu_k = W_{ik}(1 - 2\alpha)(2\beta - 1), \tag{19}$$
$$\sigma_k^2 = W_{ik}^2[\beta^2 + (1 - \beta)^2]4\alpha(1 - \alpha). \tag{20}$$

According to the Lyapunov Central Limit Theorem, if $N \to \infty$, then $\sum_{k \neq i}^{N} R_k$ is a Gaussian distribution with

$$\mu = \sum_{k \neq i}^{N} W_{ik}(1 - 2\alpha)(2\beta - 1), \tag{21}$$

$$\sigma^2 = \sum_{k \neq i}^{N} W_{ik}^2[\beta^2 + (1 - \beta)^2]4\alpha(1 - \alpha). \tag{22}$$

The above formula shows h_i is a Gaussian distribution as $x_i^m = 1$ and $N \to \infty$

$$\mu_{h_i^1} = W_{ii}(1 - 2\beta) + \sum_{k \neq i}^{N} W_{ik}(1 - 2\alpha)(2\beta - 1), \tag{23}$$

$$\sigma_{h_i^1}^2 = \sum_{k \neq i}^{N} W_{ik}^2[\beta^2 + (1 - \beta)^2]4\alpha(1 - \alpha). \tag{24}$$

When $x_i^m = -1$, and $N \to \infty$, the prove is all the same with $X_i = 1$. Since the $\sigma_{h_i^1}$ is the same with $\sigma_{h_i^{-1}}$, then it can be abbreviated as σ_{h_i}. So the bit error rate (BER) and the message error rate (MER) are as the Eq. (14).

According to this theorem, if the memory messages $\mathcal{M}$ and the noise level of the training set β are given, we can get the bound of metrics of the **TRN** protocol. The meaning is that the metrics MER and BER on the **TRN** protocol can bound by this theorem. In other words, our **TRN** protocol to writing the weight of Hopfield is feasible and controllable.

5   Experiments

We compare **TRN** with existing writing protocols by performing a number of experiments. Each experiment involves three sets of data: a message set $\mathcal{M} = \{\mathbf{x}^1, \ldots, \mathbf{x}^M\}$, a training set $\widetilde{\mathcal{P}}_{\text{train}}$, and a testing set $\widetilde{\mathcal{P}}_{\text{test}}$. The training set

$$\widetilde{\mathcal{P}}_{\text{train}} = \{(\mathbf{x}^1, \mathbf{p}^{1,k}), \ldots, (\mathbf{x}^M, \mathbf{p}^{M,k}) \mid k = 1, \ldots, K\}$$

is constructed by generating K probes for each message, where each probe is generated by flipping every bit of probe with probability β. The fraction β of corrupted probability in the message is referred to as the noise level. The testing set is generated similarly where we use γ to refer to the noise level to avoid confusion.

In the following experiments, we concentrate on the noise recovery ability and the capacity of under various protocols. In all our experiments, each message in the memory message set $\mathcal{M}$ is generated by drawing a i.i.d. Bernoulli$(\frac{1}{2})$ sequence of length N.

5.1   Noise Recovery Study

In this experiment, the number of neuron N is chosen as 100, the learning rate is set to 0.001, and the number of memory messages M takes values in $\{10, 15, 20\}$. These choices of M are based on the understanding that the capacity of Hopfield network under **HOP** is about $0.14N$ [9]. So the three choices correspond respectively to "below capacity", "around capacity", and "above capacity". For each message in $\mathcal{M}$, 10000 noisy probes are generated. In this process, we heuristically allocate the number of probes for each noise level $\gamma = 0.1$, 0.2, and 0.3

Table 1. The comparison among different protocols on metrics MER and BER under the testing set with different noise levels γ and different number of memory messages M. $N = 100$.

MER							BER						
γ	M	HOP	PSE	STO	MPF	TRN	γ	M	HOP	PSE	STO	MPF	TRN
0.1	10	0.017	0	0	0	**0**	0.1	10	0.001	0	0	0	**0**
	15	0.562	0	0	0	**0**		15	0.049	0	0	0	**0**
	20	0.893	0	0.009	0	**0**		20	0.158	0	0	0	**0**
0.2	10	0.089	0.001	0.002	0.005	**0.001**	0.2	10	0.01	0	0	0.001	**0**
	15	0.705	0.01	0.017	0.008	**0.002**		15	0.102	0.001	0.002	0.002	**0**
	20	0.952	0.058	0.11	0.021	**0.008**		20	0.23	0.007	0.012	0.004	**0.002**
0.3	10	0.353	0.103	0.111	0.143	**0.063**	0.3	10	0.079	0.025	0.027	0.043	**0.021**
	15	0.883	0.279	0.3	0.207	**0.138**		15	0.212	0.059	0.065	0.06	**0.041**
	20	0.989	0.551	0.57	0.34	**0.253**		20	0.312	0.11	0.114	0.093	**0.069**

to construct our training set and testing set. Our method **TRN** adopts 3-layer RNN to get the weight of Hopfield network.

The testing results are tabulated in Table 1. Because we just keep three figures after the decimal point, some little BER is approximate to 0. We can find the following observations.

At low noise level $\gamma = 0.1$, all protocols perform well except **HOP**. The fact that **HOP** demonstrates poor noise resilience can be explained by its simple construction of weight matrix, which only takes into account the memory message set. On the other hand, the **HOP** loses efficiency even on 15 memory messages since the MER = 0.562. It is obviously verified by experiments that **HOP** cannot handle more memory messages than $0.14N$.

At medium noise level $\gamma = 0.2$, most protocols perform well except **HOP**. There is a fact that the MER and BER are increased with the number of memory messages. It is obviously judged that there is a capacity among all the protocols. The protocol **HOP** can handle 10 memory messages, but get failed on 15 and 20 memory messages. Except that **HOP**, all other protocols can get better results among all memory messages.

At high noise level $\gamma = 0.3$, there are some errors among all protocols on all memory messages. Below the capacity of Hopfield network, all protocols except **HOP** can handle the memory task. Around the capacity of Hopfield network and above capacity of Hopfield network, there are more errors on other protocols. We can also find that along with the increase of memory messages for all the protocols, the memory ability is getting weaker.

In a word, as the noise contained in the probe increases, all protocols degrade their performance, among which the degradation of **TRN** is the slowest. On 10 messages (below capacity), most protocols perform well except **HOP**. The fact that **HOP** demonstrates poor noise resilience can be explained by its simple construction of weight matrix, which only takes into account the message set. All other messages demonstrate some level of noise resilience, among which **TRN** performs the best. Even operating above capacity, namely on 20 messages, **TRN** demonstrates an acceptable error rate.

5.2   Capacity Study

According to the outstanding results of our protocol **TRN** on the noise recovery experiments, we do more experiments on different lengths of Hopfield network: Short-Message experiments, Medium-Message experiments and Long-Message experiment, to study the capacity of our protocol **TRN** with other exiting protocols.

In the following experiments, the training $\widetilde{\mathcal{P}}_{\text{train}}$ is a mixture of probes generated using noise level β. Because the number of patterns increases with the noise level, we adopt the following equation to get the different ratio of every noise level to alleviate sampling difficulty.

$$N_\beta = \frac{1}{2} + 0.01 \cdot (1 + \beta)^{12} \tag{25}$$

$$P_{N_\beta} = \frac{N_\beta}{\sum_{\alpha \in \{\beta\}} N_\alpha} \tag{26}$$

On Short-Message experiments, the training set $\widetilde{\mathcal{P}}_{\text{train}}$ is generated by 20000 noisy probe for each message in $\mathcal{M}$, and the testing set $\widetilde{\mathcal{P}}_{\text{test}}$ is generated by 10000 noisy probe for each message. On Medium-Message and Long-Message experiments, both the training set $\widetilde{\mathcal{P}}_{\text{train}}$ and the testing set $\widetilde{\mathcal{P}}_{\text{test}}$ are generated by 10000 noisy probe for each message due to limited computing power. In this process, we heuristically allocate the number of probes for each noise level so that the number of probes grows with the noise level according to the above equation. The maximize training noise level β and testing noise level γ are 0.3 on Short-Message experiments, and for the other experiments, we allocate the maximize training noise level β and testing noise level γ as 0.1.

Short-Message Experiments. In these short-message experiments, the message length N is chosen as 200, and the number of messages M takes values between 15 and 50 with gap 1. Again noting that these choices of M covers $0.14N$. The training $\widetilde{\mathcal{P}}_{\text{train}}$ is generated using the maximize noise level $\beta = 0.3$. The training $\widetilde{\mathcal{P}}_{\text{train}}$ is a mixture of probes generated using noise level β from 0.05 to 0.3 (with spacing 0.05). Then take the above equation to calculate the exactly number of training set. For each message in $\mathcal{M}$, 20000 noisy probes are generated. For the testing $\widetilde{\mathcal{P}}_{\text{test}}$, the only difference is that we generate 10000 testing probes for each message in $\mathcal{M}$. The size of training batch is 2000 and the learning rate is 0.001. Our method **TRN** adopts 3-layer RNN to get the weight of Hopfield network.

The results of these experiments are shown in Fig. 2. First of all, as the number of the memory messages increase, all protocols degrade their performance on metric MER and BER, among which the degradation of **TRN** is the slowest.

Besides, the effective of protocol **STO** and **PSE** is almost the same. The protocol **HOP** and **MPF** have some vibration with the number of memory. So our protocol has the perfect efficiency and stability. With 40 memory messages in 200-neuron Hopfield network, the MER is below 0.2, this is rather low compared with the other previous protocols. Moreover, the tendency of BER is the same with MER from the right figure in Fig. 2. This is in accord with our intuition.

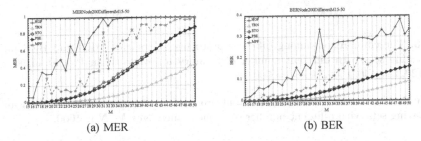

(a) MER   (b) BER

Fig. 2. The comparison among different protocols on metrics MER and BER under the testing sets with different number of memory messages M in $\{15, 16, \ldots, 50\}$ $N = 200$.

Medium-Message Experiments. In these medium-message experiments, the message length N is chosen as 500, and the number of messages M takes on different values. The training $\widetilde{\mathcal{P}}_{train}$ is a mixture of probes generated using noise level β from 0.02 to 0.1 (with spacing 0.02). Then take the above equation to calculate the exactly number of training set. For each message in $\mathcal{M}$, 10000 noisy probes are generated. Testing probes with noise level $\gamma = 0.1$. For each message, 10000 testing probes are used. The size of training batch is 2000 and the learning rate is 0.01. Our method **TRN** adopts 2-layer RNN to get the weight of Hopfield network.

The results of these experiments are shown in Fig. 3. Similarly, as the number of the memory messages increases, all protocols degrade their performance on metric MER and BER, among which the degradation of **TRN** is the slowest. With 40 messages (around the McLiece's capacity), most protocols perform well except **HOP**, this result verifies that the correctness of capacity description in McLiece paper. The fact that **STO** doesn't work on the size of 120 memory messages, and **PSE** is invalid on the size of 140 memory messages. When the size of memory messages increase to 150, all protocols collapse except our protocol **TRN**. Even on the size 200 of the memory messages, our protocol **TRN** also performs well. But our protocol gets faild on the size 250 with a low MER 0.0486.

Long-Message Experiments. In the long-message experiments, the parameter settings are the same with medium-message experiments.

All the results are similar with the Medium-Message experiments. Basically, the protocol **HOP** and **MPF** can just handle the low number of memory messages. The other three protocols **STO**, **PSE** and **TRN** can have a good efficient performance on metric MER and BER at a low number of memory messages.

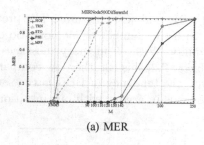
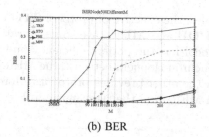

(a) MER   (b) BER

Fig. 3. The comparison among different protocols on metrics MER and BER under the testing sets with different number of memory messages M in $\{35, 40, 45, 90, 100, 110, 120, 130, 140, 150, 200\}$ $N = 500$.

Table 2. The comparison among different protocols on metrics MER and BER under the testing sets with different number of memory messages M. $N = 1000$.

M	Metric	HOP	PSE	STO	MPF	TRN
45	MER	0	0	0	0	**0**
	BER	0	0	0	0	**0**
70	MER	0.0714	0	0	0	**0**
	BER	0.0001	0	0	0	**0**
80	MER	0.1625	0	0	0	**0**
	BER	0.0002	0	0	0	**0**
190	MER	1	0	0	0.9725	**0**
	BER	0.3137	0	0	0.0159	**0**
200	MER	1	0	0.0015	0.9899	**0**
	BER	0.3332	0	0	0.0358	**0**
300	MER	1	0	0.2848	1	**0**
	BER	0.3511	0	0.0007	0.2563	**0**
350	MER	1	0.0042	0.6891	1	**0**
	BER	0.3424	0.0001	0.0061	0.3716	**0**
450	MER	1	1	0.9981	1	**0.0003**
	BER	0.3593	0.0442	0.0377	0.2761	**0**

The fact that **STO** doesn't work on 200 memory messages, and **PSE** gets failed on 350 memory messages. When the size of memory messages increase to 350, all protocols collapse except our protocol **TRN** (Table 2).

6 Conclusion

Our proposed protocol **TRN** possesses two advantages compared to the existing writing protocols for Hopfield network. On one hand, our writing protocol has a better ability of noise recovery compared to the other existing writing protocols, since our **TRN** training protocol is based on training set considering the noise recovery problem. On the other hand, the capacity of our writing protocol is bigger than other existing writing protocols from all experiments.

It should be noted that the superior performance of **TRN** does not come free of cost. The complexity of this protocol is much higher than the other protocols, particularly at long message length N. This is the number of potential noisy problems grows exponentially with N. At large N, generating the training set by sampling from the noisy probes with a decent sampling rate would result in a large training set, increasing the complexity significantly. In our experiments with $N = 1000$, it appears that the time required in **TRN** is about 5 times more than **MPF** and nearly 100 times more than **PSE**, **STO** and **HOP**.

This however does not close the possibility of using the **TRN** approach as a practical writing protocol. We believe that if one is to cleverly introduce additional structure in the connection matrix W of **TRN**, the required training examples can be significantly reduced. Moreover, the experiments are conducted on the artificial data, so we can do more experiments on some real data. Last but not least, the size of capacity of our writing protocol **TRN** should be studied in theory. We are planning to further investigate along these directions.

References

1. Anderson, J.R., Bower, G.H.: Human Associative Memory. Psychology Press, London (2014)
2. Bottou, L.: Largescale machine learning with stochastic gradient descent. In: Lechevallier, Y., Saporta, G. (eds.) Proceedings of COMPSTAT 2010, pp. 177–186. Springer, Heidelberg (2010). https://doi.org/10.1007/978-3-7908-2604-3_16
3. Cheng, K.S., Lin, J.S., Mao, C.W.: The application of competitive hopfield neural network to medical image segmentation. IEEE Trans. Med. Imaging **15**(4), 560–567 (1996)
4. Ding, J., Sun, Y.Z., Tan, P., Ning, Y.: Detecting communities in networks using competitive hopfield neural network. In: 2018 International Joint Conference on Neural Networks (IJCNN), pp. 1–7. IEEE (2018)
5. Duan, S., Dong, Z., Hu, X., Wang, L., Li, H.: Small-world hopfield neural networks with weight salience priority and memristor synapses for digit recognition. Neural Comput. Appl. **27**(4), 837–844 (2016)
6. Elman, J.L.: Finding structure in time. Cogn. Sci. **14**, 179–211 (1990)
7. Folli, V., Leonetti, M., Ruocco, G.: On the maximum storage capacity of the hopfield model. Front. Comput. Neurosci. **10**, 144 (2017)
8. Hillar, C., SohlDickstein, J., Koepsell, K.: Efficient and optimal binary hopfield associative memory storage using minimum probability flow. arXiv preprint arXiv:1204.2916 (2012)
9. Hopfield, J.J.: Neural networks and physical systems with emergent collective computational abilities. Proc. Natl. Acad. Sci. **79**(8), 2554–2558 (1982)
10. Kanter, I., Sompolinsky, H.: Associative recall of memory without errors. Phys. Rev. A **35**(1), 380 (1987)
11. Kobayashi, M.: Multistate vector product hopfield neural networks. Neurocomputing **272**, 425–431 (2018)

12. Krotov, D., Hopfield, J.J.: Dense associative memory for pattern recognition. In: Advances in Neural Information Processing Systems, pp. 1172–1180 (2016)
13. Lee, K.Y., Sode-Yome, A., Park, J.H.: Adaptive hopfield neural networks for economic load dispatch. IEEE Trans. Power Syst. **13**(2), 519–526 (1998)
14. McCulloch, W.S., Pitts, W.: A logical calculus of the ideas immanent in nervous activity. Bull. Math. Biophys. **5**(4), 115–133 (1943)
15. McEliece, R., Posner, E., Rodemich, E., Venkatesh, S.: The capacity of the hopfield associative memory. IEEE Trans. Inform. Theory **33**(4), 461–482 (1987)
16. Rebentrost, P., Bromley, T.R., Weedbrook, C., Lloyd, S.: Quantum hopfield neural network. Phys. Rev. A **98**(4), 042308 (2018)
17. Storkey, A.: Increasing the capacity of a hopfield network without sacrificing functionality. In: Gerstner, W., Germond, A., Hasler, M., Nicoud, J.-D. (eds.) ICANN 1997. LNCS, vol. 1327, pp. 451–456. Springer, Heidelberg (1997). https://doi.org/10.1007/BFb0020196
18. Wang, S.: Classification with incomplete survey data: a hopfield neural network approach. Comput. Oper. Res. **32**(10), 2583–2594 (2005)
19. Zhen, H., Wang, S.N., Zhou, H.J.: Unsupervised prototype learning in an associative-memory network. arXiv preprint arXiv:1704.02848 (2017)

Towards Efficient Convolutional Neural Networks Through Low-Error Filter Saliency Estimation

Zi Wang[1], Chengcheng Li[1]($\boxtimes$), Xiangyang Wang[2], and Dali Wang[1,3]

[1] University of Tennessee, Knoxville, TN, USA
{zwang84,cli42}@vols.utk.edu
[2] Sun Yat-sen University, Guangzhou, China
mcswxy@mail.sysu.edu.cn
[3] Oak Ridge National Laboratory, Oak Ridge, TN, USA
wangd@ornl.gov

Abstract. Filter saliency based channel pruning is a state-of-the-art method for deep convolutional neural network compression and acceleration. This channel pruning method ranks the importance of individual filter by estimating its impact of each filter's removal on the training loss, and then remove the least important filters and fine-tune the remnant network. In this work, we propose a systematic channel pruning method that significantly reduces the estimation error of filter saliency. Different from existing approaches, our method largely reduces the magnitude of parameters in a network by introducing alternating direction method of multipliers (ADMM) into the pre-training procedure. Therefore, the estimation of filter saliency based on Taylor expansion is significantly improved. Extensive experiments with various benchmark network architectures and datasets demonstrate that the proposed method has a much improved unimportant filter selection capability and outperform state-of-the-art channel pruning method.

Keywords: Network pruning · Efficient deep learning ·
Alternating direction method of multipliers (ADMM)

1 Introduction

Over the past decade, deep convolutional neural networks (DCNN) have been widely adapted in a wide range of fields [4,9,12,15,18,23,28]. However, the model size and computational requirements restrict the DCNN deployment on resource-constrained platforms. Hence, numerous approaches have been proposed to tackle this challenge. Among these approaches, channel pruning [20] has been identified as an effective technique. Compared with weight pruning [7], it can remove the entire filters as well as the corresponding feature maps, eliminating the need of customized software and hardware.

Z. Wang and C. Li—With equal contribution.

ⓒ Springer Nature Switzerland AG 2019
A. C. Nayak and A. Sharma (Eds.): PRICAI 2019, LNAI 11671, pp. 255–267, 2019.
https://doi.org/10.1007/978-3-030-29911-8_20

A typical channel pruning pipeline consists of three iterative steps, (1) training an over-parameterized neural network, (2) pruning the least important filters based on a certain criterion, and (3) fine-tuning the remained network to mitigate performance loss. An appropriate criterion plays a critical role in achieving competitive pruned models. Many reasonable criteria have been developed in recent years [19,20,25]. However, most of the criteria for filter ranking are heuristic, lacking theoretical guarantee on the sustained performance. Furthermore, lots of channel pruning methods rely on manually-crafted pruning ratio for each layer.

Saliency-based pruning methods measure the impact of each filter's removal to the training loss, i.e., the importance of each filter. The first proposed method is called Optimal Brain Damage (OBD) [17] that formulated the saliency of each weight as a Taylor series, and only used the second component to estimate training loss change. For channel pruning, [24] used the first component of Taylor expansion (i.e. Taylor series) to estimate the loss change of each filter's removal with a significantly reduced computation cost. This method has achieved outstanding performance. Compared with previous works, this channel pruning method has two significant advantages: (1) introducing a deductive filters ranking criterion with a theoretical guarantee on performance, and (2) automatically discovering the optimal structures without a pre-set pruning ratio for each layer. Our work is built upon this method.

However, the precision of saliceny estimation using Taylor expansion is influenced by many factors that are not well addressed in the original work. In specific, the importance of filters is calculated with the first order Taylor series to estimate the loss change when the filter is pruned from the network, i.e. filter's associated feature map is set as $h = 0$. Therefore, the ranking performance highly rely on how close to zero the magnitudes of the network's feature maps are and how fast and frequently the parameters' gradients change. Since fine-tuning a neural network is a dynamic process with high uncertainty, the evolutionary trend of the parameters' magnitudes and gradients largely remains untraceable. In this situation, one of the feasible ways to increase the ranking performance based on Taylor expansion is to reduce the magnitudes of the feature maps so that the estimation error can be reduced accordingly. In this paper, we propose a channel pruning approach built upon the original Taylor expansion method [24] to achieve precise saliency estimation of filters and the subsequent filter ranking. This is achieved by introducing filter level regularization constrains with both ℓ_2 and ADMM regularization. The benefits of the proposed method are three folds, (1) the magnitudes of the activation values can be largely reduced, (2) a more precise saliency estimation and the subsequent filter ranking can be achieved, and (3) the pruning performance are significantly improved accordingly. Extensive experiments on multiple benchmark network architectures (LeNet-5, AlexNet, and VGG-16) and datasets (MNIST, Cifar-10, and Cifar-100) show that our approach outperforms the state-of-the-art Taylor expansion method in terms of filter ranking and performance of the pruned models.

The rest of the paper is organized as follows. Section 2 briefly introduces several related works. Section 3 describes necessary preliminaries of channel pruning and presents our approach. Sections 4 and 5 are experimental results and discussions, respectively. Finally, Sect. 6 concludes the paper.

2 Related Work

The idea of saliency based network pruning can go back to two pioneered work, Optimal Brain Damage (OBD) [17] and Optimal Brain Surgeon (OBS) [8], which used second order Taylor expansion as the criterion for filter importance calculation. With the development of deep learning, many works for weight pruning have been proposed [3,5,7,33]. One influential work [7] zeros out weights with certain pre-set thresholds. Since weight based pruning does not actually remove the zero-value weights from the neural network, model size would not be reduced without specialized hardware [6].

For convolutional neural network acceleration, channel pruning [10,11,20,24] can prune the entire filters (convolutional kernel) and their associated feature maps, so specialized hardware is not required for the implementation. Channel pruning approaches usually use certain criteria to rank all the filters in a neural network and prune low-ranked (i.e., less important) filters. For example, [20] and [25] pruned the filters whose magnitudes of weights or feature maps are below a threshold. [24] utilized first order Taylor expansion to estimate the loss change when each filter is removed from the neural network, and achieved state-of-the-art performance. There is also another branch of methods that considered the pruning task as an optimization problem. For example, some studies minimized the reconstruction error of the next layer of the pruned filters [10], or the last fully connected layer [31].

A number of network pruning approaches introduced regularization to the neural network. [13,21] introduced a scaling factor to each filter, imposed regularization to these factors, and pruned the filters whose associated scaling factors are small. Group sparsity based regularization was also utilized to penalize and prune unimportant parameters [1,29]. ADMM was used as a dynamic regularizer to obtain sparsity in a pre-trained model before the pruning operation [19,30,33]. Although the above works added regularization to the neural network, their purpose is to impose sparsity in the network. Different from these approaches, we aim to use regularization to reduce the magnitude of the parameters in order to get better filter ranking performance with Taylor expansion.

3 Proposed Methods

In this section, we start by introducing the preliminaries of the state-of-the-art channel pruning approach based on Taylor expansion. Then we analyze the limitations of this approach and propose two potential methods to improve the performance.

3.1 Taylor Expansion Based Pruning

Consider an L-layer DCNN parameterized by $W = \{w_1^1, w_1^2, \cdots, w_1^{C_1}, w_2^1, \cdots, w_L^{C_L}\}$, where $C_i (i = 1, 2 \cdots, L)$ is the number of filters in each layer. And the associated loss function is $f(W)$. The channel pruning task can be formulated as minimizing the loss change when a desired number of filters are removed from the network (Eq. 1).

$$\underset{W'}{\text{minimize}}|f(W') - f(W)| \quad s.t. \quad ||W'||_0 \leq B, \tag{1}$$

where B is the maximal number of non-zero filters allowed in the pruned network.

Suppose $H = \{h_1^1, h_1^2, \cdots, h_1^{C_1}, h_2^1, \cdots, h_2^{C_2}, \cdots, h_L^{C_L}\}$ are the feature maps associated with W. When a feature map h_i^j is pruned from the network, the loss change can be calculated with Eq. 2. For simplicity, we replace h_i^j with h_i in the following.

$$|\Delta f(h_i)| = |f(h_i = 0) - f(h_i)|, \tag{2}$$

where $f(h_i = 0)$ is the loss when h_i is pruned, $f(h_i)$ is the original loss when h_i is present. The first order Taylor expansion at the point $h_i = 0$ can be represented as Eq. 3.

$$f(h_i = 0) = f(h_i) - \frac{\delta f}{\delta h_i} h_i + R_i(h_i = 0). \tag{3}$$

The higher order remainder $R_1 = \frac{\delta^2 f}{\delta(h_i^2 = \xi)} \frac{h_i^2}{2}$ is trivial, so it is omitted for the estimation of loss change in this approach. Combining Eqs. 2 and 3, we have:

$$|\Delta f(h_i)| = |\frac{\delta f}{\delta h_i} h_i|, \tag{4}$$

which means that we can estimate the loss change of a filter's removal with its activation value h_i and the corresponding gradient, with a forward and backward pass by feeding training samples into the DCNN. Hence, filters with the smallest $|\Delta f(h_i)|$ can removed from the DCNN since their corresponding performance degradation is trivial.

3.2   Analysis of Estimation Error

The performance of the Taylor expansion approach highly relies on the unimportant filters selection strategy, i.e., the importance estimation of each filter's removal via first order Taylor expansion. The estimation error is caused by the omission of the higher order remainder R_1. Since training/fine-tuning a neural network is a highly dynamic process, the evolutionary trend of the parameters' magnitudes and gradients is untraceable. As the magnitudes of activation values grows, the higher order remainder R_1 is likely to increase since the second term $\frac{h_i^2}{2}$ grows while the first term $\frac{\delta^2 f}{\delta(h_i^2 = \xi)}$ remains untraceable. Take the Sigmoid function $f(x) = 1/(1 + e^{-x})$ as a toy example. Using the first-degree Taylor polynomial and omitting the remainder, we have the estimation of $f(x)$ at the point $x = 0$: $\hat{f}(x) = f(0) + f'(0) \cdot x = 0.25x + 0.5$. Suppose $x = 2$, and the error can be as high as 0.12, compared with the actual value $f(2)$. As x goes away from the origin, the estimation error grows exponentially (Fig. 1).

We propose to reduce the magnitudes of the activation values h to reduce estimation error. An intuitive solution is to add ℓ_2 regularization to the DCNN during the training and/or fine-tuning phase. We will also introduce a more advanced approach to add regularization to the DCNN in the next sub-section.

3.3   ADMM-Based Regularization

In order to improve the pruning performance, we furthermore propose an advanced regularization approach based on ADMM to intelligently reduce the magnitudes of the activation values. ADMM was initially proposed as a non-convex optimization tool [2], and was recently used to obtain weight/channel level sparsity in the DCNN [19,33]. Inspired by these works, we propose to use this technology as a dynamic regularizer to achieve better unimportant filter ranking and selection.

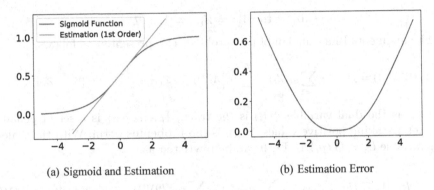

(a) Sigmoid and Estimation   (b) Estimation Error

Fig. 1. Illustration of Sigmoid function, its estimation with first order Taylor series, and the corresponding estimation error.

We first represent the DCNN training/ fine-tuning problem as Eq. 5, which introduces extra constraint to limit the parameters magnitudes:

$$
\begin{aligned}
&\underset{W}{\text{minimize}} \quad f(W) \\
&\text{subject to} \quad card(W_i) \le l_i, i = 1, ..., L,
\end{aligned} \tag{5}
$$

where $W_i = \{w_i^1, w_i^2, \cdots, w_i^{C_i}\}$ is the set of the filters in the i-th layer. The function $card(\cdot)$ gives the number of non-zero filters. l_i is the maximal number of non-zero filters allowed in the i-th layer. We rewrite this formulation as an optimization problem:

$$
\begin{aligned}
&\underset{W}{\text{minimize}} \quad f(W) \\
&\text{subject to} \quad W_i \in S_i, i = 1, ..., L,
\end{aligned} \tag{6}
$$

where $S_i = \{W_i \mid \text{card}(W_i) \leq l_i\}$. The non-convex sets $S_i(i = 1, \cdots, L)$ can be removed with an indicator function $g_i(\cdot)$:

$$\underset{W}{\text{minimize}} \quad f(W) + \sum_{i=1}^{L} g_i(W_i) \tag{7}$$

$$g_i(W_i) = \begin{cases} 0 & \text{if } \text{card}(W_i) < l_i, \\ +\infty & \text{otherwise.} \end{cases}$$

It is clear that the second term of (7) is not differentiable, and ADMM can be used to solve this problem [2,33]. Accordingly, we formulate (7) as its equivalent ADMM form:

$$\underset{W}{\text{minimize}} \quad f(W) + \sum_{i=1}^{L} g_i(Z_i) \tag{8}$$

$$\text{subject to} \quad W_i = Z_i, i = 1, ..., L.$$

The augmented Lagrangian of this problem is represented as follows:

$$L_\rho(W, Z, \Lambda) = f(W) + \sum_{i=1}^{L} g_i(Z_i) + \sum_{i=1}^{L} tr\left[\Lambda_i^T(W_i - Z_i)\right] + \sum_{i=1}^{L}(\rho_i/2)\|W_i - Z_i\|_F^2, \tag{9}$$

where Λ is the dual variable, $tr(\cdot)$ is the trace, $\{\rho_i, ..., \rho_N\}$ is a set of penalty parameters taking positive values, $\|\cdot\|_F^2$ is the Frobenius norm. With the scaled dual variable $U_i = (1/\rho_i)\Lambda_i$, Eq. 9 can be rewritten as:

$$L_\rho(W, Z, U) = f(W) + \sum_{i=1}^{L} g_i(Z_i) + \sum_{i=1}^{L}(\rho_i/2)\|W_i - Z_i + U_i\|_F^2. \tag{10}$$

[2] demonstrated that Eq. 10 can be decomposed into two sub-problems:

$$\underset{W}{\text{minimize}} \quad f(W) + \sum_{i=1}^{L}(\rho_i/2)\|W_i - Z_i^k + U_i^k\|_F^2. \tag{11}$$

$$\underset{W}{\text{minimize}} \quad \sum_{i=1}^{L} g_i(Z_i) + \sum_{i=1}^{L}(\rho_i/2)\|W_i^{k+1} - Z_i + U_i^k\|_F^2. \tag{12}$$

In (11), the first term is just the loss function and the second term can be considered as a special regularizer which is differentiable. This problem can be solved with an iterative procedure where k represents the index of iteration. According to [2,19,33], the solution of (12) can be obtained as:

$$Z_i^{k+1} = \Pi_{S_i}(W_i^{k+1} + U_i^k),$$

where $\Pi_{S_i}(\cdot)$ is the Euclidean projection onto S_i. Z_i^{k+1} can be acquired by zeroing out the desired number of filters in the ith layer. In this study, ℓ_1 norm is used as the criterion for this purpose, i.e., the filters with the smallest ℓ_1 norms are zeroed out. After solving (11) and (12), U_i^{k+1} is updated as $U_i^k + W_i^{k+1} - Z_i^{k+1}$. And the ADMM algorithm is completed.

The ADMM can be considered as a smart regularizer which changes the regularization coefficient dynamically [33]. With ADMM, the magnitudes of the activation values in the DCNN can be significantly reduced while sustaining better performance compared with the ℓ_2 regularization. More details are presented in the experiment and discussion sections. After the training phase with ADMM, the network can be pruned with the vanilla Taylor expansion approach.

4   Experiments

4.1   Setup

We carry out our experiments with the following benchmark network architectures and datasets: LeNet-5 [16] on MNIST, AlexNet [15] on Cifar-10 [14], and VGG16 [26] on Cifar-100 for classification purpose, respectively. For each set of experiments, we pre-train three individual networks, i.e., training a network (1) without any regularization, (2) with ℓ_2-regularization, and (3) with ADMM regularization, respectively. During the pruning and fine-tuning phases, we prune 1, 10 and 40 filters, and fine-tune the remaining sub-structures for 20, 100, and 500 updates, for LeNet-5, AlexNet, and VGG-16, respectively. For all scenarios, a learning rate of 0.0001, a batch size of 64, and an SGD optimizer with a momentum 0.9 are used for both training and fine-tuning phases. We conduct each experiment five times and report the average performance and associated standard deviations.

4.2   Evaluation of the Proposed Method

We evaluate the performance of pruning the networks without regularization (baseline), with ℓ_2, and ADMM regularization for each classification task. The results are shown in Fig. 2. In all scenarios, the propose method with ADMM regularization outperforms the baseline significantly. The networks with ℓ_2 regularization achieve slightly better performance than the baseline in LeNet-5 and AlexNet, and in VGG-16, the performance are comparable with the baseline. It is worth noting that after pre-training, the accuracy of the networks with ADMM regularization is slightly lower than those without regularization in AlexNet and VGG-16, due to the extra constrains introduced by ADMM. However, as the pruning process continues, the performance of the networks with ADMM regularization degrade much less than those without it, and outperform the baseline shortly after a few number of filters are removed from the networks. These observations validate the effectiveness of our proposed approach.

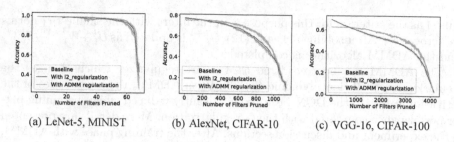

(a) LeNet-5, MINIST   (b) AlexNet, CIFAR-10   (c) VGG-16, CIFAR-100

Fig. 2. Performance comparison of the proposed method and baseline.

4.3   Study of Hyperparameter Selection

In this sub-section, we study the performance curves when introducing different levels of regularization, also refered to as ADMM rates, during network
pre-training. From the results in Sect. 4.2 we find that (1) training LeNet-5 on
MNIST is not a challenging task, and (2) the contribution of the ℓ_2 regularization is not as significant as the ADMM regularization. Therefore, in the following
experiments, we study the effect of introducing ADMM regularization in AlexNet
on Cifar-10 and VGG-16 and Cifar-100, respectively.

For both scenarios, we introduce the following levels of sparsity via ADMM
regularization during the pre-training phase: 12.5%, 25%, 50%, 75%, and 87.5%.
The results are shown in Fig. 3. We observe that for both AlexNet and VGG-16,
a larger proportion of sparsity introduced into a structure results in a higher
accuracy. In specific, with a larger level of sparsity by ADMM regularization,
a better performance can be achieved during almost the whole pruning process
for AlexNet. For VGG-16, when adding a larger sparsity, a lower accuracy is
observed after the pre-training phase because of the extra regularization introduced by ADMM as explained in Sect. 4.2. This inferiority disappears shortly
after the pruning phase begins.

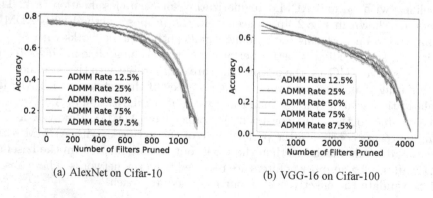

(a) AlexNet on Cifar-10   (b) VGG-16 on Cifar-100

Fig. 3. Performance comparison with different ADMM rate.

4.4   Regularization Helps Find Better Structure

Recent studies indicate that the essence of network pruning is actually structure optimization, i.e., finding efficient compact structures [22]. Therefore, in this sub-section, we investigate if the remaining sub-structure after pruning the model pre-trained with ADMM is more efficient. We still use the vanilla Taylor expansion approach as the baseline.

The experiments are conducted on both AlexNet and VGG-16, with and without ADMM regularization. For each experiment, we record the number of filters remained in each layer when 25%, 50%, 75%, and 87.5% of the total number of filters are pruned, and train these sub-networks from scratch to convergence. The results are shown in Table 1. For all cases, the sub-structures discovered with the proposed method outperform the counterparts with the baseline. In specific, our proposed approach outperforms the baseline significantly on AlexNet. When pruning 87.5% of the filters, our approach achieves an accuracy of 68.68%, which is 8.51% more than the baseline. These results indicate that by introducing ADMM regularization in network pruning, better sub-structures can be discovered.

Table 1. Performance comparison of the proposed method and baseline with varying pruning ratios.

Model	Pruning ratio	Methods	
		Ours	Baseline
AlexNet, Cifar-10	25%	77.55%	77.05%
	50%	76.71%	75.74%
	75%	73.85%	70.22%
	87.5%	68.68%	60.17%
VGG-16, Cifar-100	25%	62.71%	62.33%
	50%	59.59%	59.12%
	75%	49.68%	49.15%
	87.5%	36.57%	36.19%

5   Supplementary Analysis and Discussions

5.1   Visualization of Mean Activation Values

We continue to analyze the effectiveness of our proposed approach by visualizing the activation values of the neural networks. With AlexNet and VGG-16, we calculate average values of the feature maps in each layer and all layers of the three networks, which are pretrained normally (considered as baseline), with ℓ_2 and ADMM regularization during the whole pruning process, respectively. The results are shown in Fig. 4, where horizontal axis is the percentage of pruned filters. We observe that the curves of ℓ_2 regularization look similar with the baseline, and the values are slightly smaller than the baseline. For ADMM curves, the mean activation values are significantly reduced during the pruning procedure. These results indicate that our proposed approach can successfully reduce the magnitudes of the activation map, which can facilitate the importance estimation of filters via Taylor expansion.

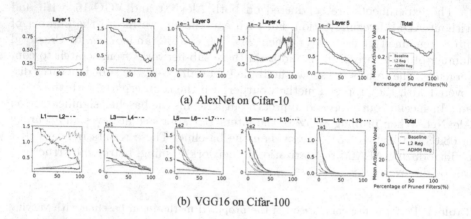

(a) AlexNet on Cifar-10

(b) VGG16 on Cifar-100

Fig. 4. Visualization of mean activation with the proposed method and baseline.

It is also worth mentioning that in the first two layers of VGG-16 pre-trained with ADMM, the mean activation values increase as more filters are pruned, which is different from other layers where the values decrease or remain similarly small during the process. The reason of this phenomenon might be that the shallower layers play a more important role for feature extraction and the importance of the remaining filters increases as the network gets smaller.

5.2 Correlation with Oracle Pruning

To further validate the proposed method's capability of improving ranking accuracy, we introduce the concept of *oracle ranking* [24]. The oracle ranking is obtained by pruning one filter from the neural network each run, and calculate the corresponding loss change, which is considered as the optimal criterion for filter ranking (small loss change corresponds to less important/low ranked filters). The result of oracle ranking can be considered as the ground truth when estimating filter ranks. In this analysis, we also use the vanilla Taylor expansion approach as the baseline. We compare the ranking results from the baseline and our proposed approach with oracle ranking. We use the Spearman's rank correlation coefficient [32] as the measurement (Eq. 13). A larger value indicates higher correlation.

$$r_s = 1 - \frac{6 \sum_{i=1}^{N} d_i^2}{N(N^2 - 1)}, \tag{13}$$

It is necessary to point out that, the ranking correlations are highly related to the hyper-parameters of a neural network, such as the number of filters remaining in the network, the batch size and number of samples used in the ranking phase, etc. In our experiments, we rank all the filters in the neural network before the first pruning operation, using a batch size of 64, and the whole training set for the estimation of filters' importance with Taylor expansion.

The result is shown in Table 2. With the proposed approach, a correlation of 0.34 with the oracle ranking can be achieved on AlexNet, while the corresponding result with the baseline is only 0.15. For VGG-16 on Cifar-100, our ranking results perform better than the baseline as well (0.28 vs. 0.19). In summary, our proposed approach can achieve a more precise ranking accuracy.

Table 2. Correlation with oracle pruning

Model	Our approach	Baseline (TE)
AlexNet, Cifar-10	0.34	0.15
VGG-16, Cifar-100	0.28	0.19

5.3 Regularization in Training vs. in Fine-Tuning

Regularization can be implemented into the pre-training, fine-tuning, or both phases. Our empirical study shows that the best performance can be achieved when the regularization is added only in the pre-training phase. Adding regularization during fine-tuning do further reduces the magnitude of activation values and improves the accuracy of ranking. However, in the meantime, the introduction of regularization in this phase hurts the performance recovery. Since only a limited number of updates are conducted during the fine-tuning phase as compared with the pre-training phase, this influence is often lethal.

5.4 Effect of Ranking Accuracy

Recent studies have showed that a precise ranking is not necessary for channel pruning, since comparable performance can be achieved with a coarse ranking [27]. Specifically, in their study, they use a certain criterion to rank filters. Different filters pruning strategies are conducted, including pruning the least important (lowest ranked) filters, and pruning filters with relatively low ranks (e.g., pruning the filters with ranks between 11 to 20, rather than 1 to 10). Comparable performances are achieved with two strategies. Significantly different with this study, our study showed that the pruning performance can be improved with an improved ranking performance. A reasonable explanation is that similar performance can be achieved only when the filters whose ranks are in a certain range are pruned. The selected filters are not necessary to be the least important ones, but cannot be too far away from them. Our proposed approach significantly improve the ranking accuracy, which is powerful enough to improve the pruning performance.

6   Conclusion

In this paper, we presented a channel pruning approach which adds regularization in the pre-training phase via ADMM. Our approach significantly improve the performance of identifying unimportant filters in a neural network, and thus improve the pruning performance. We applied the approach to three networks (LeNet-5, AlexNet and VGG-16) and tested the pruning performance with three datasets (MNIST, Cifar-10, and Cifar-100). Experimental results demonstrated that our approach outperforms the state-of-the-art channel pruning approach significantly.

References

1. Alvarez, J.M., Salzmann, M.: Learning the number of neurons in deep networks. In: Advances in Neural Information Processing Systems, pp. 2270–2278 (2016)
2. Boyd, S., Parikh, N., Chu, E., Peleato, B., Eckstein, J., et al.: Distributed optimization and statistical learning via the alternating direction method of multipliers. Found. Trends® Mach. Learn. **3**(1), 1–122 (2011)
3. Dai, X., Yin, H., Jha, N.K.: NeST: a neural network synthesis tool based on a grow-and-prune paradigm. arXiv preprint arXiv:1711.02017 (2017)
4. Goodfellow, I., et al.: Generative adversarial nets. In: Advances in Neural Information Processing Systems. pp. 2672–2680 (2014)
5. Guo, Y., Yao, A., Chen, Y.: Dynamic network surgery for efficient DNNs. In: Advances in Neural Information Processing Systems, pp. 1379–1387 (2016)
6. Han, S., et al.: EIE: efficient inference engine on compressed deep neural network. In: 2016 ACM/IEEE 43rd Annual International Symposium on Computer Architecture (ISCA), pp. 243–254. IEEE (2016)
7. Han, S., Pool, J., Tran, J., Dally, W.: Learning both weights and connections for efficient neural network. In: Advances in Neural Information Processing Systems, pp. 1135–1143 (2015)
8. Hassibi, B., Stork, D.G.: Second order derivatives for network pruning: optimal brain surgeon. In: Advances in Neural Information Processing Systems, pp. 164–171 (1993)
9. He, K., Gkioxari, G., Dollár, P., Girshick, R.: Mask R-CNN. In: Proceedings of the IEEE International Conference on Computer Vision, pp. 2961–2969 (2017)
10. He, Y., Zhang, X., Sun, J.: Channel pruning for accelerating very deep neural networks. In: Proceedings of the IEEE International Conference on Computer Vision, pp. 1389–1397 (2017)
11. Hu, H., Peng, R., Tai, Y.W., Tang, C.K.: Network trimming: a data-driven neuron pruning approach towards efficient deep architectures. arXiv preprint arXiv:1607.03250 (2016)
12. Huang, G., Liu, Z., Van Der Maaten, L., Weinberger, K.Q.: Densely connected convolutional networks. In: Proceedings of the IEEE Conference on Computer Vision and Pattern Recognition, pp. 4700–4708 (2017)
13. Huang, Z., Wang, N.: Data-driven sparse structure selection for deep neural networks. In: Ferrari, V., Hebert, M., Sminchisescu, C., Weiss, Y. (eds.) ECCV 2018. LNCS, vol. 11220, pp. 317–334. Springer, Cham (2018). https://doi.org/10.1007/978-3-030-01270-0_19

14. Krizhevsky, A., Hinton, G.: Learning multiple layers of features from tiny images. Technical report, Citeseer (2009)
15. Krizhevsky, A., Sutskever, I., Hinton, G.E.: ImageNet classification with deep convolutional neural networks. In: Advances in Neural Information Processing Systems, pp. 1097–1105 (2012)
16. LeCun, Y., Bottou, L., Bengio, Y., Haffner, P.: Gradient-based learning applied to document recognition. Proc. IEEE **86**(11), 2278–2324 (1998)
17. LeCun, Y., Denker, J.S., Solla, S.A.: Optimal brain damage. In: Advances in Neural Information Processing Systems, pp. 598–605 (1990)
18. Li, C., Wang, Z., Qi, H.: Fast-converging conditional generative adversarial networks for image synthesis. In: 2018 25th IEEE International Conference on Image Processing (ICIP), pp. 2132–2136. IEEE (2018)
19. Li, C., Wang, Z., Wang, X., Qi, H.: Single-shot channel pruning based on alternating direction method of multipliers. arXiv preprint arXiv:1902.06382 (2019)
20. Li, H., Kadav, A., Durdanovic, I., Samet, H., Graf, H.P.: Pruning filters for efficient ConvNets. arXiv preprint arXiv:1608.08710 (2016)
21. Liu, Z., Li, J., Shen, Z., Huang, G., Yan, S., Zhang, C.: Learning efficient convolutional networks through network slimming. In: 2017 IEEE International Conference on Computer Vision (ICCV), pp. 2755–2763. IEEE (2017)
22. Liu, Z., Sun, M., Zhou, T., Huang, G., Darrell, T.: Rethinking the value of network pruning. arXiv preprint arXiv:1810.05270 (2018)
23. Mnih, V., et al.: Human-level control through deep reinforcement learning. Nature **518**(7540), 529 (2015)
24. Molchanov, P., Tyree, S., Karras, T., Aila, T., Kautz, J.: Pruning convolutional neural networks for resource efficient inference. arXiv preprint arXiv:1611.06440 (2016)
25. Polyak, A., Wolf, L.: Channel-level acceleration of deep face representations. IEEE Access **3**, 2163–2175 (2015)
26. Simonyan, K., Zisserman, A.: Very deep convolutional networks for large-scale image recognition. arXiv preprint arXiv:1409.1556 (2014)
27. Wang, Z., Li, C., Wang, D., Wang, X., Qi, H.: Speeding up convolutional networks pruning with coarse ranking. arXiv preprint arXiv:1902.06385 (2019)
28. Wang, Z., Wang, D., Li, C., Xu, Y., Li, H., Bao, Z.: Deep reinforcement learning of cell movement in the early stage of C. elegans embryogenesis. Bioinformatics **34**(18), 3169–3177 (2018)
29. Wen, W., Wu, C., Wang, Y., Chen, Y., Li, H.: Learning structured sparsity in deep neural networks. In: Advances in Neural Information Processing Systems, pp. 2074–2082 (2016)
30. Ye, S., et al.: Progressive weight pruning of deep neural networks using ADMM. arXiv preprint arXiv:1810.07378 (2018)
31. Yu, R., et al.: NISP: pruning networks using neuron importance score propagation. In: Proceedings of the IEEE Conference on Computer Vision and Pattern Recognition, pp. 9194–9203 (2018)
32. Zar, J.H.: Significance testing of the spearman rank correlation coefficient. J. Am. Stat. Assoc. **67**(339), 578–580 (1972)
33. Zhang, T., et al.: A systematic DNN weight pruning framework using alternating direction method of multipliers. arXiv preprint arXiv:1804.03294 (2018)

Momentum Acceleration of Quasi-Newton Training for Neural Networks

Shahrzad Mahboubi[1]($\boxtimes$), S. Indrapriyadarsini[2], Hiroshi Ninomiya[1], and Hideki Asai[2]

[1] Shonan Institute of Technology, 1-1-25 Tsujido-nishikaigan,
Fujisawa, Kanagawa 251-8511, Japan
18T2012@sit.shonan-it.ac.jp, ninomiya@info.shonan-it.ac.jp
[2] Shizuoka University, 3-5-1 Johoku, Naka-ku,
Hamamatsu, Shizuoka 432-8011, Japan
{s.indrapriyadarsini.17,asai.hideki}@shizuoka.ac.jp

Abstract. This paper describes a novel acceleration technique of quasi-Newton method (QN) using momentum terms for training in neural networks. Recently, Nesterov's accelerated quasi-Newton method (NAQ) has shown that the momentum term is effective in reducing the number of iterations and in accelerating its convergence speed. However, the gradients had to calculate two times during one iteration in the NAQ training. This increased the computation time of a training loop compared with the conventional QN. In this research, an improvement to NAQ is done by approximating the Nesterov's accelerated gradient used in NAQ as a linear combination of the current and previous gradients. Then the gradient is calculated only once per iteration same as QN. The performance of the proposed algorithm is evaluated through computer simulations on a benchmark problem of the function modeling and real-world problems of the microwave circuit modeling. The results show the significant acceleration in the computation time compared with conventional training algorithms.

Keywords: Neural networks · Training algorithm ·
Quasi-Newton method · Nesterov's accelerated quasi-Newton method ·
Momentum terms

1 Introduction

Neural network (NN) technique has been recognized as a useful tool for modeling of data with high-nonlinearity (Zhang et al. 2003; Haykin 2009). For example, NN can be trained from Electro-Magnetic (EM) data over a range of geometrical parameters and trained networks become models providing fast solutions of the EM behavior it learned (Zhang et al. 2003; Ninomiya et al. 2008). This is useful for modeling where formulas are not available or original models are computationally too expensive. However, these models have strong nonlinearities to themselves and need a robust training algorithm.

© Springer Nature Switzerland AG 2019
A. C. Nayak and A. Sharma (Eds.): PRICAI 2019, LNAI 11671, pp. 268–281, 2019.
https://doi.org/10.1007/978-3-030-29911-8_21

Training is the most important step in developing NN's models. In this research the following optimization problem of the error function $E(\mathbf{w})$ given by the mean squared error (MSE) is considered for the training of NNs.

$$\min_{\mathbf{w} \in R^n} E(\mathbf{w}) = \frac{1}{|T_r|} \sum_{p \in T_r} E_p(\mathbf{w}), \quad E_p(\mathbf{w}) = \frac{1}{2}\|\mathbf{d}_p - \mathbf{o}_p\|^2, \tag{1}$$

where $\mathbf{o}_p$, $\mathbf{d}_p$ and $\mathbf{w}$ be the p-th output, p-th desired and weight vectors, respectively. T_r denotes a training data set $\{\mathbf{x}_p, \mathbf{d}_p\}, p \in T_r$ and $|T_r|$ is the number of training samples. Note that, the MSE is often used for the neural modeling of highly nonlinear function, but the algorithm of this research can be applied to any error function. The gradient-based algorithms have been utilized for NN training. Most of gradient-based algorithms minimize (1) using the following iterative formula,

$$\mathbf{w}_{k+1} = \mathbf{w}_k + \mathbf{v}_{k+1} \quad \text{and} \quad \mathbf{v}_{k+1} = -\eta_k \nabla E(\mathbf{w}_k), \tag{2}$$

where k is the iteration count and $\mathbf{v}_{k+1}$ is the update vector which is individually defined in each gradient algorithm with the learning rate η_k. Gradient based algorithms can be divided into two categories by the form of η_k: first-order methods and second or super-linear order methods (Haykin 2009). First-order methods are often used because each technique uses a scalar as η_k and has the simple calculation of $\mathbf{v}_{k+1}$. Popular first-order algorithms with the adaptive η_ks which are determined by an exponentially decaying average of past squared gradients are AdaGrad (Duchi et al. 2011), AdaDelta (Zeiler 2013) and RMSprop (Tieleman and Hinton 2012). Furthermore, the accelerated algorithms are Classical Momentum (CM), Nesterov's Accelerated Gradient (NAG) (Sutskever et al. 2013) and Adam (Kingma and Ba 2015) using the inertia or moment term of $\mu_k \mathbf{v}_k$ in (2) where μ_k is the momentum coefficient. Especially, Adam is the most famous and effective first-order algorithm with the adaptive η_k and the momentum acceleration scheme. However, when applied to highly-nonlinear function modeling, these first-order methods still converge too slowly and optimization error cannot be effectively reduced within finite time in spite of its advantage.

Typically, the second or super-linear order methods have been used to deal with this problem in spite of the increase for computational cost. It is caused that the parameter η_k of (2) is determined by the curvature information of the error function like Hessian or the approximated one in each algorithm. Quasi-Newton method (QN) which is one of the most efficient optimization algorithm has been widely utilized as a robust training algorithm (Zhang et al. 2003; Nocedal and Wright 2006) for the purpose of this research. Furthermore several improvements for QN have been done. One of the improvements is Multi-step quasi-Newton (multiQN) which uses past steps data for updating the curvature information (Ford and Moghrabi 1993; Moghrabi 2018). On the other hand, the acceleration of QN using the momentum term was proposed as Nesterov's accelerated quasi-Newton method (NAQ) (Ninomiya 2017). NAQ succeeded to drastically reduce the number of iterations and computational time compared with QN. However, NAQ has a disadvantage that the calculation of the gradient was required two

times in one iteration whereas QN was one time. Specifically, Nesterov's acceler-
ated gradient $\nabla E(\mathbf{w}_k + \mu_k \mathbf{v}_k)$ and the normal gradient $\nabla E(\mathbf{w}_k)$ were calculated
within per iteration.

In this research, a new quasi-Newton based training algorithm - Momentum quasi-Newton method (MoQ) - is proposed. The proposed MoQ accelerates
NAQ by the approximation of Nesterov's accelerated gradient vector as a linear combination of the current and previous normal gradients by assuming that
the error function is approximately quadratic function around the current position. Therefore, this approximation shows a reduction in the computation time
required for one iteration compared with NAQ keeping the total number of iterations low. The performance of the proposed algorithm is demonstrated through
computer simulations for benchmark problems of highly nonlinear function modeling and real-world problems of microwave circuit modeling compared with the
conventional training methods.

2   Related Work

This section briefly shows QN-based training algorithm and its accelerated
method. These methods have been commonly used as the training algorithms
for highly-nonlinear function modeling (Zhang et al. 2003; Ninomiya et al. 2008;
Ninomiya 2017).

2.1   Quasi-Newton Method (QN)

QN is one of the most efficient optimization algorithms using the curvature
information (Nocedal and Wright 2006; Forst and Hoffmann 2010). The learning
rate η_k in (2) is defined by the step size α_k (scalar) and the approximated inverse
Hessian, $\mathbf{H}_k^{QN}$ as $\eta_k = \alpha_k \mathbf{H}_k^{QN}$. Then the update vector of QN is

$$\mathbf{v}_{k+1} = -\alpha_k \mathbf{H}_k^{QN} \nabla E(\mathbf{w}_k), \tag{3}$$

where $\mathbf{H}_k^{QN}$ is the symmetric positive definite matrix and iteratively updated by
the following BFGS (Broyden-Fletcher-Glodfarb-Shanno) formula (Nocedal and
Wright 2006),

$$\mathbf{H}_{k+1}^{QN} = (\mathbf{I} - (\mathbf{s}_k \mathbf{y}_k^{\mathrm{T}}/\mathbf{s}_k^{\mathrm{T}}\mathbf{y}_k))\mathbf{H}_k^{QN}(\mathbf{I} - (\mathbf{y}_k \mathbf{s}_k^{\mathrm{T}}/\mathbf{s}_k^{\mathrm{T}}\mathbf{y}_k)) + (\mathbf{s}_k \mathbf{s}_k^{\mathrm{T}}/\mathbf{s}_k^{\mathrm{T}}\mathbf{y}_k), \tag{4}$$

where $\mathbf{s}_k = \mathbf{w}_{k+1} - \mathbf{w}_k$ and $\mathbf{y}_k = \nabla E(\mathbf{w}_{k+1}) - \nabla E(\mathbf{w}_k)$. Note that, the symmetric positive definiteness of $\mathbf{H}_k^{QN}$ in the update of (4) is guaranteed (Nocedal
and Wright 2006; Forst and Hoffmann 2010). This means that QN of (3) and (4)
always decreases $E(\mathbf{w})$.

2.2   Nesterov's Accelerated Quasi-Newton Method (NAQ)

NAQ was derived from the quadratic approximation of $E(\mathbf{w})$ at $\mathbf{w}_k + \mu_k \mathbf{v}_k$ as
(5) using $\Delta \mathbf{w} = \mathbf{w} - (\mathbf{w}_k + \mu_k \mathbf{v}_k)$ whereas QN approximated $E(\mathbf{w})$ at $\mathbf{w}_k$.

$$E(\mathbf{w}) \simeq \hat{E}(\mathbf{w}) = E(\mathbf{w}_k + \mu_k \mathbf{v}_k) + \nabla E(\mathbf{w}_k + \mu_k \mathbf{v}_k)^{\mathrm{T}} \Delta \mathbf{w}$$
$$+ (1/2)\Delta \mathbf{w}^{\mathrm{T}} \nabla^2 E(\mathbf{w}_k + \mu_k \mathbf{v}_k) \Delta \mathbf{w}. \tag{5}$$

The new iterate derived from $\partial \hat{E}(\mathbf{w})/\partial \mathbf{w} = 0$, was defined as

$$\mathbf{w}_{k+1} = (\mathbf{w}_k + \mu_k \mathbf{v}_k) - \nabla^2 E\left(\mathbf{w}_k + \mu_k \mathbf{v}_k\right)^{-1} \nabla E\left(\mathbf{w}_k + \mu_k \mathbf{v}_k\right). \tag{6}$$

This iteration is considered as Newton method with the momentum term $\mu_k \mathbf{v}_k$. Here the inverse of Hessian $\nabla^2 E(\mathbf{w}_k + \mu_k \mathbf{v}_k)$ was approximated by the matrix $\mathbf{H}_{k+1}^{\text{NAQ}}$ using

$$\mathbf{H}_{k+1}^{\text{NAQ}} = (\mathbf{I} - (\mathbf{p}_k \mathbf{q}_k^{\text{T}}/\mathbf{p}_k^{\text{T}} \mathbf{q}_k))\mathbf{H}_k^{\text{NAQ}}(\mathbf{I} - (\mathbf{q}_k \mathbf{p}_k^{\text{T}}/\mathbf{p}_k^{\text{T}} \mathbf{q}_k)) + (\mathbf{p}_k \mathbf{p}_k^{\text{T}}/\mathbf{p}_k^{\text{T}} \mathbf{q}_k), \tag{7}$$

where $\mathbf{p}_k = \mathbf{w}_{k+1} - (\mathbf{w}_k + \mu_k \mathbf{v}_k)$ and $\mathbf{q}_k = \nabla E(\mathbf{w}_{k+1}) - \nabla E(\mathbf{w}_k + \mu_k \mathbf{v}_k)$. Here, (7) was derived from Secant condition in NAQ of $\mathbf{q}_k = (\mathbf{H}_{k+1}^{\text{NAQ}})^{-1}\mathbf{p}_k$ and the rank-2 updating formula (Ninomiya 2017). Note that it was proved that the matrix $\mathbf{H}_{k+1}^{\text{NAQ}}$ updated by (7) holds the positive definite and symmetric properties if $\mathbf{H}_k^{\text{NAQ}}$ was a positive definite symmetric matrix. The update vector of NAQ is defined as

$$\mathbf{v}_{k+1} = \mu_k \mathbf{v}_k - \alpha_k \mathbf{H}_k^{\text{NAQ}} \nabla E(\mathbf{w}_k + \mu_k \mathbf{v}_k). \tag{8}$$

where $0 < \mu_k < 1$ and was usually chosen to be a value close to 1 such as $0.8, 0.85, 0.9$ or 0.95 (Sutskever et al. 2013; Ninomiya 2017). NAQ drastically improved the convergence speed of QN using the momentum term $\mu_k \mathbf{v}_k$ and the gradient vector $\nabla E(\mathbf{w}_k + \mu_k \mathbf{v}_k)$ called Nesterov's accelerated gradient vector (Sutskever et al. 2013; Ninomiya 2017). This indicates that the momentum term is effective in acceleration of QN. The algorithm of NAQ is shown in Algorithm 1. From this algorithm, it can be confirmed that there are two calculations of gradients $\nabla E(\mathbf{w}_k + \mu_k \mathbf{v}_k)$ and $\nabla E(\mathbf{w}_{k+1})$ shown in steps 4(b) and 4(e). This was a disadvantage of NAQ, but the algorithm could further shorten the iteration counts to cancel out the effect of the shortcoming compared with QN (Ninomiya 2017).

Algorithm 1: Nesterov's accelerated quasi-Newton method (NAQ)

---
1. $k = 1$
2. Initialize $\mathbf{w}_k =$ random$[-0.5, 0.5]$, $\mathbf{H}_k^{\text{NAQ}} = \mathbf{I}$(unit matrix) and $\mathbf{v}_k = \mathbf{0}$;
3. **While**$(\|\nabla E(\mathbf{w}_k)\| > \epsilon$ and $k < k_{max})$
    (a) Update μ_k;
    (b) Calculate $\nabla E(\mathbf{w}_k + \mu_k \mathbf{v}_k)$;
    (c) Calculate stepsize α_k;
    (d) Update $\mathbf{w}_{k+1} = \mathbf{w}_k + \mu_k \mathbf{v}_k - \alpha_k \mathbf{H}_k^{\text{NAQ}} \nabla E(\mathbf{w}_k + \mu_k \mathbf{v}_k)$;
    (e) Calculate $\nabla E(\mathbf{w}_{k+1})$;
    (f) Update $\mathbf{H}_{k+1}^{\text{NAQ}}$ using (7);
    (g) $k = k + 1$
4. **return** $\mathbf{w}_k$;

2.3 Adaptive NAQ Method (AdaNAQ)

NAQ has drastically improved the computing time but the momentum coefficient μ_k which was fixed during the training had to be chosen carefully in order to obtain a stable and fast solution. The adaptive momentum coefficient μ_k introduced in (Nesterov 2004) was applied to NAQ as Adaptive NAQ (AdaNAQ) in (Mahboubi and Ninomiya 2018). In this method, the adaptive derivation formula of the μ_k is given by

$$\mu_k = \theta_k(1 - \theta_k)/\theta_k^2 + \theta_{k+1} \quad \text{and} \quad \theta_{k+1}^2 = (1 - \theta_{k+1})\theta_k^2 + \gamma\theta_{k+1}. \tag{9}$$

where $\theta_0 = 1$ and $\gamma = 10^{-5}$. The μ_k of (9) gradually changes from 0 to 1 during the training with keeping the stabilities of the training and maintaining fast convergence speed of NAQ.

3 Proposed Algorithm - Momentum Quasi-Newton Method (MoQ)

The training loop of NAQ involves two gradient calculations - the normal gradient $\nabla E(\mathbf{w}_k)$ and Nesterov's accelerated gradient $\nabla E(\mathbf{w}_k + \mu_k\mathbf{v}_k)$ while QN is only one calculation of the normal gradient. This research focuses on the reducing the number of gradient calculation in an iteration without increasing the total number of iterations in NAQ. We proposed a novel quasi-Newton based training algorithm referred to as *Momentum quasi-Newton method* (MoQ). MoQ is realized by approximating Nesterov's accelerated gradient vector as a linear combination of the current (k-th) and previous (($k-1$)-th) normal gradients, and making it possible to calculate only one gradient per iteration. MoQ approximates the error function $E(\mathbf{w})$ by assuming that the function is approximately quadratic in the neighborhood of $\mathbf{w}_k + \mu_k\mathbf{v}_k$. This assumption is similar to the second-order Taylor expansion of $\hat{E}(\mathbf{w})$ in (5) which is commonly used for design of second-order method. Note that $\hat{E}(\mathbf{w})$ is an actual quadratic function but $E(\mathbf{w})$ is not. However, this approximation will work well in QN-based methods. This implies that $\nabla E(\mathbf{w}_k + \mu_k\mathbf{v}_k)$ is approximately linear, so

$$\nabla E(\mathbf{w}_k + \mu_k\mathbf{v}_k) \simeq \nabla E(\mathbf{w}_k) + \mu_k\nabla E(\mathbf{v}_k). \tag{10}$$

Furthermore, since $\mathbf{v}_k = \mathbf{w}_k - \mathbf{w}_{k-1}$, (10) can be rewritten as

$$\begin{aligned}\nabla E(\mathbf{w}_k) + \mu_k\nabla E(\mathbf{v}_k) &= \nabla E(\mathbf{w}_k) + \mu_k\nabla E(\mathbf{w}_k - \mathbf{w}_{k-1}) \\ &= (1 + \mu_k)\nabla E(\mathbf{w}_k) - \mu_k\nabla E(\mathbf{w}_{k-1}).\end{aligned} \tag{11}$$

From (10) and (11), it is confirmed that Nesterov's accelerated gradient can be approximated as an extrapolation of $\nabla E(\mathbf{w}_k)$ and $\nabla E(\mathbf{w}_{k-1})$ with a momentum coefficient μ_k, that is, a weighted linear combination. In this paper, $\mu_k\nabla E(\mathbf{v}_k) = \mu_k\{\nabla E(\mathbf{w}_k) - \nabla E(\mathbf{w}_{k-1})\}$ is referred to as *momentum gradient* (MoG) term. Therefore, MoQ can be regarded as a method accelerating QN using two momentum terms, $\mu_k\mathbf{v}_k$ and $\mu_k\nabla E(\mathbf{v}_k)$. The update vector $\mathbf{v}_{k+1}$ of MoQ can be defined as

$$\mathbf{v}_{k+1} = \mu_k \mathbf{v}_k - \alpha_k \mathbf{H}_k^{\mathrm{MoQ}} \{(1 + \mu_k) \nabla E(\mathbf{w}_k) - \mu_k \nabla E(\mathbf{w}_{k-1})\}. \tag{12}$$

Then the matrix $\mathbf{H}_k^{\mathrm{MoQ}}$ is updated by,

$$\mathbf{H}_{k+1}^{\mathrm{MoQ}} = (\mathbf{I} - (\mathbf{p}_k \hat{\mathbf{q}}_k^{\mathrm{T}} / \mathbf{p}_k^{\mathrm{T}} \hat{\mathbf{q}}_k)) \mathbf{H}_k^{\mathrm{MoQ}} (\mathbf{I} - (\hat{\mathbf{q}}_k \mathbf{p}_k^{\mathrm{T}} / \mathbf{p}_k^{\mathrm{T}} \hat{\mathbf{q}}_k)) + (\mathbf{p}_k \mathbf{p}_k^{\mathrm{T}} / \mathbf{p}_k^{\mathrm{T}} \hat{\mathbf{q}}_k), \tag{13}$$

where the Secant condition of $\hat{\mathbf{q}}_k = (\mathbf{H}_k^{\mathrm{MoQ}})^{-1} \mathbf{p}_k$ for MoQ is satisfied and

$$\mathbf{p}_k = \mathbf{w}_{k+1} - (\mathbf{w}_k + \mu_k \mathbf{v}_k) = \mathbf{w}_{k+1} - (1 + \mu_k) \mathbf{w}_k + \mu_k \mathbf{w}_{k-1}, \tag{14}$$

$$\hat{\mathbf{q}}_k = \nabla E(\mathbf{w}_{k+1}) - (1 + \mu_k) \nabla E(\mathbf{w}_k) + \mu_k \nabla E(\mathbf{w}_{k-1}). \tag{15}$$

The algorithm of MoQ is shown in Algorithm 2. From this algorithm, MoQ computes the gradient only once in step 4(d) within an iteration. Note that the multiQN (Ford and Moghrabi 1993; Moghrabi 2018) was also an acceleration technique of QN and used (14) and (15) for update of the approximated Hessian. The multiQN was proposed by only extending the Secant condition using the past steps $\mathbf{w}_i$ and $\nabla E(\mathbf{w}_i)$, $(i = k - 1, k - 2, \ldots)$. Therefore, the update vector $\mathbf{v}_{k+1}$ of multiQN was same as QN of (3) but the approximated Hessian was updated by (13).

Convergence of MoQ. It is shown that $\mathbf{H}_{k+1}^{\mathrm{MoQ}}$ which is derived from (13) holds symmetric and positive definite properties under the *Definition*: $\mathbf{H}_k^{\mathrm{MoQ}}$ *is the symmetric positive definite matrix.* Here the following conditions are guaranteed for the above:

(a): $\mathbf{H}_{k+1}^{\mathrm{MoQ}}$ of (13) satisfies the Secant condition of MoQ, $\hat{\mathbf{q}}_k = \left(\mathbf{H}_{k+1}^{\mathrm{MoQ}}\right)^{-1} \mathbf{p}_k$.

(b): If $\mathbf{H}_k^{\mathrm{MoQ}}$ is symmetry, $\mathbf{H}_{k+1}^{\mathrm{MoQ}}$ is also symmetry.

(c): If $\mathbf{H}_k^{\mathrm{MoQ}}$ is a positive definite matrix, $\mathbf{H}_{k+1}^{\mathrm{MoQ}}$ is also a positive definite matrix.

Proof of (a): From (13) and the Secant condition $\hat{\mathbf{q}}_k = \left(\mathbf{H}_{k+1}^{\mathrm{MoQ}}\right)^{-1} \mathbf{p}_k$:

$$\left(\mathbf{H}_{k+1}^{\mathrm{MoQ}}\right)^{-1} \mathbf{p}_k = \left((\mathbf{I} - \mathbf{p}_k \hat{\mathbf{q}}_k^{\mathrm{T}} / \mathbf{p}_k^{\mathrm{T}} \hat{\mathbf{q}}_k) \mathbf{H}_k^{\mathrm{MoQ}} (\mathbf{I} - \hat{\mathbf{q}}_k \mathbf{p}_k^{\mathrm{T}} / \mathbf{p}_k^{\mathrm{T}} \hat{\mathbf{q}}_k) + \mathbf{p}_k \mathbf{p}_k^{\mathrm{T}} / \mathbf{p}_k^{\mathrm{T}} \hat{\mathbf{q}}_k\right)^{-1} \mathbf{p}_k \tag{16}$$

Applying the Sherman-Morrison-Woodbury formula (Nocedal and Wright 2006) to (16),

$$= \left(\mathbf{B}_k^{\mathrm{MoQ}} + (\hat{\mathbf{q}}_k \hat{\mathbf{q}}_k^{\mathrm{T}} / \hat{\mathbf{q}}_k^{\mathrm{T}} \mathbf{p}_k) - (\mathbf{B}_k^{\mathrm{MoQ}} \mathbf{p}_k \mathbf{p}_k^{\mathrm{T}} \mathbf{B}_k^{\mathrm{MoQ}} / \mathbf{p}_k^{\mathrm{T}} \mathbf{B}_k^{\mathrm{MoQ}} \mathbf{p}_k)\right) \mathbf{p}_k \tag{17}$$

where $\mathbf{B}_k^{\mathrm{MoQ}} = \left(\mathbf{H}_k^{\mathrm{MoQ}}\right)^{-1}$,

$$= \mathbf{B}_k^{\mathrm{MoQ}} \mathbf{p}_k + (\hat{\mathbf{q}}_k \hat{\mathbf{q}}_k^{\mathrm{T}} / \hat{\mathbf{q}}_k^{\mathrm{T}} \mathbf{p}_k) \mathbf{p}_k - (\mathbf{B}_k^{\mathrm{MoQ}} \mathbf{p}_k \mathbf{p}_k^{\mathrm{T}} \mathbf{B}_k^{\mathrm{MoQ}} / \mathbf{p}_k^{\mathrm{T}} \mathbf{B}_k^{\mathrm{MoQ}} \mathbf{p}) \mathbf{p}_k = \hat{\mathbf{q}}_k. \qquad \square$$

Proof of (b): This is clear from (13). $\qquad \square$

Proof of (c): First, $\hat{\mathbf{q}}_k^T \mathbf{p}_k > 0$ will be shown. When the stepsize α_k is calculated by the exact line search as

$$dE\left(\mathbf{w}_{k+1}\right)/d\alpha_k = -\nabla E(\mathbf{w}_{k+1})^T \mathbf{H}_k^{\text{MoQ}} \{\nabla E(\mathbf{w}_k) + \mu_k \nabla E(\mathbf{v}_k)\}) = 0, \quad (18)$$

then,

$$
\begin{aligned}
\hat{\mathbf{q}}_k^T \mathbf{p}_k &= \{\nabla E(\mathbf{w}_{k+1}) - (\nabla E(\mathbf{w}_k) + \mu_k \nabla E(\mathbf{v}_k)))\}^T \{\mathbf{w}_{k+1} - (\mathbf{w}_k + \mu_k \mathbf{v}_k)\} \\
&= \{\nabla E(\mathbf{w}_{k+1}) - (\nabla E(\mathbf{w}_k) + \mu_k \nabla E(\mathbf{v}_k)))\}^T \{-\alpha_k \mathbf{H}_k^{\text{MoQ}} \left(\nabla E(\mathbf{w}_k) + \mu_k \nabla E(\mathbf{v}_k))\right)\} \quad (19) \\
&= \alpha_k \left(\nabla E(\mathbf{w}_k) + \mu_k \nabla E(\mathbf{v}_k)\right)^T \mathbf{H}_k^{\text{MoQ}} \left(\nabla E(\mathbf{w}_k) + \mu_k \nabla E(\mathbf{v}_k)\right) > 0,
\end{aligned}
$$

is derived where $\nabla E(\mathbf{w}_k) + \mu_k \nabla E(\mathbf{v}_k) = (1 + \mu_k)\nabla E(\mathbf{w}_k) - \mu_k \nabla E(\mathbf{w}_{k-1})$ and $\mathbf{w}_k + \mu_k \mathbf{v}_k = (1 + \mu_k)\mathbf{w}_k - \mu_k \mathbf{w}_{k-1}$. It is guaranteed in (19) that $\mathbf{H}_k^{\text{MoQ}}$ is a positive definite matrix and $\nabla E(\mathbf{w}_k) + \mu_k \nabla E(\mathbf{v}_k) \neq \mathbf{0}$.

Second, let $\mathbf{r} \neq \mathbf{0}$ be an arbitrary vector, $\mathbf{r}^T \mathbf{B}_{k+1}^{\text{MQN}} \mathbf{r} > 0$ will be shown. For simplicity of the proof, the positive definiteness of $\mathbf{B}_{k+1}^{\text{MoQ}} = \left(\mathbf{H}_{k+1}^{\text{MoQ}}\right)^{-1}$ will be shown. It is clear that if the positive definiteness of $\mathbf{B}_{k+1}^{\text{MoQ}}$ is proved, its inverse $\mathbf{H}_{k+1}^{\text{MoQ}}$ is also a positive definite matrix. Because $\mathbf{H}_k^{\text{MoQ}}$ is a positive definite matrix, $\mathbf{B}_k^{\text{MoQ}}$ is also a positive definite matrix and it can be divided as $\mathbf{B}_k^{\text{MoQ}} = \mathbf{C}\mathbf{C}^T$ using an arbitrary non-singular matrix $\mathbf{C}$. Let $\mathbf{t} = \mathbf{C}^T \mathbf{r} (\neq \mathbf{0})$ and $\mathbf{u} = \mathbf{C}^T \mathbf{p}_k (\neq \mathbf{0})$, it is shown using (17) that

$$\mathbf{r}^T \mathbf{B}_{k+1}^{\text{MoQ}} \mathbf{r} = \left(\left(\mathbf{t}^T \mathbf{t}\right)\left(\mathbf{u}^T \mathbf{u}\right) - \left(\mathbf{t}^T \mathbf{u}\right)^2\right)/\mathbf{u}^T \mathbf{u} + \left(\mathbf{r}^T \hat{\mathbf{q}}_k\right)^2 / \hat{\mathbf{q}}_k^T \mathbf{p}_k \geq 0, \quad (20)$$

with the Cauchy-Schwarz inequality (Nocedal and Wright 2006) and the condition of (19). In (20) the equality condition is satisfied, if and only if $\left(\mathbf{t}^T \mathbf{t}\right)\left(\mathbf{u}^T \mathbf{u}\right) - \left(\mathbf{t}^T \mathbf{u}\right)^2 = 0$ and $\mathbf{r}^T \hat{\mathbf{q}}_k = 0$. The former equation holds when $\mathbf{t} = \gamma \mathbf{u}$ with the arbitrary scalar $\gamma (\neq 0)$. When $\mathbf{t} = \gamma \mathbf{u}$, then $\mathbf{r} = \gamma \mathbf{p}_k$. Therefore the later equation is transformed as $\mathbf{r}^T \hat{\mathbf{q}}_k = \gamma \mathbf{p}_k^T \hat{\mathbf{q}}_k = 0$. This contradicts (19). Then the equality condition of (20) is not satisfied. As a result, $\mathbf{B}_{k+1}^{\text{MoQ}}$ holds $\mathbf{r}^T \mathbf{B}_{k+1}^{\text{MoQ}} \mathbf{r} > 0$, namely positive definiteness. Therefore, it is shown that $\mathbf{H}_{k+1}^{\text{MoQ}}$ is a symmetric positive definite matrix. $\qquad \square$

Furthermore, in order to guarantee the numerical stability and the global convergence of MoQ, a global convergence term is incorporated in $\hat{\mathbf{q}}_k$, as shown in (21), (22) and (23) (Li and Fukushima 2001). In this research, this term is applied to QN (Li and Fukushima 2001), multiQN and NAQ (Indrapriyadarsini et al. 2018) same as MoQ for fair comparison.

$$\hat{\mathbf{q}}_k = \nabla E(\mathbf{w}_{k+1}) - (1 + \mu_k)\nabla E(\mathbf{w}_k) + \mu_k \nabla E(\mathbf{w}_{k-1}) + \xi_k \mathbf{p}_k = \delta_k + \xi_k \mathbf{p}_k, \quad (21)$$

where

$$\xi_k = \omega \| (1 + \mu_k)\nabla E(\mathbf{w}_k) - \mu_k \nabla E(\mathbf{w}_{k-1}) \| + max\{-\delta_k^T \mathbf{p}_k/\| \mathbf{p}_k \|^2, 0\}, \quad (22)$$

and

$$\begin{cases} \omega = & 2 & if & \| (1 + \mu_k)\nabla E(\mathbf{w}_k) - \mu_k \nabla E(\mathbf{w}_{k-1}) \|^2 > 10^{-2}, \\ \omega = & 100 & if & \| (1 + \mu_k)\nabla E(\mathbf{w}_k) - \mu_k \nabla E(\mathbf{w}_{k-1}) \|^2 < 10^{-2}. \end{cases} \tag{23}$$

Algorithm 2: Momentum quasi-Newton method (MoQ)

1. $k = 1$
2. Initialize $\mathbf{w}_k = \text{random}[-0.5, 0.5]$, $\mathbf{H}_k^{\text{MoQ}} = \mathbf{I}$(unit matrix) and $\mathbf{v}_k = \mathbf{0}$;
3. Calculate $\nabla E(\mathbf{w}_k)$;
4. **While**($\|\nabla E(\mathbf{w}_k)\| > \epsilon$ and $k < k_{max}$)
   (a) Update μ_k;
   (b) Calculate stepsize α_k;
   (c) Update $\mathbf{w}_{k+1} = \mathbf{w}_k + \mu_k \mathbf{v}_k - \alpha_k \hat{\mathbf{H}}_k^{\text{MoQ}}\{(1 + \mu_k)\nabla E(\mathbf{w}_k) - \mu_k \nabla E(\mathbf{w}_{k-1})\}$;
   (d) Calculate $\nabla E(\mathbf{w}_{k+1})$;
   (e) Update $\mathbf{H}_{k+1}^{\text{MoQ}}$ using (13);
   (f) $k = k + 1$
5. **return** $\mathbf{w}_k$;

4   Simulation Results

Computer simulations are conducted in order to demonstrate the validity of the proposed MoQ. In the simulations the feedforward neural networks with one and two hidden layers of full connections with arbitrary number of hidden neurons are considered. Each neuron has a sigmoid function as an activation, $sig(\cdot) = 1/(1 + exp(-\cdot))$. The performance of MoQ is compared with conventional algorithms such as BP, AdaGrad, RMSprop, AdaDelta, Adam, QN, multiQN, NAQ and AdaNAQ for 3 benchmark problems. Benchmark problems used here are a function modeling problem and two microwave circuit modeling problems. Ten independent runs with $\mathbf{w}$ initialized by uniform random numbers in the range $[-0.5, 0.5]$ are conducted. Note that, the adaptive methods such as AdaGrad, AdaDelta, RMSprop and Adam are mainly utilized in the stochastic (mini-batch) mode. However, the problems in this paper need full batch methods (Zhang et al. 2003; Ninomiya 2013). Therefore, the full batch scheme is applied to all algorithms. The momentum coefficients μ_k used in NAQ and MoQ are set to fixed values $\{0.8, 0.85, 0.9$ and $0.95\}$ and the adaptive values of (9). Each trained neural network is estimated by the average, best and worst of $E(\mathbf{w})$, the average of computational time (s) and the average of iteration count (k). The errors for T_r are denoted by $E_{train}(\mathbf{w})$. The testing error shown as $E_{test}(\mathbf{w})$ is also calculated by (1) using a test data set T_e which is independent of the training data set T_r. Each element of the input and desired vectors of T_r and T_e are normalized in the range $[-1.0, 1.0]$ in the simulations. The termination conditions are set to $\epsilon = 1.0 \times 10^{-8}$ and $k_{max} = 150,000$. In the simulations, we consider the convergence rate (%) for each algorithm. This shows the rate at which the solution can be obtained without overshooting of the gradients within k_{max}. The step size α_k for each algorithm is determined according to Armijo's conditions (Nocedal et al. 2006; Ninomiya 2017).

4.1   Function Modeling Problem

First, (24) is used as a function modeling problem with high-nonlinearity (Ninomiya 2017; Indrapriyadarsini et al. 2018),

$$f(a, x) = 1 + (x + 2x^2)\sin(-ax^2). \tag{24}$$

This function has two inputs x and a. The ranges for this simulation are in $x \in [-4, 4)$ and $a \in [-1, 1)$. $|T_r|$ and $|T_e|$ include 3,320 training and 6,600 testing points, respectively. The trained network has a hidden layer with 55 neurons. Therefore, the structure of neural network is 2-55-1. In this problem, the learning rates of AdaGrad, AdaDelta, RMSprop and Adam were set to 0.01, 1.0, 0.1 and 0.1, respectively. Each value is decided by the best performance for each algorithm in our experiments. The results are summarized in Table 1. From this table it is shown that, first-order methods such as BP, AdaGrad, AdaDelta, RMSprop and Adam could not find sufficiently small training and testing errors within k_{max} whereas all QN-based methods could obtain sufficient small errors. Furthermore, it was confirmed that the momentum terms were effective for faster convergence of QN-based algorithms because the momentum-based QN such as NAQ and MoQ could obtain small iteration counts and fast computational times compared with QN and multiQN. In the viewpoint of the comparison of NAQ with the proposed MoQ, although the iteration counts of MoQ was similar to that of NAQ, the computation time of MoQ was much faster than NAQ. This confirms that (10) is a good approximation of the gradient at $\mathbf{w}_k + \mu_k \mathbf{v}_k$, resulting in reduced number of gradient computations and faster training. On the other hand, MoQ with fixed large μ_k (0.9 and 0.95) was unstable, that is the convergence rates were less than 100% for initial values of $\mathbf{w}$ because of overshooting of the gradients. However, this problem is improved in AdaMoQ using the adaptive scheme of μ_k as in (9) without loosing the fast convergence of MoQ with large fixed μ_k. It is shown that the adaptive scheme of μ_k in AdaMoQ is also effective in reducing the iteration counts of AdaNAQ. For measuring the accuracy of modeling, the output of the neural model trained with AdaMoQ is compared with the test data in Fig. 1. The input a is fixed to -1 and the error $E_{test}(\mathbf{w}) = 0.220 \times 10^{-3}$. From the figure, it is confirmed that the test error and the model show good match between them.

4.2   Microwave Circuit Modeling of Low-Pass Filter

Next, MoQ is applied to develop a neural network model of a microstrip Low-Pass Filter (LPF) illustrated in Fig. 2(a) (Ninomiya et al. 2008). The dielectric constant and height of the substrate of LPF are 9.3 and 1 mm, respectively. The length D ranges between 12–20 mm at intervals of 1 mm in which training data T_r and T_e are $D = [12, 14, 16, 18, 20]$ mm and $[13, 15, 17, 19]$ mm, respectively. Training data is illustrated in Fig. 3. The frequency range was 0.1 to 4.5 GHz. Each set of contains 221 samples. The numbers of samples $|T_r|$ and $|T_e|$ are 1,105 and 884, respectively. The inputs of NN are length D and frequency f. The outputs are $|S_{11}|$ and $|S_{12}|$ which are the magnitudes of S-parameters, S_{11} and S_{12}. The NN has a hidden layer with 45 hidden neurons. Therefore, the structure of neural network is 2-45-2. The training and testing data were generated using *Sonnet* which is Full-wave 3D Planar Electromagnetic Field Solver Software for High Frequency EM Simulation. The summary of results is shown in Table 2. The first-order methods were excluded in this table because these algorithms could not obtain sufficiently small errors. Moreover, in order to investigate the effect of the momentum coefficient for the convergence rates in detail, the value range of μ_k was expanded. From this table it is shown that the momentum acceleration was realized for QN-based algorithms even in this problem. However, NAQ and MoQ with fixed μ_k is much fast when μ_k becomes large but is unstable for the initial values of **w** because of the high-nonlinearity of the problem compared with the first example. Furthermore, these results were more pronounced in MoQ. On the other hand, NAQ and MoQ incorporating the adaptive scheme of μ_k as in (9), that is AdaNAQ and AdaMoQ could overcome this unstable problem. Therefore, the adaptive MoQ was the fastest algorithm among 100% convergence rate. As a result, it is confirmed that the proposed AdaMoQ is robust for the initial value of **w** without sacrificing the computational speed. For measuring the accuracy of modeling, the outputs of the neural model trained by AdaMoQ with $E_{test}(\mathbf{w}) = 0.472 \times 10^{-3}$ are compared with test data of $D = 17\,\mathrm{mm}$ in Fig. 4, and showing good match between them.

Table 1. Summary of simulation results of (24).

Algorithm	μ_k	$E_{test}(\mathrm{w})(\times 10^{-3})$ Ave/Best/Worst	Time (sec)	Iteration counts	$E_{test}(\mathrm{w})(\mathrm{w})(\times 10^{-3})$ Ave/Best/Worst	Convergence rate (%)
BP	-	42.29/42.23/42.31	578	150,000	41.33/41.26/41.35	-
AdaGrad	-	39.42/35.05/42.21	251	150,000	38.44/34.06/41.24	-
AdaDelta	-	72.12/42.38/92.93	250	150,000	71.16/41.42/91.98	-
RMSprop	-	33.12/32.24/33.34	250	150,000	32.28/31.41/32.49	-
Adam	-	6.83/1.80/25.17	253	150,000	6.57/1.72/24.49	-
QN	-	0.483/0.319/0.830	257	94,212	0.454/0.303/0.765	100
multiQN	-	0.662/0.408/1.21	214	78,489	0.618/0.385/1.10	100
NAQ	0.8	0.861/0.336/3.85	192	44,348	0.822/0.317/3.70	100
	0.85	0.547/0.362/1.17	165	38,171	0.517/0.341/1.10	100
	0.9	0.382/0.223/0.500	132	30,427	0.361/0.213/0.473	100
	0.95	4.26/0.291/37.85	**102**	**23,546**	4.14/0.274/36.95	100
AdaNAQ	-	0.459/0.268/0.679	120	27,701	0.434/0.254/0.611	100
MoQ	0.8	0.469/0.308/0.726	118	43,168	0.447/0.293/0.722	100
	0.85	3.01/0.327/26.06	119	43,640	2.94/0.308/25.55	100
	0.9	0.525/0.349/0.995	**75**	**27,516**	0.489/0.327/0.902	90
	0.95	0.730/0.328/2.66	80	29,204	0.639/0.313/2.55	80
AdaMoQ	-	0.457/0.220/0.842	**74**	**27,046**	0.428/0.206/0.773	100

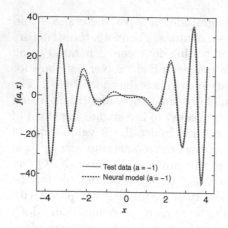

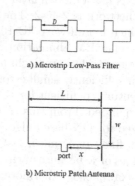

a) Microstrip Low-Pass Filter

b) Microstrip Patch Antenna

Fig. 1. Comparison between test data and neural model trained by adaMoQ.

Fig. 2. Layout of two microwave circuits.

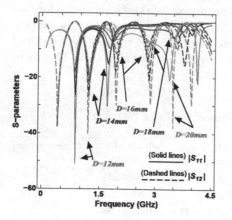

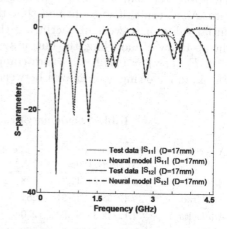

Fig. 3. Training data set for LPF.

Fig. 4. Comparison between test data and neural model trained by adaMoQ.

4.3   Microwave Circuit Modeling of Microstrip Patch Antenna

Finally the proposed algorithm is applied to develop a neural network model of a rectangular microstrip patch antenna (MPA) (Cao et al. 2009; Mahboubi and Ninomiya 2018), illustrated in Fig. 2(b). The inputs of the NN model of MPA are length L, width W, frequency f and R which is the percentage ratio of relative distance x of the microstrip feed to L. Two outputs are assigned to real and imaginary parts of S-parameter of the port S_{11}. The length L and width W ranges were 10–30 mm at intervals of 2 mm. The range of frequency f was 0.5 to 5.0 GHz at intervals of 0.5 GHz, and the range of R was 10 to 85% at intervals of 10%. The numbers of samples are 10,890. In this simulation, 10,000 and 890 samples are randomly chosen for $|T_r|$ and $|T_e|$, respectively. MPA modeling is relatively more complicated than LPF because of the large training data and inputs. Thus, MPA needs a robust training algorithm. Therefore, AdaMoQ and AdaNAQ are compared in this simulation. A NN with two hidden layers with 50 and 150 hidden neurons is chosen because a NN with one hidden layer could not obtain small training error even if the hidden layer had 1,000 or more hidden neurons. Thus the structure of the NN is 4-50-150-2. The results are shown in Table 3. The table shows that both of algorithms can obtain the small testing and training errors with high convergence rate. In addition, the numbers of iteration was the same for both methods. Therefore, the proposed AdaMoQ is faster than AdaNAQ. As a result, it is confirmed that the proposed algorithm is effective for large scale and much complicated problem such as MPA.

Table 2. Summary of simulation results of LPF modeling.

Algorithm	μ_k	$E_{test}(w)(\times 10^{-3})$ Ave/Best/Worst	Time (sec)	Iteration counts	$E_{test}(w)(w)(\times 10^{-3})$ Ave/Best/Worst	Convergence rate (%)
QN	-	0.763/0.627/0.911	120	106,287	0.901/0.534/2.01	90
multiQN	-	0.746/0.624/0.969	110	96,938	0.900/0.430/2.65	100
NAQ	0.7	0.727/0.607/0.904	126	66,133	1.87/0.466/8.94	100
	0.75	0.698/0.608/0.856	113	59,100	0.743/0.406/1.07	100
	0.8	0.791/0.570/1.08	89	46,861	8.02/0.435/65.32	100
	0.85	0.742/0.526/0.994	95	49,823	1.24/0.406/3.18	100
	0.9	0.670/0.499/0.908	84	44,149	1.10/0.442/3.60	100
	0.95	4.09/0.571/22.30	43	22,338	3.79/0.525/19.60	80
AdaNAQ	-	0.615/0.486/0.739	64	33,715	0.667/0.464/1.12	100
MoQ	0.7	0.660/0.599/0.710	81	72,090	0.965/0.566/2.18	80
	0.75	0.740/0.626/0.826	43	38,350	0.819/0.539/1.31	70
	0.8	0.649/0.569/0.727	38	34,361	0.819/0.482/1.60	50
	0.85	1.63/0.635/5.17	23	20,742	7.35/0.586/33.30	50
	0.9	0.667/0.641/0.705	16	14,262	0.636/0.488/0.761	40
	0.95	0.604/0.545/0.735	14	12,847	0.713/0.578/0.870	40
AdaMoQ	-	0.615/0.472/0.751	**31**	**27,627**	1.14/0.591/2.15	**100**

Table 3. Summary of simulation results of MPA modeling.

Algorithm	$E_{test}(w)(\times 10^{-3})$ Ave/Best/Worst	Time (sec)	Iteration counts	$E_{test}(w)(w)(\times 10^{-3})$ Ave/Best/Worst	Convergence Rate (%)
AdaNAQ	0.436/0.383/0.545	8,604	18,760	1.72/1.44/1.97	100
AdaMoQ	0.440/0.377/0.531	**4,919**	**18,573**	1.70/1.36/2.44	100

5   Conclusion

In this research a novel quasi-Newton based training with momentum terms was proposed as Momentum quasi-Newton method (MoQ). The proposed method was an improvement of Nesterov's accelerated quasi-Newton method (NAQ) so that Nesterov's accelerated gradient was approximated as a weighted linear combination of the normal gradients by assuming the error function to be a quadratic function. However, in highly-nonlinear problems, the convergence rate of MoQ with the large momentum coefficients decreased because of overshooting of the gradients. Therefore, to overcome this problem, an adaptive scheme of the momentum coefficients were applied to the proposed MoQ for stable convergence. As a result, it is confirmed that the proposed AdaMoQ is a fast training algorithm for NN, with high convergence rate compared with the conventional methods.

In the future, the adaptive scheme of the momentum parameters μ_k will be analytically studied. The convergence property of the momentum-accelerated quasi-Newton method will be clarified through this analysis. Furthermore, the validity of the proposed algorithm for much huge scale and highly nonlinear function approximation problems will be demonstrated.

References

Cao, Y., Wang, G., Zhang, Q.J.: A new training approach for parametric modeling of microwave passive components using combined neural networks and transfer functions. IEEE Trans. Microw. Theory Tech. **57**, 2727–2742 (2009)

Duchi, J., Hazan, E., Singer, Y.: Adaptive subgradient methods for online learning and stochastic optimization. J. Mach. Learn. Res. **12**, 2121–2159 (2011)

Ford, J.A., Moghrabi, I.A.: Alternative parameter choices for multi-step quasi-Newton methods. Optim. Methods Softw. **2**(3–4), 357–370 (1993)

Forst, W., Hoffmann, D.: Optimization - Theory and Practice. Springer Undergraduate Texts in Mathematics and Technology, 1st edn. Springer, New York (2010). https://doi.org/10.1007/978-0-387-78977-4

Haykin, S.S.: Neural Networks and Learning Machines, 3rd edn. Pearson, London (2009)

Indrapriyadarsini, S., Mahboubi, S., Ninomiya, H., Asai, H.: Implementation of a modified Nesterov's accelerated quasi-Newton method on tensorflow. In: Proceedings of the IEEE ICMLA 2018, pp. 1147–1154 (2018)

Kingma, D.P., Ba, J.: Adam: a method for stochastic optimization. In: Proceedings of the ICLR, pp. 1–13 (2015)

Li, D.H., Fukushima, M.: A modified BFGS method and its global convergence in nonconvex minimization. J. Comput. Appl. Math. **129**, 15–35 (2001)

Mahboubi, S., Ninomiya, H.: A novel quasi-Newton with momentum training for microwave circuit models using neural networks. In: Proceedings of the ICECS 2018, pp. 629–632 (2018)

Moghrabi, I.A.R.: Curvature-based quasi-Newton methods for optimization. IJPAM **119**(1), 131–143 (2018)

Nesterov, Y.: Introductory Lectures on Convex Optimization: A Basic Course. Applied Optimization, vol. 87, 1st edn. Springer, Boston (2004). https://doi.org/10.1007/978-1-4419-8853-9

Ninomiya, H., Wan, S., Kabir, H., Zhang, Z., Zhang, Q.J.: Robust training of microwave neural network models using combined global/local optimization techniques. In: IEEE MTT-S International Microwave Symposium (IMS) Digest, pp. 995–998 (2008)

Ninomiya, H.: Dynamic sample size selection based quasi-Newton training for highly nonlinear function approximation using multilayer neural networks. In: Proceedings of the IEEE & INNS IJCNN 2013, pp. 1932–1937 (2013)

Ninomiya, H.: A novel quasi-Newton optimization for neural network training incorporating Nesterov's accelerated gradient. IEICE NOLTA J. **E8-N**(4), 289–301 (2017)

Nocedal, J., Wright, S.J.: Numerical Optimization. Springer Series in Operations Research and Financial Engineering, 2nd edn. Springer, New York (2006). https://doi.org/10.1007/978-0-387-40065-5

Sonnet: Sonnet Software Inc. http://www.sonnetsoftware.com. Accessed 12 Mar 2019

Sutskever, I., Martens, J., Dahl, G.E., Hinton, G.E.: On the importance of initialization and momentum in deep learning. In: Proceedings of the ICML 2013 (2013)

Tieleman, T., Hinton, G.: Lecture 6.5 - RMSprop, COURSERA: neural networks for machine learning. Technical report (2012)

Zeiler, M.D.: ADADELTA: an adaptive learning rate method. arXiv print arXiv:1212.5701 (2012)

Zhang, Q.J., Gupta, K.C., Devabhaktuni, V.K.: Artifical neural networks for RF and microwave design-from theory to practice. IEEE Trans. Microw. Theory Tech. **51**, 1339–1350 (2003)

Multi-step-ahead Cyclone Intensity Prediction with Bayesian Neural Networks

Ratneel Deo[1,2(✉)] and Rohitash Chandra[2,3]

[1] School of Computing, Information and Mathematical Sciences,
University of the South Pacific, Suva, Fiji
`deo.ratneel@gmail.com`
[2] Centre for Translational Data Science, The University of Sydney, Sydney, Australia
`c.rohitash@gmail.com`
[3] School of Geosciences, The University of Sydney, Sydney, Australia

Abstract. The chaotic nature of cyclones makes track and wind-intensity prediction a challenging task. The complexity in attaining robust and accurate prediction increases with an increase of the prediction horizon. There is lack of robust uncertainty quantification in models that have been used for cyclone prediction problems. Bayesian inference provide a principled approach for quantifying uncertainties that arise from model and data, which is essential for prediction, particularly in the case of cyclones. In this paper, Bayesian neural networks are used for multi-step ahead time series prediction for cyclones in the South Pacific region. The results show promising prediction accuracy with uncertainty quantification for shorter prediction horizon; however, the challenge lies in higher prediction horizons.

1 Introduction

A tropical cyclone is a low pressure system with organized convection that forms over warm tropical waters [1]. Once formed, a cyclone can move over the ocean in the direction away from the equator that can last a few days to weeks [16]. The past decade has witnessed rise of destructive storms and cyclones with effect of climate change [22,35]. The wind-intensity and duration of cyclones are the major contributing factors of the extent of damages which can be greatly reduced with timely and precise warning [14,21,23]. The chaotic nature of cyclones makes prediction of track and wind-intensity a challenging task [36]. Statistical models have been a standard approach for predicting the intensity of the cyclones [24]. A popular method was the statistical hurricane intensity prediction scheme (SHIPS) [17] that made cyclone intensity forecasts for 12 to 120 h. SHIPS has been unsuitable for cyclones near the coast as the model was developed using cyclone data away from coastlines [18].

Machine learning methods have established themselves as complementary approaches for tropical cyclone tracking and prediction [4,13,25,27]. Amongst machine learning methods, neural networks have shown great promise due to

A. C. Nayak and A. Sharma (Eds.): PRICAI 2019, LNAI 11671, pp. 282–295, 2019.
https://doi.org/10.1007/978-3-030-29911-8_22

their prediction accuracy [6,8,20]. Baik and Huwang [3] presented of the earliest works where neural networks for tropical cyclone intensity prediction in the western North Pacific ocean for selected time-spans (12 to 72 h). Liu and Feng [30] used neural networks the prediction of the maximum potential intensity of cyclones. Chaudhuri et al. [13] considered tropical cyclones over the Bay of Bengal and the Arabian Sea for prediction of track and wind-intensity using feedforward neural networks. The method gave comparable performance with existing numerical models for 6 hour-ahead forecasts. Chandra and Dayal [8] presented a method for cyclone track prediction using coevolutionary Elman recurrent neural networks (RNNs) for the South Pacific ocean which was later improved [11]. Coevolutionary Elman RNNs was also used for cyclone wind-intensity prediction [7]. Deo and Chandra [19] presented the problem of predicting rapid intensification in wind-intensity of tropical cyclones with Elman RNNs. More recently, Zhang et al. [37] used matrix neural networks for prediction of tracks for South Indian and South Pacific oceans and found that their method performed better when compared to prominent deep learning architectures such as long-short term memory networks (LSTMs) and gated recurrent units (GRUs).

Bayesian inference accounts for uncertainties in parameter estimates and propagates it into predictions by marginalizing them out of the posterior distribution [32]. Bayesian neural networks (BNNs) use Markov Chain Monti-Carlo (MCMC) methods to sample from the posterior distribution of weights and biases [31]. MCMC methods have limitations due to the lack of scalability given the increasing size of the model and data which has been addressed by combining them with the gradient-based learning methods [10,28], simulated annealing [29], and evolutionary algorithms [26]. Bayesian methods have been used for cyclone identification problems in the past and have shown promising results [5,15].

There exists limited literature on the use of Bayesian neural methods for multiple step-ahead predictions. In the literature, cyclone wind-intensity prediction via neural networks has mostly been approached as a single-step ahead prediction problem [7,8,37]. Given dataset Joint Typhoon Warning Centre [2], this implies that single step-ahead prediction provides only a six-hour ahead prediction. This can be extended if the prediction is fed back as input to the model; however, this can reduce accuracy in prediction [33]. A limited prediction horizon lacks usefulness in giving a warning for evacuation and preparations in case the cyclone intensifies in the future. Therefore, it would be useful to increase the prediction horizon while featuring uncertainty quantification in the prediction via Bayesian inference. Moreover, there is limited work done using Bayesian inference in the area of storms and cyclones.

In this paper, Bayesian neural networks are used for multi-step ahead time series prediction for cyclones in the South Pacific region. This enables uncertainty quantification in the predictive model given multiple steps-ahead. We use two MCMC sampling methods and compare the performance with standard backpropagation network given increasing prediction horizons.

The rest of the paper is organised as follows. The proposed method is presented in Sect. 2 which is followed by results and discussion in Sect. 3. Section 4 concludes the paper with discussion of future work.

2   Bayesian Neural Networks for Cyclone Intensity Prediction

In this section, we present the Bayesian neural network (BNN) model used for multi-step ahead cyclone intensity prediction. The dynamics of a feedforward network is given in Eq. 1.

$$f(\mathbf{x}_t) = g\left(\delta_o + \sum_{h=1}^{H} v_j g\left(\delta_h + \sum_{d=1}^{D} w_{dh} y_{t-d}\right)\right) \tag{1}$$

where δ_o and δ_h are the bias weights for the output o and hidden h layer, respectively. V_j is the weight which maps the hidden layer h to the output layer. w_{dh} is the weight which maps y_{t-d} to the hidden layer h, and g is the activation function given in Eq. 2. In our case, we use the sigmoid activation function in the hidden and output layer units.

$$f(y_i) = \frac{1}{1 + e^{-y_i}} \tag{2}$$

Taken's embedding theorem [34] is used to reconstruct the univariate time series data into a phase state as given in Eq. 3.

$$Y(t) = [(x(t), x(t-T), ..., x(t(D-1)T)] \tag{3}$$

where $x(t)$ is the observed time series, T is the time delay, D is the embedding dimension, $t = 0, 1, 2, ..., N - DT - 1$ and N is the length of the original time series.

2.1   Model and Priors

Let y_t denote a univariate time series of cyclone wind-intensity:

$$y_t = f(\mathbf{x}_t) + \epsilon_t, \text{ for } t = 1, 2, \ldots, n \tag{4}$$

where $f(\mathbf{x}_t) = E(y_t|\mathbf{x}_t)$, is an unknown function, $\mathbf{x}_t = (y_{t-1}, \ldots, y_{t-D})$ is a vector of lagged values of y_t, and ϵ_t is the noise with $\epsilon_t \sim \mathcal{N}(0, \tau^2) \forall t$.

Let $\boldsymbol{\theta} = (\tilde{\mathbf{w}}, \mathbf{v}, \boldsymbol{\delta}, \tau^2)$, with $\boldsymbol{\delta} = (\delta_o, \delta_h)$, denote $L = (DH + (2*H) + O + 1)$ vector of parameters that includes weights and biases, with O number of neurons in output layer. H is the number of hidden neurons required to evaluate the likelihood for the model given by Eq. 4, with $\tilde{\mathbf{w}} = (\mathbf{w_1.}', \ldots, \mathbf{w'_D})'$, and $\mathbf{w_d.} = (w_{d1}, \ldots, w_{dH})'$, for $d = 1, \ldots, D$.

Bayesian inference via MCMC sampling is implemented by drawing samples from the posterior distribution given the prior distribution and the likelihood function that verifies how well the model fits the data. Given our model is the feedforward network given in Eq. 1, the prior distributions for the elements of $\boldsymbol{\theta}$ are given as

$$v_h \sim \mathcal{N}(0, \sigma^2) \text{ for } h = 1, \ldots, H,$$
$$\delta_0 \sim N(0, \sigma^2)$$
$$\delta_h \sim N(0, \sigma^2)$$
$$w_{dj} \sim \mathcal{N}(0, \sigma^2) \text{ for } h = 1, \ldots, H \text{ and } d = 1, \ldots, D,$$
$$\tau^2 \sim \mathcal{IG}(\nu_1, \nu_2) \tag{5}$$

where H is the number of hidden neurons. In general, the log posterior is

$$\log\left(p(\boldsymbol{\theta}|\mathbf{y})\right) = \log\left(p(\boldsymbol{\theta})\right) + \log\left(p(\mathbf{y}|\boldsymbol{\theta})\right)$$

In our particular model, the log likelihood is

$$\log\left(p(\mathbf{y}_{\mathcal{A_D,T}}|\boldsymbol{\theta})\right) = -\frac{n-1}{2}\log(\tau^2)$$
$$-\frac{1}{2\tau^2}\sum_{t\in\mathcal{A_D,T}}(y_t - E(y_t|\mathbf{x}_t))^2 \tag{6}$$

where $E(y_t|\mathbf{x}_t)$ is given by Eq. 1. We further assume that the elements of $\boldsymbol{\theta}$ are independent *apriori*; therefore, the log of the prior distributions is

$$\log\left(p(\boldsymbol{\theta})\right) = -\frac{HD+H+2}{2}\log(\sigma^2)$$
$$-\frac{1}{2\sigma^2}\left(\sum_{h=1}^{H}\sum_{d=1}^{D}w_{dh}^2 + \sum_{h=1}^{H}(\delta_h^2 + v_h^2) + \delta_o^2\right) \tag{7}$$
$$- (1+\nu_1)\log(\tau^2) - \frac{\nu_2}{\tau^2}$$

where, σ^2, ν_1, ν_2 are user chosen constants. We feature MCMC random-walk and Langevin-gradient proposals for sampling [10]. In Langevin-gradient proposals, a stochastic noise is added to one step of gradients as shown in Eqs. 8 to 11.

$$\theta^p \sim \mathcal{N}(\bar{\theta}^{[k]}, \Sigma_\theta), \text{ where} \tag{8}$$
$$\bar{\theta}^{[k]} = \theta^{[k]} + r \times \nabla E_{\mathbf{y}_{\mathcal{A_D,T}}}[\theta^{[k]}], \tag{9}$$
$$E_{\mathbf{y}_{\mathcal{A_D,T}}}[\theta^{[k]}] = \sum_{t\in\mathcal{A_D,T}}(y_t - f(\mathbf{x}_t)^{[k]})^2, \tag{10}$$
$$\nabla E_{\mathbf{y}_{\mathcal{A_D,T}}}[\theta^{[k]}] = \left(\frac{\partial E}{\partial \theta_1}, \ldots, \frac{\partial E}{\partial \theta_L}\right) \tag{11}$$

where r is the learning rate, $\Sigma_\theta = \sigma_\theta^2 I_L$ and I_L is the $L \times L$ identity matrix. The newly proposed value of θ^p consists of 2 parts:

1. A gradient descent based weight update given by Eqs. 8 to 11.
2. Add an amount of noise, from $\mathcal{N}(0, \Sigma_\theta)$.

2.2   Framework

The framework shown in Fig. 1 gives an overview of the Bayesian neural network architecture used for multi-step cyclone intensity prediction. We use a three-layer feedforward neural network and process data according to the prediction horizon using Taken's theorem.

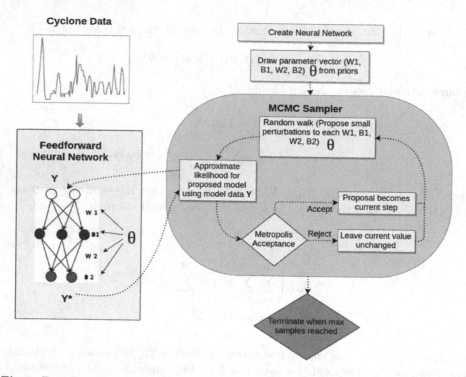

Fig. 1. Bayesian neural network for cyclone intensity prediction. The figure shows the mapping between the MCMC sampler and Bayesian neural network parameters. The three-layer feedforward neural network has four sets of parameters that make up θ; $W1$ corresponds to the network weights between the input layer and the hidden layer, $B1$ corresponds to the biases of each of the hidden neurons, and $W2$, $B2$ correspond to the weights and biases of the output layer

Algorithm 1 begins by pre-processing the data using Taken's state space reconstruction described in Eq. 3. The neural network model is then created according the specified number of input, hidden and output neurons. Note that the number of output neurons defines the steps-ahead or prediction horizon. The sampling begins where a proposal for θ that features the training neural network parameters (weights and biases) is generated either using a random-walk (RW-MCMC) or using Langevin-gradient (LG-MCMC) proposals as defined by the user. The algorithm calculates the log likelihood and then given the prior, it either accepts or rejects the proposals using the Metropolis-Hastings criterion. If the sample is accepted, it becomes part of the posterior distribution θ; otherwise, the previously accepted sample is retained. The process repeats until the maximum number of samples (max samples) is reached. Once this is done, the trained Bayesian neural network is tested using unseen data as defined by the user.

Alg. 1. Bayesian neural networks using MCMC sampling

Data: Univariate time series of cyclone intensities $\mathbf{y}$
Result: Posterior of weights and biases $p(\theta|\mathbf{y})$
Step 1: State-space reconstruction by Equation 3
Step 2: Define feedforward network as given in Equation 1
Step 3: Define θ as the set of all weights and biases
Step 4: Set parameters σ^2 ,ν_1, ν_2 for prior given in Equation 7

for *each k until max-samples* **do**
    1. Draw η from $\mathcal{N}(0, \Sigma_\eta)$
    2. Propose $\theta^* = \theta^{[k]} + \eta$
    Draw $l \sim U[0,1]$
    if *(LG is true) and (l < LG − freq)* **then**
        Conditional on m^c, propose a new value of θ
        using Langevin-gradient proposal distribution $\theta^p \sim q(\theta|\theta^c, m^c)$
        where, $q(\theta|\theta^c, m^c)$ is given in Equations 8 to 11
    else
        Conditional on m^c, propose a new value of θ
        using Random-Walk proposal distribution
    end
    3. Compute acceptance probability α
    if $u < \alpha$ **then**
        $\theta^{[k+1]} = \theta^*$
    end
    else
        $\theta^{[k+1]} = \theta^{[k]}$
    end
end

---

3   Experiments and Results

In this section, we present the experiments that are conducted to evaluate the efficiency of Bayesian neural networks for multi-step-ahead cyclone wind-intensity prediction.

3.1   Dataset and Experiment Design

The cyclone data featured the South Pacific ocean that considered cyclones from 1985 to 2013 taken from Joint Typhoon Warning Centre [2]. There are a total of 280 cyclones in the dataset with an average duration of 8 days and a standard deviation of 5.5 days for each cyclone. We concatenate the cyclones into a single time series by stacking the cyclone data in ascending order based on its start time as done in the literature [8,19]. Each cyclone was recorded at 6-h regular intervals, and therefore, the dataset consisted of 9,400 data points when concatenated. We implemented a 70:30 split ratio for our training and testing data. We normalize the univariate cyclone time series between 0 to 1 and use Taken's embedding theorem [34] from Eq. 3 to reconstruct the data where time lag of $T = 2$ and embedding dimension $D = 5$.

We use a multi-output neural network to make multiple-step ahead prediction based on the prediction horizon, where the number of outputs in each data instance represents the prediction horizon. Each output of the neural network corresponds to one step in the prediction horizon; i.e. the first output of the network maps on to the first and the second output represents the prediction horizon, and the rest in a similar manner. The root mean squared-error (RMSE) is used to measure the prediction performance of the neural network.

$$RMSE = \sqrt{\frac{1}{N} \sum_{i=1}^{N} (y_i - \hat{y}_i)^2} \tag{12}$$

where $y_i, \hat{y}_i$ are the observed data and predicted data, respectively. N is the length of the observed data.

We implemented two experimental configurations with a different number of output neurons to enable predictions over two sets of the prediction horizon.

- Experiment 1: Five step-ahead prediction with 5 input neurons, 10 hidden neurons, and 5 output neurons
- Experiment 2: Ten step-ahead prediction with 5 input neurons, 10 hidden neurons, and 10 output neurons

Bayesian neural networks with random-walk (RW-MCMC) and Langevin-gradient (LG-MCMC) sampling methods for forecasting cyclone wind-intensity with the above experimental setup. We also provide results for backpropagation neural network (BP) using gradient-descent training. In the case of RW-MCMC, each proposal of the Markov in the sampling chain (θ) added a Gaussian with mean $\mu = 0$ and standard deviation $\sigma = 0.02$. A Gaussian noise was also used for sampling η with mean $\mu = 0$ and standard deviation $\sigma = 0.2$. T The parameters for the prior given in Eq. 7 was set: $\sigma^2 = 25$, $\nu_1 = 0$, $\nu_2 = 0$. In the case of backpropagation, fixed learning rate of 0.1 and training time of 2000 epochs was used. A similar configuration was used with LG-MCMC; however, the additional parameter involved was the learning rate of 0.1 for Langevin-gradients. The maximum sampling time for the MCMC methods were set to 10,000 samples.

3.2   Results

Table 1 provides the results for the prediction accuracy for the respective methods. We observe that the three methods give a similar performance in most of the cases. There seems to be a linear relationship between the prediction horizon and prediction error; we notice a steady increase in the error in prediction

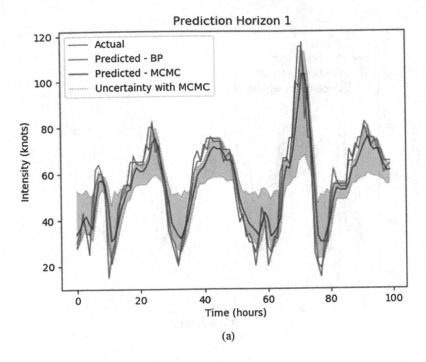

(a)

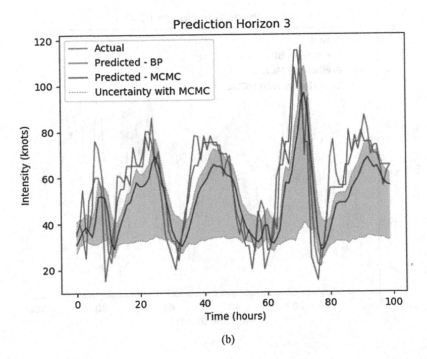

(b)

Fig. 2. (a) One step ahead prediction; (b) intensity prediction for third prediction horizon.

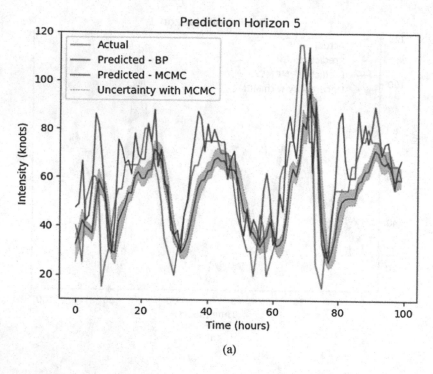

(a)

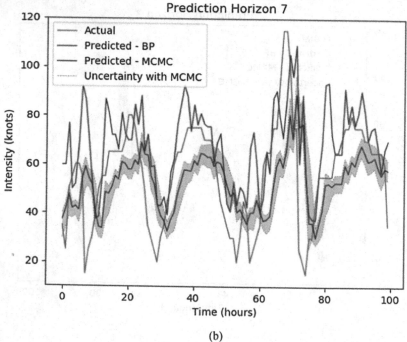

(b)

Fig. 3. (a) intensity prediction for fifth prediction horizon; (b) intensity prediction for seventh prediction horizon.

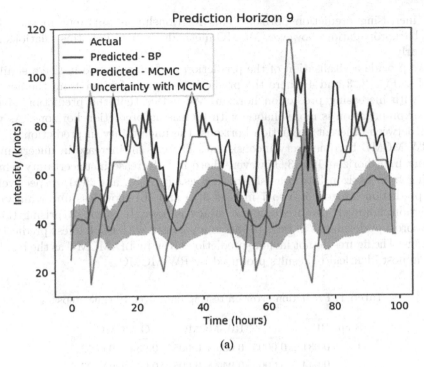

(a)

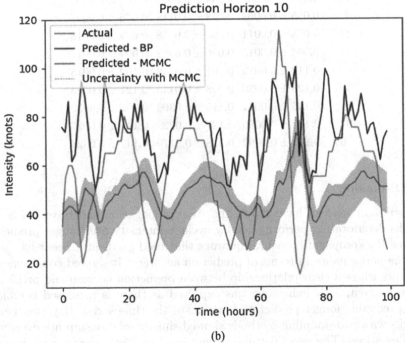

(b)

Fig. 4. (a) intensity prediction for ninth prediction horizon; (b) intensity prediction for tenth prediction horizon.

with increasing prediction horizon. This relationship is apparent in the case with backpropagation; however, MCMC methods do not show this relationship as clearly.

We provide a vitalisation of the prediction performance and notice a similar trend in Figs. 2, 3 and 4 where the predictions deviate further from the actual data with increasing prediction horizon. We notice that the prediction given by backpropagation is more chaotic with increasing prediction horizons. As we move between different prediction horizons, the uncertainty in prediction given by RW-MCMC becomes very inconsistent. There is an increase in uncertainty moving from horizon 1 to 3; however, there is a decrease in uncertainty while moving from horizon 3 to 5 as shown in Figs. 2(a), (b), and 3(a), respectively. The prediction horizon of 5 to 7 in Figs. 3(a) and (b) show less uncertainty in prediction; however, the prediction accuracy is poor. It is not surprising that, the poorest performance in terms of accuracy is seen with the highest prediction horizons. The figures do not include prediction given by LD-MCMC as the results were almost identical to results produced by RW-MCMC.

Table 1. Prediction error on testing data over 10 time-steps

Step	BP	RW-MCMC	LG-MCMC
1	0.031 ± 0.0005	0.036 ± 0.0057	0.034 ± 0.0012
2	0.044 ± 0.0005	0.044 ± 0.0061	0.045 ± 0.0007
3	0.055 ± 0.0008	0.053 ± 0.0118	0.065 ± 0.0021
4	0.078 ± 0.0011	0.067 ± 0.0238	0.079 ± 0.0018
5	0.094 ± 0.0015	0.086 ± 0.0422	0.094 ± 0.0017
6	0.112 ± 0.0022	0.101 ± 0.0442	0.102 ± 0.0018
7	0.128 ± 0.0030	0.098 ± 0.0143	0.121 ± 0.0023
8	0.145 ± 0.0041	0.115 ± 0.0309	0.132 ± 0.0030
9	0.157 ± 0.0050	0.127 ± 0.0229	0.141 ± 0.0027
10	0.173 ± 0.0062	0.128 ± 0.0170	0.147 ± 0.0027

3.3 Discussion

The results, in general, have shown that backpropagation and Bayesian neural networks deteriorating performance for cyclone intensity over longer prediction horizons. Backpropagation neural network that used gradient descent has given a notable performance in terms of prediction accuracy. It showed consistency in the results where a clear relationship between prediction horizon and prediction error was noted. This behaviour was expected as there is increased complexities of predicting longer prediction horizons of the time series. Bayesian neural networks with two sampling methods showed similar relationship however, with slight deviations. The general trend of increased prediction error with increasing horizons are seen; however, there are some outliers in the trend given the uncertainties in prediction.

The larger prediction horizons are vital. Since cyclone intensity determines the extent of damages; the better our prediction for longer prediction horizons, the more time the general public get to prepare. The 10-step ahead prediction would give 2.25 days of advance warning which is ample time to prepare or evacuate safely [14,23]. We found that increasing prediction horizons increases the complexity of the problem. This could be addressed in future work by using more advanced MCMC methods such as parallel tempering [12]. Another limitation of the experiments is in the neural network model which requires 5 data points, in order to make a prediction. This implies 1.25 days of cyclone activity before the model could be used. The limitation can be addressed in future by using a dynamic time series prediction neural network model [9]. The dynamic neural network would be able begin prediction without waiting for 5 data points.

4 Conclusions and Future Work

We have presented a Bayesian neural network approach to the prediction of wind-intensity of cyclones given multiple prediction horizons. The results show that the proposed method achieves more accurate predictions for shorter prediction horizon when compared to longer ones, which is not surprising as it is well known that the complexity of the problem increases with the horizon. Nevertheless, the proposed method has the power of rigorous uncertainty quantification that can be propagated for different prediction horizons which is helpful for extreme weather forecasting.

In future work, Bayesian neural networks can be further improved by incorporating more advanced models such as recurrent neural networks and other deep learning architectures. More datasets and input features such as distance to landfall, sea-surface temperature, and humidity can help in achieving better predictions. Furthermore, the approach can be used for trajectory or path prediction of cyclones as it provides uncertainty quantification in prediction.

Supplementary Material
The software code and dataset is given online[1].

Acknowledgements. We would like to acknowledge Prof. Sally Cripps for discussion and support during the course of this project.

References

1. Bureau of meteorology research centre (2000). http://www.bom.gov.au/cyclone/about/. Accessed 02 Jan 2018
2. JTWC tropical cyclone best track data site (2018). http://www.usno.navy.mil/NOOC/nmfc-ph/RSS/jtwc/
3. Baik, J.J., Hwang, H.S.: Tropical cyclone intensity prediction using regression method and neural network. J. Meteorol. Soc. Jpn. Ser. II **76**(5), 711–717 (1998)

[1] https://github.com/sydney-machine-learning/Bayesian-neural-networks-cyclone-intensity.

4. Carr III, L.E., Elsberry, R.L., Peak, J.E.: Beta test of the systematic approach expert system prototype as a tropical cyclone track forecasting aid. Weather Forecast. **16**(3), 355–368 (2001)
5. Chand, S.S., Walsh, K.J., Chan, J.C.: A Bayesian regression approach to seasonal prediction of tropical cyclones affecting the Fiji region. J. Clim. **23**(13), 3425–3445 (2010)
6. Chandra, R.: Multi-objective cooperative neuro-evolution of recurrent neural networks for time series prediction. In: IEEE Congress on Evolutionary Computation, Sendai, Japan, pp. 101–108, May 2015
7. Chandra, R., Dayal, K.: Cooperative coevolution of Elman recurrent networks for tropical cyclone wind-intensity prediction in the South Pacific region. In: IEEE Congress on Evolutionary Computation, Sendai, Japan, pp. 1784–1791, May 2015
8. Chandra, R., Dayal, K., Rollings, N.: Application of cooperative neuro-evolution of Elman recurrent networks for a two-dimensional cyclone track prediction for the South Pacific region. In: International Joint Conference on Neural Networks (IJCNN), Killarney, Ireland, pp. 721–728, July 2015
9. Chandra, R.: Dynamic cyclone wind-intensity prediction using co-evolutionary multi-task learning. In: Liu, D., Xie, S., Li, Y., Zhao, D., El-Alfy, E.-S.M. (eds.) ICONIP 2017. LNCS, vol. 10638, pp. 618–627. Springer, Cham (2017). https://doi.org/10.1007/978-3-319-70139-4_63
10. Chandra, R., Azizi, L., Cripps, S.: Bayesian neural learning via Langevin dynamics for chaotic time series prediction. In: Liu, D., Xie, S., Li, Y., Zhao, D., El-Alfy, E.-S.M. (eds.) ICONIP 2017. LNCS, vol. 10638, pp. 564–573. Springer, Cham (2017). https://doi.org/10.1007/978-3-319-70139-4_57
11. Chandra, R., Deo, R., Omlin, C.W.: An architecture for encoding two-dimensional cyclone track prediction problem in coevolutionary recurrent neural networks. In: 2016 International Joint Conference on Neural Networks, IJCNN 2016, Vancouver, BC, Canada, pp. 4865–4872, 24–29 July 2016
12. Chandra, R., Jain, K., Deo, R.V., Cripps, S.: Langevin-gradient parallel tempering for Bayesian neural learning. Neurocomputing (2019). http://www.sciencedirect.com/science/article/pii/S0925231219308069
13. Chaudhuri, S., Dutta, D., Goswami, S., Middey, A.: Track and intensity forecast of tropical cyclones over the North Indian Ocean with multilayer feed forward neural nets. Meteorol. Appl. **22**(3), 563–575 (2015)
14. Chowdhury, A.M.R., Bhuyia, A.U., Choudhury, A.Y., Sen, R.: The Bangladesh cyclone of 1991: why so many people died. Disasters **17**(4), 291–304 (1993)
15. Chu, P.S., Zhao, X.: A Bayesian regression approach for predicting seasonal tropical cyclone activity over the central North Pacific. J. Clim. **20**(15), 4002–4013 (2007)
16. Debsarma, S.: Cyclone and its warning system in Bangladesh. National Disaster Reduction Day (2001)
17. DeMaria, M., Kaplan, J.: A statistical hurricane intensity prediction scheme (SHIPS) for the Atlantic basin. Weather Forecast. **9**, 209–220 (1994)
18. DeMaria, M., Mainelli, M., Shay, L., Knaff, J., Kaplan, J.: Futher improvements to the statistical hurricane intensity prediction scheme (SHIPS). Weather Forecast. **20**, 531–543 (2005)
19. Deo, R., Chandra, R.: Identification of minimal timespan problem for recurrent neural networks with application to cyclone wind-intensity prediction. In: 2016 International Joint Conference on Neural Networks (IJCNN), pp. 489–496. IEEE (2016)

20. Du, W., Leung, S.Y.S., Kwong, C.K.: Time series forecasting by neural networks: a knee point-based multiobjective evolutionary algorithm approach. Expert Syst. Appl. **41**(18), 8049–8061 (2014)
21. Dvorak, V.F.: Tropical cyclone intensity analysis using satellite data, vol. 11. US Department of Commerce, National Oceanic and Atmospheric Administration, National Environmental Satellite, Data, and Information Service (1984)
22. Handmer, J., Iveson, H., et al.: Cyclone Pam in Vanuatu: learning from the low death toll. Aust. J. Emerg. Manag. **32**(2), 60 (2017)
23. Haque, C.E.: Atmospheric hazards preparedness in Bangladesh: a study of warning, adjustments and recovery from the April 1991 cyclone. Earthq. Atmos. Hazards **16**, 181–202 (1997)
24. Jarvinen, B.R., Neumann, C.J.: Statistical forecasts of tropical cyclone intensity. NOAA Techonological Memorandum. NWS NHC-10, p. 22 (1979)
25. Jin, L., Yao, C., Huang, X.Y.: A nonlinear artificial intelligence ensemble prediction model for typhoon intensity. Mon. Weather Rev. **136**, 4541–4554 (2008)
26. Kocadağlı, O., Aşıkgil, B.: Nonlinear time series forecasting with Bayesian neural networks. Expert Syst. Appl. **41**(15), 6596–6610 (2014)
27. Kovordányi, R., Roy, C.: Cyclone track forecasting based on satellite images using artificial neural networks. ISPRS J. Photogramm. Remote Sens. **64**, 513–521 (2009)
28. Li, C., Chen, C., Carlson, D., Carin, L.: Preconditioned stochastic gradient Langevin dynamics for deep neural networks. In: Thirtieth AAAI Conference on Artificial Intelligence (2016)
29. Liang, F.: Annealing stochastic approximation Monte Carlo algorithm for neural network training. Mach. Learn. **68**(3), 201–233 (2007)
30. Liu, J., Feng, B.: A neural network regression model for tropical cyclone forecast. In: Fourth International Conference on Machine Learning and Cybernetics, Guangzhou, pp. 4122–4128, 18–21 August 2005
31. MacKay, D.J.: A practical Bayesian framework for backpropagation networks. Neural Comput. **4**(3), 448–472 (1992)
32. MacKay, D.J.: Hyperparameters: optimize, or integrate out? In: Heidbreder, G.R. (ed.) Maximum Entropy and Bayesian Methods. Fundamental Theories of Physics (An International Book Series on The Fundamental Theories of Physics: Their Clarification, Development and Application), vol. 62, pp. 43–59. Springer, Dordrecht (1996). https://doi.org/10.1007/978-94-015-8729-7_2
33. Taieb, S.B., Sorjamaa, A., Bontempi, G.: Multiple-output modeling for multi-step-ahead time series forecasting. Neurocomputing **73**(10), 1950–1957 (2010)
34. Takens, F.: Detecting strange attractors in turbulence. In: Rand, D., Young, L.-S. (eds.) Dynamical Systems and Turbulence, Warwick 1980. LNM, vol. 898, pp. 366–381. Springer, Heidelberg (1981). https://doi.org/10.1007/BFb0091924
35. Tatham, P., Ball, C.M., Wu, Y., Diplas, P.: Using long endurance remotely piloted aircraft systems to support humanitarian logistic operations: a case study of cyclone winston. In: Smart Technologies for Emergency Response and Disaster Management, pp. 264–278. IGI Global (2018)
36. Zhang, F., Tao, D.: Effects of vertical wind shear on the predictability of tropical cyclones. J. Atmos. Sci. **70**(3), 975–983 (2013)
37. Zhang, Y., Chandra, R., Gao, J.: Cyclone track prediction with matrix neural networks. In: 2018 International Joint Conference on Neural Networks, IJCNN 2018, Rio de Janeiro, Brazil, pp. 1–8, 8–13 July 2018

An End-to-End Structure Aware Graph Convolutional Network for Modeling Multi-relational Data

Binling Nie[✉], Shouqian Sun, and Dian Yu

Zhejiang University, Hangzhou, China
nbl1221@zju.edu.cn

Abstract. Low-dimensional embeddings of entities and relations in large scale knowledge graphs have been proved extremely beneficial in variety of downstream tasks, e.g. entity classification and knowledge graph completion. Most of existing approaches incorporate both textual information and relation paths of triple facts for knowledge graph representation. However, they ignore rich structural information in a knowledge graph, i.e., connectivity patterns in neighboring entities and relations around a given entity. In this work, we propose a novel knowledge representation model, denoted Structure Aware Graph Convolutional Network (SAGCN), which leverages structural information for modeling the highly multi-relational data characteristic of realistic knowledge graphs. Specifically, we sample multi-hop neighboring entities and relations of a given entity as its local graph, which depicts the neighborhood topology structure. To encode features from the local graph, we introduce localized graph convolutions as a neighborhood structure encoder to generate embeddings. We further design distinct decoders for entity classification and knowledge graph completion. The proposed approach are evaluated on three public datasets and substantially outperforms state-of-the-arts.

Keywords: Knowledge graph completion ·
Graph Convolutional Networks · One-shot learning

1 Introduction

Knowledge graphs usually represent factual information as multi-relational data with enormous triples in the form of (*head entity, relation, tail entity*). Large-scale knowledge graphs, such as Freebase [1] and WordNet [16], have become useful resources to support various intelligent applications, e.g. expert system [6], web search [29,32], recommendation [37] and question answering [2,42]. Knowledge graph embedding is a nontrivial task. Common challenges stem from the

Granted by National Key Research and Development Program of China (No. 2017YFD 0700102).

A. C. Nayak and A. Sharma (Eds.): PRICAI 2019, LNAI 11671, pp. 296–308, 2019.
https://doi.org/10.1007/978-3-030-29911-8_23

large scale of knowledge graphs as well as a great many of missing and incorrect triples [17]. Due to these challenges, knowledge graphs are still far from satisfactory and have large potential to improve for practical applications.

Extensive research efforts have been made to handle these challenges. Traditional knowledge graph representation methods include translation based models [3,15,25], compositional models using a tensor/matrix product [24,30,31,43] and convolutional neural network based models [7,22]. Since they solely learn from independent fact triple, the sparsity of knowledge graphs leads to limited expressive power of learned vectors.

Recently, a growing number of methods focus on utilizing rich additional information associated with a given fact. This information, e.g., textual information and relation paths, offers more precise semantic embeddings. P-TransE [14], R-TransE [9], path-RNN [5], and CVSM [21] model multiple-step relation paths to capture rich inference patterns between entities. DKRL [39] and SSP [20] utilize textual information to promote the expressive ability of embeddings.

However, these methods ignore the vital influence of connectivity patterns in knowledge graph's structure. More recently, several researchers [23,28,41] have come to realize the importance of local graph structure. Nevertheless, they only take directed (one-hop) neighboring entities of a given entity into consideration or utilize spectral graph convolution operator as an encoder. Hence, they can not exploit the potential of local graph structure effectively.

To better utilize connectivity patterns in local graph structure, we propose Structure Aware Graph Convolutional Networks (SAGCN), a localized graph convolutional network to leverage structure information for knowledge graph representation. Specifically, we define multi-hop neighboring entities and relations of a given entity as its local graph, which describes the entity's neighborhood topological structure. Next, we design an neighborhood structure encoder for producing latent representations of entities and relations. The encoder's key computational workhorse is localized graph convolutions. Unlike traditional GCN algorithms [13,23], the convolutional operator aggregates feature information from an entity's small graph neighborhood, which alleviates the need of the full graph Laplacian during training. By stacking multiple such operators, the encoder can gain information about the local graph topology. Meanwhile, the encoding process could also be fed back to enhance the representation power of entities and relations in local graph of the learned vectors. For different tasks, we develop distinct decoders to fine-tune the latent feature representations that the encoder produce.

2   Related Works

2.1   Knowledge Graph Representation Learning

A great many of models have been proposed to model multi-relational data in low-dimensional vector spaces. These methods can be classified into two types: triple based methods and additional information enhanced methods.

Triple based methods utilize interactions in triples to model representations of entities and relations in knowledge graphs.Translation-based models [3,15,27, 38] aim to embed a knowledge graph into a continuous vector space for preserving certain information of the graph. Semantic Matching models [35,43] compute the score of each triple via similarity-based score function. Deep learning methods [7,22] introduce convolutional neural network into knowledge base completion and performs best on this branch.

Additional information enhanced embedding methods incorporate a wide variety of information, e.g., entity types [11,40], relation paths [9,14], textual descriptions [20,39,44], to further model entities and relations. The methods which leverage information about graph structures to learn entity and relation representation [28,41] are most related to our study. To take graph structure into consideration, Gmatching [41] and R-GCN [28] design distinct encoder to extract features from graph structure for entities, which are two most relevant models to our paper.

2.2   Graph Representation Learning

There is a growing literature studying graph representation learning [10,12, 13,26,33]. These methods aim to learn the low-dimensional representations of nodes in a graph. Recently, convolutional neural networks that operate on graphs [28] have been introduced, which applies spectral graph convolutions on multi-relational data to extract connectivity patterns in graph structure.

3   Problem Formulation and Notation

Similar to previous works [3,7], our model aims to generate better knowledge graph representations for downstream tasks, e.g. entity classification (assigning types or categorial properties to entities) and knowledge graph completion (recovery of missing triples). To this end, we study how to incorporate connectivity patterns in neighborhood structure of each entity to encode richer semantics. More specifically, we denote a set of triples in knowledge graphs as $(e_i, r, e_j) \in E * R * E$, where E and R are the entity set and the relation set respectively. The entities $e \in E$/relations $r \in R$ are associated with real-valued attributes, $x_e \in \mathbb{R}^d / x_r \in \mathbb{R}^d$. In general, these attributes may specify textual/visual information, pretrained embeddings of embedding models or random initialed embeddings about an entity or a relation. For an entity e_i, its neighborhood structure consists of a neighborhood entity set (N_i^e) and a neighborhood relation set (N_i^r). Our goal is to utilize neighborhood structural features and rich entity or relation features to generate high-quality embeddings.

3.1   Framework

The pipeline of SAGCN is illustrated in Fig. 1. SAGCN takes the local graph of a given entity as input to the neighborhood structure encoder, outputs representations of the given entity and items in the local graph for two tasks: entity classification and knowledge graph completion. As shown in Fig. 1(a), the local graph of an input entity e_0 is composed of a neighborhood entity set (N_i^e) and a neighborhood relation set (N_i^r). A neighborhood entity/relation set N_i^e/N_i^r is the set of a different search depth ($K = 1$, $K = 2$ or other depth) neighboring entities/relations from the given entity e_0. The two sets are used to depict the local topological structure of the given entity. After that, a relation-specific neighborhood structure encoder is designed to aggregate feature information from an entity's local graph. The encoder is an extension of traditional graph convolutional networks. Figure 1(b) describes an encoder stacks two graph convolutional layers to aggregate feature information from the entity e_0's local graph. In the encoding process, representations of neighboring entities and relations are updated in an effective way. The encoder is the main innovation of this paper, and will be detailedly introduced in Sect. 3.2. Lastly, we design distinct decoders to fine-tune the obtained embeddings respectively (Fig. 1(c)).

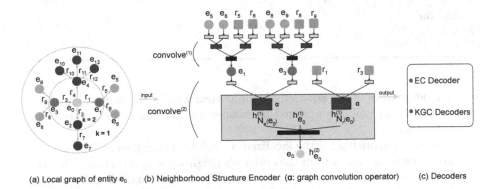

(a) Local graph of entity e_0 (b) Neighborhood Structure Encoder (α: graph convolution operator)   (c) Decoders

Fig. 1. A visual illustration showing the pipeline of SAGCN. EC Decoder: entity classification decoder, KGC Decoders: knowledge graph completion decoders.

3.2   Neighborhood Structure Encoder

Traditional GCNs [4,13] that use convolution operators over graph structures have shown beneficial to encode feature information from a node's local neighboring nodes, and have made great progress in tasks such as graph classification [8] and node classification [13]. Motivated by this, we introduce a relation-specific neighborhood structure encoder to utilize connectivity patterns of both neighboring entities and relations for better embeddings. We start with input local graph features and then transform features to compute the representations of entities and relations, which is described elaborately in Algorithm 1.

The intuition behind Algorithm 1 details the neighborhood structure encoder stacks multiple convolution iterations together to gain more information from the local graphs of entities. More specifically, at each search depth, entities encode information from their direct neighboring entities and relations, and as this process iterates, entities incrementally obtain more and more feature information

---

Algorithm 1. Neighborhood Structure Encoder (SAGCN layers)

Input: Knowledge Graph $G = (E, R)$; input feature vectors or random initialized vectors $\{x_e, x_r, \forall e \in E, \forall r \in R\}$; the ith layer's entity/relation representations h_e^i / h_r^i; depth K; weight matrices $W^k, W_e^k, W_r^k, \forall k \in 1, ..., K$; non-linearity σ; neighborhood entity function $N_e : e \rightarrow 2^e$; neighborhood relation function $N_r : e \rightarrow 2^r$

Output: Vector representations z_e for all $e \in E$ and z_r for all $r \in R$

1:   $h_v^0 = x_e, \forall e \in E$
2:   $h_r^0 = x_r, \forall r \in R$
3:   **for** $k = 1 ... K$ **do**
4:     **for all** $e \in E$ **do**
5:       $h_{N_e(e)}^k \leftarrow max(\{\sigma(W_e^k h_u^{k-1} + b_e^k), \forall u \in N_e(e)\})$
6:       $h_{N_r(e)}^k \leftarrow max(\{\sigma(W_r^k h_v^{k-1} + b_r^k), \forall v \in N_r(e)\})$
7:       $h_e^k \leftarrow \sigma(W^k \times CONCAT(h_e^{k-1}, h_{N_e(e)}^k, h_{N_r(e)}^k))$
8:     **end for**
9:     $h_e^k \leftarrow h_e^k / \|h_e^k\|_2, \forall e \in E$
10:    $h_r^k \leftarrow h_r^k / \|h_r^k\|_2, \forall r \in R$
11: **end for**
12: $z_e \leftarrow h_e^K, \forall e \in E$
13: $z_r \leftarrow h_r^K, \forall r \in R$

---

from further reaches of the knowledge graph. Meanwhile, representations of relations in the local graph are updated by feature information from further neighboring relations.

The core of Algorithm 1 is the localized convolution operation, where we learn how to encode information from the entity e's neighborhood structure. The basic idea is that we transform the representations $\forall u \in N_e(e)$ and $\forall v \in N_r(e)$ of e's neighboring entities and relations through a dense neural network and then apply max-pooling functions on the resulting set of vectors. At current step k, two max-pooling functions provide vector representations, h_e^k of e's directed neighboring entities and h_r^k of e's directed neighboring relations respectively. Notably, the kth representations depend on representations of previous iterations $(k-1)$ and the $k = 0$ representations are input features of entities and relations. The two aggregated neighborhood vector h_e^k and h_r^k are concatenated with e's current representations h_e^{k-1}. The concatenated vector then is transformed into another dense neural network layer. For notational convenience, we denote the final Kth representations as $z_e \equiv h_e^K$ and $z_r \equiv h_r^K$.

For mini-batch training, we first compute the neighboring entities and relations of each entity and then run the inner loop (line 4 in Algorithm 1). Thus, we only need to compute the representations that are essential at each step. In this work, we uniformly sample a fixed-size set of neighbor entities and relations.

3.3 Decoders

Entity Classification. This task is to infer the type of entities (e.g. person or company) in a knowledge base, which is a multi-label classification problem.

We simply link the neighborhood structure encoder with a sigmoid activation on the output of the last layer. For each entity e_i, neighborhood structure encoder outputs its embeddings $z_{e_i} = h_{e_i}^K$, which is supposed to be consistent with entity types $\hat{z}_{e_i}$. Formally, the score function is defined as

$$f_r(z_{e_i}, \hat{z}_{e_i}) = \sum_{i=1}^{|E|} \{z_{e_i} \times -log(sigmoid(\hat{z}_{e_i})) + (1 - z_{e_i}) \times -log(1 - sigmoid(\hat{z}_{e_i}))\} \quad (1)$$

Knowledge Graph Completion. We utilize one-shot knowledge graph completion and regular knowledge graph completion to evaluate the performance of our model in different aspects. For one-shot knowledge graph completion, we stack the neighborhood structure encoder with a decoder used in [41]. For regular knowledge graph completion, we use DistMult factorization [43] as the decoder.

4   Entity Classification Experiments

Entity Classification aims to predict entity types (e.g. person or company), which is essentially and widely used in many NLP and IR tasks [19]. For the multi-label classification problem, we evaluate it with micro-averaged F1 scores.

4.1   Datasets

We test the entity classification performance of SAGCN on FB15k-237. FB15k-237 is a correspondingly subset of the common datasets FB15k [34]. As mentioned in [34], FB15k may limit the credibility of performance evaluation due to inverse relation problem, i.e., a great many of test triples can be obtained simply by reversing triples in the training set. To deal with this problem, [34] remove inverse relations and create the sub-dataset FB15k-237. FB15k-237 contains 310,116 triples with 14,541 entities and 237 relations, and are randomly split into 272,115 for training, 17,535 for validation and 20,466 for testing.

4.2   Experimental Set-Up

To determine optimal parameters for SAGCN, we evaluate the parameter sensitivity of the layer number and sample size. To evaluate the sensitivity of sample size, we set $\sigma = Relu, K = 1$. For parameter sensitivity of the layer number, we set $\sigma = Relu, K = 1 \sim 3$ with neighborhood size $S_1 = 30, S_2 = 20, S_3 = 5$. Finally, we design five variants of SAGCN for comprehensive performance evaluation. These five variants are summarized in the following:

- **SAGCN-Mean.** Instead of using max-pooling function, two mean-based convolutional operators is employed to aggregate feature information from the local graph of an entity.
- **SAGCN-LSTM.** We also select two more complex graph convolutions based on LSTM architecture for encoding neighborhood structure.

- **SAGCN-MeanPooling.** The final encoder we examine is to apply two mean-pooling operations over local graphs of entities.
- **SAGCN-Entity.** In this variant, we simply takes feature information from neighboring entities into consideration.
- **SAGCN-Relation.** Compared with SAGCN, this variant only makes use of connectivity patterns in neighboring relations for training.

We train all variants of SAGCN with mini-batch Adam. As for parameters of five variants, we set $\sigma = Relu, K = 2$ with neighborhood sizes $S_1 = 30, S_2 = 20$. It was noting that the neighboring entity sample size equals the neighboring relation sample size in our work. For a fair comparison, we sweep over a same set of hyperparameters for all variants. To validate the effectiveness of SAGCN, we compare against three baselines: an unsupervised learning algorithm node2vec [10], a semi-supervised model GCN [13] and a relation-specific model R-GCN [28]. We train three models on FB15k-237 to obtain the micro F1 score. For all SAGCNs, we set initial learning rate at 0.001, dropout ratio at 0.5, entity and relation dimensions at 128, batch size at 128 and total epochs at 200.

4.3 Parameters Sensitivity

Figure 2 explores how neighborhood sample size effects the performance of SAGCN. Figure 2(a) summarizes the distribution of neighboring entities/relations for entities in FB15k-237. We can observe that the distribution is commonly quite concentrated although different entities have different number of neighbors. Thus, we choose sample size 5–50 to evaluate the model performance. Figure 2(b) shows that SAGCN yields best performance when sampling 30 neighborhoods for a given entity.

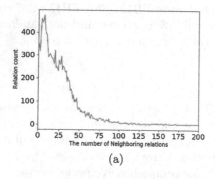 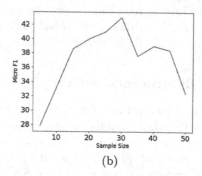

(a)   (b)

Fig. 2. (a) The distribution of neighboring entities/relations for entities in FB15k-237. (b) Model performance with the size of sampled neighborhood.

In Table 1, we illustrates the efficiency of SAGCN with different number of layers. It can be seen that stacking multiple-layers together can make an appreciable improvements of classification. We find that setting $K = 2$ provides

Table 1. Model performance with different number of layers K.

K	F1	Time
1	34.7	1.5
2	68.6	24.7
3	70.1	65.2

a consistent boost in accuracy of around 33.9% while a large increasment in time of around 20× compared to $K = 1$. Compared to $K = 3$, the balance of strong predictive accuracy and the runtime is acceptable when $K = 2$.

4.4 Summary Comparison Between the Different Graph Convolution Operators

To investigate the efficiency of our graph convolution operator, SAGCN-Mean, SAGCN-LSTM and SAGCN-MeanPooling are introduced that they couples neighborhood structure with three distinct graph convolutions. While they achieve similar results, SAGCN delivers the best performance by using max-pooling functions (Table 2). The comparison shows the superiority of max-pooling functions. Applying the max-polling operator on the local graph can be viewed as a set of functions that computer feature vectors for each of the item representations in the neighborhood set. Thus, the max-pooling operator of our model can capture diverse connectivity patterns of the local graph.

4.5 Comparison with State-of-the-arts

Table 2 summarizes the performance of SAGCN and the baselines on FB15k-237. We find that SAGCN achieves state-of-the-art by an improvement of more than 15% on average compared to node2vec and GCN. The results proves the effectiveness of our neighborhood structure encoder. In addition, both node2vec and GCN only focus on encoding features from neighboring entities, which demonstrates that the local graph containing both neighboring entities and neighboring relations characterizes an entity from a more comprehensive perspective. Compared to the relation-specific model R-GCN, we can conclude that the non-spectral graph convolution operator has more potential to explore connectivity patterns in local graph structure.

To further demonstrate that neighboring entities and neighboring relations in the local graph can complement each other to learn effective knowledge graph representations, we construct SAGCN-Entity and SAGCN-Relation to consider single neighboring entities/relations as neighborhood structure. As it can be seen in Table 2, SAGCN-Relation achieves the better performance than SAGCN-Entity, while both of them is obviously worse than SAGCN. It shows feature information in neighboring relations are more helpful to identify entity types and the combination of neighboring entities and neighboring relations can provide a

Table 2. Entity classification results for FB15k-237 (micro-averaged F1 score).

Model	F1
node2vec [10]	50.4
GCN [13]	52.3
R-GCN [28]	63.2
SAGCN-Entity	57.5
SAGCN-Relation	61.5
SAGCN-Mean	66.4
SAGCN-LSTM	65.7
SAGCN-MeanPooling	66.6
SAGCN	**68.6**

much deeper understanding of an entity. We also observe that the performance of SAGCN-Entity is better than GCN and node2vec. It verifies that the way we encoding features from neighborhood can help to improve the performance of knowledge graph completion.

5   Knowledge Graph Completion Experiments

Knowledge graph completion is to recover missing triples, i.e, inferring e_i given (r, e_j) or inferring e_j given (e_i, r). This task would rather focus on ranking a set of candidate answer than obtaining one best answer. The score of the relation fact (e_i, r, e_j) is expected to be smaller than any other corrupted triples. Follow [41], we evaluate the model with four metrics: mean reciprocal rank (MRR), Hits@1, Hits@5 and Hits@10. Lower MR, higher MRR or higher Hits@10 means better performance.

5.1   Datasets

For knowledge graph completion, we evaluate our model on three datasets: NELL-one, Wiki-one, FB15k-237. NELL-one and Wiki-one are constructed by [41] for one-shot learning. NELL-one is based on NELL [18], which contains relations with less than 500 but more than 50 triples and excludes inverse relations. In the similar way, Wiki-one is built as a larger dataset based on Wikidata [36]. NELL-one contains 181,109 triples with 68,545 entities, 358 relations and 67 task relations for one-shot learning, which is randomly split as 51/5/11 task relations for training/validation/testing. Wiki-one contains 5,859,240 triples with 4,838,244 entities, 822 relations and 183 relations for one-shot learning, which is divided as 132/16/34 task relations for training/validation/testing. FB15k-237 is the same dataset used in entity classification task.

Table 3. Knowledge graph completion results on test relations of NELL-one and Wiki-one.

Datasets	NELL-one				Wiki-one			
Model	MRR	Hits@10	Hits@5	Hits@1	MRR	Hits@10	Hits@5	Hits@1
TransE [3]	0.093	0.192	0.141	0.043	0.035	0.052	0.043	0.025
DistMult [43]	0.102	0.177	0.126	0.066	0.048	0.101	0.070	0.019
ComplEx [35]	0.131	0.223	0.086	0.086	0.069	0.121	0.092	0.040
GMatching (Random) [41]	0.171	0.255	0.210	0.122	0.219	0.328	0.269	0.163
SAGCN	0.198	0.292	0.263	0.146	0.257	0.377	0.313	0.198

5.2   Experimental Set-Up

In our experiment, we select three triple based methods and a structure aware method for one-shot learning. Three triple based methods are TransE [3], Dist-Mult [43], ComplEx [35]. The structure aware method is GMatching [41]. Experiment results of all baselines are directly reproduced from literatures [28, 41]. To contextualize the empirical results on regular knowledge graph completion task, we also compare against two kinds of methods: triple-based method and structure aware method. Triple-based method includes TransE [3], DistMult [43], ComplEx [35], Conv-E [7], Conv-KB [22]. Structure aware method contains R-GCN [28]. For this task, we set $\sigma = Relu, K = 2$ with neighborhood sizes $S_1 = 30, S_2 = 20$. We use Adam and set the initial learning rate as 0.001. We fix the batch size at 128 and set dropout ratio at 0.6, total epochs at 200. We directly take outputs from the last epoch for evaluation.

5.3   Performance Evaluation of One-Shot Knowledge Graph Completion

In Table 3, we show one-shot learning results for NELL-one and Wiki-one. We can see that SAGCN produces consistent improvement over all baselines on these one-shot relations. In more detail, SAGCN achieves a significant improvement compared to triple-based approaches, especially on larger Wiki-One dataset. The local graph including multiple-neighboring entities and relations provides a more comprehensive characterization of an entity. SAGCN further compares favorably against GMatching (Random), which utilizes a neighbor encoder to leverage one-hop neighbors of entities into their representations. This indicates that our neighborhood structure encoder can effectively recognize the local role and its global position in the graph of an entity by capturing connectivity patterns in its local graph. Additionally, SAGCN can be well generalized to any newly-added relations without fine-tuning.

5.4   Performance Evaluation of Regular Knowledge Graph Completion

Table 4 compares the regular knowledge graph completion results of our SAGCN model with other baselines. It can be observed that SAGCN outperforms all

Table 4. Knowledge graph completion results on FB15k-237.

Metrics	MRR		Hits@	
Model	Raw	Filtered	1	10
TransE [3]	0.144	0.233	0.147	0.398
DistMult [43]	0.100	0.191	0.106	0.376
ComplEx [35]	0.109	0.201	0.112	0.388
Conv-E [7]	-	0.325	0.237	0.501
Conv-KB [22]	-	0.396	-	0.517
R-GCN [28]	0.158	0.248	0.153	0.414
SAGCN	0.316	0.411	0.250	0.534

triple facts based embedding methods, in terms of MRR, Hits@1 and Hits@10 scores on FB15k-237. It proves the local graph commendably depicts diverse connectivity patterns of the given entity. Meanwhile, the embeddings of entities and relations in the local graph certainly get updated in an efficient manner and provide a useful inductive generalization on test data by encoding such connectivity patterns. To demonstrate the learning power of our localized graph convolution, we compare our model SAGCN with the most relevant model R-GCN, which introduces a relation-specific spectral graph convolution network on multi-relational data. SAGCN surpasses R-GCN, with 0.411 vs. 0.238 in Filtered MRR and 0.534 vs. 0.414 in hits@10. This indicates that our localized graph convolution is a promising operator to model relational data.

6   Conclusion

In this paper, we propose a novel model, denoted Structure Aware Graph Convolutional Networks (SAGCN), for knowledge graph representation. We introduce localized graph convolutions to capture diverse connectivity patterns in local graph of a given entity, which contains its multi-hop neighboring entities and relations. SAGCN consistently yields a better performance than state-of-the-art baselines and can be directly used to predict any newly-added relations without fine-tuning. Our future work might consider designing novel graph convolutions to make better use of graph structure in the few-shot learning case.

References

1. Bollacker, K.D., Evans, C., Paritosh, P., Sturge, T., Taylor, J.: Freebase: a collaboratively created graph database for structuring human knowledge. In: Proceedings of SIGMOD, pp. 1247–1250, June 2008
2. Bordes, A., Chopra, S., Weston, J.: Question answering with subgraph embeddings. In: Proceedings of EMNLP, pp. 615–620, October 2014

3. Bordes, A., Usunier, N., Garciaduran, A., Weston, J., Yakhnenko, O.: Translating embeddings for modeling multi-relational data. In: Proceedings of NIPs, pp. 2787–2795, December 2013
4. Bruna, J., Zaremba, W., Szlam, A., Lecun, Y.: Spectral networks and locally connected networks on graphs. In: Proceedings of ICLR, April 2014
5. Das, R., Neelakantan, A., Belanger, D., Mccallum, A.: Chains of reasoning over entities, relations, and text using recurrent neural networks. In: Proceedings of EACL, vol. 1, pp. 132–141, April 2017
6. De Kleer, J.: Building expert systems. Artif. Intell. 25(1), 105–107 (1985)
7. Dettmers, T., Pasquale, M., Pontus, S., Riedel, S.: Convolutional 2D knowledge graph embeddings. In: Proceedings of AAAI, pp. 1811–1818, February 2018
8. Duvenaud, D.K., et al.: Convolutional networks on graphs for learning molecular fingerprints. In: Proceedings of NIPs, pp. 2224–2232, December 2015
9. Garciaduran, A., Bordes, A., Usunier, N.: Composing relationships with translations. In: Proceedings of EMNLP, pp. 286–290, October 2015
10. Grover, A., Leskovec, J.: node2vec: scalable feature learning for networks. In: Proceedings of SIGKDD, pp. 855–864, August 2016
11. Guo, S., Wang, Q., Wang, B., Wang, L., Guo, L.: Semantically smooth knowledge graph embedding. In: Proceedings of IJCNLP, vol. 1, pp. 84–94 (2015)
12. Hamilton, W.L., Ying, Z., Leskovec, J.: Inductive representation learning on large graphs. In: Proceedings of NIPs, pp. 1024–1034, December 2017
13. Kipf, T.N., Welling, M.: Semi-supervised classification with graph convolutional networks. In: Proceedings of ICLR, April 2017
14. Lin, Y., Liu, Z., Luan, H., Sun, M., Rao, S., Liu, S.: Modeling relation paths for representation learning of knowledge bases. In: Proceedings of EMNLP, pp. 705–714, October 2015
15. Lin, Y., Liu, Z., Sun, M., Liu, Y., Zhu, X.: Learning entity and relation embeddings for knowledge graph completion. In: Proceddings of AAAI, pp. 2181–2187, January 2015
16. Miller, G.A.: WordNet: a lexical database for English. Commun. ACM 38(11), 39–41 (1995)
17. Min, B., Grishman, R., Wan, L., Wang, C., Gondek, D.: Distant supervision for relation extraction with an incomplete knowledge base. In: Proceedings of NAACL-HLT, pp. 777–782, June 2013
18. Mitchell, T., et al.: Never-ending learning. Commun. ACM 61(5), 103–115 (2018)
19. Neelakantan, A., Chang, M.: Inferring missing entity type instances for knowledge base completion: new dataset and methods. In: Proceedings of the 3rd Workshop on Continuous Vector Space Models and their Compositionality, pp. 515–525 (2015)
20. Neelakantan, A., Chang, M.: SSP: semantic space projection for knowledge graph embedding with text descriptions. In: Proceedings of AAAI, pp. 3104–3110 (2016)
21. Neelakantan, A., Roth, B., Mccallum, A.: Compositional vector space models for knowledge base completion. In: Proceedings of IJCNLP, vol. 1, pp. 156–166, July 2015
22. Nguyen, D.Q., Nguyen, T.D., Nguyen, D.Q., Phung, D.Q.: A novel embedding model for knowledge base completion based on convolutional neural network. In: Proceedings of NAACL-HLT, vol. 2, pp. 327–333, June 2018
23. Nguyen, D.Q., Sirts, K., Qu, L., Johnson, M.: Neighborhood mixture model for knowledge base completion. In: Proceedings of SIGNLL, pp. 40–50, August 2016
24. Nickel, M., Rosasco, L., Poggio, T.: Holographic embeddings of knowledge graphs. In: Proceedings of AAAI, vol. 1, pp. 1955–1961, February 2016

25. Nickel, M., Tresp, V., Kriegel, H.: Knowledge graph embedding by translating on hyperplanes. In: Proceedings of WWW, pp. 271–280, April 2012
26. Perozzi, B., Alrfou, R., Skiena, S.: Deepwalk: online learning of social representations. In: Proceedings of SIGKDD, pp. 701–710, August 2014
27. Schlichtkrull, M.S., Kipf, T.N., Bloem, P., Den Berg, R.V., Titov, I., Welling, M.: TransG: a generative model for knowledge graph embedding. In: Proceedings of ACL, vol. 1, pp. 2316–2325, August 2016
28. Schlichtkrull, M., Kipf, T.N., Bloem, P., van den Berg, R., Titov, I., Welling, M.: Modeling relational data with graph convolutional networks. In: Gangemi, A., et al. (eds.) ESWC 2018. LNCS, vol. 10843, pp. 593–607. Springer, Cham (2018). https://doi.org/10.1007/978-3-319-93417-4_38
29. Shen, W., Wang, J., Luo, P., Wang, M.: Linking named entities in Tweets with knowledge base via user interest modeling. In: Proceedings of SIGKDD, pp. 68–76, August 2013
30. Shi, B., Weninger, T.: ProjE: embedding projection for knowledge graph completion. In: Proceedings of AAAI, vol. 1, pp. 2181–2187, February 2017
31. Socher, R., Chen, D., Manning, C.D., Ng, A.Y.: Reasoning with neural tensor networks for knowledge base completion. In: Proceedings of NIPs, pp. 926–934, December 2013
32. Szumlanski, S.R., Gomez, F.: Automatically acquiring a semantic network of related concepts. In: Proceedings of CIKM, pp. 19–28, October 2010
33. Tang, J., Qu, M., Wang, M., Zhang, M., Yan, J., Mei, Q.: Line: large-scale information network embedding. In: Proceedings of WWW, pp. 1067–1077, May 2015
34. Toutanova, K., Chen, D.: Observed versus latent features for knowledge base and text inference. In: Proceedings of the 3rd Workshop on Continuous Vector Space Models and their Compositionality, pp. 57–66 (2015)
35. Trouillon, T., Welbl, J., Riedel, S., Gaussier, E., Bouchard, G.: Complex embeddings for simple link prediction. In: Proceedings of AAAI, pp. 2071–2080 (2016)
36. Vrandecic, D., Krotzsch, M.: Wikidata: a free collaborative knowledgebase. Commun. ACM **57**(10), 78–85 (2014)
37. Wang, H., Wang, N., Yeung, D.: Collaborative deep learning for recommender systems. In: Proceedings of SIGKDD, pp. 1235–1244, August 2015
38. Wang, Z., Zhang, J., Feng, J., Chen, Z.: Knowledge graph embedding by translating on hyperplanes. In: Proceedings of AAAI, pp. 1112–1119, July 2014
39. Xie, R., Liu, Z., Jia, J., Luan, H., Sun, M.: Representation learning of knowledge graphs with entity descriptions. In: Proceedings of AAAI, pp. 2659–2665, February 2016
40. Xie, R., Liu, Z., Jia, J., Luan, H., Sun, M.: Representation learning of knowledge graphs with entity descriptions. In: Proceedings of AAAI, pp. 2659–2665 (2016)
41. Xiong, W., Yu, M., Chang, S., Guo, X., Wang, W.Y.: One-shot relational learning for knowledge graphs. In: Proceedings of EMNLP, October 2018
42. Yahya, M., Berberich, K., Elbassuoni, S., Weikum, G.: Robust question answering over the web of linked data. In: Proceedings of CIKM, pp. 1107–1116, October 2013
43. Yang, B., Yih, W., He, X., Gao, J., Deng, L.: Embedding entities and relations for learning and inference in knowledge bases. In: Proceddings of ICLR, May 2015
44. Zhong, H., Zhang, J., Wang, Z., Wan, H., Chen, Z.: Aligning knowledge and text embeddings by entity descriptions. In: Proceedings of EMNLP, pp. 267–272, September 2015

Neural Gray-Box Identification of Nonlinear Partial Differential Equations

Riku Sasaki[1]([✉]), Naoya Takeishi[2], Takehisa Yairi[1], and Koichi Hori[1]

[1] The University of Tokyo, Tokyo, Japan
`ndutsasaki@gmail.com`, `yairi@ailab.t.u-tokyo.ac.jp`, `hori@acm.org`
[2] RIKEN Center for Advanced Intelligence Project, Tokyo, Japan
`naoya.takeishi@riken.jp`

Abstract. Many branches of the modern computational science and engineering are based on numerical simulations, for which we must prepare appropriate equations that well reflect the behavior of real-world phenomena and numerically solve them. For these purposes, we may utilize the data-driven identification and simulation technique of nonlinear partial differential equations (NPDEs) using deep neural networks (DNNs). A potential issue of the DNN-based identification and simulation in practice is the high variance due to the complexity of DNNs. To alleviate it, we propose a simple yet efficient way to incorporate prior knowledge of phenomena. Specifically, we can often anticipate what kinds of terms are present in a part of an appropriate NPDE, which should be utilized as prior knowledge for identifying the remaining part of the NPDE. To this end, we design DNN's inputs and the loss function for identification according to the prior knowledge. We present the results of the experiments conducted using three different types of NPDEs: the Korteweg–de Vries equation, the Navier–Stokes equation, and the Kuramoto–Sivashinsky equation. The experimental results show the effectiveness of the proposed method, i.e., utilizing known terms of an NPDE.

Keywords: Gray-box system identification · Nonlinear PDEs · Data-driven discovery · Machine learning

1 Introduction

The advancements in computer capabilities have enabled numerical simulations of complex phenomena in various domains such as physics, chemistry, biology, and sociology (Strang 2007). Many branches of the modern computational science and engineering depend on numerical simulations, with which we can conduct experiments *in silico* as long as the phenomena are appropriately modeled (and some numerical conditions are satisfied). To this end, there are two fundamental challenges:

© Springer Nature Switzerland AG 2019
A. C. Nayak and A. Sharma (Eds.): PRICAI 2019, LNAI 11671, pp. 309–321, 2019.
https://doi.org/10.1007/978-3-030-29911-8_24

C1 How to transform a real phenomenon into an appropriate model in a computer-friendly form such as ordinary differential equations (ODEs) and partial differential equations (PDEs)?

C2 How to perform a simulation efficiently, e.g., to obtain a meaningful solution of PDEs with a reasonable computational cost?

In the history of science, models of real-world phenomena have been obtained based on the scientific methods including observations, hypothesis formations, and experiments conducted by human scientists. Based on the theory-based models in various forms including PDEs, many types of numerical solvers have been utilized. For example, a simulation of fluid flow is performed based on the Navier–Stokes equation and different numerical integration methods, which constitute the discipline of computational fluid dynamics. However, a possible difficulty of using a theory-based model for simulations lies in misspecification of the model; conducting simulations of a damping pendulum is meaningless unless it is adequately based on equations of motion with friction terms. Moreover, numerical integration techniques are often computationally heavy.

For alleviating the issue of model misspecification, the *data-driven* approach to obtaining a model is attracting attention. In this paradigm, appropriate differential equations can be identified in a highly automated manner using data of observations. In this work, we focused on the data-driven identification of forms of nonlinear PDEs (NPDEs), which cover a variety of physical, biological, and social phenomena. The data-driven identification of NPDEs has been studied with the problem settings as follows. Now let $x \in \mathbb{R}^d$ be a state vector, $t \in \mathbb{R}$ be the time, and $u(t, x) : \mathbb{R}^{d+1} \to \mathbb{R}$ be the solution of an NPDE. Since many NPDEs concern the derivative with regard to time, i.e., $\partial u / \partial t$, in most studies, an NPDE to be identified is defined using a nonlinear map $\mathcal{N}$ as

$$u_t = \mathcal{N}(T), \quad \text{where} \quad T := \{t, x, u, u_x, u_{xx}, \dots, u_{x^k}\}, \tag{1}$$

where[1] $u_x := \partial u / \partial x$, $u_{xx} := \partial^2 u / \partial x^2$, and $u_{x^k} := \partial^k u / \partial x^k$. Thus, the problem is to estimate the map $\mathcal{N}$ in Eq. (1) using the observations of t, x, u_t, u_x, u_{xx}, and possibly higher-order derivatives.

One of the popular approaches for data-driven NPDE identification is the use of function dictionaries (Rudy et al. 2017). In this approach, $\mathcal{N}$ is represented using a set (dictionary) of functions whose elements comprise the terms in T. For example, let $d = 1$, and suppose to model $\mathcal{N}$ using a dictionary comprising monomials up to second-degree of terms in set T. That is, we model $\mathcal{N}$ by a second-degree polynomial:

$$\mathcal{N}(T) = v^\mathsf{T} A v. \tag{2}$$

where $v := [1, t, x, u, u_x, u_{xx}, \dots, u_{x^k}]^\mathsf{T}$ is a tuple of length $l := k + 4$, and $A \in \mathbb{R}^{l \times l}$ is a coefficient matrix. Now, the task is to estimate A using

---

[1] We only consider the derivatives with regard to x for ease of discussion in this paper, albeit it is straightforward to add other derivatives such as u_{tt} and u_{xt} to T.

observations. To this end, first we have to compute the empirical derivatives (u_t, u_x, u_{xx}, and so on) from the observations of u. The simplest way is the finite-difference, i.e., $u_t \approx (u(t + \Delta t) - u(t))/\Delta t$, for example. Afterward, we solve a regression problem from v to u_t under the model in Eqs. (1) and (2). The regression is straightforward to solve because the model is linear with regard to the coefficient, A. In the literature (Brunton et al. 2015; Rudy et al. 2017), a sparsity regularization was imposed on the coefficients for better generalization and interpretability. Note that more complex models than a second-degree polynomial can be used in the same manner (Rudy et al. 2017).

While the dictionary-based method provides an interpretable and straightforward way for the data-driven NPDE identification, it may pose some challenges in practice (Raissi 2018). First, the computation of the empirical derivatives tends to be numerically unstable and severely affected by observation noise. Moreover, the size of the dictionary rapidly grows against $d > 1$, which may hinder efficient computation. Furthermore, it is difficult to determine the coefficients of certain terms like $\sin(\cdot)$. To overcome these issues, the data-driven identification of NPDEs using deep neural networks (DNNs) has been studied recently (Raissi 2018; Raissi et al. 2019). It models an NPDE using a DNN-based black-box function and thus is free from the preparation of a possibly huge function dictionary. Moreover, by approximating PDE's solution also using DNNs, it avoids the direct computation of empirical derivatives. Furthermore, we can perform new simulations based on the identified neural PDE using DNNs in the same framework, which avoids numerical integration. We review this methodology, which our proposal is based upon, in Sect. 2.

The DNN-based identification and simulation of NPDEs benefit much from the expression power of DNNs, but at the same time, it may suffer from the high variance due to the complexity of DNNs in return of the low bias. This can be mitigated by incorporating prior knowledge (inductive bias) into the learning process appropriately. In this paper, we propose a simple but efficient way to incorporate prior knowledge to the DNN-based NPDE identification and simulation technique. Particularly, it is based on the *gray-box* modeling, i.e., we suppose that some terms that would exist in an ideal NPDE are known in advance. This is often the case because we can anticipate a rough form of NPDE with which the phenomena are associated. We show that such prior knowledge can be utilized by transforming a loss function accordingly in Sect. 3. Afterward, we briefly review related work in Sect. 4 and provide experimental results in Sect. 5. This paper is concluded with discussion in Sect. 6.

2 Background

For the identification of NPDEs from data, the deep hidden physics models (DHPMs) proposed by Raissi (2018) utilize DNNs in two ways: to approximate an NPDE, $\mathcal{N}$, and to approximate its solution, u. Moreover, Raissi et al. (2019) utilizes DNNs also for obtaining a solution under new initial and boundary conditions, possibly using the PDE identified by the DHPM.

2.1   Identification of NPDE Using DNNs

Suppose that we have measurements of $u(t, x)$ and the corresponding values of t and x. More formally, we have a dataset $\mathcal{D} = \{(\hat{u}^{(i)}, t^{(i)}, x^{(i)}) \mid i = 1, \ldots, n\}$, where $\hat{u}^{(i)}$ denotes the measurement of PDE's solution at $(t, x) = (t^{(i)}, x^{(i)})$. In DHPM, the solution function, $u(t, x)$, is approximated using a DNN. This is achieved by a regression from (t, x) to $\hat{u}$, i.e., learning a DNN f such that

$$\hat{u}^{(i)} \approx f(t^{(i)}, x^{(i)}), \quad \text{for} \quad i = 1, \ldots, n. \tag{3}$$

Here, we suppose that f is differentiable to some extent (as needed by application) with regard to the inputs, t and x. Then, based on the estimated f, derivatives such as

$$\tilde{u}_t := \frac{\partial f}{\partial t}, \quad \tilde{u}_x := \frac{\partial f}{\partial x}, \quad \text{and} \quad \tilde{u}_{xx} := \frac{\partial^2 f}{\partial x^2},$$

can be straightforwardly estimated through the automatic differentiation of f for arbitrary t and x. At the same time, DHPM estimates the form of the NPDE that $u(t, x)$ follows. This is done similarly as in Eq. (1), but this time, $\mathcal{N}$ is approximated using a DNN g that takes (the estimation of) the elements of T as inputs and outputs u_t. To this end, we solve a regression:

$$\tilde{u}_t \approx g(\tilde{T}), \quad \text{where} \quad \tilde{T} := \{t, x, \tilde{u}, \tilde{u}_x, \tilde{u}_{xx}, \ldots, \tilde{u}_{x^k}\}, \tag{4}$$

with $\tilde{u} := f(t, x)$.

The two types of neural networks, Eqs. (3) and (4), are trained by minimizing the following loss function:

$$\mathcal{L}_1(\theta_{f,1}, \ldots, \theta_{f,p}, \theta_g) := \frac{1}{p} \sum_{c=1}^{p} \frac{1}{n_c} \sum_{i=1}^{n_c} \left(\hat{u}^{(c,i)} - f_c(t^{(c,i)}, x^{(c,i)}) \right)^2$$

$$+ \frac{1}{m} \sum_{j=1}^{m} \left(\tilde{u}_t^{(j)} - g(\tilde{T}^{(j)}) \right)^2, \tag{5}$$

where $\mathcal{D}_c := \{(\hat{u}^{(c,i)}, t^{(c,i)}, x^{(c,i)}) \mid i = 1, \ldots, n_c\}$ denotes the dataset generated under c-th set of initial condition and boundary conditions. The first term is to estimate p copies of f, namely f_c for $c = 1, \ldots, p$, according to p different initial/boundary conditions. In contrast, g in the second term is rather equation-specific; i.e., it is commonly used for different conditions. The quantities in the second term are defined as follows; $\tilde{T}^{(j)} := \{t^{(j)}, x^{(j)}, \tilde{u}^{(j)}, \tilde{u}_x^{(j)}, \tilde{u}_{xx}^{(j)}, \ldots, \tilde{u}_{x^k}^{(j)}\}$, where $t^{(j)}$ and $x^{(j)}$ are randomly drawn from a prespecified finite range, $\tilde{u}^{(j)}$ is the value of $f_c(t^{(j)}, x^{(j)})$ (with some c), and $\tilde{u}_x^{(j)}$ and $\tilde{u}_{xx}^{(j)}$ (and higher-order ones) are the corresponding numerical derivatives of $\tilde{u}^{(j)}$. Moreover, note that $\theta_{f,c}$ and θ_g denote the parameters of f_c and g, respectively. The two terms in Eq. (5) can be optimized separately or simultaneously.

2.2   Solving the Identified NPDE Using DNNs

The above procedures are conducted during a training phase for NPDE identification. In a test phase, i.e., when one wants to run a simulation based on the identified equation, a new f, namely f_{p+1}, is learned on a new set $\mathcal{D}_{p+1}$ by minimizing

$$\mathcal{L}_2(\theta_{f,p+1}) := \frac{1}{n_{p+1}} \sum_{i=1}^{n_{p+1}} \left(\hat{u}^{(p+1,i)} - f_{p+1}(t^{(p+1,i)}, x^{(p+1,i)}) \right)^2$$

$$+ \frac{1}{m'} \sum_{j=1}^{m'} \left(\frac{\partial}{\partial t} f_{p+1}(t^{(j)}, x^{(j)}) - g(\tilde{T}^{(j)}) \right)^2, \qquad (6)$$

where the derivative, $\partial/\partial t$ can be computed using automatic differentiation. Suppose $\mathcal{D}_{p+1}$ only contains the values at the initial and boundary conditions. In this case, by minimizing the above loss we can obtain the solution of PDE $u_t = g(T)$ under conditions $\mathcal{D}_{p+1}$. This procedure is termed a physics informed neural network (PINN) by Raissi et al. (2019).

3   Proposed Method

The NPDE identification using DHPMs benefits from the expressiveness of DNNs, but its complexity may pose a problem of high variance in return for the low bias. In this paper, we propose to alleviate it by utilizing prior knowledge on phenomena on which an NPDE is identified. That is, we suppose that we know the form of some terms that will construct a part of an appropriate PDE *a priori* and employ them in the process of identification. In the area of automatic control, this type of knowledge injection technique has been termed the *gray-box* modeling for system identification. We implement the idea of gray-box system identification to the DNN-based NPDE identification.

3.1   Identification of NPDE Using DNNs with Prior Knowledge

First, we consider a partition of the term set, T, in Eq. (1) as

$$T = T_* \cup T_0, \quad \text{s.t.} \quad T_* \cap T_0 = \varnothing, \qquad (7)$$

where T_0 is the set of terms (other than u_t) for which we anticipate to be present in an appropriate PDE. In contrast, $T_* = T \setminus T_0$ is the set of remaining terms on which we do not have prior knowledge of how they appear in PDE. Accordingly, the map, $\mathcal{N}$, in Eq. (1) is decomposed as

$$\mathcal{N}(T) = \mathcal{N}_*(T_*) - \mathcal{N}_0(T_0). \qquad (8)$$

Here, $\mathcal{N}_0$ comprises the terms that we know in advance, and $\mathcal{N}_*$ comprises the terms that should be approximated. It is worth noting that T_* does not contain the terms present in T_0 (as defined in Eq. (7)), and this is important for preventing the problem from being severely ill-posed.

Once T_0 and $\mathcal{N}_0$ are defined following prior knowledge, we approximate $\mathcal{N}_*$ along with the solution, $u(t,x)$, using DNNs as done in DHPMs (Raissi 2018). First, we approximate $u(t,x)$ using a DNN as in Eq. (3). Next, given the DNN-based approximation of the solution, f, we empirically compute the terms in T_* and T_0 and calculate their numerical derivatives using the automatic differentiation. As in Sect. 2, we denote the empirical derivatives by $\tilde{u}_t$, $\tilde{u}_x$, $\tilde{u}_{xx}$, and so on. Then, we approximate $\mathcal{N}_*$ using a DNN g_* as in Eq. (4). To this end, based on the decomposition in Eq. (8), we solve a regression

$$\tilde{u}_t + \mathcal{N}_0(\tilde{T}_0) \approx g_*(\tilde{T}_*), \tag{9}$$

where $\tilde{T}_0$ and $\tilde{T}_*$ are defined analogously to $\tilde{T}$ in Eq. (4). Finally, the loss function to be minimized is defined as

$$\mathcal{L}'_1(\theta_{f,1}, \ldots, \theta_{f,p}, \theta_g) := \frac{1}{p} \sum_{c=1}^{p} \frac{1}{n_c} \sum_{i=1}^{n_c} \left(\hat{u}^{(c,i)} - f(t^{(c,i)}, x^{(c,i)}) \right)^2$$
$$+ \frac{1}{m} \sum_{j=1}^{m} \left(\tilde{u}_t^{(j)} + \mathcal{N}_0(\tilde{T}_0^{(j)}) - g_*(\tilde{T}_*^{(j)}) \right)^2, \tag{10}$$

where $\tilde{T}_0^{(j)}$ and $\tilde{T}_*^{(j)}$ are defined analogously to $\tilde{T}^{(j)}$ in Sect. 2.1.

3.2 Solving the Identified NPDE Using DNNs with Prior Knowledge

After estimating an NPDE with prior knowledge, we can perform a simulation based on it with a new initial and boundary conditions using the procedures of PINN (Raissi et al. 2019) with slight modifications. Let $\mathcal{D}_{p+1}$ be a set that contains the test-time initial and boundary conditions. Then, we can approximate the solution of the estimated PDE under new condition $\mathcal{D}_{p+1}$ by minimizing

$$\mathcal{L}'_2(\theta_{f,p+1}) := \frac{1}{n_{p+1}} \sum_{i=1}^{n_{p+1}} \left(\hat{u}^{(p+1,i)} - f_{p+1}(t^{(p+1,i)}, x^{(p+1,i)}) \right)^2$$
$$+ \frac{1}{m'} \sum_{j=1}^{m'} \left(\frac{\partial}{\partial t} f_{p+1}(t^{(j)}, x^{(j)}) + \mathcal{N}_0(\tilde{T}_0^{(j)}) - g_*(\tilde{T}_*^{(j)}) \right)^2. \tag{11}$$

Note that, in the above expression, f_{p+1} is the approximation of the solution finally obtained.

4 Related Work

We briefly review related work for completeness. In fact, the data-driven discovery of dynamics is a classical research problem (Crutchfield and McNamara 1987; Kevrekidis et al. 2003; Schmidt et al. 2011; Sugihara et al. 2012; Roberts 2015; Ye et al. 2015; Daniels and Nemenman 2015a,b). Also, the symbolic regression models (Bongard and Lipson 2007; Schmidt and Lipson 2012) have been developed using the sparsity regularization techniques (see, e.g., Hastie et al. 2018) with application to the inference of dominating dynamical systems (Brunton et al. 2015; Mangan et al. 2016; Tran and Ward 2017; Rudy et al. 2017; Schaeffer et al. 2013). Moreover, there are studies in which neural networks are utilized to deal with chaotic dynamics (Rico-Martínes et al. 1992; Anderson et al. 1996; González-García et al. 1998; Raissi et al. 2019).

5 Experiments

To examine the performance of the proposed method, we conducted experiments motivated by the previous studies (Rudy et al. 2017; Raissi 2018). For experiments, we used three different types of equations: the Korteweg–de Vries (KdV) equation, the Navier–Stokes equation, and the Kuramoto–Sivashinsky equation. Every experiment was conducted by

1. Training g and g_* using the procedures in Sects. 2.1 and 3.1 , respectively,
2. Approximating the solution of the identified PDE with new initial/boundary conditions (i.e., test sets) using the procedures in Sects. 2.2 or 3.2, and
3. Comparing the approximated solutions and the true dynamics.

We generated the training data and the true dynamics under test set conditions using Chebfun package (Driscoll et al. 2014). We conducted experiments based on the synthesized data this time, but investigating the performance on experimental data is an interesting open challenge.

5.1 KdV Equation

Dataset. The KdV equation can describe the behavior of waves on shallow water surfaces and is expressed as

$$0 = u_t + uu_x + u_{xxx}. \tag{12}$$

For a fair comparison, we followed the settings in (Raissi 2018) in generating data. That is, we set ranges $0 \leq t \leq 40$ and $-20 \leq x \leq 20$, and generated data with different initial conditions: $u_1(0, x) := -\sin(\pi x/20)$, $u_2(0, x) := -\sin(\pi x/10)$, and $u_3(0, x) := \cos(\pi x/20)$. Moreover, we used the periodic boundary condition. The training set was created by generating data with initial condition u_1 and randomly picking 10,000 points of t in $0 \leq t \leq 26.7$. For testing, we prepared two different initial conditions u_2 and u_3. The corresponding true dynamics are exemplified in the upper-left panel of Figs. 1a and b, respectively.

Prior Knowledge and Model Architecture. We suppose we know an appropriate PDE has the term u_{xxx}, i.e., $T_0 = \{u_{xxx}\}$ and $\mathcal{N}_0 = u_{xxx}$. Note that, besides u_{xxx}, u_t is assumed to be present originally. The architectures of DNNs f and g_* were set the same with ones in Raissi (2018); f was a network with fully connected two hidden layers of size 100, and g_* was with fully connected four hidden layers of size 50. We used tanh as the activation function. Moreover, we set $T_* = \{u, u_x, u_{xx}\}$.

Table 1. RMSEs between the true dynamics and the predictions for the KdV equation under the test initial conditions. The averages (and standard deviations) over 50 random trials are shown.

	DHPM (no prior knowledge)	Proposed (with u_{xxx} known)
u_2 set	0.3645 (0.254)	0.1482 (0.034)
u_3 set	0.2796 (0.279)	0.0566 (0.044)

Results. We show examples of the prediction of u based on the learned g_* and f in Figs. 1a and b. It can be observed that the proposed method generates solutions compatible with the true dynamics. In Table 1, we show the root mean squared errors (RMSEs) between the predicted solution and the true dynamics. In summary, DHPM and the proposed method can predict the true dynamics to some extent, while our model is better in terms of RMSEs.

5.2   Navier–Stokes Equation

Dataset. The Navier–Stokes equation is a well-known PDE that describes the motion of fluid flows. Here, we use the equation with conditions that the field is two-dimensional (i.e., $x = [x\ y]^\mathsf{T}$), and the flow is incompressible and has a constant viscosity, for simplicity. Under these conditions, the PDE with regard to the vorticity of flow, which we denote by u, derived from the Navier–Stokes equation is simplified as follows:

$$0 = u_t + vu_x + wu_y - \nu(u_{xx} + u_{yy}), \quad u = w_x - v_y, \tag{13}$$

where v and w represent flow's velocity along x and y axes, respectively, and ν is the viscosity coefficient.

We generated data using Eq. (13) in the same manner with the previous studies (Rudy et al. 2017; Raissi 2018). We considered the flow behind a cylinder of diameter 1 in the field of size $-1 \leq x \leq 8$ and $-2 \leq y \leq 2$. The flow comes flow the left uniformly with a constant velocity, i.e., we set boundary conditions $v = 1$ and $w = 0$ at $x = 0$. Moreover, we set the time range of simulation to be $0 \leq t \leq 30$. The flow's Reynolds number was set Re $= 100$ by setting $\nu = 0.01$. We focused on the field behind the cylinder, in which the well-known Kármán vortex street appears. Particularly, we used u in $1 \leq x \leq 7.5$ and $-1.7 \leq y \leq 1.7$. We picked up 10,000 random points of t from $0 \leq t \leq 6$ and created a training set from u at those t's. In the test phase, we used the data in $0 \leq t \leq 30$ as the true dynamics for comparison.

Prior Knowledge and Model Architecture. We supposed that $vu_x + wu_y$ was known *a priori*, i.e., $T_0 = \{u_x, u_y, v, w\}$ and $\mathcal{N}_0 = vu_x + wu_y$. We used DNNs with the architectures same as in Sect. 5.1 except that we used $\sin(\cdot)$ for the activation function. Moreover, we set $T_* = \{u, u_{xx}, u_{xy}, u_{yy}\}$.

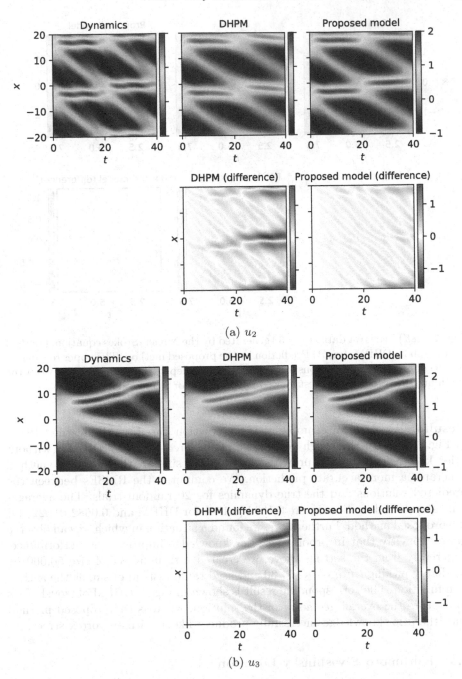

Fig. 1. (*left*) True test dynamics generated by the KdV with initial condition u_2 or u_3, (*center*) prediction by DHPM, and (*right*) prediction by the proposed method, in each of (a) and (b). The upper row depict the original data or predictions, and the lower row depict the differences between the truth and the predictions. Best viewed in color. (Color figure online)

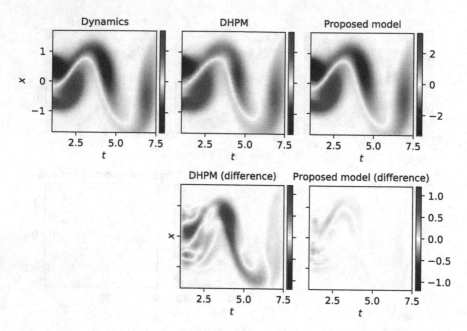

Fig. 2. (*left*) True test data at $t = 30$ generated by the Navier–Stokes equation. (*center*) Prediction by DHPM. (*right*) Prediction by the proposed method. The upper row depict the original data or predictions, and the lower row depict the differences between the truth and the predictions. Best viewed in color. (Color figure online)

Results. We show an example of the prediction based on the learned PDEs in Fig. 2. Though the rough geometries of the predictions by DHPM (without prior knowledge) and the proposed method are similar, the proposed method generates a more accurate prediction. We computed the RMSEs between the predicted solutions and the true dynamics for 20 random trials. The averages (and standard deviations) were 0.1308 (0.156) for DHPM and 0.0682 (0.022) for the proposed method. Furthermore, we found a situation in which we can observe more explicitly that incorporating prior knowledge improves the performance. Differently from the setting above, we created a training set of size 50,000 by randomly picking t from $0 \leq t \leq 30$ and used tanh, instead of sin, as the activation function. The corresponding result is shown in Fig. 3; DHPM obviously fails to capture the overall geometry of the solution, whereas the proposed method with the prior knowledge successfully produces like a Kármán vortex street.

5.3 Kuramoto–Sivashinsky Equation

Dataset. The Kuramoto–Sivashinsky equation, represented as follows, is a physics model with some chaotic behaviors:

$$0 = u_t + uu_x + u_{xx} + u_{xxxx}. \tag{14}$$

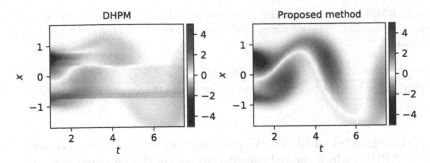

Fig. 3. Predictions for Navier–Stokes equation with the different settings of DNNs by (*left*) DHPM and (*right*) the proposed method. Best viewed in color. (Color figure online)

The data were generated following the settings in the previous studies (Rudy et al. 2017; Raissi 2018). We used experiment domain $0 \leq t \leq 50$ and $-10 \leq x \leq 10$ and initial conditions $u(0, x) = -\sin(\pi x/10)$ and and the periodic boundary condition. We created a training set of size 10,000 by randomly picking t. Unlike the two experiments above, in the test phase we used the initial/boundary conditions same as the training set; note that the test set still contains the values of u that are not in the training set. We used such test conditions for stably examining the effects of different prior knowledge given to the method.

Prior Knowledge and Model Architecture. We tried two different settings: one is $T_0 = \{u_{xx}\}$ and $\mathcal{N}_0 = u_{xx}$, and another is $T_0 = \{u_{xx}, u_{xxx}\}$ and $\mathcal{N}_0 = u_{xx} + u_{xxx}$. In both cases, we set $T_* = \{u, u_x, u_{xx}, u_{xxx}, u_{xxxx}\} \setminus T_0$. Now, remember that DHPM and the proposed method originally assumed there was term u_t in the PDE to be estimated. In other words, we originally utilize a prior knowledge that u_t exists. With this interpretation, we tried a more "knowledgeless" setting, i.e., the case where we do not premise the presence of u_t, for which we used $T = \{u, u_t, u_x, u_{xx}, u_{xxx}, u_{xxxx}\}$ with a slight modification of Eq. (5).

Results. The results of the solutions estimated via trained models are shown in Table 2. It exhibits that the smaller RMSE is achieved using a larger knowledge set, which implies that utilizing richer prior knowledge improve the performance.

6   Discussion

We proposed a simple yet efficient method for gray-box identification of NPDEs using DNNs. The proposed method is built upon the method for black-box identification of NPDEs using DNNs (Raissi 2018) and the DNN-based simulation of PDEs (Raissi et al. 2019). In the proposed method, instead of approximate all the terms (except u_t), we make some terms known as prior knowledge and model

Table 2. RMSEs between the true dynamics and the predictions for the Kuramoto–Sivashinsky equation. The averages (and standard deviations) over 10 random trials are shown.

Known terms	None	u_t (DHPM)	$T_0 = \{u_{xx}\}$	$T_0 = \{u_{xx}, u_{xxxx}\}$
RMSE	0.6274 (0.126)	0.1916 (0.137)	0.1837 (0.050)	0.1686 (0.036)

the remaining part of an NPDE. We provided the numerical examples with three different NPDEs, which showed the effectiveness of the proposed method.

There are several challenges to be addressed. For example, whether one can prepare a good prior knowledge (i.e., a set of known terms) depends on applications. In this paper, we implicitly premised that the given set of known terms is clean, that is, contains no inappropriate terms. However, does the proposed method works well if the knowledge set contains terms not present in the true PDE? If it doesn't, terms that should be utilized as prior knowledge have to be selected. Possibly this can be performed using model selection methods such as the matching pursuit and ones based on information criteria. Moreover, investigating good DNN architectures and data-gathering schemes is an issue for practical applications. Furthermore, it is interesting to analyze the complexity of the method, i.e., the amount of training data needed for specific performance.

Acknowledgements. This work was supported by JSPS KAKENHI Grant Numbers JP18H06487, JP19K21550 and JP19K12094.

References

Anderson, J.S., Kevrekidisi, I.G., Rico-Martínez, R.: A comparison of recurrent training algorithms for time series analysis and system identification. Comput. Chem. Eng. **20**, S751–S756 (1996)

Bongard, J., Lipson, H.: Automated reverse engineering of nonlinear dynamical systems. Proc. Nat. Acad. Sci. U.S.A. **104**(24), 9943–9948 (2007)

Brunton, S.L., Proctor, J.L., Kutz, J.N.: Discovering governing equations from data: sparse identification of nonlinear dynamical systems. Proc. Nat. Acad. Sci. U.S.A. **113**(15), 3932–3937 (2015)

Crutchfield, J.P., McNamara, B.: Equations of motion from a data series. Complex Syst. **1**, 417–452 (1987)

Daniels, B.C., Nemenman, I.: Automated adaptive inference of phenomenological dynamical models. Nat. Commun. **6**, 8133 (2015a)

Daniels, B.C., Nemenman, I.: Efficient inference of parsimonious phenomenological models of cellular dynamics using S-systems and alternating regression. PLoS ONE **10**(3), e0119821 (2015b)

Driscoll, T.A., Hale, N., Trefethen, L.N. (eds.): Chebfun Guide. Pafnuty Publications, Oxford (2014)

González-García, R., Rico-Martínez, R., Kevrekidis, I.G.: Identification of distributed parameter systems: a neural net based approach. Comput. Chem. Eng. **22**, S965–S968 (1998)

Hastie, T., Tibshirani, R., Wainwright, M.: Statistical Learning with Sparsity: The Lasso and Generalizations. CRC Press, Boca Raton (2018)

Kevrekidis, I.G., Gear, C.W., Hyman, J.M., Kevrekidis, P.G., Runborg, O., Theodoropoulos, C.: Equation-free multiscale computation: enabling microscopic simulators to perform system-level tasks. Commun. Math. Sci. **1**(4), 715–762 (2003)

Mangan, N.M., Brunton, S.L., Proctor, J.L., Kutz, J.N.: Inferring biological networks by sparse identification of nonlinear dynamics. IEEE Trans. Mol. Biol. Multi-Scale Commun. **2**(1), 52–63 (2016)

Raissi, M., Perdikaris, P., Karniadakis, G.: Physics-informed neural networks: a deep learning framework for solving forward and inverse problems involving nonlinear partial differential equations. J. Comput. Phys. **378**, 686–707 (2019)

Raissi, M.: Deep hidden physics models: deep learning of nonlinear partial differential equations. J. Mach. Learn. Res. **19**(25), 1–24 (2018)

Rico-Martínes, R., Kevrekidis, I.G., Kube, M.C., Hudson, J.L.: Discrete- vs. continuous-time nonlinear signal processing: attractors, transitions and parallel implementation issues. Chem. Eng. Commun. **118**(1), 25–48 (1992)

Roberts, A.J.: Model Emergent Dynamics in Complex Systems. SIAM (2015)

Rudy, S.H., Brunton, S.L., Proctor, J.L., Kutz, J.N.: Data-driven discovery of partial differential equations. Sci. Adv. **3**(4), e1602614 (2017)

Schaeffer, H., Osher, S., Caflisch, R., Hauck, C.: Sparse dynamics for partial differential equations. Proc. Nat. Acad. Sci. U.S.A. **110**(17), 6634–6639 (2013)

Schmidt, M., Lipson, H.: Distilling free-form natural laws from experimental data. Science **324**(5923), 81–85 (2012)

Schmidt, M.D., et al.: Automated refinement and inference of analytical models for metabolic networks. Phys. Biol. **8**(5), 055011 (2011)

Strang, G.: Computational Science and Engineering. Wellesley-Cambridge Press, Wellesley (2007)

Sugihara, G., et al.: Detecting causality in complex ecosystems. Science **338**(6106), 496–500 (2012)

Tran, G., Ward, R.: Exact recovery of chaotic systems from highly corrupted data. Multiscale Model. Simul. **15**(3), 1108–1129 (2017)

Ye, H., et al.: Equation-free mechanistic ecosystem forecasting using empirical dynamic modeling. Proc. Nat. Acad. Sci. U.S.A. **112**(13), E1569–E1576 (2015)

Foreground Mask Guided Network for Crowd Counting

Chun Li, Lin Shang$^{(\boxtimes)}$, and Suping Xu

State Key Laboratory for Novel Software Technology, Nanjing University,
Nanjing 210023, China
{lichun,supingxu}@smail.nju.edu.cn, shanglin@nju.edu.cn

Abstract. Crowd counting in unconstrained scenes is a challenging task due to large scale variations, complex background clutters and severe occlusions, etc. The performance of current networks utilizing multi-path based architectures for better multi-scale representation is constrained by the number of paths. In many cases, existing methods suffer from false responses background such as buildings and trees in complex scenes. To address these issues, we propose an end-to-end network, called Foreground Mask Guided Network (FMGNet), for high-quality density map generation and accurate crowd counting. By employing deep fusion in intermediate layers, the proposed network aggregates multi-scale features in a more efficient way. Moreover, foreground mask features representing the differences between crowd foreground and background are used as guidance information to suppress false responses in background. Extensive experiments on three challenging benchmarks have well demonstrated the effectiveness of the proposed method as well as the superior performance over prior state-of-the-arts.

Keywords: Crowd counting · Density map generation · Foreground mask · Dilated convolution

1 Introduction

With the rapid increase of urban population, crowd scene analysis has attracted significant attention in recent years. As an important task in crowd scene analysis, crowd counting aims to count the number of people in crowded scenes. Current crowd counting methods are developed from simple crowd counting to crowd density estimation because the estimated density map is able to demonstrate the distribution of people, thus giving us more comprehensive information about the crowd. Moreover, by simply summing up the values of all the pixels in density map, we can get the crowd count conveniently. Over the past few years, a variety of methods have been proposed to address the issues of crowd counting and density estimation. Although solid improvements have been achieved by these methods, crowd counting and density estimation are still challenging tasks in computer vision due to large scale variations, complex background clutters, non-uniform illumination and severe occlusions.

A. C. Nayak and A. Sharma (Eds.): PRICAI 2019, LNAI 11671, pp. 322–334, 2019.
https://doi.org/10.1007/978-3-030-29911-8_25

Most existing CNN-based methods of crowd counting and density estimation focus on dealing with large variations in scale. Among them, multi-path based methods using several independent CNN branches with different receptive fields [15,19] are popular for their robustness to scale variations. However, since each CNN branch only caters to a single scale due to its fixed receptive field, the ability to model multi-scale objects is severely restricted by the number of CNN branches. Although we can include more CNN branches in multi-path architectures, the increase of parameters and computational consumption is not neglectable. The inefficiency of scale aggregation limits the further development of multi-path based methods.

In addition to large scale variations, background clutter is also a major obstacle to crowd density estimation. Regrettably, due to the lack of the ability to distinguish crowd foreground from background, current networks may mistake background objects such as trees and buildings for crowd, especially in cluttered scenes. These wrong estimations decrease the quality of generated density map and result in inaccurate crowd count.

To address these issues, we propose an end-to-end network called Foreground Mask Guided Network (FMGNet) for counting crowd and generating high-quality density map. The architecture of FMGNet is shown in Fig. 1. For overcoming the drawbacks of multi-path based architectures, we design a deep fusion based Density Map Estimator (DME) for efficient multi-scale representation. Different from multi-path based networks in which fusion is only performed over the final feature representations of CNN branches, DME fuses the intermediate feature representations. Namely, we combine the features extracted by each convolutional layer which consists of several dilated convolutions, then the combined features serve as the input of different dilated convolutions at next layer and so on. By doing this, our deep fusion based DME can be regarded as an ensemble of base networks with different receptive fields, hence the representation ability of our network is greatly improved. Furthermore, dilated convolutions with increasing dilation rates may fail to aggregate features of small objects due to sparsity of the kernel, so we adopt dilated convolutions with decreasing dilation rates to alleviate this problem following the idea in [4]. Moreover, motivated by the unsatisfactory performance of current crowd counting methods on dealing with background clutter, we suggest that improving the ability to distinguish crowd foreground and background is crucial. To this end, a Mask Feature Extractor (MFE) is employed to capture mask features which indicate the differences between crowd foreground and background under the supervision of ground-truth crowd foreground mask map. Then we guide the further feature extraction process by incorporating these mask features into the input of DME. Finally, the quality of generated density map is significantly improved as false background responses obviously reduced.

To summarize, the main contributions of this paper are: (1) We employ deep fusion in our network to address the issue of scale variations in a more efficient way. (2) We propose to leverage crowd foreground mask features to guide the feature extraction process of density map estimation for reducing false responses in background. (3) Extensive experiments on three challenging benchmarks demonstrate that our method achieves superior performance compared to the state-of-the-arts.

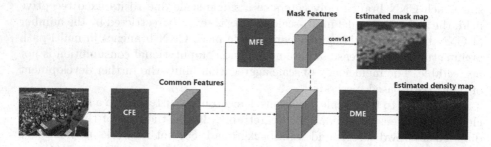

Fig. 1. Overview of the proposed FMGNet architecture.

2 Related Work

Following the idea proposed by Vishwanath et al. [13], we divide the discussion of related works into traditional approaches and CNN-based methods.

2.1 Traditional Approaches

Most of the early researches focus on detection-based approaches [3,8], where a sliding window detector is applied to detect people and this information is further used to count. Among them, body-based approaches [6,10] extract features from full bodies while part-based approaches [8] detect particular body parts such as head or shoulder. Though performing well on low density crowd scenes, these detection-based methods fail in highly congested scenes due to severe occlusions. To address these issues, regression-based methods [1,12] are proposed to learn a mapping between extracted features and crowd counts. They use low-level features such as texture features, gradient features from local image patches to calculate the number of people in crowd scenes. While regression-based methods are successful in addressing occlusion problem, most of them ignore the spatial information in crowd images. To solve this problem, Lempitsky et al. [7] propose to learn a linear mapping from local patch features to corresponding density maps. Considering the difficulty of obtaining a ideal linear mapping, Pham et al. [11] propose to learn a non-linear mapping between local patch features and density maps instead of a linear one, which achieves significant improvement on counting problem.

2.2   CNN-Based Methods

In recent years, inspired by the success of CNNs in numerous computer vision tasks, a variety of CNN-based methods have been proposed for crowd counting. Wang et al. [17] propose an end-to-end deep CNN regression model to predict crowd counts. However, this model cannot demonstrate the distribution of people, which limits its application on crowd analysis. To address the issue, Zhang et al. [18] propose to learn a mapping from images to corresponding crowd counts by alternatively training their networks on two related objectives: crowd count and density estimation. The authors of [19] propose a multi-column cnn in which several CNN branches are applied to cater to humans of different sizes. Multi-scale features captured by different columns are further fused by a convolution layer to generate final density map. Inspired by [19], Sam et al. [16] propose a switching CNN which selects an optimal CNN-based regressor suited for a particular image patch automatically. In [14], a cascaded CNN are proposed to incorporate high-level prior for boosting the density estimation performance. Recently, Sindagi et al. [15] demonstrate a method to incorporate the contextual information by learning various density levels for generating high-quality density maps. In [9], dilated convolution are employed to deliver larger receptive field, which leads to significant improvement in crowd counting and density estimation.

3   Proposed Method

In this section, we first demonstrate the architecture of our network. Then we describe the generation of ground truth. Finally, we provide the details of our training scheme.

3.1   Architecture

As is shown in Fig. 1, our FMGNet consists of three main components: Common Feature Extractor (CFE), Mask Feature Extractor (MFE) and Density Map Estimator (DME). They cooperate with each other as following: firstly, given an input crowd image, CFE extract task-independent common features which are shared by MFE and DME as input. Secondly, MFE utilizes the common features to extract mask features which represent the differences between crowd foreground and background. Finally, DME uses the common features under the guidance of mask features to generate high-quality crowd density map.

Common Feature Extractor (CFE). As is known to all, most CNN-based networks are highly data-driven, thus requiring massive labeled data for training. Regrettably, since each individual person requires to be meticulously labeled and there might be thousands of people present in a crowd image, the burden of labeling is extremely heavy, hence current crowd count datasets tend to have only a few hundred images available for training. Considering the difficulty of training a deep CNN from scratch with so little training data, we follow the similar idea in [9,15,16] and utilize a pretrained VGG-16 to build our CFE for its strong transfer learning ability. More specifically, our CFE adopts the first ten layers of a VGG-16 network pretrained on Imagenet [2], which is shown in Fig. 2. On the one hand, ten convolutional layers are appropriate to encode low-level information. On the other hand, layers closer to final objective tend to output features which are more task-related, as we want to obtain task-independent features from CFE, utilizing more layers is not wise. Moreover, different from [9,15,16], we fix all pretrained parameters in CFE rather than fine-tune them during training, by which we only need to train layers in MFE and DME. The reduction of trainable layers and parameters leads to faster convergence of our network.

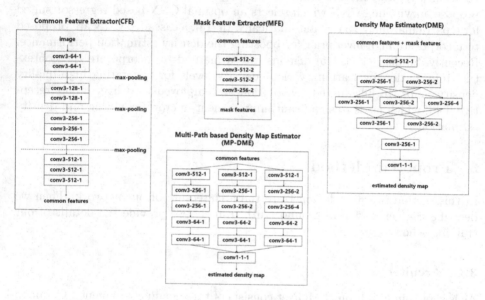

Fig. 2. Basic components. Among them, Common Feature Extractor (CFE), Mask Feature Extractor (MFE) and Density Map Estimator (DME) are main components of FMGNet while Common Feature Extractor (CFE) and Multi-Path Density Map Estimator (MP-DME) are main components of the baseline network in Sect. 4.3. A convolutional layer is denoted as "conv(kernel size)-(number of channels)-(dilation rate)"

Mask Feature Extractor (MFE). Taking common features provided by CFE as input, MFE followed by a 1×1 convolutional layer generates crowd foreground mask map under the supervision of ground truth mask map. Since the last layer of MFE is so close to mask generation objective, mask features (the output feature maps of MFE) contain abundant information about the differences between crowd foreground and background. Therefore, by incorporating mask features into the input of DME, the DME obtains massive information about how to distinguish crowd foreground from background, thus can reduce the possibility of mistaking objects in background for crowd. In other words, the mask features guide the feature extraction process in DME.

The architecture of MFE is shown in Fig. 2. We adopt dilated convolution in MFE due to its ability to support exponential expansion of the receptive field without loss of resolution or coverage. Compared to density map estimation task in which the value of different pixels varies greatly, mask map generation is a relatively simple task since we only need to determine whether the pixel belongs to crowd foreground or not. Therefore four dilated convolutional layers with all the dilation rate of 2 are capable of extracting discriminative features which help to distinguish the crowd foreground from background. Note that the sizes of generated mask map and output feature maps of MFE are 1/8 of the size of input image.

Density Map Estimator (DME). Different from MFE, the DME takes features from two sources as input: common features from CFE and mask features from MFE. The former contains low-level task-independent information and the latter contains discriminative information which helps to discriminate crowd foreground from background. Since both of them are crucial and indispensable, we concatenate them and then feed them into the deep fusion based DME for generating crowd density map.

The central idea of DME is deep fusion. Compared to current multi-path based methods which only fuse the final feature representations of CNN branches, our DME performs fusion over the intermediate feature representations. As shown in Fig. 2, the DME consists of six convolutional layers. Among them, each of the intermediate layers (the second, third and fourth layers) contains several dilated convolutions. Since the dilation rates of dilated convolutions in the same intermediate layer are varied, each intermediate layer can extract features of different scales. The output features extracted by each layer are then concatenated together and further shared by every dilated convolution at the next layer. If we consider each possible path from the first layer to the last layer of DME as a base network, the deep fusion based DME can be regarded as an ensemble of these base networks. Since the receptive fields of these base networks are varied and the number of base networks in DME is much larger than that in multi-path based networks, the multi-scale representation of our network is greatly improved in a more efficient way compared to multi-path based ones.

Moreover, in the first three layers, the dilation rate of dilated convolutions is continuously increasing for enlarging receptive fields rapidly, which, however, may results in failure to aggregate local features of small objects. To address the problem, we adopt decreasing dilation rates in the fourth and fifth layers. Again, the size of estimated density map is 1/8 of the size of input image. To guarantee the same resolution between the output and the input image, we use bilinear interpolation with the factor of 8 for scaling in test stage.

3.2   Ground Truth Generation

Since our network devotes to learning two related sub-tasks: crowd foreground mask map estimation and density map estimation, ground-truth mask maps and ground-truth density maps are required for two sub-tasks respectively.

Density Map for Training. For highly congested scenes, we follow the same scheme as in [19] to generate ground-truth density maps considering the head size variations and perspective distortions in these scenes. As one point annotation at the center of the head of each person are given in all crowd datasets, we blur each head annotation using geometry-adaptive Gaussian kernel which is normalized to 1. The geometry-adaptive kernel is defined as:

$$F(x) = \sum_{i=1}^{N} \delta(x - x_i) * G_{\sigma_i}(x), with \ \sigma_i = \beta \bar{d}^i. \tag{1}$$

For each head annotation x_i in a given crowd image, we originally represent it as a delta function $\delta(x - x_i)$. $\bar{d}^i$ denotes the average distance of its k nearest neighbors. To estimate the crowd density around the x_i, we convolve $\delta(x - x_i)$ with a Gaussian kernel with standard deviation σ_i proportional to $\bar{d}^i$. In our experiments, we follow the same configuration in [19] where $\beta = 0.3$ and $k = 3$.

For scenes with relatively sparse crowd, we adapt the Gaussian kernel to the average head size to directly blur all the annotations.

Mask Map for Training. The ground-truth mask map in our method is a binary mask in which the values of pixels located in crowd foreground regions are 1 while the values of pixels located in background regions are 0. Note that the crowd foreground in this article is a small region around each head annotation of people, which means other body parts such as the shoulder and leg are treated as background. Since the pixels of crowd foreground have non-zero values and the pixels of background have zero values in ground-truth density map according to its generation scheme, we can make use of the ground-truth density map for generating ground-truth mask map. It is natural to set the values of non-zero pixels of ground-truth density map to be 1, then we can obtain a ground-truth mask map. However, considering the property of Gaussian kernel, regions with non-zeros values in ground-truth density map are much larger than the actual crowd foreground regions. So using the above method to generate ground-truth mask map may mistake many background areas for crowd foreground. We use a threshold to alleviate this problem and define that, for each pixel in ground-truth density map, if the pixel value is greater than the threshold, the value of its corresponding pixel in ground-truth mask map is 1, otherwise, the value of corresponding pixel is 0. Generally, a higher threshold is needed in highly congested scenes while a lower threshold is needed in scenes with sparse crowd.

3.3   Training Details

We train the mask map estimation task and density map estimation task jointly. During training, we resize all input images to 1024×1024. For each input image, we use the scheme in Sect. 3.2 to generate corresponding ground-truth mask map and ground-truth density map. Then we resize the ground-truth maps to 128×128 to guarantee they share the same resolution as estimated mask map and estimated density map. Layers in CFE are fixed when that of the MFE and DME are trainable. We use a Gaussian initialization with 0.01 standard deviation to initialize the trainable layers. Adam optimizer, the learning rate of which is set to 1e−5, is used to update the parameters of these trainable layers. The Euclidean distance is used to measure the difference between ground-truth maps and estimated maps in both tasks. The loss function of density map estimation task is defined as follow:

$$L_D(\Theta_D) = \frac{1}{2N} \sum_{i=1}^{N} \left\| D(X_i; \Theta_D) - D_i^{GT} \right\|^2, \tag{2}$$

where N is the size of training batch, Θ_D is a set of learnable parameters in the DME, X_i represent the input image and $D(X_i; \Theta_D)$ is the generated density map while D_i^{GT} is the ground-truth density map of the input image X_i.

We also apply the Euclidean distance to mask map estimation task and the loss function of mask map estimation task is:

$$L_M(\Theta_M) = \frac{1}{2N} \sum_{i=1}^{N} \left\| M(X_i; \Theta_M) - M_i^{GT} \right\|^2. \tag{3}$$

Finally, the above two loss functions are added up to get the final objective:

$$L_{total} = L_D + L_M, \tag{4}$$

where the L_D and L_M are the losses of density map estimation task and mask map estimation task respectively.

4   Experiments

4.1   Evaluation Metrics

By following the convention of existing works, we evaluate different methods with the mean absolute error (MAE) and the mean squared error (MSE), which are defined as:

$$MAE = \frac{1}{N} \sum_{i=1}^{N} \left| C_i - C_i^{GT} \right|, \tag{5}$$

$$MSE = \sqrt{\frac{1}{N} \sum_{i=1}^{N} \left| C_i - C_i^{GT} \right|^2}, \tag{6}$$

where N is the number of test images, C_i^{GT} is the actual number of people in the ith image and C_i is the estimated number of people in the ith image.

4.2   Crowd Counting Datasets

We evaluate our method on three challenging crowd counting datasets, including ShanghaiTech dataset [19], UCF_CC_50 dataset [5] and WorldExpo'10 dataset [18].

ShanghaiTech Dataset. ShanghaiTech dataset contains 1198 annotated images with a total of 330165 annotated people. This dataset is divided into two parts named Part A and Part B. The former contains 482 images with highly congested scenes and the latter includes 716 images with relatively sparse crowd scenes. We use the train-test splits provided by authors for both parts and set the threshold to be 0.01 and 0.001 in Part A and Part B respectively for generating ground-truth mask map.

UCF_CC_50 Dataset. UCF_CC_50 dataset which contains 50 images from the Internet is a very challenging dataset due to the limited number of images and large variance in crowd counts. The number of annotated persons ranges from 94 to 4543 with an average of 1280 persons per image. We perform 5-fold cross-validation by following the standard setting in [5] and set the threshold to be 0.03 for generating ground-truth mask map.

The WorldExpo'10 Dataset. The WorldExpo'10 dataset consists of 1132 video sequences captured by 108 surveillance cameras. 3380 frames are used as training set, and the rest 600 frames sampled from 5 different scenes are used as testing set. The average number of people per image is 50. In this dataset, we set the threshold to be 0.001 for generating ground-truth mask map.

4.3   Ablation Study

In this subsection, we conduct ablation study on the ShanghaiTech Part A dataset to provide further analysis of relative contributions of various components of our method.

Table 1. Comparison the estimation error of different network configurations on ShanghaiTech Part A.

Model	MAE	MSE
Baseline	68.7	113.9
CSRNet [9]	68.2	115.0
DFNet	66.7	105.9
FMGNet	**62.9**	**98.9**

Deep Fusion. We design two networks to compare the performance of deep fusion based DME and multi-path based DME. On the one hand, we design a multi-path based network as our baseline. The baseline network consists of a CFE and a Multi-Path based Density Map Estimator (MP-DME) with three CNN branches. The CFE in baseline extract common features from input image and MP-DME use the common features for generating density map. The detailed architecture of MP-DME is shown in Fig. 2. On the other hand, we remove the MFE module and the following 1×1 convolutional layer of FMGNet and only use CFE and DME to build a new network. Since the DME is designed following the idea of deep fusion, we call this network Deeply-Fused Network (DFNet). To minimize the difference between the baseline network and DFNet, the depth of MP-DME is the same as that of deep fusion based DME, meanwhile, the parameters numbers of them are close (12.97M vs 12.94M).

After training on ShanghaiTech Part A dataset using the same training scheme in Sect. 3.3, we perform the evaluation metrics defined in Sect. 4.1. The detailed evaluation results are shown in Table 1. Compared to the baseline network, MAE by DFNet is decreased by 2.0 points and MSE by 8.0 points, which indicates that the deep fusion based network performs better than multi-path based networks in learning multi-scale representations.

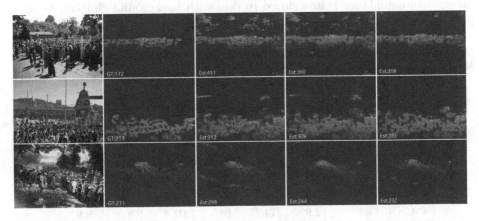

Fig. 3. Comparison of estimated density maps. First column: test image sampled from ShanghaiTech Part A; Second column: ground-truth density maps with crowd count; Third column: estimated density maps by CSRNet; Fourth column: estimated density maps by DFNet; Fifth column: estimated density map by proposed FMGNet.

Mask Feature Guidance. We also study the effectiveness of mask feature guidance. We use FMGNet and DFNet mentioned above for comparison. The difference between them is that no guidance information is used in DFNet compared to FMGNet.

Table 2. Estimation errors on ShanghaiTech dataset and UCF_CC_50 dataset.

Method	ShanghaiTech Part A		ShanghaiTech Part B		UCF_CC_50	
	MAE	MSE	MAE	MSE	MAE	MSE
Zhang et al. [18]	181.8	277.7	32.0	49.8	467.0	498.5
MCNN [19]	110.2	173.2	26.4	41.3	377.6	509.1
Cascaded-MTL [14]	101.3	152.4	20.0	31.1	322.8	397.9
Switching-CNN [16]	90.4	135.0	21.6	33.4	318.1	439.2
CP-CNN [15]	73.6	106.4	20.1	30.1	295.8	320.9
CSRNet [9]	68.2	115.0	10.6	16.0	266.1	397.5
FMGNet (ours)	**62.9**	**98.9**	**9.1**	**14.8**	**219.2**	**320.7**

After training on ShanghaiTech Part A dataset, we report the evaluation results in Table 1. We also add the result of recent state-of-the-art method: CSR-Net [9] in Table 1 for comparison. Both DFNet and FMGNet perform better than CSRNet. Compared to DFNet, FMGNet reduces the MAE error from 66.7 to 62.9 and the MSE error from 105.9 to 98.9, which indicates that the mask feature guidance also improves the performance of our network. Moreover, since the mask feature guidance is introduced to deal with background clutters, we also provide visualization results of estimated density maps by CSRNet, FMGNet and DFNet, as shown in Fig. 3. From the visualization results, we can see that the false responses in background are obviously reduced, which confirms the effectiveness of mask feature guidance.

Table 3. Estimation errors on the WorldExpo'10 dataset.

Method	Scene1	Scene2	Scene3	Scene4	Scene5	Average
Zhang et al. [18]	9.8	14.1	14.3	22.2	3.7	12.9
MCNN [19]	3.4	20.6	12.9	13.0	8.1	11.6
Switching-CNN [16]	4.4	15.7	10.0	11.0	5.9	9.4
CP-CNN [15]	2.9	14.7	10.5	**10.4**	5.8	8.9
CSRNet [9]	2.9	**11.5**	8.6	16.6	3.4	8.6
FMGNet (ours)	**2.8**	13.8	**8.5**	14.2	**3.0**	**7.9**

4.4   Comparison with the State-of-the-Art

We compare FMGNet against the state-of-the-art methods on three challenging datasets introduced in Sect. 4.2. As shown in Table 2, our method obtains the lowest MAE and MSE on both sub-datasets of ShanghaiTech. Specifically, FMGNet improves the MAE by 7.8% on Part A and 14.2% on Part B compared to the previous state-of-the-art method: CSRNet. On UCF_CC_50 dataset, our method reduces the MAE from 266.1 to 219.2, which is a significant improvement for this challenging dataset. The results on the WorldExpo'10 dataset are shown in Table 3, as can be seen, our method delivers the best accuracy in 3 out of 5 scenes and achieves the best accuracy on average. The superior performance on these datasets indicates that our method can deal with not only scenes with extremely dense crowd but also scenes with sparse crowds. We also provide sample predictions from ShanghaiTech dataset and UCF_CC_50 dataset, which are shown in Fig. 4.

Fig. 4. The first row shows the samples of the testing set in ShanghaiTech dataset and UCF_CC_50 dataset. The second row shows the ground truth for each sample while the third row presents the generated density map by FMGNet.

5   Conclusion

In this paper, we proposed a new end-to-end network called FMGNet for accurate crowd counting and high-quality density map estimation. We use deep fusion to deal with large scale variations in a more efficient way compared to current multi-path based methods. By taking mask features as guidance information, our network obtains knowledge about the differences between crowd foreground and background, which leads to significant reduction of false response in background. Extensive experiments conducted on three challenging datasets and comparisons with recent start-of-the-arts demonstrated the superior performance achieved by the proposed method.

Acknowledgments. This work is supported by the Natural Science Foundation of China (No. 61672276), Natural Science Foundation of Jiangsu Province of China (No. BK20161406).

References

1. Chen, K., Loy, C.C., Gong, S., Xiang, T.: Feature mining for localised crowd counting. In: BMVC, Vol. 1, no. 2, p. 3 (2012)
2. Deng, J., Dong, W., Socher, R., Li, L.J., Li, K., Fei-Fei, L.: Imagenet: a large-scale hierarchical image database (2009)

3. Dollar, P., Wojek, C., Schiele, B., Perona, P.: Pedestrian detection: an evaluation of the state of the art. IEEE Trans. Pattern Anal. Mach. Intell. **34**(4), 743–761 (2012)
4. Hamaguchi, R., Fujita, A., Nemoto, K., Imaizumi, T., Hikosaka, S.: Effective use of dilated convolutions for segmenting small object instances in remote sensing imagery. In: 2018 IEEE Winter Conference on Applications of Computer Vision (WACV), pp. 1442–1450. IEEE (2018)
5. Idrees, H., Saleemi, I., Seibert, C., Shah, M.: Multi-source multi-scale counting in extremely dense crowd images. In: Proceedings of the IEEE Conference on Computer Vision and Pattern Recognition, pp. 2547–2554 (2013)
6. Leibe, B., Seemann, E., Schiele, B.: Pedestrian detection in crowded scenes. In: 2005 IEEE Computer Society Conference on Computer Vision and Pattern Recognition (CVPR 2005), Vol. 1, pp. 878–885. IEEE (2005)
7. Lempitsky, V., Zisserman, A.: Learning to count objects in images. In: Advances in Neural Information Processing Systems, pp. 1324–1332 (2010)
8. Li, M., Zhang, Z., Huang, K., Tan, T.: Estimating the number of people in crowded scenes by mid based foreground segmentation and head-shoulder detection. In: 2008 19th International Conference on Pattern Recognition, pp. 1–4. IEEE (2008)
9. Li, Y., Zhang, X., Chen, D.: CSRNet: dilated convolutional neural networks for understanding the highly congested scenes. In: Proceedings of the IEEE Conference on Computer Vision and Pattern Recognition, pp. 1091–1100 (2018)
10. MGavrila, M.: Monocular pedestrian detection: survey and experiments. IEEE Trans. Pattern Anal. Mach. Intell. **31**(12), 2179–2195 (2009)
11. Pham, V.Q., Kozakaya, T., Yamaguchi, O., Okada, R.: Count forest: co-voting uncertain number of targets using random forest for crowd density estimation. In: Proceedings of the IEEE International Conference on Computer Vision, pp. 3253–3261 (2015)
12. Ryan, D., Denman, S., Fookes, C., Sridharan, S.: Crowd counting using multiple local features. In: 2009 Digital Image Computing: Techniques and Applications, pp. 81–88. IEEE (2009)
13. Sindagi, V.A., Patel, V.M.: A survey of recent advances in CNN-based single image crowd counting and density estimation. Pattern Recogn. Lett. **107**, 3–16 (2018)
14. Sindagi, V.A., Patel, V.M.: CNN-based cascaded multi-task learning of high-level prior and density estimation for crowd counting. In: 2017 14th IEEE International Conference on Advanced Video and Signal Based Surveillance (AVSS), pp. 1–6. IEEE (2017)
15. Sindagi, V.A., Patel, V.M.: Generating high-quality crowd density maps using contextual pyramid CNNs. In: Proceedings of the IEEE International Conference on Computer Vision, pp. 1861–1870 (2017)
16. Sam, D.B., Surya, S., Babu, R.V.: Switching convolutional neural network for crowd counting. In: 2017 IEEE Conference on Computer Vision and Pattern Recognition (CVPR), pp. 4031–4039. IEEE (2017)
17. Wang, C., Zhang, H., Yang, L., Liu, S., Cao, X.: Deep people counting in extremely dense crowds. In: Proceedings of the 23rd ACM International Conference on Multimedia, pp. 1299–1302. ACM (2015)
18. Zhang, C., Li, H., Wang, X., Yang, X.: Cross-scene crowd counting via deep convolutional neural networks. In: Proceedings of the IEEE Conference on Computer Vision and Pattern Recognition, pp. 833–841 (2015)
19. Zhang, Y., Zhou, D., Chen, S., Gao, S., Ma, Y.: Single-image crowd counting via multi-column convolutional neural network. In: Proceedings of the IEEE Conference on Computer Vision and Pattern Recognition, pp. 589–597 (2016)

Optimization

A Stochastic Gradient Method with Biased Estimation for Faster Nonconvex Optimization

Jia Bi and Steve R. Gunn[✉]

School of Electronics and Computer Science, University of Southampton,
Southampton, UK
jb4e14@soton.ac.uk, srg@ecs.soton.ac.uk

Abstract. A number of optimization approaches have been proposed
for optimizing nonconvex objectives (e.g. deep learning models), such as
batch gradient descent, stochastic gradient descent and stochastic variance reduced gradient descent. Theory shows these optimization methods
can converge by using an unbiased gradient estimator. However, in practice biased gradient estimation can allow more efficient convergence to
the vicinity since an unbiased approach is computationally more expensive. To produce fast convergence there are two trade-offs of these optimization strategies which are between stochastic/batch, and between
biased/unbiased. This paper proposes an integrated approach which can
control the nature of the stochastic element in the optimizer and can
balance the trade-off of estimator between the biased and unbiased by
using a hyper-parameter. It is shown theoretically and experimentally
that this hyper-parameter can be configured to provide an effective balance to improve the convergence rate.

1 Introduction

Optimization methods for nonconvex problems has become a crucial research
topic in artificial intelligence, such as in deep neural network training. The objective function for the parameter optimization can be formulated as a finite-sum
problem,

$$\min_{x \in \mathbb{R}^d} f(x), \qquad f(x) := \frac{1}{n} \sum_{i=1}^{n} f_i(x), \tag{1}$$

where the individual $f_i(i \in [n])$ and f are nonconvex but Lipschitz smooth
($\mathcal{L}$-smooth) [15,21]. We use $\mathcal{F}_n$ to denote all functions of Eq. 1 and analyse
our optimization method using the Incremental First-order Oracle (IFO) framework [1,15]. Based on complexity analysis, IFO evaluates lower bounds for finite-
sum problems [3,12]. The underlying training algorithms for nonconvex problems are still stochastic gradient descent (SGD) and its heuristic variants to
solve Eq. 1 [2]. One of the variants is variance reduced (VR) based stochastic optimization approaches (e.g. stochastic variance reduced gradient (SVRG))

© Springer Nature Switzerland AG 2019
A. C. Nayak and A. Sharma (Eds.): PRICAI 2019, LNAI 11671, pp. 337–349, 2019.
https://doi.org/10.1007/978-3-030-29911-8_26

which has been shown to accelerate the convergence rate of SGD by reducing the noise of gradients on nonconvex problems [12]. The SVRG algorithm is shown in Algorithm 1 [12].

Algorithm 1: SVRG $(x^0, \eta, \{p_i\}_{i=0}^m, m, S)$

    Input   : Epoch length m, learning rate η, number of epochs $S = T/m$ where T
               is total number of iterations, discrete probability distribution $\{p_i\}_{i=0}^m$;

1 Initialize $\tilde{x}^0 = x_m^0 = x^0$ **for** s = 0 **to** S $-$ 1 **do**

2       $x_0^{s+1} = x_m^s$; $g^{s+1} = \frac{1}{n}\sum_{i=1}^n \nabla f_i(\tilde{x}^s)$ **for** t = 0 **to** m $-$ 1 **do**

3   Randomly select i_t from $\{1,...,n\}$ $v_t^{s+1} = \nabla f_{i_t}(x_t^{s+1}) - \nabla f_{i_t}(\tilde{x}^s) + g^{s+1}$
         $x_{t+1}^{s+1} = x_t^{s+1} - \eta v_t^{s+1}$

4       $\tilde{x}^{s+1} = \sum_{i=0}^m p_i x_i^{s+1}$

  Output: $\tilde{x}^S$

VR-based stochastic algorithms have three problems. Firstly, VR schemes reduce the ability to escape local minima in later iterations due to a diminishing variance. The challenge in VR-based stochastic optimization is therefore to control the reduction in variance. Secondly, SVRG is an unbiased estimation, which can increase computation over biased estimation [13]. Thirdly, the learning rate in such an algorithm is fixed and relatively large, which has the advantage of encouraging initial points out of local minima in early iterations but can hinder optimization convergence to a local optima.

To address these three problems, we propose our method *Integrated biased SVRG* (ISVRG$^+$) which can control the variance reduction and choose the biased or unbiased estimator in each iteration to accelerate the convergence rate of nonconvex optimization.

Contributions. We summarize and list our main contributions:

- We introduce ISVRG$^+$, a well-balanced VR method for SGD. We provide a theoretical analysis of our algorithm on nonconvex problems.
- ISVRG$^+$ balances the trade-off between biased and unbiased estimation, which can provide a fast convergence rate.
- Compared with SGD and SVRG-based optimization, our method can achieve comparable or faster rates of convergence. To the best of our knowledge, we provide the first analysis about controlling the variance reduction to balance the gradient of SVRG and balance the nature of the estimator between biased and unbiased to obtain provably superior performance to SGD and its variants on nonconvex problems. Table 1 compares the theoretical rates of convergence of four methods, which shows that ISVRG$^+$ has the fastest rate of convergence.
- We show empirically that ISVRG$^+$ has faster rates of convergence than SGD, SVRG and MSVRG [15] which is a modified SVRG using an adaptive learning schedule with standard SVRG.

Table 1. Comparison of the IFO complexity of different algorithms. Generally, the learning rate schedule in SGD is decayed by increasing number of iteration. In SVRG (Algorithm 1), the learning rate is fixed. MSVRG [15] is a modified SVRG method where the learning rate in each iteration is chosen from the maximum of two terms, including a term which decays with increasing iteration and a term which is related to the number of training samples. ISVRG$^+$ adopts an adaptive learning rate similar to MSVRG.

Algorithm	IFO calls on nonconvex	The schedule of learning rate η
SGD	$\mathcal{O}(1/\varepsilon^2)$	Decayed
SVRG	$\mathcal{O}(n + (n^{2/3}/\varepsilon))$	Fixed
MSVRG	$\mathcal{O}(\min(1/\varepsilon^2, n^{2/3}/\varepsilon)$	max{Decayed, Fixed}
ISVRG$^+$	$\mathcal{O}(\min(1/\varepsilon^2, n^{1/5}/\varepsilon)$	**max{Decayed, Fixed}**

2   Preliminaries

For our analysis, we require the following background to introduce definitions for $\mathcal{L}$-smooth, ε-accuracy, and σ-bounded gradients. We assume the individual functions f_i in Eq. 1 are $\mathcal{L}$-smooth which is to say that

$$\| \nabla f_i(x) - \nabla f_i(y) \| \leq L \| x - y \|, \forall x, y \in \mathbb{R}^d. \tag{2}$$

An ε-accuracy criterion can be used to analyse the convergence of nonconvex forms of Eq. 1 [9].

Definition 1. *A point x is called ε-accurate if $\| \nabla f(x)^2 \| \leq \varepsilon$. An iterative stochastic algorithm can achieve ε-accuracy within t iterations if $\mathbb{E}[\| \nabla f(x^t) \|^2] \leq \varepsilon$, where the expectation is over the stochastic algorithm.*

Definition 2. $f \in \mathcal{F}_n$ *has σ-bounded gradient if $\| \nabla f_i(x) \| \leq \sigma$ for all $i \in [n]$ and $x \in \mathbb{R}$.*

The following theorems provides two upper bounds of complexity of standard SVRG corresponding to two cases of learning rate, which follow the results from [15] but slightly different in order to provide a consistent comparison with our algorithm. We introduce two changes: (a) re-scaling the gradient of SVRG v_t^{s+1} by a factor of 2 in Algorithm 1; (b) modifying the learning rate η and β in Theorem 3 to provide a simplified parameterization for the learning schedule. In the first case of the fixed learning rate depending on iteration number T, we use σ-bounded gradients from Definition 2 to achieve the upper bound as follows:

Theorem 1. *Suppose f has σ-bounded gradients. Let $\eta_{t_{SVRG}} = \eta_{SVRG} = C_{SVRG}/\sqrt{T}$ where $C_{SVRG} = \sqrt{\dfrac{f(x^0) - f(x^*)}{2L\sigma^2}}$, and x^* is an optimal solution to Eq. 1. Algorithm 1 satisfies*

$$\min_{0 \leq t \leq T-1} \mathbb{E}[\| \nabla f(x^t) \|^2] \leq \sqrt{2}\sqrt{\dfrac{2(f(x^0) - f(x^*))L}{T}}\sigma.$$

In the second case of the learning rate depending on the training sample size n, we can achieve an upper bound without σ-bounded gradients.

Theorem 2. *Let* $f \in \mathcal{F}_n$, *let* $c_{m_{SVRG}} = 0$, $\eta > 0$, $\beta_t = \beta > 0$ *and* $c_{t_{SVRG}} = c_{t+1}(1 + \eta\beta + 2\eta^2 L^2) + L^3\eta^2$, *so the intermediate result* $\Omega_{t_{SVRG}} = (\eta - \frac{c_{t+1}\eta}{\beta_t} - L\eta^2 - 2c_{t+1}\eta^2) > 0$, *for t from 0 to* $m - 1$. *Define the minimum value of* $\gamma_{n_{SVRG}} := \min_t \Omega_{t_{SVRG}}$. *Further let* $p_i = 0$ *where* $0 \le i < m$, $p_m = 1$, *and* T *is a multiple of* m. *Defining the output of Algorithm 1 as* x_a *we have the following upper bound:*

$$\mathbb{E}[\| \nabla f(x_a) \|^2] \le \frac{f(x^0) - f(x^*)}{T\gamma_{n_{SVRG}}},$$

where x^* *is an optimal solution to Eq. 1.*

Further, to achieve an explicit upper bound in Theorem 2 it is necessary to define the relationship between $\gamma_{n_{SVRG}}$ and n. We specify η and β following [15,16], resulting in the following theorem.

Theorem 3. *Suppose* $f \in \mathcal{F}_n$, $\eta = \frac{1}{3Ln^\alpha}$, $(0 < \alpha \le 1)$, $\beta = L/n^{\alpha/2}$, $m_{SVRG} = \lfloor\frac{9n^{\alpha/2}}{5}\rfloor$, T *is the total number of iterations which is a multiple of* m_{SVRG}, *and* $\nu_{SVRG} > 0$. *So we have* $\gamma_{n_{SVRG}} \ge \frac{\nu_{SVRG}}{18Ln^\alpha}$ *in Theorem 2. The output* x_a *of Algorithm 1 satisfies*

$$\mathbb{E}[\| \nabla f(x_a) \|^2] \le \frac{18Ln^\alpha[f(x^0) - f(x^*)]}{T\nu_{SVRG}},$$

where x^* *is an optimal solution to Eq. 1.*

3   Related Works

Many SGD-based methods have been applied to optimize functions in different domains. One approach is stochastic average gradient (SAG), which uses a memory of previous gradient values to achieve a linear convergence rate, which can be used to optimize a finite set of smooth functions in a strongly-convex domain [18]. Further, inspired from SAG and SVRG, SAGA is an incremental gradient algorithm with fast linear convergence rate that can be used in three different domains, including non-strongly convex problems [8], nonconvex but linear problems [14]. For non-smooth nonconvex finite-sum functions, proximal operators to handle nonsmoothness in the convex problem can cooperate with nonconvex optimization as ProxSGD, ProxGD, ProxSAG, ProSVRG and Prox-SAGA [16,20].

Many real-world learning scenarios such as graph deep learning models require expensive computation of the sample gradient and an unbiased estimator is usually computationally expensive or unavailable [6]. As a result, many works have proposed asymptotically biased optimizations with biased gradient estimators as an economic alternative to an unbiased version that does not converge to the minima, but to their vicinity [4–7,22]. These methods provide a good insight into the biased gradient search, however they hold under restrictive conditions which are very hard to verify for complex stochastic gradient algorithms. In this paper, we analyse the nature of biased/unbiased estimators in the optimization process on nonconvex problems, and propose a method combining the benefits of both biased and unbiased estimator to achieve a fast convergence rate.

4   Integrated SVRG with Biased Estimation

For the first challenge of SVRG, the balance of the gradient update between the full batch and stochastic estimators is fixed. We introduce a hyper-parameter λ to balance the weighting of the stochastic element with the full batch gradient to allow the algorithm to choose appropriate behaviours from stochastic, through reduced variance, to batch gradient descent. As a result, the adoption of λ in the first-order iterative algorithm can gain benefits from the stochastic estimator to speed-up computation and escape the local minimum, and reduce variance to accelerate the rates of convergence. To address the second challenge associated with the trade-off between biased/unbiased estimator, we use this hyper-parameter to choose the appropriate estimator from biased to unbiased during the whole optimization. In terms of the third challenge of SVRG associated with fixed learning rates, some research has shown that adaptive learning rates can be applied with reduced variance to provide faster convergence rates on nonconvex optimization [10,15]. We follow the work of MSVRG [15], with an adaptive learning schedule chosen to maximize between two cases of learning schedules which are based on increasing number of iterations, t, and the number of samples, n. Thus, the learning rate can be decayed by increasing the number of iterations but is also lower bounded by the data size to prevent the adaptive learning rate from decreasing too quickly.

4.1   Weighted Unbiased Estimator Analysis

We introduce a weighted SVRG shown in Algorithm 2, which can control the weight of the stochastic and batch terms by λ. Under appropriate conditions, we can achieve the following theorems for Algorithm 2.

Algorithm 2: $\text{SVRG}_{\text{unbiased}}(x^0, \{\eta_i\}_{i=0}^{T}, \{p_i\}_{i=0}^{m}, m, S)$

Input : Epoch length m, learning rate η, number of epochs $S = T/m$ where T is total number of iterations, discrete probability distribution $\{p_i\}_{i=0}^{m}$;

1 Initialize $\tilde{x}^0 = x_m^0 = x^0$ **for** s = 0 **to** S − 1 **do**

2 $\quad x_0^{s+1} = x_m^s; \ g^{s+1} = \frac{1}{n}\sum_{i=1}^{n}\nabla f_i(\tilde{x}^s)$ **for** t = 0 **to** m − 1 **do**

3 $\quad\quad$ Randomly select i_t from $\{1, ..., n\}$

$\quad\quad v_t^{s+1} = (1-\lambda)\nabla f_{i_t}(x_t^{s+1}) - \lambda(\nabla f_{i_t}(\tilde{x}^s) - g^{s+1}) \ x_{t+1}^{s+1} = x_t^{s+1} - \eta \Delta v_t^{s+1}$

4 $\quad \tilde{x}^{s+1} = \sum_{i=0}^{m}p_i x_i^{s+1}$

Output: $\tilde{x}^S$

Theorem 4. *Suppose* $f \in \mathcal{F}_n$ *have* σ*-bounded gradient. Let* $\eta_t = \eta_{\Delta_{\text{unbiased}}} = c_{\text{unbiased}}/\sqrt{\Delta + 1}$ *for* $0 \le \Delta \le T - 1$ *where* $c_{\text{unbiased}} = \sqrt{\dfrac{f(x_0) - f(x^*)}{(2\lambda^2 - 2\lambda + 1)L\sigma^2}}$ *and let* T *be a multiple of* m. *Further let* $p_m = 1$, *and* $p_i = 0$ *for* $0 \le i < m$. *Then the output* x_a *of Algorithm 2 has a bounded gradient given by*

$$\mathbb{E}[\| \nabla f(x_a)^2 \|] \le \frac{\sqrt{(2\lambda^2 - 2\lambda + 1)}}{(1 - \lambda)} \sqrt{\frac{2(f(x^0) - f(x^*))L}{T}} \sigma$$

where x^* *is the optimal solution to Eq. 1.*

In Theorem 4, we schedule a decayed learning rate $\eta_{\Delta_{\text{unbiased}}} \propto 1/\sqrt{\Delta + 1}$ [15], which can avoid knowing the total number of inner iterations across all epochs T in Algorithm 2 in advance. Compared with the upper bound in Theorem 1, we can achieve a lower upper bound in Theorem 4 if $0 \le \lambda < \frac{1}{2}$ and the optimal value of $\lambda^* = 0$.

In the second case where the learning rate η_t is fixed depending upon data size n, we can achieve the following result.

Theorem 5. *Let* $f \in \mathcal{F}_n$, *let* $c_m = 0$, $\eta_t = \eta > 0$, $\beta_t = \beta > 0$, $c_{t_{\text{unbiased}}} = c_{t+1}(1 + (1 - \lambda)\eta\beta + 2(1 - \lambda)^2\eta^2L^2) + L^3\eta^2$, *so the intermediate result* $\Omega_{t_{\text{unbiased}}} = (\eta_t - (1 - \lambda)\dfrac{c_{t+1}\eta_t}{\beta_t} - (1 - \lambda)^2L\eta_t^2 - 2(1 - \lambda)^4c_{t+1}\eta_t^2) > 0$, *for* $0 \le t \le m - 1$. *Define the minimum value of* $\gamma_{n_{\text{unbiased}}} := \min_t \Omega_{t_{\text{unbiased}}}$. *Further let* $p_i = 0$ *for* $0 \le i < m$ *and* $p_m = 1$, *and* T *is a multiple of* m. *Then the output* x_a *of Algorithm 2 has a bounded gradient given by*

$$\mathbb{E}[\| \nabla f(x_a) \|^2] \le \frac{f(x^0) - f(x^*)}{T\gamma_{n_{\text{unbiased}}}},$$

where x^* *is the optimal solution to Eq. 1.*

We use the same schedule of η and β as in Theorem 3 to determine $\gamma_{n_{\text{unbiased}}}$ in the following theorem.

Theorem 6. *Suppose* $f \in \mathcal{F}_n$, *let* $\eta = \dfrac{1}{3Ln^{a\alpha}}$ $(0 \le a \le 1$, *and* $0 < \alpha \le 1)$, $\beta = \dfrac{L}{n^{b\alpha}}$ $(b > 0)$, $m_{\text{unbiased}} = \lfloor \dfrac{3n^{(3a+b)\alpha}}{(1 - \lambda)} \rfloor$ *and* T *is the total number of iterations. Then, we can obtain the lower bound* $\gamma_{n_{\text{unbiased}}} \ge \dfrac{(1 - \lambda)v}{9n^{(2a-b)\alpha}L}$ *in Theorem 5. For the output* x_a *of Algorithm 2 we have*

$$\mathbb{E}[\| \nabla f(x_a) \|^2] \le \frac{9n^{(2a-b)\alpha}L[f(x^0) - f(x^*)]}{(1 - \lambda)Tv},$$

where x^* *is the optimal solution to Eq. 1.*

where the $\lambda \ne 0$ since the gradient in this case is not σ-bounded. As a result, compared with Theorem 3, we can achieve a lower upper bound in above theorem when $0 < \lambda < 1 - \dfrac{n^{(2a-b1)\alpha}}{2} < 1$ and the optimal value of $\lambda^* \to 0$.

4.2 Biased Estimator Analysis

In this section we theoretically analyse the performance of a biased SVRG using the same learning rate schedule with a weighted unbiased version in Algorithm 3. In the first case of the learning rate, biased SVRG can use σ-bounded gradients in Definition 2 when $0 \le \lambda \le \frac{2}{3}$.

Algorithm 3: $\text{SVRG}_{\text{biased}}(x^0, \{\eta_i\}_{i=0}^{T}, \{p_i\}_{i=0}^{m}, m, S)$

   Input : Same input parameters with Alg 1
1 Initialize $\tilde{x}^0 = x_m^0 = x^0$ for $s=0$ to $S\text{-}1$ do
2    $x_0^{s+1} = x_m^s$; $g^{s+1} = \frac{1}{n}\sum_{i=1}^{n}\nabla f_i(\tilde{x}^s)$ for $t=0$ to $m-1$ do
3   Randomly select i_t from $\{1,...,n\}$
        $v_t^{s+1} = (1-\lambda)\left(\nabla f_{i_t}(x_t^{s+1}) - \nabla f_{i_t}(\tilde{x}^s)\right) + \lambda g^{s+1}$ $x_{t+1}^{s+1} = x_t^{s+1} - \eta_\Delta v_t^{s+1}$
4    $\tilde{x}^{s+1} = \sum_{i=0}^{m} p_i x_i^{s+1}$
   Output: $\tilde{x}^S$

Proof. As the learning rate decays from 1 to T, we use Definition 2 to bound gradients v_t^{s+1} as follows:

$$
\begin{aligned}
&\mathbb{E}[\|\, v_{t^{s+1}}\|^2] \\
&= \mathbb{E}[\|\,(1-\lambda)(\nabla f_{i_t}(x_t^{s+1}) - \nabla f_{i_t}(\tilde{x}^s)) + \lambda\nabla f(\tilde{x}^s)\,\|^2] \\
&= \mathbb{E}[\|\,(1-\lambda)\nabla f_{i_t}(x_t^{s+1}) - (1-\lambda)\nabla f_{i_t}(\tilde{x}^s) + \lambda\nabla f(\tilde{x}^s)\,\|^2] \\
&\le 2(\mathbb{E}[(\|\,(1-\lambda)\nabla f_{i_t}(x_t^{s+1})\,\|^2 + \|\,(1-\lambda)\nabla f_{i_t}(\tilde{x}^s) - \lambda\nabla f(\tilde{x}^s)\,\|^2]) \\
&\le 2((1-\lambda)^2\mathbb{E}[\|\,\nabla f_{i_t}(x_t^{s+1})\,\|^2] + (1-\lambda)^2\mathbb{E}[\|\,\nabla f_{i_t}(\tilde{x}^s)\,\|^2]) \\
&\le 4(1-\lambda)^2\sigma^2,
\end{aligned}
\tag{3}
$$

where the second inequality follows from (a) the σ-bounded gradient property of f and (b) for a biased random variable ζ which has a upper bound

$$
\begin{aligned}
&\mathbb{E}[\|\,(1-\lambda)\zeta - \lambda\mathbb{E}[\zeta]\,\|^2] \\
&= \mathbb{E}[(1-\lambda)^2\,\|\,\zeta\,\|^2 - 2(1-\lambda)\lambda\zeta\mathbb{E}[\zeta] + \lambda^2\mathbb{E}^2[\zeta]] \\
&= (1-\lambda)^2\mathbb{E}[\|\,\zeta\,\|^2] - (2\lambda - 3\lambda^2)\mathbb{E}^2[\zeta] \le (1-\lambda)^2\mathbb{E}[\|\,\zeta\,\|^2],
\end{aligned}
\tag{4}
$$

where the upper bound follows from $\mathbb{E}[\|\,(1-\lambda)^2\zeta - (1-\lambda)^2\mathbb{E}[\zeta]\,\|^2] < \mathbb{E}[\|\,(1-\lambda)^2\zeta\,\|^2]$. Thus, the λ should be within the range $0 \le \lambda \le \frac{2}{3}$. We then achieve the following result.

Theorem 7. *Suppose* $f \in \mathcal{F}_n$ *has σ-bounded gradient. Let* $\eta_{t_{biased}} = \eta_\Delta = c_{biased}/\sqrt{\Delta + 1}$ *for* $0 \le \Delta \le T - 1$ *where* $c_{biased} = \sqrt{\dfrac{f(x_0) - f(x^*)}{2\lambda L \sigma^2}}$ *and let* T *be a multiple of* m. *Further let* $p_m = 1$, *and* $p_i = 0$ *for* $0 \le i < m$. *Then the output* x_a *of Algorithm 3 has a bounded gradient given by*

$$\mathbb{E}[\|\ \nabla f(x_a)^2\ \|] \le \frac{2(1 - \lambda)}{\sqrt{\lambda}} \sqrt{\frac{2(f(x^0) - f(x^*))L}{T}}\sigma$$

where x^* *is the optimal solution to Eq. 1.*

We can achieve a lower upper bound of expectation in Theorem 7 than scaled SVRG in Theorem 1 when λ satisfies the two conditions simultaneously that $0 \le \lambda \le \frac{2}{3}$ and $\frac{1}{2} < \lambda \le 1$. Consequently, the range of λ is $\frac{1}{2} < \lambda \le \frac{2}{3}$, and the optimal value of $\lambda = \lambda^* = \frac{2}{3}$.

For the second case of the learning rate, the biased version of SVRG can obtain its upper bound of expectation according to the following theorem.

Theorem 8. *Let* $f \in \mathcal{F}_n$, *let* $c_m = 0$, $\eta_t = \eta > 0$, $\beta_t = \beta > 0$, $c_{t_{biased}} = c_{t+1}(1 + \eta\beta + 2(1 - \lambda)^2\eta^2 L^2) + L^3\eta^2(1 - \lambda)^2$, *so the intermediate result* $\Omega_{t_{biased}} = (\eta_t - \dfrac{c_{t+1}\eta_t}{\beta_t} - \lambda^2 L\eta_t^2 - 2\lambda^2 c_{t+1}\eta_t^2) > 0$, *for* $0 \le t \le m - 1$. *Define the minimum value of* $\gamma_n := \min_t \Omega_{t_{biased}}$. *Further let* $p_i = 0$ *for* $0 \le i < m$ *and* $p_m = 1$, *and* T *is a multiple of* m. *Then the output* x_a *of Algorithm 3 has a bounded gradient given by*

$$\mathbb{E}[\|\ \nabla f(x_a)\ \|^2] \le \frac{f(x^0) - f(x^*)}{T\gamma_{n_{biased}}},$$

where x^* *is the optimal solution to Eq. 1.*

To determine $\gamma_{n_{biased}}$, we use same schedule of η and β from Theorems 3 and 5 and achieve the following result.

Theorem 9. *Suppose* $f \in \mathcal{F}_n$, *let* $\eta = \dfrac{1}{3Ln^{a\alpha}}$ $(0 \le a \le 1$ *and* $0 < \alpha \le 1)$, $\beta = \dfrac{L}{n^{b\alpha}}$ $(b > 0)$, $m_{biased} = \lfloor\dfrac{3n^{2a\alpha}}{2(1 - \lambda)}\rfloor$ *and* T *is the total number of iterations.*

Then, we can obtain the lower bound $\gamma_{n_{biased}} \ge \dfrac{(1 - \lambda)\lambda\nu_1}{9Ln^{(2a-b)\alpha}}$ *in Theorem 8. Then the output* x_a *of Algorithm 3 has a bounded gradient given by*

$$\mathbb{E}[\|\ \nabla f(x_a)\ \|^2] \le \frac{9Ln^{(2a-b)\alpha}[f(x^0) - f(x^*)]}{\lambda(1 - \lambda)T\nu_1},$$

where x^* *is the optimal solution to Eq. 1.*

$\lambda \ne 0$ since the gradient is not σ-bounded. In comparison to the upper bound of expectation in Theorem 3, we can achieve a lower upper bound when λ satisfies $0 < \dfrac{1 - \sqrt{1 - 4n^{(2a-b-1)\alpha}}}{2} < \lambda < \dfrac{1 + \sqrt{1 - 4n^{(2a-b-1)\alpha}}}{2} < 1$, and hence the optimal value of $\lambda^* = 0.5$.

4.3 Variance Control and Combined Biased and Unbiased Estimation

To estimate the performance of unbiased and biased estimators, we investigate the value of the upper bound for two cases of learning rate. In the first case when the learning rate decayed by iteration number, the upper bound of the biased estimator is minimized when $\lambda^* = 2/3$ in Theorem 4 and for the unbiased version is minimized when $\lambda^* = 0$ in Theorem 7. This result shows that the biased and weighted SVRG estimator can provide a tighter upper bound than unbiased SGD when the learning rate is decayed. In the second case the learning rate is fixed, the upper bound of the unbiased version is minimized when $\lambda^* \to 0$ in Theorem 5, which is lower than the biased minimum of $\lambda^* = 0.5$ in Theorem 8. When the learning rate is fixed standard SVRG is better than SGD. Therefore, it shows that unbiased and weighted SVRG is better than biased SVRG and SGD.

Consequently, these results give rise to a new optimization method, ISVRG$^+$ (Algorithm 4), which can combine biased and unbiased SVRG which controls the reduced variance so as to improve the rates of convergence. The general

---

Algorithm 4: ISVRG$^+(x^0, \{\eta_i\}_{i=0}^T, \{p_i\}_{i=0}^m, m, S)$

Input : Same input parameters with Alg 1, and learning rate
$$\eta_s = \max\{\frac{\sqrt{c_{biased}}}{ms}, \frac{1}{3Ln^{a\alpha}}\}, \lambda \to 0;$$

1   Initialize $\tilde{x}^0 = x_m^s = x^0$ for $s=0$ to $S\text{-}1$ do

2      $x_0^{s+1} = x_m^s$; $g^{s+1} = \frac{1}{n}\sum_{i=1}^n \nabla f_i(\tilde{x}^s)$ **for** $t = 0$ **to** $m-1$ **do**

3   Randomly select i_t from $\{1,...,n\}$ **if** $\eta_s = \frac{\sqrt{c_{biased}}}{ms}$ **then**

4          $\quad v_t^{s+1} = \frac{1}{3}\left(\nabla f_{i_t}(x_t^{s+1}) - \nabla f_{i_t}(\tilde{x}^s)\right) + \frac{2}{3}g^{s+1}$

5   **else if** $\eta_s = \eta = \frac{1}{3Ln^{a\alpha}}$ **then**

6          $\quad v_t^{s+1} = (1-1)\nabla f_{i_t}(x_t^{s+1}) - 1\left(\nabla f_{i_t}(\tilde{x}^s) - g^{s+1}\right)$

7        $x_{t+1}^{s+1} = x_t^{s+1} - \eta_\Delta v_t^{s+1}$

8      $\tilde{x}^{s+1} = \sum_{i=0}^m p_i x_i^{s+1}$

---

result for ISVRG$^+$ is given in the following theorem.

Theorem 10. *Let* $f \in \mathcal{F}_n$ *have* σ*-bounded gradients. Let* $\eta_t = \eta_\Delta = \max\left\{\frac{c}{\sqrt{\Delta+1}}, \frac{1}{3Ln^{a\alpha}}\right\}$ *for* Δ *from 0 to* $T-1$, $m = \lfloor 3n^{(3a+b)\alpha}\rfloor$, *and* $c = \sqrt{\frac{3f(x^0) - f(x^*)}{4L\sigma^2}}$. *Further let* T *is a multiple of* m, $p_m = 1$ *and* $p_i = 0$ *for* $0 \le i < m$. *Then, the output* x_a *of Algorithm 4 satisfies*

$$\mathbb{E}[\|\nabla f(x_a)\|^2] \le \tilde{v}\min \ \{\sqrt{3}\sqrt{\frac{(f(x^0) - f(x^*))L}{T}}\sigma, \frac{9n^{(2a-b)\alpha}L[f(x^0) - f(x^*)]}{Tv_2}\},$$

where x^* *is an optimal solution to Eq. 1,* $0 \le a \le 1$, $0 < \alpha \le 1$ *and* $b > 0$. $\tilde{v}$, v_2 *are universal constants.*

We specify the optimal value of parameters including a, b and α from Theorem 10, which give rise to the following key result of the paper (Corollary 1). In this corollary, the IFO complexity of ISVRG$^+$ is the minima between $1/\varepsilon^2$ which is equal to the IFO complexity of SGD method [9,15] and $n^{1/5}/\varepsilon$ where the optimal value of a, b and α can be found by two conditions: (a) the upper bound of ISVRG$^+$ is lower than that of scaled standard SVRG in Theorem 3 as $1 < n^{(2a-b)\alpha} \leq n^\alpha$, if $\lambda = \lambda^* = 0$; (b) $0 < \alpha = 1/(3a+b) \leq 1$ when $0 \leq a \leq 1$ and $b > 0$. Thus, we can achieve lowest upper bound when $a = 1$, $b = 2$ and $\alpha = 1/5$. Therefore its worst case IFO complexity is bounded by that of SGD.

Corollary 1. *Suppose* $f \in \mathcal{F}_n$, *the IFO complexity of Algorithm 4 (with parameters from Theorem 10) achieves an ε-accurate solution that is $\mathcal{O}(\min\{1/\varepsilon^2, n^{1/5}/\varepsilon\})$, where the number of IFO calls is minimized when $a = 1$, $b = 2$ and $\alpha = 1/5$.*

The hyper-parameter λ works with the hybrid adaptive learning rate to control the variance and to balance the trade-off between bias/unbiased estimation. For the case where the first term of the learning rate is larger than second term when t is small, larger λ with the biased estimator can reduce the variance and provide a lower upper bound than the unbiased version, accelerating the convergence in early iterations. On the other hand, when the second term becomes larger later in optimization, the value of $\lambda \to 0$ with the unbiased estimator allows the gradient to behave more stochastically. Higher variance will help gradients escape from local minimal. Meanwhile, the estimator is unbiased, which guarantees convergence. When the learning rate is decayed by increasing iteration, a biased estimation with more reduced variance will converge faster, and when the learning rate is fixed an unbiased estimation with stochastic gradient will be better.[1]

5 Application

To experimentally confirm the theoretical results and insights, we train three common deep learning topologies, including LeNet[2] and VGG-16 [19] on three datasets including MNIST, CIFAR-10 and tiny ImageNet[3]. Our method was implemented using Caffe[4]. We use SVRG as our baseline and we choose MSVRG method to compare with ISVRG$^+$; MSVRG is a leading VR scheme based on stochastic methods which can perform better than SGD and GD for nonconvex

---

[1] Proof details are at https://github.com/Bellabbbb/appendix.

[2] We choose two types of LeNet, including LeNet-300-100 which has two fully connected layers as hidden layers with 300 and 100 neurons respectively, and LeNet-5 which has two convolutional layers and two fully connected layers.

[3] Tiny ImageNet is a subset of ImageNet challenge (2012 ILSVRC [17]), which contains 500 categories. Each category has 600 training images, 200 validation images and 200 test images, each image is re-sized to 96×96 pixels.

[4] Caffe is a deep learning framework. Source code can be download: http://caffe.berkeleyvision.org.

optimization [11,15]. In our experiments the maximal value of learning rate was chosen as $\eta_t = \max\{\eta_0/\Delta, 1/(3Ln^{1/5})\}$, where the Δ from 1 to Sm and $L = 1, 10, 100$. To evaluate the performance of ISVRG$^+$, we choose the cross entropy using the softmax log loss function as the result of test error and mean squared error (MSE) to evaluate the quality of the neural networks.

In Fig. 1, we compared the performance of SGD, MSVRG and ISVRG$^+$. For SGD we set-up $\lambda = 0$ and $\eta = \eta_0/(\Delta)$ in Algorithm 2 and for MSVRG $\lambda = 0.5$ and $\eta_t = \max\{\eta_0/\Delta, 1/(3Ln^{\frac{1}{5}})\}$ in Algorithm 2. In Fig. 1, the blue lines show the SGD as baseline. The red lines show the test loss and error of ISVRG$^+$ which are all lower than the other methods. Particularly, both test error and loss of ISVRG$^+$ drop down dramatically in later epochs since the adaptive learning rate starts to depend on the data size n rather than Δ, and correspondingly λ changes from 2/3 to 0 meaning that the variance of gradients becomes higher with the unbiased estimator and can help points escape from local minima.

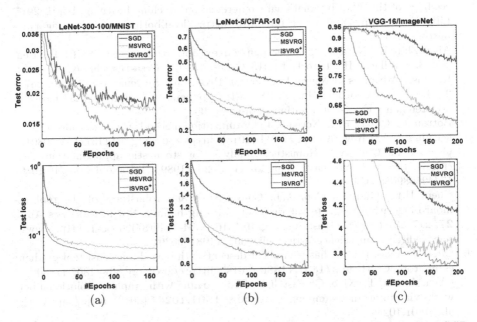

Fig. 1. Comparison of rates of convergence in three approaches, including SGD, MSVRG and ISVRG$^+$ via test loss/error. Compared with SGD and MSVRG, we can see that ISVRG$^+$ can converge faster in early epochs in both test error/loss on all three problems, and the results significantly decrease after several epochs when the learning rate changes from decaying to fixed. Thus ISVRG$^+$ has the lowest test error/loss, which can efficiently accelerate the rates of convergence.

6   Discussion

In this paper, we proposed a VR-based optimization ISVRG$^+$ for nonconvex problems. We theoretically determined that a hyper-parameter λ working with a adaptive learning rate in each iteration can control the reduced variance of SVRG and balance the trade-off between biased/unbiased estimator. Moreover, to verify our theoretical results, we experiment on different datasets on deep learning models to estimate the range of λ and compare these with other leading results. Both theoretical and experimental results show that ISVRG$^+$ can efficiently accelerate rates of convergence and is faster than SVRG and SGD for nonconvex optimization.

References

1. Agarwal, A., Bottou, L.: A lower bound for the optimization of finite sums. In: Proceedings of the 32nd International Conference on Machine Learning, ICML 2015, Lille, France, pp. 78–86, 6–11 July 2015. http://leon.bottou.org/papers/agarwal-bottou-2015
2. Allen-Zhu, Z.: Natasha 2: faster non-convex optimization than SGD. In: Bengio, S., Wallach, H., Larochelle, H., Grauman, K., Cesa-Bianchi, N., Garnett, R. (eds.) Advances in Neural Information Processing Systems, vol. 31, pp. 2675–2686. Curran Associates, Inc. (2018). http://papers.nips.cc/paper/7533-natasha-2-faster-non-convex-optimization-than-sgd.pdf
3. Bottou, L., Curtis, F.E., Nocedal, J.: Optimization methods for large-scale machine learning. SIAM Rev. 60(2), 223–311 (2018). https://doi.org/10.1137/16M1080173
4. Chen, H.F., Gao, A.J.: Robustness analysis for stochastic approximation algorithms. Stochast. Stochast. Rep. 26(1), 3–20 (1989). https://doi.org/10.1080/17442508908833545
5. Chen, H.F., Guo, L., Gao, A.J.: Convergence and robustness of the robbins-monro algorithm truncated at randomly varying bounds. Stoch. Processes Appl. 27, 217–231 (1987). https://doi.org/10.1016/0304-4149(87)90039-1, http://www.sciencedirect.com/science/article/pii/0304414987900391
6. Chen, J., Luss, R.: Stochastic gradient descent with biased but consistent gradient estimators. CoRR abs/1807.11880 (2018). http://arxiv.org/abs/1807.11880
7. Chen, J., Ma, T., Xiao, C.: FastGCN: Fast learning with graph convolutional networks via importance sampling. CoRR abs/1801.10247 (2018). http://arxiv.org/abs/1801.10247
8. Defazio, A., Bach, F.R., Lacoste-Julien, S.: SAGA: A fast incremental gradient method with support for non-strongly convex composite objectives. CoRR abs/1407.0202 (2014). http://arxiv.org/abs/1407.0202
9. Ghadimi, S., Lan, G.: Accelerated gradient methods for nonconvex nonlinear and stochastic programming. Math. Program. 156(1–2), 59–99 (2016). https://doi.org/10.1007/s10107-015-0871-8
10. Goodfellow, I., Bengio, Y., Courville, A.: Deep Learning. The MIT Press, Cambridge (2016)
11. Reddi, S.J., Sra, S., Poczos, B., Smola, A.J.: Proximal stochastic methods for non-smooth nonconvex finite-sum optimization. In: Lee, D.D., Sugiyama, M., Luxburg, U.V., Guyon, I., Garnett, R. (eds.) Advances in Neural Information Processing Systems, vol. 29, pp. 1145–1153. Curran Associates, Inc. (2016)

12. Johnson, R., Zhang, T.: Accelerating stochastic gradient descent using predictive variance reduction. In: Burges, C.J.C., Bottou, L., Welling, M., Ghahramani, Z., Weinberger, K.Q. (eds.) Advances in Neural Information Processing Systems, vol. 26, pp. 315–323. Curran Associates, Inc. (2013)
13. Liang, P., Bach, F.R., Bouchard, G., Jordan, M.I.: Asymptotically optimal regularization in smooth parametric models. In: Advances in Neural Information Processing Systems 22: 23rd Annual Conference on Neural Information Processing Systems 2009. Proceedings of a meeting held 7–10 December 2009, Vancouver, British Columbia, Canada, pp. 1132–1140 (2009). http://papers.nips.cc/paper/3693-asymptotically-optimal-regularization-in-smooth-parametric-models
14. Reddi, S.J., Sra, S., Póczos, B., Smola, A.: Fast incremental method for smooth nonconvex optimization. In: 2016 IEEE 55th Conference on Decision and Control (CDC), pp. 1971–1977, December 2016. https://doi.org/10.1109/CDC.2016.7798553
15. Reddi, S.J., Hefny, A., Sra, S., Póczós, B., Smola, A.: Stochastic variance reduction for nonconvex optimization. In: Proceedings of the 33rd International Conference on International Conference on Machine Learning ICML 2016, JMLR.org, vol. 48, pp. 314–323 (2016). http://dl.acm.org/citation.cfm?id=3045390.3045425
16. Reddi, S.J., Sra, S., Póczos, B., Smola, A.J.: Fast stochastic methods for nonsmooth nonconvex optimization. CoRR **abs/1605.06900** (2016). http://arxiv.org/abs/1605.06900
17. Russakovsky, O., et al.: ImageNet large scale visual recognition challenge. Int. J. Comput. Vis. (IJCV) **115**(3), 211–252 (2015). https://doi.org/10.1007/s11263-015-0816-y
18. Schmidt, M.W., Roux, N.L., Bach, F.R.: Minimizing finite sums with the stochastic average gradient. CoRR **abs/1309.2388** (2013). http://dblp.uni-trier.de/db/journals/corr/corr1309.html#SchmidtRB13
19. Simonyan, K., Zisserman, A.: Very deep convolutional networks for large-scale image recognition. CoRR **abs/1409.1556** (2014). http://arxiv.org/abs/1409.1556
20. Sra, S.: Scalable nonconvex inexact proximal splitting. In: Advances in Neural Information Processing Systems, pp. 539–547 (2012)
21. Strongin, R.G., Sergeyev, Y.D.: Global Optimization with Non-Convex Constraints - Sequential and Parallel Algorithms (Nonconvex Optimization and Its Applications), Vol. 45. Springer, Heidelberg (2000). https://doi.org/10.1007/978-1-4615-4677-1
22. Tadić, V.B., Doucet, A.: Asymptotic bias of stochastic gradient search. Ann. Appl. Probab. **27**(6), 3255–3304 (2017). https://doi.org/10.1214/16-AAP1272

Convex Hull Approximation of Nearly Optimal Lasso Solutions

Satoshi Hara[1(✉)] and Takanori Maehara[2]

[1] Osaka University, Osaka, Japan
satohara@ar.sanken.osaka-u.ac.jp
[2] RIKEN AIP, Tokyo, Japan
takanori.maehara@riken.jp

Abstract. In an ordinary feature selection procedure, a set of important features is obtained by solving an optimization problem such as the Lasso regression problem, and we expect that the obtained features explain the data well. In this study, instead of the single optimal solution, we consider finding a set of diverse yet nearly optimal solutions. To this end, we formulate the problem as finding a small number of solutions such that the convex hull of these solutions approximates the set of nearly optimal solutions. The proposed algorithm consists of two steps: First, we randomly sample the extreme points of the set of nearly optimal solutions. Then, we select a small number of points using a greedy algorithm. The experimental results indicate that the proposed algorithm can approximate the solution set well. The results also indicate that we can obtain Lasso solutions with a large diversity.

Keywords: Feature selection · Lasso · Diversity

1 Introduction

Background and Motivation. *Feature selection* is a procedure for finding a small set of relevant features from a dataset. It simplifies the model to make them easier to understand, and enhances the generalization performance; thus it plays an important role in data mining and machine learning [11].

One of the most commonly used feature selection methods is the *Lasso regression* [7,19]. Suppose that we have n observations of p dimensional vectors $x_1, \ldots, x_n \in \mathbb{R}^p$, and the corresponding responses $y_1, \ldots, y_n \in \mathbb{R}$. Then, the Lasso regression seeks a feature vector $\beta^* \in \mathbb{R}^p$ by minimizing the ℓ_1-penalized squared loss function

$$L(\beta) = \frac{1}{2n}\|X\beta - y\|_2^2 + \lambda\|\beta\|_1, \tag{1}$$

where $X = [x_1; \cdots; x_n] \in \mathbb{R}^{n \times p}$ and $y = [y_1; \cdots; y_n] \in \mathbb{R}^n$. Here, $\|\cdot\|_p$ denotes the ℓ_p-norm defined by $\|\beta\|_p = (\sum_j |\beta_j|^p)^{1/p}$. Since the ℓ_1 penalty induces sparsity of the solution, we may obtain a set of features from the support of the solution.

© Springer Nature Switzerland AG 2019
A. C. Nayak and A. Sharma (Eds.): PRICAI 2019, LNAI 11671, pp. 350–363, 2019.
https://doi.org/10.1007/978-3-030-29911-8_27

The Lasso regression has many desirable properties; in particular, the sparsity of the solution helps users to understand which features are important for their tasks. Hence, they are considered to be one of the most basic approaches for the cases, e.g., when models are used to support user decision making where the sparsity allows users to check whether or not the models are reliable; and, when users are interested in finding interesting mechanisms underlying the data where the sparsity enables users to identify important features and get insights of the data [11].

To further strengthen those advantages of the Lasso, Hara and Maehara [13] proposed enumerating all (essentially different) the Lasso solutions in their increasing order of the objective values. With the enumeration, one can find more reliable models from the enumerated solutions, or one can gain more insights of the data [12,13].

In this study, we aim at finding *diverse* solutions instead of the exhaustive enumeration. Hara and Maehara [13] have observed that in real-world applications, there are too many nearly optimal solutions to enumerate them exhaustively. Typically, if there are some highly correlated features, the enumeration algorithm outputs all their combinations as nearly optimal solutions; thus, there are exponentially many nearly optimal solutions. Obviously, checking all those similar solutions is too exhausting for the users, which makes the existing enumeration method less practical. To overcome this practical limitation, we consider finding diverse solutions as the representative of the nearly optimal solutions, which enables users to check "overview" of the solutions.

Contribution. In this study, we propose a novel formulation to find diverse yet nearly optimal Lasso solutions. Instead of the previous enumeration approach, we directly work on the set of nearly optimal solutions, defined by

$$B(\nu) = \{\beta \in \mathbb{R}^p : L(\beta) \leq \nu\} \tag{2}$$

where $\nu \in \mathbb{R}$ is a threshold slightly greater than the optimal objective value $\nu^* = L(\beta^*)$ of the Lasso regression.

We summarize $B(\nu)$ by a small number of points $Q \subset B(\nu)$ in the sense that the convex hull of Q approximates $B(\nu)$. We call this approach *convex hull approximation*. Section 3 describes the mathematical formulation of our approach. We illustrate this approach in the following example with Fig. 1.

Example 1. Let us consider the two-dimensional Lasso regression problem with the following loss function

$$L(\beta_1, \beta_2) = \frac{1}{2} \left\| \begin{bmatrix} 1 & 1 \\ 1 & 1+\epsilon \end{bmatrix} \begin{bmatrix} \beta_1 \\ \beta_2 \end{bmatrix} - \begin{bmatrix} 1 \\ 1 \end{bmatrix} \right\|_2^2 + \left\| \begin{bmatrix} \beta_1 \\ \beta_2 \end{bmatrix} \right\|_1 \tag{3}$$

where ϵ is a sufficiently small parameter, e.g., $\epsilon = 1/40$. Then, the optimal value ν^* is approximately $3/4$, and the corresponding optimal solution β^* is approximately $(0, 1/2)$, as shown in the green point in Fig. 1.

Now, we consider the nearly optimal solution set $B(\nu)$ for the threshold $\nu = \nu^* + \epsilon$. The boundary of this set is illustrated in the dashed line in Fig. 1.

Even if $\nu - \nu^*$ is very small, since the observations X is highly correlated, $B(\nu)$ contains essentially different solution, e.g., $\beta' = (1/2, 0)$.

We approximate $B(\nu)$ by the convex hull of a few finite points $Q \subset B(\nu)$. In this case, by taking the corners of $B(\nu)$, we can approximate this set well by the four points as shown by the blue line in Fig. 1. We note that the diversity of Q is implicitly enforced because diverse Q is desirable for approximating $B(\nu)$; we therefore do not need to add the diversity constraint such as DPP [15] explicitly.

This problem will be solved numerically in Sect. 5.   □

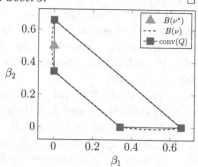

We propose an algorithm to construct a good convex hull approximation of $B(\nu)$. The algorithm consists of two steps. First, it samples sufficiently many extreme points of $B(\nu)$ by solving Lasso regressions multiple times. Second, we select a small subset Q from the sampled points to yield a compact summarization. The detailed description of our algorithm is given in Sect. 4.

Fig. 1. Illustration of our approach. The triangle shows the optimal solution $B(\nu^*) = \{\beta^*\}$, the dashed line shows the boundary of the nearly optimal solutions $B(\nu)$, and the squares with the solid line show the convex hull approximation $\mathrm{conv}(Q)$ of $B(\nu)$. (Color figure online)

We conducted numerical experiments to evaluate the effectiveness of the proposed method. Specifically, we evaluated three aspects of the method, namely, the approximation performance, computational efficiency, and the diversity of the found solutions. The results are shown in Sect. 5.

For simplicity, we describe only the method for Lasso regression in the manuscript; however it can be easily adopted to the other models such as the sparse logistic regression [16] and elastic-net [21].

2   Preliminaries

A set $C \subset \mathbb{R}^p$ is *convex* if for any $\beta_1, \beta_2 \in C$ and $\alpha \in [0, 1]$, $(1 - \alpha)\beta_1 + \alpha\beta_2 \in C$. For a set $P \subset \mathbb{R}^p$, its *convex hull*, $\mathrm{conv}(P)$, is the smallest convex set containing P. Let C be a convex set. A point $\beta \in C$ is an *extreme point* of C if $\beta = (1 - \alpha)\beta_1 + \alpha\beta_2$ for some $\beta_1, \beta_2 \in C$ and $\alpha \in (0, 1)$ implies $\beta = \beta_1 = \beta_2$. The set of extreme points of C is denoted by $\mathrm{ext}(C)$.

The Klein–Milman theorem shows the fundamental relation between the extreme points and the convex hull.

Theorem 1 (Klein–Milman Theorem; see Barvinok [2]). *Let C be a compact convex set. Then* $\mathrm{conv}(\mathrm{ext}(C)) = C$.   □

For two sets $C, C' \subset \mathbb{R}^p$, the *Hausdorff distance* between these sets is defined by

$$d(C, C') = \max \left\{ \sup_{\beta \in C} \inf_{\beta' \in C'} \|\beta - \beta'\|_2, \sup_{\beta' \in C'} \inf_{\beta \in C} \|\beta - \beta'\|_2 \right\}. \tag{4}$$

The Hausdorff distance forms a metric on the non-empty compact sets. The computation of Hausdorff distance is NP-hard in general [14].

A function $L : \mathbb{R}^p \to \mathbb{R}$ is convex if the epigraph $\mathrm{Epi}(L) = \{(\beta, \nu) \in \mathbb{R}^p \times \mathbb{R} : \nu \geq L(\beta)\}$ is convex. For a convex function L, the level set $B(\nu) = \{\beta \in \mathbb{R}^p : L(\beta) \leq \nu\}$ is convex for all $\nu \in \mathbb{R}$.

3 Formulation

In this section, we formulate our convex hull approximation problem mathematically. We assume that X has no zero column (otherwise, we can remove the zero column and the corresponding feature from the model).

Recall that the Lasso loss function $L : \mathbb{R}^p \to \mathbb{R}$ in (1) is convex; therefore, the set of nearly optimal solutions $B(\nu)$ in (2) forms a closed convex set. Moreover, since X has no zero column, $B(\nu)$ is compact.

Our goal is to summarize $B(\nu)$. By the Klein–Milman theorem (Theorem 1), $B(\nu)$ can be reconstructed from the extreme points of $B(\nu)$ as $B(\nu) = \mathrm{conv}(\mathrm{ext}(B(\nu)))$; therefore, it is natural to output the extreme points $\mathrm{ext}(B(\nu))$ as a summary of $B(\nu)$. If $\nu = \nu^*$, this approach corresponds to enumerating the vertices of $B(\nu^*)$, which forms a polyhedron [20]; therefore, we can use the existing algorithm to enumerate the vertices of a polyhedron developed in Computational Geometry [9] as in Pantazis et al. [18]. However, if $\nu > \nu^*$, $B(\nu)$ has a piecewise smooth boundary, as shown in Fig. 1; therefore, there are continuously many extreme points of $B(\nu)$, which cannot be enumerated.[1]

Therefore, we select a finite number of points $Q \subset \mathrm{ext}(B(\nu))$ as a "representative" of the extreme points such that $\mathrm{conv}(Q)$ well approximates $B(\nu)$. We measure the quality of the approximation by the Hausdorff distance (4).

To summarize the above discussion, we pose the following problem.

Problem 1. We are given a loss function $L : \mathbb{R}^p \to \mathbb{R}$ and a threshold $\nu \in \mathbb{R}$. Let $B(\nu) = \{\beta \in \mathbb{R}^p : L(\beta) \leq \nu\}$. Find a point set $Q \subset B(\nu)$ such that (1) $d(\mathrm{conv}(Q), B(\nu))$ is small, and (2) $|Q|$ is small.

The problem of approximating a convex set by a polyhedron has a long history in convex geometry (see Bronstein [5] for a recent survey). Asymptotically, for any compact convex set with a smooth boundary, the required number of points to obtain an ϵ approximation is $\Theta(\sqrt{p}/\epsilon^{(p-1)/2})$ [6,10]. Therefore, in the worst case, we may need exponentially many points to have a reasonable approximation.

On the other hand, if we focus on the non-asymptotic ϵ, we have a chance to obtain a simple representation. One intuitive situation is that the polytope $B(\nu^*)$ has a small number of vertices, as in Fig. 1. In such a case, by taking the vertices as Q, we can obtain an $O(\epsilon)$ approximation for $B(\nu)$ when $\nu = \nu^* + O(\epsilon)$.

Therefore, below, we assume that $B(\nu)$ admits a small number of representatives and construct an algorithm to find such representatives.

---

[1] Pantazis et al. [18] also consider the near optimal solutions. However, they focused only on the subset of $B(\nu)$ spanned by the support of the Lasso global solution. We do not take this approach since it cannot handle a global structure of $B(\nu)$.

4   Algorithm

In this section, we propose a method to compute a convex hull approximation conv(Q) of $B(\nu)$.

Since conv(Q) $\subseteq B(\nu)$ and the sets are compact, the Hausdorff distance between conv(Q) and $B(\nu)$ is given by

$$d(\text{conv}(Q), B(\nu)) = \max_{\beta \in B(\nu)} \min_{\beta' \in \text{conv}(Q)} \|\beta - \beta'\|_2. \qquad (5)$$

A natural approach is to minimize this quantity by a greedy algorithm that successively selects the maximizer $\beta \in B(\nu)$ of (5) and then adds it to Q. However, this approach is impractical, because the optimization problem (5) is a convex *maximization* problem.[2]

To overcome this difficulty, we use a random sampling approximation for $B(\nu)$. We first sample sufficiently many points S from ext($B(\nu)$) and then regard conv(S) as an approximation of $B(\nu)$. Once this approximation is constructed, the maximum in (5) can be obtained by a simple linear search. Therefore, this reduces our problem to a simple subset selection problem.

The overall procedure of our algorithm is shown in Algorithm 1. It consists of two steps: random sampling step and subset selection step. Below, we describe each step.

4.1   Sampling Extreme Points (Algorithm 2)

Figure 1 suggests that selecting corner points of $B(\nu)$ as Q is desirable to obtain a good approximation of $B(\nu)$. Here, to obtain a good candidate of Q, we consider a sampling algorithm that samples the corner points of $B(\nu)$.

First, we select a uniformly random direction $d \in \mathbb{R}^p$. Then, we find the extreme point $\beta \in B(\nu)$ by solving the following problem

$$\max\{d^\top \beta : \beta \in B(\nu)\}. \qquad (6)$$

We solve this problem by using the Lagrange dual with binary search as follows. With the Lagrange duality, we obtain the following equivalent problem

$$\min_{\tau \geq 0} D(\tau|d) := \max_{\beta} \left(d^\top \beta - \tau(L(\beta) - \nu)\right). \qquad (7)$$

Since the optimal solution $\beta(d)$ of (6) satisfies $L(\beta(d)) = \nu$, we seek τ by using a binary search[3] so that $L(\beta(d)) = \nu$. It should be noted that the proposed sampling algorithm can be completely parallelized.

---

[2] In our preliminary study, we implemented the projected gradient method to find the farthest point $\beta \in B(\nu)$. However, it was slow, and often converged to poor local maximal solutions.

[3] Since we have no upper bound of the search range, we actually use the exponential search that successively doubles the search range [3].

Properties of Sampling. The solution to the problem (6) tends to be sparse because of the ℓ_1 term in $L(\beta)$, which indicates that we can sample a corner point of $B(\nu)$ in the direction of d, such as the ones in Fig. 1. More precisely, the proposed algorithm samples each extreme point with probability proportional to the volume of the normal cone of each point. Because the corner points have positive volumes, the algorithm samples corner points with high probabilities.

Algorithm 1. Proposed algorithm

1: Sample sufficiently many points $S \subset B(\nu)$ by Algorithm 2.
2: Select a few points $Q \subseteq S$ by Algorithm 3.

Algorithm 2. Sampling points

1: $S = \emptyset$
2: **for** $j = 1, 2, \ldots, M$ **do**
3:     Draw $d \sim \mathcal{N}(0, I)$
4:     Solve (6) to obtain an extreme point $\beta(d)$ and add it to S
5: **end for**
6: Return S

4.2   Greedy Subset Selection (Algorithm 3)

Next, we select a small subset $Q \subseteq S$ from the sampled points $S \subset \mathbb{R}^p$ that do not lose the approximation quality.

We use the farthest point selection method, proposed in Blum *et al.* [4].[4] In this procedure, we start from any point $\beta_1 \in S$. Then, we iteratively select the point $\beta_j \in S$ by solving the sample-approximated version of (5), i.e., the farthest point from the convex hull is taken as

$$\beta_j \in \operatorname*{argmax}_{\beta \in S} \min_{\beta' \in \mathrm{conv}(\{\beta_1, \ldots, \beta_{j-1}\})} \|\beta - \beta'\|_2. \tag{8}$$

This procedure has the following theoretical guarantee.

Theorem 2 (Blum *et al.* [4]). *Let $S \subset \mathbb{R}^p$ be a finite set enclosed in the unit ball. Suppose that there exists a finite set $Q^* \subset S$ of size k^* such that $d(\mathrm{conv}(Q^*), \mathrm{conv}(S)) \leq \epsilon$. Then, the greedy algorithm finds a set $Q \subset S$ of size $k^*/\epsilon^{2/3}$ with $d(\mathrm{conv}(Q), \mathrm{conv}(S)) = O(\epsilon^{1/3})$.* □

Thus, if the number of samples $|S|$ are sufficiently large such that $d(\mathrm{conv}(S), B(\nu)) \leq \epsilon$, the algorithm finds a convex hull approximation with $O(\epsilon^{1/3})$ error.

Below, we describe how to implement this procedure. First, the distance from β to the convex hull of $\beta_1, \ldots, \beta_k$ is computed by solving the following problem:

$$\min_{\alpha} \|\beta - \textstyle\sum_j \alpha_j \beta_j\|^2 \text{ s.t. } \textstyle\sum_j \alpha_j = 1, \ \alpha_j \geq 0. \tag{9}$$

---

[4] Blum *et al.* [4] called this procedure *Greedy Clustering*.

Algorithm 3. Select points

1: Select $\beta_1 \in S$ arbitrary and let $Q = \{\beta_1\}$
2: Initialize a heap data structure H by $H[\beta] \leftarrow d(\beta, Q)$ for all $\beta \in S \setminus Q$
3: **while** $|Q| < K$ **do**
4:     Let $\beta \in H$ be the point that has the largest $H[\beta]$
5:     Update $H[\beta] \leftarrow d(\beta, Q)$
6:     **if** $H[\beta]$ is still the largest point **then**
7:         Add β to Q and remove β from the heap
8:     **end if**
9: **end while**
10: Output Q

This problem is a convex quadratic programming problem, which can be solved efficiently by using the interior point method [1].

To implement the greedy algorithm, we have to evaluate the distance from each point to the current convex hull. However, this procedure can be expensive when $|S|$ is large as we need to solve the problem (9) many times. For efficient computation, we need to avoid redundant distance evaluations.

We observe that, if we add a new point β_j to the current convex hull, the distances from other points to the convex hull decrease monotonically. Therefore, we can use the *lazy update technique* [17] to accelerate the procedure as follows.

We maintain the points S by a heap data structure whose keys are the upper bounds of the distance to the convex hull. First, we select an arbitrary point β_1, and then initialize the key of $\beta \in S$ by $d(\beta_1, \beta)$. For each step, we select the point $\beta'_j \in S$ from the heap such that β'_j has the largest distance upper bound. Then, we recompute the distance $d(\beta'_j, \text{conv}(Q))$ by solving the quadratic program (9) and update the key of β'_j. If it still has the largest distance upper bound, it is the farthest point; therefore, we select β'_j as the j-th point β_j. Otherwise, we repeat this procedure until we find the farthest point. See Algorithm 3 for the detail.

5   Experiments

We evaluate the three aspects of the proposed algorithm, namely, the approximation performance, computational efficiency, and the diversity of the found solutions. First, we visualize the results of the algorithm by using a low dimensional synthetic data (Sect. 5.1). Then, we evaluate the approximation performance and computational efficiency by using a larger dimensional synthetic data (Sects. 5.2 and 5.3). Finally, we evaluate the diversity of the obtained solutions by using a real-world dataset (Sect. 5.4).

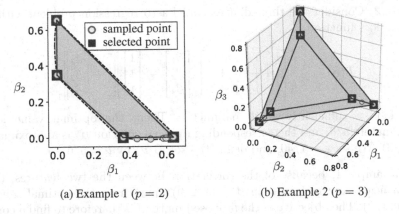

(a) Example 1 ($p = 2$)   (b) Example 2 ($p = 3$)

Fig. 2. Visual demonstrations of the proposed method in low-dimensions - (a) Result for Example 1, where $B(\nu)$ is indicated by the shaded regions, (b) Results for Example 2.

Sample Approximation of Hausdorff Distance for Evaluation. We evaluate the approximation performance by the Hausdorff distance between the obtained convex hull and $B(\nu)$. However, the exact Hausdorff distance cannot be computed since it requires solving a convex maximization problem. We therefore adopt the sample approximation of Hausdorff distance, which is derived as follows:

1. Sample M' extreme points Q^* by using Algorithm 2.
2. Define the sample approximation of $B(\nu)$ by the convex hull $\mathrm{conv}(Q^*)$.
3. Measure the Hausdorff distance $d(\mathrm{conv}(Q), \mathrm{conv}(Q^*))$ as an approximation of $d(\mathrm{conv}(Q), B(\nu))$.

Implementations. The codes were implemented in Python 3.6.[5] In Algorithm 2, to solve the problem (7), we used `enet_coordinate_descent_gram` function in `scikit-learn`. In Algorithm 3, we selected the first point $\beta_1 \in S$ as $\beta_1 = \mathrm{argmax}_{\beta \in S} \|\beta - \beta^*\|_2$. To compute the projection (9), we used `CVXOPT` library. The experiments were conducted on a system with an Intel Xeon E5-1650 3.6 GHz CPU and 64 GB RAM, running 64-bit Ubuntu 16.04.

5.1 Visual Demonstration

For visual demonstration, we consider two examples: Example 1 in Sect. 1 and Example 2 defined below.

---

[5] A sample code can be found in https://github.com/sato9hara/LassoHull.

Example 2. Consider the three-dimensional Lasso regression problem with the following loss function

$$L(\beta) = \frac{1}{2} \left\| \begin{bmatrix} 1 & 1 & 1 \\ 1 & 1+\epsilon & 1 \\ 1 & 1 & 1+2\epsilon \end{bmatrix} \begin{bmatrix} \beta_1 \\ \beta_2 \\ \beta_3 \end{bmatrix} - \begin{bmatrix} 1 \\ 1 \\ 1 \end{bmatrix} \right\|_2^2 + \left\| \begin{bmatrix} \beta_1 \\ \beta_2 \\ \beta_3 \end{bmatrix} \right\|_1 \tag{10}$$

where ϵ is a sufficiently small parameter. Then, the optimal value ν^* is approximately $5/6$, and the corresponding optimal solution β^* is approximately $(0, 0, 2/3)$. We set $\epsilon = 1/40$, and define the set $B(\nu)$ by $\nu = 5/6 + \epsilon$.

In Example 1, because of the correlation between the two features, there exists a nearly optimal solution $\beta = (1/2, 0)$ apart from the optimal solution $\beta^* = (0, 1/2)$. The objective of the proposed method is therefore to find a convex hull that covers these solutions. Similarly, in Example 2, three features are highly correlated. The objective is to find a convex hull that covers nearly optimal solutions such as $\beta = (2/3, 0, 0)$, $(0, 2/3, 0)$, and $(0, 0, 2/3)$.

Figure 2 shows the results of the proposed method for the examples. Here, we set the number of samples M in Algorithm 2 to be 50, and the number of greedy point selection $K = |Q|$ in Algorithm 3 to be four and six, respectively. Figures 2(a) and (b) show that the proposed method successfully approximated $B(\nu)$ by using a few points. Indeed, as shown in Fig. 3, the approximation errors converged to almost zeros indicating that $B(\nu)$ is well-approximated with convex hulls.

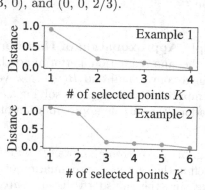

Fig. 3. Approximation errors of $B(\nu)$, measured by the Hausdorff distance ($M' = 1,000$).

5.2 Approximation Performance

We now turn to exhaustive experiments to verify the performance of the proposed algorithm in general settings. Specifically, we show that the proposed algorithm can approximate $B(\nu)$ well, even in higher dimensions.

We generate higher dimensional data by

$$x \sim \mathcal{N}(0_p, \Sigma), \quad y = x^\top \beta + \varepsilon, \quad \varepsilon \sim \mathcal{N}(0, 0.01), \tag{11}$$

where $\Sigma_{ij} = \exp(-0.1|i - j|)$, and $\beta_i = 10/p$ if $\mod(i - 1, 10) = 0$ and $\beta_i = 0$ otherwise. Because of the correlations induced by Σ, the features in x are highly correlated, which indicates that there may exist several nearly optimal β.

We set the number of observations n to be $p = 2n$, and the regularization parameter λ to be 0.1. We also define the set $B(\nu)$ by setting $\nu = 1.01 L(\beta^*)$.

Figure 4 is the result for $p = 100$. The figure shows that the proposed algorithm can approximate $B(\nu)$ well. In the figure, there are two important observations. First, as the number of samplings M increases, the Hausdorff distance decreases, indicating that the approximation performance improves. This result is intuitive in that a many greater number of candidate points lead to a better approximation.

Second, the choice of the number of samplings M is not that fatal in practice. The result shows that the difference between the Hausdorff distances for $M = 200$ and for $M = 10,000$

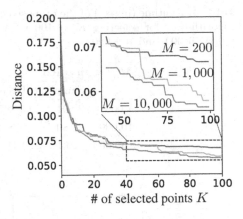

Fig. 4. # of selected points K vs. Hausdorff distance ($M' = 100,000$)

is subtle. It also shows that the Hausdorff distance for $M = 1,000$ and for $M = 10,000$ are almost identical for larger K. This indicates that we do not have to sample many points in practice.

5.3 Computational Efficiency

Next, we evaluate the computational efficiency by using the same setting (11) used in the previous section.

Table 1 shows the runtimes of the proposed method for $p = 100$ and $p = 1,000$ by fixing $K = 100$. The computational time for the sampling step increases as the number of samples M and the dimension p increases. Since the approximation performance does not improve so much as the number of samples M increases as observed in the previous experiment, it is helpful in practice to use a moderate number of samples. The computational time for the greedy selection step also increases as the number of samples M increases; however, interestingly, it *decreases* as the dimension p increases. This reason is understood by observing the number of distance evaluations as follows.

Figure 5 shows the number of distance evaluations in the greedy selection step in each K. This shows that the redundant distance computation is significantly reduced by the lazy update technique; therefore Algorithm 3 only performs a few distance evaluation in each iteration. In particular, for $p = 1,000$, the saturation is very sharp; thus the computational cost is significantly reduced. This may be because, in high-dimensional problems, adding one point to the current convex hull does not change the distance to the remaining points, and hence the lazy update helps to avoid most of distance evaluations.

Table 1. Runtime (in sec.) of the proposed algorithm (Sampling: Algorithm 2, Greedy: Algorithm 3) for selecting $K = 100$ vertices over the numbers of samplings $M = 1,000, 10,000,$ and $100,000$.

M	$p = 100$		$p = 1,000$	
	Sampling	Greedy	Sampling	Greedy
1,000	2.891	34.87	46.54	17.99
10,000	27.80	178.5	2466	66.95
100,000	279.1	1548	4586	379.9

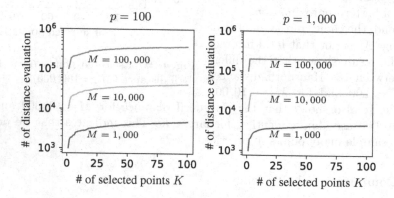

Fig. 5. # of distance evaluations in Algorithm 3

5.4   Diversity of Solutions

One of the practical advantages of the proposed method is that it can find nearly optimal solutions with a large diversity. This is a favorable property when one is interested in finding several possible explanations for a given data, which is usually the case in data mining.

Setup. We verify the diversity of the found solutions on the 20 Newsgroupsdata.[6] In this experiment, we consider classifying the documents between the two categories `ibm.pc.hardware` and `mac.hardware`. As a feature vector x, we used tf-idf weighted bag-of-words expression, with stop words removed. The dataset comprised $n = 1,168$ samples with $p = 11,648$ words. Our objective is to find discriminative words that are relevant to the classification of the documents.

Because the task is binary classification with $y \in \{-1, +1\}$, instead of the squared objective, we use the Lasso logistic regression with the objective function given as

$$L(\beta) = \frac{1}{n} \sum_{i=1}^{n} \log \left(1 + \exp(-y_i x_i^\top \beta)\right) + \lambda \|\beta\|_1. \qquad (12)$$

---

[6] http://qwone.com/~jason/20Newsgroups/.

We implemented the solver for the problem (7) by modifying `liblinear` [8]. In the experiment, we set the regularization parameter λ to be 0.001.

Baseline Methods. We compared the solution diversity of the proposed method with the two baselines in Hara and Maehara [13]. The first baseline simply enumerates the optimal solutions with different supports in the ascending order of the objective function value (12). We refer to this method as *Enumeration*. The second baseline employs a heuristics to skip similar solutions during the enumeration. It can therefore improve the diversity of the enumerated solutions. We refer to this heuristic method as *Heuristic*. Note that we did not adopt the method of Pantazis *et al.* [18] as the baseline because it enumerates only the sub-support of the Lasso global solution: it cannot find solutions apart from the global solution.

Result. With each method, we found 500 nearly optimal β, and summarized the result in Fig. 6. For the proposed method, we defined $B(\nu)$ by $\nu = 1.05L(\beta^*)$, and set the number of samplings M to be 10,000. To draw the figure, we used PCA and projected found solutions to the subspace where the variance of the solutions of Enumeration is maximum. The figure shows the clear advantage of the proposed method in that it covers a large solution region compared to the other two baselines. While the result indicates that Heuristic successfully improved the diversity of the found solutions compared to Enumeration, its diversity is still inferior to the ones of the proposed method.

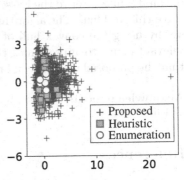

Fig. 6. Found 500 solutions in 20 Newsgroups data, shown in 2D using PCA.

We also note that the proposed method found 889 words in total within the 500 models. This is contrastive to Enumeration and Heuristic where they found only 39 and 63 words, respectively, which is more than ten times less than the proposed method. Table 2 shows some representative words found in 20 Newsgroups data. As the word "apple" is strongly related to the documents in `mac.hardware`, it is found by all the methods. However, although "macs" and "macintosh" are also relevant to `mac.hardware`, "mac" is overlooked by Enumeration, and "macintosh" is found only by the proposed method. This result also suggests that the proposed method can induce a large diversity and it can avoid overlooking informative features.

We note that the Lasso global solution attained 81% test accuracy, while the found 500 solutions attained from 77% to 83% test accuracies. This result indicates that the proposed method could find solutions with almost equal qualities while inducing solution diversities.

Table 2. Representative words found in 20 Newsgroups data

	Enumeration	Heuristic	Proposed
"apple"	✓	✓	✓
"macs"	✗	✓	✓
"macintosh"	✗	✗	✓

6 Conclusion

In this study, we considered a convex hull approximation problem that seeks a small number of points such that their convex hull approximates the nearly optimal solution set to the Lasso regression problem. We propose an algorithm to solve this problem. The algorithm first approximates the nearly optimal solution set by using the convex hull of sufficiently many points. Then, it selects a few relevant points to approximate the convex hull. The experimental results indicate that the proposed method can find diverse yet nearly optimal solutions efficiently.

Acknowledgements. Satoshi Hara is supported by JSPS KAKENHI Grant Number JP18K18106.

References

1. Achache, M.: A new primal-dual path-following method for convex quadratic programming. Comput. Appl. Math. **25**(1), 97–110 (2006)
2. Barvinok, A.: A course in convexity, vol. 54. American Mathematical Society Providence, RI (2002)
3. Bentley, J.L., Yao, A.C.C.: An almost optimal algorithm for unbounded searching. Inf. Process. Lett. **5**(3), 82–87 (1976)
4. Blum, A., Har-Peled, S., Raichel, B.: Sparse approximation via generating point sets. In: Proceedings of the Twenty-Seventh Annual ACM-SIAM Symposium on Discrete Algorithms, pp. 548–557 (2016)
5. Bronstein, E.M.: Approximation of convex sets by polytopes. J. Math. Sci. **153**(6), 727–762 (2008)
6. Bronstein, E.M., Ivanov, L.D.: The approximation of convex sets by polyhedra. Siberian Math. J. **16**(5), 852–853 (1975)
7. Chen, S.S., Donoho, D.L., Saunders, M.A.: Atomic decomposition by basis pursuit. SIAM Rev. **43**(1), 129–159 (2001)
8. Fan, R.E., Chang, K.W., Hsieh, C.J., Wang, X.R., Lin, C.J.: LIBLINEAR: a library for large linear classification. J. Mach. Learn. Res. **9**, 1871–1874 (2008)
9. Fukuda, K., Liebling, T.M., Margot, F.: Analysis of backtrack algorithms for listing all vertices and all faces of a convex polyhedron. Comput. Geom. **8**(1), 1–12 (1997)
10. Gruber, P.M.: Aspects of approximation of convex bodies. In: Handbook of Convex Geometry, Part A, pp. 319–345. Elsevier, Amsterdam (1993)
11. Guyon, I., Elisseeff, A.: An introduction to variable and feature selection. J. Mach. Learn. Res. **3**, 1157–1182 (2003)

12. Hara, S., Ishihata, M.: Approximate and exact enumeration of rule models. In: Proceedings of the 32nd AAAI Conference on Artificial Intelligence, pp. 3157–3164 (2018)
13. Hara, S., Maehara, T.: Enumerate lasso solutions for feature selection. In: Proceedings of the 31st AAAI Conference on Artificial Intelligence, pp. 1985–1991 (2017)
14. König, S.: Computational aspects of the Hausdorff distance in unbounded dimension. arXiv preprint arXiv:1401.1434 (2014)
15. Kulesza, A., Taskar, B., et al.: Determinantal point processes for machine learning. Found. Trends® Mach. Learn. 5(2–3), 123–286 (2012)
16. Lee, S.I., Lee, H., Abbeel, P., Ng, A.Y.: Efficient l1 regularized logistic regression. In: Proceedings of the 21st National Conference on Artificial Intelligence, pp. 1–9 (2006)
17. Minoux, M.: Accelerated greedy algorithms for maximizing submodular set functions. In: Stoer, J. (eds.) Optimization Techniques, vol. 7, pp. 234–243. Springer, Heidelberg (1978). https://doi.org/10.1007/BFb0006528
18. Pantazis, Y., Lagani, V., Tsamardinos, I.: Enumerating multiple equivalent lasso solutions. arXiv preprint arXiv:1710.04995 (2017)
19. Tibshirani, R.: Regression shrinkage and selection via the lasso. J. Roy. Stat. Soc. Ser. B (Methodol.) 58(1), 267–288 (1996)
20. Tibshirani, R.J., et al.: The lasso problem and uniqueness. Electron. J. Stat. 7, 1456–1490 (2013)
21. Zou, H., Hastie, T.: Regularization and variable selection via the elastic net. J. Roy. Stat. Soc. Ser. B (Stat. Methodol.) 67(2), 301–320 (2005)

Optimized Sequence Prediction of Risk Data for Financial Institutions

Ka Yee Wong, Raymond K. Wong[✉], and Haojie Huang

School of Computer Science and Engineering,
University of New South Wales, Sydney, Australia
wong@cse.unsw.edu.au

Abstract. Data quality is essential in banking industry for the compliance with the standards of banking regulation, BCBS 239. But the quality is yet to be forecasted by many financial institutions. Machine learning has been recommended by the regulator in 2018 to resolve this. To assist on this, we develop a machine learning model to train several Long Short-Term Memory ("LSTM") Recurrent Neural Networks ("RNNs") for the prediction including forward LSTM RNN, backward LSTM RNN and bi-directional LSTM RNN ("BiLSTM"). With the prediction, financial institutions will understand what data quality is going to be. The networks make sequence predictions with optimizations followed by an evaluation with heterogeneous methodologies, validation techniques and algorithms.

Keywords: Long Short-Term Memory · Recurrent Neural Network · BiLSTM

1 Introduction

Since 2013, Basel Committee on Banking Supervision ("BCBS"), a group of international banking authorities developing standards for banking regulation, issued a standard number 239 ("BCBS 239 or requirements") [1] to request for the compliance with the requirements - "principles for effective risk data aggregation and risk reporting". Financial institutions were required to meet them within a deadline.

However, many of them still find it challenging to comply with the requirements [2]. They lack a system to aggregate data from multiple sources. That's why machine learning was recommended by the Financial Stability Board, monitoring global financial system, in 2018 for the data quality improvement [3]. The key is to develop a forward-looking ability to provide warnings of any potential violations of risk limits over thresholds apart from the data quality measurement.

To predict data quality, financial institutions will understand what data quality is going to be. In the industry, the prediction be justified by the history of a sequence of the data quality. It cannot be made randomly without a consistent pattern of the data to model the data quality over time. It will be provided to the regulator - sequence prediction is made in the context of time series. In fact, the risk data is stored across years and so sequence of time series is to be taken into account.

In this paper, we develop a machine learning model to train Long Short-Term Memory ("LSTM") networks for the prediction: Forward/ Backward LSTM Recurrent

© Springer Nature Switzerland AG 2019
A. C. Nayak and A. Sharma (Eds.): PRICAI 2019, LNAI 11671, pp. 364–378, 2019.
https://doi.org/10.1007/978-3-030-29911-8_28

Neural Networks ("RNNs") and Bidirectional LSTM ("BiLSTM") RNN. We choose these networks - the aggregation of risk data in the industry requires the processing of an enormous amount of risk data in a large-scale network and both historical & future scenarios ought to be considered in the prediction over years. This is similar to a paper [4] recognizing the importance of LSTM network for data prediction over time.

In effect, BiLSTM RNN [5] models long term temporal dependencies automatically and so LSTM related network [6, 7] is suitable. Similarly, bidirectional network [8] introduces a 2nd layer to make hidden-to-hidden connections flow in opposite temporal order. This helps to exploit the information from the past and future [9] too.

The goal of this paper is to predict the data quality with respect to market risk, credit risk, operational risk, and liquidity risks. LSTM RNNs is trained with a banking dataset and then evaluated by various methodologies, validation techniques & algorithms.

1.1   The Dataset

In the dataset, we synthesize 1 million banking's customer records that capture all possible non-compliance scenarios according to BCBS 239. It has 132 data features (called "data elements") belonging to 4 risk databases, as described in Table 1.

Table 1. Data features for integrated dataset

Total number of data elements	Data elements for each risk data type	Data nature	Data quality issues
132	33 Market risk	8 Static Data (seldom changed after being recorded) & 25 Dynamic Data (which may change continually) in Each Risk Database	10 Classes
	33 Credit risk		
	33 Operational risk		
	33 Liquidity risk		

Out of 4 databases, the data features of market risk are extracted to Table 2.

Table 2. Features for Market Risk ("MR") Database (Sample)

MR	Discount rate	Cost of equity	Return on equity	Risk free rate	Systematic risk	Mkt risk premium	Equity risk premium
Mean	0.50	2.99	1.00	0.50	33.58	0.50	1.47
Min	0	0	0	0	0	0	0
Max	1	414	83	1	558	1	164

In this database, the number of issues by data quality ranks are listed in Table 3.

Table 3. Number of data quality issues by ranks ("Rating" in Table)

MR_ Segments	MR_Address_ Rating		MR_ Segments	MR_AssetAmt_ Rating		MR_ Segments	MR_CashFlow_ Rating	
0	0	6075	0	0	6075	0	0	6075
	1	13629		1	13512		1	13504
	2	150		3	267		3	275
1	0	100747	1	0	100747	1	0	100747
	1	224211		1	221979		1	221876
	2	2222		3	4454		3	4557
2	0	100665	2	0	100665	2	0	100665
	1	223551		1	221344		1	221400
	2	2310		3	4517		3	4461
3	0	100301	3	0	100301	3	0	100301
	1	223840		1	221730		1	221742
	2	2299		3	4409		3	4397

Note: 0 – no data quality issue, 1 – low issue, 2 – medium issue, 3 – high issue in the rating while segments are classified into 0, 1, 2 and 3 representing no segment, the private bank, the wholesale bank and the retail bank.

The dataset is implanted with data quality ("DQ") issues as defined in Table 4 below. These DQ issues have been aligned with the data quality principles ("DQP") of the BCBS 239: DQP# 3 - accuracy and integrity, #4 - completeness and #5 - timeliness.

Table 4. Data quality issues

	DQP# 3	DQP# 4	DQP# 5
DQ Issues	**1.1** Translation: a bank balance in foreign currency not yet converted into a local currency **1.2** Transformation: the birthday format of a banking system not yet synchronized with other systems **1.3** Redundant: potential customers not yet on-board as a true bank customer (due to a failure in the bank's customer due diligence approval process) are retained **1.4** Duplicated: an extra customer ID for the same clients not yet verified **1.6** Unreasonable: undesirable clients with a very poor credit are kept **1.7** Invalid: customers over age 150 hold an account in a bank without investigation **1.8** Data mis-match: a master data cannot be reconciled to other banking systems	**1.9** Incomplete: passport number deviates from the standard (e.g. required digits) **2.0** Missing: an amount cannot be shown in a statement for equity trading	**1.5** Stale: obsolete records over the data retention period of a bank not yet purged

1.2   Data Labelling, Scoring and Pre-processing

Prior to inputting data into the networks, we labelled them as displayed in Fig. 1.

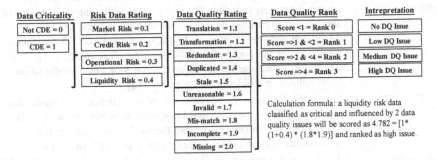

Fig. 1. Data labelling

We: (a) label data as 1 or 0 to indicate if it is critical; (b) assign a risk data rating (0.1 to 0.4) & a data quality rating (1.1 to 2) based on the types of risk data & quality issues respectively; (c) classify data quality scores (<1, =>1 & <2, =>2 & <4 & =>4) into 4 ranks (no/low/medium/high data quality issue) to be compared with the prediction.

Score is a multiplication of the rating for a quality issue. The overall score is computed as: Data Criticality Factors*(1 + Risk Data Rating)*Data Quality Rating. The ratings & ranks are usually assigned by risk experts.

For data pre-processing, we find out unusual data different from standard (e.g. null values) and score them before normalizing them into 1 or 0 by a min-max scaler.

1.3   Model and System Architecture

We deploy BiLSTM RNNs to project data quality after combining forward and backward LSTM RNNs. The network methodologies are described in Table 5 below.

Table 5. Network methodologies

Networks	Underlying methodologies of the networks
LSTM RNNs	We build a 3-dimensional LSTM based on the factors of samples, timesteps & features for sequence classification prediction. At input layer, we take 1 million samples (as sequences), leverage timesteps & input the no. of features. Then we determine the no. of memory units for hidden layer. At output layer, we generate a value for each timestep using activation function to predict the quality. In this layer, the network forms a time-distributed wrapper layer based on input sequence to forecast the output. The network weights are found by ADAM algorithm [8] and the accuracy of output is computed. Afterwards, the network generates a new input sequence to predict the quality. Those exceeding thresholds are classified. At the end, output turns out to be 0/1. This layer is the input for BiLSTM RNNs [10]

(continued)

368   K. Y. Wong et al.

Table 5. (*continued*)

Networks	Underlying methodologies of the networks
Backward LSTM RNNs	This network wraps LSTM hidden layer with backward layer to construct two sets of hidden layers – one fits in the input sequence and another one fits with a reversed input sequence. Then, the time-distributed wrapper layer around output layer will receive dual input sequences for merging before forecasting the data quality [11]. This wrapper is unlike the block processing and looka-head convolution layer utilized in a bidirectional network [12]
BiLSTM RNNs	In training this network, we revise the input sequences and import them into the LSTM as the backward input sequences before merging them. After fitting the combined one into the model, we measure the performance between them in terms of log loss [13] over epochs
Methods for BiLSTM RNN	Apart from the concatenation method ("con"), we incorporate three methods into our model to analyze the outcome of our hybrid network including multiply ("mul"), average-out ("ave") and summation (sum) giving rise to divergent outcomes in our case studies

For the network topology, the architecture is displayed in Fig. 2. The forward LSTM RNN is at the 1st layer. Turning to backward one, one layer is added such that the network is bidirectional. Then they are concatenated to generate an output at another layer, "2in1" circles, inside Fig. 2 constructing a hybrid network [22].

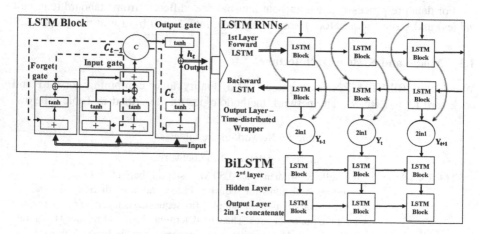

Fig. 2. System architecture

This model with a scoring approach for classifying data quality (exceeding threshold or not) in BiLSTM RNNs is called a "BCBS 239 model" which is not equivalent to the model [14] experimenting neural networks in unidirectional & bidirectional structures - built with deep bidirectional LSTM network-based sequences for classifying signals. Having said that, it is equivalent to a model [15] learning time-sequence features in a BiLSTM RNN. The variance is that we explore other methodologies to ascertain the effectiveness of our BiLSTM RNN including forward & backward & LSTM RNNs.

1.4   The Network

RNN computes the sequence of hidden state vector $(h = h_1, \ldots, h_T)$ to generate vector sequence $(y = y_1, \ldots, y_T)$ for a given input vector sequence $(x = x_1, \ldots, x_T)$, iterating the equations from $t = 1$ to T [16]:

$$h_t = \mathcal{H}(W_{xh}x_t + W_{hh}h_{t-1} + b_h)$$
$$y_t = (W_{hy}h_t + b_y)$$

where W is weight matrices, W_{xh} is weight matrix between input and hidden vectors), b is bias vector (b_h is bias vector for hidden state vector) and $\mathcal{H}$ is activation function for hidden nodes which is sigmoid in our model.

Our final network is a hybrid network constructed based on a research [12]. It covers two LSTM tracks: forward f & backward b loops. These learn from the past and previous prediction of a specific timestep to make the prediction. Thereby, the input time starts from $t - 1$, t to $t + 1$ or more and data input is read from left to right based on:

$$y_t^{f1}, h_t^{f1}, c_t^{f1} = LSTM^{f1}\left(c_{t-1}^{f1}, h_{t-1}^{f1}, x_t; W^{f1}\right)$$

The input in network is a sequence of samples $(x_1, x_2, \ldots x_t)$. It is passed to the 1st layer at a given time t $(t = 1, 2, \ldots T)$. Also, the hidden state h and internal state c of each layer l are initialized to zeros (as default) and the first layer uses input sample x at a given time t, previous hidden state h_{t-1}^1 and previous internal hidden state c_{t-1}^1 to come up with an output of the 1st layer, y, given a weight W vector. On the contrary, the sequence for backward track is read from right to left and the calculation is:

$$y_t^{b1}, h_t^{b1}, c_t^{b1} = LSTM^{b1}\left(c_{t-1}^{b1}, h_{t-1}^{b1}, x_t; W^{b1}\right)$$

In our network, the 1st layer outputs a sequence of timesteps at each epoch for forward & backward LSTM networks. They are merged into a vector to predict the timesteps as illustrated in the following equation. So, there is one output instead of two outputs, as opposed to the conventional method.

$$y = \frac{1}{T}\sum_{t=1}^{T}\left(y_t^{fL} + y_t^{bL}\right)$$

Back to LSTM RNN, it models temporal sequences and dependencies by replacing traditional nodes with memory cells such that it has internal & outer recurrence.

The cell is influenced by gates (forget, input modulation, internal state and hidden state gates) other than the input & output. The activations of units for LSTM neurons in layers at time t is computed as below:

$$i_t = \sigma(W_{xi}x_t + W_{hi}h_{t-1} + W_{ci}c_{t-1} + b_i)$$
$$f_t = \sigma(W_{xf}x_t + W_{hf}h_{t-1} + W_{cf}c_{t-1} + b_f)$$
$$c_t = f_t \odot c_{t-1} + i_t \odot \tanh(W_{xc}x_t + W_{hc}h_{t-1} + b_c)$$
$$o_t = \sigma(W_{xo}x_t + W_{ho}h_{t-1} + W_{co}c_t + b_o)$$
$$h_t = o_t \odot \tanh(c_t)$$

where input gate is i_t with weight matrix of W_{xi}, W_{hi}, W_{ci}, forget gate is f_t with weight matrix is W_{xf}, W_{hf}, W_{cf}, the cell is c_t (generated by calculating the weighted sum using previous cell state and current information generated by the cell), σ is the logistic sigmoid function, b is bias, output gate is o_t with weight matrix of W_{xo}, W_{ho}, W_{co} and output response is h_t. The input gate and forget gate govern the information flow into and out of the cell. The output gate controls how much information from the cell is passed to the output h_t. Using current input x_i, the state h_{i-1} of previous step is generated and the current state of cell c_{i-1} decides whether to take inputs, forget memory stored before and output the state generated latter [6, 7].

This is dissimilar to a bidirectional network which is a training of 2 LSTMs based on the timesteps of input sequence - on the existing input sequence and then on the reversed input sequence. This combines forward and backward outputs in the network.

Bidirectional RNN computes forward hidden sequence $\vec{h}$ & backward hidden sequence $\overleftarrow{h}$ respectively and then combines $\overrightarrow{h_t}$ and $\overleftarrow{h_t}$ to generate output y_t:

$$\overrightarrow{h_t} = H\left(W_{x\overrightarrow{h}}x_t + W_{\overrightarrow{h}\overrightarrow{h}}\overrightarrow{h_{t-1}} + b_{\overrightarrow{h}}\right)$$
$$\overleftarrow{h_t} = H\left(W_{x\overleftarrow{h}}x_t + W_{\overleftarrow{h}\overleftarrow{h}}\overleftarrow{h_{t+1}} + b_{\overleftarrow{h}}\right)$$
$$y_t = W_{\overrightarrow{h}y}\overrightarrow{h_t} + W_{\overleftarrow{h}y}\overleftarrow{h_t} + b_y$$

In forward pass [11], LSTM runs forwards from time to time once the input is feed. In the process, activations are updated and network stores all hidden layer & output activations at each time step. For each memory block, activations are updated as below:

$$\text{Input gates}: x_i = \sum_{j \in N} W_{ij}y_j(\mathcal{T} - 1) + \sum_{c \in C} W_{ic}s_c(\mathcal{T} - 1)$$
$$y_i = f(x_i)$$
$$\text{Forget gates}: x_\varnothing = \sum_{j \in N} W_{\varnothing j}y_j(\mathcal{T} - 1) + \sum_{c \in C} W_{\varnothing c}s_c(\mathcal{T} - 1)$$
$$y_\varnothing = f(x_\varnothing)$$
$$\text{Cells}: \forall_c \in C, x_c = \sum_{j \in N} W_{cj}y_j(\mathcal{T} - 1)$$
$$s_c = y_\varnothing s_c f(\mathcal{T} - 1) + y_i g(x_c)$$
$$\text{Output gates}: x_w = \sum_{j \in N} W_{wj}y_j(\mathcal{T} - 1) + \sum_{c \in C} W_{wc}s_c(\mathcal{T})$$
$$y_w = f(x_w)$$
$$\text{Cell outputs}: \forall_c \in C, y_c = y_w h(s_c)$$

In backward pass, the LSTM propagates output errors backwards via unfolded net after resetting all partial derivatives to 0. For each LSTM block, δ's is calculated as:

$$\text{Cell outputs}: \forall_c \in C, \epsilon_c = \sum_{j \in N} W_{jc} \delta_j (T+1)$$
$$\text{Output gates}: \delta_w = f'(x_w) \sum_{c \in C} \epsilon_c \, h(s_c)$$
$$\text{States}: \frac{\partial E}{\partial s_c}(T) = \epsilon_c \, y_w h'(s_c) + \sum_{c \in C} \frac{\partial E}{\partial s_c}(T+1) y_\emptyset(T+1) + \delta_i(T+1) w_{\text{ic}}$$
$$+ \delta_i(T+1) w_{\emptyset c} + \delta_w w_{\text{wc}}$$
$$\text{Cells}: \forall_c \in C, \delta_c = y_i g'(x_c) \frac{\partial E}{\partial s_c}$$
$$\text{Forget gates}: \emptyset = f'(x_\emptyset) \sum_{c \in C} \frac{\partial E}{\partial s_c} s_c (T-1)$$
$$\text{Input gates}: \delta_i = f'(x_i) \sum_{c \in C} \frac{\partial E}{\partial s_c} g(x_c)$$

This network approach is dissimilar to an assessment [17] using previous data to judge the quality of online resources before implementing a machine learning model for prediction. Our network forecasts data quality according to the past & future data.

1.5   Network Learning Methods

In BiLSTRM RNNs, there are several learning methods as below:

Sequence Prediction. The sequence of received signals are fed in the forward direction into 1 LSTM cell resulting in an output $\overrightarrow{a_k}$, and fed in backwards into another LSTM cell resulting in an output $\overleftarrow{a_k}$ [18]. Assuming $\overrightarrow{a}_k^{(l)}$ and $\overleftarrow{a}_k^{(l)}$ are outputs of final bidirectional layer, the layer with activation function is used to gain $\hat{x}_k$ as:

$$\hat{x}_k = \varnothing \left(W_{\vec{a}} \, \overrightarrow{a}_k^{(l)} + W_{\underleftarrow{a}} \, \overleftarrow{a}_k^{(l)} + b_x \right)$$

This estimated $\hat{x}_k$ is given by the following:

$$= \begin{bmatrix} \hat{p}_{model}\left(\hat{x}_k = s_1 | y_k, \overrightarrow{a}_{k-1}^{(l)}, \overrightarrow{c}_{k-1}^{(l)}, \overleftarrow{a}_{k-1}^{(l)}, \overleftarrow{c}_{k-1}^{(l)} \right) \approx \hat{p}_{model}(\hat{x}_k = s_1 | y_T, y_{T-1}, \ldots, y_1) \\ \hat{p}_{model}\left(\hat{x}_k = s_m | y_k, \overrightarrow{a}_{k-1}^{(l)}, \overrightarrow{c}_{k-1}^{(l)}, \overleftarrow{a}_{k-1}^{(l)}, \overleftarrow{c}_{k-1}^{(l)} \right) \approx \hat{p}_{model}(\hat{x}_k = s_m | y_T, y_{T-1}, \ldots, y_1) \end{bmatrix}$$

where $\hat{p}_{model}$ is probability of estimation, y_k is input to the layer, k is a sequence of transmission, W is weight, b_x is bias parameter and T is a sequence of length. The output of layer is of length m and the network considers data from previously received signals (encoded in $a_{k-1}^{(l)}$ and $c_{k-1}^{(l)}$) and from current signals.

Optimization. The Adam algorithm is computed as [19]:

$$x_t = x \cdot \frac{\sqrt{1 - \beta_2^t}}{(1 - \beta_1^t)}$$

$$x_t = \theta_t \leftarrow \theta_{t-1} - x_t \cdot m_t / (\sqrt{v_t} + \hat{\epsilon})$$

where β is delay rate, t is time step, m_t is moving average of gradient, v_t is squared gradient, θ is parameter, Assuming $f(\theta)$ is an objective function, the stochastic scalar function is differentiable with regards to the parameter. To minimize the expected value of this, $E[f(\theta)]$, we define the realization of stochastic function at timesteps $1, \ldots, t$ and the gradient (vector of partial derivatives of ft) at timestep t. Then the algorithm updates exponential moving averages of the gradient and the squared gradient whenever the hyper-parameters $\beta1, \beta2 \in [0, 1]$ control the exponential decay rates of these moving averages. ADAM has an update rule: a choice of step sizes. Assuming $\in$, the effective step taken in parameter space at timestep is Δ_t equalling to the equation: $x \cdot \hat{m}_t / \sqrt{\hat{v}_t}$.

The effective size has two upper bounds and the computation is:

$$|\Delta_t| \le x \cdot (1 - \beta_1)/\sqrt{1 - \beta_2} \text{ if } (1 - \beta_1) > \sqrt{1 - \beta_2} \text{ and } |\Delta_t| \le x$$
$$|\hat{m}_t / \sqrt{\hat{v}_t}| < 1 \text{ if } (1 - \beta_1) = \sqrt{1 - \beta_2}$$

In most scenarios, the $\left| \frac{E}{[g]} / \sqrt{E[g^2]} \right| \le 1$ gives the following:

$$\left| \hat{m}_t / \sqrt{\hat{v}_t} \right| \approx \pm 1$$

where g is gradient. The effective magnitude of the steps taken in parameter space at each time step are bounded by the step size setting x. That is $|\Delta_t| < \& \approx x$.

Regularization. We try to dropout (10% of the activations) on the LSTM layer and make regularization to see if they can alleviate overfitting. Dropout prevents co-adaptation of hidden units by randomly omitting feature detectors from the network during forward propagation. Constraining L2-norms of the weight vectors (w) by rescaling w after a gradient descent step, we obtain the cost function [7]:

$$J(\theta) = -\frac{1}{m} \sum_{i=1}^{m} t_i \log(y_i) + \lambda \|\theta\|_F^2$$

This is a negative log-likelihood of true class label y where t is time, m is number of target classes, λ is L2 regularization hyperparameter and y_i is predicted output.

Log Loss Estimation. Cross-entropy loss is used to minimize the prediction error:

$$L_1 = \sum_{(x_{df}, x_{dq})} \sum_i -y_i \log(\hat{y}_i) \tag{1}$$

where x_{df} and x_{dq} are data *elements* & *data quality* in the dataset, y is vector and $\hat{y}$ is predicted vector. A low log loss means the wrong prediction is low. Infinity is close to a perfectly correct prediction. In fact, it is capped at a maximum value of $-\log(\in)$ [20].

2 Experiment

Python v3.5 with Keras & TensorFlow backend is used on a system with the processor of i.7-7500U CPU@2.9 GHz, OS of 64-bit and Win 10 Pro. Data is synthesized dataset (available upon acceptance of this paper). 70% of data is fitted to the networks and 30% is used for the network evaluation.

2.1 Results

Utilizing ADAM algorithm, we notice that the accuracy of prediction of integrated dataset for BiLSTM RNN (100%) is superior to forward LSTM RNN (0) and backward LSTM RNN (31%), as depicted in Table 6. The high accuracy likes a BiLSTM RNN [21] solving a current problem - customers' purchase decisions by process automation.

Table 6. Loss & accuracy in 3 RNNs: forward, backward & BiLSTM

RNN	Forward LSTM		Backward LSTM		BiLSTM	
Epoch	Accuracy	Loss	Accuracy	Loss	Accuracy	Loss
1	0	0.807	30.78	0.771	52.3	**0.695**
2	0	0.799	30.78	0.770	69.4	**0.698**
3	0.1	0.791	30.78	0.770	90.2	**0.682**
4	0.2	0.783	30.78	0.769	**100**	**0.673**
5	0.4	0.775	30.78	0.768	**100**	**0.665**

The loss (in terms of prediction error) for BiLSTM RNN is constantly lower than that of other two. The loss for the former is close to 0.67% whereas that of other two is 0.78% & 0.77% respectively. So, the BiLSTM RNN is better other two RNNs.

Among them, we further compare the loss, as shown in Fig. 3. The loss of backward one is the lowest (0.55%), lower than that of the forward & hybrid ones by 0.07% to 0.08%. Nonetheless, the loss of hybrid one is lower than that of the forward one.

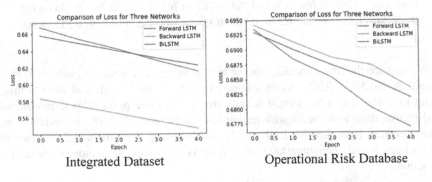

Integrated Dataset   Operational Risk Database

Fig. 3. Loss for 3 RNNs: forward, backward & BiLSTM

We confirm if the backward one is consistently better than other two networks. So, we verify this using operational risk database. The result differs, as visualized in Fig. 3 - the loss of forward & backward ones is similar (0.683%) and both are higher than that of the hybrid one (0.005% to 0.0075%). BiLSTM RNN is superior for this risk database.

To ascertain this, we validate the precision and recall of network for this database. The result, as depicted in Table 7, indicates that BiLSTM RNN outperforms others.

Table 7. Loss & accuracy for 3 RNNs: forward, backward & BiLSTM

RNN	Forward LSTM			Backward LSTM			BiLSTM		
Metrics	P	R	F	P	R	F	P	R	F
MR	48%	69%	57%	0%	0%	0%	48%	69%	56%
CR	97%	99%	98%	97%	99%	98%	97%	99%	98%
OR	99%	99%	99%	99%	99%	99%	100%	100%	100%
LR	100%	68%	81%	100%	76%	86%	100%	76%	86%
Avg	86.0%	83.8%	83.8%	74.0%	68.5%	70.8%	**86.3%**	**86.0%**	**85.3%**

Note: MR – Market Risk, CR – Credit Risk, OR – Operational Risk, LR – Liquidity Risk, P – Precision, R – Recall and F – F1-Support

2.2 Evaluation

We test the effectiveness of BiLSTM RNN by cross-validating the accuracy & loss. We identify that the accuracy of training & testing data sets for forward & BiLSTM RNNs is the same (100%) while that for backward is much lower (30.78%). This is consistent with the loss, as shown in Table 8. Training & testing loss for the former two networks decreases consistently & stabilizes at the same point, unlike backward one. This demonstrates a good fit that train loss meets with testing loss at the end.

Table 8. Cross validated loss for 3 RNNs

Epoch	1	2	3	4	5	6	7	8	9	10
Forward	0.607	0.598	0.588	0.578	0.568	0.559	0.549	0.539	0.529	0.519
Backward	0.765	0.764	0.763	0.763	0.762	0.761	0.760	0.759	0.758	0.758
BiLSTM	**0.598**	**0.588**	**0.578**	**0.568**	**0.559**	**0.549**	**0.539**	**0.529**	**0.519**	**0.509**

We can see that the accuracy rate for both training & testing data sets is 100% for forward & BiLSTM RNNs when compared with the backward, and the training & testing loss decreases consistently & stabilizes at the same point. This demonstrates a good fit that train loss meets with testing loss at the end. This cross-validation technique deviates from LSTM RNNs [22] (unidirectional, bidirectional, & cascaded architectures based) benchmarking other models (e.g. support vector machine) for a prediction.

2.3   Case Studies

To drill down into the network performance, we study three cases as below.

Case 1 - We select operational risk data to justify the accuracy & loss of integrated dataset. The accuracy is found high (over 99%) for backward & BiLSTM RNNs whereas the loss of them is as low as the integrated dataset - 0.68% for forward, 0.69% for backward & 0.66% for BiLSTM, as shown in Table 9. But the loss of BiLSTM RNN is the lowest (0.664%). So, we are in favor of this LSTM RNN for the prediction.

Table 9. Accuracy & loss of 3 RNNs for operational risk data

	Forward LSTM RNN		Backward LSTM RNN		BiLSTM RNN	
Epoch	Accuracy	Loss	Accuracy	Loss	Accuracy	Loss
1	81.8	0.693	99.3	0.694	**99.9**	**0.678**
2	99.3	0.690	99.3	0.694	99.3	**0.675**
3	**99.9**	0.687	99.3	0.693	99.3	**0.672**
4	99.3	0.684	99.3	0.693	99.3	**0.667**
5	99.3	0.680	99.3	0.691	99.3	**0.664**

To find the lowest loss, we examine 4 loss estimation methods, as compared in Fig. 4. The loss is minimized in the summation method (0.673%) whereas the highest loss is estimated by multiply method (0.691%). Other 2 methods, concatenate & average, estimate that the loss is reduced to 0.678% to 0.683% respectively.

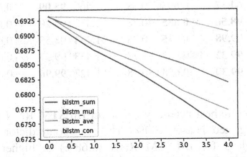

Fig. 4. Comparison of BiLSTM RNNs' performance by 4 methods

So, we prefer to use summation. These methods deviate from a paper implementing stacked bidirectional & BiLSTM network [23] measuring backward dependency.

Case 2 – We conduct an independent check to see if the prediction is convincing. Hence, we investigate under-fitting or over-fitting problem for the networks with a set of training data and a set of validation data. The outcome is visualized in Fig. 5.

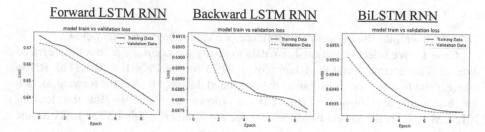

Fig. 5. Validated loss of 3 networks for operational risk data

For all LSTM RNNs, the loss of validation data is found lower than that of the training data. There is no under-fit or over-fit issue. This happens when network generalizes well or training set is large. In the result, there is a good fit for BiLSTM RNN, not the other 2 RNNs. This is the same as that of the result for integrated dataset – loss of training & validation data reduces steadily & meets at the end. Given this, we are confident of the model for data quality prediction.

Case 3 – From the integrated dataset, the accuracy & loss of prediction for BiLSTM RNN is 100% & 0.665% respectively utilizing ADAM. To explore if the loss can be improved, we apply Stochastic Gradient Descent ("SGD") algorithm to the networks. Results are displayed in Table 10.

Table 10. Accuracy & Loss in 3 RNNs (SGD)

Forward LSTM RNN		Backward LSTM RNN		BiLSTM RNN	
Epoch	Accuracy	Loss	Accuracy	Loss	Accuracy	Loss
1	64.37	0.693	30.78	1.460	**95.09**	**0.690**
2	**98.56**	**0.685**	30.78	1.453	97.20	0.688
3	**99.98**	**0.675**	30.78	1.444	98.55	0.687
4	**99.32**	**0.667**	30.78	1.433	99.27	0.683
5	99.30	**0.658**	30.78	1.427	**99.96**	0.680

Utilizing SGD, the highest accuracy occurs in BiLSTM RNN (>99.9%) which is lower than that in integrated dataset (100%). There is a contradictory result for the loss. Utilizing SGD, the loss for BiLSTM RNN (0.68%) is higher than that of the BiLSTM RNN with ADAM (0.67%). Thus, ADAM algorithm is preferable. In comparing the 3 networks under SGD, the highest accuracy happens in BiLSTM RNN but the loss for this is higher than the forward one (0.658%) and lower than the backward one (1.427%).

To confirm if ADAM is the best, we benchmark more algorithms, as made in Fig. 6. The accuracy is found high for ADAM (100%), SGD (99.96%) and ADA-GRAD (100%) but the loss is the lowest for ADAGRAD (0.452%) in comparison with ADAM, SGD, ADADELTA and RMSPROP. Consequently, ADAGRAD is better than ADAM.

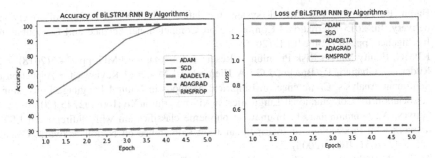

Fig. 6. Accuracy & loss for BiLSTM RNN by 5 algorithms

3 Conclusion

The experiment demonstrated an excellent performance. It assists financial institutions in the risk data quality prediction. Key contributions are the resolution of current problem by developing a model for sequence predictions with optimizations and the implementation of LSTM RNNs with divergent methodologies (forward, backward & BiLSTM RNNs) and algorithms (ADAM, SGD, ADADELTA, ADAGRAD & RMSPROP) in alignment with the BCBS 239 requirements. In future, we will automate the data remediation process (e.g. by imputation of values for quality improvement).

References

1. Bank for International Settlement (BIS), Basel Committee on Banking Supervision - Principles for Effective Risk Data Aggregation and Risk Reporting, BIS, pp. 8–23 (2013)
2. Bank for International Settlemenst (BIS), BCBS - Progress in Adopting the Principles for Effective Risk Data Aggregation and Risk Reporting, BIS, pp. 4–13 (2018)
3. Financial Stability Board (FSB), Report - Artificial Intelligence and Machine Learning in Financial Services, Market Developments and Financial Stability Implications, FSB, pp. 3–9 (2017)
4. Murad, A., Pyun, J.Y.: Deep recurrent neural networks for human activity recognition. J. Multidisciplinary Digital Publishing Inst. Sens. **17**(11), 2556 (2017)
5. Weninger, F., Bergmann, J., Schuller, B.: Introducing CURRENNT: the munich open-source CUDA RecurREnt neural network toolkit. J. Mach. Learn. Res. **2015**, 547–551 (2015)
6. Zhu, W., et al.: Co-occurrence feature learning for skeleton based action recognition using regularized deep LSTM networks. In: Proceedings of the Thirtieth AAAI Conference on Artificial Intelligence (AAAI-16), Association for the Advancement of Artificial Intelligence, pp. 3697–3702 (2016)
7. Zhou, P., et al.: Attention-based bidirectional long short-term memory networks for relation classification. In: Proceedings of the 54th Annual Meeting of the Association for Computational Linguistics, Germany, pp. 207–212 (2016)
8. Bianchi, F.M., Scardapane, S., Løkse, S., Jenssen, R.: Bidirectional deep-readout echo state networks. In: ESANN 2018 Proceedings of the European Symposium on Artificial Neural Networks, Computational Intelligence and Machine Learning, Belgium, pp. 425–430, 25–27 April 2018

9. Baran, R., Zeja, A.: The IMCOP system for data enrichment and content discovery and delivery. In: 2015 International Conference on Computational Science and Computational Intelligence, pp. 143–146. IEEE (2015)

10. KPMG, Equity Market Risk Premium – Research Summary, KPMG, pp. 3–7 (2018)

11. Ruder, S., Ghaffari, P., Breslin, J.G.: A Hierarchical Model of Reviews for Aspect-based Sentiment Analysis, Conference on Empirical Methods in Natural Language Processing – Association for Computational Linguistics, arXiv preprint arXiv:1609.02745 (2016)

12. Graves, A., Schmidhuber, J.: Framewise phoneme classification with bidirectional LSTM networks. In: Proceedings of International Joint Conference on Neural Network, Canada, pp. 2047–2051. IEEE (2005)

13. Taylor, A., Leblanc, S., Japkowicz, N.: Anomaly detection in automobile control network data with long short-term memory networks. In: 2016 IEEE International Conference on Data Science and Advanced Analytics, pp. 130–138. IEEE (2016)

14. Yildirim, O.: A novel wavelet sequence based on deep bidirectional LSTM network model for ECG signal classification. Comput. Biol. Med. **2018**(96), 189–202 (2018)

15. Yu, Z., et al.: Using bidirectional LSTM recurrent neural networks to learn high-level abstractions of sequential features for automated scoring of non-native spontaneous speech. In: 2015 IEEE Workshop on Automatic Speech Recognition and Understanding (ASRU), pp. 338–345. IEEE (2015)

16. Fan, Y.C., Qian, Y., Xie, F.L., Soong, J.K.: TTS synthesis with bidirectional LSTM based recurrent neural networks. In: Fifteenth Annual Conference of the International Speech Communication Association, Singapore, pp. 1964–1968 (2014)

17. Xie, J., Burstein, F.: Using machine learning to support resource quality assessment: an adaptive attribute-based approach for health information portals. In: Xu, J., Yu, G., Zhou, S., Unland, R. (eds.) DASFAA 2011. LNCS, vol. 6637, pp. 526–537. Springer, Heidelberg (2011). https://doi.org/10.1007/978-3-642-20244-5_50

18. Farsad, N., Goldsmith, A.: Detection Algorithms for Communication Systems Using Deep Learning, Stanford University, arXiv preprint arXiv:1705.08044 (2017)

19. Kingma, D.P., Ba, J.L.: ADAM: A Method for Stochastic Optimization, International Conference on Learning Representation, arXiv preprint arXiv:1412.6980 [cs.LG] (2014)

20. Zhou, X.J., Wan, X.J., Xiao, J.G.: Attention-based LSTM network for cross-lingual sentiment classification. In: Proceedings of the 2016 Conference on Empirical Methods in Natural Language Processing, Association for Computational Linguistics, pp. 247–256 (2016)

21. Wang, Y., Zang, J.: Keyword extraction from online product reviews based on bi-directional LSTM recurrent neural network. In: 2017 IEEE International Conference on Industrial Engineering and Engineering Management (IEEM), pp. 2241–2245. IEEE (2017)

22. Wichern, G., Lukin, A.: Low-latency approximation of bidirectional recurrent networks for speech denosing 2017. In: IEEE Workshop on Applications of Signal Processing to Audio and Acoustics (WASPAA), pp. 66–70. IEEE (2017)

23. Cui, Z.Y., Ke, R.M., Wang, Y.H.: Deep Stacked Bidirectional and Unidirectional LSTM Recurrent Neural Network for Network-wide Traffic Speed Prediction, International Workshop on Urban Computing (UrbComp) with the ACM SIGKDD, arXiv preprint arXiv (2016)

Exploiting Setup Time Constraints in Local Search for Flowshop Scheduling

Vahid Riahi[(✉)], M. A. Hakim Newton, and Abdul Sattar

Institute for Integrated and Intelligent Systems (IIIS), Griffith University,
Brisbane, Australia
vahid.riahi@griffithuni.edu.au, {mahakim.newton,a.sattar}@griffith.edu.au

Abstract. Makespan minimisation of permutation flowshop scheduling problems (PFSP) with sequence dependent setup times (SDST) is NP-Hard. PFSP-SDST has important practical applications e.g. in the paint industry. There exist several algorithms for PFSP-SDST, but they just use generic methods that lack specific structural information of the problem and so struggle with large-sized problems or find low quality solutions. In this paper, we propose a constraint-directed local search (CDLS) algorithm, which takes SDST constraints into account. SDSTs cause delays in job processing and directly affect the makespan. The PFSP-SDST solving algorithms should therefore explicitly incorporate these constraints in their search decisions. In this paper, we define a measurement of delays created by SDST constraints. The CDLS algorithm then gives priorities to the jobs that cause the highest delays since these jobs are in the most problematic parts of the solution. Our experimental results on 220 well-known instances show that the CDLS algorithm significantly outperforms the existing state-of-the-art algorithms. Moreover, it obtains new upper bounds for 163 instances out of those 220.

Keywords: Scheduling · Flowshop · Local search · Constraints

1 Introduction

Production scheduling problems have been studied greatly for more than five decades. In these problems, machines are resources that are expensive and restricted to use. So, an effective scheduling of production jobs helps increase the profitability as well as customer satisfaction. In these scheduling problems, clients' orders needed to be executed are modelled as jobs (tasks). Among different production scheduling problems, permutation flowshop is one of the most important and studied ones.

Permutation flowshop scheduling problem (PFSP) includes n jobs, and m series machines. Each job is to be processed successively by all machines in the same sequence. Also, each machine processes all jobs in the same permutation order. Each job j needs a known positive amount of processing time p_{ij} at machine i. In the classical PFSP, it is assumed that setup times are parts of

© Springer Nature Switzerland AG 2019
A. C. Nayak and A. Sharma (Eds.): PRICAI 2019, LNAI 11671, pp. 379–392, 2019.
https://doi.org/10.1007/978-3-030-29911-8_29

processing times. The goal of PFSP is to find a sequence of the given jobs such that a given objective is optimised. Among different objectives, the most common one in the PFSP literature is the minimisation of maximum completion time known as makespan. The PFSP with makespan is NP-Hard [3].

In order to capture the realistic scenarios and also to fill the gap between practical need and academic scheduling studies, different PFSP variants have been studied. One such variant is PFSPs with *sequence dependent setup times* (SDST), referred to as PFSP-SDST. Setup times are those activities that must be performed on machines to make them ready for processing the following jobs. These includes cleaning, fixing, and adjustments. On the contrary to classical PFSP, the setup times are not part of the processing times in PFSP-SDST. Furthermore, the required setup time of a machine depends not only on the next job to be processed but also does so on the job just processed by the same machine [11]. SDSTs are important in the context of flowshops since these are found in several industries such as the cider industry [11] and the paint industry [1]. In the paint industry, when a black paint is produced, the machine must be cleaned. However, the extent of cleaning is huge when the following job is a white paint, while the extent is less if the following job is a dark grey paint [14].

The PFSP-SDST with makespan objective is shown to be NP-Hard even with only one machine [4]. Considering only one machine, the PFSP-SDST is known to be a special case of the Travelling Salesman Problem (TSP) that is also well known to be NP-hard. Because of the NP-Hard nature of PFSP-SDST, researchers have focused on the incomplete algorithms to solve this problem. Although several techniques have been proposed in order to solve this problem, they still either struggle with large-sized problems or find low quality solutions. One main reason could be the typical way of employing generic algorithms that usually do not have the specific information of the problem.

In this work, we progress PFSP-SDST search by better exploiting the problem specific structural information, i.e. by using the constraints as well as the objective functions. We then utilise this information in the intensification phase of a proposed local search algorithm. Because of SDSTs, machines are delayed from processing the next jobs in the sequence. SDSTs thus directly affect the makespan. So, solving algorithms should be aware of these constraints during their search processes. Therefore, we propose a measurement to calculate the delays created by SDST constraints for each job. Then, jobs with high delay measurements get more priorities compared to the ones with lower delays. In other words, the delay measurement helps the algorithm recognise the most problematic parts of the solution and focus on them.

In the rest of the paper, Sect. 2 explains formulation of PFSP-SDST and also reviews the literature review, Sect. 3 discusses the proposed algorithm, Sect. 4 presents the experimental results, and Sect. 5 concludes the paper.

2   Preliminaries

In this section, we first formally define the PFSP-SDST, and then review some of the algorithms proposed for the problem.

2.1 PFSP-SDST Definition

There is a facility with m series machines. There are also n jobs that must be processed by all m machines in the same order, without loss of generality, machine 1 first, then machine 2, and so on until machine m. At any time, each machine $i \in [1, m]$ can process at most one job, and each job $j \in [1, n]$ can be processed by at most one machine. Each job j needs a known positive length of processing time p_{ij} at machine i. This p_{ij} does not include the setup time. There is a setup time for each machine before starting a job. The setup time depends not only on the next job to be processed but also does so on the job just processed by the same machine. The main goal of PFSP-SDST is to sequence the n jobs on the m machines so that the makespan is minimised. Basically, there are $n!$ possible job permutations at each machine. Let π be a permutation or sequence of the n jobs. The job in position k of the sequence is denoted by $[k]$. Moreover, $S_{i,[k-1][k]}$ denotes the setup time of a machine i to process job $[k]$ after processing job $[k-1]$; there is no setup time for the first job.

The completion time of job $[k]$ denotes the time when the processing of job $[k]$ on machine m is finished. The completion time $C_{i[k]}$ for the job $[k]$ on the machine i are calculated as follows:

$$C_{i[k]} = \max\{C_{i[k-1]} + S_{i,[k-1][k]}, C_{i-1[k]}\} + p_{i[k]} \quad k = 1, ..., n, \; i = 1, ..., m$$

where $C_{0[k]} = 0$, $S_{i,[0][k]} = 0$ and $C_{i0} = 0$ for all i and k. So the makespan is $C(\pi) = C_{m[n]}$.

2.2 Related Work

As already mentioned, several incomplete algorithms have been proposed in order to solve this problem. Genetic algorithms (GA) have been proposed using novel techniques such as a new crossover operator [13]. The GA algorithms out-performed other adapted algorithms that were originally proposed for classical PFSP with no SDST. Next, a local search algorithm called iterated greedy (IG) algorithm has been proposed [14]. The main idea was to use a greedy diversification technique in each iteration to extract some jobs from the permutation and to reinsert them one by one into their best possible positions. The results showed the efficiency of IG algorithm against the GAs [13]. A discrete artificial bee colony (DABC) algorithm [5] has also been proposed for PFSP-SDST. DABC uses few local search algorithm including the IG algorithm inside its framework. The results showed that DABC algorithm is competitive with the IG algorithm. Another proposed algorithm is an enhanced migrating bird optimization (EMBO) algorithm [16]. Various search operators and a tabu mechanism are used in EMBO. The authors compared the EMBO algorithm with some other adapted algorithms that were originally proposed for other PFSP variants.

3 Our Approach

In order to solve the PFSP-SDST, we propose a constraint directed local search (CDLS) algorithm, which is shown in Algorithm 1. It starts from an initial solution obtained by a constructive heuristic named NEH [7]. Then, the initial solution undergoes a constraint directed intensification procedure ConstraintDirectedIntensification() to improve its quality. The algorithm then goes through the main loop, which has three main steps. At first, a new solution is created by a random-path directed diversification procedure RandomPathDirectedDiversification(). Then, the same ConstraintDirectedIntensification() procedure will be applied to the new solution. Finally, an acceptance criterion is used to decide weather the new solution π' is to be accepted as the current solution π in the next iteration. In the proposed CDLS, we use the simulated annealing (SA) based acceptance criterion. Based on this acceptance criterion, the non-improving solution can be accepted with some probability $e^{-\Delta/T}$, where $\Delta = C(\pi') - C(\pi)$ and T is a parameter known as temperature. T starts from an initial value, and then diminishes iteratively by a given factor β.

The main difference between CDLS and other existing algorithms is the use of constraint directed approaches instead of typical random and exhaustive ones. In the following sections, the constraint directed intensification and random-path directed diversification procedures are described.

Algorithm 1. Constraint Directed Local Search

1: $\pi \leftarrow$ Initialisation()
2: $\pi' \leftarrow$ ConstraintDirectedIntensification(π')
3: **while** *termination criteria not satisfied* **do**
4:     $\pi' \leftarrow$ RandomPathDirectedDiversification(π)
5:     $\pi'' \leftarrow$ ConstraintDirectedIntensification(π')
6:     $\pi \leftarrow$ AcceptanceFunction(π, π'')
7: **return** The global best solution found so far

3.1   Constraint Directed Intensification

In the intensification phase, the algorithm moves in the neighbouring areas of the current solution in order to find better solutions. Given a current solution, if there is no better neighbouring solution, then the current solution is returned as a local optimum solution. In the PFSP literature, the main focus is on using a random or an exhaustive approach. In this paper, we propose a greedy method taking the SDST constraints into account.

Because of SDST, machines are delayed from processing the next jobs in the sequence. Thus SDSTs directly affect the makespan. So solving algorithms should be aware of these constraints during their search process. Therefore, we propose a constraint-directed approach for the job selection phase of the proposed intensification method. Our constraint-directed job selection is based on a measurement defined using the delays caused by each job. Because of the SDST constraints, machines must be set up after processing a job to become ready to process the following job. This setup time is associated with both of the jobs.

We calculate the total delays created by each job. It helps identify the problematic jobs. Given a solution π, each job $[k]$ has the total delay time $\mathsf{TDT}[k]$ that is calculated as follows:

1. For the job at the first position: $\mathsf{TDT}[1] = \sum_{i=1}^{m} S_{i,[1][2]}$
2. For the job at the last position: $\mathsf{TDT}[n] = \sum_{i=1}^{m} S_{i,[n-1][n]}$
3. For the jobs at other positions k: $\mathsf{TDT}[k] = \frac{1}{2}\sum_{i=1}^{m}(S_{i,[k-1][k]} + S_{i,[k][k+1]})$

The TDT for jobs at positions $1 < k < n$ is divided by 2 since for the jobs at the first and the last positions, there is no job before and after respectively.

Assume a solution π of an instance with 5 machines and 4 jobs is depicted in Fig. 1. As shown, the total setup times associated with the jobs $[1]$, $[2]$, $[3]$ and $[4]$ are $2+4+2+2+3 = 13$, $\frac{1}{2}((2+4+2+2+3) + (4+3+3+3+3)) = 14.5$, $\frac{1}{2}((4+3+3+3+3) + (2+2+4+4+3)) = 15.5$ and $2+2+4+4+3 = 15$ respectively. Therefore, the job ordering is π^D is $[3], [4], [2], [1]$.

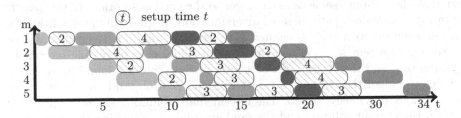

Fig. 1. An example PFSP-SDST solution

As a neighbourhood operator, we use insert-neighbourhood(π). It generates a set of sequences accumulating insert-neighbourhood(π, k) for all k. To use this operator, following three operators are defined.

- remove(π, k): Remove job $[k]$ from a given sequence π of n jobs to get a sequence π' of $n - 1$ jobs.
- insert(π', j, k): Insert job j at position k of a given sequence π' of $n - 1$ jobs to get a sequence π'' of n jobs.
- insert-neighbourhood(π, k): Remove job $j = [k]$ from a given sequence π to obtain a sequence π'. Then, produce n sequences by inserting job j at each position k' of π' separately. Each resultant sequence π'' has n jobs.

The procedure of the proposed constraint directed intensification is given in Algorithm 2. First, the total delays caused by each job is calculated. Then, jobs are sorted in a non-increasing order of their total delay times. So, the jobs in the first part of that orders are those with the highest delays created. The algorithm selects the jobs based on their order of delays. It means the algorithm gives more priorities to the jobs that are more problematic, and tries to fix their positions first. Whenever a new solution is found, the procedure will be restarted.

Algorithm 2. ConstraintDirectedIntensification

1: Let π^D be the sequence of all jobs when sorted in the non-increasing order of the total delay times $\mathsf{TDT}(k)$ for each job $[k]$ in the current solution π.
2: **for** $k = 1$ to n **do**
3:     Let k' be such that $[k']$ in π is the same as $[k]$ in π^D.
4:     Let π' be the $\pi'' \in$ insert-neighbourhood(π, k') with the lowest makespan but
5:         π'' is not the same as π.
6:     If $C(\pi') < C(\pi)$ then $\pi = \pi'$ and go to Step 1.
7: **return** π as the solution after intensification.

3.2   Diversification Method

The diversification phase is an important phase of a local search algorithm as it guides the search to the new areas in the search space and it also helps the search escape from a local optimum. In the PFSP literature, a typical diversification method applies some random moves to the current solution. In this paper, we propose a random path directed diversification. It gradually moves from the current solution to a fully generated new random solution. It creates a path between the current solution and the random solution, explores the intermediate solutions, and then selects the best intermediate solution found in the path. It helps the algorithm to have a target random solution, and do not return to the solutions previously visited. The intermediate solutions share the property of both the current solution and the random solution. Selecting the best intermediate solution also ensures the quality of the returned solution. Algorithm 3 shows the proposed random-path directed diversification method.

Algorithm 3. RandomPathDirectedDiversification(π)

---

1. $\pi_s \leftarrow \pi$
2. $\pi_t \leftarrow$ RandomTargetSolution()
3. $\pi_o \leftarrow$ RandomSelectionOrder()   // a random path
4. $\pi_* \leftarrow \pi_t$
5. for $k = 1$ to n do
    (a) $j \leftarrow$ the job at position k in π_o
    (b) $k' \leftarrow$ position of job j in π_s
    (c) $k'' \leftarrow$ position of job j in π_t
    (d) $\pi_s \leftarrow$ if $k' \neq k''$ then swap jobs at k' and k'' in π_s.
    (e) if $C(\pi_s) < C(\pi_*)$ then $\pi_* = \pi_s$
6. return π_* as the solution after diversification

Assume the current solution is $\pi = \langle 2, 6, 5, 1, 4, 3 \rangle$, the random target solution is $\pi_t = \langle 3, 5, 2, 4, 6, 1 \rangle$, and a random path represented by a job order $\pi_o = \langle 6, 2, 3, 1, 5, 4 \rangle$. The path relinking process is shown in Fig. 2. Based on π_o, the first job whose position should be fixed is job 6. Since the position of job 6 is

2 and 5 in π_s and π_t respectively, we exchange the jobs at positions 2 and 5 in π_s and get a new solution $\pi_1 = \langle 2, 4, 5, 1, 6, 3 \rangle$. This process continues until the solution π_t is obtained.

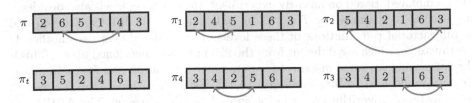

Fig. 2. Example of RandomPathDirectedDiversification()

4 Experimental Results

In this section, we are to evaluate the effectiveness of the proposed CDLS algorithm compared to various existing algorithms. We use well-known PFSP-SDST instances, called Ciavotta's instances [2]. That benchmark set is made up of 220 instances including two different SDST scenario, each with 110 instances. Setup times ($S_{i,jk}$s) are uniformly randomly distributed over the ranges of $[1, 50)$ and $[1, 125)$, and these scenarios are named as SDST50 and SDST125 respectively. Each of the SDST scenarios has 110 instances, 11 combinations of numbers of machines m and jobs n. The $n \times m$ combinations are $\{20, 50, 100\} \times \{5, 10, 20\}$, and $\{200\} \times \{10, 20\}$. Each combination has 10 different instances. In all 220 instances, the processing times are uniformly randomly generated over the ranges of $[1, 100)$.

We compare our CDLS algorithm with some of the best-performing algorithms in the literature, IG_RS [14], DABC [5], EMBO [16], ILS_PR [8], and WWO [15]. First three candidate algorithms are proposed for PFSP-SDST, however, two other candidate algorithms are from other PFSP variants and are adapted here for this problem. All candidate algorithms are reconstructed in C programming language. All algorithms are run on the same machine.

To analyse the experimental results, we use the relative percentage deviation (RPD) calculated as

$$\text{RPD} = \frac{C_A - C_{\text{Best}}}{C_{\text{Worst}} - C_{\text{Best}}} \times 100$$

where C_A is the makespan generated by a given run for a given instance by a given algorithm A. The C_{Best} and C_{Worst} are also the best and worst makespan achieved by any of the methods compared for the given problem instance. We run each search algorithm 5 times on each instance and calculate the average RPD (ARPD) over the 5 runs. We use $\rho nm/2$ ms where $\rho \in \{30, 60, 90\}$ as timeout for running the algorithms. They are the most common timeouts for this problem such as [14].

4.1 Parameter Tuning

The proposed CDLS has two parameters: T and β, both of which are in the acceptance function. To calibrate the parameters, the design of experiments method [6] is employed. Based on an early experiment, the following levels are considered for each of the parameters: $T \in \{10, 50, 100\}$, and $\beta \in \{0.99, 0.999, 0.9999\}$ and a full factorial combinations of these levels are considered. We use another 44 instances [2], which are different from the 220 instances mentioned above. This is because using the same instances for parameter calibration and for main experiments would lead to biased results [10,12]. Each algorithm is run 5 times on each instance. Algorithms are run for $\rho nm/2$ ms where $\rho = 90$. The ARPDs are calculated as defined above with C_{Best} and C_{Worst} in the ARPD is the minimum and maximum makespan obtained in this experiment.

For this experiment, the 95% Tukeys Honest Significant Difference (HSD) confidence intervals are shown in Fig. 3. We see that $T = 10$ and $\beta = 0.999$ are the best values. We will use these values in our further experiments.

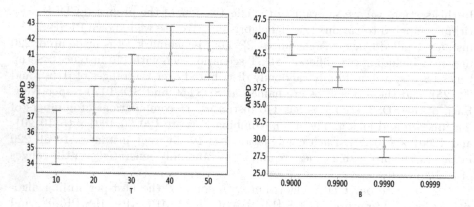

Fig. 3. 95% Tukey's HSD confidence intervals for T and β combinations in CDLS.

4.2 Analysis of Constraint-Directed Intensification

In the proposed CDLS, we use a constraint directed job selection in the intensification process (called G here). We perform an experiment to see the effectiveness of the proposed greedy approach. We consider two common approaches in the literature. The first one is the typical random one [14], and the other one is called the reference intensification process [9], which is common in the PFSP literature. Here, we called those two methods as R and Ref respectively. For method R, in Algorithm 2, π^D is constructed from a random permutation, while for method Ref, π^D is the best solution found so far in the search. The same 44 instances [2] mentioned above are also used here. The algorithm in each intensification scenario is run 5 times on each instance. Algorithms are also run for $\rho nm/2$ ms where $\rho = 90$. For this experiment, the 95% Tukey's HSD confidence intervals are shown in Fig. 4. As can be seen, the proposed constraint-directed intensification statistically significantly improves the performance of the proposed algorithm and obtains better results.

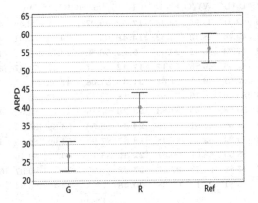

Fig. 4. 95% Tukey's HSD intervals for CDLS with different intensification approaches.

4.3   Overall Performance Comparison

We compare the proposed CDLS algorithm against 5 state-of-the-art algorithms. Each algorithm is run with timeout $\rho nm/2$ ms where $\rho \in \{30, 60, 90\}$. This timeout helps analyse the performance of the algorithms from short to long CPU times. Also, the 220 instances [2] as mentioned before are used in this section. The detailed experimental settings including instances, and candidate algorithms are already explained in Sect. 4. The ARPDs of the algorithms for each instance group are reported in Table 1. Each cell of the table, except the average row, is ARPD of 50 results over the combinations of the instances and replications of runs, i.e., $10 \times 5 = 50$, while each cell of the average row is the ARPDs of 550 results. The bold values also represent the best results. As can be seen, except in some small instances in few cases, the proposed CDLS always obtains the best results in most instance groups in all three timeouts.

To see the difference of the candidate algorithms statistically, the mean plots with 95% Tukey's HSD confidence intervals of the algorithms are also shown in Fig. 5. From this figure, we observe that the CDLS statistically significantly achieved better results compared to the other algorithms. In addition, another test, 95% confidence intervals, has been done to see the performance of the algorithms over the numbers of jobs and machines. These charts can be seen in Fig. 6. This figure confirms that the proposed CDLS is less influenced when the numbers of jobs and machines increase, even its performance improves when the numbers of jobs increase from 50 to 200. A similar investigation is done for different values of ρ and SDST and the respective charts are shown in Fig. 7.

Table 1. Comparison of algorithms on 220 instances of [2] when $\tau \in \{30, 60, 90\}$.

$\rho = 30$	SDST50						SDST125					
Ins.	ILS_PR	IG_RS	DABC	WWO	EMBO	CDLS	ILS_PR	IG_RS	DABC	WWO	EMBO	CDLS
20*5	53.75	18.56	42.31	35.94	29.93	**17.52**	49.97	14.87	32.46	44.68	25.42	**14.69**
20*10	56.54	26.77	49.76	58.13	34.32	**14.48**	65.42	29.25	52.41	44.26	32.46	**18.01**
20*20	55.13	14.42	47.33	46.42	29.06	**5.12**	50.39	23.18	51.63	42.62	24.99	**14.55**
50*5	86.95	47.74	84.94	40.85	73.17	**17.42**	84.37	44.47	74.47	37.43	72.58	**15.28**
50*10	87.33	46.91	82.01	40.95	71.61	**21.31**	87.08	47.63	78.88	40.43	72.99	**21.91**
50*20	84.01	45.58	82.40	36.15	71.87	**23.18**	89.39	46.37	80.71	41.77	71.64	**21.92**
100*5	84.75	53.64	90.68	43.05	83.83	**23.70**	87.16	47.78	84.62	42.53	84.89	**21.45**
100*10	84.50	53.70	88.68	40.91	84.76	**24.81**	86.50	53.88	85.33	41.68	82.92	**21.80**
100*20	86.36	53.10	89.34	42.18	87.48	**28.37**	87.93	54.69	86.15	40.92	86.93	**21.25**
200*10	77.90	50.68	88.63	68.07	90.51	**22.32**	83.76	50.97	89.16	63.00	91.23	**22.64**
200*20	76.89	50.37	87.88	65.75	92.37	**27.02**	81.96	53.33	90.97	67.53	90.97	**21.50**
Average	75.83	41.95	75.81	47.13	68.08	**20.48**	77.63	42.40	73.34	46.08	67.00	**19.55**

$\rho = 60$	SDST50						SDST125					
Ins.	ILS_PR	IG_RS	DABC	WWO	EMBO	CDLS	ILS_PR	IG_RS	DABC	WWO	EMBO	CDLS
20*5	44.80	14.81	34.23	34.67	16.42	**13.46**	38.01	14.39	23.94	36.51	**9.08**	11.11
20*10	51.28	16.98	40.43	44.86	23.08	**14.48**	52.18	**17.95**	36.31	41.02	20.32	20.89
20*20	39.09	14.00	37.29	33.89	17.04	**7.49**	46.04	15.73	39.83	41.23	15.31	**13.23**
50*5	85.10	39.09	75.09	34.73	62.55	**13.80**	80.01	37.26	66.93	31.36	62.54	**12.31**
50*10	82.89	42.30	74.46	36.71	63.77	**14.33**	82.26	40.30	72.52	31.73	64.53	**15.32**
50*20	80.91	39.29	73.37	33.48	61.33	**15.13**	83.55	41.20	72.27	31.97	68.26	**18.08**
100*5	83.74	46.54	79.81	33.68	75.27	**12.84**	84.59	42.76	77.05	36.14	78.52	**13.27**
100*10	84.28	46.54	81.04	31.88	79.36	**17.08**	84.58	45.34	78.44	34.07	78.11	**13.81**
100*20	84.72	46.11	78.91	30.86	79.69	**15.44**	84.51	46.47	78.30	34.01	77.92	**16.33**
200*10	75.56	45.66	81.63	45.29	86.48	**13.23**	82.95	43.93	79.90	44.50	85.24	**13.34**
200*20	75.94	43.30	81.10	45.09	87.15	**15.33**	81.32	44.53	81.14	46.23	85.20	**13.31**
Average	71.66	35.88	67.03	36.83	59.28	**13.87**	72.73	35.44	64.24	37.16	58.64	**14.64**

$\rho = 90$	SDST50						SDST125					
Ins.	ILS_PR	IG_RS	DABC	WWO	EMBO	CDLS	ILS_PR	IG_RS	DABC	WWO	EMBO	CDLS
20*5	31.91	11.98	26.87	25.71	14.47	**8.82**	36.45	**9.67**	19.80	36.41	9.63	11.14
20*10	33.08	14.66	33.19	37.42	13.57	**11.06**	40.38	15.31	33.37	37.09	13.86	**12.08**
20*20	31.42	11.13	29.89	27.40	9.00	**5.10**	37.98	16.80	24.50	31.29	12.63	**13.86**
50*5	76.91	32.80	64.90	30.89	57.63	**11.41**	81.03	32.44	57.90	26.18	58.48	**16.05**
50*10	80.76	33.55	68.30	34.74	61.04	**13.25**	83.18	35.29	67.65	30.25	58.89	**15.24**
50*20	81.92	36.32	67.78	28.28	57.38	**14.12**	81.09	36.65	68.59	30.63	63.71	**17.25**
100*5	84.24	41.67	76.43	29.87	70.77	**6.87**	86.07	39.34	73.03	29.03	74.06	**10.98**
100*10	82.04	42.72	77.86	29.15	74.77	**10.33**	84.35	41.71	74.51	31.08	73.61	**12.96**
100*20	82.91	42.69	76.28	26.17	74.30	**9.91**	86.03	43.27	76.02	26.58	73.44	**12.60**
200*10	75.65	39.73	77.71	35.96	83.00	**6.97**	83.02	40.62	75.84	34.93	82.39	**9.38**
200*20	76.53	39.45	75.64	35.85	83.46	**9.42**	81.03	41.79	76.53	37.02	81.78	**8.75**
Average	67.03	31.52	61.35	31.04	54.49	**9.75**	70.97	32.08	58.89	31.86	54.77	**12.75**

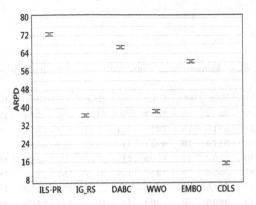

Fig. 5. 95% Tukey's HSD intervals for algorithms compared.

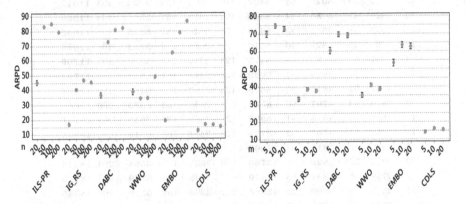

Fig. 6. 95% confidence intervals for different number of (left) jobs and (right) machines.

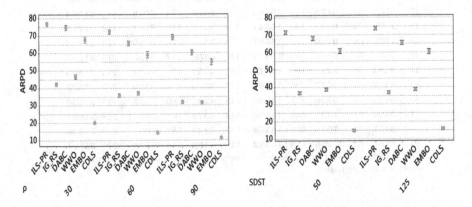

Fig. 7. 95% confidence intervals for different (left) ρ and (right) SDST values.

Table 2. Best known makespan values for 220 instances of [2].

Ins.	BKS	Ins.	BKS	Ins.	BKS	Ins.	BKS	Ins.	BKS	Ins.	BKS
SDST50		37	3352	74	7517	SDST125		147	4358	184	10095
1	1567	38	3319	75	7211	111	2065	148	4316	185	9814
2	1580	39	3174	76	6951	112	2040	149	4177	186	9487
3	1446	40	3362	77	7105	113	1933	150	4378	187	9623
4	1644	41	3934	78	7259	114	2137	151	5270	188	9773
5	1526	42	3815	79	7436	115	1979	152	5172	189	9982
6	1510	43	3803	80	7368	116	1979	153	5188	190	9953
7	1531	44	3949	81	8383	117	2002	154	5282	191	11662
8	1554	45	3946	82	8357	118	2060	155	5278	192	11599
9	1585	46	3928	83	8407	119	2005	156	5324	193	11617
10	1426	47	3985	84	8329	120	1876	157	5361	194	11526
11	2009	48	3941	85	8448	121	2656	158	5315	195	11646
12	2065	49	3829	86	8516	122	2661	159	5213	196	11614
13	1897	50	3984	87	8475	123	2515	160	5329	197	11709
14	1794	51	4984	88	8639	124	2415	161	6647	198	11794
15	1842	52	4817	89	8478	125	2502	162	6496	199	11668
16	1816	53	4767	90	8524	126	2445	163	6533	200	11684
17	1858	54	4878	91	13902	127	2485	164	6555	201	18741
18	1962	55	4765	92	13771	128	2586	165	6519	202	18595
19	1985	56	4817	93	14000	129	2588	166	6503	203	18807
20	2013	57	4829	94	13783	130	2655	167	6564	204	18544
21	2754	58	4841	95	13839	131	3498	168	6549	205	18715
22	2565	59	4869	96	13605	132	3290	169	6516	206	18345
23	2748	60	4899	97	14007	133	3475	170	6641	207	18856
24	2658	61	6532	98	13937	134	3437	171	8271	208	18755
25	2760	62	6406	99	13735	135	3514	172	8160	209	18686
26	2686	63	6352	100	13833	136	3442	173	8219	210	18696
27	2712	64	6178	101	15369	137	3452	174	8046	211	21504
28	2668	65	6399	102	15541	138	3431	175	8277	212	21715
29	2701	66	6260	103	15561	139	3456	176	8069	213	21715
30	2635	67	6373	104	15471	140	3378	177	8233	214	21585
31	3263	68	6232	105	15374	141	4261	178	8024	215	21509
32	3435	69	6577	106	15367	142	4390	179	8379	216	21538
33	3243	70	6509	107	15599	143	4241	180	8275	217	21696
34	3409	71	7425	108	15530	144	4371	181	10031	218	21691
35	3401	72	7015	109	15474	145	4347	182	9601	219	21629
36	3457	73	7258	110	15542	146	4459	183	9853	220	21701

Bold values represent the new best known solutions found by the proposed algorithm in this paper

After performing experiments, we show the better results obtained on each of 220 instances. As can be observed, for 163 out of 220 instances, the proposed CDLS obtained new best-known solutions (BKS) or upper bounds. These new upper bounds can be used by future researchers (Table 2).

5 Conclusion

In this paper, we propose a new local search algorithm for permutation flowshop scheduling problems (PFSP) with sequence-dependent setup times (SDST) and makespan objective. Although SDST constraints are the key characteristics of PFSP-SDST, existing techniques are not aware of them in their search process, and so use only in the makespan calculation. We show that further consideration of SDST constraints in the local search algorithm can improve the search performance significantly. Our experimental results on a well-known testbed of 220 instances demonstrate that the proposed algorithm significantly outperforms the existing state-of-the-art algorithms. Moreover, the proposed algorithm obtains a new upper bound for PFSP-SDST in 163 instances out of 220.

References

1. Allahverdi, A.: The third comprehensive survey on scheduling problems with setup times/costs. Eur. J. Oper. Res. **246**(2), 345–378 (2015)
2. Ciavotta, M., Minella, G., Ruiz, R.: Multi-objective sequence dependent setup times permutation flowshop: a new algorithm and a comprehensive study. Eur. J. Oper. Res. **227**(2), 301–313 (2013)
3. Garey, M.R., Johnson, D.S., Sethi, R.: The complexity of flowshop and jobshop scheduling. Math. Oper. Res. **1**(2), 117–129 (1976)
4. Gupta, J.N., Darrow, W.P.: The two-machine sequence dependent flowshop scheduling problem. Eur. J. Oper. Res. **24**(3), 439–446 (1986)
5. Ince, Y., Karabulut, K., Tasgetiren, M.F., Pan, Q.K.: A discrete artificial bee colony algorithm for the permutation flowshop scheduling problem with sequence-dependent setup times. In: 2016 IEEE Congress on Evolutionary Computation (CEC), pp. 3401–3408. IEEE (2016)
6. Montgomery, D.C.: Design and Analysis of Experiments. Wiley, New York (2017)
7. Nawaz, M., Enscore Jr., E.E., Ham, I.: A heuristic algorithm for the m-machine, n-job flow-shop sequencing problem. Omega **11**(1), 91–95 (1983)
8. Pan, Q.K., Ruiz, R.: Local search methods for the flowshop scheduling problem with flowtime minimization. Eur. J. Oper. Res. **222**(1), 31–43 (2012)
9. Pan, Q.K., Tasgetiren, M.F., Liang, Y.C.: A discrete differential evolution algorithm for the permutation flowshop scheduling problem. Comput. Ind. Eng. **55**(4), 795–816 (2008)
10. Riahi, V., Khorramizadeh, M., Newton, M.H., Sattar, A.: Scatter search for mixed blocking flowshop scheduling. Expert Syst. Appl. **79**, 20–32 (2017)
11. Riahi, V., Newton, M.H., Su, K., Sattar, A.: Local search for flowshops with setup times and blocking constraints. In: International Conference on Automated Planning and Scheduling (ICAPS), pp. 199–207 (2018)

12. Riahi, V., Newton, M.H., Su, K., Sattar, A.: Constraint guided accelerated search for mixed blocking permutation flowshop scheduling. Comput. Oper. Res. **102**, 102–120 (2019)
13. Ruiz, R., Maroto, C., Alcaraz, J.: Solving the flowshop scheduling problem with sequence dependent setup times using advanced metaheuristics. Eur. J. Oper. Res. **165**(1), 34–54 (2005)
14. Ruiz, R., Stützle, T.: An iterated greedy heuristic for the sequence dependent setup times flowshop problem with makespan and weighted tardiness objectives. Eur. J. Oper. Res. **187**(3), 1143–1159 (2008)
15. Shao, Z., Pi, D., Shao, W.: A novel discrete water wave optimization algorithm for blocking flow-shop scheduling problem with sequence-dependent setup times. Swarm Evol. Comput. **40**, 53–75 (2018)
16. Sioud, A., Gagné, C.: Enhanced migrating birds optimization algorithm for the permutation flow shop problem with sequence dependent setup times. Eur. J. Oper. Res. **264**(1), 66–73 (2018)

A Click Prediction Model Based on Residual Unit with Inception Module

Zhiwen Ni[1(✉)], Xiaohu Ma[2], Xiao Sun[1,2], and Lina Bian[1,2]

[1] School of Computer Science and Technology and Joint International Research Laboratory of Machine Learning and Neuromorphic Computing, Soochow University, Suzhou 215006, Jiangsu, China
20164227006@stu.suda.edu.cn
[2] Provincial Key Laboratory for Computer Information Processing Technology, Soochow University, Suzhou 215006, Jiangsu, China
xhma@suda.edu.cn

Abstract. The explosion in online advertisement urges to better estimate the click prediction of ads. For click prediction on single ad impression, we have access to pairwise relevance among elements in an impression, but not to global interaction among key features of elements. Moreover, the existing method on sequential click prediction treats propagation unchangeable for different time intervals. In this work, we propose a novel model, Convolutional Click Prediction Model (RES-IN), based on residual unit with inception module. RES-IN can extract local-global key feature interactions from an input instance with varied elements, which can be implemented for not only single ad impression but also sequential ad impression. Experiment results on three public large-scale datasets indicate that RES-IN is effective on click prediction.

Keywords: Click prediction · Residual unit · Inception module · Feature interactions

1 Introduction

Data representation is empirically to be a core determinant of performance of deep learning and most machine learning algorithms [1]. For that reason, much of the actual effort in deploying neural network goes into the design of feature extraction, preprocessing and data transformations. Feature engineering is important but labor-intensive and highlights the weakness of current learning algorithms [2], their inability to extract all of the juice from the data. We have two methods to get better features from the data, feature engineering is a way to take advantage of human intelligence and prior knowledge to compensate for that weakness. In order to expand the scope and ease of applicability of machine learning, it would be highly desirable to make learning algorithms less dependent on feature engineering, so that novel applications could be constructed faster, but feature engineering still can't meet our demands in some fields, for example, Image Segmentation, Automatic Speech Recognition and Big Data Forecast.

© Springer Nature Switzerland AG 2019
A. C. Nayak and A. Sharma (Eds.): PRICAI 2019, LNAI 11671, pp. 393–403, 2019.
https://doi.org/10.1007/978-3-030-29911-8_30

So more importantly, to make progress towards deep learning, that is what we called Artificial Intelligence (AI). An AI must fundamentally understand the world around us, and this can be achieved if a learner can identify and disentangle the underlying explanatory factors hidden in the observed milieu of low-level sensory data. How to extract better feature from a set of data is the core of neural network.

Online advertising has become the most popular approach to do brand promotion and product marketing for the advertiser, and contributes the overwhelming majority of income for commercial web publisher. click prediction on single ad impression has received much attention, and many different approaches have been proposed. For simplicity and effectiveness, Logistic Regression (LR) [3] has been widely used in click prediction. Representing each element (e.g. query, ad, user and other contexts) of a single ad impression by a value, LR is not capable enough to describe the latent features of an element or reveal the complicated relation among these elements. As a widely-used technique in recommendation systems, matrix factorization (MF) method in the Collaborative Filtering approach is also employed for click prediction. MF method factorizes and rebuilds the dependency matrix to learn latent semantic representations of pages and ads. Later, factorization machine (FM) [4], a extension of MF in multiple element space, obtains latent semantic information of each pairwise elements. However, MF and FM models capture relevance of pairwise elements in single ad impression and overlook the high-order interaction among these elements.

Different from traditional works taking single ad impression as input instance and overlooking dependency of historical impressions, Recurrent Neural Network (RNN) model is leveraged for click prediction of sequential ad impression. Taking full advantage of historical click sequences, the recurrent structure enhances the accuracy of click prediction further. The model takes each user's browsing history as a sequence and obtains internal sequential dependency of varied impressions. Historical click sequence of a certain user is divided by different time intervals, sequence signals of one time interval can be propagated to next interval by the recurrent connection matrix. Due to the fact that the recurrent connection matrix of a trained RNN model is a constant one, the propagations of sequence signals between every two consecutive time intervals remain all the same. However, in real-world scenarios, since users' attitudes toward ads change over time, RNN models may has its limitation for these scenarios due to using the unchangeable propagations.

In order to mine significant semantic features in complex and dynamic sceneries, deep neural network is a good choice. As stated above, for click prediction on single ad impression, the MF and FM methods only reveal the relevance between pairwise elements, but convolutional neural network (CNN) can treat varied elements in a single ad impression as a whole and obtain complex interaction among them. On the other hand, the unchangeable propagations of RNN models on sequential ad impression has the limitation in effectively modeling dynamic click predictions, while pooling and convolutional layers of a deep CNN architecture can fully extract local-global key features from sequential ad impression. In addition, some recent studies about CNN architecture have successfully model significant semantic features in varieties of fields. CNN approaches to speech recognition, image recognition, information retrieval have achieved much improvement in respective fields [5]. Moreover, proved as a effective sentence model in natural language processing, Dynamic Convolutional Neural Network (DCNN) can analyses semantic content and extracts key features of sentences [6].

We proposed a click prediction model based on residual unit with inception (RES-IN) for click prediction in sceneries of the single ad impression and sequential ad impression. An input instance of RES-IN is composed by elements of an ad impression or elements related to a sequential ad impression. Convolutional layers extract local-global features of input instances, and the dynamic pooling layers can obtain significant features. RES-IN investigates significant semantic features of an ad impression and sequential relevance of impression history into enhancing the accuracy of click prediction. Experiments are conducted to validate the RES-IN model's effectiveness in modeling different kinds of input instances and reveal that RES-IN achieves great improvement on the accuracy of click prediction comparing the state-of-the-art models such as LR, FM, RNN and DCN. RES-IN is a novel approach that attempts to leverage residual unit to improve the accuracy of click prediction.

2 RES-IN

In an event of single ad impression, there are some noticeable elements like user, query, ad, impression time, site category, device type, etc. On the other hand, sometimes system can collect sequential ad impression of each individual user, where user's behaviors on ads yield high dependency on how the user behaved along with the past time. This sequential ad impression is comprised of a series of single ad impressions. The goal of this work is to predict the click probability based on these two kinds of impressions. Our model above input instances using a convolutional architecture that alternates wide convolutional layers with flexible p-max pooling layers. The whole procedure of RES-IN is illustrated in Fig. 4. In the network the width of an intermediate feature map varies with the length of the input instance. It is remarkable to state that the proposed model can handle input instances with varied length, which make it can be used widely.

2.1 Convolution Process

The use of convolution kernel operations in click prediction scenarios is a problem. Convolutional neural networks (CNN) are mainly used to extract local features, and have achieved good results in the image and NLP fields [7], because the input of those fields is related in time or space structure. CNN's convolution operation can capture this time and space connection [8], and the biggest difficulty in the prediction field is how to construct a matrix like an image for a sample [9], so that the input can have local connections to a certain extent.

Given an input instance with n elements, to obtain the first layer of RES-IN, we take an embedding $e_i \epsilon R^d$ for each element in the instance and construct the instance matrix $s \epsilon R^{d \times n}$ as

$$\begin{bmatrix} \cdot & \cdot & \cdot \\ \cdot & & \cdot \\ e_1 & ... & e_n \\ \cdot & & \cdot \\ \cdot & \cdot & \cdot \end{bmatrix} \tag{1}$$

The values in the embedding e_i are estimated during the training process, which contributes to more suitable representations for input instances. A convolutional layer in the network is obtained by convolving a weight matrix $w \epsilon R^{d \times w}$ with the activation matrix at the layer below in an one-dimensional row-wise way. For example, the second layer is obtained by applying a convolution on the input instance matrix s. Dimension d and filter width w are hyper-parameters of input instances. The resulting matrix r has dimension $d \times (n + w - 1)$. Given $w_i \epsilon R^w$, $s_i \epsilon R^n$, and $r_i \epsilon R^{n+w-1}$ as $i - th$ row of corresponding matrix, we can obtain one-dimensional convolution as

$$r_i = w_i{}^T s_{i,j-w+1:j} \tag{2}$$

Where the index j ranges from 1 to $n+w-1$. Out-of-range values $s_{i,k}$ (where $k < 1$ or $k > n$) are set to zero.

The optimized weights in the filter w detects features and recognizes specific ranges of neighborhood in input instances. Applying one-dimensional row-wise convolution on two-dimensional matrix of activations, has the following advantage over simply using two-dimensional convolution. Usually we apply two-dimensional convolution in image identification for the reason that the detectors need to recognize special two-dimensional features, such as edges of an objective. However, in the click prediction model, each dimension of the embedding represents a distinct aspect of an element in an instance. Therefore, each row of the resulting matrix r obtains distinct features from the activation matrix.

2.2   Flexible P-Max Pooling

Here, we describe the flexible $p - max$ pooling layer. Given a vector $r_i \epsilon R^n$, $p - max$ pooling selects a sub-vector $s_i^p \epsilon R^p$, which contains the p biggest values in the original vector r_i. Due to the fact that input instances are of varied length, the vector lengths of intermediate convolutional layer change accordingly, consequently the following pooling layer need to be flexible enough to select prominent features smoothly. Considering all facts mentioned above, we let p be a function of length of the input instance and depth of the network. In spite of many possible functions, we select the following one

$$p_i = \begin{cases} (1 - (i/l)^{l-i})n, & i = 1, \ldots, l-1 \\ 3, & i = l \end{cases} \tag{3}$$

where l is the total number of convolutional layers of the network, n is the length of the input instance and p_i represents the parameter of the $i-th$ pooling layer. For example, given an input instance of length $n = 18$, in a network of three convolutional layers, whose pooling parameters are as follows: $p_1 = 16$, $p_2 = 6$ and $p_3 = 3$.

This selected function has many advantages. Firstly, the last pooling layer has a fixed parameter, so it is guaranteed that the matrix of the fully connected layer for output has a unified dimensionality, despite varied lengths of different input instances. Secondly, the power-exponential function changes slowly at first compared with linear function, which avoids losing too many important features at the beginning.

The flexible $p-max$ pooling layer can not only select the p most key features, but also preserve the relative order of those features, which plays a critical role in the sequential click prediction.

2.3 Residual Layers with Inception Module

The profound advancement of deep learning in the field of image is due to the development of convolutional neural networks [10]. This paper treats the data into a matrix form, so that the convolutional network can be applied to the prediction of click-through rate. In this paper, we combine the residual unit with Inception module, so that the model RES-IN can extract the features interactions by the multi-channel convolution operation while preserving the original information.

The residual layers [11] are constructed from the Residual Unit (see Fig. 1). The Residual Unit is the basic building block of the Residual Net that claimed the world record in the ImageNet contest. We will introduce how we combined residual net with inception module (see Fig. 2), firstly, knowing about the architecture of inception is very important. In theory, the inception module can make the width and depth of the network expand efficiently and improve the accuracy without over-fitting [12].

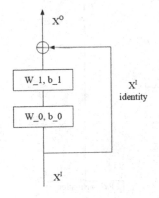

Fig. 1. Residual unit in details

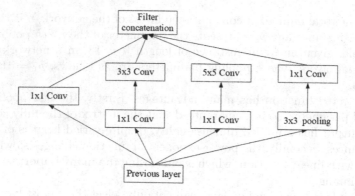

Fig. 2. The architecture of inception module

Sparse structures are a very suitable structure for neural networks, especially for large and very deep neural networks [13], such as convolutional neural networks that are sparse links. The goal is to find the optimal sparse structural unit, and this goal is supported by the Hebbian principle (the persistence and repetition of neuroreflex activity leads to increase in the ability in the stability of neuronal connections), In other words, cells that fire together, wire together.

RES-IN uses a modified Residual Unit that does not use original residual connection, its an optimized version that combined with the inception module by use sparse structural unit, the 1×1 convolution is a very good structure, which can improve the expressive power of the network while reducing the amount of computation of the network [14]. That is creative to use residual net combined inception module to solve the credit prediction and content recognition, to our knowledge this is first time to use residual unit to solve problems beyond image recognition [15], and we hope this neural network model can be used to solve more applications in other field (Fig. 3).

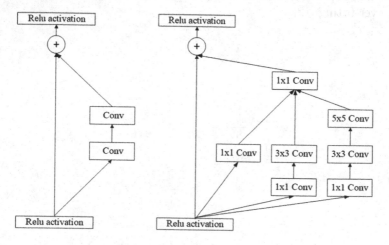

Fig. 3. On the left is the original residual net connection, on the right is the optimized residual unit with inception module

The unique property of Residual Unit is to add back the original input feature after passing it through two layers of ReLU transformations (see Fig. 1). Specifically:

$$X^O = f(X^I, \{W_0, W_1\}, \{b_1, b_1\}) + X^I \tag{4}$$

Where $W_{\{0,1\}}$ and $b_{\{0,1\}}$ are the parameters of the two layers, and f denotes the functions that maps the input X^I of the residual unit X^O. Moving X^I to the left of Eq. 4, $f(\cdot)$ is essentially fitting the residual of $X^O - X^I$. In the authors believed residual has a numerical advantage. While the actual reason why Residual Net could go as deep as 152 layers with high performance is subject to more investigations, RES-IN did exhibit a few properties that might benefit from Residual Units [16].

Before RES-IN, we tried a number of model architectures with deep layers but none of them provided significant gains over a model with two or three layers to justify the added complexity. RES-IN is our strongest model that easily beats the performance of its shallower counterparts.

RES-IN was applied to a wide variety of tasks. It was also applied to training data with large differences in sample sizes. In all case, the same model was used without any adjustment in the layers, nodes, and type of nodes. Its likely that the Residual Units are implicitly performing some kind of regularization that leads to such stability.

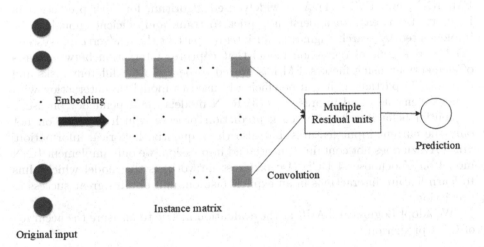

Fig. 4. The architecture of RES-IN

3   Experiment

3.1   Datasets and Baseline

To empirically evaluate the performance of our method on the click prediction with single and sequential impression data, we perform experiments on two public real-world datasets: Avazu, Yoochoose and DianPing. The Avazu dataset includes several days of ad click-through data, ordered chronologically. In each piece of click data, there are 17 data fields such as ad id, site id, click, etc. These above data fields indicate elements of a single ad impression. We use this dataset to assess the performance of click prediction on the single ad impression. Collected during several months in 2018, the Yoochoose dataset contains many sessions of browse and purchase events from an online retailer, where each session encapsulates the click events of an individual user. Some sessions contain purchase events, which means that the session ends with the user purchasing something. Here, we treat products as ads, then the browse behavior can be viewed as a single ad impression and the purchase behavior as an impression with click. This dataset is employed to evaluate the performance of click prediction on the sequential ad impression. DianPing dataset is the largest consumer review site in China. It provides diverse functions such as reviews, check-ins, and shops meta information (including geographical messages and shop attributes). We collect 6 months users check-in activities for restaurant recommendation experiments. Given a users profile, a restaurants attributes and the users last three visited POIs (point of interest), we want to predict the probability that he will visit the restaurant. For each restaurant in a users check-in instance, we sample four restaurants which are within 3 km as negative instances by POI popularity.

Four state-of-arts methods are used for empirical comparison, which are LR, FM, RNN, and DCN. (1) As a widely used algorithm for click prediction in industry, LR is easy to understand, quick to train, and efficient enough to be implemented by search engines as an integral part of their advertising system. (2) FM is a general regression model that captures interaction between pairs of elements by using factors. FM has proved to be useful in different tasks and domains. In particular, it can be efficiently used to model the interaction with various elements of ad impressions. (3) RNN models the dependency on user's sequential behaviors into the click prediction process, which depends on not only the current input features, but also the sequential historical information. Since Avazu does not contain sequential ad impression, we only implement RNN model on Yoochoose. 4 DCN (Deep&Cross network) is the model which aims to learn feature interactions in an explicit fashion, and obtains great success in prediction.

We adopt Logloss and AUC as the evaluation metric to measure the accuracy of CTR prediction.

$$logloss = -\frac{1}{n_{test}} \sum_{i=1}^{n} (y_i log(p_i) + (1 - y_i) log(1 - p_i)) \qquad (5)$$

where $p_i = P(y_i = 1|s)$ represents the predicted click probability and s denotes an ad impression. y_i is the corresponding observed label, $y_i = 1$ means the user has click the ad impression. n is the total number of input instances.

3.2   Result and Analyses

Table 1 illustrates the click prediction performance of RES-IN and other competitive compared methods on single ad impression and sequential ad impression. We identify that on both datasets, RES-IN outperform the conventional methods. Since FM can describe the latent features of an element and reveal the relation of pairwise elements, it achieves significant improvement over the that of LR on both datasets (Fig. 5).

Table 1. Experimental result of different dataset

	AVAZU		DianPing	
Model name	Logloss	AUC	Logloss	AUC
RES-IN	**0.3721**	**0.8527**	**0.3279**	**0.8634**
LR	0.4103	0.8173	0.3652	0.8210
FM	0.3988	0.8203	0.3509	0.8268
DCN	0.3767	0.8421	0.3417	0.8541

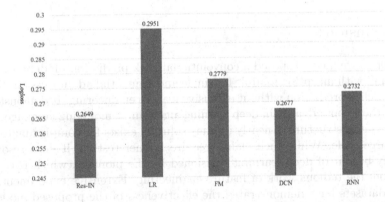

Fig. 5. Experimental results in the Yoochoose dataset

On sequential ad impression, RNN leverages sequential dependency of varied impressions, and enhance the effectiveness of click prediction further. Since RES-IN obtain underlying semantic information of input instances and extracts local-global features by using convolutional layers, and use p-max pooling to select key features, it can not only reveal the high-order interaction among various elements of a single ad impression but also capture the historical propagation pattern in sequential ad impression. In the Yoochoose dataset, we add RNN model to the experiment.

Furthermore, we compared the impact of network depth on experimental results (see Fig. 6), the dataset used is Yoochoose. We can see that after the experimental results reach saturation, continue to deepen the network. Only the experimental results of the RES-IN model have not decreased. We argue that benefits from the structure of the residual unit.

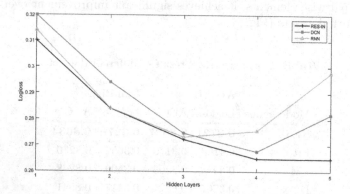

Fig. 6. Experimental results in different hidden layers

4   Conclusion

In this paper, we have proposed a convolutional click prediction model based on residual unit with inception module for single and sequential ad impression. RES-IN enables click prediction without extensive feature engineering. It demonstrate that with the recent advance in deep learning algorithms, modeling language, and GPU-based infrastructure, a nearly dummy solution exists for complex modeling task at large scale. While such claims require further testing, it does resonate with a key benefit of deep learning envisioned by the pioneers, which is to free people from the tedious work of feature engineering. Extensive experiments on different datasets have demonstrated the effectiveness of the proposed model.

Acknowledgements. This work was supported by Postgraduate Research and Practice Innovation Program of Jiangsu Province (KYCX18_2511).

References

1. Chen, Y., Shu, L., Wang, L.: Poster abstract: traffic flow prediction with big data: a deep learning based time series model. In: Computer Communications Workshops, pp. 1010–1011. IEEE (2017)
2. Abadi, M., Agarwal, A., Barham, P., et al.: TensorFlow: large-scale machine learning on heterogeneous distributed systems (2016)
3. Cucchiara, A.: Applied logistic regression. Technometrics **34**(3), 2 (2012)

4. Rendle S.: Factorization machines. In: IEEE International Conference on Data Mining (2011)
5. Yu, D., Eversole, A., Seltzer, M., et al.: An introduction to computational networks and the computational network toolkit. Microsoft Research (2014)
6. Chen, K., Huo, Q.: Scalable training of deep learning machines by incremental block training with intra-block parallel optimization and blockwise model-update filtering. In: IEEE International Conference on Acoustics, Speech and Signal Processing, pp. 5880–5884. IEEE (2016)
7. Collobert, R., Weston, J., Bottou, L., Karlen, M., Kavukcuoglu, K., Kuksa, P.: Natural language processing (almost) from scratch. J. Mach. Learn. Res. **12**, 2493–2537 (2011)
8. Krizhevsky, A., Sutskever, I., Hinton, G.E.: ImageNet classification with deep convolutional neural networks. In: International Conference on Neural Information Processing Systems, pp. 1097–1105. Curran Associates Inc. (2012)
9. Huang, P.S., He, X., Gao, J., et al.: Learning deep structured semantic models for web search using click through data. In: ACM International Conference on Conference on Information & Knowledge Management, pp. 2333–2338. ACM (2013)
10. Schmidhuber, J.: Deep learning in neural networks: an overview. Neural Netw. **61**, 85–117 (2015)
11. He, K., Zhang, X., Ren, S., Sun, J.: Deep residual learning for image recognition. arXiv preprint arXiv:1512.03385 (2015)
12. Arora, S., Bhaskara, A., Ge, R., et al.: Provable bounds for learning some deep representations, pp. 584–592 (2013)
13. Seide, F., Li, G., Chen, X., et al.: Feature engineering in Context-Dependent Deep Neural Networks for conversational speech transcription. In: Automatic Speech Recognition and Understanding, pp. 24–29. IEEE (2011)
14. Jia, Y., Shelhamer, E. et al.: Caffe: convolutional architecture for fast feature embedding, pp. 675–678 (2014)
15. Zeiler, M.D., Fergus, R.: Visualizing and understanding convolutional networks. In: Fleet, D., Pajdla, T., Schiele, B., Tuytelaars, T. (eds.) ECCV 2014. LNCS, vol. 8689, pp. 818–833. Springer, Cham (2014). https://doi.org/10.1007/978-3-319-10590-1_53
16. Srivastava, R.K., Greff, K., Schmidhuber, J.: Training very deep networks. Comput. Sci. (2015)

Efficient Identification of Critical Links Based on Reachability Under the Presence of Time Constraint

Kazumi Saito[1,2(✉)], Kouzou Ohara[3], Masahiro Kimura[4], and Hiroshi Motoda[5]

[1] Faculty of Science, Kanagawa University, Hiratsuka, Japan
k-saito@kanagawa-u.ac.jp
[2] Center for Advanced Intelligence Project, RIKEN, Tokyo, Japan
kazumi.saito@riken.jp
[3] College of Science and Engineering, Aoyama Gakuin University, Sagamihara, Japan
ohara@it.aoyama.ac.jp
[4] Department of Electronics and Informatics, Ryukoku University, Kyoto, Japan
kimura@rins.ryukoku.ac.jp
[5] Institute of Scientific and Industrial Research, Osaka University, Suita, Japan
motoda@ar.sanken.osaka-u.ac.jp

Abstract. In this paper, we focus on an emergency situation in the real-world such as disaster evacuation and propose an algorithm that can efficiently identify critical links in a spatial network that substantially degrade network performance if they fail to function. For that purpose, we quantify the network performance by node reachability from/to one of target facilities within the prespecified time limitation, which corresponds to the number of people who can safely evacuate in a disaster. Using a real-world road network and geographical information of actual facilities, we demonstrated that the proposed method is much more efficient than the method based on the betweenness centrality that is one of the representative centrality measures and that the critical links detected by our method cannot be identified by using a straightforward extension of the betweenness centrality.

1 Introduction

Identification of critical links in a large complex network is an important research issue, and has been explored from various points of view such as contamination spread, wireless sensor network, information flow and disaster evacuation [1, 8, 13, 17, 18, 20]. Recently, considerable attention has been devoted to analyzing real-world spatial networks [2, 4, 5, 10, 14, 15, 22]. We focus on spatial networks embedded in the real space, *e.g.*, urban streets, and address the problem of identifying critical links.

A critical link in a network is such a link that exerts a substantial effect on the network performance when the link fails to function properly. Thus, given a network structure and a performance measure, critical links can be found by solving the corresponding optimization problem, that is, solving the problem

A. C. Nayak and A. Sharma (Eds.): PRICAI 2019, LNAI 11671, pp. 404–418, 2019.
https://doi.org/10.1007/978-3-030-29911-8_31

of finding a link such that its blocking maximally degrades the network performance. As a motivating example, let us consider managing an urban road network from the perspective of an emergency situation such as disaster evacuation, ambulance call and fire engine dispatch. In these emergency situation, time is critical. Thus, the performance measure must take time criticalness into account. To the best of our knowledge, there has been no work that considered time criticalness in computing the performance measure.

As preliminaries, we assume that each node in the network represents the population around it, the traveling time $t(e; G)$ or the real distance $dist(e; G)$ in the real-world is assigned to each link e, and there exists a set of target nodes $\mathcal{U}$. Note that $t(e; G)$ depends on means of transportation but $dist(e; G)$ does not. In case of disaster evacuation, $\mathcal{U}$ consists of the evacuation facilities, and people living in the neighborhood of a node v evacuate to the facility $u \in \mathcal{U}$ nearest to v. In case of ambulance call, $\mathcal{U}$ consists of the emergency hospitals, and people living in the neighborhood of a node v are taken to the hospital $u \in \mathcal{U}$ nearest to v. In case of fire engine dispatch, $\mathcal{U}$ consists of the fire stations, and when fire breaks out, fire engines are dispatched from the station $u \in \mathcal{U}$ to the nearest v (nearest to the scene of the fire). Note that each node is associated with people/houses around it. Thus, the number of people/houses varies according to the node. Our previous work [18] employed the network performance measure based on node reachability, and identified critical links in the same setting, but it ignored time criticalness, *i.e.* it simply assumed that there is no time limit for going to/from $\mathcal{U}$. In this paper, we place a time limit that is allowed for the emergency actions to be completed.

Technically, in order to reflect more realistic emergency situations, given a road network G, a set of target nodes $\mathcal{U}$ and a maximum permissible time τ, we adopt the number of people/houses that are reachable from $\mathcal{U}$ within time τ as the network performance measure, and consider identifying the critical links. Here, we suppose that each node v of G represents a collection of people/houses and the traveling time $t(e; G)$ of each link e of G is given. As mentioned above, the critical links are defined by an optimization problem, where the objective function value $h(e; \tau, \mathcal{U}, G)$ for a link e measures the reduction of the number of people/houses that are reachable from $\mathcal{U}$ within time τ when e is blocked. Thus, for each link e, we can regard $h(e; \tau, \mathcal{U}, G)$ as the criticalness of e. In this paper, we refer to it as the *time-bounded criticalness centrality* of e, and consider efficiently calculating the values of $h(e; \tau, \mathcal{U}, G)$ for all the links of G.

If there is no time constraint imposed, the standard bridge detection technique [21] could be successfully applied to the efficient calculation of $\{h(e; \tau, \mathcal{U}, G) \mid e$ is a link of $G\}$. In fact, a link in a connected component is called a bridge if its deletion divides the component into two connected components, and we can expect that $\{h(e; \tau, \mathcal{U}, G)\}$ is efficiently calculated by checking whether each component intersects with $\mathcal{U}$ or not. For example, Sariyuce et al. [19] successfully utilized the bridge detection technique to efficiently calculate conventional topological centrality measures. However, calculation of $h(e; \tau, \mathcal{U}, G)$ requires both the traveling time information and the time constraint. In this paper, we propose a method that can efficiently calculate $\{h(e; \tau, \mathcal{U}, G)\}$ based on the Best-First Search consisting of two phases: Forest Construction phase and Local Update phase.

Below we summarize our contributions in this paper. (1) We formulated the problem of identifying critical links in a road network considering the traveling time needed for each link under the presence of time constraint from the viewpoint of an emergency situation. (2) We defined the concept of time-bounded criticalness centrality for a link in terms of the reachability from a set of target nodes within a maximum permissible time to identify the critical links, and proposed an efficient method of calculating the centrality for all links. (3) We experimentally demonstrated the effectiveness of the proposed method for the road network in Tokyo in case of disaster evacuation, ambulance call and fire engine dispatch, showing that the proposed method is much faster than computing the major traditional centrality measures, and the critical links cannot be properly identified by the measure derived by straightforwardly extending a traditional centrality measure. Moreover, we revealed the characteristics of the critical links by varying the maximum permissible time.

The paper is organized as follows. After briefly describing the related work in Sect. 2, we mathematically formulate the critical link detection problem in Sect. 3. We present the proposed method in Sect. 4, and report the experimental results in Sect. 5. We give our conclusion in Sect. 6.

2   Related Work

Various kinds of centrality measures have been proposed so far [3]. The centrality measure we propose in this paper is considered as an extension of vitality index that is defined as the difference of the values of a real-valued function f on a simple, undirected and unweighted graph G and on G without an element x, where x is either a node or a link in G [9]. For example, closeness vitality adopts a function that returns the total sum of distances between arbitrary pair of nodes in a given graph. Similarly, our centrality measure is defined as the difference of a real-valued function on G and on G without a link e. But, our proposed measure is different from the original vitality index in that it is defined for an weighted spatial network considering the time constraint instead of simply taking into account network topology.

As mentioned in the previous section, several studies have been made on analyzing large spatial networks. Burckhart and Martin [4] and Wang et al. [22] explored traffic usage patterns in urban streets. Crucitti et al. [5] and Park and Yilmaz [15] examined the topological properties of road networks in terms of conventional centrality measures such as degree centrality, closeness centrality and betweenness centrality. Montis et al. [10], Opsahl et al. [14] and Ohara et al. [11] analyzed road networks considering the usage frequency or the real distance for each link by extending the conventional centrality measures. Ohara et al. [12] also extended the group closeness centrality to such a road network, and investigated the problem of inserting k new links to maximize it. There are studies that are not specific to spatial network but discuss the importance of links in complex networks. Grady et al. [7] presented a notion of salient links in complex networks, which are obtained by superimposing shortest path trees for each node. Piraveenan et al. [16] proposed a new centrality based on percolation states of individual nodes, which is referred to as percolation centrality. Fang et al. [6] compared link capacities allocation models that makes a power transmission network resilient to cascading failures with limited investment costs.

In this paper, we deal with the problem of identifying critical links for emergency situations, and define the concept of time-bounded criticalness centrality. We adopt link detection methods based on the conventional centrality measures as baselines to compare with the proposed method.

There are several investigations that are related to identifying critical links in road networks. For example, Oliveira et al. [13] explored the vulnerability of links in a road network using a transportation simulation software. Saito et al. [18] examined the critical link detection problem without time constraint in a situation where links are probabilistically blocked. Our current work is different from these studies. In order to take more realistic emergency situations into account, we focus on the problem of identifying critical links in a road network that maximize the degradation of network performance measure under the time constraint considering the time needed to pass each link. To the best of our knowledge, there is no work that utilizes the number of people/houses that are reachable from a set of target nodes within a maximum permissible time as the network performance measure, and provides an efficient method of calculating the time-bounded critical centrality for a road network. Note that it is straightforward to extend the proposed method to the situation where links are probabilistically disconnected.

3   Problem Formulation

Let $G = (\mathcal{V}, \mathcal{E})$ be a given simple undirected (or bidirectional) network without self-loops, where $\mathcal{V} = \{u, v, w, \cdots\}$ and $\mathcal{E} = \{e, \cdots\}$ are sets of nodes and undirected links, respectively. We also express each link e as a pair of nodes, i.e., $e = (u, v)$. For each link $e = (u, v) \in \mathcal{E}$, we assign its traveling time $t(u, v)$ between these nodes. For each pair of nodes that does not have the direct connection, i.e., $(u, w) \notin \mathcal{E}$, we define its traveling time $t(u, w; G)$ by the minimum traveling time over all possible paths between them. In our problem setting, we assume a fixed group of nodes $\mathcal{U} \subset \mathcal{V}$ such as evacuation facilities, emergency hospitals or fire stations on a road network. Here, for each node $v \in \mathcal{V}$, we can compute the minimum traveling time $f(v; \mathcal{U}, G)$ between v and some node $u \in \mathcal{U}$ as follows:

$$f(v; \mathcal{U}, G) = \min_{u \in \mathcal{U}} t(v, u; G). \tag{1}$$

Hereafter in case that v is not reachable to any node $u \in \mathcal{U}$, we assume $f(v; \mathcal{U}, G) = \infty$ for our convention.

Now, in case of a disaster such as tsunami right after a large-scale earthquake, people living in the flooded area must evacuate to some facility before the time of tsunami arrival. Let τ be such a maximum permissible time, and for each node $v \in \mathcal{V}$, we assume that v has some weight denoted by $\rho(v)$ which is intended to represent the number of residences or houses around node v in a road network. Then, we can compute the following weighted sum of nodes whose traveling times from/to some facility are less than a maximum permissible time.

$$g(\tau; \mathcal{U}, G) = \sum_{\{v \in \mathcal{V} \mid f(v; \mathcal{U}, G) \le \tau\}} \rho(v). \tag{2}$$

Hereafter, $g(\tau; \mathcal{U}, G) / \sum_{v \in \mathcal{V}} \rho(v)$ is referred to as a success ratio for time τ.

For each graph G, let $G(e)$ be a graph constructed by deleting a link e, i.e., $G(e) = (\mathcal{V}, \mathcal{E} \setminus \{e\})$. Then, we can define the following success contribution value of a link $e \in \mathcal{E}$ over G.

$$h(e; \tau, \mathcal{U}, G) = g(\tau; \mathcal{U}, G) - g(\tau; \mathcal{U}, G(e)). \tag{3}$$

Note that the value $h(e; \tau, \mathcal{U}, G)$ can be interpreted as the weighted sum of nodes, i.e., people, who become unable to move to one of these evacuation facilities within a maximum permissible time when a link e is blocked in case of evacuation problem. Similar interpretation is possible for other problems. Hereafter, the measure defined in Eq. (3) is referred to as time-bounded criticalness centrality.

4   Proposed Method

For a given spatial network $G = (\mathcal{V}, \mathcal{E})$ with a weight $\rho(v)$ for each node $v \in \mathcal{V}$ and a traveling time $t(u, v)$ for each link $(u, v) \in \mathcal{E}$, together with a fixed group of nodes $\mathcal{U} \subset \mathcal{V}$ and a maximum permissible time τ, we describe our proposed algorithm for computing the time-bounded criticalness centrality value $h(e; \tau, \mathcal{U}, G)$ defined in Eq. (3) for each link $(v, w) \in \mathcal{E}$. Our algorithm based on the best-first search strategy consists of two phases: construction of a directed, rooted forest whose roots are nodes in $\mathcal{U}$ and computation of centrality values by locally updating the time $f(\hat{v}; \mathcal{U}, G(e))$. Below the former and latter phases are referred to as FC (forest construction) and LU (local update), respectively.

For a subset of nodes $\mathcal{W} \subset \mathcal{V}$, let $I(\mathcal{W})$ be a set of incident links from $\mathcal{W}$, i.e., $I(\mathcal{W}) = \{(w, x) \in \mathcal{E} \mid w \in \mathcal{W}, x \notin \mathcal{W}\}$. Then, we can summarize our algorithm for computing the directed, rooted forest obtained as sets of nodes and links, $\mathcal{W}$ and $\mathcal{F}$, as follows.

FC1: Initialize $\mathcal{W} \leftarrow \mathcal{U}$, $\mathcal{F} \leftarrow \emptyset$, and $f(w; \mathcal{U}, G) \leftarrow 0$ for each $w \in \mathcal{U}$.
FC2: Select the best-first link $(\hat{w}, \hat{x})$ computed by $(\hat{w}, \hat{x}) \leftarrow \text{argmin}_{(w,x) \in I(\mathcal{W})} \{f(w; \mathcal{U}, G) + t(w, x)\}$, and set $\mu \leftarrow f(\hat{w}; \mathcal{U}, G) + t(\hat{w}, \hat{x})$.
FC3: Output the forest $(\mathcal{W}, \mathcal{F})$ if $\mu > \tau$, and then terminate.
FC4: Set $\mathcal{W} \leftarrow \mathcal{W} \cup \{\hat{x}\}$, $\mathcal{F} \leftarrow \mathcal{F} \cup \{(\hat{w}, \hat{x})\}$, and $f(\hat{x}; \mathcal{U}, G) \leftarrow \mu$, and go to FC2.

Here note that the links with positive centrality values are limited to those in $\mathcal{F}$, i.e., $h(e; \tau, \mathcal{U}, G) = 0$ if $e \in \mathcal{E} \setminus \mathcal{F}$. Figure 1 illustrates construction of a directed, rooted forest from a road network, in which star shaped markers denote target nodes such as evacuation facilities. In each rooted tree in the forest, its root node is a unique target node and it is the nearest target node from the other nodes below in the tree, *i.e.*, all the nodes below can get to the target node within a given maximum permissible time. Indeed, the path between an internal/leaf node and the root node in the tree is the optimum path on the road network to reach the target node with minimum traveling time, which implies that any other link that does not appear in the forest (broken lines in Fig. 1) never affects the minimum traveling time for any node if it is blocked.

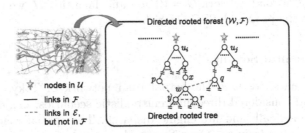

Fig. 1. Construction of a directed, rooted forest from a spatial network and local update of traveling time.

Next, let $X(w)$ be a set of descendant nodes of w over the forest $(\mathcal{W}, \mathcal{F})$. Here note that when a link $e = (w, x) \in \mathcal{F}$ is removed, we need to update the time $f(y; \mathcal{U}, G(e))$ only for $y \in X(w)$, *i.e.*, $f(y; \mathcal{U}, G(e)) = f(y; \mathcal{U}, G)$ for $y \in \mathcal{W} \setminus X(w)$. For example, if we remove link (x, w) in Fig. 1, the subtree whose root node is w consists of $X(w)$ and every node in $X(w)$ becomes unable to reach their nearest target node u_i with the minimum traveling time. But, if any node in the subtree is connected to a node in $\mathcal{W}$ with a link in $\mathcal{E} \setminus \mathcal{F}$ just like node w is connected to node q with link (w, q) in Fig. 1, some nodes in $X(w)$ may still reach a target node within a given maximum permissible time τ. The local update phase seeks such nodes while updating the minimum traveling time of each node in $X(w)$. Note that link (y, r) that is not contained in $\mathcal{F}$ has to be tested to make a path from node r to node u_i if node y can reach node u_i within τ by passing link (y, p). Then, we can summarize our algorithm for computing the centrality values for each link $e \in \mathcal{F}$ by locally updating the time $f(y; \mathcal{U}, G(e))$ for $y \in X(w)$, as follows.

LU1: Repeat the following steps described in LU2 for every link $e = (w, x) \in \mathcal{F}$.

LU2.1: Initialize $\mathcal{Y} \leftarrow X(w)$.

LU2.2: Select the best-first link $(\hat{y}, \hat{v})$ computed by $(\hat{y}, \hat{v}) \leftarrow \mathrm{argmin}_{(y,v) \in I(\mathcal{Y}) \setminus \{(x,w)\}} \{f(v; \mathcal{U}, G(e)) + t(v, y)\}$, and set $\mu \leftarrow f(\hat{v}; \mathcal{U}, G(e)) + t(\hat{v}, \hat{y})$.

LU2.3: Compute $h(e; \tau, \mathcal{U}, G) \leftarrow \sum_{y \in \mathcal{Y}} \rho(y)$ if $\mu > \tau$, and then goto LU3.

LU2.4: Set $\mathcal{Y} \leftarrow \mathcal{Y} \setminus \{\hat{y}\}$ and $f(\hat{y}; \mathcal{U}, G(e)) \leftarrow \mu$, and go to LU2.2.

LU3: Output $h(e; \tau, \mathcal{U}, G)$ for $e \in \mathcal{F}$ and 0 for $e \in \mathcal{E} \setminus \mathcal{F}$.

Evidently, the efficiency of our proposed algorithm is affected by several factors including the maximum permissible time τ, the number of nodes in $\mathcal{U}$ and so on. Thus, we evaluate the performance of our proposed algorithm which is referred to as TBC (time-bounded criticalness) in our computational experiments.

5   Experiments

Using real data of road network $G = (\mathcal{V}, \mathcal{E})$ and facilities $\mathcal{U}$, we evaluated the effectiveness of the proposed TBC algorithm.

5.1   Experimental Settings

In our experiments, we used the actual road network of Tokyo in Japan as $G = (\mathcal{V}, \mathcal{E})$, and considered three different realistic scenarios, *i.e.*, disaster evacuation, ambulance call, and fire engine dispatch. The spatial road network of Tokyo was extracted from the Open Street Map data[1]. As a matter of fact, we extracted all highways and all nodes, and constructed the spatial network by using the ends, intersections, and curve-fitting-points as nodes and the streets between them as links. The resulting network consists of $|\mathcal{V}| = 6,571,077$ nodes and $|\mathcal{E}| = 7,312,007$ links. For the facilities $\mathcal{U}$ of each scenario, we gathered geographical information about evacuation facilities, emergency hospitals, and fire stations, respectively, from the site of National Land Information Division of Ministry of Land, Infrastructure, Transport and Tourism (MLIT) of Japan[2], and mapped each of them to the nearest node in the spatial network. The numbers of evacuation facilities, emergency hospitals, and fire engines are $3,919$, 55, and 318, respectively. In this work, we assumed that a person moves at $1\,\mathrm{m}$ per second ($3.6\,\mathrm{km/h}$) on foot in the case of disaster evacuation, and that both an ambulance and a fire engine move at $10\,\mathrm{m}$ per second ($36\,\mathrm{km/h}$). We computed the traveling time $t(e; G)$ by dividing the distance $dist(e; G)$ by the velocity corresponding to each scenario. Here we should emphasize that we can arbitrary change $t(e; G)$ according to the other conditions such as road width. We used the 2015 census population aggregation data[3] for weight $\rho(v)$ setting of each node. More specifically, for a given population number n of each small region containing a subset of nodes $\mathcal{W} \subset \mathcal{V}$, we assigned to each node $v \in \mathcal{W}$ its average number as $\rho(v) = n/|\mathcal{W}|$.

Since a link between nodes having a high centrality value is considered to play an important role in the network, we used the straightforward extension of conventional link-centrality measures as the baselines to be compared with our proposed TBC centrality. More specifically, by incorporating $\mathcal{U}$ and $\rho(x)$ for $x \in \mathcal{V}$, we extended betweenness centrality and assigned a link-centrality value given by

---

[1] https://openstreetmap.jp/.
[2] http://nlftp.mlit.go.jp/ksj-e/index.html.
[3] https://www.e-stat.go.jp/gis/.

$$EBC(e) = \sum_{x \in \mathcal{V}} \frac{N^{sp}(x, y(x); e)}{N^{sp}(x, y(x))} \rho(x), \quad \text{where} \quad y(x) = \operatorname*{argmin}_{u \in \mathcal{U}} t(x, u; G). \quad (4)$$

$N^{sp}(x, y)$ stands for the number of the shortest paths from node x to node y, and $N^{sp}(x, y; e)$ denotes the number of those paths passing through a node e. Hereafter, we refer to this link-centrality as EBC. Here, we can naturally interpret $EBC(e)$ as the number of people passing through the link e during the movement to $\mathcal{U}$. All programs to compute link-centralities including TBC were implemented in C and run on a computer with a single thread (Xeon X5690 3.47 GHz CPUs) within a 192 GB main memory capacity.

5.2 Experimental Results

First, we evaluated the computational efficiency of our proposed TBC algorithm. To this end, we compared the processing time to compute the TBC centrality value for all links in $\mathcal{E}$ with the time to compute EBC for all links in $\mathcal{E}$, and the time to compute DGC and BWC for all nodes in $\mathcal{V}$, where DGC and BWC stand for standard degree centrality and betweenness centrality, respectively. Figure 2 shows the experimental results, where Figs. 2(a), (b), and (c) are cases using evacuation facilities, emergency hospitals, and fire stations as $\mathcal{U}$, respectively. To investigate the computational efficiency of the TBC algorithm more in depth, we further plotted the processing time spent for its second phase LU in each figure. In this experiment, we varied the maximum permissible time τ from 100 s to 900 s by 200 s. Note that the processing time of EBC, DGC and BWC is constant as their computation is not affected by the value of τ. It was 0.017 s for DGC and $513,525.800$ s for BWC regardless of the cases, while 50.13, 8.25, and 20.95 s for EBC with respect to the cases of evacuation facilities, emergency hospitals, and fire stations, respectively. From these results, it is obvious that the computation of DGC is the most efficient because it does not require to traverse the network to compute the centrality for every node $v \in \mathcal{V}$. The computation for EBC is modest and comparable to those of TBC. On the other hand, the computation of BWC is the most expensive. This is because its computational complexity approximately becomes a square order of the network size. Compared to BWC, the processing time for computing TBC is substantially small and less than 100 s even for a large value of the maximum permissible time τ in any scenario although it is much larger than that for DGC. This is attributed to the effect of the maximum permissible time which bounds the size of trees in the forest constructed at the first phase of the TBC algorithm. Besides, considering that the vertical axes of these figures are logarithmic, we see that most of the computation time is spent on the forest construction phase, FC, which is the difference between TBC and LU in Fig. 2, implying that the local update algorithm is quite efficient. Here, as naturally expected, the computation for EBC was comparable to those of FC. Actually, the processing time for FC depends on the size of $\mathcal{U}$, i.e., $3,919$ for evacuation facilities, 318 for fire stations, and 55 for emergency hospitals. This is because the size of $\mathcal{U}$ is equivalent to the number of trees in the forest. In short, we can say that our proposed TBC algorithm has a desirable scaling property with respect to the number of facilities and the maximum permissible time.

Next, we investigated how the success ratio defined in Sect. 3 changes as the maximum permissible time τ gets longer. Indeed, in this experiment, the success ratio is given by $|\{v \in \mathcal{V} \mid f(v; \mathcal{U}, G) \leq \tau\}|/|\mathcal{V}|$, where $f(v; \mathcal{U}, G)$ is the minimum traveling time between v and some node $u \in \mathcal{U}$ defined by Eq. (1). We plotted this value as "cumulative" in Fig. 3, where Figs. 3(a), (b), and (c) are those in case of using evacuation facilities, emergency hospitals, and fire stations as $\mathcal{U}$. Also in this experiment, we varied the maximum permissible time τ from 100 (s) to 900 (s) by 200 (s). Note that the value represented by "incremental" in Fig. 3 is the difference between the success ratios at τ and at $\tau - 200$ for $\tau \geq 300$. From these results, we can observe that the success ratio monotonically increases as the maximum permissible time τ becomes longer. It is noted that the success ratio for $\tau = 100$ is less than 0.1 in Fig. 3(a). This is because we assumed that a person moves at 1 m per second on foot in the scenario of disaster evacuation, and thus, it is difficult for most people to reach the nearest evacuation facility within 100 s. This difficulty is alleviated by setting τ to a larger value and the success ratio improves accordingly. On the other hand, the "incremental" value decreases when τ becomes larger than 500 in Fig. 3(a) due to the fact that the number of people who need such a long traveling time to reach the nearest evacuation facility is limited. Similar tendency can be observed in the cases of ambulance call and fire engine dispatch in Figs. 3(b) and (c), where we assumed that both an ambulance and a fire engine move at 10 m per second. But, the success ratios for these scenarios when $\tau = 100$ are quite different, less than 0.1 for ambulance call as shown in Fig. 3(b) and around 0.4 for fire engine dispatch as shown in Fig. 3(c) because of the difference in the number of facilities. It is 318 for fire stations, while only 55 for emergency hospitals. Thus, the time limitation of 100 s becomes harder for ambulance call. In addition, we can find that the success ratio shown in Fig. 3 somewhat correlates to the processing time for computing TBC shown in Fig. 2.

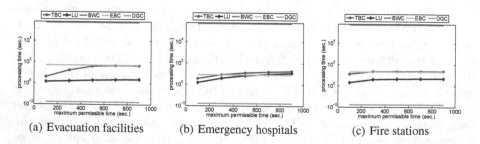

(a) Evacuation facilities   (b) Emergency hospitals   (c) Fire stations

Fig. 2. Evaluation of computational efficiency as a function of maximum permissible time.

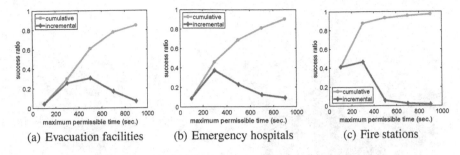

(a) Evacuation facilities   (b) Emergency hospitals   (c) Fire stations

Fig. 3. Comparison with success ratio as a function of maximum permissible time.

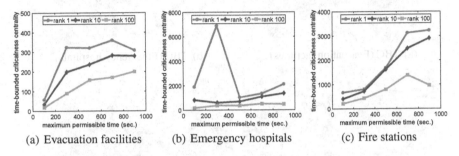

(a) Evacuation facilities   (b) Emergency hospitals   (c) Fire stations

Fig. 4. Evaluation of time-bounded criticalness centrality values of the rank 1, rank 10 and rank 100 critical links as a function of maximum permissible time.

Next, we examined how the TBC centrality values of the detected critical links fluctuate as a function of the maximum permissible time τ. Figures 4(a), (b), and (c) show the results for the scenarios of disaster evacuation, ambulance call, and fire engine dispatch, respectively. In these figures, we plotted the TBC centrality values of the rank 1, rank 10, and rank 100 critical links. Again, we adopted the same values for τ as the ones used in the previous experiments. Note that the ranking of critical links may change according to the value of τ. Roughly speaking, the TBC centrality value of the critical links tends to increase as the maximum permissible time τ gets longer, but it does not necessarily monotonically change. This is because, according to the definition of Eq. (3), the TBC centrality value for a link $e \in \mathcal{E}$ is given by $|\{v \mid f(v; \mathcal{U}, G) \leq \tau \wedge f(v; \mathcal{U}, G(e)) > \tau\}|$ in this experiment, and $|\{v \mid f(v; \mathcal{U}, G) \leq \tau\}|$ is non-decreasing with respect to the value of τ, while $|\{v \mid f(v; \mathcal{U}, G(e)) > \tau\}|$ is non-increasing with respect to the value of τ. In fact, the TBC centrality value of the highly ranked critical links is likely to largely fluctuate when the number of facilities considered is relatively small as shown in Fig. 4(b) because the number of nodes $v \in \mathcal{V}$ that satisfy the condition $f(v; \mathcal{U}, G(e)) > \tau$ may largely fluctuate depending on the actual location of each facility $u \in \mathcal{U}$ in the network.

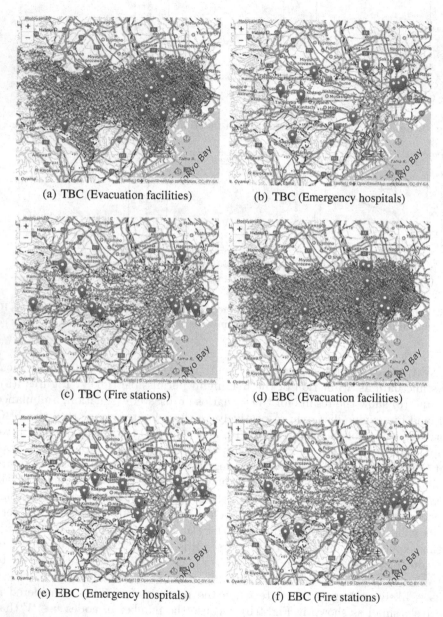

(a) TBC (Evacuation facilities)   (b) TBC (Emergency hospitals)

(c) TBC (Fire stations)   (d) EBC (Evacuation facilities)

(e) EBC (Emergency hospitals)   (f) EBC (Fire stations)

Fig. 5. Actual locations of the top-10 critical links by each of the TBC and EBC centralities.

To qualitatively compare the top-10 regions containing critical links detected by different centrality measures, we marked them on an actual map of Tokyo as shown in Fig. 5, where each marker could indicate several consecutive links. Figures 5(a), (b), and (c) respectively show the top-10 critical links detected based on the TBC centrality for the scenarios of disaster evacuation, ambulance call, and fire engine dispatch in the case of $\tau = 500$. Figures 5(d), (e) and (f) show such top-10 regions detected by the values of EBC for those scenarios, respectively. From these figures, we can say that the links detected based on EBC are substantially different from those based on the TBC centrality. This implies that EBC cannot serve as an alternative to the TBC centrality.

To quantitatively confirm our claim, we further investigated the similarity of the ranking based on TBC and EBC in case of $\tau = 100$, 500 and 900 for our three scenarios. More specifically, we measured the similarity between the top k ranked nodes based on TBC, denoted by $\mathcal{A}_k^{(\tau)} = \{v_i\}_{i=1}^{k}$, and those based on EBC, denoted by $\mathcal{B}_k = \{v_i\}_{i=1}^{k}$, by using the precision $Prec_k^{(\tau)}$ defined as follows:

$$Prec_k^{(\tau)} = \frac{|\mathcal{A}_k^{(\tau)} \cap \mathcal{B}_k|}{k}.$$

Figure 6 shows the results, where the horizontal and vertical axes denote the rank k up to top-100 and the precision $Prec_k^{(\tau)}$, respectively. Again, Figs. 6(a), (b) and (c) are the results for our three scenarios, respectively. From these results, we can see that there does not exist any similarity between TBC and EBC, especialy for disastaer evacuation and fire enging dispatch scenarios. In summary, the proposed TBC centrality can properly detect different critical links according to the task we consider.

Finally, we compare actual critical links detected based on the TBC centrality value with those based on the EBC in Fig. 7 for the scenario of ambulance call in the case of $\tau = 500$. In Fig. 7, the star shaped marker denotes the location of an emergency hospital. From Fig. 7(a) that shows the result for EBC, we can find that the nearest link from the hospital is detected as a critical link. This is natural because the number of people who pass the link is definitely larger than thoes who pass links further away when they intend to get to the hospital via the shortest pass. We observed the similar tendency for the other target nodes regardless of scenario considered. But, actually, that link is not really critical because an ambulance can easily get to the hospital within the given maximum permissible time by taking another route even if that link is blocked. On the other hand, TBC detected two bridges that are far away from the hospital as critical links as shown in Fig. 7(b) although a link near the hospital is also detected in this case. Note that such critical links, i.e., bridges, detected in Fig. 7(b) can never be identified without considering a maximum permissible time.

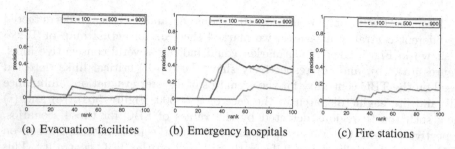

| (a) Evacuation facilities | (b) Emergency hospitals | (c) Fire stations |

Fig. 6. Precision comparison in criticalness centrality of the top-100 links obtained by each centrality measure for different maximum permissible time ($\tau = 100$, 500 and 900).

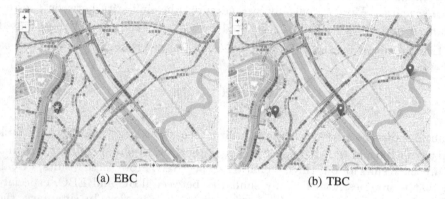

(a) EBC   (b) TBC

Fig. 7. Comparison of critical links detected by the EBC and TBC centralities in the case of ambulance call ($\tau = 500$), where the star shaped marker and the red pin marker denote the location of an emergency hospital and the detected critical link, respectively.

6 Conclusion

In this paper, we proposed an efficient algorithm to identify critical links in a spatial network based on node reachability assuming a realistic scenario in which a limitation is imposed on the traveling time from a node to the nearest target facility (or vice versa). Such time constraint is quite natural in an emergency situation such as disaster evacuation, ambulance call, and fire engine dispatch. To this end, we formalized the criticalness of a link as the reduction of the number of people that are reachable from/to one of target facilities within the maximum permissible time when the link is blocked, and named it the time-bounded criticalness centrality (TBC). The proposed algorithm can efficiently calculate the centrality by conducting tree search in two phases for a given spatial network. The first phase is forest construction (FC) that generates trees consisting of nodes reachable to one of target facilities in the spatial network within a given maximum permissible time. The second phase, local update (LU), actually calculates the time-bounded criticalness centrality of each link e by only checking a subtree isolated from the forest when e is removed. We experimentally evaluated the proposed algorithm using a real-world road network of Tokyo and the geographical information of actual evacuation facilities, emergency hospitals, and fire stations in Tokyo. The computation time of the proposed method is substantially small compared to the computation of betweenness centrality and less than 100 s even for a network having millions of nodes and links, in which the computation of FC that conducts the best first search is dominant and that of LU is much less implying the local search is quite efficient. The value of the time-bounded criticalness centrality of top-ranked critical links tends to increase as the maximum permissible time gets longer, but does not monotonically change. It depends on the number of target facilities and their locations. The critical links detected by the proposed centrality are quite different from the ones detected based on a straightforward extension of the traditional betweenness centrality and are distributed differently according to the scenario considered. Thus, the conventional centralities cannot serve as an alternative to the proposed time-bounded criticalness centrality.

Extending our algorithm so that it can handle road capacity is one future direction of this work.

Acknowledgments. This material is based upon work supported by JSPS Grant-in-Aid for Scientific Research (C) (No. 17K00314).

References

1. Akram, V.K., Dagdeviren, O.: Breadth-first search-based single-phase algorithms for bridge detection in wireless sensor networks. Sensors **13**(7), 8786–8813 (2013)
2. Barabási, A.L.: Network Science. Cambridge University Press, Cambridge (2016)
3. Brandes, U., Erlebach, T. (eds.): Network Analysis: Methodological Foundations. LNCS, vol. 3418. Springer, Heidelberg (2005). https://doi.org/10.1007/b106453
4. Burckhart, K., Martin, O.J.: An interpretation of the recent evolution of the city of barcelona through the traffic maps. J. Geogr. Inf. Syst. **4**(4), 298–311 (2012)
5. Crucitti, P., Latora, V., Porta, S.: Centrality measures in spatial networks of urban streets. Phys. Rev. E **73**(3), 036125 (2006)
6. Fang, Y.P., Pedroni, N., Zio, E.: Comparing network-centric and power flow models for the optimal allocation of link capacities in a cascade-resilient power transmission network. IEEE Syst. J. **99**, 1–12 (2014)
7. Grady, D., Thiemann, C., Brockmann, D.: Robust classification of salient links in complex networks. Nature Commun. **3**(864), 1–10 (2012)
8. Kimura, M., Saito, K., Motoda, H.: Blocking links to minimize contamination spread in a social network. ACM Trans. Knowl. Discov. Data **3**, 9:1–9:23 (2009)
9. Koschützki, D., Lehmann, K.A., Peeters, L., Richter, S., Tenfelde-Podehl, D., Zlotowski, O.: Centrality indices. In: Brandes, U., Erlebach, T. (eds.) Network Analysis. LNCS, vol. 3418, pp. 16–61. Springer, Heidelberg (2005). https://doi.org/10.1007/978-3-540-31955-9_3
10. Montis, D.A., Barthelemy, M., Chessa, A., Vespignani, A.: The structure of interurban traffic: a weighted network analysis. Environ. Plan. **34**(5), 905–924 (2007)
11. Ohara, K., Saito, K., Kimura, M., Motoda, H.: Accelerating computation of distance based centrality measures for spatial networks. In: Calders, T., Ceci, M., Malerba, D. (eds.) DS 2016. LNCS (LNAI), vol. 9956, pp. 376–391. Springer, Cham (2016). https://doi.org/10.1007/978-3-319-46307-0_24

12. Ohara, K., Saito, K., Kimura, M., Motoda, H.: Maximizing network performance based on group centrality by creating most effective k-links. In: Proceedings of the 4th IEEE International Conference on Data Science and Advanced Analytics (DSAA 2017), pp. 561–570 (2017)
13. Oliveira, E.L., Portugal, L.S., Junior, W.P.: Determining critical links in a road network: vulnerability and congestion indicators. Procedia Soc. Behav. Sci. **162**, 158–167 (2014)
14. Opsahl, T., Agneessens, F., Skvoretz, J.: Node centrality in weighted networks: generalizing degree and shortest paths. Soc. Netw. **32**(3), 245–251 (2010)
15. Park, K., Yilmaz, A.: A social network analysis approach to analyze road networks. In: Proceedings of the ASPRS Annual Conference 2010 (2010)
16. Piraveenan, M., Prokopenko, M., Hossein, L.: Percolation centrality: quantifying graph-theoretic impact of nodes during percolation in networks. PLoS ONE **8**(1), 1–14 (2013)
17. Saito, K., Ohara, K., Kimura, M., Motoda, H.: Accurate and efficient detection of critical links in network to minimize information loss. J. Intell. Inf. Syst. **51**(2), 235–255 (2018)
18. Saito, K., Ohara, K., Kimura, M., Motoda, H.: Efficient detection of critical links to maintain performance of network with uncertain connectivity. In: Geng, X., Kang, B.-H. (eds.) PRICAI 2018. LNCS (LNAI), vol. 11012, pp. 282–295. Springer, Cham (2018). https://doi.org/10.1007/978-3-319-97304-3_22
19. Sariyüce, A.E., Kaya, K., Saule, E., Çatalyürek, U.V.: Graph manipulations for fast centrality computation. ACM Trans. Knowl. Discov. Data **11**(3), 26:1–26:25 (2017)
20. Shen, Y., Nguyen, N.P., Xuan, Y., Thai, M.T.: On the discovery of critical links and nodes for assessing network vulnerability. IEEE/ACM Trans. Networking **21**(3), 963–973 (2013)
21. Tarjan, R.E.: A note on finding the bridges of a graph. Inf. Process. Lett. **2**(6), 160–161 (1974)
22. Wang, P., Hunter, T., Bayen, A.M., Schechtner, K., Gonzalez, M.C.: Understanding road usage patterns in urban areas. Sci. Rep. **2**, 1001:1–1001:6 (2012)

Adaptive Self-Sufficient Itemset Miner for Transactional Data Streams

Feiyang Tang[1(✉)], David Tse Jung Huang[1(✉)], Yun Sing Koh[1],
and Philippe Fournier-Viger[2]

[1] School of Computer Science, The University of Auckland, Auckland, New Zealand
ftan638@aucklanduni.ac.nz, dtjh@cs.auckland.ac.nz
[2] School of Humanities and Social Sciences,
Harbin Institute of Technology (Shenzhen), Shenzhen, China

Abstract. Most studies on pattern mining consider itemsets that have a high frequency of occurrence as useful, often determined by the support of the itemsets. However, current research has shown that we need to move beyond a pure "support-confidence" framework for pattern mining. Recently, there is an interest on finding statistically significant patterns and one of the most popular type of patterns is self-sufficient itemsets. One limitation is that these works do not consider concept drifts and cannot be used in a data stream. Learning in the online environment requires us to develop efficient and effective mechanisms to address the online characteristics of non-static data and non-stationary data distributions. In our research we will concentrate on detecting self-sufficient itemsets from data streams. These patterns have a frequency that is significantly different from the frequency of their subsets and supersets. We present a comprehensive framework for mining self-sufficient itemsets from data streams along with a drift detector. This supports mining self-sufficient itemsets in an online environment and provides the ability to adapt to changes in the stream. Our experimental evaluations show that our framework can mine self-sufficient itemsets faster in an online environment and with better precision and recall.

Keywords: Data stream mining · Batch processing ·
Self-sufficient itemsets · Association rule mining · Drift detection

1 Introduction

Current research in association rule mining relies on using minimum or maximum support thresholds to derive the association rules [8], which comes with many drawbacks such as not considering the statistical significance of patterns. Thus, these work may find many frequent patterns that are spurious - contains values that appear together by chance rather than having a strong correlation. To solve this drawback, Webb et al. [19,20] proposed and defined self-sufficient itemsets to produce more 'interesting' rules. Those are patterns have a frequency that is significantly different from the frequency of their subsets and supersets.

© Springer Nature Switzerland AG 2019
A. C. Nayak and A. Sharma (Eds.): PRICAI 2019, LNAI 11671, pp. 419–430, 2019.
https://doi.org/10.1007/978-3-030-29911-8_32

It has been shown that itemsets derived using a minimum support that do not also satisfy the definition of self-sufficient itemsets are unlikely to produce interesting rules. Given the infinite growth of data streams, we require the association rule mining algorithms to be workable on a data stream. While a large number of papers discussed mining interesting association rules from data streams, the non-stationary distributions problem has not been as widely dealt with in the pattern mining research domain. Changes in the underlying distribution may lead to changes in the relevant pool of itemsets over time, which will reduce the correctness of interesting rules mined. This is known as the concept drift problem.

Currently when a change is detected by the concept drift detector, the entire existing set of rules previously found are discarded and we re-mine the rules from the new data in the data stream. This is an inefficient method since there is a possibility that only a small portion of the rules have changed and discarding and re-mining entire sets to discover small changes is not ideal. There is also the problem of setting a proper interval value to discard and re-mine. If we discard and re-mine too frequently, the running cost will be high. On the other hand, if we discard and re-mine too infrequently, we risk not picking up the correct rules within the time-frame. For example, using supermarket basket analysis data, consider the situation where the supplier for Cheerios had suddenly stopped supplying Cheerios to the supermarket. As a consequence, future transactions will not contain Cheerios and this leads to a concept drift. If we discarded and re-mined at this time, the patterns containing Cheerios will be lost. If Cheerios immediately starts to restock after we re-mined, we are not able to pick up the patterns related to Cheerios again. Therefore, in this case, the disappearance of Cheerios could be identified as a regional drift. Mining regional drifts allow us to better adapt to the intricate changes in the patterns over time.

We propose a new online pattern mining framework called Adaptive Self-Sufficient Itemset Miner (ASSIM) that generates self-sufficient itemsets in non-stationary data streams containing concept drifts. To reduce inefficiency in processing time and memory use, ASSIM identifies regional drifts, which detects minor changes in the patterns of a data streams. ASSIM adapts to regional concept drifts by storing in a buffer transactions which do not contain the mined self-sufficient itemsets. Whenever a drift is reported, the buffer will be re-mined for self-sufficient itemsets. As a result, previous self-sufficient itemsets are able to be picked up again at a later time, rather than discarded completely. While this paper is focused on mining self-sufficient itemsets, the adaptive online learning structure could be used for other pattern mining techniques as well.

The structure of this paper is as follows: in Sect. 2 we discuss current research on frequent pattern mining and concept drift detection. In Sect. 3 we discuss the basic definitions of important components. In Sect. 4 we propose our Adaptive Self-Sufficient Itemset Miner (ASSIM) framework, and explain how ASSIM improves the mining results of self-sufficient itemsets. Section 5 focuses on evaluating the key components of ASSIM by evaluating their computational costs, precision and recall, and other important measures. Section 6 draws a conclusion on the work and identifies future directions.

2   Related Work

While there are large amounts of literature on identifying and discovering association rules [1–3,17]), they are all heavily reliant on using a support threshold to derive interesting association rules. The existing literature on identifying and discovering interesting rules beyond using support or frequency of occurrence is relatively sparse. Webb [18] points out that many pattern mining algorithms suffer from type-I errors which usually identifies infrequent itemsets as frequent. To deal with the drawbacks of the pure "support-confidence" framework for pattern mining, Hamalainen [8] proposed a solution which handles non-monotonicity. It also prunes redundant rules on-line. The quality of rules is estimated by the Fisher's exact test. "self-sufficient itemsets" [19] were created to solve this dilemma by contributing a set of constraints and a statistical test that can be applied during and after itemset discovery to identify itemsets significantly differ from what is expected based on higher or lower-order interactions between factors within the data.

According to [16], an important problem in the streaming scenario is classification, where data is labelled into categories or classes. As data streams are considered to be non-stationary, the distribution of data and their class labels will likely change over time. Concept drift detection methods are used to monitor classification errors from classifiers (with binary input where 0 is a correct classification and 1 is a misclassification) to identify when changes happen. In our scenario, we want to determine how frequent potential "interesting" itemsets occur in the data stream. The measure we used to feed our drift detector with is the binary occurrence of itemsets in each transaction of the data stream (0 if itemset is not present and 1 if itemset is present). Gama et al. [7] gives an overview of mainstream drift detectors used for data stream. One of the most widely used detector is ADWIN [4]. It detects concept drifts using an adaptive windowing strategy and signals drifts if the absolute value of the difference between any two windows surpasses a pre-defined threshold, derived from Hoeffding Bound.

3   Preliminaries

This section discusses the basic definitions of data streams, self-sufficient itemsets, interestingness measurements and regional concept drifts.

Data Stream. A data stream is a sequence of data instances arriving continuously. It is considered to be dynamic and unbounded in size with data generated at a very fast pace. Generally, a dynamic data stream cannot be processed in the same way as a static database. Dynamic data streams require one-pass techniques using either batch processing or online processing of data. A data stream $\mathcal{D}$ with n elements is defined as $\mathcal{D} = \{T_1, T_2, ..., T_n\}$, where by T_i represents a transaction at time i. Each transaction contains a set of items $T = \{x_1, x_2, ... x_m\}$, where by x_j represents an item.

Self-Sufficient Itemsets. The most common way to mine frequent itemsets from data streams is to define a minimum support threshold. However, it has been proven that when the data is dense, using minimum support creates a high misclassification rate where infrequent itemsets are identified as frequent. To improve this, Webb [19] defined self-sufficient itemsets using a measure called *itemset leverage*. It measures the degree of potential interest that arises naturally from the tests developed in [19] by checking their productivity and non-redundancy. We further adapted the method by using Fisher's exact test to check for the minimum support threshold as well. This has been used in previous techniques [8, 19].

In terms of quantifying interestingness, the Min Partition Measure (MPM) is used. Webb [19] suggests that itemset measures should be developed from a rule measure by selecting the least extreme value that results from applying the measure to any rule that can be created by partitioning the itemset x into an antecedent y and consequent $z = x - y$. In this work, two measures: *leverage*, δ Eq. 1 and *lift*, γ Eq. 2 have been used:

$$\delta(x) = \min_{y \subsetneq x}(sup(x) - sup(y) \times sup(x \setminus y)) \tag{1}$$

$$\gamma(x) = \min_{y \subsetneq x}(sup(x)/[sup(y) \times sup(x \setminus y)]) \tag{2}$$

Regional Concept Drift. Due to the inherent temporal aspect of data streams, the underlying data distribution of streams may change over time, known as concept drifts. Concept drift can make the machine learning model inaccurate because of the inconsistency between existing data and new data.

Most distribution based drift detection methods assume that a drift occurs abruptly at a time point, incrementally, or gradually in a time period [9]. As a result, the split time point between old and new concepts is the key solution. However, this time-oriented "one-cut" process could not adapt to the real-world scenarios well. Accordingly, the data arrived before that drift point is discarded. Thus, if a drift only occurs in a small region of the entire feature space, the other non-drifted regions may also be suspended, thereby reducing the learning efficiency of models. To retrieve non-drifted information from suspended historical data, similar to the buffer system [12] used to find the best drift time point to identify concepts, we propose a simple solution to identify regional drifts and integrate it into our self-sufficient itemset mining process.

4   Adaptive Self-Sufficient Itemset Miner (ASSIM)

To mine self-sufficient itemsets and to solve the regional concept drift problem at the same time, we propose a new technique: Adaptive Self-Sufficient Itemset Miner (ASSIM). ASSIM is able to mine self-sufficient itemsets in an online mode, and at the same time, detect regional drifts among generated self-sufficient itemsets and adapt the drifts to the self-sufficient itemset generation process.

The current self-sufficient miner [19] is designed for static databases. To use this technique unaltered on a data stream has its pitfalls. This includes regional concept drifts that may occur over time in data stream, making previously generated self-sufficient itemsets inaccurate. We can adapt self-sufficient miner by generating itemsets at fixed intervals but this is inefficient, and there may be a delay between when changes happen in the data stream to when the new set of itemsets are generated. Another possibility is that if the intervals are set too far apart we may miss out on generating those itemsets all together. Our framework is designed to overcome this problem.

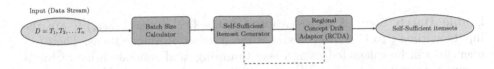

Fig. 1. Framework of adaptive self-sufficient itemset miner

An illustration of our ASSIM framework is shown in Fig. 1. It gives a general idea of the structure of ASSIM and how the data flows inside ASSIM. As transactions are fed into ASSIM, they will be processed first in the Batch Size Calculator (BSC) to get an appropriate batch size before we enter the itemset mining process. The calculation of the batch size is crucial to avoid overfitting. We realised that there are possible minor fluctuations within a data streams. Thus, a stable bucket allows for a more representative sample to be used in the mining process.

Using the calculated batch size, the Self-Sufficient Itemset Generator (SSIG) can be used to generate self-sufficient itemsets. All generated self-sufficient itemsets will be checked for potential regional concept drifts by the Regional Concept Drift Adaptor (RCDA). Once a regional drift has been detected, RCDA will check the drift type and determine whether SSIG needs to generate new self-sufficient itemsets from the drift point or not.

4.1 Batch Processing

The Batch Size Calculator (BSC) is the first part of our ASSIM framework. It was designed to handle frequency counting and batch size calculation. It provides an approximation of item frequencies. The main purpose of this is to ensure that a proper stable batch size was used before we mined for self-sufficient itemsets. As with any data streams, selecting an adequate learning window is essential to ensure the quality of the results produced. If the batch size is too small, the variance of the itemsets produced may be an issue. If the batch size is too large, then there is a lag or time delay between when transactions happen to when it is mined.

Data stream mining requires a stable and comparable batch size to represent the current state. In this case, Lossy Counting [13] has been used because of its low computational cost which improves both memory and run-time processing. As only an approximated ranking list is needed, for the expansion process we used Lossy Counting. To use Lossy Counting, we divide the incoming data stream into buckets. We keep a running histogram of the unique items for each transaction in the data stream. If items appear in a transaction within a bucket size, we increment the frequency count of those items. At the end of each bucket, we decrement each of the counters by 1. At the end, the most frequently viewed items 'survive'.

Stable Batch Size. A data stream of items $\{x_1, x_2, x_3, \ldots, x_m\}^{(t)}$ are the inputs at time t to BSC, whereby m is the number of unique items. Their frequencies will be calculated using Lossy Counting, and generate a list of top n frequent items $\{a_1, a_2, \ldots, a_n\}^{(t)}$. Meanwhile, to calculate a stable and comparable batch size for the self-sufficient itemset generator, the distribution of each frequent item $D^{(t)} = \{d_{a1}, d_{a2}, \ldots, d_{an}\}^{(t)}$ in each Lossy Counting bucket will be calculated and compared with the prior bucket of $D^{(t-b)} = \{d_{a1}, d_{a2}, \ldots, d_{an}\}^{(t-b)}$, where b is the bucket size.

When a new bucket has been processed, we average the frequency differences of top k frequent items (picked from Lossy Counting) between the current bucket and the prior one. If the average frequency difference is larger than threshold τ,

$$\frac{1}{k} \sum d_{ak}^{(t)} - \frac{1}{k} \sum d_{ak}^{(t-b)} > \tau,$$

we report the bucket number B and the first batch size will be $B \times (1/e)$ whereby e is the tolerance error rate for the approximation.

4.2 Self-Sufficient Itemset Generator (SSIG)

We adapted the OPUS Miner proposed by Webb [19], for a dynamic streaming data. For a user-specified k ($k = 100$ by default) and interest measure, OPUS Miner find the top-k productive non-redundant itemsets (also known as self-sufficient itemsets).

The original algorithm establishes a queue of items ordered in descending order on the upper bound on the value of any itemset that can include the item. However, one particular constraint with data stream algorithms is that there is only a one or limited pass through the data stream capability. This means the ability to run through an re-order of information is limited. In our self-sufficient itemset generator technique, we used the frequency counts from BSC to order the items instead.

BSC provides an approximation of frequency counts for items, which helps us replace the static counting algorithm used in the original OPUS Miner. The mining of the itemsets remains unmodified from the original version.

The new Self-Sufficient Itemset Generator (SSIG) uses the list of frequent items obtained from BSC. We check for their interestingness and start to expand them into potential self-sufficient itemsets. Each newly generated itemsets and their partitions will be passed into both Fisher's Exact Test and interestingness measure to check for productivity and non-redundancy. Finally, all itemsets that pass all required constraints are considered as self-sufficient itemsets, S.

4.3   Regional Concept Drift Adaptor (RCDA)

The Regional Concept Drift Adaptor (RCDA) plays a key role in our ASSIM framework. It detects regional concept drifts in the generated self-sufficient itemsets. It analyses concept drifts and make decisions on where and when to re-mine additional items using SSIG.

RCDA uses a well known drift detector, ADWIN [4], to detect concept drifts in the data streams. ADWIN monitors the changes in distribution between two windows, specifically, the distribution of the support of the self-sufficient itemsets found after the previous drift point, and the updated distribution of the supports that represents the current distribution. If there is a significant difference between the two windows a change is signalled.

The naïve way to adapt to concept drifts is to re-mine the itemsets each time a drift has been detected, discarding all the old itemsets. This is inefficient as we may have lost valuable itemset information that may still be current.

RCDA is designed to overcome this problem by storing previously mined self-sufficient itemsets along with its frequency. The approach works as follows. Each itemset is monitored using its own drift detector. As a transaction, T, in the data stream appears we check whether it contains any of the self-sufficient itemsets S, whereby $\exists S \in T$. If the itemsets exists, we will update the support of the itemsets. If none of the itemsets in S exist in T then we store the transaction in a buffer, B. We re-mine B using SSIG when the next drift point is signaled.

The intuition is that transactions that do not contain pre-existing itemsets may contain new knowledge on the data. Thus, by capturing and re-mining that portion of the stream, we are essentially looking for new itemsets that are just appearing in the new incoming data stream. This region of data does not contain any previously found itemsets and would not be considered to be from the same distribution.

We also remove any itemsets that are no longer found in the current data stream. For example we may have a self-sufficient itemset A that has appeared in the data stream previously but the support of this itemset has dropped significantly in the current time window measured from the previous drift point to the current point, and no longer satisfies the thresholds.

5   Experiments

In this section, we describe three groups of experiments conducted to evaluate ASSIM. The first group examines the computational costs of ASSIM, time and memory use. The second group evaluates the accuracy of BSC and RCDA by recording their precision and recall values under different circumstances. Lastly, we inject different kinds of drifts into the data streams and test the efficiency and accuracy of our drift detector. All experiments are conducted on a machine with Intel Core i7-7700 Desktop Processor 4 Cores with up to 4.2 GHz CPU with 32 GB RAM.

5.1 Descriptions of the Datasets

Table 1. Descriptions of the datasets

Dataset	Description
T10I1KD100K	Synthetic dataset with an average transaction length 10
T15I1KD1M	Synthetic dataset with an average transaction length 15
mushrooms	Prepared based on the UCI mushrooms dataset
retail	Retail market basket data from a Belgian retail store
pumsb	Census data for population and housing
chess	Prepared based on the UCI chess dataset
connect	Prepared based on the UCI connect-4 dataset
accidents	Anonymized traffic accident data
BMS_WebView	Click-stream data from a webstore used in KDD-Cup 2000
chainstore	Customer transactions from a retail store from NU-Mine Bench

We employed ten datasets including eight of the largest attribute-value datasets from the UCI machine learning [6,15] and UCI KDD [10] repositories together with the BMS-WebView [11], retail [5] and chainstore from CUCIS [14] datasets. The other two are synthetic datasets created by IBM data generator. These datasets are described in Table 1.

Each synthetic dataset configuration (*T10I1KD100K* and *T15I1KD1M*) was generated with different seed values and passed into the algorithm 30 times. The other eight real-world datasets were tested a single time each.

5.2 Runtime and Memory Performance

We ran our ten datasets on BSC and SSIG separately to record the time and memory used for each component of our technique. In this case, SSIG without batches represents the ground truth which produces the truth result of self-sufficient itemsets in each dataset.

Table 2. Runtime and memory performance

Dataset	ASSIM BSC		SSIG without batches	
	Time (s)	Memory (Mb)	Time (s)	Memory (Mb)
T10I1KD100K	1.97 ± 0.92	210.28 ± 0.89	2.85 ± 0.33	148.41 ± 0.33
T15I1KD1M	35.24 ± 1.36	642.81 ± 2.01	47.42 ± 3.64	572.22 ± 0.97
mushrooms	0.54 ± 0.04	78.36 ± 0.27	1.09 ± 0.16	55.73 ± 0.21
retail	1.64 ± 0.29	192.45 ± 0.84	2.44 ± 1.02	136.85 ± 0.76
pumsb	0.92 ± 0.05	101.34 ± 0.76	1.49 ± 0.11	74.32 ± 0.19
chess	0.19 ± 0.02	25.92 ± 0.37	0.31 ± 0.10	10.78 ± 0.14
connect	1.85 ± 0.06	168.32 ± 1.92	2.11 ± 0.21	103.27 ± 0.35
accidents	8.24 ± 0.79	385.56 ± 2.34	2.87 ± 0.67	339.14 ± 0.68
BMS_WebView	1.11 ± 0.12	119.38 ± 0.78	1.46 ± 0.40	91.25 ± 0.07
chainstore	38.21 ± 1.28	783.15 ± 2.35	51.97 ± 2.07	711.92 ± 1.06
Dataset	SSIG with fixed intervals		SSIG with batches	
	Time (s)	Memory (Mb)	Time (s)	Memory (Mb)
T10I1KD100K	3.04 ± 0.69	149.12 ± 0.30	3.05 ± 0.23	149.10 ± 0.27
T15I1KD1M	49.10 ± 2.41	574.11 ± 0.85	49.17 ± 1.94	574.12 ± 0.88
mushrooms	1.15 ± 0.11	56.09 ± 0.33	1.17 ± 0.23	56.12 ± 0.19
retail	2.69 ± 0.27	138.02 ± 0.81	2.82 ± 0.04	137.98 ± 0.84
pumsb	1.52 ± 0.11	75.65 ± 0.22	1.52 ± 0.12	75.61 ± 0.27
chess	0.39 ± 0.02	10.98 ± 0.07	0.39 ± 0.04	11.02 ± 0.08
connect	2.30 ± 0.10	104.25 ± 0.29	2.28 ± 0.09	104.23 ± 0.33
accidents	3.02 ± 0.32	321.01 ± 0.72	2.99 ± 0.17	320.88 ± 0.77
BMS_WebView	1.57 ± 0.07	92.07 ± 0.15	1.57 ± 0.12	92.05 ± 0.17
chainstore	56.39 ± 0.27	714.24 ± 0.84	56.41 ± 0.19	714.25 ± 0.86

Table 2 illustrates that BSC is stable. It has a faster runtime performance as compared from SSIG without batches. In our experiments, the tolerance error rate for the approximation $e = 0.05$ and frequency difference threshold $\tau = 25\%$. To further evaluate the efficiency of BSC, we also perform two additional experiments for each dataset. In the additional set of experiments, we feed equally divided batches into SSIG (divided into the same amount of batches as BSC but in fixed interval). This is to show how runtime and memory performance is effected given the same number of datasets. In the second set of experiments, we feed batches into SSIG separately based on the pre-determined size of the intervals found using BSC. To do this we noted the location of the batch size found in BSC and then superimposed the same exact batch sizes for SSIG. The significance level $\alpha = 0.05$ was used for performing Fisher's Exact Test in SSIG.

This experiments was to evaluate the runtime and memory if we mined at the same time point of BSC. Table 2 shows us that there is no significant difference between the time and memory consumption between SSIG with a fixed interval and with pre-calculated batches based found using BSC.

5.3 Experiments to Evaluate Precision and Recall

As a result of using Lossy Counting [13] in BSC, all the frequent items produced by BSC are true positives, as shown in Table 3. Thus producing 100% precision. Lossy Counting in BSC only provides an approximation to the frequency of an item in a batch. Some of the frequent items, which should have been included for expansion to self-sufficient itemsets may be missed. This would lead to recall being less than 100%. We use the SSIG without batches as the ground truth of the set of self-sufficient itemsets found.

Table 3. Precision and recall

Dataset	ASSIM BSC		SSIG with fixed intervals		SSIG with batches	
	Precision (%)	Recall (%)	Precision (%)	Recall (%)	Precision (%)	Recall (%)
T10I1KD100K	100% ± 0%	97% ± 2%	96% ± 1%	98% ± 2%	97% ± 2%	98% ± 1%
T15I1KD1M	100% ± 0%	98% ± 1%	93% ± 3%	95% ± 4%	96% ± 2%	99% ± 1%
mushrooms	100%	97%	97%	99%	97%	97%
retail	100%	98%	95%	96%	97%	97%
pumsb	100%	98%	96%	94%	97%	94%
chess	100%	100%	100%	98%	100%	99%
connect	100%	98%	95%	97%	95%	97%
accidents	100%	96%	93%	94%	98%	98%
BMS_WebView	100%	99%	96%	95%	99%	97%
chainstore	100%	95%	95%	97%	96%	99%

With the batch calculation from BSC, the correctly detected batches of data stream achieved better precision and recall values for self-sufficient itemset mining as compared to SSIG with fixed intervals or SSIG with batches.

5.4 Experiments to Evaluate the Regional Drift Detection

In the drift detection part, we perform two different tests: abrupt and gradual drift detection on *T10I1KD100K* dataset. The delta value $\delta = 0.002$ was set for ADWIN drift detector. For abrupt drifts, we inject different numbers of abrupt drifts, specifically 5, 10 and 20 into *T10I1KD100K*. Several indications were recorded: time and memory costs, true and false positives, and delay. Based on the results the increase of drift points, this leads to worse false positives as shown in Table 4.

To evaluate gradual drift detection, we used the same dataset *T10I1KD100K* but changed data in different rates noted as the slopes, specifically 250, 500 and 1,000. Same indications were used for this test as shown in Table 5, and it showed that higher slopes produce worse false positives and longer delay.

Table 4. Abrupt drift detection

#Drifts	Time (s)	Memory (Mb)	TP rate (%)	FP	Delay
5	6.42 ± 0.11	23.1 ± 0.07	1.0 ± 0.00	77.81 ± 0.07	184.65 ± 67.84
10	6.54 ± 0.08	23.2 ± 0.09	1.0 ± 0.00	385.42 ± 39.61	157.82 ± 39.61
20	6.59 ± 0.10	23.1 ± 0.08	1.0 ± 0.00	793.11 ± 55.28	93.11 ± 35.28

Table 5. Gradual drift detection

Slope	Time (s)	Memory (Mb)	TP rate (%)	FP	Delay
250	6.52 ± 0.14	23.1 ± 0.03	1.0 ± 0.00	174.29 ± 53.11	98.35 ± 78.25
500	6.82 ± 0.18	23.2 ± 0.07	1.0 ± 0.00	482.36 ± 42.83	164.70 ± 69.83
1000	7.01 ± 0.22	23.1 ± 0.03	1.0 ± 0.00	853.16 ± 107.28	218.65 ± 109.62

6 Conclusion and Future Work

In this paper, we first comprehensively reviewed the pure "support-confidence" framework for pattern mining and proposed a novel solution - self-sufficient itemsets. Then, we highlighted the deficiencies of the current methods. Against the shortage of current methods, we proposed Adaptive Self-Sufficient Itemset Miner (ASSIM) which makes self-sufficient itemset miner work in an online mode along with a drift detector to reduce the error brought by the non-stationary distributions. ASSIM includes a Batch Size Calculator to calculate the size of the batches, Self-Sufficient Itemset Generator to mine self-sufficient itemsets and Regional Concept Drift Adaptor to detect regional concept drifts.

Experiments demonstrated that the Batch Size Calculator provides more accurate results without substantially increasing time or memory consumption. This proves that our technique ASSIM could achieve a better result as compared to using the self-sufficient itemset miners in a static way.

Future work includes developing a more accurate method for regional drift adaptor which can retrieve location information related to drifted regions. This information can then be used to analyse in a wider picture to build a more accurate adaptive self-sufficient itemset miner that can better handle real-world data streams.

References

1. Agrawal, R., Imielinski, T., Swami, A.: Mining association rules between sets of items in large databases. In: SIGMOD Conference, vol. 22, p. 207 (1993)
2. Bayardo, R.J., Agrawal, R.: Mining the most interesting rules. In: Proceedings of the Fifth ACM SIGKDD International Conference on Knowledge Discovery and Data Mining, pp. 145–154 (1999)
3. Bayardo, R.J., Agrawal, R., Gunopulos, D.: Constraint-based rule mining in large, dense databases. Data Min. Knowl. Disc. 4(2), 217–240 (2000)

4. Bifet, A., Gavalda, R.: Learning from time-changing data with adaptive windowing. In: Proceedings of the 2007 SIAM International Conference on Data Mining, pp. 443–448 (2007)
5. Brijs, T., Swinnen, G., Vanhoof, K., Wets, G.: Using association rules for product assortment decisions: a case study. In: Proceedings of the Fifth ACM SIGKDD International Conference on Knowledge Discovery and Data Mining, pp. 254–260 (1999)
6. Dua, D., Karra Taniskidou, E.: UCI machine learning repository (2017). http://archive.ics.uci.edu/ml
7. Gama, J., Žliobaitė, I., Bifet, A., Pechenizkiy, M., Bouchachia, A.: A survey on concept drift adaptation. ACM Comput. Surv. **46**(4), 44:1–44:37 (2014)
8. Hamalainen, W.: Kingfisher: an efficient algorithm for searching for both positive and negative dependency rules with statistical significance measures. Knowl. Inf. Syst. **32**, 1–32 (2011)
9. Harel, M., Crammer, K., El-Yaniv, R., Mannor, S.: Concept drift detection through resampling. In: Proceedings of the 31st International Conference on International Conference on Machine Learning, vol. 32, pp. II-1009–II-1017 (2014)
10. Hettich, S., Bay, S.D.: Irvine, CA (1999). http://kdd.ics.uci.edu
11. Kohavi, R., Brodley, C., Frasca, B., Mason, L., Zheng, Z.: KDD-cup 2000 organizers' report. SIGKDD Explor. **2**, 86–98 (2000)
12. Liu, A., Zhang, G., Lu, J.: Fuzzy time windowing for gradual concept drift adaptation. In: Proceedings of the 2017 IEEE International Conference on Fuzzy Systems, pp. 1–6. IEEE (2017)
13. Manku, G.S., Motwani, R.: Approximate frequency counts over data streams. In: Proceedings of the 28th International Conference on Very Large Data Bases, pp. 346–357 (2002)
14. Narayanan, R., Honbo, D., Memik, G., Choudhary, A., Zambreno, J.: NU-MineBench (2018). http://cucis.ece.northwestern.edu/index.html
15. Newman, C.B.D., Merz, C.: UCI repository of machine learning databases (1998). http://www.ics.uci.edu/~mlearn/MLRepository.html
16. Nguyen, H.L., Woon, Y.K., Ng, W.K.: A survey on data stream clustering and classification. Knowl. Inf. Syst. **45**, 535–569 (2014)
17. Piatetsky-Shapiro, G.: Discovery, analysis, and presentation of strong rules. Knowl. Discovery Databases, 229–238 (1991)
18. Webb, G.: Discovering significant patterns. Mach. Learn. **68**(1), 1–33 (2007)
19. Webb, G.: Self-sufficient itemsets: an approach to screening potentially interesting associations between items. ACM Trans. Knowl. Discov. Data **4**, 1–20 (2010)
20. Webb, G.: Filtered-top-k association discovery. WIREs Data Mining Knowl. Discov. **1**(3), 183–192 (2011)

BMF: Matrix Factorization of Large Scale Data Using Block Based Approach

Prasad Bhavana[(✉)] and Vineet Padmanabhan

School of Computer and Information Sciences, University of Hyderabad,
Hyderabad, India
17mcpc14@uohyd.ac.in, vineetcs@uohyd.ernet.in

Abstract. Matrix Factorization on large scale matrices is a memory intensive task. Alternative convergence techniques are needed when the size of the input matrix and the latent feature matrices are higher than the available memory, both on a Central Processing Unit (CPU) as well as a Graphical Processing Unit (GPU). While alternating least squares (ALS) convergence on a CPU could last forever, loading all the required matrices on to a GPU memory may not be possible when the dimensions are significantly high. In this paper, we introduce a novel technique based on dividing the entire data into block matrices and make use of the Stochastic Gradient Descent (SGD) based factorization at the block level.

1 Introduction

Matrix Factorization (MF) is a well known machine learning technique with applications in domains like recommender systems, text mining, data compression and astronomy. The simplicity of the technique is based on deriving the underlying latent factors which in turn leads to an estimation of behavioural patterns by utilizing the large data of observed behaviours. Computation of MF on a CPU is not viable for large matrices as the number of computations increase with each extra row and/or column and with each additional latent feature derived. The data sets available in recommender systems domain are sparse and have marginal dimensions. The current machine learning techniques seem to work well with little extra hardware. With time, as availability of data increases, currently available techniques do not scale and/or produce sub-optimal results. MF implemented on a GPU gives substantial performance gain as the number of computations are nearly divided by the number of computational units. However, GPU memory is finite and typically low. The memory required for MF of a data matrix of dimension $m \times n$ can be calculated as $\approx (m \times n + m \times k + k \times n) \times c$ for some constant c bytes taken to represent each element. Loading part of the data into processing unit and continuing to transfer the data back and forth is a cumbersome approach that also consumes additional time. A data set of 10 million users $\times$ 1 million items, represented in dense format, consumes approximately 40 Tera Bytes of memory. Assuming 8 Giga Bytes of memory available on a given processing unit with 2 Giga bits/sec transfer rate requires a total of

© Springer Nature Switzerland AG 2019
A. C. Nayak and A. Sharma (Eds.): PRICAI 2019, LNAI 11671, pp. 431–436, 2019.
https://doi.org/10.1007/978-3-030-29911-8_33

5000 back and forth data transfers that consume ~200 h of time for data transfer alone. In [1], an alternative approach is proposed that uses memory optimization to reduce the time of data transfer into GPU for computation. While this approach provides computational gain, the approach still requires frequent data transfers for large data. In [2], a divide and conquer approach is proposed for parallelism in MF by treating factorization of each sub-matrix as a sub-problem and combining the results, an approach that resulted in noisy factorization. Similarly in [3], a localized factorization is proposed for recommendation on a block diagonal matrix. In [4], a divide and conquer strategy based Non-Negative MF (NNMF) is proposed for fast clustering and topic modeling. The approach proposes scalability from rank-2 to rank-k using binary tree structure of the data items. In [5,6] a GPU accelerated NNMF is proposed. In [7–14], different MF approaches are proposed for speed or parallelism or GPU acceleration or distributed computation but all these techniques fail to handle scale. In this paper, we propose a novel approach that divides any given matrix into a block matrix and factor the matrix in such a way that it is possible to efficiently process the data on one or more processing units. The approach can be used in the context of speed, scale, parallelism, GPU acceleration and distributed computing based on MF.

2 The Approach

Let $X \in \mathbb{R}^{\{m \times n\}}$ be a matrix with m users and n observations per user. The MF approach is an estimation of data matrix $X \approx UV^T$ where user, item latent factor matrices $U \in \mathbb{R}^{\{m \times k\}}$ and $V \in \mathbb{R}^{\{n \times k\}}$ (for some chosen k dimensions) are respectively derived from the given observations. A common formulation of MF optimization problem can be represented as:

$$\min_{U,V} \sum_{x_{ij}} (x_{ij} - u_i v_j^T)^2 + \frac{\beta}{2} \left(\sum_u ||u_i||^2 + \sum_v ||v_j||^2 \right) \tag{1}$$

$$X = \begin{bmatrix} \underline{X}_{11} & \underline{X}_{12} & \cdots & \underline{X}_{1j} & \cdots & \underline{X}_{1J} \\ \vdots & \vdots & \cdots & \vdots & \ddots & \vdots \\ \underline{X}_{i1} & \underline{X}_{i2} & \cdots & \underline{X}_{ij} & \cdots & \underline{X}_{iJ} \\ \vdots & \vdots & \cdots & \vdots & \ddots & \vdots \\ \underline{X}_{I1} & \underline{X}_{I2} & \cdots & \underline{X}_{Ij} & \cdots & \underline{X}_{IJ} \end{bmatrix} \tag{2}$$

where β is the regularization parameter. Our proposal of block matrix representation of the data matrix is based on concatenation of blocks/sub-matrices of equal dimension as shown in Eq. (2). As shown in Fig. 1, BMF considers each block as an individual matrix. It then factorizes each block for one iteration and takes the latent features of the blocks as a starting point for approximation of the latent features for the relevant blocks thereafter. Figure 2 demonstrates a simple example wherein X is divided into 4 blocks and each block is factorized individually so as to combine them together to form U, V that explain X. After the sub-matrix $\underline{X}_{ij}$ is factorized for one iteration, the resultant latent feature

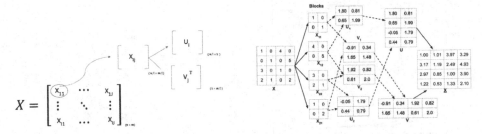

Fig. 1. Block based approach to MF   **Fig. 2.** An example of BMF

sub-matrix $\underline{U}_i$ is used further by all the sub-matrices $\underline{X}_{ij+1}, \underline{X}_{ij+2}..\underline{X}_{iJ}$ lying on the same row as that of $\underline{X}_{ij}$. Similarly, $\underline{V}_j$ is used by all the sub-matrices $\underline{X}_{i+1j}, \underline{X}_{i+2j}..\underline{X}_{Ij}$ lying on the same column as that of $\underline{X}_{ij}$. The convergence of each individual sub-matrix closely matches that of overall matrix. The optimization problem of BMF at block level can be adapted from Eq. (1) as:

$$\min_{\underline{U}_i, \underline{V}_j} ||\underline{X}_{ij} - \underline{U}_i \underline{V}_j^T|| + \frac{\beta}{2} \left(\sum_{\underline{U}} ||\underline{U}_i||_F^2 + \sum_{\underline{V}} ||\underline{V}_j||_F^2 \right) \qquad (3)$$

where $||.||_F$ denotes Frobenius norm of the matrix. The block level $\underline{U}_i$ and V_j can be factorized by alternating one block after the other for each iteration. Refer Appendix (A) for block level update equations.

Parallelism: It is possible to approximate U_i and V_j matrices simultaneously by identifying the data blocks whose latent factors do not depend on each other. Figure 4 shows one such example with a 6×6 block matrix where blocks represented with the same color (and a number placed low right corner of the cell) can be simultaneously factorized; i.e blocks on the diagonal are processed in first parallel step and then the BMF is moved on to the blocks below them while considering the entire column as a loop starting from diagonal block. A broad outline of the approach is given in Algorithm 1. The $mf()$ function in the

---

Algorithm 1: Block Matrix Factorization (BMF)

Require: Input: Data matrix $X \in \mathbb{R}^{\{m \times n\}}$, number of features k
    Init: $U \in \mathbb{R}^{\{m \times k\}}, V \in \mathbb{R}^{\{n \times k\}}$ with random values. Let I, J be two constants such
    that X is represented by $I \times J$ blocks. Represent X as block matrix with
    sub-matrices X_{ij} where $i \in 1..I$ and $j \in 1..J$. Represent U, V as block matrix with
    U_i, V_j where $i \in 1..I$ and $j \in 1..J$. Initialize STEPS (maximum iterations), α
    (learning rate), β (regularization factor) and δ (minimum deviation of error)
    for step 1 to STEPS **do**
        for each column j in block matrix X **do**
            $j \leftarrow mod((j + step), J)$
            $U_i, V_j \leftarrow mf(X_{ij}, U_i, V_j, k, \alpha, \beta)$
        end for
        Terminate if RMSE improvement is $< \delta$
    end for
    Return latent feature matrices U, V

3.00
2.75
2.50
2.25
2.00
1.75
1.50
1.25
1.00
rmse
1 BLOCK
4 BLOCKs
16 BLOCKs
0
2000
4000
6000
8000
10000
12000
time(s)

Fig. 3. RMSE comparison of different block combinations of BMF

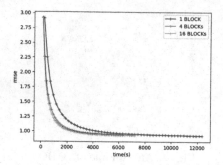

X_{11} 1
X_{12} 6
X_{13} 5
X_{14} 4
X_{15} 3
X_{16} 2
X_{21} 2
X_{22} 1
X_{23} 6
X_{24} 5
X_{25} 4
X_{26} 3
X_{31} 3
X_{32} 2
X_{33} 1
X_{34} 6
X_{35} 5
X_{36} 4
X_{41} 4
X_{42} 3
X_{43} 2
X_{44} 1
X_{45} 6
X_{46} 5
X_{51} 5
X_{52} 4
X_{53} 3
X_{54} 2
X_{55} 1
X_{56} 6
X_{61} 6
X_{62} 5
X_{63} 4
X_{64} 3
X_{65} 2
X_{66} 1

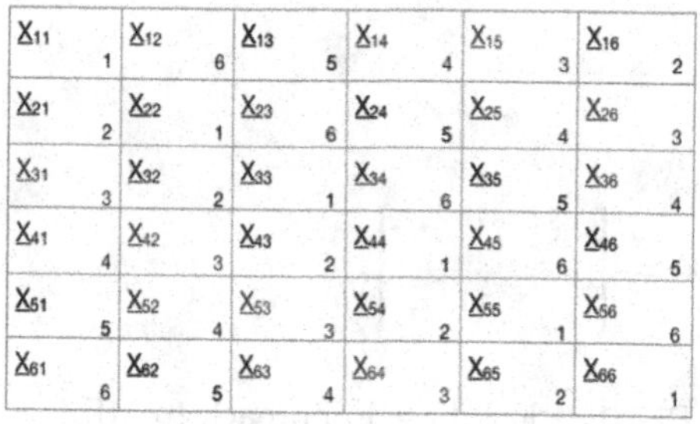

Fig. 4. Example of a parallel approach to BMF

algorithm encapsulates parallel implementation of MF at a block level for one iteration only. Considering I, k as constants and as the two for-loops (iterating STEPS number of times, and iterating for each sub-matrix) already contribute to I and size of data, hence, the time complexity of the algorithm remains same as MF. Considering the block size as constant, the space complexity per block is $\approx O(c)$ (constant).

3 Experiments

The experiments outlined below are conducted on a shared hardware with Intel(R) Xeon(R) CPU E5-2640 v3 @ 2.60 GHz. The data sets used in the experiments are split into 80% training and 20% test at random. The experiments are repeated 3 times and the results are averaged for consistency. Table 1 lists the comparative analysis of time taken per iteration and test RMSE for CPU implementation of BMF (1 Block, 4 Blocks, 16 Blocks variants). From the results presented in the table, Fig. 3, it is evident that the convergence of BMF coincides with that of MF. Different data sets are used to confirm the same observation. The RMSE of all block variants are within delta. The decrease in computational time with increase in number of blocks is achieved through parallelism. Optimization in space is also observed as each thread needs constant memory.

Table 1. Results of BMF against reference data sets. 4, 16 block variants are multi-threaded parallel implementations with 4, 16 parallel threads respectively.

	BMF num.of blocks	MovieLense 100K	MovieLense 1M	Jester 4M
Training time (sec/iteration)	1 Block	233.38	3029.63	943.84
	4 Blocks	136.22	1801.49	628.94
	16 Blocks	128.26	1741.56	614.88
Test RMSE	1 Block	0.955	0.921	2.163
	4 Blocks	0.954	0.926	2.167
	16 Blocks	0.956	0.926	2.16

4   Conclusion

Our proposed approach of BMF is a novel framework that provides computational advantage, with respect to parallel processing and with respect to runtime memory need, without compromising on RMSE. The technique could be combined with GPU acceleration, memory optimization as detailed in [1]. The technique can also be extended further for speed, scale, parallelism, distributed computation and GPU acceleration with other approaches like [2–14]. The $mf()$ function within Algorithm 1 can implement state-of-the-art kernels for better results while leveraging scale, parallelism, speed and distribution with BMF. The technique could be altered for NNMF, Maximum-Margin MF (MMMF), Probabilistic MF (PMF) and any other variants of MF. The approach can also be applied to various domains (that leverage MF) ranging from recommender systems to text mining [6].

A   Derivation of SGD Update Equations for BMF

Our objective is to find $\underline{U_i}, \underline{V_j}$ for $\underline{X_{ij}}$ such that $\underline{X_{ij}} \approx \underline{U_i}.\underline{V_j}^T$. Let $\underline{E_{ij}}$ represent the deviation of estimate $\underline{X_{ij}}'$ from actual $(\underline{X_{ij}})$. Hence, sum of squared deviations $(\mathcal{E})$ can be represented as:

$$\mathcal{E} = ||\underline{X_{ij}} - \underline{X_{ij}}'||^2 = ||\underline{X_{ij}} - \underline{U_i}\underline{V_j}^T||^2 \tag{4}$$

The goal is to find $\underline{U_i}$ and $\underline{V_j}$ such that the sum of squared deviations is minimal. The optimum value for g^{th} latent feature of $\underline{U_i}$ and $\underline{V_j}$ blocks can be obtained by minimizing Eq. (4) with respect to $\underline{U_i}$ and $\underline{V_j}$ respectively as:

$$\frac{\partial}{\partial \underline{U_i}_{*g}} \mathcal{E} = -2(\underline{X_{ij}} - \underline{X_{ij}}').\underline{V_j}_{*g} \tag{5}$$

$$\frac{\partial}{\partial \underline{V_j}_{*g}} \mathcal{E} = -2(\underline{X_{ij}} - \underline{X_{ij}}')^T \underline{U_i}_{*g} \tag{6}$$

Using the block level gradients for a latent feature, the update equations for g^{th} feature of $\underline{U_i}$ and $\underline{V_j}$ can be arrived as:

$$\underline{U_i}'_{*g} = \underline{U_i}_{*g} + \alpha \frac{\partial}{\partial \underline{U_i}_{*g}} \mathcal{E} = \underline{U_i}_{*g} + 2\alpha \underline{E_{ij}} \underline{V_j}_{*g} \tag{7}$$

$$\underline{V_j}'_{*g} = \underline{V_j}_{*g} + \alpha \frac{\partial}{\partial \underline{V_j}_{*g}} \mathcal{E} = \underline{V_j}_{*g} + 2\alpha \underline{E_{ij}}^T \underline{U_i}_{*g} \tag{8}$$

Factoring in regularization term into the Eqs. (7) and (8) gives us:

$$\underline{U_i}'_{*g} = \underline{U_i}_{*g} + \alpha(2\underline{E_{ij}}\underline{V_j}_{*g} - \beta \underline{U_i}_{*g}) \tag{9}$$

$$\underline{V_i}'_{*g} = \underline{V_j}_{*g} + \alpha(2\underline{E_{ij}}^T \underline{U_i}_{*g} - \beta \underline{V_j}_{*g}) \tag{10}$$

References

1. Tan, W., Chang, S., Fong, L.L., Li, C., Wang, Z., Cao, L.: Matrix factorization on GPUs with memory optimization and approximate computing. In: ICPP (2018)
2. Mackey, L.W., Jordan, M.I., Talwalkar, A.: Divide-and-conquer matrix factorization. In: NIPS, pp. 1134–1142 (2011)
3. Zhang, Y., Zhang, M., Liu, Y., Ma, S., Feng, S.: Localized matrix factorization for recommendation based on matrix block diagonal forms. In: WWW, pp. 1511–1520. ACM (2013)
4. Du, R., Kuang, D., Drake, B., Park, H.: DC-NMF: non-negative matrix factorization based on divide-and-conquer for fast clustering and topic modeling. J. Glob. Optim. **68**(4), 777–798 (2017)
5. Koitka, S., Friedrich, C.M.: nmfgpu4R: GPU-accelerated computation of the non-negative matrix factorization using cuda capable hardware. R J. **8**(2), 382–392 (2016)
6. Kysenko, V., Rupp, K., Marchenko, O., Selberherr, S., Anisimov, A.: GPU-accelerated non-negative matrix factorization for text mining. In: NIPS, pp. 158–163 (2012)
7. Schelter, S., Satuluri, V., Zadeh, R.: Factorbird - a parameter server approach to distributed matrix factorization. CoRR arXiv:abs/1411.0602 (2014)
8. Gemulla, R., Nijkamp, E., Haas, P.J., Sismanis, Y.: Large-scale matrix factorization with distributed stochastic gradient descent. In: SIGKDD, pp. 69–77 (2011)
9. Yun, H., Yu, H.F., Hsieh, C.J., Vishwanathan, S.V.N., Dhillon, I.: NOMAD: non-locking, stochastic multi-machine algorithm for asynchronous and decentralized matrix completion. Proc. VLDB Endow. **7**(11), 975–986 (2014)
10. Li, B., Tata, S., Sismanis, Y.: Sparkler: supporting large-scale matrix factorization. In: Joint EDBT/ICDT Conferences, pp. 625–636 (2013)
11. Zhuang, Y., Chin, W.S., Juan, Y.C., Lin, C.J.: A fast parallel stochastic gradient descent for matrix factorization in shared memory systems. In: RecSys, pp. 249–256 (2013)
12. Recht, B., Ré, C., Wright, S.J., Niu, F.: Hogwild: a lock-free approach to parallelizing stochastic gradient descent. In: NIPS, pp. 693–701 (2011)
13. Oh, J., Han, W., Yu, H., Jiang, X.: Fast and robust parallel SGD matrix factorization. In: KDD, pp. 865–874 (2015)
14. Yu, H., Hsieh, C., Si, S., Dhillon, I.S.: Scalable coordinate descent approaches to parallel matrix factorization for recommender systems. In: ICDM, pp. 765–774 (2012)

Traffic and Vehicular Automation

Pedestrian Trajectory Prediction Using a Social Pyramid

Hao Xue$^{(\boxtimes)}$, Du Q. Huynh , and Mark Reynolds

The University of Western Australia, Perth, Australia
hao.xue@research.uwa.edu.au, {du.huynh,mark.reynolds}@uwa.edu.au

Abstract. Understanding and forecasting human movement paths are vital for a wide range of real world applications. It is not an easy task to generate plausible future paths as the scenes and human movement patterns are often very complex. In this paper, we propose a social pyramid based prediction method (SPP), which includes two encoders to capture motion and social information. Specifically, we design a social pyramid map structure for the Social encoder, which can differentiate the influence of other pedestrians in nearby areas or remote areas based on their spatial locations. For the Motion encoder, a mixing attention mechanism is proposed to combine the location coordinates and velocity vectors. The two encoded features are then merged and passed to the decoder which generates future paths of pedestrians. Our extensive experimental results demonstrate competitive prediction performance from our method compared to state-of-art methods.

Keywords: Trajectory prediction · LSTM · Social pyramid

1 Introduction

Research on predicting trajectories of pedestrians has gained much attention in the past few years due to its relevance to a large number of applications such as traffic analysis [6,25], crowd management [42,44], pedestrian tracking [8], autonomous vehicles [3], and anomaly detection [24]. The prediction of pedestrians' moving paths depends on two crucial factors. First is *Motion information*: the movement of a target person (or person of interest, POI) relies on his/her own motion information. This provides the main clue for future path prediction. Second is *Social information*: a pedestrian should not be treated in isolation during the prediction process. The route of one pedestrian is often under the influence of other people in the scene. This is often referred to as *social influence* or *social interaction* in the literature.

Pedestrian trajectory prediction is not a new problem. Research work in this field dates back to the 90s. Classical prediction models [13,16,26,41] reported in the literature rely heavily on hand-crafted features and they have been shown to give poorer performance compared to more modern techniques. With a large amount of video data collected in many public areas today, we see a growing

© Springer Nature Switzerland AG 2019
A. C. Nayak and A. Sharma (Eds.): PRICAI 2019, LNAI 11671, pp. 439–453, 2019.
https://doi.org/10.1007/978-3-030-29911-8_34

Fig. 1. In a crowded scene, the immediate neighbourhood region (blue) and a remote area (green) have different degrees of *social influence* to the POI (red dot). The crowd in the blue region would affect the POI's walking pace; the crowd in the green area would affect the POI's future path if his/her destination is the exit at the upper left corner. (Color figure online)

number of data-driven deep learning methods [1,11,12,18,19,28–30,34,38] being applied to pedestrian trajectory forecasting. Social influence is known to play an important role in pedestrians' walking paths in a scene. Indeed, quite a few papers on incorporating social influence into trajectory prediction framework have already been reported in the literature. For example, social pooling layers have been used in the Social LSTM [1] network to model the social relationship between nearby neighbours; different shapes of neighbourhood regions together with scene information have been used to capture pedestrian movement patterns [40]; a social pooling module, which expands on the social pooling idea, have been used in Social GAN [11]. The pooling mechanism in this method considers all the pedestrians in the scene rather than only the surrounding neighbours.

To illustrate the complexity of social influence in a crowded scene, consider the image of the busy Central Station shown in Fig. 1. With respect to the POI (red dot), the immediate neighbourhood (blue rectangle) is likely to have more influence on his/her walking pace: generally pedestrians prefer to keep some distance from strangers in public areas. However, the more remote areas (e.g., the region marked in green) should not be ignored. When pedestrians move in a scene, remote areas serve as a guidance for their future path planning. Suppose that the POI intends to go to the exit on the top left corner of the image. He/she would more likely detour slightly to avoid the crowd in the green region rather than taking a straight-line path. In this paper, we propose to handle social influence by dividing the scene into grids and looking at the pedestrians in each grid in turn, *i.e.*, our method does not focus on just the immediate neighbourhood of the POI. However, unlike the existing methods above which model social influence using either a small neighbourhood region around the POI (*e.g.*, [1,35,40]) or all the pedestrians in the scene (*e.g.*, [11,21]), our method does not consider the exact location coordinates of pedestrians in the remote areas. Our method can be considered as between the two categories above.

To handle the motion information, we design an attention mechanism that merges the location and velocity information in our network. This is different from existing techniques which use only the location coordinates [1, 29, 30, 46] or only the displacement vectors [21, 38, 43].

We name our model SPP, which is short for Social Pyramid based Prediction. The research contributions of this work are summarized below: (i) Our SPP network embodies information from both the motion clue of pedestrians' own trajectories and the social neighbourhood. We evaluate our method on publicly available datasets with different experimental settings and compare its performance with state-of-art methods. We also justify the effectiveness of our method by comparing it with its three variants. (ii) The Motion encoder of our network includes information from location and the velocity coordinates. We also design a mixing attention mechanism to merge these two parts for each trajectory. (iii) We propose to use a novel social pyramid structure to handle the social relationship from all the other pedestrians at different levels, starting from the whole scene and gradually zooming into each person of interest.

The paper is organized as follows. Related work about different trajectory prediction methods are given in Sect. 2. Section 3 presents the proposed SPP. The datasets used for evaluation, details of our experiments, quantitative and qualitative results are discussed in Sect. 4. Finally, the last section concludes the paper.

2 Related Work

Classical Models
Traditionally, hand crafted features were widely used for human motion modelling and trajectory prediction. The Social Force model [13] (SFM), a classical and pioneer model designed to describe pedestrian behaviour, encompasses two interactive social forces: the attractive force towards the pedestrians' destinations and the repulsive force for collision avoidance. This method has been recently revisited by Pellegrini et al. [26]. The authors design a trajectory prediction model, named as Linear Trajectory Avoidance (LTA), which takes into account both simple scene information in the form of destinations or desired direction and interactions between different targets. This LTA model has also been used for tracking people in their work. Since then, further research built on top of the SFM includes: Yamaguchi et al. [41] extend the Social Force model by incorporating more factors such as damping and social interactions; Xie et al. [37] add scene context information into the cost function. The main shortcoming of these methods is that their performance highly depends on energy cost functions manually designed based on relative distances or specific rules.

Another research branch is trajectory prediction based on Gaussian Processes. Kim et al. [15] model trajectories as a continuous dense flow field and use Gaussian Process regression to classify trajectories and detect anomaly. For

442   H. Xue et al.

pedestrian trajectory prediction, Wang *et al.* [36] propose to use Gaussian Process Dynamical models to capture the motion dynamics of trajectories. Vemula *et al.* [35] design an interactive Gaussian Process model to describe the cooperative behaviour in dense human crowds, targeting at collision avoidance problems in robotics.

CNN Based Models
Convolutional Neural Networks are commonly used in classification or recognition problems that are associated with images. However, CNN models have been used successfully in prediction problems. The behaviour-CNN of Yi *et al.* [43] encodes the pedestrians' walking paths as displacement volumes, which are then used to predict future trajectories. Nikhil *et al.* [25] design a CNN that has highly parallelizable convolutional layers to deal with motion dependencies in the trajectory data. For vehicle trajectories, a convolutional social pooling structure has been used to encode the past motion of neighbouring vehicles [6] and a multiple layer CNN has been adopted to combine multi-scale trajectory patterns for trajectory prediction [23].

LSTM Based Models
Recurrent models such as the basic Recurrent Neural Network (RNN), Long Short Term Memory (LSTM) [14], and Gated Recurrent Unit (GRU) [5] have been designed and successfully applied to various sequence data tasks including speech recognition [10,27], language translation [32], action recognition [22,45] and image captioning [4]. In the last few years, several methods have also been proposed to use LSTMs to handle trajectories represented as sequences of 2D coordinates. Motivated by the sequence generation model from [9], Alahi *et al.* [1] propose the Social LSTM model which includes a social pooling layer to model the neighbourhood and to avoid collisions between pedestrians.

Since the proposal of Social LSTM [1], a tremendous number of LSTM based trajectory prediction methods have been published [31,38,39,46]. From the Social Force model [13] to Social LSTM [1] and Social GAN [11], the social influence aspect in trajectory prediction has particularly drawn much interest. Typical work includes: Gupta *et al.*'s paper [11] on using a pooling module to expand the social neighbourhood modelling to the entire scene; and Li's [20,21] handling of social information using a convolutional LSTM network to incorporate social information.

Apart from the work above, we also see attention mechanisms being incorporated into trajectory forecasting, *e.g.*, [7,34], scene context being encoded into prediction networks, *e.g.*, [2,18,40], and head pose information being used, *e.g.*, the MX-LSTM architecture of [12].

3   Proposed Method

3.1   Problem Definition and System Overview

The trajectory of pedestrian i, where $i \in [1, N]$ assuming that there are N pedestrians in the scene, is represented as a sequence of two dimensional coordinates

(x_t^i, y_t^i). The trajectory prediction problem can be described as one where we observe the coordinates from $t = 1$ to $t = T_{\mathrm{obs}}$ and make predictions for the time span $t = T_{\mathrm{obs}}+1, \cdots, T_{\mathrm{obs}}+T_{\mathrm{pred}}$. Here, T_{obs} and T_{pred} are the observation length and the prediction length, respectively.

Our proposed network is illustrated in Fig. 2. To handle both the motion and social dependencies in the trajectory prediction process, we propose to use two encoders: one for the motion information and one for the social information. The predicted trajectories are generated through the decoder which takes the output from the two encoders as input. In the subsections below, we will describe the details of these three key components of our network separately.

3.2 The Motion Encoder

This encoder focuses on the POI's own history path, which is the dominating information for generating his/her future path. Unlike other methods, both the location and velocity terms of each trajectory are taken as input in our proposed network. The velocity (u_t^i, v_t^i) is obtained from the finite differences of (x_t^i, y_t^i) with respect to time t. As the velocity term depicts the instantaneous moving direction and stride of the pedestrian, it is independent of the POI's absolute location on the ground. The velocity term therefore captures important walking pace of the pedestrian regardless of which part of the scene he/she is located. Instead of passing the coordinates and displacements directly to the LSTM encoder, a mixing attention layer is used to firstly merge the terms (x_t, y_t) and (u_t, v_t) so that our model has the attentiveness capability. The idea of adding a mixing attention layer is based on the observation that the location and velocity terms do not usually contribute equally to the trajectory prediction process. To simplify the explanation, the subscript i is dropped from hereon.

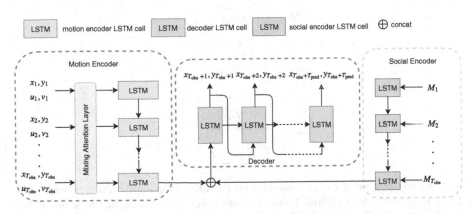

Fig. 2. The proposed SPP framework. Location (x_t, y_t) and velocity (u_t, v_t) are jointly considered through the mixing attention layer in the Motion encoder. The social pyramid tensors $M_t, \forall t$, are the input of the Social encoder. The encoded motion and social features are concatenated as input to the decoder.

Using the renowned scaled dot-product attention mechanism proposed by Vaswani *et al.* [33], an attention function can be considered as one that maps a query vector and a set of key-value pairs to an output. At each time step, our (x_t, y_t) and (u_t, v_t) terms can thus be embedded into the query vectors $\mathbf{q}_t^l$ and $\mathbf{q}_t^v$ and key vectors $\mathbf{k}_t^l$ and $\mathbf{k}_t^v$. These embedding query and key vectors are r-dimensional, where r is a chosen integer suitable for the problem.

The query vectors $\mathbf{q}_t^l$ and $\mathbf{q}_t^v$ are stacked row-wise to form a matrix $\mathbf{Q}_t \in \mathbb{R}^{2 \times r}$. Similarly, $\mathbf{k}_t^l$ and $\mathbf{k}_t^v$ are stacked row-wise to form $\mathbf{K}_t \in \mathbb{R}^{2 \times r}$. The attention matrix $\mathbf{A}_t \in \mathbb{R}^{2 \times 2}$ is then calculated as:

$$\mathbf{A}_t = \text{softmax}\left(\frac{\mathbf{Q}_t \mathbf{K}_t^\top}{\sqrt{r}}\right), \tag{1}$$

where $\sqrt{r}$ is used as a scaling factor and the softmax function is applied to the matrix in a row-wise fashion.

We use the diagonal entries of $\mathbf{A}_t$ as the weights for the location and velocity terms. That is, we let $\alpha_{t,1} = \mathbf{A}_{t,1,1}$ and $\alpha_{t,2} = \mathbf{A}_{t,2,2}$. Note that it is not necessary to normalize so that $\alpha_{t,1} + \alpha_{t,2} = 1$ as the scale would be absorbed by the downstream LSTM layer. The combined weighted output $(\hat{x}_t, \hat{y}_t)$ after the mixing attention is computed using Eq. (2) and the encoded hidden state, $\mathbf{h}_t^m$, of the Motion encoder part is defined using Eq. (3):

$$(\hat{x}_t, \hat{y}_t) = \alpha_{t,1}(x_t, y_t) + \alpha_{t,2}(u_t, v_t) \tag{2}$$

$$\mathbf{h}_{t+1}^m = \text{LSTM}_m\left(\mathbf{h}_t^m, (\hat{x}_t, \hat{y}_t); \mathbf{W}_m\right), \tag{3}$$

where $\mathbf{W}_m$ is the weight matrix of LSTM_m, the LSTM layer of the Motion encoder.

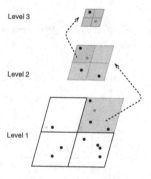

Fig. 3. An illustration of the proposed Social Pyramid Map construction process. The red dot represents the POI and black dots are other pedestrians in the scene at the same time step. In this example, the grid size n is set to 2 and the pyramid map has 3 levels. The ROI of level 1 is the whole scene. The peach colour grid at level 1 becomes the ROI at level 2. The light blue grid of level 2 becomes the ROI at level 3. (Color figure online)

3.3 The Social Encoder

To incorporate the social information, current existing prediction methods in the literature consider either the neighbours of the POI [1,35,40] or the whole scene [11,21]. However, people in remote areas do not have the same degree of influence as pedestrians in the immediate neighbourhood around a POI. Thus, we use a pyramid structure (Fig. 3) of L levels and grid size n to capture the social information around each POI at different scales. At level 1, the region of interest (ROI) containing the POI is just the entire scene. As one moves up to the next level of the pyramid structure, the size of ROI is reduced by the factor given by n. This structure can be seen as a spotlight following the POI and gradually zooming into his/her neighbourhood level by level.

With the setting of grid size n and map level L, for each pedestrian at time step t, a social pyramid tensor $M_t \in \mathbb{R}^{2 \times n^2 \times L}$ is built using Algorithm 1. For simplification, we drop superscript i but note that the social pyramid tensor is computed for each pedestrian. In the algorithm, $\mathcal{P}_t = \{(x_t^j, y_t^j)\}_{j=1}^{J_t}$ denotes a set of pedestrians' location coordinates, where J_t is the total number of pedestrians inside the boundary of the ROI at the current level at time t. At the beginning, $\mathcal{P}_t$ is initialized to contains all the pedestrians in the whole scene. The 3D entities $g_t^l \in \mathbb{R}^{2 \times n \times n}$, for $l = 1, \cdots, L$, are the social map tensors for the construction of M_t. At the grid indexed by $[a, b]$, the entity $g_t^l[a, b]$ is a $\mathbb{R}^2$ vector holding information at that region at level l of the scene. We use $\mathcal{I}_{ab}^l(x, y)$ to denote the

---

Algorithm 1. Building the Social Pyramid Map for a POI at location (x_t, y_t) at time t

Input: n: grid size; L: maximum map level; (x_t, y_t): location of POI; ROI: region of interest containing the POI; $\mathcal{P}_t$: $\{(x_t^j, y_t^j)\}_{j=1}^{J_t}$, set of pedestrians' coordinates in ROI
Output: Social pyramid map tensor M_t at time step t

1: **for** $1 \leq l \leq L$ **do**
2:      divide ROI into $n \times n$ grids
3:      **for** each grid $[a, b]$ at level l in ROI **do**
4:          **if** $\mathcal{I}_{ab}^l(x_t, y_t) = 1$ **then**
5:              $g_t^l[a, b] \leftarrow (x_t, y_t)$
6:              $\mathcal{P}_t \leftarrow \{(x_t^j, y_t^j) \in \mathcal{P}_t, \forall j \mid \mathcal{I}_{ab}^l(x_t^j, y_t^j) = 1\}$
7:              update ROI using grid $[a, b]$
8:          **else**
9:              **if** $\sum_{j=1}^{J} \mathcal{I}_{ab}^l(x_t^j, y_t^j) = 0$ **then**
10:                 $\bar{x}_{a,b}^l \leftarrow 0, \bar{y}_{a,b}^l \leftarrow 0$
11:             **else**
12:                 $\bar{x}_{a,b}^l \leftarrow \dfrac{\sum_{j=1}^{J_t} \mathcal{I}_{ab}^l(x_t^j, y_t^j) x_t^j}{\sum_{j=1}^{J_t} \mathcal{I}_{ab}^l(x_t^j, y_t^j)}$
13:                 $\bar{y}_{a,b}^l \leftarrow \dfrac{\sum_{j=1}^{J_t} \mathcal{I}_{ab}^l(x_t^j, y_t^j) y_t^j}{\sum_{j=1}^{J_t} \mathcal{I}_{ab}^l(x_t^j, y_t^j)}$
14:             $g_t^l[a, b] \leftarrow (\bar{x}_{a,b}^l, \bar{y}_{a,b}^l)$
15: $M_t \leftarrow g_t^1 \oplus g_t^2 \oplus \cdots \oplus g_t^L$
16: **return** M_t

indicator function which returns 1 if the coordinates (x, y) fall inside the grid $[a, b]$ at the lth level of the social map tensor, and returns 0 otherwise.

The way M_t is constructed is based on the observation that, with respect to a POI, the exact coordinates of each pedestrian in those remote areas are not important. To the POI, each remote area at different parts of the scene is perceived to have a small group of pedestrians scattering around. Only until the POI moves into one of these areas, more detailed information about the pedestrians in that area would become relevant. As a result, for those grids $g_t^l[a, b]$ that do not contain the POI, the algorithm computes only the mean coordinates $(\bar{x}_{a,b}^l, \bar{y}_{a,b}^l)$ (lines 12–13 of Algorithm 1). At each level, the grid containing the POI becomes the ROI for the next level. The social pyramid map M_t is finally formed by the concatenation of the 3D tensors $g_t^l, \forall l$.

The grid size n and the total number of levels L are two related parameters that define the size of M_t. Let H and W be the height and width of the scene in pixels. As it is impossible for two persons to fall onto the same pixel, once n is determined, it is necessary that $n^L / \min(H, W) \geq 1$. This means that

$$L \geq \lceil \log \min(H, W) / \log n \rceil, \tag{4}$$

where $\lceil . \rceil$ denotes rounding up to the nearest integer. Since the size of the ROI needs to shrink by a factor of n when moving up one level of the social pyramid tensor M_t, the only constraint on n is $n \geq 2$. For large n, fewer levels (smaller L) would be needed to zoom into the POI. In the case where n becomes so large that each grid contains at most 1 pedestrian only, M_t would collapse to a degenerate 1-level tensor. This would be undesirable as it would not be able to distinguish remote areas versus immediate neighbourhood any more. So, for the social pyramid tensor to be useful, n should not be too large. In Sect. 4.3, we explore various values of n and the associated prediction errors.

The constructed social pyramid tensor M_t is finally passed to the Social encoder LSTM_s for encoding the hidden state $\mathbf{h}_t^s$ as:

$$\mathbf{h}_{t+1}^s = \text{LSTM}_s\left(\mathbf{h}_t^s, M_t; \mathbf{W}_s\right), \tag{5}$$

where $\mathbf{W}_s$ is the weight matrix of LSTM_s.

3.4 Generating Predictions

We apply a straightforward encoder-decoder architecture for the trajectory prediction process. The input to the decoder LSTM_{dec} is the concatenated encoded hidden states $(\mathbf{h}_t^m \oplus \mathbf{h}_t^s)$. The predicted trajectory coordinates are calculated using Eq. (7) below:

$$\mathbf{h}_{t+1}^{\text{dec}} = \text{LSTM}_{\text{dec}}\left(\mathbf{h}_t^{\text{dec}}, \mathbf{h}_t^m \oplus \mathbf{h}_t^s; \mathbf{W}_{\text{dec}}\right), \tag{6}$$

$$\left(x_t^i, y_t^i\right) = \mathbf{W}_o \mathbf{h}_t^{\text{dec}} + \mathbf{b}_o, \tag{7}$$

where $\mathbf{W}_{\text{dec}}$ is the weight matrix of the LSTM decoder, and $\mathbf{W}_o$ and $\mathbf{b}_o$ are the weight matrix and bias term of the output layer.

Our proposed network is implemented using the Pytorch framework in Python. The dimension of each LSTM layer is set to 128 and the dimension r of the query and key vectors for the mixing attention layer in the Motion encoder is 64. The mean squared error (MSE) loss function is used to train the network and the Adam optimizer [17] is used for optimization. The initial learning rate is set to 0.001, which is decreased by half at every 1000 epochs.

4   Experiments

4.1   Datasets, Baselines and Evaluation Metrics

The Central Station dataset [44] contains over 10,000 trajectories represented in pixel coordinates. The resolution of the videos is 720 (width) × 480 (height) pixels. For the sake of fair comparison, we follow the same setting as in [46] and set $T_{obs} = 9$ and $T_{pred} = 8$. Short trajectories are firstly filtered out and then the rest trajectories are split into the training set (80%) and the test set (20%). Our SPP and its variants were trained on the training set only. We report the prediction results on the test set for all experiments. We also preprocess the dataset by normalizing the coordinates of each trajectory so that all the coordinates in the dataset are within $[0, 1]$.

We compare the prediction performance of our SPP network with the following baselines and state-of-art methods:

- *Constant Velocity*: A linear prediction method that assumes each pedestrian keeping the same velocity for the whole journey.
- *Social Force Model (SFM)* [13]: Prediction based on the pioneer Social Force model.
- *Linear Trajectory Avoidance (LTA)* [26]: Prediction based on energy minimization to avoid collision.
- *Behaviour-CNN* [43]: A CNN based method for pedestrian trajectory prediction.
- *Vanilla LSTM:* This is the basic vanilla LSTM using only the location information as input.
- *SA-GAIL* [46]: Social-Aware Generative Adversarial Imitation Learning, a generative adversarial network designed for trajectory prediction.

Our proposed SPP method has three variants for the ablation study:

- *SPP-social-only*: The Motion encoder is removed in this simplified version of SPP. Only the Social encoder is connected to the decoder for prediction.
- *SPP-motion-only*: This variant of SPP does not use any social pyramid tensors and does not include the Social encoder in the network.
- *LV-vanilla*: This variant is a simplified version of SPP-motion-only, with the mixing attention layer removed.

We adopt two common metrics used in evaluating trajectory prediction: Average Displacement Error (ADE) and Final Displacement Error (FDE). Where appropriate, the normalized ADE (normADE), which scales the ADE with respect to the size of the image, is also used.

Table 1. Prediction errors (in pixels) on the Central Station dataset.

Method	normADE	ADE	FDE
Constant velocity[a]	5.86%	-	-
SFM[a] [13]	4.45%	-	-
LTA[a] [26]	4.35%	-	-
Behaviour CNN[a] [43]	2.52%	-	-
LSTM[a]	2.39%	14.57	27.78
SA-GAIL[a] [46]	1.98%	11.98	23.05
SPP (ours)	1.67%	10.05	18.48
SPP-social-only (ours)	1.76%	10.65	20.64
SPP-motion-only (ours)	1.89%	11.46	22.54
LV-vanilla (ours)	2.31%	14.27	24.74

[a] Results taken from [46].

4.2 Quantitative Results

The results on the Central Station dataset are shown in Table 1. We follow the same experimental settings (*e.g.*, same T_{obs} and T_{pred} values) and take some of their reported results for comparison. As the most straightforward method, using constant velocity for trajectory prediction gives the worst result. Small improvements are evident when more factors, such as collision avoidance in the LTA or the attractive/repulsive forces in the SFM, are included in the prediction model. Compared to the above classical methods that use manually designed energy functions, there is a large gain in prediction accuracy from data-driven deep learning methods. All LSTM based methods, including the vanilla one, have better accuracy than the Behaviour CNN method. This makes perfect sense as the LSTM architecture is specifically designed for analyzing sequence data. The results show that our proposed SPP algorithm outperforms other methods on all the three metrics.

4.3 Ablation Study

The numerical results of our ablation study on the Central Station dataset are shown on the last four rows of Table 1. The better predication result of SPP over SPP-social-only and SPP-motion-only demonstrates the importance of having the Motion and Social encoders working together. Compared to the Motion encoder part, the Social encoder and the social pyramid tensors appear to have more contributions to the improvement of prediction. Our variant LV-vanilla only performs slightly better than Vanilla LSTM. The much poorer performance of LV-vanilla versus that of SPP-motion-only confirms the significance of the mixing attention layer in the Motion encoder.

Table 2. Prediction errors (in pixels) of using different grid sizes.

Method	SPP			SPP-social-only		
n	3	5	7	3	5	7
normADE	1.72%	1.67%	1.65%	1.82%	1.76%	1.74%
ADE	10.45	10.05	9.97	10.94	10.65	10.48
FDE	20.12	18.48	19.24	21.19	20.64	20.43

Different Grid Sizes

The grid size n is an important parameter in SPP as it determines the size of the social pyramid tensor. Table 2 shows the performance of SPP and SPP-social-only on the Central Station dataset for $n = 3$, 5, and 7. The value of L is computed accordingly using Eq. (4) (by replacing the $\geq$ sign by $=$). With larger n, the prediction errors are smaller for both methods. The results are not surprising as a larger n value gives finer grids and reveals more detailed information of the neighbourhood. However, it also results in more entries in the social pyramid tensor M_t and would require longer time to train and predict. Table 2 shows that there is a larger gain in performance from $n = 3$ to $n = 5$ compared to that from $n = 5$ to $n = 7$. So we choose $n = 5$ and set L to 4 (the smallest value computed from Eq. (4)) for a trade-off between speed and accuracy. We use these as the default values for n and L in all the experiments reported in this paper.

Different Prediction Lengths

Table 3 shows how our proposed method performs on predicting trajectories of different lengths. We train two SPP models using the $T_{obs} = 9$ setting in the training phase: **SPP-p8**, trained with $T_{pred} = 8$; and **SPP-p16**, trained with $T_{pred} = 16$. In the testing phase, these two models can be used to predict trajectories of any lengths. In our experiments, we use them to generate trajectories of 8, 12 and 16 frames long. Table 3 shows that SPP-p8 performs slightly better for 8-frame prediction. However, SPP-p16 is clearly the winner in predicting longer trajectories.

Table 3. ADE/FDE (in pixels) on different prediction lengths. SPP-p8 is trained with $T_{pred} = 8$; SPP-p16 is trained with $T_{pred} = 16$.

Model	Prediction length		
	8	12	16
SPP-p8	10.05/18.48	16.43/34.47	23.25/49.36
SPP-p16	10.27/19.91	15.52/31.47	21.69/45.62

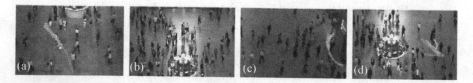

Fig. 4. Comparison of predicted trajectories generated by SPP (pink), SPP-motion-only (red) and SPP-social-only (yellow) on the Central Station dataset. Input observed trajectories are shown in blue; ground truth trajectories are in green. (Color figure online)

(a) Examples of trajectories that are almost straight lines

(b) Examples of pedestrians taking slight turns

(c) Examples of pedestrians leaving the scene

(d) Examples of pedestrians making an abrupt change of walking direction

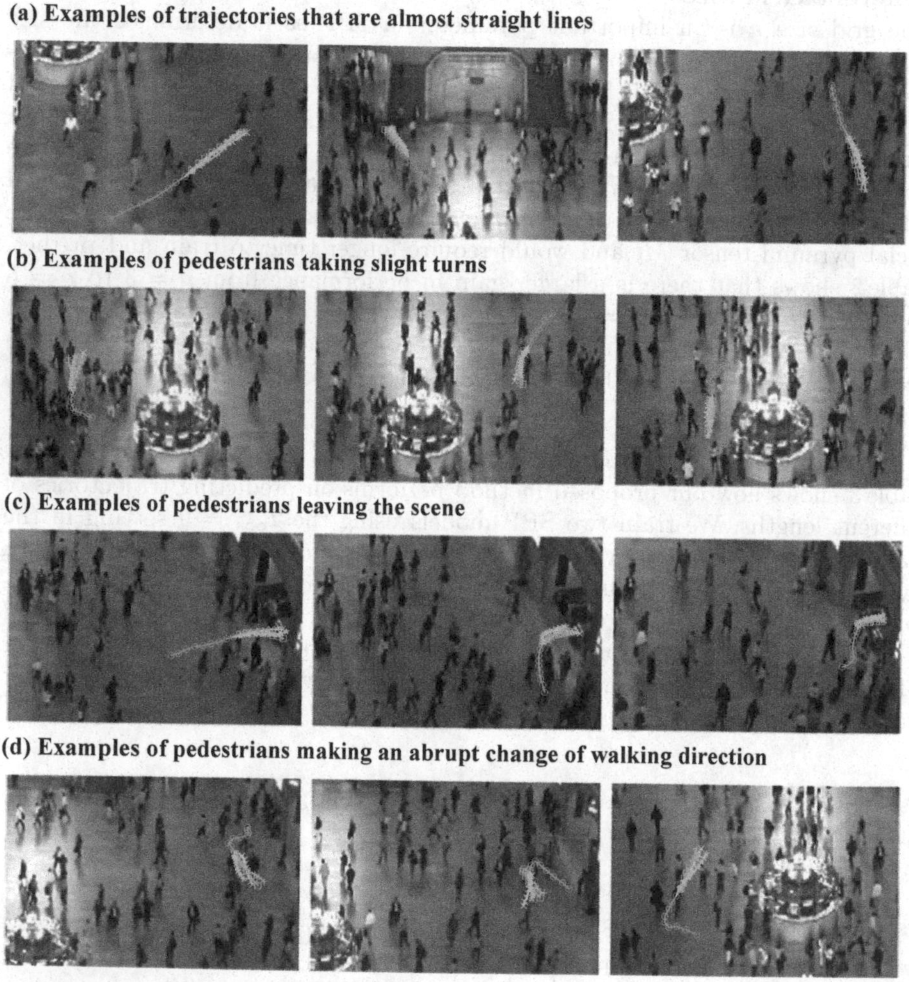

Fig. 5. Comparison of predicted trajectories generated by SPP on the Central Station dataset for grid size $n = 3$ (yellow), $n = 5$ (red), and $n = 7$ (pink). Input observed trajectories are shown in blue; ground truth trajectories are in green. (Color figure online)

4.4 Qualitative Results

We illustrate in Fig. 4 some qualitative prediction results generated by SPP (pink curves), SPP-social-only (red), and SPP-motion-only (yellow) for the 8-frame prediction length. The observed and ground truth trajectories are shown in blue and green, respectively. In the first three relative simple cases (parts (a)–(c)), the trajectories are of the form of a straight path and two slight turning paths. In these 3 examples, all the methods exhibit similar prediction results and are very close to the ground truth trajectories. Figure 4(d) shows the case of an abrupt turn of a pedestrian. With both the Motion and Social encoders incorporated, SPP clearly gives a better predicted trajectory compared to its two variants.

In Fig. 5, we compare the predicted trajectories of SPP when different grid sizes are used. We set the grid size n to 3 (shown as yellow trajectories), 5 (red) and 7 (pink). Figure 5(a) shows simple prediction cases where the trajectories are almost straight lines. In these examples, it appears that the value of n does not have much effect on the prediction results. For slightly turning examples (Fig. 5(b)), the SPP method trained for the 3 grid sizes can also generate plausible trajectories. In Fig. 5(c), three POIs respectively leave the scene with an almost straight line path, abrupt 90° change of direction, and an S-turn. For these cases, all the three settings are still working fine, but $n = 7$ is slightly better. More abrupt turning examples are shown in Fig. 5(d). Compared to smaller grid sizes, the SPP model with $n = 7$ gives the best predicted trajectories.

5 Conclusion

We have presented an LSTM based method for pedestrian trajectory prediction which combines both motion and social information. Our proposed SPP method has a Motion encoder and a Social encoder. The former merges the location and velocity terms of the input trajectories through a mixing attention layer while the latter analyzes the social information captured in a social pyramid tensor. Our SPP method has been evaluated on different real world datasets and the effectiveness of the two encoders has been analyzed in an ablation study on three variants of SPP. Both quantitative and qualitative results in our experiments demonstrate competitive prediction accuracy from our method compared to state-of-art trajectory prediction methods.

References

1. Alahi, A., Goel, K., Ramanathan, V., Robicquet, A., Li, F.F., Savarese, S.: Social LSTM: human trajectory prediction in crowded spaces. In: CVPR, pp. 961–971, June 2016
2. Bartoli, F., Lisanti, G., Ballan, L., Del Bimbo, A.: Context-aware trajectory prediction. arXiv preprint arXiv:1705.02503 (2017)
3. Bhattacharyya, A., Fritz, M., Schiele, B.: Long-term on-board prediction of people in traffic scenes under uncertainty. In: CVPR, June 2018

4. Chen, M., Ding, G., Zhao, S., Chen, H., Liu, Q., Han, J.: Reference based LSTM for image captioning. In: AAAI, pp. 3981–3987 (2017)
5. Chung, J., Gulcehre, C., Cho, K., Bengio, Y.: Empirical evaluation of gated recurrent neural networks on sequence modeling. arXiv preprint arXiv:1412.3555 (2014)
6. Deo, N., Trivedi, M.M.: Convolutional social pooling for vehicle trajectory prediction. In: CVPR, June 2018
7. Fernando, T., Denman, S., Sridharan, S., Fookes, C.: Soft+ hardwired attention: an LSTM framework for human trajectory prediction and abnormal event detection. arXiv preprint arXiv:1702.05552 (2017)
8. Fernando, T., Denman, S., Sridharan, S., Fookes, C.: Tracking by prediction: a deep generative model for mutli-person localisation and tracking. In: IEEE Winter Conference on Applications of Computer Vision (WACV), pp. 1122–1132. IEEE (2018)
9. Graves, A.: Generating sequences with recurrent neural networks. arXiv preprint arXiv:1308.0850 (2013)
10. Graves, A., Jaitly, N.: Towards end-to-end speech recognition with recurrent neural networks. In: ICML, vol. 14, pp. 1764–1772 (2014)
11. Gupta, A., Johnson, J., Fei-Fei, L., Savarese, S., Alahi, A.: Social GAN: socially acceptable trajectories with generative adversarial networks. In: CVPR, June 2018
12. Hasan, I., Setti, F., Tsesmelis, T., Del Bue, A., Galasso, F., Cristani, M.: MX-LSTM: mixing tracklets and vislets to jointly forecast trajectories and head poses. In: CVPR, June 2018
13. Helbing, D., Molnar, P.: Social force model for pedestrian dynamics. Phys. Rev. E 51(5), 4282 (1995)
14. Hochreiter, S., Schmidhuber, J.: Long short-term memory. Neural Comput. 9(8), 1735–1780 (1997)
15. Kim, K., Lee, D., Essa, I.: Gaussian process regression flow for analysis of motion trajectories. In: ICCV, pp. 1164–1171. IEEE (2011)
16. Kim, S., et al.: BRVO: predicting pedestrian trajectories using velocity-space reasoning. Int. J. Robot. Res. 34(2), 201–217 (2015)
17. Kingma, D.P., Ba, J.: Adam: a method for stochastic optimization. arXiv preprint arXiv:1412.6980 (2014)
18. Lee, N., Choi, W., Vernaza, P., Choy, C.B., Torr, P.H.S., Chandraker, M.: DESIRE: distant future prediction in dynamic scenes with interacting agents. In: CVPR (2017)
19. Li, S., Li, W., Cook, C., Zhu, C., Gao, Y.: Independently Recurrent Neural Network (IndRNN): building a longer and deeper RNN. In: CVPR, June 2018
20. Li, Y.: A deep spatiotemporal perspective for understanding crowd behavior. IEEE Trans. Multimed., 1–8 (2018). https://doi.org/10.1109/TMM.2018.2834873
21. Li, Y.: Pedestrian path forecasting in crowd: a deep spatio-temporal perspective. In: Proceedings of the ACM on Multimedia Conference, pp. 235–243. ACM (2017)
22. Liu, J., Wang, G., Hu, P., Duan, L.Y., Kot, A.C.: Global context-aware attention LSTM networks for 3D action recognition. In: CVPR, pp. 1647–1656 (2017)
23. Lv, J., Li, Q., Sun, Q., Wang, X.: T-CONV: a convolutional neural network for multi-scale taxi trajectory prediction. In: 2018 IEEE International Conference on Big Data and Smart Computing (BigComp), pp. 82–89. IEEE (2018)
24. Mehran, R., Oyama, A., Shah, M.: Abnormal crowd behavior detection using social force model. In: CVPR, pp. 935–942. IEEE (2009)
25. Nikhil, N., Morris, B.T.: Convolutional neural network for trajectory prediction. arXiv preprint arXiv:1809.00696 (2018)

26. Pellegrini, S., Ess, A., Schindler, K., Van Gool, L.: You'll never walk alone: modeling social behavior for multi-target tracking. In: ICCV, pp. 261–268. IEEE (2009)
27. Ren, J.S., et al.: Look, listen and learn - a multimodal LSTM for speaker identification. In: AAAI, pp. 3581–3587 (2016)
28. Sadeghian, A., Kosaraju, V., Sadeghian, A., Hirose, N., Savarese, S.: SoPhie: an attentive gan for predicting paths compliant to social and physical constraints. arXiv preprint arXiv:1806.01482 (2018)
29. Su, H., Dong, Y., Zhu, J., Ling, H., Zhang, B.: Crowd scene understanding with coherent recurrent neural networks. In: IJCAI, pp. 3469–3476 (2016)
30. Su, H., Zhu, J., Dong, Y., Zhang, B.: Forecast the plausible paths in crowd scenes. In: IJCAI, pp. 2772–2778 (2017)
31. Sun, L., Yan, Z., Mellado, S.M., Hanheide, M., Duckett, T.: 3DOF pedestrian trajectory prediction learned from long-term autonomous mobile robot deployment data. arXiv preprint arXiv:1710.00126 (2017)
32. Sutskever, I., Vinyals, O., Le, Q.V.: Sequence to sequence learning with neural networks. In: NIPS, pp. 3104–3112 (2014)
33. Vaswani, A., et al.: Attention is all you need. In: NIPS, pp. 5998–6008 (2017)
34. Vemula, A., Muelling, K., Oh, J.: Social attention: modeling attention in human crowds. In: ICRA, pp. 1–7, May 2018. https://doi.org/10.1109/ICRA.2018.8460504
35. Vemula, A., Muelling, K., Oh, J.: Modeling cooperative navigation in dense human crowds. In: IEEE International Conference on Robotics and Automation (ICRA), pp. 1685–1692. IEEE (2017)
36. Wang, J.M., Fleet, D.J., Hertzmann, A.: Gaussian process dynamical models for human motion. IEEE Trans. Pattern Anal. Mach. Intell. **30**(2), 283–298 (2008)
37. Xie, D., Todorovic, S., Zhu, S.C.: Inferring "dark matter" and "dark energy" from videos. In: ICCV, December 2013
38. Xu, Y., Piao, Z., Gao, S.: Encoding crowd interaction with deep neural network for pedestrian trajectory prediction. In: CVPR, June 2018
39. Xue, H., Huynh, D., Reynolds, M.: Bi-Prediction: pedestrian trajectory prediction based on bidirectional LSTM classification. In: International Conference on Digital Image Computing: Techniques and Applications (DICTA), pp. 307–314 (2017)
40. Xue, H., Huynh, D.Q., Reynolds, M.: SS-LSTM: a hierarchical LSTM model for pedestrian trajectory prediction. In: IEEE Winter Conference on Applications of Computer Vision (WACV), pp. 1186–1194. IEEE (2018)
41. Yamaguchi, K., Berg, A.C., Ortiz, L.E., Berg, T.L.: Who are you with and where are you going? In: CVPR, pp. 1345–1352. IEEE (2011)
42. Yi, S., Li, H., Wang, X.: Understanding pedestrian behaviors from stationary crowd groups. In: CVPR, pp. 3488–3496 (2015)
43. Yi, S., Li, H., Wang, X.: Pedestrian behavior understanding and prediction with deep neural networks. In: Leibe, B., Matas, J., Sebe, N., Welling, M. (eds.) ECCV 2016. LNCS, vol. 9905, pp. 263–279. Springer, Cham (2016). https://doi.org/10.1007/978-3-319-46448-0_16
44. Zhou, B., Wang, X., Tang, X.: Understanding collective crowd behaviors: learning a mixture model of dynamic pedestrian-agents. In: CVPR, pp. 2871–2878. IEEE (2012)
45. Zhu, W., et al.: Co-occurrence feature learning for skeleton based action recognition using regularized deep LSTM networks. In: AAAI, pp. 3697–3703 (2016)
46. Zou, H., Su, H., Song, S., Zhu, J.: Understanding human behaviors in crowds by imitating the decision-making process. In: AAAI (2018)

Deep Global-Relative Networks for End-to-End 6-DoF Visual Localization and Odometry

Yimin Lin[1]([⊠])[iD], Zhaoxiang Liu[1][iD], Jianfeng Huang[1][iD], Chaopeng Wang[1][iD], Guoguang Du[1][iD], Jinqiang Bai[2][iD], and Shiguo Lian[1][iD]

[1] AI Department, CloudMinds Technologies Co. Ltd., Beijing, China
{anson.lin,robin.liu,jianfeng.huang,chaopeng.wang,george.du,
scott.lian}@cloudminds.com
[2] School of Electronic Information Engineering, Beihang University, Beijing, China
baijinqiang@buaa.edu.cn

Abstract. Although a wide variety of deep neural networks for robust Visual Odometry (VO) can be found in the literature, they are still unable to solve the drift problem in long-term robot navigation. Thus, this paper aims to propose novel deep end-to-end networks for long-term 6-DoF VO task. It mainly fuses relative and global networks based on Recurrent Convolutional Neural Networks (RCNNs) to improve the monocular localization accuracy. Indeed, the relative sub-networks are implemented to smooth the VO trajectory, while global sub-networks are designed to avoid drift problem. All the parameters are jointly optimized using Cross Transformation Constraints (CTC), which represents temporal geometric consistency of the consecutive frames, and Mean Square Error (MSE) between the predicted pose and ground truth. The experimental results on both indoor and outdoor datasets show that our method outperforms other state-of-the-art learning-based VO methods in terms of pose accuracy.

Keywords: Deep Learning · Visual localization · Visual Odometry · Robotics

1 Introduction

The problem of visual localization has drawn significant attention from many researchers over the past few decades. Solutions for overcoming this problem come from computer vision and robotic communities by means of Structure from Motion (SfM) and visual Simultaneous Localization and Mapping (vSLAM) [1, 2]. Many variants of these solutions have started to make an impact in a wide range of applications, including autonomous navigation and augmented reality.

During the past few years, most of traditional visual localization techniques have been proposed and grounded on the estimate of the camera motion among

© Springer Nature Switzerland AG 2019
A. C. Nayak and A. Sharma (Eds.): PRICAI 2019, LNAI 11671, pp. 454–467, 2019.
https://doi.org/10.1007/978-3-030-29911-8_35

a set of consecutive frames with geometric methods. For example, the feature-based method uses the projective geometry relations between 3D feature points of the scene and their projection on the image plane [3, 4], or the direct method minimizes the gradient of the pixel intensities across consecutive images [5, 6]. However, these techniques are critical to ideal and controlled environments, e.g., with a large amount of texture, unchanged illumination and without dynamic objects. Obviously, their performance drops quickly when facing those challenging and unpredicted scenarios.

Recently, a great breakthrough has been achieved in the Deep Learning (DL), through the application of Convolutional Neural Networks (CNNs) and Recurrent Neural Networks (RNNs), e.g., for the object recognition and scene classification tasks. Therefore, learning-based visual odometry in the past few years has seen an increasing attention of the computer vision and robotic communities [7]. This is due to its potentials in learning capability and the robustness to camera parameters and challenging environments. However, so far they are still unable to outperform most state-of-the-art feature-based localization methods. The drift from the true trajectory due to accumulation of errors over time is inevitable in those learning based VO system. This is due to the fact that such approaches cannot exploit high-capacity learning 3D structural constraints from limited training datasets. Recent work [8] concluded that global place recognition and camera relocalization plays a significant role in reducing these global drifts. As demonstrated in another relevant VLocNet [9], the global and Siamese-type relative networks are designed for inferring global poses with the great help of relative motion. Nevertheless, VO drift problem still exists since its global and relative networks are separately optimized and regressed by a multitask alternating optimization strategy.

To solve the drift problem completely, this paper extends VLocNet to fuse both relative and global networks, and considers more temporal sequences with LSTM incorporated in each networks for accurate pose prediction. Furthermore, we also employ a geometric consistency of the adjacent frames for regressing the relative and global networks at the same time. This proposed method brings two advantages: one is obviously that we leverage the camera re-localization to improve the accuracy of 6-DoF VO. On the other hand, relative motion information from odometry can also be used to improve the global pose regression accuracy. In summary, our main contributions are as follows:

(1) We demonstrate the architecture consisting of the CNN-based feature extraction sub-networks (CNN1), the RCNNs-type relative and global pose regression sub-networks (named RCNN1 and RCNN2 respectively), and finally Fully-connected fusion layers (FCFL) fuse the global and relative poses by connecting these sub-networks to each other.
(2) The training strategy: we firstly train the feature extraction and relative pose estimation sub-networks from a sequence of raw RGB images, and then the whole architecture is trained in an end-to-end manner to fill the rest of the pose regression sub-networks according to different scenes.

(3) We design two loss functions to improve the accuracy of our networks. For training the relative sub-networks, the CTC is employed to enforce the temporal geometric consistency between each other within a batch of frames. For training the whole networks, we minimize both CTC and the pose MSE.
(4) We evaluate our networks using 7-Scenes and KITTI datasets, and the results show it achieves state-of-the-art performance for learning-based monocular camera localization.

2   Related Work

Over the past years, there are numerous approaches that have been proposed for visual localization. In this section, we discuss traditional geometry-based and recent learning-based localization approaches.

2.1   Geometry-Based Localization

Geometry-based localization estimates the camera motion among a set of consecutive frames with geometric methods. A variety of geometric methods can be classified into feature-based and direct methods.

Feature-Based Methods: Most feature-based methods work by detecting feature points and matching them between consecutive frames. To improve pose accuracy, they minimize the projective geometry errors between 3D feature points of the scene and their projection on the image plane, e.g., PTAM [4] is a classical vSLAM system. However, it may suffer from drift since it does not address the principle of loop closing. More recently, the ORB-SLAM algorithm by Mur-Artal et al. [3] is state-of-the-art vSLAM system designed for sparse feature tracking and reached impressive robustness and accuracy. In practice, it also suffers from a number of problems such as the inconsistency in initialization, and the drift caused by pure rotation.

Direct Methods: In contrast, direct methods estimate the camera motion by minimizing the photometric error over all pixels across consecutive images. Engel et al. [5] developed LSD-SLAM, which is one of the most successful direct approaches. Direct methods do not provide better tolerance towards changing lighting conditions and often require more computational costs than feature-based methods since they work a global minimization using all the pixels in the image.

2.2   Learning-Based Localization

Even though Deep Neural Networks (DNNs) are not a novel concept, their popularity has grown in recent years due to a great breakthrough that has been achieved in the computer vision community. Inspired by these achievements, lots of learning-based visual relocalization and odometry systems have been widely proposed to improve the 6-DoF pose estimation.

Visual Relocalization: Learning-based relocalization systems are designed to learn from recognition to relocalization with very large scale classification datasets. For example, Kendall et al. proposed PoseNet [10], which was the first successful end-to-end pre-trained deep CNNs approach for 6-DoF pose regression. In addition, Clark et al. [11] introduced deep CNNs with Long-Short Term Memory (LSTM) units to avoid overfitting to training data while PoseNet needs to deal with this problem with careful dropout strategies.

Visual Odometry: Learning-based visual odometry systems are employed to learn the incremental change in position from images. LS-VO [12] is a CNNs architecture proposed to learn the latent space representation of the input Optical Flow field with the motion estimate task. SfM-Net [13] is a self-supervised geometry-aware CNNs for motion estimation in videos that decomposes frame-to-frame pixel motion in terms of scene and object depth, camera motion and 3D object rotations and translations. Recently, most state-of-the-art deep approaches to visual odometry employ not only CNNs, but also sequence-models, such as long-short term memory (LSTM) units [14], to capture long term dependencies in camera motion.

More recently, learning-based global and relative networks are designed for 6-DoF global pose regression and odometry estimation from consecutive monocular images. Clark et al. [8] have presented a CNNs+Bi-LSTMs approach for 6-DoF video-clip relocalization that exploits the temporal smoothness of the video stream to improve the localization accuracy of the global pose estimation. Brahmbhatt et al. [15] proposed a MapNet that enforces geometric

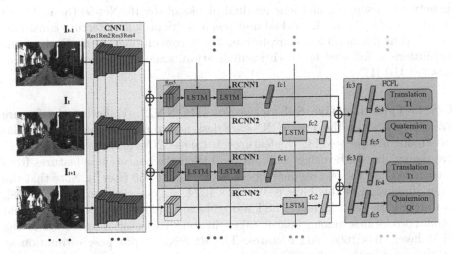

Fig. 1. Architecture of the proposed learning-based monocular VO system. CNN1 determines the most discriminative feature as an input for the next two RCNNs; RCNN1 estimates the egomotion of the camera and constrict the motion space while regressing the global localization; RCNN2 is competent to model the 3D structural constraints of the environment while learning from the first two assistant networks; Fully-connected fusion layers (FCFL) fuse relative and global networks to improve the VO accuracy.

constraints between relative poses and absolute poses in network training. Our work is extended to VLocNet [9], which incorporated a global and a relative sub-networks. More precisely, even though it has the joint loss function designed for global and relative sub-networks, it is just used to improve the global predictions. Conversely, the global regression results are unable to totally benefit relative networks since its unshared weights are optimized independently without consider the global constraints. Moreover, it considers only a single image as global networks input, which greatly impedes the ability of CNNs to achieve accurate poses. In contrast, we fuse these two streams from both global and relative RCNNS-type sub-networks with joint optimization to benefit the pose prediction.

3   Proposed Model

In this section, we detail our learning-based global and relative fusion framework for jointly estimating global pose and odometry from consecutive monocular images. The proposed networks are shown in Fig. 1.

3.1   Network Architecture

CNN-Based Feature Extraction Networks (CNN1). In order to learn effective features that are suitable for the global and relative pose estimation problem automatically, CNN-based feature extraction networks are developed to perform feature extraction on the monocular RGB image. We build upon this networks using the first four residual blocks of the ResNet-50 (named from Res 1 to Res 4) [16]. Each residual unit has a bottleneck architecture consisting of 1×1 convolution, 3×3 convolution, 1×1 convolution layers. Each of the convolutions is followed by batch normalization, scale and Exponential Linear Units (ELUs) [17].

RCNNs-Type Relative Sub-networks (RCNN1). Following the feature extraction networks, the deep RCNNs are designed to model dynamics and relations among a sequence of CNNs features. It takes CNNs features from a consecutive monocular RGB images as input, and then the concatenate features from them are fed into the last residual blocks of the ResNet-50 (Res 5). Note that the output dimension of this layer is W × H × 1024. As described in DeepVO [18], two Long Short-Term Memory (LSTMs) [19] are employed as RNNs to find and exploit correlations among images taken in long trajectories and each of the LSTM layers has 1000 hidden states. The RCNNs output pose estimation at each time step with a fully-connected layer fc1 whose dimension is 1024.

RCNNs-Type Global Sub-networks (RCNN2). We also feed the previous CNNs features to the last residual blocks of the ResNet-50 (Res 5) and reshape LSTM′s output to a fully-connected layer fc2, whose dimension is 1024. It corresponds in shape to the output of the relative RCNNs unit before the fusion stage. Note that the cell of LSTM stores the past few global poses and therefore it is able to improve the predicted pose accuracy of current image.

Fully-Connected Fusion Layers (FCFL). Finally, the following fusion stage concatenates features from the two relative and global sub-networks, and reshapes its output to 1024, namely fc3. We also add two inner-product layers for regressing the translation T_k and quaternion Q_k, namely fc4 and fc5. Obviously, the dimensions of fc4 and fc5 layers are 3 and 4, respectively.

3.2   Temporal Geometric Consistency Loss

Here, we introduce CTC that are based on the fundamental concepts of composition of rigid-body transformations. Figure 2 shows a sequential set of frames $F = (I_0, I_1, I_2, I_3, I_4)$, where we note that temporal length K = 5. Note that $P_i = (Q_i, T_i)$ is a 6-DoF predicted pose, where T_i and Q_i denote the translation and quaternion of frame i, respectively. We train the networks to predict the transforms between each other. As an example, the predicted transform P_{01} from I_0 to I_1 should be equal to the product of the two $\widehat{P}_0$ and $\widehat{P}_1$ transforms, where $\widehat{P}_i$ indicates the ground truth of frame i, thus:

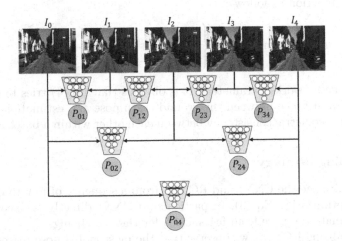

Fig. 2. Architecture of CTC. It represents temporal geometric consistency of the consecutive frames.

$$P_{01} = \widehat{P}_1 \widehat{P}_0^{-1} = \widehat{P}_{01} \tag{1}$$

Note that using Eq. (1) in practice, there exist errors in the predicted and ground truth, so we have CTC functions:

$$L_0 = \left\| P_{01} - \widehat{P}_{01} \right\|_2^2, L_1 = \left\| P_{12} - \widehat{P}_{12} \right\|_2^2$$

$$L_2 = \left\| P_{23} - \widehat{P}_{23} \right\|_2^2, L_3 = \left\| P_{34} - \widehat{P}_{34} \right\|_2^2$$

$$L_4 = \left\| P_{02} - \widehat{P}_{02} \right\|_2^2, L_5 = \left\| P_{24} - \widehat{P}_{24} \right\|_2^2 \tag{2}$$

$$L_6 = \left\| P_{04} - \widehat{P}_{04} \right\|_2^2$$

where $\|\cdot\|_2^2$ is MSE. So the relative loss function which consists of Eq. (2) are shown as:

$$\theta = \arg\min_{\theta} \frac{1}{N} \sum_{i=1}^{N} \sum_{k=0}^{6} (L_k^i) \tag{3}$$

where θ is the relative or global RCNNs parameters and N is the number of samples. We use this optimization Eq. (3) to train our RCNNs sub-networks. Note that, these constrains can be equal to a Local Bundle Adjustment in traditional vSLAM system [3], also known as windowed optimization. It is an efficient way to maintain a good quality pose over a local number of frames. So the CTC here are better strategies to learn about spatial relations of the environment. To train our 6-DoF end-to-end pose regression system, we can jointly use the global and relative loss function as follows:

$$ww = \arg\min_{w} \frac{1}{N} \sum_{i=1}^{N} \left\{ \sum_{k=0}^{6} (L_k^i) + \sum_{j=0}^{4} \left\| P^i_j - \widehat{P}^i_j \right\|_2^2 \right\} \tag{4}$$

where ω is the networks parameters. It is obvious that Eq.(4) tries to minimize the Euclidean distance between the ground truth pose and estimated one while enforcing the geometric consistency between each other within a batch of frames.

3.3   Training Strategy

We firstly initialize the CNN1 and RCNN1 from a sequence of raw RGB images using the optimization Eq. (3). In particular, RCNN1 directly replace fc3 with fc1 and estimate the pose from fc4 and fc5 for the time being.

For initializing RCNN2, we observe that the most global pose regression [10] can only be determined in a known training environment. So it is time consuming to retrain the whole networks according to different scenes. As shown in Fig. 3, in order to retrain our deep model faster, different scenes are fed into the common CNN1 to produce an effective feature in the monocular image, which is then passed through individual RCNN2 to learn for saving their landmark Si. Thereby, we only need to retrain the RCNN2 for different scenes and each image still yields an accurate pose estimate at each Si through the networks. Note that, RCNN2 also directly replaces fc3 with fc2 and regress the pose using the optimization Eq. (4).

Up to now, we achieve pretrained weights for CNN1, RCNN1 and RCNN2. Finally, the whole architecture is trained and refined in an end-to-end manner via the optimization Eq. (4).

4 Experimental Evaluation

In this section, we evaluate our proposed networks in comparison to the state-of-the-art algorithms on both indoor and outdoor datasets, followed by detailed analysis on the architectural decisions and finally, we demonstrate the best temporal length.

4.1 Evaluation Datasets

We evaluate our networks on two well-known datasets: Microsoft 7-Scenes [20] and KITTI Visual Odometry benchmark [21]. We follow the original train and test splits provided by other literatures to facilitate comparison and benchmarking.

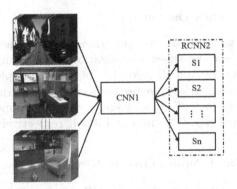

Fig. 3. Illustration of training for the global networks from different scenes. CNN1 determines the most discriminative feature and RCNN2 learns from different scenes for saving their landmark Si.

Microsoft 7-Scenes. It is a dataset that collect RGB-D images from seven different scenes in an indoor office environment. All scenes were recorded from a handheld Kinect RGB-D camera at 640 × 480 resolution. The dataset provides the ground truth poses extracted using KinectFusion. Each sequence was recorded with motion blur, perceptual aliasing and textureless features in the room, thereby making it a challenging dataset for relocalization and tracking.

KITTI Visual Odometry Benchmark. It consists of 22 stereo sequences and they provide 11 sequences (00–10) with ground truth trajectories for training and 11 sequences (11–21) without ground truth for evaluation. This high-quality dataset was recorded with long sequences of varying speed, including a set of 41000 frames captured at 10 fps and a total driving distance of 39.2 km with frequent loop closures which are of interest in SLAM. So it is very popular for the monocular Visual Odometry algorithms.

4.2   Network Training

The network models were implemented with the TensorFlow framework and trained with NVIDIA GTX 1080 GPUs and Intel Core i7 2.7 GHz CPU. Adam optimizer was employed to train the networks for up to 2000 epochs with parameter $\beta_1 = 0.9$ and $\beta_2 = 0.999$. The learning rate started from 0.001 and decreased by half for every 1/5 of total iterations. The temporal length K fed to the relative and global pose estimator is 5. The size of image used by the networks is 224×224 pixel. Thus, our per-frame runtime for each pose inference is between 45 ms and 65 ms.

4.3   Microsoft 7-Scenes Datasets

In this experiment, we compare the performance of our networks with other state-of-the-art deep learning-based relocalization and tracking methods, namely PoseNet [10], DeepVO [22] and VLocNet [9]. In order to implement fair qualitative and quantitative comparison, we use the same 7-Scenes datasets for training and testing as described in [9]. For each scene, we show their median translational t_{rel}: (m) and rotational r_{rel}: $(°)$ errors in Table 1, respectively.

Table 1. Median Errors on Microsoft 7-Scenes

Scene	PoseNet		DeepVO		VLocNet		Ours	
	t_{rel}	r_{rel}	t_{rel}	r_{rel}	t_{rel}	r_{rel}	t_{rel}	r_{rel}
Chess	0.32	8.12	0.06	2.61	0.036	**1.70**	**0.016**	1.72
Fire	0.47	14.4	0.10	4.33	0.039	5.33	**0.011**	**2.19**
Heads	0.29	12.0	0.35	7.11	0.046	6.64	**0.017**	**3.56**
Office	0.48	7.68	0.10	3.11	0.039	**1.95**	**0.024**	1.95
Pumpkin	0.47	8.42	0.11	3.30	0.037	2.28	**0.022**	**2.27**
RedKitchen	0.59	8.64	0.10	2.58	0.039	2.20	**0.018**	**1.86**
Stairs	0.47	13.8	0.45	9.18	0.097	6.47	**0.017**	**4.79**
Average	0.44	10.4	0.18	4.60	0.048	3.80	**0.018**	**2.62**

It shows that our networks outperform previous CNN-based PoseNet by 95.9% in positional error and 74.8% in orientation error. Taking Pumpkin as an example, we achieve a positional error reduction from 0.47 m for PoseNet to 0.022 m for our method. The reason is that PoseNet always results in noisy predictions on single image. In contrast, the RCNNs in our networks constrict the motion space while using sequential images to improve global relocalization accuracy. Therefore, this experiment results validate that our networks have the effectiveness of using geometric constraints from consecutive images for improving relocalization accuracy. Furthermore, it can be seen that the proposed networks significantly outperform the DeepVO approach in all of the test scenes, resulting in a 90% and 43% boost in position and orientation accuracy, respectively. The DeepVO network tries to regress the VO but probably suffers from high drifts. The reason is that the orientation changes in the training data are usually small and orientation is more prone to overfitting. However, our system reduces the drift over time due to the global pose regression strategy as done in the traditional visual SLAM system. In addition, our networks also perform better than VLocNet, and the orientation and positional errors are reduced by more than 31% and 62%, respectively. The main reason we find from VLocNet is that their global pose regression and visual odometry networks are predicted independently. But in our framework, we do fuse the results from global regression and relative pose estimation. In summary, these experimental results validate that our strategy is able to filter out the noises by fusing a series of measurements observed from global and relative networks over time.

4.4   KITTI Datasets

Next, we additionally deploy experiments in an outdoor environment for analyzing the large-scale VO performance. KITTI is much larger than typical indoor datasets like 7-Scenes, where sequence 00, 02, 08 and 09 are used for training the RCNNs-type relative sub-networks. As described in [18], the trajectories are segmented to different lengths to generate almost 7410 samples in total for training. The trained models are tested on the sequence 03, 04, 05, 06, 07 and 10. As shown in Table 2, the performance of the our networks is analyzed according to

Table 2. Results on KITTI Sequences

Seq.	DeepVO		L-VO3		Ours	
	t_{rel}	r_{rel}	t_{rel}	r_{rel}	t_{rel}	r_{rel}
03	6.72	6.46	3.18	**1.31**	**1.93**	1.95
04	6.33	6.08	2.04	0.81	**0.10**	**0.25**
05	3.35	4.93	**2.59**	0.99	2.51	**0.91**
06	7.24	7.29	1.38	**0.95**	**0.30**	0.99
07	3.52	5.02	2.81	2.54	**1.53**	**2.11**
10	9.77	10.2	4.38	3.12	**3.63**	**3.00**
Average	6.15	6.66	2.73	1.62	**1.67**	**1.54**

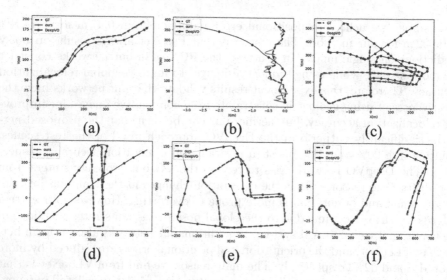

Fig. 4. Trajectories of results on the testing Sequence (a) 03, (b) 04, (c) 05, (d) 06, (e) 07 and (f) 10 of the KITTI VO benchmark.

the KITTI VO/SLAM evaluation metrics, where t_{rel}: (%) and r_{rel}: (°/100 m) are averaged Root Mean Square Errors (RMSE) of the translational and rotational drifts for all subsequences of lengths ranging from 100 to 800 m with different speeds.

Table 2 shows quantitative comparison against two state-of-the-art VO approaches including L-VO3 [23] and RCNNs-type DeepVO [18]. The proposed method significantly outperforms the DeepVO approach in all of the test sequences, resulting in a 71% and 76% boost in translation and rotation accuracy, respectively. As shown in Fig. 4, DeepVO suffers from high drifts as the length of the trajectory increases and the errors of the rotation significantly increase because of significant changes on rotation during car driving. Unlike that, our networks produce relatively accurate and consistent trajectories against to the ground truth. These owe to the global and relative architecture with the proposed CTC loss. In addition, it is able to overcome the performance of state-of-the-art learning-based L-VO3. Although some errors are slightly worse than that of the L-VO3, this may be due to the fact that our networks are trained without enough data to cover the velocity and orientation variation. Finally, we can see that the absolute scale to each sequence is completely maintained during the end-to-end training.

4.5   Ablation Studies

In this section, we present additional ablation studies on performances with respect to considering various architectural components and temporal length K.

In order to validate the effectiveness of our joint architecture, we compare our networks against relative-only (RCNN1) and global-only (RCNN2) architectures.

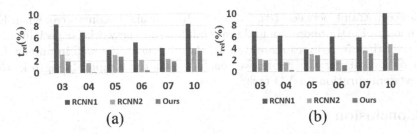

Fig. 5. Comparative analyses of average (a) translation and (b) rotation RMSE using various architectures on KITTI sequences.

The quantitative rules can be found in Sect. 4.4. In particular, RCNN1 directly replaces fc3 with fc1 and estimates the pose from consecutive images. While RCNN2 also directly replaces fc3 with fc2 and regresses the pose. They are trained using the loss function Eqs. (3) and (4) respectively, and temporal length K equals to 5 as well. It is observed that compared with the RCNN1, the pose generated from RCNN2 is more accurate. A possible explanation is that the global networks reduce the serious drift since it has the ability to relocalization with previous observation for the long-term prediction. While the relative networks only focus on motion from 2D or 3D optical flow, which is hard to efficiently model 3D structural constraints with limited training samples in complex environments. Compared to the RCNN1 and RCNN2 as shown in Fig. 5, our approach predicts more precise pose. This is more evident if we fuse streams from both global and relative sub-networks to benefit the long-term pose prediction.

In addition, we provide a performance comparison with respect to various temporal lengths. Figure 6 shows our networks with different K values changed from 2 to 11 and their corresponding average translation and rotation RMSE of the six KITTI sequences. We observe that the localization errors descend as the length of the sequential frames increases. However, the accuracy seems to be stable when K is larger than 5. This phenomenon is due to the fact that the

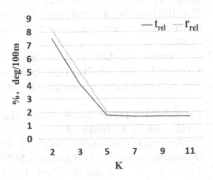

Fig. 6. Comparation of average translation t_{rel} and rotation r_{rel} RMSE with respect to various temporal length K.

covisible constraint between 1-th frame and K-th frame become weak when K is large enough. Furthermore, we find that training such networks, especially when K is larger than 5, requires more training data to generalize well in unseen data and avoid overfitting. Therefore, we conclude that the temporal length k = 5 is the best configuration for VO task.

5 Conclusion

In this paper, we addressed the challenge of learning-based visual localization of a camera or an autonomous system with the novel networks. It mainly consists of CNN-based feature extraction sub-networks that determine the most discriminative feature as an input for the next two RCNNs, RCNNs-type relative sub-networks that estimate the egomotion of the camera and constrict the motion space while regressing the global localization, and RCNNs-type global sub-networks that are competent to model the 3D structural constraints of the environment while learning from the first two assistant networks. Finally, it fuses and jointly optimizes the relative and global networks to improve VO accuracy. Furthermore, we employ the CTC loss function for training the relative and global RCNNs. The indoor and outdoor experimental evaluations indicate that our networks can produce accurate localization and be adopted to maintain a large feature map for drift correction under long range pose estimation. In the next step, we plan to extend the ability of global networks to work under any unknown environment and promote the robustness of place recognition in cases where illumination and appearance change dramatically.

References

1. Cadena, C., et al.: Past, present, and future of simultaneous localization and mapping: toward the robust-perception age. IEEE Trans. Rob. **32**(6), 1309–1332 (2016)
2. Özyeşil, O., Voroninski, V., Basri, R., Singer, A.: A survey of structure from motion. Acta Numerica **26**, 305–364 (2017)
3. Mur-Artal, R., Montiel, J.M.M., Tardos, J.D.: ORB-SLAM: a versatile and accurate monocular slam system. IEEE Trans. Rob. **31**(5), 1147–1163 (2015)
4. Klein, G., Murray, D.: Parallel tracking and mapping for small AR workspaces. In: 6th IEEE and ACM International Symposium on Mixed and Augmented Reality (ISMAR), pp. 225–234 (2007)
5. Engel, J., Schöps, T., Cremers, D.: LSD-SLAM: large-scale direct monocular SLAM. In: Fleet, D., Pajdla, T., Schiele, B., Tuytelaars, T. (eds.) ECCV 2014. LNCS, vol. 8690, pp. 834–849. Springer, Cham (2014). https://doi.org/10.1007/978-3-319-10605-2_54
6. Engel, J., Koltun, V., Cremers, D.: Direct sparse odometry. IEEE Trans. Pattern Anal. Mach. Intell. (TPAMI) **40**(3), 611–625 (2018)
7. Li, R., Wang, S., Gu, D.: Ongoing evolution of visual SLAM from geometry to deep learning: challenges and opportunities. Cogn. Comput. **10**(6), 875–889 (2018)
8. Clark, R., Wang, S., Markham, A., Trigoni, N., Wen, H.: VidLoc: a deep spatio-temporal model for 6-DoF video-clip relocalization. In: Proceedings of the IEEE Conference on Computer Vision and Pattern Recognition (CVPR), vol. 3, pp. 2652–2660 (2017)

9. Valada, A., Radwan, N., Burgard, W.: Deep auxiliary learning for visual localization and odometry. arXiv preprint arXiv:1803.03642 (2018)
10. Kendall, A., Grimes, M., Cipolla, R.: PoseNet: a convolutional network for real-time 6-DoF camera relocalization. In: Proceedings of the IEEE International Conference on Computer Vision (ICCV), pp. 2938–2946 (2015)
11. Walch, F., Hazirbas, C., Leal-Taixe, L., Sattler, T., Hilsenbeck, S., Cremers, D.: Image-based localization using LSTMS for structured feature correlation. In: Proceedings of the IEEE International Conference on Computer Vision (ICCV), pp. 627–637 (2017)
12. Costante, G., Ciarfuglia, T.A.: LS-VO: learning dense optical subspace for robust visual odometry estimation. IEEE Robot. Autom. Lett. $3(3)$, 1735–1742 (2018)
13. Vijayanarasimhan, S., Ricco, S., Schmid, C., Sukthankar, R., Fragkiadaki, K.: SfM-Net: learning of structure and motion from video. arXiv preprint arXiv:1704.07804 (2017)
14. Iyer, G., Murthy, J.K., Gunshi Gupta, K., Paull, L.: Geometric consistency for self-supervised end-to-end visual odometry. arXiv preprint arXiv:1804.03789 (2018)
15. Brahmbhatt, S., Gu, J., Kim, K., Hays, J., Kautz, J.: Geometry-aware learning of maps for camera localization. In: Proceedings of the IEEE Conference on Computer Vision and Pattern Recognition (CVPR), pp. 2616–2625 (2018)
16. He, K., Zhang, X., Ren, S., Sun, J.: Deep residual learning for image recognition. In: Proceedings of the IEEE Conference on Computer Vision and Pattern Recognition (CVPR), pp. 770–778 (2016)
17. Clevert, D.A., Unterthiner, T., Hochreiter, S.: Fast and accurate deep network learning by exponential linear units (ELUs). arXiv preprint arXiv:1511.07289 (2015)
18. Wang, S., Clark, R., Wen, H., Trigoni, N.: End-to-end, sequence-to-sequence probabilistic visual odometry through deep neural networks. Int. J. Robot. Res. $37(4–5)$, 513–542 (2018)
19. Zaremba, W., Sutskever, I.: Learning to execute. arXiv preprint arXiv:1410.4615 (2014)
20. Shotton, J., Glocker, B., Zach, C., Izadi, S., Criminisi, A., Fitzgibbon, A.: Scene coordinate regression forests for camera relocalization in RGB-D images. In: Proceedings of the IEEE Conference on Computer Vision and Pattern Recognition (CVPR), pp. 2930–2937 (2013)
21. Geiger, A., Lenz, P., Urtasun, R.: Are we ready for autonomous driving? The KITTI vision benchmark suite. In: IEEE Conference on Computer Vision and Pattern Recognition (CVPR), pp. 3354–3361 (2012)
22. Mohanty, V., Agrawal, S., Datta, S., Ghosh, A., Sharma, V.D., Chakravarty, D.: DeepVO: a deep learning approach for monocular visual odometry. arXiv preprint arXiv:1611.06069 (2016)
23. Zhao, C., Sun, L., Purkait, P., Duckett, T., Stolkin, R.: Learning monocular visual odometry with dense 3D mapping from dense 3D flow. arXiv preprint arXiv:1803.02286 (2018)

Optimizing DNN Architectures for High Speed Autonomous Navigation in GPS Denied Environments on Edge Devices

Prafull Prakash[1]([✉]), Chaitanya Murti[1], Saketha Nath[2], and Chiranjib Bhattacharyya[1,3]

[1] Robert Bosch Centre for Cyber-Physical Systems, Indian Institute of Science, Bengaluru, India
{prafull,mchaitanya,chiru}@iisc.ac.in
[2] Department of Computer Science and Engineering, Indian Institute of Technology, Hyderabad, India
saketha@iith.ac.in
[3] Department of Computer Science and Automation, Indian Institute of Science, Bengaluru, India

Abstract. We address the challenge of high speed autonomous navigation of micro aerial vehicles (MAVs) using DNNs in GPS-denied environments with limited computational resources; specifically, we use the ODROID XU4 and the Raspberry Pi 3. The high computation costs of using DNNs for inference, particularly in the absence of powerful GPUs, necessitates negotiating a tradeoff between accuracy and inference. We address this tradeoff by employing sparsified neural networks. To obtain such architectures, we propose a novel algorithm to find sparse "sub networks" of existing pre trained models. Contrary to existing pruning-only strategies, our proposal includes a novel exploration step that efficiently searches for a different, but identically sparse, architecture with better generalization abilities. We derive learning theoretic bounds that reinforce our empirical findings that the optimized network achieves comparable generalization to the original network. We show that using our algorithm it is possible to discover models which, on average, have upto 19x fewer parameters than those obtained using existing state of the art pruning methods on autonomous navigation datasets, and achieve upto 6x improvements on inference time compared to existing state of the art shallow models on the ODROID XU4 and Raspberry Pi 3. Last, we demonstrate that our sparsified models can complete autonomous navigation missions with speeds upto 4 m/s using the ODROID XU4, which existing state of the art methods fail to do.

We gratefully acknowledge the Robert Bosch Centre for Cyber-Physical Systems, Indian Institute of Science, Bangalore, for their support via grant RBCO-0018.

Electronic supplementary material The online version of this chapter (https://doi.org/10.1007/978-3-030-29911-8_36) contains supplementary material, which is available to authorized users.

© Springer Nature Switzerland AG 2019
A. C. Nayak and A. Sharma (Eds.): PRICAI 2019, LNAI 11671, pp. 468–481, 2019.
https://doi.org/10.1007/978-3-030-29911-8_36

1   Introduction

Micro Aerial Vehicles (MAVs), or drones, exemplify the notion of mobile edge computing, as they are required to interact with data from a variety of sources while navigating independently. They are increasingly being used in a variety of applications, including delivery, videography, surveillance, and search-and-rescue (Giusti et al. 2016). A key requirement for many MAV applications is the ability to react autonomously in a variety of challenging environments, including those where GPS availability is limited. Additionally, drones are required to complete missions as quickly as possible, given their limited power envelope, and the steep power consumption profile of the motors. In particular, this necessitates high speed autonomous navigation to optimize their effectiveness (Boroujerdian et al. 2018). Moreover, because of the adversarial impact of latency on the MAV's decision making, it is better to use onboard compute devices instead of offboard systems, even if the onboard options have limited computing capabilities (Genc et al. 2017); some typical examples of such devices are listed in (Delmerico and Scaramuzza 2018). Also, in such resource scarce set-ups, monocular cameras are ideal sensors for empowering autonomous navigation on MAVs.

The recent success of deep neural network (DNN) based methods on computer vision tasks has fostered a growing movement towards applying DNNs to empower drones with a variety of autonomous navigation capabilities (Giusti et al. 2016; Loquercio et al. 2018). While DNN models outperform other techniques in terms of accuracy, typically the associated inference time is prohibitive for high speed navigation. As a result, the extremely challenging task of enabling high speed navigation by deploying DNNs on resource constrained platforms becomes crucial to their application on MAVs (Mohta et al. 2018). Significant efforts have gone into developing efficient, customized hardware to enable high speed inference; see (Quigley et al. 2018) and the references therein. Another approach is algorithmic, wherein DNN models are optimized to enable faster inference and lower storage requirements.

This paper proposes using a highly optimized sparse DNN that achieves the right accuracy vs. inference time trade-off as prescribed for high-speed autonomous navigation in such resource-constrained environments. Specifically, our contributions are as follows.

- We empirically establish that existing deep as well as shallow neural network architectures have prohibitively high inference times for deployment on resource constrained platforms like the ODROID XU4 and the Raspberry Pi 3, to enable high speed, vision based autonomous navigation. We observe that unless the inference time is reduced to ≈ 23 ms per image, it is difficult to achieve high-speed navigation.
- The key technical contribution is a novel algorithm, FeatherDrop, that efficiently optimizes a given (state-of-the-art) network's structure to achieve the right accuracy vs. inference time trade-off. Unlike existing prune-only algorithms, this algorithm includes a new exploration step that searches for an alternate sub-network with same sparsity but better generalization.

- We analyze the algorithm for convergence and show that it achieves a particular kind of sub-optimality. We also present learning bounds that explicitly illustrate the trade-off with the inference time.
- We empirically establish that the new exploration step can be used along with any existing pruning strategy to improve its efficacy.
- We demonstrate that FeatherNet enables a Parrot Bebop 2 drone to autonomously navigate on semi-structured roads at speeds upto 4 m/s, using an Odroid XU4. Furthermore, architectures proposed in (Giusti et al. 2016) and (Loquercio et al. 2018) fail to do so. In addition, we also establish the efficacy of our sparsified model on the Raspberry Pi 3.

All proofs, and further experimental detail, is available in the supplementary material[1].

2   Related Work

2.1   Autonomous Navigation of MAVs

Vision Based Autonomous Navigation. Cameras are generally considered to be ideal sensors for autonomous navigation for drones (Giusti et al. 2016). The success of deep learning algorithms for image processing tasks has naturally led to their application toward enabling autonomous navigation capabilities in drones where explicit structure is unavailable, as classical image processing techniques fail in such conditions, see (Giusti et al. 2016; Loquercio et al. 2018) and the references therein.

Low Power MAVs. A crucial drawback to using DNNs on MAVs is the fact that they require significant computational resources. Typically, MAVs are equipped with small, low power compute platforms (Delmerico and Scaramuzza 2018). However, the limited power available to drones, and the high power demand of motors means that to optimize power usage, it is critical that missions be completed as quickly as possible; an ideal solution to this problem is to enable the drone to navigate autonomously at high speeds (Boroujerdian et al. 2018). When navigation is empowered by DNNs, the flight speed of the MAV is bottlenecked by the inference rate of the DNN (Loianno et al. 2018). Efforts to enable efficient inference for DNNs typically involve developing custom hardware (Quigley et al. 2018). Our approach involves algorithmically improving the inference rate of the DNN using model compression.

2.2   Sparse Architecture Search with Pruning

Pruning refers to the sparsification of the model itself. As noted in (Frankle and Carbin 2018), for every neural network, there exists an initialization which, when trained therefrom, results in a model with far fewer parameters. The aim

---

[1] at: https://tinyurl.com/y2dzss44.

of pruning techniques is to find such sparsified models, either by compressing a pre-trained model or by inducing sparsity during training. Moreover, it was proposed in (Liu et al. 2018) that all pruning techniques are essentially algorithms to search for sparsified architectures. Pruning techniques can be further classified into structured pruning and unstructured pruning. Weight pruning refers to processes by which individual weights are removed the model, such as (LeCun et al. 1990; Iandola et al. 2016). As noted in (Iandola et al. 2016), unstructured pruning algorithms can achieve remarkably high levels of compression in terms of the number of parameters removed from the model. We don't employ such methods since the drawback to using them is that there is no guarantee that entire filters or neurons are removed; thus, to fully exploit the benefits of highly sparse (but potentially numerous) filters, efficient implementations of sparse matrix multiplications and convolutions are necessary.

Searching for Sparse Architectures. Searching for sparse architectures of neural networks, sometimes referred to as structured pruning (Molchanov et al. 2016), refers to processes by which entire filters or neurons (which we collectively refer to as *artifacts*) are removed from the model to obtain sparse "sub networks" of the original model. The methods proposed in (Li et al. 2016) and similar works search for architectures that meet a preselected level of sparsity; the problems solved by those methods can be formulated as

$$\min \ \{f(\mathbf{w})| \ \text{number of artifacts} \ = K\}$$

for some natural number K. We do not adopt such methods since we know of no rigorous mechanism by which the sparsity level K can be chosen while also satisfying an accuracy constraint. Another approach to solve the structured pruning problem is to automatically search for compressed architectures. This can be formulated as the following optimization problem:

$$\min \{\text{number of artifacs} \ | \ f(\mathbf{w}) \leq t\}$$

for some test error threshold t, which can be chosen based upon empirically determined constraints. One way to solve such problems is to utilize regularization during training to induce sparsity, such as (Zhang et al. 2018) and similar work; we discount such methods since our goal is to compress existing pre-trained models. Another class of methods iteratively remove filters based on "saliency scores", and then "fine-tune", or retrain, the model, such as (Li et al. 2016; Molchanov et al. 2016). In (Li et al. 2016), filters are pruned based on saliency scores derived from the ℓ_1 norm of the vectorized weights of each filter; note that in the paper, a predefined target architecture is provided, but this can easily be adapted to the setting where an accuracy constraint must be met. In (Molchanov et al. 2016), saliency scores are used to determine which filters can be removed with the least impact on the loss function. Our approach using *basis exploration*, described in Sect. 3, is by design an algorithm to improve upon architecture search methods; employing our algorithm alongside an iterative architecture search strategy results in models that are at least as sparse as those obtained without using basis exploration.

3 Searching for Sparse DNN Architectures

Motivated by the constraints on accuracy and inference time, we propose a novel technique for optimizing neural network architectures. We observe that the search for sparse neural network architectures can be broadly thought of as searching for the minimum support of the model. We then propose *Greedy Minimum Support (GMS)*, an iterative algorithm that finds the minimum support of a function, which utilizes a novel exploration step. We adapt the GMS algorithm to finding sparse neural architectures. The specific algorithm thus obtained is called `FeatherDrop`, an iterative pruning algorithm for efficient architecture search. `FeatherDrop` enables significant sparsification, while systematically satisfying an accuracy constraint.

3.1 Preliminaries and Notation

Lower case letters such as, x, denote scalars, bold lower case letters such as, $\mathbf{x}$, denote vectors, uppercase letters like X denote sets, and bold uppercase letters, such as $\mathbf{X}$, denote matrices. $[n] = \{1, ..., n\}$ for $n \in \mathbb{N}$. For a finite set A, let $|A|$ denote the cardinality of A. $\mathbf{x}_i$ denotes the ith entry of $\mathbf{x}$. Let $\nabla_i f(\mathbf{x}) = \frac{\partial f}{\partial \mathbf{x}_i}$ for any $\mathbf{x} \in \mathbb{R}^n$. For $\mathbf{x} \in \mathbb{R}^n$, let $\text{sort}_i(\mathbf{x})$ denote the ith largest absolute element of $\mathbf{x}$. Define $\text{sparse}_k(\mathbf{x}) \in \mathbb{R}^d$ as a vector with its jth element defined as:

$$(\text{sparse}_k(\mathbf{x}))_j = \begin{cases} \mathbf{x}_j & |\mathbf{x}_j| \geq \text{sort}_k(\mathbf{x}) \\ 0 & \text{otherwise} \end{cases}$$

We define the loss function of a neural network as follows.

Definition 1. *Let $\mathcal{Y} = \{y_1, .., y_l\}$ be a set of labels for data from set $\mathcal{D}$. Let $g : \mathcal{D} \times \mathcal{W} \rightarrow [0,1]^{|\mathcal{Y}|}$ define the output of the neural network G, with vectorized parameters belonging to $\mathcal{W}$. We define the categorical cross entropy loss of G over samples $\{D_i \in \mathcal{D}\}_{i=1}^{N}$, given $\mathbf{w} \in \mathcal{W}$ as*

$$f(\mathbf{w}) = -\frac{1}{N|\mathcal{Y}|} \sum_{i=1}^{N} \sum_{j=1}^{|\mathcal{Y}|} \bar{y}_{ij} \log(g_j(\mathbf{w}, D_i)) \tag{1}$$

where each $\bar{y}_{ij}$ is the ground-truth score for class j of sample D_i.

Parameters of filters in convolutional layers and incoming weight vectors in feed forward layers are collectively referred to as *artifacts*. For notational convenience, we assume that the network has N artifacts, each of which has m parameters, thus giving us a network with $n = mN$ parameters and $\mathbf{w} \in \mathbb{R}^n$. Let $\mathbf{w}_{[i]}$ denote the ith block of m parameters corresponding to the ith artifact. Let $\text{supp}(\mathbf{w})$ denote the set of indexes for blocks/artifacts with non-zero parameter values in $\mathbf{x}$. Thus $\text{supp}(\mathbf{w}) \subseteq [N]$.

3.2   Formulation

We pose the objective of architecture optimization as follows. Given a neural network loss function f defined in Definition 1, and $t \in \mathbb{R}$ such that $t > \min f(\mathbf{w})$ for $\mathbf{w} \in \mathbb{R}^n$, we wish to solve

$$\min_{A \subset [N]} |A| \text{ subject to } \min_{\{\mathbf{w}|\text{supp}(\mathbf{w})=A\}} f(\mathbf{w}) \le t \tag{OPT}$$

The choice of t is crucial to ensure that the feasibility set of (OPT) is non-empty:

Lemma 1. *Let $\mathbf{w}^{(0)}$ be an unconstrained local minimum of any $f : \mathbb{R}^n \to \mathbb{R}$ and let the gradient of f be L-Lipschitz, and suppose $f_0 = f(\mathbf{w}^{(0)}) > 0$. Then there exists $\mathbf{w} \in \mathbb{R}^n$ such that*

$$f(\mathbf{w}) \le f_0(1 + \delta), \quad \|\mathbf{w}\|_0 = k \in \mathbb{N} \le n - 1,$$

whenever $\delta \ge \delta_0$,

$$\delta_0 = \frac{L}{2} \frac{1}{f_0} \sum_{i=0}^{n-k-1} \left(\text{sort}_{n-i}(\mathbf{w}^{(0)}) \right)^2. \tag{2}$$

For a given $t = f_0(1 + \delta)$, where $\delta \ge \delta_0$, defined in (2), the optimal A^* of problem OPT satisfies the following property:

$$A \subset [d], |A| < |A^*| \Rightarrow \min_{\{\mathbf{w}|\text{supp}(\mathbf{w})=A\}} f(\mathbf{w}) > t. \tag{3}$$

Now, define $\mathbf{w}^* \equiv \arg\min_{\{\mathbf{w}|\text{supp}(\mathbf{w})=A^*\}} f(\mathbf{w})$. To achieve better generalization, from all the optimal solutions, we would like to select that special solution A^* such that:

$$f(\mathbf{w}^*) = \min_{\{\mathbf{w} \mid |\text{supp}(\mathbf{w})|=|A^*|\}} f(\mathbf{w}). \tag{4}$$

In general, verifying whether a candidate $\hat{A}$ is indeed optimal would require solving $O(2^{|\hat{A}|})$ minimization problems. Instead, we opt for a special (sub-optimal) greedy solution: a feasible candidate, $(\mathbf{w}^*, A^* = \text{supp}(\mathbf{w}^*))$ is said to be greedy-optimal iff it satisfies the following:

G1 As a consequence of (3), for all $i \in A^*$, $\min_{\{\mathbf{w} \mid \text{supp}(\mathbf{w})=A^*-\{i\}\}}$ $f(\mathbf{w}) > f_0(1 + \delta)$.

G2 Similarly, a consequence of (4), for every $l \in A^*$ and every $m \in \bar{A}^*$, $f(\mathbf{w}^*) \le f_{lm} = \min_{\{\mathbf{w} \mid \text{supp}(\mathbf{w})=A^*-\{l\}\cup\{m\}\}} f(\mathbf{w})$. We call this **Basis Exploration**.

The above conditions suggest that for a greedy optimal point, it is neither possible to improve the sparsity by removing a single artifact nor possible to improve the loss with a strategy of exchanging a single artifact.

3.3   The GMS Algorithm

We use these conditions to derive an iterative algorithm, stated in Algorithm 1, which is guaranteed to converge to a greedy-optimal point. This is because Algorithm 1 does not enter a cycle due to the strict inequality condition for an exchange.

Infact, the proposed algorithm can be efficiently implemented by noting that the identities of the artifacts within a layer do not matter, assuming each layer consists of the same type of artifacts. Hence verifying condition **G1** can be performed by solving $O(h)$ minimization problems, where h is the number of hidden layers in the network. And, condition **G2** can be verified by solving $O(h(h-1))$ minimization problems.

Algorithm 1. Greedy Minimum Support (GMS)

1: **Input:** t
2: **Initialize:** Find $\mathbf{w}^*$ a local minimum of

$$\min_{\mathbf{w}} f(\mathbf{w})$$

   such that $f(\mathbf{w}^*) \leq t$.
3: $A = \mathrm{supp}(\mathbf{w}^*)$, $\mathbf{w}_{sparse} = \mathbf{w}^*$.
4: **while** True **do**
5:    **if** there exists $l \in A$ such that $\min_{\mathrm{supp}(\mathbf{w})=A-\{l\}} f(\mathbf{w}) \leq t$ **then**
6:       $\mathbf{w}_{sparse} = \arg\min_{\mathrm{supp}(\mathbf{w})=A-\{l\}} f(\mathbf{w})$ and $A \to A - \{l\}$
7:    **else if** Find $l \in A$ and $m \in \bar{A}$ such that $f_{lm} \leq t$

$$f_{lm} = \min_{\mathrm{supp}(\mathbf{w})=A-\{l\}\cup\{m\}} f(\mathbf{w})$$

      then
8:       $A \to A - \{l\} \cup \{m\}$ and $\mathbf{w}_{sparse} = \arg\min_{\mathrm{supp}(\mathbf{w})=A} f(\mathbf{w})$
9:    **else**
10:      End
11:   **end if**
12: **end while**
13: **Output:** $\mathbf{w}_{sparse}, A$

The pursuit of a greedy-optimal solution is justified because, in the general case, the original problem is NP-hard. The algorithm, as described above, is an instance of an algorithm which searches for a 1-opt solution, as defined in (Park and Boyd 2018). This greedy search algorithm can be used to search for network architectures, as we show in the next section.

3.4   Applying GMS to Network Architecture Search

We begin with a heuristic for avoiding the $O(h)$ retraining cycles during the pruning phase of the proposed Algorithm 1.

For ease of exposition, we define a score function for each artifact to evaluate its importance. These scores are then normalized and the artifact with the lowest score is pruned, instead of $O(h)$ retrainings. More specifically, for any parameter vector $\mathbf{w}$, and the jth artifact in the lth layer, we define

$$\mathtt{select}(\mathbf{w}) \equiv \mathrm{argmin}_{j\in\mathtt{supp}(\mathbf{w})} \frac{g_j(\mathbf{w})}{\max_{k\in\mathtt{Layer}(\mathbf{w},l)} g_k(\mathbf{w})} \tag{5}$$

where $\mathtt{Layer}(\mathbf{w}, l)$, is the set of all artifacts in the lth layer and in $\mathtt{supp}\mathbf{w}$, and $g_j(\mathbf{w})$ is a positive artifact specific score function. We use this normalization as at least one artifact in each layer has score 1, thereby ensuring that at least 1 artifact remains in each layer. In this paper we experiment with two different score functions. We call $\mathtt{select}_{\ell_2}(\mathbf{w})$, the selection criterion obtained by applying the following score function

$$g_j(\mathbf{w}) = \|\mathbf{w}_{(j)}\| \tag{ℓ_2}$$

to Eq. (5). This criterion can be useful at saddle points where the gradient vanishes. However, whenever the gradient exists then one can build a more refined model of the objective function value, $f(\mathbf{w})$, when we remove the jth artifact through the first order Taylor expansion. Indeed, from the first order Taylor expansion, we obtain the following approximation $f(\mathbf{w} - \mathbf{w}_{(j)}) - f(\mathbf{w}) \approx \langle \mathbf{w}_{(j)}, \nabla_{(j)} f(\mathbf{w}) \rangle$. This motivates the alternate selection criterion, $\mathtt{select}_{FS}(\mathbf{w})$, which is defined by using the score function

$$g_j(\mathbf{w}) = \left| \langle \mathbf{w}_{(j)}, \nabla_{(j)} f(\mathbf{w}) \rangle \right| \tag{FS}$$

in (5). We refer to the variant of GMS, that uses (ℓ_2) and (FS) used in lines 5 and 7, as $\mathtt{FeatherDrop}$[2].

Learning Bounds

In the reminder of this section we present a learning bound that explicitly incorporates the inference time budget. If N_i is the number of (non-pruned) artifacts in the ith hidden layer, n_i, n_o are the input and output dimensions of the network, then the inference time is proportional to $n_i N_1 + N_1 N_2 + \ldots + N_{D-1} N_D + N_D n_o$, which we assume is less than some budget, B. Then, the following theorem holds.

Theorem 1. *With probability atleast* $1 - \delta$, *we have:*

$$\mathcal{R}[\mathbf{w}] \leq \hat{\mathcal{R}}[\mathbf{w}] + 2\sqrt{\frac{4^d \log n_i R \Pi_{l=1}^d B_l}{m}} + 3\sqrt{\frac{1}{2m}\left(\log\frac{2}{\delta} + d\log\frac{B}{2}\right)}, \tag{6}$$

where $\|W_l\|_{1_{N_l},\infty}^2 \leq B_l, \mathcal{R}, \hat{\mathcal{R}}$ *denote the true, empirical risk with employing the pruned classifier respectively. Here,* $\|x\|_{1_N}$ *denotes the sum of the absolute values*

---

[2] In the analogy of flight of birds, we drop unnecessary feathers, hence $\mathtt{FeatherDrop}$.

of the largest (in magnitude) N entries of x. If $N = dim(x)$, then this is same as 1-norm. For a matrix W, $\|W\|_{1_N,\infty}$ denotes the maximum of the 1_N-norms of the columns of W.

This learning bound provides the following insights into the generalization ability of the pruned classifier:

1. As inference rate increases (B decreases), the confidence terms decrease. Hence the guarantees become better and better as long as the empirical risk is upper bounded (like in our algorithm by t).
2. The above phenomenon has more pronounced effect for deep networks. In other words, the benefits of pruning are more prominent for deep networks.

4   Experimental Results

In this section, we motivate and detail our experiments. We investigate two different areas, namely the efficacy of the pruning algorithm, and the utility of compressed models for autonomous navigation.

4.1   Experimental Methodology

Our aim is to address the question- can drones be made to autonomously navigate at high speeds of upto 4 m/sec in GPS denied environments, using CPU on lightweight compute platforms? Here, we detail how we established inference time constraints on the Odroid XU4 and Raspberry Pi 3, our reactive navigation scheme, and our dataset collection scheme.

Establishing Inference Time Constraints. In particular, we have used Odroid XU4 for running algorithms, and Parrot Bebop 2 drone as our testing platform. Parrot Bebop 2 driver running in ROS on the Odroid XU4 board receives data from the drone at 30 Hz i.e. approximately every 33 ms (refer to supplemental). Using the CvBridge package in ROS, the raw data conversion to OpenCv image takes on average 10 ms (refer to supplemental) on Odroid XU4. This leaves approximately 23 ms to process each frame for autonomous navigation.

Thus, we cast the problem as searching for sufficiently accurate neural networks which require less than 23 ms for inference, using only the Odroid XU4 CPU. Our approach to finding such networks is to search for a sparse subnetwork of existing neural network architectures that are capable of satisfying our given test-set accuracy requirements. We conduct similar experiments with the Raspberry Pi 3, as detailed in our supplemental material.

Navigation Technique. We use the strategy proposed in (Giusti et al. 2016). Utilizing the semi-structured settings of urban roads, we formulate the problem of autonomous navigation as a three class classification problem, where each input image is labelled as- (1) Turn Left, (2) Go Straight, or (3) Turn Right, corresponding to a control command taken when an image is classified as such. For further details, refer to the supplemental material.

Dataset Collection. We collected two datasets. We construct the first dataset, called CampusRoads, out of images of roads in the university campus, annotated with TurnRight, TurnLeft, or GoStraight. We collected a total of 60042 frames, of which 40200 are for training, 9000 are for validation of architecture search algorithms, and 10842 are for testing. We construct a similar dataset of the data provided in (Giusti et al. 2016), which we call Forest Trails (20316, 3765 and 5361 frames for training, validation and testing). For a more detailed description of our data collection process, refer to the supplemental material.

4.2   Experimental Setup

Training and Sparsification of Models. We train our models, and sparsify them on desktop computers equipped with an Nvidia 1080Ti and an Intel Xeon workstation processor. The models are trained on the CampusRoads and ForestTrails datasets we have constructed.

Computational Board. We use the ODROID XU4 and Raspberry Pi 3 as our compute platforms. The ODROID XU4 and Raspberry Pi 3 are both small, low power computing devices (Delmerico and Scaramuzza 2018), and are thus ideal for use on MAVs.

Navigation Stack. We use the Parrot Bebop 2 as our MAV. These MAVs are retail products, and more importantly, have drivers that integrate with the Robot Operating System (ROS). The rate of image acquisition from the drone is limited to 30 Hz. Thus, we achieve autonomous navigation at high speeds of upto 4 m/sec by optimizing the entire stack to run at rate at least as high as 30 Hz. For a full description of our navigation stack, and the establishment of inference rate constraints, refer to the supplementary material.

All accuracies are reported on the testing set defined in Sect. 3. Lastly, we conduct our flight tests at two locations in the university campus.

4.3   Comparison of FeatherDrop with Other Pruning Schemes

In this section, we establish the effectiveness of FeatherDrop as compared to the algorithms proposed in (Molchanov et al. 2016) and (Li et al. 2016). We begin with pre trained models with the architecture proposed in (Giusti et al. 2016), trained separately on the CampusRoads and ForestTrails datasets. We then apply a variety of architecture search algorithms to obtain sparsified architectures. The algorithms we chose for comparision are FeatherDrop, FeatherDrop without basis exploration, (Molchanov et al. 2016; Li et al. 2016), as well as randomly selecting artifacts for pruning to obtain sparsified architectures. In order to demonstrate the utility of basis exploration, we append the random pruning strategy and the strategy proposed in (Li et al. 2016) with basis exploration. We then compare the degree of sparsification obtained by models

478   P. Prakash et al.

trained on the CampusRoads and ForestTrails datasets for different values of t chosen a priori.

Results and Discussion. We compare the extent of pruning for different constraint values of t as test set accuracy using `FeatherDrop` algorithm versus naive strategy of pruning without any basis exploration. The results are tabulated in Table 1.

- Table 1 shows that `FeatherDrop` leads to much more pruned architectures than the naive pruning technique without basis exploration, random pruning without basis exploration, and the algorithms proposed in (Li et al. 2016) without basis exploration and (Molchanov et al. 2016).
- We observe that using basis exploration significantly improves the sparsification when applied to models pruned using (Li et al. 2016), and random pruning. Appending both the random strategy and the strategy in (Li et al. 2016) with basis exploration results in a significant increase in sparsification. This supports our conjecture that any iterative weight-based pruning scheme can be improved, potentially significantly, by utilizing basis exploration.
- We notice `FeatherDrop` is comparably less susceptible to change in extent of pruning with change in t constraint. In particular, as t increases we obtain the same pruned architectures although the number of basis exploration steps increase.

Table 1. Percentage reduction in the number of parameters obtained by different iterative pruning algorithms. BE refers to Basis Exploration, CR refers to CampusRoads, FT refers to ForestTrails.

Test set accuracy \dataset	FeatherDrop	Naive strategy	Random without BE	Random with BE	Li et al. 2016	Li et al. 2016 with BE	Molchanov et al. 2016
92% on CR	**98.69**	96.24	89.85	98.57	85.85	93.05	93.43
93% on CR	**97.98**	87.08	36.79	89.11	72.42	91.75	93.43
94% on CR	**96.68**	79.69	0.41	90.86	5.54	72.82	66.81
95% on CR	**94.74**	3.41	1.19	90.42	1.58	70.05	66.81
81% on FT	87.29	69.98	4.59	84.54	3.56	**90.04**	9.96
82% on FT	**80.08**	63.18	1.98	72.59	9.1	70.02	2.19
83% on FT	82.52	16.77	8.65	60.15	3.96	**90.5**	1.4
84% on FT	71.72	1.62	0.83	56.09	0.40	**87.51**	1.01
85% on FT	**36.06**	3.41	3.06	3.45	0.39	0.79	0.0

4.4   Using Sparse Models for Autonomous Navigation

The goal of these experiments is to demonstrate that drones are capable of autonomously navigating roads at speeds upto 4 m/s with sparsified models.

1. We show that existing DNN architectures for autonomous navigation proposed in (Giusti et al. 2016) and (Loquercio et al. 2018) are unsuitable for deployment on the ODROID XU4 and the Raspberry Pi 3. Then, we show that the sparsified model is able to achieve sufficient inference rates on the ODROID XU4 and the Raspberry Pi 3 (see supplemental material).
2. We compare the performance of the networks proposed in (Giusti et al. 2016) and (Loquercio et al. 2018) with the sparsified architectures obtained using FeatherDrop. Specifically, we deploy each model on the ODROID XU4, and attempt to complete two challenging road following tasks wherein the roads have unclear boundaries, while flying at speeds upto 4 m/s.

Results and Discussion

1. We compared the inference rates of the models proposed in (Giusti et al. 2016) and (Loquercio et al. 2018) with the sparsified model we obtained using FeatherDrop on both the ODROID XU4 and the Raspberry Pi 3. We observed that on average the former two models achieve 61 ms and 50 ms inference times, and thus fail to meet the inference rate constraints established previously. Moreover, we observe that the sparsifed model obtained with FeatherDrop achieves an average inference time of 10 ms, a 5x increase in inference rate over (Loquercio et al. 2018) and a 6x increase in inference rate over the model proposed in (Giusti et al. 2016) on the ODROID XU4; similarly, the sparsified model achieves a 12 ms inference time on the Raspberry Pi 3 (5x and 4x improvements). For a more detailed description of these results, refer to the supplementary material.
2. Last, we compared the performance of each network on challenging autonomous road following missions at speeds upto 4 m/s with an ODROID XU4 using a Parrot Bebop2 drone as the platform. The missions we chose were to follow two challenging roads inside the university campus- one with two turns and the other as an unseen straight road. We observe that the models proposed in (Giusti et al. 2016) and (Loquercio et al. 2018) are incapable of regularly completing missions, whereas the sparsified model obtained using FeatherDrop finished all but 1 trial. This corresponds to failures occurring only when the entire system is unable to keep up with the inference rate requirement and significant environmental noise. These results are tabulated in Table 2.

Table 2. Comparison of mission success rates (3 attempts) of our sparsified architecture with architectures proposed in (Giusti et al. 2016) and (Loquercio et al. 2018) using an ODROID XU4 for computation.

Network	Mission status on unseen straight road	Mission status on road with 2 turns
(Giusti et al. 2016)	1	0
(Loquercio et al. 2018)	0	0
Sparse model	**3**	**2**

5   Conclusions

In this work, we have addressed the problem of autonomous navigation of MAVs at high speeds using DNNs in GPS-denied environments with limited computational resources. This problem naturally requires trading off accuracy and inference rate; our proposed solution negotiates this tradeoff by deploying neural networks with sparse architectures with good generalization ability. We obtain such models by searching for "sub networks" of existing pre trained models. We propose a novel algorithm to find such sparse sub networks which utilizes an exploration step. We show that this algorithm achieves superior sparsity to state of the art iterative pruning methods. Furthermore, we show that our algorithm can be used to improve the efficacy of any iterative pruning method. Lastly, we demonstrate that small, sparsified models obtained by applying our network search algorithm to a network based on (Giusti et al. 2016), are able to complete real world, autonomous flight missions at high speed that models proposed in (Giusti et al. 2016) and (Loquercio et al. 2018) cannot.

References

Boroujerdian, B., Genc, H., Krishnan, S., Faust, A., Reddi, V.J.: Why compute matters for UAV energy efficiency? (2018)

Delmerico, J., Scaramuzza, D.: A benchmark comparison of monocular visual-inertial odometry algorithms for flying robots. Memory **10**, 20 (2018)

Frankle, J., Carbin, M.: The lottery ticket hypothesis: training pruned neural networks. arXiv preprint arXiv:1803.03635 (2018)

Genc, H., Zu, Y., Chin, T.W., Halpern, M., Reddi, V.J.: Flying IoT: toward low-power vision in the sky. IEEE Micro **37**(6), 40–51 (2017)

Giusti, A., et al.: A machine learning approach to visual perception of forest trails for mobile robots. IEEE Robot. Autom. Lett. **1**(2), 661–667 (2016)

Iandola, F.N., Han, S., Moskewicz, M.W., Ashraf, K., Dally, W.J., Keutzer, K.: Squeezenet: Alexnet-level accuracy with 50x fewer parameters and¡ 0.5 mb model size. arXiv preprint arXiv:1602.07360 (2016)

LeCun, Y., Denker, J.S., Solla, S.A.: Optimal brain damage. In: Advances in neural information processing systems. pp. 598–605 (1990)

Li, H., Kadav, A., Durdanovic, I., Samet, H., Graf, H.P.: Pruning filters for efficient convnets. arXiv preprint arXiv:1608.08710 (2016)

Liu, Z., Sun, M., Zhou, T., Huang, G., Darrell, T.: Rethinking the value of network pruning. arXiv preprint arXiv:1810.05270 (2018)

Loianno, G., Scaramuzza, D., Kumar, V.: Special issue on high-speed vision-based autonomous navigation of uavs. Journal of Field Robotics **35**(1), 3–4 (2018)

Loquercio, A., Maqueda, A.I., del Blanco, C.R., Scaramuzza, D.: Dronet: Learning to fly by driving. IEEE Robotics and Automation Letters **3**(2), 1088–1095 (2018)

Mohta, K., Sun, K., Liu, S., Watterson, M., Pfrommer, B., Svacha, J., Mulgaonkar, Y., Taylor, C.J., Kumar, V.: Experiments in fast, autonomous, gps-denied quadrotor flight. In: 2018 IEEE International Conference on Robotics and Automation (ICRA). pp. 7832–7839. IEEE (2018)

Molchanov, P., Tyree, S., Karras, T., Aila, T., Kautz, J.: Pruning convolutional neural networks for resource efficient transfer learning. arXiv preprint arXiv:1611.06440 (2016)

Park, J., Boyd, S.: A semidefinite programming method for integer convex quadratic minimization. Optimization Letters **12**(3), 499–518 (2018)

Quigley, M., Mohta, K., Shivakumar, S.S., Watterson, M., Mulgaonkar, Y., Arguedas, M., Sun, K., Liu, S., Pfrommer, B., Kumar, V., et al.: The open vision computer: An integrated sensing and compute system for mobile robots. arXiv preprint arXiv:1809.07674 (2018)

Zhang, D., Wang, H., Figueiredo, M., Balzano, L.: Learning to share: Simultaneous parameter tying and sparsification in deep learning (2018)

Social Cost Guarantees in Smart Route Guidance

Paolo Serafino[1(✉)], Carmine Ventre[2], Long Tran-Thanh[3], Jie Zhang[3], Bo An[4], and Nick Jennings[5]

[1] Gran Sasso Science Institute, L'Aquila, Italy
paolo.serafino@gssi.it
[2] University of Essex, Colchester, UK
c.ventre@essex.ac.uk
[3] University of Southampton, Southampton, UK
{ltt08r,jie.zhang}@soton.ac.uk
[4] Nanyang Technological University, Singapore, Singapore
boan@ntu.edu.sg
[5] Imperial College London, London, UK
n.jennings@imperial.ac.uk

Abstract. We model and study the problem of assigning traffic in an urban road network infrastructure. In our model, each driver submits their intended destination and is assigned a route to follow that minimizes the social cost (i.e., travel distance of all the drivers). We assume drivers are strategic and try to manipulate the system (i.e., misreport their intended destination and/or deviate from the assigned route) if they can reduce their travel distance by doing so. Such strategic behavior is highly undesirable as it can lead to an overall suboptimal traffic assignment and cause congestion. To alleviate this problem, we develop moneyless mechanisms that are resilient to manipulation by the agents and offer provable approximation guarantees on the social cost obtained by the solution. We then empirically test the mechanisms studied in the paper, showing that they can be effectively used in practice in order to compute manipulation resistant traffic allocations.

1 Introduction

Recent years have witnessed increasing interest in the development of efficient traffic control systems [9,15,19]. This is motivated by the significant negative impact on the quality of life of both road users and residents caused by heavy traffic congestion levels in large cities such as London, Beijing, and Los Angeles. Indeed, heavy congestion is known to be a major cause of air and noise pollution, which are widely recognized as the main cause of many health issues [14,23]. Adding to this is the economic cost associated with the large amount of time spent in traffic jams, which reduces the productivity of the economy [13]. Moreover, the situation is expected to become significantly worse in the future when the population, and thus the traffic flow, in large cities will be much bigger

© Springer Nature Switzerland AG 2019
A. C. Nayak and A. Sharma (Eds.): PRICAI 2019, LNAI 11671, pp. 482–495, 2019.
https://doi.org/10.1007/978-3-030-29911-8_37

than at present. Unfortunately, conventional traffic control systems have proven unable to efficiently decrease congestion levels, as they are not designed to be adaptive to the dynamics of city traffic, which changes over space and time. On the other hand, it has been shown [16,21] that by putting some sort of intelligence/smartness into traffic control systems, we can make them adapt to the changes of the traffic flow. A key objective within these smart traffic control systems is to address the so-called *traffic assignment problem* (TAP), in which mobile agents (i.e., typically drivers) declare their intended destination to the system, perhaps via their satellite navigation systems, and are then assigned a route to follow, in such a way that some objective function of the overall traffic flow in the system is optimized (i.e., minimizing the total traveled distance or maintaining an efficient traffic load balance). As these agents are typically self-interested and strategic (i.e., they try to maximize their own utility, disregarding whether this is detrimental to the global optimization goal), they may manipulate the system whenever they can benefit from doing so [16,25]. This kind of opportunistic behavior is highly undesirable as it will increase the total social cost (i.e., decreasing the total load balance or increasing the total congestion level). As such, incentivizing agents not to be strategic is a key design objective of these traffic assignment systems [16,21,25]. Given this, we focus on *strategyproof* TAP mechanisms, which guarantee that it is in the agent's best interest to always report her true destination and follow the assigned route. Furthermore, we assume that money transfers between the mechanism and the agents are not available. This is a common assumption in many domains [20] that will facilitate the likely real-world deployment of the system by lowering set up costs (i.e., avoiding the construction of tolling booths).

The remainder of the paper is organized as follows. In Sect. 2 we discuss related works. In Sect. 3 we introduce our model for TAP and prove that Pareto optimal allocations theoretically guarantee that agents will follow their assigned paths (Theorem 1). We then move to study deterministic (Sect. 4) and randomized (Sect. 5) Pareto optimal mechanisms for our problem. We show that the approximation ratio of *deterministic* strategyproof mechanisms is lower bounded by 3 (Theorem 2), while the Serial Dictatorship mechanism can achieve an upper bound of $2^n - 1$ and it is Pareto-optimal and non-bossy (Theorems 4 and 5), where n is the number of agents (Theorems 4 and 5). Furthermore, if we require non-bossiness and Pareto optimality, we are able to close this approximation ratio gap by showing that the Bipolar Serial Dictatorship mechanism is the *only* strategyproof mechanism. For *randomized* mechanisms, we show that the approximation ratio is lower bounded by $\frac{11}{10}$ (Theorem 7). In addition, the Random Serial Dictatorship mechanism can achieve an n-approximation (Theorems 8 and 9), while still preserving the desired properties of Pareto-optimality and non-bossiness. In addition to these theoretical results, we present an extensive experimental evaluation on traffic networks generated from real road network data, which show how the mechanisms studied in the paper provide good performance in practice, despite the high theoretical worst case approximation guarantee.

2   Related Work

There is a large body of literature on traffic network modelling and assignment [2,7,8,22]. However, these works typically ignore the strategic behaviour of participating agents. Nevertheless, they can be useful to model the underlying traffic network in our work. In particular, we follow the widely used traffic model proposed in [2].

To tackle the strategic behaviour of the agents, several researchers have suggested employing mechanism design with money and auction theory for traffic control [4,16,21,25]. These works typically rely on the computation of the VCG auction in order to assign vehicles to paths. However, they require monetary incentives, and typically focus on a local control level, such as intersection management (as VCG is typically computationally hard, and thus, not readily scalable [6]).

A number of researchers have focused on mechanism design without money [5,20]. However, none of these mechanisms can be easily applied to the traffic assignment problem, as they do not take into account the features of the underlying traffic network structure. As we will show, TAP bears some resemblance to the problem of assigning indivisible objects [3,10,24], although these results are not directly applicable to our scenario. Indeed TAP has a much more complex structure (mainly due to the underlying traffic network topology) which traditional assignment mechanisms fail to address.

3   Model and Preliminary Definitions

A *traffic assignment problem* (TAP) consists of a set of agents $A = \{a_1, \ldots, a_n\}$ and a road network infrastructure, represented as a directed graph $G = (V, E)$, where: (*i*) $V = \{v_1, \ldots, v_{|V|}\}$ is the set of nodes representing the junctions of the road network infrastructure; and (*ii*) $E \subseteq V \times V$ is the set of directed edges representing one-way road segments. Each edge $e \in E$ has a *capacity* $c : E \to \mathbb{N}^+$, which determines the maximum number of agents that can travel through the edge at any given time, and a *weight function* $w : E \to \mathbb{R}^+$ which represents the cost incurred by the agent traveling through the edge (i.e., travel distance). Furthermore, each edge is associated to a *transit time* $\tau : E \to \mathbb{Z}^+$ which represents the *free travel time of the edge* (i.e., the minimum travel time needed to travel through the road at maximum allowed speed). This means that agent a_i setting off at time t from node v_o and heading to node v_d through the edge (v_o, v_d) will reach node v_d at time $t + \tau(v_o, v_d)$, and will occupy edge (v_o, v_d) only in the time interval $[t, t + \tau(v_o, v_d)]$. Unless stated otherwise, we assume that edges (u, v) and (v, u) are *symmetrical*: for all $(u, v), (v, u) \in E$ $c(u, v) = c(v, u)$, $w(u, v) = w(v, u)$ and $\tau(u, v) = \tau(v, u)$.

As in [17], we assume that if the flow of traffic through an edge does not exceed its capacity, then no congestion occurs and the traveling time equals the free travel time. Initially, at time $t = 0$, agents reside on a (publicly known) set

$O \subseteq V$ of nodes[1] of the graph, O_i being the initial location of agent a_i. Each agent $a_i \in A$ wants to reach an intended destination $D_i \in V$, which is the agent's private information and will be referred to in the remainder as her *type*.

Agents submit (or *bid*) a destination to an *allocation mechanism*, which then assigns each agent a path in order to optimize a certain objective function. More formally, let $\mathcal{P}$ be the set of all possible simple paths between any two nodes in G. Let $\mathbf{D} = (D_1, \ldots, D_n) \in V^n$ be a *vector of declarations* (also referred to as *bids*) by the agents and $\mathbf{D}_{-i}$ be the vector of declarations of all agents but a_i. A *mechanism* $M^{G,O} : V^n \to \mathcal{P}^n$ maps a vector of declarations to *feasible paths* (i.e., not exceeding the capacity of the edges at any given time) on G, given the initial locations O of the agents. We write $M(\mathbf{D})$ instead of $M^{G,O}(\mathbf{D})$ when G and O can be deduced from the context. The path associated to agent a_i is denoted as $M_i(\mathbf{D})$.

A traffic assignment $S = M(\mathbf{D})$ induces a *flow over time*[2] $f_S : E \times \mathcal{T} \to \mathbb{N}^+$, where $\mathcal{T}$ is a suitable discretization of time w.r.t. the transit times of the edges of G (for simplicity we will assume that $\mathcal{T} = \{0, 1, \ldots, T\}$, where T is a time horizon sufficient for the network to clear. Thus, $f_S(u, v; t) = |\{a_i \in A | (u, v) \in S_i\}|$ is the number of agents that are assigned a path that contains edge (u, v) at time $t \in \mathcal{T}$. Feasibility constraints imply that $f_S(u, v; t) \leq c(u, v)$ for all $t \in \mathcal{T}$.

In the remainder, without loss of generality, we will study the problem on the *time-expanded network* [11,12] of G and consider the *static* flow through it (i.e, the transit of an agent over and edge is instantaneous). A time-expanded network is a properly constructed directed graph with cost and capacity functions on the edges just like G, but no transit time (i.e. travel time is instantaneous through all the edges). This is without loss of generality from the point of view of SP, Pareto-optimality, non-bossines and approximation guarantee since it is well known (see [11,12]) that a flow over time is equivalent to a static flow on the corresponding time-expanded network.

Let $f_S^{-i} : E \to \mathbb{N}$ be the flow induced by traffic assignment S generated by agents $A \setminus \{a_i\}$, formally for all $e \in E$, $f_S^{-i}(e) = |\{a_j \in A : e \in S_j, j \neq i\}|$. The *residual graph* G_f^{-i} is a graph such that: (i) G_f^{-i} has the same nodes and edges as G; (ii) each edge $e \in E$ of G_f^{-i} has capacity $c(e) - f_S^{-i}(e)$. For any two nodes $u, v \in V$, let $\mathcal{P}_{u,v}$ denote the set of simple paths in G connecting u to v. Furthermore, for all traffic assignments $S = M(\mathbf{D})$ and all agents a_i, let $\mathcal{P}_{u,v}^i(S) = \{P \in \mathcal{P}_{u,v} | \forall e \in P, c(e) > f_S^{-i}(e)\}$. Informally, $\mathcal{P}_{u,v}^i(S)$ is the set of paths connecting u and v that have spare capacity from the perspective of agent a_i (i.e., they can be used by

---

[1] Restricting origins/destinations of journeys to road junctions is without loss of generality since fictitious nodes that serve the sole purpose of acting as starting/ending point of a journey can always be created by edge splitting operations.

[2] Sometimes also referred to as *dynamic flow* in the literature. We prefer the term *flow over* time as the adjective *dynamic* has often been used in many algorithmic settings to refer to problems where the input data arrive online or change over time. We assume that all the agents are present at time $t = 0$ and the network is cleared after the last agent reaches their destination.

agent a_i) when the other agents implement S. Then, the set of reactions available to agent a_i having type D_i at allocation S is defined as $R_i(S) = \mathcal{P}^i_{O_i,D_i}(S)$.

Agents are not constrained to follow their assigned path but can choose a different one, subject to capacity constraints[3]. To model this, as per [18], we assume that, after the mechanism computes a traffic allocation, the agents can *react* by choosing an action from a set $R_i \subseteq \mathcal{P}$. Hence, the actual *cost function* of an agent depends on: (*i*) her true type D_i; (*ii*) the allocation S chosen by the mechanism on input the bids reported by the agents; and (*iii*) the reactions chosen by the agents.

We can now formally define the cost function of an agent. Given an allocation $S' = M(D'_i, \mathbf{D}_{-i})$, the cost of an agent of type D_i with respect to S' is defined as: $cost_i(S', D_i) = \min_{P \in R_i(S')} w(P)$ where $w(P) = \sum_{(u,v) \in P} w(u,v)$ denotes the cost of P. We assume that agents are risk-neutral. In what follows, we define a set of desiderata for our allocation mechanism, namely: (*i*) strategyproofness, (*ii*) Pareto optimality and (*iii*) non-bossiness.

A deterministic mechanism M is *strategyproof* (SP for short) if, for all agents a_i, for all declarations D_i and D'_i and all declarations of the other agents $\mathbf{D}_{-i}$, agent a_i cannot decrease her cost by misreporting her true type, namely:

$$cost_i(M(\mathbf{D}), D_i) \leq cost_i(M(D'_i, \mathbf{D}_{-i}), D_i) \tag{1}$$

A randomized mechanism is *strategyproof in expectation* if (1) holds in expectation (i.e., over the random choices of the mechanism). A randomized mechanism is *universally strategyproof* if agents cannot gain by lying regardless of the random choices made by the mechanism, i.e., the output of the mechanism is a distribution over strategyproof deterministic allocations.

The *social cost* of an allocation S is defined as $SC(S, \mathbf{D}) = \sum_{a_i \in A} cost_i(S, D_i)$. A mechanism OPT is *optimal* for TAP if $OPT(\mathbf{D}) \in \arg\min_{S \in \mathcal{P}^n} SC(S, \mathbf{D})$ for all $\mathbf{D}$. A mechanism M is an α–approximation (w.r.t the optimal social cost) with $\alpha \in \mathbb{R}$, $\alpha \geq 1$, being referred to as the *approximation ratio* of M, if, for all $\mathbf{D}$, $SC(M(\mathbf{D}), \mathbf{D}) \leq \alpha \cdot SC(OPT(\mathbf{D}), \mathbf{D})$.

A traffic allocation $S \in \mathcal{P}^n$ is *Pareto optimal* if there exists no other feasible traffic allocation S' such that $cost_j(S', D_j) \leq cost_j(S, D_j)$ for all a_j, and $cost_k(S', D_k) < cost_k(S, D_k)$ for some a_k. Pareto optimal allocations are of particular interest in our scenario, because, as proven in Theorem 1, they are a min-cost response in the available reactions $R_i(S)$ of an agent. This gives us a theoretical guarantee that agents will actually implement Pareto optimal solutions returned by the mechanism.

---

[3] We do not prevent agents from using edges other than the ones belonging to their assigned paths, as doing so would result in a waste of public resources (i.e., road capacity). To avoid congestion, though, we assume that agents not following their assigned route can be disincentivized from using an edge that, according to the scheduled traffic, is filled to capacity. This can be easily implemented in a smart traffic control system through the use of traffic cameras that check cars' number plates.

Theorem 1. *Let $S = M(\mathbf{D})$ be a traffic assignment and let $R_i(S)$ be the set of reactions available to a_i at S. If S is Pareto optimal, then $M_i(\mathbf{D}) \in \arg\min_{P \in R_i(S)} w(P)$.*

Finally, a mechanism M is *non-bossy* if $M_i(\mathbf{D}) = M_i(D_i', \mathbf{D}_{-i})$ implies that $M_j(\mathbf{D}) = M_j(D_i', \mathbf{D}_{-i})$, for all $a_i, a_j \in N$ and all $\mathbf{D}$ and D_i'. In other words, non-bossiness excludes (arguably undesirable) mechanisms that allow one agent to change the allocation of other agents without changing her own too. In the remainder of this paper, we focus on strategyproof mechanisms for TAP that approximately achieve the optimal social cost. In particular, we are interested in mechanisms that are also Pareto-optimal and non-bossy.

4   Deterministic Mechanisms

In this section, we discuss deterministic mechanisms for TAP. In particular, we first provide a lower bound on the approximation ratio of SP deterministic mechanisms.

Theorem 2. *There is no α-approximate deterministic SP mechanism for the traffic assignment problem with $\alpha < 3 - \varepsilon$, for any $\varepsilon > 0$.*

These impossibility results suggest that in order to achieve strategyproofness we have to give up on optimality. This naturally leads to asking to what extent can we approximate the optimal social welfare while satisfy the desired properties. As a first step to answer this question, we examine the well-known Serial Dictatorship mechanism that is deterministic and notoriously satisfies our three desiderata (i.e., strategyproofness, Pareto optimality and non-bossiness).

Definition 1. *Mechanism Serial Dictatorship (SD), given an ordering $a_1 \prec, \ldots, \prec a_n$ of the agents, allocates paths to agents in n stages such that at stage i agent a_i is allocated her minimum cost path in the residual graph $G_f^{-\{a_1,\ldots,a_{i-1}\}}$.*

The following theorem proves that SD is indeed feasible under some mild conditions:

Theorem 3. *If G is K-edge-connected[4], mechanism SD is feasible for K agents.*

Next we provide an upper bound on the approximation ratio of SD, and thus, on its worst case performance. In order to prove our result, we make the following assumption:

Definition 2. *The deviation on capacious path assumption (DoCP) assumes that whenever the SD mechanism allocates to an agent a path that is different from the one that the optimal mechanism would allocate, the assigned path has sufficient capacity to potentially be allocated to all the remaining agents.*

---

[4] A graph is K-edge-connected if it remains connected when strictly fewer than K edges are removed.

To better understand this assumption, consider the following example. With reference to Fig. 1, let a_i be an agent and P_i^* be the path she is assigned in the optimal allocation (i.e., $OPT_i = P_i^*$). If agent a_i is not assigned P_i^* by SD, there must be an agent a_j, where $j \prec i$ in the ordering used by SD, such that: (i) $SD_j = P_j \neq OPT_j$ and (ii) $P_j \cap P_i^* \neq \emptyset$ and (iii) at least one edge of P_i^* is saturated after a_j is assigned P_j. In such a situation, we say that agent a_i is blocked by agent a_j. Let $\alpha_i \in P_j \cap P_i^*$ ($\beta_i \in P_j \cap P_i^*$, respectively) be the first (last, respectively) node of P_i^* in P_j. The DoCP assumption postulates that if a_j blocks a_i, then the *alternative path of blocked agent a_i through blocking agent a_j* $\Gamma_i^j = (O_i, \alpha_i, O_j, D_j, \beta_i, D_i)$ has at least capacity $n - |\{a_k \in A | a_j \prec a_k\}|$ in the residual graph $G_f^{-\{a_1,\dots,a_j\}}$. That is, all agents yet to be assigned by SD after a_j can be accommodated on this path. We note that, by construction, if agent a_i is blocked by agent a_j then path Γ_i^j always exists, although unless we assume DoCP, it might not have spare capacity to be assigned to agent a_i. It is not difficult to see that if we relax the DoCP assumption, then the approximation ratio of SD is not bounded by any function of the number of agents on certain pathological TAP instances.

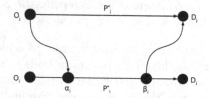

Fig. 1. Deviation on capacious paths

Theorem 4. *Under the DoCP assumption, SD is at most $(2^n - 1)$-approximate.*

Proof (Proof sketch). We prove the claim by induction on the number of players. Let OPT_i denote the cost and solution (with a slight abuse of notation) of the optimal allocation that only considers bids of agents $j \leq i$. Similarly, let SD_i denote the cost and solution of SD on input all the bids of agents $j \leq i$. Base of the induction ($i = 1$): trivially $OPT_1 = SD_1$. Now assume that the claim is true for $i - 1$ and, for $j \leq i$, let P_j^* (P_j, respectively) be the path assigned to agent j by OPT_i (SD_i, respectively). For a path P, we let $w(P)$ denote the cost of the path in the given graph G. We want to prove that under the DoCP assumption, the following holds:

$$w(P_i) \leq OPT_i + SD_{i-1}. \tag{2}$$

If $P_i^* = P_i$ then we are done. Therefore, we can assume that $P_i^* \neq P_i$. This means that the paths P_j allocated to agents $j < i$ by SD_i saturate some of the edges of P_i^*. Now, for at least one of these agents, say $\bar{j}$, $P_{\bar{j}}^* \neq P_{\bar{j}}$ for otherwise also in OPT_i path P_i^* would be unavailable to i. But then $w(P_i) \leq w(\Gamma_i^{\bar{j}})$, $\Gamma_i^{\bar{j}}$ being the path that connects O_i to D_i through $O_{\bar{j}}$, as per the definition of DoCP. Note that, under the DoCP assumption, $\Gamma_i^{\bar{j}}$ is always feasible. Since $\Gamma_i^{\bar{j}}$ uses only edges in $OPT_i \cup SD_{i-1}$ (i.e. P_i^* and P_j^* are in OPT_i, paths (O_i, α_i) and (β_i, D_j) belong to SD_{i-1}), (2) is proven. We finally observe that (2) and the inductive hypothesis yield:

$$SD_i = SD_{i-1} + w(\Gamma_i^{\bar{j}}) \leq 2SD_{i-1} + OPT_i$$
$$\leq 2((2^{i-1} - 1)OPT_{i-1}) + OPT_i \leq (2^i - 1)OPT_i.$$

As the $(2^n - 1)$-approximation ratio can be prohibitively large for large n, we ask ourselves whether we can further improve this upper bound. Unfortunately, the following theorem answers this question in the negative.

Theorem 5. *Under the DoCP assumption, the bound of Theorem 4 is tight.*

We now provide a characterization of SP, Pareto-optimal, and non-bossy mechanisms for a subset of instances of TAP, named TAP$^+$and we prove that the family of all mechanisms satisfying the above properties is comprised by a generalization of SD, namely *Bi-polar Serial Dictatorship* (BSD). Such a characterization extends naturally to TAP instances. TAP$^+$ is subset of instances of TAP having a peculiar structure: (i) every agent has the same source node O; (ii) O has outgoing edges with unitary capacity and no ingoing edges, let $E_O = \{(O, v_1), \ldots, (O, v_m)\}$ denote the set of outgoing edges of O; and (iii) the set of possible destinations that the agents can declare is restricted to a given subset $\mathcal{D} \subset V$.

Definition 3. *Given an ordering of the agents $\{i_1, i_2\} \prec i_3 \prec \ldots \prec i_n$ and a bipartition $\{X_1, X_2\}$ of the set of alternatives X (i.e., paths in the case of TAP) such that $X_1 \cap X_2 = \emptyset$ and $X_1 \cup X_2 = X$, a BSD mechanism executes SD with ordering $i_2 \prec i_1 \prec \ldots \prec i_n$ if $\min_{x \in X} cost_1(x) = \min_{x \in X} cost_2(x) = x \in X_2$; otherwise SD with ordering $i_1 \prec i_2 \prec \ldots \prec i_n$ is executed.*

Theorem 6. *A traffic allocation mechanism for TAP$^+$is Pareto-optimal, SP and non-bossy if and only if it is a Bi-polar Serially Dictatorial Rule.*

Proof (Proof sketch). We reduce an instance of the problem of *assigning indivisible objects* with general ordinal preferences [3] (AIO for short) to TAP$^+$. In an instance of AIO, a set of objects $X = \{x_1, \ldots, x_m\}$ has to be assigned to a set of agents $A = \{a_1, \ldots, a_n\}$, such that every agent receives at most one object and no agent is left without an object if there are objects still available. Agents have ordinal general preferences $\succeq_i$, where $x \succeq_i y$ for $x, y \in X$ means that agent i (weakly) prefers object x to object y. From an instance of AIO, we build an instance of TAP$^+$ as follows. TAP$^+$ has the same set of agents A as AIO. Graph G of TAP$^+$ has a node O such that $O_i = O$ for all $a_i \in A$. For every object $x_j \in X$ we construct in G a node v_j and an edge (O, v_j) such that $c(O, v_j) = 1$ and $w(O, v_j) = \varepsilon$ for $0 < \varepsilon \ll 1$. Let Ψ be the set of all possible preference relations over X. We construct $|\Psi|$ destination nodes D_k, one for each preference relation $\succeq \in \Psi$ and for each $k \in 1, \ldots, |\Psi|$. For each $j \in \{1, \ldots, m\}$ we add an edge (v_j, D_k) having capacity 1 and weight $w(v_j, D_k)$ equal to the *ranking* of x_j

according to $\succeq$. We can now transform an instance of the so-constructed TAP$^+$ problem to an instance of the AIO problem, and vice versa. In [3] it is proved that BSD is the only Pareto optimal, SP and non-bossy mechanism for AIO. This characterization transfers to TAP$^+$ due to the reduction sketched above.

Next, we investigate the performance of BSD and show that it does not asymptotically perform better than SD. In particular, we state that:

Lemma 1. *BSD cannot achieve an approximation ratio lower than $\Omega(2^n)$ for TAP.*

5   Randomized Mechanisms

Given the undesirable approximation guarantees of deterministic mechanisms, we now turn to randomization. Randomized mechanisms can often be interpreted as fractional mechanisms for the deterministic solutions, under mild conditions. We start by proving the following inapproximability lower bound:

Theorem 7. *There is no α-approximate universally truthful randomized mechanism for the traffic assignment problem with $\alpha < 11/10$.*

In the remainder of this section, we study the randomized version of SD for TAP, which is universally strategyproof, (ex-post) Pareto optimal and non-bossy.

Definition 4. *The Randomized Serial Dictatorship (RSD) mechanism computes uniformly at random an ordering σ over the agents and returns the output of SD over ordering σ.*

The following results gives a tight bound on the approximation ratio of RSD.

Theorem 8. *Under the DoCP assumption, RSD is at most n-approximate.*

Proof (Proof sketch). We are going to prove the claim by induction on the number of agents. As above, let OPT_i denote the cost of the optimal solution with paths assigned only to agents a_j, with $j \leq i$. With a slight abuse of notation we also let OPT_i denote the solution itself. Similarly, RSD_i denotes the expected cost of RSD on input all the bids of agents a_j, $j \leq i$. For the base of the induction with $i = 1$, it is clear that RSD_1 is the optimal solution. Now assume that the claim is true for $i - 1$ and consider an instance with i agents. Let $I_{-k}(P)$, P being a path from O_k to D_k, be the instance of the problem without agent a_k and with the capacity of the directed edges in P diminished by one (i.e., as if the path P were used by a_k). Note that by the DoCP assumption, one of the agents a_j, with $j \neq k$, is guaranteed to be able to use the edges of P in the opposite direction than a_k. We now let $OPT_{-k,P}$ and $RSD_{-k,P}$ be the cost of the optimum and expected cost of RSD on $I_{-k}(P)$, respectively. Moreover, let

π_j be the path minimizing the cost of agent a_j (i.e., the path that SD would assign to a_j if she was the first to choose). We then have

$$RSD_i = \frac{1}{i} \sum_{k=1}^{i} \left(w(\pi_k) + RSD_{-k,\pi_k} \right) \leq \frac{1}{i} \sum_{k=1}^{i} \left(w(\pi_k) + (i-1)OPT_{-k,\pi_k} \right)$$

$$\leq \frac{1}{i} \sum_{k=1}^{i} w(\pi_k) + \frac{1}{i} \sum_{k=1}^{i} \left((i-1)(OPT_i + w(\pi_k)) \right) \leq \frac{1}{i}OPT_i + (i-1)OPT_i + \frac{i-1}{i}OPT_i$$

$$= i \cdot OPT_i$$

where the first equality follows from the definition of RSD, i.e., with probability $1/i$ each agent k will have the first choice. As for the inequalities, we note that the first follows from the inductive hypothesis whilst the last from the observation that $OPT_i \geq \sum_{k=1}^{i} w(\pi_k)$. We are left with the second inequality. That is, we prove that under the DoCP $OPT_{-k,\pi_k} \leq OPT_i + w(\pi_k)$. If OPT_i allocates π_k to agent a_k then we are done. Otherwise, let P_k be the path that a_k gets in OPT_i and note that the paths P_j allocated to agents a_j $j \neq k$ by OPT_i saturates some of the edges of P_k; let $a_{\bar{j}}$ be one of these agents. Consider now the solution S to $I_{-k}(\pi_k)$ where all agents but $a_{\bar{j}}$ are allocated the same path as in OPT_i and agent $a_{\bar{j}}$ is given, instead of $P_{\bar{j}}$, the alternative path $\Gamma_{\bar{j}}^k$ through agent a_k. Observe that $\Gamma_{\bar{j}}^k$ uses the same directed edges of $P_{\bar{j}}$ and P_k and the edges of π_k in opposite direction and, as observed above, under the DoCP assumption, is a feasible path for $a_{\bar{j}}$ and S a feasible solution to $I_k(\pi_k)$, whose social cost is denoted $SC(S)$. But then:

$$OPT_{-k,\pi_k} \leq SC(S) = OPT_i - w(P_j) - w(P_k) + w(P) \leq OPT_i + w(\pi_k)$$

where the last inequality follows from the fact that the edges in $P \setminus (P_k \cup P_j)$ are a subset of the edges in π_k.

Theorem 9. *The approximation ratio of RSD is $\Omega(n)$.*

This means that by allowing randomness in the allocation mechanism, we can improve the exponential approximation ratio of the deterministic case to a linear one.

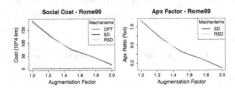

	Rome-99	NY-4000	NY-10000
$|V|$	3000	4000	10000
$|E|$	8859	10027	312594
δ_{AVG}^+	2.6	2.5	31
c_{AVG}	27.3	20.5	30

Fig. 2. Experimental results on Rome99

Fig. 3. Structural characteristics of test graphs

6   Experimental Results

In this section we present the results of the experimental evaluation we conducted in order to assess whether the theoretical inapproximability lower bounds impose a high approximation cost on real-life instances. In short, we will show that they do not. In particular, we have measured the approximation ratio obtained by SD and RSD on three real-life graphs extracted from the DIMCAS 99 shortest path implementation challenge benchmark datasets [1]. In particular, Rome99 represents a large portion of the directed road network of the city of Rome, Italy, from 1999. The graph contains 3353 vertices and 8870 edges. Vertices correspond to intersections between roads and edges correspond to roads or road segments. NY-4000 and NY-10000 are two subgraphs extracted from NY-d, a larger distance graph (with 264,346 nodes and 733,846 edges) representing a large portion the road network infrastructure of New York City, USA. The two graphs were obtained by taking a subset, respectively, of the first 4000 and 10000 nodes of the graph while ensuring that the connectivity was preserved by adding edges representing paths through nodes of the original graph not included in the subgraph. In Fig. 3 some statistics related to the structural characteristics of our test graphs are reported, where δ_{AVG}^{+} represents the average outdegree of a node (i.e. the average number of edges originating from a node) and c_{AVG} is the average capacity of the outgoing edges of a node. In our experimental assessment, we studied the variation of the approximation ratio of SD and RSD on the test graphs while varying the *resource augmentation factor*. The resource augmentation factor is the key parameter of the resource augmentation framework [5], a novel comparison framework where a truthful mechanism that allocates "scarce resources" is evaluated by its worst-case performance on an instance where such "scarce resources" are augmented, against the optimal mechanism on the same instance with the original amount of resources. In [5] it is argued that this is a fairer comparison framework than the traditional approximation ratio, which compares the performance of a mechanism that is severely limited by the requirement of truthfulness to that of an omnipotent mechanism that operates under no restrictions and has access to the real inputs of the agents. An equivalent resource augmentation framework is often also used in the analysis of online algorithms. In the TAP scenario, the natural resource to be augmented is the capacity of the existing edges, modelled by the augmentation factor γ, which in our framework is defined as the factor by which the average capacity of the edges departing from

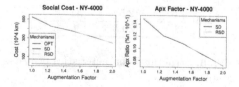

Fig. 4. Experimental results on NY-4000

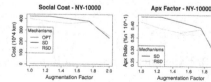

Fig. 5. Experimental results on NY-10000

a node is multiplied, spreading the excess capacity evenly among the outgoing edges of the node. More formally, if $c_{AVG}(v)$ is the average capacity of node v, then the augmented average capacity $c^{\gamma}_{AVG}(v) = \gamma \cdot c_{AVG}$, and the capacity of each outgoing edge is set as $\frac{c_{AVG}(v)}{\delta^+(v)}$, where $\delta^+(v)$ is the outdegree of v. In our experiments we ranged the augmentation factor γ in the interval $[1, 2]$, which means increasing the initial capacity until it is doubled. To run our experiments, we generated three separate populations of agent-origin-destination triplets, one population for each test graph, each comprising a number of triplets roughly equal to $1/3$ of the nodes of the graph. The size of the population of triplets was empirically tailored to let the competition for popular links arise without making the allocation problem unfeasible. For each agent-origin-destination triplet in the population, both the origin and the destination were independently drawn uniformly at random from the set of the nodes of the graph, with replacement (i.e. the same node can be the origin/destination of multiple triplets).

Figures 2, 4 and 5 show the results of our experimental analysis, respectively on graph Rome99, NY-4000 and NY-10000. In particular, the left hand side plot represents the absolute value of the social cost for the optimal mechanism, expressed in kilometers, for SD and for RSD, whereas the right hand side plot represents the approximation ratio for SD and RSD. From our experimental analysis we can see that the actual approximation ratio of both SD and RSD is much lower than the predicted theoretical worst-case approximation. In particular, our experiments show that the approximation ratios of SD and RSD are quite similar and strongly $o(n)$ on the investigated road networks. This is due to the fact that such theoretical approximation lower bounds rely on pathological instances that are quite unlikely to occur in real life graphs. It is also worth noting the beneficial effect that augmenting the capacity of existing roads has on the approximation ratio: increasing the augmentation factor steadily decreases the approximation ratio on both Rome99 and NY-4000. On the other hand a marked decrease is noticeable only if we increase the augmentation factor to 1.8 in the case of NY-10000. This phenomenon is due to the already reach topological structure of NY-10000, which necessitates less augmentation to yield good performances.

7   Conclusions

In this paper we investigate the problem of strategyproof traffic assignment without monetary incentives. We study two SP mechanism for our problem, namely Serial Dictatorship and its randomized counterpart Random Serial Dictatorships. For deterministic mechanisms we prove that Serial Dictatorship is $2^n - 1$ under some mild assumptions, and characterize Bipolar Serial Dictatorship as the only SP, Pareto optimal and non-bossy deterministic mechanism for our problem. In the randomized case, we prove that Random Serial Dictatorship is n-approximate. Finally we assess the performance of Serial Dictatorship and Random Serial Dictatorship on real road network infrastructure, and show that they exhibit good approximation guarantees. In particular, RSD is almost indistinguishable from SD, which means that the instances giving rise to the inapproximability results rarely occur in practice.

Note that our work is the first that addresses the problem of moneyless strategyproof traffic assignment. Although it ignores a number of properties that occur in real-world scenarios (e.g., dynamic network behavior, or asynchronous bid submissions), it still serves as a proof of concept for the existence of moneyless strategyproof assignment mechanisms.

References

1. 9th DIMACS Implementation Challenge - Shortest Paths (1999). http://www.diag. uniroma1.it/challenge9/download.shtml
2. Beckmann, M., McGuire, C., Winsten, C.B.: Studies in the economics of transportation. Technical report (1956)
3. Bogomolnaia, A., Deb, R., Ehlers, L.: Strategy-proof assignment on the full preference domain. J. Econ. Theor. **123**(2), 161–186 (2005). https://doi.org/10.1016/j.jet.2004.05.004
4. Brenner, J., Schäfer, G.: Online cooperative cost sharing. In: Calamoneri, T., Diaz, J. (eds.) CIAC 2010. LNCS, vol. 6078, pp. 252–263. Springer, Heidelberg (2010). https://doi.org/10.1007/978-3-642-13073-1_23
5. Caragiannis, I., Filos-Ratsikas, A., Frederiksen, S.K., Hansen, K.A., Tan, Z.: Truthful facility assignment with resource augmentation: an exact analysis of serial dictatorship. In: WINE 2016, pp. 236–250 (2016)
6. Conitzer, V., Sandholm, T.: Failures of the VCG mechanism in combinatorial auctions and exchanges. In: AAMAS 2006, pp. 521–528. ACM (2006)
7. Coogan, S., Arcak, M.: A compartmental model for traffic networks and its dynamical behavior. IEEE Trans. Autom. Control **60**(10), 2698–2703 (2015)
8. Daganzo, C.F.: The cell transmission model: a dynamic representation of highway traffic consistent with the hydrodynamic theory. Transp. Res. Part B: Methodol. **28**(4), 269–287 (1994)
9. Djahel, S., Salehie, M., Tal, I., Jamshidi, P.: Adaptive traffic management for secure and efficient emergency services in smart cities. In: PERCOM 2013, pp. 340–343. IEEE (2013)
10. Filos-Ratsikas, A., Frederiksen, S.K.S., Zhang, J.: Social welfare in one-sided matchings: random priority and beyond. In: SAGT 2014, pp. 1–12 (2014)
11. Ford, L.R., Fulkerson, D.R.: Constructing maximal dynamic flows from static flows. Oper. Res. **6**(3), 419–433 (1958). https://doi.org/10.1287/opre.6.3.419
12. Ford, L.R., Fulkerson, D.R.: Flows in Networks. Princeton University Press, Princeton (1962). http://www.jstor.org/stable/j.ctt183q0b4
13. Goodwin, P.: The economic costs of road traffic congestion (2004)
14. Krzyzanowski, M., Kuna-Dibbert, B., Schneider, J.: Health effects of transport-related air pollution. WHO Regional Office Europe, pp. 1–190 (2005)
15. Leontiadis, I., Marfia, G., Mack, D., Pau, G., Mascolo, C., Gerla, M.: On the effectiveness of an opportunistic traffic management system for vehicular networks. IEEE Trans. Intell. Transp. Syst. **12**(4), 1537–1548 (2011)
16. Levin, M.W., Fritz, H., Boyles, S.D.: On optimizing reservation-based intersection controls. IEEE Trans. Intell. Transp. Syst. **18**(3), 505–515 (2017)

17. Nesterov, Y., de Palma, A.: Stationary dynamic solutions in congested transportation networks: summary and perspectives. Netw. Spat. Econ. **3**(3), 371–395 (2003). https://doi.org/10.1023/A:1025350419398
18. Nissim, K., Smorodinsky, R., Tennenholtz, M.: Approximately optimal mechanism design via differential privacy. In: ITCS 2012, pp. 203–213 (2012)
19. Osorio, C., Nanduri, K.: Urban transportation emissions mitigation: coupling high-resolution vehicular emissions and traffic models for traffic signal optimization. Transp. Res. Part B: Methodol. **81**, 520–538 (2015)
20. Procaccia, A.D., Tennenholtz, M.: Approximate mechanism design without money. ACM TEAC **1**(4), 18:1–18:26 (2013). https://doi.org/10.1145/2542174.2542175
21. Raphael, J., Maskell, S., Sklar, E.: From goods to traffic: first steps toward an auction-based traffic signal controller. In: Demazeau, Y., Decker, K.S., Bajo Pérez, J., de la Prieta, F. (eds.) PAAMS 2015. LNCS (LNAI), vol. 9086, pp. 187–198. Springer, Cham (2015). https://doi.org/10.1007/978-3-319-18944-4_16
22. Skabardonis, A., Dowling, R.: Improved speed-flow relationships for planning applications. Transp. Res. Rec.: J. Transp. Res. Board **1572**, 18–23 (1997)
23. Stansfeld, S.A., Matheson, M.P.: Noise pollution: non-auditory effects on health. Oxf. J. Med. Health Br. Med. Bull. **68**(1), 243–257 (2003)
24. Svensson, L.G.: Strategy-proof allocation of indivisible goods. Soc. Choice Welfare **16**(4), 557–567 (1999). https://doi.org/10.1007/s003550050160
25. Vasirani, M., Ossowski, S.: A market-inspired approach for intersection management in urban road traffic networks. JAIR **43**, 621–659 (2012)

Router Node Placement in Wireless Mesh Networks for Emergency Rescue Scenarios

Mariusz Wzorek[1](✉)(iD), Cyrille Berger[1](✉)(iD), and Patrick Doherty[1,2](✉)(iD)

[1] Department of Computer and Information Science,
Linköping University, Linköping, Sweden
{mariusz.wzorek,cyrille.berger,patrick.doherty}@liu.se
[2] School of Intelligent Systems and Engineering,
Jinan University (Zhuhai Campus), Zhuhai, China
https://www.ida.liu.se/divisions/aiics/

Abstract. The focus of this paper is on base functionalities required for UAV-based rapid deployment of an ad hoc communication infrastructure in the initial phases of rescue operations. The general idea is to use heterogeneous teams of UAVs to deploy communication kits that include routers. These kits will then be used in the generation of ad hoc Wireless Mesh Networks. A fundamental problem, known as the Router Node Placement problem (RNP) is to determine how one can optimally place such routers. An extended version of the RNP problem is specified that takes into account additional constraints that arise in actual field usage. This extended problem is solved with a new algorithm, RRT-WMN, based on a novel use of the Rapidly Exploring Random Trees (RRT) algorithm used in motion planning. A comparative empirical evaluation between RRT-WMN and existing techniques, CMA-ES and PSO, shows that the RRT-WMN algorithm has far better performance both in time and coverage as the extended RNP problem scales to realistic scenarios.

Keywords: Robotics · UAV deployed ad hoc networks ·
Wireless Mesh Networks · Router node placement · Emergency rescue

1 Introduction

The importance of effective communication among disaster relief organizations, ranging from governmental and non-governmental relief organizations (NGOs) to actual emergency responders on the ground, is essential for the coordination of life-saving activities in regions affected by natural or man-made disasters.

Supported by the ELLIIT network organization for Information and Communication Technology, and the Swedish Foundation for Strategic Research (Smart Systems: RIT 15-0097), and Autonomous Systems and Software Program (WASP) funded by Knut and Alice Wallenberg Foundation.

© Springer Nature Switzerland AG 2019
A. C. Nayak and A. Sharma (Eds.): PRICAI 2019, LNAI 11671, pp. 496–509, 2019.
https://doi.org/10.1007/978-3-030-29911-8_38

Fig. 1. Example mission scenario for deployment of an ad hoc communication network in a search and rescue environment.

Recent disasters such as the hurricanes in Texas and Puerto Rico have made this very clear. Denning [5], pointed out the importance of establishing "hastily formed networks" in the larger sense as "the ability to form multi-organizational networks rapidly" and as being crucial to disaster relief.

The work presented in this paper is part of a larger infrastructural framework being developed with the goal of leveraging the use of heterogeneous teams of Unmanned Aerial Vehicles (UAVs) in providing services and supplies to rescuers on the ground in collaboration with other human resources in disaster relief scenarios. In many disaster scenarios such as earthquakes, floods or hurricanes, existing communication infrastructures are knocked out either partially or wholly. One of the first tasks at hand is to rapidly restore or set-up ad hoc communication networks in affected areas, in particular in those areas where rescuers have to rapidly enter, in order to acquire first-response situation awareness and convey this information to operations centers for additional decision support.

The focus of this paper is on base functionalities required for UAV-based rapid deployment of an ad hoc communication infrastructure in the initial phases of rescue operations. Figure 1 presents an example of such a mission scenario where a fleet of UAVs is tasked to deliver a set of communication nodes which would serve as the physical communication infrastructure for a specific region. The idea is that teams of UAVs can be used to dynamically deliver router nodes via air delivery, which are then used in an ad hoc network. A proof of concept design of a UAV deliverable communication node prototype has been developed for this purpose [17]. It also includes efficient deployment technology based on autonomous release mechanisms and airdrop by a parachute.

Assuming this technology, the important question, and one that is answered in this paper, is how to determine the optimal or semi-optimal placement of router nodes in a physical region to form a viable ad hoc wireless mesh network.

Wireless Mesh Networks (WMNs) are an emerging technology that is well suited for applications where ad hoc network infrastructure needs to be deployed rapidly. WMNs offer advantages over many other technologies (e.g. satellite links) by being cost efficient, robust, and easy to expand or repair on demand. In short, a WMN consists of a set of router nodes (RNs) organized in a mesh topology that can be seen as a backbone of the network. The connection between the RNs is realized using radio waves, thus no cable connections are required. A WMN client connected to the network is able to communicate with other clients of the network. Additionally, some of the RNs may act as gateways to other networks, for example to provide Internet access to the entire network.

Designing efficient and robust WMNs is a challenging task with many aspects to consider, among them two network performance measures: the *network connectivity* and the *client coverage*. Network connectivity measures the degree of connectivity between router nodes and client coverage measures the number of client nodes connected to the WMN. Finding router node placement (RNP) in a specific geographical area for a WMN that optimizes both performance measures has been the focus of several recent research publications, although not in the context of UAV deployment.

The ongoing research in the field of WMNs [14] focuses on solving many practical challenges associated with the design and deployment of WMNs. The topics include, but are not limited to, frequency channel assignment [15,16], gateway placement [2,8] and routing algorithms [1]. Naturally, the RNP problem has been extensively studied as well. The RNP problem is a complex multi-objective combinatorial optimization problem most commonly solved with evolutionary algorithms. In [3,4,9,11,18,19] various metaheuristic algorithms have been proposed for the RNP problem in different application contexts such as genetic algorithms, tabu search, and simulated annealing, all assuming that routers are placed on grids. The latter assumption limits the flexibility as to where they are placed as positions are calculated using a set of fixed grid positions. The closest related work to the problem addressed in this paper is presented in [12,13], where a dynamic WMN is considered, in which a Particle Swarm Optimization (PSO) technique is used to calculate router node positions in continuous state space. The reason evolutionary algorithms are appealed to is that the RNP problem has certain characteristics that make the problem less amenable for using classical optimization techniques as will be considered in the problem statement in Sect. 2.

In this paper we focus on solving the RNP problem with a different set of assumptions than found in the current literature that we believe are important from the practical application perspective of deploying WMNs in emergency rescue scenarios. In fact, this new set of assumptions was derived through actual experimentation with UAV-deployed WMNs.

One strong assumption used in previous work was knowledge of the client positions beforehand. Although in some environments typical client positions could be assumed or estimated (e.g. populated urban areas) due to urban structure, this cannot be assumed in emergency rescue scenarios where the environments are often unstructured and the network clients (rescuers or victims) are highly mobile and where responders are usually required to perform an exhaustive search of the disaster area in question. This leads to an alternative network coverage performance measure that is expressed as the total area covered by the WMN.

Another assumption used in previous work relates to *network connectivity*, where obstacles in the environment are not dealt with at all. The signal strength of a mesh router depends not only on the distance to another router, but also on any physical structures (i.e. obstacles) present in the space between them. Therefore, in order to fully utilize the range of a mesh router, obstacles in the environment have to be taken into account when calculating the RNP. For that reason we propose to use two additional constraints when calculating a solution for a RNP problem: (1) enforce line-of-sight requirement between two connected mesh routers, and (2) exclude obstacles from possible node placements. The latter constraint relates to the example mission scenario depicted in Fig. 1, where one wants to avoid delivery of mesh router nodes on possibly collapsed building structures or dense vegetation areas (e.g. trees) in order to increase the robustness of the network connections.

Given these additional constraints, the RNP problem becomes fundamentally more difficult, but its solution radically more applicable in real-life scenarios. One major part of the solution to this problem is to develop an algorithm for RNP that is incremental in nature and appeals to intuitions derived from the motion planning domain where we combine the optimization problem with the use of the Rapidly Exploring Random Trees (RRT) [10] algorithm used in motion planning. This algorithm is generic in nature in that it can be viewed as searching through a search space, RNP graphs in our case, both incrementally and with random exploration of that search space.

1.1   Contributions

This paper makes the following contributions:

- It provides a new definition of the RNP problem taking into account both technical constraints associated with WMNs and structural constraints commonly associated with areas affected by disasters.
- It provides a novel algorithm, RRT-WMN, for solving the extended RNP problem that uses the Rapidly Exploring Random Trees (RRT) [10] algorithm used in motion planning, as a basis for solving this problem.
- It provides a detailed experimental evaluation, where the proposed algorithm is compared to two popular optimization techniques (CMA-ES [7] and PSO [6,13]), with the latter being used in previous work for the RNP problem. The results of the experimentation show that the new algorithm has far better performance in terms of both time and coverage as the RNP problem scales to realistic scenarios.

The remainder of the paper is structured as follows. In the next section our RNP domain formulation is presented. The RRT-WMN algorithm is described in Sect. 3. Empirical evaluation of the algorithms is presented in Sect. 4, followed by conclusions in Sect. 5.

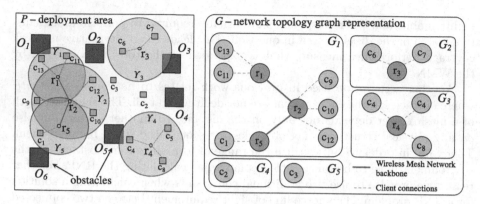

Fig. 2. Wireless Mesh Network example. Overview of the WMN deployed in an area P with obstacles (left). Topology graph representation of the WMN (right). (Color figure online)

2   Problem Definition

In this section, a mathematical model of the RNP problem is provided that is specified as a constrained optimization problem. A WMN is composed of a set of mesh router nodes (RNs) and mesh clients. RNs serve as access points for mesh clients (rescuers or victims in our domain) and are interconnected with point-to-point wireless links creating a backbone for the network. In Fig. 2, an example of a deployed WMN is shown consisting of five mesh routers r with their respective radio coverage Υ (green circles), and ten mesh clients c (orange), deployed in the area P with six obstacles O (blue polygons). For each WMN generated, a network topology graph, $G = (V, E)$, can be constructed and used for analysis. In the literature for RNPs (e.g. [12,13]), the set of vertices (V) in a graph consists of mesh clients and mesh routers. The edges (E) represent connectivity, where: (1) for two router nodes to be connected they have to be in their communication range, and (2) the client/router edge is added when the client is in communication range of a router. In our approach, we extend the definition of edge connectivity by introducing additional constraints that relate to the handling of obstacles and line-of-sight requirements.

Formally, a WMN for the RNP problem (Fig. 2) [18], is defined as a set of interconnected devices in a universe $U = R \cup C$, where $R = \{r_1, \ldots, r_n\}$ is a set of n mesh router nodes and $C = \{c_1, \ldots, c_m\}$ is a set of m mesh clients. Each r_i represents the ith mesh router and consists of a tuple $\langle r_i^X, \gamma_i, \Upsilon_i \rangle$ where $r_i^X = (x_i, y_i) \in \mathbb{R}^2$, is the position of the router node, γ_i is its nominal communication range, and Υ_i is the circle representing its radio coverage centered at the r_i^X position with radius γ_i for $i \in \{1, \ldots, n\}$. C is the client set, where each c_j for $j \in \{1, \ldots, m\}$, represents the jth client. In our problem formulation, we assume the client positions are unknown, so $C = \emptyset$. Consequently, the network topology graph $G = (R, E)$ will consists of vertices from R, with a graph edge connectivity constraint on members of E defined as:

$$e(r_i, r_j) \in E(G) \iff \left(\overline{r_i^X r_j^X} \cap O = \emptyset \right) \wedge \left(\|r_i^X - r_j^X\| < \min(\gamma^i, \gamma^j) \right). \quad (1)$$

This states that for any edge in $E(G)$, between a pair of router nodes r_i and r_j in R, the line segment between their positions, $\overline{r_i^X r_j^X}$, is not in collision with any obstacle, and the distance between them is smaller than the minimum of their radio coverage radius (e.g. r_1 and r_2 in Fig. 2). The latter connectivity constraint used in our approach is different from previous work where two nodes were considered to be connected when their coverage circles overlap (i.e. $\varUpsilon_i \cap \varUpsilon_j \neq \emptyset$). Our formulation is motivated by pragmatic constraints, since most commercially available devices have the same radio range for both inter-router mesh connections as well as clients. Therefore, a pair of connected routers will always have an overlap in their respective coverage areas, but additional constraints may be needed for the connectivity to actually work in practice.

The deployment area for an ad hoc network is defined as a set P specified by a polygon. Within the area, an obstacle set is the union of all obstacle regions specified by polygons, i.e. for m obstacles $O = O_1 \cup O_2 \cup \ldots O_m$.

Based on the definitions introduced so far, the extended RNP problem considered in this paper can be specified as the following non-convex constrained optimization problem. Find n mesh router positions r_i^X where $i \in \{1, \ldots, n\}$, that maximize a cost function $f(\mathcal{X})$ given a target deployment set P, obstacle set O, and a network topology graph $G = (R, E)$. The objective function is defined as the proportion between the geographical area covered by the WMN and the deployment set P without obstacles:

$$f(\mathcal{X}) = \psi(G, P, O) = \frac{Area\left(\left(\left(\bigcup_{i=1}^{n} \varUpsilon_i\right) \cap P\right) \setminus O\right)}{Area\,(P \setminus O)}, \tag{2}$$

where $f : R^n \mapsto \mathbb{R}$ (each $x \in \mathcal{X}$ is a tuple $\langle r_1^X, \ldots, r_n^X \rangle$). Intuitively, when $\psi(G, P, O) = 1$, the WMN defined by the graph G fully covers the entire deployment area excluding obstacles, and at $\psi(G, P, O) = 0$, there is no coverage of the area. Using *network coverage* $\psi(G, P, O)$, as an objective function rather than *client coverage* used in other approaches, allows us to search for solutions that are not dependent on knowledge of client positions. Details of the area coverage calculations are presented in Sect. 2.1.

Another important measure of WMN performance is *network connectivity* which quantifies how well the routers are interconnected. Since the connections between router nodes depend on their radio ranges and line-of-sight constraints, a network topology graph G for a particular set of RN positions may not be fully connected (i.e. may consists of several subgraph components) as shown in the example WMN in Fig. 2. There the graph G consists of 3 subgraphs (G_1, G_2, G_3) in the WMN backbone case (i.e. excluding client connections). The size of the greatest subgraph component in $G = G^1 \cup G^2 \cup \ldots G^h$ is defined as:

$$\phi(G) = \max_{i \in \{1, \ldots, h\}} \{|G^i|\} \tag{3}$$

Typically, in other work (e.g. [12,18]), the *network connectivity* (also called *size of the greatest component*) is considered as part of the objective function. In this case, there is always a trade-off between finding solutions that maximize both objectives. Such problems are often solved using the bi-objective optimization technique, where each objective is multiplied with a weight parameter emphasizing the importance of each separate objective. Generally, *network connectivity* is considered more important than *client or network coverage*. Consequently, in our formulation it is considered as a very strong requirement that the RNP solution guarantees a fully connected network. For that reason network connectivity is treated as a constraint rather than an objective to be maximized.

The general optimization problem formulation for the extended RNP problem, which includes the objective function and all the constraints considered in our approach, is defined as:

$$\max_{\mathcal{X}} \quad f(\mathcal{X}) \tag{4a}$$

$$\text{s.t.} \quad r_i^X \in P \setminus O \qquad\qquad \forall i \in \{1, \ldots, n\} \tag{4b}$$

$$e(r_i, r_j) \in E(G) \iff \overline{r_i^X r_j^X} \cap O = \emptyset \wedge \left(\|r_i^X - r_j^X\| < \min(\gamma^i, \gamma^j) \right)$$

$$\forall i \neq j; i, j \in \{1, \ldots, n\} \tag{4c}$$

$$\phi(G) = n \tag{4d}$$

The goal of our optimization problem is to maximize the geographical area which is covered by the WMN (Eq. 4a) and the constraints enforce three important features of solutions we are aiming at finding in our approach. First, all router positions should be within the deployment area P with exclusion of obstacle regions (Eq. 4b). Second, connections between any two routers that are considered as valid have a direct line-of-sight (Eq. 4c). Finally, the topology graph G is fully connected, i.e. consists of a single graph (Eq. 4d). In practice solving this nonconvex non-smooth high-dimensional constrained optimization problem directly is infeasible. An alternative to solving such a problem is to use penalty function methods in which the constraints are replaced with a penalty function that is a cumulative measure of constraint violations. The penalty function is added to the objective function thus discouraging the search algorithm from visiting infeasible parts of the search space.

Penalty methods with binary constraints still require parameter tuning and there are no guarantees for convergence to the global optimum. In an attempt to alleviative this problem, we use a penalty function that also includes a distance measure indicating how infeasible a particular solution is. The objective function, including penalties for different constraint violations, is calculated as follows:

$$\max_{\mathcal{X}}(f(\mathcal{X}) - \pi(\mathcal{X})); \quad \pi(\mathcal{X}) = \sum_{p=1}^{4}(\pi_c \cdot \pi_p(\mathcal{X}))^2 \tag{5}$$

where π_c is a penalty coefficient chosen empirically. Four π_p penalty functions are used in our RNP problem formulation, where in the case of no constraint violations the value of $\pi(\mathcal{X}) = 0$.

$$\pi_1(\mathcal{X}) = \sum_{i=1}^{n} \begin{cases} r_i^X \in P \to 0 \\ r_i^X \notin P \to d(P, r_i^X) \end{cases} \tag{6}$$

$$\pi_2(\mathcal{X}) = \sum_{i=1}^{n} \begin{cases} r_i^X \notin O \to 0 \\ r_i^X \in O \to \exists k \left(r_i^X \in O^k \right) \to d(O^k, r_i^X) \end{cases} \tag{7}$$

$$\pi_3(\mathcal{X}) = \sum_{e(r_i, r_j) \in E(G)} \begin{cases} \overline{r_i^X r_j^X} \cap O = \emptyset \to 0 \\ \overline{r_i^X r_j^X} \cap O \neq \emptyset \to 1 \end{cases} \tag{8}$$

$$\pi_4(\mathcal{X}) = \sum_{\substack{j>1}}^{h} \min_{\substack{r_i \in G^1 \\ r_j \in G^j}} \|r_i^X - r_j^X\| - \min(\gamma_i, \gamma_j) \tag{9}$$

Otherwise, penalties π_1 and π_2 correspond to the first constraint (Eq. 4b) and if violated they are calculated as a distance measure to the closest border of the deployment area or obstacle, respectively. Line-of-sight constraints (Eq. 4d) are imposed by penalty π_3. Full graph connectivity constraints are enforced by penalty π_4 which in case of a violation (i.e. graph G consists of several subgraphs) is equal to the sum of the minimum distances between the largest subgraph component G^1 in the graph G and the remaining subgraphs. This penalty will decrease as the number of subgraphs decreases or the remaining smaller subgraphs are moved closer to the largest subgraph component G^1.

Note, that although solving the extended RNP problem using penalty functions bears some similarities to bi-objective optimization, where constraints are a part of the objective function with much higher negative values, in our case, a feasible solution is one that meets all the constraints, thus our penalty in the objective function is $\pi(\mathcal{X}) = 0$.

2.1 Network Coverage Calculation

Network coverage calculations are an essential part of the RNP algorithm described in Sect. 3. This has to be done efficiently, so we use grid representations to do this. Two types of network coverage calculations are used in the algorithm. The first, $\psi(G, P, O)$, assesses the total geographical area covered by a WMN over a given deployment set P, excluding obstacles O. It is used as the objective function (Eq. 2) when applying optimization algorithms. The second variant, $\mu(G, P, O, r_{new})$, assesses an area coverage improvement due to a particular router node r_{new}, when selecting a new router node position in the process of finding a final network topology graph incrementally.

Both area calculations are approximated using grid representations encoded as three two-dimensional matrices. This allows us to leverage very efficient image processing algorithms to calculate network coverage.

3   RRT-WMN Algorithm

In this subsection, a description of the proposed RRT-WMN algorithm is presented. The algorithm incorporates an extension to the Rapidly Exploring

---

Algorithm 1: RRT-WMN

Input: G, R, *timeout*
Parameters : P, O, N_B, ψ_{min}

1 **if** $G = \emptyset$ **then**
2     $r_{init} \leftarrow$ removeFirst(R)
3   **if** $r_{init}^X = \emptyset$ **then**
4        $r_{init}^X \leftarrow$ randomState(P, O)   ▷ select random state s.t.: $r_{init}^X \in P \setminus O$
5     $G \leftarrow G \cup r_{init}$
6     $G_{best} \leftarrow \emptyset$
7 **if** *timeout* **then** return G_{best}
8 **if** $|R| > 0 \wedge \psi(G) \leq \psi_{min}$ **then**
9     $candidates \leftarrow$ getConstrainedStates(G, R, N_B)   ▷ rejection sampling
10   sort $candidates$ according to score
11   **for** (r_{new}, r_{score}) **in** $candidates$ **do**
12       $G \leftarrow G \cup r_{new}$
13   remove(R, r_{new})
14       $G_{best} \leftarrow$ RRT-WMN(G, R)   ▷ recursive call
15 **else**
16   **if** $\psi(G)/\phi(G) > \psi(G_{best})/\phi(G_{best})$ **then**
17       $G_{best} \leftarrow G$ ▷ the current graph is a better solution
18 **return** G_{best}

Random Trees (RRT) [10] motion planning technique that is capable of finding efficient solutions to the motion planning problem in multi-dimensional state spaces that take into account state constraints. The original version of the RRT algorithm iteratively builds a tree rooted in an initial state by extending it towards a randomly selected state. This expansion procedure is biased towards covering unexplored parts of the state space and that is the key feature exploited in our algorithm when applied to the RNP domain. The RRT and its variants are predominantly applied to finding motion plans that connect an initial state to a goal state, i.e. building a single graph or a tree structure to solve the motion planning query.

The RRT-WMN algorithm uses the same state exploration principle for calculating router node positions, but instead of generating a single graph, the algorithm creates multiple graphs in parallel, each of which is a feasible RNP solution. A recursive process is used to compute these graphs where, at each step, a number of potential new router positions are considered for addition to one of the existing partial graphs. All router position candidates are ranked according to an area coverage improvement score, i.e. $\mu(G, P, O, r_{rew})$. The pseudo-code for the algorithm is presented in Algorithms 1 and 2. The input to the RRT-WMN is a graph G (i.e. current partial solution) and a set R (i.e. list of router nodes as tuples, see Sect. 2). The parameters used during the calculations include polygons specifying the deployment area P and obstacles O, a limit for number of candidates considered at each iteration N_B, a *timeout* constant and a minimum area coverage value ψ_{min}. The last parameter is used for finding a minimum set of router nodes that yields at least ψ_{min} network coverage.

Algorithm 2: GETCONSTRAINEDSTATES

Input: G, R, N_B - number of candidates,
Output: $candidates = \{(r_{cand}, r_{score})\}$
Parameters : P, O

1 $candidates \leftarrow (\emptyset, \emptyset)$
2 **while** $|candidates| \leq N_B$ **do**
3       $x_{rand} \leftarrow$ randomState(P, O) ▷ sampling for positions to expand towards
4   **if** $inRange(x_{rand}, G)$ **then continue**   ▷ already in WMN range
5       $r_{near} \leftarrow$ NearestVertex(x_{rand}, G)
6       $r_{new} \leftarrow$ random(R)
7       $d = min(\gamma_{near}, \gamma_{new})$ ▷ find minimum distance to expand
8       $x_{new} \leftarrow$ NewState$(x_{rand}, r_{near}^X, d)$
9   **if** $\neg CollisionFree(P, O, x_{new}, r_{near}^X)$ **then continue**
10      $r_{new}^X \leftarrow x_{new}$
11      $r_{score} \leftarrow \mu(G, P, O, r_{new})$ ▷ calculate area coverage improvment
12      $candidates \leftarrow candidates \cup \{(r_{new}, r_{score})\}$

13 **return** $candidates$

An initialization step is performed (in Lines 1–6) that either assigns a pre-defined router node position, already given as an input to the algorithm (i.e. $r_1^X \neq \emptyset$ in $r_1 \in R$), or selects the first position by random state sampling, subject to constraints (i.e. Eq. 4b). A *timeout* termination condition is checked in Line 7 (i.e. has the algorithm run for the specified time?) and if true, the current best solution is returned. In the main loop of the algorithm, a condition for a feasible solution is evaluated in Line 8. It checks if there are any more nodes in R to be added to the solution graph, or if the current solution has reached a specified minimum network coverage (ψ_{min}). If any of these two conditions are true, a comparison between the current solution graph and the best graph found so far is performed (Line 16–17). Otherwise, a set of N_B candidate nodes are generated by performing rejection sampling according to Algorithm 2. The candidate nodes are then sorted according to their score and the one with the highest score is added first to the solution graph G and removed from the set R. The updated solution graph G and the set of unassigned router nodes R are then used in the recursive call to the algorithm (Line 14).

The rejection sampling algorithm (Algorithm 2) generates a random state x_{rand}, in Line 3, subject to the constraints specified in Eq. 4b. In case the selected random state is already in range of the current solution graph G, a new random state is generated. Next, the closest router r_{near} in the graph to the random sample is selected (Line 5). In order to enforce the full network connectivity constraint specified in Eq. 4d, a distance d used for graph extension is calculated. Its value is based on the minimum radio coverage radiuses of r_{near} and one of the unassigned router nodes in R that is selected randomly (Lines 6–7). A new state is then calculated (x_{new}) as a point on a line between the positions of x_{new} and r_{near}^X located at the distance d from r_{near}^X (Line 8). A line-of-sight check, accord-

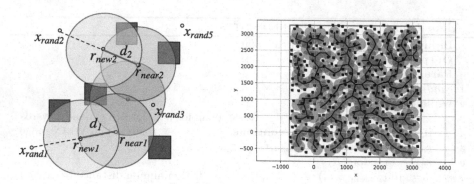

Fig. 3. Generation of candidate router positions in the RRT-WMN algorithm (left). Example solution generated by the RRT-WMN in Case 3 scenario (right).

ing to the edge connectivity constraint specified in (Eq. 4c), between the points is then performed (Line 9). If successful, the new state is used as a candidate with its score calculated using the area coverage improvement $\mu(G, P, O, r_{new})$. The procedure is repeated until N_B candidates are created. Figure 3 presents an example of two successfully generated candidates (r_{new1} and r_{new2}) and some rejected state samples, x_{rand3}, which is already in range of the WMN (rejected in Line 4), and x_{rand5}, where the potential new extended state would not have a line-of-sight to its nearest node r_{near2} (rejected in Line 9).

4   Experimental Evaluation

In this section, results of a comparative experimental evaluation are provided for the extended RNP problem. The performance of the RRT-WMN algorithm is compared with two optimization techniques, Particle Swarm Optimization (PSO) [6] and Covariance Matrix Adaptation Evolution Strategy (CMA-ES) [7]. The criteria used for comparison between the algorithms are based on the computational time and quality of the solutions, i.e. the coverage of the WMN.

The PSO algorithm variant used for comparison, proposed in [13], includes use of a constriction coefficient and local search. It has been successfully applied to a different RNP problem specification. The CMA-ES algorithm is an evolutionary optimization technique that has grown in popularity in recent years due to its success in solving many problems where the objective function is non-convex, multi-modal, non-smooth, discontinuous, noisy, or ill-conditioned. All the evaluated algorithms were implemented in the Python programming language and the experiments were run on a computer equipped with an Intel Core i7 (I7-6820HQ) processor. Three cases of different complexity were designed for the evaluation. The first two are based on setups previously used in the evaluation of other approaches [12,13,19], and include a relatively small limit on the number of router nodes used. These cases are used for comparison between the two optimization techniques, PSO and CMA-ES, and the RRT-WMN algorithm. The third case has a significantly larger complexity and is used to show

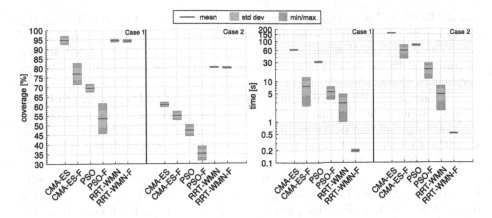

Fig. 4. Experimental evaluation results for Case 1 and Case 2.

the scalability of our approach in comparison to the non-scalability of the other approaches.

- *Case 1*: 16 mesh router nodes with a circular radio coverage range with radius of 6 are to be deployed in an area of size 32×32. The area includes 10 randomly distributed obstacles with size 3×3.
- *Case 2*: 32 mesh router nodes with a circular radio coverage range with radius of 7.5 are to be deployed in an area of size 64×64. The area includes 10 randomly distributed obstacles with size 6×6.
- *Case 3*: 200 mesh router nodes with a circular radio coverage range with radius of 183 are to be deployed in the area of size 4000×4000. The area includes 320 randomly distributed obstacles with size 50×50.

Parameters used for algorithms in our evaluation were chosen empirically and were set as follows. The PSO: 100 particles, 50 iterations limit, $v_{max} = 3.5$ for the particle velocity. The CMA-ES: 15000 iterations limit, $\sigma = 0.01$, no adaptive σ strategy was used. The RRT-WMN: *timeout* $= 10s$ ($30s$), $N_B = 10$ (20) and $\psi_{min} = 0.99$ (values in the brackets for Case 3). Additionally, since all three algorithms can be run iteratively and in anytime fashion, the first valid solution with its execution time was recorded as well and it is marked in the results by a capital letter F at the end of an algorithm name (e.g. PSO-F).

For each of the cases, 10 instances of an environment were generated using a uniform distribution. The algorithms were executed 10 times per each instance. Figure 4 presents statistics for Cases 1–2. The coverage measurement is the percentage of the overall deployment area covered i.e. $f(\mathcal{X})$ (see Sect. 2).

In general, for Case 1, the best results were obtained using the CMA-ES and RRT-WMN algorithms, where solutions reached the average coverage of 94.7% and 94.5%, respectively. The CMA-ES algorithm reached a maximum of 97.3% coverage on average which is around 2% better than the best coverage in the RRT-WMN case. However, the average calculation time was slower by a factor of 12, where average CMA-ES times were 62 s compared to 4.8 s for the RRT-WMN. Interestingly, the first solutions calculated by the RRT-WMN are quite close in quality to the final ones and are computed at an average of 0.2 s. The PSO algorithm performed quite poorly in our extended RNP domain as compared to the other two algorithms, providing solutions with an average coverage of 69.6%.

For Case 2, the RRT-WMN outperformed both the CMA-ES and PSO algorithms with average solutions reaching 80% coverage while still maintaining very short average calculation times of 4.8 s. In this case, the CMA-ES and PSO algorithms require 16–30 times more computational time than RRT-WMN and provides solutions with lower coverages between 31–62%.

The RRT-WMN performed even better on more complex and realistic problems. In Case 3, it reached an average coverage of $80.9 \pm 0.5\%$ with computation times at 20.1 ± 3.4 s. Figure 3 presents a sample solution for Case 3 from the experiments. The two other algorithms, CMA-ES and PSO, were not anywhere near feasible for this case due to the amount of time required for finding a solution.

5   Conclusions

In this paper, a novel algorithm for computing router node placement in Wireless Mesh Networks has been proposed with the intent of utilizing the algorithm with UAVs in emergency rescue applications. An extended formulation of the RNP is provided that takes into account pragmatic constraints that arise from our application domain. In particular, a set of constraints is added for handling obstacles and line-of-sight requirements that we believe is essential from a practical perspective. The RRT-WMN algorithm proposed has been experimentally evaluated on a set of problems with different complexities and compared to two popular evolutionary algorithms (PSO and CMA-ES). The results very clearly show that the RRT-WMN algorithm outperforms both PSO and CMA-ES and also scales well to more complex problems reflected in realistic scenarios.

References

1. Alotaibi, E., Mukherjee, B.: A survey on routing algorithms for wireless Ad-Hoc and mesh networks. Comput. Netw. **56**(2), 940–965 (2012). https://doi.org/10.1016/j.comnet.2011.10.011
2. Aoun, B., Boutaba, R., Iraqi, Y., Kenward, G.: Gateway placement optimization in wireless mesh networks with QoS constraints. IEEE J. Sel. Areas Commun. **24**(11), 2127–2136 (2006). https://doi.org/10.1109/JSAC.2006.881606
3. Barolli, A., Oda, T., Ikeda, M., Barolli, L., Xhafa, F., Loia, V.: Node placement for wireless mesh networks: analysis of WMN-GA system simulation results for different parameters and distributions. J. Comput. Syst. Sci. **81**(8), 1496–1507 (2015). https://doi.org/10.1016/j.jcss.2014.12.024
4. Benyamina, D., Hafid, A., Gendreau, M.: Wireless mesh network planning: a multi-objective optimization approach. In: 2008 5th International Conference on Broadband Communications, Networks and Systems, pp. 602–609, September 2008. https://doi.org/10.1109/BROADNETS.2008.4769149

5. Denning, P.J.: Hastily formed networks. Commun. ACM **49**(4), 15–20 (2006). https://doi.org/10.1145/1121949.1121966
6. Eberhart, R., Kennedy, J.: A new optimizer using particle swarm theory. In: Proceedings of the Sixth International Symposium on Micro Machine and Human Science, MHS 1995, pp. 39–43, October 1995. https://doi.org/10.1109/MHS.1995.494215
7. Hansen, N.: The CMA evolution strategy: a comparing review. In: Lozano, J.A., Larrañaga, P., Inza, I., Bengoetxea, E. (eds.) Towards a New Evolutionary Computation. Studies in Fuzziness and Soft Computing, vol. 192, pp. 75–102. Springer, Heidelberg (2006). https://doi.org/10.1007/3-540-32494-1_4
8. Hu, Z., Verma, P.K.: Gateway placement in backbone wireless mesh networks using directional antennas. In: 2011 Ninth Annual Communication Networks and Services Research Conference, pp. 175–180, May 2011. https://doi.org/10.1109/CNSR.2011.33
9. Kolici, V., Barolli, L., Sakamoto, S., Oda, T., Xhafa, F., Uchida, K.: Optimization of giant component and number of covered users in wireless mesh networks: a comparison study. In: 2015 IEEE 29th International Conference on Advanced Information Networking and Applications, pp. 215–222, March 2015. https://doi.org/10.1109/AINA.2015.188
10. Kuffner, J.J., LaValle, S.M.: RRT-connect: an efficient approach to single-query path planning. In: Proceedings IEEE International Conference on Robotics and Automation (2000). https://doi.org/10.1109/ROBOT.2000.844730
11. Lin, C., Shu, L., Deng, D.: Router node placement with service priority in wireless mesh networks using simulated annealing with momentum terms. IEEE Syst. J. **10**(4), 1402–1411 (2016). https://doi.org/10.1109/JSYST.2014.2341033
12. Lin, C.C.: Dynamic router node placement in wireless mesh networks: a PSO approach with constriction coefficient and its convergence analysis. Inf. Sci. **232**, 294–308 (2013). https://doi.org/10.1016/j.ins.2012.12.023
13. Lin, C.C., Chen, T.H., Chin, H.H.: Adaptive router node placement with gateway positions and QoS constraints in dynamic wireless mesh networks. J. Netw. Comput. Appl. **74**, 149–164 (2016). https://doi.org/10.1016/j.jnca.2016.05.005
14. Pathak, P.H., Dutta, R.: A survey of network design problems and joint design approaches in wireless mesh networks. IEEE Commun. Surv. Tut. **13**(3), 396–428 (2011). https://doi.org/10.1109/SURV.2011.060710.00062
15. Rad, A.H.M., Wong, V.W.: Congestion-aware channel assignment for multi-channel wireless mesh networks. Comput. Netw. **53**(14), 2502–2516 (2009). https://doi.org/10.1016/j.comnet.2009.05.006
16. Ramamurthi, V., Reaz, A.S., Ghosal, D., Dixit, S., Mukherjee, B.: Channel, capacity, and flow assignment in wireless mesh networks. Comput. Netw. **55**(9), 2241–2258 (2011). https://doi.org/10.1016/j.comnet.2011.03.007
17. Wzorek, M., Berger, C., Rudol, P., Doherty, P.: Deployment of ad hoc network nodes using UAVs for search and rescue missions. In: IEEE International Electrical Engineering Congress (iEECON) (2018)
18. Xhafa, F., Sánchez, C., Barolli, L.: Genetic algorithms for efficient placement of router nodes in wireless mesh networks. In: 2010 24th IEEE International Conference on Advanced Information Networking and Applications, pp. 465–472, April 2010. https://doi.org/10.1109/AINA.2010.41
19. Xhafa, F., Sánchez, C., Barolli, A., Takizawa, M.: Solving mesh router nodes placement problem in wireless mesh networks by Tabu search algorithm. J. Comput. Syst. Sci. **81**(8), 1417–1428 (2015). https://doi.org/10.1016/j.jcss.2014.12.018

MotionRFCN: Motion Segmentation Using Consecutive Dense Depth Maps

Yiling Liu and Hesheng Wang[✉]

Department of Automation, Shanghai Jiao Tong University, Shanghai, China
{yilingliu,wanghesheng}@sjtu.edu.cn

Abstract. It is important to enable autonomous robots to detect or segment moving objects in dynamic scenes as they must perform collision-free navigation. Motion segmentation from a moving platform is challenging due to the dual motion caused by the background and the moving objects. Existing approaches for motion segmentation either have long multistage pipelines which are inefficient for real-time application or utilize optical flow which is sensitive to environment. In this paper, this challenging task is tackled by constructing spatiotemporal features from two consecutive dense depth maps. Depth maps can be generated either by LiDaR scans data or stereo vision algorithms. The core of the proposed approach is a fully convolutional network with inserted Gated-Recurrent-Units, denoted as MotionRFCN. We also create a publicly available dataset (KITTI-MoSeg) which contains more than 2000 frames with motion annotations. Qualitative and quantitative evaluation of MotionRFCN are presented to demonstrate its state-of-the-art performance on the KITTI dataset. The basic MotionRFCN can run in real time and segment moving objects whether the platform is stationary or moving. To the best of our knowledge, the proposed method is the first to implement motion segmentation with only dense depth maps inputs.

Keywords: Deep learning · Motion segmentation · Autonomous driving

1 Introduction

Parsing dynamic scenes has always been a crucial component in outdoor robotic activities. The ability to detect or segment moving objects such as cars and pedestrians can improve robotics perception, enable autonomous robots to reason in dynamic environment and perform collision-free navigation. Motion segmentation has a wide range of application areas including autonomous driving and traditional robotics [33–36]. It is a challenging problem because the camera

Supported in part by the Natural Science Foundation of China under Grant U1613218 and 61722309.

motion and the motion of independent objects are mixed. However, spatiotemporal cues behind consecutive frames significantly help motion segmentation. For example, it is hard to recognize a moving object in one single frame, but it is obvious considering its position change relative to the surrounding areas in consecutive frames.

Typically, motion features are extracted from optical flow through geometric models [5–8,10,12,17,20,21] or deep learning methods [13,24,25,27–29]. However, optical flow-based approaches have many drawbacks. First, optical flow is susceptible to occlusion, illumination change, and color change in environment. It also suffers from aperture problem, noise, and large camera displacement. Second, camera distortion may result in inevitable wrong optical flow values. Finally, objects at different depths from the camera can exhibit different optical flows even though they share the same motion states. These problems limit the applications and precision of optical flow-based methods.

In this paper, a novel framework for motion segmentation from either a stationary or moving platform is proposed. The motion cues are extracted from consecutive dense depth maps which can be obtained from multiple sources such as laser scanner, stereo camera, and RGB-D camera. Compared with optical flow-based approaches, the proposed method, called MotionRFCN, is more robust in real-world circumstances and has a wider range of applications (e.g., night scene, rainy scene). Moreover, the values of depth map generated by LiDaR scans data or calibrated stereo camera has higher precision without distortion. And depth variation is more intrinsically related to actual object motion because depth variation (i.e., velocity) of a moving object is inconsistent with that of its surrounding background in terms of direction and magnitude. To the best of our knowledge, the proposed method is the first to implement motion segmentation with only dense depth maps inputs. The contributions of this paper are as follows:

- A gated recurrent fully convolutional network architecture that performs motion segmentation utilizing two consecutive dense depth maps is proposed.
- 10 sequences from KITTI raw dataset [9] are manually annotated with motion mask to evaluate the proposed MotionRFCN approach. The results show MotionRFCN achieves state-of-the-art performance both in accuracy and efficiency.

The rest of this paper is organized as follows. Section 2 reviews the related work for motion segmentation. Section 3 details the proposed method. Section 4 presents the experimental results and discussion. Finally, conclusion is drawn in Sect. 5.

2   Related Work

In this section, the contributions of works most related to ours are reviewed. First, there are numerous approaches that have been proposed in recent years for motion detection or segmentation from a moving camera. These methods can be categorized into optical flow based, background modeling based, and tracking based approaches.

Optical flow-based approaches typically utilize the deviations of the moving objects' radial optical flows from that of the surrounding areas. Lenz et al. [5] use disparity and optical flow to compute the scene flow. They detect moving rigid objects through clustering points describing a similar scene flow. Namdev et al. [6] integrate optical flow and geometry cues to provide for a dense segmentation through a graph-based clustering algorithm. Narayana et al. [7] only use optical flow orientation in motion segmentation to avoid the over-segmentation of the scene into depth-dependent entities. In [8,10], the difference between the predicted flow of camera and optical flow is regarded as motion likelihood. Ochs et al. [12] compute point trajectories via optical flow, then segment moving objects using trajectories spanning hundreds of frames. Kao et al. [17] recover 3D motion using depth and optical flow, then apply spectral clustering to obtain motion segmentation. In [20], the inconsistency between the histogram of oriented optical flow of the object and its surrounding background is measured for the object-level motion detection. Bideau et al. [21] utilize optical flow to model camera motion, then use motion component priors and negative log likelihoods to implement motion segmentation. In recent work [27], deep learning architecture is introduced to segment moving objects directly from optical flow. Fragkiadaki et al. [13] train a moving objectness detector operating on both image and optical flow map. They rank segment proposals according to moving objectness and get final motion segmentation result. However, the method is computationally inefficient and do not scale well on outdoor scenes. In [24,25,28,29], they use CNN to do joint semantic and motion segmentation with optical flow and image inputs. Integrating semantic constraints incredibly improves the performance of motion segmentation. Besides, Haque et al. [28] add a 3D fully connected CRF in the end to introduce temporal constraints including optical flow and long-term tracks which brings further improved performance along with substantially increased inference time.

Background modeling-based approaches segment moving foreground objects by explicitly modeling the motion of the background, as in [1,4,26]. Elhamifar et al. [2] formulate motion segmentation as clustering the trajectories into subspaces. It is elegant in formulation but fails to address real world challenges such as motion degeneracy. Tourani et al. [19] use in-frame shear constraints to generate and merge affine models which performs well when facing degenerate motion scenarios.

Tracking-based approaches segment moving objects by localizing objects across sequential frames and track their movement trajectories. Kundu et al. [3] utilize recursive Bayes filter to assign the probability of a feature being stationary or moving based on epipolar and focus of expansion constraints. Lin et al. [11] incorporate the tracked moving points and the learned spatiotemporal features as inputs to recursive neural network that performs motion segmentation. Qiu et al. [16] use RANSAC to classify the matched features extracted from two consecutive stereo image pairs into inliers caused by the camera and outliers caused by moving objects. They cluster outliers in a U-disparity map to generate motion mask. Drayer et al. [18] use tracked detections from R-CNN denoted as tubes, then apply a spatiotemporal graph to segment objects. A major disadvantage of these approaches is their long processing pipelines and inference time which make them inefficient for real time applications.

Second, motion segmentation using LiDaR scans data can be broadly subdivided into model-free and model-based approaches. Occupancy modelling using Dempster-Shafer theory [22] or probability is a popular approach to implement motion segmentation. It models the occupancy information of the space and detects moving objects by monitoring the changes of occupancy states. However, these approaches are computation costly and cannot generalize to objects of different categories. To overcome these problems, Dewan et al. [23] propose a model-free method which detects motions by sequentially using RANSAC and a Bayesian approach. But it requires multi-sensor fusion to operate. To the best of our knowledge, no literature exploits deep learning method to implement motion segmentation on LiDaR scans data.

3   MotionRFCN Approach

In this section, the problem statement for motion segmentation is formulated first. Then the detailed network architecture is presented.

Let $D = \{d_t, t = 1, ..., N\}$ and $Y = \{y_t, t = 1, ..., N\}$ represent the training set. Since the motion states of objects at different times are different, we only segment objects which are moving during $[t-1, t]$. Given two consecutive depth maps, $I_t = \{d_{t-1}, d_t\} \subset D$, along with the corresponding ground truth motion mask $M_t = \{y_t^j, j = 1, ..., |d_t|\} \subset Y, y_t^j \in \{0, 1\}$, where 0 denotes a static pixel and 1 denotes a moving pixel (when d_{t-1} does not exist, assign d_t to d_{t-1}). Let w be the network parameters. The aim of learning is to find a prediction function $f_w : D \rightarrow Y$ which directly predicts the motion segmentation in depth map d_t. the employed loss function, denoted as $L(f_w(I), M)$, is the pixel-wise cross-entropy loss and the number of classes is set to 2 in our case. The two classes are equally weighted because class balancing is found unnecessary in improving performance even though the two classes are very unbalanced in dataset. Using stochastic gradient descent, we then solve

$$w^* = \underset{w}{argmin} \sum_{t=1}^{N} L(f_w(I_t), M_t) \tag{1}$$

A gated recurrent fully convolutional network architecture that extracts the spatiotemporal information from consecutive dense depth maps is proposed to take the role of f_w. Figure 1 depicts the detailed architecture. The proposed MotionRFCN is primarily adapted from FCN-8s [14], with inserted recurrent units to utilize temporal information. The deployed gated recurrent units can get variation information over time by differentiating consecutive frames. Instead of simply feeding the combined feature maps into dense layers, gated recurrent units pay more attention to the motion segmentation of the current frame.

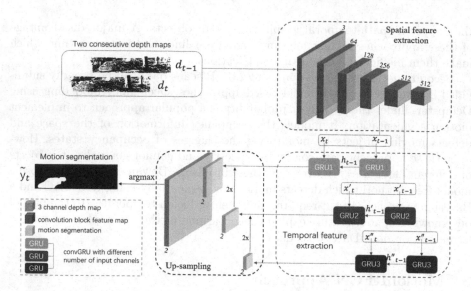

Fig. 1. MotionRFCN architecture. x_t, x_t', and x_t'' represent the output feature maps of the 3rd, 4th, and 5th convolution block operated on current frame d_t. x_{t-1}, x_{t-1}', and x_{t-1}'' represent the corresponding feature maps obtained from previous frame d_{t-1}.

The process of MotionRFCN can be divided into 3 steps. The first step is spatial feature extraction. The first 5 sequential convolution blocks of VGG16 are utilized to generate feature maps of multiple sizes. Each convolution block is a stack of 2 or 3 convolution layers followed by a maxpooling layer. The output feature maps of the 3rd, 4th, and 5th convolution block are given to the corresponding recurrent unit as inputs respectively. To benefit from the pretrained VGG16 weights which require the input to be 3 channel RGB image, an additional convolution layer is added at the beginning of MotionRFCN to transform 1 channel depth map into 3 channel input. The resulting 3 channel input is simply a depth map encoded linearly in a RGB space. Compared to simple colormap approaches, this formulation can learn a mapping method that best fit our case.

The second step is employing recurrent units to implement temporal feature extraction. Unlike 3D convolution which requires large memory and long training time, recurrent units are convenient to use but can still exploit temporal information. In addition, it can be easily inserted into existing architecture. Conventional recurrent units are designed for processing text data and they only work with vectors. Thus, they do not preserve spatial information in images. To overcome this problem, convolutional recurrent units extend inputs from vectors to matrices by replacing dot products with convolutions. Convolutional Gated-Recurrent-Unit [15], denoted as convGRU, is employed in MotionRFCN. It has similar performance compared to convLSTM but with reduced number of gates thus fewer parameters. convGRU, defined by the following equations, takes its operation result of previous frame as initial state and the current frame as input.

When previous frame does not exist, zero matrix is used to represent initial state.

$$z_t = \sigma(W_{hz} * h_{t-1} + b_{hz} + W_{xz} * x_t + b_{xz}) \tag{2}$$

$$r_t = \sigma(W_{hr} * h_{t-1} + b_{hr} + W_{xr} * x_t + b_{xr}) \tag{3}$$

$$h_t' = tanh(W_h * (r_t \odot h_{t-1}) + W_x * x_t + b) \tag{4}$$

$$h_t = (1 - z_t) \odot h_{t-1} + z_t \odot h_t' \tag{5}$$

Where $*$ denotes the convolution operation, $\odot$ the Hadamard product, σ the sigmoid function, $tanh$ the hyperbolic tangent function. z_t the update gate matrix, r_t the reset gate matrix, h_t the output matrix, x_t the input matrix, W the parameter matrices and b the bias vectors. Through such gating mechanism, information from previous frame can be selected to help motion segmentation in current frame.

The third step is up-sampling the coarse segmentation to the original size of the input depth map. The outputs of convGRUs are passed through convolution layers to generate coarse segmentation of different sizes. Semantic information from a deep, coarse layer and appearance information from a shallow, fine layer are combined through merging multiple coarse segmentation to produce better results. The merged coarse segmentation is up-sampled through deconvolution layers to the original size of the input depth map.

It is worthy noting that the proposed network architecture is fully convolutional, allowing the network to accommodate different input sizes since it is not restricted to a fixed output size.

Since common depth maps completed from projected raw LiDaR scans or computed through stereo vision algorithms do not preserve fine contours of objects and usually have some invalid regions, the motion segmentation results of MotionRFCN gives only rough locations, even some incorrectly labeled moving pixels. Due to this inevitable fact, the semantic mask produced by Mask R-CNN [30] are leveraged to implement motion segmentation refinement. The steps for postprocessing are as follows.

First, considering motion masks and semantic masks jointly. Only the motion masks that has the potential to be moving according to the corresponding semantic labels is preserved. Here car, person, bicycle, motorcycle, bus, etc. are considered as potential moving objects. Second, motion masks are projected onto semantic masks. Then the ratio of overlapping areas to total areas is used to determine whether replacing motion masks boundaries with semantic mask boundaries or not.

Introducing semantic constraints results in a further boost in performance. Since it is just a postprocessing procedure, one can choose not to use them depending on the timing requirements, sacrificing accuracy for inference time. A quantitative evaluation of this tradeoff is presented in Sect. 4.

4 Experiments

In this section, the datasets used, experimental results, and the comparison to the state-of-the-art are presented. The standard metric of pixel intersection over union is employed to evaluate experiment results, which can be calculated as $IoU = TP/(TP+FP+FN)$, where TP, FP, and FN represent true positives, false positives, and false negatives respectively.

4.1 Dataset

A large dataset with ground truth annotations is significantly important to train a neural network. However, for the task of motion segmentation using dense depth maps, there exists no public dataset. Even though there are several public datasets for motion segmentation, it is hard to generate high quality dense depth maps from the raw data. To implement training of neural networks for motion segmentation using dense depth maps and to allow for credible quantitative evaluation, 10 sequences from KITTI raw dataset [9] which contain multiple moving objects and challenging scenarios such as acute illumination change, complex camera motion, and occlusion are selected. The corresponding dense depth maps provided in Annotated Depth Maps (generated through depth completion algorithm using projected raw LiDaR scans data) are chosen as inputs for MotionRFCN. We follow the motion segmentation definition in [21] to manually annotate the images with pixel-wise motion labels considering two consecutive RGB images. The created dataset is denoted as KITTI-MoSeg in this paper. To compare with optical flow-based approaches, PWC-Net [31] is used to generate optical flow for them.

To provide credible evaluation, the proposed method is also evaluated on other motion segmentation dataset based on KITTI: KITTI MOD Dataset [29]. Since it only assign motion label to vehicle categories, other categories in our motion segmentation results are removed using semantic constraints.

We also evaluate MotionRFCN on Cityscapes [32] dataset to demonstrate its performance on depth maps generated by stereo vision algorithms.

4.2 Training Details

For the network implementation, we use PyTorch with cuDNN backend for acceleration. We train the network on a system with an Intel i7-8700K CPU and one NVIDIA 1080Ti with initial learning rate $\lambda_0 = 5e^{-4}$. Initial weights of the convolution blocks are copied from the weights of the convolution layers in VGG16 pretrained on ImageNet. The deconvolution layer is initialized to bilinear distribution, and then learned. The rest layers including convGRUs and depth mapping layer are initialized with Xavier distribution.

In order to create additional training data, apply the augmentations composed of random horizontally flip and random rotate on the training data.

4.3 Qualitative Evaluation

KITTI-MoSeg dataset is split into three subsets: train, val, and test. Figure 2 shows qualitative results on frames from test subset with MotionRFCN trained on train subset. The red masks denote moving objects.

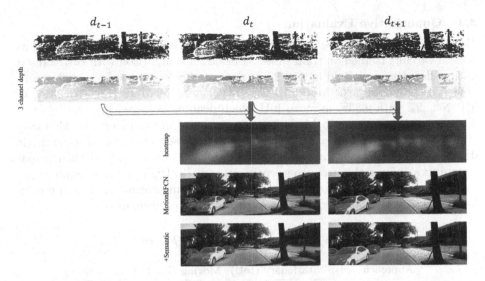

Fig. 2. Qualitative evaluation. Top to Bottom: (1) Consecutive dense depth maps inputs. (2) Learned 3 channel dense depth maps. (3) Motion likelihood. (4) Motion segmentation obtained from MotionRFCN. (5) Motion segmentation obtained from MotionRFCN with semantic constraints. Given d_{t-1} and d_t, y_t(the motion segmentation on d_t) is predicted. Given d_t and d_{t+1}, y_{t+1} is predicted. (Color figure online)

In Fig. 2, note that the basic MotionRFCN roughly segments moving objects when the sensor is also moving. However, due to lots of invalid depth values caused by the limited LiDaR channels, depth maps cannot maintain fine object contour. Thus, MotionRFCN can only predicts rough locations of moving objects. Introducing semantic constraints produced by semantic segmentation can significantly improve its performance. However, commonly used method, Fully Connected CRF, is time consuming which makes it impractical for outdoor navigation. So, simple and fast formulation described in Sect. 3 is employed to refine motion segmentation, but also achieve ideal result. Besides semantic segmentation, detection results can also undertake the task of introducing semantic constraints which require less inference time and bring limited performance improvement.

Specially, increasing the number of input depth maps is found not only take much longer inference time but also make no improvements since motion varies at different times. So, we choose to input only two consecutive depth maps.

In general, MotionRFCN with semantic constraints can well handle multiple challenging outdoor circumstances including complex camera motion, undesirable weather condition, and occlusion.

4.4   Quantitative Evaluation

Table 1 shows quantitative results on test subset with MotionRFCN as well as several variants trained on train subset. Besides, a comparison with two popular optical flow-based method in [13,27] is presented, whose code is publicly available. The proposed basic MotionRFCN outperforms STMOP [13] with 11.41%, MP-Net [27] with 9.33% in mean IoU which denotes averaged IoU over classes. There are three reasons behind the performance improvement: (1) Manually annotated KITTI-MoSeg enable better feature representation than the synthetic dataset used in [27] when applied in real world circumstances. (2) Utilizing spatiotemporal information from consecutive frames. (3) High precision input depth maps. In addition, both preprocessing (i.e., data augmentation) and postprocessing (i.e., semantic constraints) can further improve performance.

Table 1. Comparison on Motion-MoSeg

Approach	Stationary (IoU)	Moving (IoU)	Mean IoU
STMOP [13]	82.34	46.52	64.43
MP-Net [27]	83.79	49.21	66.51
MotionRFCN	99.18	52.51	75.84
+aug	99.20	53.04	76.12
+aug+Semantic	99.32	63.07	81.19

+aug: introducing data augmentation in MotionRFCN
+Semantic: introducing semantic constraints in MotionRFCN

Fast inference is one of the most critical requirements for environment perception in real-world robotic navigation. Several state-of-the-art approaches for motion segmentation are listed in Table 2 to demonstrate the outstanding efficiency of MotionRFCN. For a fair comparison, all methods use input whose resolution is 768 × 384. The proposed basic MotionRFCN takes 138 ms to predict motion segmentation of a single frame which is much faster than the first three algorithms. Unlike SMSnet which can only segment moving cars, the proposed MotionRFCN can segment non-rigid moving objects (e.g., pedestrian) in slightly less inference time. MotionRFCN enables real-time processing speed which is a prerequisite for robotic navigation.

Many of the aforementioned approaches do not provide open source code. Thus, comparison with them is difficult. To make credible evaluation on KITTI MOD [29], semantic cues are utilized to remove moving objects except vehicle categories from motion segmentation results. As the comparison results presented in Table 3, the proposed basic MotionRFCN outperforms MODNet [29] with 25.44% in mean IoU.

4.5   Evaluation of Generality

The generality of the proposed MotionRFCN is demonstrated in Fig. 3. We select a short sequence in Cityscapes [32] dataset and compute disparity using

Table 2. Comparison of inference time

Approach	Time
CRF-M [10]	240,000 ms
U-Disp-CRF-FCN [16]	1,060 ms
CMD [20]	900 ms
SMSnet [25]	153 ms
MotionRFCN	138 ms
+aug	277 ms
+aug+Semantic	602 ms

Table 3. Comparison on KITTI MOD [29]

Approach	Mean IoU
MODNet	45.41
MotionRFCN	70.85

semi-global matching on stereo images. Then the disparity is turned into depth map in KITTI-MoSeg format. Figure 3 shows the MotionRFCN trained on LiDaR scans data can generalize well to depth maps computed through stereo vision algorithm. However, MotionRFCN cannot segment some tiny moving objects which have already been smoothed in disparity computing process.

Disparity   Motion segmentation (+semantic)

Fig. 3. Motion segmentation on disparity using MotionRFCN trained on KITTI-MoSeg with semantic constraints.

Overall, one can note that the proposed MotionRFCN applies to depth map from multiple resources.

5 Conclusion

In this paper, a novel framework for motion segmentation using two consecutive dense depth maps is proposed. The main motivation is the extensive sources of depth maps compared to optical flow. The developed deep architecture, Motion-RFCN, constructs features from both spatial and temporal dimensions by inserting Gated-Recurrent-Unit into FCN. Semantic constraints are utilized to further boost the model performance. We also introduce a large dataset with manually annotated ground truth, called KITTI-MoSeg, that enables training of Motion-RFCN. Comprehensive qualitative and quantitative evaluations are presented to demonstrate that the proposed MotionRFCN achieves state-of-the-art performance and can inference in real time.

Motion segmentation from either a stationary or moving platform is still far from being solved and applied in real world. Our future work is compensating for indistinct object contour in depth maps by introducing semantic constraints in network architecture instead of in postprocessing.

References

1. Xiao, J., Shah, M.: Motion layer extraction in the presence of occlusion using graph cut. IEEE Trans. Pattern Anal. Mach. Intell. **27**, 1644–1659 (2005)
2. Elhamifar, E., Vidal, R.: Sparse subspace clustering. In: Computer Vision and Pattern Recognition (2009)
3. Kundu, A., Krishna, K.M., Sivaswamy, J.: Moving object detection by multi-view geometric techniques from a single camera mounted robot. In: International Conference on Intelligent Robots and Systems (2009)
4. Sheikh, Y., Javed, O., Kanade, T.: Background subtraction for freely moving cameras. In: International Conference on Computer Vision (2009)
5. Lenz, P., Ziegler, J., Geiger, A., Roser, M.: Sparse scene flow segmentation for moving object detection in urban environments. In: Intelligent Vehicles Symposium (2011)
6. Namdev, R.K., Kundu, A., Krishna, K.M., Jawahar, C.V.: Motion segmentation of multiple objects from a freely moving monocular camera. In: International Conference on Robotics and Automation (2012)
7. Narayana, M., Hanson, A., Learned-Miller, E.: Coherent motion segmentation in moving camera videos using optical flow orientations. In: International Conference on Computer Vision (2013)
8. Romero-Cano, V., Nieto, J.I.: Stereo-based motion detection and tracking from a moving platform. In: Intelligent Vehicles Symposium (2013)
9. Geiger, A., Lenz, P., Stiller, C., Urtasun, R.: Vision meets robotics: the KITTI dataset. Int. J. Robot. Res. **32**, 1231–1237 (2013)
10. Reddy, N.D., Singhal, P., Krishna, K.M.: Semantic motion segmentation using dense CRF formulation. In: Proceedings of the Indian Conference on Computer Vision Graphics and Image Processing (2014)
11. Lin, T.H., Wang, C.C.: Deep learning of spatio-temporal features with geometric-based moving point detection for motion segmentation. In: International Conference on Robotics and Automation (2014)
12. Ochs, P., Malik, J., Brox, T.: Segmentation of moving objects by long term video analysis. IEEE Trans. Pattern Anal. Mach. Intell. **36**, 1187–1200 (2014)
13. Fragkiadaki, K., Arbelaez, P., Felsen, P., Malik, J.: Learning to segment moving objects in videos. In: Computer Vision and Pattern Recognition (2015)

14. Long, J., Shelhamer, E., Darrell, T.: Fully convolutional networks for semantic segmentation. In: Computer Vision and Pattern Recognition (2015)
15. Ballas, N., Yao, L., Pal, C., Courville, A.: Delving deeper into convolutional networks for learning video representations. arXiv preprint arXiv:1511.06432 (2015)
16. Qiu, F., Yang, Y., Li, H., Fu, M., Wang, S.: Semantic motion segmentation for urban dynamic scene understanding. In: International Conference on Automation Science and Engineering (2016)
17. Kao, J.Y., Tian, D., Mansour, H., Vetro, A., Ortega, A.: Moving object segmentation using depth and optical flow in car driving sequences. In: International Conference on Image Processing (2016)
18. Drayer, B., Brox, T.: Object detection, tracking, and motion segmentation for object-level video segmentation. arxiv:1608.03066 (2016)
19. Tourani, S., Krishna, K.M.: Using in-frame shear constraints for monocular motion segmentation of rigid bodies. J. Intell. Robotic Syst. **82**(2), 237–255 (2016)
20. Chen, T., Lu, S.: Object-level motion detection from moving cameras. IEEE Trans. Circuits Syst. Video Technol. **27**, 2333–2343 (2016)
21. Bideau, P., Learned-Miller, E.: It's moving! a probabilistic model for causal motion segmentation in moving camera videos. In: Leibe, B., Matas, J., Sebe, N., Welling, M. (eds.) ECCV 2016. LNCS, vol. 9912, pp. 433–449. Springer, Cham (2016). https://doi.org/10.1007/978-3-319-46484-8_26
22. Postica, G., Romanoni, A., Matteucci, M.: Robust moving objects detection in lidar data exploiting visual cues. In: International Conference on Intelligent Robots and Systems (2016)
23. Dewan, A., Caselitz, T., Tipaldi, G.D., Burgard, W.: Motion-based detection and tracking in 3D LiDAR scans. In: International Conference on Robotics and Automation (2016)
24. Haque, N., Reddy, N.D., Krishna, K.M.: Joint semantic and motion segmentation for dynamic scenes using deep convolutional networks. In: International Conference on Computer Vision Theory and Applications (2017)
25. Vertens, J., Valada, A., Burgard, W.: SMSnet: semantic motion segmentation using deep convolutional neural networks. In: International Conference on Intelligent Robots and Systems (2017)
26. Wehrwein, S., Szeliski, R.: Video segmentation with background motion models. In: British Machine Vision Conference (2017)
27. Tokmakov, P., Alahari, K., Schmid, C.: Learning motion patterns in videos. In: Computer Vision and Pattern Recognition (2017)
28. Haque, N., Reddy, N.D., Krishna, M.: Temporal semantic motion segmentation using spatio temporal optimization. In: Pelillo, M., Hancock, E. (eds.) EMMCVPR 2017. LNCS, vol. 10746, pp. 93–108. Springer, Cham (2018). https://doi.org/10.1007/978-3-319-78199-0_7
29. Siam, M., Mahgoub, H., Zahran, M., Yogamani, S., Jagersand, M.: Motion and appearance based moving object detection network for autonomous driving. arXiv:1709.04821v2 (2017)
30. He, K.M., Gkioxari, G., Dollar, P., Girshick, R.: Mask R-CNN. In: International Conference on Computer Vision (2017)
31. Sun, D., Yang, X., Liu, M., Kautz, J.: PWC-Net: CNNs for optical flow using pyramid, warping, and cost volume. In: Computer Vision and Pattern Recognition (2018)
32. Cordts, M., Omaran, M., Ramos, S., Rehfeld, T., Enzweiler, M., Benenson, R.: The cityscapes dataset for semantic urban scene understanding. In: Computer Vision and Pattern Recognition (2016)

33. Zheng, L., Wang, H., Chen, W.: A fast 3D object recognition pipeline in cluttered and occluded scenes. In: Huang, Y.A., Wu, H., Liu, H., Yin, Z. (eds.) ICIRA 2017. LNCS (LNAI), vol. 10463, pp. 588–598. Springer, Cham (2017). https://doi.org/10.1007/978-3-319-65292-4_51
34. Yang, B., Wang, H., Chen, W., Liang, Y.: Vision-based automatic hair follicular unit separation. In: Liu, H., Kubota, N., Zhu, X., Dillmann, R., Zhou, D. (eds.) ICIRA 2015. LNCS (LNAI), vol. 9246, pp. 273–284. Springer, Cham (2015). https://doi.org/10.1007/978-3-319-22873-0_24
35. Xu, L., Wang, H., Chen, W., Wang, J.: Light intensity optimization in trajectory planning of inspection robot. In: Liu, H., Kubota, N., Zhu, X., Dillmann, R., Zhou, D. (eds.) ICIRA 2015. LNCS (LNAI), vol. 9245, pp. 297–308. Springer, Cham (2015). https://doi.org/10.1007/978-3-319-22876-1_26
36. Wang, H., Lai, Y., Chen, W.: The time optimal trajectory planning with limitation of operating task for the Tokamak inspecting manipulator. Fusion Eng. Des. **113**, 57–65 (2016)

SAF: Semantic Attention Fusion Mechanism for Pedestrian Detection

Ruizhe Yu, Shunzhou Wang, Yao Lu$^{(\boxtimes)}$, Huijun Di, Lin Zhang, and Lihua Lu

Beijing Laboratory of Intelligent Information Technology, School of Computer Science and Technology, Beijing Institute of Technology, Beijing 100081, China
{2120171090,shunzhouwang,vis_yl,ajon,zhanglin,lulihua}@bit.edu.cn

Abstract. Benefiting from deep learning methods, pedestrian detection has witnessed a great progress in recent years. However, many pedestrian detectors are prone to detect background instances, especially under urban scenes, which results in plenty of false positive detections. In this paper, we propose a semantic attention fusion mechanism (SAF) to increase the discriminability of detector. The SAF includes two key components, attention modules and reverse fusion blocks. Different from previous attention mechanisms which use attention modules for re-weighting the top features of network directly, the outputs of our attention modules are fused by reverse fusion blocks from high level layers to low level layers step by step, which aims at generating strong semantic features for pedestrian detections. Experiments on CityPersons dataset demonstrate the effectiveness of our SAF.

Keywords: Pedestrian detection · Semantic attention · Background errors

1 Introduction

Pedestrian detection is the fundament of many computer vision tasks, such as pose estimation, multiple pedestrian tracking, and action recognition. Benefiting from the deep learning method, pedestrian detection has got a significant progress such as [7,11–13,15,18,20,21]. However, there still exist many issues to be solved, such as the occluded pedestrian detections, the small scale pedestrian detections, background errors and so on [19]. Specially, background errors are the main source of false positive detections [19], especially under the urban street scenes.

There are some approaches for decreasing background errors. One way [18] is that adding the boosted forests after the top of network to refine the output detections, the other way [11] is that adding more predictors to improving detection results. The above methods all employ two or more classification steps for filtering out background errors, but some small background objects are still detected as pedestrian wrongly due to the low layers of network lacking of enough pedestrian semantic information. Attention mechanism can be used

© Springer Nature Switzerland AG 2019
A. C. Nayak and A. Sharma (Eds.): PRICAI 2019, LNAI 11671, pp. 523–533, 2019.
https://doi.org/10.1007/978-3-030-29911-8_40

for suppressing background information and Zhang et al. [21] develop different attention modules for guiding the network pay more attention to different pedestrian parts. However, they do not consider the fact that some background instances will also have high detection responses and are tend to be detected as pedestrians. In a word, the pedestrian semantic information is not utilized effectively in [11,18,21].

(a)   (b)

Fig. 1. The visualization results of ALFNet without (a) and with (b) the semantic attention fusion mechanism (SAF) from *CityPersons* validation set. The green and red rectangles represent detection results and the ground truth results respectively. The comparison indicates that our semantic attention fusion mechanism decreases background errors effectively. (Color figure online)

In order to decrease background errors effectively, we propose a Semantic Attention Fusion mechanism (SAF), which consists of attention modules(AM) and reverse fusion blocks(RFB) [6,8,10]. Different from previous attention mechanisms [21] which use attention modules for re-weighting the top features of network directly, the outputs of attention modules are fused by reverse fusion blocks from high level layers to low level layers step by step, which aims at generating strong semantic features for pedestrian detections. Moreover, we place our SAF on ALFNet [11] and Fig. 1 shows the visualization results of the ALFNet without and with our SAF. The number of background errors in Fig. 1(b) decreases indeed comparing with that in Fig. 1(a), which indicates that our SAF works effectively.

The rest of our paper is organized as follows. Section 2 introduces some related works about pedestrian detections and attention modules. Section 3 represents our proposed SAF and how to apply the SAF on ALFNet [11]. In Sect. 4, we perform some experiments on CityPersons dataset for evaluating effectiveness of our method. In Sect. 5, we conclude the paper.

2   Related Work

In this section, we will review some related works from the following.

Pedestrian Detection. In recent years, there are a lot of works improving pedestrian detection performance from different aspects. Zhang et al. [20] did five modifications of the Faster R-CNN and made the Faster R-CNN achieve the state of the art results on Caltech dataset [2]. Mao et al. [12] analysed how different features affect the final detection results and designed a HyperLearner combining with extra features. Zhang et al. [21] added attention mechanism to the Faster R-CNN for detecting occluded pedestrians. Lin et al. [7] designed a graininess attention mask and proposed a zoom-in-zoom-out mechanism to detect small and occluded pedestrians. Wang et al. [15] proposed the PCN network, which used part semantic information and contextual information to detect occluded pedestrians. While the above works [7,12,15,20,21] mainly focus on solving the small scale pedestrians detection and occluded pedestrians detection, our SAF is proposed for decreasing false background errors and increasing the ability of the network to distinguish pedestrians from hard background instances.

Attention Module. Some attention modules have been proposed in recent years. Hu et al. [5], Squeeze and Excitation module(SE) were proposed for reweighting channel weights of different layers and after that SE module were applied in different computer vision problems. Zhang et al. [21] chose the SE module as the network component for detecting occluded pedestrians accurately. Yu et al. [17] used the SE module for helping the network to select discriminative features for semantic segmentation. However, SE module only considered channel relationship of network layer and the spatial information of feature map was also important. Therefore, Woo et al. [16] designed convolutional block attention module(CBAM), which helped Faster-RCNN [14] to get performances improvement on MS COCO detection dataset and VOC 2007 detection dataset. In this work, CBAM [16] is chosen as our attention module and the outputs of different attention modules are fused step by step from high level layers to low level layers with the help of reverse fusion blocks for generating strong semantic features.

3   Proposed Method

We apply our proposed SAF on ALFNet [11] and the architecture of all network is shown in Fig. 2. It can be divided into three parts: Backbone Network, Semantic Attention Fusion (SAF) and Asymptotic Localization Fitting Module (ALF) [11]. Each input image is processed by the three parts sequentially to get final detection results. Backbone Network is used for extracting the convolutional features of each input image. The SAF is used for outputting strong semantic features for pedestrian detection and the ALF is used for outputting the final detection results.

3.1   Backbone Network

MobileNet [4], which has been pretrained on the ImageNet dataset, is chosen as our backbone. As shown in Fig. 2, we select feature maps from the backbone network for different scale pedestrian detections and these feature maps are named

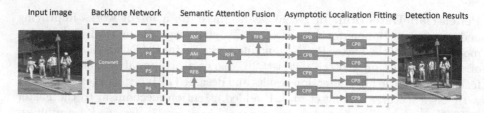

Input image   Backbone Network   Semantic Attention Fusion   Asymptotic Localization Fitting   Detection Results

Fig. 2. Illusion of the ALFNet with SAF. Each input image is firstly processed by the backbone network (Sect. 3.1). Then, the output features are processed by the semantic attention fusion (Sect. 3.2) for generating more strong semantic features. Finally, asymptotic localization fitting modules (Sect. 3.3) receive all refined features and output the final pedestrian detections.

as P3, P4, and P5, whose size are 1/8, 1/16, and 1/32 of the original input image respectively. Especially, P6 is a new added convolutional layer, which is used for making pre-trained backbone adapt pedestrian detection task [11], and acquiring high level semantic information as well as global contextual information during training stage [17].

3.2   Semantic Attention Fusion

Different from the work [21] whose attention modules are directly used for re-weighting the top features of network, in this paper, our semantic attention fusion helps the network to learn more strong semantic features via fusing features from high level layers to low level layers step by step. The diagram of the semantic attention fusion is shown in Fig. 2.

The proposed semantic attention fusion includes two key components: attention modules and reverse fusion blocks. Attention modules are used for helping the network to concentrate on more pedestrian relevant features and suppressing background object responses. Reverse fusion blocks are employed to fuse features from high level layers to low level layers step by step for generating more strong semantic features. Combining with attention modules and reverse fusion blocks, our SAF outputs features with more semantic information layer by layer. Specially, our attention modules are only attached to P3 and P4. The reason is that P3 and P4 include lots of low level object detailed features and only some of the features represent pedestrians. Therefore, attention modules help P3 and P4 to filter out irrelevant background information and pay more attention to relevant pedestrian features. P5 and P6 have owned abundant high level semantic features for pedestrian detection so it is not necessary to add attention modules after P5 and P6.

Convolutional block attention module (CBAM) [16] is chosen as the AM and its structure is shown in Fig. 3. The CBAM has two parts, channel attention module and spatial attention module. The channel attention module focuses on finding whether the feature map including pedestrians or not and the spatial attention module focuses on looking for where pedestrians are. The channel

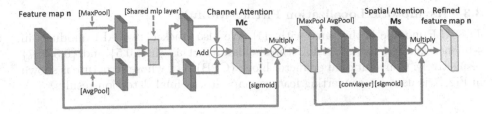

Fig. 3. Convolutional block attention module is chosen as our attention module. The feature maps are processed by the channel attention module and the spatial attention module in sequence.

attention module is followed by spatial attention module, which is the same as [16]. The attention process can be presented as follows:

$$F' = M_c(F) \otimes F$$
$$F'' = M_s(F') \otimes F' \tag{1}$$

where $\otimes$ represents element-wise multiplication. M_c is the channel attention vector generated by the channel attention module and M_s is the spatial attention vector generated by the spatial attention module. F, F' and F'' stand for original feature maps, feature maps processed by the channel attention module and feature maps processed by the CBAM module respectively.

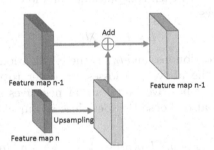

Fig. 4. The diagram of reverse fusion block. The feature map of Stage n is up-sampled to the same size of Stage n-1 and above feature maps are processed element-wise add with each other to generate new feature map for Stage n-1.

The kernel size of the spatial attention module should be set manually. We find that the detection accuracy is the best when the kernel size was set to 3. Effects of different spatial kernel size value on the final detection results will be discussed in Sect. 4.2.

Following AM, the RFB workflow is shown in Fig. 4. Feature maps of Stage n are firstly up-sampled to the same spatial size of Stage n-1. Then, the above two feature maps will do element-wise add to generate the new feature maps of Stage n-1.

3.3 Asymptotic Localization Fitting Module

The ALF module is the same with [11]. We also stacked two ALF modules in sequence and the two steps IoU thresholds are set as {0.3, 0.5} and {0.5, 0.7} respectively. Convolutional predictor block (CPB) [11], whose structure is shown in Fig. 5, is used for converting feature maps to the final detection results.

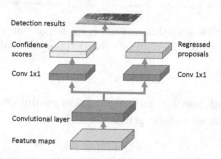

Fig. 5. The workflow of convolutional prediction block. Each feature map will be processed by the classification branch and regression branch for getting the final detection results.

3.4 Loss Functions

Being the same with [9,11], each convolutional predictor is optimized with the multi-task loss as follows:

$$L = l_{cls} + \lambda l_{loc} \qquad (2)$$

where l_{cls} is the classification loss and l_{loc} is the localization loss. λ is the weight parameter to balance the above two losses. In order to decrease the impact of imbalanced amount of positive samples and negatives samples on the final detection accuracy, we also choose the focal loss as our classification loss. The focal loss is formulated as:

$$l_{cls} = -\alpha \sum_{i \in S_+} (1 - p_i)^\gamma log(p_i) - (1 - \alpha) \sum_{i \in S_-} p_i{}^\gamma log(1 - p_i) \qquad (3)$$

where S_+ presents the samples whose IoUs with ground truth are larger than u_{high} and S_- presents the samples whose IoUs with ground truth are smaller than u_{lower}. The values of u_{high} and u_{high} are set according to the description in Sect. 3.3. Following [9], p_i stands for the likelihood of sample i to be positive. α and γ are hyper-parameters, which are set to 0.25 and 0.75 respectively.

The $smooth_{L_1}$ loss [3] is chosen as the localization loss, which is formulated as:

$$l_{loc} = \sum_{i \in x,y,w,h} smooth_{L_1}(t_i{}^u - v_i) \qquad (4)$$

$$smooth_{L_1} = \begin{cases} 0.5x^2, & if |x| < 1. \\ |x| - 0.5, & otherwise. \end{cases} \qquad (5)$$

where t^u is the predicted bounding box of pedestrian class and v is the ground truth bounding box. x and y represent the left corner location of the bounding box. w and h are the width and height of the bounding box.

4   Experiments

4.1   Experiments Setup

CityPersons dataset [20] is chosen to evaluate the performance of our proposed method. The CityPersons dataset is derived from the *Cityscapes* dataset [1], which is one of the most Challenging semantic segmentation dataset. The CityPersons dataset includes 5000 images recorded from 27 different cities. There are 35016 persons and 13172 ignore regions annotated. The CityPersons dataset is divided into training subset, validation subset and test subset, which includes 2975 images, 500 images and 1525 images respectively. MR^{-2} [20] is chosen as the evaluation metric. Data augumentation strategies are used, such as random cropping, horizontal flipping and color distortion. The Adam is chosen as our network optimizer. Less than 240k iterations of ALFNet training setting [11], our method only need 40k iterations to be convergent. The initial learning rate is set to 0.0001 and after 20k iterations the learning rate is divided by 10. All experiments is under the Ubuntu 14.04 system, with the Intel Core i5-4430, 32 G RAM and only one GTX Titan X card. In addition, all experiments are performed with the original image size, whose the width of image is 2048 and the height of image is 1024.

4.2   Ablation Studies

In this part, some experiments are performed on the validation set for analyzing the effect of different spatial kernel size of spatial attention module on the final detection accuracy. We also compare our method with ALFNet based on Mobilenet backbone [11] to prove effectiveness of our SAF.

Different Spatial Kernel Size. There is a hyper-parameter about kernel size of spatial attention module in the CBAM. To find the best value of the kernel size, we have done experiments on the validation set. The results are shown in Table 1. When the kernel size is set to 3, our method achieves the best result, no matter what different IoU thresholds are. The results of kernel size with 5 and kernel size with 1 are not better than the results of kernel size with 3, which means that too large or too small kernel size of the spatial attention module doesn't help the low layers for acquiring semantic information from the high layers. Small kernel size can't acquire enough features and large kernel size may introduce noise features, which harms the final pedestrian detection.

Table 1. Comparison of the different spatial kernel sizes under different IoU thresholds on CityPersons validation set.

Spatial kernel size	Test time	R	HO	R+HO
1	0.24 s/img	16.67	46.96	31.39
3	0.24 s/img	**16.25**	**45.12**	**29.81**
5	0.24 s/img	16.85	46.92	31.52

Semantic Attention Fusion Improvement. To validate effectiveness of our semantic attention fusion, we perform experiments on the validation set of CityPersons. The results are shown in Table 2. From Table 2, we find that when IoU threshold is equal to 0.5, the performances of ALFNet with RFB and our proposed method are lower than the original ALFNet, which decreases **1.12%** point and **0.80%** point respectively. But when IoU threshold is equal to 0.75, the results of above two methods are better than original ALFNet. Specially, our method gets a **3.55%** point gain under more restrict threshold comparing with the original ALFNet. The detection accuracy improvement can be attributed to the semantic attention fusion, which makes our network pay more attention to pedestrian relevant features.

Table 2. Semantic attention fusion improvement evaluated under different IoU thresholds on CityPersons validation set. *ALF* represents two stacked asymptotic localization fitting modules. *RFB* represents reverse fusion blocks and *SA* represents that attention modules used for semantic attention fusion.

Backbone	ALF	RFB	SA	MR^{-2}	
				IoU = 0.5	IoU = 0.75
ResNet-50 [11]				16.01	48.94
MobileNet [11]				18.88	56.26
MobileNet [11]	√			**15.45**	47.42
MobileNet	√	√		16.57	44.24
MobileNet	√	√	√	16.25	**43.87**

Meanwhile, the visualization results of different methods are shown in Fig. 6. The first row shows that original ALFNet detects instances from background, such as wall or car, as pedestrian by mistake. The detection results of ALFNet with RFB are shown in the second row and some background errors are reduced. The results of our proposed method are shown in the last row and we find that the number of background errors is the least among the above three methods. The above comparisons demonstrate the effectiveness of our semantic attention fusion and efficiency of our method in handling background errors.

Table 3. Comparison of our method with the other attention networks on CityPersons validation set. All experiments are done with the original image size of the validation set. **R** represents reasonable occlusion level. **HO** represents heavy occlusion level. **R+HO** represents occlusion level includes reasonable occlusion situation and heavy occlusion situation.

Method	Attention part	R	HO	R+HO
Faster-RCNN (VGG-16) [21]	-	15.52	64.83	41.45
Faster-RCNN (VGG-16)+ATT-self [21]	Self attention	20.93	58.33	40.83
Faster-RCNN (VGG-16)+ATT-vbb [21]	vbb supervision	16.40	57.31	39.49
Faster-RCNN (VGG-16)+ATT-part [21]	Part detections	15.96	56.66	38.23
ALFNet (MobileNet) [11]	-	**15.46**	47.40	31.11
Ours (MobileNet)	Semantic attention	16.25	**45.12**	**29.81**

Fig. 6. The visualization of detection results. The first row((a)) displays the outputs of original ALFNet [11]. The second row((b)) displays the outputs of ALFNet with RFB. The third row((c)) displays the outputs of our proposed method. The green and red rectangles represent detection results and the ground truth results respectively. (Color figure online)

4.3 Comparing with the Other Attention Networks

Our method is also compared with the other attention networks on the validation set of CityPersons. The results of different occlusion levels are shown in Table 3. Comparing with Faster-RCNN(VGG-16)+ATT-part [21], our proposed method achieves **11.54%** point improvement under heavy occlusion subset(**HO**) and **8.42%** point improvement under reasonable plus heavy occlusion subset(**R+HO**). Comparing with ALFNet [11], our method also achieve **2.28%** point and **1.30%** point improvement under **HO** subset and **R+HO** subset respectively. The above comparisons indicate two facts. On one hand, our SAF is more practical than the other attention modules because we don't need external information as attention guidance. On the other hand, the results also show that semantic attention fusion mechanism is important for pedestrian detection, especially for occluded pedestrian detection.

5   Conclusions

In this paper, we propose a semantic attention fusion mechanism for pedestrian detection. We use the convolutional block attention module as our attention module and we choose the reverse fusion block to fuse and transmit semantic information from the high layers to the low layers step by step. The above two components construct the semantic attention fusion, which makes the network own more strong semantic features for pedestrian detection. To validate our method, some experiments are performed on CityPersons dataset. The effects of different kernel sizes of the spatial attention module are compared and our proposed method achieve a 6.85% point gain than the ALFNet without the SAF under the strict IoU threshold. We also compare our method with the other attention networks on the validation set of CityPersons and our method also achieves more superior results than theirs. In the future, we can extend our semantic attention fusion mechanism to another pedestrian detectors, such as the Faster R-CNN and so on.

Acknowledgments. This work is in part supported by the National Nature Science Foundation of China (No. 61273273), by the National Key Research and Development Plan, China (No. 2017YFC0112001).

References

1. Cordts, M., et al.: The cityscapes dataset for semantic urban scene understanding. In: Proceedings of the IEEE Conference on Computer Vision and Pattern Recognition, pp. 3213–3223 (2016)
2. Dollar, P., Wojek, C., Schiele, B., Perona, P.: Pedestrian detection: an evaluation of the state of the art. IEEE Trans. Pattern Anal. Mach. Intell. **34**(4), 743–761 (2011)
3. Girshick, R.: Fast R-CNN. In: Proceedings of the IEEE International Conference on Computer Vision, pp. 1440–1448 (2015)
4. Howard, A.G., et al.: Mobilenets: Efficient convolutional neural networks for mobile vision applications. arXiv preprint arXiv:1704.04861 (2017)
5. Hu, J., Shen, L., Sun, G.: Squeeze-and-excitation networks. In: Proceedings of the IEEE Conference on Computer Vision and Pattern Recognition, pp. 7132–7141 (2018)
6. Kong, T., Sun, F., Yao, A., Liu, H., Lu, M., Chen, Y.: Ron: reverse connection with objectness prior networks for object detection. In: Proceedings of the IEEE Conference on Computer Vision and Pattern Recognition, pp. 5936–5944 (2017)

7. Lin, C., Lu, J., Wang, G., Zhou, J.: Graininess-aware deep feature learning for pedestrian detection. In: Ferrari, V., Hebert, M., Sminchisescu, C., Weiss, Y. (eds.) ECCV 2018. LNCS, vol. 11213, pp. 745–761. Springer, Cham (2018). https://doi.org/10.1007/978-3-030-01240-3_45

8. Lin, T.Y., Dollár, P., Girshick, R., He, K., Hariharan, B., Belongie, S.: Feature pyramid networks for object detection. In: Proceedings of the IEEE Conference on Computer Vision and Pattern Recognition, pp. 2117–2125 (2017)

9. Lin, T.Y., Goyal, P., Girshick, R., He, K., Dollár, P.: Focal loss for dense object detection. In: Proceedings of the IEEE International Conference on Computer Vision, pp. 2980–2988 (2017)

10. Liu, L., et al.: Deep learning for generic object detection: A survey. arXiv preprint arXiv:1809.02165 (2018)

11. Liu, W., Liao, S., Hu, W., Liang, X., Chen, X.: Learning efficient single-stage pedestrian detectors by asymptotic localization fitting. In: Ferrari, V., Hebert, M., Sminchisescu, C., Weiss, Y. (eds.) Computer Vision – ECCV 2018. LNCS, vol. 11218, pp. 643–659. Springer, Cham (2018). https://doi.org/10.1007/978-3-030-01264-9_38

12. Mao, J., Xiao, T., Jiang, Y., Cao, Z.: What can help pedestrian detection? In: Proceedings of the IEEE Conference on Computer Vision and Pattern Recognition, pp. 3127–3136 (2017)

13. Noh, J., Lee, S., Kim, B., Kim, G.: Improving occlusion and hard negative handling for single-stage pedestrian detectors. In: Proceedings of the IEEE Conference on Computer Vision and Pattern Recognition, pp. 966–974 (2018)

14. Ren, S., He, K., Girshick, R., Sun, J.: Faster R-CNN: towards real-time object detection with region proposal networks. In: Advances in Neural Information Processing Systems, pp. 91–99 (2015)

15. Wang, S., Cheng, J., Liu, H., Tang, M.: PCN: Part and context information for pedestrian detection with CNNs. arXiv preprint arXiv:1804.04483 (2018)

16. Woo, S., Park, J., Lee, J.-Y., Kweon, I.S.: CBAM: convolutional block attention module. In: Ferrari, V., Hebert, M., Sminchisescu, C., Weiss, Y. (eds.) ECCV 2018. LNCS, vol. 11211, pp. 3–19. Springer, Cham (2018). https://doi.org/10.1007/978-3-030-01234-2_1

17. Yu, C., Wang, J., Peng, C., Gao, C., Yu, G., Sang, N.: Learning a discriminative feature network for semantic segmentation. In: Proceedings of the IEEE Conference on Computer Vision and Pattern Recognition, pp. 1857–1866 (2018)

18. Zhang, L., Lin, L., Liang, X., He, K.: Is faster R-CNN doing well for pedestrian detection? In: Leibe, B., Matas, J., Sebe, N., Welling, M. (eds.) ECCV 2016. LNCS, vol. 9906, pp. 443–457. Springer, Cham (2016). https://doi.org/10.1007/978-3-319-46475-6_28

19. Zhang, S., Benenson, R., Omran, M., Hosang, J., Schiele, B.: How far are we from solving pedestrian detection? In: Proceedings of the IEEE Conference on Computer Vision and Pattern Recognition, pp. 1259–1267 (2016)

20. Zhang, S., Benenson, R., Schiele, B.: Citypersons: a diverse dataset for pedestrian detection. In: Proceedings of the IEEE Conference on Computer Vision and Pattern Recognition, pp. 3213–3221 (2017)

21. Zhang, S., Yang, J., Schiele, B.: Occluded pedestrian detection through guided attention in CNNs. In: Proceedings of the IEEE Conference on Computer Vision and Pattern Recognition, pp. 6995–7003 (2018)

Clique-Based Traffic Control Strategy Using Vehicle-To-Vehicle Communication

Lauren M. Gee$^{(\boxtimes)}$ and Mark Reynolds

The University of Western Australia, Crawley, WA 6009, Australia
lauren.gee@research.uwa.edu.au, mark.reynolds@uwa.edu.au
https://www.uwa.edu.au/ems/research

Abstract. Vehicular communication systems can be used to create more efficient traffic control systems at road intersections. This paper presents a new clique-based traffic control strategy, which uses communication between vehicles to control the flow of traffic through an intersection. A traffic simulation is used to compare the proposed strategy with existing strategies, including traditional traffic lights, and virtual traffic lights. The results show that the proposed traffic control strategy creates very efficient traffic flow, outperforming both of the existing strategies.

Keywords: Smart transportation system · Autonomous vehicle · Virtual traffic lights · Agent-based modelling

1 Introduction

The aim of this paper is to develop a decentralised controller, which improves the efficiency of traffic flow through a road network. We propose a *clique-based traffic controller*, which uses vehicle-to-vehicle communication to coordinate traffic at each intersection of the road network.

We have also developed a traffic simulation to test the proposed strategy experimentally, and compare it against two other strategies. The first strategy is traditional *traffic lights*, which uses a static cycle of changing lights to direct traffic. The second strategy is *virtual traffic lights*, proposed by Bazzi, Zanella, and Masini [2].

2 Related Work

In recent years, there has been a lot of research interest in vehicular communication systems as a platform for smart transportation systems [3,5–7,9]. Smart traffic control strategies are often based around intersections and fall into two categories: centralised approaches [4,8], with a separate controller, and decentralised approaches [1,2], relying on vehicle-to-vehicle protocols only.

Bazzi, Zanella, and Mansini's *virtual traffic lights* algorithm [2] is the state of the art for decentralised traffic control strategies. In an intersection controlled

A. C. Nayak and A. Sharma (Eds.): PRICAI 2019, LNAI 11671, pp. 534–538, 2019.
https://doi.org/10.1007/978-3-030-29911-8_41

by *virtual traffic lights*, queues of cars will take turns crossing the intersection, similar to traditional traffic lights. However, rather than using physical traffic lights, the intersection is controlled by messages sent between cars using wireless vehicle-to-vehicle communication.

3 Methodology

The simulation consists of a network of roads and intersections on a two dimensional plane. Cars drive around the road network, with some simple car physics to determine how they move. Each car is controlled by an intelligent agent[1] (Fig. 1).

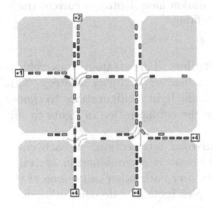

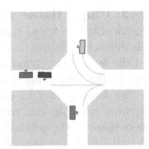

Fig. 1. Traffic simulation using a generated road network.

Fig. 2. Traffic simulation using *traffic lights* controller. None of the cars are crossing because the green light is active for an empty lane. (Color figure online)

3.1 Traffic Control Strategies

Strategy 1: Traffic Lights. For this strategy, each intersection in the scenario runs a repeating cycle of traffic lights. The queues of cars around the intersection take turns being active. The active queue receives a green light signal for n seconds, then an amber light signal for 1 s, and then a red light for 1 s. All inactive queues receive a red light signal while they wait their turn (Fig. 2).

Strategy 2: Virtual Traffic Lights. Bazzi et al. [2]'s *virtual traffic lights* algorithm was implemented for this strategy. In this strategy, a green light token is passed between cars, and holding this token indicates that the car has permission to cross. The green light token starts at the leader of a queue of cars, and is passed backwards along the queue for n steps, before it is passed to the leader of the next queue. Read their paper for more details on how their algorithm works (Fig. 3).

---

[1] Link to code: https://github.com/nightglyde/traffic-simulation.

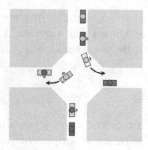
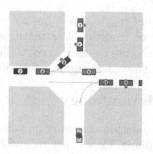

Fig. 3. Traffic simulation using *virtual traffic lights* controller. Cars with green circles have permission to cross the intersection. (Color figure online)

Fig. 4. Traffic simulation using *clique-based traffic controller*. Traffic light configuration has adapted to current traffic conditions.

Strategy 3: Clique-Based Traffic Controller. This strategy uses vehicular communication systems, similar to the *virtual traffic lights* strategy. This strategy is different because there are many traffic light configurations to choose from, and the leader can dynamically change the configuration of lights to suit the current traffic conditions (Fig. 4).

There are twelve ways of crossing a four-road intersection, as each entry road has three possible exit roads. A valid clique is a combination of traffic lights where none of the activated paths cross over each other, and none of the activated paths have the same exit. Valid cliques indicate safe combinations of lights, where the cars cannot crash into each other.

Rules: Cars waiting at an intersection vote to decide who the leader is. The elected leader will control the intersection until they leave, or are voted out and replaced. A car will cross if the leader sends them a green light message.

Voting strategy: Vote for whoever has the most votes. If there is a tie, vote for the car with the lexicographically smallest name. If there are no votes, vote for yourself.

Leadership strategy: Give each queue of cars a priority, based on how long the cars have been driving; the queue containing the car that has been driving longest is given first priority. Iterate through each of the queues in order of priority, checking if the car at the front of the queue is allowed to cross. A car is only allowed to cross if adding that car's path would result in a valid clique; otherwise, that car will have to wait. If the car is allowed to cross, send a green light message to that car and add its path to the current traffic light configuration.

The *clique-based traffic controller* was implemented so that voting and leadership strategies could easily be swapped out for more complex strategies. However, for our purposes, only simple deterministic strategies were used.

3.2   Experimental Methodology

Each trial of the experiment involves a randomly generated schedule of cars, representing one hour of traffic with a given traffic density. Each car in the schedule is given a start time and an intended route through the road network. To ensure that the different traffic control strategies are tested under the same conditions, the same test data is used for each strategy.

4   Results and Discussion

Figure 5 shows how traffic density affects traffic flow for each of the traffic control strategies. In general, average journey duration increases with traffic density; if there are more cars on the road, each car spends more time waiting at intersections and waiting behind other cars, which increases journey duration. The results show that the *clique-based traffic controller* and *virtual traffic lights* have significantly lower mean journey durations, compared to the more traditional *traffic lights*. This suggests that their use of vehicular communication systems cuts down on wait time, creating more efficient traffic flow. The *clique-based traffic controller* had the lowest mean journey duration: its ability to micromanage and adapt to changing conditions gives it an advantage over *virtual traffic lights*.

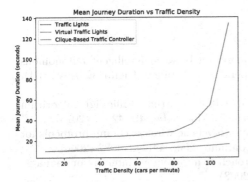

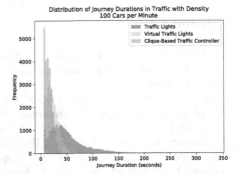

Fig. 5. Mean journey duration for each traffic control strategy, over a range of traffic densities. The results shown are the average of five trials.

Fig. 6. Distribution of journey durations for each traffic control strategy, in test scenarios with a traffic density of 100 cars per minute. Ten trials are included.

However, it is not enough for a strategy to be more efficient on average; there is a risk that a strategy might benefit the majority, but leave some cars waiting a lot longer than others. Figure 6 shows the distribution of journey durations for test cases with a particular traffic density, in this case 100 cars per minute. For each strategy, the distribution of cars' journey durations is shaped like a normal distribution. This indicates that most cars have a journey duration similar to the average journey duration. The distribution for the *clique-based traffic controller* has the lowest mean and variance, while the distribution for *traffic lights* has the highest mean and variance. This suggests that more efficient traffic control strategies lead to less variance in journey durations, and benefits all cars.

5   Conclusion and Future Work

We developed a decentralised traffic control strategy, and compared it against some other strategies. The results show that the *clique-based traffic controller* is a very efficient traffic control strategy, outperforming both the traditional *traffic lights*, and *virtual traffic lights*.

The simulation presents a simplified version of reality, limiting the reliability of these findings. In real life, road networks contain many different types of roads and intersections, arranged in many ways. Also, roads are affected by weather and time of day, different types of vehicles, pedestrians and cyclists, and unexpected hazards. Further work is needed to generalise the *clique-based traffic controller* for different road conditions.

We also need to consider the possible ramifications of vehicular communication systems. In real life, there are limitations on how quickly and accurately cars can communicate over a wireless network. Also, rogue vehicles could spoof the network, send erroneous messages, or simply refuse to follow the rules. Additionally, the cars' on-board controllers must be protected against cyber threats.

References

1. Bahnes, N., Kechar, B., Haffaf, H.: Cooperation between intelligent autonomous vehicles to enhance container terminal operations. J. Innov. Digital Ecosyst. **3**(1), 22–29 (2016)
2. Bazzi, A., Zanella, A., Masini, B.M.: A distributed virtual traffic light algorithm exploiting short range v2v communications. Ad Hoc Netw. **49**, 42–57 (2016)
3. Biswas, S., Tatchikou, R., Dion, F.: Vehicle-to-vehicle wireless comm. protocols for enhancing highway traffic safety. IEEE Commun. Mag. **44**(1), 74–82 (2006)
4. Dresner, K., Stone, P.: A multiagent approach to autonomous intersection management. J. Artif. Intell. Res. **31**, 591–656 (2008)
5. Papadimitratos, P., De La Fortelle, A., Evenssen, K., Brignolo, R., Cosenza, S.: Vehicular communication systems: enabling technologies, applications, and future outlook on intelligent transportation. IEEE Commun. Mag. **47**(11), 84–95 (2009)
6. Petrov, T., Dado, M., Ambrosch, K.E.: Computer modelling of cooperative intelligent transportation systems. Procedia Eng. **192**, 683–688 (2017)
7. Sommer, C., Joerer, S., Segata, M., Tonguz, O.K., Cigno, R.L., Dressler, F.: How shadowing hurts vehicular communications and how dynamic beaconing can help. IEEE Trans. Mobile Comput. **14**(7), 1411–1421 (2015)
8. Tachet, R., et al.: Revisiting street intersections using slot-based systems. PLoS ONE **11**(3), e0149607 (2016)
9. Yang, X., Liu, L., Vaidya, N.H., Zhao, F.: A vehicle-to-vehicle communication protocol for cooperative collision warning. In: The First Annual International Conference on Mobile and Ubiquitous Systems: Networking and Services 2004. MOBIQUITOUS 2004, pp. 114–123. IEEE (2004)

Social and Information Networks

Multi-type Relational Data Clustering for Community Detection by Exploiting Content and Structure Information in Social Networks

Tennakoon Mudiyanselage Gayani Tennakoon[1(✉)], Khanh Luong[1],
Wathsala Mohotti[1], Sharma Chakravarthy[2], and Richi Nayak[1]

[1] Queensland University of Technology, 2 George Street, Brisbane, Australia
{gayani.mudiyanselage,khanh.luong,
wathsalaanupama.mohotti}@hdr.qut.edu.au, r.nayak@qut.edu.au
[2] University of Texas at Arlington, 701 S Nedderman Dr, Arlington, TX 76019, USA
sharma@cse.uta.edu

Abstract. Social Networks popularity has facilitated the providers with an opportunity to target specific user groups for various applications such as viral marketing and customized programs. However, the volume and variety of data present in a network challenge the identification of user communities effectively. The sparseness and heterogeneity in a network make it difficult to group the users with similar interests whereas the high dimensionality and sparseness in text pose difficulty in finding content focused groups. We present this problem of discovering user communities with common interests as the multi-type relational data (MTRD) learning with the content and structural information, and propose a novel solution based on non-negative matrix factorization with added regularization. We empirically evaluate the effectiveness of the proposed method on real-world Twitter datasets benchmarking with the state-of-the-art community discovery and clustering methods.

Keywords: Twitter · Community discovery ·
Multi-type relational data clustering · NMF ·
Non-negative matrix factorization · Social media

1 Introduction

Social networks such as Twitter have become a popular source of sharing information and opinions. A large volume of data is continuously generated on these networks that create many opportunities for political parties, businesses, and government organizations to target certain audience groups for their campaigns, marketing strategies, and customized programs and events. Community discovery is a well-studied research problem that can facilitate these applications. A large proportion of this research has been focused on using graph models which

A. C. Nayak and A. Sharma (Eds.): PRICAI 2019, LNAI 11671, pp. 541–554, 2019.
https://doi.org/10.1007/978-3-030-29911-8_42

represent *how* users are connected [3,7,24]. However, these structure-based community discovery methods have shown to be ineffective in identifying the users with similar interests due to the network sparseness and heterogeneity. On the contrary, clustering users based on *what* content they share [10,21] allows identifying the user communities that reflect in written media posts. However, these short texts are noisy and extremely sparse. Consequently, these content-based community detection methods produce inferior outcomes due to the curse of dimensionality [9].

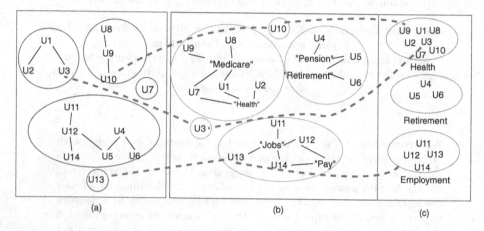

(a)   (b)   (c)

Fig. 1. An example of (a) structure-based, (b) content-based, and (c) structure and content based communities

In this paper, we conjecture that exploiting both the structure and content information effectively to identify user groups will achieve accurate solution. As shown in Fig. 1, due to the sparseness and noise, it is challenging to decide the communities of some users (e.g., $U13$ and $U3$) using a single type of input only. However, utilizing both structure and content together can produce more accurate results. A naive approach will be to concatenate all this information into a single feature matrix and apply clustering [25,26]. Clustering on the concatenated data can embed all available information from all types into the learning process. However, this process usually results in poor outcomes as it ignores the inter-relatedness between sample objects and different feature objects, or between the sample objects, or between the feature object types [16,30]. We present the community discovery problem as the multi-type relational data (MTRD) learning, which simultaneously groups all data object types (e.g., users, tweets, etc.) considering all possible relationships existing between objects.

Community discovery in multiplex networks [20,29] is one of the related research areas which tries to identify communities using heterogeneous user relationships (e.g. friend, colleague). However, these methods do not take noisy and high dimensional text data as input which makes the community discovery process more challenging and complex. Some community discovery methods [1,22,23] discover groups of users by taking both content and structure into the learning process. However they require label information or impose many constraints. We propose a novel approach based on non-negative matrix factorization (NMF) in the unsupervised MTRD learning framework, named as Multi-Type Community Discovery (MTCD). We propose the MTRD learning with the added regularization to ensure that the global structure is preserved in the learned low-rank representations, i.e., two users who are similar (or dissimilar) in the original data should be kept close (or far) in the new low-dimensional space [17]. We empirically evaluate MTCD using three real-world Twitter datasets and benchmark with the state-of-the-art community discovery and clustering methods. The empirical analysis shows that MTCD can handle sparse datasets (both structural and content wise) and produce more accurate clusters than the benchmark methods. We also explore the different data representation and integration approaches and how they affect the outcome.

2 Related Work

Community discovery is a popular research problem which facilitates several real-world applications. In this paper, we propose to combine the structural relationship among users with the content similarity to generate meaningful user groups. With this objective, we categorize the related work as (1) Single-type and (2) Multi-type methods.

2.1 Single-Type Data Methods

Researchers have predominately focused on exploiting graph models, derived from structural (user-user relationship) information, to form communities [3, 7,24]. These methods are based on the theories behind network formation or system behavior which highlight *how* users are connected. However, in a sparse network, there can be many disconnected user groups interested in the same topic. Unfortunately, these structure-based methods identify these groups as distinct. Moreover, in a heterogeneous social network, user links are formed by different types of connections, e.g., being friends, relatives or colleagues, which lead to identifying user groups with mixed interests.

A very few researchers have analyzed the media content similarity to group common users [10,21]. The traditional text analytic methods based on distance, density or probability face difficulties due to the noise and extreme sparseness of short text media data [19]. These methods result in poor outcome due to negligible distance differences in higher dimensionality [11] or information loss in lower dimensional projection [19].

In this paper, we propose to overcome these issues faced by using the structure or content data alone by combining these multiple types of data and finding the latent relationships among users.

2.2   Multi-type Data Methods

Multiplex Network Methods: In recent years, multiplex networks have been used to represent different relationships between the same set of users in a multi-layer network and various methods have been proposed for community discovery [20,29]. Although these methods can handle the heterogeneity of networks, the sparseness issue remains unsolved. Moreover, multiplex networks focus on representing different types of relationships among the same type of objects (ex. user-user). They ignore the relationships among different types of objects (ex. user-hashtag, user-term) that are significant for grouping users based on similar interest. Although it is possible to transform user-term relationships into a user-user relationship and derive multi-layer networks, the transformation process is time-consuming and looses some useful information in the process.

MTRD-Clustering Methods: Due to the easy availability of MTRD data such as in computer vision, bio-informatics, web-based system, a new area of multi-type relational data (MTRD) clustering has emerged [16,18,30]. These methods incorporate relationships between objects of different object types in the process. Object types can be data sample or different data features. MTRD methods based on non-negative matrix factorization (NMF) framework have known to produce effective result when dealing with high dimensional and sparse data [17]. In this paper, we deem the community discovery problem as MTRD clustering and propose to simultaneously groups users by exploiting relatedness using both the content and structure information inherent in social media data. Prior researchers have used the NMF framework (but not in MTRD setting) to combine content and structure information [1,22,23]. Unfortunately, methods in [1,23] require the community label information to learn the commonality amongst users. Method in [22] is unsupervised; however, it imposes many constraints as well as it requires many factor matrices to update. Imposing many constraints can help in achieving a meaningful solution but it makes the learning process too complex and time consuming. It may also bring adverse effect to the learning process if coefficients are not set correctly. To the best of our knowledge, there exists no effective MTRD based community mining method.

3   Multi-type Relational Data Learning for Community Discovery (MTCD)

3.1   MTCD: Problem Definition

Suppose $\mathcal{D} = \{X_1, X_2, ..., X_m\}$ be a MTRD dataset with m data types where X_h denotes the h-th data type. Examples of data types in Twitter dataset can be retweet, reply, mention, tweet text, hash tags and URLs. Suppose $\{R_{hl} \in \mathbb{R}_+\}$ is a set of pairwise relationship matrices where $R_{hl} = \{r_{ij}\}^{n_h \times n_l}$, r_{ij} denotes the relationship (e.g., the tf-idf weight of a term in a tweet) between i-th object and j-th object of X_h and X_l respectively, $R_{lh}^T = R_{hl}$.

The task in this paper is to simultaneously group m object types into c clusters by considering the relationships between objects of different types in the dataset. The NMF-based objective function for MTRD can be written as [16,30],

$$J = \min \sum_{1 \leq h < l \leq m} \|R_{hl} - G_h S_{hl} G_l^T\|_F^2, G_h \geq 0, G_l \geq 0 \qquad (1)$$

where $\|.\|_F$ denotes the Frobenius norm and $G_h \in \mathbb{R}_+^{n_h \times c}$ and $G_l \in \mathbb{R}_+^{n_l \times c}$ are low-rank representations of object types X_h and X_l, respectively. Since G_h and G_l are being simultaneously optimized to be the low-rank representations of object types X_h and X_l, S_{hl} plays the role of a trade-off matrix that provides additional degree of freedom for the factorizing process [6].

The objective function in Eq. (1) will simultaneously learn the low-rank representations of sample object type and all feature object types. As reported in many high-order co-clustering methods [5,12], the process of clustering of sample objects is benefited by using information of clusters of feature objects. Due to simultaneously learning the factor matrices of all feature object types and the sample object type during the learning process, the objective function creates an effective learning process for learning the meaningful sample object clustering. The new low-rank representations are able to capture the cluster structures of all object types.

This objective function incorporates all inter type relationships between the users and other types such as content they post. In social networking sites, there also exist many relationships between users, showing how they are connected. These relationships will return in symmetric input data matrices. Directly applying the objective function in Eq. (1), designed for an asymmetric matrix, will lead to impractical results. Therefore, we propose to add the second term to deal with the symmetric data matrices [13]. These two terms will learn the inter and intra multi-relationships present in the data respectively. However, prior research has shown that the NMF framework may need to include manifold learning to guide the learning process so that the global structure of the data remain preserved in the learned low-rank presentation [17].

In order to have accurate communities, we propose to implement the manifold learning by including an affinity matrix that will help in preserving the global structure for the learned low-rank representations, i.e., two users who are similar (or dissimilar) in the original data should be kept close (or far) in the new low-dimensional space. A third term is added in Eq. (1) to indicate this. Finally, we propose to add the pseudo-orthogonal constraints on factor matrices $(G_h^T D_h G_h = I)$ that has shown to force the factor matrices to learn the optimal solution by learning the association among clusters of different object types [17]. The novel objective function for community discovery problem can be defined as follows:

$J = \min$

$$\sum_{1 \leq h < l \leq m} \|R_{hl} - G_h S_{hl} G_l^T\|_F^2 + \sum_{h=1..m, i=1..q} \|R_{hi} - G_h G_h^T\|_F^2 - \sum_{h=1}^m Tr(G_h^T W_h G_h), \quad (2)$$

s.t., $G_h \geq 0, G_l \geq 0, S_{hl} \geq 0, G_h^T D_h G_h = I$

Including the second term, the objective function learns that there exists q symmetric data matrices between members of object type h, corresponding to different q extents. Note that q can be zero when there exists no symmetric data matrix in the problem. The third term will ensure all the important distances of data in the original space will be maintained in the new low-dimensional space. W_h is the affinity matrix built by using both the k nearest neighbour (kNN) and p farthest neighbour (pFN) graph with the purpose of encoding both close and far distance information [17], D_h is the diagonal matrix, $(D_h)_{ii} = \sum_j (W_h)_{ij}$.

3.2   Proposed Solution

We provide the solution for the objective function in Eq. (2) with respect to S_{hl}, G_h, G_l. We use multiplicative update rule [14] where each variable will be separately updated while fixing others as constants until converged [8,15,30].

1. *Update rule for S_{hl}:* When fixing h, l and tHus fixing G_h, G_l, Eq. (2) is reduced to minimizing

$$J_{S_{hl}} = \left\| R_{hl} - G_h S_{hl} G_l^T \right\|_F^2, \ S_{hl} \geq 0 \quad (3)$$

By setting the derivative of $J_{S_{hl}}$ to be zero and using the condition for non-negative constraint [6], we have the update rule for S_{hl},

$$S_{hl} = (S_{hl})_{ij} \left[\frac{(G_h^T R_{hl} G_l)_{ij}}{(G_h^T G_h S_{hl} G_l^T G_l)_{ij}} \right]^{1/2} \quad (4)$$

2. *Update rule for G_h, G_l:* When fixing h, fixing $S_{hl}, G_l, h < l \leq m$, fixing $S_{lh}, G_l, 1 \leq l < h$, optimizing Eq. (2) with respect to G_h is equivalent to optimizing the following,

$$J_{G_h} = \sum_{h < l \leq m} \left\| R_{hl} - G_h S_{hl} G_l^T \right\|_F^2 + \sum_{1 \leq l < h} \left\| R_{lh} - G_l S_{lh} G_h^T \right\|_F^2$$

$$+ \sum_{1 \leq i < q} \left\| R_{hi} - G_h G_h^T \right\|_F^2 - Tr(G_h^T W_h G_h) \quad (5)$$

$$G_h \geq 0, G_h^T D_h G_h = I,$$

With the pseudo-orthogonal constraint $G_h^T D_h G_h = I$, we introduce the Lagrangian multiplier. We take the first deviation on the Lagrangian function before using the Karush-Kuhn-Tucker (KKT) condition [4] for the non-negative constraint $G_h \geq 0$ to infer the update rule for G_h as well as for G_l [17].

4   Empirical Analysis

We used three Twitter datasets obtained from TrISMA[1] focusing on Cancer, Health and Sports domains as reported in Table 1. We have chosen the set of groups under a domain where we can identify Twitter accounts to collect posts and interaction information. Each group in each domain is considered as the ground-truth community to benchmark the algorithmic outcome. For all the datasets, the user interaction networks are very sparse as shown by low-density values in Table 1. The conductance metric measures the fraction of total edge strength that points outside the ground truth communities. The conductance values of these datasets show the existence of different levels of inter-community interactions where sports and health datasets report the lowest and highest values respectively.

Table 1. Dataset description

Dataset	U	I	N	C	Tw	Te	Co
DS1: Cancer	1585	1174	0.0005	0.152	8260	2975	8
DS2: Health	2073	2191	0.0005	0.274	19758	5444	6
DS3: Sports	5531	19699	0.0006	0.098	12044	3558	6

U: #Users, I: #Interactions, N: Network density
C: Conductance, Tw: #Tweets, Te: #Terms
Co: #Communities

A clustering solution (or community) is evaluated by the standard pairwise F1-score which calculates the harmonic average of precision and recall, and Normalized Mutual Information (NMI) which measures the purity against the number of clusters [28].

The empirical analysis was carried out with two objectives; (1) Identify an effective data representations for the proposed MTCD method and (2) Evaluate the effectiveness of MTCD by benchmarking the state-of-the-art community discovery and clustering methods.

4.1   Identify the Effective Data Representation

In social media, two users can be similar based on their follower/friendship network or/and based on the people they interact and the content they share.

---

[1] https://trisma.org/.

The follower/friendship network is an outcome of heterogeneous relationships such as family, friend, colleague or fan. This network cannot be considered as a strong input for discovering communities based on common interests as it could yield communities with mixed interests. Moreover, extracting a complete follower/friendship network is a difficult task because of the data unavailability. Therefore in this paper, we propose to utilize the relationship between users with regard to their interactions as the structural input and the relationship between the user and media posts as the content input.

Interaction-Centric Relationships. In social media, users can interact with each other in many ways such as sharing others' posts, replying to other messages and mentioning others within their posts. We use three types of Twitter interactions and explore how these interactions should be represented as structural input in MTCD. For each pair of users, we count the total number of interactions between them and derive the relationship matrices R_{urt}, R_{ure}, R_{umt} and R_{us} which represent retweets, replies, mentions and combination respectively. The combined R_{us} matrix is created as follows,

$$R_{us(ij)} = R_{urt(ij)} + R_{ure(ij)} + R_{umt(ij)} \tag{6}$$

where $R_{urt(ij)}$, $R_{ure(ij)}$ and $R_{umt(ij)}$ are the number of times users i and j retweet each others posts, reply to each other and mention each other respectively. R_{us} represents the relationships between objects of the same type, i.e., between users, covering the different types of interactions between users. R_{us} becomes the defined symmetric matrix R_{hi} in the proposed model in Eq. (2).

We test these different types of structural data to determine the effective structural representation in the NMF framework. Figure 2(a) shows that the accuracy of NMF based clustering (measured as NMI) is highest with the combined interaction matrix (R_{us}). These results ascertain that all these interaction types indicate a similar community membership which makes the combination more effective. Therefore, we use the combined relationship matrix as the structural input to MTRD learning.

Content-Centric Relationships. We consider three kinds of Twitter content information for a user: text, hashtags, and URLs. Due to the post length restriction and high dimensionality, social media text are short in length and sparse in nature respectively [9]. Additionally, the external information (i.e., hashtags and URLs) in social media and unstructured phrases in text create new challenges in data representation for clustering purpose [9]. We use the standard pre-processing steps of stop words removal and lemmatizing for the text content. In order to deal with the unstructured nature and presence of abbreviations, we used a dictionary-based slang removal and word standardization.

The user-Hashtag R_{uh} and user-URL R_{ul} matrices are generated based on the count-based Bag-of-Words (bow) model (binary weighting scheme) as this information is rarely present. To represent the text content in media posts, the user-term matrix R_{ut} is generated with different term weighting schemes such as bow, term frequency *(tf)*, inverse document frequency *(idf)* and *(tf*idf)* [27].

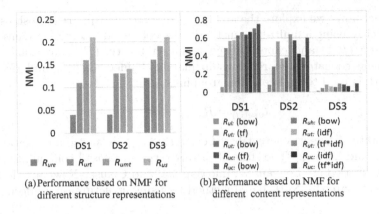

(a) Performance based on NMF for different structure representations

(b) Performance based on NMF for different content representations

Fig. 2. Performance based on NMF for different representations

To explore the effectiveness of combining content in a media post all the terms, urls and hash tags are considered as general terms and the user-content matrix R_{uc} is created as follows,

$$R_{uc(ij)} = w_{ij} \qquad (7)$$

where w_{ij} represents the weight of ith user having the jth term. This value can be represented using different weighting schemes such as bow, tf, idf and tf*idf. All these representations are tested in order to identify the best representation for MTCD. The R_{uc} matrix can be considered as the inter-relationship between user and content as denoted by R_{hl} in the proposed model in Eq. (2).

Figure 2(b) presents the accuracy of NMF based clustering (measured as NMI) with these different content representations. The *(tf*idf)* weighting scheme gives best NMI and makes the combined content representation R_{uc} represented with *(tf*idf)* as the best candidate to represent content relationship. This confirms the capacity of *(tf*idf)* in assigning high weight to discriminative words in a document.

4.2 Evaluate the Effectiveness of MTCD

Benchmarks. We extensively benchmark MTCD with methods that can utilise both structure and content information, as well as methods that can utilise either structure or content only information. For the immediate comparison, we compare with the traditional MTRD-NMF [30] method as well as the state-of-the-art multiplex network methods GenLouvain [20] and PMM [29]. These two multiplex network methods however only accept the symmetric user-user relationships as input. In order to represent content relationship (i.e., user-content matrix) which is not symmetric with the symmetric interaction relationship (i.e.,user-user matrix), we construct a user-user matrix from R_{uc}. This matrix R'_{uc} takes the number of overlapping terms between user i and user j using the respective vectors of users.

$$R'_{uc(ij)} = \sum (R_{uc(i)} \cap R_{uc(j)}) \qquad (8)$$

Furthermore, we explore the ability to combine multiple relationships without explicitly using a multi-type method. The combined interaction relationship information (R_{us}) and content-based user-user matrix (R'_{uc}) are combined to get a single concatenated relationship matrix defined as R_{usc} and the NMF framework is used to find common groupings.

$$R_{usc(ij)} = R_{us(ij)} + R'_{uc(ij)} \tag{9}$$

The state-of-the-art content-based clustering methods used are k-means [11], NMF [14] and LDA [2]. The state-of-the-art structure-based community discovery methods used are Louvain [3], InfoMap [24] and Clauset-Newman-Moore [7]. We also compare the NMF based method by using structure only information.

Accuracy Analysis. Results in Table 2 confirm that the proposed MTCD method is able to learn the most accurate and meaningful user communities. MTCD outperforms MTRD-NMF due to the inclusion of both the association relationship learning and the complete geometric structure learning. The performance gap is significant in DS2 where both content and structure representation is sparse as shown in Table 1. This confirms the suitability of MTCD in dealing with sparse multi-type data. It indicates that, for the heterogeneous dataset such as Twitter, the embedded regularizations used in MTCD with NMF help to obtain the improved outcome. It can be noted that both MTCD and MTRD-NMF methods perform substantially better than the conventional NMF (except NMF content only). Since MTRD methods discover user communities by considering the relationships of users with other feature object types, i.e., interaction and content, they achieve more accurate user groups. Though NMF on concatenated R_{usc} matrix considers all related information in the learning process, yet it is unable to learn the latent features in both object types within the higher dimensional matrix. Thus it fails to bring a satisfactory result. Although the multiplex network based GenLouvain method outperforms single type-structure based methods most of the time, it produces inferior results to both MTCD and MTRD-NMF methods, showing its ineffectiveness in handling sparse and high dimensional text data.

Within the content only methods, NMF which forms groups by factoring sparse matrix into lower dimension performs better than the centroid-based partitional (k-means) and generative probabilistic (LDA) clustering methods. Due to the nature of social media, this (short text) data presents extreme sparseness and results in much higher dimensional term vectors with less term co-occurrence where distance calculations in partitional methods, as well as probability calculation in probabilistic methods, are not able to succeed.

Structure-based methods are unable to outperform MTCD except in DS3 where the number of inter-community interactions is comparably high as indicated by the conductance value. Mostly, MTCD outperforms single-type content and structure-based methods by complimenting information given by each other. In DS3, as shown by the very poor performance of single-type content methods,

Table 2. Performance comparison of different community discovery methods

Method	Complexity	DS1		DS2		DS3	
		NMI	F1	NMI	F1	NMI	F1
Multi type - content and structure							
MTCD # (R_{us} and R_{uc})	$O(vn^2)$	**0.79**	**0.79**	**0.76**	**0.83**	**0.31**	**0.41**
MTRD-NMF # (R_{us} and R_{uc})	$O(vn^2)$	0.67	0.69	0.37	0.45	0.27	0.39
NMF # (R_{usc})	$O(n^2)$	0.34	0.42	0.27	0.41	0.03	0.33
GenLouvain (R_{us} and R'_{uc})	$O(nlogn)$	0.52	0.50	0.46	0.62	0.48	0.53
PMM (R_{us} and R'_{uc})	$O(n^3)$	0.26	0.38	0.18	0.33	0.14	0.37
Single type - content							
k-means # (R_{uc})	$O(n^{dk})$	0.72	0.74	0.50	0.59	0.07	0.36
LDA* (R_{uc})	$O(nd^2)$	0.41	0.47	0.38	0.60	0.0	0.32
NMF# (R_{uc})	$O(n^2)$	0.76	0.79	0.60	0.69	0.09	0.37
Single type - structure							
NMF (R_{us})	$O(n^2)$	0.21	0.38	0.14	0.44	0.39	0.52
Louvain (R_{us})	$O(nlogn)$	0.32	0.40	0.24	0.40	0.44	0.49
InfoMap (R_{us})	$O(nlog^2 n)$	0.32	0.40	0.26	0.43	0.45	0.47
Clauset-Newman-Moore (R_{us})	$O(m)$	0.32	0.42	0.25	0.43	0.53	0.58

Notes: # and * represent the methods with inputs as tf-idf and bow representations
n: *number of users,* d: *number of features in a term matrix*
m: *number of edges in the network,* k: *number of communities,* v: *number of types*
The matrix(s) input to each method is given within the parentheses.

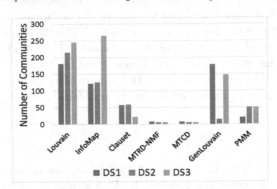

Fig. 3. Number of communities detected in different community discovery methods

they could not complement the structural information in community discovery process and MTCD results in inferior performance than structure only methods.

Nevertheless, the structure-methods give a low-level picture of the network structure. As shown in Fig. 3, when the network is sparse these methods generate a high number of communities, and they are not suitable for identifying high-level user communities with common interests. On the other hand, MTRD and other content based methods were able to identify the smaller number of communities as per ground-truth. These content-based methods show better performance in identifying communities with comparably dense content representations. The proposed MTCD shows the capability of balancing the effects of content and structure, and able to form meaningful communities in datasets where both structure and content are sparse.

Computational Complexity. Results in complexity column of Table 2 show that all the NMF related methods have $O(n^2)$ complexity or its' linear multiplication including MTCD. These are lesser complex than k-means and LDA clustering. In comparison, structure-based community discovery methods have less computational complexity. However, trade-off by achieving higher accuracy in terms of F1-score and NMI with MTCD as in Table 2 is well-justified for datasets with higher sparsity.

5   Conclusion and Future Work

In this paper, we present a novel approach of NMF-based MTRD learning to identify communities using both the structural and content information inherent in social media networks. This paper explores how the various types of information present on social media including media post as well as user interaction can be combined and included in the community discovery process. The proposed approach is evaluated on three Twitter datasets and benchmarked with several state-of-the-art methods. The experiment results show the importance of considering the community discovery problem in the heterogeneous context and learn it as multi-relational model, in order to achieve the accurate community groups and understand the behavior among user groups. The user-user relationship is considered as a special relationship in the proposed MTRD model. However, this important relationship should be paid more attention to obtain a more understanding. In the future, we will explore the applicability of MTRD learning for solving the overlapping community discovery problem.

References

1. Akbari, M., Chua, T.S.: Leveraging behavioral factorization and prior knowledge for community discovery and profiling. In: Proceedings of the Tenth ACM International Conference on Web Search and Data Mining, pp. 71–79. ACM (2017)
2. Blei, D.M., Ng, A.Y., Jordan, M.I.: Latent dirichlet allocation. J. Mach. Learn. Res. **3**(Jan), 993–1022 (2003)
3. Blondel, V.D., Guillaume, J.L., Lambiotte, R., Lefebvre, E.: Fast unfolding of communities in large networks. J. Stat. Mech.: Theory Exp. **2008**(10), P10008 (2008)
4. Boyd, S., Vandenberghe, L.: Convex Optimization. Cambridge University Press, Cambridge (2004)
5. Dhillon, I.S.: Co-clustering documents and words using bipartite spectral graph partitioning. In: Proceedings of the Seventh ACM SIGKDD International Conference on Knowledge Discovery and Data Mining, pp. 269–274. ACM (2001)

6. Ding, C., Li, T., Peng, W., Park, H.: Orthogonal nonnegative matrix t-factorizations for clustering. In: Proceedings of the 12th ACM SIGKDD International Conference on Knowledge Discovery and Data Mining, pp. 126–135. ACM (2006)
7. Girvan, M., Newman, M.E.: Community structure in social and biological networks. Proc. Natl. Acad. Sci. **99**(12), 7821–7826 (2002)
8. Gu, Q., Zhou, J.: Co-clustering on manifolds. In: Proceedings of the 15th ACM SIGKDD International Conference on Knowledge Discovery and Data Mining, pp. 359–368. ACM (2009)
9. Hu, X., Liu, H.: Text analytics in social media. In: Aggarwal, C., Zhai, C. (eds.) Mining text Data, pp. 385–414. Springer, Boston (2012). https://doi.org/10.1007/978-1-4614-3223-4_12
10. Iyer, R., Wong, J., Tavanapong, W., Peterson, D.A.: Identifying policy agenda sub-topics in political tweets based on community detection. In: Proceedings of the 2017 IEEE/ACM International Conference on Advances in Social Networks Analysis and Mining 2017, pp. 698–705. ACM (2017)
11. Jain, A.K.: Data clustering: 50 years beyond K-means. Pattern Recogn. Lett. **31**(8), 651–666 (2010)
12. Jing, L., Yun, J., Yu, J., Huang, J.: High-order co-clustering text data on semantics-based representation model. In: Huang, J.Z., Cao, L., Srivastava, J. (eds.) PAKDD 2011. LNCS (LNAI), vol. 6634, pp. 171–182. Springer, Heidelberg (2011). https://doi.org/10.1007/978-3-642-20841-6_15
13. Kuang, D., Ding, C., Park, H.: Symmetric nonnegative matrix factorization for graph clustering. In: Proceedings of the 2012 SIAM International Conference on Data Mining, pp. 106–117. SIAM (2012)
14. Lee, D.D., Seung, H.S.: Algorithms for non-negative matrix factorization. In: Advances in Neural Information Processing Systems, pp. 556–562 (2001)
15. Li, P., Bu, J., Chen, C., He, Z.: Relational co-clustering via manifold ensemble learning. In: Proceedings of the 21st ACM International Conference on Information and Knowledge Management, pp. 1687–1691. ACM (2012)
16. Long, B., Zhang, Z.M., Wu, X., Yu, P.S.: Spectral clustering for multi-type relational data. In: Proceedings of the 23rd International Conference on Machine Learning, pp. 585–592. ACM (2006)
17. Luong, K., Nayak, R.: Learning association relationship and accurate geometric structures for multi-type relational data. In: 2018 IEEE 34th International Conference on Data Engineering (ICDE), pp. 509–520. IEEE (2018)
18. Luong, K., Nayak, R.: Clustering multi-view data using non-negative matrix factorization and manifold learning for effective understanding: a survey paper. In: P, D., Jurek-Loughrey, A. (eds.) Linking and Mining Heterogeneous and Multi-view Data. USL, pp. 201–227. Springer, Cham (2019). https://doi.org/10.1007/978-3-030-01872-6_9
19. Mohotti, W.A., Nayak, R.: Corpus-based augmented media posts with density-based clustering for community detection. In: 2018 IEEE 30th International Conference on Tools with Artificial Intelligence (ICTAI), pp. 379–386. IEEE (2018)
20. Mucha, P.J., Richardson, T., Macon, K., Porter, M.A., Onnela, J.P.: Community structure in time-dependent, multiscale, and multiplex networks. Science **328**(5980), 876–878 (2010)
21. Park, A., Conway, M., Chen, A.T.: Examining thematic similarity, difference, and membership in three online mental health communities from reddit: a text mining and visualization approach. Comput. Hum. Behav. **78**, 98–112 (2018)

22. Pei, Y., Chakraborty, N., Sycara, K.: Nonnegative matrix tri-factorization with graph regularization for community detection in social networks. In: Proceedings of the 24th International Conference on Artificial Intelligence, IJCAI 2015, pp. 2083–2089. AAAI Press (2015)
23. Qin, M., Jin, D., Lei, K., Gabrys, B., Musial-Gabrys, K.: Adaptive community detection incorporating topology and content in social networks. Knowl.-Based Syst. **161**, 342–356 (2018)
24. Rosvall, M., Bergstrom, C.T.: Maps of random walks on complex networks reveal community structure. Proc. Natl. Acad. Sci. **105**(4), 1118–1123 (2008)
25. Ruan, Y., Fuhry, D., Parthasarathy, S.: Efficient community detection in large networks using content and links. In: Proceedings of the 22nd International Conference on World Wide Web, pp. 1089–1098. ACM (2013)
26. Sachan, M., Contractor, D., Faruquie, T.A., Subramaniam, L.V.: Using content and interactions for discovering communities in social networks. In: Proceedings of the 21st International Conference on World Wide Web, pp. 331–340. ACM (2012)
27. Salton, G., Buckley, C.: Term-weighting approaches in automatic text retrieval. Inform. Process. Manage. **24**(5), 513–523 (1988)
28. Schütze, H., Manning, C.D., Raghavan, P.: Introduction to Information Retrieval, vol. 39. Cambridge University Press, Cambridge (2008)
29. Tang, L., Wang, X., Liu, H.: Community detection via heterogeneous interaction analysis. Data Min. Knowl. Discov. **25**(1), 1–33 (2012)
30. Wang, H., Huang, H., Ding, C.: Simultaneous clustering of multi-type relational data via symmetric nonnegative matrix tri-factorization. In: Proceedings of the 20th ACM International Conference on Information and Knowledge Management, pp. 279–284. ACM (2011)

Predicting Scientific Impact via Heterogeneous Academic Network Embedding

Chunjing Xiao[1]([✉]), Jianing Han[1], Wei Fan[1], Senzhang Wang[2], Rui Huang[1], and Yuxiang Zhang[1]

[1] School of Computer Science and Technology, Civil Aviation University of China, Tianjin, China
chunjingxiao@163.com
[2] School of Computer Science and Technology, Nanjing University of Aeronautics and Astronautics, Nanjing, China

Abstract. Predicting the scientific impact of literatures and researchers has been widely studied for a long time, and prevailing graph-based methods mainly rely on the *global structure* of the academic network. However, systematically integrating the *local structural information* of academic network and the *text information* of articles into a *unified model* to *jointly predict* the future impact of *published articles* and future potential of *researchers* is relatively unexplored. In this paper, we focus on how to effectively leverage these aforementioned information to predict the future impact of articles and researchers. Specifically, we first design a novel network embedding model which can simultaneously learn the local structural information of heterogeneous academic network and the text information of articles into a low-dimensional vector. Then a multivariate random-walk model is proposed to mutually rank the future impact of articles and researchers by leveraging such learned embeddings. We conduct extensive experiments on the AMiner dataset and the ACL Anthology Network, and the results demonstrate that the proposed method significantly outperforms existing state-of-the-art ranking approaches.

Keywords: Scientific impact · Heterogeneous academic networks · Network embedding · Multivariate random walk

1 Introduction

Accurately assessing the potential importance of literatures and researchers is one of the centric research issues in scientometrics, which can suggest many useful directions for future research, and provide a reference for policy makers in faculty recruitment and funding allocation [5,16]. So far, remarkable efforts have been devoted to ranking the *current importance* of articles and researchers [5], and some complicated metrics are proposed. However, how to accurately identify

© Springer Nature Switzerland AG 2019
A. C. Nayak and A. Sharma (Eds.): PRICAI 2019, LNAI 11671, pp. 555–568, 2019.
https://doi.org/10.1007/978-3-030-29911-8_43

influential papers and researchers and predict their future impact is less touched upon, especially for new papers and young researchers.

The *graph-based models* (i.e., random-walk models) are widely used for ranking the importance of articles and predict their future impact [12,15,16], and considered as the state-of-the-arts. These graph-based models first build a single paper citation network or heterogeneous academic network (which consists of the paper citation network, paper-author network and co-author network). Then the univariate or multivariate random walk techniques are used on these academic networks to rank articles or authors. However, almost all existing graph-based models focus on capturing the global structural information of the academic network in a shallow way in which the ranking scores of nodes are recursively computed from the entire network, and cannot directly integrate the *local structural information* of the academic network (i.e., local proximity between nodes) and the *text information of papers* (i.e., topical information of articles). Thus, these two types of information are largely ignored in existing approaches.

In fact, these two types of information are very important to improve the accuracy of predicting scientific impact of articles and researchers, especially for new articles and young researchers. Specifically, the local structural information can enhance the accuracies of links of the academic network. Similarly, the text information can help us better discover potentially popular research topics. Recent advances on network embedding [7,17,19] have shed light on this problem, which makes it possible to learn representations of different types of nodes in a shared common representation space and preserve the local network structures and semantic relationships between nodes in the original space.

In this paper, we make the first attempt to propose a heterogeneous academic network embedding model to capture the local structural information of the academic network and the text information of articles to improve the accuracy of scientific impact prediction. More specifically, we first design a *heterogeneous academic network embedding model* to capture these two major types of information simultaneously, and then integrate the learned embeddings of various entities (including articles, researchers, topics and words) and global structural information of the heterogeneous academic network into a multivariate random walk algorithm to comprehensively predict the future impact of scientific literatures and researchers. We conduct extensive experiments on the AMiner dataset and the ACL Anthology Network to evaluate the effectiveness of the proposed method. The experimental results demonstrate that our method significantly outperforms existing state-of-the-art predicting algorithms.

2   Related Work

Our work is mainly related to graph-based approaches which have been proved to be effective in the scientific impact prediction. The earlier methods [2,9] directly applied univariate random-walk algorithm (i.e., PageRank algorithm) to the paper citation network to rank the importance of articles. Similarly, some researches [3,8] directly utilized the PageRank algorithm on the co-author network to rank the impact of researchers.

In fact, the academic network is heterogeneous and contains several different types of networks, including the paper citation network, co-author network and venue-article network [5]. Thus, some studies began trying to apply multivariate random-walk techniques to heterogeneous scientific networks to rank an entity or rank different entities (such as articles, researches) simultaneously [5,12,15, 20]. Zhou et al. [20] first combined the paper citation network and co-author network to improve the ranking results for both articles and authors. Jiang et al. [5] proposed a mutual reinforcement ranking model that involved intra- and internetwork information for ranking papers, authors and venues.

Following these studies, numerous extensions integrate various types of information into the multivariate random-walk framework to enhance the predicting accuracy on the heterogeneous academic network. Sayyadi et al. [12] assumed that recently published papers are more likely to obtain more citations than old ones, and added the publication time of the articles to the multivariate random-walk ranking model. Wang et al. [15] guessed that text may provide important clues to improve the predicting results, and simply incorporated the text information into the ranking model. However, these graph-based methods do not consider the local structural information of the heterogeneous academic network and fined-grained text information extracted from articles.

Recently, network embedding has been widely recognized as effective network representation learning, and aims to learn low-dimensional vectors for nodes by preserving the structural information of networks. Different methods have been successfully applied in many tasks, such as node classification [13], link prediction [17,18] and community detection [1]. However, these existing methods cannot be directly applied to predict the scientific impact. In this work, we develop a novel network embedding model for learning the local structural information and fine-grained text information from the heterogeneous academic network.

3   Methodology

The aim of this work is to learn effective latent representations for the heterogeneous academic network, which can capture the local structural information of the academic network and the rich text information of articles, and then use these learned representations to predict future impact of articles and researchers. Figure 1 shows the overview of our proposed method, which can be divided into three parts: (1) constructing the heterogeneous academic network (HAN); (2) learning the effective latent representations for the HAN, in which the various types of important information are preserved; (3) co-ranking the future impact of articles and researchers by leveraging such representations.

3.1   Heterogeneous Academic Network Definition

Definition 1. *Paper citation network with text information (PCNT).*
Let P, Z, W be the set of papers, topics and words of papers, respectively, E_{pp},

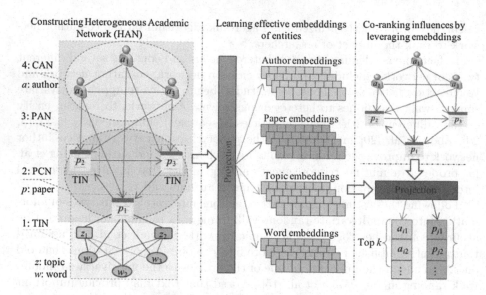

Fig. 1. A overview of the proposed approach. The heterogeneous academic network (HAN) consists of the text information network (TIN), paper citation network (PCN), paper-author network (PAN) and co-author network (CAN).

E_{pz}, E_{pw} and E_{zw} be the set of edges between papers and their references, topics, words, and between topics and words, respectively. The PCNT is defined as $G_p = (V_p, E_p, F_p)$, where $V_p = \{P \cup Z \cup W\}$, $E_p = \{E_{pp} \cup E_{pz} \cup E_{pw}\}$, and $F_p = \{F_{pp} \cup F_{pz} \cup F_{pw}\}$ is a set of weights of the corresponding edges.

The PCNT captures the text semantic similarities between articles, which can be helpful to accurately predict newly published papers with few citations. In order to capture collaboration patterns among researchers and relationships between papers and their authors, we introduce the co-author network denoted as $G_a = (V_a, E_a, F_a)$ and paper-author network denoted as $G_{pa} = (P \cup V_a, E_{pa}, F_{pa})$, where V_a is a set of authors, and the descriptions of other notations is similar to that defined in PCNT.

Definition 2. *Heterogeneous academic network (HAN).* *The three types of networks above can be further integrated into one heterogeneous academic network (HAN), which is denoted as $G = (V_p \cup V_a, E, F)$, where $E = \{E_p \cup E_a \cup E_{pa}\}$ and $F = \{F_p \cup F_a \cup F_{pa}\}$.*

3.2 Heterogeneous Academic Network Embedding

PCNT Embedding. As aforementioned, the PCNT G_p is composed of paper citation network G_{pp}, paper-topic network G_{pz} and paper-word network G_{pw}, where the paper vertices are shared across the three networks.

Let $\hat{\mathcal{P}}(\cdot|p_i)$ uniformly represent the different types of empirical distributions of paper p_i over its different types of neighbor vertices in G_{pp}, G_{pz} and G_{pw}, and let $\mathcal{P}(\cdot|p_i)$ represent the corresponding conditional distributions specified by the low-dimensional representations in the latent space. To learn the vector representations $\mathbf{p}_i$ of paper p_i, $\mathbf{z}_i$ of topic z_i, and $\mathbf{w}_i$ of word w_i, which supports the scientific impact prediction, we minimize the KL-divergence of two probability. By simplifying this KL-divergence, the corresponding objective function can be given as:

$$\mathcal{L}_p = - \sum_{(i,j)\in E_p} \lambda_p^i \hat{\mathcal{P}}(v_j|p_i) \log \mathcal{P}(v_j|p_i), \tag{1}$$

where v_j is one of p_j, and z_j and w_j, λ_p^i is a weight of paper p_i representing the importance of p_i in G_{pp}, G_{pz} and G_{pw} and will be defined below. $\mathcal{P}(v_j|p_i)$ is the conditional probability of v_j given paper p_i, and it is estimated by such a softmax function:

$$\mathcal{P}(v_j|p_i) = \frac{\exp(\mathbf{v}_j^\top \cdot \mathbf{p}_i)}{\sum_{k\in V_p} \exp(\mathbf{v}_k^\top \cdot \mathbf{p}_i)}, \tag{2}$$

where $\mathbf{p}_i \in \mathcal{R}^d$ and $\mathbf{v}_j \in \mathcal{R}^d$ are d-dimensional embedding vectors of p_i and v_j, respectively.

$\hat{\mathcal{P}}(v_j|p_i)$ is defined as $\hat{\mathcal{P}}(v_j|p_i) = \frac{\omega_{ij}}{\sum_{k\in R(p_i)} \omega_{ik}}$, where ω_{ij} is the weight of edge (p_i, v_j), and $R(p_i)$ is the set of neighbors of paper p_i. As with λ_p^i, these two variables will be defined in terms of different types of networks.

For the paper citation network G_{pp}, $R(p_i)$ is the set of references of paper p_i, and ω_{ij} ($\omega_{ij} \in F_{pp}$) is used to capture the dynamic properties of the citation relationship between two papers, and is calculated by the following exponentially decaying equation:

$$\omega_{ij} = e^{-\rho(T_c - T_{i\to j})}, \tag{3}$$

where ρ is a predefined decaying parameter, T_c is the current time, and $T_{i\to j}$ is the time of paper p_i citing paper p_j. Here, we assign higher weights to the more recent citations. In addition, we set $\lambda_p^i = \sum_{k\in C(p_i)} \omega_{ki}$, where $C(p_i)$ is the set of papers that cite paper p_i.

For the paper-topic network G_{pz}, $R(p_i)$ is the set of topics that are included in paper p_i. ω_{ij} ($\omega_{ij} \in F_{pz}$) is the probability that the topic z_j occurs in a given paper p_i (i.e., $\mathcal{P}(z_j|p_i)$), calculated by LDA model. And λ_p^i is defined as $\lambda_p^i = \sum_{k\in R(p_i)} \omega_{ik}$.

For the paper-word network G_{pw}, $R(p_i)$ represents the set of words that occur in paper p_i. ω_{ij} ($\omega_{ij} \in F_{pw}$) is the importance of word w_j in paper p_i, and computed by the tf-idf score of word w_j in paper p_i. And λ_p^i is also formally defined as $\lambda_p^i = \sum_{k\in R(p_i)} \omega_{ik}$.

CAN Embedding. The co-author network G_a captures the collaboration relationship among authors, and can reflect the impact of authors. Thus, to preserve this local structural information and learn the vector representations $\mathbf{a}_i$ of author a_i, we minimize the KL-divergence of the empirical distribution $\hat{P}(\cdot|a_i)$ in G_a and conditional distribution $P(\cdot|a_i)$ in latent space. By simplifying this KL-divergence, the corresponding objective function can be defined as:

$$\mathcal{L}_a = - \sum_{(i,j) \in E_a} \lambda_a^i \hat{P}(a_j|a_i) \log P(a_j|a_i). \tag{4}$$

where $\hat{P}(a_j|a_i)$ is defined as $\hat{P}(a_j|a_i) = \frac{\omega_{ij}^a}{\sum_{k \in N(a_i)} \omega_{ik}^a}$, where $N(a_i)$ is the set of co-authors of author a_i, and ω_{ik}^a is the weight of co-author relationship. λ_a^i is the weight of author a_i representing the impact of a_i in G_a, and is calculated as $\lambda_a^i = \sum_{j \in N(a_i)} \omega_{ij}^a$. The conditional probability $P(a_j|a_i)$ is estimated by the softmax function used in Eq. (2).

PAN Embedding. For each pair of paper p_i and author a_j linked by an edge, let $\hat{P}(p_i, a_j)$ be the empirical probability representing the closeness between p_i and a_j which is estimated by the edge weight ω_{ij}^{pa}, and $P(p_i, a_j)$ be the joint probability between paper p_i and author a_j in the latent space. To learn the vector representations $\mathbf{p}_i$ of author p_i and $\mathbf{a}_j$ of author a_j,

We minimize the KL-divergence of these two probability distributions. By simplifying this KL-divergence, the corresponding objective function can be defined as:

$$\mathcal{L}_{pa} = - \sum_{(i,j) \in E_{pa}} \omega_{ij}^{pa} \log P(p_i, a_j), \tag{5}$$

where $P(p_i, a_j)$ is defined as $P(p_i, a_j) = \frac{1}{1 + \exp(-\mathbf{p}_i^\top \cdot \mathbf{a}_j)}$, $\mathbf{P}_i \in \mathcal{R}^d$ and $\mathbf{a}_j \in \mathcal{R}^d$ are d-dimensional embedding vectors of paper p_i and author a_j, respectively.

HAN Embedding. The heterogeneous academic network HAN can simultaneously capture all the information appeared in three networks aforementioned. To learn the embeddings of HAN, an intuitive approach is to collectively embed three networks, which can be achieved by minimizing the objective function:

$$\mathcal{L} = \mathcal{L}_p + \mathcal{L}_a + \mathcal{L}_{pa}. \tag{6}$$

Model Optimization and Algorithm. It is computationally expensive and not practical for directly calculating the softmax function as shown in Eq. (2) [13]. To improve the training efficiency, we adopt negative sampling approach [10]. Maximizing the probability of positive edges while minimizing the probability of negative samples. In addition, we use L2-norm to avoid overfitting.

By omitting some constants and combining similar terms of $\mathcal{L}_p$ and $\mathcal{L}_a$, the loss function $\mathcal{L}$ can be rewritten as follows:

$$
\begin{aligned}
\mathcal{L} = & - \sum_{(i,j)\in E'} \lambda_v^i \hat{\mathcal{P}}(v_j|v_i) \log(\sigma(\mathbf{v}_j^\top \cdot \mathbf{v}_i)) - \sum_{(i,j)\notin E'} \lambda_v^i \log(\sigma(-\mathbf{v}_j^\top \cdot \mathbf{v}_i)) \\
& - \sum_{(i,j)\in E_{pa}} \omega_{pa}^{ij} \log(\sigma(\mathbf{p}_i^\top \cdot \mathbf{a}_j)) + \lambda \sum_{n=1}^{|P|} ||\mathbf{p}_n||_2 + \beta \sum_{n=1}^{|V_a|} ||\mathbf{a}_n||_2,
\end{aligned}
\tag{7}
$$

where λ, $\beta \in \mathcal{R}$ are regularization coefficients, $\sigma(x) = \frac{1}{1+exp(-x)}$ is the sigmoid function. The first term in Eq. (7) models the observed edges, and the second term models the negative edges. We use $(i,j) \notin E'$ to represent the set of negative samples, where $E' = \{E_{pp} \cup E_{pz} \cup E_{pw} \cup E_a\}$. Here, v_i and v_j represent vertices in HAN and (i,j) represents the corresponding edge.

We adopt the stochastic gradient descent algorithm to optimize the model Eq. (6). Thu the gradients of the object function $\mathcal{L}$ with respect to $\mathbf{p}_i$ and $\mathbf{a}_i$ can be obtained as follows.

$$
\begin{aligned}
\frac{\partial \mathcal{L}}{\partial \mathbf{p}_i} = & - \sum_{(i,j)\in E_p} \lambda_p^i \frac{\hat{\mathcal{P}}(v_j|p_i)exp\{-\mathbf{v}_j^\top \mathbf{p}_i\}}{1+exp\{-\mathbf{v}_j^\top \mathbf{p}_i\}} \mathbf{v}_j + \sum_{(i,j)\notin E_p} \frac{\lambda_p^i}{1+exp\{-\mathbf{v}_j^\top \mathbf{p}_i\}} \mathbf{v}_j \\
& - \sum_{(i,j)\in E_{pa}} \omega_{pa}^{ij} \frac{exp\{-\mathbf{p}_i^\top \mathbf{a}_j\}}{1+exp\{-\mathbf{p}_i^\top \mathbf{a}_j\}} \mathbf{a}_j + \lambda \sum_{r=1}^{d_p} 2(\mathbf{p}_i^r),
\end{aligned}
\tag{8}
$$

$$
\begin{aligned}
\frac{\partial \mathcal{L}}{\partial \mathbf{a}_i} = & - \sum_{(i,j)\in E_a} \lambda_a^i \frac{\hat{\mathcal{P}}(a_j|a_i)exp\{-\mathbf{a}_j^\top \mathbf{a}_i\}}{1+exp\{-\mathbf{a}_j^\top \mathbf{a}_i\}} \mathbf{a}_j + \sum_{(i,j)\notin E_a} \frac{\lambda_a^i}{1+exp\{-\mathbf{a}_j^\top \mathbf{a}_i\}} \mathbf{a}_j \\
& - \sum_{(j,i)\in E_{pa}} \omega_{pa}^{ji} \frac{exp\{-\mathbf{p}_j^\top \mathbf{a}_i\}}{1+exp\{-\mathbf{p}_j^\top \mathbf{a}_i\}} \mathbf{p}_j + \beta \sum_{r=1}^{d_a} 2(\mathbf{a}_i^r),
\end{aligned}
\tag{9}
$$

where d_p and d_a are the dimensions of embeddings of papers and authors, respectively, which are set to be equal (i.e., $d_p = d_a = d$). Due to space limitation, we omit the gradients of $\mathbf{z}_i$ and $\mathbf{w}_i$, which can be easily derived.

The detailed learning algorithm is presented in Algorithm 1. The backtracking line search [18] is used to learn an appropriate learning rate for each iteration. The overall time complexity of our model is $O(|E|d \times dt)$, where $|E|$ is the number of edges, d is the dimension of embeddings, and t is the iteration times. Accordingly, the proposed embedding model can be solved in polynomial time.

3.3 Predicting the Future Scientific Impact

In this section, we introduce how to integrate the learned **Embeddings** and global **Structure** of heterogeneous academic network into a unified mutual reinforcement **Multivariate Random-walk** model (**ESMR**) to predict the future impact

---

Algorithm 1. Algorithm for HAN Embedding.

Input: $G(V, E, F)$, embedding dimension d, learning rate η, negative samples ratio k, regularization coefficients λ and β

Output: Embeddings of papers and authors

 1: initialization embeddings $\mathbf{p}, \mathbf{z}, \mathbf{w}$ and $\mathbf{a}$;

 2: **while** (not converge) **do**

 3:    Compute gradient $\frac{\partial \mathcal{L}_p}{\partial \mathbf{p}_i}$ for all P;

 4:    Step size $\eta_i \leftarrow$ backtracking line search;

 5:    Update $\mathbf{p}$, for all P ;

 6:    Update $\mathbf{p}, \mathbf{z}$ for all P and Z;

 7:    Update $\mathbf{p}, \mathbf{w}$ for all P and W;

 8: **end while**

 9: pre-training $\mathbf{a}$ for all V_a;

10: **while** (not converge) **do**

11:    find the optimal $V_p(\mathbf{p}, \mathbf{z}, \mathbf{w})$ with gradient descent based on Eq. (8) and gradient $\frac{\partial \mathcal{L}}{\partial \mathbf{z}_i}, \frac{\partial \mathcal{L}}{\partial \mathbf{w}_i}$ when fix V_a;

12:    find the optimal $V_a(\mathbf{a})$ with gradient descent based on Eq. (9) when fix V_p;

13: **end while**

14: **return** Embeddings $\mathbf{p}, \mathbf{z}, \mathbf{w}$ and $\mathbf{a}$

---

of articles and authors. We first use the cosine similarity between two learned representation vectors to measure the similarity between corresponding entities, including articles and authors. Then, the corresponding transition matrix in the multivariate random-walk model is calculated. For example, the transition matrix in the paper citation network PCN is calculated as follows:

$$M_{pp}(j, i) = \begin{cases} \gamma \frac{Sim(p_i, p_j)}{\sum_{p_k \in N(p_i)} Sim(p_i, p_k)} + (1 - \gamma) \frac{\lambda_{pp}^i}{deg(p_i)}, & e_{pp}^{ij} \in E_{pp} \\ 0, & otherwise \end{cases} \quad (10)$$

where λ_{pp}^i is a specific description of λ_p^i in paper citation network, $N(p_i)$ is a set of neighbors of paper p_i in PCN, $Sim(p_i, p_j)$ is the cosine similarity based on learned embedding vectors of two papers, $deg(p_i)$ is the out-degree of paper p_i, and γ is a adjustment parameter used to balance the proportion of potential similarity between nodes in the process of random walk. Similarly, the transition matrices M_{aa}, M_{pa}, M_{ap} of co-author network and paper-author network can be obtained.

Finally, we use the intra-network as well as inter-network multivariate random-walk technique on the heterogeneous academic network to predict the future impact of papers and authors simultaneously. We define the following equations for each iterative process:

$$\mathbf{p}^{(t+1)} = \alpha_{pp} M_{pp} \mathbf{p}^{(t)} + \beta_{pa} M_{pa} \mathbf{a}^{(t)}, \quad (11)$$

$$\mathbf{a}^{(t+1)} = \alpha_{aa} M_{aa} \mathbf{a}^{(t)} + \beta_{ap} M_{ap} \mathbf{p}^{(t)}, \quad (12)$$

where $\mathbf{p}^{(t)}$ and $\mathbf{a}^{(t)}$ are probability distribution vectors representing the future impact of papers and authors at time t. α_{pp} and β_{pa} control how much influence the papers can receive from other papers and authors. α_{aa} and β_{ap} control how much influence the authors can receive from other authors and papers. Thus, we can obtain the stationary probability distribution vectors by iteratively running Eqs. (11) and (12) until converge.

4 Experimental Results

4.1 Dataset

We evaluate the proposed model on two publicly available dataset, the first one is the Academic Social Network of AMiner Dataset[1] [14]. It contains 2,092,356 papers published before 2014 and 8,024,869 citations among these papers. The second one is the ACL Anthology Network (AAN), which contains 23,766 papers and 18,862 authors and 124,857 citations[2].

We first preprocess the dataset as follows. As we focus on the prediction of the future impact of papers and researchers, we select the papers published after 1998 for evaluation. Then we remove the papers with incomplete metedata and extract authors from these selected papers and predict the impact of them.

4.2 Experiment Setup

Ground Truth. How to evaluate the prediction results itself is challenging for almost all the related works because of the lack of gold standard. Following most previous works [15,16], we use the future citation number as the ground truth to evaluate the future impact of papers and authors.

We divide the papers published before 2009 and after 2009 as the training set and testing set. Then we choose three time periods 2010, 2010–2012, and 2010–2014 to calculate the future citations, and compare the future citations obtained in the three time periods by papers published before 2009. The results show that the paper impact rankings in 2010 are obviously not conducive to the newly published papers. But between three and five years, the stability of the prediction will be good across time. In this paper, we use the citations of these papers obtained in the period of 2010–2014 as the ground truth.

Evaluation Metric. We use the following two metrics for evaluation, one is the widely used Normalized Discounted Cumulative Gain (NDCG) [6], and the other is Recommendation Intensity (RI) [4,5]. The larger the two metrics, the better the performance of the algorithm.

4.3 Baselines

We compare our method with the following baselines.

(1) **MRCoRank(MR).** MRCoRank ranks the future impact of multiobjects simultaneously, which integrates time, network structure and text information into a unified framework [15]. (2) **FutureRank(FR).** FutureRank combines

---

[1] https://www.aminer.cn/aminernetwork.

[2] http://clair.eecs.umich.edu/aan/index.php.

the information of citations, authors and publication time to predict the future ranking of papers [12]. (3) **PageRank(PR).** We compare with PageRank [11] in ranking the future impact of papers and authors, and the weights of edges are set the same as ESMR. (4) **LINE+CoRank (LCR)** LINE is one of the most representative homogeneous network embedding methods [13]. So we use LINE to learn paper embeddings in paper citation network and learn author embeddings in Co-author network. And then combine the embeddings with our ranking algorithm described in Sect. 3.3 as a baseline.

Additionally, we also compare our model with the following two variations of ESMR: ESMR-T is used to verify whether the text information is helpful for prediction results, and ESMR-NE is used to study how much performance can be improved by the embedding process.

4.4 Parameter Settings

For the implementation of ESMR, we set the ratio of negative sampling as 5. We use the commonly used settings for backtracking line search. The coefficients for regularization terms λ and β are both set to 1. The effect of the embedding dimension on the performance of ESMR on the AAN dataset is shown in Fig. 2. One can see that the performance of ESMR is not remarkably sensitive to the dimension. It shows that 100 is a reasonable choice of the dimension of the representation vector. Thus, in the following experiments we use 100 as the default dimension setting.

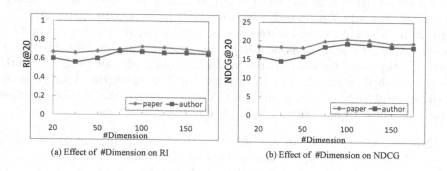

(a) Effect of #Dimension on RI   (b) Effect of #Dimension on NDCG

Fig. 2. Parameter sensitivity analysis

The parameter γ in Eq. (10) is set to 0.3 for the AAN dataset and 0.6 for the AMiner dataset. In addition, there are four parameters in the ranking part of ESMR, α_{pp}, α_{aa}, β_{pa} and β_{ap}. For the AAN dataset, the best performance is achieved when $\alpha_{pp} = 0.3$, $\alpha_{aa} = 0.15$, $\beta_{pa} = 0.3$ and $\beta_{ap} = 0.85$. And for the AMiner dataset, we set $\alpha_{pp} = 0.6$, $\alpha_{aa} = 0.2$, $\beta_{pa} = 0.35$ and $\beta_{ap} = 0.8$ as the default parameter settings. The parameters of the baselines are set following their setting in the corresponding papers.

4.5   Prediction Results of Paper Impact

We quantitatively compare the performance of the proposed approach with baselines. The Fig. 3 shows that for paper rankings, our proposed ESMR outperforms all the baselines over various k on the AAN dataset. ESMR outperforms MRCoRank by 33% and 42% for NDCG@50 and RI@50, and outperforms LINE+CoRank by 36% and 40% for NDCG@50 and RI@50.

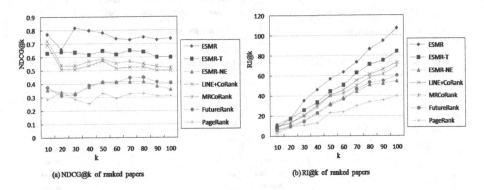

(a) NDCG@k of ranked papers   (b) RI@k of ranked papers

Fig. 3. NDCG@k and RI@k of the paper rankings on the AAN dataset

Next, we select the papers published in the same year and same research community to evaluate the prediction results on the Aminer dataset. It is based on the following two considerations. (1) The ground truth inevitably biases towards the old papers. (2) There is a wide gap among the number of citations for the papers published in different research communities. Therefore, to make an unbiased comparison for different research communities, we give the prediction results of papers that are published in different years and communities separately. Due to space limitation, we select the years of 2001, 2003, 2005 and 2007 to report the prediction results of papers of Artificial Intelligence (AI) Fig. 4(a)–(b) show the NDCG@20 and RI@20 of the ranked papers in the research community of AI.

For the prediction results in AI, LINE+CoRank generally performs better than MRcoRank and FutureRank, but inferior to the ESMR. ESMR-T also performs well and its performance is comparable to LINE+CoRank in most years. ESMR outperforms MRCoRank by 31% and 40% for NDCG@20 and RI@20 in the year of 2003, and outperforms LINE+CoRank by 21% and 29% for NDCG@20 and RI@20 in the year of 2007, which demonstrates the effectiveness of the proposed embedding model on heterogeneous networks. The performance of ESMR is much better than ESMR-T in general. It is mainly because ESMR benefits from exploiting the text information.

4.6   Prediction Results of Author Impact

The prediction results of authors on AAN dataset is shown in Fig. 5, it shows that ESMR outperforms all the baselines over various k on the AAN dataset. ESMR outperforms FutureRank by 41% and 42% for NDCG@50 and RI@50, and outperforms LINE+CoRank by 45% and 55% for NDCG@50 and RI@50.

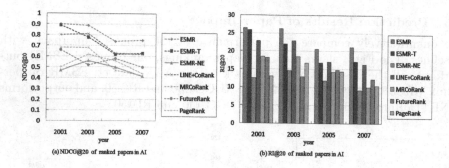

Fig. 4. NDCG@20 and RI@20 of the paper rankings on the AMiner dataset

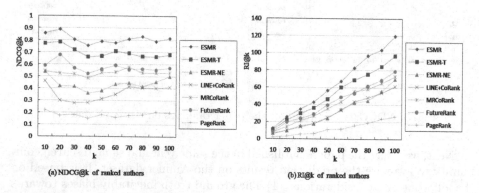

Fig. 5. NDCG@k and RI@k of the author rankings on the AAN dataset

Then we rank the authors who start to publish papers at the same year and in the same research community on the AMiner dataset to avoid a biased prediction. We select the years of 2002, 2004, 2006 and 2008 to report the prediction results of authors in AI . Figure 6(a)–(b) show NDCG@20 and RI@20 of the ranked authors of AI in the four years, respectively.

Figure 6 shows that ESMR outperforms all the baselines in all the cases. ESMR outperforms FurureRank by 20% and 26% for NDCG@20 and RI@20 in the year of 2004, and outperforms all the baselines by a large margin in the year of 2008. For the comparison between ESMR and ESMR-T, the results of the two methods are similar in 2002 and 2004, but ESMR outperforms ESMR-T in the year of 2008. The reasonable explanation is that the text information transfers the impact of papers to authors through the paper-author network, and it is conducive to rank authors especially for the authors who start to publish papers in a more recent year.

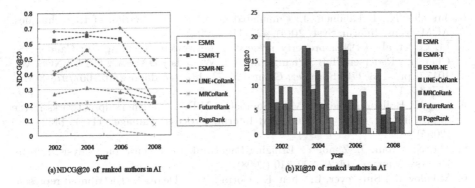

Fig. 6. NDCG@20 and RI@20 of the author rankings on the AMiner dataset

5 Conclusion

In this paper, we proposed a new model to predict the future impact of scientific articles and researchers. We first designed a network embedding model for the heterogeneous academic network, which could learn the local structural information of this academic network and the rich text information of articles. And these two types of information could support the scientific impact prediction. Then, we integrated the learned embeddings and the global structure of heterogeneous academic network into a unified mutual reinforcement multivariate random-walk model to predict the future impact of articles and researchers simultaneously. The experimental results on AMiner dataset and the ACL Anthology Network demonstrated that the proposed model outperforms the state-of-the-art methods. In future, we plan to extend our model to the comprehensive heterogeneous academic network, including authors, articles, text information, publication venue and institution of authors.

Acknowledgements. This work was supported by the Fundamental Research Funds for the Central Universities (No. ZXH2012P009).

References

1. Cavallari, S., Zheng, V.W., Cai, H., Chang, K.C.C., Cambria, E.: Learning community embedding with community detection and node embedding on graphs. In: Proceedings of CIKM, pp. 377–386 (2017)
2. Chen, P., Xie, H., Maslov, S., Redner, S.: Finding scientific gems with Google's PageRank algorithm. J. Inform. **1**(1), 8–15 (2007)
3. Ding, Y., Yan, E., Frazho, A., Caverlee, J.: PageRank for ranking authors in co-citation networks. J. Assoc. Inform. Sci. Technol. **60**(11), 2229–2243 (2009)
4. Jiang, X., Sun, X., Hai, Z.: Graph-based algorithms for ranking researchers: not all swans are white!. Scientometrics **96**(3), 743–759 (2013)
5. Jiang, X., Sun, X., Zhuge, H.: Towards an effective and unbiased ranking of scientific literature through mutual reinforcement. In: Proceedings of CIKM, pp. 714–723 (2012)

6. Järvelin, K., Kekäläinen, J.: Cumulated gain-based evaluation of IR techniques. ACM Trans. Inform. Syst. **20**(4), 422–446 (2002)
7. Li, C., et al.: PPNE: property preserving network embedding. In: Candan, S., Chen, L., Pedersen, T.B., Chang, L., Hua, W. (eds.) DASFAA 2017. LNCS, vol. 10177, pp. 163–179. Springer, Cham (2017). https://doi.org/10.1007/978-3-319-55753-3_11
8. Liu, X., Bollen, J., Nelson, M.L., Sompel, H.V.D.: Co-authorship networks in the digital library research community. Inform. Process. Manage. **41**(6), 1462–1480 (2005)
9. Ma, N., Guan, J., Zhao, Y.: Bringing PageRank to the citation analysis. Inform. Process. Manage. **44**(2), 800–810 (2008)
10. Mikolov, T., Sutskever, I., Chen, K., Corrado, G., Dean, J.: Distributed representations of words and phrases and their compositionality. In: Proceedings of NIPS, pp. 3111–3119 (2013)
11. Page, L.: The PageRank citation ranking: bringing order to the web. Stanford Digit. Libr. Work. Paper **9**(1), 1–14 (1999)
12. Sayyadi, H., Getoor, L.: FutureRank: ranking scientific articles by predicting their future PageRank. In: Proceedings of SDM, pp. 533–544 (2009)
13. Tang, J., Qu, M., Wang, M., Zhang, M., Yan, J., Mei, Q.: LINE: large-scale information network embedding. In: Proceedings of WWW, pp. 1067–1077 (2015)
14. Tang, J., Zhang, J., Yao, L., Li, J., Zhang, L., Su, Z.: ArnetMiner: extraction and mining of academic social networks. In: Proceedings of KDD, pp. 990–998 (2008)
15. Wang, S., Xie, S., Zhang, X., Li, Z., He, Y., He, Y.: Coranking the future influence of multiobjects in bibliographic network through mutual reinforcement. ACM Trans. Intell. Syst. Technol. **7**(4), 64 (2016)
16. Wang, Y., Yunhai, T., Zeng, M.: Ranking scientific articles by exploiting citations, authors, journals, and time information. In: Proceedings of AAAI, pp. 933–939 (2013)
17. Wang, Z., Chen, C., Li, W.: Predictive network representation learning for link prediction. In: Proceedings of SIGIR, pp. 969–972 (2017)
18. Xu, L., Wei, X., Cao, J., Yu, P.S.: Embedding of embedding (EOE): joint embedding for coupled heterogeneous networks. In: Proceedings of WSDM, pp. 741–749 (2017)
19. Yang, D., Wang, S., Li, C., Zhang, X., Li, Z.: From properties to links: deep network embedding on incomplete graphs. In: Proceedings of CIKM, pp. 367–376 (2017)
20. Zhou, D., Orshanskiy, S.A., Zha, H., Giles, C.L.: Co-ranking authors and documents in a heterogeneous network. In: Proceedings of ICDM, pp. 739–744 (2007)

Hint-Embedding Attention-Based LSTM for Aspect Identification Sentiment Analysis

Murtadha Ahmed[1,2](✉), Qun Chen[1,2](✉), Yanyan Wang[1,2](✉), and Zhanhuai Li[1,2](✉)

[1] School of Computer Science, Northwestern Polytechnical University,
Xi'an, Shaanxi, People's Republic of China
{a.murtadha,wangyanyan}@mail.nwpu.edu.cn, {chenbenben,lizhh}@nwpu.edu.cn
[2] Key Laboratory of Big Data Storage and Management,
Northwestern Polytechnical University,
Ministry of Industry and Information Technology,
Xi'an, Shaanxi, People's Republic of China

Abstract. Aspect identification became an important task for aspect-based sentiment analysis. Previous approaches realized the importance of aspect identification in aspect-level sentiment analysis task. To this aim, there are different approaches proposed including rule-based and supervised learning based. Rule-based methods introduce rule mining based on features engineering, while supervised methods consider it as multi-task text classification problem. However, aspect identification is still a challenge from two perspectives: detecting the implicit aspect and mapping aspect-term into category. In this paper, we propose a novel neural network approach with Hint-embedding that aims at exploring the connection between an aspect and its semantic content in the sentence. Attention mechanism is designed to focus on different parts of a sentence based on aspects' indicators. We experiment on benchmark datasets (SemEval 2014 task 4 restaurant and SemEval 2016 task 5 laptop), and results show that our model achieves considerable performance on aspect identification task.

Keywords: Sentiment analysis · Aspect-level sentiment analysis · Aspect category identification

1 Introduction

In recent years, social networks and many online platforms (such as TripAdvisor, Yelp, Amazon, etc.) allowed people to express their opinions towards entities or topics (e.g., products and services). An entity, usually represents names such as products, services, individuals, events and organizations, while the aspect describes the attributes and components of entities. The task of the entity and aspect extraction is also called opinion target extraction in sentiment analysis, where both entity and aspect come up together to form the opinion target.

© Springer Nature Switzerland AG 2019
A. C. Nayak and A. Sharma (Eds.): PRICAI 2019, LNAI 11671, pp. 569–581, 2019.
https://doi.org/10.1007/978-3-030-29911-8_44

Aspect identification is a fundamental task in aspect-based sentiment analysis (ABSA), which consists of identifying the evaluated aspects in a given sentence [14]. For example, *"it is an expensive restaurant"*, emphasizes the *"price"* by the word *"expensive"* for the entity *"restaurant"*. Note that the evaluation is aspect-level rather than the restaurant as a whole. The aspect identification task consists of two sub-tasks: (1) Extracting the indicators of an aspect in a given sentence. (2) Grouping those contributions accordingly into categories in order to predict the aspect category.

The proposed approaches to address the aspect category identification commonly face two main challenges: (1) How to detect the aspect when it is expressed implicitly in a text. For example, in the sentence *"it is very expensive"* the category *"price"* is absent explicitly whereas the sentiment word *"expensive"* confirms its presence implicitly. (2) Mapping aspect-relevant parts, also called aspect-terms, into categories. For example, *"I highly recommend it for not just its superb cuisine, but also for its friendly owners and staff."* includes the aspect-relevant parts *"cuisine, friendly, owners and staff"*, which should be mapped to food and service categories respectively.

Previous approaches of aspect identification could be summarized in three main categories rule-based methods, supervised models, and topic model-based methods. For rule-based approaches, the authors in [8] attempt to focus on uncovering entity features words without taking into consideration the connection between an entity features itself at aspect-level. However, rule-based approaches rely on the quality of rules, which cannot be applicable in the explicit cases. However, the authors in [9] proposed Hidden Markov Model(HMM) to extract aspects. SVM-based approaches, [4,11] considered the aspect identification as multi-class text classification. These methods usually suffer from heavy feature engineering, which is labor intensive.

Inspired by the way that human beings think to identify an aspect. We firstly begin by finding out the aspects' representatives (e.g., expensive, delicious, staff etc.), then mapping them into different categories (e.g., price, food etc.). In this paper, we propose a novel deep neural network approach, called Hint-Embedding Attention-based Long-short Term Memory (HEA-LSTM), to address the two challenges mentioned previously. Although standard LSTM achieved good performance in semantic representation, but it remains a challenge in aspect identification, where the sentence review as whole is not useful to identify the evaluated aspect. In a given sentence, we are interested only in the parts that are semantically related to the aspect. To this end, we first extract the linguistic indicators which can be considered as the prior knowledge of an aspect. We then design an attention mechanism utilizes those indicators to encourage the model to weight-up the important parts towards an aspect. We finally group the aspect's candidates into aspect categories in a fully connected layer to deal with aspect identification as multi-class classification problem.

In contrast to SVM-based models which rely on heavy feature engineering, our proposed method captures the meaningful parts of the output of LSTM using the weighted vector obtained from the attention layer.

The main contributions of our work can be summarized as follows:

- We model the semantic representation of the sentence using Long Short-Term Memory (LSTM).
- We propose an attention mechanism aims at capturing the important parts in a sentence toward an aspect based on prior knowledge. To the best of our knowledge, we are the first to employ the indicators of an aspect in a sentence. Results show that the attention mechanism is effective.
- Experimental results show that our approach achieves considerable performance for aspect identification task, and the attention mechanism with the hint-embedding can encourage the model to predict the true aspect.

The rest of this paper is structured as follows: Sect. 2 discusses related work, Sect. 3 gives a detailed description of our attention-based model with hint embedding, Sect. 4 presents extensive experiments to demonstrate the effectiveness of our approach, and Sect. 5 summarizes this work.

2 Related Work

2.1 Rules-Based

The authors in [8] proposed a rule-based approach to capture the product features, for that they counted the occurrence frequencies of some terms (e.g., noun and phrase) using an association rule mining algorithm. OPINE proposed in [22] to extract product features by computing Point-wise Mutual Information (PMI) between the phrase and estimated discriminators associated with the entity. Following their approach, many frequency-based methods have been introduced [15,23]. Rule-based methods are generally based on predefined rules, which may not work well in explicit cases due to the coherence and ambiguity of aspect-relevant words.

2.2 Supervised Learning

Many supervised learning methods considered aspect identification as a specific information extraction problem. Sequential learning (or sequential labeling) is the most dominant methods. The authors in [9] applied Hidden Markov Models, HMM for short, and CRF [12], with Support Vector Machines, SVMs for short, to deal with the aspect extraction as a sequential learning. In [9], they introduced modeling the problem as an information extraction task and trained the CRF model on review sentences from different domains. The authors in [33] developed an approach to aspect-term extraction based on unsupervised learning of distributed representations of words and dependency paths to automatically learn features for CRF-based aspect extraction. SVM-based in [4,11], they addressed aspect-category detection as a multi-task text classification problem using one-vs-all SVM classifier, with different features as ngrams, non-contiguous ngrams, lexicon features. NLANGP is proposed in [30] based on a variety of features engineering (word, name list word embedding). Addition to these features, they used the probability of CNN as a new feature to be fed for binary classification process. Deep neural networks in [25,28] proposed to cast aspect identification as a multi-task classification problem. Both methods are designed for multilingual data, the best performance achieved by [25] was with English. Despite the effectiveness of supervised learning approaches, they heavily rely on feature engineering and the quality of extracted rules as well as all of the words share the same importance degree due to the absence of attention mechanism.

2.3   Unsupervised Learning

In unsupervised approaches, Topic Modeling is the most dominating approach, which consists of determining the topics in text by estimating the proportion of each topic in the document. Many existing unsupervised approaches are basically improvements of two topic models, probabilistic Latent Semantic Analysis, pLSA for short, and Latent Dirichlet Allocation, LDA for short. The authors in [29] explained that using LDA may not be suitable for detecting aspects due to the dependency of topic distribution over the word. For that, they initially used both LDA and pLSA to review the text for aspect extraction. Following LDA, many methods and extensions were proposed in [14,17]. Other variants of topic models-based approaches joined both aspect and sentiment for addressing sentiment analysis problem. Extensions of LDA in [10,34] proposed two models called ASUM and MaxEnt-LDA respectively, which address the aspect and sentiment prediction. The main difference of these two models is the separation of aspect and sentiment. Restricted Boltzmann Machines, RBM for short, based model proposed in [13] to jointly tackle Aspect extraction and sentiment analysis of reviews tasks. More recently, [5] introduced a neural approach to uncover coherent aspects by exploiting the distribution of word co-occurrences through the use of neural word embedding.

2.4   Attention-Based Neural Network

In the era of deep neural networks, attention mechanism achieved good performance. It has been proposed in many domains including image processing, translation and sentiment analysis. The authors in [19] proposed visual attention to extract information from images. It has been integrated encoder-decoder architectures in machine translation to encourage the model to look for the relatedness in the source text to predict the target word in [1]. Moreover, the authors of [24] proposed reasoning to determine entailment of two sentences using an attention neural network as well as abstractive sentence summarization [26]. In addition, teaching the machine to read a text and understand the content to be able to answer the question posed on this content [6]. Recently, attention mechanism is also introduced to sentiment analysis tasks in [31] proposed Attention-based Recurrent Neural Network (ATAE) to predict the polarity of an aspect in the sentence. Unsupervised model in [16], which designed an attention mechanism that aimed to model targeted sentiment in the sentence.

3 The Approach

3.1 Hints Extraction

Hints are key words that indicate the aspect in a given sentence. For instance, *"It is only for two dollars"*, even though the *"price"* is expressed in an ambiguous way, but the word *"dollars"* is a helpful hint to predict the aspect.

For each aspect, we generate a seed list of representatives. We thus refer to two methods to generate the seed list: (1) Topic Modeling, which consists of computing the distribution of topics over the vocabulary. (2) We use an unsupervised neural model proposed in [5], which called ABAE. The idea is to exploit the distribution of word co-occurrences through the use of neural word embedding to discover the representative words of aspect. The output of these models are a list of representative words for each aspect in the corpus, where each aspect is identified by at least 100 words. For example, the aspect *"food"* is expressed by the name of dishes or by the sentiment words (e.g. delicious, tasty, etc.). After generating the seed list, we then expand the list with synonyms and antonyms as well as the sentiment words using WordNet and SentiWordNet dictionaries. In addition, we manually generate a small seed list of representative words.

For a given domain, we first extract the aspect indicators in the dataset, then we map them to different hints, each aspect category is represented by one and only one hint. Each hint is embedded to a pre-specified length, we then come up with a matrix of hint-embedding. Our goal is to learn the hint-embedding via attention mechanism in order to encourage the model to weight-up the aspect-related parts.

3.2 Long Short-Term Memory (LSTM)

LSTM model is a basic version of our approach. Unlike feed-forward neural networks, recurrent neural networks, RNNs for short, are designed to read back only a few steps, thus it does not work well for long term dependencies. To this end, Long Short-Term Memory (LSTM) was introduced to improve the performance of long term dependency problem by adding a cell state and three gates layers: *"input gate layer, forget gate layer and output gate layer"*. These gates functionally encourage the cell state to remember information for a long period of time [7].

We begin by associating each word w in our vocabulary with a real-valued embedding $w_v \in \mathbb{R}^d$ where w_v is the dimension of word vector. All words in the vocabulary are embedded in a matrix $L_x \in \mathbb{R}^{|V| \times w_v}$, where $|V|$ is the vocabulary size. Since our objective is to learn hint-embedding, we then require a second matrix $h_e \in \mathbb{R}^{k \times d}$, where k is the number of hints extracted from the corpus and d is the pre-specified length. Each input to the model is a list of indexes of a input sentence in the vocabulary. The representation of the input sentence is first computed using LSTM. The model's input is:

$$x_t = [w_v \oplus h_{e_i} \oplus h_{t-1}] \tag{1}$$

where $\oplus$ stands for point-wise element concatenation, w_v is the word embedding, h_{e_i} is the hint-embedding corresponding to the input sentence and $i = 1, ..., k$, while h_{t-1} is the previous hidden layer output. The input is a low dimensional representations $M_x \in \mathbb{R}^{|V| \times (w_v + h_{e_i} + h_{t-1})}$, where $|V|$ is the length of input sentence.

LSTM cell is computed as follows:

$$f_t = \sigma(W_f \bullet [h_{t-1}; x_t] + b_f) \tag{2}$$

$$i_t = \sigma(W_i \bullet [h_{t-1}; x_t] + b_i) \tag{3}$$

$$y_t = tanh(W_y \bullet [h_{t-1}; x_t] + b_y) \tag{4}$$

$$o_t = \sigma(W_o \bullet [h_{t-1}; x_t] + b_o) \tag{5}$$

$$c_t = f_t \odot c_{t-1} + i_t \odot y_t \tag{6}$$

$$h_t = o_t \odot tanh(c_t) \tag{7}$$

where σ is sigmoid function, $\odot$ stands for point-wise element multiplication, $\bullet$ is point-wise element dot product. W and b are the parameters of gates layers, where $W \in \mathbb{R}^{w_v + h_{e_i} + h_{t-1}}$. The previous hidden layer h_{t-1} is required to compute the first hidden state, by default it is initialized to zero. Once the representations h_t of the input sentence is done, it is then fed to the attention mechanism to compute a new vector representations of the input sentence based on prior knowledge.

3.3 Attention-Based with Hints Embedding

In this part, we describe the proposed attention mechanism that combines the hint embedding with the LSTM output to capture the relevant information towards an aspect. Detecting related parts and mapping them into an aspect are the main contributions of our approach to tackle the aspect identification problem. Standard LSTM usually ignores the degree of importance of each part in response to an aspect. To this end, we design an attention mechanism shown in Fig. 1 that aims at computing a new representation of an input sentence given a prior knowledge about the sentence. In the attention layer, we aim to compute a learnable weight vector over the output of LSTM h_t obtained in the Eq. 7. This weight is computed according to the relevance of each hidden state's h_i in h_t towards a hint. We begin by expanding the hint-embedding h_{e_i} to the length of hidden layers h_t, we then concatenate h_{e_i} with each hidden layer's output h_t obtained in the Eq. 7,

$$t = [h_t \bullet W_h \oplus h_{e_i} \bullet W_e] \tag{8}$$

where $\oplus$ stands for point-wise element concatenation, while W_h and W_e are the parameters and $t \in \mathbb{R}^{|V| \times (w_v + h_{e_i})}$. We reduce t to d-dimensional vector and then apply a softmax non-linearity to yield non-negative weights,

$$s = Softmax(m) \tag{9}$$

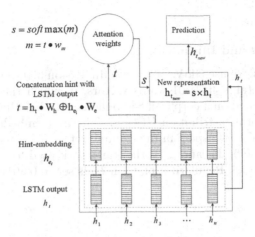

Fig. 1. An example of HEA-LSTM, s is the probability of each word to be an aspect-related, $h_{t_{new}}$ is the new representation of input sentence given a hint.

$$m = t \bullet W_m \tag{10}$$

where W_m is the parameter learned during the training, which can be read as the degree of importance of each word. The reduced vector $m \in \mathbb{R}^d$, where d is the length of input sentence, contains a weight for each word. The weighted vector s can be read as the probability that a word is an aspect-related information. Since we get a probability for each word to be the right word to focus on, we thus use it to compute a new representation of the input sentence. To do that, we simply multiply the weighted vector s and the output of LSTM h_t in the Eq. 7,

$$h_{t_{new}} = s \times h_t \tag{11}$$

where $h_{t_{new}}$ is the new representation of the input sentence. By feeding the new presentation to softmax in order, we get the probability of an input sentence for each aspect in the prediction layer,

$$p = softmax(W_p.h_{t_{new}} + b_p) \tag{12}$$

where W_p and b_p are the parameters, and p is probability of cach predicted aspect. We train the model in an end-to-end supervised learning way by back-propagation in order to minimize the cross-entropy between marked aspect y and predicted aspect $\hat{y}$,

$$loss = - \sum_i y^i \times log(\hat{y}^i) + \lambda ||\theta||^2 \tag{13}$$

where θ is the set of parameters, i is the index of sentence, λ is a regularization hyper-parameter.

4   Experiment

4.1   Parameters and Initialization

In our experiments, we use GloVe[1] [20] with dimension 300 to initialize the word vectors. GloVe contains 4000001 words vectors, in which the word embedding vectors are pre-trained on a corpus of 840 billions. All the others parameters are initialized by uniform distribution $U(-\epsilon, \epsilon)$. The hint embedding matrix $h_e \in \mathbb{R}^{a \times d}$, a is the number of aspect in the training set and d is set to 100. Dropout keep probability is 0.5. Theano [2] is the framework used for implementing our neural networks model. Regularization term L_2 is set to 0.001 with batch size of 25 sentences.

4.2   Datasets

To validate our approach, we rely on benchmark datasets. SemEval (Semantic Evaluation) is an ongoing series of evaluations of computational semantic analysis systems. We evaluate our approach with Aspect Based Sentiment Analysis (ABSA) task in 2014 and 2016. We are asked in this task to identify the entity E and attribute A pairs towards an opinion expressed in a given sentence. More details are in [18,21]. The detailed statistics are summarized in Table 1.

Table 1. Datasets statistics, SemEval 2014 restaurant and SemEval 2016 laptop.

Dataset	Train (sentence)	Test (sentence)	Total
Restaurant	3041	800	3841
Laptop	2500	808	3308

4.3   Comparative Methods

We validate the performance by comparing our model with the methods that achieved best performance in aspect identification as well as the successful methods in competition:

1. **UNITOR:** The authors of [4] proposed UNITOR to tackle aspect category identification in SemEval 2014 Task 4. They linearly combined multiple Kernels to generalize linguistic information using SVM-framework to deal with aspect category detection as a text classification problem. However, UNITOR is an unconstrained system that relied on additional training data and relied on the feature engineering which is labor intensive.
2. **SUACD:** SUACD in [27] proposed two methods unsupervised and supervised for aspect identification, we compare with the supervised method. The authors introduced to mine the detection rules using conditional probability, which are calculated by some features including word co-occurrence, grammatical relation triples and the annotated aspect category.

---

[1] Pre-trained model of GloVe is available from stanford.

3. **NRC-Can:** NRC-Can [11] proposed SVM-based approach to detect aspects in customer reviews. The input of their model is a set of generated features such as ngrams, non-contiguous ngrams and lexicon features, etc.
4. **NLANG:** NLANG proposed in [30], which aims at improving aspect based sentiment analysis using neural network features. It referred to set of features including (names, proper name and component, embedding and the output of a CNN layer). It used a binary classifiers trained using single layer feed-forward network where the input is these collected features.
5. **AUEB-ABSA:** AUEB-ABSA proposed in [32]. They used multiple ensembles based on SVM classifiers to address the aspect category identification task in laptop domain. The features are hand-crafted and word embedding based.

In addition to the comparative methods mentioned previously, we also compared with two approaches SYSU and XRCE [3,21] to ensure the compression with top three performances in the competition.

4.4   Results

Table 2. Results of restaurant domain. The results of XRCE, UNITOR and NRC-Can are taken from [18], while SUACD is from [27]. Best scores are in bold.

Domain	Method	F_1
Restaurant	XRCE	82.28
	SUACD	83.8
	UNITOR	85.26
	NRC-Can	88.57
	HEA-LSTM	**92.31**

Table 3. Results of laptop domain. The results of SYSU, NLANG and AUEB-ABSA are taken from [21]. Best scores are in bold.

Domain	Method	F_1
Laptop	SYSU	49.07
	AUEB-ABSA	49.105
	NLANG	51.93
	HEA-LSTM	**59.65**

We conduct experiments on benchmark datasets summarized in the Table 1 to evaluate the performance of our approach. However, we follow experimental settings of the previous works measuring the model by F_1 scores. As it is shown in the Tables 2 and 3, our approach achieves best performance in both restaurant and laptop datasets, with 92.31 and 59.65 respectively. In the Table 4, we compare the standard LSTM with HEA-LSTM, the results prove the improvement of attention mechanism over standard LSTM.

4.5   Qualitative Analysis

While experiment on benchmark datasets, we end up with several observations that can be summarized as follows: (1) The dataset of restaurant is annotated with only five gold aspect categories. In such case, each aspect is provided with

Table 4. Improvement of HEA-LSTM over standard LSTM, measured by F_1.

Dataset	LSTM	HEA-LSTM
Restaurant	87.52	**92.31**
Laptop	52.65	**59.65**

Table 5. Recall, precision and F1 for the five gold aspect-categories of restaurant dataset.

Category	Precision	Recall	F_1
Food	93.65	94.67	94.15
Service	92.91	95.89	94.37
Ambiance	88.95	89.70	89.32
Price	92.82	97.29	95.00
Miscellaneous	89.51	87.92	88.70

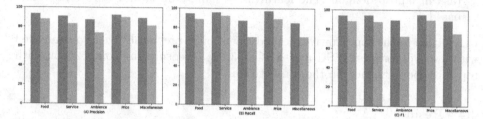

Fig. 2. Gold aspect-categories of restaurant domain. Blue and green represent the proposed approach HEA-LSTM and SUACD [27] respectively. (Color figure online)

enough examples to be learned. Therefore, the existing work already achieved good performance, as it is shown in the Table 2. (2) In the Table 3 the provided dataset is very small compared with the high number of evaluated aspects. The learning based approaches cannot build a good knowledge for each aspect from few examples. However, we referred to extra knowledge, such as the aspect's indicators, which can encourage the model to learn better. (3) In laptop dataset, we observe that an indicator may refer to different aspects. For example, the representative phrase *"battery life"* stands for two aspects *"battery#quality"* and *"operation#performance"*. In the sentence, *"the battery issue and the battery life does not last too long"* is annotated with *"operation#performance"* while our model predicts *"battery#quality"*.

To analyze the errors, we supervised the performance for each aspect, as reported in Table 5. However, we figured out that our approach could not perform very well with the aspects *"ambience"* and *"miscellaneous"* compared to the other aspects. The reasons behind that are the coherence of aspect-representatives and the aspect *"miscellaneous"* poses a challenge (i.e., it is unclear what exactly belongs in this category). The true label of the sentence review *"the restaurant is rather small but we were lucky to get a table quickly"* is *"ambience"*, *"small"* alone is not enough to evaluate the *"ambiance"* with the presence of *"quickly"*, which expresses the service (i.e.; *"staff"*). The representative word *"place"* significantly stands for *"ambiance"*, but it also evaluates the restaurant generally and different aspects. For example, the sentence *"you do not want to miss this place"* evaluates *"miscellaneous"*. As it is shown in the

Fig. 2, our proposed model outperforms SUACD [27] in term of recall, precision and f1-score for all aspects category in the dataset.

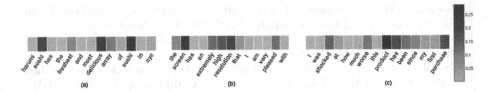

Fig. 3. Attention layer visualization (a) for *"Food"*, (b) for *"display#quality"* and (c) for *"laptop#general"*. The important parts of the sentence are represented by the color depth according to their weights assigned by the attention mechanism.

The proposed attention mechanism aims at computing the importance of each part in a sentence towards the expressed aspect. Equation 9 provides the probability for each part of being an aspect-relevant. Thus, as it is shown in Fig. 3, we use plotly[2] to visualize this importance the more depth colored parts the more important ones. It illustrates the effectiveness of the proposed attention mechanism, which can be interpreted as follows: In (a), the true label aspect is *"food"*, the parts (*"sushi, delicious, freshest and array"*) obtain higher probability than the other ones. In (b), the true label aspect is *"display#quality"*, the aspect-relevant parts (*"screen and high resolution"*) are weighted-up. In (c), the true label *"laptop#general"* represented by (*"product, purchase and shocked"*).

5 Conclusion

In this paper, we presented Hint-embedding Attention-based Long-short Term Memory for Aspect Identification, HEA-LSTM. It first extracts the representative words of aspects from the corpus, which are considered as aspects' hints. It then computes the aggregation of hints and the output of LSTM via an attention mechanism. In contrast to SVM-based models, HEA-LSTM can more focus on the aspect-related information by embedding its indicators in the sentence. Our experiment results show that HEA-LSTM obtains superior performance over the existing approaches. To the best of our knowledge, HEA-LSTM is the first to combine hints with LSTM via an attention mechanism to deal with the aspect identification problem.

Acknowledgment. This work was supported by the Ministry of Science and Technology of China, National Key Research and Development Program (2016YFB1000703), NSF of China (61732014 and 61672432).

---

[2] Tool for data visualization, it is available on plotly.

580   M. Ahmed et al.

References

1. Bahdanau, D., Cho, K., Bengio, Y.: Neural machine translation by jointly learning to align and translate. arXiv preprint arXiv:1409.0473 (2014)
2. Bastien, F., et al.: Theano: new features and speed improvements. In: Deep Learning and Unsupervised Feature Learning NIPS 2012 Workshop (2012)
3. Brun, C., Popa, D.N., Roux, C.: XRCE: hybrid classification for aspect-based sentiment analysis. In: SemEval@ COLING, pp. 838–842 (2014)
4. Castellucci, G., Filice, S., Croce, D., Basili, R.: UNITOR: aspect based sentiment analysis with structured learning. In: SemEval@ COLING, pp. 761–767 (2014)
5. He, R., Lee, W.S., Ng, H.T., Dahlmeier, D.: An unsupervised neural attention model for aspect extraction. In: Proceedings of the 55th Annual Meeting of the Association for Computational Linguistics (Volume 1: Long Papers), vol. 1, pp. 388–397 (2017)
6. Hermann, K.M., et al.: Teaching machines to read and comprehend. In: Advances in Neural Information Processing Systems, pp. 1693–1701 (2015)
7. Hochreiter, S., Schmidhuber, J.: Long short-term memory. Neural Comput. 9(8), 1735–1780 (1997)
8. Hu, M., Liu, B.: Mining and summarizing customer reviews. In: Proceedings of the Tenth ACM SIGKDD International Conference on Knowledge Discovery and Data Mining, pp. 168–177. ACM (2004)
9. Jakob, N., Gurevych, I.: Extracting opinion targets in a single-and cross-domain setting with conditional random fields. In: Proceedings of the 2010 Conference on Empirical Methods in Natural Language Processing, pp. 1035–1045. Association for Computational Linguistics (2010)
10. Jo, Y., Oh, A.H.: Aspect and sentiment unification model for online review analysis. In: Proceedings of the Fourth ACM International Conference on Web Search and Data Mining, pp. 815–824. ACM (2011)
11. Kiritchenko, S., Zhu, X., Cherry, C., Mohammad, S.: NRC-Canada-2014: detecting aspects and sentiment in customer reviews. In: SemEval@ COLING, pp. 437–442 (2014)
12. Lafferty, J., McCallum, A., Pereira, F.C.: Conditional random fields: probabilistic models for segmenting and labeling sequence data (2001)
13. Wang, L., Liu, K., Cao, Z., Zhao, J., De Melo, G.: Sentiment-aspect extraction based on restricted Boltzmann machines. In: ACL, vol. 1, pp. 616–625 (2015)
14. Liu, B.: Sentiment analysis and opinion mining. Synth. Lect. Hum. Lang. Technol. 5(1), 1–167 (2012)
15. Liu, B., Hu, M., Cheng, J.: Opinion observer: analyzing and comparing opinions on the web. In: Proceedings of the 14th International Conference on World Wide Web, pp. 342–351. ACM (2005)
16. Liu, J., Zhang, Y.: Attention modeling for targeted sentiment. In: EACL 2017, p. 572 (2017)
17. Chen, Z., Mukherjee, A., Liu, B.: Aspect extraction with automated prior knowledge learning. In: Proceedings of the 52nd Annual Meeting of the Association for Computational Linguistics, pp. 347–358 (2014)
18. Maria, P., Dimitrios, G., John, P., Haris, P., Ion, A., Suresh, M.: SemEval-2014 task 4: aspect based sentiment analysis, pp. 27–35 (2014)
19. Mnih, V., Heess, N., Graves, A., et al.: Recurrent models of visual attention. In: Advances in Neural Information Processing Systems, pp. 2204–2212 (2014)

20. Pennington, J., Socher, R., Manning, C.: GloVe: global vectors for word representation. In: Proceedings of the 2014 Conference on Empirical Methods in Natural Language Processing (EMNLP), pp. 1532–1543 (2014)
21. Pontiki, M., et al.: SemEval-2016 task 5: aspect based sentiment analysis. In: ProWorkshop on Semantic Evaluation (SemEval-2016), pp. 19–30. Association for Computational Linguistics (2016)
22. Popescu, A.M., Etzioni, O.: Extracting product features and opinions from reviews. In: Kao, A., Poteet, S.R. (eds.) Natural Language Processing and Text Mining, pp. 9–28. Springer, London (2007). https://doi.org/10.1007/978-1-84628-754-1_2
23. Qiu, G., Liu, B., Bu, J., Chen, C.: Opinion word expansion and target extraction through double propagation. Comput. Linguist. $37(1)$, 9–27 (2011)
24. Rocktäschel, T., Grefenstette, E., Hermann, K.M., Kočiský, T., Blunsom, P.: Reasoning about entailment with neural attention. arXiv preprint arXiv:1509.06664 (2015)
25. Ruder, S., Ghaffari, P., Breslin, J.G.: INSIGHT-1 at SemEval-2016 task 5: deep learning for multilingual aspect-based sentiment analysis. arXiv preprint arXiv:1609.02748 (2016)
26. Rush, A.M., Chopra, S., Weston, J.: A neural attention model for abstractive sentence summarization. arXiv preprint arXiv:1509.00685 (2015)
27. Schouten, K., van der Weijde, O., Frasincar, F., Dekker, R.: Supervised and unsupervised aspect category detection for sentiment analysis with co-occurrence data. IEEE Trans. Cybern. $48(4)$, 1263–1275 (2018)
28. Tamchyna, A., Veselovská, K.: UFAL at SemEval-2016 task 5: recurrent neural networks for sentence classification. In: Proceedings of the 10th International Workshop on Semantic Evaluation (SemEval-2016), pp. 367–371 (2016)
29. Titov, I., McDonald, R.: Modeling online reviews with multi-grain topic models. In: Proceedings of the 17th International Conference on World Wide Web, pp. 111–120. ACM (2008)
30. Toh, Z., Su, J.: NLANGP at SemEval-2016 task 5: improving aspect based sentiment analysis using neural network features. In: SemEval@ NAACL-HLT, pp. 282–288 (2016)
31. Wang, Y., Huang, M., Zhu, X., Zhao, L.: Attention-based LSTM for aspect-level sentiment classification. In: EMNLP, pp. 606–615 (2016)
32. Xenos, D., Theodorakakos, P., Pavlopoulos, J., Malakasiotis, P., Androutsopoulos, I.: AUEB-ABSA at SemEval-2016 task 5: ensembles of classifiers and embeddings for aspect based sentiment analysis. In: Proceedings of the 10th International Workshop on Semantic Evaluation (SemEval-2016), pp. 312–317 (2016)
33. Yin, Y., Wei, F., Dong, L., Xu, K., Zhang, M., Zhou, M.: Unsupervised word and dependency path embeddings for aspect term extraction. arXiv preprint arXiv:1605.07843 (2016)
34. Zhao, W.X., Jiang, J., Yan, H., Li, X.: Jointly modeling aspects and opinions with a MaxEnt-LDA hybrid. In: Proceedings of the 2010 Conference on Empirical Methods in Natural Language Processing, pp. 56–65. Association for Computational Linguistics (2010)

Sparsity Constraint Nonnegative Tensor Factorization for Mobility Pattern Mining

Thirunavukarasu Balasubramaniam[1](✉), Richi Nayak[1](✉), and Chau Yuen[2]

[1] School of Electrical Engineering and Computer Science, Queensland University of Technology, Brisbane, Australia
{thirunavukarasu.balas,r.nayak}@qut.edu.au
[2] Engineering Product Development, Singapore University of Technology and Design, Singapore, Singapore

Abstract. Despite the capability of modeling multi-dimensional (such as spatio-temporal) data, tensor modeling and factorization methods such as Nonnegative Tensor Factorization (NTF) is in infancy for automatically learning mobility patterns of people. The quality of patterns generated by these methods gets affected by the sparsity of the data. This paper introduces a Sparsity constraint Nonnegative Tensor Factorization (SNTF) method and studies how to effectively generate mobility patterns from the Location Based Social Networks (LBSNs) usage data. The factorization process is optimized using the element selection based factorization algorithm, Greedy Coordinate Descent algorithm. Empirical analysis with real-world datasets shows the significance of SNTF in automatically learning accurate mobility patterns. We empirically show that the sparsity constraint in NTF improves the accuracy of patterns for highly sparse datasets and is able to identify distinctive patterns.

Keywords: Nonnegative Tensor Factorization · Sparsity constraint · Mobility pattern mining · Spatiotemporal · Greedy Coordinate Descent

1 Introduction

People migration from rural areas to urban cities for various reasons is a common and growing phenomenon [6]. Despite the increasing population growth, cities should be able to provide necessary infrastructure such as well-connected transportation [10]. Understanding the (spatio-temporal) mobility patterns of people assists the city planners to plan and respond proactively in applications such as modeling traffic controlling and easy transportation.

Recent advancements in Information and Communication Technologies such as smartphones, sensors, and Internet of Things (IoT) enable data collection with location information for further analyses [19]. For example, people mobility can be tracked using the Global Positioning System (GPS) [16]. Smartphones with inbuilt sensors generate a massive amount of data. Consequently, there is a

© Springer Nature Switzerland AG 2019
A. C. Nayak and A. Sharma (Eds.): PRICAI 2019, LNAI 11671, pp. 582–594, 2019.
https://doi.org/10.1007/978-3-030-29911-8_45

growing interest in utilizing mobile generated sensor data and data collected by
LBSNs to understand the mobility patterns of people and use them in making
the smart cities intelligent [5].

Data generated by smartphones and LBSNs is multi-dimensional. Tensor
modelling [14], that has been successfully applied in diverse fields of image processing, telecommunications, chemometrics, Recommender systems, and pattern
mining for modelling multi-dimensional data, becomes a natural choice to represent them. Factorization methods such as Tucker and CP [15] are applied to the
populated tensor model to project higher-dimensional data to lower-dimension
matrices. The lower-order mapping enables the factor matrices to learn the latent
relationships that can be investigated for pattern mining [4]. For example, a
third-order tensor (user × location × time) can be used to represent users'
spatio-temporal data collected by a LBSNs. This tensor can be factorized into
the lower-order representation of three factor matrices. The location and temporal factor matrices will reveal the location and temporal patterns respectively.
The temporal patterns can be derived for different periods by varying the time
dimension scaling such as hourly, daily, etc. as per the data suitability.

While multi-type relationships present in a multi-dimensional dataset can be
captured using tensor factorization, the sparsity prevailing in the mobile and
LBSNs generated data needs a special attention [3]. The existing factorization
methods fail to learn the associations under this condition as the objective function formulated for the factorization process is not able to learn sparse factor
matrices. The factorization process results into the dense factor matrices, hence
the learned patterns can not reveal the real relationships [11]. Tensor factorization of sparse multi-dimensional datasets is a challenging task.

This paper proposes a Sparsity constraint Nonnegative Tensor Factorization (SNTF) method using the $L_{2,1}$ norm and half-quadratic minimization.
We extend the popular Greedy Coordinate Descent (GCD) factorization algorithm, developed for matrix [12], to tensor to generate the sparse metrics effectively and automate the process of pattern mining. Two real-world datasets are
used to evaluate the proposed SNTF method: (1) the Singapore senior citizens
dataset recording their check-in behavior with smartphones; and (2) the Tokyo
foursquare dataset which records the users' check-in behavior at various locations
via the LBSNs. We evaluate SNTF for identifying distinctive spatiotemporal patterns in comparison to the state-of-the-art NTF based spatiotemporal pattern
mining methods. The spatiotemporal patterns are effectively used to cluster the
users according to their mobility patterns. Experimental results show the significant pattern elicitation achieved using SNTF.

2   Related Work

Every instance in spatiotemporal datasets is associated with both spatial and
temporal information. This makes the tensor model [14] as the clear choice to
represent this type of data. We present related works in the areas of spatiotemporal pattern finding with tensor modeling and factorization models.

The application of tensor modeling in smart city data is in infancy. Tensor
modeling was applied to model the (location × noise category × time-slot) data

to understand the noise pollution across New York City to inform people about the better environment [22]. Results show that the traditional tensor factorization fails to predict most of the missing entries due to the data being sparse. Another example of traditional NTF can be seen in modeling the spatiotemporal information and predicting the site-selection recommendation [8]. This study understands the patterns of local commute in the Great East Japan Earthquake. The spatiotemporal mobility data were modeled and factorized using probabilistic tucker factorization to understand the mobility of users to model the urban structure [20]. However, the tucker factorization is known to be very expensive, different from the one as proposed in the paper. The spatiotemporal patterns derived with tensor factorization were used to understand network events [13]. However, this method formulates the objective function to deal with the denser log data, hence it is not suitable to understand the spatiotemporal user patterns in the smart city under sparse condition.

Existing state-of-the-art tensor model based methods focus on deriving spatiotemporal patterns by representing the data as (location × day × time) tensor and report not to have high accuracy due to sparsity [2]. More importantly, these methods do not focus on identifying users' clusters based on spatiotemporal patterns. While most of the methods propose how to use spatial and temporal contexts naively, this paper proposes to incorporate spatial and temporal contexts in a non-linear fashion and focus on users' usage patterns and clusters.

With the popularity of multi-dimensional data, researchers have designed NTF with different regularizations and constraints to learn meaningful patterns. For example, a graph laplacian Regularization based NTF (RNTF) uses the regularization to maintain the geometrical structure of the original data in its lower dimensional representation to learn the transportation network's traffic dynamics [9]. Though RNTF can maintain the geometrical structure for better patterns, it may have no effect when the dataset is sparse. The orthogonal constraint NTF (ONTF) has been introduced to incorporate the orthogonal constraint to identify independent patterns with highly distinctive patterns [2]. However, the orthogonal constraint imposed is rigorous and results in slower convergence. The strictness of each factor to be distinctive will also make the method to lose the true nature. To our best of knowledge, a NTF method does not exist that can work for sparse LBSNs datasets.

3   Nonnegative Tensor Factorization: Background

Tensor Factorization (TF) is a dimensionality reduction technique that learns the latent relationships inherent in the multi-dimensional dataset. A third order TF factorizes a three dimensional tensor into three factor matrices representing the latent features of each dimension. These latent features become the patterns and regularities that occur in the data. The basic idea of NTF is factorizing the tensor into n factor matrices with the nonnegative constraint, i.e., all values in the matrices should be positive [14]. NTF can be solved using a traditional Tucker or CP factorization model by imposing the constraint to maintain the nonnegative values in a factor matrix. CP factorization has been proved to be more efficient than Tucker [1]. Alternating Least Square (ALS) is one of the most commonly used factorization algorithm to learn the factor matrices [21]. Table 1 details the notations used throughout this paper.

Table 1. Notations

Symbol	Definition
$\mathcal{X}$	Tensor (Euler script letter)
$\mathbf{U}$	Matrix (upper case. bold letter)
$\mathbf{u}$	Vector (lower case, bold letter)
u	Scalar (upper case, italic letter)/element
$\mathbf{X_n}$	Mode-n matricization of tensor
$\odot$	Khatri-Rao product
$*$	Hadamard product
$\circ$	Outer product
$\|\cdot\|$	Frobenius norm

The objective function of NTF of a third-order tensor $\mathcal{X} \in \mathbb{R}^{M \times N \times O}$ based on the CP model with tensor rank R is formulated as follows:

$$f(\mathbf{U}, \mathbf{L}, \mathbf{T}) = \|\mathcal{X} - [\![\mathbf{U}, \mathbf{L}, \mathbf{T}]\!]\|^2, s.t. \mathbf{U}, \mathbf{L}, \mathbf{T} \geq 0 \qquad (1)$$

where $[\![\mathbf{U}, \mathbf{L}, \mathbf{T}]\!] = \sum_{r=1}^{R} \mathbf{u}_r \circ \mathbf{l}_r \circ \mathbf{t}_r$, $\mathbf{U} \in \mathbb{R}^{M \times R}$, $\mathbf{L} \in \mathbb{R}^{N \times R}$, and $\mathbf{T} \in \mathbb{R}^{O \times R}$.

4 Sparsity Constraint Nonnegative Tensor Factorization

Figure 1 details the overall process of the proposed SNTF method for spatiotemporal pattern mining. The factor matrices $\mathbf{U}, \mathbf{L}$, and $\mathbf{T}$ are randomly initialized, and the optimization process starts with gradient calculation. With the calculated gradient values, the important elements of factor matrices are updated using the GCD factorization algorithm [12]. The sparsity constraint is incorporated into the process, and the update is conducted until convergence. The learned factor matrices are then used to derive the spatiotemporal patterns and users' clusters.

Sparsity constraint is usually incorporated into NTF using a norm to produce meaningful interpretations of the factor matrices. L_1 norm is the commonly used sparsity constraint that generates sparser factor matrices when compared to NTF alone. However, it does not guarantee successful model outcome due to the fact that it penalizes the features individually (column-wise) and is incapable to deal with simultaneous elimination [23]. Simultaneous elimination is a process where a set of features are eliminated considering correlations among the features. $L_{1,2}$

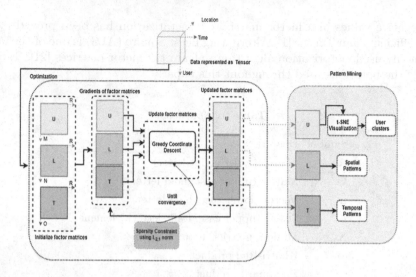

Fig. 1. The overall process of SNTF

norm is also used as sparsity constraint which can generate even more sparser factor matrices, but it is also reported to disregard simultaneous elimination due to column-wise sparsity constraint [17].

Our prior research has shown that $L_{2,1}$ norm is a suitable unbiased choice to impose sparsity constraint in non-negative matrix factorization [3]. It imposes sparsity constraint row-wise and takes into account the feature correlation during the process. Moreover, the row-wise sparsity constraint can facilitate simultaneous elimination and result in successful model outcome. In this paper, we apply $L_{2,1}$ norm sparsity constraint on the factor matrices that can facilitate to learn the sparser tensor factor matrices effectively.

Using $L_{2,1}$ norm, we introduce the sparsity constraint row-wise. This way of constraint application makes only the insignificant features to be zero. Each row of factor matrices corresponds to a feature in the original space, and insignificant rows are set to be zero to preserve the sparsity. As mobility pattern involves all the factor matrices to be analyzed, we propose to set the sparsity constraint on all factor matrices.

The $L_{2,1}$ norm NTF objective function can be formulated as,

$$f(\mathbf{U}, \mathbf{L}, \mathbf{T}) = \|\mathcal{X} - [\![\mathbf{U}, \mathbf{L}, \mathbf{T}]\!]\|^2 + \|\mathbf{U}\|_{2,1} + \|\mathbf{L}\|_{2,1} + \|\mathbf{T}\|_{2,1}, s.t. \mathbf{U}, \mathbf{L}, \mathbf{T} \geq 0 \quad (2)$$

where $\|\mathbf{U}\|_{2,1}$, $\|\mathbf{L}\|_{2,1}$, and $\|\mathbf{T}\|_{2,1}$ are $L_{2,1}$ norms of $\mathbf{U}$, $\mathbf{L}$, and $\mathbf{T}$ respectively.

This Objective function is based on Euclidean loss function, non-quadratic and non-convex, hence will be difficult to be solved. The half-quadratic minimization technique converts the non-quadratic function into an augmented objective function that eases the minimization process [7]. Hence, we propose to calculate $L_{2,1}$ norm of factor matrices using an auxiliary variable based on half-quadratic minimization as,

$$\|\mathbf{U}\|_{2,1} = Tr(\mathbf{U}^T \mathbf{Q_U} \mathbf{U}) \tag{3}$$

$$\|\mathbf{L}\|_{2,1} = Tr(\mathbf{L}^T \mathbf{Q_L} \mathbf{L}) \tag{4}$$

$$\|\mathbf{T}\|_{2,1} = Tr(\mathbf{T}^T \mathbf{Q_T} \mathbf{T}) \tag{5}$$

where $\mathbf{Q_U}, \mathbf{Q_L}, \mathbf{Q_T} \in \mathbb{R}^{R \times R}$ are diagonal matrices which impose insignificant rows to be zero making the factor matrices sparse.

For instance, the ith diagonal elements of $\mathbf{Q_U}$ is calculated [7] as,

$$\mathbf{Q_{U_{ii}}} = \frac{1}{2\|\mathbf{U}_i\|_1} \tag{6}$$

where $\mathbf{U}_i$ indicates the ith row of $\mathbf{U}$. Similarly, other diagonal matrices can be calculated.

We now apply the Greedy Coordinate Descent algorithm to solve the regularized objective function defined in Eq. (2).

4.1 Greedy Coordinate Descent (GCD) Factorization Algorithm

GCD is an element selection based coordinate descent factorization algorithm. It has shown to converge faster for NMF and learn better patterns in a data [4,12]. We apply GCD to update one factor matrix at a time by fixing all other factor matrices in the tensor factorization as defined in the non-convex objective function Eq. (2). We first show the update process of $\mathbf{U}$ by fixing the values of factor matrices $\mathbf{L}$ and $\mathbf{T}$.

$$\underset{\mathbf{U} \geq 0}{\operatorname{argmin}} \|\mathbf{X}_1 - \mathbf{U}(\mathbf{T} \odot \mathbf{L})^T\|^2 + \|\mathbf{U}\|_{2,1} \tag{7}$$

GCD follows the coordinate descent update rule and the gradients are calculated as,

$$\frac{\partial f}{\partial \mathbf{U}} = \mathbf{G} = -\mathbf{X}_1(\mathbf{T} \odot \mathbf{L}) + \mathbf{U}(\mathbf{L}^T \mathbf{L} * \mathbf{T}^T \mathbf{T}) + \mathbf{Q_U} \mathbf{U} \tag{8}$$

The second order derivatives of Eq. (8) can be calculated as,

$$\frac{\partial^2 f}{\partial \mathbf{U}} = \mathbf{H} = \mathbf{L}^T \mathbf{L} * \mathbf{T}^T \mathbf{T} + \mathbf{Q_U} \tag{9}$$

With the calculated gradients and second order derivatives, the element-wise update rule is formulated as,

$$u_{ij} = u_{ij} + \left[\max\left(0, u_{ij} - \frac{-\mathbf{X}_1(\mathbf{T} \odot \mathbf{L}) + \mathbf{U}(\mathbf{L}^T \mathbf{L} * \mathbf{T}^T \mathbf{T}) + \mathbf{Q_U} \mathbf{U}}{\mathbf{L}^T \mathbf{L} * \mathbf{T}^T \mathbf{T} + \mathbf{Q_U}}\right) - u_{ij} \right] \tag{10}$$

where u_{ij} is ij^{th} element of factor matrix $\mathbf{U}$.

Similarly, the factor matrices $\mathbf{L}$ and $\mathbf{T}$ are updated by calculating gradients and second order derivatives as,

$$\frac{\partial f}{\partial \mathbf{L}} = \mathbf{G} = -\mathbf{X_2}(\mathbf{T} \odot \mathbf{U}) + \mathbf{L}(\mathbf{U}^T\mathbf{U} * \mathbf{T}^T\mathbf{T}) + \mathbf{Q_U}\mathbf{L} \tag{11}$$

$$\frac{\partial^2 f}{\partial \mathbf{L}} = \mathbf{H} = \mathbf{U}^T\mathbf{U} * \mathbf{T}^T\mathbf{T} + \mathbf{Q_L} \tag{12}$$

$$l_{ij} = l_{ij} + \left[\max(0, l_{ij} - \frac{-\mathbf{X_2}(\mathbf{T} \odot \mathbf{U}) + \mathbf{L}(\mathbf{U}^T\mathbf{U} * \mathbf{T}^T\mathbf{T}) + \mathbf{Q_U}\mathbf{L}}{\mathbf{U}^T\mathbf{U} * \mathbf{T}^T\mathbf{T} + \mathbf{Q_L}}) - l_{ij} \right] \tag{13}$$

$$\frac{\partial f}{\partial \mathbf{T}} = \mathbf{G} = -\mathbf{X_3}(\mathbf{L} \odot \mathbf{U}) + \mathbf{T}(\mathbf{U}^T\mathbf{U} * \mathbf{L}^T\mathbf{L}) + \mathbf{Q_T}\mathbf{T} \tag{14}$$

$$\frac{\partial^2 f}{\partial \mathbf{T}} = \mathbf{H} = \mathbf{U}^T\mathbf{U} * \mathbf{L}^T\mathbf{L} + \mathbf{Q_T} \tag{15}$$

$$t_{ij} = t_{ij} + \left[\max(0, t_{ij} - \frac{-\mathbf{X_3}(\mathbf{L} \odot \mathbf{U}) + \mathbf{T}(\mathbf{U}^T\mathbf{U} * \mathbf{L}^T\mathbf{L}) + \mathbf{Q_T}\mathbf{T}}{\mathbf{U}^T\mathbf{U} * \mathbf{L}^T\mathbf{L} + \mathbf{Q_T}}) - t_{ij} \right] \tag{16}$$

Element Selection. With the update rules defined, the objective of GCD is to select important elements row-wise and update it. This helps to converge faster and learning significant features as only important elements are updated. Moreover, simultaneous elimination becomes easier. We first calculate each element's importance which is the difference between the objective function with and without element being updated as,

$$e_{ij} = -(u_{ij} * g_{ij}) - 0.5 * (h_{jj} * u_{ij} * u_{ij}) \tag{17}$$

where e_{ij} is the ij^{th} element importance $\mathbf{E}$.

For each row (say i^{th} row), an element is selected with the higher value of $e \in \mathbf{e_{i*}}$ to be updated. Algorithm 1 details the process. The spatial and temporal patterns are derived from the learned factor matrices $\mathbf{L}$ and $\mathbf{T}$ respectively and the users' clusters based on spatiotemporal patterns are derived using the learned factor matrix $\mathbf{U}$.

5   Experiments and Discussion

Experiments are conducted to answer the following questions.

Q1. What is the performance of SNTF and other baseline methods for identifying distinctive patterns?

Q2. How the SNTF derived patterns can be used to understand the mobility patterns?

Q3. How to cluster users based on their spatio-temporal patterns?

The datasets used for the experiments and the experimental setups are detailed in Sects. 5.1 and 5.2. The Q1, Q2 and Q3 are addressed in Sects. 5.3, 5.4 and 5.5 respectively.

Algorithm 1. The GCD Algorithm for SNTF

Input: Tensor $\mathbf{X}$, Randomly Initiated factor matrices $\mathbf{U} \in \mathbb{R}^{M \times R}$, $\mathbf{L} \in \mathbb{R}^{N \times R}$, $\mathbf{T} \in \mathbb{R}^{O \times R}$, Rank R, maxiters, maxiniters.
Output: Learned $\mathbf{U} \in \mathbb{R}^{M \times R}$, $\mathbf{L} \in \mathbb{R}^{N \times R}$, $\mathbf{T} \in \mathbb{R}^{O \times R}$

1: **while** iters $\leq$ maxiters **do**
2:      **for** i $= 1{:}M$ **do**
3:          **for** j $= 1{:}R$ **do**
4:              calculate element importance using Eq. (17)
5:          **end for**
6:      **end for**
7:      **for** p $= 1{:}$ M **do**
8:          **while** inters $\leq$ maxiniters **do**
9:              identify the most importance element $\max(\mathbf{u_p})$
10:             update the element of $\mathbf{U}$ using Eq.(10)
11:         **end while**
12:     **end for**
13:     repeat steps 2 to 12 to update $\mathbf{L}$ and $\mathbf{T}$ using Eq. (13) and Eq. (16) respectively
14:     **return** $\mathbf{U}, \mathbf{L},$ and $\mathbf{T}$
15: **end while**

5.1 Datasets

Two real-world datasets are used to evaluate SNTF. The Singapore elderly people's mobility data is generated using smartphones. It consists of 37 users' check-in behavior at 1295 locations. The check-in activities are associated with a timestamp, and hence we generate two variations of datasets D1 and D2 with 24 h and 7 days time slots respectively. The Tokyo foursquare dataset is check-in behavior of 2294 users at 25000 locations with the relevant timestamp. Two variations, D3 and D4 are generated by setting 24 h and 7 days as time slots respectively. Table 2 shows the statistics of datasets used.

Table 2. Datasets

Dataset	Unique users	Unique locations	Time slot	Tensor size	Density
D1	37	1295	24	$37 \times 1295 \times 24$	0.00200
D2	37	1295	7	$37 \times 1295 \times 7$	0.00700
D3	2294	25000	24	$2294 \times 25000 \times 24$	0.00010
D4	2294	25000	7	$2294 \times 25000 \times 7$	0.00030

5.2 Experimental Setup and Benchmarks

Choosing a tensor rank (R) is a NP-hard problem and data specific. We identify a suitable R by empirically testing different rank values. For D1 and D4, we set the rank of tensor to 4 and 2 respectively as setting higher ranks does not provide any unique patterns. For D2 and D3, we set it to 3 as setting of higher ranks tends to identify fine grain clusters.

Table 3. Pattern distinctiveness and runtime

Method	D1	D2	D3	D4	Avg. PD	Avg. runtime (secs)
NTF	0.46	0.39	0.38	0.53	0.44	**0.33**
ONTF	**0.42**	0.36	0.73	0.77	0.57	8.57
RNTF	0.99	0.99	0.73	0.50	0.80	0.44
SNTF	0.47	**0.29**	**0.20**	**0.35**	**0.33**	23.91

The proposed SNTF method is compared against the following baseline methods. The state-of-the-art **NTF** [14] using ALS updating algorithm is used. Orthogonal Constraint NMF **ONTF** [2] imposes orthogonal constraint on any of the factor matrix so that the factor matrices derived can be highly distinctive to each other. This distinctive factors tends to provide distinctive patterns. Regularized NTF **RNTF** [9] is based on Graph Laplacian regularization which regularizes the factor matrices to maintain the geometrical structure of the high dimensional data to achieve better patterns.

For fair comparison, we start all the methods with the same randomly initialized factor matrices. The experiments are repeated five times with different initialization and the average value is reported.

5.3   Pattern Distinctiveness

The quality of a factor matrix can be calculated using Pattern Distinctiveness (PD), which measures the similarity among the patterns. A factor matrix is a low-order representative of a dimension in the tensor model and includes the number of columns as set by the R rank. Each column of a factor matrix is called as a pattern representing a hidden feature. As the objective is to find unique patterns and the inter-pattern similarity should be less, lower the value of PD, better the quality. PD of the column i of factor matrix **U** can be calculated as,

$$PD_i = \frac{1}{R-1} * \sum_{i=1,j=1}^{R} < \mathbf{u_i}, \mathbf{u_j} > s.t, \ i \neq j \qquad (18)$$

where PD_i is the pattern distinctiveness of ith pattern, and $< \mathbf{u_i}, \mathbf{u_j} >$ indicates the similarity between pattern i and j of factor matrix **U**.

In Eq. (18), the average similarity between the pattern i with all other patterns is calculated. This is repeated for all other patterns of **U** and the average is indicated as $PD_\mathbf{U}$ (PD of the factor matrix **U**). Similarly, the PD of all other factor matrices are calculated and the average is reported. Table 3 shows the PD of all the datasets. It can be seen that on average, SNTF can generate more distinctive patterns when compared to the benchmarking methods. While ONTF performs well for D1 and D2 where there are more patterns, it fails to identify any patterns when there are fewer patterns as in D3 and D4. On the other hand, RNTF performs well for D4 but fails to identify patterns for D1,

D2, and D3. Only NTF and SNTF performs consistently in all the cases where SNTF outperforms NTF with 11% higher PD. Due to frequent gradient updates involved in GCD, the average runtime of SNMF is higher as shown in Table 3.

5.4   Mobility Pattern Mining

Figures 2 and 4 show the temporal and spatial patterns derived from the factor matrices T and L respectively. Each color indicates a pattern and is the column of each factor matrix. For instance, in Fig. 2a, the red color indicates the first column of the temporal factor matrix T and red color marks in Fig. 4a indicates the first column of the location factor matrix L. As we set the rank to 4, we have four columns, each representing a pattern. We also report the patterns derived using NTF on D2 and D3 in Fig. 3. It can be noted that NTF fails to detect a few peaks (red color) on D2 and does not derive any unique patterns for D3 when compared to the patterns derived using SNTF.

To understand the mobility pattern, we have to relate Figs. 2 and 4. The blue pattern in Fig. 2a shows the higher activity from 1 pm to 11 pm, and this happens in the locations marked blue in Fig. 4a. Similarly, multiple mobility patterns can be understood. Another example is Fig. 2d, where people are highly active during the weekdays and are less active on weekends.

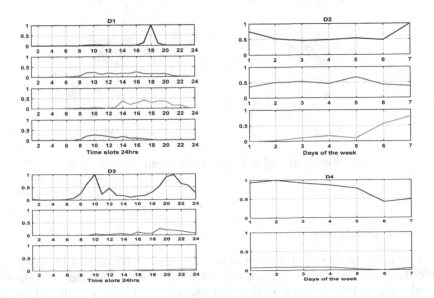

Fig. 2. Temporal patterns using SNTF (Color figure online)

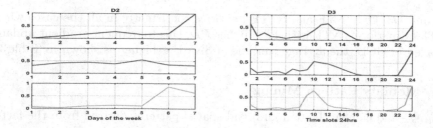

Fig. 3. Temporal patterns using NTF (Color figure online)

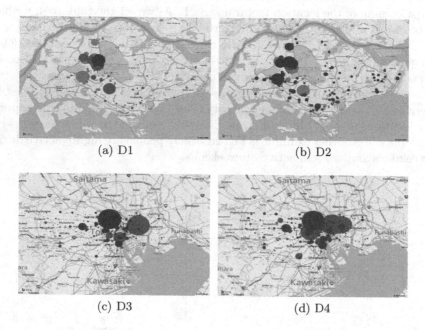

(a) D1   (b) D2

(c) D3   (d) D4

Fig. 4. Spatial patterns (Color figure online)

5.5 User Clustering

Figure 5 shows the user clusters derived from the user factor matrix $\mathbf{U}$. The factor matrix $\mathbf{U}$ have the columns (dimensions) ≥ 2. In order to visualize the clusters derived using NTF, we use *t-SNE* [18], a visualization technique based on distance measures where higher dimensional data is projected into two-dimensions. It becomes easy to visualize two-dimensional representation of factor matrix data points as shown in Fig. 5, rather than visualizing R-dimensional factor matrix. For instance, in Fig. 5b, the people generating red patterns of Figs. 2b and 4b are clustered together. This reveals the set of users who are following that particular spatiotemporal patterns.

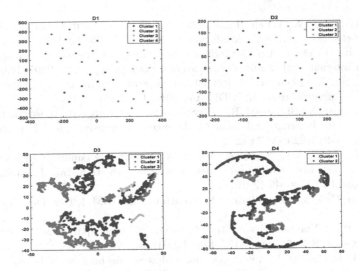

Fig. 5. User clusters - SNTF

6   Conclusion

This paper presents an effective tensor-based factorization method for mobility pattern mining. The proposed SNTF method imposes a sparsity constraint into NTF where factor matrices are learned using the GCD algorithm. The experimental results with two real-world datasets show the effectiveness of SNTF in learning the mobility patterns more distinctly. In the future, we would like to extend SNTF for joint factorization, which can facilitate pattern mining for multi-context data.

Acknowledgments. This research was partly supported by the Lee Kuan Yew Centre for Innovative Cities under Lee Li Ming Programme in Aging Urbanism.

References

1. Acar, E., Dunlavy, D.M., Kolda, T.G., Mørup, M.: Scalable tensor factorizations for incomplete data. Chemometr. Intell. Lab. Syst. **106**(1), 41–56 (2011)
2. Afshar, A., et al.: CP-ORTHO: an orthogonal tensor factorization framework for spatio-temporal data. In: SIGSPATIAL International Conference on Advances in Geographic Information Systems, p. 67. ACM (2017)
3. Balasubramaniam, T., Nayak, R., Yuen, C.: Understanding urban spatio-temporal usage patterns using matrix tensor factorization. In: IEEE International Conference on Data Mining Workshops, pp. 1497–1498 (2018)
4. Balasubramaniam, T., Nayak, R., Yuen, C.: Nonnegative coupled matrix tensor factorization for smart city spatiotemporal pattern mining. In: Nicosia, G., Pardalos, P., Giuffrida, G., Umeton, R., Sciacca, V. (eds.) Machine Learning, Optimization, and Data Science, pp. 520–532. Springer, Cham (2019). https://doi.org/10.1007/978-3-030-13709-0_44

5. Bao, J., Zheng, Y., Wilkie, D., Mokbel, M.: Recommendations in location-based social networks: a survey. GeoInformatica **19**(3), 525–565 (2015)
6. Chourabi, H., et al.: Understanding smart cities: an integrative framework. In: Hawaii International Conference on System Sciences, pp. 2289–2297. IEEE (2012)
7. Du, L., Li, X., Shen, Y.D.: Robust nonnegative matrix factorization via half-quadratic minimization. In: ICDM, pp. 201–210. IEEE (2012)
8. Fan, Z., Song, X., Shibasaki, R.: CitySpectrum: a non-negative tensor factorization approach. In: International Joint Conference on Pervasive and Ubiquitous Computing, pp. 213–223. ACM (2014)
9. Han, Y., Moutarde, F.: Analysis of large-scale traffic dynamics in an urban transportation network using non-negative tensor factorization. Int. J. Intell. Transp. Syst. Res. **14**(1), 36–49 (2016)
10. Harrison, C., et al.: Foundations for smarter cities. IBM J. Res. Dev. **54**(4), 1–16 (2010)
11. Hoyer, P.O.: Non-negative matrix factorization with sparseness constraints. J. Mach. Learn. Res. **5**(Nov), 1457–1469 (2004)
12. Hsieh, C.J., Dhillon, I.S.: Fast coordinate descent methods with variable selection for non-negative matrix factorization. In: SIGKDD, pp. 1064–1072. ACM (2011)
13. Kimura, T., et al.: Spatio-temporal factorization of log data for understanding network events. In: INFOCOM, pp. 610–618. IEEE (2014)
14. Kolda, T.G., Bader, B.W.: Tensor decompositions and applications. SIAM Rev. **51**(3), 455–500 (2009)
15. Kruskal, J.B.: Three-way arrays: rank and uniqueness of trilinear decompositions, with application to arithmetic complexity and statistics. Linear Algebra Appl. **18**(2), 95–138 (1977)
16. Lau, B.P.L., et al.: Extracting point of interest and classifying environment for low sampling crowd sensing smartphone sensor data. In: PerCom Workshops, pp. 201–206. IEEE (2017)
17. Luo, P., Peng, J., Fan, J.: l2, 1 norm and hessian regularized non-negative matrix factorization with discriminability for data representation. Appl. Sci. **7**(10), 1013 (2017)
18. Maaten, L.V.D., Hinton, G.: Visualizing data using t-SNE. J. Mach. Learn. Res. **9**(Nov), 2579–2605 (2008)
19. Marakkalage, S.H., et al.: Understanding the lifestyle of older population: mobile crowdsensing approach. IEEE TCSS (2018)
20. Sun, L., Axhausen, K.W.: Understanding urban mobility patterns with a probabilistic tensor factorization framework. Transp. Res. Part B Methodol. **91**, 511–524 (2016)
21. Takane, Y., Young, F.W., De Leeuw, J.: Nonmetric individual differences multidimensional scaling: an alternating least squares method with optimal scaling features. Psychometrika **42**(1), 7–67 (1977)
22. Zheng, Y., Liu, T., Wang, Y., Zhu, Y., Liu, Y., Chang, E.: Diagnosing New York city's noises with ubiquitous data. In: UbiComp, pp. 715–725. ACM (2014)
23. Zou, H., Yuan, M.: The f∞-norm support vector machine. Statistica Sinica, 379–398 (2008)

Short-Term Memory Variational Autoencoder for Collaborative Filtering

Hangbin Zhang[1], Raymond K. Wong[1(✉)], and Victor Chu[2]

[1] University of New South Wales, Sydney, Australia
hangbin.zhang@unsw.edu.au, wong@cse.unsw.edu.au
[2] Nanyang Technological University, Singapore, Singapore
wchu@ntu.edu.sg

Abstract. Recommender systems have been widely used by online service providers to conduct targeted marketing. However, since user behaviour and preferences are fluid and dynamic, predicting users' online actions is indeed a very difficult task. Variational Autoencoders (VAEs) have been recently proposed to improve the prediction accuracy of user preferences. Although classic VAEs go beyond linear modeling, they suffer from underfitting problem when the underlying datasets are sparse. Moreover, we found that classic VAEs are ineffective for dynamic user preferences. To address these deficiencies, we propose Short Term Memory Variational Autoencoder (STMVAE) to overcome the underfitting issue and to better handle the dynamics. This is achieved by capturing users' short term preferences to generate near term predictions. The validity and efficacy of our proposed model are evaluated comprehensively using three datasets in our experiments.

1 Introduction

There are three major approaches for recommender systems: (i) content-based filtering, (ii) collaborative filtering and (iii) hybrid filtering. Content-based filtering uses the profiles of users and items, and hypothesizes that if a user is interested in some items in the past, they will prefer the items once again in the future. The issue of content-based filtering is that the recommendations are limited, since the recommender system is specialized to a set of items. Collaborative filtering is among the most widely applied approaches in recommender systems. Collaborative filtering makes use of historical interactions data, such as ratings on items, purchasing and like items, to construct model. It predicts what items a user may prefer by discovering similarities between users and items. The latent factor model is largely studied and applied in the collaborative filtering research and industries as it is simple and effective. However, because it is a linear model, it is limited in dealing with data sparsity and cold-start problems on large and sparse datasets. In recent years, the advance of neural networks in image analysis, speech recognition and natural language processing have gained significant attention. Meanwhile, recent studies demonstrate its effectiveness in recommendation tasks.

A. C. Nayak and A. Sharma (Eds.): PRICAI 2019, LNAI 11671, pp. 595–607, 2019.
https://doi.org/10.1007/978-3-030-29911-8_46

Hybrid filtering seeks to find the best approach by combining content filtering and collaborative filtering. Because of privacy concerns, it becomes hard to collect user profile. Collaborative filtering also has its limitations. When a dataset is sparse, the performance drops down dramatically. The hybrid filtering solves this problem by combining content-based data and the explicit data. In addition, the hybrid filtering has two sub-categories. The first one is loosely coupled methods and the second one is tightly coupled methods. One instance of the loosely coupled methods is described in [13]. The drawback of the methods is that the feature information cannot feedback to the extraction of features because the flow is one-way. To make improvements in this sub-category, the common method is manually test and trial the feature extraction process. However, this method is useful to improve the prediction accuracy of the collaborative filtering models such as matrix factorization. The tightly coupled methods can learn features from the auxiliary information with two-way interaction. Therefore, the tightly coupled methods usually have better performance than the loosely coupled methods [14].

On the other hand, VAEs have been studied extensively in image and natural language processing with satisfactory results, but there are only a few researches on VAEs in the field of recommender systems. In our studies, we extend VAEs to collaborative filtering for implicit feedback and temporal factors. Typically, VAEs rely on high quality input data to generate latent factors through an inference model, but only a few researches studied the improvement of input data to the models. In this paper, we propose Short Term Memory Variational Autoencoder (STMVAE) as a better solution for collaborative filtering. It is a neural temporal model cooperating with VAE. While most studies on VAEs used normalized bag-of-words vectors as input data, we found that although VAE is capable to handle sparsity, the processed input helps improve VAE's generated recommendations.

STMVAE is built to be a probabilistic latent factor model to avoid overfitting and can better make use of information from users. STMVAE explores an improved way to deal with temporal features in latent factor from other literature. While VAE is claimed to suffer from underfitting [5], we address this by introducing Short Term Memory (STM) model that learns temporal features. STMVAE is a Bayes based model, which is proved to be more robust regardless of the scarcity of the data [6]. We evaluate STMVAE on variety of real-world datasets and the results show that our proposed model outperforms competing collaborative filtering approaches. To the best of our knowledge, STMVAE is the first Bayesian generative model that provides a unified framework for recommender systems with temporal factors.

2 Problem Statement

Suppose there are U users $\mathbf{U} = \{1, 2, .., U\}$, I items $\mathbf{I} = \{1, 2, .., I\}$. Let $\mathbf{R} \in \mathbb{R}^{U \times I}$ denote the ratings or interests, where R_{ui} is the rating of user u on item i. If the rating is unknown, we mark unk. We construct the user-item interaction matrix $\mathbf{Y} \in \mathbb{R}^{U \times I}$ from R with implicit feedback as Eq. (1).

$$\mathbf{Y}_{ui} = \begin{cases} 0 \text{ if } R_{ui} = unk \\ 1 \ \ otherwise \end{cases} \tag{1}$$

Note that although we binarize the ratings in this study, STMVAE still works on explicit ratings. Recommender systems are commonly formulated as the problem of estimating probabilities of each unobserved entry in $\mathbf{Y}$, which are used for ranking items. VAE assumes that there is an underlying model that can generate probabilities from the latent variables $\mathbf{z}$ as Eq. (2) [1].

$$p(\mathbf{X}) = f(\mathbf{z}; \theta) \tag{2}$$

Where $\mathbf{z}$ is latent variables in high dimensional space $\mathbb{Z}$ that we can sample according to probability density function $p(\mathbf{z})$ defined over $\mathbb{Z}$. Function $f(\cdot)$ is parameterized by θ in space Θ. Based on this function, we can generate the probability of item i for the user u, and achieve the goal of recommending a set of items for an user u to maximize the user's satisfaction.

3 The Proposed Model

Our proposed Short Term Memory Variational Autoencoder (STMVAE) model is built upon VAE. In this section, we firstly introduce the VAE briefly, and then present our proposed STMVAE model.

Our notations are summarized as follows. We use $u \in \{1, 2, ..., \mathbf{U}\}$ to index users and $i \in \{1, 2, ..., \mathbf{I}\}$ to index items. $\mathbf{z}_u \in \mathbb{R}^K$ denotes the K-dimensional latent space representations and $\mathbf{x}_u \in \mathbb{N}^{\mathsf{T}}$ is a bag-of-words vector with the binary value that equals to 1 if the user liked or clicked an item or equals to 0 otherwise. $\mathbf{X}_u = \{\mathbf{x}_{u1}, \mathbf{x}_{u2}, ..., \mathbf{x}_{u|\mathbf{V}|}\}$ denotes the embedding vectors with respect to the u's interested item set $\mathbf{V}$.

3.1 Variational Autoencoder

Variational Autoencoder (VAE) is composed of two processes: (i) generative process and (ii) inference process.

The generative process is similar to what was discussed in [6]. For each user u, the generative network samples K-dimensional latent representation $\mathbf{z}_u$ from a Gaussian prior. Then the latent representation $\mathbf{z}_u$ is transformed through a multilayer perceptron $f_\theta(\cdot)$ to produce the probability distribution $\pi(\mathbf{z}_u)$ over $\mathbf{I}$ items. Then, $\mathbf{x}_u$ is drawn from the multinomial distribution.

$$\mathbf{z} \sim N(0, \mathbf{I}_K) \tag{3}$$

$$\pi(\mathbf{z}_u) \propto exp\{f_\theta(\mathbf{z}_u)\} \tag{4}$$

$$\mathbf{x}_u \sim \mathbf{Mult}(\mathbf{N}_u, \pi(\mathbf{z}_u)) \tag{5}$$

Note that the generative process can be reduced to classic matrix factorization when $f_\theta(\cdot)$ is a linear function. The log-likelihood for user u conditioned on the latent representation is as Eq. (6).

$$\log p_\theta(\mathbf{x}_u|\mathbf{z}_u) = \sum_i x_{ui} \cdot \log \pi_i(\mathbf{z}_u) \qquad (6)$$

Then we use inference network to learn Eq. (3). Because $p(\mathbf{z}_u|\mathbf{x}_u)$ is intractable, we approximate the post prior with a variational distribution $q(\mathbf{z}_u)$ that is set to be a factorized Gaussian distribution, as shown in Eq. (7).

$$q(\mathbf{z}_u) = N(\mu_u, diag\{\sigma_u^2\}) \qquad (7)$$

Optimizing the variational inference is equivalent to optimizing the variational parameters μ and σ in Eq. (7), i.e., minimizing the Kullback-leiber divergence $\mathrm{KL}(q(z_u)\|p(z_u|x_u))$. VAE avoids the increment of the weighting parameters when optimizing $\{\mu_u, \sigma_u^2\}$ by using so-called inference model as Eq. (8) to replace the data-dependent function.

$$q_\phi(\mathbf{z}_u|\mathbf{x}_u) = N(\mu_\phi(\mathbf{x}_u), diag\{\sigma_\phi^2(\mathbf{x}_u)\}) \qquad (8)$$

The inference model outputs the variational parameters for $q_\phi(\mathbf{z}_u|\mathbf{x}_u)$. In this way, when optimizing $q_\phi(\mathbf{z}_u|\mathbf{x}_u)$, the intractable $p_\theta(\mathbf{z}_u|\mathbf{x}_u)$ is approximated. With the inference model $q_\phi(\mathbf{z}_u|\mathbf{x}_u)$ and the generative model $p_\theta(\mathbf{x}_u|\mathbf{z}_u)$, the VAE model is constructed. The lower bound of the log marginal likelihood of the data is given as Eq. (9). In Eq. (9), The first term is the reconstruction error, and the second term is Kullback-leiber divergence, which play a role of regularization in the formula, where β controls the regularization level.

$$\log p(x_u; \theta) \geq \mathbf{E}_{q_\phi(z_u|x_u)} \log p_\theta(x_u|z_u) - \beta \cdot \mathrm{KL}(q_\phi(z_u|x_u)\|p(z_u)) \qquad (9)$$

3.2 The STMVAE Model

Inspired by the approach taken by [7] and by teacher-student model [12], we develop STMVAE based on VAE. Considering that users are only interested in a small subset of items [6], we argue that simply use bag-of-words vector as input leads to underfitting since the data is sparse. Classic VAE uses sparse vector as input, which limits the capability of VAE. In STMVAE, the input of VAE is the probability for each item, which includes more information.

The structure of STMVAE model is shown in Fig. 1. STMVAE is composed of two models: (i) STM model and (ii) VAE model. STM extracts the temporal features and generates the score vector. Specifically, the embedding layer in STM model is trained to embed each item $i \in \mathbf{V}$. $\mathbf{X}_u$ is the set of items that the user is interested in. $\mathbf{x}_{ul}$ represents the last interested record in $\mathbf{X}_u$, and in this study, this represents user's current interests, and $\mathbf{x}_{ug}$ represents the general interests of the user u, which is defined as the average of the external memory.

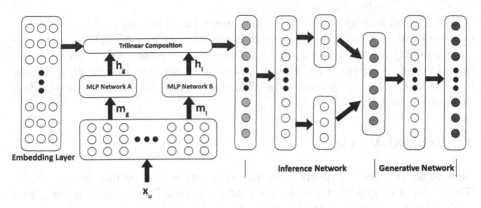

Fig. 1. The proposed Short Term Memory Variational Autoencoder (STMVAE)

$$m_g = \frac{1}{|\mathbf{V}|} \sum_{v=1}^{\mathbf{V}} \mathbf{x}_{uv} \tag{10}$$

$$m_l = \mathbf{x}_{ul} \tag{11}$$

Then, the general interests m_g and the last interest m_l are processed through two Multilayer Perceptron (MLP) networks with n hidden layers respectively. Two MLP networks have the same number of hidden layers, but the weights and biases are independent. The operation on each hidden layer is defined as Eq. (12), where $\mathbf{h}_n \in \mathbb{R}^d$ denotes the output state for each hidden layer. $\mathbf{W}_n \in \mathbb{R}^{d \times d}$ is the weight matrix and $\mathbf{b}_n \in \mathbb{R}^d$ is the bias vector. $g(\cdot)$ is the non-linear activation function, and we choose *tanh* function in this study.

$$\mathbf{h}_n = g(\mathbf{W}_n \mathbf{h}_{n-1} + \mathbf{b}_n) \tag{12}$$

At the trilinear composition layer, the score function for item $i \in \mathbf{I}$ is defined as Eq. (13), where $\mathbf{r}_i$ denotes the score for item i, $\sigma(\cdot)$ denotes the sigmoid function and $\odot$ denotes the element-wise product between two vectors.

$$\mathbf{r}_i = \sigma(\mathbf{h}_g^\top (\mathbf{h}_l \odot \mathbf{x}_i)) \tag{13}$$

For a set of user's interested items $\mathbf{V}$, the loss function for STM model is defined as the cross-entropy of r as Eq. (14).

$$\mathcal{L}(r) = -\sum_{v=1}^{|V|} y_v \cdot \log(r_v) + (1 - y_v) \cdot \log(1 - r_v) \tag{14}$$

STM model is connected to VAE model by feeding the output of STM model to VAE. Since the score provides more latent features than bag-of-words vectors, the inference model in VAE tends to learn more robust latent variables. In addition, during the training process, the feedback is flowed back to STM to train the embedding parameters. The loss function for STMVAE is defined as Eq. (15).

$$\mathcal{L} = \mathcal{L}(r) + \mathbb{E}_{q_\phi(z_u|x_u)} \log p_\theta(x_u|z_u) - \beta \cdot \mathrm{KL}(q_\phi(z_u|x_u)||p(z_u)) \tag{15}$$

For a given history of user u, we rank items based on the predicted multinomial probability $f_\theta(\mathbf{z}_u)$. It is obvious that the advantage of STMVAE is that we can effectively address the sparsity problem and generate robust recommendations by evaluating the STM model. Classic VAE simply use raw click history to train VAE, while $\mathbf{r}_u$ generated by STM model contains more knowledge than raw click history.

4   Related Work

General approaches to capture users' interests can be divided into two categories [7]: (i) global models that focused on identifying users' interests in general, and (ii) localized models that emphasized that emphasized users' temporal interests. More recent approaches are neighborhood methods [11], which make recommendations by calculating item similarities from co-occurrences of items, and Markov chain based models, explore either general interests or current interests. However, these models can hardly adapt users' interests to users' recent activities.

Different from the other approaches, our proposed STMVAE model explores users' both general and recent interests, adapting recommendations to users' activities. It is proved to be more robust and effective than state-of-art models. The number of parameters in STMVAE grows linearly with the number of items, and STM model transformed sparse data by learning temporal factors, which is proved to effectively improve the performance on sparse dataset. Also, STMVAE uses multinomial distribution to sample probabilities of users' interests, which is proved to significantly more robust in recommender system than Gaussian and logistic likelihood loss function [6].

4.1   VAE

VAE has been widely used since it was proposed by Kingma and Welling [4]. VAE on images was studied by [2,10]. VAE on natural language processing was used in [9]. Liang et al. [6] suggested that when a dataset is large and sparse, VAE suffers from underfitting, so they worked around the issue by controlling the regularization level (i.e. β). STMVAE model solves the issue by transforming the sparse data through STM model, and we also set $\beta < 1$ to avoid underfitting as shown in Eq. (15). We will show from our experiment results that STM model address the data sparsity problem effectively.

4.2   Neural Network Based Collaborative Filtering

Early works on collaborative filtering focused on explicit data and evaluate ratings. With the importance of implicit feedback being gradually recognized, some researches turned to non-linear neural network. Xue et al. [17] proposed a deep matrix factorization (DMF) model that transformed the traditional matrix factorization to a non-linear model by learning user and item vectors via MLP. Although the model is non-linear, it is trained by explicit data (e.g. ratings) and the loss function is explicit data based. Also, the number of parameters grows linearly related to the number of users and items, which will lead to overfitting. Wu et al. [16] proposed collaborative denoising autoencoder. Comparing with standard denoising autoencoder, CDAE adds a latent vector for each user, which leads to the same issue as DMF that the parameters grows linearly with the number of users and items. Moreover, CDAE requires additional optimization to training.

5   Experiments

In this section, we conduct experiments on three datasets to demonstrate the effectiveness of our model. We provide insights into the performance by exploring the resulting fits. STMVAE achieves state-of-art results on three real-world datasets in the comparison with various baselines, which are recently proposed neural network based collaborative filtering models.

5.1   Datasets and Data Preparation

We evaluate the proposed model on three widely used datasets in recommender systems: MovieLens 100K (ML-100K), MovieLens 1M (ML-1M) and Netflix Prize (Netflix).

Movielens datasets are user-movie ratings collected from a movie recommendation service. We do not process Movielens datasets because they are already filtered. For ML-100k, there are 944 users, 1,683 items and 100,000 ratings. For ML-1M, there are 6,040 users, 3,706 movies and 1M ratings.

Netflix dataset is the user-movie ratings data from the Netflix Prize. We binarized the data in the same way as in [15] that only keeps positive ratings (rating 5) for training, validating and testing. After filtering users with less than 20 interactions and items with less than 20 interactions, we have 252,827 users, 15,563 movies and 21M ratings in the final dataset.

On three datasets, we randomly split users in the ratio of 8:1:1 for training, validating and testing respectively.

5.2   Metrics

We evaluate our results by ranking-based metrics: Recall@R and the truncated normalized discounted cumulative gain (NDCG@R). For each user, both metrics compare the predicted rank of the held-out items with the true rank. While Recall@R considers all items ranked within the first R to be equally important, NDCG@R emphasize the importance that the high rank versus low rank [6].

The Recall@R for each user is defined as Eq. (16), where $\omega(r)$ is the item at rank r, $\mathbb{I}[\cdot]$ is the indicator function, and I_u is the set of items that user u clicked on. The expression in the denominator is the minimum of R and the number of items that the user u clicked. The Recall@R is normalized with the maximum value of 1, so the items are ranked in this way.

$$Recall@R(u,\omega) = \frac{\sum_{r=1}^{R} \mathbb{I}[\omega(r) \in I_u)]}{min(M,|I_u|)} \tag{16}$$

The NDCG@R is defined as 17. NDCG@R is figured out by normalizing DCG@R after dividing by the best possible DCG@R.

$$NDCG@R(u,\omega) = \frac{\sum_{r=1}^{R} 2^{\mathbb{I}[\omega(r) \in I_u)]]} - 1}{log(r+1)} \tag{17}$$

5.3 Baselines

In this section, we compare our proposed model with the following methods. As STMVAE is a neural network based model that aims to learn the relationship between users and items, we mainly compare with neural network based user-item models. The models included in our comparison are listed as follows:

- Collaborative Denoising Autoencoder (**CDAE**) is a model that using denoising autoencoder for collaborative filtering [16]. This model learns latent representations and implicit relationships between items and users.
- Deep Matris Factorization model (**DMF**) [17] is a state-of-art collaborative filtering model that utilizes the neural network for matrix factorization.
- Neural Collaborative Filtering model (**NCF**) [3] is a non-linear collaborative filtering Bayesian model. The model ranks items by the possibility generated from matrix.
- Multinomial Variational Autoencoder (**Mult-VAE**) is a state-of-art multinomial conditional likelihood based collaborative filtering model [6]. This model utilizes the multinomial likelihood for the data distribution in collaborative filtering. Mult-VAE is a strong baseline and achieves the best performance among our baseline methods.

5.4 Parameters

We study the performance of models under strong generalization [8]. The hyperparameters are optimized via grid search on the validation set. To evaluate, we take part of the records from test set to learn the representation for the model and compute the metrics on the rest of unseen records from test set.

We choose the embedding dimension d as 100, reference and generative model are symmetrical with one hidden layer. The latent representation K and the hidden layer are set to 200 and 400 respectively. We train STMVAE models by Adam with the batch size of 500 and keep the model with the best validation NDCG@10 and report test set metrics with it.

5.5 Experimental Results

The results of the comparison are summarized in Table 1. They demonstrate the effectiveness of our proposed architecture on all datasets in both metrics of NDCG and recall. We can find that Mult-VAE is a strong baseline that beats CDAE, DMF and NCF on dense and sparse datasets. The good performance of Mult-VAE demonstrates that variational autoencoder is able to handle sparse dataset when choosing appropriate hyper-parameters and latent distribution. CDAE is a denoising autoencoder based model that trains the users' latent variables, which is the same as Mult-VAE. NCF and DMF are two models that can be treated as neural network based matrix factorization. The two models learns the user latent variables and item variables respectively through non-linear functions. The experiment results from DMF and NCF show that the performances of two models vary on various datasets. In addition, since two models are based on matrix factorization, they suffer from sparsity problem, which is reflected in our results. DMF performs well on dense dataset, where the performance is similar to CDAE, but its performance drops down on sparse dataset. Our proposed STMVAE model achieves the best performance among baselines because it models the temporal factor and the influence of the last records for each user.

5.6 Effects of the Last Click

In this section, we compare our proposed model with a modified version that does not use the last click records to verify the validity of modeling of the last click information.

- **STMVAE :** The STMVAE model proposed in this paper.
- **STMVAE-:** On the basis of STMVAE, not using the last click item embedding in the trilinear layer.

The results in Table 2 shows that the model that the last click combines with the long term preferences has better performance than without. In addition, when a dataset is dense, the performance of two models are similar, and the last click model only has an improvement of 0.8%. However, STMVAE has 5.22% improvement on Netflix, which is a sparse dataset. This is because the last click history helps to narrow down the alternatives when the dataset is sparse.

The results prove that the last click history positively contributes to the recommendations. Our model is able to capture long term and short term preferences while weighting more on short term. The reason behind the results is the last click represents users' most recent interests, therefore the users' following preferences may be more related to the last click.

Table 1. Comparison between various baselines and our proposed model. Our proposed STMVAE model outperforms the baselines across datasets and metrics.

(a) ML-100k

	Recall@10	NDCG@10
STMVAE	0.4350	0.4559
CDAE	0.4033	0.4093
DMF	0.4122	0.4010
NCF	0.3309	0.3737
Mult-VAE	0.4258	0.4552

(b) ML-1M

	Recall@10	NDCG@10
STMVAE	0.4436	0.4627
CDAE	0.3584	0.3307
DMF	0.3525	0.3755
NCF	0.3102	0.3018
Mult-VAE	0.3601	0.3756

(c) Netflix

	Recall@10	NDCG@10
STMVAE	0.3030	0.3144
CDAE	0.1985	0.1864
DMF	0.1501	0.1375
NCF	0.2102	0.2018
Mult-VAE	0.2564	0.2705

Table 2. Impacts of the last click

	ML-100k		ML-1M		Netflix	
	Recall	NDCG	Recall	NDCG	Recall	NDCG
STMVAE	0.4350	0.4599	0.4436	0.4627	0.3030	0.3144
STMVAE-	0.4339	0.4559	0.4283	0.4453	0.2810	0.2988

5.7 Sensitivity to Hyper-parameters

Size of Embedding Layer. In STM, we need to map items to vectors through an embedding layer. We conduct an extensive experiment to apply various sizes of embedding layer on ML dataset to test the performance. As shown in Fig. 2, the size of the embedding layer influence the performance. The performances of two models on the dense dataset are similar to what are shown on the left side. In contrast, the size of the embedding layer influence the performance significantly on dense dataset, which is shown on right side. We argue that it is because size 50 leads to underfitting while size 200 leads to overfitting.

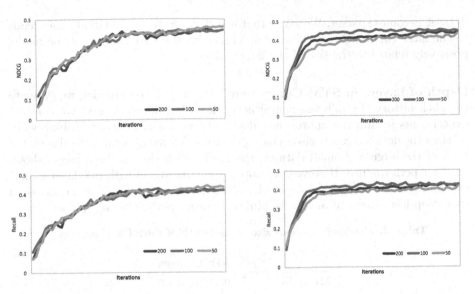

Fig. 2. Metrics for various size of the embedding layer. Left: ML-100K, Right: ML-1M

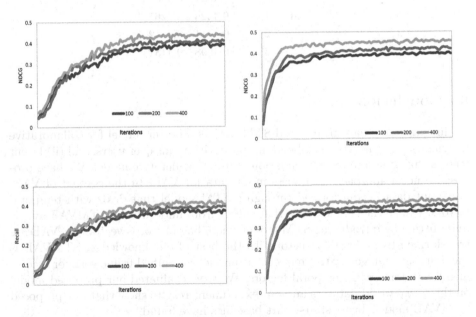

Fig. 3. Metrics for various size of the latent factor. Left: ML-100K, Right: ML-1M

Size of the Latent Factor. The size of the latent space is another factor that controls the performance. We conduct experiments and compare the performance with various sizes (i.e. 100, 200, 400) on ML datasets. As shown in Fig. 3, the performance is better with higher latent spaces, and the gap increases as the dataset becomes sparser. We argue that it is because the large latent space leads to the large capabilities of the model. Therefore, the performance of the model positively relates to the size of the latent space.

Depth of Layers in STM Component. In our proposed model, we evaluate the click history through the neural network with multiple layers. We conduct experiments to find the appropriate depth of the neural network. Table 3 summarizes the detailed comparison among the range of layers (i.e. one to three). On both of the large and small dataset, the model with three hidden layers shows the best performance. However, we notice that the model with one layer is better than with two on large dataset ML-1M. Therefore, we can draw a conclusion that deep layers are not always helpful to improve performance.

Table 3. Metrics for various size of the depth of the STM component

	Depth	NDCG	Recall
ML-100K	1	0.4476	0.426
	2	0.4539	0.433
	3	0.4627	0.439
ML-1M	1	0.4526	0.4267
	2	0.4411	0.4312
	3	0.4598	0.4431

6   Conclusion

In this paper, we have introduced STMVAE as a better model for collaborative filtering that learns: (i) an embedding space with items over users, and (ii) latent factors that generate recommendations through generative model. We have proposed a novel approach to process input data for VAE. In the context of VAE, the input data is transformed through a STM model that deals with temporal factors. Unlike the classic VAEs that suffers from underfitting, STMVAE avoids underfitting by introducing STM model where bag-of-words vectors for VAE are transformed to probability vectors. To the best of our knowledge, STMVAE is the first Bayesian generative model that provides a unified framework for recommender systems with temporal factors. We have evaluated our proposed model on three real world datasets and our experiment results show that our proposed STMVAE models beats state-of-art baselines have found.

References

1. Doersch, C.: Tutorial on variational autoencoders. arXiv preprint arXiv:1606.05908 (2016)
2. Gulrajani, I., et al.: PixelVAE: a latent variable model for natural images. arXiv preprint arXiv:1611.05013 (2016)

3. He, X., Liao, L., Zhang, H., Nie, L., Hu, X., Chua, T.S.: Neural collaborative filtering. In: Proceedings of the 26th International Conference on World Wide Web, pp. 173–182. International World Wide Web Conferences Steering Committee (2017)
4. Kingma, D.P., Welling, M.: Auto-encoding variational bayes. arXiv preprint arXiv:1312.6114 (2013)
5. Krishnan, R.G., Liang, D., Hoffman, M.: On the challenges of learning with inference networks on sparse, high-dimensional data. arXiv preprint arXiv:1710.06085 (2017)
6. Liang, D., Krishnan, R.G., Hoffman, M.D., Jebara, T.: Variational autoencoders for collaborative filtering. arXiv preprint arXiv:1802.05814 (2018)
7. Liu, Q., Zeng, Y., Mokhosi, R., Zhang, H.: STAMP: short-term attention/memory priority model for session-based recommendation. In: Proceedings of the 24th ACM SIGKDD International Conference on Knowledge Discovery & Data Mining, pp. 1831–1839. ACM (2018)
8. Marlin, B.: Collaborative Filtering: A Machine Learning Perspective. University of Toronto, Toronto (2004)
9. Miao, Y., Yu, L., Blunsom, P.: Neural variational inference for text processing. In: International Conference on Machine Learning, pp. 1727–1736 (2016)
10. Pu, Y., et al.: Variational autoencoder for deep learning of images, labels and captions. In: Advances in Neural Information Processing Systems, pp. 2352–2360 (2016)
11. Sarwar, B., Karypis, G., Konstan, J., Riedl, J.: Item-based collaborative filtering recommendation algorithms. In: Proceedings of the 10th International Conference on World Wide Web, pp. 285–295. ACM (2001)
12. Sau, B.B., Balasubramanian, V.N.: Deep model compression: distilling knowledge from noisy teachers. arXiv preprint arXiv:1610.09650 (2016)
13. Sevil, S.G., Kucuktunc, O., Duygulu, P., Can, F.: Automatic tag expansion using visual similarity for photo sharing websites. Multimedia Tools Appl. **49**(1), 81–99 (2010)
14. Wager, S., Wang, S., Liang, P.S.: Dropout training as adaptive regularization. In: Advances in Neural Information Processing Systems, pp. 351–359 (2013)
15. Wang, H., Wang, N., Yeung, D.Y.: Collaborative deep learning for recommender systems. In: Proceedings of the 21th ACM SIGKDD International Conference on Knowledge Discovery and Data Mining, pp. 1235–1244. ACM (2015)
16. Wu, Y., DuBois, C., Zheng, A.X., Ester, M.: Collaborative denoising auto-encoders for top-n recommender systems. In: Proceedings of the Ninth ACM International Conference on Web Search and Data Mining, pp. 153–162. ACM (2016)
17. Xue, H.J., Dai, X., Zhang, J., Huang, S., Chen, J.: Deep matrix factorization models for recommender systems. In: IJCAI, pp. 3203–3209 (2017)

On Facilitating Large-Scale Online Discussions

Daichi Shibata, Ahmed Moustafa(✉), Takayuki Ito, and Shota Suzuki

Department of Computer Science, Nagoya Institute of Technology, Nagoya, Japan
{afmed,ito.takayuki}@nitech.ac.jp

Abstract. Since various opinions are openly discussed on the Web and there is a growing need to facilitate such discussions, discussion-support systems have been attracting attention. In this regard, human facilitator plays an important role for leading constructive discussions on the Web. However, human facilitation for large-scale Web discussions is limited in terms of the available resources. For proper facilitation, it is necessary to understand the content of a discussion to effectively lead the discussion and build consensus. Towards this end, we propose an automated facilitator for supporting large-scale online discussions. Specifically, the proposed automated facilitator structures online discussions using the issue-based information system in order to make these discussions easy to understand for both humans and intelligent agents. In addition, the proposed automated facilitator employs several strategies that encourage participants to conduct discussions appropriately. The experimental results demonstrate the efficiency of the proposed automated facilitator in promoting the progress of large-scale online discussions, and thus enabling open and constructive discussions to be conducted.

Keywords: Discussion support system · Automated facilitator · Intelligent facilitation

1 Introduction

Online discussion platforms have attracted great attention due to their suitability for gathering a variety of opinions [9,13,16]. In this regard, it becomes important for separate participants to express diverse opinions during the course of their discussions. However, it grows inefficient to conduct these discussions on classical open platforms, such as a conventional bulletin board, because (1) online discussions often become too complicated and (2) flaming, i.e., throwing personal insults to others, usually occurs [20]. Therefore, these factors stunt the constructive exchange of ideas among online participants. One approach to alleviate these issues is involving a human facilitator [5,6,21] in these discussions. This human facilitator plays the following roles: (1) supporting collective activities, such as discussion planning and idea generation, and (2) assisting participants in reaching a certain level of agreement. Towards this end, he/she gathers the participants' opinions and

© Springer Nature Switzerland AG 2019
A. C. Nayak and A. Sharma (Eds.): PRICAI 2019, LNAI 11671, pp. 608–620, 2019.
https://doi.org/10.1007/978-3-030-29911-8_47

leads the discussion towards consensus by summarizing these opinions. In fact, so important is the role of facilitation that facilitators are seen on many occasions to coordinate discussions, e.g., for general public debate, consensus development conferences, and scientific workshops. In this context, Ito [11] reported that there was no abuse among participants in the presence of human facilitators that coordinated workshops and social experiments. In addition, the results of this study suggest that participants gained a sense of social presence [2,8] during the discussions that involved a human facilitator.

Nonetheless, human facilitation has several limitations including bias, human resources constrains, and time restrictions. These limitations make it difficult to control discussions and achieve large-scale consensus for online discussions that involve more than 1000 participants. Therefore, automated facilitation becomes essential for coping with such large-scale discussions. In this regard, several efforts have been made towards developing automated facilitators [1,7,10,24]. However, till the moment very little effort has been made to understand the meaning of the participants' comments and to provide the relevant facilitation. To fill this gap, we propose an automated facilitator that improves the quality of online facilitation through the analysis of online discussions. In order to analyze these discussions, we model the discussion structure using the issue-based information system (IBIS) [18]. The difference from argumentation mining [3,17] is that the IBIS includes an Issue element, which is important for supporting discussions. We implemented the proposed automated facilitator on a cloud service and constructed an architecture that can handle large-scale discussions. We conducted experiments in which the general public participated in discussions. We confirmed that the proposed automated facilitator encourages participants' opinions.

The remainder of this paper is organized as follows. In Sect. 2, we introduce preliminary research. In Sect. 3, we present extracting discussion structures. In Sect. 4, we introduce the proposed automated facilitator. In Sect. 5, we discuss the experiments we conducted. Finally, we summarize in Sect. 6.

2   Preliminaries

2.1   IBIS Structure

The IBIS [18] is a system of structuring discussions to promote decision-making in complicated problems by making the discussion structures easy to understand. The elements of the IBIS structure are classified into the following three categories; "Issue", "Idea", and "Argument". Issues are questions that need to be answered, ideas are answers for these questions, and arguments support or oppose a given idea, respectively. Arguments that support an idea are called "Pros", while arguments that oppose an idea are called "Cons". IBIS elements are usually represented as nodes, and the relations among these elements are represented as directed edges called links.

2.2 D-Agree (COLLAGREE)

D-Agree is a system that extends the API function of the large-scale discussion support system COLLAGREE [12,13]. This system has been used in order to gather opinions from citizens regarding Nagoya city planning. As a mechanism to support online discussions, incentives, keyword clouds, and human facilitation are introduced in COLLAGREE. In this context, human facilitators support discussions, making it possible to conduct constructive online discussions. In this research, we evaluate the proposed automated facilitator on D-Agree.

2.3 Motivating Example

The outline of the proposed automated facilitator is illustrated in Fig. 1 as follows. Firstly, participants post messages A and B, i.e., A: "How can we deal with river flooding?" and B: "We should introduce technology such as a sensor network." Then, the manager agent obtains the discussion log and requests the discussion structure from the discussion-structure-extraction agent. In turn, the discussion-structure-extraction agent conducts node classification (A is Issue, B is Idea) and link extraction (B responds to A). In the next step, the post-generation agent generates candidate suggested posts, as shown in Fig. 1(b). Finally, the manager agent chooses the selected posts from the group of suggested posts.

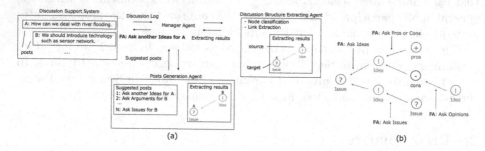

Fig. 1. Outline of the proposed automated facilitator (FA). (a) Example of how the proposed facilitator functions. (b) Automated facilitator generating posts based on IBIS structure.

3 Extracting Discussion Structure

To extract the structure of the online posts on a discussion-support system, we divided this extraction task into two steps, i.e., node-classification and link-extraction.

Node-classification: This step divides the online posts into sentences and classifies them as elements of the IBIS structure (Issue, Idea, Pros, Cons). It is assumed that one sentence and one element of the IBIS structure are paired.

Link-extraction: This step extracts the link relations among the elements after conducting node classification. In this step, we assume the IBIS structure then conduct link extraction.

3.1 Node-Classification Model

We used Doc2Vec [15] and cosine similarity in order to create a baseline node-classification model. With the Doc2Vec model, we are able to calculate the similarity among the elements of the IBIS structure. For example, it is possible to obtain a representative vector of an issue from the sentences that were tagged as Issue. Similarly, it is possible to obtain representative vectors of Idea, Pros, and Cons from the discussion data. By obtaining the cosine similarity between these representative vectors and the vectorized sentences of different posts, we are able to calculate the similarity between different vectors.

By assuming that similar postings are classified into the same class, we are also able to classify the sentences into the elements of the IBIS structure. Finally, the cosine similarity of each class is multiplied by the softmax function. This node classification model is described by Algorithm 1.

Algorithm 1. Node Classification Model

Input: Discussion Log D; *model*.
Parameter: *epoch*; *batchsize*.
Output: trained *model*
1: **for all** thread $T \in D$ **do**
2:      **for all** post $P \in T$ **do**
3:          **for all** sentence $s \in P$ **do**
4:              remove noises from s
5:              perform a morpheme analysis on s
6:              acquire embedded representations of morphemes in s
7:          **end for**
8:      **end for**
9: **end for**
10: **for each** *epoch* **do**
11:     **for** select *batchsize* data from set of $(s, type)$ **do**
12:         train *model* with the data
13:     **end for**
14: **end for**
15: **return** *model*

3.2 Link-Extraction Model

For the link-extraction model, we employ the model that is developed as part of this research project. This model extracts the links using fastText [4] and bidirectional long short-term memory [14, 22]. In the learning phase, we use the extracted links from the discussion data, and train this model by regression

Algorithm 2. Link Extraction Model

Input: set of source nodes *Tail*; set of target nodes *Head*; *model*.
Parameter: *epoch*; *batchsize*.
Output: trained *model*
 1: **for all** *tail* ∈ *Tail* **do**
 2:    perform a morpheme analysis on *tail*
 3:    acquire embedded representations of morphemes in *tail*
 4: **end for**
 5: **for all** *head* ∈ *Head* **do**
 6:    perform a morpheme analysis on *head*
 7:    acquire embedded representations of morphemes in *head*
 8: **end for**
 9: **for each** *epoch* **do**
10:    **for** select *batchsize* data from set of (*Tail*, *Head*) **do**
11:       train *model* with the data
12:    **end for**
13: **end for**
14: **return** *model*

analysis with the input as the link source and the output as the link target. And using this model, we are able to calculate the similarity among the elements. Finally, the link relations are extracted by similarity. This link-extraction model is described by Algorithm 2.

4   Automated Facilitator Based on IBIS Structure

In this section, we present the proposed automated facilitator. The proposed automated facilitator consists of three agents, i.e., manager agent, post-generation agent, and discussion-structure-extraction agent.

4.1   Architecture

Figure 2 shows the architecture of the proposed automated facilitator. We used the Web API to establish communication among the three agents. Please note that the proposed automated facilitator can easily scale up according to the given number of participants in the discussion because of its deployment in a cloud service. In addition, it becomes easy to switch agents or models by separating the implementation for each role in the proposed automated facilitator.

4.2   Manager Agent

The manager agent receives the suggested posts from the post-generation agent and selects the posts to be posted to the discussion-support system.

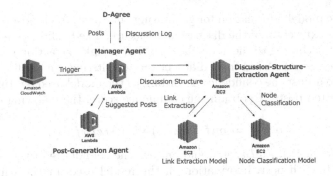

Fig. 2. Proposed automated facilitator architecture

Algorithm 3. Manager-agent

Input: *theme_id; system_url*
Parameter: threshold *th*; confidence of each model *cm*
Output: None

1: get discussion log *d* from *theme_id, system_url*.
2: request discussion structure *x* from Discussion-structure-extraction agent by *d*.
3: extract new posts *ns* from *d*.
4: **if** count(*d*) > *th* **then**
5:    *c* ← ["*req_nodes*"]
6:    request suggested posts *sp* from post-generation agent by *x, c, ns*.
7:    **for** each *p* of *sp* **do**
8:        *p.score* ← *p.confidence* * *cm*(*p.srcInfo*)
9:    **end for**
10:   *i* ← *argmax*(*sp.score*)
11:   posts *sp*(*i*) to system by *theme_id, system_url*.
12: **end if**

The manager agent functions as described in Algorithm 3. It has two arguments, theme_id and system_url which determine the url of the discussion. It is important to note that the manager agent obtains the discussion log by using the Web API of D-agree (Line 1). Firstly, the manager agent requests the discussion structure from the discussion-structure-extraction agent (Line 2). In the next step, it extracts new posts from the discussion log (Line 3). When the number of new posts is larger than a certain threshold, the automated facilitator creates a reply post (Line 4). For example, if the threshold is set to 3, the facilitator returns one reply each time participants post three different opinions. The manager agent sends information of the discussion structure, category, post IDs of new posts to the post-generation agent (Lines 5–6). In this context, the category is different for each sort of posts. By specifying the category, the manager agent can generate sentences with the desired meaning.

Then, the manager agent calculates the confidence scores (Lines 7–8). The suggested posts include the following information; confidence and srcInfo. Confidence is the confidence of the discussion structure for generating a post, while srcInfo is the model information for generating that post. Each post is generated based on the extraction of the discussion structure. The confidence is calculated for each post according to the node-classification or link-extraction model. When the confidence is calculated from different models, its measure will be different. Therefore, to adjust the confidence according to the model used, srcInfo is added to the suggested posts. To obtain the confidence score, the following equation is used.

$$score(i) = confidence(i) * cm(srcInfo(i)) \tag{1}$$

where $confidence(i)$, $srcInfo(i)$, and cm are the confidence of the model used to generate the ith post, information on the model used for the ith post, and the parameter value for each srcInfo, respectively. Finally, the manager agent selects posts with the maximum confidence scores (Line 10) and posts them to the discussion-support system (Line 11).

4.3 Post-generation Agent

The post-generation agent first receives the estimation results and generates the suggested posts using a set of predefined rules. The following template presents the post-generation agent that is implemented in the proposed automated facilitator. The template includes the following information; target, source, category, and text are the type of node, type of link-source node attached to the target, the type of reply sentence, and the text of post, respectively. Based on the above template, it becomes possible to generate appropriate comments on posts.

This process is described in Algorithm 4. When the category is a reply to a post, the node information that correspond to the new post are extracted (Lines 2–4). Then, the post-generation agent generates posts using the extracted node information (Lines 5–12). This agent then generates general-purpose posts in order to post these posts when the confidence of extracting the discussion structure is low (Lines 13–16). In addition, to generate more specific posts, this agent extracts the link relations corresponding to the extracted node (Line 17), and then generates posts using the link relations (Lines 18–25). Finally, the post-generation agent returns the suggested posts to the manager agent (Line 30).

4.4 Discussion-Structure-Extraction Agent

The discussion-structure-extraction agent manages the node-classification and the link-extraction models.

The work of this agent is described in Algorithm 5. Firstly, the agent counts the number of posts from the log (Line 1) then creates a unique key from theme_id, system_url (Line 2). If the key of estimation results was generated in the past (Line 3) and there is no change in the number of posts (Line 4), the past estimation results are returned (Lines 5–6). Otherwise, the agent requests the estimation results from the node-classification and link-extraction models (Lines 9–10). Finally, the agent saves these results and returns them to the manager agent (Lines 11–13).

Algorithm 4. Post-generation agent

Input: discussion structure x; category c; new posts ns
Parameter: *thresholds*
Output: sp

  1: initialize sp with empty list.
  2: **if** c equals "*req_nodes*" **then**
  3:   **for** each n of ns **do**
  4:     extract *nodes* from x matching n.
  5:     **for** each *node* of *nodes* **do**
  6:       $target \leftarrow node.type$
  7:       $source \leftarrow None$
  8:       generate posts ps matching the category with $target$, $source$, c from the template.
  9:       select p from ps
 10:       $confidence \leftarrow node.confidence$
 11:       $srcInfo \leftarrow$ name of the node-classification model.
 12:       append $\{p, confidence, srcInfo\}$ to sp.
 13:       generate posts sp matching the category with c from the template.
 14:       select p from ps.
 15:       $confidence \leftarrow thresholds(node.type)$
 16:       append $\{p, confidence, srcInfo = "None"\}$ to sp.
 17:       extract *links* from x matching *node*.
 18:       **for** each *link* of *links* **do**
 19:         $target \leftarrow link.targetnode.type$
 20:         $source \leftarrow link.sourcenode.type$
 21:         generate posts ps matching the category with $target$, $source$, c from the template.
 22:         select p from ps.
 23:         $confidence \leftarrow link.confidence$
 24:         $srcInfo \leftarrow$ name of the link-extraction model.
 25:         append $\{p, confidence, srcInfo\}$ to sp.
 26:       **end for**
 27:     **end for**
 28:   **end for**
 29: **end if**
 30: **return** sp

---

5   Experiments

We conducted two experiments in order to evaluate the proposed automated facilitator. The first experiment examines whether the proposed automated facilitator can properly lead large-scale discussions. In the second experiment, we compare the proposed automated facilitator agent with a human facilitator, and examine the effectiveness of the proposed automated facilitator.

Algorithm 5. Discussion-structure-extraction agent

Input: discussion log d; *theme_id*; *system_url*
Parameter: None
Output: discussion structure x

1: $n \leftarrow$ number of posts in d.
2: make *key* from *theme_id*, *system_url*.
3: **if** key in *old_cnt* **then**
4:    **if** n equals *old_cnt*[*key*] **then**
5:      $x \leftarrow$ *old_x*[*key*]
6:      **return** x
7:    **end if**
8: **end if**
9: request node result *nodes* from node-classification model by d.
10: request discussion structure x from link-extraction model by *nodes*.
11: *old_cnt*[*key*] $\leftarrow n$
12: *old_x*[*key*] $\leftarrow x$
13: **return** x

5.1 Experimental Setup

We generated a Doc2Vec model that learns the distributed representation of online discussions using the discussion data collected on D-Agree. In this regard, we used the Gensim package [19] for Python. Table 1 shows the number of elements included in the dataset. The parameters settings of Doc2Vec are shown in Table 2. After creating the model using these parameters, we constructed the node-classification model according to cosine similarity.

The accuracy of the constructed model was measured by k-cross validation [23]. Table 3 shows the results. In this context, Issue and Idea show relatively high F values. Since the automated facilitator, that is implemented in this research, creates posts to correctly guide the discussion, extracting the discussion structure of Issue and Idea is particularly important, so that the role of Doc2Vec as a baseline node-classification model is fulfilled.

Table 1. Dataset

Class	Num
Issue	169
Idea	864
Pros	451
Cons	440

Table 2. Doc2Vec parameter settings

Parameter	Value
vector_size	400
window	20
min_count	20
workers	11
alpha (learning rate)	0.05
min_alpha	0.025
epochs	1000

Table 3. Node-classification results (k = 5)

	Issue	Idea	Pros	Cons
precision	0.672	0.706	0.436	0.447
recall	0.858	0.702	0.299	0.540
f_value	0.751	0.703	0.353	0.486

5.2   Experiment One: Large-Scale Discussion

We conduct an experiment involving a large-scale online discussion about Nagoya city planning from November 1st to December 7th, 2018. This Experiment was conducted on D-Agree. The conducted experiment has the following metrics. The number of page views is 15199, the number of visited participants is 798, the number of registered participants is 157, the total number of posts is 452. It is important to note that these participants are able to see whether the facilitator is human or the proposed automated facilitator.

Table 4 lists the number of posts and the number of participants per theme. The human facilitator facilitated Themes 1 and 2, the automated facilitator facilitated Themes 3 and 4, and Theme 5 was facilitated by both the human and the automated facilitators.

Table 4. Number of posts

Theme	Posts	Participants
Theme 1 (Human facilitator)	81	38
Theme 2 (Human facilitator)	56	35
Theme 3 (Automated facilitator)	88	64
Theme 4 (Automated facilitator)	70	52
Theme 5 (Automated and Human facilitators)	137	99
Sum	432	288

Figure 3 shows an example of the discussions held during this social experiment. Firstly, participants present the issue of the name recognition of Nagoya city. Since the automated facilitator correctly recognizes this issue, it posts on how to address it. In response to the posting, one participant issues an idea. In turn, the automated facilitator, which has correctly recognized the idea, posts a request for a task to the idea and what is necessary for realization. Participants respond to these posts from the automated facilitator and issue a proposal to materialize the idea; thus, the automated facilitator is able to correctly guide the discussion.

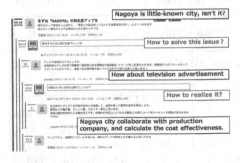

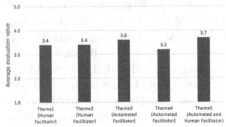

Fig. 3. Successful case of proposed automated facilitator

Fig. 4. Are you satisfied with the discussion of the city plan? (N=20)

We conduct a questionnaire after this experiment. The results of the item "Are you satisfied with the discussion of city plan?" are shown in Fig. 4. Twenty people respond to the questionnaire. The evaluation is based on a five-point scale. As you can see from the figure, the same value as human facilitator is obtained by the automated facilitator; thus, the proposed automated facilitator works effectively.

5.3 Experiment Two: Comparison with Human Facilitator

We conduct 10 experiments to compare the automated facilitator with the human facilitator. The discussion time is set to either 45 or 60 min according to the number of generated ideas, and there exist 5 discussion themes, the number of participants is set to 10. To quantitatively evaluate the proposed automated facilitator, we conduct the same discussion with both human and automated facilitators. Participants take part in the experiments without knowing whether the facilitator is human or automated.

Table 5. Facilitation results

	Human facilitator	Automated facilitator
Ave number of posts	156.8	165.6
Ave number of facilitators' posts	25.2	34
Ave time of facilitation	399.9 s	**53.9 s**
Total number of Issues	28	32
Total number of Ideas	374	344
Total number of Pros	144	138
Total number of Cons	139	146
Total number of N/A	91	110

Table 5 shows the total number of elements of the IBIS structure that are included in the extracted participants' posts. In this context, N/A represent the elements that are not applicable to the IBIS structure. The total number of elements is shown for each facilitator, and the number of each element type is almost equal for both human and automated facilitators, even though the automated facilitator extracted these elements dynamically. In addition, it is important to note that the automated facilitator takes shorter time (53.9 s) to facilitate almost the same number of issues that the human facilitator took (399.9 s) in order to facilitate them.

On the other hand, Tables 6 and 7 show the number of elements derived from the participants by the human facilitator and automated facilitator, respectively. It is clear that the automated facilitator encourages the participants to express their opinions. However, when it fails in extracting the discussion structure, the number of N/As increases because the participants had reacted to these failed posts.

Table 6. Human facilitator

Human facilitator		Type of participant posts				
Type	N	Issue	Idea	Pros	Cons	N/A
Response	32	0	9	7	6	3
Issue	4	0	4	1	3	0
Idea	46	0	52	2	1	1
Pros	8	0	1	6	0	0
Cons	12	0	2	2	15	0
Pros or Cons	5	0	0	2	2	0
Total	107	0	68	20	27	4

Table 7. Automated facilitator

Automated facilitator		Type of participant posts				
Type	N	Issue	Idea	Pros	Cons	N/A
Response	35	0	6	6	7	3
Issue	3	0	0	0	2	1
Idea	77	0	65	0	4	8
Pros	13	0	1	7	1	2
Cons	35	1	1	1	21	2
Pros or Cons	3	0	0	0	0	0
Total	166	1	73	14	35	16

6 Conclusions

This paper proposes an automated facilitator that aims to support open online discussions. The proposed automated facilitator structures online discussions based on the IBIS style in order to create the appropriate posts. The proposed automated facilitator is implemented and deployed on a cloud service to handle large-scale discussions. The experimental results show that the proposed automated facilitator succeeds in encouraging online participants to express their opinions.

References

1. Adla, A., Zarate, P., Soubie, J.L.: A proposal of toolkit for GDSS facilitators. Group Decis. Negot. **20**(1), 57–77 (2011)
2. Aragon, S.R.: Creating social presence in online environments. New Dir. Adult Continuing Educ. **100**, 57–68 (2003)
3. Bench-Capon, T.J., Dunne, P.E.: Argumentation in artificial intelligence. Artif. Intell. **171**(10–15), 619–641 (2007)
4. Bojanowski, P., Grave, E., Joulin, A., Mikolov, T.: Enriching word vectors with subword information. Trans. Assoc. Comput. Linguist. **5**, 135–146 (2017)
5. Chalidabhongse, J., Chinnan, W., Wechasaethnon, P., Tantisirithanakorn, A.: Intelligent facilitation agent for online web-based group discussion system. In: Hendtlass, T., Ali, M. (eds.) IEA/AIE 2002. LNCS (LNAI), vol. 2358, pp. 356–362. Springer, Heidelberg (2002). https://doi.org/10.1007/3-540-48035-8_35
6. Eastmond, D.V.: Effective facilitation of computer conferencing. Continuing High. Educ. Rev. **56**(1), 23–34 (1992)
7. Gu, W., Moustafa, A., Ito, T., Zhang, M., Yang, C.: A case-based reasoning approach for automated facilitation in online discussion systems. In: The Thirteenth International Conference on Knowledge, Information and Creativity Support Systems (KICSS-2018), Pattaya, Thailand, pp. 15–17 (2018)
8. Gunawardena, C.N., Zittle, F.J.: Social presence as a predictor of satisfaction within a computer-mediated conferencing environment. Am. J. Distance Educ. **11**(3), 8–26 (1997)
9. Iandoli, L., Klein, M., Zollo, G.: Can we exploit collective intelligence for collaborative deliberation? the case of the climate change collaboratorium (2007)

10. Ikeda, Y., Shiramatsu, S.: Generating questions asked by facilitator agents using preceding context in web-based discussion. In: 2017 IEEE International Conference on Agents (ICA), pp. 127–132. IEEE (2017)
11. Ito, T.: Towards agent-based large-scale decision support system: the effect of facilitator. In: Proceedings of the 51st Hawaii International Conference on System Sciences (2018)
12. Ito, T., et al.: Collagree: a faciliator-mediated large-scale consensus support system. Collective Intelligence 2014 (2014)
13. Ito, T., et al.: Incentive mechanism for managing large-scale internet-based discussions on collagree. Collective Intelligence 2015 (2015)
14. Lample, G., Ballesteros, M., Subramanian, S., Kawakami, K., Dyer, C.: Neural architectures for named entity recognition. arXiv preprint arXiv:1603.01360 (2016)
15. Le, Q.V., Mikolov, T.: Distributed representations of sentences and documents. CoRR abs/1405.4053 (2014)
16. Malone, T.W., Klein, M.: Harnessing collective intelligence to address global climate change. Innovations Technol. Gov. Globalization 2(3), 15–26 (2007)
17. Modgil, S., Prakken, H.: A general account of argumentation with preferences. Artif. Intell. 195, 361–397 (2013)
18. Noble, D., Rittel, H.W.: Issue-based information systems for design (1988)
19. Řehůřek, R., Sojka, P.: Software framework for topic modelling with large corpora. In: Proceedings of the LREC 2010 Workshop on New Challenges for NLP Frameworks, pp. 45–50. ELRA, Valletta, Malta, May 2010
20. Rice, R.E., Shepherd, A., Dutton, W.H., Katz, J.E.: Social interaction and the internet. In: Oxford Handbook of Internet Psychology (2007)
21. Rovai, A.P.: Facilitating online discussions effectively. Internet High. Educ. 10(1), 77–88 (2007)
22. Schuster, M., Paliwal, K.K.: Bidirectional recurrent neural networks. IEEE Trans. Signal Process. 45(11), 2673–2681 (1997)
23. Stone, M.: Cross-validatory choice and assessment of statistical predictions. J. Roy. Stat. Soc. Ser. B (Methodol.) 36, 111–147 (1974)
24. Wong, Z., Aiken, M.: Automated facilitation of electronic meetings. Inf. Manag. 41(2), 125–134 (2003). http://www.sciencedirect.com/science/article/pii/S0378720603000429

A Label-Based Nature Heuristic Algorithm for Dynamic Community Detection

Chunyu Wang, Yue Deng, Xianghua Li, Yingchu Xin, and Chao Gao[✉]

School of Computer and Information Science,
Southwest University, Chongqing 400715, China
cgao@swu.edu.cn

Abstract. The evolving patterns of the real-world can be tracked and captured by the dynamic network community structure. Some existing methods such as the multi-objective particle swarm optimization (MOPSO) use the evolutionary clustering model to detect the dynamic network community. However, the MOPSO has defects that are undesirable premature convergence and insufficient diversity of particles due to a high selection pressure. Therefore, a label-based heuristic algorithm based on the evolutionary clustering model is proposed for overcoming those shortcomings. The label propagation algorithm is adopted to initialize community structure and restrict the condition of the mutation process. The operations of crossover and mutation are used to increase the diversity of solutions and maintain the quality of community structure simultaneously. Experimental results demonstrate that the proposed method is effective and outperforms other methods in synthetic and real-world datasets.

Keywords: Label propagation · Nature-inspired algorithm ·
Dynamic networks · Community structure

1 Introduction

Many real-world complex systems can be formulated as networks, in which nodes denote the entities of the real world and edges represent connections of entities [1]. In this field, studies of community detection can help us understand the topology of a network and predict the evolution of a network [2]. Although some algorithms have been proposed for detecting community structure, most of them just focus on the static community detection [3]. In fact, a real-world system has dynamic characteristics. For instance, the community structure of a traffic flow network will change with the movement of people [2], and relationships among users in social networks will vary with time [4].

Nowadays community detection algorithms for dynamic networks can be classified into two main categories: incremental clustering [5] and evolutionary clustering [6]. The incremental clustering is not flawless because of the highly variable community structure. To be more robust for networks, the evolutionary

© Springer Nature Switzerland AG 2019
A. C. Nayak and A. Sharma (Eds.): PRICAI 2019, LNAI 11671, pp. 621–632, 2019.
https://doi.org/10.1007/978-3-030-29911-8_48

clustering defines two metrics for community detection [6]. One is the *snapshot cost (SC)*, which is evaluated by the current network topology, and the other one is the *temporal cost (TC)*, which is measured by the difference between the current clustering result and the previous one. Currently, the particle swarm optimization based on the evolutionary clustering framework, is proposed for detecting dynamic community structure [7]. However, due to the high selection pressure, such method often falls into the undesirable premature convergence and insufficient diversity [8].

The label propagation algorithm has a good clustering quality and the near-linear time complexity simultaneously [9]. The one-way crossover and mutation operations can improve the diversities of population and lessen the premature convergence [10]. Inspired by these advantages, a label-based dynamic multi-objective nature heuristic algorithm (denoted as L-DMGAPSO) is proposed to explore dynamic structures with two objectives, i.e., Q and *NMI*. The main contributions of L-DMGAPSO are summarized as follows:

(1) Node degree is used to improve the clustering quality of the label propagation algorithm and solve the problem of unstable iterations.
(2) The genetic algorithm is implemented to preserve excellent community structure and increase the diversities of particles.

The rest of the paper is organized as follows: Sect. 2 describes the related work. Section 3 designs a framework including encoding and decoding procedures, the proposed algorithm and complexity analysis. Section 4 presents experimental results in both synthetic and real-life datasets. Section 5 concludes the whole work.

2   Related Work

A dynamic network is formulated as a temporal graph $\{G_t(V_t, E_t)\,|t = 1, 2, ...\}$, where V_t and E_t denote a set of nodes and edges, respectively, and G_t is a network snapshot at t. A division for each snapshot $C_t = \{c_i|c_i \neq \phi, c_i \cap c_j = \phi, c_i \neq c_j\}$ is detected by the dynamic network algorithm, where c_i and c_j denote the ith and j^{th} community, respectively. Figure 1 shows the dynamic changes of a network from $t - 1$ to t. V_1, E_{12} and E_{13} are removed at $t - 1$. V_7, E_{57} and E_{67} are added at t. Currently, the evolutionary clustering framework is a popular method for solving the dynamic community detection [6]. Specifically, the cost function, as defined in Eq. (1), is used to measure the efficiency of evolutionary clustering [6].

$$Cost = \alpha * SC(C_t, G_t) + (1 - \alpha) * TC(C_{t-1}, C_t) \tag{1}$$

where $SC(C_t, G_t)$ is the *snapshot cost*, $TC(C_{t-1}, C_t)$ is the *temporal cost*, and α stands for a preset weight coefficient whose value is 0 or 1. The result of the function is the same as the previous time step when $\alpha = 0$, and the function is not smooth when $\alpha = 1$.

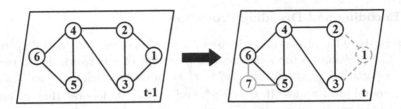

Fig. 1. A sample dynamic network graphic. It describes the change of nodes and edges from time step $t-1$ to t.

Existing research shows that dynamic community detection can be turned into a multi-objective optimization problem [11]. Q and NMI are adopted for estimating the quality of community detection [12,13]. The aim of dynamic community detection algorithm is maximizing two objectives simultaneously, as defined in Eq. (2).

$$C_t^* = \arg\max_{C_t}\{Q\left(C_t\right), NMI\left(C_{t-1}, C_t\right)\}, t \geq 2 \tag{2}$$

Q is used to optimize the object *snapshot cost*, as defined in Eq. (3). More specifically, k and m are the number of communities and edges, respectively. d_s represents the degrees of all nodes in C_s and l_s is the number of internal links in C_s. NMI is used to optimize the other object *temporal cost* as defined in Eq. (4), where A and B denote divisions $A = \{A_1, A_2, ..., A_a\}$ and $B = \{B_1, B_2, ..., B_b\}$, respectively. C is a confusion matrix. C_{ij} denotes the number of nodes belonging to i^{th} community of A and j^{th} community of B. C_A and C_B are the number of communities of A and B, respectively. N is the number of nodes. $C_{i.}$ and $C_{.j}$ represent the sum of C in a row i and a column j, respectively.

$$Q = \sum_{s=1}^{k}\left[\frac{l_s}{m} - \left(\frac{d_s}{2m}\right)^2\right] \tag{3}$$

$$NMI(A, B) = \frac{-2\sum_{i=1}^{C_A}\sum_{j=1}^{C_B} C_{ij} \log(\frac{C_{ij}N}{C_{i.}C_{.j}})}{\sum_{i=1}^{C_A} C_{i.} \log(\frac{C_{i.}}{N}) + \sum_{j=1}^{C_B} C_{.j} \log(\frac{C_{.j}}{N})} \tag{4}$$

Therefore, the main task of an optimization-based algorithm is to ensure two objectives as large as possible for solving the problem of the dynamic community detection.

3   Proposed Framework

This section proposes an improved multi-objective particle swarm optimization for dynamic networks, denoted as L-DMGAPSO, through combining label propagation and genetic algorithm. The coding procedure is introduced in Sect. 3.1. Detailed formulations of L-DMGAPSO are provided in the following subsections.

3.1   Encoding and Decoding Procedure

The string-based representation is used for the encoding and decoding procedures. The position vector x denotes the partition of a network. For a particle i and its partition $x_i = \{x_i^1, x_i^2, ..., x_i^n\}$, x_i^j is an integer belonging to $[1, n]$ and n is the number of nodes. If $x_i^j == x_i^k$ and $j \neq k$, it denotes that v_j and v_k belong to the same community. Figure 2 illustrates the encoding and decoding procedures in which a network is coded as a string of integers and each node corresponds to a label. The clustering result is shown in Fig. 2(b), where v_1, v_2 and v_3 belong to the same community.

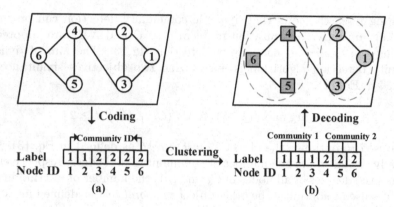

Fig. 2. An example of encoding and decoding processes. Each node is labeled by an integer which denotes a community ID. The different community labels are generated and decoded into a network after a series of operations.

3.2   Initialization

In order to improve the computational efficiency, RAK algorithm framework [9] is adopted to community detection because of the linear time complexity. According to this framework, v_i has a unique c_i which is updated on the basis of neighbor nodes. The iteration stops when labels of nodes remain unchanged. However, if there is more than one possible label as updating candidates, the algorithm will choose one of candidates as the result randomly. The higher the degree of a node is, the greater influence it has on the neighbor nodes. Therefore, the node with the largest degree and a synchronous updating rule are chosen for the proposed method. More specifically, v_i is updated at t based on the label of the highest-degree neighbor nodes at $t - 1$. The initialization process is shown in Algorithm 1.

Algorithm 1: The initialization process

Input: The number of particle n. The set of neighbor N_i. The degree D_i.
Output: A particle position vector $x_i = \{x_i^1, x_i^2, ..., x_i^n\}$, $x_i^j \in [1, n]$.
1 A unique label is assigned to each node randomly ;
2 A neighbor node label is selected randomly as the current nonisolated node label, $x_i = \{x_i^1, x_i^2, ..., x_i^n\}$, $x_i^j \in N_i$ (j);
3 Use the synchronous updating rule and select N_i with the largest D_i;
4 Return a particle position vector $x_i = \{x_i^1, x_i^2, ..., x_i^n\}$;

3.3 Genetic Operation

There are two important operations in genetic algorithm, i.e., one-way crossover and mutation operations. In this paper, the one-way crossover scheme [10] is applied to maintain a good community structure during the crossover process. Based on this scheme, a roulette algorithm is used to choose the partition of "Source" and "Destination" in the first time. Then, the one-way crossover operation is implemented as plotted in Fig. 3. When v_1 is chosen, v_1, v_2 and v_4 are in the same community in "Source". The labels of these nodes propagate to v_1, v_2 and v_4 in "Destination". Then, c_1, c_2 and c_4 in "Destination" are updated to 1. Such a approach creates a new partition.

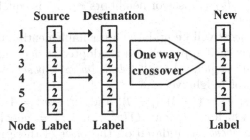

Fig. 3. The one-way crossover of community detection algorithm. The labels of nodes propagate from "Source" to "Destination".

The mutation operation is designed to enhance the quality of community structure and the convergence speed of the algorithm. When a random number is less than the mutation rate, the synchronous updating rule updates the label of a node based on the label of neighbor nodes at $t - 1$.

3.4 Particle Swarm Optimization

Particle swarm optimization is adopted to improve the convergence rate and avoid to fall into the local optimum [7]. The updating rules are defined in Eqs. (5) and (6).

$$v_i = \omega v_i \oplus (c_1 r_1 (pbest_i \ominus x_i) + c_2 r_2 (gbest \ominus x_i)) \tag{5}$$

$$x_i = x_i \otimes v_i \tag{6}$$

where $pbest_i = \{pbest_i^1, pbest_i^2, ..., pbest_i^n\}$ is the best personal position of ith particle and $gbest = \{gbest^1, gbest^2, ..., gbest^n\}$ is the best global position of population, c_1 and c_2 are learning factors; ω is the inertia weight; r_1 and r_2 are random number between 0 and 1. In Eq. (5), $\ominus$ is an XOR operator. For instance, $pbest_i \ominus x_i$ presents that if $pbest_i$ is equal to x_i, the value is 0; otherwise the value is 1. $\oplus$ adds two velocity vectors to create a new velocity vector. For example, if $v_1 = \{v_1^1, v_1^2, ..., v_1^n\}$ and $v_2 = \{v_2^1, v_2^2, ..., v_2^n\}$, $v_1 \oplus v_2 = v_3 = \{v_3^1, v_3^2, ..., v_3^n\}$. The operation of $\oplus$ is defined in Eq. (7).

$$\begin{cases} v_3^i = 0, \ if \ rand(0,1) \geq \frac{1}{1+e^{-(v_1^i+v_2^i)}} \\ v_3^i = 1, \ if \ rand(0,1) < \frac{1}{1+e^{-(v_1^i+v_2^i)}} \end{cases} \tag{7}$$

In Eq. (6), the velocity and position vector are combined by $\otimes$ to form a new position vector. More specifically, an old position vector $x_{old} = \{x_{old}^1, x_{old}^2, ..., x_{old}^n\}$ and a velocity vector $v = \{v_1, v_2, ..., v_n\}$ are provided for $x_{old} \otimes v = x_{new} = \{x_{new}^1, x_{new}^2, ..., x_{new}^n\}$. The operation of $\otimes$ is defined in Eq. (8).

$$\begin{cases} x_{new}^i = x_{old}^i, & if \ v_i == 0 \\ x_{new}^i = \arg\max_r \sum_{j \in L_i} \varphi(x_{old}^j, r), & if \ v_i == 1 \end{cases} \tag{8}$$

where $L_i = \{l_1, l_2, ..., l_k\}$ is a set of neighbors n_i, if i is equal to j, $\varphi(i, j) = 1$; otherwise, $\varphi(i, j) = 0$.

The $pbest_i$ and $gbest$ will be updated after implementing the particle updating rules. The Tchebycheff approach [14] is adopted to determine whether $pbest_i$ updates or not. If $g^{te}(x_i|w_i, z^*) < g^{te}(pbest_i|w_i, z^*)$, $pbset_i = x_i$. Based on the Euclidean distance of weight vectors $W = \{w_1, ..., w_i, ..., w_p\}$, where p is the number of particles, $w_i^1 = (i-1)/(p-1)$, and $w_i^1 + w_i^2 = 1$. $z^* = (z_1^*, z_2^*)$ is a reference point in which $z_1^* = \max(Q(x_i^t))$ and $z_2^* = \max(NMI(x_i^{t-1}, x_i^t))$. The global position $gbest_j$ is updated on the basis of these neighbor particles. If $g^{te}(x_i|w_j, z^*) < g^{te}(gbest_j|w_j, z^*)$, $gbset_j = x_i$, where $j \epsilon b_i$, and b_i is a set of neighbor nodes.

3.5   L-DMGAPSO Algorithm

The core components of L-DMGAPSO algorithm are provided in Algorithm 2. The L-DMGAPSO algorithm optimizes an objective in $G_{t=1}$ and two objectives in the rest of networks. Such method aims to improve the clustering quality, through increasing the diversities of particle swarm positions and maintaining the quality of community structure. The positions of particles are created by the improved label propagation operation. Then particles execute one-way crossover and mutation operations. Next the particle updating rule generates new particles, and creates the solutions of the Pareto Front with corresponding to the tradeoff between two objectives (Q and NMI). Finally the largest value of NMI is chosen from the set of solutions.

Algorithm 2: The L-DMGAPSO process

Input: The dynamic network $G = \{G_1, G_2, ..., G_t\}$, time step T, the number of nodes n.

Output: Community division results for each network G_t are
$$C_t = \{C_{t1}, C_{t2}, ..., C_{tk}\}.$$

1   Generate an initial clustering C_1 of a network G_1 by optimizing only the first objective;

2   **for** $t = 1 : T$ **do**

3   **while** *termination condition is not satisfied* **do**

4   Initialize the particle swarm position vectors x_i based on Alg. 1;

5   Perform one-way crossover and mutation operations for $x_i = \{x_i^1, x_i^2, ..., x_i^n\}$;

6   Q and NMI are used for assessing the fitness of particles;

7   Particle swarm updating rule creates a new position x_i and updates $pbset_i$ and $gbest$;

8   Return the solution C_t of the Pareto Front with the maximum NMI value;

---

4 Experiments

The L-DMGAPSO algorithm is implemented in MATLAB. All experiments are repeated 10 times both on synthetic and real-world datasets. Following a general guideline, the high crossover rate is set to 0.9 and the low mutation rate is set to 0.1. ω, $c1$ and $c2$ are set to typical values of 0.7298, 1.4961 and 1.4961 based on [7]. Besides, the number of particles and iterations is 100, and the neighbor size is 40.

Four well-known community detection algorithms for dynamic networks including DYN-MODPSO [7], sE-NMF [15], FacetNet [16] and DYN-MOGA [11] are selected as benchmark algorithms. The parameters of these benchmark algorithms are specified according to their papers.

4.1 Evaluation Metrics

Two evaluation metrics, i.e., NMI and *Error Rate* are verified community structure. NMI has been introduced in Sect. 2. *Error Rate* measures the distance from a community Z to a real community G [17] as defined in Eq. (9).

$$Error\ Rate = \left\| ZZ^T - GG^T \right\| \tag{9}$$

$Z = n * k$ represents the algorithmic indicator matrix, where n and k are the number of nodes and communities, respectively. The formulation of G is same with Z.

4.2 Datasets

SYN [17] is a benchmark dynamic network including 128 nodes based on a Girvan and Newman rule [18]. Z denotes the number of nodes associated with other communities, and $nC\%$ represents the percent of removing nodes from communities.

SYN-EVENT refers to four main events including 1000 nodes in dynamic networks [19]. Besides, two real-world datasets with unknown community structure are used for comparisons. The one is *Cellphone Calls*[1] which includes 400 nodes, the other one is *Enron Mail*[2] which contains 150 nodes. Using the DYNMOGA, such community structure is detected as the ground truth according to [17].

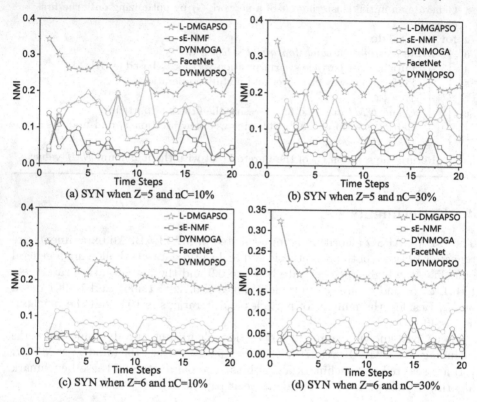

Fig. 4. Comparisons of *NMI* among different algorithms on (a) $Z = 5$ and $nC = 10\%$ (b) $Z = 5$ and $nC = 30\%$ (c) $z = 6$ and $nC = 10\%$ (d) $z = 6$ and $nC = 30\%$. Although Z and $nC\%$ increase the complexity of algorithms, L-DMGAPSO can still better recognize community structure than other algorithms.

4.3 Results

Figures 4 and 5 compare L-DMGAPSO with other algorithms on synthetic datasets. The L-DMGAPSO shows a better performance for community detection even when the fuzziness of networks increases. The reason is that the

[1] http://www.cs.umd.edu/hcil/VASTchallenge08/download/Download.htm.
[2] http://www.cs.cmu.edu/~enron/.

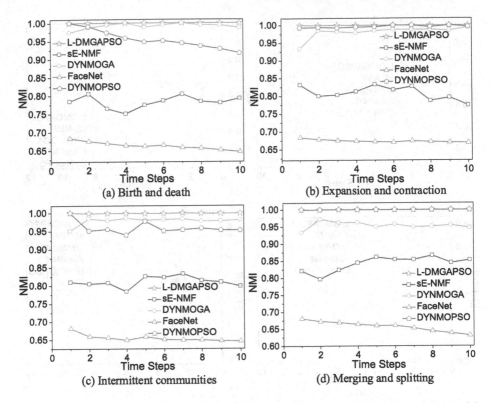

Fig. 5. Comparisons of *NMI* among different algorithms on (a) *Birth and death* (b) *Expansion and contraction* (c) *Intermittent communities* (d) *Merging and splitting*. The L-DMGAPSO values of NMI are higher than other algorithms at all steps. More specifically, the accuracy of L-DMGAPSO remains stable all the time.

improved label propagation algorithm enhances the quality of clustering and the genetic operations increase the diversities of particles. Figure 5 shows that the accuracy of FacetNet tends to decrease with time, while the accuracy of L-DMGAPSO and DYNMOGA remain stable, because they both obtain the current communities based on the previous ones.

The conclusion of NMI are consistent with results of synthetic datasets. Obviously, the low *Error Rate* indicates that L-DMGAPSO is able to obtain a stable and accurate community structure in Figs. 6(c), (d) and (f).

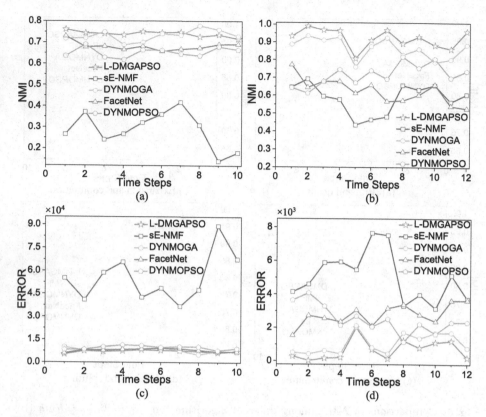

Fig. 6. Comparisons of *NMI* and *Error Rate* among other algorithms on (a) and (c) *Cellphone Calls*, (b) and (d) *Enron Mail* respectively. The L-DMGAPSO is superior than other algorithms in most steps, and the distance between this community and the ground truth is smaller than other algorithms.

5   Conclusion

A novel multi-objective optimization algorithm is proposed to detect community structure in dynamic networks. The main idea integrates genetic operation and the label propagation into the particle swarm optimization framework. Moreover, it balances the multi-objective optimization of problem. The one maximizes the quality of community structure at current time step, the other one minimizes the difference of community structure between the previous time step and the current time step. Experimental results in synthetic and real-word datasets show our proposed method can identify dynamic community structure with a good performance.

Acknowledgement. This work is supported by National Natural Science Foundation of China (Nos. 61602391, 61402379, 61403315), Natural Science Foundation of Chongqing (No. cstc2018jcyjAX0274), and Southwest University Training Programs of Innovation and Entrepreneurship for Undergraduates (No. X201910635045)

References

1. Rai, S., Chaturvedi, S., Jain, A.: Community detection on social media: A review. Int. J. Sci. Res. Eng. Technol. **3**(2), 29–33 (2018)
2. Li, X., Kurths, J., Gao, C., Zhang, J., Wang, Z., Zhang, Z.: A hybrid algorithm for estimating origin-destination flows. IEEE Access **6**, 677–687 (2017)
3. Gao, C., Liang, M., Li, X.: Network community detection based on the physarum-inspired computational framework. IEEE/ACM Trans. Comput. Biol. Bioinf. **15**(6), 1916–1928 (2018)
4. Gao, C., Liu, J.: Network-based modeling for characterizing human collective behaviors during extreme events. IEEE Trans. Syst. Man Cybern. B Cybern. **46**(1), 171–183 (2017)
5. Mansoureh, T., Reihaneh, R., Osmar, R.Z.: Incremental local community identification in dynamic social networks. In: Proceedings of 2013 IEEE/ACM International Conference on Advances in Social Networks Analysis and Mining, pp. 90–94 (2013)
6. Chakrabarti, D., Kumar, R., Tomkins, A.: Evolutionary clustering. In: Proceedings of 12th ACM SIGKDD International Conference on Knowledge Discovery and Data Mining, pp. 554–560 (2006)
7. Gao, C., Chen, Z., Li, X., Tian, Z., Li, S., Wang, Z.: Multiobjective discrete particle swarm optimization for community detection in dynamic networks. Europhys. Lett. **122**(2), 28001 (2018)
8. Zaina, M.Z.M., Kanesana, J., Chuaha, J.H., Dhanapal, S., Kendall, G.: A multiobjective particle swarm optimization algorithm based on dynamic boundary search for constrained optimization. Appl. Soft Comput. **70**, 680–700 (2018)
9. Raghavan, U.N., Albert, R., Kumara, S.: Near linear time algorithm to detect community structures in large-scale networks. Phys. Rev. E **76**(3), 036106 (2007)
10. Tasgin, M., Herdagdelen, A., Bingol, H.: Community detection in complex networks using genetic algorithms. Comput. Res. Repository **2005**(3120), 1067–1068 (2007)
11. Folino, F., Pizzuti, C.: An evolutionary multiobjective approach for community discovery in dynamic networks. IEEE Trans. Knowl. Data Eng. **26**(8), 1838–1852 (2014)
12. Newman, M.E.J., Girvan, M.: Finding and evaluating community structure in networks. Phys. Rev. E **69**(2), 026113 (2004)
13. Leon, D., Albert, D.-G., Jordi, D., Alex, A.: Comparing community structure identification. J. Stat. Mech: Theory Exp. 09008 (2005)
14. Zhang, Q., Li, H.: MOEA/D: a multiobjective evolutionary algorithm based on decomposition. IEEE Trans. Evol. Comput. **11**(6), 712–731 (2007)
15. Ma, X., Dong, D.: Evolutionary nonnegative matrix factorization algorithms for community detection in dynamic networks. IEEE Trans. Knowl. Data Eng. **29**(5), 1045–1058 (2017)
16. Lin, Y.-R., Chi, Y., Zhu, S., Hari, S., Belle, L.T.: FacetNet: A framework for analyzing communities and their evolutions in dynamic networks. In: Proceedings of 17th International Conference on World Wide Web, pp. 685–694 (2008)
17. Lin, Y.-R., Chi, Y., Zhu, S., Sundaram, H., Tseng, B.L.: Analyzing communities and their evolutions in dynamic social networks. ACM Trans. Knowl. Discov. Data **3**(2), 8:1–8:31 (2009)

18. Girvan, M., Newman, M.E.J.: Community structure in social and biological net-
    works. Proc. Nat. Acad. Sci. U.S.A. **99**(12), 7821–7826 (2002)
19. Greene, D., Doyle, D., Cunningham, P.: Tracking the evolution of communities
    in dynamic social networks. In: Proceedings of 2010 International Conference on
    Advances in Social Networks Analysis and Mining, pp. 176–183 (2010)

Time-Efficient Network Monitoring Through Confined Search and Adaptive Evaluation

Qifu Hu[1,2]([✉]), Angsheng Li[3], Jiamou Liu[4][ID], and Jun Liu[1,2]

[1] State Key Laboratory of Computer Science, Institute of Software,
Chinese Academy of Sciences, Beijing, China
huqf@ios.ac.cn
[2] University of Chinese Academy of Sciences, Beijing, China
[3] State Key Laboratory of Software Development Environment,
School of Computer Science, Beihang University, Beijing, China
[4] The University of Auckland, Auckland, New Zealand

Abstract. The network monitoring problem, crucial to many applications from outbreak prevention to online rumor management, demands an optimal set of monitors to detect the spreading of infections or rumors over a network. We tackle this problem through solving a type of facility location problem where the monitored nodes are selected to minimize their distance to other nodes. Existing methods for this problem either consume prohibitively long time for large networks, lack of reasonable theoretical performance guarantees, or are very difficult to implement. We propose a new algorithm, csav, which combines a novel technique to reduce the search space with an iterative improvement mechanism. Our algorithm outputs a logarithmic number of monitors in $\tilde{O}(|E|)$ time. We perform empirical analysis over both synthesized and real-world networks as well as three propagation models. The results show that csav achieves superior performance over a number of benchmark algorithms. In particular, it produces outputs that are comparable to the well-established local search at only a fraction of its running time. Our approach is hence a scalable and time-efficient method for the network monitoring problem.

Keywords: Network monitoring problem · k-median facility location · Search algorithms · Heuristic · Social network

1 Introduction

The recent decades have seen great progress towards methods for processing large and complex social networks. The progress attests the increasing interconnectedness and interdependency of the modern society as interpersonal links enable effective spread of knowledge and ideas. While an important theme of

This work was supported by the National Natural Science Foundation of China (61772503).

© Springer Nature Switzerland AG 2019
A. C. Nayak and A. Sharma (Eds.): PRICAI 2019, LNAI 11671, pp. 633–646, 2019.
https://doi.org/10.1007/978-3-030-29911-8_49

the research has been focusing on identifying key individuals who facilitate the propagation of information – a problem generally known as *influence maximization* – other situations arise where influence should be monitored and controlled. For example, a viral infection may quickly spread via the network and cascade from a handful of affected individuals to a wide-spread outbreak. On the other hand, the rumor spreaders disseminate misinformation which has the potential to cause fear and social unrest. The monitoring problem, which seeks for the most efficient means to stay alert of potential outbreak through a network, thus becomes pivotal in many applications where the network effect is of concern.

The premises of the problem involve social actors and their links which form a complex network. There is also an explicit or implicit mechanism of infection propagation. The problem asks for a selection of a set of nodes, i.e., a *monitor placement*, so that any diffusion process may be captured by a monitor soon after it appears.

For a more precise problem formulation, we make some assumptions: (a) We use the aforementioned probability-based propagation mechanism, which encompasses many well-known network diffusion models such as SIR, independent cascade, and forest fire models. (b) To reflect resource limitation, we constrain the number of monitors and assume that each node costs equally to be monitored. (c) By *detection time*, we mean the steps it takes for the first monitor to be infected during an outbreak. The *network monitoring problem* thus asks for a monitor placement with minimum expected detection time during random outbreaks.

As measuring the detection time often involves expensive data gathering or simulations over heterogeneous networks, it is natural and cost-effective to approximate detection time using the distance between where the infection starts and the closest monitor. The problem can thus be conveniently expressed as a form of *k-median facility location problem*, a well-known NP-hard problem [10]. The problem asks for a selection of k nodes in a graph which minimize the total distance from all other nodes to the closest selected node. For this problem, there has been a long-running effort in combinatorial optimization and artificial intelligence which aims to find efficient approximation.

The existing algorithms can be broadly classified into three classes: The first class contains methods that are based on linear programming (LP) [2–4], the second class contains rule-of-thumb heuristics that are based on local structural indices such as degree and local centrality [5], and the third class utilizes iterative local searches [1]. However, applying these existing algorithms to real-world networks poses many limitations: (1) While the LP-based methods are proved to have small approximation ratio, they consume too much computation cost. The constraints of LP require $\Omega\left(n^3\right)$ space where n is the number of nodes. Moreover, these algorithms also require the provision of a table that stores the all-pair distance between any two locations in the network as part of the input. This input is necessary to achieve a sub-quadratic time complexity. For our problem though, such a distance table is not given and must be computed from the network structure. This adds $\Omega\left(n^2\right)$ to both the running time and space.

(2) The rule-of-thumb heuristics trade solution quality with time. While they can be applied to very large networks and run extremely fast, they do not have provable performance guarantee. (3) The local search algorithm iteratively improves a solution by searching for nodes that could reduce the penalty function until reaching a local optimum. Even though the algorithm does not rely on the all-pair distance table, this method nevertheless lacks of a reasonable running time guarantee. It is thus important to ask whether an algorithm exists that balances computation time with solution quality and can scale to very large networks.

Contributions. This paper proposes a new algorithm, named *Confined Search with Adaptive eValuation* (csav), which solves the network monitoring problem and fulfills the goal above. Firstly, our algorithm guarantees to terminate in $\tilde{O}(k^2|E|)$ where $|E|$ is the number of edges in the network. The algorithm runs efficiently in practice on large networks. E.g., for a road network with $\sim 175,000$ nodes the algorithm runs in merely ~ 160 min as opposed to ~ 6000 min for local search giving a 36-time speedup. Secondly, our algorithm produces solutions that are on a par with the solutions of local search which has an approximation ratio of 5. In practice, the algorithm achieves less than 0.2% higher penalty score than the solutions of local search in most cases, whereas solutions of the best rule-of-thumb heuristic with a better running time have significantly higher penalty (See Experiment). Thirdly, as shown in our experiments, solutions found by the algorithm correspond to good monitor placements for the network monitoring problem.

csav adopts a two-phase structure, each of which constitutes a search procedure: The first phase searches for an initial k-node solution and the second phase iteratively looks for nodes to swap into the solution for further improvement. This makes the algorithm conceptually similar to local search, but we introduce two novel algorithmic techniques which make csav remarkably different:

1. (ℓ-confined search) As opposed to local search which examines the entire network in each iteration, csav only adds a fixed number of new nodes to the search space. This balances the level of "greediness" of the search with time costs and potentially leads to a sharp drop in time consumption while not affecting much the solution quality.
2. (Adaptive evaluation) While iteratively building up and improving the solution, the algorithm needs to constantly evaluate the marginal reward of nodes in the network. csav utilizes an adaptive mechanism that performs two graph traversals in the network to quickly update the penalty score. This further reduces the running time without affecting the solution outcome.

2   Problem Definition and Related Work

A *network* is a connected undirected graph $G = (V, E)$ with node set V and edge set E; an edge $\{u, v\}$ represents a dyadic link such as a contact or message channel and is expressed as uv for short. The *distance* $d(u, v)$ between u and v is the length of a shortest path between the two nodes. For any $S \subseteq V$, let $d(u, S) = \min_{v \in S} d(u, v)$.

Contact relationships between individuals provide pivotal information on the spreading of infectious diseases. A *propagation model* specifies the spread of virus over a network G. An *outbreak* starts from a *source* $u \in V$ and generates a sequence of sets $U_0 = \{u\} \subseteq U_1 \subseteq U_2 \subseteq \cdots \subseteq V$ where U_i denote the set of nodes that are infected at or before the ith time step. A classical example is the *SIR model* which partitions V into three mutually-exclusive sets at any time step i ($i \geq 0$): S_i (susceptible), I_i (infected) and R_i (recovered). A node $v \in S_i$ may move into I_{i+1} in the next time instance through a neighbor $v' \in I_i$ with probability $q \in [0,1]$. Any node $v \in I_i$ may move to R_{i+1} with probability $p \in (0,1]$ and stop being infectious. The process eventually stops when $I_i = \varnothing$. The outbreak can be represented by the sequence $U_i = \cup_{j \leq i} I_j$. Another well-known propagation model is *independence cascade (IC)* which resembles information diffusion through a social network. Here each edge uv in the graph is assigned an activation probability $p(uv) \in [0,1]$. If a node $u \notin U_{i-1}$ moves into U_i at time step i and $v \notin U_i$, then with probability $p(uv)$ v will move into U_{i+1}. A special case of the IC model is the *forest fire (FF)* model where $p(uv) = 1$ for any edge uv.

The *network monitoring problem* aims to detect, e.g., the spreading of computer virus [7,20], or the spread of messages via online social media [15]. More formally, we assume that a propagation mechanism is applied on the network $G = (V, E)$. Instead of assuming a specific source set, we assume that all nodes are potential sources from which infection may start. A *placement* is a nonempty subset $M \subseteq V$. A monitor $v \in M$ would report an outbreak once it is infected.

Definition 1. *During an outbreak, T_v is the least $i \in \mathbb{N} \cup \{\infty\}$ when node v becomes an element of I_i. For a placement $M \subseteq V$, the detection time T_M is $\min_{v \in M} T_v$.*

Let $\mathbf{E}(T_M|s)$ denote the expected detection time of M given source s. The *expected detection time* $\mathbf{E}(T_M)$ is thus $\sum_{s \in V} \mathbf{E}(T_M|s) p_s$, where p_s is the probability of s being the source. Assuming equiprobability amongst all nodes to be the source, $\mathbf{E}(T_M) = \frac{1}{|V|} \sum_{s \in V} \mathbf{E}(T_M|s)$. The network monitoring problem (NMP) is formulated as follows: Given a network $G = (V, E)$ and $k \in \mathbb{N}$, find a placement $M \subseteq V$ such that $|M| \leq k$ and $\mathbf{E}(T_M)$ is minimized.

Note that the expectation $\mathbf{E}(T_M)$ can be thought of as a "penalty" to the placement M. In the FF model, for example, this penalty can be defined as:

Definition 2. *Penalty function $\rho \colon 2^V \to \mathbb{R}$ is defined by $\rho(M) = \sum_{u \in V} d(u, M)$ if $M \neq \varnothing$; and set $\rho(\varnothing) = |V|^2$.*

In this case, NMP can be rephrased as a form of *k-median problem*: Find $\arg\min_{|M|=k} \rho(M)$. There are several advantages to using the penalty function as an objective function for our purpose. Firstly, evaluating $\rho(M)$ of a specific M is generally much more efficient than evaluation $\mathbf{E}(T_M)$, which normally would require expensive simulation. Secondly, the original formulation of NMP depends on a propagation mechanism. Adopting a unifying objective function like $\rho(M)$ makes the problem independent of the mechanism and conceptually simpler.

Thirdly, as we will shown in the experiments below, over the mentioned propagation mechanisms and many network structures, the monitor placement with smaller $\rho(M)$ tends also to have smaller $\mathbf{E}(T_M)$.

There are many works that address the k-median problem and its variants. Algorithms with constant approximations can be achieved with LP [2–4]. [16] proposed a $12 + o(1)$ approximation algorithm, which is in $\tilde{O}(|E|)$ time and $\tilde{O}(|E|)$ space. However, it is of theoretical interests only and its implementation would face many obstacles.

The local search approach is widely known in operation research. [1] proved that the approximation ratio of local search with p-swap is $3+2/p$. In particular, local search with single swap, also referred to as *partition around medoids* (pam), is often used due to its relative fast speed. An empirical analysis conducted by [14] compared different approximation algorithms and concluded that pam performs better than the 4-approximation greedy algorithm proposed in [9]. Due to this proven good quality and relative efficiency, we will use pam as a benchmark algorithm to compare with our method. The procedure of pam contains two phases: (1) compute an initial k-node set S and (2) iteratively improve S if it is possible to do so by swapping a node in S with an outside node. Our proposed method has a similar conceptual framework.

3   csav: Confined Search with Adaptive Evaluation

We propose the csav algorithm to compute a set M of nodes in $G = (V, E)$ with small penalty $\rho(M)$. Define the *reward function* $R: 2^V \to \mathbb{R}$ by

$$R(M) = \rho(\varnothing) - \rho(M). \tag{1}$$

Clearly, minimizing $\rho(M)$ is equivalent to maximizing $R(M)$.

The algorithm performs two phases of operations. We next give a high-level description of each of the phases.

Phase one. For a given set $M \subseteq V$, and $u \notin M$, the *marginal reward* of u with respect to M is

$$\delta_M(u) = R(M \cup \{u\}) - R(M).$$

When the set M is clear, we abuse the notion writing it simply as $\delta(u)$. A *forward greedy solution* is a k-node placement M defined by iteratively adding into M a node $u \notin M$ with maximum marginal reward $\delta_M(u)$. The first phase of csav aims to approximate a forward greedy solution.

It is easy to prove that R is *sub-modular*, i.e., $\forall A \subseteq B \forall u \notin B \colon R(A \cup \{u\}) - R(A) \geq R(B \cup \{u\}) - R(B)$. We thus modify the well-known cost-effective lazy forward (celf) scheme, which exploits submodularity of R [11]. In csav, a method is implemented to speedup celf and output a near-forward greedy solution. The detail is stated in the next section.

Phase two. Let $M = \{m_1, \ldots, m_k\}$ be a placement. A *coordinate ascension* of M is $M' = \{m'_1, \ldots, m'_k\}$, which is defined by iteratively solving the single-variable optimization problem: For each $j = 1$ to k, set

$$m'_j = \arg\max_{u \in V} R(\{m'_1, \ldots, m'_{j-1}, u, m_{j+1}, \ldots, m_k\}). \tag{2}$$

The second phase aims to improve the initial solution produced by Phase one through iteratively improving it using the coordinate ascent method above.

In the subsequent sections, we introduce the two novel algorithmic techniques introduced in csav (1) confined search and (2) adaptive evaluation, which play a key part in the algorithm.

4   Confined Search

Both phases consist of searching for nodes $u \notin M$ that maximize the reward of adding (as in Phase one) or swapping (as in Phase two) u into the solution set M. This requires scanning through all nodes in $V \backslash M$. To speed-up the search process, a natural idea is to confine the search space by leaving some nodes out of the search space, so that only a bounded number of elements are examined. We call such a scheme *confined search*.

4.1 ℓ-Confined celf

In Phase one, We modify the celf algorithm to build a near-forward greedy solution to the k-median problem. Similar to celf, we use a priority queue to store nodes to be added to M. Essentially, the priority queue corresponds to the search space.

In the original formulation of celf, the priority queue contains all nodes in $V \backslash M$. In comparison, we put into the priority queue only a subset of $V \backslash M$. We refer to nodes that have been inserted into the priority queue as *candidates*. Here we use a parameter $\ell \in \mathbb{N}$ to indicate the number of candidates that we insert at each iteration. The result scheme is called ℓ-confined celf:

- At the first iteration, M initiates to $\varnothing$. We approximate $R(\{u\})$ for each node $u \in V$ using the approx-pen(G) subroutine and select the ℓ nodes with the highest approximated value as the initial candidates.
- At all subsequent iterations, we approximate the marginal reward $\delta(u)$ with respect to M of all nodes $u \in V \backslash M$ using the score(G, M) subroutine and select the ℓ nodes with the highest score as candidates.

The ℓ-confined celf is shown in Algorithm 1. The algorithm initializes an empty priority queue and assigns a flag f_u to every node $u \in V$.

Subroutine approx-pen(G). The approx-pen(G) subroutine approximates the penalty of each singleton $\{u\}$ for all $u \in V$. Here we use an efficient approach rand, introduced in [18], to approximate $\rho(\{u\})$. The method relies on sampling

---

Algorithm 1. The ℓ-confined celf algorithm

INPUT $G = (V, E), k \in \mathbb{N}$

OUTPUT Placement $M \subseteq V$

    Initialize empty max-priority queue H; Set $M \leftarrow \varnothing$

                                                   ▷ Select initial candidates.

    Run approx-pen(G) and obtain $\rho'(u)$ for all $u \in V$.

    $S_{\text{init}} \leftarrow \ell$ nodes with the smallest value of ρ'

    Run add-candidate(S_{init})

    repeat

        $\langle u, \delta_u \rangle \leftarrow H.\text{remove}()$

        if f_u *is* true **then**

            Run add-candidate($\{u\}$); **continue**

        end if

        $M \leftarrow M \cup \{u\}$

        for $u \in V \setminus M$ **do** $f_u \leftarrow$ true

        end for

        Run score(G, M) to compute $\sigma(v)$ for all $v \in V \setminus M$

        $C \leftarrow$ the set of ℓ nodes with maximum σ-score in $V \setminus M$

        Run add-candidate(C)

    until $|M| = k$

---

random nodes, called *pivots*, and solving the single-sourced shortest path (SSSP) problem from these pivots. With pivots $u_1, u_2, \ldots, u_r$, the *approximated penalty* of a node $v \in V$ is $\rho'(v) = \sum_{i=1}^{r} (n \cdot d(v, u_i))/r$.

Theorem 1. *[18, Thm3] With high probability,* rand *approximates* $\rho(\{u\})$ *of all* $u \in V$ *with an additive error of* $\epsilon(n-1)\mathrm{diam}(G)$ *using* $\Theta\left(\log |V|/(\epsilon^2)\right)$ *pivots. In particular, with polylogarithmically many pivots,* rand *achieves* $\epsilon(n-1)$ *additive error in time* $\tilde{O}(|E|)$.

Subroutine add-candidate(X). This subroutine loops through nodes in the input set $X \subseteq V$, updating marginal reward $\delta(u)$ for each $u \in X$ and then adding the key-value pair $\langle u, \delta_u \rangle$ to the heap H (if the key u is not in H already), and changes the f_u flag to false. We will discuss how marginal reward $\delta(u)$ will be updated using adaptive evaluation in the next section.

Subroutine score(G, M). Nodes that have already been added into M guide us to approximate the marginal reward of other nodes. Define the set $L_i = \{u \in V | d(u, M) = i\}$ for all $i \geq 0$. For node $u \in L_i$, define X_u, Y_u, Z_u as the set of u's neighbors who lie in L_{i-1}, L_i, L_{i+1}, respectively.

Definition 3. *Given set* $M \subseteq V$, *define the* σ-score

$$\sigma(u) = |X_u| \times I(d(u, M) - 2) + |Y_u| \times I(d(u, M) - 1) + \left(\sum_{v \in Z_u} t_v + 1\right) \times d(u, M) \quad (3)$$

where t_v *is number of descendants of* v *in* $\mathcal{T}_M$ *and* $I(x) = 1_{\mathbb{N}}(x) \cdot x \; \forall x \in \mathbb{Z}$.

Observe that the marginal rewards $\delta(u) = \rho(M) - \rho(M \cup \{u\}) \geq \sigma(u)$. As $\sigma(u)$ is a lowerbound on the marginal reward of u, We pick new candidates guided by this score. Starting from $M \subseteq V$, we run a BFS-like traversal treating all nodes in M as roots and generate a collection of trees, called the *BFS forest* from M. We represent the BFS forest by a data structure $\mathcal{T}_M = \{L_0, \ldots, L_d\}$ where d is the maximum level. The σ-scores are then computed from processing $\mathcal{T}_M$ bottom-up.

4.2 ℓ-Confined Coordinate Ascent

Phase two iteratively finds nodes that may swap into the current solution M to improve the reward. The search space involves all nodes outside of M. To speed-up the process, we again use ℓ-confined search to select a set C of *candidates*. Intuitively speaking, these candidates should have high marginal reward. Therefore, we select the candidates by the σ-scores of nodes. Each round tries to swap k nodes into M. We repeat the process for s rounds or until we reach a local optimal solution, for some given $s \in \mathbb{N}$. See Algorithm 2.

Algorithm 2. CoordinateAscent(G, M, s)

INPUT $G, M = \{m_1, \ldots, m_k\}, s \in \mathbb{N}$
OUTPUT Improved solution set $M' \subseteq V$
  $M' \leftarrow M; i \leftarrow 0$
  repeat
    $R' \leftarrow R(M')$
    for $j = 1$ to k **do**
      Run score(G, M') to obtain $\sigma(u)$ for all $u \in V \setminus M'$
      Set $C \leftarrow$ top ℓ nodes by $\sigma(u)$
      $m_j \leftarrow \arg\max_{v \in (C \cup \{m_j\})} R(\{m_1, \cdots, m_{j-1},$
        $v, m_{j+1}, \cdots, m_k\})$
    end for
    $i \leftarrow i + 1$
  until $i > s$ or $R(M') - R' = 0$

In implementation of csav, we set parameters ℓ and s to be in $\Theta\left(\log^2 |V|\right)$.

Theorem 2. *With ℓ and s in $O\left(polylog(|V|)\right)$, the* csav *algorithm computes a k-node placement $M \subseteq V$ in time $\tilde{O}\left(k^2 |E|\right)$[1].*

5   Adaptive Evaluation

The confined celf procedure described above iteratively builds a k-node placement M by calling add-candidate(X) subroutine at each iteration. One crucial

---

[1] [https://github.com/networkmonitor2019/appendix/blob/master/cplex-proof.pdf].

task done in this sub-routine is to update the marginal reward of a node u. A *static algorithm* would compute $R(M \cup \{u\})$ using a traversal of the entire network. Instead, we define an *adaptive evaluation* technique that dynamically updates the marginal reward of nodes. Throughout, the technique maintains (i) $d(v, M)$ of all nodes $v \in V$ and (ii) the penalty $\rho(M)$. To preserve these information, it is sufficient to run a BFS starting from nodes in M every time when M is changed.

The adaptive evaluation algorithm takes a node $u \in V$ and outputs the marginal reward $\delta(u)$ with respect to the current M. For any node $u \notin M$, observe that the marginal reward $\delta(u) = \sum_{v \in D} (d(v, M) - d(v, u))$, where the set $D = \{v \in V | d(u, v) < d(v, M)\}$. Thus, to obtain $\delta(u)$ given $d(v, M)$ of all $v \in V$, it is sufficient to compute the set D and $d(u, v)$ for all $v \in D$. Therefore, the algorithm performs a traversal starting from the node u and searches for all v with $d(u, v) < d(v, M)$. The following fact is easy to prove.

Lemma 1. *Take any $v \in V$. If there exists a node s that lies on a shortest path between u and v and $s \notin D$. Then $v \notin D$*

By Lemma 1, during the second BFS, once we have encountered a node s where $d(s, u) \geq d(s, M)$, all descendants from s on the BFS tree do not need to be examined, and thus we can prune this branch of the BFS search tree away. As The add-candidate procedure is frequently called throughout Phase one, this technique can potentially save a lot of computation time and space. The adaptive evaluation algorithm is shown in Algorithm 3.

Algorithm 3. Adaptive-Eval(G,M,u)

INPUT $G = (V, E), M, u, \rho(M)$. Assume that $d(v, M)$ is stored with all $v \in V$.
OUTPUT $\delta(u)$
    $L \leftarrow \{u\}$;lev $\leftarrow 0$;$\delta \leftarrow 0$;visited $\leftarrow \varnothing$;
    while $L \neq \varnothing$ **do**
        Up $\leftarrow \varnothing$;
        for $v \in L$ **do**
            visited $\leftarrow$ visited $\cup \{v\}$
            if $d(v, M) >$ lev **then**
                Up $\leftarrow$ Up $\cup \{v\}$; $\delta \leftarrow \delta + (d(v, M) -$ lev$)$
            end if
        end for
        lev $\leftarrow$ lev $+ 1$; next $\leftarrow \varnothing$;
        for $v \in$ Up **do**
            for neighbor w of v in G **do**
                Add w to next if $w \notin$ visited and $w \notin$ next
            end for
        end for
        $L \leftarrow$ next
    end while
    Set $\rho(M \cup \{u\}) \leftarrow \rho(M) - \delta$
    return δ

---

6   Methods, Results and Analysis

Alternative Methods. We compare csav with three methods: (1) Firstly, pam will serve as a baseline method due to its guaranteed performance. To reduce its running time, adaptive evaluation is adopted in implementation. (2) clc (combinatorial local centrality) is based on the notion of **local centrality** proposed in [5]. For a given node v and a distance l, $N_v(l) = \{u : d(u,v) \leq l\}$. Local centrality of v is defined as $C_L(v) = \sum_{u \in N_v(1)} \sum_{w \in N_u(1)} |N_w(2)|$. $C_L(v)$ is a upper bound of the number of nodes within a 4-step circle. [12] extended the definition to set M as $C_L(M) = \sum_{u \in \cup_{v \in M} N_v(1)} \sum_{w \in N_u(1)} |N_w(2)|$. The intuition of maximizing $C_L(M)$ is to find a M with more nodes within 4-step, which is consistent with our goal on some level. Thus we adopt it and the near-optimal heuristic introduced in [12]. (3) deg (degree discount heuristic) which applies a maximum degree-based heuristic [6]. In fact, the set chosen by deg is a $1 - 1/e$ approximation of choosing k nodes to cover as more neighbor nodes as possible. It can be regarded as local monitoring strategy.

Data Sets. We use synthetic networks that are generated using well-known random graph models as well as real-world networks. The first model is Kleinberg's small-world networks (KL). Starting from an $n \times n$ grid H, build $\alpha \in \mathbb{N}$ edges for every node u with the chance of adding an edge uv being proportional to $(d_H(u,v))^{-\beta}$, where $d_H(u,v)$ is the distance between u and v in H. For our experiments, we set $\alpha = 2$ and $\beta \in \{3,4\}$ and create KL with $|V| = 50,000$.

The second model is Random Euclidean Model (RE), which is generated in the plane. Cartesian coordinates on nodes will be generated at random. There will be an edge between any two nodes, for which Euclidean distance between them below some threshold T. Due to high density when T is large, we create RE with a small $T = 0.02$ and $|V| = 10,000$ [8].

We take 12 real-world networks: 1 infrastructure network (powergrid), 3 collaboration networks of scientists (ca-GrQc, ca-HepPh and astro-ph), 4 road networks (OL_road, TG_road, CA_road and San_road), 2 social networks (soc-douban, Enron), 1 citation network (ca-citeseer) and 1 web network (NotreDame)[2].

Evaluation Metrics. We compare algorithms with respect to different performance metrics: penalty, average detection time and the running time. To facilitate comparisons between algorithms, we define the stretch ratio of penalty as below. The definition of the stretch ratio of average detection time is similar. And we always take result of pam, if any, as baseline in our experiments.

---

[2] Power grid, soc-douban are available in [konect.uni-koblenz.de/networks]; ca-GrQc, ca-HepPh, astro-ph, Enron, NotreDame are available in [snap.stanford.edu]; OL_road, TG_road, CA_road, San_road are available in [www.cs.utah.edu/~lifeifei]; ca-citeseer is available in [www.networkrepository.com].

Definition 4. *Given set $M \subseteq V$ as a baseline, for any set $X \subseteq V$, the* stretch ratio of penalty $r_\rho(X) = \frac{(\rho(X) - \rho(M))}{\rho(M)}$.

For each parameter combination of network model we average the results over 10 network instances. We choose $k = \Theta \left(\log^2 |V| \right)$ nodes to monitor. We set $q = 0.6, p = 0.2$ in SIR model and $p(uv) = 0.6$ for each edge uv in IC model. Our results of average detection time are based on $10,000$ rounds of simulation. We stop the algorithm if the running time exceeds $10,000$ mins. In the following we discuss penalty and running time before presenting average detection time over various network data sets.

Result Set 1: Penalty and Running Time. We compare the penalty of monitors selected by different algorithms and the running time [3] of pam and csav in Table 1. We take csav as baseline on NotreDame because pam cannot finish in $10,000$ mins. The results show that: (1) csav performs comparatively well as pam, specifically the stretch ratios of csav are negligible($< 0.2\%$) on most networks and less than 2% on all networks. (2) The performance of csav is far more better than clc and deg, especially on road networks. (3) With $k = \Theta \left(\log^2 |V| \right)$, csav runs invariably faster than pam, with around 20–36 times the speed over networks with ≥ 20000 nodes. Therefore, csav balances computation time with solution quality. An illustrative example is provided to further compare the algorithms[4].

Table 1. Network statistics, penalty and running time. The table lists network statistics, monitor number, stretch ratio of penalty, and the comparison of running time.

Graph			k	r_ρ			Time (mins)		Speedup
Type	$|V|$	$|E|$		csav	clc	deg	pam	csav	
KL, $\beta = 3$	50,000	198,470	300	1.77%	12.07%	23.43%	621.34	84	7.4
KL, $\beta = 4$	50,000	198,470	300	1.68%	27.53%	35.32%	494.26	53.6	9.22
RE, $T = 0.02$	10,000	61,885	200	0.16%	17.97%	62.53%	32.15	4.38	7.34
powergrid	4,941	6,594	200	−0.02%	29.08%	28.00%	2.22	0.53	4.19
ca-GrQc	5,242	14,496	200	0.00%	12.47%	32.96%	1.47	0.61	2.41
OL_road	6,105	7,035	200	0.05%	64.59%	49.27%	3.58	0.84	4.26
ca-HepPh	12,008	118,521	200	0.04%	9.45%	42.49%	36.94	5.15	7.17
astro-ph	14,845	239,303	200	0.00%	10.89%	29.11%	47.06	6.74	6.98
TG_road	18,263	23,874	200	1.31%	209.03%	61.8%	46.19	5.88	7.86
CA_road	21,048	21,693	200	0.88%	287.72%	251.76%	85.41	4.13	20.68
Enron	36,692	183, 831	200	0.00%	5.98%	10.46%	177.22	9.07	19.54
soc-douban	154,908	327,162	400	0.04%	8.42%	12.25%	2590.06	126.50	20.48
San_road	174,956	223,001	400	1.91%	254.06%	127.67%	5994.57	165.90	36.13
ca-citeseer	227,320	814,134	400	0.13%	6.73%	13.43%	9792.11	335.40	29.20
NotreDame	325,729	1,497,134	400	604647	23.46%	27.49%	>10,000	346.46	>28.86

---

[3] Running times are based on experiments performed on a server with a 96 Core Intel Xeon CPU E7540 2.40 GHz. Algorithms are implemented using Python 2.6.6, which is available at [https://github.com/networkmonitor2019/Code].

[4] [https://github.com/networkmonitor2019/appendix/blob/master/KL-400.pdf].

Result Set 2: Average Detection Time. We compare the penalty and detection performance of the monitors selected by different algorithms in Fig. 1. In general, the result shows that: (1) Penalty and average detection time are consistent in that the monitor placement with smaller penalty tends also to have smaller average detection time[5]. (2) In terms of average detection time, csav performs comparatively well as pam and outperforms all other alternative methods.

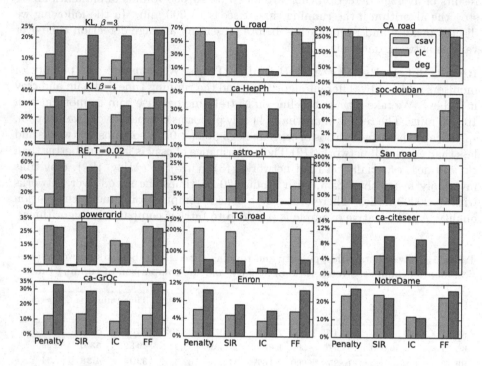

Fig. 1. Stretch ratio of penalty and average detection time.

In addition, to demonstrate the conclusions above are robust, we study penalty and average detection time with various k. The result is provided in a link here[6].

7 Conclusion

The extension of csav to weighted networks is straight forward. To balance the quality of solution and cost, we can (1) Adjust the number of candidates. (2) Compute tighter lower bound of marginal reward through sampling multiple BFS forests. This framework is also applicable to other problems. For example,

---

[5] Abundant linear topologies in CA_road or San_road prevent IC from outbreaking, which makes all algorithms indistinguishable.

[6] [https://github.com/networkmonitor2019/appendix/blob/master/vary-k.pdf].

to solve *network building problem* with eccentricity [13,19], all we need is to modify each node to gather distance distribution of the subtree in the subroutine score(G, M).

There are several future directions building on this work, the first is to obtain theoretical results of confined search; the second is to put it under the framework of game theory [17], in which one player intends to spread rumor in the network while the other player attempts to detect the rumor as soon as possible. Another is to investigate ways to monitor outbreaks over dynamic networks.

References

1. Arya, V., Garg, N., Khandekar, R., Meyerson, A., Munagala, K., Pandit, V.: Local search heuristics for k-median and facility location problems. SIAM J. Comput. **33**(3), 544–562 (2004)
2. Awasthi, P., Bandeira, A.S., Charikar, M., Krishnaswamy, R., Villar, S., Ward, R.: Relax, no need to round: Integrality of clustering formulations. In: Proceedings of the 2015 Conference on Innovations in Theoretical Computer Science, pp. 191–200. ACM (2015)
3. Charikar, M., Guha, S., Tardos, É., Shmoys, D.B.: A constant-factor approximation algorithm for the k-median problem. In: Proceedings of the Thirty-First Annual ACM Symposium on Theory of computing, pp. 1–10. ACM (1999)
4. Charikar, M., Li, S.: A dependent LP-rounding approach for the k-median problem. In: Czumaj, A., Mehlhorn, K., Pitts, A., Wattenhofer, R. (eds.) ICALP 2012. LNCS, vol. 7391, pp. 194–205. Springer, Heidelberg (2012). https://doi.org/10. 1007/978-3-642-31594-7_17
5. Chen, D., Lü, L., Shang, M.S., Zhang, Y.C., Zhou, T.: Identifying influential nodes in complex networks. Phys. A **391**(4), 1777–1787 (2012)
6. Chen, W., Wang, Y., Yang, S.: Efficient influence maximization in social networks. In: Proceedings SIGKDD 2009, pp. 199–208. ACM (2009)
7. Chen, Z., Gao, L., Kwiat, K.: Modeling the spread of active worms. In: Proceedings INFOCOM 2003, vol. 3, pp. 1890–1900. IEEE (2003)
8. Gilbert, E.N.: Random plane networks. J. Soc. Ind. Appl. Math. **9**(4), 533–543 (1961)
9. Jain, K., Mahdian, M., Markakis, E., Saberi, A., Vazirani, V.V.: Greedy facility location algorithms analyzed using dual fitting with factor-revealing LP. J. ACM (JACM) **50**(6), 795–824 (2003)
10. Kariv, O., Hakimi, S.L.: An algorithmic approach to network location problems. i: the p-centers. SIAM J. Appl. Math. **37**(3), 513–538 (1979)
11. Leskovec, J., Krause, A., Guestrin, C., Faloutsos, C., VanBriesen, J., Glance, N.: Cost-effective outbreak detection in networks. In: Proceedings of the 13th ACM SIGKDD International Conference on Knowledge Discovery and Data Mining, pp. 420–429. ACM (2007)
12. Moores, G., Shakarian, P., Macdonald, B., Howard, N.: Finding near-optimal groups of epidemic spreaders in a complex network. PLoS ONE **9**(4), e90303 (2014)
13. Moskvina, A., Liu, J.: How to build your network? a structural analysis. In: Proceedings IJCAI-16, pp. 2597–2603. AAAI Press (2016)
14. Nagarajan, C., Williamson, D.P.: An experimental evaluation of incremental and hierarchical k-median algorithms. In: Pardalos, P.M., Rebennack, S. (eds.) SEA 2011. LNCS, vol. 6630, pp. 169–180. Springer, Heidelberg (2011). https://doi.org/ 10.1007/978-3-642-20662-7_15

15. Nekovee, M., Moreno, Y., Bianconi, G., Marsili, M.: Theory of rumour spreading in complex social networks. Phys. A **374**(1), 457–470 (2007)
16. Thorup, M.: Quick k-median, k-center, and facility location for sparse graphs. SIAM Journal on Computing **34**(2), 405–432 (2005)
17. Tsai, J., Nguyen, T.H., Tambe, M.: Security Games for Controlling Contagion. AAAI (2012)
18. Wang, D.E.J.: Fast approximation of centrality. Graph Algorithms. Appl. **5**(5), 39 (2006)
19. Yan, B., Chen, Y., Liu, J.: Dynamic relationship building: exploitation versus exploration on a social network. In: Bouguettaya, A., et al. (eds.) WISE 2017. LNCS, vol. 10569, pp. 75–90. Springer, Cham (2017). https://doi.org/10.1007/978-3-319-68783-4_6
20. Zou, C.C., Gao, L., Gong, W., Towsley, D.: Monitoring and early warning for internet worms. In: Proceedings CCS 2003, pp. 190–199. ACM (2003)

Autoencoding Binary Classifiers
for Supervised Anomaly Detection

Yuki Yamanaka[1]([⊠]), Tomoharu Iwata[2], Hiroshi Takahashi[3],
Masanori Yamada[1], and Sekitoshi Kanai[3,4]

[1] NTT Secure Platform Laboratories, Musashino-shi, Japan
{yuuki.yamanaka.kb,masanori.yamada.cm}@hco.ntt.co.jp
[2] NTT Communication Science Laboratories, Kyoto, Japan
tomoharu.iwata.gy@hco.ntt.co.jp
[3] NTT Software Innovation Center, Musashino-shi, Japan
{hiroshi.takahashi.bm,sekitoshi.kanai.fu}@hco.ntt.co.jp
[4] Keio University, Minato City, Japan

Abstract. We propose the Autoencoding Binary Classifiers (ABC), a
novel supervised anomaly detector based on the Autoencoder (AE).
There are two main approaches in anomaly detection: supervised and
unsupervised. The supervised approach accurately detects the known
anomalies included in training data, but it cannot detect the unknown
anomalies. Meanwhile, the unsupervised approach can detect both known
and unknown anomalies that are located away from normal data points.
However, it does not detect known anomalies as accurately as the supervised approach. Furthermore, even if we have labeled normal data points
and anomalies, the unsupervised approach cannot utilize these labels.
The ABC is a probabilistic binary classifier that effectively exploits the
label information, where normal data points are modeled using the AE as
a component. By maximizing the likelihood, the AE in the proposed ABC
is trained to minimize the reconstruction error for normal data points,
and to maximize it for known anomalies. Since our approach becomes
able to reconstruct the normal data points accurately and fails to reconstruct the known and unknown anomalies, it can accurately discriminate
both known and unknown anomalies from normal data points. Experimental results show that the ABC achieves higher detection performance
than existing supervised and unsupervised methods.

Keywords: Anomaly detection · Supervised machine learning ·
Autoencoder

1 Introduction

Anomaly detection is one of the most important tasks in artificial intelligence
and is widely performed in many areas, such as cyber security [10], complex
system management [12], and material inspection [19].

© Springer Nature Switzerland AG 2019
A. C. Nayak and A. Sharma (Eds.): PRICAI 2019, LNAI 11671, pp. 647–659, 2019.
https://doi.org/10.1007/978-3-030-29911-8_50

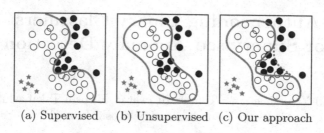

(a) Supervised   (b) Unsupervised   (c) Our approach

Fig. 1. (a) Supervised, (b) unsupervised and (c) our approaches. White circles, black circles, and red stars represent normal data points, known anomalies, and unknown anomalies, respectively. Red lines show the decision boundary. (Color figure online)

Anomaly detection methods can be categorized into supervised and unsupervised approaches. A supervised approach learns a classification rule that discriminates anomalies from normal data points [15]. Figure 1(a) shows the image of the supervised approach. This approach utilizes the label information, which indicates whether each data point is an anomaly or not, and can achieve high detection performance for known anomalies included in a dataset. However, a supervised approach is effective only for limited applications for two reasons. First, it cannot detect the unknown anomalies not included in the dataset. Generally, it is difficult to obtain a training dataset that covers all types of possible anomalies in advance. For example, in malware detection, unknown anomalies will appear one after another. Second, the standard supervised approaches do not work well when there are much fewer number of anomalies than normal data points. This is called a class imbalance problem. Since the anomalies rarely occur, it is difficult to collect a sufficient number of them.

On the other hand, an unsupervised approach does not require anomalies for training, since it tries to model only the normal data points. Figure 1(b) shows the image of the unsupervised approach. Since this approach detects anomalies by using the difference between normal and test data points, it can detect both known anomalies and unknown anomalies that are away from normal data points. This difference is frequently called the anomaly score. To detect anomalies in high-dimensional and complex data, various methods based on deep learning techniques have been presented. One of the major unsupervised approaches based on deep learning is the autoencoder (AE) [13,17]. The AE is composed of two neural networks: the encoder and the decoder. The encoder compresses data points into low-dimensional latent representations. The decoder reconstructs data points from latent representations. The parameters of the encoder and decoder are optimized by minimizing the error between data points and reconstructed data points, which is called the reconstruction error. Since the AE is trained with normal data points, it becomes able to reconstruct normal data points and fails to reconstruct anomalies. Therefore, the reconstruction error can be used as the anomaly score. However, an unsupervised approach performs inferiorly to a supervised approach at detecting known anomalies since it does not utilize the label information. Furthermore, even if anomalies are obtained in advance, an unsupervised approach cannot utilize these anomalies for improving detection performance. To handle this problem, the limiting reconstruction capability (LRC), which is the simple extension of the AE, has been presented [14]. The LRC maximizes the reconstruction error for the anomaly data points, in addition to minimizing the reconstruction error for normal data points. As a result, the LRC can detect the known anomalies close to normal data points. However, the LRC has a serious drawback: the training of AE in the LRC is unstable. Since the reconstruction error is bounded below but not bounded above, the LRC tends to maximize the reconstruction error for known anomalies rather than to minimize the reconstruction error for normal data points. As a result, the LRC cannot reconstruct the normal data points well.

In this paper, we propose the Autoencoding Binary Classifier (ABC), which is a novel supervised approach to exploit the benefits of both supervised and unsupervised approaches. In the ABC, we regard the conditional probability of the label variable given a data point as the Bernoulli distribution. Its negative log likelihood is modeled by the reconstruction error of the AE. Thus, by minimizing the negative log likelihood, the AE in the ABC is trained so as to minimize the reconstruction error for normal data points and to maximize the reconstruction error for known anomalies. Although the behavior of the AE in the ABC is similar to the LRC, the training of the ABC is stable since its objective function is bounded below and above with respect to reconstruction error. After the training, we can obtain the conditional probability of the label variable given a data point, which is more reasonable anomaly score than the reconstruction error. As shown in Fig. 1(c), the ABC can detect the anomalies located away from normal data points and detect the anomalies that are close to the known anomalies. In addition, even if training dataset does not contain the known anomalies enough, the ABC can outperform the supervised approaches since the ABC behaves as the unsupervised approach.

2   Preliminaries

First, we review the autoencoder (AE) [6] and limiting reconstruction capability method (LRC) [14].

The AE is a dimensionality reduction algorithm using neural networks. The AE consists of two parts of neural networks: the encoder and the decoder. The encoder $E(x)$ compresses data point x into low-dimensional latent representation z. The decoder $D(z)$ reconstructs data points from latent representation z. In the AE, the objective function for each data point is given by

$$\mathcal{L}_{AE}(x) = ||x - D(E(x))||, \tag{1}$$

where $||\cdot||$ denotes an arbitrary distance function. The ℓ_2-norm is usually used. This objective function is called the reconstruction error. The parameters of the encoder and decoder are optimized by minimizing the sum of the reconstruction error for all data points.

One of the most widely used variants of the AE is the Denoising autoencoder (DAE) [21], which tries to reconstruct original data points from the noisy input data. The DAE is estimated by minimizing the following objective function

$$\mathcal{L}_{DAE}(x) = ||x - D(E(x + \epsilon))||, \tag{2}$$

where ϵ is a noise from an isotropic Gaussian distribution. Since the DAE is robust against the noise, it is useful in noisy environments. The AE and DAE can be optimized with stochastic gradient descent (SGD) [7].

There are various anomaly detectors based on the AEs [13,17,22,23]. As a simple way, the reconstruction error can be used for anomaly detection [17]. If we trained the AE on normal data points, the reconstruction error for anomalies can be larger than that for normal data points. Therefore, we can detect the anomalies by using the reconstruction error as anomaly score. However, this approach is likely to fail to detect the anomalies near the normal data points. Furthermore, even if anomalies are obtained in advance, the AE cannot utilize the label information.

The LRC is the simple extension of the AE. The LRC tries to minimize the reconstruction error of the AE for normal data points and to maximize the reconstruction error for known anomalies. Suppose that we are given a training dataset $\{(x_1, y_1), (x_2, y_2), \cdots, (x_N, y_N)\}$, where x_i represents the i-th data point, $y_i \in \{0, 1\}$ denotes its label, $y_i = 1$ represents a normal data point and $y_i = 0$ represents an anomaly. The objective function of the LRC to be minimized is

$$y_i \mathcal{L}_{AE}(x_i) - (1 - y_i)\mathcal{L}_{AE}(x_i), \tag{3}$$

where $\mathcal{L}(x_i)$ represents the reconstruction error of the AE for data point x_i. By using reconstruction error as anomaly score, the LRC can detect both known and unknown anomalies. However, the training of the LRC is unstable. As shown in Eq. (3), the LRC tries to maximize the reconstruction error for known anomalies and minimize the reconstruction error for normal data points. Since the reconstruction error is bounded below but not bounded above, the LRC tends to maximize the reconstruction error for known anomalies rather than to minimize the reconstruction error for normal data points. As the result, the LRC cannot reconstruct the normal data points well.

3   Proposed Methods

We propose a new supervised anomaly detector based on the AE, the Autoencoding Binary Classifiers (ABC), which can accurately detect known and unknown anomalies.

The ABC uses a probabilistic binary classifier for anomaly detection. The probabilistic binary classifier predicts the label y_i from the data point x_i. We assume that the conditional probability of y_i given x_i follows the Bernoulli distribution,

$$p(y_i|x_i) = [\eta(x_i)]^{y_i} [1 - \eta(x_i)]^{1-y_i}, \tag{4}$$

Algorithm 1. Autoencoding Binary Classifiers

---
while not converged **do**

   Sample minibatch $\{(x_1, y_1), \cdots, (x_K, y_K)\}$ from dataset

   Compute the gradient of θ with respect to (8):

   $\quad g_\theta \leftarrow \frac{1}{K} \sum_{i=1}^{K} \nabla_\theta \left[-\log p_\theta(y_i|x_i) \right]$

   Perform SGD-update for θ with g_θ

end while

---

where $\eta(x_i) = p(y_i = 1|x_i) = E[y_i|x_i]$ is called the regression function, and its output range is $[0, 1]$. We can regard $p(y_i = 0|x_i) = 1 - \eta(x_i)$ as the probability that x_i is anomaly. Since the regression function gives low values for known anomalies and high values for normal data points by maximizing the likelihood of Eq. (4), the ABC can detect known anomalies. To detect unknown anomalies, we want to make the regression function give low values for unknown anomalies. The ABC uses the reconstruction error of the AE for the regression function as follows:

$$\eta_\theta(x_i) \equiv e^{-\mathcal{L}_\theta(x_i)}, \tag{5}$$

where θ is the parameter of the AEs. The ABC can use the reconstruction error of the AE (Eq. (1)) or the DAE (Eq. (2)) for $\mathcal{L}_\theta(x_i)$. This function takes one when the reconstruction error is zero, and becomes close to zero asymptotically when the reconstruction error goes to infinity. The range of this regression function is $[0, 1]$. Since this regression function is based on the AE, it gives low values for unknown anomalies.

   Under this definition, we minimize the sum of the following negative log-likelihood of the conditional probability

$$-\log p_\theta(y_i|x_i) \tag{6}$$

$$= -y_i \log e^{-\mathcal{L}_\theta(x_i)} - (1 - y_i) \log(1 - e^{-\mathcal{L}_\theta(x_i)}) \tag{7}$$

$$= y_i \mathcal{L}_\theta(x_i) - (1 - y_i) \log(1 - e^{-\mathcal{L}_\theta(x_i)}). \tag{8}$$

This objective function is equal to that of the AE (Eq. (1)) when the input data is normal ($y_i = 1$). Therefore, if the training dataset consists of only normal data points, this model is identical to the AE. On the other hand, when the input data is anomaly ($y_i = 0$), this model tries to maximize the reconstruction error $\mathcal{L}_\theta(\cdot)$. The reason is that $-\log(1 - e^{-\mathcal{L}_\theta})$ is monotonically decreasing for the reconstruction error $\mathcal{L}_\theta \geq 0$. Note that the reconstruction errors for normal and anomaly data points are reasonably balanced by using the likelihood (Eq. (8)), and thus, we can stably train the ABC, unlike the LRC. Furthermore, the ABC also works well for imbalanced data since it exploits the reconstruction error of the unsupervised AE.

   Our model can be optimized with SGD by minimizing sum of Eq. (8) for all data points. Algorithm 1 shows pseudo code of the proposed ABC, where K is the minibatch size and θ is the parameters of the AE in our model. After the training, this model can detect anomalies by using the conditional probability $p(y_i|x_i)$ for each data point.

4   Related Work

There is a large literature on anomaly detection. Here, we briefly review anomaly detection methods by categorizing them into supervised and unsupervised. In this paper, we define a supervised approach as a method that requires labeled anomalies for training, an unsupervised approach as a method that can be learned without labeled anomalies.

If the label information is given perfectly, anomaly detection can be regarded as a binary classification problem. In this situation, supervised classifiers such as support vector machines [5], gradient tree boosting [4] and feed-forward neural networks [3] are usually used. However, these standard supervised classifiers cannot detect unknown anomalies accurately and do not work well in the class imbalance situations. There are several approaches for imbalanced data such as cost-sensitive and ensemble approaches such as random undersampling boost [18] although these approaches do not aim to detect unknown anomalies. Our ABC also works well for imbalanced data and can detect unknown anomalies since it exploits the reconstruction error of the unsupervised AE. To achieve high detection performance when label information is available for part of the dataset, semi-supervised approaches that utilize both labeled and unlabeled data have been presented. Positive-unlabeled (PU) learning and positive-negative-unlabeled (PNU) learning are the main methods that utilize unlabeled data. The PU learning uses normal and unlabeled data [9]. The PNU learning assume that the normal, anomaly, and unlabeled data can be used for training [16]. We can train our ABC in the case of normal data points containing a small amount of unlabeled anomalies. Thus, our proposed ABC can be used in such cases of both PU and PNU anomaly detection settings.

Since the label information is rarely given perfectly in real situation, unsupervised approaches such as the local outlier factor [1], one-class support vector machines [20], and the isolation forest method [12] are usually used. Especially, neural network based methods, typically the AE and the variational autoencoder (VAE) [8], have succeeded in detecting anomalies for high-dimensional datasets. However, the unsupervised approaches do not detect known anomalies as accurately as the supervised approach. To solve this problems, the LRC has been presented as shown in Sect. 2. This is similar approach to ours. However, the training of the LRC becomes unstable since the reconstruction error of the AE in the LRC is bounded below but not bounded above. Opposite to this, our ABC can be trained stably since the objective function of the ABC is bound above with respect to reconstruction error as described in Sect. 3.

5   Experiments

5.1   Datasets

We used the following four datasets.

2D-Toy. In order to explain the strengths of our approach, we use the simple two-dimensional dataset consisting of normal data points, known anomalies that

Table 1. Details of the datasets used in experiments. $\mathcal{D}$, $\mathcal{N}$, $\mathcal{A}$, and $\mathcal{U}$ are the numbers of attributes, normal data points, known anomalies, and unknown anomalies, respectively.

	2D-Toy	MNIST	KDD'99	CIFAR10
$\mathcal{D}$	2	784	38	3,072
$\mathcal{N}$ (train)	10,000	17,791	87,721	5,000
$\mathcal{A}$ (train)	10,000	13,797	47,869	5,000
$\mathcal{N}$ (test)	10,000	17,791	47,905	1,000
$\mathcal{A}$ (test)	10,000	13,797	17,797	1,000
$\mathcal{U}$ (test)	10,000	6,824	2,926	1,000

are close to normal data points, and unknown anomalies that are away from normal data points. Figure 2(a) shows this dataset. We generated two interleaving half-circle distribution near the $(0,0)$. We regarded samples from the upper and lower distributions as normal data points and known anomalies, respectively. For unknown anomalies, we generated samples from a Gaussian distribution with a $(-3,3)$ mean and a standard derivation of 0.3.

MNIST. The MNIST consists of hand-written images of digits from 0–9 [11]. In this data, we used the digits $1,3,5,7,9$ for normal data points, $0,2,6,8$ for known anomalies, and 4 for unknown anomalies. We used 50% of this dataset for training and the remaining 50% for testing.

KDD'99. The KDD'99 data was generated using a closed network and hand-injected attacks for evaluating the performance of supervised network intrusion detection. The dimensionality of the data point was 41. We used '10 percent dataset' for training and 'corrected dataset' for test. For simplicity, we removed three categorical features ('protocol type', 'service' and 'flag') and duplicated data points. We used 'neptune', which is the largest anomaly class, for known anomalies, and used attacks included in 'R2L' for unknown anomalies.

CIFAR10. The CIFAR10 is a collection of images that contains 60,000 32×32 color images in 10 different classes. We used 'data_batch_1-5' for training, and 'test_batch' for testing. We used a set of 'automobile' images for normal data points, 'truck' for known anomalies, and 'dog' for unknown anomalies.

The details of datasets are listed in Table 1. We designed the experiments so that detecting unknown anomalies is more difficult than detecting known anomalies in unsupervised fashion except for 2D-Toy dataset.

5.2 Comparison Methods

We compared our approach with the following methods:

Supervised Methods. As the supervised approaches, we used the LRC, Support Vector Machine (SVM) classifier [5], Gradient Tree Boosting (GTB) [2],

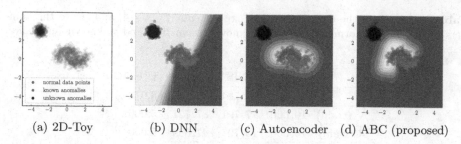

(a) 2D-Toy   (b) DNN   (c) Autoencoder   (d) ABC (proposed)

Fig. 2. (a) Visualization of 2D toy data. Green, red, and black data points represent normal data points, known anomalies, and unknown anomalies, respectively. (b)-(d) Heatmap of anomaly scores on 2D-toy data in setting 1. (Color figure online)

Deep Neural Network (DNN) [3], and Random undersampling boost (RUS-Boost) [18]. For the SVM, we used the radial basis function (rbf) kernel. For the DNN, we used a network that had three fully-connected layers and sigmoid cross entropy as a loss function.

Unsupervised Methods. As the unsupervised approaches, we used the AE, DAE, One-class SVM (OCSVM) [20], and Isolation Forest (IF) [12]. For the OCSVM, we used the rbf kernel.

Semi-supervised Method. As the semi-supervised approach, we used the Non-Negative Positive-Unlabeled learning (nnPU) [9]. We used three-layer perceptron as the classifier and sigmoid function for all tasks.

5.3 Setup

We did experiments in following three settings:

Setting 1. To evaluate detection performance for both known and unknown anomalies, we divided datasets into three subsets: normal data points, known anomalies and unknown anomalies. The normal data points and known anomalies were used for training supervised methods, and only normal data points were used for training unsupervised methods. We do not test the semi-supervised methods in this setting. The unknown anomalies were only used for testing. In this setting, we regard the unknown anomalies as novel anomalies.

Setting 2. This is the same as setting 1 except that 100 unknown anomalies were included in the normal data points. This is the more realistic setting than setting 1. The remaining unknown anomalies were used for test.

Setting 3. To measure the detection performances of supervised and semi-supervised approaches in class imbalance situations, we evaluated their performances when the number of known anomalies is changed in setting 1. Note that we tested the nnPU in positive-unlabeled situation; that is, known anomalies that were removed in this setting were used as unlabeled data for training.

We evaluated the detection performance by using the area under the receiver operating characteristic curve (AUROC).

For our approach, we used neural networks with two hidden layer (10–10 hidden units for 2D-Toy, and 300–100 hidden units for other datasets) for the encoder and the decoder. We used ℓ_2-norm as the distance function of Eq. (1) and Eq. (2). We also evaluated our ABC with the DAE with noise from a Gaussian distribution with a standard deviation of 0.2. We used a hyperbolic tangent for the activation function. As the optimizer, we used Adam with batch size 100 [7]. The number of latent variables was changed in accordance with the datasets: we set the dimension of z to one for 2D-Toy and the dimension of z to 20 for the other datasets. The maximum number of epochs was set to 300 for all datasets, and we used early-stopping on the basis of the validation data. We use same network architecture for the AE, DAE and LRC. We used 20% of the training dataset as validation data. Each attribute was linearly normalized into a range [0, 1] by min-max scaling expect for 2D-Toy. We ran all experiments five times each.

5.4   Results

Figures 2(b)–(d) show the heatmap of anomaly scores of 2D-Toy by the DNN, the AE and our ABC in setting 1. Table 2 show the AUROC with the proposed method and comparison methods in setting 1 and 2. We used bold to highlight the best result and the results that are not statistically different from the best result according to a pair-wise t-test. We used 5% as the p-value.

First, we focus on the supervised approaches: DNN, SVM, GTB, and RUS-Boost. Figure 2(b) shows the heatmap of anomaly scores by the DNN, which achieved the highest performance among supervised approaches for detecting known anomalies. This result indicates that supervised approaches can discriminate known anomalies from normal data points accurately. However, these approaches failed to detect unknown anomalies on the opposite side of the known anomalies. Table 2 also show that these approaches can detect known anomalies but not unknown anomalies accurately on various datasets. In contrast to these approaches, our ABC can detect known anomalies as accurately as supervised approaches and unknown anomalies better than these approaches.

Second, we focus on the unsupervised approaches: AE, DAE, OCSVM, and IF. Figure 2(c) shows the heatmap of anomaly scores by the AE, which achieved the highest performance among unsupervised approaches. In contrast to supervised approaches, unsupervised approaches can detect unknown anomalies that are located away from normal data points. However, these approaches cannot detect known anomalies as accurately as supervised approaches: they are likely to fail to detect anomalies close to normal data points since these approaches use the difference between normal and observed data points for detection. Table 2 also show that these approaches can detect unknown anomalies but not known anomalies accurately. Furthermore, for CIFAR10 datasets, these approaches perform poorly because this dataset is most complicated and heavily overlapping dataset in our experiments. Meanwhile, our ABC achieved high detection performances for both known and unknown anomalies on all datasets.

Third, we focus on the LRC. The LRC shows the same performance tendency as our ABC. The LRC can detect both known and unknown anomalies. However, the variance of performance is larger than that of the ABC and sometimes it cannot detect both known and unknown anomalies at all. Furthermore, it performed inferiorly to our ABC in all situations. To compare the stability of training of the LRC and ABC, we plotted in Fig. 4 the reconstruction error for normal data points and the known anomalies on 2D-Toy dataset. Figure 4(a) shows the mean reconstruction error of the LRC. As the training proceeds the LRC does not reconstruct normal data points. The reason is the LRC tends to maximize the reconstruction error for known anomalies rather than to minimize the reconstruction error for normal data points. This result indicates that the training of the AE in the LRC is unstable. Opposite to this, the ABC can minimize the reconstruction error for normal data points and maximize the reconstruction error for known anomalies as show in Fig. 4(b). This indicates the training of the AE in the ABC is stable.

Fourth, we focus on our ABC. Figure 2(d) shows the heatmap of anomaly scores by our ABC. In contrast to the AE, the anomaly scores by our ABC are low for normal data points and high for known anomalies. The reason is that we train the AE in our ABC to minimize the reconstruction error for normal data points and maximize the reconstruction error for known anomalies. On the other hand, the anomaly scores of our ABC for unknown anomalies are also high since our approach fails to reconstruct data points not included in the training dataset. Therefore, our ABC can detect both known and unknown anomalies accurately. Table 2 shows that our ABC achieved the almost equal to or better performance than the other approaches. These results indicate that our ABC is useful in various tasks.

Figures 3 shows the relationship between the AUROC and the number of known anomalies for training in setting 3. Our ABC maintains a high detection performance, whereas the other supervised approaches perform poorly as the number of known anomalies decreases, even RUSBoost, which is designed to work well in class imbalance situations. The semi-supervised learning nnPU shows the same performance tendency as the supervised approaches. This is because nnPU learning aims to work well on partially labeled datasets and does not aims to work well in class imbalance situations. This result indicates that our ABC is useful when we cannot obtain enough anomalies.

These results indicate that our approach is a good alternative to other approaches: our approach can detect both known and unknown anomalies accurately, and it works well when the number of known anomalies are not enough.

Table 2. Summary of the experiment results AUROC. The standard deviation is in parentheses. For convenience of space, it is written up to 3 decimal points (e.g., 0.1234 is expressed as 123).

Setting 1	2D-Toy		MNIST		KDD'99		CIFAR10	
	Known	Unknown	Known	Unknown	Known	Unknown	Known	Unknown
ABC(AE)	0.965(004)	**1.000(000)**	**0.998(000)**	0.835(030)	**1.000(000)**	**0.884(017)**	**0.847(008)**	**0.793(028)**
ABC(DAE)	0.966(001)	0.999(000)	**0.999(000)**	0.856(016)	**1.000(000)**	0.788(013)	**0.842(010)**	**0.785(026)**
LRC	0.914(002)	0.857(044)	0.972(006)	0.630(055)	0.999(001)	0.781(018)	0.658(123)	0.624(097)
DNN	**0.972(000)**	0.000(001)	0.998(000)	0.758(033)	**1.000(000)**	0.624(180)	0.780(006)	0.613(041)
SVM	0.970(000)	0.907(000)	0.985(000)	0.705(009)	**1.000(000)**	**0.893(000)**	0.788(000)	0.550(000)
GTB	0.972(000)	0.005(000)	0.991(000)	0.704(009)	1.000(000)	0.621(000)	0.826(000)	0.628(000)
RUSBoost	0.961(002)	0.006(002)	0.958(001)	0.663(041)	**1.000(000)**	0.735(044)	0.656(027)	0.557(052)
AE	0.859(005)	**1.000(000)**	0.968(001)	**0.892(011)**	0.998(002)	0.841(041)	0.534(002)	0.465(003)
DAE	0.888(005)	**1.000(000)**	0.970(001)	**0.886(010)**	0.998(001)	0.793(009)	0.533(001)	0.465(002)
OCSVM	0.833(000)	**1.000(000)**	0.805(001)	0.623(002)	1.000(000)	0.762(000)	0.490(000)	0.495(000)
IF	0.895(006)	**1.000(000)**	0.817(014)	0.662(012)	0.999(001)	0.842(015)	0.498(010)	0.531(009)

Setting 2	2D-Toy		MNIST		KDD'99		CIFAR10	
	Known	Unknown	Known	Unknown	Known	Unknown	Known	Unknown
ABC(AE)	0.965(002)	**0.988(019)**	0.999(000)	0.799(013)	**1.000(000)**	0.845(019)	**0.836(009)**	**0.727(029)**
ABC(DAE)	0.967(001)	0.997(001)	**0.999(000)**	0.823(016)	**1.000(000)**	0.781(016)	**0.844(004)**	**0.700(031)**
LRC	**0.836(171)**	0.762(125)	0.972(004)	0.645(058)	1.000(000)	0.786(040)	0.602(138)	0.544(070)
DNN	**0.972(000)**	0.000(001)	0.998(000)	0.708(059)	**1.000(000)**	0.598(185)	0.780(005)	0.575(024)
SVM	0.970(000)	0.755(000)	0.985(000)	0.685(009)	**1.000(000)**	**0.892(001)**	0.787(000)	0.521(005)
GTB	0.972(000)	0.001(000)	0.991(000)	0.689(013)	1.000(000)	0.622(001)	0.823(002)	0.600(007)
RUSBoost	0.964(001)	0.001(001)	0.955(002)	0.655(031)	**1.000(000)**	0.763(049)	0.660(013)	0.514(015)
AE	0.839(026)	**0.767(214)**	0.969(002)	**0.862(011)**	0.998(000)	0.844(030)	0.532(002)	0.458(002)
DAE	0.848(040)	**0.750(228)**	0.970(001)	**0.857(010)**	0.998(001)	0.794(010)	0.531(001)	0.458(002)
OCSVM	0.833(000)	**1.000(000)**	0.805(001)	0.619(002)	1.000(000)	0.762(000)	0.492(000)	0.494(003)
IF	0.893(006)	**1.000(000)**	0.821(008)	0.660(013)	1.000(000)	0.840(009)	0.503(16)	0.533(014)

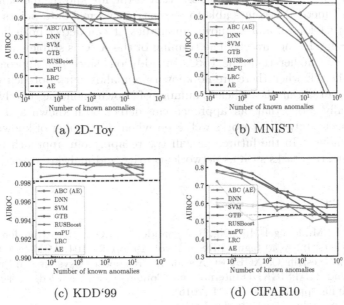

(a) 2D-Toy   (b) MNIST

(c) KDD'99   (d) CIFAR10

Fig. 3. Detection performance comparison when number of known anomalies is reduced. For comparison, the dashed line plots the AUROC of the AE that does not use any known anomalies for training.

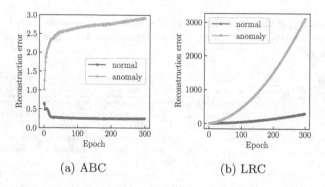

Fig. 4. Mean training loss for normal data points and anomalies on the 2D-Toy dataset.

6   Conclusion

In this paper, we introduced a new anomaly detector Autoencoding Binary Classifiers (ABC). We modeled normal data points with the unsupervised approach, and made it fail to model known anomalies by the supervised approach. We assumed that labels follow a Bernoulli distribution, and modeled its negative log likelihood of the normal label given a data point by using the reconstruction error of the AE. By maximizing the likelihood of the conditional probability, our AE was trained so as to minimize the reconstruction error for normal data points, and to maximize the reconstruction error for known anomalies. Since the proposed method becomes able to reconstruct normal data points and does not reconstruct known and unknown anomalies, it can detect both known and unknown anomalies accurately. The training of the ABC is stable and detection performance is higher than the LRC. In addition, since our approach corresponds to the AE when there are no known anomalies, our approach work well when we do not obtain the sufficient number of known anomalies in advance. We experimentally shows that our approach can detect both known and unknown anomalies accurately and it works well even when the number of known anomalies is not enough. In the future, we will try to apply our approach to various anomaly detection tasks such as network security and malware detection.

References

1. Breunig, M.M., Kriegel, H.P., Ng, R.T., Sander, J.: LOF: identifying density-based local outliers. In: ACM Sigmod Record, vol. 29, pp. 93–104. ACM (2000)
2. Chen, T., Guestrin, C.: XGBoost: A scalable tree boosting system. In: Proceedings of the 22nd ACM SIGKDD International Conference on Knowledge Discovery and Data Mining, pp. 785–794. ACM (2016)
3. Dreiseitl, S., Ohno-Machado, L.: Logistic regression and artificial neural network classification models: a methodology review. J. Biomed. Inform. **35**(5–6), 352–359 (2002)

4. Friedman, J.H.: Stochastic gradient boosting. Comput. Stat. Data Anal. **38**(4), 367–378 (2002)
5. Hearst, M.A., Dumais, S.T., Osuna, E., Platt, J., Scholkopf, B.: Support vector machines. IEEE Intell. Syst. Appl. **13**(4), 18–28 (1998)
6. Hinton, G.E., Salakhutdinov, R.R.: Reducing the dimensionality of data with neural networks. Science **313**(5786), 504–507 (2006)
7. Kingma, D.P., Ba, J.: Adam: A method for stochastic optimization. arXiv preprint arXiv:1412.6980 (2014)
8. Kingma, D.P., Welling, M.: Auto-encoding variational bayes. arXiv preprint arXiv:1312.6114 (2013)
9. Kiryo, R., Niu, G., du Plessis, M.C., Sugiyama, M.: Positive-unlabeled learning with non-negative risk estimator. In: Advances in Neural Information Processing Systems, pp. 1675–1685 (2017)
10. Kwon, D., Kim, H., Kim, J., Suh, S.C., Kim, I., Kim, K.J.: A survey of deep learning-based network anomaly detection. Cluster Comput, pp. 1–13 (2017)
11. LeCun, Y., Bottou, L., Bengio, Y., Haffner, P.: Gradient-based learning applied to document recognition. Proc. IEEE **86**(11), 2278–2324 (1998)
12. Liu, F.T., Ting, K.M., Zhou, Z.H.: Isolation forest. In: Eighth IEEE International Conference on Data Mining 2008. ICDM 2008, pp. 413–422. IEEE (2008)
13. Lyudchik, O.: Outlier detection using autoencoders. Tech. rep. (2016)
14. Munawar, A., Vinayavekhin, P., De Magistris, G.: Limiting the reconstruction capability of generative neural network using negative learning. In: 2017 IEEE 27th International Workshop on Machine Learning for Signal Processing (MLSP), pp. 1–6. IEEE (2017)
15. Nasrabadi, N.M.: Pattern recognition and machine learning. J. Electron. Imaging **16**(4), 049901 (2007)
16. Sakai, T., du Plessis, M.C., Niu, G., Sugiyama, M.: Semi-supervised classification based on classification from positive and unlabeled data. arXiv preprint arXiv:1605.06955 (2016)
17. Sakurada, M., Yairi, T.: Anomaly detection using autoencoders with nonlinear dimensionality reduction. In: Proceedings of the MLSDA 2014 2nd Workshop on Machine Learning for Sensory Data Analysis, p. 4. ACM (2014)
18. Seiffert, C., Khoshgoftaar, T.M., Van Hulse, J., Napolitano, A.: Rusboost: a hybrid approach to alleviating class imbalance. IEEE Trans. Syst. Man Cybern. Part A Syst. Hum. **40**(1), 185–197 (2010)
19. Tagawa, T., Tadokoro, Y., Yairi, T.: Structured denoising autoencoder for fault detection and analysis. In: Asian Conference on Machine Learning, pp. 96–111 (2015)
20. Tax, D.M., Duin, R.P.: Support vector data description. Mach. Learn. **54**(1), 45–66 (2004)
21. Vincent, P., Larochelle, H., Bengio, Y., Manzagol, P.A.: Extracting and composing robust features with denoising autoencoders. In: Proceedings of the 25th International Conference on Machine Learning, pp. 1096–1103. ACM (2008)
22. Zhou, C., Paffenroth, R.C.: Anomaly detection with robust deep autoencoders. In: Proceedings of the 23rd ACM SIGKDD International Conference on Knowledge Discovery and Data Mining, pp. 665–674. ACM (2017)
23. Zong, B., et al.: Deep autoencoding Gaussian mixture model for unsupervised anomaly detection. In: International Conference on Learning Representations (2018)

Contourlet Transform Based Seismic Signal Denoising via Multi-scale Information Distillation Network

Yu Sang[1](✉), Jinguang Sun[1], Simiao Wang[1], Xiangfu Meng[1],
and Heng Qi[2]

[1] School of Electronic and Information Engineering,
Liaoning Technical University, Huludao 125105, China
sangyu2008bj@sina.com
[2] School of Computer Science and Technology,
Dalian University of Technology, Dalian 116023, China

Abstract. Recently, convolutional neural network (CNN) based models have achieved great success in many multimedia applications. Seismic signals as one kind of important multimedia resources are often interfered by noise in practice, which bring difficulties for utilizing these resources effectively. To this end, this paper presents a novel CNN architecture in the contourlet transform (CT) domain for seismic signal denoising. First of all, we propose multi-scale information distillation (MSID) module to fully exploit features from seismic signals. And then, a series of MSIDs are cascaded in a coarse-to-fine manner to restore the noisy seismic signals, which is named as deep multi-scale information distillation network (D-MSIDN). In addition, we propose to formulate the denoising problem as the prediction of CT coefficients, which is able to make D-MSIDN further remove noise and preserve richer structure details than that in spatial domain. We use synthetic seismic signals and public Society of Exploration Geophysicists (SEG) and European Association of Geoscientists & Engineers (EAGE) salt and overthrust seismic data to demonstrate the superior performance of the proposed method over other state-of-the-art methods. From some qualitative and quantitative results, we find that our method is capable of obtaining data with higher quality assessment and preserving much more useful signals than other methods. In particular, our denoising performances are more considerable for seismic data with lower signal-to-noise ratio.

Keywords: Seismic signal · Denoising · Convolutional neural network · Multi-scale information distillation network · Contourlet transform

1 Introduction

In seismic exploration, the noise seriously distorts and interferes with effective seismic signals. Noise attenuation is a very important step for obtaining high-quality seismic data, which can directly affect the success rate of oil/gas exploration.

Many seismic denoising methods have been proposed [1–9], in which the sparse transform based methods [2, 3, 5–7] and dictionary learning based methods [8, 9] are

© Springer Nature Switzerland AG 2019
A. C. Nayak and A. Sharma (Eds.): PRICAI 2019, LNAI 11671, pp. 660–672, 2019.
https://doi.org/10.1007/978-3-030-29911-8_51

most effective methods currently. However, denoising seismic data with low signal-to-noise ratio has always been a challenging task. Due to the powerful learning ability, CNN-based methods [10–18] are widely used to address multimedia processing tasks, i.e., nature image super-resolution (SR), and have achieved impressive results. We will attempt to establish appropriate CNN models to solve seismic signal denoising problem with the aim to satisfy high precision seismic exploration.

In this paper, we present a novel CNN architecture in the CT domain for seismic signal denoising. The main contributions are as follows:

(1) We propose multi-scale information distillation (MSID) module to fully exploit features from seismic signals; and D-MSIDN is formed to effectively restore the noisy seismic signals.
(2) We formulate the denoising problem as the prediction of CT coefficients, which is able to make D-MSIDN further remove noise and preserve richer detail information than that in spatial domain.
(3) We evaluate the proposed method with synthetic seismic signals and SEG/EAGE salt and overthrust seismic data. The qualitative and quantitative results confirm that our method is capable of obtaining data with higher PSNR values and preserving much more useful signals than other state-of-the-art methods. Most of all, our denoising performances are more considerable for seismic data with lower signal-to-noise ratio.

2 Related Work

So far lots of seismic denoising methods have been developed. Initially, Canales [1] proposed random noise reduction method for seismic data, which achieves a potential result. But, with the analysis of its deficiencies, some effective random noise attenuation methods were presented such as nonlocal means algorithm [4], the sparse transform based methods and dictionary learning based methods. The sparse representation of seismic data has gained its popularity. Traditionally, most denoising operations are conducted in a transform domain [2, 3, 5–7]. Learning based methods [8, 9] infer an over complete dictionary from a set of examples. The dictionary is typically represented as an explicit matrix and a training procedure is required to adapt the matrix to the examples.

In recent years, deep learning (DL) has attracted wide attention as a method to overcome the defects of traditional learning based methods. It leverages convolutional neural network (CNN) architecture and demonstrates superb power in many machine learning and multimedia applications. For low-level vision task SR, a series of CNN-based methods [10–18] have been presented from the first SRCNN [10] to the latest RCAN [18], which are significantly better than conventional SR methods. The number of convolutional layer for these networks increases from 3 to 400, which proves that depth of network does count and deeper networks can obtain better SR results. Recently, some CNN-based SR methods construct the entire network by connecting a series of identical feature extraction modules [15–18], indicating the capability of each block plays a crucial role.

The above SR methods are conducted in the spatial domain. By contrast, SR in the transform domain can preserve the image's context and texture information in different layers to produce better SR results. With that in mind, Guo et al. [19] designed a deep wavelet super-resolution (DWSR) network to acquire HR image by predicting "missing details" of wavelet coefficients of the LR image. Later, the same team [20] integrated discrete cosine transformation (DCT) into CNN and put forward an orthogonally regularized deep network. In addition, Huang et al. [21] applied wavelet transform to CNN-based face SR to validate that this method can accurately capture global topology information and local textural details of faces.

Based on the above analysis, we propose a novel D-MSIDN architecture in the CT domain for seismic signal denoising. We will detail our method in next section.

3   Method

In this section, we will first describe the proposed the architecture of our D-MSIDN. After that, we will provide a brief introduction to the proposed MSID block, followed by the description of CT domain prediction.

3.1   Network Structure

As shown in Fig. 1, our D-MSIDN consists of two parts, the shallow feature extraction (SFE) module and the deep feature extraction (DFE) module. Let's denote the I^L and I^H as the noised signals and clean signals respectively, we solve the following problem:

$$\hat{\theta} = \arg \min_{\theta} \frac{1}{N} \sum_{i=1}^{N} L(I_i^L, I_i^H), \tag{1}$$

where θ denotes the parameter set, N is the number of training samples. L is the loss function for minimizing the difference between the I^L and I^H.

The mean square error (MSE) function is the most widely-used objective optimization function in image super-resolution [11, 13, 14]. However, Lim et al. [22] have experimentally demonstrated that training with MSE loss is not a good choice. In order to avoid introducing unnecessary training tricks and reduce computations, we use the mean absolute error (MAE) function L_1 as a better alternative, as defined below

$$L_1 = \frac{1}{N} \sum_{i=1}^{N} \left\| I_i^L - I_i^H \right\|_1. \tag{2}$$

Specially, we use two convolution layers to extract the shallow feature F_0 from the noisy seismic signals. So we can have

$$F_0 = H_{SFE1}\left(H_{SFE2}\left(I^L\right)\right), \tag{3}$$

where H_{SFE1} and H_{SFE2} denote the convolution operation of the two layers in SFE module respectively. After shallow feature module, the shallow feature F_0 is used for DFE module, which contains a set of cascaded MSID blocks. Each MSID block can gather more information as much as possible and distill more useful information. After that we use a 1×1 convolutional layer to adaptively control the output information. We name this operation as feature fusion formulated as

$$F_{GF} = H_{GFF}([F_1, F_2, \cdots, F_D]),\tag{4}$$

where $[F_1, F_2, \cdots, F_D]$ denotes the concatenation of feature maps produced by MSID blocks 1, 2, ..., D. H_{GFF} is a composite function of 1×1 convolutional layer. Global residual learning is utilized after feature fusion to obtain the feature maps F_{DF}, which can be formulated as

$$F_{DF} = F_{GF} + F_0.\tag{5}$$

In our D-MSIDN, all convolutional layers have 64 filters, except that in feature fusion, whose has 128 filters.

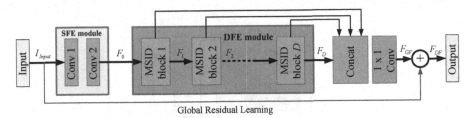

Fig. 1. The architecture of our proposed D-MSIDN.

3.2 MSID Block

The proposed MSID block is shown in Fig. 2. Each MSID block can be divided into two parts, which are used for exploiting short and long-path features. Different from the IDN model [15], we construct two-bypass network in each part and different bypass use different convolutional kernels. In this way, our model can adaptively detect the short and long-path features at different scales.

Supposing the input and output of the first part are F_{d-1} and F_{M1}, we have

$$F_{M1} = \sigma\big(Y_{1\times1}^3\big(\big[\sigma\big(Y_{3\times3}^1(F_{d-1})\big) + \sigma\big(Y_{5\times5}^2(F_{d-1})\big)\big]\big)\big),\tag{6}$$

where $Y_{1\times1}^3$, $Y_{3\times3}^1$ and $Y_{5\times5}^2$ refers to the function of 1×1, 3×3, and 5×5 convolutional layers in the first part respectively. [•] indicates the concatenation of feature maps by different convolutional kernels. σ denotes the ReLU function. After that, the feature maps with 64 dimensions of F_{M1} and the input F_{d-1} are concatenated in the channel dimension,

$$R = C(S(F_{M1}, 64), F_{d-1}),\tag{7}$$

where C and S indicate concatenation operation and slice operation respectively. Therefore, the 64 dimensional features are fetched from S. The purpose is to combine the current multi-scale information with the previous information. It can be regarded as retained short path information. And then, we take the rest of 64 dimensional feature maps as the input of the second part, which mainly further extracts long path information,

$$F_{M2} = \sigma\big(Y^6_{1\times1}\big(\big[\sigma\big(Y^4_{3\times3}(F_{M1}, 64)\big) + \sigma\big(Y^5_{5\times5}(F_{M1}, 64)\big)\big]\big)\big), \qquad (8)$$

where $Y^6_{1\times1}$, $Y^4_{3\times3}$ and $Y^5_{5\times5}$ refers to the function of 1×1, 3×3, and 5×5 convolutional layers in the second part respectively. Finally, the input information, the short path information and the long path information are aggregated, which can be formulated as follows:

$$F_d = R + F_{M2}. \qquad (9)$$

where F_d indicates the output of the MSID block.

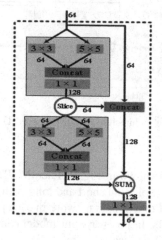

Fig. 2. The architecture of MSID block.

3.3   Contourlet Transform (CT) Prediction

It is well known that many signal processing tasks benefit from having a sparse representation of signals. Do and Vetterli [23] developed CT, which aimed at improving the representation sparsity of signals compared to the wavelet transform [24]. The main properties of CT are the directionality and anisotropy. The advantage over other geometrically-driven representations, i.e. curvelets and bandelets, is the relatively simple and efficient wavelet-like implementation using iterative filter banks.

We analyze the sparsity of CT here. The effect of noise suppression depends on the degree of approximation of the decomposed effective signals [25]. The better the sparsity of the method is, the better the effect of suppressing noise is. Figure 3 gives the reconstruction errors on synthetic data (Fig. 5(a)) in three transform domains: wavelet transform, curvelet transform and CT domains. We can see obviously that the approximation error of CT can be close to zero while only retaining 6% coefficients, and it presents the smallest reconstruction error while retaining the same percentage coefficients, which shows its optimal sparsity.

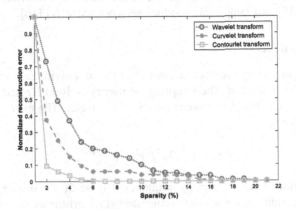

Fig. 3. Reconstruction errors in three transform domains.

In this paper, we formulate the seismic denoising problem as the prediction of CT coefficients as show in Fig. 4, which is able to make D-MSIDN further remove noise and preserve richer structure detail than that in spatial domain. It is worth mentioning that CT can be used in different seismic denoising networks, which is a simple and effective way to improve the performance. Speaking of the role of CT, it is to take further experiment in Sect. 4.4. The detailed process of CT implementation can be found in [23].

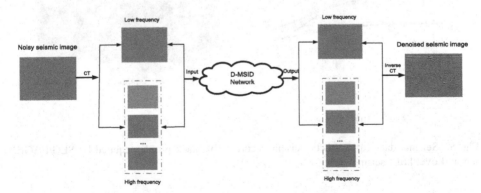

Fig. 4. CT domain coefficients prediction.

4   Experiments

In the experiments, the performance of the proposed method is evaluated on both qualitative and quantitative aspects. The contrasting methods are selected in this section as follows: traditional seismic denoising methods—wavelet-based threshold denoising and curvelet-based threshold denoising; DL-based methods—information distillation network (IDN) [15] and multi-scale residual network (MSRN) [16].

4.1   Seismic Datasets

We synthesize some seismic records composed of linear, curvilinear, various dip angle and fault events as basic data. The sampling frequency is 1000 Hz and the number of traces is 150. We select Ricker wavelet as seismic wavelet. The expression of Ricker wavelet is as follows:

$$x(t) = \left(1 - 2\pi^2 f^2 t^2\right) \cdot e^{-\pi^2 f^2 t^2}, \tag{10}$$

where t denotes time, f is the sampling frequency. Figure 5(a) is one example of these synthetic data. In addition, we acquire immigrated stack profile by the SEG/EAGE salt and overthrust seismic data [26] as shown in Fig. 5(b). Meanwhile, we respectively rotate the above two types of seismic data by 45°, 90°, 135°, 180°, 270°, and 360° inspired by [12, 13], and add Gaussian white noise of different levels to original and rotated data, obtaining additional expanded versions. 80% versions are selected as training sets; the rest is as test sets.

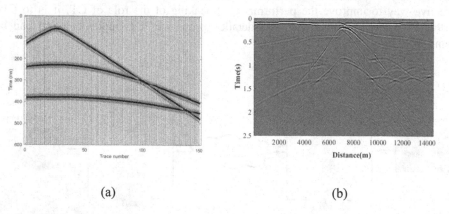

(a)   (b)

Fig. 5. Seismic data. (a) Synthetic seismic records; (b) Stack profile acquired by SEG/EAGE salt and overthrust seismic data.

4.2 Implementation Details

Our D-MSIDN contains 12 MSID blocks. Training seismic data are passed through the 1-level CT to produce one low-frequency sub-band and four high-frequency sub-bands. These sub-bands are then cropped to 48×48 patches with 24 pixels overlapping for training. We set 64 as the batch size. The learning rate in initialized to 10^{-4} for all layers and decreases half for every 50 epochs. Training our model takes roughly 18 h with Tesla k80 GPUs.

4.3 Evaluation of Results

In this section, we evaluate the performance of our method on synthetic seismic signals and SEG/EAGE salt and overthrust seismic data. For fair comparison, we use the released codes of the above models and train all models with the same training set. PSNR [27] is used as a quantitative evaluation metric to justify the denoising results. PSNR is an engineering term for the ratio between the maximum possible power of a signal and the power of corrupting noise that affects the fidelity of its representation. PSNR (dB) between the denoised seismic data X' and clear seismic data X of size $M \times N$ is calculated as:

$$PSNR\left(X', X\right) = 10 \log_{10} \frac{\sum_{i=1}^{M} \sum_{j=1}^{N} MAX_I^2}{\sum_{i=1}^{M} \sum_{j=1}^{N} \left(X'(i,j) - X(i,j)\right)^2}, \qquad (11)$$

where MAX_I is the maximum possible pixel intensity value. $X'(i,j)$ and $X(i,j)$ denote the pixel values at locate (i,j) of X' and X, respectively.

In order to evaluate the denoising performance, we first evaluate the performance of our method on synthetic seismic records compared with traditional curvelet-based threshold denoising method and DL-based IDN model as shown in Fig. 6, which shows that our method has achieved better result with higher PSNR value.

Next, we evaluate the performance of our method on SEG/EAGE salt and over-thrust seismic data. The PSNR (dB) values for comparison are shown in Table 1; values in bold font indicate optimal values. The table shows that when evaluated on seismic data, our proposed method obtains higher PSNR than other methods by a large margin quantitatively. In particular, our denoising performances are more considerable for seismic data with higher noise level. The noise level in Table 1 denotes the intensity of noise added to original seismic data. That is, the higher the noise level is, the lower the signal-to-noise ratio is. In addition, we compare our model with DL-based methods [15, 16] qualitatively. As shown in Fig. 7(a), we add Gaussian white noise to the clean seismic signals. Examine the denoised results in Fig. 7(b), (c), and (d). We find that our method is an ideal denoising method for removing random noises while keeping coherent details.

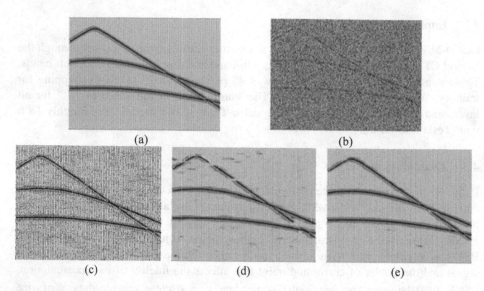

Fig. 6. The performance of seismic signal denoising. (a) Synthetic seismic signals. (b) The seismic signals with added strong Gaussian white noise (PSNR: 68.1429 dB). (c) Denoised seismic signals by curvelet-based threshold denoising (PSNR: 83.1584 dB). (d) Denoised seismic signals by IDN (PSNR: 89.8992 dB). (e) Denoised seismic signals by our method (PSNR: 92.4105 dB).

Table 1. Comparison of PSNR for different methods on the salt and overthrust seismic data.

Noise level	Traditional methods		DL-based methods		
	Wavelet	Curvelet	IDN	MSRN	Ours
0.05	91.25	92.35	95.03	95.48	**97.68**
0.10	83.95	85.66	87.62	88.25	**91.85**
0.20	77.34	78.25	82.35	83.59	**86.23**
0.30	72.41	72.59	75.85	77.62	**82.04**
Average	81.24	82.21	85.21	86.34	**89.45**

4.4 Ablation Study

Given that in this paper, we introduce to predict CT coefficients in the field of seismic signal denoising, we evaluate the effect of the contribution. We use three methods (MSRN, IDN and D-MSIDN) and integrate them with CT prediction. Figure 8(a) shows the comparison results of D-MSIDN across seismic data with different noise level. Figure 8(b) shows the average comparison result of MSRN and IDN. From Fig. 8, we can see both methods improve significantly when integrated with CT. Experimental results demonstrate that CT prediction is superior to spatial domain; the improvements are consistent across various networks and benchmarks.

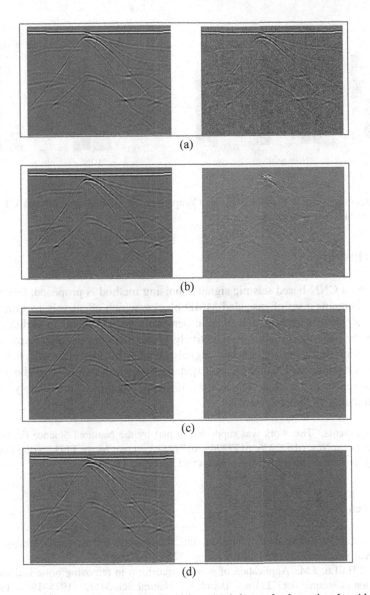

Fig. 7. Visual results of seismic signal denoising. (a) left panel: clean signals without noise, right panel: the signals with added white noise; (b) left panel: denoised signals by IDN, right panel: differences between the clean signals and the denoised signals on the left. (c) left panel: denoised signals by MSRN, right panel: differences between the clean signals and the denoised signals on the left. (d) left panel: denoised signals by our method, right panel: differences between the clean signals and the denoised signals on the left.

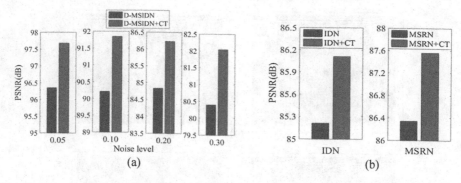

Fig. 8. Effectiveness of CT prediction. (a) Comparison for spatial domain and CT domain. (b) CT prediction using different networks.

5   Conclusions

In this paper, a CNN-based seismic signal denoising method is proposed. Our network D-MSIDN contains a set of cascaded MSID blocks, which effectively exploit features of seismic signals to improve the seismic denoising performance. In addition, CT is applied to the network structure to effectively preserve richer detail information than spatial domain in the noisy seismic signals, which further improves the seismic denoising performance. Qualitative and quantitative results show that the proposed method is much better than other state-of-the-art methods, remarkably boosting restoration ability of seismic signals.

Acknowledgements. This work was supported in part by the National Science Foundation of China under Grant Nos. 61602226, 61772249, 61772112; in part by the PhD Startup Foundation of Liaoning Technical University of China under Grant No. 18-1021.

References

1. Canales, L.L.: Random noise reduction. In: 54th Annual International Meeting of SEG Technical Program Expanded Abstracts, pp. 525–527 (1984)
2. Zhang, J.H., Lu, J.M.: Application of wavelet transform in removing noise and improving resolution of seismic data. J. Univ. Petrol. Ed. Natural Sci. **31**(12), 1975–1981 (1997)
3. Neelamani, R., Baumstein, A., Gillard, D., Hadidi, M., Soroka, W.: Coherent and random noise attenuation using the curvelet transform. Lead. Edge **27**, 240–248 (2008)
4. Bonar, D., Sacchi, M.: Denoising seismic data using the nonlocal means algorithm. Geophysics **77**(1), A5–A8 (2012)
5. Xu, J., Wang, W., Gao, J.H., Chen, W.C.: Monochromatic noise removal via sparsity-enabled signal decomposition method. IEEE Geosci. Remote Sens. Lett. **10**(3), 533–537 (2013)
6. Chen, Y., Fomel, S.: EMD-seislet transform. In: 85th Annual International Meeting of SEG Technical Program Expanded Abstracts, pp. 4775–4778 (2015)

7. Liu, W., Cao, S., Chen, Y., Zu, S.: An effective approach to attenuate random noise based on compressive sensing and curvelet transform. J. Geophys. Eng. **13**, 135–145 (2016)
8. Beckouche, S., Ma, J.W.: Simultaneous dictionary learning and denoising for seismic data. Geophysics **79**(3), A27–A31 (2014)
9. Chen, Y.K.: Fast dictionary learning for noise attenuation of multidimensional seismic data. Geophys. J. Int. **209**(1), 21–31 (2017)
10. Dong, C., Loy, C.C., He, K., Tang, X.: Learning a deep convolutional network for image super-resolution. In: Fleet, D., Pajdla, T., Schiele, B., Tuytelaars, T. (eds.) ECCV 2014. LNCS, vol. 8692, pp. 184–199. Springer, Cham (2014). https://doi.org/10.1007/978-3-319-10593-2_13
11. Dong, C., Loy, C.C., Tang, X.: Accelerating the super-resolution convolutional neural network. In: Leibe, B., Matas, J., Sebe, N., Welling, M. (eds.) ECCV 2016. LNCS, vol. 9906, pp. 391–407. Springer, Cham (2016). https://doi.org/10.1007/978-3-319-46475-6_25
12. Kim, J., Lee J.K., Lee, K.M.: Accurate image super-resolution using very deep convolutional networks. In: Proceedings of the IEEE Conference on Computer Vision and Pattern Recognition (CVPR), pp. 1646–1654 (2016)
13. Tai, Y., Yang, J., Liu, X.M.: Image super-resolution via deep recursive residual network. In: Proceedings of the IEEE Conference on Computer Vision and Pattern Recognition (CVPR), pp. 3147–3155 (2017)
14. Tai, Y., Yang, J., Liu, X.M., Xu, C.Y.: MemNet: a persistent memory network for image restoration. In: Proceedings of the IEEE Conference on Computer Vision and Pattern Recognition (CVPR), pp. 4539–4547 (2017)
15. Hui, Z., Wang, X.M., Gao, X.B.: Fast and accurate single image super-resolution via information distillation network. In: Proceedings of the IEEE Conference on Computer Vision and Pattern Recognition (CVPR), pp. 723–731 (2018)
16. Li, J., Fang, F., Mei, K., Zhang, G.: Multi-scale residual network for image super-resolution. In: Ferrari, V., Hebert, M., Sminchisescu, C., Weiss, Y. (eds.) ECCV 2018. LNCS, vol. 11212, pp. 527–542. Springer, Cham (2018). https://doi.org/10.1007/978-3-030-01237-3_32
17. Zhang, Y.L., Tian, Y.P., Kong, Y., Zhong, B.N., Fu, Y.: Residual dense network for image super-resolution. In: The IEEE Conference on Computer Vision and Pattern Recognition (CVPR) (2018)
18. Zhang, Y., Li, K., Li, K., Wang, L., Zhong, B., Fu, Y.: Image super-resolution using very deep residual channel attention networks. In: Ferrari, V., Hebert, M., Sminchisescu, C., Weiss, Y. (eds.) ECCV 2018. LNCS, vol. 11211, pp. 294–310. Springer, Cham (2018). https://doi.org/10.1007/978-3-030-01234-2_18
19. Guo, T.T., Mousavi, H.S., Vu, T.H., Monga, V.: Deep wavelet prediction for image super-resolution. In: The IEEE Conference on Computer Vision and Pattern Recognition Workshops (CVPRW), pp. 104–113 (2017)
20. Guo, T.T., Mousavi, H.S., Monga, V.: Orthogonally regularized deep networks for image super-resolution. arXiv preprint arXiv:1802.02018 (2018)
21. Huang, H.B., He, R., Sun, Z.N., Tan, T.N.: Wavelet-SRNet: a wavelet-based cnn for multi-scale face super resolution. In: Proceedings of the IEEE Conference on Computer Vision and Pattern Recognition (CVPR), pp. 1689–1697 (2017)
22. Lim, B., Son, S., Kim, H., Nah, S., Lee, K.M.: Enhanced deep residual networks for single image super-resolution. In: Proceedings of the IEEE Conference on Computer Vision and Pattern Recognition Workshop (CVPRW), pp. 136–144 (2017)
23. Do, M.N., Vetterli, M.: The contourlet transform: an efficient directional multiresolution image representation. IEEE Trans. Image Process. **14**(12), 2091–2160 (2005)
24. Mallat, S.: A Wavelet Tour of Signal Processing: the Sparse Way. Academic Press, Boston (2008)

25. Shahdoosti, H.R., Khayat, O.: Image denoising using sparse representation classification and non-subsampled shearlet transform. SIViP **10**(6), 1–7 (2016)
26. Aminzadeh, F., Burkhard, N., Kunz, T., Nicoletis, L.: 3-D modeling project: 3rd report. Lead. Edge **14**, 125–128 (1995)
27. Wang, Z., Bovik, A.C., Sheikh, H.R., Simoncelli, E.: Image quality assessment: from error visibility to structural similarity. IEEE Trans. Image Process. **13**(4), 600–612 (2004)

Network Embedding by Resource-Allocation for Link Prediction

Xinghao Song[1], Chunming Yang[1,4](✉), Hui Zhang[2], Xunjian Zhao[1], and Bo Li[1,3]

[1] School of Computer Science and Technology,
Southwest University of Science and Technology,Mianyang 621010, Sichuan, China
yangchunming@swust.edu.cn
[2] School of Science, Southwest University of Science and Technology,
Mianyang 621010, Sichuan, China
[3] School of Computer Science and Technology,
University of Science and Technology of China, Hefei 230027, Anhui, China
[4] Sichuan Civil-military Integration Institute, Mianyang 621010, Sichuan, China

Abstract. In network embedding, the analysis of the relationship between nodes has a great influence on the link prediction. In this paper, we re-examine the role of network topology in predicting missing links from the perspective of node embedding, and proposed a practical algorithm based on the resource allocation of nodes in network. Experiments on six different data sets show that this method has better performance in link prediction than other methods.

Keywords: Network embedding · Link prediction · Node similarity · Resource allocation

1 Introduction

Inferring the behavior of network link by predicting missed or future relationships based on currently observed connections is called link prediction. In the prediction, topological properties of networks are widely applied. The network is usually represented by a *graph* data structure, so link prediction in networks is the probability of predicting vertex connections in graphs. It includes both the unknown links and the future links in the network. This problem has important significance and value in both theory and application, such as predicting interaction in protein networks, recommending friends in social networks, etc. [11].

The existing method mainly predicts the possibility of links by computing similarity between nodes. The methods include common neighbors [8], local paths between nodes [10] and random walk [2]. These methods need to traverse

Supported by the Ministry of education of Humanities and Social Science project (17YJCZH260), CERNET Innovation Project (NGII20170901, NGII20180403), the Fund of Fundamental Sichuan Civil-military Integration (18sxb017, 18sxb028).

© Springer Nature Switzerland AG 2019
A. C. Nayak and A. Sharma (Eds.): PRICAI 2019, LNAI 11671, pp. 673–683, 2019.
https://doi.org/10.1007/978-3-030-29911-8_52

the entire network, and it is difficult to deal with large-scale real sparse networks. In recent years, researchers began to study the learning method of low-dimensional vector representation of nodes in networks, called network embedding. It uses the low-dimensional dense vector represent the nodes instead of the sparse vector of traditional adjacency matrices, so as to improve the efficiency of the algorithm [6]. The typical method is to regard nodes in the network as words, form a sequence of nodes by random or traversal method, and regard the sequence as sentences, and use Word2vec [12] to learn the vector representation of nodes in the network. This method is a general learning framework, and the learning node vectors are better than the existing methods in node classification and link prediction tasks.

In the link prediction task, similar nodes usually have a similar structure, and contains the relationship between node position and edge, which is more complicated than the context of word to sentence. We propose a Network Embedding for Link Prediction (NELP) based on the similarity between nodes in the network structure. The method first calculates the similarity between nodes by resource allocation between nodes, and then randomly initializes the vector representation of nodes; finally we learn the node representation through minimizing the square error between pair node similarity and vectors distance.

2   Related Work

Network Embedding is an effective method to map sparse and high-dimensional networks to dense and low-dimensional vectors and ensure that the characteristics of nodes in the network remain unchanged. It can be applied to the tasks of node classification and link prediction. Current methods can be divided into random walk-based method, neighbor node-based coding method and matrix factorization method. Random walk-based approach mainly refers to the word vector learning model in natural language processing [1]. It is believed that nodes with similar network often have similar nodes and similar contexts (sequences) with natural language. For example, DeepWalk [15] uses random walk to generate a *sequence* of nodes from the network, regards the nodes as the *words* processed by natural language, and then uses Skip-Gram in Word2vec to process *sentences* and generate the node vectors. Node2vec [7] improves DeepWalk by expanding depth-first and breadth-first and setting roaming weights, which provides more flexibility in generating node context. HARP [5] generates new graphs by merging nodes and random walks on new graphs. Struc2vec [16] expresses graph weight through original network. The new construction extends a random walk to a multilevel graph for a multilayer complete graph.

The method based on neighbor node coding uses the neighbor information of the node to encode the node. For example, LINE [18] describes the neighbor information of the node by defining the first-order and second-order relationship of the node. The first-order relationship refers to the node relationship directly connected in the network, and the second-order relationship refers to the node relationship connected through the common neighbor. It establishes an objective function for the first-order and second-order relations of nodes respectively.

The vector representation of nodes is learned by minimizing the KL distance between the first-order and second-order probability distribution and the empirical distribution of nodes as a whole objective function.

The method of matrix factorization models the relationship between nodes by considering the probability transfer matrix between nodes. The typical method GraRep [4] first normalizes the adjacent matrix A, and then calculates the k-order relation matrix of nodes by calculating A^k. Each cell in the relational matrix corresponds to the probability of the random walk between two nodes through the k step. By summing up the relational matrices corresponding to different k value, a more abundant relational matrix is formed and the node representation with stronger expressive ability is obtained by SVD decomposition. HOPE [13] constructs different asymmetric relation matrices, and then uses JDGSVD algorithm to describe two different representations for each node.

Random Walk has achieved good results in node classification and link prediction, but considering the linear relationship between nodes, while the relationship between neighbors in the network cannot be simply described by the linear relationship; and with the complexity of walk method, the efficiency of the algorithm is also decreasing. The method based on neighbor node coding does not consider all the common neighbors among the nodes in its second-order relationship, and does not analyze all the nodes with links, and only analyzes the partially sampled strategy instead of all the nodes with links. Although the method of matrix decomposition has strong expressive power, it is inefficient in computing A^k.

Although a large number of network embedding methods have been proposed, the direct application of these methods to link prediction has the above problems. According to the characteristics of link prediction, a network embedding algorithm for link prediction is proposed in this paper. This method describes the relationship between nodes by resource allocation of all the common neighbors of nodes, so as to solve the problem of linearity and incompleteness of the relationship between nodes in random walk and neighbor node coding methods. At the same time, this method avoids the efficiency problem through only considering the second-order relationship between the common neighbors of nodes.

3   Network Embedding for Link Prediction

3.1   Problem Definition

Given a network $G = (V, E)$, where $V = \{v_1, v_2, ..., v_n\}$ is the set of vertexes, E is the set of edges. The problem of Network Embedding aims to represent each vertex $v \in V$ into a low-dimensional space R^d, i.e., learning a function $f_G : V \to R^d$ or embedding matrix $U_{|V| \times d}$, where $d \ll |V|$.

3.2   Structural Similarity Based on Node Common Neighbors

The basic idea of the link prediction algorithm is to calculate the possibility of a link between two nodes by calculating the similarity of the two unconnected nodes. The most direct way to describe the structural similarity between the two nodes is the common neighbor node. Here we define $N(i) = \{v_j | e_{ij} \, or \, e_{ji} \in E\}$ as the set of neighbors of node v_i. However, the importance of different nodes in the neighbor nodes of two nodes is different. In [14], it is assumed that each node in the network has a certain *resource*, and the nodes pass the resource through the common neighbor as a medium, and each node equally allocates its own resource to the neighbors. For example, the personal wealth of financial network, the number of passengers in airport network, the throughput of power grid and so on; these resource are constantly flowing in the network, from one node to another; therefore, the importance of a neighbor can be determined by the resource, so that the resource obtained from the large degree node is less. As shown in Figs. 1a and b, both u and v have a common neighbor w, but w in 1a is more important for u, v, and its more likely to generate link for u, v in 1a. Therefore, we use the idea of *resource allocation* and the weight of edges, that is, not to distribute resources equally, but to assign it according to the weight of edge. We use weighted resource allocation to characterize the similarity between two nodes, it defined as:

$$s_{uv} = \sum_{k \in N(u) \cap N(v)} \frac{w_{uk} + w_{kv}}{2d_k |N(u) \cap N(v)|} \tag{1}$$

where d_k is the degree of node k, $w_{uk} \leq 1$ and $w_{kv} \leq 1$ is the weight of edge. The higher similarity of the two nodes, the larger s_{ij}. The Eq. (1) shows that the similarity of the two nodes is symmetric, that is, $s_{ij} = s_{ji}$.

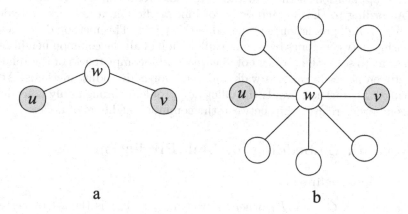

a   b

Fig. 1. Node neighbors in different conditions

3.3   NELP

NELP Model. After calculating the similarity of the nodes by the Eq. (1), the basic idea of the vector representation of the learning node is to make the distance of the node vector with similarity in the vector space small, and the distance of the node vector with small similarity is large, that is, making node similarity is equal to the vector similarity. The distance and the similarity here show the opposite relationship, so the distance between the vectors needs to be converted into the similarity between the vectors and positively correlated with the similarity of the nodes. The similarity of node vectors is defined as follows:

$$s(\boldsymbol{u}_i, \boldsymbol{u}_j) = \frac{1}{1 + \|\boldsymbol{u}_i - \boldsymbol{u}_j\|} \tag{2}$$

Where $\boldsymbol{u}_i \in \boldsymbol{R}^d$ is the low-dimensional vector representation of vertex v_i, and also the i-th row of embedding matrix $\boldsymbol{U}$. Our objective is to minimize the error between the $s(\boldsymbol{u}_i, \boldsymbol{u}_j)$ and s_{ij} that formulate by Eqs. (2) and (1), we can learn $\{\boldsymbol{u}_i\}_{i=1,\ldots,|V|}$ by optimizing the problem:

$$\min_{U} \mathcal{L}(\boldsymbol{U}) = \frac{1}{2} \sum_{v_i, v_j \in V} (s_{ij} - s(\boldsymbol{u}_i, \boldsymbol{u}_j))^2 \tag{3}$$

Optimization Method. To solve this optimization problem efficiently, a popular approach is Stochastic Gradient Descent (SGD). In contrast to traditional methods that require time-consuming gradient computation, SGD takes only a small number of random samples to compute the gradient. SGD is also natural to online algorithms in real-time streaming applications, where instead of retraining the model with all the data, parameters might be updated incrementally when new data comes in. If a pair node (v_i, v_j) is sampled, the gradient w.r.t. the represent vectors $\boldsymbol{u}_i$ and $\boldsymbol{u}_j$ will be calculated as:

$$\frac{\partial \mathcal{L}(\boldsymbol{U})}{\partial \boldsymbol{u}_i} = (s_{ij} - s(\boldsymbol{u}_i, \boldsymbol{u}_j)) \frac{\boldsymbol{u}_i - \boldsymbol{u}_j}{\|\boldsymbol{u}_i - \boldsymbol{u}_j\| [s(\boldsymbol{u}_i, \boldsymbol{u}_j)]^2} = \ell(i, j) \tag{4}$$

$$\frac{\partial \mathcal{L}(\boldsymbol{U})}{\partial \boldsymbol{u}_j} = (s_{ij} - s(\boldsymbol{u}_i, \boldsymbol{u}_j)) \frac{\boldsymbol{u}_j - \boldsymbol{u}_i}{\|\boldsymbol{u}_j - \boldsymbol{u}_i\| [s(\boldsymbol{u}_i, \boldsymbol{u}_j)]^2} = -\ell(i, j) \tag{5}$$

Now, we can update the following variable by rules from Eqs. (4), (5):

$$\boldsymbol{u}_i := \boldsymbol{u}_i - \eta \ell(i, j), \ \boldsymbol{u}_j := \boldsymbol{u}_j + \eta \ell(i, j) \tag{6}$$

Here, η is the learning rate. For a large network, to reduce training time, the training data sets can be generated by sampling part of the node pairs instead of all the node pairs. The number of $e_{ij} \in E$ and $e_{ij} \notin E$ should be close to each other when sampling.

The NELP Algorithm. The pseudo code for NELP is given in Algorithm 1. Before we train our model, we need to calculate s_{ij} for each pair nodes in the network. Then use SGD to train the model. If we use whole network, calculating s_{ij} step needs to calculate $C_{|V|}^2$ pairs, and it takes $O(|V|^2)$ time. If we use sampling pairs, for calculating s_{ij} just takes $O(K^2)$ time and $O(K)$ time for sampling the pairs $e_{ij} \notin E$

Algorithm 1. NELP

Input: Graph G, learning rate η, epoch n, batch size s, dimension d
Output: embedding matrix U
 1: **Initialize** $U^{n \times d}$
 2: **for** $(v_i, v_j) \in \{(v_i, v_j) | v_i \neq v_j\}$ **do**
 3:     calculate s_{ij} by Eq. (1)
 4: **end for**
 5: **for each** epoch **do**
 6:     **for each** pair (v_i, v_j) **do**
 7:         calculate $s(\boldsymbol{u}_i, \boldsymbol{u}_j)$ by Eq. (2)
 8:         $\boldsymbol{u}_i := \boldsymbol{u}_i - \eta\ell(i,j)$
 9:         $\boldsymbol{u}_j := \boldsymbol{u}_j + \eta\ell(i,j)$
10:     **end for**
11: **end for**

---

4   Experiment

4.1   Experiment Setup

Data Sets. The experimental evaluate the feature representations obtained through NELP on standard supervised learning task: link prediction for edges by six data from real world networks. Blogcata [19] is a directory of social blogs that manages blogs and blogs. It contains information about contact networks and selected group members. Facebook [9] is a network of friends from Facebook, a social networking site. Power [17] is an American power network, Router [17] is a routing network composed of routes on the Internet, USAir [17] is an American flight route network, and Yeast [17] is a protein interaction network. The specific information of the data is as follows (Table 1):

Baselines. We compare the NELP with several existing network embedding methods and a traditional link prediction method. For all NE methods, we set the embedding dimension $d = 128$. And we use AUC [3] value which indicates the probability that the score of an unobserved link is higher than that of a nonexistent link as our evaluation metric and select the scoring function with best performance for each baseline.

Table 1. Information of datasets.

Network	Node	Edge	Avg-degree	Avg-clustering
Blogcata	10312	333983	64.77	0.4632
Facebook	4039	88234	43.69	0.6055
Power	4941	6594	2.67	0.0801
Router	5022	6258	2.49	0.0115
USAir	332	2126	12.81	0.6252
Yeast	2375	1163	9.85	0.3057

- DeepWalk [15]. A network embedding method based on random walk. In the experiment, we set the –number-walks = 10, –walk-length = 80, –window-size = 10.
- LINE [18]. A network embedding method based on node first-order and second-order relations. In the experiment, we set the –negative-ratio = 0.5, –order = 3.
- GraRep [4]. A network embedding method based on matrix decomposition. In the experiment, we set the –kstep = 4.
- CN (Common Neighbors). A traditional co-neighbor-based link prediction method.

For the NE methods we first learn the representation vector of each node, then score each pair of vertices given their vectors. For each pair of node vector, we try score function, i.e. cosine similarity and inverse L_2-distance to score the possibility of a connection between two nodes. For CN just counts the common neighbors to score the possibility.

Parameter Settings. In the experiment we divided the edge set into train set E^{train} and test set E^{p_test}. In dividing edge set, we need to ensure that E^{train} is also a connected graph. During the test, to generate negative examples E^{n_test}, we randomly sample an equal number of node pairs from the network which have no edge connecting them, so the $E^{test} = E^{p\_test} + E^{n\_test}$. For the detail of experiment, we divided E train into 90%, and set the parameters learning-rate $\eta = 0.001$, train-epochs = 10.

4.2   Experiment Results Analysis

From Table 2, NELP achieves better results on AUC in four of the six datasets, which shows that NELP is better than other network embedding algorithms by mapping nodes with similar structures into similar vector spaces. Most of the representational learning algorithms have achieved good results compared with traditional link prediction, which also shows that the analysis of network data by representational learning is an effective method. But it can also be seen that NELP's results on Power and Router datasets are not ideal, which is worse than Deepwalk and GraRep. According to the characteristics of the data set itself, Power and Router are obviously sparse networks. From Fig. 2, we can see that the degree of most nodes in two networks is in the range of 0–5, and the number of nodes with degree 1 and 2 is much larger than that of other nodes. This means that there are a large number of nodes in two networks with the same similarity, which makes NELP algorithm unable to separate nodes in vector space by similarity. Because the distance between most vectors is the same, it is impossible to predict the existence possibility of nodes correctly when predicting links. DeepWalk and GraRep related to random walk outperform NELP on Power and Router, which indicates that random walk can better characterize the similarity between nodes on sparse networks.

Table 2. The AUC value of 5 methods on datasets.

	Blogcata	Facebook	Power	Router	USAir	Yeast
NELP	**0.9202**	**0.9812**	0.7043	0.8064	**0.9208**	**0.9632**
DeepWalk	0.9168	0.9806	0.7748	**0.8505**	0.8079	0.9288
LINE	0.4580	0.8596	0.6911	0.3787	0.5898	0.6462
GraRep	0.7676	0.9420	**0.7825**	–	0.7806	0.8362
CN	0.6952	0.6828	0.5272	0.5423	0.6689	0.5444

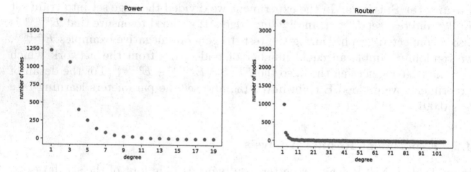

Fig. 2. Degree distribution of Power and Router

4.3   NELP Based on Random Walk

From the experiment, we can see that random walk has a good result on sparse network, and we further consider using random walk to define the similarity of nodes. $P = AD^{-1}$ is the first-order random walk matrix, where A is the adjacency matrix of the network and D is the degree matrix of the network; then P_{ij} denotes the probability that node v_i walks to node v_j in one step, and P^k is the k-order random walk matrix. We define random walk similar matrix as

$$S = \sum_{i=1}^{k} P^i \tag{7}$$

S_{ij} denotes the similarity between node v_i and v_j, and replaces it with s_{ij} in algorithm 1 to learn the representation of node vector based on random walk

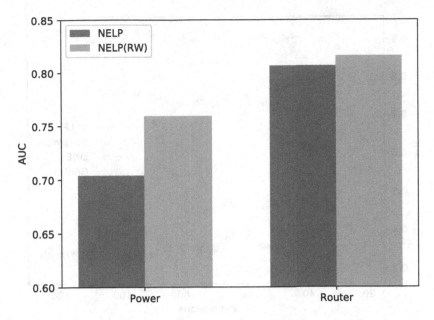

Fig. 3. Comparison between NELP and NELP (RW, $k = 5$) in AUC results.

similarity. We compare the similarity of random walk in Power and Router data with the method of Eq. (7), we can see from Fig. 3 that the similarity of random walk in sparse network has a certain improvement.

In sparse network data, most nodes have only one or two neighbors, and most of them have only one common neighbor. At this time, the difference between them cannot be distinguished by resource allocation. Random walk can enlarge the difference between nodes by walk, so random walk is more efficient in computing the similarity of nodes in sparse network. On the dense data, the nodes have more co-neighbors and random walks can only be related to one neighbor and lose other neighbors, resulting in missing information when computing node similarity.

4.4   Parameter Sensitivity

The performance about the parameter dimension d on the Blogcata network. Figure 4 reports the performance of the DeepWalk, LINE, GraRep and NELP model w.r.t. the dimension d. We can see that the performance of NELP is more stable. The NELP determines the distance between vectors by the similarity of nodes when learning the node vector, so the change of the vector dimension is insensitive to the distance between vectors, and it can also get better results on low-dimensional vectors.

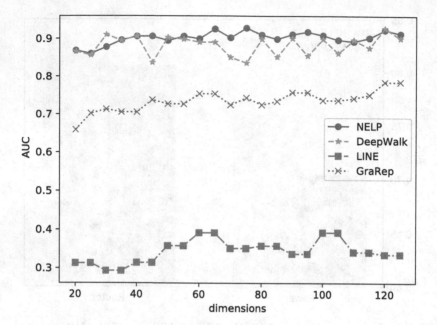

Fig. 4. The influence of dimension d on different methods.

5   Conclusion

In this paper, we propose a network embedding algorithm for link prediction based on the similarity of node structure. It shows good performance on the experimental data set. Compared with traditional methods and other embedding algorithms, it has better results. From the experimental results, it can be seen that there are still some works need to do on sparse network data. The next step is to consider detecting the sparseness of data and use different similarity for different data.

References

1. Bengio, Y., Senécal, J.S.: Adaptive importance sampling to accelerate training of a neural probabilistic language model. IEEE Trans. Neural Networks **19**(4), 713–722 (2008). https://doi.org/10.1109/TNN.2007.912312
2. Brin, S., Page, L.: The anatomy of a large-scale hypertextual web search engine. Comput. Netw. ISDN Syst. **30**(1–7), 107–117 (1998). https://doi.org/10.1016/S0169-7552(98)00110-X
3. Brown, C.D., Davis, H.T.: Receiver operating characteristics curves and related decision measures: a tutorial. Chemometr. Intell. Lab. Syst. **80**(1), 24–38 (2006)
4. Cao, S., Lu, W., Xu, Q.: GraRep: learning graph representations with global structural information. In: Proceedings of the 24th ACM International on Conference on Information and Knowledge Management, pp. 891–900. ACM (2015). https://doi.org/10.1145/2806416.2806512

5. Chen, H., Perozzi, B., Hu, Y., Skiena, S.: HARP: hierarchical representation learning for networks, pp. 2127–2134 (2018)
6. Cunchao, T.U., et al.: Network representation learning: an overview. Sci. Sinica **47**, 980–996 (2017). https://doi.org/10.1360/N112017-00145
7. Grover, A., Leskovec, J.: node2vec: scalable feature learning for networks. In: Proceedings of the 22nd ACM SIGKDD International Conference on Knowledge Discovery and Data Mining, pp. 855–864. ACM (2016). https://doi.org/10.1145/2939672.2939754
8. Jiehua, W.: Link prediction based on partitioning com-munity and differentiating role of common neighbors. Appl. Res. Comput. **30**(10), 2954–2957 (2013)
9. Leskovec, J., Mcauley, J.J.: Learning to discover social circles in ego networks. In: Advances in Neural Information Processing Systems, pp. 539–547 (2012)
10. Lü, L., Jin, C.H., Zhou, T.: Similarity index based on local paths for link prediction of complex networks. Phys. Rev. E **80**(4), 046122 (2009)
11. Martinez, V., Berzal, F., Cubero, J.: A survey of link prediction in complex networks. ACM Comput. Surv. **49**(4), 69 (2017). https://doi.org/10.1145/3012704
12. Mikolov, T., Sutskever, I., Kai, C., Corrado, G., Dean, J.: Distributed representations of words and phrases and their compositionality. In: Advances in Neural Information Processing Systems, vol. 26, pp. 3111–3119 (2013)
13. Ou, M., Cui, P., Pei, J., Zhang, Z., Zhu, W.: Asymmetric transitivity preserving graph embedding. In: Proceedings of the 22nd ACM SIGKDD International Conference on Knowledge Discovery and Data Mining, pp. 1105–1114. ACM (2016). https://doi.org/10.1145/2939672.2939751
14. Ou, Q., Jin, Y.D., Zhou, T., Wang, B.H., Yin, B.Q.: Power-law strength-degree correlation from resource-allocation dynamics on weighted networks. Phys. Rev. E **75**(2), 021102 (2007)
15. Perozzi, B., Al-Rfou, R., Skiena, S.: DeepWalk: online learning of social representations. In: Proceedings of the 20th ACM SIGKDD International Conference on Knowledge Discovery and Data Mining, pp. 701–710. ACM (2014). https://doi.org/10.1145/2623330.2623732
16. Ribeiro, L.F., Saverese, P.H., Figueiredo, D.R.: struc2vec: learning node representations from structural identity. In: Proceedings of the 23rd ACM SIGKDD International Conference on Knowledge Discovery and Data Mining, pp. 385–394. ACM (2017). https://doi.org/10.1145/3097983.3098061
17. Rossi, R.A., Ahmed, N.K.: The network data repository with interactive graph analytics and visualization. In: Proceedings of the Twenty-Ninth AAAI Conference on Artificial Intelligence (2015). http://networkrepository.com
18. Tang, J., Qu, M., Wang, M., Zhang, M., Yan, J., Mei, Q.: LINE: large-scale information network embedding. In: Proceedings of the 24th International Conference on World Wide Web, pp. 1067–1077. International World Wide Web Conferences Steering Committee (2015). https://doi.org/10.1145/2736277.2741093
19. Tang, L., Liu, H.: Relational learning via latent social dimensions. In: Proceedings of the 15th ACM SIGKDD International Conference on Knowledge Discovery and Data Mining, pp. 817–826. ACM (2009). https://doi.org/10.1145/1557019.1557109

Rectified Encoder Network for High-Dimensional Imbalanced Learning

Tao Zheng[1,2], Wei-Jie Chen[3], Ivor Tsang[2], and Xin Yao[1(✉)]

[1] Shenzhen Key Laboratory of Computational Intelligence,
University Key Laboratory of Evolving Intelligent Systems of Guangdong Province,
Department of Computer Science and Engineering,
Southern University of Science and Technology, Shenzhen 518055, China
`xiny@sustech.edu.cn`
[2] Centre for Artificial Intelligence (CAI),
University of Technology Sydney, Ultimo, Australia
[3] Zhijiang College, Zhejiang University of Technology, Hangzhou Shi, China

Abstract. Many existing works have studied the learning on imbalanced data, however, it is still very challenging to handle high-dimensional imbalanced data. One key challenge of learning on imbalanced data is that most learning models usually have a bias towards the majority and its performance will deteriorate in the presence of under-represented data and severe class distribution skews. One solution is to synthesize the minority data to balance the class distribution, but it may lead to more overlapping, especially in the high-dimensional setting. To alleviate the above challenges, in this paper, we present a novel Rectified Encoder Network (REN) for high-dimensional imbalanced learning tasks. The main contribution is that: (1) To deal with high-dimensionality, REN encodes high-dimensional imbalanced data into low dimensional latent codes as a latent representation. (2) To obtain a discriminative representation, we introduce a Rectifier to match the latent codes with our proposed Predefined Codes, which disentangles the overlapping among classes. (3) During rectification, in the Predefined Latent Distribution, we can efficiently identify and generate informative samples to maintain the balance of class distribution, so that the minority classes will not be neglected. The experimental results on several high-dimensional and image imbalanced data sets indicate that our REN obtains good representation code for classification and visualize the reason why REN gets better performance in high-dimensional imbalanced learning.

Keywords: Imbalanced learning · High-dimensionality · Representation learning · Characteristics extraction

1 Introduction

Many existing works have studied class imbalanced learning [10], where the number of a class of data is severely less than others. However, it is still very

© Springer Nature Switzerland AG 2019
A. C. Nayak and A. Sharma (Eds.): PRICAI 2019, LNAI 11671, pp. 684–697, 2019.
https://doi.org/10.1007/978-3-030-29911-8_53

challenging to learn from high-dimensional imbalanced data, since the high-dimensionality [11] of data affects the treatment of imbalanced learning. One key challenge is that most learning models usually have a bias towards the majority and its performance will deteriorate in the presence of underrepresented data and severe class distribution skews. One important approach is data pre-processing including Random Oversampling (RoS) [5] and Synthetic Oversampling Techniques, as they are dedicated to preparing, sampling and cleaning the imbalanced data set to make the data set appropriate for most learning models. Nonetheless, RoS will cause over-fitting [20], and the traditional synthetic techniques suffer from the negative effect due to the high-dimensionality of data. Unfortunately, high-dimensional and imbalanced data are more and more unavoidable in the modern applications, such as image processing, video analysis, text learning, user preference classification and autonomous driving. This issue inevitably degenerates the performance of traditional imbalanced learning including the synthetic oversampling techniques.

There are several main synthetic oversampling techniques such as SMOTE [4], ADASYN [9] and MWMOTE [3]. They have become the most prevalent imbalanced learning approaches because of its two merits. First, synthetic oversampling techniques alter the class distribution before the data are fed into the following model, which is a type of data pre-processing. This merit lets it appropriate to cooperate with most learning models. Second, some synthetic oversampling techniques analyze the class structure, identify seed samples [3,9] and then generate new samples. This merit reduces the over-fitting with new samples rather than duplicating samples like RoS. As a result, some main stream software tools [13,14] apply these synthetic oversampling techniques in imbalanced learning. However, given that high-dimensionality of data degrade the performance of conventional synthetic oversampling techniques due to ineffective synthetic samples (e.g. two images of digit 1 may synthesize an image of number 11), this begs a new challenge: can we reduce the negative effect caused by the high-dimensionality of data?

To address this challenge, we propose a latent synthetic network call Rectified Encoder Network (REN), which integrates the auto-encoder with a rectification and the synthetic oversampling technique of imbalanced learning. Specifically, the framework of REN involves Encoder, low dimensional Predefined Latent Code, Decoder, and Rectifier. To sum up, REN leverages Encoder to represent the high-dimensional data by a low-dimensional latent code, which are used to synthesize more codes and generate more minority data to balance the distribution. With the balanced data made of both original ones and generative ones, rectifier assists the REN to disentangle the overlapping due to the synthetic samples. In the sub-sequenced epochs, REN further rectifies the codes to the Predefined Codes, where REN can further identify, synthesize the informative samples and disentangle the overlapping to obtain a discriminative, balanced, and low-dimensional representation. The contributions of this paper are listed as follow:

1. To deal with high-dimensionality, we encode high-dimensional imbalanced data into low dimensional latent codes as a representation. REN is the first attempt to leverage the generative models to tackle the high-dimensional imbalanced problem.
2. To obtain a discriminative representation, we introduce a Rectifier to match the latent codes to our proposed Predefined Codes, which disentangles the overlapping among classes.
3. During rectification, in the predefined latent distribution, we can identify and synthesize informative samples to maintain the balance of class distribution, so that the minority classes will not be neglected. To illustrate the reason why REN can improve the performance of imbalanced learning, we conduct a visualization to interpret that the trained REN has emphasized extracting the minority classes, informative samples, and key characteristics.

The rest of this paper is organized as follows. In the Sect. 2, we will briefly review some re-sampling methods, cost-sensitive methods, generative models, and recent papers using deep neural networks for the imbalanced learning. Then we will describe our model, Rectified Encoder Network (REN) in Sect. 3. We will first demonstrate the framework and mechanism, and then one implement of the model. The experiment results, analyses and visualization of REN will be in Sect. 4. Finally, we conclude this paper and discuss the future works in Sect. 5.

2   Related Works

The challenges in learning from high-dimensional imbalanced data can not comprehensively solved by exiting related works. This first kinds of related works are existing re-sampling methods for imbalanced learning, which alter the class distribution to make the train set balanced. For example, Random over Sampling (RoS) randomly duplicates the minority class samples, which will cause over-fitting [20]. On the contrary, Random under Sampling (RuS) removes the majority class samples randomly [7], but it degrades the prediction performance for the majority class. SMOTE [4] is a basic Synthetic Oversampling Technique, which randomly identifies seed samples of minority, and generates new related monitory samples via convex combination of the seed samples. The variants of Synthetic Oversampling Technique like ADASYN [9], MWMOTE [3], and SMOM [22], further identify some informative samples and assign different weights to the samples to emphasize the boundary, prevent overlapping, and over-generalization problem. Nevertheless, in the case of high-dimensional feature data or image data, it is not proper for above methods to align all the dimensions to calculate the distances or to convexly combine the pixel-wise of two images to synthesize a new image. But our REN learns a latent representation, then synthesizes and generates samples.

Our work is also related to cost-sensitive methods, which manipulate at the algorithmic level by adjusting misclassification costs. Cost-sensitive boosting

[16,17] introduces the misclassification costs into AdaBoost for the distribution update in each iteration. However, it is also a problem to define the costs matrix before training. But our REN will update the cost autonomously during rectification.

Our work can be compared with the ensemble learning approach [18,20], as the samples that are not correctly classified by the current base classifier will be emphasized more in the next base classifier. But REN emphasizes such samples in the same neural network to rectify the representation in the next training epoch. Our work is also slightly related to generative models, like GAN, VAE [8,12], and their variants. WAE [19] proposed a different regularizer from VAE, and the regularizer encourages the encoded distribution to match a Gaussian prior. Our work is also inspired by [1] which operates samples in a deep feature space. The above models are used for learning the distribution of training data and then generating new samples, but not for imbalanced learning, where these models usually neglect the minority class. But our work focus on improving the performance of the class prediction of the minority class. In addition, some deep learning works [6,10] for imbalanced learning involved with quintuplet maintenance or other hard-sample mining technique, which is very time-consuming in searching samples. But our work designs a high-efficient mining trick for the informative samples and even extraction on key characteristics.

3   Rectified Encoder Network

In this section, we propose Rectified Encoder Network framework (Fig. 1), which is composed of Encoder, Rectifier, Predefined Distribution, Synthesizer and Decoder. Encoder maps high-dimensional data (images) into low-dimension latent codes (knowledge). Synthesizer chooses latent codes and synthesize more, and Decoder converts a set of chosen latent codes into get new high-dimensional data (images), which also assist the original data to balance the class distribution. Rectifier is the key step to cooperate the representation (Encoder) with generation (Synthesizer&Decoder). It rectifies the latent codes to the Predefined Code Distribution (pre-knowledge). Via such rectification, REN adjusts and improves the representation and generation. At the same time, latent codes with balanced distribution from original and new samples are further refined to acquire a discriminative representation for following classification.

3.1   Preliminary

Consider we have a high-dimensional imbalanced data set: $\mathscr{D} : \{(x_1, y_1), ..., (x_M, y_M)\}$, where each tuple consists of one sample and its label. x_m can be a high-dimensional feature vector or image. $y_m \in \mathbb{R}^K$ is a K-dimensional binary vector indicating the class, and K is the number of classes. In the imbalanced case, y_m is sampled from a high-skewed distribution. Among data pre-processing approaches, oversampling techniques from $\mathscr{D}$ synthesize $\mathscr{S} : \{(\tilde{x}_1, \tilde{y}_1), (\tilde{x}_2, \tilde{y}_2), ..., (\tilde{x}_S, \tilde{y}_S)\}$ consisting of the same form of tuple, to obtain the union $\mathscr{D} \cup \mathscr{S} = \mathscr{B} :$ $\{(x_1, y_1), (x_2, y_2), ..., (x_N, y_N)\}$ what has balanced distribution.

3.2 Encoding into Low Dimensional Space

In our model, before synthesizing $\mathcal{O}$ from $\mathcal{D}$, Encoder obtains low dimensional latent vector Z from instance X. We model such representation process as $Q(Z|X)$. In the generation process $P(X|Y,Z)$, the X is generated based on the latent code and the label. Since it is intractable directly maximize the log-likelihood, we construct an evidence lower bound (ELBO) [12,15] as follows:

$$
\begin{aligned}
\log P(X|Y) &= KL(q(z|x,y)\|p(z|x,y)) + E_{q(z|x,y)}[-\log q(z|x,y) + \log p(x,z|y)] \\
&\geq E_{q(z|x,y)}[-\log q(z|x,y) + \log p(x,z|y)] \\
&= E_{q(z|x,y)}[-\log q(z|x,y) + \log p(z|y)] + E_{q(z|x,y)}[\log p(z|x,y) \\
&= -KL(q(z|x,y)\|p(z|y)) + E_{q(z|x,y)}[\log p(x|z,y)]
\end{aligned}
\tag{1}
$$

where variational distribution $q(z|x,y)$ is to approximate the true distributions of Z. After maximizing the ELBO, we obtain low dimensional latent code z from instance x.

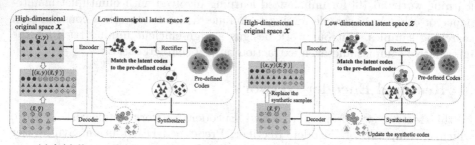

(a) initially, synthesize new samples   (b) sequencially, update the synthetic samples

Fig. 1. The Overview of the Rectified Encoder Network (REN). REN aims to obtain low dimensional, discriminative and balanced representation. The Encoder maps the training set from the high-dimensional original space $\mathcal{X}$ to the low dimensional latent space $\mathcal{Z}$; The Rectifier matches the latent codes to the Predefined Codes. The right hand side shows a simple Predefined Latent Code distribution, truncated Gaussian Mixture Distribution with three components for three classes. Synthesizer creates new latent codes $(\tilde{z}, \tilde{y})$ and the Decoder generates new samples $(\tilde{x}, \tilde{y})$, which join the training set to make the original class distribution balanced. Then, REN encodes and rectifies the balanced input data to the Predefined Codes again, updating the synthetic and generative samples and refining the latent representation.

3.3 Predefined Latent Code and Rectifier

The goal of these two components is to overcome the overlapping problem during learning the representation, so that we can obtain discriminative representation for following classification.

The purpose of the former component, Predefined Code distribution, is to scatter the latent codes with certain constraints, which helps to discover the relationships among the classes and codes, so that REN can identify certain codes for further generating new samples. In our setting, we use the mixture of multivariate truncated Gaussian distribution as the latent class-conditional distribution. Our model does not directly converge all the samples of each class from the training set into a one-hot vector as traditional network classifiers do. Instead, our model only maps them into a certain area, which is the corresponding Predefined Code distribution in the latent space as a stage of learning representation.

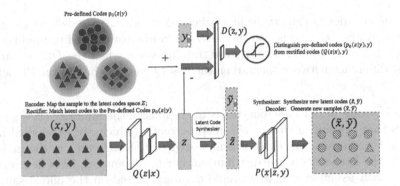

Fig. 2. One network architecture implementation of the Rectified Encoder Network. The Encoder $Q(z|x)$ maps instance x to latent code z, which is also rectified by network D. Predefined distribution $p_0(x|y)$, Q and D composed a GAN, so the Q ultimately maps (x, y) to the Predefined distribution $p_0(x|y)$. The Synthesizer does not contain trained parameters. The decoder $P(x|z, y)$ is trained to generate informative samples to balance the distribution.

To implement this, the Predefined Code should not impose any bias on the relation among class, such as class A is similar to B, but different from C; B is between A and C; or any of them are closer to the output of the initialized network then others. Therefore, our Predefined Code distribution should meet the following criteria:

- Centers of the codes of all class are symmetrical to the original point O;
- The distances between centers of the codes of any two classes are equal;
- The variances on any dimensions of any class are equal.

One simplest Predefined Code with 3 classes meeting these three requirements is like the top-right corner of Fig. 1 showing. The centers of the three classes in the prior latent space are $(\sin 0, \cos 0)$, $(\sin 2\pi/3, \cos 2\pi/3)$, $(\sin 4\pi/3, \cos 4\pi/3)$ respectively. As for 2 classes, it can be $N(1, 1)$ and $N(-1, 1)$. As for a Predefined Code for $K > 3$ classes, we find a compatible method to define them:

Lemma 1: Assume an $n \times n$ identity matrix I_n, where each column is a point $p_i, i \in \{1, 2, .., n\}, p_i \in \mathcal{R}^n$, and PCA [21] is conducted on them. Then for the point p_i, the distance between a pair of them d_{ij}, and the distance from any of

$\tilde{p}_i$ to original point d_{0i}, satisfies: $\forall i, j, k, l \in \{1, 2, .., n\}$, we have $\tilde{p}_i \in \mathcal{R}^{n-1}, d_{ij} = d_{kl}, d_{0i} = d_{0j}$

The purpose of the latter component, the Rectifier, is to match the latent codes to mimic the Predefined Code distribution. To learn a distribution, GAN is a good option:

$$\begin{cases} \max_D \mathbb{E}_{z \sim p_0} log(D(z, y)) + \mathbb{E}_{z \sim Q} log(1 - D(z, y)) \\ \min_Q -\mathbb{E}_{x \sim P_{data}} log(D(Q(x), y)) \end{cases} \tag{2}$$

where the encoder Q that maps input data to mimic the Predefined Code distribution $p_0(z|y)$. $D(z, y)$ is also the GAN discriminator trained to conditionally distinguish $z \sim p_0$ from $z \sim Q$. As the training goes, when the $D(z, y)$ can not find the difference between them, then the $z \sim Q$ has matched to the Predefined Codes $z \sim p_0$.

The key task of both components is to emphasize the minority class and the samples that are difficult to be classified correctly, which are also called hard-samples. For the minority class, it is allocated to the same area as the majority class's in the Predefined Code distribution. For hard-samples, REN detects such samples with assigned weights (sample mining). Based on the mined samples, REN synthesizes more codes to let them be discriminative from samples of other classes. In next subsection, we will introduce a novel way for high-efficient sample mining.

3.4 High Efficient Sample Mining

As for conventional SMOTE, randomly choosing samples for synthesis may not obtain the informative samples. Discovering the sample relationship among classes and choosing seed samples are called sample mining. As for more advanced traditional Synthetic Oversampling Techniques, sample mining by k-NN has large time computational complexity. To make the best use of the Predefined Code, REN can apply a high efficient sample mining. Via the Predefined distribution, how informative a samples is can be measured. In addition, the time computational complexity is much lower than the traditional sample mining of the Synthetic Oversampling Techniques.

When it comes to measuring how informative a sample is, time complexity of conventional Synthetic Oversampling Technique using K-NN is $O(dn^2)$, where d is the dimension, and n is the number of samples. In contrast, REN uses the absolute distance. Then the destination point of each class should be defined. The closer distance from the destination point of a sample, the less informative this sample is. In this case, the Predefined Distribution is a reference system, and the destination point can be regarded as pivot points. The REN only needs to calculate how far away the sample from the destination point of the class, thus the time complexity is only $O(dn)$.

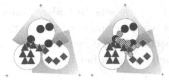

Fig. 3. The cross stars are the destination points of the classes, relatively

The destination points are two times far away of the centers of classes from original point as Fig. 3 shows. Any sample will never reach $2\mu_k$ in latent space, but the closer to it, the easier to be classified correctly, so it is treated to be less informative.

Here, we denote the i-th sample of the k-th class as x_{ki}, so as the corresponding distance w_{ki}, weight w_{ki} and latent code z_{ki}. The distance of a latent code from the destination point is $d_{ki} = \|Q(x_{ki}) - 2\mu_k\|_2$. We weight the sample based on the distance, and normalize it as $w_{ki} = d_{ki}/\Sigma_i d_{ki}$.

After the difficulty of every sample is measured and the sample is assigned with a normalized weight. The number of synthetic samples assign the certain seed latent code z_{ki} is $S_{ki} = N w_{ki}$. To build the classification boundary, the Synthesizer synthesizes a new sample based on the original sample and another one that has the similar distances from the destination. To build the boundary precisely, the encoder-decoder should penalize the reconstruction error of the difficult sample. Since the difficulty measurement is based on the distance, we can multiple this distance d_{ki} as a weight in the reconstruction loss function directly.

$$\frac{1}{K}\sum_{k=1}^{k} W_k \frac{1}{N_k}\sum_{i=1}^{N_k} \|x_{ki}, P(Q(x_{ki}))d_{ki}\|_2^2 \tag{3}$$

To find the nearest samples, we sort the d_{ki} as d'_{ki} and change the index of the z_{ki}, S_{ki} to the same index order as d'_{ki}, so it is much more effective to search the nearest neighbors of a latent code. For z_{ki}, we sample S_{ki} times from the K nearest samples $\bar{z}_{ki}$ of z_{ki} based on the sorted distances d'_{ki} to get $\hat{z}_{ki}$. With S_{ki} random numbers λ_{ki} between 0 and 1, the new latent code is $\tilde{z}_{ki} = \lambda_{ki}z_{ki} + (1 - \lambda_k)\hat{z}_{ki}$. Finally, REN generates new samples based on sample i-th samples of class k: $\tilde{x}_{ki} = P(\tilde{z}_{ki}, y = k)$ to make the class distribution balanced.

With the new balanced date set, REN encodes, rectifies, mines, synthesizes and decodes samples until it learn a discriminative, balanced representation in the low dimensional latent space. Using such a representation, a simple classifier can get a better performance than the based methods in the following experiments.

4   Experimental Analyses

To evaluate the REN's performance for high-dimensional imbalanced learning, we not only conduct comprehensive experiments on 3 multi-class UCI high-dimensional and imbalanced data sets but also image data sets (MNIST and 3D chairs). In all data sets, we can make a systematic comparison with typical imbalanced learning approaches. In the last data set, we visualize and interpret the features of REN that help to get a better performance. We use the following compared methods:

1. No-Sampling (NoS) is a baseline using original training without any re-sampling process set for comparisons;
2. Random Over Sampling (ROS) [5] is a basic sampling method in which examples are randomly duplicated;
3. Synthetic Minority Oversampling Technique (SMOTE) [4] can generate new synthetic samples for the minority class, while the previous baseline methods only remove or repeat old samples.
4. Adaptive Synthetic Sampling (ADASYN) [9] adapts the number of synthetic examples for every minority example according to the level of difficulty in classification, which focuses on these difficult samples.
5. Adaptive Boosting Negative Correction (AdaBoost.NC) [20] is a recent ensemble-type method for multi-class imbalanced learning. It not only considers the misclassified samples by assigning larger weights on them in the next base classifier, but also carries a penalty on the similar base classifiers, so as to encourage the ensemble diversity.

Note: This baseline ranges from very simple methods to elaborated methods that are in common used. In the same data set, the numbers of cells in neural networks of all baselines and REN are the same or very close.

We evaluate classification performance via the overall accuracy (OA) and geometric means of classification of every class(G-mean). Accuracy is an elementary performance of classification: TR/N, where N is the number of all the testing samples, and TR is the number of samples that are classified correctly. But it is not a systematic metric, because it can not effectively show the accuracy of the minority data. Therefore, the geometric means [16] of the classification accuracy for all classes (G-mean) will be employed as another performance metric in our

Table 1. Average of Overall Accuracy, G-means and Average of Ranking

Dataset	Dimensions classes	NoS Accuracy G-mean	RoS Accuracy G-mean	SMOTE Accuracy G-mean	ADASYN Accuracy G-mean	AdaBoost.NC Accuracy G-mean	REN-code Accuracy G-mean
Satellite	36	85.257	85.741	85.119	85.406	**86.781**	86.634
	6	78.949	82.876	82.431	81.441	82.972	**83.611**
Musk2	166	81.596	**92.376**	80.398	79.538	91.489	91.651
	2	76.891	87.627	78.341	78.391	**87.078**	88.167
Arrhythmia	279	60.286	71.389	65.971	68.823	**76.264**	77.519
	7	55.892	63.592	62.721	**64.461**	68.473	73.287
MNIST	28*28	85.530	**86.588**	84.001	83.754	85.075	86.236
	10	82.404	**83.976**	80.888	81.025	82.537	84.706
3D chair	58*58	**92.000**	88.500	87.500	90.500	89.000	97.000
	5	87.663	**87.851**	87.584	87.238	87.429	95.089

experimental study. G-mean is defined as $(\Pi_{k=1}^{K} \frac{tr_k}{n_k})^{\frac{1}{K}}$, where K is the number of classes, n_k is the number of examples in class k, and tr_k is the number of correctly classified examples in class k. Poor value of G-mean indicates that the classifier has poor performance at least one class, usually the minority class. The OA and G-means were calculated and the average values over 20 times independent five-fold cross-validation on each data set are presented.

4.1   UCI Datasets

All the UCI data sets we used are available from the UCI Repository[1]. Table 1 shows our REN outperforms other methods. The performance of SMOTE and ADASYN is not as good as the simple oversampling method, because examples that they synthesize near the boundary can cause more overlapping in the hidden layer of neural network. The reason that REN is better than other methods is because it not only synthesizes difficult examples but also maps them into the Predefined Code where each class has its area, which is a dynamical process of disentangling the overlapping.

4.2   MNIST

We ran experiments on the MNIST data set to determine whether REN would result in better performance than the baseline for image data. This imbalanced MNIST data set is customized to be imbalanced distribution, 4:5:6:7:8:9:10:11:12:13. Table 1 shows the two tradition Synthetic Oversampling Technique did not get good results because they synthesize the image in the pixel level, which is not suitable. The base classifier of ensemble learning is usually the decision tree, which is effective in the UCI like datasets, but is not proper to apply on image datasets. Thus, here we use CNN as the base classifier of ensemble learning. REN has better performance because the design of REN is more suitable for imbalanced image datasets.

4.3   3D Chair

We conducted a set of experiments on 3D chair [2] data set to show the difference of our model as an Over-sampling method for real-world imbalanced image data set. Table 1 shows the REN outperforms other methods.

In addition, to globally visualize what characteristic the REN mainly learns from the original imbalanced training set with the capacity-limited neural networks, a direct way is to compare all of the original training samples with corresponding reconstructed generative samples after completing the training of Encoder and Decoder Networks. The training of the Encoder is to extract the feature of the image into latent codes, while the Decoder recovers images from the code via the network cells, which means the cells of the Encoder and Decoder storage the classes, samples, and characteristics of the image data set. The Fig. 4

---

[1] http://archive.ics.uci.edu/ml/index.php.

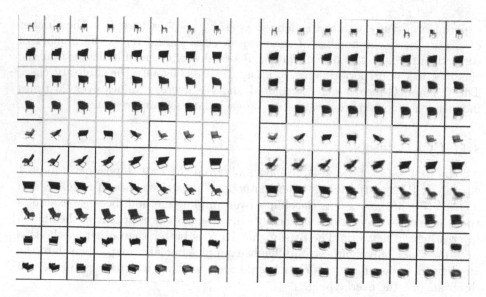

Fig. 4. Visualization:the original training images and the corresponding reconstructed image. The class distribution is 1:3:1:3:2, corresponding to the rows. The 3th and 4th classes have some similar samples (overlapping). We can check what class, sample and characteristic that REN emphasizes extracting and recovering in the imbalanced dataset. (Color figure online)

is the original data (x, y) and the reconstructing data $\tilde{x} = P(Q(x), y)$ (no synthetic process). Via this reconstructing process, we can directly check what kind of classes, samples, and characteristics that REN tries to extract and recover, so as to improve the performance of imbalanced learning. Note that Q and P are only 3 convolution and 3 transposed-convolution layers with limited cells, so they must make the better use of the capacity of the limited networks cells. This visualization (Fig. 4) shows that after training the REN:

4.3.1   The Minority Class is Emphasized More Than Majority Class

In the reconstructing images, The 1st kind of chairs (the 1st row, red frame, 8 samples) is more clear than the 2nd kind of chairs (the 2nd-4nd row, blue frame, 24 samples). Because REN assigns more weight in reconstructing the minority since there more synthetic samples for the minority. On the other hand, even though the 2nd kind of chairs is vague, it is still sharp enough to help to be distinguished from other classes. This is because when the majority latent codes are not discriminative enough, the reconstructing weight will also increase till it is sufficient.

4.3.2   The Samples that Are Difficult to Be Classified Are Emphasized More Than Other Samples

In the original images, half of the 4th (the 6–8th rows, 24 samples) and most of the 5th (the last 2 rows, 16 samples) kinds of chairs are easy to be classified directly. But the back side of the 4th chair (green frame) and the front side of the 5th (purple frame) chair are still a little bit difficult to distinguish from the corresponding sides of the 3rd kind of chairs (yellow and orange frame). We can see that in the reconstructing images, these difficult/informative samples are clearer than other samples in the same class. Because these sample are far way from the pivot point, they get larger weights. Therefore, REN emphasizes more on extracting samples that are difficult to be classified.

4.3.3   The REN Can Extract and Recover the Key Characteristic Used to Distinguish Similar Samples Among Different Classes

Several samples in 3rd class (the 2nd to 5th chairs in the 5th row, yellow frame) are extremely similar to the some samples in 4th class (last 4 chairs in the 6th row and the first 4 chairs in the 7th row, green frame) because the "backrest" is nearly identical. These samples lead to the classification performance degeneration of the baseline methods. But REN can handle it by focusing on the key characteristic used to distinguish them – the "chair legs". The "chair legs" of these samples are much more clear than the other parts, and than those "chair legs" of other samples within the classes. The reason is that in the mining process, REN tries to capture samples and characteristics. When the right characteristics are not captured, REN keep updating new ones until disentangles the overlapping. Therefore, we can see REN extract key characteristic to distinguish among different classes.

5   Conclusion and Future Works

This paper explored a novel adversarial deep learning framework for imbalanced learning, which not only gets good performance in classification but also generates new samples including attribution data and image. The experiments were conducted on the traditional UCI datasets and the real-world image datasets where the performance is systematically tested regarding Accuracy and G-mean. The visible effects of learning the image data show our model can (1) emphasize the minority class; (2) emphasize the samples that are difficult to be classified correctly; (3) extract and recover the key characteristic used to distinguish similar samples among different classes, also resist the interference from the similar characteristic that causes misclassification. The last effects will be explored and investigated more in our future works.

Acknowledgment. This work was supported by the National Key R&D Program of China (Grant No. 2017YFC0804003), the Program for Guangdong Introducing Innovative and Entrepreneurial Teams (Grant No. 2017ZT07X386), Shenzhen Peacock Plan (Grant No. KQTD2016112514355531), the Science and Technology Innovation Committee Foundation of Shenzhen (Grant Nos. ZDSYS201703031748284, JCYJ20180504165652917), the Program for University Key Laboratory of Guangdong Province (Grant No. 2017KSYS008), the ARC Future Fellowship ARC LP150100671, DP180100106, and National Natural Science Foundation of China (Grant Nos. 61603338, 61866010, 61703370).

References

1. Ashby, F.G., Maddox, W.T.: Capturing human category representations by sampling in deep feature spaces, pp. 1–10 (2018)
2. Aubry, M., Maturana, D., Efros, A.A., Russell, B.C., Sivic, J.: Seeing 3D chairs: exemplar part-based 2D–3D alignment using a large dataset of cad models. In: Proceedings of the IEEE Conference on Computer Vision and Pattern Recognition, pp. 3762–3769 (2014)
3. Barua, S., Islam, M.M., Yao, X., Murase, K.: MWMOTE-majority weighted minority oversampling technique for imbalanced data set learning. IEEE Trans. Knowl. Data Eng. **26**(2), 405–425 (2014)
4. Chawla, N.V., Bowyer, K.W., Hall, L.O., Kegelmeyer, W.P.: SMOTE: synthetic minority over-sampling technique. J. Artif. Intell. Res. **16**, 321–357 (2002)
5. Chawla, N.V., Japkowicz, N., Kotcz, A.: Special issue on learning from imbalanced data sets. ACM SIGKDD Explor. Newsl. **6**(1), 1–6 (2004)
6. Dong, Q., Gong, S., Zhu, X.: Imbalanced deep learning by minority class incremental rectification. IEEE Trans. Pattern Anal. Mach. Intell. **41**(6), 1367–1381 (2018)
7. Drummond, C., Holte, R.C., et al.: C4. 5, class imbalance, and costsensitivity: why under-sampling beats over-sampling. In: Workshop on Learning from Imbalanced Datasets II. vol. 11, pp. 1–8. Citeseer (2003)
8. Goodfellow, I., et al.: Generative adversarial nets. In: Advances in Neural Information Processing Systems, pp. 2672–2680 (2014)
9. He, H., Bai, Y., Garcia, E.A., Li, S.: ADASYN: Adaptive synthetic sampling approach for imbalanced learning. In: IEEE International Joint Conference on Neural Networks 2008. IJCNN 2008. IEEE World Congress on Computational Intelligence), pp. 1322–1328. IEEE (2008)
10. He, H., Garcia, E.A.: Learning from imbalanced data. IEEE Trans. Knowl. Data Eng. **9**, 1263–1284 (2008)
11. Jimenez, L.O., Landgrebe, D.A.: Supervised classification in high-dimensional space: geometrical, statistical, and asymptotical properties of multivariate data. IEEE Trans. Syst. Man Cybern. Part C Appl. Rev. **28**(1), 39–54 (1998)
12. Kingma, D.P., Welling, M.: Auto-encoding variational bayes. arXiv preprint arXiv:1312.6114 (2013)
13. Lemaître, G., Nogueira, F., Aridas, C.K.: Imbalanced-learn: a python toolbox to tackle the curse of imbalanced datasets in machine learning. J. Mach. Learn. Res. **18**(1), 559–563 (2017)
14. Pedregosa, F., et al.: Scikit-learn machine learning in python. J. Mach. Learn. Res. **12**, 2825–2830 (2011)

15. Sohn, K., Lee, H., Yan, X.: Learning structured output representation using deep conditional generative models. In: Advances in Neural Information Processing Systems, pp. 3483–3491 (2015)
16. Sun, Y., Kamel, M.S., Wang, Y.: Boosting for learning multiple classes with imbalanced class distribution. In: Sixth International Conference on Data Mining 2006. ICDM 2006, pp. 592–602. IEEE (2006)
17. Sun, Y., Kamel, M.S., Wong, A.K., Wang, Y.: Cost-sensitive boosting for classification of imbalanced data. Pattern Recogn. **40**(12), 3358–3378 (2007)
18. Sun, Y., Tang, K., Minku, L.L., Wang, S., Yao, X.: Online ensemble learning of data streams with gradually evolved classes. IEEE Trans. Knowl. Data Eng. **28**(6), 1532–1545 (2016)
19. Tolstikhin, I., Bousquet, O., Gelly, S., Schoelkopf, B.: Wasserstein auto-encoders, pp. 1–16 (2018). http://arxiv.org/abs/1711.01558
20. Wang, S., Yao, X.: Multiclass imbalance problems analysis and potential solutions. IEEE Trans. Syst. Man Cybern. Part B Cybern. **42**(4), 1119–1130 (2012)
21. Wold, S., Esbensen, K., Geladi, P.: Principal component analysis. Chemom. Intell. Lab. Sys. **2**(1–3), 37–52 (1987)
22. Zhu, T., Lin, Y., Liu, Y.: Synthetic minority oversampling technique for multiclass imbalance problems. Pattern Recogn. **72**, 327–340 (2017)

Network Alignment by Representation Learning on Structure and Attribute

Thanh Trung Huynh[1]([✉]), Van Vinh Tong[2], Chi Thang Duong[3],
Thang Huynh Quyet[2], Quoc Viet Hung Nguyen[1], and Abdul Sattar[1]

[1] Griffith University, Brisbane, Australia
{h.thanhtrung,henry.nguyen,a.sattar}@griffith.edu.au
[2] Hanoi University of Science and Technology, Hanoi, Vietnam
thanghq@soict.hust.edu.vn
[3] EPFL, Lausanne, Switzerland
thang.duong@epfl.ch

Abstract. Network alignment is the task of recognizing similar network nodes across different networks, which has many applications in various domains. As traditional network alignment methods based on matrix factorization do not scale to large graphs, a variety of representation learning based approaches has been proposed recently. However, these techniques tend to focus on topology consistency between two networks while ignoring other valuable information (e.g. network nodes attribute), which makes them susceptible to structural changes. To alleviate this problem, we propose RAN, a representation-based network alignment model that couples both structure and node attribute information. Our framework first constructs multi-layer networks to represent topology and node attribute information, then computes the alignment result by learning the node embeddings for source and target network. The experimental results show that our method is able to outperform other techniques significantly even on large datasets.

Keywords: Network alignment · Network embedding

1 Introduction

Networks are natural but powerful structures that capture relationships between different entities in many domains, such as social networks, citation networks, bioinformatics, chemistry. In many applications that involves multiple networks analysis, network alignment, the task of recognizing node correspondence across different networks, plays an important role. For example, by detecting accounts from the same user in different social networks, information of that user in one site can be exploited to perform better downstream functions (e.g. friend suggestion or content recommendation) in the other site [20]. In computer vision, network alignment helps to match images without human supervision [19]. In bioinformatics, analysis of protein-protein interactions networks across species makes remarkable improvement for gene prioritization [7].

© Springer Nature Switzerland AG 2019
A. C. Nayak and A. Sharma (Eds.): PRICAI 2019, LNAI 11671, pp. 698–711, 2019.
https://doi.org/10.1007/978-3-030-29911-8_54

Despite its ubiquity, network alignment is challenging as it is an NP-hard problem [3]. There have been several works aiming to deal with this problem using matrix factorization to directly achieve the alignment result, such as Iso-Rank [17], NetAlign [3], UniAlign [10], FINAL [20], REGAL [8]. However, these methods fail to deal with large networks since their computation time grows exponentially with network size.

In order to handle large networks, several alignment techniques [11,12,21] attempt to integrate latent representation learning [5,6,15] to make their models scalable. Although representation based methods can handle large-scale datasets, most of them focus only on topology consistency, which states that neighborhood relationship between any two nodes is maintained across different networks. However, this assumption can be incorrect in many contexts, for example, a person might have more connections in one social network (e.g. Facebook, Twitter) than others (e.g. LinkedIn, MySpace). When this assumption does not hold, the performance of these methods is adversely affected.

To alleviate this problem, we propose a representation-based network alignment model that couples both topology and node attribute information to enhance the result. Our framework first converts the given networks to multi-layered networks to represent topology and node attribute information, then retrieves the alignment result through learning the node embeddings for source and target network. The experimental results show that our method outperform other techniques significantly even on large datasets.

Our contributions may be stated as follows:

- We formulate the attributed network alignment problem which takes into account the alignment of multiple networks where node attribute information is available.
- We propose a representation-based alignment on attributed network framework (RAN) which identifies node alignments by learning node embeddings for each network and obtaining node pairs having similar embedding across networks after reconciling the embedding spaces.
- Within our framework, we transform the original attributed network into a multi-layer graph to represent both topology and attribute neighborhood and use these information simultaneously in representation learning stage. To the best of our knowledge, we are the first to do so to tackle network alignment problem.
- Experiments on real-world graphs show that our model outperforms state-of-the-art network alignment methods and more robust to structural and attribute noise.

Our paper is organized as follows. Section 2 introduces some necessary preliminaries to our work. Section 3 provides an overview of our approach and the attributed network alignment problem. Section 4 discusses why and how to transform the original networks to multi-layer graphs while Sect. 5 gives details of representation learning strategy with random walk on generated networks. Section 6 describes how to reconcile the embedding spaces and achieve the alignment result. The empirical results are shown in Sect. 7 while Sect. 8 surveys the related works and Sect. 9 concludes the paper.

2   Background

Attributed Network. Network (or graph, we use these terms interchangeably in this paper) is an omnipresent data structure appearing in applications in various fields such as computer science, social science, biology. Basically, a network is presented by a pair $G = (V, E)$ comprising a set V of vertices together with a set E of edges. However, in many applications, network nodes associate with valuable information called node attributes. Node attributes can be presented as a matrix $N \in \mathbb{R}^{nxd}$ with n is the number of node in the network and d is the size of feature vector; each node $v \in V$ associates with a feature vector $N(v) \in \mathbb{R}^d$. An network combining with node attribute can now be presented as a triplet $G = (V, E, N)$.

Network Embedding. Network embedding is an emerging technique in graph analysis due to the ubiquity of large-scale networks in real-world applications. The goal of network embedding is to map network nodes to a low-dimensional embedding space so that similarity of any two nodes reflects their similarity in the original network. Given a graph $G = (V, E)$, learning node embeddings requires three main steps:

- Define an encoder $\phi : V \to \mathbb{R}^{n \times d}$ associates each network node to a low-dimensional vectorial representation.
- Define an similarity function $\mathbf{sim} : V \times V \to \mathbb{R}$ in the original network that measures the relation between any two nodes.
- Optimize the parameters of the encoder so that similarity function $\mathbf{sim}$ of two nodes approximates the distance between their representation vectors:

3   Model and Approach

3.1   Model

Network alignment is the task of identifying corresponding nodes across two different networks. In this work, we address attributed networks as we use both topology and nodes' feature of the networks to enhance the performance of our proposed network alignment model. Given two attributed networks, without loss of generality, we select one network as source network and the other as target network, denoted by G_s and G_t respectively. For each node in the source network, we aim to recognize, if any, its counterpart in the target network. To achieve this goal, network alignment techniques often calculate an alignment matrix S, which is technically a cross-network similarity matrix: $S(u, v)$ represents the similarity between a node $u \in V_s$ and $v \in V_t$. This can be formally formulated as follow:

Problem 1. *Given two attributed networks* $G_s = (V_s, E_s, N_s)$ *and* $G_t = (V_t, E_t, N_t)$ *where* V_s, V_t *are sets of nodes,* E_s, E_t *are sets of edges and* N_s, N_t *are node attribute matrices, the problem of network alignment is to return an alignment matrix* S *where* $S(u, v)$ *represents the similarity between a node* $u \in V_s$ *and* $v \in V_t$.

Matching node pairs across source and target network then can be inferred by applying heuristics on this alignment matrix [8,9] to learn $\mathbf{M} : \mathbf{V}_s \times \mathbf{V}_t \rightarrow \{0,1\}$ such that $\mathbf{M}(u,v) = 1$ if two nodes $u \in \mathbf{V}_s$, $v \in \mathbf{V}_t$ share the same identity; otherwise $\mathbf{M}(u,v) = 0$.

3.2 Approach

Solving the delineated problem is a complex task. Real-world networks often have significant amount of nodes, therefore constructing the potential matching between two networks can be costly, requires the solution method being time efficient and scalable. Besides, in many cases, networks contain structural noises, for example two nodes are neighbors in one network do not always maintain the neighborhood relation in other network. In such case, using topology information alone is insufficient and can mislead to poor alignment result. In our work, therefore, we study an alignment approach that integrating attribute of network nodes into multi-layer network structure.

Figure 1 presents an overview of our model. We start by transforming each given source and target network into a two-layer network. The first layer, namely *structure layer*, corresponds to the structure of the origin network without any node attribute information. The second layer, named *attribute layer*, is constructed by generating pseudo nodes corresponding to nodes feature, called *attribute node*. The intuition behind creating this layer is to capture the relationship between network nodes based on feature through forming links between their attribute nodes. Attribute node of one node also links to its node in structure layer to represent the relationship between topology and feature characteristic of that node. Designing this two-layer network allows us to unify the structure and attribute property of the network and leverage node feature information to facilitate the process of generating nodes representation.

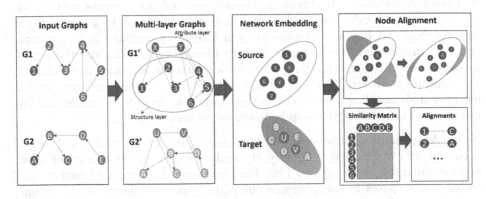

Fig. 1. Overview of RAN model

To learn latent representations of network nodes, we employ a biased random walk and language modeling technique approach. The embedding approach exploits properties of the multi-layer network by adopting random paths over the two layers as nodes' context, enriches the context with both topology and attribute information. Then, the popular skip-gram model is applied on the random walks to learn nodes' embedding by considering walks as the equivalent of sentences in language modeling.

After the embedding step, each network is presented by a low-dimensional space which reflects the characteristic of network nodes through distance: similarity in the embedding space approximates similarity in the original network, which helps to identify the nodes across source and target networks. Because latent space of source and target networks are independently learned, a mapping function is produced in the next step to map the spaces of source and target network into a shared space where the alignment result can be achieved by mapping pairs of nodes that have close embeddings.

Following this structure, our model requires the realization of the following steps:

Multi-layer Network Construction. This step extends each given network to a two-layer network that represents its structure and attribute information. The structure layer maintains the original network topology while the attribute layer captures the attribute neighborhood relationship of network nodes. To construct the attribute layer, first we group the node feature vectors into k clusters, then we generate the attribute nodes presenting each cluster. The attribute node of clusters having close centroids will be linked together to capture nodes feature similarity. Using clustering result makes our model more robust to small changes in attribute introduced by noise and reduces the computation time needed. The detailed process of constructing structure attribute multi-layer networks is described in Sect. 4.

Network Embedding. In this stage, low-dimensional latent spaces are created based on the networks produced in the last step. We want to leverage both topology and attribute information to learn latent representations for network nodes so that more information are used to identify and distinguish the nodes across the networks. As a result, random walks are generated over the two layers and contains both attribute node and structure node. Then, skip-gram model with negative sampling is employed on the random walks to learn embedding for the nodes. The detail of this step is described in Sect. 5.

Node Alignment. As the vectorial embedding spaces for the source and target networks are obtained independently, the embeddings might belong to different and incomparable vector spaces. Therefore, we produce a mapping function that reconcile the spaces by mapping one embedding space to the other. We adopt a supervised algorithm for learning the mapping function inspired by cross-language dictionary building. After being mapped to the common space, nodes from source and target network that have similar representation will be chosen to form the alignment pairs. Node alignment is described in Sect. 6.

4   Multi-layer Network

First we discuss the preprocessing step that convert each source and target network to a multi-layered network. Given the attributed network $G = (V, E, N)$, we divide the network into two layers. The first layer corresponds to the structure, and the second layer is for the content of the network.

4.1   Structure Layer

This layer is designed to capture the topology information of the original network. To this purpose, we replicate the topology of the original network and discards nodes attribute information in this layer. Mathematically, given the input network $G = (V, E, N)$, the structure layer is a graph $G_{st} = (V_{st}, E_{st})$, with $V_{st} = V$ and $E_{st} = E$. There are some reasons for constructing the structure layer this way. First, this helps to avoid losing topology information because any two neighbor nodes in the original network will be connected in the structure layer of the new network. Otherwise, if any two nodes lose their neighborhood relationship during the transformation, they will become undesirable structure noise and consequently adversely affects the final performance of the model due to the homophily principle assumption. Secondly, separating topology and attribute information in two different layers allows us to manage and unify these information easier. While similarity in topology between nodes is presented in this layer, the relation related to attribute will be specified in the attribute layer.

4.2   Attribute Layer

This layer is a directed graph which captures the similarity between nodes in terms of their respective features. Constructing the layer requires two sub-steps:

Creating Attribute Nodes. In this sub-step, we generate pseudo node to represent features of the original network nodes. To prevent the explosion in the amount of pseudo nodes that are generated and taken into account, we bin node features together into k groups, with $k << n$, then create one *attribute node* for each group. The grouping strategy depends on the type of node attributes. For categorical node attributes where node feature vectors are in the form of one-hot vectors, we propose using the number of category features as k. For multi-categorical or real-valued node attributed, a variety of popular clustering algorithm can be employed accordingly (K-mean algorithm is used in our work). It is worth noting that this process not only reduces the amount of attribute node, it also makes our model more resistant to small changes in feature vectors introduced by noise as their representing *attribute node* remain the same.

Connecting Attribute Nodes. After forming the attribute nodes, we assign the edges between these nodes to simulate the attribute similarity between network nodes. For each attribute node $v_i \in V$, initially we compute the similarity or weight to all other nodes $v_j, (j \neq i)$ based on the similarity of the presenting feature vector of the group. But in this case, the attribute graph can be close to a complete graph and consequently it would increase the computational time. To avoid this problem, we propose to use a threshold for average degree of the attribute graph based on that of structure layer. Let average degree of the structure layer is avg_{st}, we only keep top avg_{st} edges that have the highest weight. Using avg_{st} has two advantages: (1) avg_{st} is determined value and (2) leveraging it allows us to maintain the balance between the size of structure layer and attribute layer. At the end, we get the attribute layer in the form of a graph $\mathbf{G}_{at} = (\mathbf{V}_{at}, \mathbf{E}_{at})$.

4.3   Connect Attribute and Structure Layer

Next, we complete the multi-layer network by adding the edges that connects structure layer and attribute. For any node v_i in the original network, suppose it corresponds to node v_i^{st} in the structure layer and node v_i^{at} in the attribute layer, we join v_i^{st} and v_i^{at} together by an edge which associated with four transition weights as follows:

$$w_i^{ss} = ln(e + |\Gamma_i^{ss}|) \mid \Gamma_i^{ss} = \{(v_i^{st}, v_j^{st}), v_j^{st} \in \mathbf{V}_{st}\} \tag{1}$$

$$w_i^{sa} = w_i^{as} = ln(e + |\Gamma_i^{at}|) \mid \Gamma_i^{at} = \{(v_i^{at}, v_j^{st}), v_j^{st} \in \mathbf{V}_{st}\} \tag{2}$$

$$w_i^{aa} = ln(e + |\Gamma_i^{aa}|) \mid \Gamma_i^{aa} = \{(v_i^{at}, v_j^{at}), v_j^{at} \in \mathbf{V}_{at}\} \tag{3}$$

This weights are determined based on the number of direct neighbors in terms of topology and attribute. The intuition behind these weights is to guide the random walk generation process to the layer which have more information in each walk step. The detail of usage of these weights will be discussed later at Sect. 5.1.

We have generated a multi-layered graph $\mathbf{G}_{mul} = (\mathbf{V}_{mul}, \mathbf{E}_{mul})$ using network structure and attribute. Next, we leverage this graph to learn the latent representations for network nodes.

5   Structure Attribute Network Embedding

In this step, each network is embedded into a low-dimensional space by combining structure and attribute information where each node v_i is represented as a d-dimensional vector z_i. First we describe a biased random walks generator on the multi-layered graph, then we address the latent representation learning strategy.

5.1   Biased Random Walks

Algorithm 1 depicts how the random walks are generated. Given the multi-layer network from the previous step, we would want to produce a random walks set which plays the same role as corpus in language modelling. There are r random walks starting from each node in the multi-layered graph as root, each random walk has the length l.

Algorithm 1. Random walks construction

1: Input: The network $\mathbf{G}_{mul} = (\mathbf{V}_{mul}, \mathbf{E}_{mul})$,
      r: Number of random walk starting form each vertex,
      l: Length of each random walk
2: Output: Random walks set C
3: $C = []$ ▷ Initialize the corpus
4: **for** $n \in [1, r]$ **do**
5:     **for** $v \in \mathbf{V}_{mul}$ **do**
6:         $W = [v]$, $v_0 = $ v   ▷ Initialize the walk
7:         **for** $i \in [1, l]$ **do**
8:             $v_i = WALKSTEP(v_{i-1})$ ▷ Determine the next node in walk step
9:             Append v_i to W
10:       Append W to C
11: **return** C

Lines 4–9 shows the basis of the generator. Line 4, line 5 specifies the loops with r and l. For each iteration, line 6 first initialize the walk. Then, given at a particular time step i of the random walk, we are at node v_i, with v_i either in the structure layer or in the content layer; the $WALKSTEP$ function calculates to choose v_{i+1} to perform the next walk step in line 8. The function first calculate the probability of taking that step either into the structure layer or into the attribute layer, with the goal is to move to a layer which is more informative using the weights specified in Sect. 4.3. The transition probabilities are defined as:

$$p(v_{i+1} \in \mathbf{V}_{st} | v_i \in \mathbf{V}_{st}) = \frac{w_i^{ss}}{w_i^{ss} + w_i^{sa}} \tag{4}$$

$$p(v_{i+1} \in \mathbf{V}_{at} | v_i \in \mathbf{V}_{st}) = \frac{w_i^{sa}}{w_i^{ss} + w_i^{sa}} \tag{5}$$

$$p(v_{i+1} \in \mathbf{V}_{st} | v_i \in \mathbf{V}_{at}) = \frac{w_i^{as}}{w_i^{as} + w_i^{aa}} \tag{6}$$

$$p(v_{i+1} \in \mathbf{V}_{at} | v_i \in \mathbf{V}_{at}) = \frac{w_i^{aa}}{w_i^{as} + w_i^{aa}} \tag{7}$$

After selecting the layer, the $WALKSTEP$ function pick randomly a node from neighbor set of the current node v_i in that layer to move to. The chosen node v_{i+1} then is appended to the walk in line 9. The loop continues until the length of the walk reaches l and the walk is added to the corpus in line 10. When all random walks are generated, the corpus is returned in line 11.

5.2 Latent Representation Learning

After having the random walk set generated, we leverage Skip-Gram with Negative Sampling (SGNS) technique [14] in language modelling to learn the embedding for network nodes. In language modelling, the main goal is to maximize the likelihood of a sequence of words appearing in a document. In our work, generated biased random walks play the same role as short sentences in language modelling and the goal is to maximize the co-occurrence probability of all vertices $v_1, .., v_n$ in the walk given the observing vertex v_0. Mathematically, it can be written in the following form:

$$\underset{v_0}{\text{maximize}} \ Pr(v_1, .., v_n \mid v_0) \tag{8}$$

Skip-Gram model can be used to produce embedding for nodes given the random walk corpus C. For a vertex v_i, $\phi(v_i)$ represents the embedding of the node, we would like to maximize the probability of its neighbors in the walk. Given w being the window size of the node, the embeddings ϕ can be found by maximizing the following objective:

$$\underset{\phi}{\text{maximize}} \ \log(Pr\{v_{i-w}, ..., v_{i+w} \mid v_i\} \mid \phi(v_i)) \tag{9}$$

6 Node Alignment

To reconcile two latent representation spaces that are learned independently, we construct a pairwise mapping between two embedding spaces. The idea behind this technique is to facilitate reconciliation based on a part of groundtruth given as seed dictionary, called anchor nodes, denoted by A. Because we construct embedding for source and target network separately, these anchor nodes will be assigned to different embedding spaces, even if they are related to the same entities. As a result, these anchor nodes play an important role to align one embedding space to the other.

Let $\mathbf{Z}_s$ and $\mathbf{Z}_t$ denote the embedding matrices for source and target network, we learn the mapping function $\Theta : \mathbf{Z}_s \longrightarrow \mathbf{Z}_t$ such that the embeddings of the anchor nodes A are closed in the common space. Our objective can be determined by the following loss function:

$$L = \sum_{v \in A} ||\Theta(z_v^s) - z_v^t||_F \tag{10}$$

where $||.||_F$ is the Frobenius norm.

The mapping function Θ can be either a linear function [2] or a multilayer perceptron [12]. Although the linear function $\Theta(\mathbf{Z}) = \mathbf{Z} \times \mathbf{W}$ is a simple model, we apply this model into our work because of the two reasons. First, according to [12], it is sufficient to obtain a good mapping. Second, with the linear mapping, the optimized solution can be found in an exact manner. It is worth noting that better mapping comes with the addition of orthogonality constraint to the mapping matrix $\mathbf{W}$, because orthogonal matrix helps to maintain distance between any two nodes across networks. The optimized orthogonal matrix $\mathbf{W}^*$ can be obtained by using singular value decomposition. In more detail, let

$$\mathbf{U}\Sigma\mathbf{V}^T = \mathbf{E}_s\mathbf{E}_t^T \tag{11}$$

be the SVD decomposition of the matrix $\mathbf{E}_s\mathbf{E}_t^T$. Then the mapping matrix $\mathbf{W}$ is calculated from $\mathbf{U}, \mathbf{V}$

$$\mathbf{W} = \mathbf{U}\mathbf{V}^T \tag{12}$$

After reconciling the two representation spaces, we calculate the alignment matrix $\mathbf{S}$ by:

$$\mathbf{S}(u, v) = \mathbf{sim}(\phi(u), \phi(v)), u \in \mathbf{V}_s, v \in \mathbf{V}_t \tag{13}$$

with $\mathbf{sim}$ is the similarity measure, for our work we choose cosine similarity. Then, we adopt a heuristic greedy algorithm [9] on the similarity matrix to obtain one-to-one alignments between the source and target networks.

7 Experiments

7.1 Experimental Setup

Datasets. In the experiments, we employ three real-world datasets to evaluate the performances of our model, including protein-protein interaction (ppi) [6], economic network (econ) [16] and brain network (bn) [1]. Starting from each real-world network $\mathbf{G}_s = (\mathbf{V}_s, \mathbf{E}_s, \mathbf{N}_s)$ with adjacency matrix $\mathbf{D}_s$ as source network, we produce a permuted network $\mathbf{G}_p = (\mathbf{V}_p, \mathbf{E}_p, \mathbf{N}_p)$ with adjacency matrix $\mathbf{D}_p$ by the following equation:

$$\mathbf{D}_p = \mathbf{P}\mathbf{D}_s\mathbf{P}^T \tag{14}$$

where $\mathbf{P}$ is the permutation matrix, with $\mathbf{P}_{ij} = 1$ means that node i from the source network corresponds to node j in the target network, otherwise $\mathbf{P}_{ij} = 0$.

Baseline Methods. We compare against four well-known existing network alignment methods: (1) UniAlign, which applies alternating projected gradient descent on formulated bipartie network alignment model [10]; (2) FINAL, which defines a model with three criteria namely structure consistency, node feature consistency and edge feature consistency to tackle alignment problem on attributed networks [20]; (3) REGAL, which models alignment matrix using topology and nodes' feature similarity then employs low-rank matrix factorization approximation to speed up calculation [8]. (4) DeepLink, which generates the embeddings using skip-gram model then using auto-encoder and MLP to construct mapping function [21]. Besides, we use one variant of our method that using only structure layer to verify the effectiveness of the construction of the multi-layer graph. We name it as RAN_so (RAN with structure layer only).

Settings. Due to the randomness, we run 50 times for each dataset to compute the average results. For our algorithm, we use following hyperparameters: number of random walks = 100, walk lengths = 5, window size = 2. For other algorithms, we try our best to tune the parameters to have the best experiment performance. We use alignment accuracy as the evaluation metric to measure the performance. All the experiments are conducted on an AMD Ryzen Thread-Ripper 3.8 GHz system with 64 GB of main memory and four GTX Titan X graphic cards.

7.2   Alignment Performance Analysis

Robustness to Structural Noise. Network alignment methods exploit the topology consistency in its model, which assumes that the two node neighbors tends to maintain their relationship across the networks. Therefore, it would be important to learn about the effect of structural noise to these state-of-the-art alignment algorithms. To stimulate structural noise, we permute the original graph then remove edge from the original network with probability p_e ranging from 0 to 0.2 as described in 7.1

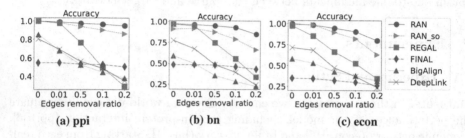

Fig. 2. Robustness of algorithms to structural noise

Figure 2 illustrates the accuracy results on the datasets. In general, all algorithms suffer accuracy drop when the noise level increased. RAN outperforms all four existing methods in all scenarios. It achieves 20–40% accuracy improvement over the state-of-the-art method REGAL when the noise level is at around from 0.05 to 0.1. This is because while both algorithm use network structure and attribute information, REGAL adopt a strict assumption on topology consistency that two nodes are similar when their neighbor's degree are the same, which make its model susceptible to considerable level of structure noise. Furthermore, RAN is more robust to structural noise as the accuracy gap between it and other methods becomes larger when noise grows. The performance of FINAL also witnesses a slight decrease but remains stable at average level, around 50% for ppi and bn dataset and 40% for econ dataset. By contrast, the accuracy of REGAL, BigAlign and DeepLink drop sharply when the level of noise goes high. Last but not least, the alignment accuracy of RAN is 10–30% better than its variant RAN_so, which verifies the importance of the construction of multi-layer graph.

Robustness to Attribute Noise. In this experiment, we study the effect of attribute noise to the performance of RAN and other baseline methods. Figure 3 shows the effect of attribute noise on alignment algorithms with the attribute changing p_a probability ranging from 0 to 0.5 while the structural noise p_s fixing at 0.05. We only consider RAN, REGAL, FINAL and BigAlign because the others do not utilize attribute information.

It can be seen from the diagram that REGAL and FINAL performance deteriorate with similar rate when level of attribute noise rises, while BigAlign's

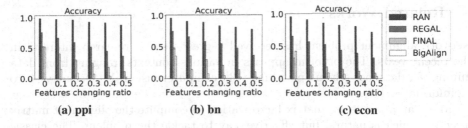

Fig. 3. Robustness of algorithms to attribute noise

accuracy declines with slightly faster pace. RAN performs the best not only on the accuracy but also on the stability when the level of attribute noise increased for all three datasets. On the other hand, performance of FINAL and BigAlign decrease significantly when attribute noise arises, drop below 10% accuracy at the noise level of 0.5 for all datasets. This is expected due to FINAL and BigAlign heavy reliance on attribute consistency.

Robustness to Graph Size Imbalance. This experiment investigates the effect of the difference between the size of two network to the accuracy of all models. Figure 4 shows the experiment result with the removal ratio of nodes p_n increases from 0 to 0.5.

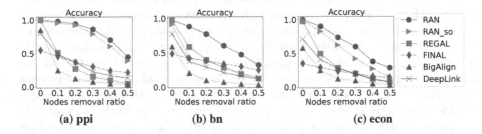

Fig. 4. Robustness of algorithms to graph size imbalance

It can be observed from the diagram that representation based method such as RAN, RAN_so and REGAL are sensitive to graph size imbalance factor. On the other hand, FINAL, a matrix-factorization based method, is more stable than the other when the level of imbalance increased. This is because size imbalance between source and network make the corresponding representation vector space harder to reconcile. It is worth notice that RAN is not the winner on the stability of performance when the number of removal nodes increased but it performs the best in accuracy on all datasets.

8 Related Works

Network alignment problem has received a great deal of research interests in the recent years. The problem appears in various contexts, ranging from data mining [3], database schema matching [13], computer vision [19], security [4] to bioinformatics [17].

Many approaches use matrix factorization to compute the alignment matrix directly, which is natural but effective way to tackle the problem. The classic and well-known IsoRank algorithm [17], inspired by PageRank [18], propagates the pairwise node similarity along the network with the assumption that two corresponding nodes in two networks connect to similar characteristic neighbors. NetAlign [3] models the alignment problem as an integer quadratic programing problem and adopts a belief propagation heuristic to solve. UniAlign [10] then applies alternating projected gradient descent on formulated bipartie network alignment model. FINAL [20] defines a model with structure, node feature and edge feature consistency to tackle alignment problem. REGAL [8] employs low-rank matrix factorization approximation to speed up calculation.

While matrix factorization based methods prove their efficiency in many scenario, they struggle to deal with large-scale networks due to the sparsity and massive size of their adjacency matrix. With the appearance of network embedding techniques [5,6,15]; alignment techniques leverage their scalability to deal with large-size network. PALE [12] learns nodes embedding by maximizing the co-occurrence likelihood of edge's vertices then applies linear or multilayer perceptron (MLP) as mapping function. IONE [11] uses the same mapping function as PALE but its embedding process is more complicated as it takes into account second-order node similarity. DeepLink [21] employs unbiased random walk to generate embeddings using skip-gram then using auto-encoder and MLP to construct mapping function. While these methods put in solid performance in some large datasets, they rely only topology information and therefore remain vulnerable to structure noise, which is very common in real-world networks. In this paper, in our end-to-end setting, we integrate both structure and attribute information to mitigate this problem and enhance the alignment result.

9 Conclusion

This paper proposed a representation learning based technique to align two attributed networks. The main novelty of our work is to transform the given networks into a multi-layer network to integrate both topology and attribute information before mapping network nodes to latent representation vector space. Then, the alignment matrix is retrieved by reconciling the two embedding spaces through a mapping function and eventually matching heuristic is applied on the matrix to retrieve the corresponding node pairs. Experiments on different benchmark datasets, different settings and numerous alignment methods verify the efficiency of our method on real-world large scale networks.

References

1. Amunts, K., et al.: BigBrain: an ultrahigh-resolution 3D human brain model. Science **340**, 1472–1475 (2013)
2. Artetxe, M., Labaka, G., Agirre, E.: Learning bilingual word embeddings with (almost) no bilingual data. In: ACL, pp. 451–462 (2017)
3. Bayati, M., Gerritsen, M., Gleich, D.F., Saberi, A., Wang, Y.: Algorithms for large, sparse network alignment problems. In: ICDM, pp. 705–710. IEEE (2009)
4. Bayati, M., Gleich, D.F., Saberi, A., Wang, Y.: Message-passing algorithms for sparse network alignment. ACM Trans. Knowl. Discov. Data (TKDD) **7**(1), 3 (2013)
5. Grover, A., Leskovec, J.: node2vec: scalable feature learning for networks. In: KDD, pp. 855–864. ACM (2016)
6. Hamilton, W., Ying, Z., Leskovec, J.: Inductive representation learning on large graphs. In: NIPS, pp. 1024–1034 (2017)
7. Hashemifar, S., Xu, J.: HubAlign: an accurate and efficient method for global alignment of protein-protein interaction networks. Bioinformatics **30**(17), i438–i444 (2014)
8. Heimann, M., Shen, H., Safavi, T., Koutra, D.: REGAL: representation learning-based graph alignment. In: CIKM, pp. 117–126 (2018)
9. Kollias, G., Mohammadi, S., Grama, A.: Network similarity decomposition (NSD): a fast and scalable approach to network alignment. TKDE **24**(12), 2232–2243 (2012)
10. Koutra, D., Tong, H., Lubensky, D.: BIG-ALIGN: fast bipartite graph alignment. In: ICDM, pp. 389–398 (2013)
11. Liu, L., Cheung, W.K., Li, X., Liao, L.: Aligning users across social networks using network embedding. In: IJCAI, pp. 1774–1780 (2016)
12. Man, T., Shen, H., Liu, S., Jin, X., Cheng, X.: Predict anchor links across social networks via an embedding approach. In: IJCAI, vol. 16, pp. 1823–1829 (2016)
13. Melnik, S., Garcia-Molina, H., Rahm, E.: Similarity flooding: a versatile graph matching algorithm and its application to schema matching. In: ICDE, pp. 117–128 (2002)
14. Mikolov, T., Sutskever, I., Chen, K., Corrado, G.S., Dean, J.: Distributed representations of words and phrases and their compositionality. In: NIPS, pp. 3111–3119 (2013)
15. Perozzi, B., Al-Rfou, R., Skiena, S.: DeepWalk: online learning of social representations. In: KDD (2014)
16. Rossi, R.A., Ahmed, N.K.: The network data repository with interactive graph analytics and visualization. In: AAAI (2015). http://networkrepository.com
17. Singh, R., Xu, J., Berger, B.: Global alignment of multiple protein interaction networks with application to functional orthology detection. In: Proceedings of the National Academy of Sciences, pp. 12763–12768 (2008)
18. Xing, W., Ghorbani, A.: Weighted PageRank algorithm. In: CNSR, pp. 305–314. IEEE (2004)
19. Yang, H., Song, D., Liao, L.: Image captioning with relational knowledge. In: Geng, X., Kang, B.-H. (eds.) PRICAI 2018. LNCS (LNAI), vol. 11013, pp. 378–386. Springer, Cham (2018). https://doi.org/10.1007/978-3-319-97310-4_43
20. Zhang, S., Tong, H.: Final: fast attributed network alignment. In: KDD, pp. 1345–1354 (2016)
21. Zhou, F., Liu, L., Zhang, K., Trajcevski, G., Wu, J., Zhong, T.: DeepLink: a deep learning approach for user identity linkage. In: INFOCOM, pp. 1313–1321 (2018)

Subject-Specific-Frequency-Band for Motor Imagery EEG Signal Recognition Based on Common Spatial Spectral Pattern

Shiu Kumar[1,2(✉)] , Alok Sharma[2,3,4,5,6(✉)] ,
and Tatsuhiko Tsunoda[4,5,6]

[1] School of Electrical and Electronics Engineering,
Fiji National University, Suva, Fiji
shiu.kumar@fnu.ac.fj
[2] The University of the South Pacific, Laucala Campus, Suva, Fiji
[3] IIIS, Griffith University, Brisbane, QLD 4111, Australia
alok.sharma@griffith.edu.au
[4] RIKEN Center for Integrative Medical Sciences, Yokohama, Kanagawa, Japan
[5] Department of Medical Science Mathematics, Medical Research Institute,
Tokyo Medical and Dental University, Tokyo, Japan
[6] CREST, JST, Tokyo 113-8510, Japan

Abstract. Over the last decade, processing of biomedical signals using machine learning algorithms has gained widespread attention. Amongst these, one of the most important signals is electroencephalography (EEG) signal that is used to monitor the brain activities. Brain-computer-interface (BCI) has also become a hot topic of research where EEG signals are usually acquired using non-invasive sensors. In this work, we propose a scheme based on common spatial spectral pattern (CSSP) and optimization of temporal filters for improved motor imagery (MI) EEG signal recognition. CSSP is proposed as it improves the spatial resolution while the temporal filter is optimized for each subject as the frequency band which contains most significant information varies amongst different subjects. The proposed scheme is evaluated using two publicly available datasets: BCI competition III dataset IVa and BCI competition IV dataset 1. The proposed scheme obtained promising results and outperformed other state-of-the-art methods. The findings of this work will be beneficial for developing improved BCI systems.

Keywords: Brain-computer-interface (BCI) · Motor imagery (MI) · EEG signal recognition

1 Introduction

Machine learning has gained widespread attention in this modern era due to technological advancements over the last few decades. These advancements in technology have provided means to high computational power and speed. As a result, machine learning has been widely applied in various applications, one of which is pattern

© Springer Nature Switzerland AG 2019
A. C. Nayak and A. Sharma (Eds.): PRICAI 2019, LNAI 11671, pp. 712–722, 2019.
https://doi.org/10.1007/978-3-030-29911-8_55

recognition. Manually recognizing patterns in different types of complex signals is time consuming and a difficult task. Machine learning techniques help us to tackle these problems.

Brain-computer-interface (BCI) has recently gained increased attention with applications in gaming [1], stroke rehabilitation [2–6], emotion recognition [7–12], sleep stage classification [13–16], seizure detection/diagnosing epilepsy [17–23] and other applications [2, 24–27]. The use of non-invasive sensors is preferred over invasive sensors due to the fact that it does not require any surgery, is low cost, portable and simple to use. In a BCI system, usually non-invasive sensors are used to capture the brain activities. The patterns of the brain activities acquired are then recognized using machine learning and pattern recognition techniques. A BCI system involves three basic steps: signal acquisition, feature extraction and signal classification/recognition as shown in Fig. 1. Once the signal is recognized, it is then appropriately translated to control signals for communication with external devices. It is very much desirable that a BCI system has the ability to correctly recognize the signals as accurately as possible. Therefore, obtaining high recognition rate or classification accuracy for a BCI application is driving more and more research to be carried out with various methods being proposed.

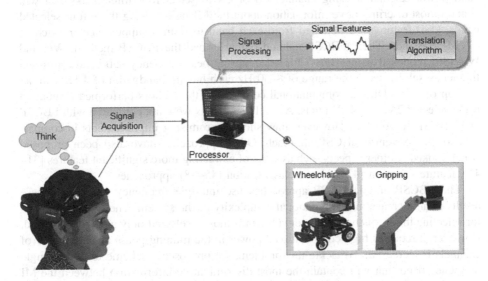

Fig. 1. Conceptual overview of a BCI system

The EEG signals for the same MI task varies from one subject to another due to different skull size, skin thickness, age and due to the fact that the way subjects think about the same task differs amongst different subjects. Although subject independent BCI systems would be highly desirable, due to the factors mentioned above, subject specific BCI systems have been usually proposed. Furthermore, these factors also affect the frequency range in which the signals are significantly discriminative for each of the subjects. Manually finding or tuning the filter band parameters is a difficult and time consuming exercise. Therefore, to tackle these problems many researchers have proposed various methods for autonomously finding the filter bands. This would provide signals that are as discriminative as possible between different tasks thereby boosting the ability to correctly recognize different categories of MI tasks. Filter bank common spatial pattern (FBCSP) [28], discriminative FBCSP (DFBCSP) [29], and binary particle swarm optimization (BPSO) for frequency band selection [30] are some of the methods proposed to tackle this problem. In the FBCSP approach [28], the raw EEG signal is filtered using multiple zero-phase Chebyshev Type II Infinite Impulse Response (IIR) filter banks in the range of 4–40 Hz, each having a bandwidth of 4 Hz. There was no overlap in the frequencies of the different filter banks. CSP spatial filters were computed using the filtered signal for each of the filter banks. The CSP features obtained from each filter bank were then concatenated and several methods of feature selection were used to select the significant features. A number of classifiers were also evaluated and promising results were obtained. To further improve the FBCSP approach, DFBCSP was proposed. In DFBCSP [29], the raw EEG signal is filtered using multiple filters in the range of 6–40 Hz. The filter banks have a bandwidth of 4 Hz with an overlap of 2 Hz. Instead of extracting features from the filtered signals of all the filter banks the authors have proposed using fisher's ratio of the single channels band power calculated using channel C3 or C4 to select four filter banks that will contain most discriminative information about the MI tasks. Using these four selected bands, CSP features are obtained from each band to train a support vector machine (SVM) classifier. The DFBCSP method outperformed the FBCSP method. Wei and Wei [30] proposed using BPSO for selecting the best frequency sub-bands from ten frequency sub-bands in the range of 8–30 Hz each having bandwidth of 4 Hz with an overlap of 2 Hz. Due to computational complexity, the authors performed evaluation using selected 24 and 14 channels. As such the results were not compared with FBCSP or DFBCSP approaches. However, they showed promising improvements in comparison to the conventional CSP approach. Other approaches have also been proposed which looked at other aspects such as ways of extracting more significant features [31–41], feature selection [42–44] and classification [45–48] approaches.

The FBCSP and DFBCSP approaches use multiple frequency bands and these results in an increase in computational complexity of the system. The BPSO approach for selecting the frequency bands or sub-bands mostly selected only a single sub-band. However, it requires high computational power in the training phase as the number of channels is increased. To tackle this problem, we proposed a scheme to find a single frequency band that will contain the most discriminative information between the MI tasks [49]. Genetic algorithm (GA) was employed for this purpose. In this work, we extend our previous work [49] by proposing the use of common spatial spectral pattern (CSSP) instead of CSP to further improve the scheme. This is a simple yet an effective approach (mostly ignored by researchers in this field) that improves the spatial resolution of the signal resulting in improved performance. We achieved promising results using the proposed scheme.

The remainder of this paper is organized as follows: in Sect. 2 we present our proposed scheme in detail. Section 3 presents the description of the datasets used together with the results. Discussion of the results and future works are presented in Sect. 4 while conclusions are presented in the last section.

2 Methodology

BCI has become a hot topic of research. One of the major challenges faced by researchers is the low signal-to-noise ratio (SNR) of the EEG signals acquired using non-invasive sensors. The SNR is improved to some extent by using non-invasive sensors. However, since non-invasive sensors require surgery, they are not preferred for majority of BCI applications. As such, more and more approaches are proposed by researchers with the aim to improve the classification accuracy of a BCI system. A major solution to the low SNR is to filter out the unwanted signal. Finding the frequency range which contains the most important information about the MI tasks is quite challenging. While use of multiple sub-bands has been a key to the improved performance, it also increased the computational complexity. Keeping this in mind, we propose a scheme based on CSSP that autonomously finds a single frequency band which provides maximum information to distinguish between different MI tasks. This results in an increased recognition ability of our proposed scheme and is the major contribution of this work. Our proposed scheme is presented in detail in the following sub-sections.

2.1 The Proposed Scheme

The overall framework of our proposed scheme is shown in Fig. 2. In our proposed scheme, the filter parameters of a bandpass filter are optimized using optimization algorithm. Once the parameters are determined, the training data is filtered using the filter parameters. CSSP spatial filters are determined using the filtered data and the filtered data is transformed using the learned spatial filters. The variance based features are then extracted, which are used to train a support vector machine (SVM) classifier. The test data also undergoes the same procedure except that the learned parameters are used for bandpass filtering, spatial filtering and classification is done using the trained classifier.

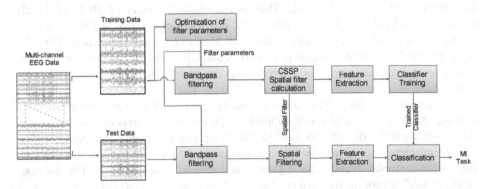

Fig. 2. Overall framework of the proposed scheme

2.2   Common Spatial Spectral Pattern (CSSP)

CSSP is a simple method that was proposed to increase the spatial resolution of the signal, which results in the signal containing more information that helps in the recognition of the MI EEG signals with higher accuracies. The only difference between CSP and CSSP is the training and test samples. In CSSP a temporal delayed signal is inserted to the raw signal, which in turn doubles the dimension of the signal. All other processes are the same for CSP and CSSP approaches. The spatial filters W_{CSP} are learned from the training data, and the training and test data are transformed to a new time series using (1). The variance based features are then extracted from the spatially filtered data.

$$Z = W_{CSP}X \tag{1}$$

2.3   Optimization of Filter Parameters

Filtering the signal using appropriate temporal filter to obtain as much important information as possible is a vital step in a BCI system. Here, we employ the method proposed in our previous work [49]. The three main parameters of a Butterworth bandpass filter (filter order, lower cutoff frequency and upper cutoff frequency) are optimized. Any optimization algorithm can be used for this purpose. However, we used genetic algorithm (GA) as used in [49]. 10-fold cross validation method has been used to evaluate the performance of the filter parameters during the optimization phase.

3   Results and Discussion

In order to validate our work, we have evaluated the proposed scheme on two publicly available datasets, BCI Competition III Dataset IVa and BCI Competition IV Dataset 1 referred to as dataset 1 and dataset 2, respectively from here onwards. These datasets have been widely used in this field. Dataset 1 contains 2 classes of MI EEG signals recorded from 5 subjects. We have utilized the down sampled signal at 100 Hz as used in other works. Dataset 2 contains 2 classes of MI EEG signals sampled at 1000 Hz, however, the down sampled signal at 100 Hz is used. It contains signals recorded from 7 subjects. A detailed description of the datasets can be obtained at http://www.bbci.de/competition/.

We have utilized 10×10-fold cross validation approach to evaluate our proposed scheme. The 10×10-fold cross validation results are also reported for all other competing methods in order to make a fair comparison between the methods. The average misclassification rates and their kappa coefficient values for different methods are shown in Tables 1 and 2 for dataset 1 and dataset 2, respectively. For the conventional CSP approach, we have used a 7–30 Hz frequency band. Parameters such as the number of spatial filters and the number of bands used are adopted from the respective works as initially proposed by the respective authors. It can be seen from Tables 1 and 2 that our proposed scheme outperformed all other competing methods achieving the lowest misclassification rate of 9.95% and 18.72%, and also achieved highest average kappa coefficient values of 0.801 and 0.624 for dataset 1 and dataset 2, respectively. Subjects *al* and *aw* of dataset 1 and subjects *b*, *e* and *f* of dataset 2 obtained the lowest misclassification rates using the proposed scheme. Compared to the conventional CSP approach and the GA based filter optimization approach using CSP (GA-CSP) [49], the proposed scheme achieved reduction in the misclassification rate by 3.52% and 0.80% for dataset 1 and, 5.52% and 1.52% for dataset 2, respectively. Our method also outperformed the scheme proposed in [42], which utilized sparse Bayesian learning to obtain the sparse feature vectors (SBLFB).

Table 1. The average misclassification rates and their kappa coefficient values (given in brackets) for different methods evaluated using dataset 1

Subject	CSP	CSSP	FBCSP	DFBCSP	SBLFB	GA-CSP	Proposed
aa	21.00 (0.613)	17.00 (0.659)	19.93 (0.601)	**9.21** (0.816)	16.79 (0.664)	16.96 (0.661)	14.77 (0.705)
al	3.86 (0.927)	3.07 (0.940)	1.50 (0.970)	1.21 (0.976)	1.36 (0.973)	1.79 (0.964)	**1.07** (0.979)
av	28.29 (0.426)	28.86 (0.423)	30.79 (0.384)	33.57 (0.329)	28.07 (0.439)	**24.82** (0.504)	26.67 (0.467)
aw	10.36 (0.800)	8.43 (0.837)	8.14 (0.837)	4.71 (0.890)	5.57 (0.889)	5.36 (0.943)	**3.21** (0.936)
ay	**3.86** (0.903)	4.29 (0.926)	5.93 (0.881)	7.64 (0.847)	11.00 (0.780)	4.82 (0.904)	4.05 (0.919)
Average	13.47 (0.734)	12.16 (0.757)	13.26 (0.735)	11.27 (0.771)	12.56 (0.749)	10.75 (0.795)	**9.95** (0.801)

Table 2. The average misclassification rates and their kappa coefficient values (given in brackets) for different methods evaluated using dataset 2

Subject	CSP	CSSP	FBCSP	DFBCSP	SBLFB	GA-CSP	Proposed
a	13.20 (0.736)	13.65 (0.727)	19.10 (0.618)	16.80 (0.664)	19.10 (0.618)	**12.67** (0.747)	13.30 (0.723)
b	42.80 (0.144)	42.70 (0.146)	44.70 (0.106)	42.90 (0.142)	41.50 (0.170)	43.67 (0.127)	**41.17** (0.177)
c	43.70 (0.126)	39.95 (0.201)	35.70 (0.286)	35.20 (0.290)	33.20 (0.336)	**33.00** (0.340)	34.20 (0.316)
d	22.40 (0.552)	14.60 (0.708)	22.20 (0.556)	23.50 (0.530)	**11.50** (0.770)	20.50 (0.590)	12.70 (0.746)
e	18.00 (0.640)	18.05 (0.639)	14.00 (0.720)	18.30 (0.634)	11.60 (0.768)	10.50 (0.790)	**8.30** (0.834)
f	22.50 (0.550)	18.55 (0.629)	19.60 (0.608)	14.30 (0.714)	21.20 (0.576)	14.02 (0.720)	**14.00** (0.720)
g	7.10 (0.858)	6.35 (0.873)	6.90 (0.862)	9.00 (0.820)	**5.90** (0.882)	7.33 (0.853)	7.40 (0.852)
Average	24.24 (0.515)	21.98 (0.560)	23.17 (0.537)	22.86 (0.542)	20.57 (0.589)	20.24 (0.595)	**18.72** (0.624)

As mentioned earlier, using CSSP instead of CSP improves the spatial resolution of the signal and thus the signal contains more important information. This results in a reduction in the misclassification rate. Figure 3 shows the distribution of the best 2 features for one of the trial runs of subject d (of dataset 2) for CSP, GA-CSP and the proposed scheme. It is clearly evident from Fig. 3 that the features learned by the proposed scheme contains more information about the different MI tasks and is due to the increased spatial resolution. Thus, the proposed method takes advantage of the spatial resolution and filter optimization for achieving improved performance.

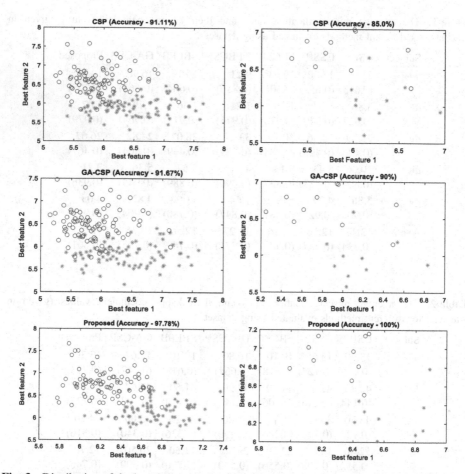

Fig. 3. Distribution of the best 2 features for one of the trial runs of subject d (of dataset 2). On the left is the distribution of training data and on the right is the distribution of the test data.

It should also be noted that the proposed scheme did not achieve the lowest misclassification rate for all subjects. However, in such cases the misclassification rate of the subjects using the proposed scheme was within 1.85% of the lowest misclassification rate for that particular subject except for subject aa of dataset 1. Subject aa of dataset 1 achieved lowest misclassification rate of 9.21% using DFBCSP approach, while the proposed scheme achieved the second lowest misclassification rate of 14.77%, a difference of 5.56%. This is because the important information about the different MI tasks for this subject was around two different frequency bands and DFBCSP was successfully able to select those frequency bands. On the other hand, the proposed scheme only finds a single wide band. This is evident from [33], where it is shown that the wide band was not selected. This also paves way for future works to test the proposed scheme for tuning multiple filters. With multiple filters we can also employ dimensionality reduction techniques [50–54], feature selection [55, 56] and clustering methods [57, 58], and classifiers [41, 59, 60]. Furthermore, in this work we have utilized a single sample point delay in the CSSP approach. In future, we will consider multiple sample point delays and develop methods to select the best number of sample point delays for each subject in a quest to try and further improve the performance of the proposed scheme.

4 Conclusions

In this paper we have proposed a scheme that utilizes CSSP and filter optimization using GA. The proposed scheme achieved the lowest misclassification rate and highest kappa coefficient values outperforming all other competing methods. Another advantage of the scheme is that any optimization algorithm can be used for optimizing the filter parameters. It is recommended that future works be carried out to test and evaluate the effects of parameter optimization of multiple filter bands. Also, future works may consider optimizing the number of sample point delays for each of the subject that would give optimal results. The proposed scheme would prove vital for developing improved BCI systems.

References

1. Li, T., et al.: Development of a novel motor imagery control technique and application in a gaming environment. Comput. Intell. Neurosci. **2017**, 16 (2017)
2. Yanyan, X., Xiaoou, L.: A brain controlled wheelchair based on common spatial pattern. In: International Symposium on Bioelectronics and Bioinformatics (ISBB) (2015)
3. Ang, K.K., et al.: A randomized controlled trial of EEG-based motor imagery brain-computer interface robotic rehabilitation for stroke. Clinincal EEG Neurosci. **46**(4), 310–320 (2015)
4. Alonso-Valerdi, L.M., Salido-Ruiz, R.A., Ramirez-Mendoza, R.A.: Motor imagery based brain–computer interfaces: an emerging technology to rehabilitate motor deficits. Neuropsychologia **79**(Part B), 354–363 (2015)
5. Ramos-Murguialday, A., et al.: Brain–machine interface in chronic stroke rehabilitation: a controlled study. Ann. Neurol. **74**(1), 100–108 (2013)
6. Ortner, R., et al.: A motor imagery based brain-computer interface for stroke rehabilitation. Stud. Health Technol. Inform. **181**, 319–323 (2012)
7. Spezialetti, M., et al.: Towards EEG-based BCI driven by emotions for addressing BCI-Illiteracy: a meta-analytic review. Behav. Inf. Technol. **37**(8), 855–871 (2018)

8. Zheng, W.L., et al.: EEG-based emotion classification using deep belief networks. In: 2014 IEEE International Conference on Multimedia and Expo (ICME) (2014)
9. Jirayucharoensak, S., Pan-Ngum, S., Israsena, P.: EEG-based emotion recognition using deep learning network with principal component based covariate shift adaptation. Sci. World J. **2014**, 10 (2014)
10. Jatupaiboon, N., Pan-Ngum, S., Israsena, P.: Emotion classification using minimal EEG channels and frequency bands. In: 10th International Joint Conference on Computer Science and Software Engineering (JCSSE) (2013)
11. Nie, D., et al.: EEG-based emotion recognition during watching movies. In: 5th International IEEE/EMBS Conference on Neural Engineering (NER), Cancun, Mexico (2011)
12. Yuan-Pin, L., et al.: EEG-based emotion recognition in music listening. IEEE Trans. Biomed. Eng. **57**(7), 1798–1806 (2010)
13. Yulita, I.N., et al.: Multi-layer perceptron for sleep stage classification. J. Phys. Conf. Ser. **1028**(012212) (2018)
14. Fonseca, P., et al.: A comparison of probabilistic classifiers for sleep stage classification. Physiol. Measur. **39**(5), 055001 (2018)
15. Chambon, S., et al.: A deep learning architecture for temporal sleep stage classification using multivariate and multimodal time series. IEEE Trans. Neural Syst. Rehabil. Eng. **26**(4), 758–769 (2018)
16. Crespo-Garcia, M., Atienza, M., Cantero, J.L.: Muscle artifact removal from human sleep EEG by using independent component analysis. Ann. Biomed. Eng. **36**(6), 467–475 (2008)
17. Zhou, M., et al.: Epileptic seizure detection based on EEG signals and CNN. Frontiers Neuroinformatics **12**(95) (2018)
18. Li, Y., et al.: Epileptic seizure detection based on time-frequency images of EEG signals using gaussian mixture model and gray level co-occurrence matrix features. Int. J. Neural Syst. **28**(07), 1850003 (2018)
19. Baumgartner, C., Koren, J.P., Rothmayer, M.: Automatic computer-based detection of epileptic seizures. Frontiers Neurol. **9**, 639 (2018)
20. Zahra, A., et al.: Seizure detection from EEG signals using multivariate empirical mode decomposition. Comput. Biol. Med. **88**, 132–141 (2017)
21. Samiee, K., Kovcs, P., Gabbouj, M.: Epileptic seizure detection in long-term EEG records using sparse rational decomposition and local Gabor binary patterns feature extraction. Know. Based Syst. **118**, 228–240 (2017)
22. Janjarasjitt, S.: Epileptic seizure classifications of single-channel scalp EEG data using wavelet-based features and SVM. Med. Biol. Eng. Compu. **55**(10), 1743–1761 (2017)
23. Alotaiby, T.N., et al.: Epileptic seizure prediction using CSP and LDA for scalp EEG Signals. Comput. Intell. Neurosci. **2017**, 1240323 (2017)
24. Cao, L., et al.: A hybrid brain computer interface system based on the neurophysiological protocol and brain-actuated switch for wheelchair control. J. Neurosci. Methods **229**, 33–43 (2014)
25. Reshmi, G., Amal, A.: Design of a BCI system for piloting a wheelchair using five class MI based EEG. In: Third International Conference on Advances in Computing and Communications (2013)
26. Naveen, R.S., Julian, A.: Brain computing interface for wheel chair control. In: Fourth International Conference on Computing, Communications and Networking Technologies (ICCCNT) (2013)
27. Lopes, A.C., Pires, G., Nunes, U.: Assisted navigation for a brain-actuated intelligent wheelchair. Rob. Auton. Syst. **61**(3), 245–258 (2013)

28. Ang, K.K., et al.: Filter bank common spatial pattern (FBCSP) in brain-computer interface. In: IEEE International Joint Conference on Neural Networks (IEEE World Congress on Computational Intelligence), Hong Kong (2008)
29. Thomas, K.P., et al.: A new discriminative common spatial pattern method for motor imagery brain computer interfaces. IEEE Trans. Biomed. Eng. **56**(11), 2730–2733 (2009)
30. Wei, Q., Wei, Z.: Binary particle swarm optimization for frequency band selection in motor imagery based brain-computer interfaces. Bio-Med. Mater. Eng. **26**(s1), S1523–S1532 (2015)
31. Wang, J., et al.: An information fusion scheme based common spatial pattern method for classification of motor imagery tasks. Biomed. Signal Process. Control **46**, 10–17 (2018)
32. Gaur, P., et al.: A multi-class EEG-based BCI classification using multivariate empirical mode decomposition based filtering and Riemannian geometry. Expert Syst. Appl. **95** (Supplement C), 201–211 (2018)
33. Kumar, S., Sharma, A., Tsunoda, T.: An improved discriminative filter bank selection approach for motor imagery EEG signal classification using mutual information. BMC Bioinf. **18**(16), 545 (2017)
34. Kumar, S., Mamun, K., Sharma, A.: CSP-TSM: optimizing the performance of Riemannian tangent space mapping using common spatial pattern for MI-BCI. Comput. Biol. Med. **91** (Supplement C), 231–242 (2017)
35. El Bahy, M.M., Hosny, M., Mohamed, W.A., Ibrahim, S.: EEG signal classification using neural network and support vector machine in brain computer interface. In: Hassanien, A.E., Shaalan, K., Gaber, T., Azar, A.T., Tolba, M.F. (eds.) AISI 2016. AISC, vol. 533, pp. 246–256. Springer, Cham (2017). https://doi.org/10.1007/978-3-319-48308-5_24
36. Yang, B., et al.: Subject-based feature extraction by using fisher WPD-CSP in brain–computer interfaces. Comput. Methods Programs Biomed. **129**, 21–28 (2016)
37. Raza, H., et al.: Adaptive learning with covariate shift-detection for motor imagery-based brain–computer interface. Soft. Comput. **20**(8), 3085–3096 (2016)
38. Mingai, L., et al.: A novel EEG feature extraction method based on OEMD and CSP algorithm. J. Intell. Fuzzy Syst., 1–13 (2016)
39. Li, X., Lu, X., Wang, H.: Robust common spatial patterns with sparsity. Biomed. Signal Process. Control **26**, 52–57 (2016)
40. Kumar, S., et al.: Decimation filter with common spatial pattern and fishers discriminant analysis for motor imagery classification. In: 2016 International Joint Conference on Neural Networks (IJCNN), Vancouver, Canada (2016)
41. Kumar, S., et al.: A deep learning approach for motor imagery EEG signal classification. In: 3rd Asia-Pacific World Congress on Computer Science and Engineering, Denarau, Island, Fiji (2016)
42. Zhang, Y., et al.: Sparse bayesian learning for obtaining sparsity of EEG frequency bands based feature vectors in motor imagery classification. Int. J. Neural Syst. **27**(02), 1650032 (2017)
43. Miao, M., Wang, A., Liu, F.: A spatial-frequency-temporal optimized feature sparse representation-based classification method for motor imagery EEG pattern recognition. Med. Biol. Eng. Compu. **55**(9), 1589–1603 (2017)
44. Luo, J., et al.: Dynamic frequency feature selection based approach for classification of motor imageries. Comput. Biol. Med. **75**, 45–53 (2016)
45. Zhang, Y., et al.: Multi-kernel extreme learning machine for EEG classification in brain-computer interfaces. Expert Syst. Appl. **96**, 302–310 (2018)
46. Dong, E., et al.: Classification of multi-class motor imagery with a novel hierarchical SVM algorithm for brain–computer interfaces. Med. Biol. Eng. Compu. **55**(10), 1809–1818 (2017)

47. Zhang, Y., et al.: Sparse bayesian classification of EEG for brain computer interface. IEEE Trans. Neural Netw. Learn. Syst. **27**(11), 2256–2267 (2016)
48. Ma, Y., et al.: Classification of motor imagery EEG signals with support vector machines and particle swarm optimization. Comput. Mathe. Methods Med. **2016**, 8 (2016)
49. Kumar, S., Sharma, A.: A new parameter tuning approach for enhanced motor imagery EEG signal classification. Med. Biol. Eng. Compu. **56**(10), 1861–1874 (2018)
50. Sharma, A., Paliwal, K.K.: A deterministic approach to regularized linear discriminant analysis. Neurocomputing **151**(Part 1), 207–214 (2015)
51. Sharma, A., et al.: Principal component analysis using QR decomposition. Int. J. Mach. Learn. Cybernet. **4**(6), 679–683 (2013)
52. Paliwal, K.K., Sharma, A.: Improved direct LDA and its application to DNA microarray gene expression data. Pattern Recogn. Lett. **31**(16), 2489–2492 (2010)
53. Sharma, A., Paliwal, K.K.: Fast principal component analysis using fixed-point algorithm. Pattern Recogn. Lett. **28**(10), 1151–1155 (2007)
54. Sharma, A., Paliwal, K.K.: A gradient linear discriminant analysis for small sample sized problem. Neural Process. Lett. **27**(1), 17–24 (2008)
55. Sharma, A., et al.: A feature selection method using improved regularized linear discriminant analysis. Mach. Vis. Appl. **25**(3), 775–786 (2014)
56. Sharma, A., et al.: Null space based feature selection method for gene expression data. Int. J. Mach. Learn. Cybernet. **3**(4), 269–276 (2012)
57. Sharma, A., Kamola, P.J., Tsunoda, T.: 2D–EM clustering approach for high-dimensional data through folding feature vectors. BMC Bioinform. **18**(16), 547 (2017)
58. Sharma, A., et al.: Hierarchical maximum likelihood clustering approach. IEEE Trans. Biomed. Eng. **64**(1), 112–122 (2017)
59. Saini, H., et al.: Protein fold recognition using genetic algorithm optimized voting scheme and profile bigram. J. Softw. **11**(8), 756–767 (2016)
60. Sharma, A., Paliwal, K.K., Onwubolu, G.C.: Class-dependent PCA, MDC and LDA: a combined classifier for pattern classification. Pattern Recogn. **39**(7), 1215–1229 (2006)

Author Index

Printed in the United States
By Bookmasters